Third Edition

COBOL for Today

Third Edition

J. Wayne Spence
University of North Texas

John C. Windsor
University of North Texas

WEST PUBLISHING COMPANY

St. Paul • New York • Los Angeles • San Francisco

Composition: Carlisle Publishers Services

Text Art: Carlisle Graphics

Part Opener Art: Randy Miyake

Cover Photo: Pete Turner

50 W. Kellogg Boulevard
P.O. Box 64526
St. Paul, MN 55164-1003

Printed in the United States of America
96 95 94 93 92 91 90 89 8 7 6 5 4 3 2 1 0

Library of Congress Cataloging-in-Publication Data
Spence, J. Wayne.
COBOL for today/J. Wayne Spence, John C. Windsor.—3rd ed.
p. cm.
Rev. ed. of: COBOL for the 80's. 2nd. c1985.Includes index.
ISBN 0-314-68967-2
1. COBOL (Computer program language) I. Windsor, John C., (John Clayton), 1946-
II. Spence, J. Wayne. COBOL for the 80's.
III. Title.
QA76.73.C25S657 1989
005. 13'3—dc19 88-38582
CIP

To Jan, Pat, and Cari
(Congratulations to each of you on *your* accomplishments)
J.W.S.

To Eileen, Laura, and Raeld
(Your accomplishments are greater)
J.C.W.

Contents

Preface to the Instructor

COBOL for Today has been designed with you in mind. The text is divided into four parts: (1) *Introductory Concepts* that explain the basic nucleus of COBOL, (2) *More Advanced COBOL Concepts* that explain the student's understanding and build on the basic nucleus, (3) *Fundamental File Processing Concepts* that introduce the student to sequential, indexed, relative, and virtual files (as well as other support for file operations including report writer and the sort verb), and (4) *Special Usage COBOL Concepts* that describes features of COBOL that are useful but not frequently used.

This text has been organized to provide both flexibility for classroom use (since most chapters are independent of each other) and increasing levels of rigor. The text begins with relatively simple concepts and gradually increases the level of difficulty to provide a more realistic picture of how COBOL is used in a commercial environment. Because of its breadth of content and level, this text could easily be used in an introductory, advanced, (or single accelerated) course in COBOL.

All of the materials presented in this text have been classroom tested, from the general discussion of each concept, the illustrations presented in each chapter, and the problems presented at the end of many of the chapters. Beyond explaining the basic concepts and syntax of COBOL, this text also presents descriptions and illustrations of coding style and embellishes on this style through sections labeled *Notes on Programming Style*.

To supplement the text, additional support materials are available. The first element of this support material is an *Instructor's Manual*. This manual describes the objectives, concepts, and answers to questions for each chapter, and it acts as a key to the other support materials. Second, over 200 *Transparency Masters* are available that illustrate basic to advanced statements and concepts. Third, *Program Support* is available. This feature includes a tested copy of each program identified in the text, whether a figure or a problem. Thus, you may customize the programs to your installation or make your own transparency masters illustrating particular programming statements or concepts. In addition, this feature also includes a sample data set and a copy of the printed results of each program. This feature also includes a *Test Bank* of approximately 1000 items. These materials are available to qualified adoptors on 5¼ inch or 3½ inch diskettes, or in printed form.

The authors view this text and its support materials as living documents. Although the authors have used this material in a classroom environment and continually strive to improve the presentation of it, your *suggestions and comments for improving this work are always welcome*.

Thank you for considering this text and we hope you find its presentation useful for both you and your students.

J. Wayne Spence
University of North Texas

John C. Windsor
University of North Texas

Preface to the Student

You are about to embark upon an area of study in computing that is the lifeblood of the commercial applications programmer. The COBOL programming language is a vital part of most business data-processing environments. Nationwide, as much as 80 percent of all new applications are written in COBOL. Thus, a knowledge of COBOL and a skill in writing programs are the single most important talents to those seeking an entry-level position in commercial processing.

COBOL is *not* the easiest language to learn. However, if it were easy, there would be no reason for a company to want to pay you handsomely for your programming talents and skills. Although you may find yourself frustrated at times, perseverance generally pays off in the long run. Of course, you will make mistakes. Even the "expert" programmer makes them, but what separates the "expert" from the "also rans" is that the expert doesn't usually make the same mistake twice. Thus, you should try to learn something from each mistake. Next, you should allow yourself plenty of time to complete each assignment. Many students find it difficult to complete assignments when they wait until the last minute. While you might be able to construct a solution to a problem on a short-term basis, you will frequently find that there is "one more error" to fix. So, allow yourself time to fix that "one more error." Finally, you should plan what you do. Not only should you plan the time you spend working on a solution to an assignment, but you should also plan the solution as well! Unless you are already an "expert" programmer, this "up front" time is usually well worth the effort and frequently reduces the amount of time spent coding and correcting errors.

We encourage you not only to learn COBOL, but to learn it well. Not only will you find your efforts immediately rewarding, but you will find that it pays off in terms of a successful career in data processing as well. We wish you success in this endeavor and good luck with your future.

J. Wayne Spence

John C. Windsor

Preface to the Student

Acknowledgments

The following acknowledgment has been reproduced from COBOL Edition, U.S. Department of Defense, at the request of the Conference on Data Systems Languages.

> Any organization interested in reproducing the COBOL report and specifications in whole or in part, using ideas taken from this report as the basis for an instruction manual or for any other purpose is free to do so. However, all such organizations are requested to reproduce this section as part of the introduction to the document. Those using a short passage, as in a book review, are requested to mention ''COBOL'' in acknowledgment of the source, but need not quote this entire section.
>
> COBOL is an industry language and is not the property of any company or group of companies, or of any organization or group of organizations.
>
> No warranty, expressed or implied, is made by any contributor or by the COBOL Committee as to the accuracy and functioning of the programming system and language. Moreover, no responsibility is assumed by any contributor, or by the committee, in connection therewith.
>
> Procedures have been established for the maintenance of COBOL. Inquiries concerning the procedures for proposing changes should be directed to the Executive Committee of the Conference on Data Systems Languages.
>
> The authors and copyright holders of the copyrighted material used herein:
>
> FLOW-MATIC (Trademark of Sperry Rand Corporation), Programming for the Univac (R) I and II, Data Automation Systems copyrighted 1958, 1959, by Sperry Rand Corporation: IBM Commercial Translator Form No. F 28-8013, copyrighted 1959 by IBM: FACT, DSI 27 A5260-2760, copyrighted 1960 by Minneapolis-Honeywell have specifically authorized the use of this material in whole or in part, in the COBOL specifications. Such authorization extends to the reproduction and use of COBOL specifications in programming manuals or similar publications.

Finally, we would like to express my deepest appreciation to those individuals whose considerable efforts, helpful suggestions, and professional expertise aided the authors in the development of this text. For the first edition, these individuals were:

Gary Block, Onondaga Community College—New York
Marilyn Bohl, Scientific Research Associates (SRA)—California

John B. Crawford, California Polytech Institute—Pomona
Tom Dart, Valdosa State University—Georgia
Robert W. Duvall, Virginia Commonwealth University—Richmond
Robert J. Fedrick, El Camino State University—California
David Greenblatt, Queens College—New York
Robert B. Kirklin, L.A. Harbor Community College—California
James L. Landre, California State University—Sacramento
J. David Naulmann, University of Minnesota
Ruth Schwartz, Arizona State University

For the second edition, these individuals were:

Barry Barlow
University of Southern Mississippi

Joseph J. Cebula
Community College of Pennsylvania
William G. Dey
Central Missouri State University

Mary Jane Fedor
Community College of Allegheny, South Campus
Pennsylvania

Kathleen Geletko
Community College of Allegheny, South Campus

Lillian E. Peters Hupert
Loyola University of Chicago

John E. Martin
University of Wisconsin, Milwaukee

Carl F. Slemmer
Frostburg State College
Maryland

For the third edition, these individuals were:

Professor Debra Burton
Southwest Texas State University

Professor Jim Hampson
Allegany Community College
Maryland

Professor Tim Holland-Davis
Orangeburg-Calhoun Technical College
South Carolina

Professor Ron McNeilly
Kishwaukee College
Illinois

Professor Timothy J. Rolfe
Gonzaga University
Washington

Professor Mary Sapp
DeKalb Area Technical School
Georgia

Professor Laura W. Swaney
Xavier University of Louisiana

Professor Julian Wade
DeKalb Area Technical School
Georgia

In addition, we would like to thank our collegues at the University of North Texas for their assistance and helpful suggestions. Finally, a special note of thanks goes to our wifes Jan and Eileen for their encouragement and assistance in the preparation of the manuscript.

While acknowledging the assistance of others, the authors assume full responsibility for any errors or omissions in this text.

PART I

INTRODUCTORY CONCEPTS

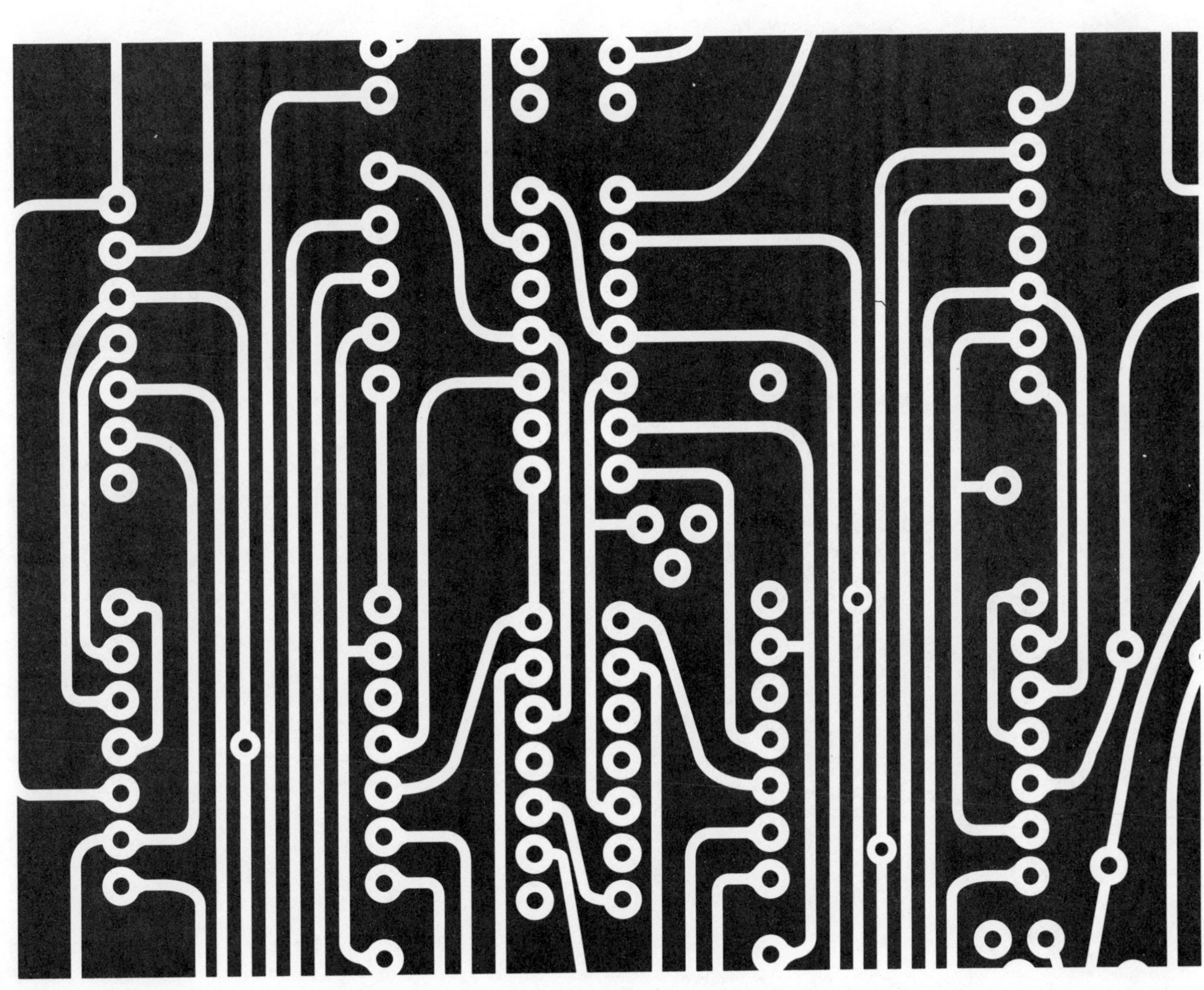

CHAPTER

1

Introduction

COBOL (COmmon Business-Oriented Language) is a high-level programming language. COBOL began to be developed in 1959 as a standard programming language that could be used on several different computers. Thus, the word *common* should be taken literally. COBOL is common to commerically oriented large- and medium-sized computers, many minicomputers, and some microcomputers.

Because COBOL is business oriented, it is particularly well suited to commercial data-processing applications. Compared to scientific applications, business applications require limited mathematical manipulations and many input and output operations. Thus, COBOL handles input and output operations efficiently, but its mathematical capabilities are somewhat limited.

COBOL: The Past

During the late 1950s, the Department of Defense was awarding many contracts to companies throughout the United States. To document contract progress, costs, and many other control factors, each company had its own computer programs. Before long, the Department of Defense found it impossible to verify these figures because of the wide variety of programming languages used [some high-level and some low-level]. Thus, the Defense Department either had to train its investigators (auditors) to work with a variety of programming languages or require all companies under contract to use a common language.

Consequently, the idea of one language for all government contracts was adopted. But no existing language could be adopted by all of these companies, primarily because of the differences in their equipment. In addition, most available languages were ill-suited to the task. To address the problem, CODASYL (Committee On DAta SYstems Language) was created in 1959 to study the problems of business computer applications. The committee included representatives of U.S. government agencies (primarily the Department of Defense), computer manufacturers, universities, and computer users. CODASYL decided to create a new language with common elements for all computers. The language was to be understandable by people with very little computer training.

The results of the CODASYL Conference were produced in April, 1960. They included the initial specifications for COBOL. (The language came to be known as COBOL-60, after the year of its inception.) Later revisions were produced in 1963 and 1965. As COBOL started to change, computer manufacturers recognized the importance of new capabilities, with each manufacturer taking a different approach to implementation. It soon became apparent that if computer manufacturers were not encouraged to standardize, COBOL would no longer be a common language. Consequently, in 1968, the American National Standards Institute (ANSI) published suggestions for making COBOL a standard programming language, making one standard for the construction of COBOL compilers. COBOL compilers that *generally* conform to the ANSI recommendations are often referred to as Standard COBOL or ANSI COBOL compilers. (Recently, ANSI COBOL has been shortened to ANS COBOL.) In 1974, ANSI revised the standard COBOL specifications. The 1974 specifications had a limited impact on the language, with relatively few additions and changes. However, in 1985, the specifications for the most recent version of COBOL were approved. As a result, substantial changes and several additions have been incorporated into the language, most of which are designed to either enhance its structure or provide additional capabilities.

1985 COBOL Standards

COBOL: The Present

Currently, COBOL is the most widely used language for business data-processing applications. Some estimate that COBOL is used for as much as 80 percent of new business applications. One widely known study supporting this claim was performed by Andreas Phillippakis (*Datamation,* December, 1977) and has been supported by other surveys.

Why is COBOL so widely used? There are five reasons. First, many government contractors adopted the language because of the urging of the Defense Department. This resulted in a ripple effect—from contractor to subcontractor, down the long chain of companies involved in large government contracts. Thus, because COBOL was widely used during its infancy, it was somewhat easier for other companies to adopt. Some companies adopted COBOL as they changed computer systems, and others adopted it as their primary language when they went from manual to computer procedures.

Second, COBOL was designed to be a common language, that is, machine independent. Because of the standardization of COBOL by ANSI, it *should* be a very simple matter to convert a program written for one manufacturer's computer to run on another manufacturer's computer.

Third, in keeping with the initial requirements for the language, COBOL is said to be "self-documenting." That is, very little of COBOL is symbolic or cryptic. Many of the statements in COBOL are English-like sentences. For the programming novice, it is not as difficult to read as many other programming languages.

Fourth, COBOL is one of the most efficient high-level languages for data handling. It possesses extensive data-editing features and more importantly, excellent file management capabilities.

Finally, COBOL is not a "dead" language. It is being continually updated, modified, and improved to meet the demands of a business-oriented programming language. Both CODASYL and ANSI continue to monitor changing demands on COBOL. For example, in the early 1970s, CODASYL suggested a new series of capabilities for COBOL so that it might be more easily used as a *host* programming language in a database environment. Some computer manufacturers have extended COBOL to handle these new demands; however, these extensions are not yet standard.

A recent major development, which has promoted the continued use of COBOL, was the birth and adoption of *structured programming*. This concept (discussed in Chapter 2) does not require any changes to the current version of COBOL, but rather requires a new look at the capabilities of the language. Structured programming is a disciplined approach to the programming of medium to large projects (although it may be applied to projects of any size).

With all these advantages, why is COBOL not the universal language? First, the most critical shortcoming is its limited mathematical capabilities. Thus, for mathematical or scientific applications, COBOL is ill suited. More scientifically oriented languages, such as FORTRAN, have extensive mathematical capabilities. Second, COBOL is "wordy." That is, due to its "self-documenting" nature, COBOL requires more coding and keying (e.g., key-punching) time than most other languages. BASIC and APL are much more concise languages that require comparatively little program preparation time. Third, COBOL is both comprehensive and coherent. It is comprehensive in that a programmer must know a great deal about COBOL before attempting to construct a COBOL program. It is coherent in that simply knowing the parts of COBOL is not sufficient; the programmer must know the relationships of the parts. COBOL is not for the individual interested in occasional use or in a language that can be quickly mastered. Finally, COBOL is not considered the best language for a structured approach. Both PL/I and ALGOL contain all the "structures" used in structured programming, and both are modular in design.

In this text COBOL has been broken into major topical areas. The remaining chapters in Part 1 present the basic framework (nucleus) of COBOL. Only the essential details are presented in these chapters so that the programmer can begin writing programs. The topics in Part 2 present other details that may be inserted into the basic framework to extend the programmer's ability to solve certain types of program-related problems. In Part 3 COBOL is described in a file processing environment. Finally, Part 4 presents those aspects of COBOL that tend to be less frequently used.

COBOL: The Future

The basic framework of COBOL, as presented in this text, should be the same for several years, partly because many currently used commmercial programs are written in COBOL. To redesign or rewrite these programs would be a monumental (if not insurmountable) task.

The future of COBOL's file-handling capabilities, however, is not so certain, for two reasons. First, file handling (management) is the least consistent aspect of COBOL. Each firm producing a COBOL compiler has a different viewpoint on the physical manipulations of each file-oriented statement, even though the statements themselves may look the same from one system to another. Thus, for COBOL to become a truly standard language, a consensus must be reached with regard to file handling.

The second reason is the concept of *database systems* which became a reality in the early 1970s. This approach abandons the "file" in favor of a "pooled data source." Although many database systems are now in use, continuing research will probably result in new and more efficient methods of handling data. Thus, files (and database systems) as we know them today may become obsolete in the future.

COBOL: The Environment

Although this text is devoted to the COBOL programming language, there are other elements in any data-processing installation of which the programmer must be aware. Among these other elements are *hardware, system software, application software,* a *job control language,* and *data.* Of these, hardware is probably the most easily identifiable.

Hardware is generally any and all equipment in a data-processing installation, that is, central processing units (computers), internal storage (primary memory or ''core''), and peripheral devices (terminals, line printers, tape drives, and disk drives—the latter two are often referred to as *secondary* or *mass storage* units). These devices can be referred to as hardware, either collectively or individually. Collectively, they can be referred to as the *computer system.* Of course, there are other hardware elements in computer systems, such as input-output channels, which connect the peripheral devices to the central processing unit, or telecommunication devices, which permit the transmission of data over telephone lines, but knowledge of these is not necessary to understand how a programmer uses a programming language.

Software, in general, encompasses all programs regardless of their nature or purpose. System software and application software are separated above because of their different functions. A *program* is simply a list of commands to which the computer system reacts. Specifically, a program (or algorithm) is a set of nonambiguous, step-by-step instructions that direct the computer to fulfill a specified objective. System software is the set of programs that directs the overall activity of the computer—it controls the computer. Computer operating systems fall into this category.

Operating systems vary in both name and capability from one manufacturer to another. For example, IBM produces three basic types of operating systems, which are referred to as DOS (disk operating system), OS (operating system), and OS/VS (operating system for virtual storage machines). This is not an exhaustive list of the operating systems produced by IBM, but it gives you an idea of the variability of operating systems from just one manufacturer.

System software also includes *assemblers, compilers,* and *interpreters.* These programs translate programming languages (such as COBOL) into machine-understandable (computer) instructions. COBOL is a compiler-oriented language. Before the computer can react to a program written in COBOL, the program must be compiled (translated) from a *source program* (a program written in a high-level programming language such as COBOL) into an *object program* (a set of instructions in machine language). Only after the compilation process is completed can the program be executed by the computer.

Application software are programs written to perform a specific function needed by a user, such as payroll, accounts receivable, and inventory control programs. Programs written in COBOL fall into this category. Utility programs and processors are also considered to be application software. Utility programs generally sort data, copy data from one medium to another (e.g., from magnetic disk to a printer), or format reports. It is the development of the various types of application software that occupies most of the programmer's time.

The distinction among hardware, system hardware, and application software becomes blurred in a relatively new area called *firmware.* Firmware is a component (integrated-circuit chips) of a piece of hardware (generally the central processor). However, these chips may contain operating systems and utility programs, and under some circumstances may be programmed by a programmer.

Job Control Language (JCL) is used by the programmer to communicate with the operating system to interface his or her program with the operating system. Generally, it is not used to write application programs. JCL instructions act as flags to the operating system. They may be used to communicate accounting information to the operating system, indicate the types of resources needed to execute an application program, invoke a compiler, specify the location of data, and terminate a procedure. All these functions may be called to execute a single program. However, since JCL instructions are a direct function of the operating system, further explanation is beyond the scope of this text. Consult your installation for information regarding job control language. Many installations will provide "canned" (previously written) JCL instructions for the novice user.

The last element, *data,* is the entity to be manipulated. Data may be composed of names, addresses, quantities, dollar amounts, and so on. These numeric or character "values" are accepted by application software and manipulated to a useful end—perhaps a report. The data may represent information about a customer, an employee, or an inventory item.

Here is a scenario of the interaction of some of these elements using the framework of this text. The programmer begins creating a COBOL application program, which is supposed to perform a definable task. To this application program, the programmer adds JCL and data to create a group of elements (a *job*) arranged in the sequence illustrated in Figure 1.1. Notice that the COBOL program and the data are concentrated into units, and JCL (in this case identified by "//" in the first two columns) is spread throughout the job stream.

After the job stream has been prepared, the programmer submits it to the computer by having the job stream read into the computer system by an input device (e.g., a disk file). Within the computer system, each element of the procedure is identified, examined, and acted upon by the computer. The job card (the first JCL command) is accessed, and information on the record is examined for accuracy (e.g., a valid account number,

Figure 1.1 Illustration of a Job Stream

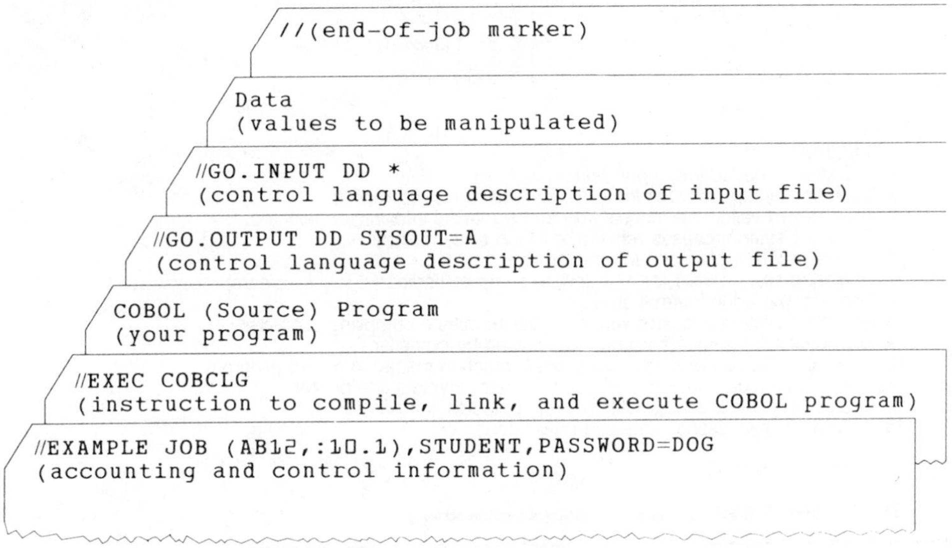

```
//(end-of-job marker)

Data
(values to be manipulated)

//GO.INPUT DD *
(control language description of input file)

//GO.OUTPUT DD SYSOUT=A
(control language description of output file)

COBOL (Source) Program
(your program)

//EXEC COBCLG
(instruction to compile, link, and execute COBOL program)

//EXAMPLE JOB (AB12,:10.1),STUDENT,PASSWORD=DOG
(accounting and control information)
```

correct format, etc.). If the job card is acceptable, the operating system begins collecting job statistics (e.g., elapsed job time, compile time, execution time, number of records read, etc.) and in many cases assigns a job number to the procedure. The job card may also call for specific computer resources—amount of internal storage, expected compilation and execution time, specific print forms, and so on—and if the resources are available, the procedure takes the next step (see Figure 1.2a). The second JCL command calls for the COBOL compiler. The compiler (or at least elements of the compiler) are copied into the computer's internal storage to begin the translation process. Once the compiler is available, the COBOL (source) program is placed in internal storage, and the translation process begins. The COBOL instructions are examined one at a time by the compiler, under the supervision of the operating system. As each instruction is examined, the compiler produces the machine language equivalent in the object program area. When compilation has been completed, the *object* program will be the essence of the source program but in machine language. (*Machine language* is an extremely ele-

Figure 1.2a Illustration of Source Program Compilation

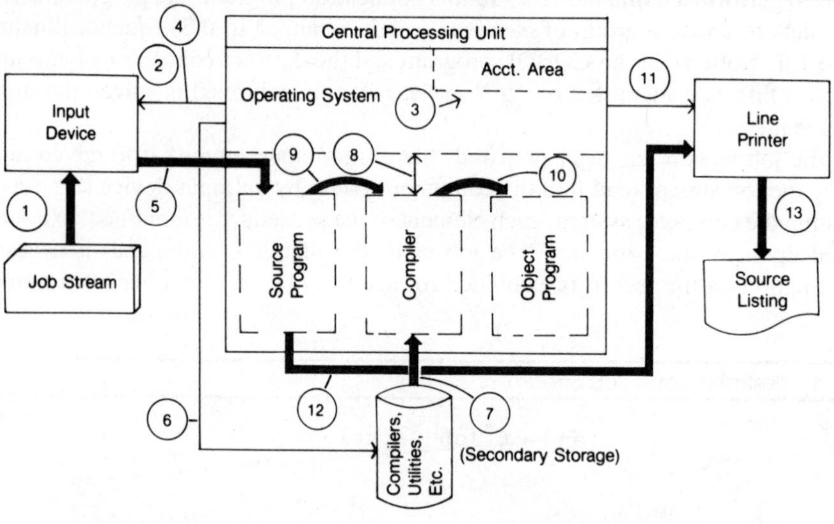

LEGEND
1. Job stream loaded into input device.
2. Operating system initiates input device and reads job record.
3. If job record valid, user accounting and statistical information initiated.
4. Operating system causes remainder of job stream to be read.
5. Source program placed in internal storage.
6. Operating system calls for appropriate compiler (indicated in job stream).
7. Compiler placed in internal storage.
8. Operating system interacts with compiler to initiate compiling process.
9. Instructions from source program examined by compiler.
10. Translated version of source-program instruction placed in object program.
11. After compilation complete, operating system invokes line printer.
12. Source program (perhaps with errors) copied to line printer.
13. Source program listing produced on printout.

Control Operations: ⟶

Data Transfer Operations: ➡

mentary language peculiar to particular computers and is understood by the computer without additional interpretation.)

After the object program has been produced, "linking" takes place (see Figure 1.2b). Linking, or linkage editing is basically a housekeeping process, wherein loose ends, such as external references, internal address locations, and so forth are resolved. Finally, the program is linked to the devices called for and the program executes. It is only during execution that data will be accepted and manipulated by the program. Eventually, the program terminates. Program termination causes the last of the JCL commands to be encountered—generally a marker declaring the end of the job stream.

To review, the general procedure required to complete a job stream containing an application program is: (1) compile the source program into an object program, (2) link the object program, and (3) execute the object program and accept data. These steps are often termed "compile-link-and-go."

Figure 1.2b Illustration of Program Execution

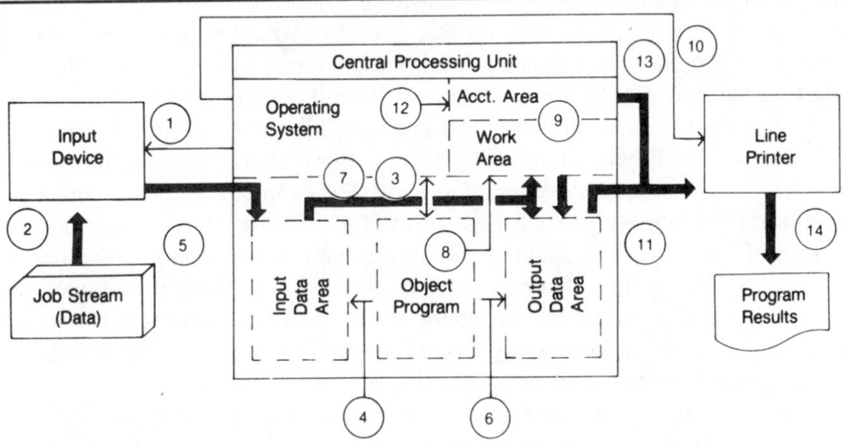

LEGEND
1. After object program is created, operating system checks job stream for "load" and "execute" JCL commands and data availability.
2. Records from job stream made available.
3. Operating system initiates object program execution.
4. Object program requests input of data (READ operation).
5. Data is transferred from input device to input data area (internal storage) under control of operating system.
6. Object program requests output of data (WRITE operation).
7. Data transferred from input data area to output data area.
8. Object program requests movement of data to work area. (Step 7 repeated, but data transferred to work area.)
9. Data transferred from work area to output data area. (Step 8 precedes this operation when object program requests movement of data from work area to output data area.)
10. Operating system checks printer availability and initiates output sequence.
11. Data transferred from output data area to the line printer.
12. End-of-job-stream data collected under operating system control.
13. Job statistics transmitted to line printer.
14. Line printer produces program results (printout).

Control Operations: ⟶

Data Transfer Operations: ➡

Creation of a Keyed File

In the preceding illustration, a *batch* job stream was developed and submitted to the computer system via an input device, such as a card reader, with all the elements necessary to process a program (JCL, source language statements, and data) being submitted as a single unit.

Today, many computer systems, indeed most larger commercial installations, do not develop programs in the batch mode because it is not the most productive use of programmer time. In these installations, *on-line* facilities permit the programmer to develop, modify, and often execute a program via a remote terminal. This means the programmer is in direct communication with the computer system through a *CRT* (cathode ray tube—a video display unit with an integral keyboard) or a microcomputer. As in the batch mode of operation, the programmer must have a means of modifying or correcting the program. In the batch mode this may mean correcting and moving records within a program card deck. In the on-line mode, however, the programmer develops a *program* or *procedure* file—a system reference point that contains the ''images'' of records that might otherwise exist in a card form.

The program file created through on-line operations may be called a *source* file, a *keyed* file, or a *text editor* file depending on the computer system in use. However, all program files have characteristics in common: they all contain images of program statements. Each record (line of the program) is accessible, and individual records can be inserted, deleted, modified, or moved. Beyond these characteristics, however, commonality between computer systems often ends. For example, some systems attach an addressable record number to each line (record) in the procedure; others do not. The significance of line numbers is that individual lines may be addressed by number without having to address those lines that precede the specified line. Without the line numbers, one must sequentially search the procedure file until the desired record is located. In addition, some systems automatically ''save'' or retain for future reference the records as they are entered; others must be instructed to save the records. Some systems automatically incorporate any changes made to the file in the file itself; others provide for a primary (original) file and a secondary (working) file for the purpose of making changes. In a system that does not automatically save a procedure file when it is addressed, the programmer normally is provided with a command like ''SAVE file-name,'' permitting the existing program to be copied and retained for future reference.

Finally, some systems permit the programmer to compile and execute a program only by submitting it to the batch system; others provide the capability for compiling and executing the program in both the batch mode and an *interactive* mode. (*Interactive* means that the program is compiled and executed on-line so that the programmer can ''converse'' with the program as it is executing.)

All computer systems permit programs to be executed in the batch mode. However, in many computer systems it is possible to develop a procedure file, through the use of a terminal. In this situation, program compilation and execution is accomplished by a command such as ''BATCH file-name,'' thus causing the procedure file to be placed in the batch job queue (or waiting line) of the computer system. The procedure file in this case would likely include JCL, COBOL statements, and perhaps even data.

As an additional capability, many computer systems permit compilation and execution of programs on-line. Although on-line operations in systems vary, the procedure file might contain only the statements of a COBOL program. The programmer may call for on-line compilation of this program by entering a command such as ''COBOL file-name.'' During the compiling process, diagnostic messages (e.g., errors) and other operator prompts may be displayed on the terminal that initiated the compilation. Then, after the program has been successfully compiled, it could be executed immediately, or the object program could be saved in a separate file and executed later by using commands such as ''RUN file-name'' or ''EXECUTE file-name.''

The variability of on-line program development in today's environment makes it virtually impossible to describe the process in detail without addressing individual computers, support equipment, and operating systems. You will have to rely on your instructor and computer center support personnel for assistance in this area. You will find that learning this mode of program development will be well worth the effort, especially when you modify or change a program.

Summary

COBOL, which was conceived by the CODASYL committee in 1959, is the most widely used language for programming commercial applications. COBOL is common to a wide variety of computers and, to a large extent, it has been standardized by the American National Standards Institute.

Since COBOL's inception, it has been frequently updated and expanded. COBOL has also been enhanced so that it may be used as a host programming language in a database system environment.

COBOL is not *the* universal language, yet it has been widely adopted. COBOL is more English-oriented than other languages, it handles input-output operations efficiently, and is capable of supporting the structured approach to programming. However, COBOL's mathematical capabilities are limited. It is not one of the easiest languages to learn and is not the *best* language for structured programming.

COBOL (as well as other programming languages) is used in a data-processing environment composed of hardware, system software, application software, a job control language, and data. Each of these elements of a data-processing installation interacts with the others to become a useful tool for solving business data-processing problems.

Questions

Below, fill in the blank(s) with the appropriate word, words, or phrases.

1. COBOL is an acronym for ____ .
2. COBOL is referred to as a common language because ____ .
3. COBOL is intended for use in ____ applications (programs).
4. Unlike scientific data processing, commercial data processing requires ____ calculations and ____ input-output operations.
5. CODASYL is an acronym for ____ .
6. CODASYL's purpose was ____ .
7. The CODASYL committee had representatives from ____ , ____ , and ____ .
8. The latest version of COBOL is referred to as ____ .
9. ANSI is an acronym for ____ .
10. Standard COBOL is also referred to as ____ COBOL.

11. The programming language currently most widely used for commercial applications is _____ .

12. A host programming language is one that is used in a(n) _____ environment.

13. Structured programming is a(n) _____ approach to programming.

14. Another term for equipment or devices is _____ .

15. Internal storage or primary memory resides within the _____ and secondary storage resides on _____ .

16. The total of all combined devices within a data-processing installation may be called a _____ .

17. A collection of all programs in a data-processing installation is known as _____ .

18. A list of commands to which the computer reacts or a set of nonambiguous, step-by-step instructions aimed at a specific objective is the definition of a(n) _____ or a(n) _____ .

19. One of the primary entities in the system software group is a(n) _____ .

20. A program written in a language such as COBOL may also be referred to in general terms as a(n) _____ program.

21. A program written in machine language is known as a(n) _____ program.

22. A(n) _____ translates a source program into an object program.

23. _____ software are programs written to satisfy a specific user-oriented function and when written in COBOL usually satisfy a business need.

24. Firmware is _____ , _____ , and _____ .

25. _____ is used by the programmer to communicate with the operating system and to interface the program to the operating system.

26. A compiler is generally invoked by a(n) _____ command.

27. _____ are generally manipulated by application programs in data-processing installations.

28. What are the advantages of using COBOL?

29. What are the disadvantages of using COBOL?

30. List the components (elements) of a computer system. Of a data-processing installation.

31. List the steps that JCL controls to take a COBOL program from its original form to a form manipulated by a user.

32. Briefly describe the major differences in developing job streams in a batch environment and an on-line/interactive environment.

CHAPTER

2

Programming: The Traditional Versus a Structured Approach

Two primary considerations related to running a computer installation are the cost of computer *hardware* (equipment) and the cost of *software* (programs) or program development within an organization. The cost of hardware is declining, whereas the cost of software development is increasing, and this trend is likely to continue for the foreseeable future. To combat the rising cost of program development, three techniques have been developed to reduce the amount of time required from program initiation to program completion. These techniques are called *flowcharting, pseudocode,* and *structured programming*. Before discussing these, we will look briefly at the program development process.

The development of programs follows a pattern with at least three distinct phases. The first phase is generally called program *analysis* (often referred to as analysis, design, and planning). In the analysis phase, the requirements of the program are determined (e.g., types of input and output, decisions, calculations, etc.). Once these requirements have been identified, the programmer (or analyst) may begin the design and planning of the program. The programmer must begin to develop the logical flow of the program, which is often done with the aid of a program *flowchart* and *pseudocode*.

Beginning programmers often overlook the importance of planning a program solution before attempting to write the program. Perhaps this is because beginning programmers start with simple programs so they can remember all the details. With larger programs, however, even the best programmers need a way to keep track of where they have been and where they are going. Program planning is similar to coding a program—the more you practice, the better you get. Do not wait until an extremely complex program comes along to start thinking about program planning; practice program planning in order to have the necessary skills when they are needed.

The second phase of program development is *implementation*. During this phase, the program is organized and coded in a programming language. After coding is complete, *testing* and *debugging* begin, which involve attempting to execute the program. Most programs will not execute properly the first time. Usually they contain keying or program-planning errors. Thus, testing and debugging are the repetitive processes of correcting errors or ''bugs'' (debugging) and verifying the correctness of results of the program (testing). Once these are satisfactorily concluded, implementation is complete and the program is executed under "real life" conditions.

The third phase is called *modification and maintenance,* which involves altering or enhancing an existing program to keep it up to date, to correct a previously undiscovered error, or to expand its ability to handle more operations. Often, the person responsible for creating a program is *not* the individual who performs the modification and maintenance work. Thus, one step in this phase is to understand at least the portion of the program that will be changed. After this step is complete, modification and maintenance activities continue with a repeat of the analysis and implementation phases.

Flowcharting

Flowcharting is a technique for diagraming a procedure. More specifically, *program flowcharting* is the technique of planning a program by expressing a program's logic in terms of symbols or blocks prior to coding. The flowchart consists of symbols or blocks, which represent types of operations (presented in Figure 2.1), notations, which identify the operations to be performed; and flowlines, which represent the logical relationship of one operation to another.

There are several advantages to flowcharting programs before coding. First, by logically arranging the program's sequence of events, the program designer can trace through

Figure 2.1 Program Flowcharting Symbols

Symbol	Description
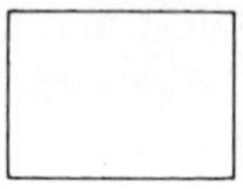	Any processing function; operation(s) causing change in value, form, or location of data.
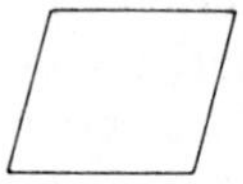	General input/output function; data available for processing (input), or recording of processed data (output).
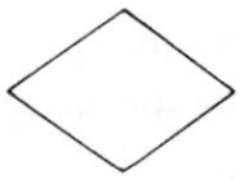	A decision or switching-type operation that determines which of a number of alternative paths is followed.
	A terminal point in a flowchart—start, stop, halt, delay, or interrupt; may show entry to or exit from a closed subroutine.
	Connector used to demonstrate the exit to or entry from another part of the flowchart on the same page. Often used to eliminate flowlines.
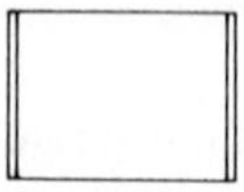	Predefined process, used to indicate one or more named operations or program steps specified in a subroutine or another set of flowcharts.
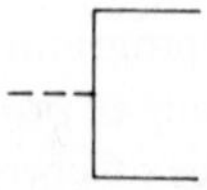	Annotation or comment, used to provide additional descriptive clarification. Attached to another symbol by a dotted line.

the flowchart to determine if the procedure performs as anticipated. If not, the flowchart can be modified and retested. Second, drawing flowcharts is usually less time-consuming than coding. In case of error, it is easier to redraw the flowchart than it is to modify the program code. Third, the flowchart acts as documentation. Someone unfamiliar with programming should be able to comprehend the program's sequence of events through the flowchart. In large corporations the individual responsible for program implementation may not be the individual who performs the analysis. Then, the flowchart can be used to communicate program requirements from the analyst to the program coder.

The flowchart should be written independent of the programming language, primarily to avoid "coding" of the flowchart. Each MOVE statement should *not* be represented by a block in the flowchart. Rather, each block should capture the essence of the operation to take place at that point in the process. The details are added during coding.

Figure 2.2 presents a program flowchart for the program presented in Chapter 7 (Figure 7.15). In this problem a report and column heading were to be produced, records were to be used from a file, the data contained in the records were to be reorganized, and the data were to be printed on a line printer. The reading and writing cycle was to

Figure 2.2 A Simple Program Flowchart

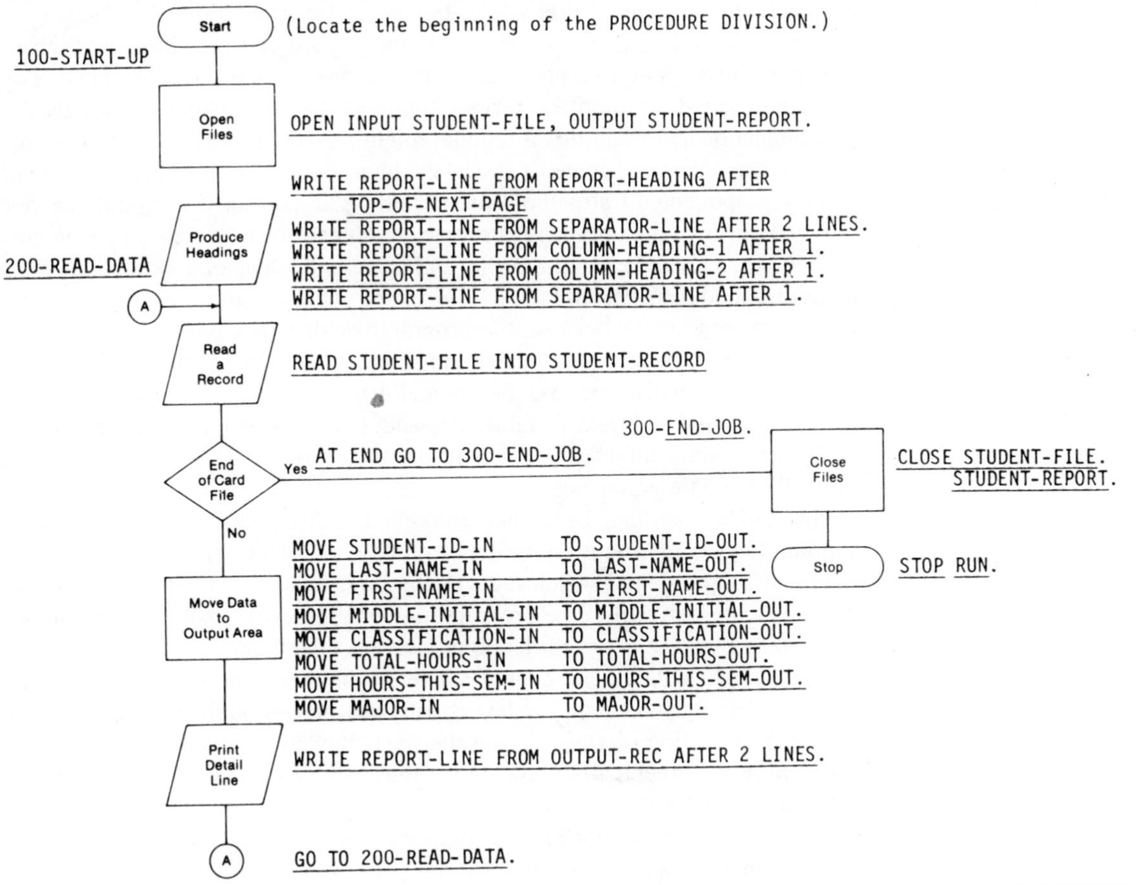

continue until all records had been processed. (When flowlines go from left to right or from top to bottom, arrowheads are normally omitted; this is a standard convention in flowcharting. Further, notice the connector symbol used to eliminate the flowline that could have been drawn from the "Print Detail Line" block to the area just above the "Read a Record" block.) As an aid to understanding the relationship between the flowchart and the program, the corresponding COBOL statements are shown where they relate to the flowchart.

Structured Programming

Although the program flowchart in Figures 2.2 is concise and solves the problem for which it is intended, it violates almost every rule of structured programming. Imagine increasing the complexity of the second problem by a factor of 10. The flowchart for such a problem would be extremely difficult to construct and next to impossible to understand. This is due to flowcharting's attempt to solve the entire problem in one giant step.

The most significant advantage of structured programming is that the programmer no longer has to consider all the details of a problem with the idea of solving it in one step. The program is viewed as a series of *modules* (a collection of program statements) connected through "driving" or control routines. Each module should be *clearly defined* and *functionally oriented,* if possible. In a payroll-computation procedure, for example, one module could be dedicated to handle the payroll computations, and other modules could perform the functions necessary to get the process started and stopped. The payroll-computation module might be further subdivided into modules to calculate taxes and other deductions. An additional module might be used to interface all other modules in the same way a table of contents shows the interrelationship between chapters of a book.

Many proponents of structured programming argue that if a module cannot be adequately described in a one-page narrative, the function should be further subdivided. In addition, each module should permit only one entry and one exit point. *Single-entry, single-exit* modules greatly facilitate program understanding and the location of logic errors in programming because the programmer does not have to worry that the code may be executed from some other point later in the block, thereby jumping the code that would "normally" be executed first. Furthermore, the programmer knows exactly where the module ends and therefore does not have to worry that one or more statements within the module might cause a jump to some other part of the program before the end of the module is reached.

What advantages can be gained through the structured approach to developing a program? Most important, large and complex problems can be attacked as smaller, simplified subproblems, which reduces the time required to develop a program. If the project is extremely large, the programming effort can be easily divided among several individuals. Because program functions can be isolated into specific modules, execution errors and logical bugs can be located and eliminated more quickly. Portions of the program code may be tested independently of other modules or functions. This may call for the insertion of *stubs* during the development process. Stubs are nothing more than dummy statements that indicate the presence of modules that are to be more fully coded at a later time.

Structured programming also encourages and supports a *standardized style,* which facilitates maintenance and modification. This standardized style uses three basic approaches to module design:

1. The *sequence*
2. The *if-then-else*
3. The *do-while*

Each of the three structures, shown in flowcharts in Figure 2.3, is supported by COBOL. The sequence structure is a series of process (or input/output) operations that are executed sequentially from the first statement to the last. In COBOL, this type of structure could be written as a series of READ, WRITE, MOVE, and arithmetic statements.

The function of the if-then-else is provided through the COBOL IF statement (see Chapter 9). Often, structured programs incorporate nested IF statements. That is, on the basis of one decision, another decision is made. An illustration of this operation is shown in Figure 2.4. For example, suppose a programmer wants to determine a customer discount from purchases on the following schedule:

Purchase	Discount
Up to $500	0%
$501 to $1,000	5
$1,001 to $2,000	10
Over $2,000	20

One approach to the problem would be to examine the conditions in a ''*tree*'' form. Condition-1 might determine if the amount of purchase is $1000 or less. If the first answer is ''true,'' condition-2 might determine if the purchase is $500 or less. If this is true, the discount would be zero percent. However, if condition-2 is false, the discount

Figure 2.3 Three Forms Used in Structured Programming

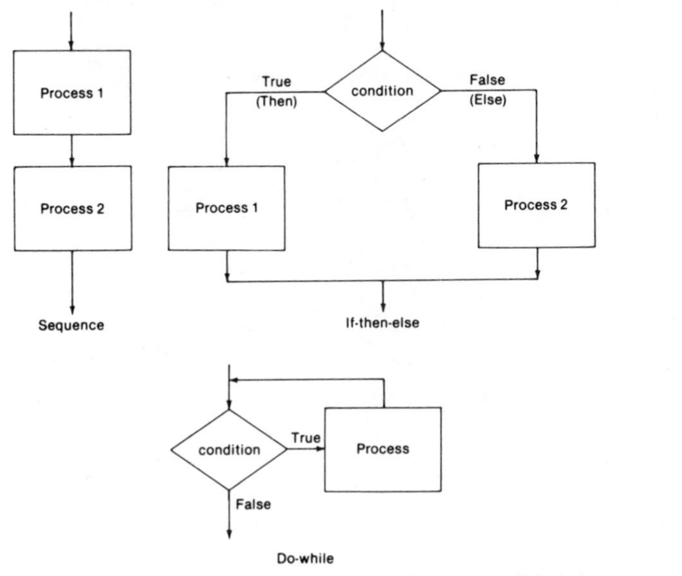

Figure 2.4 Nested IF Statement in a "Tree" Form

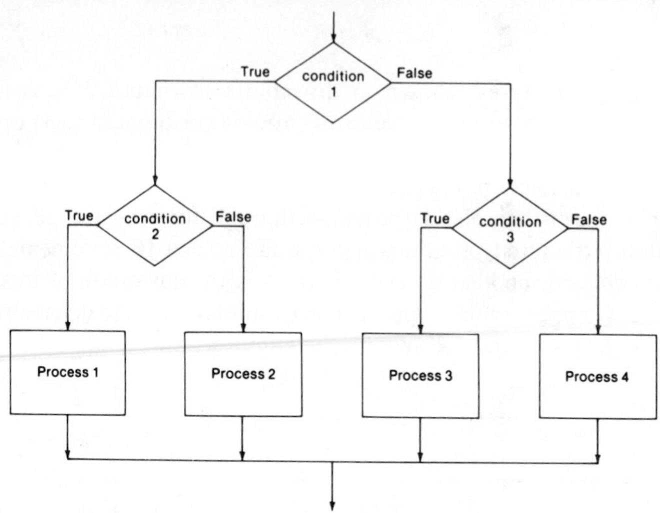

would be 5 percent. If the first test (condition-1) was false, condition-3 might determine if the purchase was $2000 or less. If this is true, the discount would be 10 percent; but if false, the discount would be 20 percent.

Another way to view this series of decisions is to check each category in *staged* or *"stair-step"* form. Figure 2.5 provides this type of decision process. For example, condition-1 might determine if the amount of purchase is $500 or less. If this condition is true, the discount would be zero and a structure exit would occur; if false, the second

Figure 2.5 Nested IF Statements in a "Staged" Form

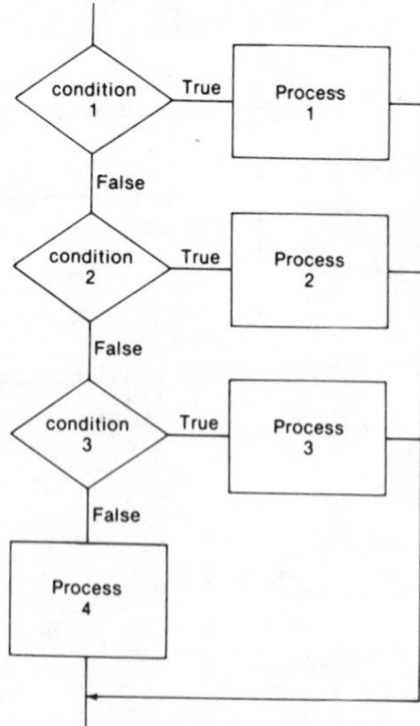

condition would determine if the amount of purchase was $1000 or less. If condition-2 is true, the discount would be 5 percent and a structure exit would occur; if false, the third condition would determine if the amount of purchase was $2000 or less. If condition-3 is true, the discount would be 10 percent and a structure exit would occur; if false, the discount would be 20 percent by default.

These two approaches to decision logic are frequently used; however, both examples suffer from the same problem—they require the programmer to remember a sequence of events in a testing cycle. Although the example is easy to understand, as testing complexity increases, so does the programmer's difficulty in understanding and programming the decision logic. Furthermore, complex decision logic requires more indepth study when it becomes necessary to modify the program. For this reason, *simple independent testing procedures are generally preferred.*

For example, the same series of decisions presented above could be redesigned into individual tests executed in serial fashion. (See Figure 2.6.) Condition-1 determines if the purchase amount is $500 or less, and if true, it assigns a discount of zero. Condition-2 determines if the purchase amount is greater than $500 and less than $1001, and if true, it sets the discount to 5 percent. Condition-3 determines if the purchase amount is greater than $1000 and less than $2001, and if true, it sets the discount at 10 percent. Finally, condition-4 determines if the purchase amount is greater than $2000, and if true, it sets the discount to 20 percent. In this form, one of the tests could be altered without altering other tests. For example, suppose another category is added, say, if the amount of purchase was $3001 or more, the discount would be 25 percent. It would only be necessary to add a fifth condition and a fifth process to the tests to incorporate the new category into the program.

To alter the decision "tree" form of nested IFs would require an "unbalanced tree," and exact placement of the new test would require careful study and the alteration of existing statements. In the "stair-step" form of nested IFs the "default" value would

Figure 2.6 Independent IF Statements

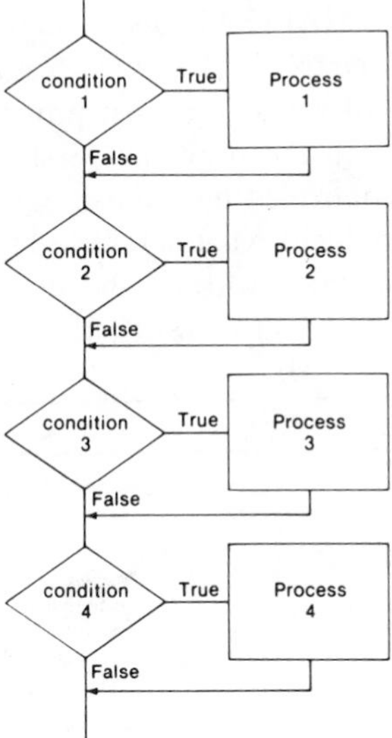

probably no longer be valid, and the existing structure would have to be altered to incorporate the new test. Independent IF statements, however, are simpler, easier to modify, and less prone to new logic errors as a program is modified.

The last of the fundamental structures of structured programming is the do-while. Although COBOL does not totally embrace the do-while structure, the structure can be approximated by the PERFORM statement (see Chapter 7). The PERFORM statement incorporates a *do-until* structure, illustrated in Figure 2.7. The do-while structure specifies that a process is to be repeated so long as the indicated condition is *true*. The do-until structure indicates that a process is to be repeated so long as the specified condition is *false*. Thus, the control of *looping* operations (the repetitive execution of a series of statements) is geared to a positive response to a condition with a do-while and to a negative response to a condition with do-until. Although there is a fundamental difference between the two structures, most programmers can easily translate the do-while structure to the do-until structure.

Figure 2.8 illustrates structured programming in the context of a program. The module flowchart and program illustrated demonstrate a redesign of the student list program from Chapter 7. The flowchart *decomposes* (divides) the procedure into several small, single-function modules. Included in this list of modules are CONTROL PROCEDURE, INITIALIZATION, WRITE REPORT HEADING, READ AND PRINT DETAILS, and TERMINATION.

The CONTROL PROCEDURE represents a new paragraph relative to the program illustrated in Chapter 7; however, its addition is significant. One of the primary purposes of structured programming is to isolate the control of the program within a very few procedures. CONTROL PROCEDURE serves this function in the new version of the student list program. It controls the execution of all other modules (paragraphs) within the PROCEDURE DIVISION. For the most part, CONTROL PROCEDURE can be viewed as a simple sequence structure. That is, each of the indicated procedures are executed, in turn, one after the other. However, note that the procedures are identified in the flowchart with *predefined process* symbols. This means that although each module is identified in the CONTROL PROCEDURE module, the actual details of these modules are more clearly spelled out in another part of the flowchart with a corresponding label. Thus, for example, although INITIALIZATION is identified in the CONTROL PROCEDURE module, the details of the INITIALIZATION module may be found elsewhere.

Another significant alteration of the student list program is based on the procedure used to control looping activity. In the previous version of the student list program, looping activity was primarily controlled by the use of a series of GO TO statements. However, the previous design produces what is referred to as *linear code*—a single line of logic runs throughout the program without the benefit of any global control (as

Figure 2.7 Do-while Versus Do-until (PERFORM)

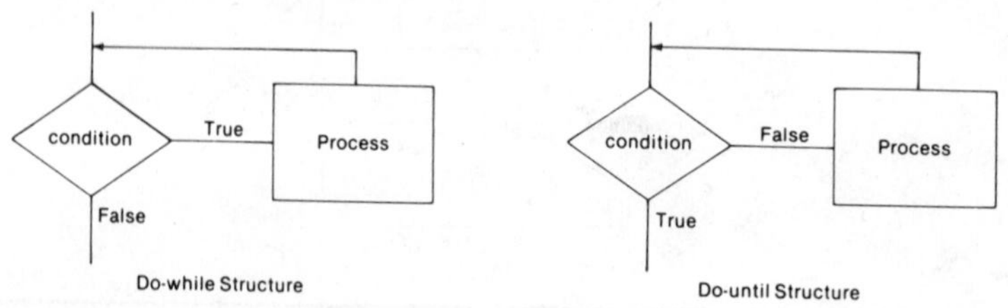

represented in the new version by the CONTROL PROCEDURE). Linear code is generally more difficult to understand, debug, and modify than structured code because of the lack of isolated functions. In the new version of the student list program a do-until structure is used to control looping activity. Thus, the looping activity for the READ AND PRINT DETAILS module is initiated, controlled, and terminated by the do-until structure in the CONTROL PROCEDURE module. Therefore, the READ AND PRINT DETAILS module is repeated until the EOF (end-of-file) indicator (FILE-STATUS)

Figure 2.8 Student List Program (Structured Flowchart)

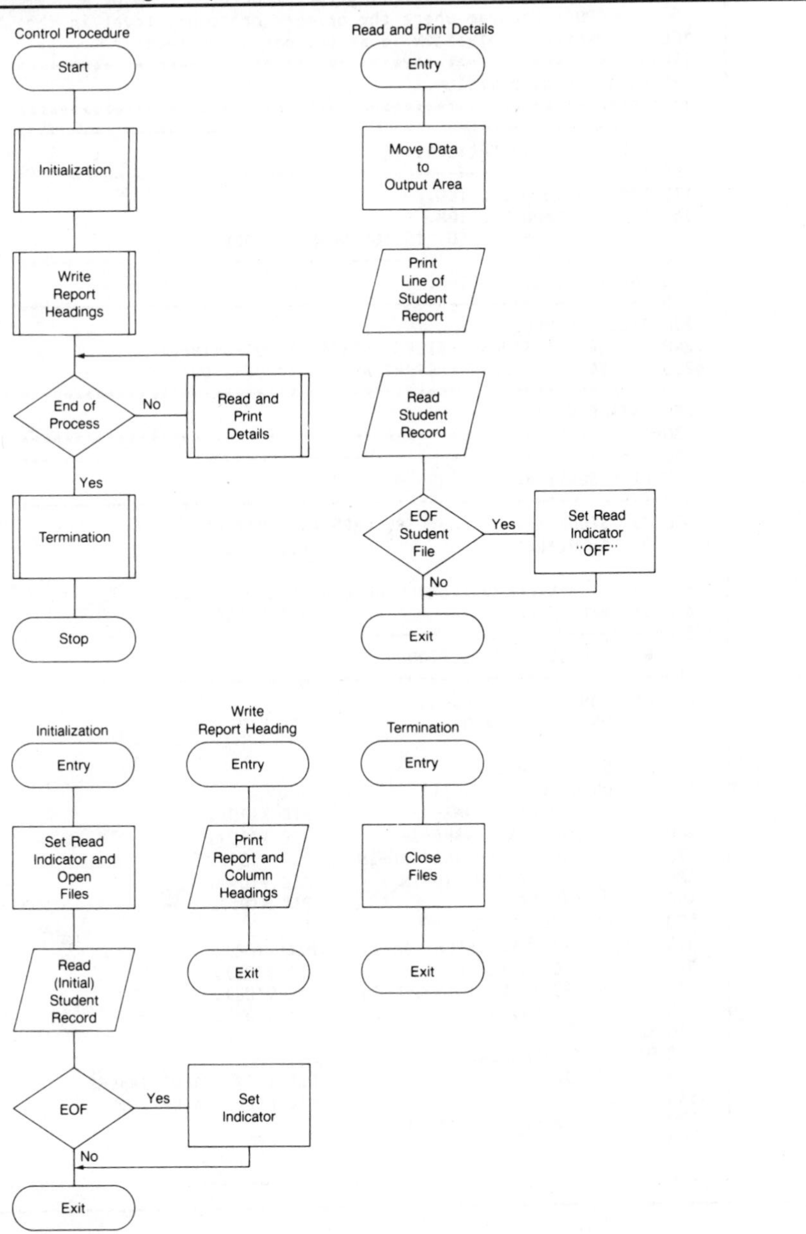

Figure 2.8 *Continued* Student List Program (Structured)

```
         1   1   2   2   2   3   3   4   4   4   5   5   6   6   6   7
 4   8   2   6   0   4   8   2   6   0   4   8   2   6   0   4   8   2
*****************************************************************
 IDENTIFICATION DIVISION.
*****************************************************************
 PROGRAM-ID.     STUDENT-LIST.
 AUTHOR.         J. WAYNE SPENCE.
 DATE-WRITTEN.   JANUARY 1, 1989.
 DATE-COMPILED.  JANUARY 1, 1989.
*     This program illustrates the structured form of a
*     COBOL program where the primary procedure level in the
*     PROCEDURE DIVISION is at the paragraph level.
*****************************************************************
 ENVIRONMENT DIVISION.
*****************************************************************
*---------------------------------------------------------------*
 CONFIGURATION SECTION.
*---------------------------------------------------------------*
 SOURCE-COMPUTER. IBM.
 OBJECT-COMPUTER. IBM.
 SPECIAL-NAMES.   C01 IS TOP-OF-NEXT-PAGE.
*---------------------------------------------------------------*
 INPUT-OUTPUT SECTION.
*---------------------------------------------------------------*
 FILE-CONTROL.
     SELECT STUDENT-FILE   ASSIGN TO UT-S-INPUT.
     SELECT STUDENT-REPORT ASSIGN TO UT-S-OUTPUT.
*****************************************************************
 DATA DIVISION.
*****************************************************************
*---------------------------------------------------------------*
 FILE SECTION.
*---------------------------------------------------------------*
 FD  STUDENT-FILE LABEL RECORDS ARE OMITTED.
 01  DUMMY-RECORD                   PIC X(80).
 FD  STUDENT-REPORT LABEL RECORDS ARE OMITTED.
 01  REPORT-LINE                    PIC X(133).
*---------------------------------------------------------------*
 WORKING-STORAGE SECTION.
*---------------------------------------------------------------*
 01  WORKING-RECORD.
     05  FILE-STATUS                PIC X(05).
 01  STUDENT-RECORD.
     05 STUDENT-IDENTIFICATION.
         10 LAST-NAME-IN            PIC X(10).
         10 FIRST-NAME-IN           PIC X(10).
         10 MIDDLE-INITIAL-IN       PIC X(01).
         10 STUDENT-ID-IN           PIC 9(09).
     05 FILLER                      PIC X(05).
     05 ENROLLMENT-INFO.
         10 CLASSIFICATION-IN       PIC X(02).
         10 TOTAL-HOURS-IN          PIC 9(03).
         10 HOURS-THIS-SEM-IN       PIC 9(02).
         10 MAJOR-IN                PIC X(03).
 01  REPORT-HEADING.
     05 FILLER                      PIC X(29) VALUE SPACES.
     05 FILLER                      PIC X(21) VALUE
     'Semester Student List'.
```

Figure 2.8 *Continued* Student List Program (Structured)

```
                1   1   2   2   2   3   3   4   4   4   5   5   6   6   6   7
    4   8   2   6   0   4   8   2   6   0   4   8   2   6   0   4   8   2
--------------------------------------------------------------------------------
    01  SEPARATOR-LINE.
        05 FILLER                     PIC X(01)  VALUE SPACE.
        05 FILLER                     PIC X(79)  VALUE ALL '-'.

    01  COLUMN-HEADING-1.
        05 FILLER                     PIC X(01) VALUE SPACE.
        05 FILLER                     PIC X(79) VALUE '|        Student
-       'Name        | Student ID. | Class | Major |  Current    | Tota
-       'l |'.

    01  COLUMN-HEADING-2.
        05 FILLER                     PIC X(28) VALUE ' |'.
        05 FILLER                     PIC X(14) VALUE '|    Number'.
        05 FILLER                     PIC X(08) VALUE '|'.
        05 FILLER                     PIC X(08) VALUE '|'.
        05 FILLER                     PIC X(22) VALUE '| Enrollment | H
-       'ours |'.

    01  OUTPUT-RECORD.
        05 FILLER                 PIC X(03) VALUE ' |'.
        05 FIRST-NAME-OUT         PIC X(11).
        05 MIDDLE-INITIAL-OUT     PIC X(01).
        05 FILLER                 PIC X(02) VALUE '.'.
        05 LAST-NAME-OUT          PIC X(10).
        05 FILLER                 PIC X(04) VALUE ' |'.
        05 STUDENT-ID-OUT         PIC 9(09).
        05 FILLER                 PIC X(05) VALUE '  |'.
        05 CLASSIFICATION-OUT     PIC X(02).
        05 FILLER                 PIC X(06) VALUE '   |'.
        05 MAJOR-OUT              PIC X(03).
        05 FILLER                 PIC X(08) VALUE '  |'.
        05 HOURS-THIS-SEM-OUT     PIC 9(02).
        05 FILLER                 PIC X(08) VALUE '     |'.
        05 TOTAL-HOURS-OUT        PIC 9(03).
        05 FILLER                 PIC X(03) VALUE '  |'.
   ******************************************************************
    PROCEDURE DIVISION.
   ******************************************************************
    000-CONTROL-PROCEDURE.
        PERFORM 100-INITIALIZATION.
        PERFORM 200-WRITE-REPORT-HEADING.
        PERFORM 300-READ-AND-PRINT-DETAILS
            UNTIL FILE-STATUS = 'DONE'.
        PERFORM 400-TERMINATION.
        STOP RUN.

    100-INITIALIZATION.
        MOVE 'START' TO FILE-STATUS.
        OPEN INPUT STUDENT-FILE, OUTPUT STUDENT-REPORT.
        READ STUDENT-FILE INTO STUDENT-RECORD
            AT END MOVE 'DONE' TO FILE-STATUS.

    200-WRITE-REPORT-HEADING.
        WRITE REPORT-LINE FROM REPORT-HEADING AFTER
            TOP-OF-NEXT-PAGE.
        WRITE REPORT-LINE FROM SEPARATOR-LINE AFTER 2 LINES.
        WRITE REPORT-LINE FROM COLUMN-HEADING-1 AFTER 1.
        WRITE REPORT-LINE FROM COLUMN-HEADING-2 AFTER 1.
        WRITE REPORT-LINE FROM SEPARATOR-LINE AFTER 1.

    300-READ-AND-PRINT-DETAILS.
```

Figure 2.8 *Continued* Student List Program (Structured)

```
          1   1   2   2   2   3   3   4   4   4   5   5   6   6   6   7
  4   8   2   6   0   4   8   2   6   0   4   8   2   6   0   4   8   2
------------------------------------------------------------------------
           MOVE STUDENT-ID-IN          TO STUDENT-ID-OUT.
           MOVE LAST-NAME-IN           TO LAST-NAME-OUT.
           MOVE FIRST-NAME-IN          TO FIRST-NAME-OUT.
           MOVE MIDDLE-INITIAL-IN      TO MIDDLE-INITIAL-OUT.
           MOVE CLASSIFICATION-IN      TO CLASSIFICATION-OUT.
           MOVE TOTAL-HOURS-IN         TO TOTAL-HOURS-OUT.
           MOVE HOURS-THIS-SEM-IN      TO HOURS-THIS-SEM-OUT.
           MOVE MAJOR-IN               TO MAJOR-OUT.
           WRITE REPORT-LINE FROM OUTPUT-RECORD AFTER 2 LINES.
           READ STUDENT-FILE INTO STUDENT-RECORD
               AT END MOVE 'DONE' TO FILE-STATUS.

       400-TERMINATION.
           CLOSE STUDENT-FILE, STUDENT-REPORT.
```

specifies that all data have been read. Thereafter, the TERMINATION module is executed, and finally, the procedure is terminated by the STOP operation in the CONTROL PROCEDURE module. The CONTROL PROCEDURE module, then, initiates, controls, and terminates the entire overall logic of the new version of the student list program.

Another alteration of the student list program is first noticed in the INITIALIZATION module. As before, this module is responsible for opening all files used by the procedure. However, a READ statement has been added to this procedure. The purpose of this input operation is to retrieve the first or *initial* record from the input file. This serves two functions. First, if the input file is empty (no data in the file), the input control indicator (FILE-STATUS) is set so that the READ AND PRINT DETAILS module is bypassed upon returning to the CONTROL PROCEDURE. Second, this initial input operation provides the *first* input record for later processing by the READ AND PRINT DETAILS module. Thus, regardless of whether or not a record is actually read, initialization is invoked by the control procedure module, and when the INITIALIZATION

Figure 2.8 *Continued* Student List Program (Structured) Data

```
      |         1         2         3         4         5
Record|12345678901234567890123456789012345678901234567890
------------------------------------------------------------
     1|Anderson  Jimmy     Q343564321     Gr21900Csc
     2|Booker    John      A555667777     Fr03515Mgt
     3|Carter    Matt      N456789012     Jr09408Mgt
     4|Davidson  Anthony   R353492761     Sr13816Eco
     5|Eldridge  David     Q376495268     So04712Fin
     6|Franklin  Rose      V000000001     Gr18912Gbu
     7|Garrison  Kenneth   A537903251     So02816Mgt
     8|Hamilton  Mark      C486762389     Jr09618Csc
     9|Issacs    Matt      H474653790     Sr12018Eco
    10|Jefferson Harold    Q502326955     Fr01818Mkt
    11|Kennedy   Floyd     R476329092     Jr06012Mkt
    12|Lincoln   Steven    O442648942     So04515Mkt
    13|Monroe    Jeff      V546677219     Sr09918Csc
```

Figure 2.8 *Continued* Student List Program (Structured) Output

Semester Student List

Student Name		Student ID. Number	Class	Major	Current Enrollment	Total Hours
Jimmy	Q. Anderson	343564321	Gr	Csc	00	219
John	A. Booker	555667777	Fr	Mgt	15	035
Matt	N. Carter	456789012	Jr	Mgt	08	094
Anthony	R. Davidson	353492761	Sr	Eco	16	138
David	Q. Eldridge	376495268	So	Fin	12	047
Rose	V. Franklin	000000001	Gr	Gbu	12	189
Kenneth	A. Garrison	537903251	So	Mgt	16	028
Mark	C. Hamilton	486762389	Jr	Csc	18	096
Matt	H. Issacs	474653790	Sr	Eco	18	120
Harold	Q. Jefferson	502326955	Fr	Mkt	18	018
Floyd	R. Kennedy	476329092	Jr	Mkt	12	060
Steven	O. Lincoln	442648942	So	Mkt	15	045
Jeff	V. Monroe	546677219	Sr	Csc	18	099

module has been completed, control is returned to the CONTROL PROCEDURE module. The same pattern is followed by all other modules invoked by the CONTROL PROCEDURE module.

The second module executed by the CONTROL PROCEDURE module is the WRITE REPORT HEADING module. This module is exactly the same as previously shown in the student list program in Chapter 6. However, the execution of this module is controlled differently. In the previous illustration of this program, the WRITE REPORT HEADING module was executed as a result of a *fall through*—a condition that exists when one procedure (paragraph) is executed immediately after the completion of a previous procedure. That is, a fall through is a result of sequentially executing one procedure after the completion of another without benefit of any intervening control. It is executed simply because it is next. In the new version of the program, WRITE REPORT HEADING is executed if, and only if, it is invoked by another part of the procedure. In the new version of the program, it is called by the CONTROL PROCEDURE.

The third module executed by the CONTROL PROCEDURE is the READ AND PRINT DETAILS module, which is controlled by a do-until structure. The operations performed in this module are essentially the same as those shown in the previous version of this procedure. However, because of the requirements of structured logic, some of the operations have been moved. In the previous version of the program, the sequence of events was *"read-move-write."* Now, the sequence is *"move-write-read."* Recall that the INITIALIZATION procedure retrieved the first record from the input file. This being the case, the beginning sequence in the READ AND PRINT DETAILS module must be to process data that have been previously supplied. Thus, data from the first input record are moved to the output record and written to the line printer. After these operations are completed, the procedure is ready for the next input record. The result of this sequencing is that the READ statement becomes the *last* instruction in the READ AND PRINT DETAILS module. Furthermore, this placement also ensures that as soon as an end-of-file condition is encountered, the indicator is set to EOF and control is returned to the CONTROL PROCEDURE module. If EOF is not encountered, the CONTROL PROCEDURE simply indicates a repeat of the read and print details module.

When control is finally returned to the CONTROL PROCEDURE module (after the end-of-file has been encountered), the TERMINATION module is executed. This module closes all files. However, as opposed to our previous version of this program, it *does not* stop the program. The stop operation is performed only upon a return to the CONTROL PROCEDURE.

Although Figure 2.8 is organized in a manner that would please even the structured programming purist, it is not the only approach to ''structured'' program design. Why have more than one approach to a problem? The first reason is that many beginning programmers would examine the READ AND PRINT DETAILS module and become confused over the fact that the first input operation *appears* to follow the activity associated with its processing. Although this is not true (the initial input operation occurred in the INITIALIZATION module), this approach may not be so logically ''natural'' as is an *explicit* input operation prior to processing. Second, the ''purist'' approach typically causes at least some minimal level of code duplication (as seen in the duplication of READ statements in the INITIALIZATION and READ AND PRINT DETAILS modules). Third, as you will find later in the text, when a series of interdependent conditions are placed together, it is often difficult to construct the logic of such a complex process. These ''decisions'' frequently have to be *nested* to state correctly the series of conditions. The issue is *not* whether or not the conditions *can* be nested correctly, but whether the logic of the process is easier to understand, produce, debug, and modify in these situations. It is my *opinion* (which is shared by a number of industrial computer installations with which I am familiar) that structure *clarity* should not be sacrificed at the expense of structure *purity.* With this in mind, an alternate approach to structured programming is possible.

Figure 2.9 illustrates a second solution to the student list program. Since it is intended to solve the same problem as that examined in Figure 2.8, both illustrations are highly similar. In fact, the IDENTIFICATION, ENVIRONMENT, and DATA DIVISIONs of these two programs are essentially the same. The difference lies in the PROCEDURE DIVISION. However, even in the PROCEDURE DIVISION, the logic of the CONTROL PROCEDURE, WRITE REPORT HEADING, and TERMINATION modules are the same for the two solutions. An examination of the PROCEDURE DIVISION of the COBOL program in Figure 2.9 reveals that each of these procedures is coded at the SECTION level rather than as paragraphs. The difference, however, does not lie in the fact that the use of SECTIONs makes the two procedures different. (All paragraphs of the PROCEDURE DIVISION in Figure 2.8 could be converted to SECTIONs without modifying the fundamental logic of the solution.) The difference is in how the SECTIONs are used.

The first logical difference between the procedures stated in Figure 2.8 and that of Figure 2.9 is in the INITIALIZATION module. Note that although this module opens files in both illustrations, it *does not* require an initial input operation in Figure 2.9—all input operations are a part of the READ DATA module. The second difference is in

Figure 2.9 Student List Program (A Structured Flowchart Alternative)

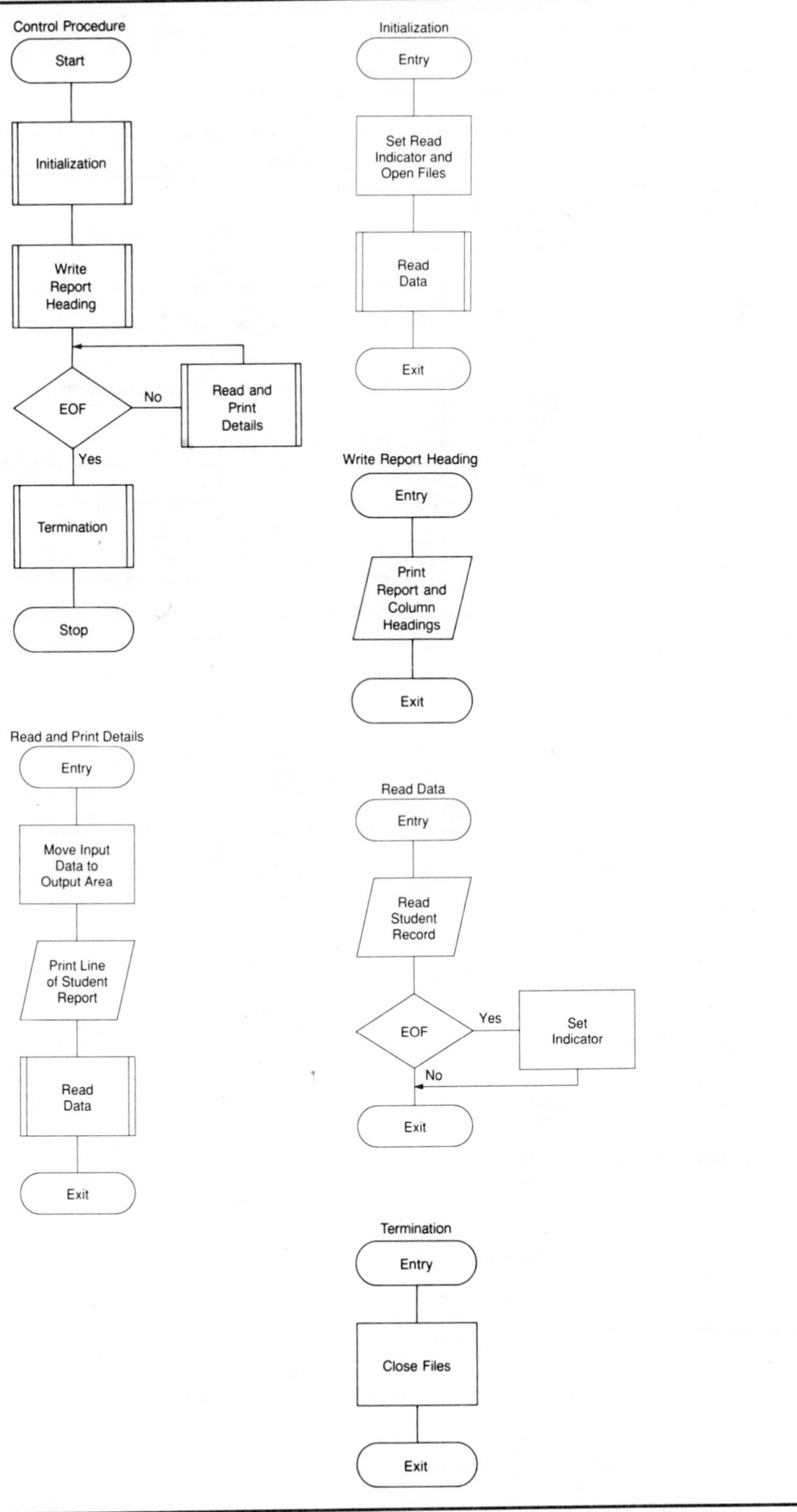

Figure 2.9 Student List Program (Structured Alternative)

```
           1   1   2   2   2   3   3   4   4   4   5   5   6   6   6   7
   4   8   2   6   0   4   8   2   6   0   4   8   2   6   0   4   8   2
*************************************************************
 IDENTIFICATION DIVISION.
*************************************************************
 PROGRAM-ID.     STUDENT-LIST.
 AUTHOR.        J. WAYNE SPENCE.
 DATE-WRITTEN.  JANUARY 1, 1989.
 DATE-COMPILED. JANUARY 1, 1989.
*    This program illustrates the structured form of a
*    COBOL program where the primary procedure level in the
*    PROCEDURE DIVISION is at the SECTION level.
*************************************************************
 ENVIRONMENT DIVISION.
*************************************************************
*-----------------------------------------------------------*
 CONFIGURATION SECTION.
*-----------------------------------------------------------*
 SOURCE-COMPUTER. IBM.
 OBJECT-COMPUTER. IBM.
 SPECIAL-NAMES.   C01 IS TOP-OF-NEXT-PAGE.
*-----------------------------------------------------------*
 INPUT-OUTPUT SECTION.
*-----------------------------------------------------------*
 FILE-CONTROL.
     SELECT STUDENT-FILE   ASSIGN TO UT-S-INPUT.
     SELECT STUDENT-REPORT ASSIGN TO UT-S-OUTPUT.
*************************************************************
 DATA DIVISION.
*************************************************************
*-----------------------------------------------------------*
 FILE SECTION.
*-----------------------------------------------------------*
 FD  STUDENT-FILE LABEL RECORDS ARE OMITTED.
 01  DUMMY-RECORD                    PIC X(80).

 FD  STUDENT-REPORT LABEL RECORDS ARE OMITTED.
 01  REPORT-LINE                     PIC X(133).
*-----------------------------------------------------------*
 WORKING-STORAGE SECTION.
*-----------------------------------------------------------*
 01  WORKING-RECORD.
     04  FILE-STATUS                 PIC X(05).

 01  STUDENT-RECORD.
     05 STUDENT-IDENTIFICATION.
        10 LAST-NAME-IN             PIC X(10).
        10 FIRST-NAME-IN            PIC X(10).
        10 MIDDLE-INITIAL-IN        PIC X(01).
        10 STUDENT-ID-IN            PIC 9(09).
     05 FILLER                       PIC X(05).
     05 ENROLLMENT-INFO.
        10 CLASSIFICATION-IN        PIC X(02).
        10 TOTAL-HOURS-IN           PIC 9(03).
        10 HOURS-THIS-SEM-IN        PIC 9(02).
        10 MAJOR-IN                 PIC X(03).

 01  REPORT-HEADING.
     05 FILLER                       PIC X(29) VALUE SPACES.
     05 FILLER                       PIC X(21) VALUE
     'Semester Student List'.

 01  SEPARATOR-LINE.
     05 FILLER                       PIC X(01)  VALUE SPACE.
     05 FILLER                       PIC X(79)  VALUE ALL '-'.

 01  COLUMN-HEADING-1.
     05 FILLER                       PIC X(01) VALUE SPACE.
     05 FILLER                       PIC X(79) VALUE '|       Student
-    'Name        | Student ID. | Class | Major |  Current    | Tota
-    'l |'.
```

Figure 2.9 *Continued* Student Lift Program (Structured Alternative)

```
          1   1   2   2   2   3   3   4   4   4   5   5   6   6   6   7
   4   8  2   6   0   4   8   2   6   0   4   8   2   6   0   4   8   2

        01  COLUMN-HEADING-2.
            05 FILLER                   PIC X(28) VALUE ' |'.
            05 FILLER                   PIC X(14) VALUE '|    Number'.
            05 FILLER                   PIC X(08) VALUE '|'.
            05 FILLER                   PIC X(08) VALUE '|'.
            05 FILLER                   PIC X(22) VALUE '| Enrollment | H
        -   'ours |'.

        01  OUTPUT-RECORD.
            05 FILLER               PIC X(03) VALUE ' |'.
            05 FIRST-NAME-OUT       PIC X(11).
            05 MIDDLE-INITIAL-OUT   PIC X(01).
            05 FILLER               PIC X(02) VALUE '.'.
            05 LAST-NAME-OUT        PIC X(10).
            05 FILLER               PIC X(04) VALUE ' |'.
            05 STUDENT-ID-OUT       PIC 9(09).
            05 FILLER               PIC X(05) VALUE '  |'.
            05 CLASSIFICATION-OUT   PIC X(02).
            05 FILLER               PIC X(06) VALUE '   |'.
            05 MAJOR-OUT            PIC X(03).
            05 FILLER               PIC X(08) VALUE '  |'.
            05 HOURS-THIS-SEM-OUT   PIC 9(02).
            05 FILLER               PIC X(08) VALUE '    |'.
            05 TOTAL-HOURS-OUT      PIC 9(03).
            05 FILLER               PIC X(03) VALUE '  |'.
       ************************************************************
        PROCEDURE DIVISION.
       ************************************************************
       *----------------------------------------------------------*
        000-CONTROL-PROCEDURE SECTION.
       *----------------------------------------------------------*
            PERFORM 100-INITIALIZATION.
            PERFORM 200-WRITE-REPORT-HEADING.
            PERFORM 300-READ-AND-PRINT-DETAILS
                UNTIL FILE-STATUS = 'DONE'.
            PERFORM 400-TERMINATION.
            STOP RUN.
       *----------------------------------------------------------*
        100-INITIALIZATION SECTION.
       *----------------------------------------------------------*
            MOVE 'START' TO FILE-STATUS.
            OPEN INPUT STUDENT-FILE, OUTPUT STUDENT-REPORT.
            PERFORM 310-READ-DATA SECTION.
       *----------------------------------------------------------*
        200-WRITE-REPORT-HEADING SECTION.
       *----------------------------------------------------------*
            WRITE REPORT-LINE FROM REPORT-HEADING AFTER
                TOP-OF-NEXT-PAGE.
            WRITE REPORT-LINE FROM SEPARATOR-LINE AFTER 2 LINES.
            WRITE REPORT-LINE FROM COLUMN-HEADING-1 AFTER 1.
            WRITE REPORT-LINE FROM COLUMN-HEADING-2 AFTER 1.
            WRITE REPORT-LINE FROM SEPARATOR-LINE AFTER 1.
       *----------------------------------------------------------*
        300-READ-AND-PRINT-DETAILS SECTION.
       *----------------------------------------------------------*
        300-ENTRY.
            MOVE STUDENT-ID-IN         TO STUDENT-ID-OUT.
            MOVE LAST-NAME-IN          TO LAST-NAME-OUT.
            MOVE FIRST-NAME-IN         TO FIRST-NAME-OUT.
            MOVE MIDDLE-INITIAL-IN     TO MIDDLE-INITIAL-OUT.
            MOVE CLASSIFICATION-IN     TO CLASSIFICATION-OUT.
            MOVE TOTAL-HOURS-IN        TO TOTAL-HOURS-OUT.
            MOVE HOURS-THIS-SEM-IN     TO HOURS-THIS-SEM-OUT.
            MOVE MAJOR-IN              TO MAJOR-OUT.
            WRITE REPORT-LINE FROM OUTPUT-RECORD AFTER 2 LINES.
            PERFORM 310-READ-DATA SECTION.
```

Figure 2.9 *Continued* Student List Program (Structured Alternative)

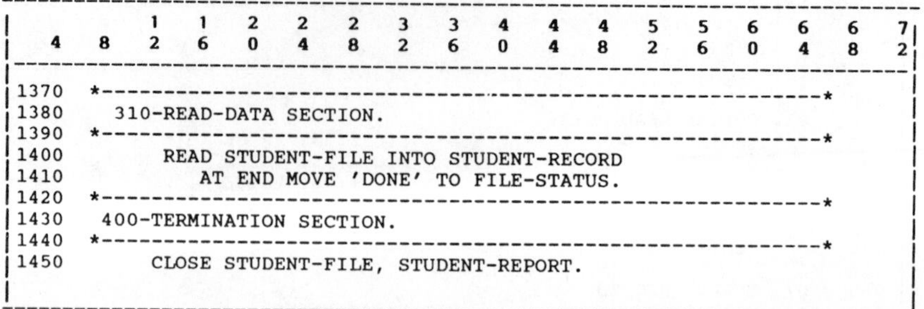

```
      *-----------------------------------------------------------*
       310-READ-DATA SECTION.
      *-----------------------------------------------------------*
           READ STUDENT-FILE INTO STUDENT-RECORD
               AT END MOVE 'DONE' TO FILE-STATUS.
      *-----------------------------------------------------------*
       400-TERMINATION SECTION.
      *-----------------------------------------------------------*
           CLOSE STUDENT-FILE, STUDENT-REPORT.
```

the READ AND PRINT DETAILS module. In Figure 2.9 this module PERFORMs READ DATA, the input operation. Thus there is only one READ instruction for the STUDENT-FILE. After the data are moved to the output area and written to the line printer, the data are read and the entire procedure is repeated. The sequence of events is then ''move-write-read.'' This process continues until an end-of-file condition is detected. When this occurs, the indicator is set and process is terminated by the UNTIL phrase in the PERFORM 300-READ-AND-PRINT-DETAILS statement.

Although some programmers have very strong feelings about the use of SECTION structure it can make programming simpler. You should check with your instructor to determine which style is preferred. If you are planning to write computer programs for a commercial installation, you should check the programming standards for the installation to determine the appropriate style for writing COBOL programs. Since the style preferred by your instructor may differ from the style used by the commercial installation by which you may later be employed, both styles demonstrated in this chapter will be utilized in the remainder of the text. I believe that you should be familiar and comfortable with both!

Pseudocode

Program flowcharting as a technique for designing and documenting programs has been around for over 40 years. Structured programming as a common practice is less than half that old. As a result, many of the rules that had been developed for flowcharting had to be changed to handle the concepts of structured program design. Because these changes made flowcharts difficult to use when planning a program, another method was needed to represent the logical flow through a structured program. *Pseudocode* was specifically designed to perform this function.

Pseudocode is the technique for planning a program by expressing a program's logic in terms of English-like phrases. While there are very few set rules for the use of pseudocode there are some guidelines that must be followed for the tool to be useful. Pseudocode is read from the top to bottom with indentations (much like an outline) used to represent the *superior-subordinate relationship* of actions to be taken in the program. Each line of pseudocode should begin with an action, indicated by a verb, followed by a description of the action. Finally, the beginning and end of a logical (control) structure must be clearly labeled. In addition to these guidelines, pseudocode should not list *all* of the details in a program, and should be language free.

There are several advantages to using pseudocode to plan a program. Beyond the advantages already presented for flowcharting, pseudocode is faster and easier to work

Figure 2.10 Three Forms Used in Structured Programming (Pseudocode)

```
SEQUENCE STURCTURE        IF-THEN-ELSE              DO-WHILE (UNTIL)

START                     START                     START
     Process 1                 IF Condition              DO Action UNTIL Condition
     Process 2                      Process 1                  Process 1
     Process 3                 ELSE                            IF Condition
END                                 Process 2                       Process 2
                               ENDIF                           ENDIF
                          END                             ENDDO
                                                    END
```

with. This further reduces the time needed to plan and develop a program. In addition because pseudocode is so free of formal rules, the English used can closely resemble the structure and syntax of the language in which the program is to be written. Thus, the process of converting from pseudocode to the final program is much faster than converting from a flowchart.

The ability to write pseudocode that uses the structure and syntax of the programming language to be used for the program is also a major disadvantage. Often programmers will write pseudocode that is more detailed and longer than the actual program. This misuse of pseudocode can result in increased cost and time required to develop programs.

Since pseudocode was developed as a tool for structured programming it supports and encourages a standardized style, which facilitates maintenance and modification. This standardized style uses the same three basic logic or control structures to module design that were explained earlier in this chapter: the *sequence,* the *if-then-else,* and the *do-while (until).*

Each of the three structures, shown in Figure 2.10, is supported by COBOL. The sequence structure is a series of process (or input/output) operations that are executed sequentially from the first statement to the last. The if-then-else structure is used to execute a series of process operations *depending on the tested relationship.* The do-while (until) structure is used to control a looping operation, *the repetitive execution of a series of statements.*

The use of these structures can easily be seen in Figure 2.11. This is the pseudocode for the Student List program shown in Figure 2.9. Notice that these structures all use indentation to show the superior-subordinate relationships and that each line of pseudocode begins with an action verb. Unfortunately, as can be seen from Figure 2.11, pseudocode suffers from at least one of the same problems as flowcharting. The more complex a program becomes, the more difficult it is to place all of the pseudocode on a single sheet of paper in an easily readable form. One solution to this problem is to decompose the pseudocode into modules in much the same manner as the flowchart in Figure 2.8 was divided. This division, shown in Figure 2.12, is easy to read and contains all of the information needed to create a program. The module pseudocode also has the advantage of not repeating the READ DATA module each time it is to be executed.

The Hierarchy Chart

Figure 2.13 illustrates a structured version of the student list procedure in Figure 2.9. A *hierarchy chart* (sometimes called a *Visual Table of Contents*—VTOC) is used to get a grasp of the overall logic of the problem while identifying the major modules of the program. The hierarchy chart shows a *logic tree* of a process. That is, the blocks of the chart indicate the logical relationships between operations and the sequence in which

Figure 2.11 Student List Program (Pseudocode)

```
START
    DO initialization
        SET file indicator
        OPEN files
        DO read data
            READ next record
            IF end of file
                SET indicator
            ENDIF
        ENDDO
    DO write and report heading
        PRINT page heading
    DO read and print details UNTIL end of file
        MOVE input data to output data
        PRINT details
        DO read data
            READ next record
            IF end of file
                SET indicator
            ENDIF
        ENDDO
    DO termination
        CLOSE files
    ENDDO
END
```

the operations are to be executed. Normally, the tree is "executed" from top to bottom, traversing each branch of the tree from left to right. Tracing the hierarchy chart of the student list procedure produces the sequence in Table 2.1.

Note that when a module is being "continued," rather than "started," the completion of the routine will cause control to be returned to the module that originally "called" it. Thus, when the CONTROL PROCEDURE module invokes the INITIALIZATION module (Step 2), the sequence will ultimately return to the MAIN CONTROL module when the INITIALIZATION module has been completed (Step 5).

Again look at Figure 2.13, and notice the series of numbers recorded at the upper right-hand corner of each block. This numbering system is used to provide an understanding of the *superior-subordinate relationship* between modules. Each identifying

Figure 2.12 Student List Program (A Pseudocode Alternative)

```
START
    DO initialization
    DO write report heading
    DO read and print details
        UNTIL end of file
    DO termination
END

INITIALIZATION
    SET file indicator
    OPEN files
    DO read data
END

WRITE REPORT HEADING
    PRINT headings
END

READ AND PRINT DETAILS
    MOVE input data to output data
    PRINT detail line
    DO read data
END

READ DATA
    READ next record
    IF end of file
        SET indicator
    ENDIF
END

TERMINATION
    CLOSE files
END
```

Figure 2.13 Student List Program (Hierarchy Chart)

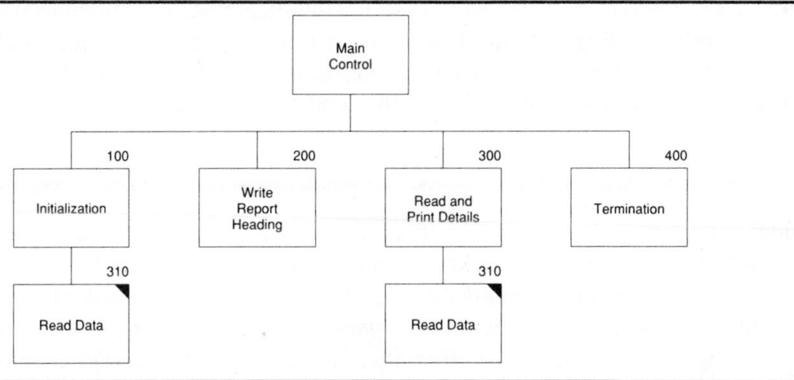

number is composed of three digits (although four- and five-digit numbers could be used on more complex problems). The first module (CONTROL PROCEDURE) should be unnumbered or numbered "000." One level below the PROCEDURE CONTROL module, all "hundred" series modules are recorded. The numbers are not necessarily consecutive to permit later addition of other modules. All remaining numbers in the hierarchy chart should be from the same series as those at the first level. For example, all blocks subordinate to READ AND PRINT DETAILS (300) should be from the 300 series—320, 340, and 360, and so on. Thus, not only is each block uniquely identified by name and number, but the numbering system helps to determine the relationships between modules and the order in which the modules should appear in the PROCEDURE DIVISION. Although other numbering systems may be used in the hierarchy chart, the numbering system presented is both meaningful and concise. Its biggest limitation is that it permits only nine (1–9) different modules to be subordinated to a single superior module.

Table 2.1 Sequence of Events in the Student List Program Hierarchy Chart

Step	Module Number	Start/Continue*	Called From/Return to
1	—	MAIN CONTROL (S)	
2	100	INITIALIZATION (S)	MAIN CONTROL
3	310	READ-DATA (S)	INITIALIZATION
4	100	INITIALIZATION (C)	—
5	—	MAIN CONTROL (C)	—
6	200	WRITE REPORT HEADING (S)	MAIN CONTROL
7	—	MAIN CONTROL (C)	—
8	300	READ AND PRINT DETAILS (S)	MAIN CONTROL
9	310	READ DATA (S)	READ AND PRINT DETAILS
10	300	READ AND PRINT DETAILS (C)	—
11	—	MAIN CONTROL (C)	
12	400	TERMINATION (S)	—
13	–	MAIN CONTROL (C) - STOP	MAIN CONTROL

*S = start processing module
C = continue processing module.

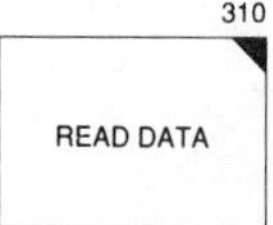

As with all procedures, there are exceptions to the rules. In the hierarchy chart in Figure 2.13, module 310 (READ DATA) is duplicated under modules 100 and 300. Because module 310 is not unique to a single branch of the logic tree, it is a *utility* or *service* module. For purposes of visual clarity, utility modules are often drawn with a shaded upper right-hand corner. Thus, the module might appear as shown here.

The Case Structure

Besides the three fundamental structures already discussed, one additional structure—the *case*—is often added to make it easier to represent and code a certain class of problems. In some situations a decision is to be made on the basis of a known set of alternatives. This set is referred to as a *mutually exclusive, collectively exhaustive set.* By choosing one alternative, all other alternatives are excluded. Furthermore, a list of all the alternatives in the set would contain all possibilities.

With the case structure, after the appropriate alternative has been selected, one and only one process is executed. Figure 2.14 illustrates the case structure.

The first mechanism in the case structure performs switching operations. One such mechanism is provided in COBOL through the GO TO/DEPENDING ON statement and the EVALUATE statement in COBOL 85 (See Chapter 21). Thus, depending upon the data provided to the selection mechanism, one (and only one) of the processes is performed. After the process is performed, the structure is complete.

Figure 2.15 illustrates how the case structure might be used in a structured flowchart. Again, using the student list procedure, suppose we wanted to know the number of undergraduate and the number of graduate students in the list. The case structure would permit the selection of one of the categories followed by the appropriate process (in this case, a summation).

Approaches to Procedure Design

Now that you have seen examples of structured flowcharting and pseudocode, you are probably wondering how to begin the design of the diagrams. There are several recommended approaches to structured-program design. The most popular one is the *top-down* approach. A flowchart and pseudocode designed from the top down begins with the major aspects of the problem and progresses to the level of least importance. In

Figure 2.14 The Case Structure

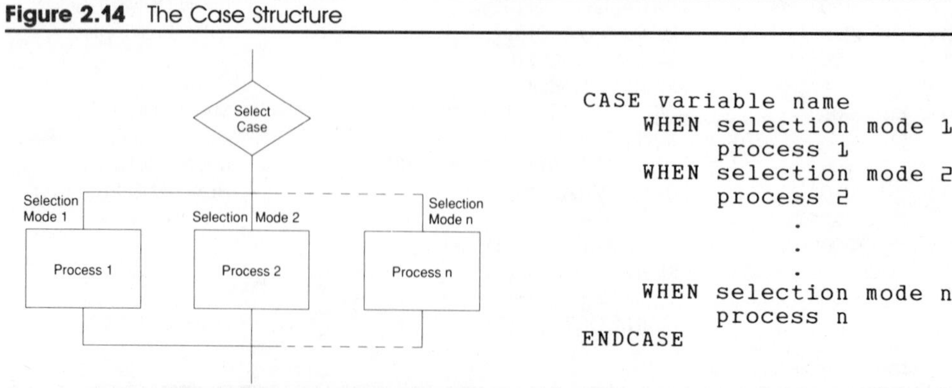


```
CASE variable name
    WHEN selection mode 1
         process 1
    WHEN selection mode 2
         process 2
              .
              .
              .
    WHEN selection mode n
         process n
ENDCASE
```

Figure 2.15 An Illustration of the Case Structure (Class Count)

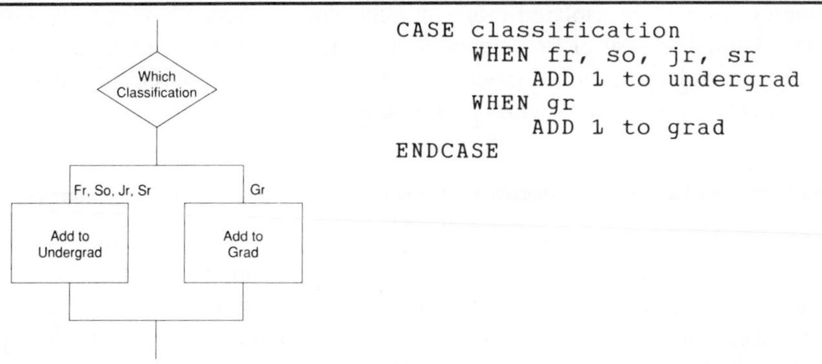


```
CASE classification
     WHEN fr, so, jr, sr
          ADD 1 to undergrad
     WHEN gr
          ADD 1 to grad
ENDCASE
```

Figure 2.9, for example, this would mean that the CONTROL PROCEDURE routine is designed first. The INITIAL modules would be designed next, and so on.

Other alternatives are the *bottom-up* approach and the *critical-event* approach. The bottom-up approach is simply a reversal of the top-down method. The critical-event approach begins with the most important module, regardless of its level. Work then begins on superior and subordinate routines, which either drive or service the critical-event routine. For example, in Figure 2.9 the routine may be viewed as the most important. The subordinate modules that service this routine are identified when the module is complete. The final module to be designed might be the routine that determines when the module is to be executed.

Regardless of which alternative is selected to begin the design of procedures, the guidelines of structured program development should be followed. The result will be easily implemented, maintainable, and clear programs.

Summary

As program development has become more costly, tools and techniques have been developed that aid the programmer in program development. The program-development cycle generally includes at least three distinct (but perhaps overlapping) phases—analysis, implementation, and modification and maintenance. During the analysis phase, both program flowcharting and structured programming have been used as planning and cost-reduction tools.

Program flowcharting and pseudocode are means of representing the logic of a problem in a block diagram form which includes blocks or symbols, notations, and flowlines or in pseudocode. The intent of the flowchart or pseudocode is to demonstrate the operation to be performed and the interrelationships between operations. Flowcharts and pseudocodes have many advantages, including the capability for the programmer to trace his or her logic through the diagram, the conservation of programmer time, and enhanced documentation.

The discipline of structured programming is enforced through three fundamental program structures: (a) simple sequence, (b) if-then-else, and (c) do-while. The do-while structure is translated into a do-until in COBOL (COBOL 85 has implemented a do-while structure). These three structures may be augmented by the case structure when the program involves a ''select one from a set'' situation.

The structured approach also provides several advantages, including the division of the procedure into small concise subproblems; functional orientation of modules; and the ability to easily divide programming among several programmers. Also, execution and logic errors may be isolated more quickly, and the procedure may be coded and tested in stages. For ease of implementation, hierarchy charts are available to provide the overall interrelationships of modules, and program flowcharts are redesigned into module flowcharts with single entry and exit points.

Notes on Programming Style

Beyond raw intelligence, three factors seem to play a role in learning how to write programs. The first factor is experience—on-the-job training. Learning from mistakes is admittedly painful at times and time-consuming, but individuals rarely make the same mistake twice, and a certain amount of knowledge gained in the solution to one problem can be directly applied to the next problem, and so on.

The second factor is planning. ''Playing computer'' (tracing the process step by step as the computer will do when it executes your solution) to determine strengths and weaknesses, even before committing to code, is a good method of planning a solution. Do not measure your progress toward solving a problem in lines of COBOL code, but rather, in finding solutions to elements of the overall problem. Determine the shortcomings and pitfalls of each element of your solution and plan contingencies for each.

It is often said that ''he who codes last, codes best.'' So planning has an additional advantage—it helps you avoid a vested interest in work performed. Unfortunately, it is human nature to avoid scrapping a product in which a great deal of time (or money) is invested. When we spend a lot of time writing a computer program and later realize that our solution is not viable, we often attempt to ''patch'' it. Unfortunately, the more we patch a program, the less manageable it becomes. And, as we continue, it becomes increasingly harder to give up and try a new angle. Appropriate planning should help you avoid ever approaching this stage.

The third factor is closely related to planning. It is in essence a planning methodology called *recursive decomposition* or *stepwise refinement*. Recursive decomposition consists of breaking larger (perhaps more poorly defined) problems into smaller, more clearly defined subproblems. One decomposing pass is made on each subproblem until each subproblem is clearly understood.

When viewed from the programming perspective, the process is referred to as stepwise refinement. That is, a partial solution to the problem is devised, providing the basic structure for the ultimate solution. After the first partial solution has been implemented and tested, a new element is added to solve an additional aspect of the problem. The process continues one step at a time until all aspects of the problem have been incorporated into the solution.

Questions

Below, fill in the blank(s) with the appropriate word, words, or phrases.

1. The program development phase in which the procedure requirements are determined is called the ____ phase.

2. The process of transforming a planned approach to a problem into program code is called ____ .

3. Program errors are called ____ .

4. The implementation step in which the programmer determines whether or not his program will work is called _____ .

5. A(n) _____ is a technique for expressing the logic of a program in a block diagram form.

6. Flowcharting a problem has many advantages including (a) _____ , (b) _____ , and (c) _____ .

7. When flowlines on a flowchart go from top to bottom or from left to right, _____ are generally omitted.

8. One of the advantages of _____ is that the programmer does not have to ''solve'' a problem in one step.

9. In a structured flowchart, a module should be _____ oriented.

10. Each module should have _____ entry and exit point(s).

11. The three basic structures used to design modules are (a) _____ , (b) _____ , and (c) _____ .

12. A(n) _____ is simply a representation in a procedure that will exist but has not yet been coded.

13. Among the advantages of structured programming are (a) _____ , (b) _____ , and (c) _____ .

14. A sequence structure describes processes that are in _____ form to be executed one after the other.

15. Decisions made in either a(n) _____ or a(n) _____ form suffer some type of limitation when compared to simple decision logic using independent tests.

16. A do-while structure repeats a process so long as a specified condition is _____ , whereas the do-until structure repeats the process so long as the condition is _____ .

17. A program variable used to control looping operations is often called a(n) _____ .

18. An overview of a procedure in logic-tree form is called a(n) _____ .

19. When a control module invokes (calls) an initialization module, execution resumes with the _____ module when the initialization module has been completed.

20. A subordinate module invoked by two or more superior modules is often referred to as a(n) _____ module.

21. Superior-subordinate relationship are shown by _____ in pseudocode.

22. A(n) _____ should be used to start a line of pseudocode.

23. The structure indicating that one of a series of choices is to be selected is called the _____ structure.

Answer the following questions by circling either ''T'' for true or ''F'' for false.

T F **24.** In most computer installations the cost of hardware exceeds the expenditure on software.

T F **25.** Programs generally ''work'' the first time they are executed.

T F **26.** A program flowchart is a tool used by a programmer to plan a program.

T F **27.** Each block of a flowchart should contain a single program statement such as a MOVE statement.

T F **28.** In a flowchart, a MOVE operation is normally represented by a parallelogram symbol.

T F **29.** Structured flowcharts are oriented toward modules.

T F **30.** A module should encompass as many functions as possible.

T F **31.** Each module should have a specific beginning point, although multiple ending points are desirable.

T F 32. The intent of the do-while structure is to test conditions.

T F 33. The overall logic of a structured program may be gained from a control module.

T F 34. A hierarchy chart is not used to show relationships between modules, but rather, the functional elements of each module.

T F 35. Flowlines of a flowchart indicate the interrelationships between blocks.

T F 36. The logical flow of pseudocode is from left to right.

T F 37. Development of a program in a structured form from the highest-level to the lowest-level modules is called the _____ approach.

CHAPTER

3

COBOL: A Matter of Form

The COBOL programming language is one of the most structured programming languages in general use today. Initially, the programmer may think some of the structure of COBOL is unnecessary especially if he or she had been exposed to other programming languages. However, as the programmer becomes familiar with the structure of COBOL, he or she will begin to understand the principles behind this structure.

Overall Organization of COBOL

COBOL is organized much like a book. A book is broken into major segments called chapters. COBOL's major segments are called *divisions*. Some chapters in books have subparts that might be called sections. Likewise, most of the COBOL divisions have subparts called *sections*. Within major sections of a book, one also finds paragraphs. Similarly, each section of a COBOL program may have a *paragraph* or a similar division. Paragraphs in books, generally comprise one or more sentences. Paragraphs in a COBOL program also comprise *sentences* (or *entries*). Finally, a sentence in a book might have one or more statements. In a COBOL program, a sentence also has one or more *statements* (and an entry is represented by one or more *clauses*).

A COBOL program is always composed of four divisions—IDENTIFICATION, ENVIRONMENT, DATA, and PROCEDURE. The divisions always appear in this order. The IDENTIFICATION, ENVIRONMENT, and DATA DIVISIONS are composed of sections, paragraphs, entries, and clauses (except for the IDENTIFICATION DIVISION, which has no sections). This is the hierarchy (from highest level to lowest) of these three divisions. The PROCEDURE DIVISION hierarchy consists of sections, paragraphs, sentences, and statements.

Each division is responsible for a specific function within a COBOL program. The IDENTIFICATION DIVISION (shown as lines 20 through 90 in Figure 3.1) identifies the program. It gives the program a name and other basic information. The ENVIRONMENT DIVISION (lines 110 through 240 in Figure 3.1) is *responsible* for identifying the type of computers used to compile and execute the program (the CONFIGURATION SECTION) and the types of equipment used to provide data and

Figure 3.1 A Sample COBOL Program

```
                 1   1   2   2   2   3   3   4   4   4   5   5   6   6   6   7
    4   8   2   6   0   4   8   2   6   0   4   8   2   6   0   4   8   2
      ******************************************************************
       IDENTIFICATION DIVISION.
      ******************************************************************
       PROGRAM-ID.        SAMPLE-PROGRAM.
       AUTHOR.            J. WAYNE SPENCE.
       DATE-WRITTEN.      JANUARY 1, 1989.
       DATE-COMPILED.     JANUARY 1, 1989.
      *    The purpose of this program is to demonstrate the parts
      *    of a COBOL program.
      ******************************************************************
       ENVIRONMENT DIVISION.
      ******************************************************************
      *----------------------------------------------------------------*
       CONFIGURATION SECTION.
      *----------------------------------------------------------------*
       SOURCE-COMPUTER.  IBM.
       OBJECT-COMPUTER.  IBM.
       SPECIAL-NAMES.    C01 IS TOP-OF-PAGE.
      *----------------------------------------------------------------*
       INPUT-OUTPUT SECTION.
      *----------------------------------------------------------------*
       FILE-CONTROL.
           SELECT STUDENT-FILE   ASSIGN TO UT-S-INPUT.
           SELECT STUDENT-REPORT ASSIGN TO UT-S-OUTPUT.
      ******************************************************************
       DATA DIVISION.
      ******************************************************************
      *----------------------------------------------------------------*
       FILE SECTION.
      *----------------------------------------------------------------*
       FD      STUDENT-FILE  LABEL RECORDS ARE OMITTED.
       01      STUDENT-RECORD.
               05  STUDENT-IDENTIFIICATION.
                   10  STUDENT-ID-IN         PIC 9(09).
                   10  LAST-NAME-IN          PIC X(10).
                   10  FIRST-NAME-IN         PIC X(10).
                   10  MIDDLE-INITIAL-IN     PIC X(01).
                   10  SEX-IN                PIC 9(01).
               05  ENROLLMENT-INFO.
                   10  MAJOR-IN              PIC X(03).
                   10  CLASS-IN              PIC 9(01).
                   10  PREVIOUS-HOURS-IN     PIC 9(03).
                   10  HOURS-THIS-SEM-IN     PIC 9(02).

       FD      STUDENT-REPORT  LABEL RECORDS ARE OMITTED.
       01      OUTPUT-RECORD                 PIC X(133).
      *----------------------------------------------------------------*
       WORKING-STORAGE SECTION.
      *----------------------------------------------------------------*
       01      WORKING-VARIABLES.
               05  FILE-STATUS               PIC X(05) VALUE 'START'.

       01      DETAIL-RECORD-OUT.
               05  FIRST-NAME-OUT            PIC X(11).
               05  MIDDLE-INITIAL-OUT        PIC X(02).
               05  LAST-NAME-OUT             PIC X(10).
               05  FILLER                    PIC X(05) VALUE SPACES.
               05  STUDENT-ID-OUT            PIC 9(09).
               05  FILLER                    PIC X(05) VALUE SPACES.
               05  SEX-OUT                   PIC X(06).
               05  FILLER                    PIC X(05) VALUE SPACES.
               05  CLASS-OUT                 PIC X(10).
               05  FILLER                    PIC X(05) VALUE SPACES.
               05  MAJOR-OUT                 PIC X(03).
               05  FILLER                    PIC X(05) VALUE SPACES.
               05  TOTAL-HOURS-OUT           PIC Z(03).
      ******************************************************************
       PROCEDURE DIVISION.
      ******************************************************************
```

Figure 3.1 *Continued* A Sample COBOL Program

```
          1   1   2   2   2   3   3   4   4   4   5   5   6   6   6   7
  4   8   2   6   0   4   8   2   6   0   4   8   2   6   0   4   8   2

 700    000-CONTROL-LOGIC.
                PERFORM 100-START-UP.
 710            PERFORM 200-READ-AND-PRINT
 720
 730                UNTIL FILE-STATUS = 'DONE'.
 740            PERFORM 300-END-OF-JOB.
 750            STOP RUN.
 760
 770    100-START-UP.
 780            OPEN INPUT STUDENT-FILE, OUTPUT STUDENT-REPORT.
 790            MOVE 'Student Records list' TO OUTPUT-RECORD.
 800            WRITE OUTPUT-RECORD AFTER ADVANCING TOP-OF-PAGE.
 810            MOVE SPACES TO OUTPUT-RECORD.
 820            WIRTE OUTPUT-RECORD AFTER ADVANCING 2 LINES.
 830            READ STUDENT-FILE
 840                AT END MOVE 'DONE' TO FILE-STATUS.
 850
 860    200-READ-AND-PRINT.
 870            MOVE STUDENT-ID-IN TO STUDENT-ID-OUT.
 880            MOVE LAST-NAME-IN TO LAST-NAME-OUT.
 890            MOVE FIRST-NAME-IN TO FIRST-NAME-OUT.
 900            MOVE MIDDLE-INITIAL-IN TO MIDDLE-INITIAL-OUT.
 910            MOVE MAJOR-IN TO MAJOR-OUT.
 920            IF SEX-IN = 1
 930                MOVE 'Male' TO SEX-OUT
 940            ELSE
 950                MOVE 'Female' TO SEX-OUT.
 960            PERFORM 250-DETERMINE-CLASS.
 970            ADD PREVIOUS-HOURS-IN, HOURS-THIS-SEM-IN
 980                GIVING TOTAL-HOURS-OUT.
 990            WRITE OUTPUT-RECORD FROM DETAIL-RECORD-OUT
1000                AFTER ADVANCING 1 LINES.
1010            READ STUDENT-FILE
1020                AT END MOVE 'DONE' TO FILE-STATUS.
1030
1040    250-DETERMINE-CLASS.
1050            IF CLASS-IN = 1
1060                MOVE 'Freshman' TO CLASS-OUT.
1070            IF CLASS-IN = 2
1080                MOVE 'Sophmore' TO CLASS-OUT.
1090            IF CLASS-IN = 3
1100                MOVE 'Junior' TO CLASS-OUT.
1110            IF CLASS-IN = 4
1120                MOVE 'Senior' TO CLASS-OUT.
1130            IF CLASS-IN = 5
1140                MOVE 'Graduate' TO CLASS-OUT.
1150
1160    300-END-OF-JOB.
1170            MOVE 'End of Student Records List' TO OUTPUT-RECORD.
1180            WRITE OUTPUT-RECORD AFTER ADVANCING 2 LINES.
1190            CLOSE STUDENT-FILE, STUDENT-REPORT.


Legend:   Divisions  -- Boldface and Underline
          Sections    -- Boldface
          Paragraphs  -- Underline
          Entries or Sentences -- Italics
          Comments    -- None
```

accept output from the program (the INPUT-OUTPUT SECTION). The DATA DIVISION, the third major part, describes data items to be used in the program. It is generally one of the larger segments of a COBOL program (see lines 260 through 660 in Figure 3.1). The DATA DIVISION is generally composed of at least two sections. The FILE SECTION is used to describe the form in which data will be either input to the program or output from the program. The last major part of a COBOL program, the PROCEDURE

DIVISION (lines 680 through 1190 in Figure 3.1), provides the process to be performed (e.g., the records to be read, the data to be manipulated, the output to be written, etc.).

Figure 3.1 illustrates one approach to program design, the *structured approach,* which will be discussed in more detail in Chapter 2. In this program, comments have been added to assist you in locating the primary parts. In addition, the legend at the bottom of Figure 3.1 indicates which parts of this program are divisions, sections, paragraphs, entries, or sentences.

Developing and Using a Hierarchy Chart

Examine Figure 3.2—a hierarchy chart for the sample COBOL program. The chart provides a global overview of the structure of the PROCEDURE DIVISION. In figure 3.2, the *Control Logic* module (lines 700–750 of Figure 3.1) represents the beginning and end of the program. The Control Logic module initiates the execution of three subordinate modules—*Start Up* (lines 770–840), *Read and Print* (lines 860–1020), and *End of Job* (lines 1160–1190). Their order of execution is left-to-right from the Control Logic module to the Start Up module. When the Start Up module is completed, control returns to the Control Logic module, and so on until all of the subordinate modules have been executed.

The *Determine Class* (lines 1040–1140) module will be executed during the execution of the Read and Print module. After the Determine Class module has completed its execution, control returns to the Read and Print module (which subsequently returns control to the Control Logic module).

Developing and Using Module Flowcharts

Additional support for module relationships may be in the form of module flowcharts, as in Figure 3.3, or pseudocode, as in Figure 3.4.

The module flowcharts in Figure 3.3 represent a logic diagram for each process indicated in the hierarchy chart. For each process indicated in the hierarchy chart, a module flowchart should exist. The Control Logic module flowchart in Figure 3.3 is a combination of a simple sequence structure and a do-until structure. Notice the correspondence between the flowchart and PROCEDURE DIVISION statements of the sample

Figure 3.2 A Hierarchy Chart for the Sample Program

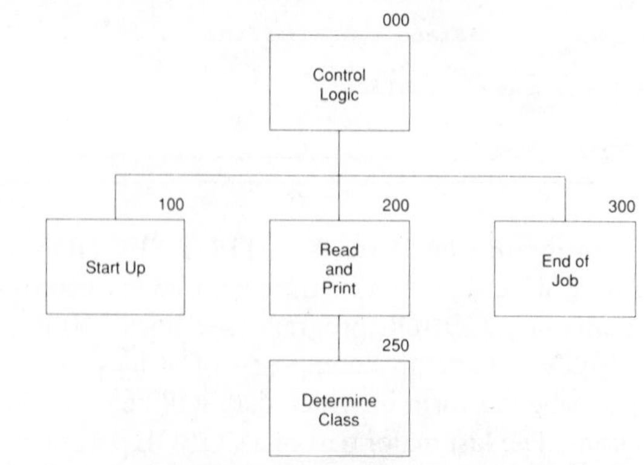

Figure 3.3 Module Flowcharts for the Sample Program

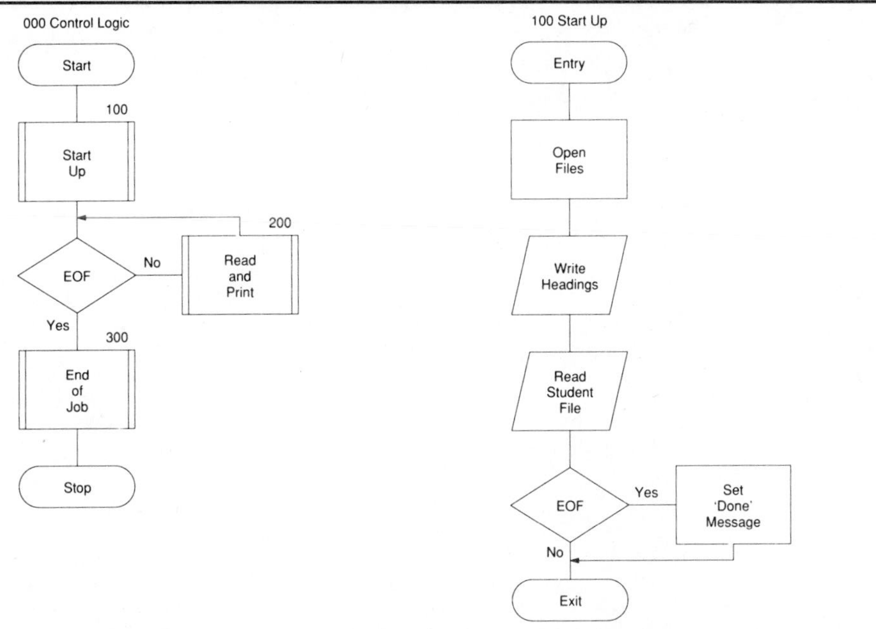

COBOL program. No corresponding COBOL statement for the Start terminal symbol exists in the Control Logic module (as well as Entry terminal symbols in the remaining module flowcharts); each block of the flowchart corresponds to a statement in the program. The Start Up module (a predefined process as a simple sequence) corresponds to line 170 of the program. The Read and Print predefined process is connected to an end-of-file decision and corresponds to lines 720 and 730. This combination of predefined process and decision is a do-until structure. Finally, the End of Job predefined process corresponds to line 740 and the Stop terminal symbol corresponds to line 750.

Now notice the correspondence between symbol type, program structure, and COBOL statement. Predefined processes are most frequently represented in COBOL programs by PERFORM statements. Predefined processes preceded by decisions creating a do-until structure are also represented by PERFORM statements, but with an attached UNTIL phrase. The Stop terminal symbol is represented by the STOP RUN statement in COBOL. (Sometimes the Exit terminal symbol, as shown in the other module flowcharts, is represented by an EXIT statement in COBOL).

The second module in the flowchart, Start Up, is responsible for procedure initialization operations. Start Up is first indicated in the Control Logic module in a format (predefined process) indicating that the details are located "elsewhere." The "elsewhere" is the module flowchart for Start Up. The predominant structure in the Start Up module flowchart, is a simple sequence (with a trailing decision). The block types used in the simple sequence include both process and input-output symbols, although still a simple sequence. Comparing this module flowchart with the sample COBOL program, the Entry terminal symbol is simply a beginning marker and does not correspond to a COBOL statement. However, the Open Files process corresponds to line 780, the Write Headings output operation corresponds to lines 790–820, and the Read Student File input operation corresponds to line 830. Thus, combinations of OPEN,

Figure 3.3 *Continued* Module Flowcharts for the Sample Program

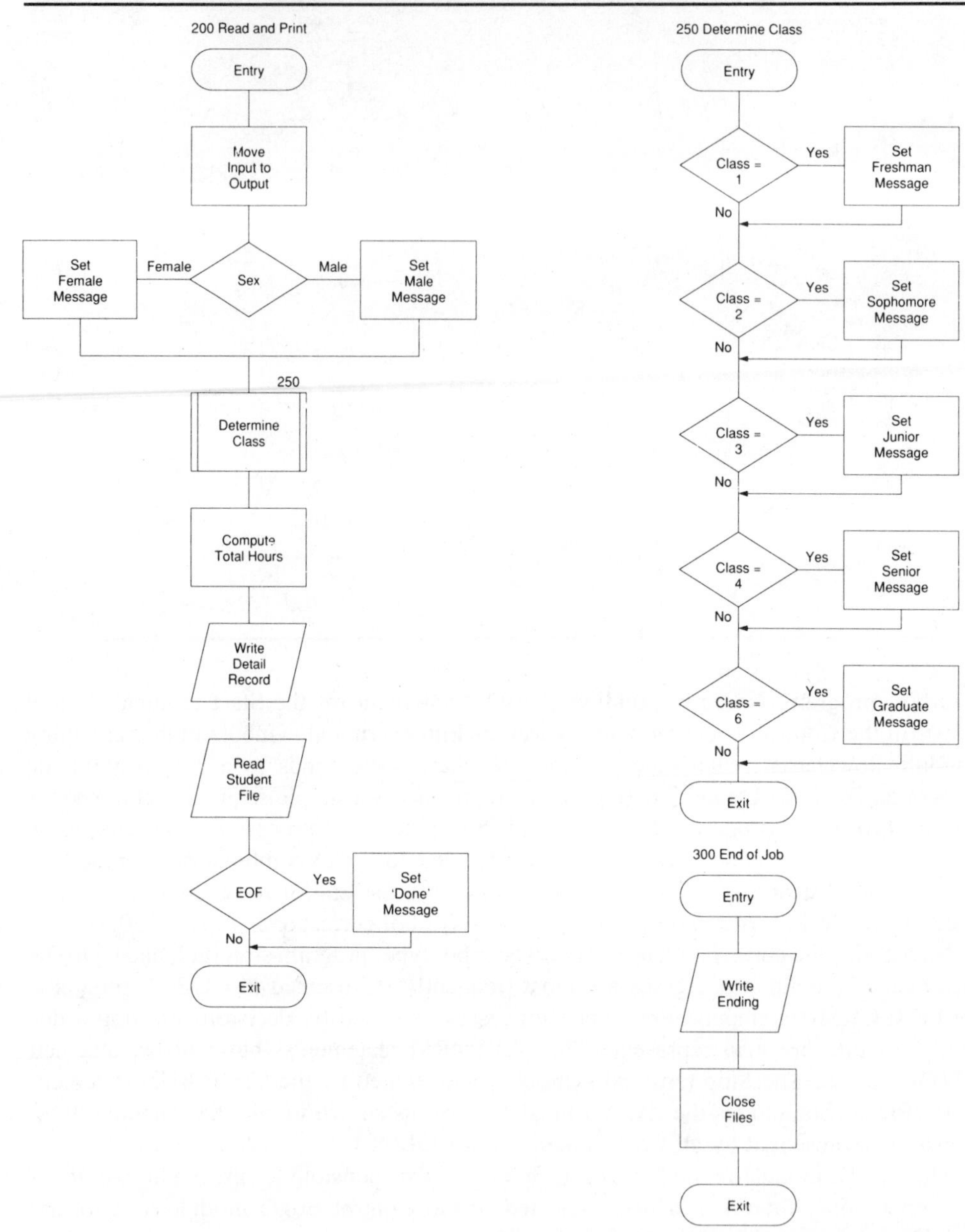

WRITE, and READ statements may comprise a simple sequence structure. The end-of-file decision that appears at the end of this module flowchart, like the end-of-file decision in the middle of the Control Logic flowchart, is not represented by an IF statement in the COBOL program. Rather, it is represented by a special phrase (AT END), which can be attached to a READ statement, as shown in line 840.

Read and Print module, linked to the Control Logic module through the do-until structure, represents the major activity that takes place during the procedure. The Read

Figure 3.4 Pseudocode for the Sample COBOL Program

```
DO start-up
     OPEN files
     PRINT page heading
     READ first record
DO read and print until end of file
     MOVE input data to output area
     IF male
          MOVE "male" to output area
     ELSE
          MOVE "female" to output area
     DO determine class
          WHEN class is freshman
               MOVE "freshman" to output area
          WHEN class is sophomore
               MOVE "sophomore" to output area
          WHEN class is junior
               MOVE "junior" to output area
          WHEN class is senior
               MOVE "senior" to output area
          WHEN class is graduate
               MOVE "graduate" to output area
     COMPUTE total hours
     PRINT results
     READ next record
     IF end of file
          EXIT DO
DO end-of-job
     PRINT footing
     CLOSE files
STOP
```

and Point module combines simple sequences and if-then-else structures. The Move Input to Output simple sequence, which begins this module flowchart, corresponds to lines 870–910 of the COBOL program. A single process operation represents a series of statements in a COBOL program. A group of statements, however, such as ''Move Input to Output'' may be represented by a single symbol in the module flowchart, thereby improving the simplicity and clarity.

The process symbol in the Read and Print module is a good example of the if-then-else structure. This decision and affiliated processing operations correspond to lines 920–950 of the sample program. Regardless of the path through the if-then-else sequence, the module continues with a simple sequence composed of Determine Class (a PERFORM statement in line 960), Compute Total Hours (an ADD statement in lines 970–980), and Read Student File (a READ statement in line 1010). A decision is then made (the AT END phrase in line 1020) to determine if the end-of-file has been encountered. If the end-of-file has not been reached, an exit occurs. However, the Read and Print module is controlled by the do-until structure in the Control Logic module; therefore, the Read and Print module will repeat unless the end-of-file has been encountered and designated.

While completing the Read and Print module, a subordinate module - Determine Class - is encountered. The Determine Class module is composed of if-then-else structures. Specifically, Determine Class is a simple sequence of ''if-then'' structures. Based on this structure, the objective of the module is to select one operation based on the classification of the student, thus only one of the decisions will be true. Therefore, although the structure is the Determine Class module (and lines 1050–1140 of the program) indicating a sequence of if-then structures, this procedure is also a good

1985 COBOL Standards 

example of how a case structure could be used (as represented in COBOL 85 by the EVALUATE statement).

The final module in the flowchart is End of Job. End of Job is a simple sequence structure composed of the Write Ending output operation (lines 1170–1180) and the Close Files process (line 1190).

In this illustration a certain correspondence exists between structure, symbol type, and COBOL statement. Comparing Figures 3.1 and 3.3, note that simple sequence structures can be comprised of process, predefined process, and input/output symbols. Process symbols may be used to represent OPEN, MOVE, ADD, and CLOSE statements. In fact, most COBOL statements are represented by the process symbol. Consequently, they can only be represented by a simple sequence structure. Input/Output symbols are represented by READ and WRITE statements. The if-then-else structure is a combination of the decision symbol with other symbols (e.g., process or predefined process symbols). The if-then-else structure is often associated with the COBOL IF statement. However, as you have seen, special phrases (such as AT END attached to the READ statement) may also represent an if-then type of structure. Finally, the do-until structure is represented by the PERFORM-UNTIL statement in COBOL.

Developing and Using Pseudocode

Figure 3.4, pseudocode, provides an alternate format to the module flowcharts illustrated in Figure 3.3. The boldbase lines extending to the left correspond to lines 710–750 of the PROCEDURE DIVISION in Figure 3.1. The lines in Figure 3.4 at the right indicate that they are part of corresponding procedures. For example, ''DO start-up'' is composed of OPEN files, PRINT page heading, and READ first record. Thus, ''DO start up'' is a simple sequence structure, meaning that pseudocode verbs such as OPEN, PRINT, and READ can be used to create a simple sequence.

The next process is controlled by a do-until structure. ''Do read and print until end of file'' is composed of MOVE input data to output area, IF male, DO determine class, COMPUTE total hours, PRINT results, READ next record, and IF end-of-file (lines 870–1020 in Figure 3.1). Thus, this procedure combines simple sequence and if-then-else structures. The simple sequence portion of the pseudocode is composed of the verbs MOVE, DO, COMPUTE, PRINT, and READ. The if-then-else structures are composed of ''IF male . . .'' and ''IF end-of-file.'' An examination of the DO determine class line of the pseudocode shows that the lines following it are indented, meaning that they are subordinate to this DO structure. The subsequent lines represent a case structure, through which only one of the classes will be picked - freshman, sophomore, junior, and senior. The last structure in the DO read and write block is IF end-of-file. If the end-of-file is encountered, EXIT DO is executed, which terminates the DO read and write block.

The final structure represented by DO end of job is a simple sequence (lines 1170–1190 in Figure 3.1). Composed of the verbs PRINT and CLOSE, the procedure terminates with the appearance of STOP, the last line in the pseudocode.

Now compare Figures 3.1 and 3.4. Notice that pseudocode resembles more closely the actual statements in the COBOL program than do the module flowcharts. Also, pseudocode tends to be quicker to develop and more compact. However, it does not quickly identify the lack of closure, as do module flowcharts. In module flowcharts, each block (except for terminal blocks) has definite entry and exit points, as identified by flowlines. Thus, the formal structure of flowcharts has its advantages, while pseudocode is more abbreviated.

The COBOL Coding Form

Most programming languages have specific rules for each line. The COBOL coding form is presented in Figure 3.5. The body of the form (eliminating the top portion, which includes nonprogramming entries) provides specific column designations for the COBOL entries. These designations represent five parts of COBOL lines (statements)—sequence numbers, continuation and comment, Area A, Area B, and identification (shown in the upper right-hand corner of the form).

The sequence numbers occupy columns 1 through 6. The numbers act only as a means of recording the sequence of lines from coding forms. Most COBOL compilers, unless directed otherwise, will ignore the numbers placed in these columns. They may be omitted without detriment. However, they can be an effective means of ensuring that the statements (or records) are in the prescribed sequence. COBOL compilers, if directed, will check the sequence of these numbers during the compiling process and will mark (with a warning message) any lines out of sequence. To be acceptable, the sequence numbers must be in an ascending order, but not necessarily in fixed increments.

Many coding forms subdivide these six columns so that columns 1 through 3 represent page numbers and columns 4 through 6 represent serial numbers. This procedure provides slightly better control. The page number represents the page number of the coding form from which the line was taken. The serial number represents the specific line on that page. Thus, a programmer could return to the original coding form for a program. Serial or line numbers are generally printed on the coding form in increments of 10 to allow for later insertion of new lines while continuing to maintain the ascending order.

The second part of the coding form serves a dual function. Column 7 may be used for indicating the continuation of a COBOL statement (entry) from one line to the next, or it may be used for entering a comment entry, as shown in Figure 3.1. If a continuation

Figure 3.5 The COBOL Coding Form

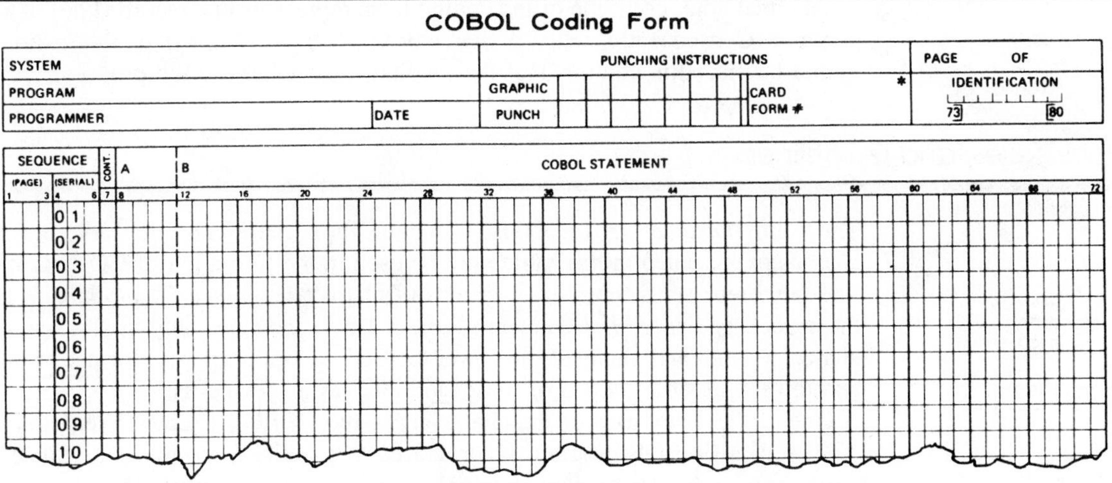

COBOL Coding Form

SYSTEM
PROGRAM
PROGRAMMER
DATE
PUNCHING INSTRUCTIONS
GRAPHIC
PUNCH
CARD FORM #
PAGE OF
IDENTIFICATION
73 80

SEQUENCE (PAGE) (SERIAL) 1 3 4 6
CONT. 7
A 8
B 12
COBOL STATEMENT
16 20 24 28 32 36 40 44 48 52 56 60 64 68 72

01
02
03
04
05
06
07
08
09
10

is necessary, the programmer enters a hyphen (-) in column 7 of each line following the start of the statement and for every additional line needed to complete the statement. This is necessary because the COBOL compiler assumes a space between column 72 of one line and column 12 of the line immediately following it. The significance of this will become more apparent after reading the discussion on Area B.

A continuation is usually required *only* if (1) a reserved word is being continued from one line to another, (2) a programmer-supplied name cannot be completed on one line, or (3) a literal does not begin and end on the same line. Therefore, just because a statement, entry, or clause is not completed on one line *does not* mean a continuation is needed. A statement may take two or more lines with no continuations. Conversely, two or more statements may be recorded on the same line. This will be discussed more fully later in this chapter under COBOL punctuation.

Column 7 is also used for comment entries. Any line in a COBOL program with an asterisk (*) in column 7 will be ignored by the compiler. Thus, comments or a verbal commentary on the purpose of specific segments of the program require an asterisk in column 7 of each of the affected lines.

Area A of the coding form, columns 8 through 11, is used to record the major segments of a COBOL program. All DIVISION headings, SECTION headings, paragraph names, FD entries, and level numbers 01, 66, and 77 should begin in columns 8 through 11. (Some of these terms are new but they will be discussed in later chapters). Only these items should appear in Area A. It is *desirable* to record these entries in a special way to make them easy to locate. Examine Figure 3.1. Notice that some of the lines extend more to the left than others. All these entries are major segments.

Area B, columns 12 through 72, is the portion of the coding form where statements and clauses are recorded. Notice that the bulk of the coding in Figure 3.1 begins four positions to the right of the DIVISION headings (in column 12).

The final part of the coding form lies in columns 73 through 80, which is not scanned by the COBOL compiler. The programmer can put any information in these columns he or she desires or leave it blank. Generally, this area is used to identify the program by placing a code or series of symbols in these columns on all lines. Because this area is not checked by the compiler, the programmer should be careful not to use it for any portion of a COBOL clause or statement.

One final note, each line of the coding form represents one record (line) in a COBOL program. Consequently, when a character appears in column 1 of the coding form, it should be placed in column 1 of the medium used to record the program.

Definitions, Rules, and Guidelines

The valid *character set* for COBOL statements is represented in Table 3.1. Only the characters presented in this table may be used in the formation of COBOL statements. The table represents three basic groups of characters—*numeric, alphabetic* (including the space), and *special characters*. Table 2.1 also indicates only upper case alphabetic characters, although many of the newer COBOL compilers permit the use of both upper- and lowercase letters. Each of these symbols has a specific use.

One of the many uses of the characters in the COBOL character set is *punctuation*. As noted, a COBOL program is structured to parallel a written text. Since there are punctuation rules for textual material, there are also punctuation rules for COBOL programs. The punctuation characters are as follows.

Character	Meaning
	space
,	comma
;	semicolon
:	colon
.	period
"or'	quote characters
(	Left (open) parenthesis
)	right (close) parenthesis

Remember that the hierarchy of COBOL is DIVISION, SECTION, paragraph, sentence (or entry), and statement (or clause). Each of these parts is shown in Figure 3.1. The required punctuation for both DIVISION and SECTION headings (within the scope of this text) is that each *must* be coded on a line by itself and followed immediately by a period. Although it *may* be coded on a line by itself, each paragraph is terminated by a period and followed by at least one space. Sentences and entries follow the same rules as paragraphs. (However, they must be recorded in Area B—columns 12 through 72—and there may be one or more sentences (or entries) on one line.) Other rules related to punctuation are listed here.

1. Any punctuation shown in the format of clauses or statements in subsequent chapters is required of that clause or statement.
2. As with a period, a space must appear after any use of a comma or semicolon. However, there should not be a space immediately before these characters.
3. Two successive words in COBOL are required to have at least one space separating them. This rule applies equally to reserved words, programmer-supplied-names, literals, and figurative constants (each of which is discussed shortly).

Table 3.1 The COBOL Character Set

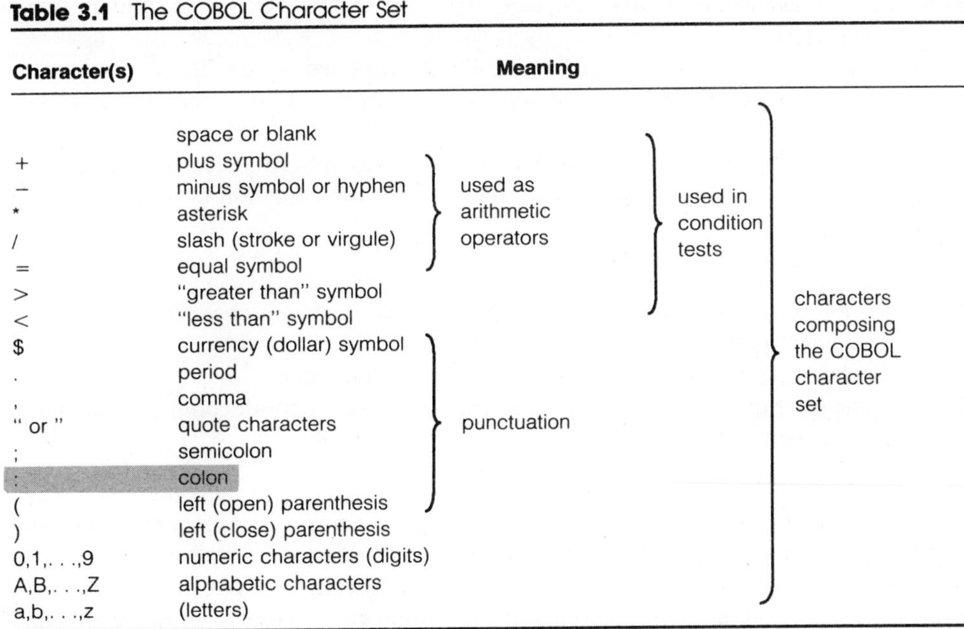

Character(s)	Meaning			
	space or blank			characters composing the COBOL character set
+	plus symbol	used as arithmetic operators	used in condition tests	
−	minus symbol or hyphen	used as arithmetic operators	used in condition tests	
*	asterisk	used as arithmetic operators	used in condition tests	
/	slash (stroke or virgule)	used as arithmetic operators	used in condition tests	
=	equal symbol		used in condition tests	
>	"greater than" symbol		used in condition tests	
<	"less than" symbol			
$	currency (dollar) symbol	punctuation		
.	period	punctuation		
,	comma	punctuation		
" or "	quote characters	punctuation		
;	semicolon	punctuation		
:	colon	punctuation		
(	left (open) parenthesis	punctuation		
)	left (close) parenthesis			
0,1,. . .,9	numeric characters (digits)			
A,B,. . .,Z	alphabetic characters			
a,b,. . .,z	(letters)			

4. Any arithmetic operator (a symbol indicating the operation of adding, subtracting, multiplying, or dividing) or an equal sign is required to have at least one space before and after the symbol. (See the COMPUTE statement and the IF statements.)
5. A left parenthesis should be preceded by a space and must not be followed by a space. The right parenthesis should not be preceded by a space but must be followed by either a space or some other form of punctuation such as a period. (See the COMPUTE and IF statements and table handling.)
6. A comma may be used to separate multiple operands in a statement. (See, for example, the MOVE statement.)
7. A comma or semicolon is always optional and may be used to separate several clauses that form an entry or several statements that form a sentence. They should be followed by a space.

1985 COBOL Standards

8. In COBOL 85, periods may be considered optional in the PROCEDURE DIVISION, especially when a "capstone" statement (e.g., END-IF, END-PERFORM, and so on) is present.
9. In COBOL 85, a colon is used to separate the character position specifier from the length indicator for substring operations.

The first nonpunctuation use of the COBOL character set is in the formation of *words* in COBOL. A *word* is a combination of numeric and alphabetic characters and the special character hyphen (-) to form a reference symbol that has meaning to the COBOL compiler and the programmer. There are two types of words—*reserved words* and *programmer-supplied-names*. A reserved word is a symbol with which the COBOL compiler associates special meaning. The first two words found in any COBOL program are the symbols IDENTIFICATION and DIVISION. Both are reserved words and should be used only in the context permitted (or established) by the COBOL compiler. For example, all division names, and the word DIVISION itself, are reserved words. A reserved word has special connotation to the COBOL compiler and its use should be avoided except as directed by the language. Table 3.2 is provided to aid in identifying the reserved words.

A word of caution—all compilers have additional reserved words. To avoid incorrect use of a reserved word, review the reserved-word list for the COBOL compiler available at your installation.

Programmer-supplied-names, the second class of words in COBOL, includes all names in a program that are *not* reserved words. The rules for the creation of a programmer-supplied-name follow:

1. It may not exceed a total of thirty (30) consecutive nonblank characters.
2. The characters in the name must be alphabetic or numeric or a hyphen.
3. The hyphen may not be the first or last character in a name.
4. The name is terminated by the first occurrence of a space, period, comma, semicolon, or right (open) parenthesis.

There are three basic classes of programmer-supplied-names—*data-names, condition-names*, and *procedure-names*. Data-names have one additional requirement over standard programmer-supplied-names. All *data-names must include at least one alphabetic character.* Data-names are used to represent data. The following types of names are all data-names.

file-names
record-names
group-names
elementary-item-names
independent-elementary-item-names
index-names
index-data-items
report-names
sort-file-names
sort-record-names
mnemonic-names

All data names must be described (or defined) in the DATA DIVISION of a COBOL program, except for mnemonic-names, which are described in the ENVIRONMENT DIVISION (SPECIAL-NAMES paragraph). They can also be referenced in the PROCEDURE DIVISION.

Table 3.2 ANS COBOL Reserved Words**

ACCEPT	CHARACTER	DEBUG-SUB-2	END-SUBTRACT
ACCESS	CHARACTERS	DEBUG-SUB-3	END-UNSTRING
ADD	CLOCK-UNITS*†	DEBUGGING	END-WRITE
ADVANCING	CLOSE	DECIMAL-POINT	END-OF-PAGE
AFTER	COBOL*†	DECLARATIVES	ENTER
ALL	CODE*	DELETE	ENVIRONMENT
ALPHABETIC	CODE-SET*	DELIMITED	EOP
ALPHANUMERIC	COLLATING*	DELIMITER	EQUAL
ALPHANUMERIC-	COLUMN	DEPENDING	ERROR
EDITED	COMMA	DESCENDING	ESI*
ALPHABETIC-	COMMUNICATION*	DESTINATION*	EVALUATE
LOWER	COMP	DETAIL	EVERY
ALPHABETIC-	COMPUTATIONAL	DISABLE*	EXCEPTION*
HIGHER	COMPUTE	DISPLAY	EXIT
ALSO*	CONFIGURATION	DIVIDE	EXTEND
ALTER*	CONTAINS	DIVISION	
ALTERNATE	CONTINUE	DOWN	FALSE
AND	CONTROL	DUPLICATES	FD
ANY	CONTROLS	DYNAMIC	FILE
ARE	CONVERTING		FILE-CONTROL
AREA	COPY	EGI*	FILLER
AREAS	CORR*	ELSE	FINAL
ASCENDING	CORRESPONDING*	EMI*	FIRST
ASSIGN	COUNT	ENABLE*	FOOTING
AT	CURRENCY	END	FOR
AUTHOR		END-ADD	FROM
	DATA	END-CALL	
BEFORE	DATE	END-COMPUTE	GENERATE
BINARY	DATE-COMPILED	END-DELETE	GIVING
BLANK	DATE-WRITTEN	END-DIVIDE	GO
BLOCK	DAY	END-EVALUATE	GREATER
BOTTOM*	DAY-OF-WEEK	END-IF	GROUP
BY	DE	END-MULTIPLY	
	DEBUG-	END-PERFORM	HEADING
CALL	CONTENTS	END-READ	HIGH-VALUE
CANCEL*	DEBUG-ITEM	END-RETURN	HIGH-VALUES
CD*	DEBUG-LINE	END-REWRITE	
CF	DEBUG-NAME	END-SEARCH	I-O
CH	DEBUG-SUB-1	END-START	I-O-CONTROL*

*Reserved words and mentioned or discussed in this text.
**Additional non-ANS COBOL reserved words are listed in Appendix A.
†COBOL-74 Reserved words not used in COBO-85.

Table 3.2 *Continued* ANS COBOL Reserved Words**

IDENTIFICATION	NO	REFERENCES	SUB-QUEUE-1*
IF	NOT	RELATIVE	SUB-QUEUE-2*
IN	NUMBER	RELEASE	SUB-QUEUE-3*
INDEX	NUMERIC	REMAINDER	SUBTRACT
INDEXED	NUMERIC-EDITED	REMOVAL*	SUM
INDICATE		RENAMES	SURPRESS*
INITIAL*	OBJECT-	REPLACING	SYMBOLIC
INITALIZE	COMPUTER	REPORT	SYNC
INITIATE	OCCURS	REPORTING	SYNCHRONIZED
INPUT	OF	REPORTS	
INPUT-OUTPUT	OFF*	RERUN†	TABLE*
INSPECT	OMITTED	RESERVE	TALLY
INSTALLATION	ON	RESET	TALLYING
INTO	OPEN	RETURN	TAPE*
INVALID	OPTIONAL*	REVERSED	TERMINAL*
IS	OR	REWIND	TERMINATE
	ORGANIZATION	REWRITE	TEST
JUST	OUTPUT	RF	TEXT*
JUSTIFIED	OVERFLOW	RH	THAN
		RIGHT	THROUGH
KEY	PACKED-	ROUNDED	THRU
	DECIMAL	RUN	TIME
LABEL	PAGE		TIMES
LAST	PAGE-COUNTER	SAME*	TO
LEADING	PERFORM	SD	TOP*
LEFT	PF	SEARCH	TRAILING
LENGTH	PH	SECTION	TRUE
LESS	PIC	SECURITY	TYPE
LIMIT	PICTURE	SEGMENT*	
LIMITS	PLUS	SEGMENT-LIMIT*	UNIT
LINAGE*	POINTER	SELECT	UNSTRING
LINAGE-	POSITION*	SEND*	UNTIL
COUNTER*	POSITIVE	SENTENCE	UP
LINE	PRINTING*	SEPARATE*	UPON
LINE-COUNTER*	PROCEDURE	SEQUENCE*	USAGE
LINES	PROCEDURES	SEQUENTIAL	USE
LINKAGE	PROCEEDING*	SET	USING
LOCK	PROGRAM	SIGN	
LOW-VALUE	PROGRAM-ID	SIZE	VALUE
LOW-VALUES		SORT	VALUES
	QUEUE*	SORT-MERGE*	VARYING
MEMORY*†	QUOTE	SOURCE	
MERGE*	QUOTES	SOURCE-	WHEN
MESSAGE*		COMPUTER	WITH
MODE	RANDOM	SPACE	WORDS*
MODULES*†	RD	SPACES	WORKING-
MOVE	READ	SPECIAL-NAMES	STORAGE
MULTIPLE*	RECEIVE*	STANDARD	WRITE
MULTIPLY	RECORD	STANDARD-1*	
	RECORDS	START	ZERO
NATIVE*	REDEFINES	STATUS	ZEROES
NEGATIVE	REEL*	STOP	ZEROS
NEXT		STRING	

*Reserved words and mentioned or discussed in this text.
**Additional non-ANS COBOL reserved words are listed in Appendix A.
†COBOL-74 Reserved words not used in COBO-85.

The second type of programmer-supplied-name, a condition-name, is assigned a particular value or set of values provided through an associated data-name. It is used solely in testing operations and cannot be used to reference data as can data-names. A condition-name must also contain at least one alphabetic character; it is described in the DATA DIVISION, and may be referenced in the PROCEDURE DIVISION (see Chapter 11).

The last type of programmer-supplied-name, a procedure-name is used to reference segments of the PROCEDURE DIVISION. Procedure-names do not reference data but rather reference the location of one or more statements in the PROCEDURE DIVISION. Procedure-names, commonly referred to as paragraph or SECTION names in the PROCEDURE DIVISION, need *not* contain an alphabetic character.

Table 3.3 lists some possible programmer-supplied-names. Note that in some cases, the name does not conform to the rules for name formation. The next category of items used in COBOL are *constants*. Unlike data-names, constants retain the same "value" from the beginning of the program to the end. Three classes of constants are used in COBOL—*numeric, literals, nonnumeric literals,* and *figurative constants*. Numeric and nonnumeric literals, as a group, are sometimes simply referred to as *literals*.

A numeric literal is what we generally think of as a constant. It is a numeric value. The digits in the numeric literal represent its numeric value. A numeric literal must conform to the following rules:

1. It must contain one or more of the characters Ø through 9.
2. It may have a leading plus or minus sign.

Table 3.3 Sample Programmer-Supplied-Names

Programmer-supplied-name	Valid-data-name* or condition-name	Valid procedure-name*
EMPLOYEE-NAME	YES	YES
NUMBER	NO[1]	NO[1]
GO-TO	YES[2]	YES[2]
DATE-COMPILED	NO[3]	NO[3]
1ST-NAME	YES	YES
RATE-PER-HOUR	YES	YES
475	NO[4]	YES
HOURS-WORKED	NO[5]	NO[5]
ANNUAL-INTEREST-RATE	YES[6]	YES[6]

1. NUMBER is a COBOL reserved word. Instead of NUMBER, an abbreviation such as NUM or NUMB could be used. (NO is another reserved word.)
2. Even though the words GO and TO are reserved words, when a hyphen is placed between them, they no longer fall into the reserved word category. There are relatively few reserved words containing a hyphen. Thus, hyphenated words are often used as programmer-supplied-names.
3. DATE-COMPILED is an ANS COBOL reserved word. Note that it also contains a hyphen.
4. A data-name or condition-name must contain at least one alphabetic character.
5. Programmer-supplied-names must not begin or end with a hyphen.
6. Even though the name is rather long, it falls within the 30-character limit. (Hyphens are included in the character count.)

*It is assumed that the same name is not being used as both a data-name (or condition-name) and a procedure-name in the same program.

3. If a portion of the number represents a decimal fraction, it may contain a decimal point in any position except following the last character of the value.
4. It may generally be from 1 to 18 digits in length. (The sign and decimal point characters are not considered a part of this length.)

Generally, a nonnumeric literal is a textual string of characters, (e.g., column headings). A nonnumeric literal must conform to the following rules:

1. It may contain any character acceptable to the computer being utilized, (e.g., characters in the EBCDIC or ASCII coding systems larger than the COBOL character set in Table 3.1.).
2. It must be contained within quotes; it begins and ends with a quote character. The quote characters are not part of the nonnumeric literal. The quote character may be either a quote mark ('') or an apostrophe ('). Check at your installation to determine which character is assumed by default by your compiler. In most cases it is the apostrophe.
3. It may contain reserved words.
4. Each space (or blank) represents a character.
5. The length of the nonnumeric literal may generally be from 1 to 120 characters (excluding the quote character). COBOL 85 permits nonnumeric literals of up to 160 characters.

The final category in the constant group is the figurative constant, a COBOL reserved word which represents the value(s) signified by the word. As reserved words, no other special designation is necessary. The figurative constants, their alternate spellings, and meanings are below. The meaning is the same whether the singular or plural form of the word is used.

ZERO ZEROS ZEROES SPACE SPACES	One or more occurrences of the number zero. (This is the only figurative constant that can be used in conjunction with a numeric data item.) One or more occurrences of a space (or blank).
HIGH-VALUE HIGH-VALUES	One or more occurrences of the character considered to be the highest in a particular computer's collating (character-value) sequence.
LOW-VALUE LOW-VALUES	One or more occurrences of the character considered to be the lowest in a particular computer's collating (character-value) sequence.
QUOTE QUOTES	One or more occurrences of the quote character, that is, either the quote mark ('') or the apostrophe ('). The figurative constant QUOTE(S) is not intended to replace the quote character in nonnumeric literals.
ALL literal	One or more occurrences of the character string that composes the literal. The literal must be either a nonnumeric literal or a figurative constant. (In the case of figurative constants, the word ALL is redundant.)

Table 3.4 Sample Numeric and Nonnumeric Literals

Text of literal*	Type of literal (comments)
12345	Numeric
123.45	Numeric
.12345	Numeric
12345.	Illegal numeric—a decimal point cannot appear as the last character in a numeric literal
– 12345	Numeric—all previous numeric literals are treated as positive, although no sign is shown
'END OF JOB'	Nonnumeric—10 characters in length
'12345'	Nonnumeric—even though the literal is composed entirely of digits, the literal is treated as nonnumeric
'ED'S PLACE'	Illegal nonnumeric—one of the characters in the literal is the quote character
'12,345.56—BALANCE'	Nonnumeric—18 characters in length

*In these examples, it is assumed that the apostrophe (') is the character used by the compiler to represent the quote character.

In the case of HIGH-VALUE(S) and LOW-VALUES(S), the particular internal representation used depends on the coding system used by the computer (EBCDIC or ASCII). Several examples of numeric and nonnumeric literals are presented in Table 3.4.

It is possible to code literals as portions of entries or statements that do not lie totally within Area B of one line. For example, when coding a nonnumeric literal, it is possible for one literal, which could reach 120 characters, to exceed the space provided in Area B, which is only 61 characters. If it is necessary to continue a nonnumeric literal from one line to another, the continuation character (hyphen) should be placed in column 7 of all additional lines. It is also necessary to *repeat* the quote character in Area B (column 12) of each line for which the literal continues. A continued nonnumeric literal might appear in Figure 3.6. No continuation character is necessary on the first line containing the literal. However, on the second line a hyphen is placed in column 7, and the quote character is repeated in column 12. The literal includes any remaining spaces (up to and including column 72) from the first line. Therefore, to continue a nonnumeric literal, as much of the literal as possible should be written on the first line before it is continued on subsequent lines. This ensures that no unanticipated spaces are "added" to the literal. Continuation of lines containing numeric literals, figurative constants, other reserved words, and programmer-supplied-names is a simpler task, as demonstrated in Figure 3.6. Only the hyphen in column 7 is necessary for a continuation. However, remember that all these items (with the possible exception of a lengthy nonnumeric literal) may be placed on a following line if preceded by one or more spaces on the first line.

The final set of rules and guidelines are not rules for the COBOL language but rather an aid to understanding the form of the language. The following rules have been widely adopted to describe COBOL clauses and statements. The rules are provided here to make the transition from this text to other manuals or texts simpler.

1. Any reserved word in a statement or clause will appear in capital letters.
2. Any underlined reserved word is a required reserved word. If an underscored reserved word appears in an optional portion of a statement or clause, the word is required only if the option is used. A reserved word not underscored may be employed at the programmer's discretion.

Figure 3.6 Examples of Continuations

COBOL Coding Form

SYSTEM An Introduction to ANS COBOL		PUNCHING INSTRUCTIONS	PAGE 1 OF 1
PROGRAM Illustrations of Statement Continuation		GRAPHIC	CARD FORM # FIG 3.6
PROGRAMMER J. Wayne Spence	DATE 01/01/89	PUNCH	

```
SEQUENCE  CONT  A   B   COBOL STATEMENT                                     IDENTIFICATION
01        *     CONTINUATION OF A NON-NUMERIC LITERAL
02                                                          ... 'GENERALLY S
03        -     "PEAKING, SOMETHING WOULD PRECEED THIS LITERAL'.
04
05
06        *     CONTINUATION OF A NUMERIC LITERAL
07                                                                   ... 12
08
09        -     3456.
10
11        *     CONTINUATION OF RESERVED WORDS (SUCH AS FIGURATIVE CONSTANTS)
12        *         AND PROGRAMMER-SUPPLIED-NAMES
13
14                                                                    ... Z
15        -     EROES.
16
17
```

3. Any word in lowercase letters is a programmer-supplied-name (e.g., data-name, condition-name, etc.). It is the programmer's responsibility to supply these words in an appropriate context.
4. Words in brackets ([ ]) indicate that this portion of the statement or clause is optional. It may be included in the statement or clause at the programmer's discretion.
5. An option followed by an ellipsis (. . .) indicates that the option may be repeated at the programmer's discretion.
6. Any portion of a statement or clause within braces ({ }) indicates that the programmer must make a selection between (or among) the items. This is a forced choice unless the braces are shown within a set of brackets.

Summary

COBOL is based upon a hierarchical structure. This structure from the highest level to the lowest, includes DIVISION headings, SECTION headings, paragraphs, entries or sentences, and clauses or statements. There are four divisions in every COBOL program—IDENTIFICATION, ENVIRONMENT, DATA, and PROCEDURE—and they must be recorded in that order. Each division satisfies a particular purpose within the program.

IDENTIFICATION—general documentation and definition
ENVIRONMENT—definition of equipment (hardware) used by the program
DATA—definition and description of all data items used in the program and interrelationships of data items
PROCEDURE—definition of the process to be executed

Like most programming languages, COBOL conforms to a series of coding rules. Columns 1 through 6 of each line are reserved for sequence numbers; column 7 may be used for continuations or comments; columns 8 through 11, Area A, is used for recording major headings; columns 12 through 72, Area B, is used to record entries and sentences; and columns 73 through 80 may be used for additional program identification.

Entries and sentences are composed of reserved words, programmer-supplied-names, punctuation, and perhaps constants. Reserved words have special meaning to the COBOL compiler and should only be used in the prescribed context. Programmer-supplied-named are those names selected by the programmer and include data-names, condition-names, and procedure-names. Programmer-supplied-names must conform to specific formation rules, and each name type has a specific use. Punctuation—periods, commas, and semicolons—is necessary for the completion of entries and sentences. Commas may be used to separate clauses within an entry, although the entry itself is terminated by a period. Finally, some clauses and statements require the use of constants. The three categories of COBOL constants are—numeric literals, nonnumeric literals, and figurative constants. Thus, through hierarchical design and sublevel components of clauses and statements, COBOL becomes a highly structured programming language.

Notes on Programming Style

Although COBOL compilers allow entries and statements to appear on the same line as paragraph names, most commercial programmers record paragraph-names on a line by themselves as an additional visual cue.

COBOL compilers also permit multiple statements (and clauses) *per line*. However, multiple statements per line is not advisable for three reasons. First, program modifications become more difficult, especially when other statements need to be inserted between existing statements. Secondly, debugging (logical error correcting) is often more difficult because of each statement's lack of isolation. Finally, statements are more readable when recorded one per line. In addition, since all compilers ignore blanks in Area B (except in nonnumeric literals), the programmer may choose to indent certain segments of the program to improve readability.

Comments are helpful in explaining a certain approach or the significance of a particular procedure. Furthermore, as shown in Figure 2.1, they may be helpful as visual markers for certain portions of a program. However, work cautiously! Too many comments distract from otherwise readable code. Furthermore, comments that are too specific should be avoided. Historically, when programs are modified after extended use, the comments are rarely modified to reflect the changes. Thus, after modification, the original comments may no longer be accurate. Finally, never use comments to try to "improve" or make up for poorly written procedures! The procedure should speak for itself if at all possible.

Questions

Below, fill in the blank(s) with the appropriate word, words, or phrases.

1. The largest (most encompassing) segment of a COBOL program is at the ____ level.

2. Within a COBOL program there are ____ (number) divisions.

3. Divisions are subdivided into segments called ____, which are in turn broken into ____.

4. Sentences are composed of one or more ____, whereas entries are composed of one or more ____.
5. The first division of a COBOL program is always the ____ DIVISION, and the last division is always the ____ DIVISION.
6. The ____ DIVISION contains no sections.
7. Sentences appear only in the ____ DIVISION.
8. The function of the IDENTIFICATION DIVISION is to ____.
9. The function of the ENVIRONMENT DIVISION is to ____.
10. All data items are described in the ____ DIVISION.
11. The FILE SECTION may be found in the ____ DIVISION.
12. The INPUT-OUTPUT SECTION may be found in the ____ DIVISION.
13. The process to be performed by a COBOL program is provided in the ____ DIVISION.
14. Columns 1 through 6 of a COBOL coding form are reserved for ____.
15. If a COBOL statement is to be continued, a(n) ____ should appear in column(s) ____.
16. When an asterisk appears in column 7, the line is treated as a(n) ____.
17. Paragraph names should begin in Area ____.
18. Clauses should begin in Area ____.
19. The COBOL character set is composed of ____, ____, and ____ characters.
20. Both ____ and ____ must be recorded on a line by themselves and be followed by a period.
21. An entry is terminated by a(n) ____.
22. Clauses in an entry may be separated by ____ or ____.
23. There are two types of words in COBOL, ____ which have special meaning to the COBOL compiler and ____ which have special meaning to the programmer.
24. A data-name differs from a procedure-name in that it must include at least one ____ character.
25. All data-names must appear in the ____ DIVISION.
26. A programmer-supplied-name is a generic term that includes, ____, ____, and ____.
27. Numeric literals, nonnumeric literals, and figurative constants are all generically known as ____.
28. The maximum length of a numeric literal is____ digits.
29. The maximum length of a nonnumeric literal is ____ characters.
30. The figurative constant associated with the maximum quantity of a computer is ____.
31. All figurative constants are ____ words.

Respond to the following questions by circling either "T" for true or "F" for false.

T F 32. The proper order of divisions in a COBOL program is ENVIRONMENT, IDENTIFICATION, DATA, AND PROCEDURE.
T F 33. All divisions may contain sections.
T F 34. Paragraphs are always composed of sentences.
T F 35. The lowest-level item in the PROCEDURE DIVISION is the clause.
T F 36. The WORKING-STORAGE SECTION may be a part of the DATA DIVISION.
T F 37. Sequence numbers (in columns 1 through 6) are necessary on each line of a COBOL program.

T F **38.** A hyphen is the only character permitted in column 7 of a COBOL statement.
T F **39.** Each time a COBOL statement requires two or more lines to record, continuation (a hyphen in column 7) is required.
T F **40.** Division headings must begin in column 8.
T F **41.** Section headings should begin in Area A.
T F **42.** Entries and sentences should begin in Area A.
T F **43.** In COBOL, there is a distinction between alphabetic and special characters.
T F **44.** In COBOL, only one statement may be recorded per line.
T F **45.** Paragraph names must be recorded on a line by themselves.
T F **46.** A period must be followed by a space.
T F **47.** A sentence may be terminated by a semicolon.
T F **48.** A data-name may be selected for use by the programmer from the list of reserved words.
T F **49.** All programmer-supplied-names are used to reference data values.
T F **50.** All programmer-supplied-names must contain at least one alphabetic character.
T F **51.** Numeric literals may contain digits.
T F **52.** Nonnumeric literals may contain digits.
T F **53.** Figurative constants may contain digits.
T F **54.** The value −12.5 could be used as a numeric literal.
T F **55.** The value 147. could be used as a numeric literal.

Exercises

1. Below is a list of programmer-supplied-names. Identify those names that are legal names. If the name is illegal, indicate the reason it is illegal.

a. ANNUAL-SALES
b. DOLLAR-INVESTMENT
c. W2-FORM
d. 1040
e. MONTH-OF-THE-WEEK
f. DAY OF THE WEEK
g. FEDERAL-WITHHOLDING-TAX-DEDUCTION
h. F.I.C.A.
i. DATE-COMPILED
j. TAX

2. In the program that follows, identify at least one of each of the following:
division heading
paragraph-name
clause
statement
data-name
numeric literal
figurative constant
section heading
entry
sentence

programmer-supplied-name
procedure-name
nonnumeric literal
comment

Problems

3.1 With the help of your instructor, run the program shown below. You will need the necessary job control language (JCL) instructions for compiling and executing a COBOL program that requires no external data. You will need to supply your name adjacent to the AUTHOR paragraph in line 50. Also, you may need to modify the ASSIGN clause provided in line 180 of the program so that it conforms to the type of compiler and equipment available at your installation.

```
               1   1   2   2   2   3   3   4   4   4   5   5   6   6   6   7
   4   8   2   6   0   4   8   2   6   0   4   8   2   6   0   4   8   2
 10***************************************************************
 20 IDENTIFICATION DIVISION.
 30***************************************************************
 40 PROGRAM-ID.      PROBLEM-1.
 50 AUTHOR.          (supply your name here).
 60***************************************************************
 70 ENVIRONMENT DIVISION.
 80***************************************************************
 90*-------------------------------------------------------------*
100 CONFIGURATION SECTION.
110*-------------------------------------------------------------*
120 SOURCE-COMPUTER. IBM.
130 OBJECT-COMPUTER. IBM.
140*-------------------------------------------------------------*
150 INPUT-OUTPUT SECTION.
160*-------------------------------------------------------------*
170 FILE-CONTROL.
180     SELECT PRINT-FILE ASSIGN TO UT-S-OUTPUT.
190***************************************************************
200 DATA DIVISION.
210***************************************************************
220*-------------------------------------------------------------*
230 FILE SECTION.
240*-------------------------------------------------------------*
250 FD  PRINT-FILE LABEL RECORDS ARE OMITTED.
260 01  PRINT-RECORD.
270     05  FILLER                     PIC X(01).
280     05  FIELD-1-OUT                PIC X(10).
290     05  FILLER                     PIC X(05).
300     05  FIELD-2-OUT                PIC 9(10).
310     05  FILLER                     PIC X(107).
320*-------------------------------------------------------------*
330 WORKING-STORAGE SECTION.
340*-------------------------------------------------------------*
350 01  WORKING-RECORD.
360     05  FIELD-1-WS                 PIC X(10) VALUE 'FIELD NO 1'.
370     05  FIELD-2-WS                 PIC 9(05) VALUE 145.
380***************************************************************
390 PROCEDURE DIVISION.
400***************************************************************
410 000-PROCEDURE-CONTROL.
420     PERFORM 100-OPENING-COMMANDS.
430     PERFORM 200-LINES-OF-OUTPUT.
440     PERFORM 300-CLOSING-COMMANDS.
450     STOP RUN.
460
```

```
-----------------------------------------------------------------------
|          1   1   2   2   2   3   3   4   4   4   5   5   6   6   6  7|
|  4   8   2   6   0   4   8   2   6   0   4   8   2   6   0   4   8  2|
|---------------------------------------------------------------------|
|  470 100-OPENING-COMMANDS.                                          |
|  480     OPEN OUTPUT PRINT-FILE.                                    |
|  490     MOVE SPACES              TO PRINT-RECORD.                  |
|  500                                                                |
|  510 200-LINES-OF-OUTPUT.                                           |
|  520     MOVE FIELD-1-WS          TO FIELD-1-OUT.                   |
|  530     MOVE FIELD-2-WS          TO FIELD-2-OUT.                   |
|  540     WRITE PRINT-RECORD AFTER ADVANCING 2 LINES.                |
|  550     MOVE ALL '-'             TO PRINT-RECORD.                  |
|  560     WRITE PRINT-RECORD AFTER ADVANCING 2 LINES.                |
|  570     MOVE SPACES              TO PRINT-RECORD.                  |
|  580     MOVE 'END REPORT'        TO FIELD-1-OUT.                   |
|  590     WRITE PRINT-RECORD AFTER ADVANCING 2 LINES.                |
|  600                                                                |
|  610 300-CLOSING-COMMANDS.                                          |
|  620     CLOSE PRINT-FILE.                                          |
-----------------------------------------------------------------------
```

3.2 With the help of your instructor, run the following program. You will need to supply the JCL instructions used by your computer, your name in line 50, device specifications in the ASSIGN clauses in lines 180 and 190, and an additional record containing your name in the location specified by your instructor.

```
-----------------------------------------------------------------------
|          1   1   2   2   2   3   3   4   4   4   5   5   6   6   6  7|
|  4   8   2   6   0   4   8   2   6   0   4   8   2   6   0   4   8  2|
|---------------------------------------------------------------------|
|   10*****************************************************************|
|   20 IDENTIFICATION DIVISION.                                       |
|   30*****************************************************************|
|   40 PROGRAM-ID.     PROBLEM-2.                                     |
|   50 AUTHOR.         (supply your name here).                       |
|   60*****************************************************************|
|   70 ENVIRONMENT DIVISION.                                          |
|   80*****************************************************************|
|   90*-------------------------------------------------------------* |
|  100 CONFIGURATION SECTION.                                         |
|  110*-------------------------------------------------------------* |
|  120 SOURCE-COMPUTER. IBM.                                          |
|  130 OBJECT-COMPUTER. IBM.                                          |
|  140*-------------------------------------------------------------* |
|  150 INPUT-OUTPUT SECTION.                                          |
|  160*-------------------------------------------------------------* |
|  170 FILE-CONTROL.                                                  |
|  180     SELECT NAME-FILE  ASSIGN TO UT-S-INPUT.                    |
|  190     SELECT PRINT-FILE ASSIGN TO UT-S-OUTPUT.                   |
|  200****************************************************************|
|  210 DATA DIVISION.                                                 |
|  220****************************************************************|
|  230*-------------------------------------------------------------* |
|  240 FILE SECTION.                                                  |
|  250*-------------------------------------------------------------* |
|  260 FD  NAME-FILE  LABEL RECORDS ARE OMITTED.                      |
|  270 01  NAME-RECORD                      PIC X(80).                |
|  280                                                                |
|  290 FD  PRINT-FILE LABEL RECORDS ARE OMITTED.                      |
|  300 01  PRINT-RECORD                     PIC X(133).               |
|  310*-------------------------------------------------------------* |
|  320 WORKING-STORAGE SECTION.                                       |
|  330*-------------------------------------------------------------* |
|  340 01  OUTPUT-RECORD.                                             |
|  350     05  FILLER                       PIC X(01) VALUE SPACES.   |
|  360     05  FILLER                       PIC X(11) VALUE 'MY NAME IS'. |
|  370     05  NAME-OUT                     PIC X(80).                |
-----------------------------------------------------------------------
```

```
          1   1   2   2   2   3   3   4   4   4   5   5   6   6   6   7
  4   8   2   6   0   4   8   2   6   0   4   8   2   6   0   4   8   2
--------------------------------------------------------------------------
   ***************************************************************
    PROCEDURE DIVISION.
   ***************************************************************
   *-------------------------------------------------------------*
    000-PROCEDURE-CONTROL SECTION.
   *-------------------------------------------------------------*
    000-START.
        PERFORM 100-OPEN-FILES.
        PERFORM 300-PRODUCE-NAME.
        PERFORM 500-CLOSE-FILES.
        STOP RUN.

   *-------------------------------------------------------------*
    100-OPEN-FILES SECTION.
   *-------------------------------------------------------------*
    100-ENTRY.
        OPEN INPUT NAME-FILE, OUTPUT PRINT-FILE.

   *-------------------------------------------------------------*
    300-PRODUCE-NAME SECTION.
   *-------------------------------------------------------------*
    300-ENTRY.
        READ NAME-FILE INTO NAME-OUT.
        MOVE ALL '-'               TO PRINT-RECORD.
        WRITE PRINT-RECORD AFTER ADVANCING 2 LINES.
        WRITE PRINT-RECORD FROM OUTPUT-RECORD AFTER 1 LINES.
        MOVE ALL '-'               TO PRINT-RECORD.
        WRITE PRINT-RECORD AFTER ADVANCING 1 LINES.

   *-------------------------------------------------------------*
    500-CLOSE-FILES SECTION.
   *-------------------------------------------------------------*
    500-ENTRY.
        CLOSE NAME-FILE, PRINT-FILE.
```

CHAPTER

4

The IDENTIFICATION DIVISION

Purpose of the Division

The IDENTIFICATION DIVISION is always present in a COBOL program or routine and is always the first division. As its name implies, the IDENTIFICATION DIVISION identifies the program by providing documentation. It provides information about the program, such as the title of the program, who wrote it, when it was written, the date it was *compiled* (translated) from the *source program* (a high-level language program such as COBOL) into an *object program* (a program in the computer's language), whom it was written for, whether it is to be protected from unauthorized use or access, and its purpose. Thus, to become familiar quickly with a program in COBOL, you need only refer to the IDENTIFICATION DIVISION.

Overall View of the IDENTIFICATION DIVISION

The permitted entries in the IDENTIFICATION DIVISION are shown in Figure 4.1. The IDENTIFICATION DIVISION heading is always the first entry of the division. The one major difference between the structure of this division and that of the other divisions is that no SECTION names are permitted. The IDENTIFICATION DIVISION is composed totally of *paragraph names*.

The paragraph names (which are reserved words) should be coded in the order shown in Figure 4.1. The paragraph names should begin in Area A of the COBOL coding form, be spelled exactly as shown, and be terminated with a period and at least one space. The entries following the paragraph names may follow on the same line or start on a new line beginning in Area B. Each entry terminates with the next paragraph-name (or division heading) but should end with a period.

Of the paragraph names, only the PROGRAM-ID paragraph is required. The program-name provides an external name by which the program is recognized by the computer's *operating system* (a program that controls the overall operation of the computer). The program-name is a programmer-supplied-name and must, at a minimum, conform to the rules for the creation of programmer-supplied-names (see Chapter 3). Following

Figure 4.1 Format of the IDENTIFICATION DIVISION

```
IDENTIFICATION DIVISION.

PROGRAM-ID.  program-name.

[AUTHOR.  [comment entry.]. . .]

[INSTALLATION. [comment entry.]. . .]

[DATE-WRITTEN. [comment entry.]. . .]

[DATE-COMPILED.[comment entry.]. . .]

[SECURITY. [comment entry.]. . .]
```

these rules will provide a satisfactory program-name for any COBOL compiler (although some compilers will truncate and/or translate the program-name into a form acceptable to the operating system). Additional uses of the program-name are discussed in Chapter 20.

All other paragraph names in the IDENTIFICATION DIVISION are optional; however, many installations encourage programmers to use them to improve their documentation. All "comment entries" give the programmer complete freedom of content. The entries may be English sentences or paragraphs and may contain numbers, special characters and symbols, and reserved words. All comment entries must appear totally within Area B.

The only special benefit of including optional paragraph names in the IDENTIFICATION DIVISION is that any comment entries that appear after the DATE-COMPILED paragraph will be replaced by the current date by some computer systems; the month, day, and year the program was last compiled (see Figure 4.2).

A note about Figure 4.2—the area of the coding form labeled "Punching Instructions" is used to avoid misinterpretation of characters printed on the coding form. The area marked "Graphic" identifies specific characters that may be similar in physical appearance (e.g., S and 5). The area marked "Punch" demonstrates the hexadecimal codes that correspond to the characters. This information is especially useful if the person coding the information is not the individual keying the information into a machine media form.

Summary

The IDENTIFICATION DIVISION is the first division of each COBOL program. Its purpose is to provide information to someone unfamiliar with the program. The division has one required paragraph—PROGRAM-ID—as well as other paragraphs, which are designed to provide information about the author of the program, the date the program was written, the date the program was last compiled, and so forth. Thus, there are very few functional components in the IDENTIFICATION DIVISION.

Notes on Programming Style

Documentation is the primary purpose of the IDENTIFICATION DIVISION. Little effort is required to program this division, yet the effort is well worth the rewards. Assume

Figure 4.2 An Illustration of the IDENTIFICATION DIVISION

COBOL Coding Form

SYSTEM INTRODUCTION TO COBOL		PUNCHING INSTRUCTIONS						PAGE 1 OF 1
PROGRAM IDENTIFICATION DIVISION		GRAPHIC	1	1	Ø	5	S	CARD FORM -
PROGRAMMER R. D. WILLIAMS	DATE 1/1/89	PUNCH	1	12/4	Ø	11/6	5	0/2

```
SEQUENCE          A   B                                           COBOL STATEMENT                                  IDENTIFICATION
(PAGE)(SERIAL)
      01      IDENTIFICATION DIVISION.
      02      PROGRAM-ID. PAYROLL-CHECKS
      03      AUTHOR. ORIGINAL CODE -- J. WAYNE SPENCE -- 5/31/86.
      04                  REVISED CODE -- ROBERT D. WILLIMAS -- 4/2/88.
      05      INSTALLATION.
      06              KLINGON ENTERPRISES, INC.
      07      DATE-WRITTEN.
      08              JANUARY 1, 1986.
      09      DATE-COMPILED.  7/25/89.
      10      SECURITY.
      11              THIS PROGRAM UTILIZES CONTROLLED DOCUMENTS (PAYCHECK FORMS)
      12                  AND SENSITIVE DATA INVOLVING POSSIBLE VIOLATIONS OF
      13                  PERSONAL PRIVACY OF EMPLOYEES. EXECUTE APPROPRIATE
      14                  SAFEGUARDS AS DIRECTED BY THE COMPTROLLERS OFFICE IN
      15                  POLICY STATEMENT SGP-1793, DATED SEPTEMBER 1, 1980.
      16
      17
      18
      19
      20
```

for the moment that you are required to change a program that is unfamiliar to you and that was written by someone else more than two years ago. Wouldn't you like to have most, if not all, of the information allowed in this division before beginning your work?

Questions

Below, fill in the blank(s) with the appropriate word, words, or phrases.

1. The first division of a COBOL program is the ____ DIVISION.
The purpose of the IDENTIFICATION DIVISION is to provide ____ .
3. Although there are paragraphs in the IDENTIFICATION DIVISION, the division permits no ____ headings.
4. The only paragraph the COBOL compiler requires to be present in the IDENTIFICATION DIVISION is the ____ paragraph.
5. All paragraph names in the IDENTIFICATION DIVISION should begin in Area _ of the COBOL coding form.
6. All entries following the paragraph names in the IDENTIFICATION DIVISION should appear in Area ____ .
7. The only paragraph that will have its comment entry modified when executed is the comment entry following the ____ paragraph.

8. The entry following the PROGRAM-ID paragraph at a minimum must conform to the rules for a(n) ____ .

9. Comment entries in the IDENTIFICATION DIVISION should be terminated by a(n) ____ .

10. Comment entries may include ____ .

Answer the following questions by circling either "T" for true or "False" for false.

T F **11.** The paragraph names in the IDENTIFICATION DIVISION may be written (listed in the program) in any order desired by the programmer.

T F **12.** If the DATE-WRITTEN paragraph is present in the IDENTIFICATION DIVISION, the DATE-COMPILED paragraph must also be present.

T F **13.** It is possible for the DATE-WRITTEN paragraph to be the first paragraph in a COBOL program.

T F **14.** It is possible for the DATE-WRITTEN paragraph to be the second paragraph in a COBOL program.

T F **15.** Division names must be coded on a line by themselves.

T F **16.** Entries following paragraph names in the IDENTIFICATION DIVISION may be coded on a separate line from the paragraph name itself.

T F **17.** A paragraph name must be followed by a period.

T F **18.** In the comment entry following the AUTHOR paragraph, more than one period may be present.

T F **19.** Comment entries that follow paragraph names may be several lines long and appear anywhere between columns 8 and 72.

T F **20.** PROGRAM-ID is a section name.

Exercises

1. Below is the IDENTIFICATION DIVISION of a COBOL program. Locate the errors and correct them.

```
IDENTIFICATION DIVISION
AUTHOR. JOHN DOE
DATE COMPILED. JANUARY 1, 1980.
DATE-WRITTEN.
01/-1/80.
SECURITY . PART-1: EXAMINE THIS PROBLEM CLOSELY.
PART-II: CORRECT ALL ERRORS.
```

2. Write the code for an IDENTIFICATION DIVISION that gives the following details:

Comments:	This procedure provides the basic computational requirements for demand forecasting based on historical data collected over the past 12 months.
Programmer:	(insert your name)
Original coding:	(insert the current date)
Procedure name:	DFCM214
Precautionary measures:	Procedure requires history tapes, which should be returned to the tape vault after use.

3. Rewrite the code provided in question 2 so that it conforms to the minimum requirements of the COBOL compiler.

CHAPTER

5

The ENVIRONMENT DIVISION

Purpose of the Division

The ENVIRONMENT DIVISION is the second COBOL division. It documents the types of hardware used and the types and number of input and output files, such as disk files and line printers. The division also includes several functional entries.

Because of the differences in COBOL compilers, even between those labeled "standard" ANS COBOL, the programmer must know what hardware is to be used to compile and execute the program. The differences between types of computers (e.g., between IBM and CDC) are definite and very distinct, but the differences between ANS COBOL compilers are minimal and more subtle. At times a program may have to be changed before it will run on two different computer models made by the same manufacturer. Therefore, although COBOL is called a machine-independent language, it is not completely so. Where it is practical throughout the rest of this text, differences among COBOL compilers will be mentioned.

Overall View of the ENVIRONMENT DIVISION

The ENVIRONMENT DIVISION heading is the first entry of the division. It should be followed immediately by the CONFIGURATION SECTION heading, the first section of a COBOL program. The CONFIGURATION SECTION has been designated as optional in COBOL 85. The CONFIGURATION SECTION heading is then followed, in order, by two required paragraphs, SOURCE-COMPUTER and OBJECT-COMPUTER and one optional paragraph, SPECIAL-NAMES. The SOURCE-COMPUTER and OBJECT-COMPUTER paragraphs are followed by "comment-entries," which show both the type of computer used to compile the source program and the type used to execute the object program. In most cases, these "comment-entries" are nonfunctional and are treated as comments. They differ slightly from the comment entries of the IDENTIFICATION DIVISION, however, in that they are required and should take the form of a programmer-supplied-name. The format of the ENVIRONMENT DIVISION is shown in Figure 5.1. [The ENVIRONMENT DIVISION in this part of the text will

Figure 5.1 The Format of the ENVIRONMENT DIVISION

```
ENVIRONMENT DIVISION.*
CONFIGURATION SECTION.
SOURCE-COMPUTER.  comment-entry.
OBJECT-COMPUTER.  comment-entry.
[SPECIAL-NAMES.   system-name-1 IS mnemonic-name-1.**
    [system-name-2 IS mnemonic-name-2.] . . .]
[INPUT-OUTPUT SECTION.
 FILE-CONTROL.
     SELECT file-name ASSIGN TO system-name
               {NO      }            [AREA ]
    [RESERVE   {integers} ALTERNATE  [AREAS]  ]
    [ACCESS MODE IS SEQUENTIAL**]
     [PROCESSING MODE IS SEQUENTIAL] . . . .]
```

*The division, as shown, is incomplete.
**The paragraph, as shown, is incomplete.

be discussed only to the extent it is needed for simple record input and line-printer output.]

SPECIAL-NAMES

The SPECIAL-NAMES paragraph is optional, but it is the first paragraph that contains information related to specific COBOL compilers. The clause(s) that follows the paragraph heading is of the form.

```
system-name IS mnemonic-name
```

The system-name, an *external name* known to the COBOL compiler, must conform to the requirements of the computer being used. The mnemonic-name, an *''internal name,''* is known to the COBOL program, is a programmer-supplied name, and must conform to the rules for data-name formation in Chapter 3. Thus, the clause allows a COBOL program to ''communicate'' with a COBOL compiler.

The SPECIAL-NAMES clause has a variety of uses; all are generally related to input or output commands. The clause can be used with the ACCEPT statement [discussed in the Chapter 7 supplement], the DISPLAY statement [discussed in the Chapter 7 supplement and Appendix E, and the WRITE statement [discussed in Chapter 7]. The clause is most often used with the WRITE statement [as one means of indicating vertical spacing or carriage control on the line printer].

WRITE statements used for a line printer are generally limited [without the use of the SPECIAL-NAMES clause] to advancing a specified number of lines from the last written. Often, it is desirable to advance to either the top of the page or a fixed number of lines from the top of a page [e.g., to produce page headings]. Then the SPECIAL-NAMES clause is used.

Two of the more popular system-names that indicate top-of-page are CØ1 [used by IBM machines] and '1' [used by CDC, Honeywell, and others]. The SPECIAL-NAMES clause for an IBM machine might be

```
CØ1 IS TOP-OF-PAGE.
```

The same clause for a CDC machine might be

```
'1' IS TOP-OF-PAGE
```

where "TOP-OF-PAGE" represents the mnemonic-name that appears in the PROCEDURE DIVISION and WRITE statements. These are not the only system-names applicable to most computers. Check with your computer installation for the system-names it permits.

INPUT-OUTPUT SECTION

The INPUT-OUTPUT SECTION heading appears next in the ENVIRONMENT DIVISION. It appears in all programs, except where the routine is a subprogram, without input-output capability. [See Chapter 20.] For purposes of this text, the INPUT-OUTPUT SECTION appears in almost all programs.

The FILE-CONTROL paragraph follows the INPUT-OUTPUT SECTION heading. Within the FILE-CONTROL paragraph, each file used is described by the clauses shown in Figure 5.1. If a program requires input *and* output, two sets of descriptions are presented. Like the SPECIAL-NAMES clause, part of the description of each five uses *external-system-names,* and some of the entries use *internal-names*.

SELECT and ASSIGN Clauses

The only entries required to indicate the presence of a file are the SELECT and ASSIGN clauses. The SELECT clause is used to provide an *internal-name* for a file. This internal-name must conform to the rules for formation of data-names presented in Chapter 3. A SELECT clause might appear as

```
SELECT INPUT-FILE
```

or

```
SELECT OUTPUT-FILE
```

The file-names, INPUT-FILE and OUTPUT-FILE, become internal-file-names and would appear later in other entries and statements of the program. [INPUT-FILE would likely appear in a file description entry of the DATA DIVISION and OPEN, READ, and CLOSE statements in the PROCEDURE DIVISION. The file-name OUTPUT-FILE would likely appear in a file description entry of the DATA DIVISION and OPEN and CLOSE statements of the PROCEDURE DIVISION.]

The ASSIGN clause is used to provide and *enternal-system-name* for the type of external peripheral device (e.g., a disk file or a line printer) to be associated with a file. Since these are external-names, they must conform to the names used by the computer manufacturer. These differences are shown in Table 5.1 for simple input devices [disk file] and line printers of the many popular computer manufacturers. For example, the ASSIGN statements for a disk file and a line printer in a system using an IBM computer using the OS, VS, or VM operating system might be

```
...ASSIGN UT-S-INPUT
```

and

```
...ASSIGN UT-S-OUTPUT
```

where INPUT and OUTPUT are further described in the program job control language.

The ASSIGN clause for a CDC computer might be

```
...ASSIGN INPUT,
```

and

```
...ASSIGN OUTPUT.
```

Table 5.1 Device Designations for Popular Computer Manufacturers

Software Vendor	Input Device Designation	Line Printer Designation
IBM (OS or VS)	{UR, UT, DA}-[1442R, 2501, 2520R, 2540R]-S[-name].	{UR, UT, DA}-[1132, 1403, 1404, 1443]-S[-name].
IBM (YM)	name	name
IBM (DOS)	SYSnnn-{UR, UT, DA}-[1442R, 2501, 2520R, 2540R]-S	SYSnnn-{UR, UT, DA}-[1132, 1403, 1404, 1443]-S.
Honeywell	CARD-READER	PRINTER
CDC	INPUT or SYSTEM-INPUT	OUTPUT or SYSTEM-OUTPUT
UNISYS (UNIVAC) DEC/PDP	CARD-READER Literal	PRINTER Literal
Burroughs	READER	PRINTER
Ryan-McFarland Corporation (RM-COBOL)*	INPUT {literal, data-name}	PRINT OUTPUT {literal, data-name}
Microsoft Corporation (MS-COBOL)**	DISK	PRINTER

*RM-COBOL is a copyrighted software product of Ryan-McFarland Corporation. (The literal or data-name may be used to specify a disk file-name.) Versions of this compiler are available on computers such as the Texas Instruments 990 series minicomputer and the Radio Shack TRS80 series microcomputers.

**MS-COBOL is a copyrighted software product of Microsoft Corporation. (Although a device type is specified in the ASSIGN clause, the specific assignment is made in the FD description of the associated file in the FILE SECTION of the DATA DIVISION. This is done by supplying a VALUE OF FILE-ID entry. This entry concludes with an identification of either a literal or a data-name. It is not required for a PRINTER file.) Versions of this compiler are available on the IBM-PC and compatible microcomputers.

where INPUT represents the system input device and OUTPUT represents the system line printer.

Note from Table 5.1, that with IBM external device names under the OS and VS operating systems, the optional name at the end of the ASSIGN clause entry may or may not be required. With IBM systems under DOS, the system addresses may be other than those shown in the example. Regardless of the type of system to be used, it is wise to consult with your computer installation for any special requirements.

Those systems that employ specific names in the ASSIGN clause (e.g., IBM) generally require that those files be further described through JCL. Those systems that employ generic names (e.g., CDC) may require a more complete description of those files in the DATA DIVISION.

Sample ENVIRONMENT DIVISIONS Entries

Now look at the examples in Figure 5.2. The examples illustrate the different forms of the ENVIRONMENT DIVISION, but they are not the only approaches to the formation of the division. The first example shows the most frequently required entries of the ENVIRONMENT DIVISION. The entries include the division heading, the section headings, and three paragraph names [SOURCE-COMPUTER, OBJECT-COMPUTER,

Figure 5.2 Examples of the ENVIRONMENT DIVISION

COBOL Coding Form

SYSTEM INTRODUCTION TO ANS COBOL — PUNCHING INSTRUCTIONS — PAGE 1 OF 1

PROGRAM ENVIRONMENT DIVISION EXAMPLES — GRAPHIC — CARD FORM -

PROGRAMMER PATRICK THOMAS SPENCE — DATE 1/1/89 — PUNCH

SEQUENCE (PAGE) (SERIAL) — CONT. — A — B — COBOL STATEMENT — IDENTIFICATION

```
       ENVIRONMENT DIVISION.
       CONFIGURATION SECTION.
       SOURCE-COMPUTER, HONEYWELL-200.
       OBJECT-COMPUTER, HONEYWELL-200.
       INPUT-OUTPUT SECTION.
       FILE-CONTROL.
           SELECT PAYROLL-FILE            ASSIGN CARD-READER.
           SELECT PAY-CHECK-FILE          ASSIGN PRINTER.


       ENVIRONMENT DIVISION.
       CONFIGURATION SECTION.
       SOURCE-COMPUTER, IBM.
       OBJECT-COMPUTER, IBM.
       SPECIAL-NAMES.
           C01 IS TOP-OF-PAGE.
       INPUT-OUTPUT SECTION.
       FILE-CONTROL
           SELECT MASTER-FILE             ASSIGN TO UT-S-SYSIN.
           SELECT REPORT-FILE             ASSIGN TO UT-S-SYSOUT.
```

and FILE-CONTROL]. The FILE-CONTROL paragraph indicates that a punched-card input file and a line printer will be used. The computer name suggests that a Honeywell computer will be used to compile and execute the program, so the ASSIGN clauses conform to the external device names used by Honeywell equipment.

The second example uses an optional clause of the ENVIRONMENT DIVISION. The optional clause is the SPECIAL-NAMES paragraph, which provides a new-page carriage control. In the FILE-CONTROL paragraph, the ASSIGN clauses conform to the format for IBM systems. The input file uses a model card-image reader. The output is ASSIGNed to a line printer. Both the input and output files are further described by the additional labels of SYSIN and SYSOUT.

After looking at the ENVIRONMENT DIVISION, you might think it will be difficult to learn COBOL. This is true for the ENVIRONMENT DIVISION because you must specify the types of devices used, but there are few differences in the other three divisions from one ANS COBOL compiler to another. Most of the code in a COBOL program is in the DATA and PROCEDURE DIVISIONs, making COBOL a ''standardized'' language, aside from the ENVIRONMENT DIVISION. The ''programming'' of COBOL is in the DATA DIVISION and the PROCEDURE DIVISION, to which the remainder of this text is devoted.

Summary

The ENVIRONMENT DIVISION, the second division of a COBOL program, defines the computer resources needed by a program. Although COBOL is known as a ''standard'' language, the ENVIRONMENT DIVISION provides the means for tailoring a program to specific hardware. The ENVIRONMENT DIVISION comprises two sections, the CONFIGURATION SECTION [which specifies the computer to be used to compile and execute a program] and the INPUT-OUTPUT SECTION [which enumerate the files and peripheral devices to be used by a program]. Establishing files and devices in a program is done with SELECT and ASSIGN clauses.

Although there are several special clauses possible in the ENVIRONMENT DIVISION, the clauses associated with the SPECIAL-NAMES paragraph are probably the most often used. In the SPECIAL-NAMES paragraph, an entry may establish a top-of-form carriage control for output statements in the PROCEDURE DIVISION.

Notes on Programming Style

Two points should be emphasized about the ENVIRONMENT DIVISION. First, you should not feel that mastering COBOL is going to be impossible because of the variability you see in the ENVIRONMENT DIVISION. On the contrary, after you have completed your first few programs, you will find that coding the first *two* divisions is relatively automatic when compared to the DATA and PROCEDURE DIVISIONs.

Second, understanding the concept of file processing is vital to understanding why COBOL is so frequently used for commercial application programs. However, this is often forgotten, even by experienced programmers, because COBOL tends to ''take care of you.'' COBOL is more efficient in handling input and output operations than are most high-level languages. As programmers, we should never forget that input and output efficiency is more critical in commercial applications than internal processing efficiency. Therefore, we should avoid coding situations that hamper I/O handling.

Questions

Below, fill in the blank(s) with the appropriate word, words, or phrases.

1. The purpose of the ENVIRONMENT DIVISION is to describe ____ .
2. The ENVIRONMENT DIVISION is composed of the ____ SECTION and the ____ SECTION.
3. The two required paragraphs of the CONFIGURATION SECTION are ____ and ____ .
4. In the SPECIAL-NAMES paragraph an external ____ name is assigned to a program-oriented ____ name.
5. The system names CØ1 or '1' are used to represent ____ .
6. A mnemonic-name can appear in the SPECIAL-NAMES paragraph of the ENVIRONMENT DIVISION and in the ____ DIVISION.
7. All files and devices used in a program appear in the ____ SECTION.
8. The clause that is used to assign a file-name to a program is the ____ clause.
9. The clause that is used to assign a device to a file is the ____ clause.
10. One ____ clause and one ____ clause will appear in the FILE-CONTROL paragraph for each file used in a COBOL program.

Respond to the following questions by circling either "T" for true or "F" for false.

T F **11.** The ENVIRONMENT DIVISION of a COBOL program is the same regardless of the type of computer used to compile and execute the program.

T F **12.** COBOL is independent of the computer upon which it is executed.

T F **13.** The ENVIRONMENT DIVISION provides information concerning the types of peripheral devices needed by a program.

T F **14.** The CONFIGURATION SECTION is an optional section and may be omitted from the ENVIRONMENT DIVISION of a COBOL program.

T F **15.** The entries that appear in the SPECIAL-NAMES paragraph are comment entries and have no functional purpose.

T F **16.** It is possible to conduct input-output operations in a COBOL program without an INPUT-OUTPUT SECTION.

T F **17.** The same file may be assigned to two different devices in the same program.

T F **18.** The external device names are the same regardless of the computer being used.

Exercises

1. Below is the ENVIRONMENT DIVISION of a program. The coding of the division contains errors. Locate the error and demonstrate what correction is necessary.

```
ENVIRONMENT DIVISION.
CONFIGURATION-SECTION.
SOURCE-COMPUTER.  UNKNOWN.
OBJECT COMPUTER  IBM.
    SPECIAL-TERMS.  CØ 1  IS NEXT-PAGE
INPUT-OUTPUT.
    SELECT MY-INPUT-FILE.   ASSIGN TO UT-S-CARDIN.
SELECT MY-PRINT-FILE ASSIGN UT-S-PROUT.
```

2. Write the ENVIRONMENT DIVISION of a program on the basis of the following information:

FILE INFORMATION—

File Name	Device Designation
BANK BALANCE	UT-S-INPT
ACCOUNT BALANCE REPORT	UT-S-RPTOUT

COMPUTER INFORMATION—

The program will be compiled and executed on an IBM computer utilizing the OS operating system. The term to be used in the program to represent the top-of-form for the printer will be NEXT-ACCOUNT-HEADING.

CHAPTER

6

The DATA/DIVISION

Purpose of the Division

The DATA DIVISION provides a description of the characteristics of *all* data items that will be used in a program as well as the groupings of those items and other data interrelationships. This chapter is an initial examination of the DATA DIVISION. Many of the chapters in Parts 2, 3, and 4 deal with additional specific details of the DATA DIVISION not covered in this chapter.

Overall Description of the DATA DIVISION

The DATA DIVISION generally comprises at least two parts—the FILE SECTION and the WORKING-STORAGE SECTION. The FILE SECTION presents a detailed description of the input and output files and records. The WORKING-STORAGE SECTION provides the description of data items or records to be used within the program but which are not directly connected to either an input or an output file. A very basic description of the DATA DIVISION is provided in Figure 6.1.

The coding of the DATA DIVISION requires patience and planning. These are sometimes neglected by beginning COBOL programmers, with the result being later correction and longer debugging time. Many of the entries in the DATA DIVISION are also used in the PROCEDURE DIVISION. So the DATA DIVISION should be coded such that the programmer can remember the structure and characteristics of the DATA DIVISION entries without continued reference. The programmer can then code the PROCEDURE DIVISION more easily. Thus, the choices for data references, groupings, and so on should have meaning (both to the programmer and to the problem).

FILE SECTION

The FILE SECTION of the DATA DIVISION provides a description of all files to be used in the program. There is a direct association between the FILE-CONTROL paragraph of the ENVIRONMENT DIVISION and the FILE SECTION of the DATA DI-

Figure 6.1 Basic Format of the DATA DIVISION

```
DATA DIVISION.*
FILE SECTION.
FD  file description entries.
Ø1  record description entries.
    .
    .
    .
WORKING-STORAGE SECTION.
Ø1   record description entries.
    .
    .
    .
```

*DATA DIVISION is incomplete as shown; only the basic framework of the division is shown.

VISION. In the FILE-CONTROL paragraph (in Chapter 5) all files to be used in a program were ASSIGNED to their external devices. The SELECT clause coupled with *each* ASSIGN clause provided a file-name. In the FILE SECTION of the DATA DIVISION there are a series of entries associated with each file-name specified in the SELECT clauses. Thus, if two SELECT clauses appear in the ENVIRONMENT DIVISION, two sets of file describing entries appear in the FILE SECTION.

The first part of the description of each file is a series of entries and clauses showing the characteristics of the file. A list of some of these clauses, in their appropriate format, is presented in Figure 6.2. The first entry following the FILE SECTION heading is an FD (File Description) entry, which is coded in AREA A. All other entries and clauses should be coded in AREA B. Following the FD entry, one of the file-names from a SELECT clause is coded. After the file-name, on the same line or on another line, the other clauses may be entered in any order. The only ''required'' clause is the LABEL RECORDS clause, which may use either of the combinations of words shown in Figure 6.2. Although the LABEL RECORDS clause is ''required,'' some compilers will assume it to be present if it is omitted. Furthermore, this clause is optional in COBOL 85. The LABEL RECORDS clause is not particularly useful when files are using only punched-

1985 COBOL Standards

Figure 6.2 Format of the File Description Entries and Clauses

```
FILE SECTION.*
FD  file-name
      LABEL {RECORD IS  } OMITTED**
            {RECORDS ARE}
      [RECORD CONTAINS integer CHARACTERS]
      [DATA {RECORD IS  } data-name-1  [data-name-2 . . .] .
            {RECORDS ARE}
Ø1 record description entries.
```

*FILE SECTION is incomplete as shown; only references to card readers and line printers are shown.
**Clause is incomplete as shown.

card input and line-printer output. (When magnetic tape or disk is utilized, however, it is possible for the programmer to have record labeling information within the file itself. For example, additional security may be provided to make sure the correct tape or disk file is used with a program. An additional discussion of this clause is provided in Chapter 17.)

The RECORD CONTAINS clause is also generally more useful when employed with tape or disk files. It is used to specify the number of characters in a record description. If the clause does not reflect the sum of all PICTURE string lengths, the compiler will respond with at least a warning message.

The DATA RECORDS clause is used to provide the record-name(s) of all records used with a file. It is not a functional clause and therefore is only used for documentation.

As mentioned in Chapter 5, the ASSIGN clause used by some compilers indicates a specific external name that is to be associated with the file-name indicated in the SELECT clause. In this environment, the file is further defined in the JCL used by that computer system. However, some operating systems utilize limited JCL or no JCL at all. In this environment, frequently including mini- and microcomputer systems, a generic name is attached to the ASSIGN clause. To further describe the file in the FILE SECTION FD, a non-ANS COBOL entry is used to describe the file. The entry is:

```
VALUE-ID IS "literal"
```

where the literal (enclosed in quotes) is an actual file name on disk. Thus, it is the VALUE-ID clause, not JCL, which establishes the connection between the COBOL file-name and the actual data file.

One final note before leaving the file description clauses: all major portions of the descriptions are clauses. As such, *only one period is permitted from the beginning of the file description entries (the FD) to the beginning of the (first) record description (the 01 level);* however, other types of punctuation (commas and semicolons) are permitted.

Record Descriptions

Record descriptions follow a specific order. Figure 6.3 illustrates their form. The description begins with the name of the record itself. Records are composed of groups (possibly at several levels) and *elementary-items*. The elementary-items describe data

Figue 6.3 Format of a Record Description

```
Ø1  record-name.*
    [[Ø2 - 48] group-name.]
    [[Ø2 - 49] elementary-item-name {PICTURE} field-description-entry.]
                                    {PIC    }
    [[Ø2 - 49] FILLER {PICTURE} field-description-entry.]
                      {PIC    }
          .
          .
          .
```

*Record description is incomplete as shown. Only essential elements are included.

(fields), as indicated by PICTURE clauses. Collections of elementary-items are called *groups* (which may be collected into other groups).

Record descriptions are presented in an outline or hierarchical form similar to that used in division organization. However, since record-names, group-names, and elementary-item-names are data-names, a data-name itself does not distinguish among different levels of inclusiveness. (Data-names must follow the rules in Chapter 3 on data-name formation.) Therefore, *level numbers* are coupled with data-names to indicate different levels of inclusiveness. The permitted level numbers are 01 through 49. The lower the level number is, the higher is the level of inclusiveness.

Since the 01 level is the most inclusive level of a record description it is always associated with the record-name. It should be coded in AREA A, with the record-name itself in AREA B. The record-name can be used as a data reference in other portions of a program, and if used, it will refer to all groups and elementary-items subordinate to it (all data-names at a lower level). Thus, by using the record-name as a data reference, it is possible to jointly address all data-items associated within the record.

The level numbers 02 through 48 may be used for either group or elementary-item designations. The lowest level number, 49, cannot represent a group; it must be an elementary-item. A group represents a series of entries in a record begun by an entry without a PICTURE clause and ended by the next entry that has an equal or higher level number. By definition, a record-name is also a group-name. In addition, however, records may contain groups, and groups may contain groups.

For example, look at the illustration in Figure 6.4. By definition, any entry *with* a PICTURE clause cannot be a group-name and must be an elementary-item. ITEM-3, ITEM-4, ITEM-5, ITEM-8, ITEM-9, ITEM-10, and ITEM-11 are elementary-items. Those data-names *without* PICTURE clauses are, by definition, group-names at various levels. MASTER-RECORD is a group-name (and a record-name), and it may be used to reference all data items from ITEM-1 through ITEM-11. ITEM-1 is a group-name. It has a level number of 03. Thus, all data items listed under it until the next occurrence of an 01, 02, or 03 level are part of this group (and subordinate to ITEM-1). ITEM-2 through ITEM-10 are part of ITEM-1. ITEM-2 is also a group-name. It includes all entries until the next occurrence of a level number less than or equal to 05 (down to, but not including, ITEM-5). Thus, ITEM-3 and ITEM-4 are part of group ITEM-2.

Figure 6.4 An Illustration of a Record Description

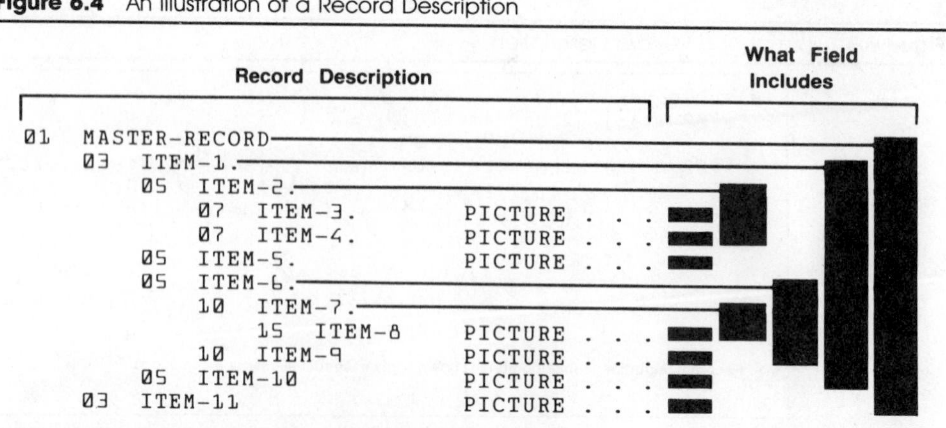

Recall that ITEM-3 and ITEM-4 are elementary-items. This might generally mean that the next level number that is lower than 07 would be another group-name. Such is not the case, however; ITEM-5 is the next higher level number, but it is an elementary-item. Thus, level numbers by themselves *do not* necessarily indicate the grouping of data items. PICTURE clauses are the primary means of identifying elementary-items. ITEM-6 is at the same level as ITEM-5, but it is a group-name. It contains ITEM-7 through ITEM-9. ITEM-7 is a group-name containing ITEM-8. ITEM-8 through ITEM-11 all contain PICTURE clauses and are therefore elementary-items.

Two more conclusions can be drawn from Figure 6.4. First, it is not necessary to use consecutive level numbers. Notice that level numbers 02, 04, 06, and so on, do not appear in the example. The only requirement is that the higher the number used in a record description, the less data it describes in that record. (However, the reverse is not also true, as is illustrated by ITEM-11.) Second, level numbers do not have to occur at any specific interval. For example, ITEM-2 is an 05 level, and its subordinate items are 07 levels. On the other hand, ITEM-6 is an 05 level, but its subordinate items are 10 and 15 levels.

Four additional points need to be made. First, every entry (line) should end with a period because compilers react differently to their omission. Second, the indention shown in the example is not required. It simply reflects a popular convention used by most COBOL programmers so that different levels can be seen easily. (This is one of the tenets of structured programming, discussed in Chapter 2.) Third, it is a good idea to use nonconsecutive level numbers. Although the record description is carefully planned, unforeseen circumstances are not unusual (at least in the beginning) and may necessitate adding groups to a record description. If consecutive level numbers are used (e.g., 01, 02, 03, etc.), it is impossible to add new group-names without renumbering some items. However, if a nonconsecutive numbering system is used (e.g., 01, 05, 10, 15, etc.), several new groupings could be inserted between existing items without renumbering.

Finally, the reserved word, FILLER, as indicated in Figure 6.3, may be placed in a record description at any level number except 01 and is always used *with* a PICTURE clause. It follows the same basic characteristics of an elementary-item-entry, except that FILLER is used in place of a data-name. FILLER is used to represent one or more spaces or data that are not to be accessed. Thus, when data fields are noncontiguous in an input record or spacing is desired in an output line, FILLER is generally used. In addition, FILLER is generally characterized as being an alphanumeric data-type and cannot be referenced in the PROCEDURE DIVISION (even if it should happen to contain data). Under the COBOL 85 standards, whenever a PICTURE clause is used without an elementary-item-name, the field is assumed to be a FILLER. Thus, the name FILLER *may* be omitted from the record description (although this practice should be avoided) without affecting the execution of a program.

PICTURE Clauses

PICTURE clauses are used to describe the characteristics of a field whether the field internally describes a data item or a field connected with an input or output medium (e.g., disk files or print lines). An accompanying PICTURE clause distinguishes an elementary-item from a group-name. Every elementary-item will have a PICTURE clause.

The PICTURE-clause field-description entries discussed here are limited to nonedited (DISPLAY) PICTURE character strings. Other types of PICTURE characters are presented in Chapter 8, and other forms of data representation are presented in Chapter 23.

The nonedited PICTURE characters and their meanings are presented in Table 6.1. The table shows the three different types of data representation allowed in COBOL. The first is *alphabetic* data. A programmer may input, output, or internally store alphabetic data using the PICTURE character "A" for every alphabetic character in the field. Alphabetic characters are the characters A through Z and blanks. The allowable character set for alphabetic fields is not universal, however. A few compilers permit any allowable character for an alphanumeric field to be placed in an alphabetic field. Check your installation to determine the restrictions on "A" fields.

Alphanumeric PICTURE clauses are created with the character X. Thus, a number of consecutive Xs (a string) is a representation of alphanumeric data. Any character that means something to the computer may be recorded in an X field. Modern computers use one of two popular character codes, either EBCDIC (Extended Binary Coded Decimal Interchange Code) or ASCII (American Standard Code for Information Interchange). These character sets are shown in Table 6.2. Since this set of characters includes alphabetic characters, X PICTURE fields are sometimes substituted for A fields.

The PICTURE character 9 is used to represent *numeric* data, whether or not computation is planned for the data item. For every 9 in the character string describing a numeric item, one digit position is reserved. The allowable characters in a numeric field are the digits Ø through 9. Spaces are not allowed. Consequently, in a numeric field, any column not containing a digit must contain a zero.

Table 6.1 Nonedited (DISPLAY) PICTURE Characters

Character	Meaning	Use	Maximum Size for Data
A	Alphabetic	Elementary-items used to represent or store alphabetic data (not for computational purposes)	30 characters
X	Alphanumeric	Elementary-items used to represent or store alphabetic, numeric, and special characters. All group-names are treated as alphanumeric even though they do not have a PICTURE clause. Not for computational purposes.	30 characters*
9	Numeric	Elementary-items used to represent or store numbers. May be used for computation purposes.	18 digits
S	Operational Sign	Numeric elementary-items for which the capability to store a sign (+ or −) is desired.	no space used
V	Implied Decimal	Numeric elementary-item for which decimal positions are desired.	no space used
P	Scaling Factor	Numeric elementary-item to which zeros are to be added when transferred from an external medium to the computer's internal storage.	no space used

1985 COBOL Standards

*The maximum length of an alphanumeric data item, when used to represent nonnumeric literals, is 120 characters (160 characters for COBOL 85). FILLER items are permitted to be as long as is required to describe a given data area (within practical limitations of approximately 32,000 characters on most computers).

Table 6.2 The COBOL Character Sets (in Collating-Sequence Order from Lowest Value to Highest Value)

EBCDIC		ASCII	
	space		space
.	period or decimal point	"	quote symbol
<	less than symbol	$	currency symbol
(	left parenthesis	'	apostrophe
+	plus symbol	(	left parenthesis
$	currency symbol	)	right parenthesis
*	asterisk	*	asterisk
)	right parenthesis	+	plus symbol
;	semicolon	,	comma
-	hyphen or minus symbol	-	hyphen or minus symbol
/	slash	.	period or decimal point
,	comma	/	slash
>	greater than symbol	0–9	numeric characters (digits)
'	apostrophe	;	semicolon
=	equal symbol	<	less than symbol
"	quote symbol	=	equal symbol
A–Z	alphabetic characters (letters)	>	greater than symbol
0–9	numeric characters (digits)	A–Z	alphabetic characters (letters)

Another problem with numeric input data is recording negative values. If negative numeric data is to be entered, a negative sign should be over-punched in the last column of the field. Then the digit in the last column will appear with a minus sign. If the number −123 were to be entered in a four-column field, it would have to be entered as Ø123. The last position requires both the digit "3" and a minus sign. The combination of these is the EBCDIC Code representation for the character L. Thus, −123 could be entered as 012L, where the character L in a numeric field is treated as a minus sign *and* the digit 3. A list of all "negative digit representations" for the last column of a negative field is shown in Table 6.3.

In addition, unless the PICTURE string contains the operational sign (the character S), the sign of the number will not be stored within the computer. Any numeric field

Table 6.3 Negative Data Representations

Numeric Value	EBCDIC CODE	Character Representation
1	D1	J
2	D2	K
3	D3	L
4	D4	M
5	D5	N
6	D6	O
7	D7	P
8	D8	Q
9	D9	R
Ø	DØ	}

Table 6.4 Illustrations of Nonedited (DISPLAY) PICTURE Clause Characters

Data Class	PICTURE String	Meaning	Number of Columns Represented on an Input Record or a Line of Print
Alphabetic	A	A single alphabetic character of storage	1
	AAAA or A(4)	Four characters of alphabetic storage	4
	A(20)	Twenty characters of alphabetic storage	20
Alphanumeric	X	A single alphanumeric character of storage	1
	XXXX or X(4)	Four characters of alphanumeric storage	4
	X(20)	Twenty characters of alphanumeric storage	20
Numeric	9	An unsigned single digit of numeric storage	1
	9999 or 9(4)	A 4-digit integer storage position	4
	9(18)	An 18-digit integer (the maximum) storage position	18
	99V99	A 4-digit numeric field with 2 digits preceding the implied decimal point and 2 digits after	4
	9(5)V99	An unsigned, 7-digit storage position with 5 digits preceding the implied decimal point and 2 digits after	7
	9(4)V9(5)	An unsigned, 9-digit storage position with 4 digits preceding the implied decimal point and 5 digits after	9
	V99	An unsigned, 2-digit numeric storage position with both digits following the implied decimal point	2
	999V	Illegal use of an implied decimal point (V should be omitted)	—
	S9(6)	A 6-digit integer storage position capable of recording a sign	6
	S9V9(8)	A 9-digit numeric storage position capable of storing 1 digit preceding the implied decimal point, 8 digits after, and a sign	9
	VPPP99	An unsigned 5-digit numeric storage position with all 5 digits following the implied decimal point. The 9s represent digit storage positions that in general come from an external medium (e.g., punched cards), with the Ps replaced by zeros. The internal data storage would appear as .000nn where n is replaced by a digit from an external source.	2
	S9(4)P(5)	A signed, 9-digit storage position where Ps are replaced by zeros. This yields an internally stored value of nnnn00000 where ns are replaced by digits.	4

that does not contain the operational sign treats the numeric data it contains as unsigned, regardless of the sign actually in the data. The character S, if used, can appear only once per PICTURE clause as the leftmost character. It does not occupy space either internally or externally.

The character V is used to indicate an implied decimal point. Without this character in a numeric PICTURE clause, all numbers are treated as integers (whole numbers). Thus, to record data with decimal-fraction storage capability, the character V must appear in the PICTURE string. The character V can appear only once in a PICTURE string and cannot be the rightmost character. It does not occupy internal or external space.

The last of the nonediting PICTURE characters is the P. The least used of the nonediting characters, P is used to insert additional zeros either before or after a string of 9s. That is, a number may be either scaled up (by adding zeros after the last digit taken from an external medium) or scaled down (by adding zeros before the first digit, assuming an implied decimal point is the leftmost character).

Table 6.4 illustrates the use of each of these nonedited PICTURE characters. The complete PICTURE clause requires coding the reserved word *PICTURE* (or its abbreviation *PIC*), followed by at least one space and the character string representing the data field, without any intervening spaces. Provided no additional clauses are attached to the elementary-item, the entry is terminated with a period.

Two additional comments should be made about PICTURE clauses. First, although A, X, and 9 are generally used exclusively of one another, combinations of these characters in one PICTURE clause are permitted. When this is done, however, the entire field is treated as being alphanumeric. Second, if several consecutive positions include the same PICTURE character, the character may be shown by repeating it (e.g., a five-character alphabetic field could be recorded as AAAAA), or a *replication factor* could be used. A replication factor is an integer number placed in parentheses following the character to be repeated. Thus, to show a five-character alphabetic field, we could use the code A(5)—meaning five consecutive A characters. PICTURE clauses may also contain multiple replication factors if warranted, that is, S9(4)P(5).

Examples of FILE SECTION Entries

The following examples will help you fully understand how the FILE SECTION entries are used in context. First, look at Figure 6.5. It shows the type of input record one might expect to see in a banking application: initial deposit slip for opening a checking account. The relevant information from this record includes:

1. The account number—a nine-digit numeric field appearing in columns 1 through 9
2. Customer's last name—a ten-character alphabetic field appearing in columns 10 through 19
3. Customer's first name—a ten-character alphabetic field appearing in columns 20 through 29
4. Customer's middle initial—a one-character alphabetic field appearing in column 30
5. Customer's street address—a ten-character alphanumeric field appearing in columns 31 through 40
6. Customer's city address—a ten-character alphabetic field appearing in columns 41 through 50

Figure 6.5 Graphic Sample of an Input Record

MULTIPLE-CARD LAYOUT FORM

Company LEARNING COBOL, INC.

Application EXAMPLE RECORD DESCRIPTION by J. WAYNE SPENCE Date 01/01/89 Job No Sheet No 1

ACCOUNT NUMBER	CUSTOMER NAME			CUSTOMER ADDRESS				DEPOSIT DATE			SIGNATURE CARD NUMBER		AMOUNT OF DEPOSIT
	LAST	FIRST	MI	STREET	CITY	STATE	ZIP	DAY	MONTH	YEAR			

1 2 3 4 5 6 7 8 9 10 11 12 13 14 15 16 17 18 19 20 21 22 23 24 25 26 27 28 29 30 31 32 33 34 35 36 37 38 39 40 41 42 43 44 45 46 47 48 49 50 51 52 53 54 55 56 57 58 59 60 61 62 63 64 65 66 67 68 69 70 71 72 73 74 75 76 77 78 79 80

7. Customer's state name abbreviation—a two-character alphabetic field appearing in columns 51 and 52

8. Customer's zip code—a five-digit numeric field appearing in columns 53 through 57

9. The day of the date of deposit—a two-digit numeric field appearing in columns 58 and 59

10. The month of the date of deposit—a two-digit numeric field appearing in columns 60 and 61

11. The year of the date of deposit—a two-digit numeric field appearing in columns 62 and 63

12. Customer's signature-card number—a five-digit numeric field appearing in columns 64 through 68

13. A blank field consisting of five card columns and appearing in columns 69 through 73

14. The amount of deposit (in dollars and cents)—a seven-digit numeric field appearing in columns 74 through 80

Compare Figure 6.5 with Figure 6.6. The FILE SECTION begins with an FD entry; subsequent clauses describe the characteristics of the file. The file-name is DEPOSIT-FILE (and would also appear in a SELECT clause in the FILE-CONTROL paragraph of the ENVIRONMENT DIVISION). The one required clause after the file-name is the LABEL RECORDS clause (which could have been coded on the same line as the file-name). The RECORD CONTAINS clause and the DATA RECORDS clause are optional. The RECORDS CONTAINS clause shows that the record description that follows is 80 characters long. The DATA RECORDS clause is only for documentation; it shows the record-names that follow. Note that only one period appears in the entire file description entry—after the last clause.

The record description (which begins with 01) should match, column by column, the record description given in Figure 6.5. The results of this record description in Figure 5.6 are given in Table 6.5. Any data-name listed in this table references data and may be used in the PROCEDURE DIVISION.

Suppose you want to describe an output file that might be used to print some of the data from the input record of the previous example. Examine Figures 6.7 and 6.8. In Figure 6.8 note the multiple uses of the reserved word FILLER which provides spaces between data fields. Obviously, FILLER is not limited to a single occurrence within a record description, and it is likely to appear in the DATA DIVISION several times.

The FD entry for this file is the minimum requirement. As Figure 6.8 indicates, only the file-name (NEW-CUSTOMER-FILE) and the LABEL RECORDS clause are used.

Table 6.5 Data Description Results

Data Name	Type of Data-Name Record (R); Group (G); Elementary-Item (E)	Number of Characters Represented	Type of Data Represented
DEPOSIT-RECORD	R/G	80	Alphanumeric
ACCOUNT-NUMBER-IN	E	9	Numeric
CUSTOMER-NAME-IN	G	21	Alphanumeric
LAST-NAME-IN	E	10	Alphanumeric
FIRST-NAME-IN	E	10	Alphanumeric
MIDDLE-INITIAL-IN	E	1	Alphanumeric
CUSTOMER-ADDRESS-IN	G	27	Alphanumeric
STREET-IN	E	10	Alphanumeric
CITY-IN	E	10	Alphanumeric
STATE-IN	E	2	Alphanumeric
ZIP-CODE-IN	E	5	Numeric
DATE-OF-DEPOSIT	G	6	Alphanumeric
DEPOSIT-DAY-IN	E	2	Numeric
DEPOSIT-MONTH-IN	E	2	Numeric
DEPOSIT-YEAR-IN	E	2	Numeric
SIGNATURE-NUMBER-IN	E	5	Numeric
(FILLER)	-	5	Alphanumeric
AMOUNT-OF-DEPOSIT-IN	E	7	Numeric (with 2 decimal positions)

Figure 6.6 A Sample of FILE SECTION Entries for an Input File

COBOL Coding Form

SYSTEM FILE SECTION ENTRIES (INPUT) | PUNCHING INSTRUCTIONS | PAGE 1 OF 1
PROGRAM INITIAL BANK DEPOSIT | GRAPHIC | CARD FORM #
PROGRAMMER M. JANET WILLIAMS | DATE 01/01/89 | PUNCH

SEQUENCE (PAGE) (SERIAL) | A | B | COBOL STATEMENT | IDENTIFICATION

```
       FILE SECTION.
       FD  DEPOSIT-FILE.
           LABEL RECORDS ARE OMITTED
           RECORD CONTAINS 80 CHARACTERS
           DATA RECORD IS DEPOSIT-RECORD.
       01  DEPOSIT-RECORD.
           05  ACCOUNT-NUMBER-IN               PIC 9(09).
           05  CUSTOMER-NAME-IN.
               10  LAST-NAME-IN                PIC X(10).
               10  FIRST-NAME-IN               PIC X(10).
               10  MIDDLE-INITIAL-IN           PIC X(01).
           05  CUSTOMER-ADDRESS-IN.
               10  STREET-IN                   PIC X(10).
               10  CITY-IN                     PIC X(10).
               10  STATE-IN                    PIC X(02).
               10  ZIP-CODE-IN                 PIC 9(05).
           05  DATE-OF-DEPOSIT-IN.
               10  DEPOSIT-DAY-IN              PIC 9(02).
               10  DEPOSIT-MONTH-IN            PIC 9(02).
               10  DEPOSIT-YEAR-IN             PIC 9(02).
           05  SIGNATURE-NUMBER-IN             PIC 9(05).
           05  FILLER                          PIC X(05).
           05  AMOUNT-OF-DEPOSIT-IN            PIC 9(05)V99.
```

Figure 6.7 A Graphic Description of a Desired Report

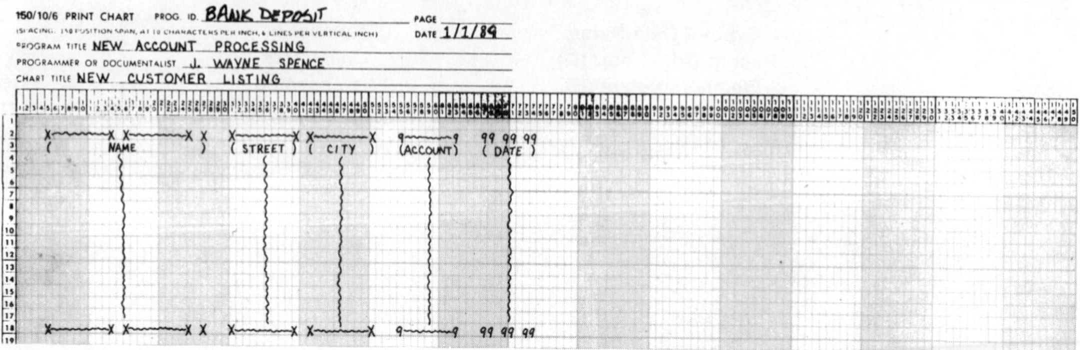

In a program, the FD might immediately follow the last entry shown in Figure 6.5; that is, the input-file description may precede the output-file description. However, this is not required, and FDs do not have to appear in the same order as the SELECT clauses in the ENVIRONMENT DIVISION—they are independent of each other.

As with the input-record description, the output-record descriptions in Figures 6.7 and 6.8 should correspond, column by column. The major differences between the input-record description and the output-record description are that different data-names are used so that unique storage positions are addressed (this is not a requirement), the number of data-names is different, and the output is longer (the output line shown is for 133 characters—a standard print-line length). Another difference not shown in the diagram is that output-record descriptions may contain edited data fields (see Chapter 8).

Other entries related to the FILE SECTION will be discussed in later chapters.

The WORKING-STORAGE SECTION

The WORKING-STORAGE SECTION is utilized to provide storage space for those data items not directly related to an input or an output file. As Figure 6.9 indicates, the WORKING-STORAGE SECTION is an optional section, but when used it must follow the FILE SECTION. The entries in the WORKING-STORAGE SECTION take the form of record descriptions. Record descriptions in the WORKING-STORAGE SECTION are structurally no different from those in the FILE SECTION, except that they are not connected with a file.

One other difference between data items described in the FILE SECTION and those described in the WORKING-STORAGE SECTION is that in the WORKING-STORAGE SECTION, each record requires additional internal storage space, unless explicitly REDEFINED. This is covered in greater depth in Chapter 22.

Another major difference between data items in the FILE SECTION and those in the WORKING-STORAGE SECTION is that VALUE clauses are permitted in the latter. As indicated in Figure 6.9, a VALUE clause may be used in conjunction with elementary-items of record descriptions in the WORKING-STORAGE SECTION. VALUE clauses

Figure 6.8 A Sample of FILE SECTION Entries for a Printed Output Line

COBOL Coding Form

SYSTEM FILE SECTION ENTRIES (OUTPUT)		PUNCHING INSTRUCTIONS	PAGE 1 OF 1
PROGRAM INITIAL BANK DEPOSIT		GRAPHIC	CARD FORM #
PROGRAMMER M. JANET WILLIAMS	DATE 01/01/89	PUNCH	

```
FD  NEW-CUSTOMER-FILE
    LABEL RECORDS ARE OMITTED.
Ø1  NEW-CUSTOMER-RECORD.
    Ø5  FILLER                          PIC X(Ø4).
    Ø5  CUSTOMER-NAME-OUT.
        1Ø  LAST-NAME-OUT               PIC X(1Ø).
        1Ø  FILLER                      PIC X(Ø1).
        1Ø  FIRST-NAME-OUT              PIC X(1Ø).
        1Ø  FILLER                      PIC X(Ø1).
        1Ø  MIDDLE-INITIAL-OUT          PIC X(Ø1).
    Ø5  FILLER                          PIC X(Ø3).
    Ø5  ACCOUNT-NUMBER-OUT              PIC 9(Ø9).
    Ø5  FILLER                          PIC X(Ø3).
    Ø5  DATE-OF-DEPOSIT-OUT.
        1Ø  DEPOSIT-DAY-OUT             PIC 9(Ø2).
        1Ø  FILLER                      PIC X(Ø1).
        1Ø  DEPOSIT-MONTH-OUT           PIC 9(Ø2).
        1Ø  FILLER                      PIC X(Ø1).
        1Ø  DEPOSIT-YEAR-OUT            PIC 9(Ø2).
    Ø5  FILLER                          PIC X(59).
```

are used for initial (or constant) values for elementary-items in records and FILLERs. As indicated in Figure 6.9, the VALUE of an elementary-item could be a figurative constant (e.g., SPACE or ZERO), a numeric literal (a constant composed of digits and a possible decimal point and sign), a nonnumeric literal (a character string), or the figurative constant ALL followed by a nonnumeric literal.

Figure 6.10 includes some examples of how the VALUE clause might be used in the WORKING-STORAGE SECTION. Obviously, the examples do not list all of its uses. Also, the VALUEs created in this WORKING-STORAGE SECTION may be assigned in the PROCEDURE DIVISION. Finally, although every item shown in the example utilizes a VALUE clause, it is not required.

In Figure 6.10, the figurative constant ZERO used as a VALUE for CUSTOMER-COUNT-WS (and ZEROS used with AVERAGE-DEPOSIT-WS) places the number Ø in each position of the field. The same result is achieved by using the numeric literal Ø with TOTAL-DEPOSITS-WS. In the case of PAGE-COUNT-WS, the VALUE 1 is a numeric constant, which is placed in the *last* digit position with the other digit position(s) filled with zero(s). TOTAL-SERVICE-CHARGE-WS has a value of 4.5 which is aligned on the (implied) decimal point to result in Ø4$_\wedge$5Ø (the same alignment as with PAGE-COUNT-WS since the decimal point is assumed to be located after the last digit).

The other record descriptions entries in the WORKING-STORAGE SECTION, are provided as headings to the output shown in Figure 6.7. YEAR-BEGINNING-RECORD is used to illustrate one very important point: the type of VALUE used should be consistent with the field description; that is, a numeric field should only be VALUED

Figur 6.9 Format of the WORKING-STORAGE SECTION

```
[WORKING-STORAGE SECTION.*

[01  record-description.

   [[02 - 48] group-name.]

    [02 - 49] {elementary-item-name} {PICTURE}  field-description-entry
              {FILLER              } {PIC    }

                       {figurative-constant  }
                       {numeric-literal      }
     [VALUE IS         {non-numeric-literal  }  ]]]
                       {ALL literal          }
```

*Section, as shown, is incomplete. Only basic elements are included.

with a numeric-oriented figurative constant or numeric literals; alphabetic fields, with alphabetic-oriented figurative constants and nonnumeric literals; and alphanumeric field, with figurative constants and nonnumeric literals. The VALUE 01/01/88 is a nonnumeric literal because it is enclosed in the ''quote'' character (apostrophe). It would be a nonnumeric literal even if the slash characters were eliminated.

Figure 6.10 An Illustration of the WORKING-STORAGE SECTION

COBOL Coding Form

SYSTEM WORKING-STORAGE SECTION
PROGRAM INITIAL BANK DEPOSIT (WORKING-STORAGE)
PROGRAMMER M. JANET WILLIAMS DATE 01/01/89
PUNCHING INSTRUCTIONS — GRAPHIC — PUNCH
PAGE 1 OF 1
CARD FORM -

```
01 01  YEAR-BEGINNING-RECORD.
02        05  FILLER           PIC X(08)       VALUE '01/01/88'.
03 01  PAGE-HEADING-RECORD.
04        05  FILLER           PIC X(27)       VALUE SPACES.
05        05  FILLER           PIC X(20)       VALUE
06                             'NEW CUSTOMER LISTING'.
07 01  COLUMN-HEADING-RECORD.
08        05  FILLER           PIC X(09)       VALUE SPACES.
09        05  FILLER           PIC X(13)       VALUE
10                             'CUSTOMER NAME'.
11        05  FILLER           PIC X(12)       VALUE SPACES.
12        05  FILLER           PIC X(13)       VALUE
13                             'LOCAL ADDRESS'.
14        05  FILLER           PIC X(08)       VALUE SPACES.
15        05  FILLER           PIC X(07)       VALUE 'ACCOUNT'.
16        05  FILLER           PIC X(06)       VALUE SPACES.
17        05  FILLER           PIC X(04)       VALUE 'DATE'.
18 01  UNDERLINE-RECORD.
19        05  FILLER           PIC X(77)       VALUE ALL'*'.
20
```

The record descriptions YEAR-BEGINNING-RECORD, PAGE-HEADING-RECORD, COLUMN-HEADING-RECORD, and UNDERLINE-RECORD all have FILLER as the elementary-item description. The only data-name reference that may be used to access these descriptions are the record-names. Note that in the last three record descriptions FILLER may contain SPACE (or SPACES) and nonnumeric literals. Those FILLER items that contain SPACES have a blank character in every position of the field and are used to provide horizontal spacing. The other FILLER items are used to provide "message-oriented" output.

Field descriptions may be either longer or shorter than the VALUE to be placed in the field. If the VALUE is shorter than the field length, the compiler will place the data in the leftmost positions of alphanumeric or alphabetic fields (left-justify). Enough blanks will be added in the trailing positions to fill the field with data. If the VALUE is too long for the field, it will be truncated (characters dropped off) from the right until it is exactly the same size as the field. (Most compilers will generate a WARNING message when truncation occurs.) SPACE or SPACES will always fill the field, as will the use of "ALL literal." A literal character(s) will be generated to fill the field exactly. In the example, the FILLER of UNDERLINE-RECORD contains exactly 77 asterisks (because the PICTURE size is 77 characters).

Summary

The DATA DIVISION, the third division of a COBOL program, provides for the descriptions of all data-names. Because each data-name is described, the DATA DIVISION is generally one of the more time-consuming to construct. The DATA DIVISION may be divided into several sections; the most common are the FILE SECTION and the WORKING-STORAGE SECTION.

In the FILE SECTION, each file-name defined in the ENVIRONMENT DIVISION with a SELECT clause is further described. The file description (FD) entries include record descriptions. Each record is defined with level number Ø1. Subparts of records (groups and elementary-items) may be described using a hierarchy of level numbers (Ø2 through 49). Only elementary-items describe fields. PICTURE clauses are utilized to describe the characteristics of fields and may be classified as alphabetic (A), alphanumeric (X), or numeric (9). Only numeric fields may be used for computation. Numeric fields may be further defined with the PICTURE characters S (operational sign) and V (implied decimal point).

The second section—the WORKING-STORAGE SECTION—provides for the description of those data-items *not* directly related to input-output activities, that is, internal or working variables. The WORKING-STORAGE SECTION also permits the use of VALUE clauses at the elementary-item level to assign initial values to data-names.

Notes on Programming Style

Several programming conventions are commonly employed to record DATA DIVISION entries. The most widely used convention is appropriate indention. For example, level numbers dictate the hierarchy of the record description. However, the grouping of data items may be easier to see if subordinate items are indented to the right of "superior" items. For example, the syntax of the two record descriptions below is equivalent, but the record description to the right is easier to understand at a glance because it is more visually appealing.

```
01 INVOICE.                          01 INVOICE.
   05 INV-NUM...                        05 INV-NUM...
   05 CUST-ID.                          05 CUST-ID.
   10 CUST-NO...                           10 CUST-NO...
   10 CUST-NAME...                         10 CUST-NAME...
   05 DATE-OF-SALE.                     05 DATE-OF-SALE.
   10 SALE-MONTH...                        10 SALE-MONTH...
   10 SALE-DAY...                          10 SALE-DAY...
   SALE-YEAR...                            10 SALE-YEAR...
```

PICTURE clauses of elementary-items are also indented, usually to column 40, to make it easy to locate the characteristic of each item.

The second convention is sometimes used in the FILE SECTION. Although the programmer is permitted to record extremely detailed record descriptions with each FD, only minimal definition of records is really necessary in the FILE SECTION. More detailed descriptions can be coded in the WORKING-STORAGE SECTION. Thus,

```
FD INPUT-FILE LABEL RECORDS ARE OMITTED.
01 INPUT-RECORD.
   05 IN FIELD-1          PIC 9(02).
   05 IN-FIELD-2          PIC X(10).
   05 IN-FIELD-3          PIC 9(02)V9(02).
```

could become

```
FD INPUT-FILE LABEL RECORDS ARE OMITTED.
01 INPUT-RECORD           PIC X(16).
    .
    .
    .
WORKING-STORAGE SECTION.
01 WORKING-INPUT-RECORD.
   02 WS-FIELD-1          PIC 9(02).
   02 WS-FIELD-2          PIC X(10).
   02 WS-FIELD-3          PIC 9(02)V9(02).
```

The purpose of such a change is to remove "special cases" in favor of more uniform definitions (even though the latter requires additional internal storage). Thus, *all* useful definitions of data appear in the WORKING-STORAGE SECTION. Data placed in the input-record (FD) description would simply be copied INTO its WORKING-STORAGE definition and output-record (FD) descriptions would be filled by copying its contents FROM a WORKING-STORAGE record description.

In conjunction with more extensive uses of the WORKING-STORAGE SECTION (and more comprehensive applications), the creation of meaningful and unique data-names for two or more fields that represent the same data sometimes becomes a problem. The convention employed to overcome this problem is to tag each data name with a prefix (or suffix) denoting the function it is to serve. For example, if we used the letter I to denote input and O to denote output, we might develop the following data-names:

```
I-CUSTOMER-NUMBER
O-CUSTOMER-NUMBER
I-QUANTITY
O-QUANTITY
```

It is immediately obvious that data-names preceded by I are from the input record and those preceded by O are from the output record. Furthermore, if a third or fourth name is necessary, it may be developed without modifying the "root" data-names. For example, data-names that appear in the WORKING-STORAGE SECTION could begin with the prefix W or WS. Suffixes have been chosen for use in this text. (Perhaps you have noticed by now!)

The most recently developed coding convention is to make PICTURE clauses as uniform as possible. This convention goes beyond the simple alignment previously mentioned. Consider for a moment the following PICTURE descriptions:

```
...PIC XXX.
...PIC X(3).
...PIC X(03).
```

The data described in all three PICTURE descriptions are the same. Now consider the following sequence of PICTURE clauses taken from Figure 6.6:

```
Existing             Possible
PIC 9(9).            PIC 9(09).
PIC X(10).           PIC X(10).
PIC X(10).           PIC X(10).
PIC X.               PIC X (01).
PIC X(10).           PIC X(10).
PIC X(10).           PIC X(10).
PIC XX.              PIC X(02).
PIC 9(5).            PIC 9(05).
PIC 99.              PIC 9(02).
PIC 99.              PIC 9(02).
PIC 99.              PIC 9(02).
PIC 9(5).            PIC 9(05).
PIC X(5).            PIC X(05).
PIC 9(5)V99.         PIC 9(05)V9(02).
```

Again, the data described in both records are exactly the same; however, it is much easier to verify the record length represented by the second column (by summing the length specifications) since they are all in the same columns (except for implied decimal fields). In addition, this format is somewhat easier to use when it is necessary to identify the data types (X or 9) of each field or to alter field lengths.

Questions

Below, fill in the blank(s) with the appropriate word, words, or phrases.

1. The DATA DIVISION may contain both a(n) ____ SECTION and a(n) ____ SECTION.

2. All files defined in the INPUT-OUTPUT SECTION of the ENVIRONMENT DIVISION are described in detail in the ____ SECTION of the DATA DIVISION.

3. Data items not directly related to input-output operations are described in the ____ SECTION.

4. For each FD entry, the file-name and the ____ clause must be specified before the first level 01.

5. A punched-card record is assumed to be ____ (number) columns long.

6. The ____ clause serves only as documentation in the FD entry.

7. Records may contain ____ , which are always treated as alphanumeric fields, and ____ , which may be represented by PICTURE clauses.

8. ____ determines the inclusiveness of a data-name.

9. The level number ____ is always associated with a record-name.

10. The level number(s) ____ always appear in Area A, and the level number(s) ____ always appear in Area B.

11. All elementary-item-descriptions include a level number, a data-name, and a(n) ____ clause.

12. The three different types of data items that can be described with a PICTURE clause are ____ , ____ , and ____ .

13. ____ data may be described with the PICTURE character A, ____ with the PICTURE character X, and ____ , with the PICTURE character 9.

14. When an area of an input record contains no data, that area may be referred to as the reserved word ____ in the record description.

15. When negative numeric data are required, the PICTURE should contain a(n) ____ character in the ____ position of the PICTURE string, and the data itself should contain a(n) ____ in the ____ position (column).

16. Anytime a decimal fraction is anticipated in a numeric field, the PICTURE string should contain the character ____ .

17. When a series of the same PICTURE character appear adjacent to each other, the character could be repeated in the PICTURE string, or a single PICTURE character could be written followed by a(n) ____ .

18. In the WORKING-STORAGE SECTION, data may be described within the context of a record or as a(n) ____ .

19. Two 80-byte record descriptions associated with a single file in the FILE SECTION require ____ (number) bytes of internal storage, whereas two 80-byte records in the WORKING-STORAGE SECTION require ____ (number) bytes of internal memory.

20. VALUE clauses are permitted only in the ____ SECTION and only at the ____ level.

Answer the following questions by circling either "T" for true or "F" for false.

T F **21.** A description of all data items used in a program may be found in the DATA DIVISION.

T F **22.** All COBOL programs require a WORKING-STORAGE SECTION.

T F **23.** For every SELECT clause in the FILE-CONTROL paragraph, there should be an FD entry in the FILE SECTION.

T F **24.** The FDs in the FILE SECTION must be in the same order as the SELECT clauses in the INPUT-OUTPUT SECTION.

T F **25.** In a record description, one group may appear within another group.

T F **26.** Elementary-items are composed of groups.

T F **27.** Within a record description the level numbers Ø1 through 1ØØ may be used.

T F **28.** The level number Ø2 is always used to indicate a group.

T F **29.** The level number Ø2 may be used in the representation of an elementary-item.

T F **30.** When used in a record description, level numbers must appear in a consecutive sequence (Ø1, Ø2, Ø3, etc.).

T F **31.** Each item within a record (whether a record, a group, or an elementary-item) should appear on a line by itself and should be followed by a period.

T F **32.** Both alphanumeric and numeric fields may be used for computation.

T F **33.** All group items are treated as though they were defined as alphanumeric data items.

T F 34. The operational sign character (S) should be used in a PICTURE clause anytime negative numeric data are anticipated.

T F 35. The character V can appear anywhere in a numeric PICTURE string.

T F 36. Multiple replication factors could be used in one PICTURE string.

T F 37. The reserved word FILLER may appear in a record description more than once.

T F 38. A level-77 item is permitted in the FILE SECTION.

T F 39. The level numbers Ø1 through 49 may appear in the WORKING-STORAGE SECTION.

T F 40. The WORKING-STORAGE SECTION is required in every COBOL program.

T F 41. Elementary-items may follow record descriptions in the WORKING-STORAGE SECTION.

T F 42. In the WORKING-STORAGE SECTION, a VALUE clause may be used in conjunction with a FILLER.

T F 43. A numeric elementary-item may have a value of SPACES assigned through a VALUE clause.

T F 44. The values assigned to an alphanumeric field may be shorter than the field length.

T F 45. An alphanumeric field of 20 characters with a VALUE ALL '-' will produce 20 hyphens (or dashes) in the field.

Exercises

1. Below is a record description associated with a file in the FILE SECTION. Complete a table with the indicated headings using the information presented within the record description.

```
Ø1 INVOICE-RECORD.
   Ø5 DESCRIPTIVE-INFORMATION.
      1Ø INVOICE-NUMBER             PIC 9(Ø5).
      1Ø CUSTOMER-NUMBER.
         15 CUSTOMER-GROUP          PIC 9(Ø2).
         15 CUSTOMER-SUFFIX         PIC 9(Ø7).
      1Ø ITEM-INFORMATION.
         15 ITEM-NUMBER             PIC 9(1Ø).
         15 ITEM-DESCRIPTION        PIC X(3Ø).
         15 QUANTITY-PURCHASED      PIC 9(Ø5).
         15 PRICE-PER-UNIT          PIC 9(Ø3)V9(Ø2).
         15 COST-PER-UNIT           PIC 9(Ø3)V9(Ø2).
         15 UNIT-MEASUREMENT        PIC X(Ø1).
   Ø5 FILLER                        PIC X(Ø5).
```

RECORD DESCRIPTION

DATA NAME	GROUP OR ELEMENTARY ITEM	LENGTH	COLUMNS OR POSITIONS

2. The following is a record that might be associated with a record description in the FILE SECTION. Complete a table with the indicated headings using the information presented within the record description.

```
Ø1 PAYROLL-SUMMARY-RECORD.
   Ø3 INDIVIDUAL-IDENTIFICATION.
      Ø5 EMPLOYEE-NUMBER                    PIC X(Ø4).
      Ø5 DEPARTMENT                         PIC 9(Ø3).
      Ø5 EMPLOYEE-NAME.
         1Ø LAST-NAME                       PIC X(1Ø).
         1Ø FIRST-NAME                      PIC X(1Ø).
         1Ø MIDDLE-NAME                     PIC X(1Ø).
      Ø5 MONETARY-BASE-DATA.
         1Ø RATE-PER-HOUR                   PIC 9(Ø4)V9(Ø2).
         1Ø SALARIED-HOURLY                 PIC X(Ø1).
         1Ø FEDERAL-TAX-INFORMATION.
            15 MARRIED-SINGLE               PIC X(Ø1).
            15 NO-DEPENDENTS                PIC 9(Ø2).
            15 EXTRA-DEDUCTION              PIC 9(Ø3)V9(Ø2).
```

RECORD DESCRIPTION			
DATA NAME	GROUP OR ELEMENTARY ITEM	LENGTH	COLUMNS OR POSITIONS

3. The graphic record layout shown in this exercise contains three records. Write the DATA DIVISION entries necessary to describe these records. (Assume each record is independent of the others.)

MULTIPLE-CARD LAYOUT FORM

Company LEARNING COBOL, INC.

Application DATA DIVISION EXAMPLES by M. JANET SPENCE Date 01/01/89 Job No. ____ Sheet No. 1

a) NAME/ADDRESS LABELS

CONTACT NAME (Alphanumeric--A/N)	BUSINESS NAME (A/N)	STREET ADDRESS/P.O. BOX (A/N)	CITY (Alphabetic--A)	ST. (A/N)	ZIP CODE (A/N)
1–20	21–38	39–59	60–73	74–75	76–80

b) INVENTORY RECORD

IDENTIFICATION INFORMATION		CURRENT INFORMATION				STATISTICAL INFO.		
ITEM NUMBER (Numeric--N)	ITEM DESCRIPTION (A/N)	PRICE GROUP (N)	UNIT PRICE (N)	UNIT COST (N)	ON HAND (N)	MONTH TO DATE SALES (N)	YEAR TO DATE SALES (N)	
1–9	10–39	40–44	45–50 (^ after 48)	51–56 (^ after 54)	57–62	63–70	71–78	79–80

c) STUDENT GRADE RECORD

STUDENT NAME (A/N)	STUDENT ID NUMBER (N)	EXAM GRADES				COURSE DATA		
		EXAM 1 (N)	EXAM 2 (N)	EXAM 3 (N)	EXAM 4 (N)	PRE-FIX (A/N)	NUM-BER (N)	COURSE TITLE (A/N)
1–20	21–29	30–33 (^ after 32)	34–37 (^ after 36)	38–41 (^ after 40)	42–45 (^ after 44)	46–49	50–53	54–80

4. Given the following information about a record, write the record description. The record-name is to be PAYMENT-RECORD. Use your discretion in the coding of groups and subgroups.

Column	Description	Type*
1–8	Customer number	N
10–19	Amount of payment (dollars and cents)	N
20–21	Month of payment	N
22–23	Day of payment	N
24–25	Year of payment	N
30–31	Month of receipt	N
32–33	Day of receipt	N
34–35	Year of receipt	N
40–45	Check number	N
50–52	Receipt clerk	A/N
60–80	Special notes	A/N

*N-numeric field; A/N-alphanumeric field

5. The layout below represents a report and column headings for output to be created by a program. Write the record description(s) necessary to create this form. Assume the record description(s) appear in the WORKING-STORAGE SECTION, and use VALUE clauses (where appropriate) to load the text of the heading. The numbers that appear in the layout represent column numbers. The "99" designations indicate the location of data fields. Use your own data-names as appropriate.

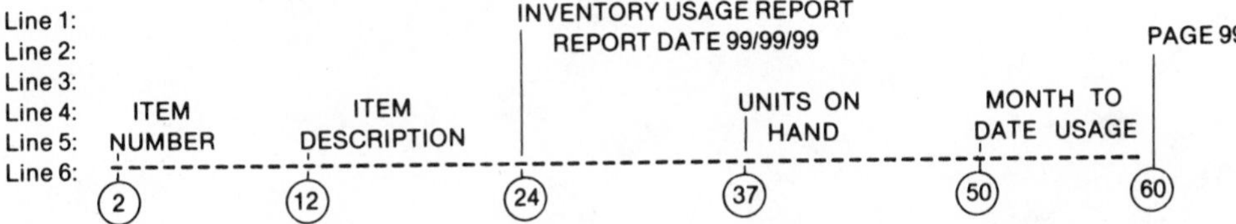

6. Assume the report layout below represents the form of an output report. Write the record description(s) necessary to form both the column headings and data record(s). The numbers that appear on the layout represent column locations and the names in parentheses should be used to represent data-names in the output description.

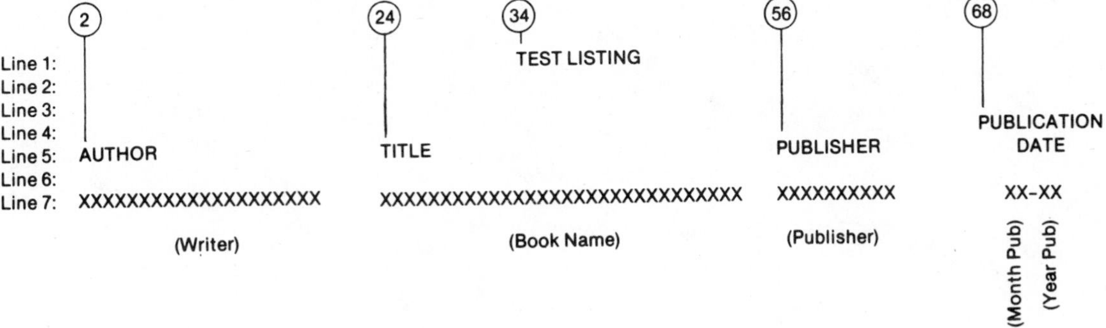

CHAPTER

7

The PROCEDURE DIVISION

Purpose of the Division

The PROCEDURE DIVISION is the portion of a COBOL program that provides the procedure, process, or algorithm to be executed. Thus, it is the ''doing'' part of the program. All input and output operations, data manipulation and movement, and decisions (testing of data values) occur during the execution of this division. The PROCEDURE DIVISION is logically the most complex portion of a COBOL program. Although the IDENTIFICATION, ENVIRONMENT, and DATA DIVISIONs may be very similar between programs, there may be little similarity between the PROCEDURE DIVISION of one program and another. Therefore, the PROCEDURE DIVISION, unlike the first three divisions, has no general format, that is, required section and paragraph names, entries, and clauses. (This chapter is limited to those commands necessary to process input and output records. Additional capabilities of the PROCEDURE DIVISION are discussed in Parts 2, 3, and 4.)

Overall Structure of the PROCEDURE DIVISION

The lack of a required structure in the PROCEDURE DIVISION may be disconcerting at first; however, it gives the programmer the benefit of a rather wide latitude in structure choice. The programmer structures the PROCEDURE DIVISION with selection, organization, and use of the section names, paragraph names, sentences, and statements that may be included in the division. To form a section or paragraph name, refer to the rules for the creation of data-names in Chapter 3. Remember that the principal difference between data-names and procedure-names is that section and paragraph names do not require an alphabetic character. Little difference exists for creating these names, but a vast difference exists in employing them. Data-names, presented in both the DATA and PROCEDURE DIVISIONs, are used to refer internally to data-storage positions. Section and paragraph names in the PROCEDURE DIVISION are used to reference or mark the location of one or more statements. For instance, to perform a branching operation (go from one location in the PROCEDURE DIVISION to somewhere other than the next sequential statement), you may use section or paragraph names to indicate the destination of the branching instruction.

As data-names should indicate the type of data the name represents, section and paragraph names in the PROCEDURE DIVISION indicate their functions. If a part of the PROCEDURE DIVISION is responsible for accepting data from an external data source (e.g., reading data records into the computer's internal storage, the paragraph name DATA-INPUT might be used. DATA-INPUT should include only those statements necessary for the acquisition of data. (This isolation of functions may require paragraph names that are seemingly useless. However, in Chapter 2 you saw that this approach makes a program easier to modify or *debug* (to correct errors in logic) and adds to the "structure" of the program.)

So far, section names have not been discussed. In the PROCEDURE DIVISION, the programmer may have section names, paragraph names, or both. Sections are not required if paragraphs are used. The differences between section names and paragraph names are: (1) a section name must be followed by the word *SECTION;* and (2) sections, as in the other divisions, may include one or more paragraphs. (*Note:* Some compilers *require* paragraphs within sections.)

One final comment about the structure of the PROCEDURE DIVISION. Some COBOL compilers require a procedure-name immediately following the division heading (on another line). Other compilers do not. All compilers, however, *permit* a procedure-name to follow the division heading. Because the additional name also improves program clarity, a procedure-name should follow the PROCEDURE DIVISION heading.

OPEN and CLOSE Statements

In COBOL, a program's access to a file may be localized. If a file is not needed from the beginning of the procedure to the end, the programmer, by using OPEN and CLOSE statements, may make a file available only during certain segments of the procedure (e.g., when reading data or producing printed output). This releases resources (e.g., disk files, line printers, etc.) to other programs that might also be requesting their use.

The OPEN statement (see Figure 7.1) is responsible for "preparing" a file for use by a program. Following the required reserved word OPEN, either INPUT (reading operations) or OUTPUT (writing operations) must be declared. The word INPUT or OUTPUT can appear only once in a single OPEN STATEMENT; however, a program could have many OPEN statements. After the reserved word INPUT (or OUTPUT), one or more file-names are listed—the same file-names used in SELECT clauses in the ENVIRONMENT DIVISION and in FD entries in the DATA DIVISION. Once a file has been opened, it cannot be reopened, unless it has previously been *closed*.

Figure 7.1 Format of the OPEN Statement. (Only clauses used in conjunction with a simple input device, or a line printer are shown.)

```
OPEN {INPUT } file-name-1 [file-name-2]...
     {OUTPUT}

     [{OUTPUT} *  file-name-m  [file-name-n]...]
     [{INPUT }                                 ]
```

*The reserved word used in the first set of braces cannot be repeated in the second set of braces.

Figure 7.2 Format of the CLOSE Statement. (Only clauses used in conjunction with a simple input device or a line printer are shown.)

```
CLOSE file-name-1  [file-name-2] ...
```

The CLOSE statement, shown in Figure 7.2, complements the OPEN statement. The CLOSE statement "disconnects" the file-names listed in the statement from the program. It is not necessary to indicate whether the file was being used for input or output operations, only that the files are no longer needed. A CLOSE statement should not be executed for a file until it has been opened, and the file should not be closed again until it has been reopened.

Figure 7.3 illustrates the use of OPEN and CLOSE statements to "localize" input or output resources. Notice that the file-names are "tied together" through the ENVIRONMENT, DATA, and PROCEDURE DIVISIONs. EMPLOYEE-FILE appears in the first SELECT clause and is ASSIGNed to an input device (e.g., disk file, in the ENVIRONMENT DIVISION). For the remainder of the program, the description of EMPLOYEE-FILE should be consistent with the device being employed. Regardless of the input device used, the input record description should *not* reflect edited data (as described in Chapter 8). In the PROCEDURE DIVISION, EMPLOYEE-FILE should be opened as an input file—UT-S-INPUT signifies an input device. In the PROCEDURE

Figure 7.3 Nonoverlapping INPUT and OUTPUT Operations

COBOL Coding Form

SYSTEM LEARNING COBOL, INC. — PUNCHING INSTRUCTIONS — PAGE 1 OF 1
PROGRAM SAMPLE OPEN AND CLOSE OPERATIONS — GRAPHIC — CARD FORM - FIG. 7.3
PROGRAMMER JOHN WINDSOR — DATE 01/01/89 — PUNCH

```
               SELECT EMPLOYEE-FILE ASSIGN TO UT-S-INPUT.
               SELECT PAYCHECK-FILE ASSIGN TO UT-S-OUTPUT.
           DATA DIVISION.
           FILE SECTION
           FD EMPLOYEE-FILE ...

           FD PAYCHECK-FILE ...


           PROCEDURE DIVISION.
           000-PROCEDURE-CONTROL
               OPEN INPUT EMPLOYEE-FILE
          * DATA INPUT PHASE.


          * DATA INPUT COMPLETE -- PRINTING STARTS.
               CLOSE EMPLOYEE-FILE.
               OPEN OUTPUT PAYCHECK-FILE.


          * PRINTING COMPLETE.
               CLOSE PAYCHECK-FILE.
```

DIVISION, EMPLOYEE-FILE is opened, all input is presumed to occur, and the file is closed before PAYCHECK-FILE is referenced. Presumably the requirements for this program never call for the input device to be available at the same time as the output device. (Your initial programs will generally require some overlap of input and output operations.) The characteristics of PAYCHECK-FILE must be consistent with an output device (e.g., line printer). The data should be described in character form, could be edited (as explained in Chapter 8), and should generally not be over 133 characters in length. In addition, a line printer is always used for OUTPUT.

Figure 7.4 illustrates how the OPEN and CLOSE operations may be performed when input and output operations are needed in the same segment of a program. Using the same SELECT clauses and FD entries as presented in Figure 7.3, EMPLOYEE-FILE and PAYCHECK-FILE are both available during the same phase of the program. Since EMPLOYEE-FILE and PAYCHECK-FILE are opened and closed together, at any point between the OPEN and CLOSE statements, data could be retrieved from the input device or output could be transmitted to the output device. In both examples, files were opened and closed in the same manner. This does not mean that you are forced to OPEN and CLOSE files using a consistent form of OPEN and CLOSE statements. Several files could be opened in the same statement and each closed separately, or vice versa. Also, the order of the SELECT clauses in the ENVIRONMENT DIVISION is not related to the order files are opened or closed in the PROCEDURE DIVISION. However, for purposes of clarity, ordering of SELECTs often establishes the logical order for file use in the PROCEDURE DIVISION.

Figure 7.4 Overlapped INPUT and OUTPUT Operations

COBOL Coding Form

SYSTEM LEARNING COBOL, INC. PUNCHING INSTRUCTIONS PAGE 1 OF 1
PROGRAM OVERLAPPED INPUT=OUTPUT OPERATIONS GRAPHIC
PROGRAMMER JOHN WINDSOR DATE 01/01/89 PUNCH CARD FORM - FIG. 7.6

```
01 PROCEDURE DIVISION
02 000-PROCEDURE-CONTROL.
03         OPEN INPUT EMPLOYEE-FILE. OUTPUT PAYCHECK-FILE.
04 *   INPUT AND OUTPUT OPERATIONS PERFORMED.
05
06
07 *   INPUT AND OUTPUT COMPLETED.
08         CLOSE EMPLOYEE-FILE. PAYCHECK-FILE.
09
10
11
12
13
14
15
16
17
18
19
20
```

READ Statement

Once a file has been OPENed as an INPUT file, the file is available for the retrieval of records via the READ statement. When a READ statement is executed, data in one record will be transferred into the computer's internal storage. The data in the record will then be available for use by the program by referencing the data-names of the FD record description.

The format of the READ statement is presented in Figure 7.5. The keyword READ is required, followed by the *file-name* from which a record is to be read. The file-name must appear in an OPEN statement prior to the execution of the first READ statement for that file. The keyword RECORD is not required. The INTO identifier phase is also optional. INTO makes it possible to read a record to an ''alternate'' record description outside the FD description for this file. During the execution of the READ statement, data are automatically placed in the record description that appears in the FD for that file. However, if INTO is specified, data from the input record will also be placed in a second description provided by the programmer. The alternate description is generally in the WORKING-STORAGE SECTION. The READ statement with an INTO option is equivalent to a READ statement followed by a ''MOVE'' statement (discussed shortly) which moves the entire record into the alternate description.

The AT END phrase should be used when reading from a simple input device. The phrase indicates (in the imperative statement) the procedure to be executed when an end-of-file (EOF) condition is found. When repetitive READ operations are executed, eventually the list of data records will be exhausted. At that time the imperative statement is executed.

1985 COBOL Standards

COBOL 85 provides two additional options for the READ statement. The NOT AT END clause may be used to indicate (in the imperative-statement) a procedure to be executed when an end-of-file condition is *not* found. The second additional option is the END-READ clause. This clause, a *structured delimiter,* is used to indicate the end of the READ instruction. A period at the end of the instruction performs the same function. However, the READ instruction may be used as a part of a longer, more complex sentence. In this instance, the END-READ clause would be necessary.

Remember that, in COBOL, a statement is one executable instruction. However, the imperative *statement* shown with the AT END phrase is really an imperative *sentence;* that is, one or more statements could be used. The imperative statement directs what happens when the end-of-file is reached. If the imperative statement includes a GO TO statement (discussed in Chapter 9), the GO TO should be the *last* statement in the imperative statement. Any statement following an unconditional branch in a sentence will not be executed.

Figure 7.6 illustrates the use of a READ statement in a program. In this example, when the first READ statement is executed, data from the first record of EMPLOYEE-

Figure 7.5 Format of the READ Statement

```
READ file-name [NEXT] RECORD [INTO identifier]

 {AT END imperative-statement-1      }
 {NOT AT END imperative-statement-2  }
```

Figure 7.6 Illustration of the READ Statement

COBOL Coding Form

SYSTEM LEARNING COBOL, INC.	PUNCHING INSTRUCTIONS		PAGE 1 OF 2
PROGRAM SAMPLE INPUT OPERATIONS	GRAPHIC		CARD FORM # FIG. 7.6
PROGRAMMER JOHN WINDSOR	DATE 01/01/89	PUNCH	

```
           SELECT EMPLOYEE-FILE ASSIGN TO UT-S-INPUT.
       DATA DIVISION.
       FILE SECTION.
       FD  EMPLOYEE-FILE
           LABEL RECORDS ARE OMITTED.
       01  EMPLOYEE-RECORD.                                    LOCATION
           05  EMPLOYEE-NUMBER-IN          PIC X(05).             .15
           05  EMPLOYEE-NAME-IN            PIC X(20).            6.25
           05  RATE-PER-HOUR-IN            PIC S9(04)V9(02).    26.31
           05  HOURS-WORKED-IN             PIC 9(03).           32.34


       WORKING-STORAGE SECTION
       01  EMPLOYEE-RECORD-WS.
           05  EMPLOYEE-NUMBER-WS.
               10  DEPARTMENT-CODE-WS      PIC 9(02).              12
               10  SERIAL-NUMBER-WS        PIC 9(03).              25
           05  EMPLOYEE-NAME-WS.
               10  LAST-NAME-WS            PIC X(10).            6.15
               10  FIRST-NAME-WS           PIC X(10).           16.25
           05  RATE-PER-HOUR-WS            PIC 9(04)V9(02).     26.31
           05  HOURS-WORKED-WS             PIC 9(02)V9(02).     32.34
```

FILE are placed in the EMPLOYEE-RECORD record description. The data in columns 1 through 5 of the input record would be placed in EMPLOYEE-NUMBER-IN; columns 6 through 25, in EMPLOYEE-NAME-IN; columns 26 through 31, in RATE-PER-HOUR-IN; and columns 32 through 34, in HOURS-WORKED-IN. If no data were available when an attempt was made to read from EMPLOYEE-FILE, the FILE-STATUS identifier is set to indicate EOF.

When the second READ statement is executed, the same data alignment would be made for EMPLOYEE-NUMBER-IN through HOURS-WORKED-IN. In *addition,* the contents of EMPLOYEE-NUMBER-IN would also be placed in EMPLOYEE-NUMBER-WS), EMPLOYER-NAME-WS (which is made up of DEPARTMENT-NUMBER-WS and SERIAL-NUMBER-WS), EMPLOYEE-NAME-WS (which is composed of LAST-NAME-WS and FIRST-NAME-WS) and would be the same as EMPLOYEE-NAME-IN; RATE-PER-HOUR-WS. It would also be the same as RATE-PER-HOUR-IN, and HOURS-WORKED-IN and HOURS-WORKED-WS would contain the same digits. Note the minor differences in the PICTURE clauses of EMPLOYEE-RECORD and EMPLOYEE-RECORDS-WS. It is unnecessary for the PICTURE clauses to be the same or for the fields to align on the same columns of the input record.

The presence of an alternate description has three important advantages. First, the alternate may be used to describe the data fields differently from the FD record description. Second, changes made to the data fields in EMPLOYEE-RECORD, which is independent

Figure 7.6 *Continued* Illustration of the READ Statement

COBOL Coding Form

SYSTEM LEARNING COBOL, INC. — PUNCHING INSTRUCTIONS — PAGE 2 OF 2
PROGRAM SAMPLE INPUT OPERATIONS — GRAPHIC — CARD FORM #
PROGRAMMER JOHN WINDSOR — DATE 01/01/89 — PUNCH

SEQUENCE (PAGE) (SERIAL) | CONT. | A | B | COBOL STATEMENT | IDENTIFICATION

```
       PROCEDURE DIVISION.
       000-PROCEDURE-CONTROL.
           OPEN INPUT EMPLOYEE-FILE.


           READ EMPLOYEE-FILE
               AT END MOVE 'DONE' TO FILE-STATUS.


           READ EMPLOYEE-FILE INTO EMPLOYEE-RECORD-WS
               AT END MOVE 'Input Phase Completed' TO PRINT-LINE
                      WRITE PRINT-LINE AFTER ADVANCING 1 LINES.
```

of EMPLOYEE-RECORD-WS, will not affect the contents of the data in EMPLOYEE-RECORD-WS; the reverse is also true. Third, the FD description is a "buffer" description (further described in Chapter 17) that should not be changed except by data from an external source. The EMPLOYEE-RECORD-WS description is a WORKING-STORAGE record and is not directly associated with any file (although in the example the INTO option is an indirect reference). Thus, the WORKING-STORAGE record description may be used for purposes other than holding input data. The contents of the elementary-items could be manipulated and changed without causing processing problems.

In the example (Figure 7.6), the AT END phrase includes a sentence, not a simple statement. The execution of the imperative statement will cause the nonnumeric literal input phase complete to be moved to an output line and the output line to be written.

WRITE Statement

A WRITE statement takes data that have been stored internally and records it on an external medium. Within the scope of this part of the text, the WRITE statement causes lines of printed output to be created. Each time a WRITE statement is executed, one record (line of output) is printed. Prior to the first execution of a WRITE, the file used in conjunction with the WRITE statement must be OPENed in an OUTPUT mode.

The format of the WRITE statement appears in Figure 7.7. Within this statement the reserved word WRITE is followed by the name of the record to be written. *A record-*

name, not the file-name, is used in WRITE statements. The record-name to be written must appear in the FD for the output file. There may be one or more record descriptions (depending upon the requirements of the output) within a single FD.

The FROM option of the WRITE statement can be used to move an alternate record description—referenced by identifier-1—into the output record before the WRITE statement takes place. The record description, referenced by identifier-1, is generally located in the WORKING-STORAGE SECTION.

The next optional clause (BEFORE/AFTER ADVANCING) specifies the carriage control or vertical spacing for printed output. The programmer chooses whether the vertical positioning can take place BEFORE or AFTER the line is printed. If BEFORE, the line is written before any vertical movement takes place. If AFTER, the carriage control is invoked, and then the line of output is produced. Once BEFORE or AFTER has been specified, all other WRITE statements to the same file must contain the same reserved word. The word ADVANCING is not required but is provided for clarity. The programmer then has a choice of entries for specifying the line to which the printer is to be positioned. If identifier-2 is specified, identifier-2 must be described as an integer, nonedited-numeric field. The field should not contain an integer value less than zero or greater than 100. The value associated with identifier-2 will cause that number of lines to be advanced on the line printer. If the value is zero, no advance takes place (provided your printer supports this option). When either identifier-2 or integer is specified, the optional word LINE or LINES may follow.

Most compilers support the use of a mnemonic-name as one of the options indicating the number of lines to be advanced. Remember the SPECIAL-NAMES paragraph in the ENVIRONMENT DIVISION. One of the entries in the SPECIAL-NAMES paragraph is "system-name IS mnemonic-name." Most compilers provide a series of system-names that indicate a particular location or channel on a printer carriage-control tape or electronic vertical forms control unit. To use system-names to indicate paper advancement, SPECIAL-NAMES is used with the WRITE statement. The most used system-names for indicating top-of-the page are C01 (IBM) and '1' (e.g., CDC). Other system-names could be used for other methods of line advancement, but this is the only practical means for advancing to the top of a new page without regard to the present location on the previous page.

Figure 7.7 Format of the WRITE Statement. (Statement, as shown, is designed for printed output only.)

```
WRITE record-name [FROM identifier-1]

[ { BEFORE }  ADVANCING  { { integer        } [ LINES ] } ]
[ {        }             { { identifier-2   } [ LINE  ] } ]
[ {        }             {   mnemonic-name      *       } ]
[ { AFTER  }             {   PAGE *                     } ]

[        { END-OF-PAGE }                          ] *
[   AT   {             }   imperative-statement   ]
[        { EOP         }                          ]

   [END-WRITE]
```

* ANS standard, but not always implemented

The final option that indicates paper advancement on a line printer is PAGE. In Figure 7.7 note that PAGE is an American National Standard (ANS) option but is not always implemented. Not all implementations are uniform. Sometimes PAGE is used to indicate a top-of-page advancement (e.g., UNISYS and RM-COBOL), and in other cases it is replaced with TO *TOP* OF PAGE (e.g., Honeywell).

The next clause associated with the WRITE statement is the END-OF-PAGE clause. As noted in Figure 7.7, it is among the ANS options but is not always implemented. It is implemented in a large number of COBOL compilers; however, they differ widely in how the END-OF-PAGE condition is detected.

COBOL 85 provided an additional option for the WRITE statement. The option is the END-WRITE clause. This clause is a *structured delimiter* used to clearly indicate the end of the WRITE instruction. A period at the end of the instruction performs the same function. However, the WRITE instruction may be used as a part of a longer, more complex sentence. In this instance the END-WRITE clause would be necessary.

Figure 7.8 illustrates the use of WRITE statements in a COBOL program. The first WRITE statement of the illustration produces a ''page heading.'' In this statement, the record-name to be printed is PAYCHECK-RECORD. PAYCHECK-RECORD is described in general terms in the FILE SECTION. The FROM option provides more detailed information from a record (identifier-1) labeled HEADING-LINE. The description of HEADING-LINE in the WORKING-STORAGE SECTION indicates that a series of nonnumeric literals are to be written with interspersed blank columns (indicated by FILLER). This output record is placed at the top of the next page of print. NEXT-PAGE is the mnemonic-name identified in the SPECIAL-NAMES paragraph.

The next line of output created by the program is located four lines below the top of the page. This WRITE statement produces ''column headings.'' The record-name PAYCHECK-RECORD signifies the output line; and, the FROM option provides the text for the output line. In this instance, however, a data-name (identifier-2) is used to indicate the number of lines to be advanced. In the WORKING-STORAGE SECTION, the data item HEADING-SPREAD-WS contains a value of 4, signifying that four lines are to be advanced. Since a data item is used, the value of the variable could be changed later to provide variably spaced output.

The last line of output is produced from DETAIL-LINE. DETAIL-LINE is moved to PRINT-LINE prior to the execution of the WRITE statement so that individual data items will be printed. A procedure for placing data into each of the elementary items of DETAIL-LINE prior to the execution of this WRITE statement is assumed. In this final example the integer value 2 is specified, indicating that two lines are to be advanced. Thus, if the third WRITE statement were executed repeatedly the output would be double-spaced.

In the example the AFTER ADVANCING option is also employed. Thus, all of the WRITE statements in the program using PAYCHECK-RECORD must use the AFTER keyword to indicate when vertical position is to take place.

The MOVE Statement

The MOVE statement provides the means for moving data from one location to another within internal storage. Although the MOVE statement appears to be ''simple,'' it is one of the most powerful operations in COBOL. The format of the MOVE statement is provided in Figure 7.9. It is composed of two parts, the sending field and the receiving field(s). The ''sending'' field in the statement is either identifier-1, a literal, or a figurative

Figure 7.8 An Illustration of the WRITE Statement

```
                    .
                    .
                    .
ENVIRONMENT DIVISION.
CONFIGURATION SECTION.
SOURCE-COMPUTER.  IBM.
OBJECT-COMPUTER.  IBM.
SPECIAL-NAMES.    C01 IS NEXT-PAGE.
INPUT-OUTPUT SECTION.
FILE-CONTROL.
    SELECT PAYCHECK-FILE  ASSIGN TO UT-S-OUTPUT.
                    .
                    .
                    .
DATA DIVISION.
FILE SECTION.
FD  PAYCHECK-FILE  LABEL RECORDS ARE OMITTED.
01  PAYCHECK-RECORD              PIC X(133).
                    .
                    .
                    .
WORKING-STORAGE SECTION.
01  WORKING-VARIABLES.
    05  HEADING-SPREAD-WS        PIC 9(02) VALUE 4.
01  HEADING-LINE.
    05  FILLER                   PIC X(46) VALUE SPACES.
    05  FILLER                   PIC X(17) VALUE
                                 'Paycheck Register'.
01  COLUMN-HEADINGS.
    05  FILLER                   PIC X(01) VALUE SPACES.
    05  FILLER                   PIC X(25) VALUE 'Employee Name'.
    05  FILLER                   PIC X(20) VALUE
                                 'Employee Number'.
    05  FILLER                   PIC X(17) VALUE 'Check Number'.
    05  FILLER                   PIC X(18) VALUE 'Regular Hours'.
    05  FILLER                   PIC X(14) VALUE 'Overtime Hours'.
01  DETAIL-LINE.
    05  FILLER                   PIC X(01) VALUE SPACES.
    05  EMPLOYEE-NAME-OUT        PIC X(20).
    05  FILLER                   PIC X(10) VALUE SPACES.
    05  EMPLOYEE-NUMBER-OUT      PIC 9(05).
    05  FILLER                   PIC X(15) VALUE SPACES.
    05  CHECK-NUMBER-OUT         PIC 9(06).
    05  FILLER                   PIC X(12) VALUE SPACES.
    05  REGULAR-HOURS-OUT        PIC 9)03).
    05  FILLER                   PIC X(17) VALUE SPACES.
    05  OVERTIME-HOURS-OUT       PIC 9(03).
                    .
                    .
                    .
PROCEDURE DIVISION.
000-PROCEDURE-CONTROL.
    OPEN OUTPUT PAYCHECK-FILE.
    WRITE PAYCHECK-RECORD FROM HEADING-LINE
        AFTER ADVANCING NEXT-PAGE.
    WRITE PAYCHECK-RECORD FROM COLUMN-HEADINGS
        AFTER ADVANCING HEADING-SPREAD-WS LINES.
                    .
                    .
                    .
    MOVE DETAIL-LINE TO PAYCHECK-RECORD.
    WRITE PAYCHECK-RECORD AFTER ADVANCING 2 LINES.
                    .
                    .
                    .
    CLOSE PAYCHECK-FILE.
```

Figure 7.9 Format of the MOVE Statement

```
       ⎧identifier-1       ⎫
MOVE   ⎨literal            ⎬  TO identifier-2 [identifier-3]...
       ⎩figurative constant⎭
```

constant. The sending field acts as the source of the data to be transmitted. The receiving field(s) are those identifiers listed after the reserved word TO.

Valid movements of data from a sending field to a receiving field are listed in Table 7.1. Sending fields are classified by the types of data represented. The same approach is used for the receiving fields. The content of the sending field is not affected by this movement. The (new) content of the receiving field is determined by the sending field.

A fundamental difference exists between alphanumeric data (including record- and group-names), alphabetic data, and numeric data. Alphanumeric and alphabetic data in a sending or a receiving field are generally *left-justified* (occupy the leftmost positions of the field); unused positions (to the right) are filled with spaces. If the sending field is longer than the receiving field, data are truncated from right to left as much as necessary to fit the PICTURE description of the receiving field.

The rules are different for numeric data. Normally, data from the sending field are aligned on the (implied) decimal point of the receiving field. In the absence of a decimal point, it is presumed to follow the *right-most* digit. If the sending field is too long for the PICTURE description of the receiving field, the data may be truncated to the size of the receiving field from either the right or the left based upon the decimal point alignment. If there are not enough digit positions to the left of the decimal point in the

Table 7.1 Permissable Moves of Nonedited Data

	Receiving Fields			
		Elementary Items		
Sending Fields	**Records or Groups**	**Alphaneumeric (X)**	**Alphabetic (A)**	**Numeric (9)**
Record of Group	YES	YES	YES[1]	YES[3]
Alphanumeric (X)	YES	YES	YES[1]	YES[3]
Alphabetic (A)	YES	YES	YES	NO
Numeric (9)	YES[3]	YES[4]	NO	YES
Figurative Constants				
ZEROS	YES	YES	NO	YES
SPACES	YES	YES	YES	NO
HIGH-VALUE LOW-VALUE and QUOTES	YES	YES	NO	NO
ALL Literal	YES	YES	YES[1]	YES[2]
Numeric Literal	YES[3]	YES[4]	NO	YES
Nonnumeric Literal	YES	YES	YES[1]	YES[2]

[1]When the field contains only alphabetic charactrers and spaces.
[2]When the field contains only numeric characters. The field is treated as a numeric integer.
[3]The movement of data is treated the same as an alphanumeric to alphanumeric move.
[4]When the numeric data item represents an integer number.

Figure 7.10 Illustrations of the MOVE Statement

The results of "MOVE ITEM-1 TO ITEM-2," when ITEM-1 and ITEM-2 are described as follows (each example should be considered separately):

ITEM-1		ITEM-2	
Picture Clause	**Contains***	**PICTURE Clause**	**After MOVE* Contains**
X(Ø5)	ABCDE	X(Ø5)	ABCDE
X(Ø5)	ABCDE	X(Ø3)	ABC
X(Ø5)	ABCDE	X(Ø7)	ABCDEƀƀ
X(Ø5)	ABCDE	A(Ø4)	ABCD
X(Ø5)	ƀ1234	9(Ø5)	ƀ1234
A(Ø4)	ABƀƀ	A(Ø3)	ABƀ
A(Ø4)	ABCD	A(Ø6)	ABCDƀƀ
A(Ø4)	ABCD	X(Ø8)	ABCDƀ
9(Ø5)	12345	9(Ø5)	12345
9(Ø5)	12345	9(Ø4)	2345
9(Ø5)	12345	9(Ø6)	Ø2345
9(Ø3)V9(Ø2)	123∧45	9(Ø2)	23
9(Ø3)V9(Ø2)	123∧45	9(Ø4)	Ø123
9(Ø3)V9(Ø2)	123∧45	V9(Ø2)	∧45
9(Ø3)V9(Ø2)	123∧45	9(Ø1)V9(Ø1)	3∧4
9(Ø4)	1234	X(Ø4)	1234
9(Ø4)	1234	X(Ø5)	1234ƀ

The results of "MOVE—TO ITEM-2." when the sending field is described as follows:

Sending Field		ITEM-2*	
Type	**Form**	**PICTURE Clause**	**After MOVE Contains**
Figurative constant	ZERO	9(Ø4)	ØØØØ
Figurative constant	SPACES	X(Ø5)	ƀƀƀƀƀ
Figurative constant	ALL(*)	X(Ø7)	*******
Numeric literal	1234	9(Ø4)	1234
Numeric literal	1234	9(Ø3)V9(Ø2)	234∧ØØ
Numeric literal	123.4	9(Ø3)V9(Ø2)	123∧4Ø
Nonnumeric literal	'ENDƀOFƀJOB'	X(1Ø)	ENDƀOFƀJOB
Nonnumeric literal	'1234'	9(Ø4)	1234
Nonnumeric literal	'A'	A(Ø3)	Aƀƀ

*The symbol ƀ represents a blank; the symbol Ø represents a zero.

receiving field to accommodate the data from the sending field, high-order (leading) digits will be truncated. If there are not sufficient positions following the decimal location in the receiving field, data will be truncated from the low-order (trailing) digit positions. If the sending field is larger than the receiving field (either to the left or right or both), zeros will replace unused digit positions.

The examples in Figure 7.10 show some results of the MOVE statement.

PERFORM Statements in General

The PERFORM statement allows a programmer to execute one or more contiguous procedures (paragraphs or sections), which are not necessarily physically close to the location of the PERFORM statement itself. Initially, the PERFORM statement causes a temporary transfer of control to the procedure specified. Therefore, the PERFORM statement regains control of execution after the procedure or procedures have been completed. When all operations within the procedure are completed, execution continues from a point immediately after the PERFORM statement. Thus, the PERFORM statement permits a programmer to "go to" a particular procedure or set of procedures and "return" to the location of the PERFORM statement after the procedure has been completed.

Although there are four formats of the PERFORM statement, only the two most frequently used in structured programs are described in this chapter (see Figure 7.11). The remaining two are discussed in Chapter 12. All PERFORM formats have one phrase in common—the name(s) of the procedure(s) to be executed. In Figure 7.11, Format 1 of the PERFORM statement (and the other formats, as well) shows that, at a minimum, procedure-name-1 must be specified. A procedure-name is a paragraph or SECTION name located in the PROCEDURE DIVISION. The procedure may be located either above or below the PERFORM statement. The PERFORM statement should never specify the procedure-name containing itself unless precautions are taken to avoid an endless loop.

If the optional phrase THROUGH (THRU) procedure-name-2 is specified, procedure-name-2 is a paragraph or SECTION name that is physically below (but not necessarily immediately below) procedure-name-1. The THROUGH option should be avoided to improve program clarity and maintenance. The statements in either procedure-name-1 or procedure-name-2 may be any COBOL statements, including other PERFORM statements.

The optional phrase END-PERFORM is provided by the COBOL 85 standards. This phrase is a structured delimiter, which indicates the end of a set of imperative-statements used by the PERFORM instruction. This use of the PERFORM instruction, called an *inline-perform* along with other advanced options of the PERFORM instruction are discussed in Chapter 12.

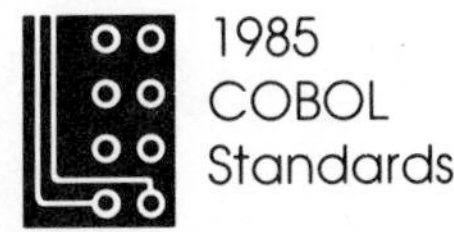

Figure 7.11 Formats of the PERFORM Statement

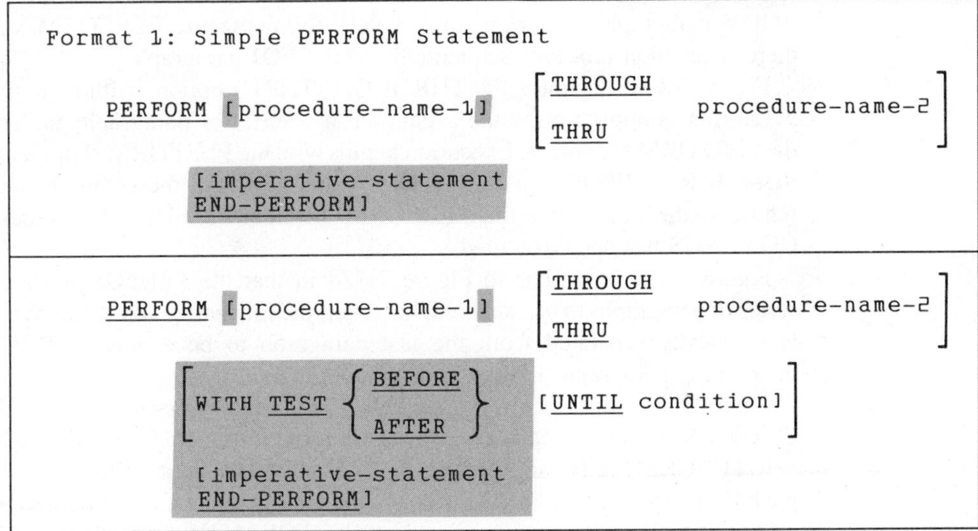

The Simple PERFORM Statement

The Format-1 PERFORM statement is terminated (control passes to the statement following the PERFORM statement) when the last statement in the specified set of procedures is executed, resulting in the logical effect of the insertion of the statements in the set of procedures at the location of the PERFORM statement. The same PERFORM statement could appear at several locations in a program (e.g., a utility or service module) without repeating the procedure. The PERFORM statement may be placed anywhere in the PROCEDURE DIVISION, even embedded in sentences or imperative statements.

Figure 7.12 illustrates how the simple PERFORM statement might be used in a program. This figure presents a series of PERFORM statements. Remember, when a PERFORM has completed execution, *control* of the program returns to the statement immediately following the PERFORM statement. Thus, unless some provision is placed in a program to avoid reexecution of procedures following the PERFORM statement they will be executed again.

In Figure 7.12a the TERMINATION paragraph is invoked by a PERFORM statement. When the next paragraph name is encountered (or the physical end of the program is reached), procedural control is passed to the statement following the PERFORM statement. The STOP RUN statement is executed, and the program is halted. In this example the TERMINATION paragraph may include operations such as report footings, a summary report, or file closings.

Figure 7.12b illustrates what happens when a PERFORM operation is not protected from fall through. The sequence indicates that GET-A-RECORD is executed twice—once as a result of the PERFORM, and once because GET-A-RECORD immediately follows the PERFORM statement.

In Figure 7.12c the sequence of paragraphs executed begins with a series of paragraphs. Only after the PROCEDURE-BODY paragraph is encountered is a PERFORM statement executed. However, in this case the paragraph being performed is located above the PERFORM statement. Thus, when the PAGE-HEADING paragraph is invoked by the PERFORM statement, execution will remain in the paragraph until the next paragraph (PROCEDURE-BODY) is reached. Then execution continues in the PROCEDURE-BODY paragraph at a point immediately following the PERFORM statement. From there, execution proceeds sequentially to the EOJ paragraph.

Figure 7.12d illustrates the THROUGH (THRU) option. Although similar to Figure 7.12a this example causes the execution of a series of paragraphs under the control of the PERFORM statement. Execution begins with the PERFORM statement, which causes SUMMARY-REPORT to be invoked. Control, under these circumstances, does not return to the point after the PERFORM statement until the last statement of FILE-CLOSINGS has been executed.

Figure 7.12e is similar to Figure 7.12d in that the PERFORM statement causes a series of paragraphs to be executed; however, the first paragraph (FED-WITHHOLDING) is physically separated from the last paragraph to be executed (DEDUCTS) by an intervening paragraph (FICA-CALCULATIONS).

Figure 7.12f illustrates multiple PERFORM statements in one procedure. The first PERFORM statement caused the execution of three paragraphs (READ-A-RECORD, WRITE-A-RECORD, and MOVE-DATA). After the first PERFORM has been completed, the second PERFORM invokes the READ-A-RECORD paragraph. Despite the reference to the paragraph in a previous PERFORM statement, the use of the paragraph

Figure 7.12 Illustrations of the Simple PERFORM Statement

PROCEDURE DIVISION STRUCTURE	SEQUENCE OF PARAGRAPHS EXECUTED
a) PERFORM TERMINATION. STOP RUN TERMINATION.	TERMINATION
b) PERFORM GET-A-RECORD. GET-A-RECORD.	GET-A-RECORD (fall through) GET-A-RECORD
c) PAGE-HEADING. PROCEDURE-BODY. PERFORM PAGE-HEADING. EOJ.	(fall through) { PAGE-HEADING PROCEDURE-BODY PAGE-HEADING (fall through) EOJ
d) PERFORM SUMMARY-REPORT THRU FILE-CLOSINGS. STOP RUN. SUMMARY-REPORT. FILE-CLOSINGS.	{ SUMMARY-REPORT FILE-CLOSINGS
e) PERFORM FED-WITHHOLDING THROUGH DEDUCTS. STOP RUN. FED-WITHHOLDING. FICA-CALCULATION. DEDUCTS.	{ FED-WITHHOLDING FICA-CALCULATION DEDUCTS
f) PERFORM READ-A-RECORD THRU MOVE-DATA. PERFORM READ-A-RECORD. PERFORM WRITE-A-RECORD. READ-A-RECORD. WRITE-A-RECORD. MOVE-DATA. EOJ.	{ READ-A-RECORD WRITE-A-RECORD MOVE-DATA READ-A-RECORD WRITE-A-RECORD (fall through) { READ-A-RECORD WRITE-A-RECORD MOVE-DATA EOJ
g) PERFORM UNIT-1. PERFORM UNIT-4. STOP RUN. UNIT-1. PERFORM UNIT-2 THRU UNIT-3. UNIT-2. PERFORM UNIT-4. UNIT-3. UNIT-4. PERFORM UNIT-3.	UNIT-1 UNIT-2 UNIT-4 UNIT-3 UNIT-3 UNIT-4 UNIT-3

name is not restricted in other PERFORM statements even though the context of its use may be different. Thus, when READ-A-RECORD has been completed, the third PERFORM statement is executed, and WRITE-A-RECORD is invoked. Finally, once WRITE-A-RECORD has been completed, a fall through causes the repeated execution of all four remaining paragraphs.

The final illustration, Figure 7.12g, demonstrates PERFORM statements being performed within paragraphs. When UNIT-1 is executed as a result of the first PERFORM statement, another PERFORM statement is encountered. The second PERFORM statement (PERFORM UNIT-2 THRU UNIT-3) invokes UNIT-2. While UNIT-2 is being executed, a third PERFORM statement is encountered, which causes UNIT-4 to be invoked. Finally, during the execution of UNIT-4, a fourth PERFORM is discovered, causing the execution of UNIT-3 to begin. At this point, all four PERFORM statements are "active" and an "unfolding" operation begins. When UNIT-3 is completed, execution of UNIT-4 resumes. When UNIT-4 is completed, execution of UNIT-2 resumes. When UNIT-2 is completed, execution of UNIT-3 begins (for the second time) because the PERFORM which originated this operation was PERFORM UNIT-2 THRU UNIT-3. When UNIT-3 is completed for the second time, execution of UNIT-1 resumes. When UNIT-1 is completed, execution proceeds with the statement that originally caused UNIT-1 to be invoked. Thus, the statement PERFORM UNIT-4 is executed, causing UNIT-4 to be invoked. Again, during the execution of UNIT-4, a PERFORM statement invoking UNIT-3 is encountered. UNIT-3 is completed; UNIT-4 is resumed and completed, and the original PERFORM statement is thus completed; and finally, STOP RUN is encountered.

The PERFORM/UNTIL Statement

The second format of the PERFORM statement, the PERFORM/UNTIL, allows the programmer to control, within the procedure, the number of times a procedure is executed. As indicated in Format 2 of Figure 7.11, the PERFORM/UNTIL statement provides for the testing of a specified condition. The condition may be any condition or combination of conditions permitted within the context of an IF statement. (See Chapters 9 and 11 for more details about IF statement conditions). The condition is tested by the PERFORM statement *when the PERFORM statement is encountered and prior to each repeated execution of the procedure* specified in the PERFORM statement.

1985 COBOL Standards

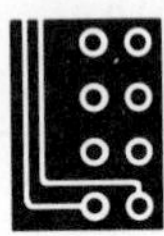

There are times when it may be more efficient to test agreement with the UNTIL condition after the execution of a procedure. COBOL 85 uses a TEST option to provide this capability. The WITH TEST BEFORE option works exactly the same as the PERFORM statement without the option. With the WITH TEST AFTER option, the condition is tested by the PERFORM *after the procedure specified in the PERFORM statement has been executed, and after each repeated execution of the procedure.*

Figure 7.13 illustrates the PERFORM/UNTIL statement. Note that where the PERFORM/UNTIL statement is used, a statement (or combination of statements) in some way affects the condition specified in the PERFORM/UNTIL statement.

In Figure 7.13a the data-name DAYS is used to control the performed activity. DAYS is initialized in a MOVE statement (DAYS = 1) and the PERFORM statement is encountered. If, at this point, DAYS is greater than 5, WEEKDAYS is not performed at all. However, since DAYS is equal to 1, the PERFORM statement invokes WEEKDAYS, which is repeatedly executed until DAYS is greater than 5. While WEEKDAYS is executed, an ADD statement is encountered (The ADD statement is discussed in

Figure 7.13 Illustrations of the PERFORM/UNTIL Statement

PROCEDURE DIVISION STRUCTURE	SEQUENCE OF PARAGRAPHS EXECUTED
a) MOVE 1 TO DAYS. PERFORM WEEKDAYS UNTIL DAYS GREATER THAN 5. STOP RUN. WEEKDAYS. ADD 1 TO DAYS	WEEKDAYS WEEKDAYS WEEKDAYS WEEKDAYS
b) MOVE 4 TO NUM. PERFORM FIRST-PROCESS UNTIL NUM = ZERO. MOVE 4 TO NUM. FIRST-PROCESS. PERFORM SECOND-PROCESS UNTIL NUM = 1. SUBTRACT 1 FROM NUM. SECOND-PROCESS. SUBTRACT 1 FROM NUM. FINAL-PROCESS.	FIRST-PROCESS SECOND-PROCESS SECOND-PROCESS SECOND-PROCESS FIRST-PROCESS SECOND-PROCESS SECOND-PROCESS SECOND-PROCESS SECOND-PROCESS FINAL-PROCESS
c) MOVE 1 TO LINE-COUNT PERFORM WRITE-LINE WITH TEST AFTER UNTIL LINE-COUNT = 1 STOP RUN WRITE-LINE. WRITE PRINT-LINE AFTER 1 LINES.	WRITE-LINE (WRITE-LINE performed 1 times.)
d) DATA DIVISION. FILE SECTION. FD PROCESS-FILE . . . 01 PROCESS-RECORD. 05 PROCESS-INDICATOR PIC 9. PROCEDURE DIVISION. PERFORM TYPE-1-PROCESS UNTIL PROCESS-INDICATOR=1. PERFORM TYPE-2-PROCESS UNTIL PROCESS-INDICATOR=2 OR 3. PERFORM TYPE-3-PROCESS UNTIL PROCESS-INDICATOR > 4. STOP RUN. TYPE-1-PROCESS. TYPE-2-PROCESS. TYPE-3-PROCESS.	TYPE-1-PROCESS until PROCESS-INDICATOR contains the value 1, then TYPE-2-PROCESS until PROCESS-INDICATOR contains the value 2 or 3, and then TYPE-3-PROCESS until PROCESS-INDICATOR contains a value greater than 3.

detail in Chapter 10) and DAYS is incremented by 1. At this point, DAYS is equal to 2, thus WEEKDAYS is repeated. When DAYS = 6 and the end of the WEEKDAYS paragraph is encountered, the condition is true; the PERFORM statement is terminated, and the STOP RUN statement is encountered.

The second illustration, Figure 7.13b, demonstrates the use of multiple PERFORM/UNTIL statements. The sequence begins when NUM is initialized to 4. The first PERFORM statement is then encountered. In this instance, the condition uses a test based on the value of NUM. Thus, FIRST-PROCESS continues until NUM has been decremented (reduced) to zero. However, while FIRST-PROCESS is being executed for the first time, PERFORM SECOND-PROCESS is encountered. The condition necessary for the termination of SECOND-PROCESS is for NUM to be equal to 1. While SECOND-PROCESS is being executed, a SUBTRACT statement is encountered, which decrements the value of NUM each time SECOND-PROCESS is executed. (The SUBTRACT statement is described in detail in Chapter 10.) As a consequence, SECOND-PROCESS will be executed three times before NUM is equal to 1 at the end of the paragraph. After SECOND-PROCESS has been completed, execution of FIRST-PROCESS resumes, where NUM is again decremented (and NUM should contain a value of zero). Thus, the first time the end of FIRST-PROCESS is encountered, the condition specified for no longer executing the paragraph is true. Again, the value of 4 is moved to NUM and execution falls through to the FIRST-PROCESS paragraph. Within FIRST-PROCESS, SECOND-PROCESS is again repeated three times. However, when the PERFORM SECOND-PROCESS has been completed, the procedure falls through SECOND-PROCESS to the FINAL-PROCESS paragraph.

In Figure 7.13b, it is not desirable to have several perform statements controlled in a "nested" arrangement, especially when all the procedures have the opportunity to modify the same "control" data-name. The nested control structure is generally difficult to properly construct; it rarely works the first time, and it is a nightmare to maintain. Second, the conditions "NUM-ZERO" and "NUM-1" are dangerous. If the SUBTRACT statement were eliminated accidentally from the illustration, the procedure would be executed until it was canceled by the computer operator or the program time limit was exceeded. To make the procedure self-checking, the first condition could be stated in terms of "LESS THAN OR EQUAL TO 0," and the second condition could test for "LESS THAN OR EQUAL TO 1." Finally, procedure fall through, used extensively in this illustration, should be reduced (if not totally eliminated) in favor of more explicit control structures. For example, the execution sequence achieved in this illustration could be created by totally separating the execution of FIRST-PROCESS from SECOND-PROCESS (e.g., PERFORM FIRST-PROCESS and then PERFORM SECOND-PROCESS).

The third illustration, Figure 7.13c, is controlled by an interrelationship between two items.—LINE-COUNT and the WITH TEST AFTER phrase. LINE-COUNT is initialized to 1 to start the procedure. The next statement initiates the execution of the WRITE-LINE paragraph. When LINE-COUNT is equal to 1 the UNTIL condition is true. If the TEST BEFORE option had been used (or if the TEST option had been left off), the WRITE-LINE paragraph would not have been performed and no output printed. However, because the TEST AFTER option is used, the UNTIL condition is not evaluated until after the WRITE-LINE paragraph is performed and one line of output is printed.

Figure 7.13d is the final example. Because the content of input records is not shown, the precise number of iterations (repetitions) of each process cannot be determined. However, this much can be determined: (1) until the data-name PROCESS-INDICATOR is equal to 1, TYPE-1-PROCESS is executed; (2) until PROCESS-INDICATOR contains a value of 2 or 3, TYPE-2-PROCESS is executed; and (3) TYPE-3-PROCESS is executed until PROCESS-INDICATOR contains a value greater than 3.

The STOP Statement

The STOP statement terminates the execution of a program. The format of the statement is shown in Figure 7.14. The STOP statement is placed at the *logical* termination point of a program, not necessarily at the last statement in a program. If a program has several logical termination points, several STOP statements could be used.

When the statement is coded as STOP RUN, the program is permanently terminated. If STOP RUN appears in a sentence (such as in the imperative statement of the READ statement), it should be the last statement. The programmer is responsible for closing all active files prior to the execution of the STOP RUN statement. All programs in this text assume a permanent termination of program execution, so only the STOP RUN form of the statement is used.

The second form of the STOP statement temporarily halts a program. Direct intervention by the computer operator is required before the program will continue. Then, execution continues with the statement immediately following the STOP. The literal used in this form of the STOP may be numeric or nonnumeric or any figurative constant except ALL. During the learning/experimenting process, this form of the STOP statement should be avoided.

Figure 7.14 Format of the STOP Statement

```
STOP  {RUN    }
      {literal}
```

A Comprehensive Example

The program presented in Figure 7.15 incorporates many of the features of COBOL presented in Part 1. The function of the program is to accept data records and produce a listing of the records on a printed output form. The design of the input records is shown in Figure 7.15 (Record Layout). The desired output from the program is shown in Figure 7.15 (Report Layout). Note that the output data items are determined by the input data items. The difference between the input-record description and the output record is that the order of the STUDENT-IDENTIFICATION data items and of the ENROLLMENT-INFO are slightly different. The only added information on the output is the report and column headings.

The Record Layout of Figure 7.15 is described in lines 490 through 600 of the COBOL program. Each field is described in the input-record description of STUDENT-RECORD. In addition, group data items (STUDENT-IDENTIFICATION and ENROLLMENT-INFO) have been added. Finally, the blank fields in the input record are described by

Figure 7.15 Hierarchy Chart

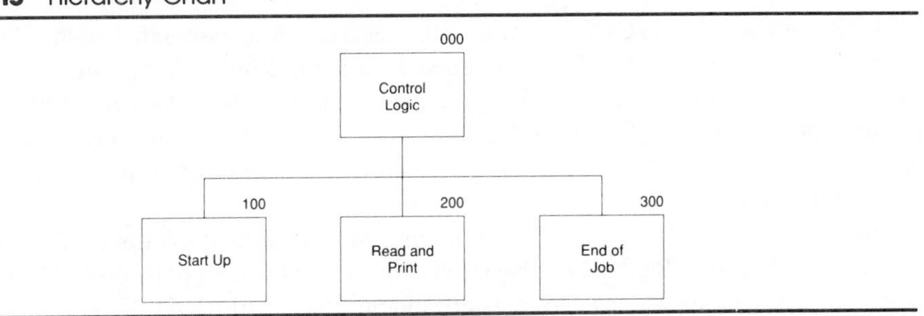

Figure 7.15 *Continued* Module Flowcharts

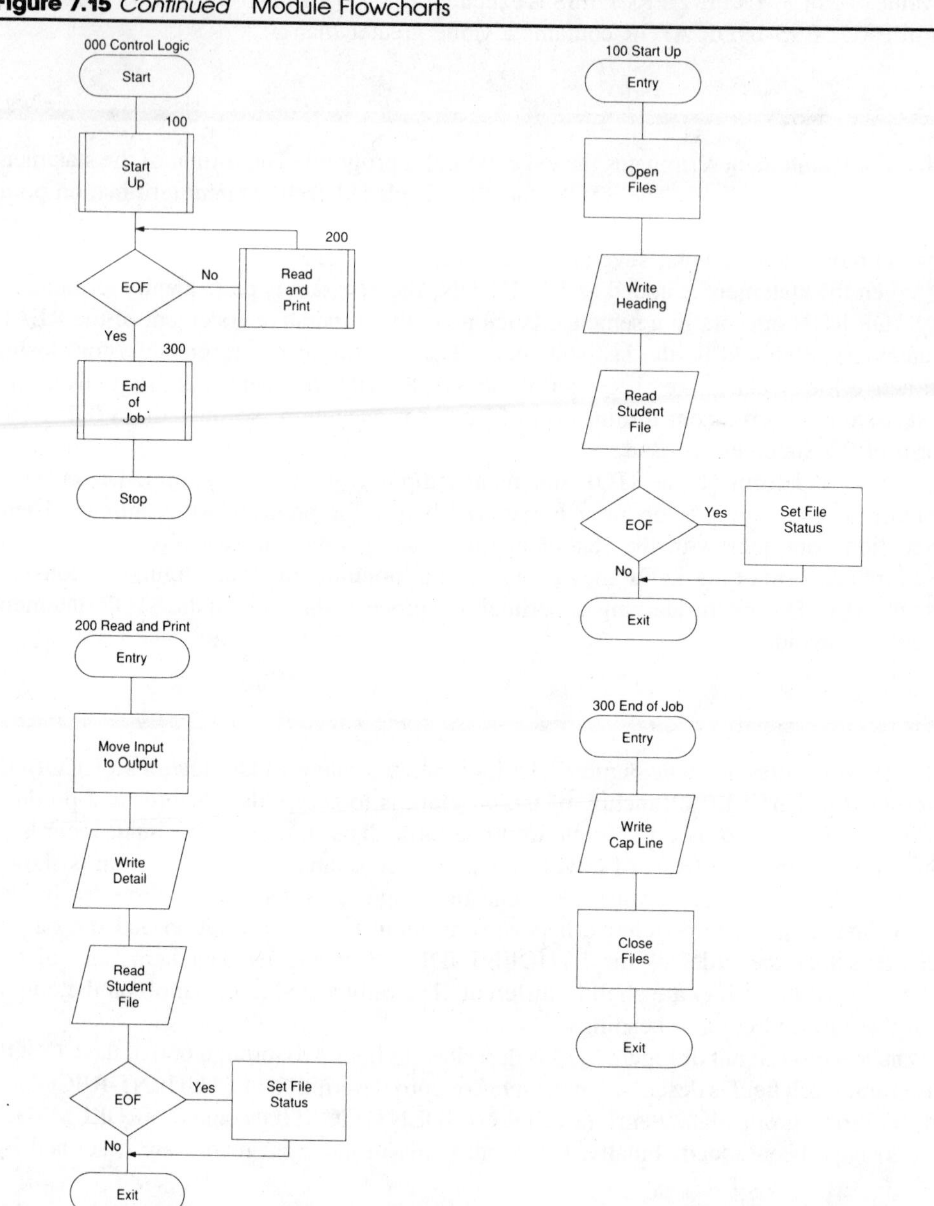

FILLER entries. The STUDENT-RECORD description is associated with STUDENT-FILE (line 360), which has been assigned to a simple input device in line 280. The second file description in the program is STUDENT-REPORT. This file will be used to produce printed output. STUDENT-REPORT is assigned to a line printer (line 290), and the output REPORT-RECORD is provided with a utility (general) description (lines 400 through 420).

The WORKING-STORAGE SECTION provides additional details of the description of the printed output. REPORT-HEADING (lines 620 through 650) provides the record description needed to produce ''Semester Student List.'' SEPARATOR-LINE (Lines 670

Figure 7.15 *Continued* Pseudocode

```
START
     DO start up
     DO read and print
          UNTIL end of file
     DO end of job
END

START UP
     OPEN files
     PRINT page headings
     READ next record
     IF end of file
          SET indicator
     ENDIF
END

READ AND PRINT
     MOVE input data to output data
     PRINT detail line
     READ next record
     IF end of file
          SET indicator
     ENDIF
END

END OF JOB
     PRINT last line
     CLOSE files
END
```

through 690) is used to produce a row of dashes above and below the column headings and at the end of the report. COLUMN-HEADING-1 (lines 710 through 750) provides the first line of column headings. Note the use of continuation of the nonnumeric literal message producing this part of the column headings. It was necessary to use three records (lines) to make a "message" 79 characters in length. Thus, lines 740 and 750 have a hyphen in column 7 (the continuation character and column), and the nonnumeric literal is restarted with each new line. (The apostrophe in column 12 of lines 740 and 750 is required to continue the nonnumeric literal.) The second line of the column headings is presented in COLUMN-HEADING-2 (lines 770 through 810). The final record description (lines 830 through 950) provides data-names that closely resemble those in the input-record description.

The PROCEDURE DIVISION begins at line 970. The 100-START-UP paragraph is responsible for opening the files needed by the program (the OPEN statement in line 1070 and 1080) and producing the report and column headings indicated on the Report Layout. The WRITE statement appearing in line 1090 produces the report heading "Semester Student List." A WRITE statement using the FROM option causes the REPORT-HEADING record description to be moved to the REPORT-LINE. (All output produced by the program must be directed through REPORT-LINE, since this is the record description that is directly associated with the line printer.) Furthermore, the mnemonic-name TOP-OF-NEXT-PAGE is used to indicate the appropriate carriage control. TOP-OF-NEXT-PAGE is described in the SPECIAL-NAMES paragraph (line 230). The remainder of the WRITE statements in the 100-START-UP paragraph are responsible for producing the column headings. The primary difference between these WRITE statements and the previous WRITE statement involves each indicating a specified (integer) number of lines to be advanced before the output is printed. The statement

Figure 7.15 *Continued* Student List Program (Record Layout)

MULTIPLE-CARD LAYOUT FORM

Company ABC MANUFACTURING COMPANY

Application SAMPLE PROGRAM by J. WAYNE SPENCE Date 01/01/89 Job No. ____ Sheet No. 1

STUDENT IDENTIFICATION					ENROLLMENT INFO				
LAST NAME	FIRST NAME	MI	STUDENT ID		CLASS	TOTAL HOURS	ENROL.	MAJOR	
X(10)	X(10)	X	9(09)		XX	999	99	XXX	
1–10	11–20	21	22–30	31–35	36–37	38–40	41–42	43–45	46–80

Figure 7.15 *Continued* Student List Program

```
          1   1   2   2   2   3   3   4   4   4   5   5   6   6   6   7
   4  8   2   6   0   4   8   2   6   0   4   8   2   6   0   4   8   2
***************************************************************
 IDENTIFICATION DIVISION.
***************************************************************
 PROGRAM-ID.       SAMPLE-PROGRAM.
 AUTHOR.           J. WAYNE SPENCE.
 DATE-WRITTEN.  JANUARY 1, 1989.
 DATE-COMPILED. JANUARY 1, 1989.
*    This program illustrates a complete COBOL program.
*    It primarily demonstrates record descriptions
*    in the FILE SECTION and WORKING-STORAGE SECTION of
*    the DATA DIVISION and the use of PERFORM,OPEN, READ,
*    MOVE, WRITE, CLOSE and STOP RUN statements in the
*    PROCEDURE DIVISION.  Record descriptions in the WORKING-
*    STORAGE SECTION employ VALUE clauses.
***************************************************************
 ENVIRONMENT DIVISION.
***************************************************************
*-------------------------------------------------------------*
 CONFIGURATION SECTION.
*-------------------------------------------------------------*
 SOURCE-COMPUTER. IBM.
 OBJECT-COMPUTER. IBM.
 SPECIAL-NAMES.  C01 IS TOP-OF-NEXT-PAGE.
*-------------------------------------------------------------*
 INPUT-OUTPUT SECTION.
*-------------------------------------------------------------*
 FILE-CONTROL.
     SELECT STUDENT-FILE    ASSIGN TO UT-S-INPUT.
     SELECT STUDENT-REPORT  ASSIGN TO UT-S-OUTPUT.
***************************************************************
 DATA DIVISION.
***************************************************************
*-------------------------------------------------------------*
 FILE SECTION.
*-------------------------------------------------------------*
 FD  STUDENT-FILE
     LABEL RECORDS ARE OMITTED.
 01  DUMMY-RECORD                     PIC X(45).

 FD  STUDENT-REPORT
     LABEL RECORDS ARE OMITTED.
 01  REPORT-LINE                      PIC X(133).
*-------------------------------------------------------------*
 WORKING-STORAGE SECTION.
*-------------------------------------------------------------*
 01  WORKING-RECORD.
     05 FILE-STATUS                   PIC X(05) VALUE SPACES.

 01  STUDENT-RECORD.
     05 STUDENT-IDENTIFICATION.
          10 LAST-NAME-IN             PIC X(10).
          10 FIRST-NAME-IN            PIC X(10).
          10 MIDDLE-INITIAL-IN        PIC X(01).
          10 STUDENT-ID-IN            PIC 9(09).
     05 FILLER                        PIC X(05).
     05 ENROLLMENT-INFO.
          10 CLASSIFICATION-IN        PIC X(02).
          10 TOTAL-HOURS-IN           PIC 9(03).
          10 HOURS-THIS-SEM-IN        PIC 9(02).
          10 MAJOR-IN                 PIC X(03).

 01  REPORT-HEADING.
     05 FILLER                        PIC X(29) VALUE SPACES.
     05 FILLER                        PIC X(21) VALUE
     'Semester Student List'.

 01  SEPARATOR-LINE.
     05 FILLER                        PIC X(01)  VALUE SPACE.
     05 FILLER                        PIC X(79)  VALUE ALL '-'.
```

Figure 7.15 *Continued* Student List Program

```
          1   1   2   2   2   3   3   4   4   4   5   5   6   6   6   7
  4   8   2   6   0   4   8   2   6   0   4   8   2   6   0   4   8   2
--------------------------------------------------------------------------
       01  COLUMN-HEADING-1.
           05 FILLER                       PIC X(01)  VALUE SPACE.
           05 FILLER                       PIC X(79) VALUE '         Student
      -    'Name          Student ID.   Class   Major     Current      Tota
      -    'l  '.

       01  COLUMN-HEADING-2.
           05 FILLER                       PIC X(32) VALUE SPACE.
           05 FILLER                       PIC X(28) VALUE 'Number'.
           05 FILLER                       PIC X(20) VALUE
              'Enrollment   Hours'.

       01  OUTPUT-RECORD.
           05 FILLER                       PIC X(03)  VALUE SPACE.
           05 FIRST-NAME-OUT               PIC X(11).
           05 MIDDLE-INITIAL-OUT           PIC X(01).
           05 FILLER                       PIC X(02)  VALUE '.'.
           05 LAST-NAME-OUT                PIC X(14).
           05 STUDENT-ID-OUT               PIC 9(09).
           05 FILLER                       PIC X(05)  VALUE SPACE.
           05 CLASSIFICATION-OUT           PIC X(08).
           05 MAJOR-OUT                    PIC X(11).
           05 HOURS-THIS-SEM-OUT           PIC 9(02).
           05 FILLER                       PIC X(08)  VALUE SPACE.
           05 TOTAL-HOURS-OUT              PIC 9(03).
      *****************************************************************
       PROCEDURE DIVISION.
      *****************************************************************
       000-CONTROL-LOGIC.
           PERFORM 100-START-UP.
           PERFORM 200-READ-AND-PRINT
               UNTIL FILE-STATUS = 'DONE'.
           PERFORM 300-END-OF-JOB.
           STOP RUN.

       100-START-UP.
           OPEN INPUT STUDENT-FILE,
                OUTPUT STUDENT-REPORT.
           WRITE REPORT-LINE FROM REPORT-HEADING AFTER
               TOP-OF-NEXT-PAGE.
           WRITE REPORT-LINE FROM SEPARATOR-LINE AFTER 2 LINES.
           WRITE REPORT-LINE FROM COLUMN-HEADING-1 AFTER 1.
           WRITE REPORT-LINE FROM COLUMN-HEADING-2 AFTER 1.
           WRITE REPORT-LINE FROM SEPARATOR-LINE AFTER 1.
           READ STUDENT-FILE INTO STUDENT-RECORD
               AT END MOVE 'DONE' TO FILE-STATUS.

       200-READ-AND-PRINT.
           MOVE STUDENT-ID-IN          TO STUDENT-ID-OUT.
           MOVE LAST-NAME-IN           TO LAST-NAME-OUT.
           MOVE FIRST-NAME-IN          TO FIRST-NAME-OUT.
           MOVE MIDDLE-INITIAL-IN      TO MIDDLE-INITIAL-OUT.
           MOVE CLASSIFICATION-IN      TO CLASSIFICATION-OUT.
           MOVE TOTAL-HOURS-IN         TO TOTAL-HOURS-OUT.
           MOVE HOURS-THIS-SEM-IN      TO HOURS-THIS-SEM-OUT.
           MOVE MAJOR-IN               TO MAJOR-OUT.
           WRITE REPORT-LINE FROM OUTPUT-RECORD AFTER 1 LINES.
           READ STUDENT-FILE INTO STUDENT-RECORD
               AT END MOVE 'DONE' TO FILE-STATUS.

       300-END-OF-JOB.
           WRITE REPORT-LINE FROM OUTPUT-RECORD AFTER 1 LINES.
           CLOSE STUDENT-FILE, STUDENT-REPORT.
```

Figure 7.15 *Continued* Student List Program (Data)

```
-------------------------------------------------------------
|      |         1         2         3         4         5|
|Record|12345678901234567890123456789012345678901234567890|
|-----------------------------------------------------------|
|     1|Anderson  Jimmy     Q343564321       Gr21900Csc   |
|     2|Booker    John      A555667777       Fr03515Mgt   |
|     3|Carter    Matt      N456789012       Jr09408Mgt   |
|     4|Davidson  Anthony   R353492761       Sr13816Eco   |
|     5|Eldridge  David     Q376495268       So04712Fin   |
|     6|Franklin  Rose      V000000001       Gr18912Gbu   |
|     7|Garrison  Kenneth   A537903251       So02816Mgt   |
|     8|Hamilton  Mark      C486762389       Jr09618Csc   |
|     9|Issacs    Matt      H474653790       Sr12018Eco   |
|    10|Jefferson Harold    Q502326955       Fr01818Mkt   |
|    11|Kennedy   Floyd     R476329092       Jr06012Mkt   |
|    12|Lincoln   Steven    O442648942       So04515Mkt   |
|    13|Monroe    Jeff      V546677219       Sr09918Csc   |
-------------------------------------------------------------
```

(the READ statement in line 1150) causes data to be accepted from the input device. Thus, a data record in STUDENT-FILE is transferred into the input-record description (STUDENT-RECORD). From this point forward, the program has access to the data of the first data record, until a READ statement is again executed.

The 200-READ-AND-PRINT paragraph (lines 1130 through 1290) represents the body of the program. That is, the majority of the ''work'' done by the program occurs within the 200-READ-AND-PRINT paragraph. The procedure first transfers the data from the input record to the output record with a series of MOVE statements (lines 1190 through 1260). Notice that each field name in STUDENT-RECORD is moved to a similar representation of that data item in the OUTPUT-RECORD description. The WRITE statement in line 1270 causes the data represented by the OUTPUT-RECORD description to be placed in the REPORT-LINE. The REPORT-LINE IS WRITTEN. Finally, another READ statement (line 1280) is executed, providing data from next record. The process just described is repeated until all data records have been read. When the end of the STUDENT-FILE is reached, the AT END phrase of the READ statement is executed, resulting in DONE being moved to FILE-STATUS. This results in completing the condition specified in the PERFORM statement in line 1010.

Figure 7.15 *Continued* Student List Program (Output)

```
                          Semester Student List
------------------------------------------------------------------------------
         Student Name              Student ID.   Class   Major    Current     Total
                                     Number                      Enrollment   Hours
------------------------------------------------------------------------------
   Jimmy        Q. Anderson        343564321      Gr      Csc       00         219
   John         A. Booker          555667777      Fr      Mgt       15         035
   Matt         N. Carter          456789012      Jr      Mgt       08         094
   Anthony      R. Davidson        353492761      Sr      Eco       16         138
   David        Q. Eldridge        376495268      So      Fin       12         047
   Rose         V. Franklin        000000001      Gr      Gbu       12         189
   Kenneth      A. Garrison        537903251      So      Mgt       16         028
   Mark         C. Hamilton        486762389      Jr      Csc       18         096
   Matt         H. Issacs          474653790      Sr      Eco       18         120
   Harold       Q. Jefferson       502326955      Fr      Mkt       18         018
   Floyd        R. Kennedy         476329092      Jr      Mkt       12         060
   Steven       O. Lincoln         442648942      So      Mkt       15         045
   Jeff         V. Monroe          546677219      Sr      Csc       18         099
```

When the 300-END-OF-JOB paragraph is encountered, the requirements of the program have been fulfilled. First, a line is written (line 1320). Then the input device (STUDENT-FILE) and the line printer (STUDENT-REPORT) files are released from the program (line 1330). This completes the 300-END-OF-JOB procedure, and terminates the PERFORM statement in line 1030. The next statement is STOP RUN (line 1040), which terminates the program. The results of this program are shown in Figure 6.13 (Output).

Summary

The PROCEDURE DIVISION is the last division in a COBOL program. The PROCEDURE DIVISION establishes the process or algorithm to be executed. The procedure is supported by entries, especially by the data definitions in the DATA DIVISION. No structure is prescribed in the PROCEDURE DIVISION, and the programmer has complete latitude with SECTION and paragraph names.

Several types of statements are permitted in the PROCEDURE DIVISION. The statements described in this chapter include:

- The OPEN statement, which "enables" files to the procedure
- The CLOSE statement, which "disconnects" files from the procedure
- The READ statement, which causes records from an input file to be placed in internal storage
- The WRITE statement, which causes internally stored data to be placed on an output medium
- The MOVE statement, which copies data from one field to another
- The PERFORM statement, which causes temporary interruption of the sequential execution of statements.
- The STOP RUN statement, which permanently terminates the execution of the program.
- Other statements will be discussed later in this text.

Notes on Programming Style

As mentioned in the notes at the end of Chapter 6, record descriptions that could appear in the FILE SECTION are frequently transferred to the WORKING-STORAGE SECTION. Printed output in the form of headings is frequently developed in the WORKING-STORAGE SECTION and moved to the output-record description by using a "WRITE record-name FROM identifier" form of the statement. In fact, all WRITE statements may be written in this form. Likewise, the READ-INTO form of the input statement may be used to conform to the same style by reading the data into the input-record description and moving the input data into a WORKING-STORAGE record description.

From a program design standpoint, your first objective should be to obtain an overall grasp of the program requirements. The next step should be to identify the general functions to be performed, e.g. a start-up or initialization function, a repetitive-processing function, and a termination function. After the general functions have been isolated, you should examine each to determine its suitability for further subdivision. Try to isolate each separate, identifiable, functional element of the problem. Only when you have broken the problem into its most basic elements should you begin coding statements and clauses.

Questions

Below, fill in the blank(s) with the appropriate word, words, or phrases.

1. The structure of the PROCEDURE DIVISION includes a division heading, sections, paragraphs, _____, and _____.

2. In the PROCEDURE DIVISION, section and paragraph names are also referred to as _____ names.

3. Data-names appear in both the _____ and the _____ division, but procedure-names appear only in the _____ division.

4. A procedure-name that is also a SECTION name may be composed of one or more _____ names.

5. A file-name that appears in an OPEN statement in the PROCEDURE DIVISION must also appear in a(n) _____ clause in the ENVIRONMENT DIVISION and in a(n) _____ entry in the DATA DIVISION.

6. In the OPEN statement, a file processing mode of _____ must be declared for read-oriented files, while the file must be opened _____ for write-oriented files.

7. Each file-name that appears in an OPEN statement should also appear in a(n) _____ statement before the program is terminated.

8. Data from an external medium are available for use within the program (in internal storage) once a(n) _____ statement has been executed.

9. A READ statement causes one _____ (logical/physical) input operation to be executed.

10. When an end-of-file condition is detected for an input file, the _____ phrase of the READ statement is executed.

11. In a READ statement, an imperative statement is really an imperative _____.

12. When a file has been assigned to a line printer it should be opened as a(n) _____ file.

13. A single WRITE statement will cause _____(number) lines to be printed.

14. For an output file, the WRITE statement should reference the output file _____ name.

15. The READ statement may use an INTO option to place data from an input record into an alternate area, whereas the WRITE statement may use a(n) _____ option to move data from an alternate area to an output record.

16. The BEFORE/AFTER clause of the WRITE statement is used for _____.

17. Carriage control may be specified in a WRITE statement through _____ LINES, _____ LINES, or a(n) _____.

18. If a WRITE statement is always to advance to the top of the next page a(n) _____ should be used in the WRITE statement.

19. When a mnemonic-name appears in a WRITE statement, the mnemonic-name should also appear in the _____ paragraph of the _____ DIVISION.

20. The COBOL statement that causes data from one field to be copied to another field is the _____ statement.

21. In a MOVE statement, the field that contains the data to be moved to another location is often called the _____ field.

22. The field that has its value altered as a result of a MOVE statement is the _____ field.

23. Numeric data are generally _____-justified in an integer field, whereas alphanumeric data are generally _____-justified.

24. The PERFORM statement permits the execution of a(n) ____ name or a(n) ____ name.
25. After the procedure(s) indicated in the PERFORM statements have been executed, execution continues with/at ____.
26. A simple PERFORM statement is completed only when ____.
27. With a simple PERFORM statement, the indicated procedure is executed ____ (number) time(s).
28. A PERFORM/UNTIL statement is completed only when ____ and ____.
29. With a PERFORM/UNTIL, when the condition is true upon encountering the PERFORM statement, the procedure is executed ____ (number) time(s).
30. The ____ statement causes the termination of a program and should be placed at the ____ termination point of a program.

Answer the following questions by circling either ''T'' for true or ''F'' for false.

T F **31.** A READ operation may be referred to as destructive, that is, the data accessible by the first READ operation are replaced (destroyed) by the data assessed by the second READ operation.
T F **32.** READ statements read a record, and WRITE statements write a file.
T F **33.** When the AFTER option is used in a WRITE statement, the output line is printed and then carriage control takes place.
T F **34.** When an identifier is used to indicate vertical spacing of printed output, the identifier is permitted to contain zero as its value.
T F **35.** There is no condition under which a group-item may be moved to an elementary-item.
T F **36.** An elementary-item can always be moved to a group.
T F **37.** To be able to move data from one field to another, the lengths of the two fields must be the same.
T F **38.** The PROCEDURE DIVISION may be omitted from some COBOL programs.
T F **39.** The PROCEDURE DIVISION may appear prior to the DATA DIVISION in a COBOL program.
T F **40.** The algorithm or process to be performed by a program is presented in the PROCEDURE DIVISION.
T F **41.** The PROCEDURE DIVISION has a number of required SECTIONS and paragraphs.
T F **42.** The PROCEDURE DIVISION does not require the use of section names.
T F **43.** The word ''SECTION'' must follow each section name in the PROCEDURE DIVISION.
T F **44.** In COBOL, data files are available for input/output operations at any location within the PROCEDURE DIVISION without any kind of preparatory operation.
T F **45.** The word ''INPUT'' may appear more than once in a single OPEN statement.
T F **46.** Only a single file may be opened in a single OPEN statement.
T F **47.** Multiple OPEN statements are permitted in a single COBOL program.
T F **48.** The same file-name may be opened as both INPUT and OUTPUT at the same time.
T F **49.** A particular file may be opened several times without ever being closed.
T F **50.** A file may be read from or written to after it has been closed.

T F **51.** A file that was opened in an output mode must be closed in an output mode; that is, the word "OUTPUT" must appear in the CLOSE statement preceding the file-name.

T F **52.** Files must be opened in the same order as the SELECT clauses in the ENVIRONMENT DIVISION.

T F **53.** Once a file has been opened in an input mode, records may be read from that file.

T F **54.** More than one logical record can be accessed by the program with a single execution of one READ statement.

T F **55.** An input file-name always appears in a READ statement.

T F **56.** With a READ statement, it is possible to have input data stored in two separately addressable areas of internal storage.

T F **57.** Any statements following an unconditional branch in a sentence will not be executed.

T F **58.** To be able to move data from one field to another, the field types of the two fields must be the same (e.g., both must be numeric).

T F **59.** The PERFORM statement may be used to invoke a paragraph, so long as that paragraph appears physically below the PERFORM statement itself in the PROCEDURE DIVISION.

T F **60.** With the PERFORM statement, the programmer is permitted to invoke a procedure and return to the location of the PERFORM when the procedure has been completed.

T F **61.** The PERFORM statement only permits the execution of one paragraph or section.

T F **62.** When a THROUGH option is used in a PERFORM statement, the second procedure-name does not necessarily have to follow the first procedure-name.

T F **63.** If the THROUGH option is used in a PERFORM, the procedure-names listed must be paragraphs.

T F **64.** A PERFORM statement may invoke a procedure containing another PERFORM statement.

T F **65.** Once a paragraph has been executed by one PERFORM statement, it may not be reexecuted by another PERFORM statement in another part of the program.

T F **66.** A program that contains PERFORM statements is also permitted to include GO TO statements.

T F **67.** A PERFORM statement could appear in the imperative statement portion of an IF statement.

T F **68.** A PERFORM statement could appear in the imperative statement portion of a READ statement.

T F **69.** In a PERFORM/UNTIL, the only condition permitted is a relational condition.

T F **70.** In a PERFORM/UNTIL, compound conditions are permitted.

Exercises

1. The following are an input-record description, PROCEDURE DIVISION statements, and two data records. After each input operation, record the values associated with each data-name of the input record.

```
          ENVIRONMENT DIVISION.
                                          .
                                          .
                                          .
          INPUT-OUTPUT SECTION.
          FILE-CONTROL.
              SELECT INSURANCE-POLICY-FILE  ASSIGN TO UT-S-INPUT.
                                          .
                                          .
                                          .
          DATA DIVISION.
          FILE SECTION.
          FD  INSURANCE-POLICY-FILE  LABEL RECORDS ARE OMITTED.
          01  INSURANCE-POLICY-RECORD.
              05  POLICY-NUMBER-IN          PIC X(10).
              05  CLIENT-NUMBER-IN          PIC 9(08).
              05  ANNIVERSARY-DATE-IN.
                  10 ANNIVERSARY-MONTH-IN PIC 9(02).
                  10 ANNIVERSARY-DAY-IN   PIC 9(02).
              05  EXPIRATION-DATE-IN.
                  10 EXPIRATION-MONTH-IN  PIC 9(02).
                  10 EXPIRATION-DAY-IN    PIC 9(02).
                  10 EXPIRATION-YEAR-IN   PIC 9(02).
              05  PREMIUM-AMOUNT-IN         PIC 9(05)V9(02).
              05  COMMISSION-AMOUNT-IN      PIC 9(03)V9(02).
              05  SALESMAN-CODE-IN          PIC X(03).
              05  STATE-CODE-IN             PIC X(02).
              05  FILLER                    PIC X(35).
                                          .
                                          .
                                          .
          PROCEDURE DIVISION.
                                          .
                                          .
                                          .
              OPEN INPUT INSURANCE-POLICY-FILE.
                                          .
                                          .
                                          .
          100-READ-INSURANCE-POLICY.
              READ INSURANCE-POLICY-FILE
                  AT END GO TO 200-EXERCISE-COMPLETE.
                                          .
                                          .
                                          .
          200-EXERCISE-COMPLETE.
              CLOSE INSURANCE-POLICY-FILE.
              STOP RUN.

Record 1: AX-14293-40 05021480415022682007238808690JWSTX ----- blank -----
Record 2: R44219-C  108521020831102881019117611612DEWIL ----- blank -----
```

DATA-NAME	VALUE FROM FIRST READ	VALUE FROM SECOND READ

2. The following procedure produces a printed output form. Describe (using a printer layout form, if available), the output created by the program.

```
IDENTIFICATION DIVISION.
PROGRAM-ID.    EXERCISE-2.
ENVIRONMENT DIVISION.
CONFIGURATION SECTION.
SOURCE-COMPUTER.    IBM.
```

```
OBJECT-COMPUTER.    IBM.
SPECIAL-NAMES.      C01 IS NEXT-PAGE.
INPUT-OUTPUT SECTION.
FILE-CONTROL.
    SELECT PATIENT-FILE        ASSIGN TO UT-S-INPUT.
    SELECT CASE-REPORT-FILE    ASSIGN TO UT-S-OUTPUT.
DATA DIVISION.
FILE SECTION.
FD  PATIENT-FILE                    LABEL RECORDS ARE OMITTED.
01  PATIENT-RECORD.
    05  PATIENT-NUMBER-IN           PIC 9(05).
    05  PATIENT-NAME-IN             PIC X(20).
    05  DATE-OF-SERVICE-IN          PIC X(06).
    05  DIAGNOSIS-CODE-IN           PIC X(04).
    05  PROCEDURE-TIME-IN.
        10  HOURS-IN                PIC 9(02).
        10  MINUTES-IN              PIC 9(02).
    05  DIAGNOSIS-COMMENTS-IN       PIC X(40).
    05  VERIFICATION-CODE-IN        PIC X(01).
FD  CASE-REPORT-FILE                LABEL RECORDS ARE OMITTED.
01  REPORT-RECORD.
    05  FILLER                      PIC X(01).
    05  PATIENT-NUMBER-OUT          PIC 9(05).
    05  FILLER                      PIC X(05).
    05  PATIENT-NAME-OUT            PIC X(20).
    05  FILLER                      PIC X(05).
    05  DIAGNOSIS-CODE-OUT          PIC X(04).
    05  FILLER                      PIC X(05).
    05  DIAGNOSIS-COMMENTS-0UT      PIC X(40).
    05  FILLER                      PIC X(05).
    05  HOURS-OUT                   PIC 9(02).
    05  TIME-SEPARATOR-OUT          PIC X(01).
    05  MINUTES-OUT                 PIC 9(02).
    05  FILLER                      PIC X(05).
    05  SERVICE-DAY-OUT             PIC 9(02).
    05  DASH-1-OUT                  PIC X(01).
    05  SERVICE-MONTH-OUT           PIC 9(02).
    05  DASH-2-OUT                  PIC X(01).
    05  SERVICE-YEAR-OUT            PIC 9(02).
    05  FILLER                      PIC X(25).
WORKING-STORAGE SECTION.
01  WORKING-VARIABLES.
    05  FILE-STATUS                 PIC X(04) VALUE 'WORK'.
01  DATE-REC0RD-WS.
    05  DAY-WS                      PIC 9(02).
    05  MONTH-WS                    PIC 9(02).
    05  YEAR-WS                     PIC 9(02).
01  REPORT-HEADING.
    05  FILLER                      PIC X(46) VALUE SPACES.
    05  FILLER                      PIC X(28) VALUE
                                   Daily Cases for the Date of.
    05  DAY-OUT                     PIC 9(02).
    05  FILLER                      PIC X(01) VALUE '/'.
    05  MONTH-OUT                   PIC 9(02).
    05  FILLER                      PIC X(01) VALUE '/'.
    05  YEAR-OUT                    PIC 9(02).
01  COLUMN-HEADING-1.
    05  FILLER                      PIC X(01) VALUE SPACES.
    05  FILLER                      PIC X(07) VALUE 'Patient'.
    05  FILLER                      PIC X(28) VALUE SPACES.
    05  FILLER                      PIC X(04) VALUE 'Diag'.
    05  FILLER                      PIC X(50) VALUE SPACES.
    05  FILLER                      PIC X(16) VALUE
    05  FILLER                      '***** Service *****'.
```

```
Ø1  COLUMN-HEADING-2.
    Ø5  FILLER                      PIC X(11) VALUE 'Number'.
    Ø5  FILLER                      PIC X(25) VALUE 'Patient Name'.
    Ø5  FILLER                      PIC X(Ø9) VALUE 'Code'.
    Ø5  FILLER                      PIC X(45) VALUE 'Comments'.
    Ø5  FILLER                      PIC X(12) VALUE 'Time.'
    Ø5  FILLER                      PIC X(Ø4) VALUE 'Date'.
PROCEDURE DIVISION.
ØØØ-INITIAL-DRIVER.
    PERFORM 1ØØ-OPEN-FILES.
    PERFORM 2ØØ-HEADING-PRODUCTION.
    PERFORM 4ØØ-READ-PATIENT-FILE.
    PERFORM 3ØØ-BØDY-OF-REPORT
            UNTIL FILE-STATUS / 'DONE'.
    PERFORM 5ØØ-PROCEDURE-TERMINATION.
    STOP  RUN.
1ØØ-OPEN-FILES.
    OPEN INPUT PATIENT-FILE, OUTPUT CASE-REPORT FILE.
    READ PATIENT-FILE INTO DATE-RECORD-WS
        AT END MOVE 'DONE' TO FILE-STATUS.
2ØØ-HEADING-PRODUCTION.
    MOVE DAY-WS                 TO DAY-OUT.
    MOVE MONTH-WS               TO MONTH-OUT.
    MOVE YEAR-WS                TO YEAR-OUT.
    WRITE REPORT-RECORD FROM REPORT-HEADING AFTER NEXT-PAGE.
    WRITE REPORT-RECORD FROM COLUMN-HEADING-1 AFTER 2 LINES.
    WRITE REPORT-RECORD FROM COLUMN-HEADING-2 AFTER 1 LINES.
    MOVE ALL '-'                TO REPORT-RECORD.
    WRITE REPORT-RECORD AFTER 1 LINES.
    MOVE SPACES                 TO REPORT-RECORD.
    MOVE '-'                    TO DASH-1-OUT, DASH-2-ØUT.
    MOVE ':'                    TO TIME SEPARATOR-OUT.
3ØØ-BODY-OF-REPORT.
    MOVE PATIENT-NUMBER-IN      TO PATIENT-NUMBER-OUT.
    MOVE PATIENT-NAME-IN        TO PATIENT-NAME-OUT.
    MOVE DATE-OF-SERVICE-IN     TO DATE-RECORD-WS.
    MOVE DAY-WS                 TO SERVICE-DAY-OUT.
    MOVE MONTH-WS               TØ SERVICE-MONTH-OUT.
    MOVE YEAR-WS                TO SERVICE-YEAR-OUT.
    MOVE DIAGNOSIS-CODE-IN      TO DIAGNOSIS-CODE-OUT.
    MOVE HOURS-IN               TØ HOURS-OUT.
    MOVE MINUTES-IN             TO MINUTES-OUT.
    MOVE DIAGNOSIS-COMMENTS-IN TØ DIAGNOSIS-COMMENTS-OUT.
    WRITE REPORT-RECORD AFTER ADVANCING 2 LINES.
    PERFORM 4ØØ-READ-PATIENT-FILE.
4ØØ-READ-PATIENT-FILE.
    READ PATIENT-FILE
        AT END MOVE 'DONE' TO FILE-STATUS.
5ØØ-PROCEDURE-TERMINATION.
    CLOSE PATIENT-FILE, CASE-REPORT-FILE.
(DATA)

19Ø58Ø ----- blank -----
14827PHILLIPƀHARRISTONƀƀƀ14Ø58AØ471Ø245REMOVALƀOFƀFOREIGNƀBODYƀƀƀƀƀƀƀƀƀƀƀƀƀƀƀƀR
29884ELIZABETHƀFREDERICKS15Ø58ØNØ46Ø115TREATMENTƀOFƀSEVEREƀINSULT--LEFTƀHANDƀƀJ

(END OF FILE)
```

3. Assume the following items are situations in which the statement "MOVE FIRST-FIELD TO SECOND-FIELD." is to be executed. Indicate what the result of each movement of data would be. Be sure to indicate the location of blanks and zeros, where applicable.

First-field		Second-field	
Data Value	**Picture String**	**Picture String**	**Result**
482	9(03)	9(03)	______
3976	9(04)	9(03)	______
1872	9(04)	9(05)	______
Ø672^88	9(04)V9(02)	9(03)	______
2118^69	9(04)V9(02)	9(03)V9(02)	______
Ø	9(01)	9(04)	______
112^ØØ4	9(03)V9(02)	9(05)V9(02)	______
SAVE	X(04)	X(04)	______
MONIES	X(06)	X(03)	______
UNITS	X(05)	X(07)	______
ONE	X(03)	X(01)	______
1234	X(04)	9(04)	______
2417	9(04)	X(04)	______
Ø8271	9(05)	X(03)	______
4Ø5	X(03)	9(04)	______
5Ø4	X(03)	9(02)	______
JOHN	A(04)	A(05)	______
ƀ	A(01)	X(04)	______
OUT	X(03)	A(03)	______
FOUR	X(04)	A(02)	______

Problems

7.1 Your company periodically performs a manual count of all items in inventory. Although there are records for the sale and purchase of each item, sometimes mistakes are made, items are returned and not accounted for, and items are damaged, lost, or stolen. Thus, the actual count is necessary. A report (as shown) is needed on which the inventory clerks can record items present in the specified locations. The record format (as shown) contains the following fields:

1. Item number—8-digit number to be split into two parts (group and item) when printed
2. Item description—30 characters
3. Item location—5 characters composed of
   a. Aisle—2 characters and
   b. Bin number—3 digits
4. Lot size (e.g., per foot, pound, etc.)—3 chararters
5. Estimated contents (what we think should be in the bin)—5 digits

The report format should be followed as closely as possible. Each data record should be reflected on the report. A blank area (flanked by less than and greater than symbols) should appear under the actual location column so clerks can record an item's actual location in the event it has been moved. Likewise, a blank area should appear under the actual contents column to record the corrected count. Finally, a hyphen is to appear between the group and item numbers. All detail lines should be double-spaced (as shown) and the report should begin at the top of a page.

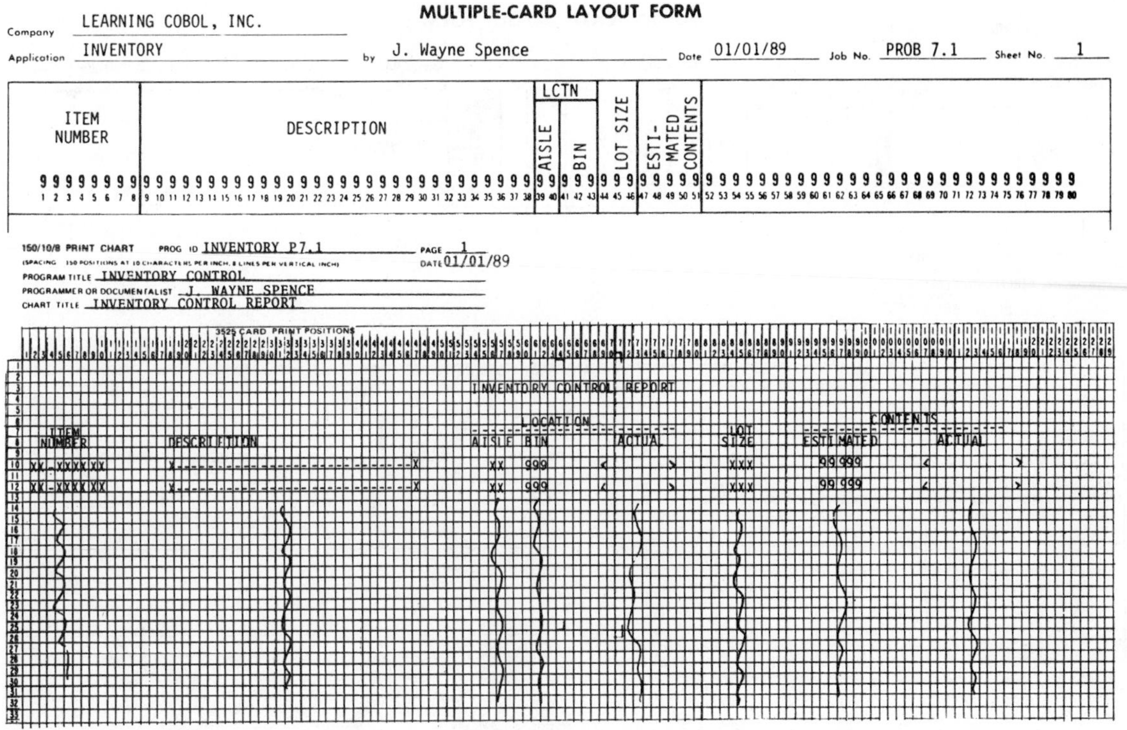

MULTIPLE-CARD LAYOUT FORM

Company LEARNING COBOL, INC.

Application INVENTORY by J. Wayne Spence Date 01/01/89 Job No. PROB 7.1 Sheet No. 1

ITEM NUMBER	DESCRIPTION	LCTN: AISLE	LCTN: BIN	LOT SIZE	ESTI-MATED CONTENTS	
1–8	9–38	39–40	41–43	44–46	47–51	52–80

150/10/8 PRINT CHART PROG ID INVENTORY P7.1 PAGE 1 DATE 01/01/89

PROGRAM TITLE INVENTORY CONTROL

PROGRAMMER OR DOCUMENTALIST J. WAYNE SPENCE

CHART TITLE INVENTORY CONTROL REPORT

```
                                  INVENTORY CONTROL REPORT
                                       LOCATION                           CONTENTS
  ITEM                                                           LOT
 NUMBER       DESCRIPTION           AISLE BIN      ACTUAL       SIZE    ESTIMATED   ACTUAL
XX-XXXX-XX   X-----------------X     XX   999   <        >      XXX     99,999   <        >

XX-XXXX-XX   X-----------------X     XX   999   <        >      XXX     99,999   <        >
```

7.2 During the course of business, passengers make reservations for flights on our airline. We keep a permanent record of all reservation information for each passenger in a printed-report form for future reference. Therefore, even though the computer records may be replaced, modified, or destroyed, we will have a record of the reservation. Each reservation request contains the following information (also see the graphic record layout):

1. Ticket number—5 digits (appears on our records but is not printed on the report)
2. Passengers name:
   a. First name—10 characters (to be printed second on the report)
   b. Middle initial—1 character (to be printed last)
   c. Last name—10 characters (to be printed first)
3. Date of the flight—6 digits in the format MMDDYY (2 digits each for the month, day, and year)
4. Flight number—3 digits
5. Passenger class—1 character (e.g., first class, tourist, economy, etc.)
6. Estimated time of departure— 4 digits in the format HHMM (2 digits each for hours and minutes)
7. Departure gate number—3 characters
8. Flight status—2 characters (e.g., delayed, canceled, on time, etc.)
9. Estimated time of arrival— 4 digits in the format HHMM
10. Comments—10 characters (status spelled out plus other entries)

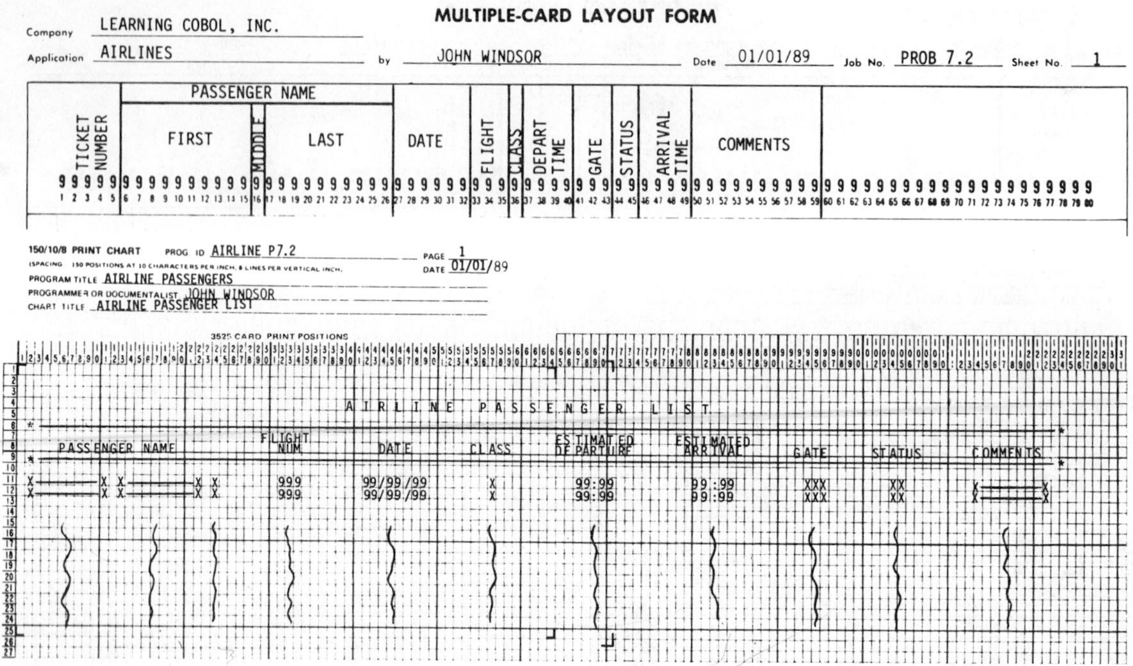

MULTIPLE-CARD LAYOUT FORM

Company LEARNING COBOL, INC.

Application AIRLINES by JOHN WINDSOR Date 01/01/89 Job No. PROB 7.2 Sheet No. 1

TICKET NUMBER	PASSENGER NAME: FIRST	MIDDLE	LAST	DATE	FLIGHT	CLASS	DEPART TIME	GATE	STATUS	ARRIVAL TIME	COMMENTS	
1–5	6–15	16	17–26	27–32	33–35	36	37–40	41–43	44–45	46–49	50–59	60–80

150/10/8 PRINT CHART PROG ID AIRLINE P7.2 PAGE 1 DATE 01/01/89

PROGRAM TITLE AIRLINE PASSENGERS

PROGRAMMER OR DOCUMENTALIST JOHN WINDSOR

CHART TITLE AIRLINE PASSENGER LIST

AIRLINE PASSENGER LIST

PASSENGER NAME	FLIGHT NUM	DATE	CLASS	ESTIMATED DEPARTURE	ESTIMATED ARRIVAL	GATE	STATUS	COMMENTS
X—X X—X X X	999	99/99/99	X	99:99	99:99	XXX	XX	X—X
X—X X—X X X	999	99/99/99	X	99:99	99:99	XXX	XX	X—X

On the report, column headings are to be printed flanked (above and below) by a row of asterisks. The passenger's name is to be printed in the format of last, first, middle. The date of the flight should have a slash (/) between the month-day and the day-year. The departure and arrival times should have a colon(:) between the hours and minutes. All detail lines are to be single-spaced (as shown), and the report should begin at the top of a page.

7.3 The personnel department has requested a status report on all company employees. Records in an applicable format have been constructed in the format shown, and each record contains the following fields:

1. Employee number—3 digits (not used on the report)
2. Employee name—20 characters
3. Job classification—4 digits
4. Job title—20 characters
5. Department—10 characters
6. Date of employment—6 digits in the format MMDDYY
7. Date of last promotion—6 digits in the format MMDDYY
8. Employee status—10 characters (e.g., vacation, on leave, laid off, etc.)

On the printed Status Report, the employee number is not to be printed. However, a field called "Hourly/Salaried" has been added. The data to be placed in this field are the first digit of the job classification. (The job classification report field should include all 4 digits.) In addition, the two dates are to be edited as shown and should be printed in the format of DD/MM/YY. The report should begin at the top of a page, and the detail lines should be double-spaced.

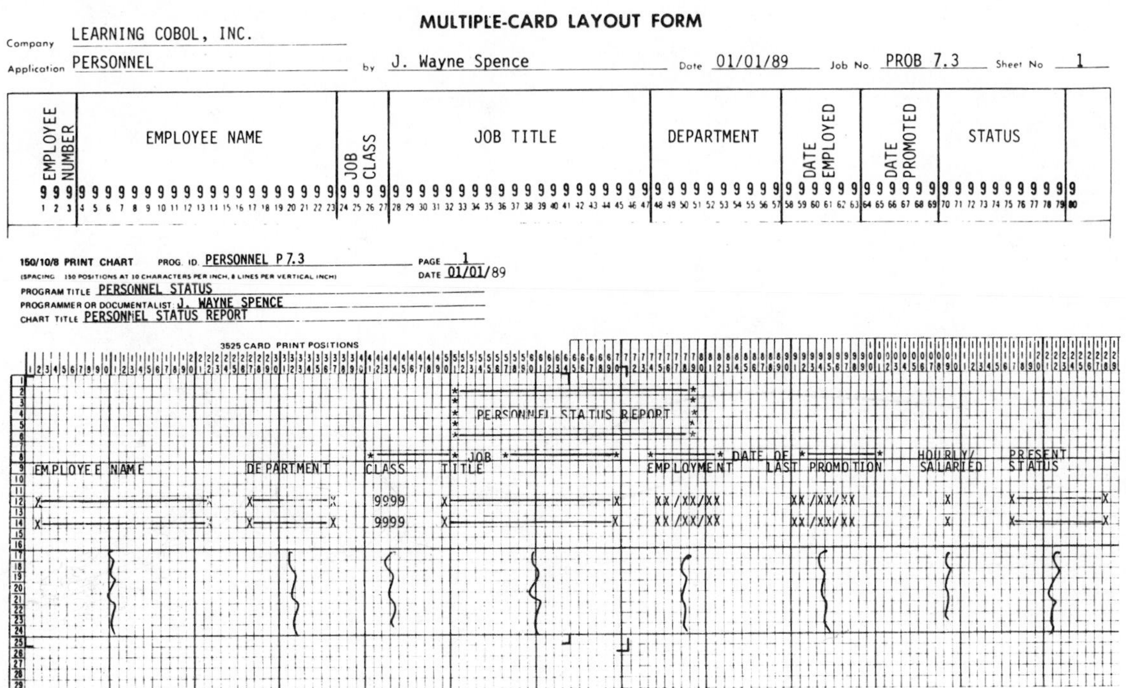

MULTIPLE-CARD LAYOUT FORM

Company LEARNING COBOL, INC.
Application PERSONNEL by J. Wayne Spence Date 01/01/89 Job No. PROB 7.3 Sheet No. 1

EMPLOYEE NUMBER	EMPLOYEE NAME	JOB CLASS	JOB TITLE	DEPARTMENT	DATE EMPLOYED	DATE PROMOTED	STATUS	
1–3	4–23	24–27	28–47	48–57	58–63	64–69	70–79	80

150/10/8 PRINT CHART PROG. ID PERSONNEL P 7.3 PAGE 1
(SPACING: 150 POSITIONS AT 10 CHARACTERS PER INCH, 8 LINES PER VERTICAL INCH) DATE 01/01/89
PROGRAM TITLE PERSONNEL STATUS
PROGRAMMER OR DOCUMENTALIST J. WAYNE SPENCE
CHART TITLE PERSONNEL STATUS REPORT

```
PERSONNEL STATUS REPORT

EMPLOYEE NAME        DEPARTMENT   CLASS  JOB TITLE         DATE OF EMPLOYMENT  LAST PROMOTION  HOURLY/SALARIED  PRESENT STATUS

X------------------X  X--------X   9999  X----------------X  XX/XX/XX           XX/XX/XX         X               X--------X
X------------------X  X--------X   9999  X----------------X  XX/XX/XX           XX/XX/XX         X               X--------X
```

Supplement for Chapter 7

Using the ACCEPT and DISPLAY Statements for Input and Output

The previous discussion in this chapter has been aimed at reading and writing records (using READ and WRITE statements). Although this is typically the most common form of attaining data from an external source or production written lines of printed output, the advent of the computer terminal has changed how data are entered into a program and how results are produced. Computer terminals (also called video display devices—VDTs or cathode ray tubes—CRTs) provide a level of flexibility not previously found when dealing with record input and output. Generally, terminals are field-rather than record-oriented. That is, if a terminal keyboard is used to supply data, the input data values are usually supplied one field at a time. When output is produced on a terminal, the output may be one or more fields at a time.

By using the additional flexibility provided by using a terminal, a programmer may employ input and output statements to ''interact'' with a program. Since the programmer determines the location of input and output statements in the PROCEDURE DIVISION, and since the execution of each of the statements produces visible results on the terminal display, the programmer should be able to determine exactly at what step the program is executing. Thus, by employing interactive input and output statements, the programmer should be capable of more easily developing the logic of a program, as well as more rapidly detecting errors during the execution of the program. Although both these functions are possible, we focus in this section on the use of the input and output statements to provide data values. The use of these statements for debugging purposes is presented in Appendix E.

The ACCEPT Statement

The ACCEPT statement may be employed to provide input data of relatively low volume to a COBOL program. Although the ACCEPT statement may appear in a multitude of forms, only two forms are presently part of ANS COBOL. The first of these formats, the simple ACCEPT statement, is shown in Figure 7.16. The identifier associated with the ACCEPT statement specifies the data item into which a value is to be placed. Normally, this would be an elementary-item. Once executed, the terminal user should

Figure 7.16 The Simple Format of the ACCEPT Statement

```
ACCEPT identifier [FROM mnemonic-name]
```

then use the terminal keyboard to enter the data value. If fewer characters are keyed than is indicated by the description of the identifier, the Enter (or Return) key on the keyboard is used to transmit the data value. Otherwise, when the field is exactly full, that is, when the final character to be placed in the field is supplied, normally the COBOL program containing the statement would automatically proceed to the next available statement.

The mnemonic-name entry is used to identify the device from which data are to be accepted. As previously demonstrated, the mnemonic-name clause is associated with the

```
system-name IS mnemonic-name
```

entry in the SPECIAL-NAMES paragraph of the ENVIRONMENT DIVISION. This entry has been previously used to identify the system name for top-of-form. In the case of an ACCEPT statement, used in an IBM environment, the entry

```
SYSIN IS TERMINAL-TYPE
```

might have meaning. However, this is a highly variable requirement from one system to another. Check with your computer installation to determine the requirements for this entry or whether or not it is needed.

To illustrate how this statement might be used, suppose the following instruction was placed in a program:

```
ACCEPT STUDENT-NAME-IN.
```

Each time the statement is executed, it would cause a question mark symbol (?) to appear on the terminal display. This signifies that the program is waiting for the user to key in data. As characters are pressed on the terminal keyboard, they would usually appear adjacent to the question mark symbol generated by the ACCEPT statement. Thus, the user should be able to establish (1) when the program is expecting data to be entered (by the appearance of the ? symbol) and (2) the data value supplied from the keyboard. Therefore, the user's response to the execution of our sample ACCEPT statement might be:

```
?JOHN Q. ADAMS
```

assuming, of course, that the description of STUDENT-NAME-IN is alphanumeric (or alphabetic) and at least as long as the data value entered.

If we were to redesign the program presented in Figure 7.15 to use ACCEPT statements to enter data rather than the READ statement, we might approach the problem by eliminating all entries related to STUDENT-FILE (in the ENVIRONMENT DIVISION, DATA DIVISION, and PROCEDURE DIVISION). Then we could remove STUDENT-RECORD from the WORKING-STORAGE SECTION. (We no longer need the input-record description. We can enter the data directly into the output-record field descriptions.) Finally, in the PROCEDURE DIVISION, the READ statement and the MOVE statements previously required to place the input data into the output data items are replaced by the following:

```
ACCEPT FIRST-NAME-OUT.
ACCEPT MIDDLE-INITIAL-OUT.
ACCEPT LAST-NAME-OUT.
ACCEPT ID-NUMBER-OUT.
ACCEPT CLASSIFICATION-OUT.
ACCEPT MAJOR-OUT.
ACCEPT CURRENT-HOURS-OUT.
ACCEPT TOTAL-HOURS-OUT.
```

The dialogue between the user and the program would be similar to the following for the first set of data:

```
?JOHN
?Q
?ADAMS
?343564321
?GR
?CSC
?00
?219
```

Thereafter, the first line of output would be produced and the set of ACCEPT statements would be repeated.

Figure 7.17 illustrates another standard form of the ACCEPT statement. Note that in this form of the statement, we can get the current DATE, DAY, or TIME into a programmer-specified identifier. For ease of use, the identifier should be specified, either implicitly or explicitly, as alphanumeric. When the DATE is specified as the source of data, the current date is retrieved from the computer system in a YYMMDD (year-month-day) format. Thus, a value such as ''850125'' would be placed into the identifier. When DAY is specified, the computer places a five-digit numeric value in the format YYDDD (year and number of days elapsed from the beginning of the year) into the identifier. This format represents the ''Julian date'' with COBOL 85, when DAY-OF-WEEK a numeric value for the day of the week (1 for Monday, 2 for Tuesday, and so on) is placed into the identifier. Finally, if TIME is specified, an eight-digit number in the format HHMMSSCC (hours, minutes, seconds, and fractions of seconds) is returned. This value is stated in terms of a 24-hour clock; that is, hours may be a value between 0 and 23. Minutes and seconds will be between 0 and 59, and fractions of seconds will be between 0 and 99.

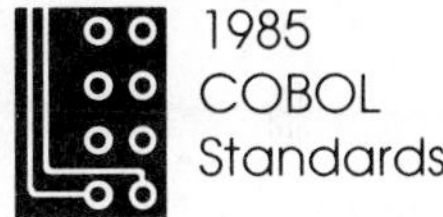
1985
COBOL
Standards

To illustrate this form of the ACCEPT statement, suppose you wished to utilize the current date in the heading of a program. You might employ the following code in the DATA and PROCEDURE DIVISIONs:

Figure 7.17 Second Format of the ACCEPT Statement

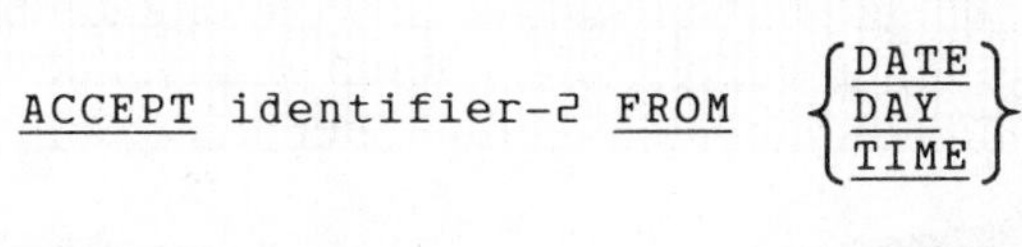
ACCEPT identifier-2 FROM
DATE
DAY
TIME

```
       .
       .
       WORKING-STORAGE SECTION.
       01  ENTRY-DATE.
           05  ENTRY-YEAR          PIC 9(02).
           05  ENTRY-MONTH         PIC 9(02).
           05  ENTRY-DAY           PIC 9(02).
       .
       .
       .
       PROCEDURE DIVISION.
       .
       .
       .
            ACCEPT ENTRY-DATE FROM DATE.
       .
       .
       .
```

After the ACCEPT statement has been executed, the current date may be rearranged into a more convenient format for further processing.

Among the most varied types of ACCEPT statements is the format that is used to build and manipulate "display screens." The programmer is permitted to design programs fully by saying the capabilities of a video terminal; then the display area of the screen can be viewed as a matrix of character positions, as illustrated in Figure 7.18. This matrix typically consists of 24 lines, each capable of producing 80 characters, that is, a 1920 (24 × 80) character display area. Furthermore, some compilers permit what is called *cursor addressing*. Cursor addressing is the capability, via program control, to access any position in the 24 × 80 display screen matrix. Thus, the programmer, using this capability, can map out where information is to be placed and accessed on the

Figure 7.18 Video Display Screen Layout

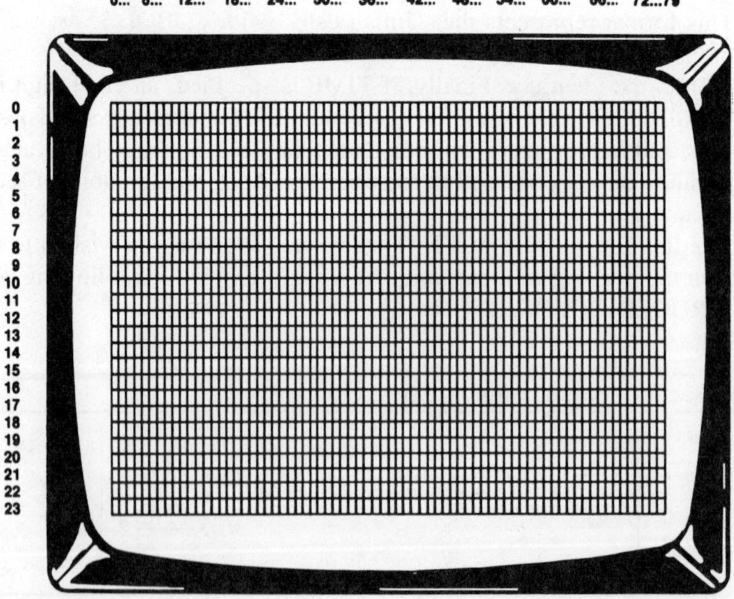

screen. In addition, unlike record input or printed output that generally runs from first to last (or top to bottom), information may be placed on the screen or accessed from the screen in any order. This capability is available on many large computers and is almost always available on mini-and microcomputers with COBOL compilers.

This type of capability obviously calls for a much more sophisticated form of the ACCEPT statement. In addition, to illustrate the variability of this statement format, let us examine two different versions of this type of ACCEPT statement. Figure 7.19 provides the format of an enhanced version of the ACCEPT statement in MS-COBOL (a product of Microsoft, Incorporated), which may be used on the IBM-PC microcomputer and other compatible machines. The ACCEPT statement illustrated in Figure 7.20 is available in RM-COBOL (a product of Ryan-McFarland, Incorporated) and may be used on machines such as the minicomputers manufactured by Texas Instruments, Incorporated and AT&T. In both formats, identifier-1 is the field into which data are placed as a result of executing the statement. The UNIT clause in the RM-COBOL version permits data to be accepted from a terminal other than the one running the program.

The next characteristic of both statements is a location specification. Thus, if we wished to have data accepted from the tenth character position on the 5th line of the screen, the statements would be:

```
ACCEPT (5, 10) FIRST-INPUT-FIELD
```

in the MS-COBOL system, and

```
ACCEPT FIRST-INPUT-FIELD LINE 5 POSITION 10
```

in the RM-COBOL version. Although the actual cursor position for both may be specified as an integer (as shown) or through the value of a numeric, nonedited, integer identifier, MS-COBOL also permits relative cursor positioning; that is, the cursor position is relative to its previous location on the screen. Thus, assuming that the previous statement had been executed and the statement

Figure 7.19 Format of the MS-COBOL Enhanced ACCEPT Statement

```
ACCEPT

[   { LIN { + }  integer-1 }   { COL  +   integer-3 }   ]
[ ( {     { - }            } , {      -             } ) ]
[   { integer-2            }   {   integer-4        }   ]

identifier-1

[ WITH

    [ { SPACE-FILL } ]   [ { LEFT-JUSTIFY  } ]
    [ { ZERO-FILL  } ]   [ { RIGHT-JUSTIFY } ]

    [ TRAILING-SIGN ] [ PROMPT ] [ UPDATE ]

    [LENGTH-CHECK] [ AUTO-SKIP ] [ BEEP ] . . . ]
```

Figure 7.20 Format of the RM-COBOL Enhanced ACCEPT Statement

```
ACCEPT identifier-1  [ UNIT { identifier-2 } ]
                            { literal-1    }

  [ LINE { identifier-3 } ] [ POSITION { identifier-4 } ]
         { literal-2    }              { literal-3    }

  [ SIZE { identifier-5 } ] [ PROMPT      [ literal-5 ] ]
         { literal-4    }

  [ ECHO ] [ CONVERT ] [ TAB ] [ ERASE ] [ NO BEEP ]

  [ [ OFF ] ]   [ { HIGH } ]   [ BLINK ] [ REVERSE ]
                [ { LOW  } ]

  [ ON EXCEPTION identifier-6 imperative-statement] . . .
```

```
ACCEPT (LINE - 2, COL + 10) SECOND-INPUT-FIELD
```

immediately followed, the location referenced into which data could be entered would be the twentieth character position on the third line, that is, go up (5 — 2) and right (10 + 10).

Among the other features of the MS-COBOL version of the statement are SPACE-FILL to fill unused positions of an alphabetic or alphanumeric field with spaces (the default for these field types if omitted), ZERO-FILL to fill the unused positions of a numeric or numeric-edited field with zeros (the default for these field types if omitted), LEFT-JUSTIFY to have data placed in the leftmost positions of a field (treated as a comment), RIGHT-JUSTIFY to have data placed in the rightmost positions of a field, TRAILING-SIGN to have the sign of a numeric field placed at the end of the field, PROMPT to have a row of periods (".") completely fill the field to indicate its length (the default is spaces), UPDATE to show the current value of a field before the input operation (in place of the PROMPT character), LENGTH-CHECK to require the field to be completely filled with characters entered from the keyboard, AUTO-SKIP to proceed automatically to the next statement when the last character of the field is entered, and BEEP to sound an audible alarm when the ACCEPT statement begins execution.

Among the other features of the RM-COBOL ACCEPT statement are SIZE to specify the number of characters to be accepted from the keyboard into the field (default is field length), PROMPT (without an identifier or literal) to cause the accepted field area to be blank (default is an underscore in each character position), PROMPT (with an identifier or literal) to specify a particular character to be placed in each position of the accepted field, ECHO to have the current value of the accepted identifier displayed in the field in place of the prompt character, CONVERT to manipulate the characters entered into a numeric field so that they conform to the characteristics of that field (e.g. right-justified, zero-filled, etc.), TAB to force the system to wait for the RETURN key to be pressed prior to completing the statement (this allows the TAB key to reposition at the beginning of the field, if pressed, and permits the BACKSPACE key to be used to make corrections), ERASE to cause the display screen to be cleared prior to the execution of the ACCEPT statement, NO BEEP to suppress the sounding of an audible alarm when the ACCEPT statement is executed, OFF to turn off the echoing of keyboard strokes to the display screen area, HIGH/LOW to set screen intensity for the field to full or partial brightness, BLINK to cause the prompt and data characters to appear in blinking mode, REVERSE to produce the field image in reverse video mode (the normal mode is usually light letters on a dark background), and ON EXCEPTION which causes an imperative statement to be executed in the event the data do not conform to the field type.

These are only two illustrations of the format used for the enhanced version of the ACCEPT statement. You should check with your instructor to determine the form of the ACCEPT statement in your installation or whether or not it is available to you.

The DISPLAY Statement

The previous discussion has centered on getting data into a program on an interactive basis. However, there is another side to this problem. If data are to be entered into several fields via the ACCEPT statement, we may quickly lose track of which ACCEPT statement is being executed. One way to overcome this problem is to produce textual messages on the screen to assist the user in determining for which field data are being sought. The DISPLAY statement may also be employed to produce the known data values of previously used fields.

The standard form of the DISPLAY statement is shown in Figure 7.21. Note that either an identifier or a literal (or combinations of identifiers and literals) may be produced by this statement. However, you should be cautioned about totally replacing the WRITE statements of a program with DISPLAY statements. First, the DISPLAY statement is not so efficient at producing printed output as is the WRITE statement. Second, when a data value is displayed, it is not converted from its internal form. That is, if a nonedited field or a COMPUTATIONAL data item is displayed, the computer will attempt to produce the character representations of those fields. In other words, this type of data may not be displayable. We overcome this problem when WRITE statements are used by first moving the data to print-oriented fields before the output operation is performed. See Chapter 23 for additional details about noncharacter data representations.

To illustrate the use of this statement, suppose we again revise the program previously presented in Figure 7.15. When we modified this program to accept data from the keyboard (rather, the READ a record), we eliminated all references to the input file, as well as several MOVE statements. However, the result is less than acceptable because we cannot now determine exactly which ACCEPT statement is requesting what data. If we modify the code to be:

Figure 7.21 Format of the DISPLAY Statement

```
          { identifier-1 }   [ { identifier-2 } ]
DISPLAY   {              }   [ {              } ] . . .
          { literal-1    }   [ { literal-2    } ]

     [UPON mnemonic-name]
```

```
DISPLAY 'ENTER STUDENT INFORMATION AS INDICATED BELOW:'.
DISPLAY 'WHAT IS THE FIRST NAME?'.
ACCEPT FIRST-NAME-OUT.
DISPLAY 'WHAT IS THE MIDDLE INITIAL?'.
ACCEPT MIDDLE-INITIAL-OUT.
DISPLAY 'WHAT IS THE LAST NAME?'.
ACCEPT LAST-NAME-OUT.
DISPLAY 'WHAT IS THE ID NUMBER?'.
ACCEPT ID-NUMBER-OUT.
DISPLAY 'WHAT IS THE CLASSIFICATION (E.G. "JR", "SR", ETC.)?'.
ACCEPT CLASSIFICATION-OUT.
DISPLAY 'WHAT IS THE MAJOR (E.G. "SC," "MKT", ETC.)?'.
ACCEPT MAJOR-OUT.
DISPLAY 'FOR HOW MANY HOURS IS THE STUDENT CURRENTLY ENROLLED?'.
ACCEPT CURRENT-HOURS-OUT.
DISPLAY 'WHAT IS THE TOTAL NUMBER HOURS THE STUDENT HAS TAKEN?'.
ACCEPT TOTAL-HOURS-OUT.
```

then the dialogue between the program and the user might be similar to the following for the first set of data:

```
ENTER STUDENT INFORMATION AS INDICATED BELOW:
WHAT IS THE FIRST NAME?
?JOHN
WHAT IS THE MIDDLE INITIAL?
?Q
WHAT IS THE LAST NAME?
?ADAMS
WHAT IS THE ID NUMBER?
?343564321
WHAT IS THE CLASSIFICATION (E.G. "JR", "SR", ETC.)?
?GR
WHAT IS THE MAJOR (E.G. "CSC", "MKT", ETC.)?
?CSC
FOR HOW MANY HOURS IS THE STUDENT CURRENTLY ENROLLED?
?00
WHAT IS THE TOTAL NUMBER HOURS THE STUDENT HAS TAKEN?
?219
```

The sequence would then repeat for entry of the second, third, and subsequent sets of data. The difference now is that we can easily determine what type of data is to be entered into each field.

As with the ACCEPT statement, a nonstandard form of the DISPLAY statement is frequently available on systems that utilize video display terminals as output devices. Again, you should be reminded that this form of the DISPLAY statement is typically highly variable from one component to the next. To illustrate some of these differences, examine Figure 7.22—the MS-COBOL enhanced DISPLAY statement—and Figure 7.23—the RM-COBOL enhanced DISPLAY statement. In the MS-COBOL and RM-COBOL versions of the DISPLAY statement, cursor positioning is achieved in the same manner as the corresponding ACCEPT statement. Thus, if you wanted to produce a heading at the top of a display screen, you might employ a statement such as

```
DISPLAY (3, 20) 'STUDENT DATA ENTRY SCREEN'
```

in MS-COBOL or the statement

```
DISPLAY 'STUDENT DATA ENTRY SCREEN' LINE 3
                    POSITION 20
```

in RM-COBOL. As before, the MS-COBOL version supports relative cursor positioning (with the LIN and COL option), where the RM-COBOL version has no such option.

Figure 7.22 Format of the MS-COBOL Enhanced DISPLAY Statement

```
DISPLAY
                   +                               +
[ ( { LIN  {   } integer-1 }, { COL  {   } integer-3 } ) ]
                   -                               -
    { integer-2            }  { integer-4            }

   { identifier-1 }
   { literal-1    }  . . .
   { ERASE        }

   [UPON mnemonic-name]
```

Figure 7.23 Format of the RM-COBOL Enhanced DISPLAY Statement

```
DISPLAY { identifier-1 }        [ UNIT { identifier-2 } ]
        { literal-1    }        [      { literal-2    } ]

  [ LINE { identifier-3 } ]     [ POSITION { identifier-4 } ]
  [      { literal-3    } ]     [          { literal-4    } ]

  [ SIZE { identifier-5 } ]
  [      { literal-5    } ]

                HIGH
  [ BEEP ]                 [ BLINK ] [ REVERSE ] [ ERASE ]
                LOW
```

Another common characteristic of both DISPLAY statements is the use of the ERASE clause to clear the screen. In the MS-COBOL version, ERASE is used in place of an identifier or literal. In RM-COBOL the ERASE clause is an additional clause (which is acted upon prior to the output of data).

Furthermore, the RM-COBOL version supports a number of additional clauses. The UNIT option is used to identify a terminal for the output other than the one executing the program. The SIZE option is used to control the number of characters displayed on the screen, if different from the description of the data to be displayed. The BEEP option causes an audible tone to sound, HIGH/LOW causes a variation in full/half intensity, the BLINK option causes the field to blink, and the REVERSE option causes the output to be produced in a reverse video mode.

A Screen Input-Output Program

As has been illustrated, enhanced versions of the ACCEPT and DISPLAY statements may be used to create a dialogue between a program and its user. Therefore, designing an interactive program is somewhat different from writing conventional code. Think of the display screen as a two-dimensional work area on which you can record and erase information at will. To illustrate one application of ACCEPT and DISPLAY statements that create a screen format and enter data into that format, examine Figure 7.24.

The interactive COBOL program incorporates three major activities. First, the program places a screen format on the display screen, as shown in Figure 7.25. This screen format is produced by the DISPLAY statements in lines 660–790. Note that the sequence of events is such that the screen is cleared of all previously displayed material, a title

Figure 7.24 An Interactive COBOL Program

```
       1   1   2   2   2   3   3   4   4   4   5   5   6   6   6   7
   4   8   2   6   0   4   8   2   6   0   4   8   2   6   0   4   8   2
 10*****************************************************************
 20 IDENTIFICATION DIVISION.
 30*****************************************************************
 40 PROGRAM-ID.    INTERACTIVE-PROGRAM.
 50 AUTHOR.        J. WAYNE SPENCE.
 60 DATE-WRITTEN.  JANUARY 1, 1989.
 70 DATE-COMPILED. JANUARY 1, 1989.
 80*     This program illustrates how COBOL may interact with
 90*     the user of the program.  The program illustrates
100*     ACCEPT and DISPLAY statements as they are implemented
110*     within MS-COBOL.
120*****************************************************************
130 ENVIRONMENT DIVISION.
140*****************************************************************
150*-------------------------------------------------------------*
160 CONFIGURATION SECTION.
170*-------------------------------------------------------------*
180 SOURCE-COMPUTER. IBM-PC.
190 OBJECT-COMPUTER. IBM-PC.
200 SPECIAL-NAMES.   '1' IS TOP-OF-NEXT-PAGE.
210*-------------------------------------------------------------*
220 INPUT-OUTPUT SECTION.
230*-------------------------------------------------------------*
240 FILE-CONTROL.
250     SELECT STUDENT-REPORT  ASSIGN TO PRINTER.
260*****************************************************************
270 DATA DIVISION.
280*****************************************************************
290*-------------------------------------------------------------*
300 FILE SECTION.
310*-------------------------------------------------------------*
320
330 FD  STUDENT-REPORT LABEL RECORDS ARE OMITTED.
340 01  REPORT-LINE.
350     05 FILLER                   PIC X(03).
360     05 FIRST-NAME-OUT           PIC X(11).
370     05 MIDDLE-INITIAL-OUT       PIC X(02).
380     05 LAST-NAME-OUT            PIC X(10).
390     05 FILLER                   PIC X(04).
400     05 STUDENT-ID-OUT           PIC 9(09).
410     05 FILLER                   PIC X(05).
420     05 CLASSIFICATION-OUT       PIC X(02).
430     05 FILLER                   PIC X(06).
440     05 MAJOR-OUT                PIC X(03).
450     05 FILLER                   PIC X(08).
460     05 HOURS-THIS-SEM-OUT       PIC 9(02).
470     05 FILLER                   PIC X(08).
480     05 TOTAL-HOURS-OUT          PIC 9(03).
490     05 FILLER                   PIC X(03).
500*-------------------------------------------------------------*
```

is produced, and an identification of each data field is provided. The screen itself, based on the line and character position entries of the DISPLAY statements, is produced from top to bottom. For example, the "Student's Name" message on the left half of the screen is produced and then the "Classification" message on the right half of the screen is displayed. By adjusting the sequence of DISPLAY statements, we can produce all the messages on the left half of the screen and then the messages on the right half.

The second function of the program is to accept data into the fields of the student record. This is performed by the series of ACCEPT statements in lines 850–920. Note

Figure 7.24 *Continued* An Interactive COBOL Program

```
-----------------------------------------------------------------------
|       1   1   2   2   2   3   3   4   4   4   5   5   6   6   6   7|
|   4   8   2   6   0   4   8   2   6   0   4   8   2   6   0   4   8   2|
|---------------------------------------------------------------------|
| 510 WORKING-STORAGE SECTION.
| 520*---------------------------------------------------------------*
| 530****************************************************************
| 540 PROCEDURE DIVISION.
| 550****************************************************************
| 560 100-START-UP.
| 570       OPEN OUTPUT STUDENT-REPORT.
| 580       MOVE SPACES TO REPORT-LINE.
| 590
| 600 200-READ-DATA.
| 610
| 620*=-=-=-=-=-=-=-=-=-=-=-=-=-=-=-=-=-=-=-=-=-=-=-=-=-=-=-=-=-=-=-*
| 630*            Screen Format Portion of Procedure                *
| 640*=-=-=-=-=-=-=-=-=-=-=-=-=-=-=-=-=-=-=-=-=-=-=-=-=-=-=-=-=-=-=-*
| 650
| 660       DISPLAY (1, 1)     ERASE.
| 670       DISPLAY (1, 25)    "============================".
| 680       DISPLAY (2, 25)    "= Student Data Entry Screen =".
| 690       DISPLAY (3, 25)    "============================".
| 700       DISPLAY (5, 5)     "Student's Name:".
| 710       DISPLAY (5, 40)    "Classification (e.g. JR, SR, etc)--".
| 720       DISPLAY (6, 10)    "First Name--".
| 730       DISPLAY (7, 10)    "Middle Initial--".
| 740       DISPLAY (7, 40)    "Major (e.g. CSC, MKT, etc)--".
| 750       DISPLAY (8, 10)    "Last Name--".
| 760       DISPLAY (9, 40)    "Hours:".
| 770       DISPLAY (10, 5)    "Student ID Number:".
| 780       DISPLAY (10, 45)   "Current--".
| 790       DISPLAY (11, 45)   "Total--".
| 800
| 810*=-=-=-=-=-=-=-=-=-=-=-=-=-=-=-=-=-=-=-=-=-=-=-=-=-=-=-=-=-=-=-*
| 820*         Screen Data Entry Portion of Procedure               *
| 830*=-=-=-=-=-=-=-=-=-=-=-=-=-=-=-=-=-=-=-=-=-=-=-=-=-=-=-=-=-=-=-*
| 840
| 850       ACCEPT (6, 22)     FIRST-NAME-OUT.
| 860       ACCEPT (7, 26)     MIDDLE-INITIAL-OUT.
| 870       ACCEPT (8, 21)     LAST-NAME-OUT.
| 880       ACCEPT (10, 24)    STUDENT-ID-OUT.
| 890       ACCEPT (5, 75)     CLASSIFICATION-OUT.
| 900       ACCEPT (7, 68)     MAJOR-OUT.
| 910       ACCEPT (10, 54)    HOURS-THIS-SEM-OUT.
| 920       ACCEPT (11, 52)    TOTAL-HOURS-OUT.
| 930
| 940       WRITE REPORT-LINE AFTER 2 LINES.
| 950       GO TO 200-READ-DATA.
| 960
| 970 300-END-JOB.
| 980       CLOSE STUDENT-FILE, STUDENT-REPORT.
| 990       STOP RUN.
-----------------------------------------------------------------------
```

Figure 7.25 The Display Screen (before data entry)

```
                              ==============================
                              - Student Data Entry Screen -
                              ==============================

Student's Name:                         Classification (e.g. JR, SR etc)--
     First Name--
     Middle Initial--                   Major (e.g. CSC, MKT, etc)--
     Last Name--
                                        Hours:
Student ID Number--                          Current--
                                             Total--
```

that data are accepted into the fields in the same order as previously seen (e.g., in the program illustrated in Figure 3.1). This means that although the screen format was developed from top to bottom, data are entered into the screen on the basis of the left half first and then the right. Thus, after data have been entered into all fields, the screen would appear as shown in Figure 7.26. The programmer must be conscious of how the screen is designed so that it might be easily used ''user friendly''.

The final activity of the program is to produce a printed record of the contents of the data fields. This is performed by the WRITE statement in line 940. Thereafter, the procedure begins to repeat itself by first clearing the screen and producing the screen format, entering data into the fields, and producing a line of printed output. All these activities are performed without using a single READ statement or any support for an input file in the ENVIRONMENT or DATA DIVISIONs.

As a final note, we should be aware of a couple of problems associated with the program illustrated in Figure 7.24. First, the program will loop continuously, since there is no apparent test for an end-of-file condition. For now, this problem may be overcome by using the BREAK key on the keyboard to terminate the program. Later (in Chapter 9), we will see that other statements may be used to control this looping activity, which ultimately causes the termination of the program. Second, most interactive data entry programs allow for the changing of data entered into a field. Subsequently we will find (via the CASE structure) that a program may be designed to perform selective activity and, relative to interactive programming, identify a particular field to be changed.

Figure 7.26 The Display Screen (after data entry)

```
                              ==============================
                              - Student Data Entry Screen -
                              ==============================

Student's Name:                         Classification (e.g. JR, SR, etc)--GR
     First Name--JOHN
     Middle Initial--Q                  Major (e.g. CSC, MKT, etc)--CSC
     Last Name--ADAMS
                                        Hours:
Student ID Number--343564321                 Current--00
                                             Total--219
```

PART

II

MORE ADVANCED COBOL CONCEPTS

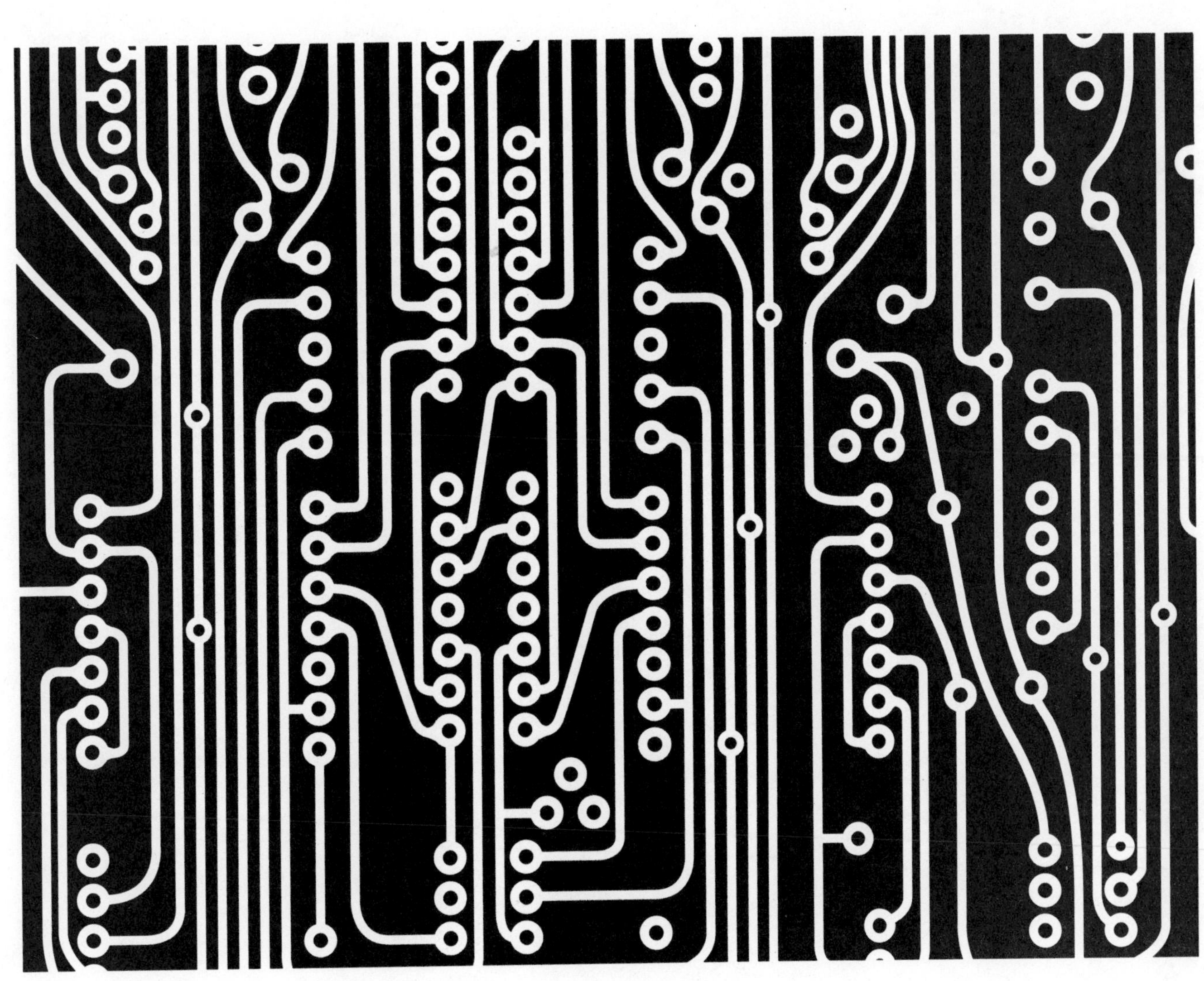

CHAPTER

8

Editing Data for Printed Output

In Chapter 6 (The DATA DIVISION), the basic PICTURE characters—A, X, 9, V, S, and P—were presented. These characters are sufficient for the internal description of input data or data items needed for internal purposes only; however, printed output should be easy for users to read. To improve its readability, we can edit printed output, using PICTURE characters specifically designed for that purpose.

The PICTURE characters used for editing are presented with their meanings in Table 8.1. Editing PICTURE characters fall into three categories: *fixed-insertion, floating - insertion,* and *replacement* characters. Some characters fall into two of these categories. Each category has a precise set of rules for its use.

Fixed Insertions

A fixed-insertion character is printed on the output in the position it occupies in the PICTURE string. The fixed-insertion characters are shown below at the left. However, +, –, and $ also fall into the floating-insertion category. These three characters are considered to be fixed-insertion characters if they appear only once in a PICTURE string.

The rules for the fixed-insertion category are as follows:

1. The +, –, CR, and DB symbols are mutually exclusive. If one of the characters appears in a PICTURE string, the other three symbols must not appear in that PICTURE string.
2. The + or – symbol may appear only once per PICTURE string. It must appear as either the leftmost or rightmost character in the PICTURE string.
3. The CR and DB symbol may appear only once in a PICTURE string. It must appear to the right of the least- significant-digit position in the PICTURE string.
4. The $ symbol may appear only once in a PICTURE string. It must appear to the left of the most-significant-digit position in the PICTURE string.
5. The . symbol may appear only once in a PICTURE string. It must not appear as the rightmost character of the PICTURE string.

1. –
2. —
3. $
4. .
5. ,
6. 0
7. B
8. CR
9. DB

Table 8.1 Editing PICTURE Characters

Character	Meaning	Editing Category	Data type Used With
+	The plus symbol causes either a plus or minus sign to be printed, depending on the algebraic value of the data item.	Fixed Insertion Floating Insertion	Numeric
–	The minus symbol causes only the minus sign to be printed if the algebraic value of the data item is negative.	Fixed Insertion Floating Insertion	Numeric
$	The currency symbol causes the "dollar sign" to be printed. It may be printed at the beginning of a PICTURE string or it may be used as a floating character (the symbol appears adjacent to the most significant digit in a numeric field).	Fixed Insertion Floating Insertion	Numeric
.	The decimal point causes a decimal point to be printed at the point where it is located in a PICTURE string, it may appear only once in a PICTURE string.	Fixed Insertion	Numeric
,	The comma causes a comma to be printed at the point(s) where it is located in a PICTURE string. Although a fixed-insertion character, it may be replaced by floating or replacement characters.	Fixed Insertion	Numeric
Ø	The zero causes a zero to appear on the output in every position it occupies in a PICTURE string.	Fixed Insertion	Numeric Alphanumeric Alphabetic
B	The blank symbol causes a blank to be printed on the output at the point(s) where it is located in a PICTURE string.	Fixed Insertion	Numeric Alphanumeric Alphabetic
CR	The "credit" symbol appears on the printed output if the field it is in contains a negative value.	Fixed Insertion	Numeric
DB	The "debit" symbol appears on the printed output if the field it is in contains a negative value.	Fixed Insertion	Numeric
Z	The zero-suppression symbol causes leading zeros to be replaced with blanks (spaces) on the printed output.	Replacement	Numeric
*	The "check protection" character causes leading zeros to be replaced with asterisks(*).	Replacement	Numeric

6. The , symbol may appear several times in a PICTURE string. It must never be the leftmost or rightmost character in a PICTURE string, and two commas should not be adjacent to each other.
7. The Ø symbol may be used in numeric-, alphabetic-, or alphanumeric-edited fields. Zeros may be adjacent and may appear as either the leftmost or rightmost characters in a PICTURE string.
8. The B symbol may be used in numeric-, alphabetic-, or alphanumeric-edited fields. Blanks may be inserted in adjacent positions, as the left-most characters or the rightmost characters in a PICTURE string.

Table 8.2 shows how fixed-insertion characters can be used.

Table 8.2 Examples of the Use of Fixed-Insertion Characters

Data Value	Output PICTURE String	PICTURE String Output Length	Resulting Output	Comments
123456	+9(6)	7	`+123456`	Length of the output field is 7 columns; unsigned source field is interpreted as containing a positive value.
−123456	9(6)+	7	`123456-`	Note that the + symbol may be recorded on the right and that it produces a minus sign when the data are negative.
$+1234_{\wedge}56$	−9(5).99	9	` Ø1234.56`	The length of the output field is 9 characters, the minus sign does not cause the sign to be printed (consequently leaving a blank), and data are aligned on the decimal point in the PICTURE string such that a zero is added to the output.
$-1234_{\wedge}56$	9(4)−	5	`1234-`	The minus sign is recorded at the rightmost position of this 5-character output field, and since the assumed decimal position follows the last digit, the fractional portion of the source field is truncated.
$+123_{\wedge}45$	$99.99B	7	`$23.45 `	A high-order digit is truncated, but the dollar sign and the blank of the PICTURE string are printed—a digit cannot replace a fixed-insertion character.
−123456	99B99B99BØØ	11	`12 34 56 ØØ`	The length of the output field is 11 characters, multiple nonadjacent B's are used, and adjacent 0's are inserted at the rightmost character positions of the PICTURE string. Note that the minus sign is ignored.
$12345_{\wedge}67$	$999,999.99CR	13	`$Ø12,345.67  `	The output field is 13 characters long, and several fixed-insertion characters appear—note that since the data are not negative, the CR symbol is not produced, but it does require two spaces.
−1234	$9999.ØØBDB	11	`$1234.ØØ DB`	Again, several fixed-insertion characters are used—since the data are negative, the DB symbol is produced.
$-1234_{\wedge}56$	−$9(4).99	9	`-$1234.56`	Both the dollar sign and the minus sign appear in the PICTURE string.
$_{\wedge}1234$	.999ØØB(4)	10	`.123ØØ    `	The decimal point may appear as the leftmost character; the field is not sufficiently large to accommodate the "4," and editing characters may use replication factors (such as B in the example).
ABCDEF	AAABBAAA	8	`ABC  DEF`	Example shows the use of blank insertion in an alphabetic field.
123 ABC	XXBBØX(5)	10	`12  Ø3 ABC`	Example shows the use of blank and zero insertion in an alphanumeric field. Note that the first two blanks are caused by the blank insertion, and the single blank is part of the data field.

Floating-Insertion

The second category of editing characters is floating-insertion characters. Floating insertion gives the appearance that the field is exactly large enough to accommodate the number. As the name implies, these characters "float" from left to right and appear adjacent to the most significant digit (assuming the floating character is coded to the most significant digit position of the PICTURE string). The floating-insertion characters are +, −, and $. To be interpreted as a floating character, two or more of the same floating-insertion characters must be recorded adjacent to each other. In other words, a

Table 8.3 Examples of the Use of Floating-Insertion Characters

Data Value	Output PICTURE String	PICTURE String Output Length	Resulting Output	Comments
+12345	+++++9	6	+123456	No "floating" is apparent because the number exactly fills the field.
+123	+(6)	6	□□+123	The + symbol is floated two positions to the right to appear adjacent to the most-significant-digit position, and the field may be composed totally of an insertion character.
−12345	+(5)	5	-2345	The field is not sufficiently large to accommodate the data value. Consequently, the data are decimal-point aligned (assumed to be after the rightmost digit) and placed in the field. *Note:* the floating-insertion character must be written in the output field, even to the exclusion of a significant digit.
−123456∧78	- - - -, - - -.- -	11	-123.456.78	The floating-insertion character may be interspersed with fixed-insertion characters.
+123∧45	- - - -,- - -.- -	11	□□□□□123.45	Note the disappearance of the comma as the − sign is floated from left to right (except the sign of the number is positive so the − symbol is not printed).
+12345∧67	$$$,$$$,$$$.$$B+	16	□□□□$12.345.67□+	The length of the output field is 16 characters, the $ symbol floats from left to right to become adjacent to the most significant digit—it is replaced by blanks as it moves.
Ø	$(5).$$	8	□□□□□□□□	If the field contains zero, the field on the output will be blank.
∧Ø1	$(5).$$	8	□□□□$.Ø1	If there is a significant digit to the right of the decimal point, the floating character will be printed adjacent to the decimal point.

single + recorded adjacent to a single $ in a PICTURE string is not floating-insertion, but is rather two fixed-insertion characters recorded together. Two different floating-insertion characters are not allowed in the same PICTURE string; however, a floating character could be preceded by, followed by, or interspersed with other PICTURE characters. (Remember that when one "sign-oriented" character is used in a PICTURE string, no other "sign-oriented" character can be used. Thus, if + is used as a floating-insertion character, –, CR, and DB cannot also be used as a fixed-insertion character in that PICTURE clause).

All floating-insertion characters are used with numeric data fields. Since floating-insertion characters are placed adjacent to the most-significant-digit position of a numeric field, a floating-insertion character may not appear to the right of a 9 in a PICTURE string. If a fixed-insertion character (e.g., comma) is used in conjunction with a floating-insertion character, the floating-insertion character is capable of either replacing the fixed insertion character or causing the fixed-insertion character to be replaced with a blank. Examples of floating-insertion characters are presented in Table 8.3

Replacement

The final category of editing characters is replacement characters. These characters (* and Z) are used to replace insignificant zeros (from left to right) in an output field. The

Table 8.4 Examples of the Use of Replacement Characters

Data Value	PICTURE String Used for Output	PICTURE String Ouput Length	Resulting Output	Comments
1234	ZZZZ9	5	[ ][1][2][3][4]	The first character of the output, which would normally be a zero, is replaced with a blank.
123	Z(5)	5	[ ][ ][1][2][3]	The first two positions are replaced with blanks.
12345	Z(5)	5	[1][2][3][4][5]	Unlike a floating-insertion character, the replacement character does not always have to be used.
−1234‸56	+ZZZ,ZZZ.ZZ	11	[−][ ][ ][1][,][2][3][4][.][5][6]	Fixed-insertion characters may be used in conjunction with replacement characters.
12‸34	$***,***.99	11	[$][*][*][*][*][*][1][2][.][3][4]	The fixed-insertion comma is replaced by an asterisk, and 9's are used in conjunction with the replacement character.
Ø	$***,***.**	11	[*][*][*][*][*][*][*][*][*][*][*]	All characters are replaced with the replacement characters.
‸Ø1	$***,***.**	11	[*][*][*][*][*][*][*][*][.][Ø][1]	The zero in the output field occupies a significant position.
−1234	$*****.ØØCR	11	[$][*][1][2][3][4][.][Ø][Ø][C][R]	The zero-insertion character may be used with a zero-suppression (replacement) character, as can other fixed-insertion characters.
Ø	Z,ZZZ	5	[ ][ ][ ][ ][ ]	All zeros are replaced by blanks (insertion characters are replaced with blanks, if passed).

* replaces zeros with asterisks, and the Z replaces zero with blanks. Since replacement characters and floating-insertion characters are for somewhat the same purpose, both replacement and floating-insertion characters cannot appear in the same PICTURE string. And the same two replacement characters cannot appear in the same PICTURE string; however, replacement characters can be interspersed with fixed-insertion characters.

The replacement characters, like floating-insertion characters, are used only with numeric fields. A replacement character cannot appear after a 9 in a PICTURE string. The replacement character will cause a fixed-insertion character (e.g., comma or period) to be replaced by an asterisk or a blank if there is not a significant digit to the left of the fixed-insertion character. Table 8.4 gives examples of the use of replacement characters.

Edited Data and the MOVE Statement

The use of edited data (numeric-edited, alphabetic-edited, and alphanumeric-edited fields) affects the use of the COBOL statements previously discussed, primarily the MOVE statement. There are specific rules for the movement of data into and from edited data fields. Table 8.5 shows the permitted movements of edited data.

One note of caution: beginning programmers sometimes forget that numeric data are not the same as numeric-*edited* data. In terms of data manipulation (e.g., adding, subtracting, etc.) numeric- edited data fields are more limited than simple numeric fields. Often, the beginning programmer temporarily forgets that, in a numeric PICTURE string, the decimal point is an editing character. Thus, *use the decimal point* (as well as other editing characters) *only in a data field that will be directly written a "printing" device.* Otherwise, you may spend a great deal of time trying to trace insignificant data errors. Chapter 10 (Arithmetic Statements) discusses, in detail, the use of numeric-edited versus

Table 8.5 Permissible Moves of Data**

	Receiving Fields						
		Elementary-Items					
Sending Fields	**Record or Group**	**Alpha-numeric (X)**	**Alpha-numeric-Edited**	**Alphabetic (A)**	**Alphabetic-Edited***	**Numeric (9)**	**Numeric-Edited**
Record or groups	YES	YES	YES	YES[1]	YES[1]	YES[3]	YES[3]
Alphanumeric (X)	YES	YES	YES	YES[1]	YES[1]	YES[3]	YES[3]
Alphanumeric-edited	YES	YES	YES	YES[1]	YES[1]	NO	NO
Alphabetic (A)	YES	YES	YES	YES	YES	NO	NO
Alphabetic-edited	YES	YES	YES	YES	YES	NO	NO
Numeric (9)	YES[3]	YES[4]	YES[4]	NO	YES[4]	YES	YES
Numeric-edited	YES	YES[3]	YES[3]	NO	YES[3]	NO	NO
Figurative Constants							
ZEROS	YES	YES	YES	NO	YES	YES	YES
SPACES	YES	YES	YES	YES	YES	NO	NO
HIGH-VALUES, LOW-VALUES, and QUOTES	YES	YES	YES	NO	YES	NO	NO
ALL literal	YES	YES	YES	YES[1]	YES	YES[2]	YES[2]
Numeric literal	YES[3]	YES[4]	YES[4]	NO	YES	YES	YES
Non-numeric literal	YES	YES	YES	YES[1]	YES	YES[2]	YES[2]

[1]So long as the field contains only alphabetic characters and spaces.
[2]So long as the field contains only numeric characters. The field is treated as a numeric integer.
[3]The movement of data is treated the same as an alphanumeric to alphanumeric move.
[4]So long as the numeric data item represents as integer number.
*Alphabetic-edited data are treated the same as alphanumeric-edited data.
**The permissible moves of COMPUTATIONAL data items and INDEX data items are not presented in this table.

numeric-nonedited fields. If you should have difficulty with edited data causing execution errors in your program, refer to Appendix E for an explanation of how the error may be located.

Inventory Listing Program (with Edited Output)

Figure 8.1 provides an additional program example of the use of editing characters. The program is designed to input a series of records and produce from these records a master list of inventory items. Because the first digit of the item number is used to indicate the product category, on the output, the first digit of the item number is separated from the

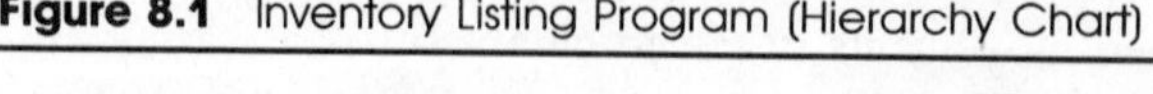

Figure 8.1 Inventory Listing Program (Hierarchy Chart)

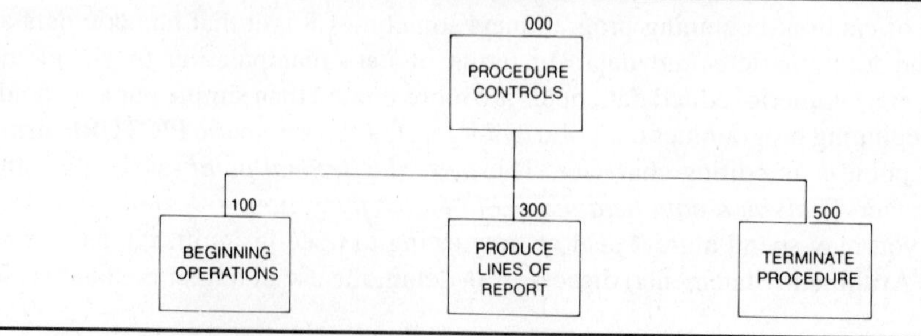

Figure 8.1 Inventory Listing Program (Pseudocode)

```
START
     DO Beginning operations
     DO Produce lines of report UNTIL eof
     DO Termination procedure
END

BEGINNING OPERATIONS
     OPEN files
     PRINT heading
     READ input
          IF eof
               SET file indicator
          ENDIF
END

PRODUCE LINES OF REPORT
     MOVE input to output
     WRITE output
     READ input
          IF eof
               SET file indicator
          ENDIF
END

TERMINATE PROCEDURE
     CLOSE files
END
```

Figure 8.1 *Continued* Inventory Listing Program

```
        1   1   2   2   2   3   3   4   4   4   5   5   6   6   6   7
4   8   2   6   0   4   8   2   6   0   4   8   2   6   0   4   8   2

*****************************************************************
 IDENTIFICATION DIVISION.
*****************************************************************
 PROGRAM-ID.      MASTER-LIST.
 AUTHOR.         J. WAYNE SPENCE.
 DATE-WRITTEN.  JANUARY 1, 1989.
 DATE-COMPILED. JANUARY 1, 1989.
*     This problem produces a master inventory list for ABC
*     Building Supply Company.  Tje program illustrates the use
*     of edited output and the use of VALUE clauses with
*     non-numeric literals in the WORKING-STORAGE SECTION.
*****************************************************************
 ENVIRONMENT DIVISION.
*****************************************************************
*---------------------------------------------------------------*
 CONFIGURATION SECTION.
*---------------------------------------------------------------*
 SOURCE-COMPUTER. IBM.
 OBJECT-COMPUTER. IBM.
 SPECIAL-NAMES.
                  C01 IS TOP-OF-NEXT-PAGE.
*---------------------------------------------------------------*
 INPUT-OUTPUT SECTION.
*---------------------------------------------------------------*
 FILE-CONTROL.
     SELECT INVENTORY-ITEM LIST ASSIGN TO UT-S-INPUT.
     SELECT MASTER-LIST FILE    ASSIGN TO UT-S-OUTPUT.
*****************************************************************
 DATA DIVISION.
*****************************************************************
*---------------------------------------------------------------*
 FILE SECTION.
*---------------------------------------------------------------*
 FD  INVENTORY-ITEM-FILE
     LABEL RECORDS ARE OMITTED.
```

Figure 8.1 *Continued* Inventory Listing Program

```
            1   1   2   2   2   3   3   4   4   4   5   5   6   6   6   7
    4   8   2   6   0   4   8   2   6   0   4   8   2   6   0   4   8   2
------------------------------------------------------------------------
       01  INVENTORY-ITEM-RECORD          PIC X(60).

       FD  MASTER-LIST-FILE
           LABEL RECORDS ARE OMITTED.
       01  MASTER-LIST-RECORD             PIC X(133).
      *--------------------------------------------------------------*
       WORKING-STORAGE SECTION.
      *--------------------------------------------------------------*
       01  WORKING-VARIABLES.
           04  FILE-STATUS                PIC X(05) VALUE 'START'.

       01  ITEM-RECORD.
           05 ITEM-DESCRIPTION-IN         PIC X(24).
           05 FILLER                      PIC X(12).
           05 ITEM-NUMBER-IN              PIC 9(06).
           05 FILLER                      PIC X(04).
           05 NUMBER-OF-UNITS-IN          PIC 9(03).
           05 FILLER                      PIC X(02).
           05 PACKING-UNIT-IN             PIC X(03).
           05 FILLER                      PIC X(02).
           05 PRICE-PER-UNIT-IN           PIC 9(02)V9(02).

       01  TITLE-LINE-1.
           05 FILLER                      PIC X(22) VALUE SPACES.
           05 FILLER                      PIC X(27) VALUE
           'ABC Building Supply Company'.

       01  TITLE-LINE-2.
           05 FILLER                      PIC X(25)  VALUE SPACE.
           05 FILLER                      PIC X(29)  VALUE
              'Master Inventory List'.

       01  HEAD-LINE-1.
           05 FILLER                      PIC X(04) VALUE SPACE.
           05 FILLER                      PIC X(15) VALUE 'Item'.
           05 FILLER                      PIC X(21) VALUE 'Description'.
           05 FILLER                      PIC X(11) VALUE 'Packing'.
           05 FILLER                      PIC X(13) VALUE 'Price Per'.
           05 FILLER                      PIC X(06) VALUE 'Number'.

       01  HEAD-LINE-2.
           05 FILLER                      PIC X(03) VALUE SPACES.
           05 FILLER                      PIC X(38) VALUE 'Number'.
           05 FILLER                      PIC X(12) VALUE 'Unit'.
           05 FILLER                      PIC X(10) VALUE 'Unit'.
           05 FILLER                      PIC X(08) VALUE 'of Units'.

       01  ITEM-RECORD-2.
           05 FILLER                      PIC X(03) VALUE SPACES.
           05 ITEM-NUMBER-OUT             PIC 9B9(05).
           05 FILLER                      PIC X(03) VALUE SPACES.
           05 ITEM-DESCRIPTION-OUT        PIC X(28).
           05 PACKING-UNIT-OUT            PIC XBXBX(07).
           05 PRICE-PER-UNIT-OUT          PIC $$$.99.
           05 FILLER                      PIC X(08) VALUE SPACES.
           05 NUMBER-OF-UNITS-OUT         PIC ZZ9.
      ****************************************************************
       PROCEDURE DIVISION.
      ****************************************************************
       000-PROCEDURE-CONTROLS SECTION.
           PERFORM 100-BEGINNING-OPERATIONS.
           PERFORM 300-PRODUCE-LINES-OF-REPORT
               UNTIL FILE-STATUS = 'DONE'.
           PERFORM 500-TERMINATION-PROCEDURE.
           STOP RUN.

       100-BEGINNING-OPERATIONS SECTION.
           OPEN INPUT INVENTORY-ITEM-FILE
                OUTPUT MASTER-LIST-FILE.
           WRITE MASTER-LIST-RECORD FROM TITLE-LINE-1
               AFTER TOP-OF-PAGE.
```

Figure 8.1 *Continued* Inventory Listing Program

```
                1   1   2   2   2   3   3   4   4   4   5   5   6   6   6   7
    4   8   2   6   0   4   8   2   6   0   4   8   2   6   0   4   8   2

           WRITE MASTER-LIST-RECORD FROM TITLE-LINE-2 AFTER 1 LINES.
           WRITE MASTER-LIST-RECORD FROM HEAD-LINE-1 AFTER 1 LINES.
           WRITE MASTER-LIST-RECORD FROM HEAD-LINE-2 AFTER 1 LINES.
           MOVE SPACES TO MASTER-LIST-RECORD.
           WRITE MASTER-LIST-RECORD AFTER ADVANCING 1 LINES.
           READ INVENTORY-ITEM-FILE INTO ITEM-RECORD
               AT END MOVE 'DONE' TO FILE-STATUS.

       300-PRODUCE-LINES-OF-REPORT SECTION.
           MOVE ITEM-NUMBER-IN            TO ITEM-NUMBER-OUT.
           MOVE ITEM-DESCRIPTION-IN       TO ITEM-DESCRIPTION-OUT.
           MOVE PACKING-UNIT-IN           TO PACKING-UNIT-OUT.
           MOVE PRICE-PER-UNIT-IN         TO PRICE-PER-UNIT-OUT.
           MOVE NUMBER-OF-UNITS-IN        TO NUMBER-OF-UNITS-OUT.
           MOVE SPACES                    TO MASTER-LIST-RECORD.
           WRITE MASTER-LIST-RECORD FROM ITEM-RECORD-2 AFTER 1.
           READ INVENTORY-ITEM-FILE INTO ITEM-RECORD
               AT END MOVE 'DONE' TO FILE-STATUS.

       500-TERMINATE-PROCEDURE SECTION.
           CLOSE INVENTORY-ITEM-FILE, MASTER-LIST-FILE.
```

Figure 8.1 *Continued* Inventory Listing Program (Output)

ABC Building Supply Company
Master Inventory List

Item Number	Description	Packing Unit	Price Per Unit	Number of Units
1 31139	1/2 in. Finishing Nails	B o x	$.75	120
1 76414	Stove Bolts--2 in.	B o x	$1.60	65
1 88217	1/2 in. Roofing Nails	B o x	$.60	30
1 91192	Die Cast Alum. Bolts--2"	B o x	$1.95	275
2 21570	8 ft. 2 X 4 -- Redwood	E a	$3.75	40
6 15523	8 ft. 2 X 4 -- Pine	E a	$2.20	500
6 65227	8 ft. 1 X 6 -- Pine	E a	$2.05	115
6 81874	8 ft. 4 X 4 -- Pine	E a	$5.95	15
7 21250	Split Cedar Shingles	B u n	$52.50	80
7 94825	Composition Shingles	B u n	$31.95	120

other digits by the blank insertion. Also notice that a blank insertion has been used with the packing unit field. The output also shows the price per unit for each item. This is produced on the output with a floating dollar sign and a decimal-point insertion. The last column of the report represents the number of units available. Zero suppression is used to eliminate leading zeros in the field; however, if no units are available, zero is printed as a single digit.

Summary

In this chapter, you have been introduced to a means for improving the readability of printed reports—edited data fields. Although any elementary-item may be described by using editing characters, only those fields that are to be printed should include them.

Editing characters fall into three categories, as indicated here.

Fixed-Insertion	Floating-Insertion	Replacement
+	+	*
−	−	Z
$	$	
.		
,		
0		
B		
CR		
DB		

Fixed-insertion characters are printed on output where they appear in the edited PICTURE string. Floating-insertion characters are used to suppress leading zeros in numeric fields. Replacement characters are similar to floating characters in that they react to nonsignificant (leading) zeros in numeric fields. Unlike floating characters, however, replacement characters replace leading zeros with another character.

Although all editing characters are permitted in numeric fields, the zero insertion (0) and blank insertion (B) characters may also be used in the description of alphabetic- and alphanumeric-edited fields. COBOL permits the mixing of fixed- and floating-insertion characters *or* fixed-insertion and replacement characters in the numeric-edited field.

Notes on Programming Style

Typically, the beginning programmer overuses editing characters, and this improper use tends to detract from readability. A case in point is the overuse of the currency symbol ($). Examine the following columns of figures.

```
$123.45     $123.45     123.45
$   6.78      $6.78       6.78
$  90.12     $90.12      90.12
$    .34       $.34        .34
```

The left column uses a fixed-insertion dollar symbol and zero suppression. The center column uses a floating-insertion dollar symbol. The right column uses zero suppression only. Ask yourself which column you would rather look at if you were spending the day reading printed reports containing one of the three. You probably chose the right column, because *without* the dollar symbol the values are easier to read. When designing reports, especially when edited output is to be included, always ask yourself if the part the user reads is in its most usable form.

Remember also that editing characters may not appear in a numeric field if that field is to be used in mathematical processing. The most frequent violation of this requirement is the use of decimal-point insertion character (.) in place of the implied decimal character (V).

Recall also, when program requirements call for the use of negative data, it is the programmer's responsibility to incorporate that into the program and report design. Signed internal fields should be used, and a reflection of the sign should be incorporated into printed report formats. It is also the programmer's responsibility to be aware of the possibility of field truncation, especially in numeric fields.

The printed report is frequently the only visible product of a program. The printed report, more than any other single factor, may mean the success or failure of a given application system. It is the programmer's responsibility to ensure that the reports are meaningful, in the most useful format, and *accurate!* The printed report is your "window to the world" outside the commercial programming environment. *Treat is accordingly!*

Questions

Below fill in the blank(s) with the appropriate word, words, or phrases.

1. An editing character that will occupy a specific position in a field (regardless of the magnitude of the numeric value placed in the field) is referred to as a(n) ____ character.
2. The fixed-insertion character (symbol) that causes a sign (+ or –) to be printed regardless of the sign of a numeric field is the ____ character (symbol).
3. The fixed-insertion character (symbol) that causes a sign to be printed only if a numeric value is negative is the ____ character (symbol).
4. The only editing characters considered to be both fixed- and floating-insertion characters are ____ , ____ and ____ .
5. The asterick (check protection) character is considered to be a(n) ____ insertion character and is used to replace leading zeros in numeric fields.
6. The editing picture characters ____ must never appear as the rightmost character.
7. The editing picture characters ____ and ____ may be used in numeric-, alphabetic-, and alphanumeric-edited fields.
8. The three floating-insertion characters are ____ , ____ , and ____ .
9. The replacement characters are ____ and ____ .

Answer the following questions by circling either "T" for True or "F" for False.

T F **10.** It is only possible to edit numeric fields.
T F **11.** Each picture character falls into a single-use category.
T F **12.** The fixed-insertion character + may be used only with numeric-edited fields and may produce either the plus or minus sign in the output field depending upon the sign of the numeric value.
T F **13.** The fixed-insertion character + may appear in a picture string only as the leftmost character.
T F **14.** The editing character + is a fixed-insertion character only.
T F **15.** All fixed-insertion characters are also floating-insertion characters.
T F **16.** Only one sign-oriented picture character is permitted per picture string.
T F **17.** The currency symbol ($) must appear to the left of the most-significant-digit position as a fixed-insertion character.
T F **18.** The comma (,) editing character may appear more than once per picture string, but the decimal-point character may appear only once.

T F **19.** Only one fixed-insertion character may appear in a picture string.

T F **20.** To be considered a floating-insertion character, a currency symbol ($) must appear more than once in a picture string.

T F **21.** Two floating characters may appear in the same picture string.

T F **22.** A picture string may contain both a floating-insertion character and a fixed-insertion character.

T F **23.** Floating-insertion characters may be used in conjunction with numeric fields only.

T F **24.** A floating-insertion character may appear only to the left of a 9 in the same picture string.

T F **25.** It is possible for a floating-insertion character to replace a comma in a numeric-edited picture string.

T F **26.** It is possible for a floating-insertion character to replace a decimal point in a numeric-edited picture string.

T F **27.** It is permitted to have a fixed-insertion character flanked by floating-insertion characters.

T F **28.** Replacement characters may suppress zeros to the right of a significant digit position.

T F **29.** Both replacement and floating-insertion characters may appear in the same picture string.

T F **30.** Replacement characters should be used only in numeric-edited fields.

T F **31.** If the first significant digit in a numeric field appears to the right of a fixed-insertion character, the fixed-insertion character may be replaced with a blank if replacement characters are in use.

Exercises

1. Below is a series of source data fields, with PICTURE clauses, blank receiving fields with PICTURE clauses. For each, indicate the result of the movement of data, and show the length (number of columns) the field would occupy if it appeared in a printed report.

SOURCE FIELD		RECEIVING FIELD		
DATA*	**PICTURE**	**PICTURE**	**RESULT**	**LENGTH**
a. 69274	9(5)	99,999	________	________
b. 3192∧88	9(4)V99	99,999.99	________	________
c. −24∧76	S99V99	+9(4).99	________	________
d. −627	S999	−9(3).00	________	________
e. +821∧62	S9(3)V99	+99	________	________
f. +677∧44	S999V99	9(3).99CR	________	________
g. −7621∧88	S9(4)V99	$9,999.99B−	________	________
h. 4562∧894	9999V999	$$$,$$$.$$	________	________
i. 000∧97	9(3)V99	$(4).$$	________	________
j. 4855∧97	9(4)V99	$(4).99	________	________
k. −9884∧60	S9(4)V99	−$$$,$$$.$$	________	________
l. 000	9(3)	$(4).$$	________	________
m. 462∧88	S9(4)V99	+$*,***.**	________	________
n. 1286	9(4)	99B99B00	________	________
o. HELPME	X(6)	X(4)BBXX	________	________

*∧ denotes the location of the implied decimal point. Signs are shown in leading characters for visual identification.

2. Create an edited output-record description that accommodates the following situation:

An output line is to consist of an employee number, hourly rate, hours worked, total deductions, gross pay, and net pay. The employee number is six digits long, the first two of which indicate the employee's department. The field is to be printed with one space separating the department number from the remainder of the employee number. The hourly rate is recorded as dollars and cents. The total field width is five digits. Print the field to suppress all insignificant zeros. The field should be blank for salaried employees (rate per hour is equal to zero). In the hours-worked field only whole hours are recorded; suppress unnecessary zeros in this three-digit field, and insert a decimal point followed by two zeros at the end of the field. It is conceivable that total deductions (a dollars-and-cents field) could be a negative value or could exceed $1000. Thus, this field should be printed such that the sign (if negative) should appear adjacent to the most-significant-digit position. Commas and decimal points should also appear in the field, as appropriate. However, the field (at a minimum) should be printed as ".00." Gross pay is a seven-digit, dollars-and-cents field. Use commas and decimal points as appropriate, and print a dollar sign adjacent to the most-significant-digit position. Finally, the seven-digit (dollars-and-cents) net pay field should contain a dollar sign, a decimal point, and commas, as appropriate. Leading zeros should appear as a check protection character.

Supply your own data-names for this record, and reserve at least five columns (containing spaces) between fields.

Problems

8.1 The personnel department has asked you to create a data-verification sheet containing employee data. Because these reports are to be distributed to individual departments, when the department name changes, a new page is to begin (indicating the department name). You may assume the data have been ordered by department name and employee name. The records contain these fields as well as the fields indicated below (see multiple-card layout form):

1. Employee number— 4 digits
2. Employee name—30 characters
3. Social security number—9 digits
4. Employment date—6 digits in the format MMDDYY
5. Department name—10 characters
6. Hourly/Salaried code—1 character
7. Rate for regular time—8 digits, 2 of which are decimal positions (contains either the rate per hour or salary amount)
8. Overtime rate—6 digits, 2 of which are decimal positions (contains either overtime rate per hour or zeros for salaried employees)
9. Number of dependents—2 digits
10. Medical plan code—1 character
11. Retirement plan code—1 character
12. Savings plan code—1 character

From these data you are to produce the report indicated on the print chart that meets the following requirements:

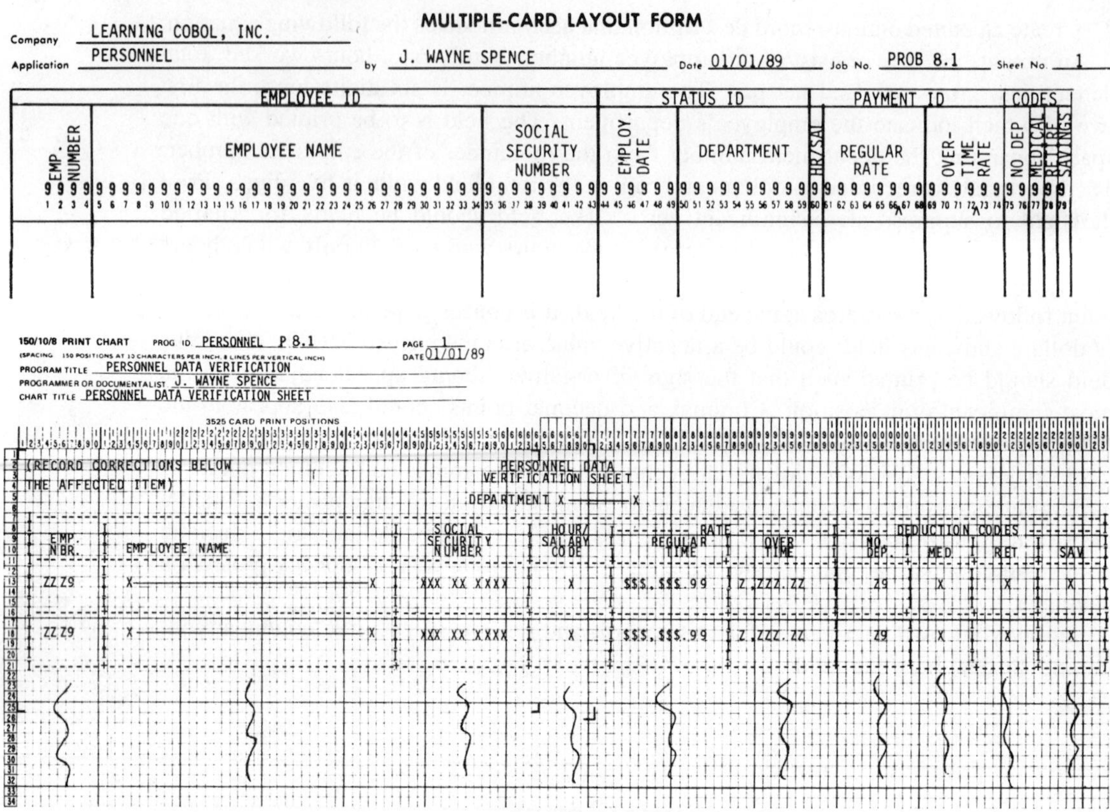

MULTIPLE-CARD LAYOUT FORM

Company LEARNING COBOL, INC.
Application PERSONNEL by J. WAYNE SPENCE Date 01/01/89 Job No. PROB 8.1 Sheet No. 1

EMPLOYEE ID: EMP. NUMBER (1–4), EMPLOYEE NAME (5–34), SOCIAL SECURITY NUMBER (35–43)
STATUS ID: EMPLOY. DATE (44–49), DEPARTMENT (50–59)
PAYMENT ID: HR/SAL (60), REGULAR RATE (61–67), OVER-TIME RATE (68–74)
CODES: NO DEP (75–76), MEDICAL (77), RETIRE (78), SAVINGS (79)

150/10/8 PRINT CHART PROG ID PERSONNEL P 8.1 PAGE 1
DATE 01/01/89
PROGRAM TITLE PERSONNEL DATA VERIFICATION
PROGRAMMER OR DOCUMENTALIST J. WAYNE SPENCE
CHART TITLE PERSONNEL DATA VERIFICATION SHEET

(RECORD CORRECTIONS BELOW
THE AFFECTED ITEM)
PERSONNEL DATA
VERIFICATION SHEET
DEPARTMENT X———X

EMP. NBR.	EMPLOYEE NAME	SOCIAL SECURITY NUMBER	HOUR/ SALARY CODE	RATE: REGULAR TIME	RATE: OVER TIME	NO. DEP.	DEDUCTION CODES: MED	RET	SAV
ZZZ9	X———X	XXX XX XXXX	X	$$$,$$$.99	Z,ZZZ.ZZ	Z9	X	X	X
ZZZ9	X———X	XXX XX XXXX	X	$$$,$$$.99	Z,ZZZ.ZZ	Z9	X	X	X

1. The employee number should have leading digits suppressed.
2. The social security number should have blanks inserted at the appropriate positions of the number (should be treated as *one* field).
3. The regular rate per hour should have the dollar symbol printed adjacent to the most-significant-digit position.
4. The overtime rate per hour should be zero suppressed.
5. The number of dependents should be zero suppressed.

Both the regular and overtime rate per hour should have a decimal point (except the overtime rate should be blank when the field contains zero). The regular rate per hour should have a comma inserted between hundreds and thousands (since a monthly salary could appear in this field).

8.2 Your company has decided to implement a computer-generated payroll check procedure. The procedure that develops the actual monetary amounts to be printed by the check-writing program is the responsibility of another programmer; however, she has indicated to you that the data will be provided in two formats—a single-data record, which will precede the remainder of the file, and a payment record for each employee to receive a paycheck. The date record is composed of the following fields (see multiple-card layout form):

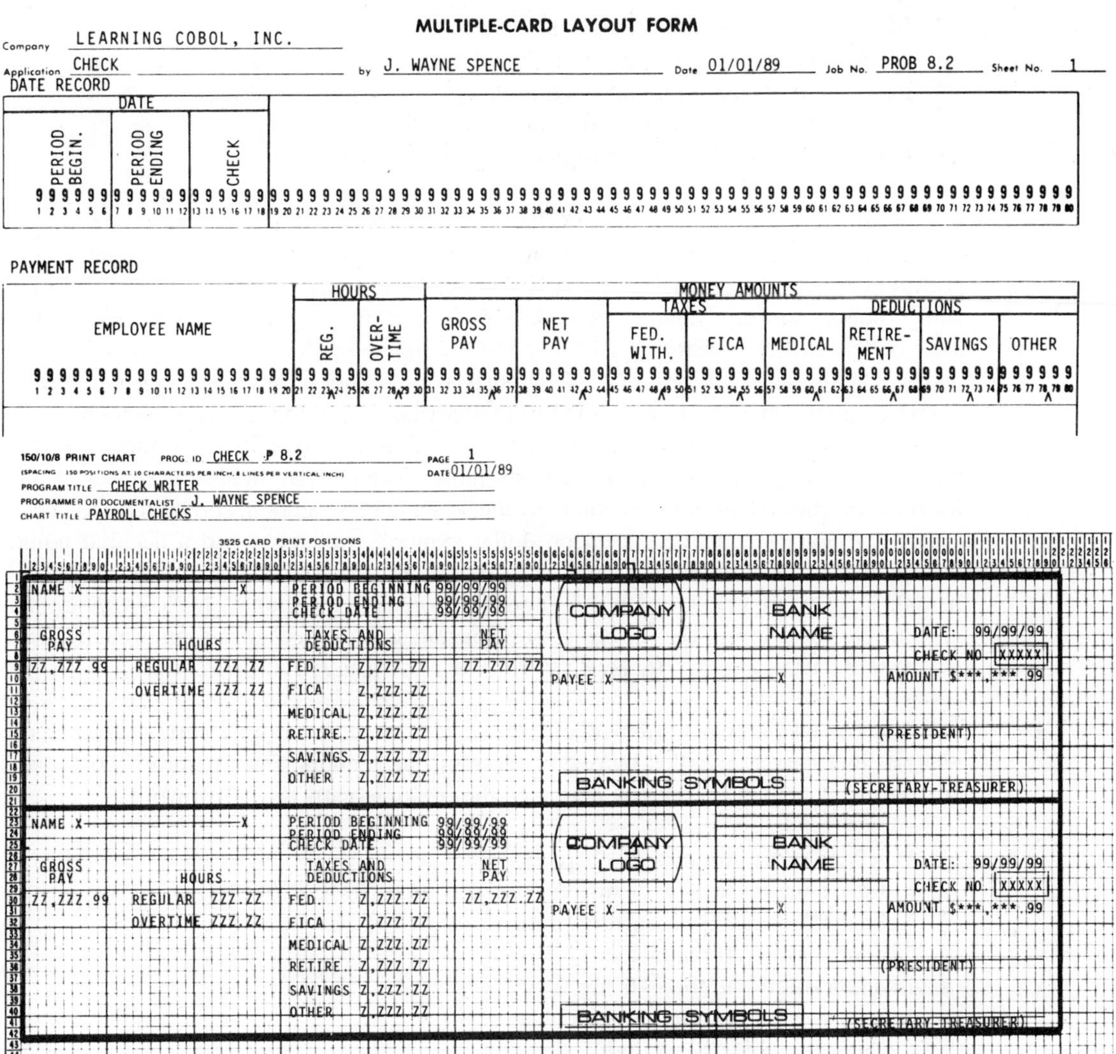

MULTIPLE-CARD LAYOUT FORM

Company LEARNING COBOL, INC.

Application CHECK by J. WAYNE SPENCE Date 01/01/89 Job No. PROB 8.2 Sheet No. 1

DATE RECORD

DATE			
PERIOD BEGIN.	PERIOD ENDING	CHECK	
999999	999999	999999	9999…9
1–6	7–12	13–18	19–80

PAYMENT RECORD

EMPLOYEE NAME	HOURS: REG.	HOURS: OVER-TIME	MONEY AMOUNTS: GROSS PAY	NET PAY	TAXES: FED. WITH.	TAXES: FICA	TAXES: MEDICAL	DEDUCTIONS: RETIRE-MENT	DEDUCTIONS: SAVINGS	DEDUCTIONS: OTHER
99999999999999999999	99999	99999	9999999	9999999	999999	99999	99999	999999	999999	99999
1–20	21–25	26–30	31–37	38–44	45–50	51–56	57–62	63–68	69–74	75–80

150/10/8 PRINT CHART PROG ID CHECK P 8.2 PAGE 1 DATE 01/01/89

PROGRAM TITLE CHECK WRITER

PROGRAMMER OR DOCUMENTALIST J. WAYNE SPENCE

CHART TITLE PAYROLL CHECKS

```
NAME X-----------------X    PERIOD BEGINNING 99/99/99
                            PERIOD ENDING    99/99/99
                            CHECK DATE       99/99/99    COMPANY LOGO      BANK NAME
  GROSS                      TAXES AND          NET                                      DATE:  99/99/99
   PAY           HOURS       DEDUCTIONS         PAY                                      CHECK NO. XXXXX
ZZ,ZZZ.99  REGULAR  ZZZ.ZZ  FED.     Z,ZZZ.ZZ  ZZ,ZZZ.ZZ   PAYEE X------------X          AMOUNT $***,***.99
           OVERTIME ZZZ.ZZ  FICA     Z,ZZZ.ZZ
                            MEDICAL  Z,ZZZ.ZZ
                            RETIRE.  Z,ZZZ.ZZ                                            (PRESIDENT)
                            SAVINGS  Z,ZZZ.ZZ
                            OTHER    Z,ZZZ.ZZ              BANKING SYMBOLS               (SECRETARY-TREASURER)
```

1. Payment period beginning date—6 digits in the format MMDDYY
2. Payment period ending date—6 digits in the format MMDDYY
3. Check date (date on which the check is to be printed)—6 digits in the format MMDDYY

The payment record consists of the following fields (see multiple-card layout form):

1. Employer name—20 characters
2. Number of regular hours worked—5 digits with 2 decimal positions
3. Number of overtime hours worked—5 digits with 2 decimal positions
4. Gross pay amount—7 digits with 2 decimal positions
5. Net pay amount–7 digits with 2 decimal positions
6. Federal withholding tax—6 digits with 2 decimal positions

7. FICA amount—6 digits with 2 decimal positions
8. Medical deduction amount—6 digits with 2 decimal positions
9. Retirement deduction amount—6 digits with 2 decimal positions
10. Savings deduction amount—6 digits with 2 decimal positions
11. Other deduction amount—6 digits with 2 decimal positions

The information contained in the DATE and PAYMENT records are to be printed in the format indicated on the print chart. Note that this is a preprinted form—spacing should be followed *exactly.* Furthermore, as is the case with most preprinted forms, only the name, hours monetary amount, and date fields are to be printed by your procedure. That is, ''NAME,'' ''PERIOD BEGINNING,'' and so forth are already printed on the paper to be used by your program. (Obviously you will not have these preprinted forms, but assume you do.) As shown on the print chart, all hours and monetary amount fields are to be zero suppressed and to include a decimal point. In addition, comma insertion is to be used in the gross pay and net pay fields. The net pay field will appear in this form on the check stub; on the actual paycheck the net pay amount should use the check protection character, a fixed-insertion dollar symbol, a comma, and a decimal point. Also notice that the employee name is to be printed twice (''NAME'' and ''PAYEE'' fields). Finally, the check number is preprinted on each individual check—you are not responsible for printing this information. Spacing is indicated on the preprinted form. *DO NOT ADVANCE TO THE TOP OF FORM FOR EACH PAYCHECK!*

8.3 A series of purchase order records have been prepared from a series of purchase requests that have been filled by one or more of our vendors. Each record is composed of a series of fields as indicated here (see the multiple-card layout form):

1. Purchase order number—5 characters
2. Purchase order date—6 characters in the format MMDDYY
3. Vendor ID code—3 characters (initials)
4. Vendor name—20 characters
5. Inventory item number—6 digits
6. Inventory item description—20 characters
7. Quantity purchased— 4 digits
8. Cost per item purchased—6 digits (dollars and cents)
9. Tax on item purchased—5 digits (dollars and cents)
10. Discount on item purchased—5 digits (dollars and cents)

From these records, you are to produce the report presented on the print chart. The Purchase Order Listing is to begin at the top of a new page. Since each purchase order contains several line items (multiple items purchased), several records in sequence will contain the same purchase order number. The print editing to be performed should be as follows:

1. Purchase order number should be printed such that the first digit is separated from the other four digits by a single space.
2. Purchase order date should be printed such that a single space appears between the month and day and a single space appears between the day and year.
3. Vendor ID code should be printed with a single space between each of the individual characters in the field.

4. Inventory item number should be printed as three digits, a single space and the remaining three digits.

5. Quantity purchased should be printed such that leading zeros are suppressed; however, zeros should be printed if the quantity is zero.

6. Cost per item purchased should contain a dollar sign, a comma between the thousands and hundreds positions, a decimal point, and nonsignificant zeros (excluding cents) should be suppressed.

7. Tax on items purchased should be zero suppressed, with a decimal point (such that the field is blank if no tax is charged on the purchase).

8. Discount on items purchased should have the same field characteristics as 7 above.

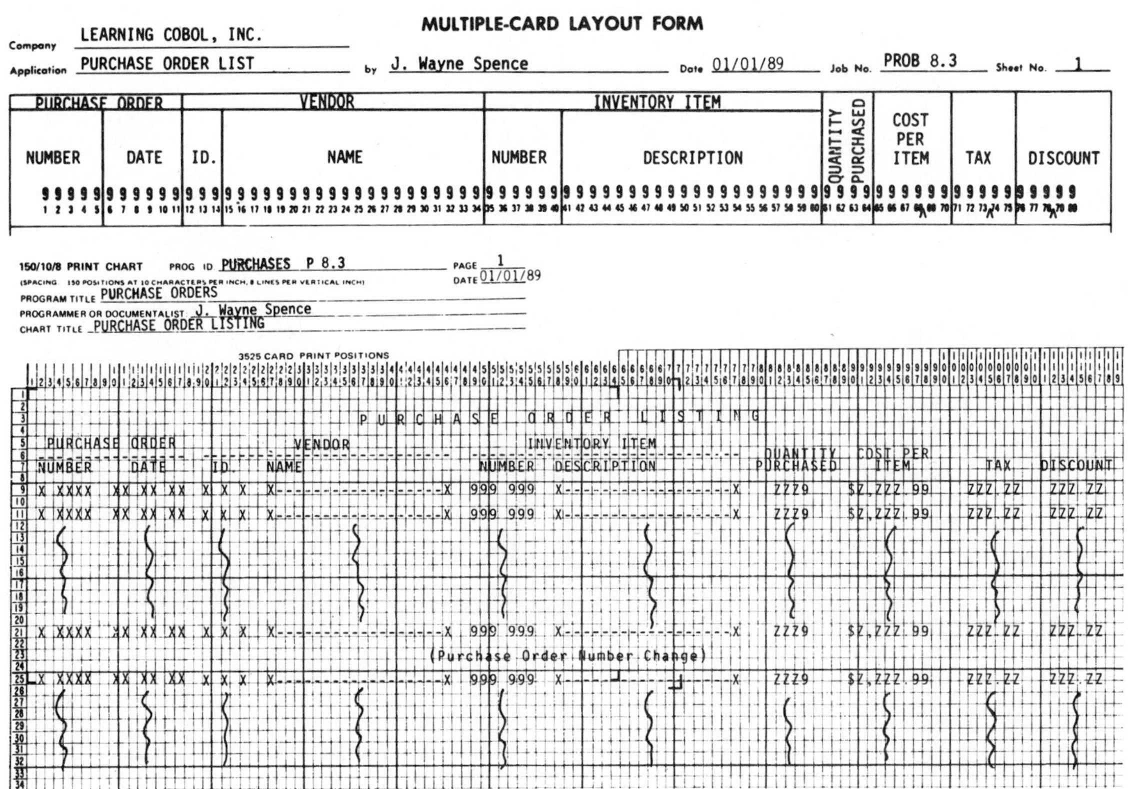

MULTIPLE-CARD LAYOUT FORM

Company LEARNING COBOL, INC.

Application PURCHASE ORDER LIST by J. Wayne Spence Date 01/01/89 Job No. PROB 8.3 Sheet No. 1

PURCHASE ORDER		VENDOR		INVENTORY ITEM					
NUMBER	DATE	ID.	NAME	NUMBER	DESCRIPTION	QUANTITY PURCHASED	COST PER ITEM	TAX	DISCOUNT
1–5	6–11	12–14	15–34	35–40	41–60	61–64	65–70	71–75	76–80

150/10/8 PRINT CHART PROG ID PURCHASES P 8.3 PAGE 1

(SPACING 150 POSITIONS AT 10 CHARACTERS PER INCH, 8 LINES PER VERTICAL INCH) DATE 01/01/89

PROGRAM TITLE PURCHASE ORDERS

PROGRAMMER OR DOCUMENTALIST J. Wayne Spence

CHART TITLE PURCHASE ORDER LISTING

3525 CARD PRINT POSITIONS

```
                                     P U R C H A S E   O R D E R   L I S T I N G

 PURCHASE ORDER            VENDOR                           INVENTORY ITEM
                                                                                      QUANTITY    COST PER
 NUMBER      DATE      ID.   NAME                       NUMBER    DESCRIPTION        PURCHASED     ITEM         TAX     DISCOUNT
 X XXXX   XX XX XX   X X X   X--------------------X    999 999   X-----------------X    ZZZ9     $Z,ZZZ.99     ZZZ.ZZ   ZZZ.ZZ
 X XXXX   XX XX XX   X X X   X--------------------X    999 999   X-----------------X    ZZZ9     $Z,ZZZ.99     ZZZ.ZZ   ZZZ.ZZ

 X XXXX   XX XX XX   X X X   X--------------------X    999 999   X-----------------X    ZZZ9     $Z,ZZZ.99     ZZZ.ZZ   ZZZ.ZZ
                                            (Purchase Order Number Change)
 X XXXX   XX XX XX   X X X   X--------------------X    999 999   X-----------------X    ZZZ9     $Z,ZZZ.99     ZZZ.ZZ   ZZZ.ZZ
```

CHAPTER

9

The Relational IF Statements and Other Structures

This chapter will discuss the if-then-else structure through the use of the relational IF statement. After completing this chapter, you will be acquainted with how the three structures (sequence, *if-then-else,* and *do-until*), typically used in a structured program, are implemented in COBOL. Combinations of statements, including OPEN, CLOSE, READ, WRITE, and MOVE statements, form the simple sequence structure. The PERFORM statements form the do-until structure, and the IF statement forms the if-then-else structure.

IF Statements in General

Many programming applications require portions of a program to be executed under one set of circumstances, and other statements, under other circumstances. This "selective" execution of statements is made possible through IF statements. IF statements are capable of determining the relationships between data values and selecting "paths" of execution on the basis of those relationships. For example, if the programmer wants to perform one set of operations when data-value-1 is greater than data-value-2, an IF statement can be employed to "test" for this relationship.

Although there are four categories of conditions used to describe the test to be performed, only the relational form of the IF statement will be discussed in this chapter. The *relational test* examines the relationship between two or more data values (in less than, equal to, or greater than form). The other forms of the IF statement (presented in Chapter 11) are referred to as the sign test, the class test, and the *condition-name test*. The sign test is used to determine whether a data value (represented by an identifier or an expression) is algebraically positive, negative, or zero. The class test is used to determine the type of data (numeric or alphabetic) contained in an identifier. The condition-name test is used to determine whether a preset condition is true or false, that is, the presence or absence of a particular value associated with a condition-name.

The Relational Test

The format of the relational test, presented in Figure 9.1, includes a number of parts. The identifiers in the relational IF statement may be any type of data item (e.g., an

Figure 9.1 Format of the Relational IF Statement

```
    ⎧identifier-1            ⎫                           ⎧identifier-2        ⎫
IF  ⎨literal-1               ⎬  relational-operator      ⎨literal-2           ⎬
    ⎩arithmetic-expression-1 ⎭                           ⎩arithmetic-operator ⎭

         ⎧imperative-statement-1⎫  ⎡       ⎧imperative-statement-2⎫⎤
[THEN]   ⎨                      ⎬  ⎢ ELSE  ⎨                      ⎬⎥
         ⎩NEXT SENTENCE         ⎭  ⎣       ⎩NEXT SENTENCE         ⎭⎦

[END-IF]
```

elementary-item, group-name, or record-name), and elementary-items can be numeric, alphabetic, and alphanumeric. The literals may be numeric, nonnumeric, or figurative constants. The arithmetic expressions must conform to the format for arithmetic expressions (see Chapter 10, the COMPUTE statement). Thus, the relationships that can be tested are numerous.

A relational operator must be specified between the items being compared. The relational operator indicates the relationship to be evaluated. The allowable relational operators are:

```
IS [NOT] GREATER THAN           or   IS ]NOT] >
IS [NOT] EQUAL TO               or   IS [NOT] =
IS [NOT] LESS THAN              or   IS [NOT] <
IS GREATER THAN OR EQUAL TO     or   IS >=
IS LESS THAN OR EQUAL TO        or   IS <=
```

The reserved word IS is not required. The reserved word *NOT* is optional. *NOT* represents the logical negation of the statement. For example, if the relational operator *NOT GREATER* is indicated, the test could be considered to be equivalent to "less than or equal to." After the reserved word *NOT,* the relation to be tested is specified i.e., GREATER, EQUAL TO, LESS, or their equivalent symbols. The new COBOL 85 standards provide for two new relational operators. The GREATER OR EQUAL relational operator is equivalent to NOT LESS, and the LESS OR EQUAL relational operator is equivalent to NOT GREATER. Notice that these two relational operators do not allow the use of the reserved word *NOT*.

1985 COBOL Standards

The portion of the IF statement that follows the second set of items is used to indicate the process(es) to be executed. Imperative-statement-1 (or NEXT SENTENCE) will be executed if the result of the comparison is *true*. Imperative-statement-2 (or NEXT SENTENCE) will be executed when the result is *false*. Each of the imperative statements may be either simple (single) statements or compound (multiple) statements. However, note that *only one period* should appear in the IF statement—at the end. When NEXT SENTENCE is provided in the place of an imperative statement, the statement that immediately follows the IF statement is executed. The NEXT SENTENCE phrase may be used for either the true or the false "branch"; however, there is no practical reason for the ELSE NEXT SENTENCE phrase as a false branch. (The next statement in the program will be executed by default in the event that the result of the comparison is false. Thus, the ELSE phrase could be omitted.) Furthermore, if either the true or the false branch is not an unconditional branching statement, a GO TO (discussed later in this chapter) statement, after the true or false branch is executed, the next sequential statement will be executed.

There are two additional reserved words provided by COBOL 85 standards, The reserved word THEN is used to make the IF-THEN-ELSE structure of the IF statement easier to read and understand. The use of THEN is optional. The reserved word END-IF is also optional. This reserved word is used as a *structure deliminter* to indicate the end of an IF statement. Like the reserved word THEN, the use of END-IF is optional.

An example will help to clarify these points. Assume we wish to execute the statement MOVE ZERO TO A if the value of A exceeds the value of B. If the value of A is not greater than B, the programmer may wish to execute the statement MOVE 1Ø TO A. Figure 9.2 illustrates the program steps necessary to perform this operation. In Case 1 an unconditional branch is executed on either the true condition or the false condition, thereby executing the appropriate statement. However, after the unconditional branch takes place (GO TO ZERO-A or GO TO MOVE-TO-A is executed), the flow of the program proceeds from two separate points. This could be desirable in some circumstances, but generally, it is better to maintain a *singular flow* through the program, as in Case 2. In this IF statement the operations to be executed on a true or a false condition are entered as imperative statements in the IF statement rather than as separate statements. After either the true or false branch is executed, the next operation is indicated by the statement immediately following the IF statement. Consequently, the major difference between Cases 1 and 2 is that Case 1 concludes with two possible directions (which could ultimately cause an error), whereas Case 2 yields only one, which, for the sake of program simplicity and control, is the type recommended.

Case 3 of Figure 9.2 demonstrates the use of NEXT SENTENCE. The result of this sequence is different from those in the two previous cases. In Case 3, if A is greater than B, A will be modified to zero. Otherwise, the value 1Ø is placed in A. The difference is that after the false branch is executed, the next operation is MOVE ZERO TO A—destroying the result produced by the false branch, obviously not the intent of the program. This form of the IF statement should be used only if the true and false branches do not modify the same data item.

The last case presented in Figure 9.2 provides a structured programming approach using the PERFORM statement. In this IF statement the operations to be executed on a true or a false condition are entered through the PERFORM statements. Upon completion of the paragraphs entered through the PERFORM statements control is returned to the statement immediately after the IF statement. Consequently, the result of Case 4 is the same as the result of Case 2. While both Case 2 and Case 4 satisfy the guidelines for structure programming, Case 2 is preferred because of its simplicity and ease of understanding.

Figure 9.3 illustrates the use of relational IF statements in a program. Assume the problem is to determine the letter grade for a course from a numeric average. For the purposes of this problem, any student averaging over 89.4 should receive an A. A student scoring between 89.4 and 79.5 (inclusive) should receive a B; between 79.4 and 69.5, a C; and so forth. (See Chapter 10 for the complete program.)

In Figure 9.3, IF statements capable of making the proper letter-grade assignments based on the preceding information are shown. The sequence of statements shown is based on *default logic*. That is, when *all* possible outcomes for a set of decisions can be stated, it is necessary to test for all but one possible situation. In the case of letter-grade assignments, five grades are possible (A, B, C, D, and F). If a student is not assigned one of the first four grades he or she must have received the fifth grade.

Figure 9.2 Illustrations of the Relational IF Statement

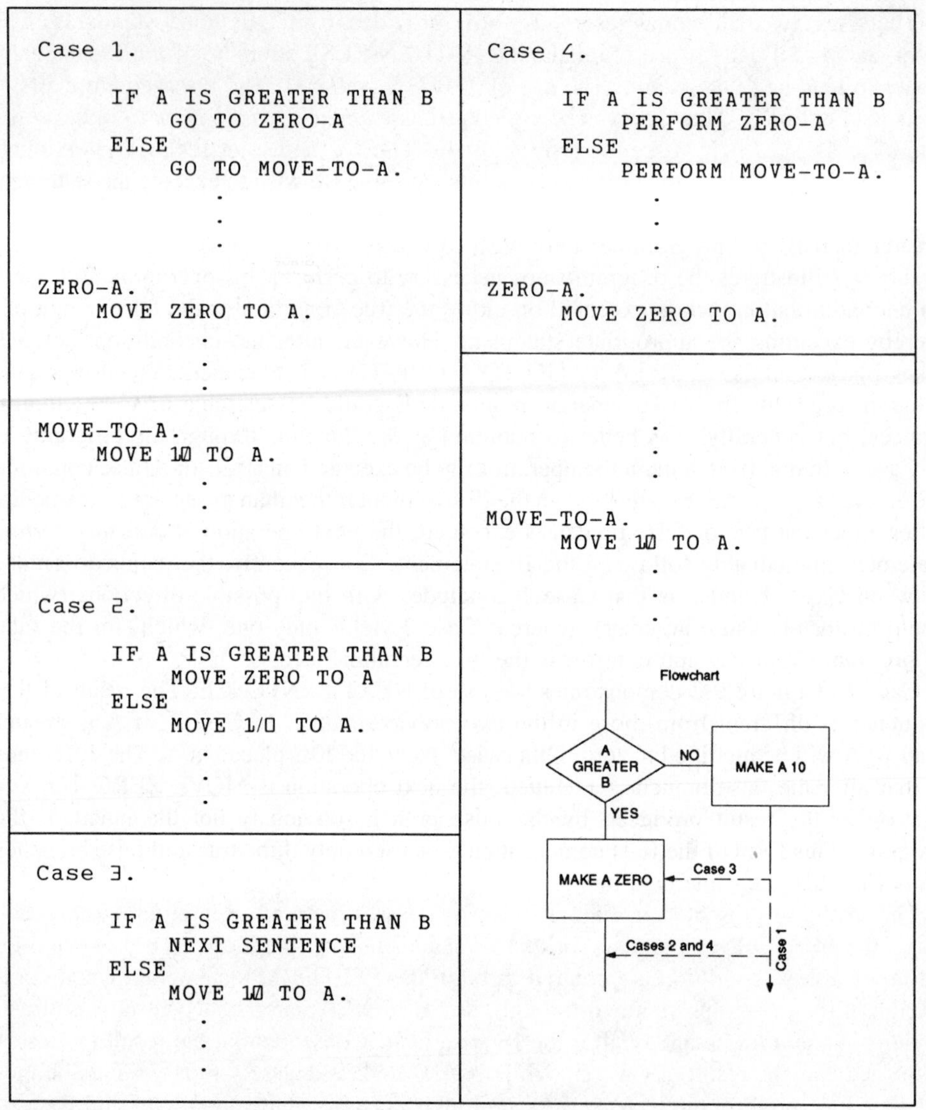

Case 1.
IF A IS GREATER THAN B
GO TO ZERO-A
ELSE
GO TO MOVE-TO-A.
ZERO-A.
MOVE ZERO TO A.
MOVE-TO-A.
MOVE 1Ø TO A.
Case 2.
IF A IS GREATER THAN B
MOVE ZERO TO A
ELSE
MOVE 1/0 TO A.
Case 3.
IF A IS GREATER THAN B
NEXT SENTENCE
ELSE
MOVE 1Ø TO A.
Case 4.
IF A IS GREATER THAN B
PERFORM ZERO-A
ELSE
PERFORM MOVE-TO-A.
ZERO-A.
MOVE ZERO TO A.
MOVE-TO-A.
MOVE 1Ø TO A.
Flowchart
A
GREATER
B
NO
MAKE A 10
YES
MAKE A ZERO
Case 3
Cases 2 and 4
Case 1

In Figure 9.3, the student is assigned a letter grade of A until subsequent decisions determine that the grade assignment should have been lower. The first IF statement may override the original letter-grade assignment if the average is less than 89.5. The letter-grade B then becomes the default grade until subsequent IF statements prove the assignment is incorrect. Consequently, the student is assigned successively lower letter grades until the appropriate grade is reached. After the correct assignment, all remaining

Figure 9.3 Relational IF Statements for Letter Grade Assignment

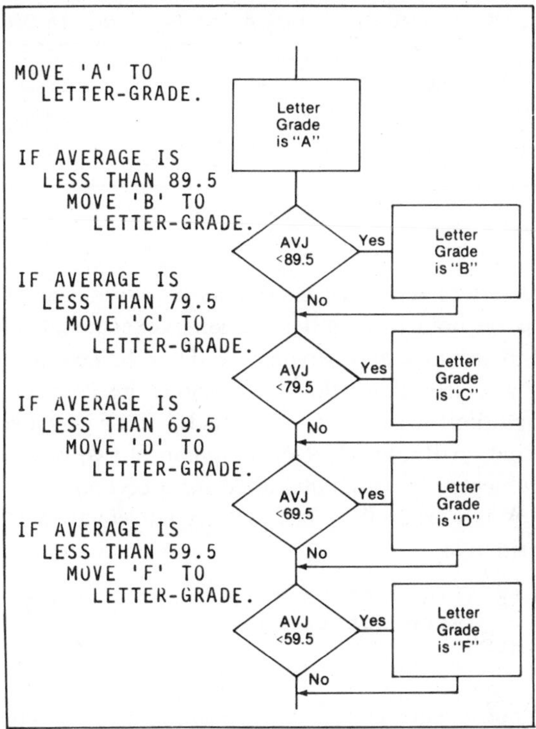
MOVE 'A' TO
LETTER-GRADE.
IF AVERAGE IS
LESS THAN 89.5
MOVE 'B' TO
LETTER-GRADE.
IF AVERAGE IS
LESS THAN 79.5
MOVE 'C' TO
LETTER-GRADE.
IF AVERAGE IS
LESS THAN 69.5
MOVE 'D' TO
LETTER-GRADE.
IF AVERAGE IS
LESS THAN 59.5
MOVE 'F' TO
LETTER-GRADE.
Letter Grade is "A"
AVJ <89.5
Yes
Letter Grade is "B"
No
AVJ <79.5
Yes
Letter Grade is "C"
No
AVJ <69.5
Yes
Letter Grade is "D"
No
AVJ <59.5
Yes
Letter Grade is "F"
No

IF statements will be false. For example, if the student's average was 75, the following sequence would be executed.

Test	Test Results	Letter Grade
—	—	A
Average <89.5	True	B
Average <79.5	True	C
Average <69.5	False	—
Average <59.5	False	—

Thus, the last assigned letter grade would be a C.

Compound IF Statements

Under some circumstances it is desirable to make a comparison between (or among) several data items. Perhaps a program requires two separate operations depending on the outcome of several comparisons. To allow several sets to be compared within one IF statement, COBOL includes two logical operators—the reserved words AND and OR.

Table 9.1 Results of the Evaluation of Logical Operators

A	B	A AND B	A OR B	NOT A	NOT (A AND B)	NOT A AND B	NOT (A OR B)	NOT A OR B
True	True	True	True	False	False	False	False	True
True	False	False	True	False	True	False	False	False
False	True	False	True	True	True	True	False	True
False	False	False	False	True	False	False	True	True

When two or more sets of relational conditions are combined using AND, and all conditions are true, the true branch of the IF statement is executed. (This type of operation is sometimes referred to as a logical or Boolean AND or the *intersection* of two or more sets.) When two or more sets of relational conditions are connected by the reserved word OR, and *any* conditions is true, the true branch will be executed. (This is referred to as a logical, inclusive, or Boolean OR or the *union* of two or more sets.)

Suppose the requirements of a program called for a certain set of instructions to be executed when *both* A is greater than B and C is not equal to D. The COBOL IF statement could be written as

```
IF A IS GREATER THAN B AND C NOT = D
    true-instructions
ELSE
    false-instructions.
```

By the same token, suppose that a certain set of instructions was to be executed if *either* of the two relations stated above was true. Then this series of conditions could be written as two separate IF statements or a single statement, such as

```
IF A IS GREATER THAN B OR C NOT = D
    true-instructions
ELSE
    false-instructions.
```

In some cases the coding of an IF statement becomes so complex, a programmer becomes confused about how the compiler will interpret the instruction. For that reason, there is a six-step operation sequence for IF statements that indicates the order in which the statement will be evaluated. First, the programmer may specify the sequence of relationships to be evaluated by enclosing within parentheses those relationships to be examined first. The second component of the IF statement to be examined is arithmetic expressions, if present. Third, relational operators are examined. Fourth, NOT conditions are evaluated. Fifth, the portions of IF statements connected with the logical operator AND are analyzed. And finally, any relationship connected by the logical operator OR is checked. If more than one AND or OR is present in a logical expression, the expression is evaluated from left to right.

The meaning of these relationships (using AND, OR, NOT, and parentheses) is presented in Table 9.1. In this table, two logical expressions are presented in conjunction with AND, OR, NOT, and parentheses. Suppose that the first logical expression is of the form ITEM1 LESS THAN ITEM2 (expression A), and the second logical expression is of the form ITEM3 EQUAL TO ITEM4 (expression B). Given these logical expressions, there are four possible outcomes. These combinations are:

Expression A	Expression B
True	True
True	False
False	True
False	False

Implied Subjects and Relational Operators

Often it is unnecessary to repeat the *subject* of an IF statement. In those circumstances where the same identifier, literal, or arithmetic expression (subject) is compared to two or more objects, there is no need to repeat the subject; this is called an *implied* subject. For example, the statement

```
IF A LESS THAN B AND A GREATER THAN C . . .
```

has the same subject for two comparisons—A is the subject of two relationships. In this case the statement could also be coded as

```
IF A LESS THAN B AND GREATER THAN C . . .
```

Thus, the subject (A) was not repeated for the second relationship—it is assumed to be the same as for the previous relationship.

If the subject and relational operator are the same for several conditions, both the subject and the relational operator may be implied. For example, the statement

```
IF A IS EQUAL TO B AND A IS EQUAL TO C . . .
```

could be written such that both the subject and relational operator are assumed for the second relationship; that is,

```
IF A IS EQUAL TO B AND C . . .
```

Obviously, if the same subject and relational operator are used for three or more relationships, they may also be implied. However, the logical operator is not implied. This is true whether the logical connective is AND or OR.

Figure 9.4 illustrates the use of compound IF statements with a repeat of the letter-grade assignment process. In this series of statements each numeric average is placed in a bracket much the same as in the original statement of the problem. That is, the first IF statement examines the average to determine whether or not it is greater than 89.4. This statement could have been written as

```
IF AVERAGE IS GREATER THAN 89.5 OR AVERAGE IS EQUAL TO 89.5
                    MOVE 'A' TO LETTER-GRADE.
```

However, the same result is achieved by the noncompound IF statement in the example (assuming the PICTURE description of AVERAGE can contain no more than one digit following the decimal point—e.g., 9(Ø3)V9). Other IF statements in the example utilize the logical operator AND. For example, for a letter grade of B to be assigned, the average must be between (but should not include) 89.5 and 79.4. And, since each letter grade is placed in its own specific bracket, a fifth IF statement must be added to the sequence of tests. Thus, a letter grade of F is assigned in the last IF statement if the average is below 59.5.

Figure 9.4 Compound IF Statements

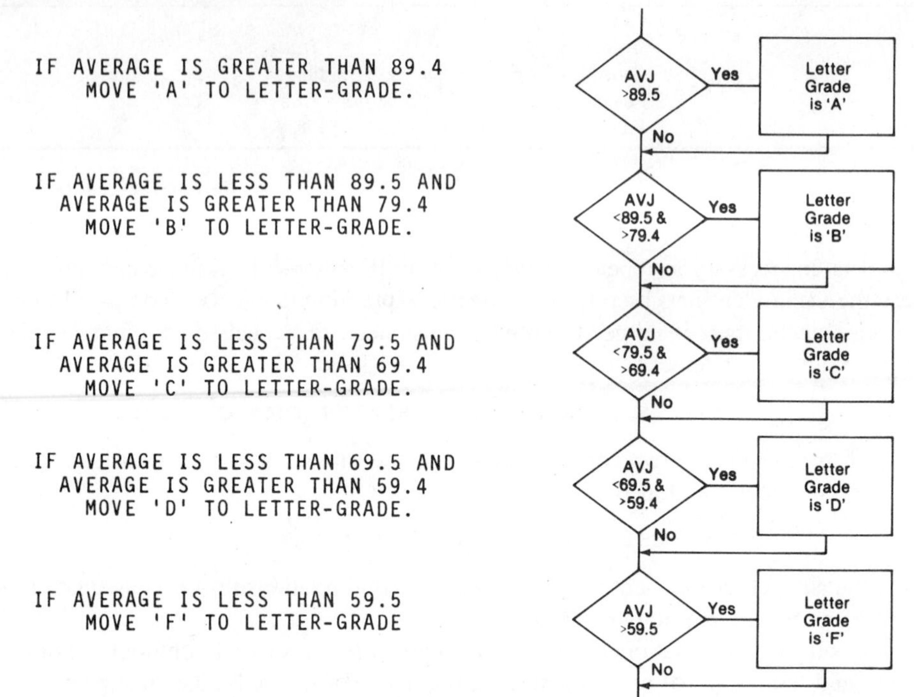
IF AVERAGE IS GREATER THAN 89.4
MOVE 'A' TO LETTER-GRADE.
IF AVERAGE IS LESS THAN 89.5 AND
AVERAGE IS GREATER THAN 79.4
MOVE 'B' TO LETTER-GRADE.
IF AVERAGE IS LESS THAN 79.5 AND
AVERAGE IS GREATER THAN 69.4
MOVE 'C' TO LETTER-GRADE.
IF AVERAGE IS LESS THAN 69.5 AND
AVERAGE IS GREATER THAN 59.4
MOVE 'D' TO LETTER-GRADE.
IF AVERAGE IS LESS THAN 59.5
MOVE 'F' TO LETTER-GRADE
AVJ >89.5
Yes
Letter Grade is 'A'
No
AVJ <89.5 & >79.4
Yes
Letter Grade is 'B'
No
AVJ <79.5 & >69.4
Yes
Letter Grade is 'C'
No
AVJ <69.5 & >59.4
Yes
Letter Grade is 'D'
No
AVJ >59.5
Yes
Letter Grade is 'F'
No

Comparing Figure 9.3 with Figure 9.4, notice the different number of IF statements—four and five, respectively. However, use of compound IF statements, even with the extra IF statement, is more efficient because no erroneous letter grades are assigned in the progression from one IF statement to the next. Only one grade is assigned—the correct one!

Nested IF Statements

The imperative statements used as the true and false branches of an IF statement may contain any type of statement in the COBOL language. True and false imperative statements may even contain other IF statements. A combination of IF statements leads to the *nested IF statement*. A nested IF statement is an IF statement that appears as the imperative statement of another IF statement.

This combination of IF statements is illustrated in Figure 9.5. In the letter-grade problem the relational IF statements (of Figure 9.3) can be replaced with one nested IF statement. Case 1 of Figure 9.5 presents the nesting of IF statements on false branches. In this case, as long as the responses to the conditions remain false, the next level of the statement (the next false branch) is examined. If, at any point in the chain of IF statements, a true branch is taken, the entire statement is terminated with the appropriate MOVE statement, and other false branches are not examined. This is the *affirmative* approach to the nesting of IF statements—that is, the positive action (or true branch) is closely coupled with the IF statement, which causes the completion of the ''decision-making'' process. This type of nested IF statement is very easy to understand and code. If an indention convention is used to begin the reserved words IF and ELSE in the same

Figure 9.5 Nested Relational IF Statements

Case 1:

```
IF AVERAGE IS GREATER THAN 89.4
    MOVE 'A' TO LETTER-GRADE
ELSE
    IF AVERAGE IS GREATER THAN 79.4
        MOVE 'B' TO LETTER-GRADE
    ELSE
        IF AVERAGE IS GREATER THAN 69.4
            MOVE 'C' TO LETTER-GRADE
        ELSE
            IF AVERAGE IS GREATER THAN 59.4
                MOVE 'D' TO LETTER-GRADE
            ELSE
                MOVE 'F' TO LETTER-GRADE.
```

Case 2:

```
IF AVERAGE IS LESS THAN 89.5
    IF AVERAGE IS LESS THAN 79.5
        IF AVERAGE IS LESS THAN 69.5
            IF AVERAGE IS LESS THAN 59.5
                MOVE 'F' TO LETTER-GRADE
            ELSE
                MOVE 'D' TO LETTER-GRADE
        ELSE
            MOVE 'C' TO LETTER-GRADE
    ELSE
        MOVE 'B' TO LETTER-GRADE
ELSE
    MOVE 'A' TO LETTER-GRADE.
```

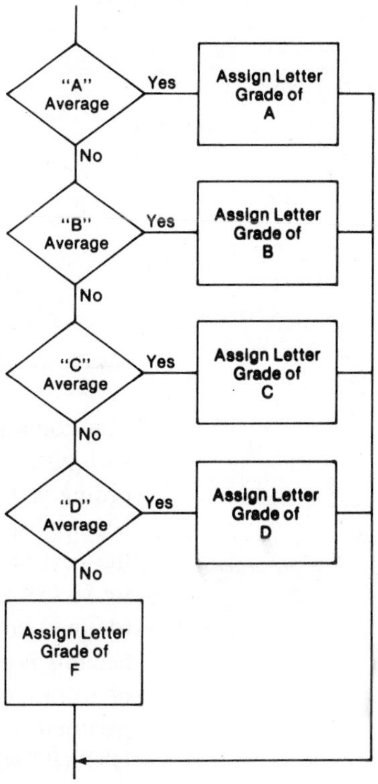

column, this grouping of IF statements should create a stair-step appearance in the program code. This approach makes understanding the nested IF statements and their relationship to each other a more manageable task.

The second method of nesting IF statements is to use the true branch for coding embedded IF's (Case 2 of Figure 8.5). In this form, one IF statement is immediately followed by another. This is the *negative* approach to coding nested IF statements, since the false branch of each statement is separated from the true branch by one or more intervening IF statements. This nested IF statement appears much like brackets, where one IF statement falls totally within the code of another. If the code indention procedure illustrated in Case 2 of Figure 9.5 is used, the connection between true and false branches of the parent IF statement is somewhat more easily determined; however, this type of nesting of IF statement is still much more difficult to code properly and understand than the form presented in Case 1. If coded correctly, and all true and false branches are present, the code should appear as a V-shape.

The Control Break

A process common to many programs is the *control break*. The control break is a process through which an *unusual* programming situation is executed. For example, examine Figure 9.6. This program produces a simple listing of employees. However, the employees are to be listed by department. So, the data must be arranged by department.

Figure 9.6 Employee Report by Department (Hierarchy Chart)

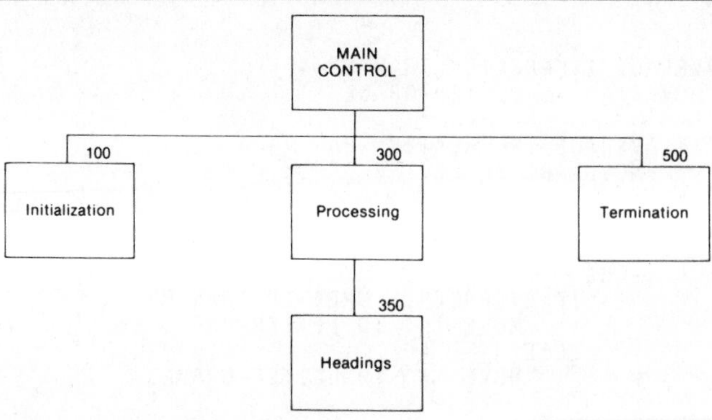

The control break is executed when the value in the department field *changes*. Thus, so long as the department values stays the same, the program does nothing out of the ordinary. Examine the COBOL program for a moment. The control-break process is accomplished by the statement on lines 930 and 940. Upon encountering this statement the first time, note that DEPARTMENT-NO-IN (defined at line 330) contains a value by virtue of the READ statement at line 890. However, PREVIOUS-DEPARTMENT (defined at line 460) contains no previously defined value. As a result, the first page heading is produced. Thus, this control break produces output *ahead* of the actual printing of information regarding the department. To perform the control break *after* the department changes (e.g., subtotals by department), all that is necessary is to move the DEPARTMENT-NO-IN value to the PREVIOUS DEPARTMENT field immediately after the READ statement at line 890.

To avoid reproducing the heading each time line 930 is encountered, notice that while the new heading is being produced, the value in DEPARTMENT-NO-IN is moved to PREVIOUS-DEPARTMENT. Thus, these two fields contain the same value so long as the value of DEPARTMENT-NO-IN does not change; however, when this value does

Figure 9.6 *Continued* Employee Report by Department (Pseudocode)

```
START
     DO initialization
     DO processing UNTIL eof
     DO termination
END

INITIALIZATION
     OPEN files
     READ  employee file
          IF eof
               SET indicator
          ENDIF
END

TERMINATION
     CLOSE files
END

PROCESS
     IF department not equal
        previous department
          DO heading
     ENDIF
     MOVE input to output
     WRITE output
     READ employee file
          IF eof
               SET indicator
          ENDIF
END

HEADING
     MOVE titles to output
     WRITE output
END
```

Figure 9.6 *Continued* Employee Report by Department

```
        1   1   2   2   2   3   3   4   4   4   5   5   6   6   6   7
4   8   2   6   0   4   8   2   6   0   4   8   2   6   0   4   8   2
-----------------------------------------------------------------------
*****************************************************************
 IDENTIFICATION DIVISION.
*****************************************************************
 PROGRAM-ID.      DEPARTMENT-BREAK.
 AUTHOR.          J. WAYNE SPENCE.
 DATE-WRITTEN.    JANUARY 1, 1989.
 DATE-COMPILED.   JANUARY 1, 1989.
*****************************************************************
 ENVIRONMENT DIVISION.
*****************************************************************
*---------------------------------------------------------------*
 CONFIGURATION SECTION.
*---------------------------------------------------------------*
 SOURCE-COMPUTER. IBM.
 OBJECT-COMPUTER. IBM.
 SPECIAL-NAMES.
                  C01 IS PAGE-TOP.
*---------------------------------------------------------------*
 INPUT-OUTPUT SECTION.
*---------------------------------------------------------------*
 FILE-CONTROL.
     SELECT EMPLOYEE-FILE     ASSIGN TO UT-S-INPUT.
     SELECT DEPARTMENT-REPORT ASSIGN TO UT-S-OUTPUT.
*****************************************************************
 DATA DIVISION.
*****************************************************************
*---------------------------------------------------------------*
 FILE SECTION.
*---------------------------------------------------------------*
 FD  EMPLOYEE-FILE
     LABEL RECORDS ARE OMITTED.
 01  EMPLOYEE-RECORD.
     05  DEPARTMENT-NO-IN        PIC X(05).
     05  EMPLOYEE-NO-IN          PIC X(05).
     05  EMPLOYEE-NAME-IN        PIC X(20).
     05  FILLER                  PIC X(50).

 FD  DEPARTMENT-REPORT
     LABEL RECORDS ARE OMITTED.
 01  REPORT-LINE.
     05  FILLER                  PIC X(133).
*---------------------------------------------------------------*
 WORKING-STORAGE SECTION.
*---------------------------------------------------------------*
 01  WORKING-VARIABLES.
     05 PREVIOUS-DEPARTMENT      PIC X(05).
     05 FILE-STATUS              PIC X(04) VALUE SPACES.

 01  HEADING1-RECORD.
     05  FILLER                  PIC X(49) VALUE SPACES.
     05  FILLER                  PIC X(20) VALUE
     'Learning COBOL, Inc.'.

 01  HEADING2-RECORD.
     05  FILLER                  PIC X(51) VALUE SPACES.
     05  FILLER                  PIC X(10) VALUE 'Department'.
     05  FILLER                  PIC X(01) VALUE SPACES.
     05  DEPARTMENT-HEADING-OUT  PIC X(05).

 01  HEADING3-RECORD.
```

Figure 9.6 *Continued* Employee Report by Department

```
          1   1   2   2   2   3   3   4   4   4   5   5   6   6   6   7
  4   8   2   6   0   4   8   2   6   0   4   8   2   6   0   4   8   2
           05  FILLER                    PIC X(30) VALUE SPACES.
           05  FILLER                    PIC X(10) VALUE 'Department'.
           05  FILLER                    PIC X(10) VALUE SPACES.
           05  FILLER                    PIC X(15) VALUE
                                         'Employee Number'.
           05  FILLER                    PIC X(10) VALUE SPACES.
           05  FILLER                    PIC X(13) VALUE 'Employee Name'.

       01  OUTPUT-LINE.
           05  FILLER                    PIC X(32) VALUE SPACES.
           05  DEPARTMENT-NO-OUT         PIC X(05).
           05  FILLER                    PIC X(17) VALUE SPACES.
           05  EMPLOYEE-NO-OUT           PIC X(05).
           05  FILLER                    PIC X(15) VALUE SPACES.
           05  EMPLOYEE-NAME-OUT         PIC X(20).
      *****************************************************************
       PROCEDURE DIVISION.
      *****************************************************************
       000-MAIN-CONTROL.
           PERFORM 100-INITIALIZATION.
           PERFORM 300-PROCESSING
               UNTIL FILE-STATUS = 'DONE'.
           PERFORM 500-TERMINATION.
           STOP RUN.

       100-INITIALIZATION.
           OPEN INPUT EMPLOYEE-FILE
                OUTPUT DEPARTMENT-REPORT.
           READ EMPLOYEE-FILE
               AT END MOVE 'DONE' TO FILE-STATUS.

       300-PROCESSING.
           IF DEPARTMENT-NO-IN NOT EQUAL TO PREVIOUS-DEPARTMENT
               PERFORM 350-HEADINGS.
           MOVE DEPARTMENT-NO-IN     TO DEPARTMENT-NO-OUT.
           MOVE EMPLOYEE-NO-IN       TO EMPLOYEE-NO-OUT.
           MOVE EMPLOYEE-NAME-IN     TO EMPLOYEE-NAME-OUT.
           WRITE REPORT-LINE FROM OUTPUT-LINE
               AFTER ADVANCING 2 LINES.
           READ EMPLOYEE-FILE
               AT END MOVE 'DONE' TO FILE-STATUS.

       350-HEADINGS.
           MOVE DEPARTMENT-NO-IN     TO DEPARTMENT-HEADING-OUT,
                                        PREVIOUS-DEPARTMENT.
           WRITE REPORT-LINE FROM HEADING1-RECORD
               AFTER ADVANCING PAGE-TOP.
           WRITE REPORT-LINE FROM HEADING2-RECORD
               AFTER ADVANCING 1 LINES.
           WRITE REPORT-LINE FROM HEADING3-RECORD
               AFTER ADVANCING 3 LINES.

       500-TERMINATION.
           CLOSE EMPLOYEE-FILE,
                 DEPARTMENT-REPORT.
```

Figure 9.6 *Continued* Employee Report by Department

```
--------------------------------------
|      |         1         2         3|
|Record|123456789012345678901234567890|
|-------------------------------------|
|     1|1412910001Mary Kay Griffin    |
|     2|1412911200John Baker          |
|     3|1412920050George Montgomery   |
|     4|1412940095Linda Johnson       |
|     5|1412975500Lonnie Anderson     |
|     6|1412995220Harold Williams     |
|     7|2058310500Howard Phelps       |
|     8|2058325000Michael Reed        |
|     9|2058329850Donna Edwards       |
|    10|2058330045William Hargrove    |
|    11|2058335025Karla Saunders      |
|    12|2058365300Ronald McVey        |
|    13|2058395225DeWayne Richardson  |
|    14|3593712399Andrea Krumwell     |
|    15|3593730005Janice Trimble      |
|    16|3593735422Laura Wellington   |
|    17|3593740030Jerry Dobson        |
|    18|3593755550Andrew Knight       |
|    19|3593764900Herman Yarborough   |
|    20|3593775400Brenda Smith        |
|    21|3593788505Gary Jamison        |
|    22|3593799950Thomas Whittington  |
--------------------------------------
```

Figure 9.6 *Continued* Employee Report by Department (Data)

Learning COBOL, Inc.
Department 14129

Department	Employee Number	Employee Name
14129	10001	Mary Kay Griffin
14129	11200	John Baker
14129	20050	George Montgomery
14129	40095	Linda Johnson
14129	75500	Lonnie Anderson
14129	95220	Harold Williams

Learning COBOL, Inc.
Department 20583

Department	Employee Number	Employee Name
20583	10500	Howard Phelps
20583	25000	Michael Reed
20583	29850	Donna Edwards
20583	30045	William Hargrove
20583	35025	Karla Saunders
20583	65300	Ronald McVey
20583	95225	DeWayne Richardson

Learning COBOL, Inc.
Department 35937

Department	Employee Number	Employee Name
35937	12399	Andrea Krumwell
35937	30005	Janice Trimble
35937	35422	Laura Wellington
35937	40030	Jerry Dobson
35937	55550	Andrew Knight
35937	64900	Herman Yarborough
35937	75400	Brenda Smith
35937	88505	Gary Jamison
35937	99950	Thomas Whittington

change (as is the case when record number 7 is read), a new heading is produced and the PREVIOUS-DEPARTMENT field is updated.

The Simple GO TO Statement

The simple GO TO statement is often referred to as an *unconditional branch* instruction. The execution of a GO TO statement causes the execution sequence to begin again with th statement immediately below or adjacent to the paragraph or SECTION name provided in the GO TO statement. The instruction to be executed may be either above or below the GO TO statement itself. Be careful not to go immediately to the GO TO statement being executed or to another series of statements that would cause a *closed* or *continuous loop* (a series of statements with no mechanism for terminating itself, so the program ''spins its wheels''). In many installments, a closed loop will cause an execution time limit error.

Figure 9.7 Format of the GO TO Statement

```
GO TO procedure-name.
```

As noted in Figure 9.7, the GO TO statement provides a branch to either a paragraph- or SECTION-name. For this reason, paragraph names must be unique within the PROCEDURE DIVISION—at least within SECTIONs of the PROCEDURE DIVISION. The differences between paragraph and SECTION names are that [1] paragraphs are less inclusive than SECTIONs, (2) a SECTION name is alwasy followed with the reserved word SECTION, and (3) paragraph names can be qualified by SECTION names.

THE EXIT Statement

Some problems may require many possible paths through a set of procedures, while some systems (e.g., IBM) often require a PERFORM procedure to be terminated in a special manner. To satisfy both requirements for the use of the PERFORM statement, a common ending point is required. That is, regardless of the logical processes in several paragraphs or sections being performed, the procedure must have a single point at which it begins (procedure-name-1) and a single point at which it ends (procedure-name-2). COBOL provides a common ending point through the EXIT statement and the END-PERFORM discussed in Chapter 7. The EXIT statement is composed of a single reserved word—EXIT. To qualify as a common reference point, the EXIT statement must be *a single-statement sentence* and *must appear in a paragraph by itself* (see Figure 9.8). The EXIT statement serves no function other than as a common ending point for a series of procedures. Thus, it is possible to use the paragraph name containing the EXIT statement in a PERFORM statement as procedure-name-2. To complete a single execution of the procedure, we need to encounter procedure-name-2 (by branching to it or by encountering it serially) and execute the statement in procedure-name-2.

Figure 9.8 The EXIT Statement

```
EXIT.
```

Control Break with Sections

Thus far, most of the programs illustrated have used only paragraphs in the PROCEDURE DIVISION. Such is also the case in Figure 9.6. The procedure from Figure 9.6 is illustrated again in Figure 9.8. The hierarchy chart for these two procedures is the same, the data are the same, and the output is the same. Yet there is only one paragraph in the PROCEDURE DIVISION of Figure 9.9—the 300-EXIT paragraph on line 1150—which is directly referenced. The differences between these two programs are worth noting. All other active procedures are at the SECTION level. The next difference is

Figure 9.9 Employee Report by Department [with SECTIONS] (Pseudocode)

```
START
     DO initialization
     DO processing UNTIL eof
     DO termination
END

INITIALIZATION
     OPEN files
END

TERMINATION
     CLOSE files
END

PROCESSING
     READ employee file
        IF eof
           SET indicator
           GO TO exit
        ENDIF
     IF department not equal
        previous department
          DO heading
     ENDIF
     MOVE input to output
     WRITE output
     EXIT
END

HEADING
     MOVE titles to output
     WRITE output
END
```

that a READ statement *does not* appear in the 100-INITIALIZATION procedure. Next, 300-PROCESSING begins (rather than ends) with a READ statement, and the AT END phrase transfers control to 300-EXIT upon encountering the end-of-file condition. This style has been widely adopted in industry because statements need not be duplicated (as has been the case with the READ statements). Therefore, if input-related changes are necessary (e.g., the file type changes), only one READ statement has to be located and modified.

Figure 9.9 *Continued* Employee Report by Department [with SECTIONs]

```
       1   1   2   2   2   3   3   4   4   4   5   5   6   6   6   7
   4   8   2   6   0   4   8   2   6   0   4   8   2   6   0   4   8   2
------------------------------------------------------------------------
 ****************************************************************
 IDENTIFICATION DIVISION.
 ****************************************************************
 PROGRAM-ID.      DEPARTMENT-BREAK.
 AUTHOR.          J. WAYNE SPENCE.
 DATE-WRITTEN.    JANUARY 1, 1989.
 DATE-COMPILED.   JANUARY 1, 1989.
 ****************************************************************
 ENVIRONMENT DIVISION.
 ****************************************************************
 *--------------------------------------------------------------*
 CONFIGURATION SECTION.
 *--------------------------------------------------------------*
 SOURCE-COMPUTER. IBM.
 OBJECT-COMPUTER. IBM.
 SPECIAL-NAMES.
                  C01 IS PAGE-TOP.
 *--------------------------------------------------------------*
 INPUT-OUTPUT SECTION.
 *--------------------------------------------------------------*
 FILE-CONTROL.
     SELECT EMPLOYEE-FILE     ASSIGN TO UT-S-INPUT.
     SELECT DEPARTMENT-REPORT ASSIGN TO UT-S-OUTPUT.
 ****************************************************************
 DATA DIVISION.
 ****************************************************************
```

Figure 9.9 *Continued* Employee Report by Department [with SECTIONs]

```
                 1   1   2   2   2   3   3   4   4   4   5   5   6   6   6   7
     4   8   2   6   0   4   8   2   6   0   4   8   2   6   0   4   8   2
------------------------------------------------------------------------------
*-----------------------------------------------------------*
 FILE SECTION.
*-----------------------------------------------------------*
 FD  EMPLOYEE-FILE
     LABEL RECORDS ARE OMITTED.
 01  EMPLOYEE-RECORD.
     05  DEPARTMENT-NO-IN          PIC X(05).
     05  EMPLOYEE-NO-IN            PIC X(05).
     05  EMPLOYEE-NAME-IN          PIC X(20).
     05  FILLER                    PIC X(50).

 FD  DEPARTMENT-REPORT
     LABEL RECORDS ARE OMITTED.
 01  REPORT-LINE.
     05  FILLER                    PIC X(133).
*-----------------------------------------------------------*
 WORKING-STORAGE SECTION.
*-----------------------------------------------------------*
 01  WORKING-VARIABLES.
     05 PREVIOUS-DEPARTMENT        PIC X(05).
     05 FILE-STATUS                PIC X(04) VALUE SPACES.

 01  HEADING1-RECORD.
     05  FILLER                    PIC X(49) VALUE SPACES.
     05  FILLER                    PIC X(20) VALUE
     'Learning COBOL, Inc.'.

 01  HEADING2-RECORD.
     05  FILLER                    PIC X(51) VALUE SPACES.
     05  FILLER                    PIC X(10) VALUE 'Department'.
     05  FILLER                    PIC X(01) VALUE SPACES.
     05  DEPARTMENT-HEADING-OUT    PIC X(05).

 01  HEADING3-RECORD.
     05  FILLER                    PIC X(30) VALUE SPACES.
     05  FILLER                    PIC X(10) VALUE 'Department'.
     05  FILLER                    PIC X(10) VALUE SPACES.
     05  FILLER                    PIC X(15) VALUE
                                   'Employee Number'.
     05  FILLER                    PIC X(10) VALUE SPACES.
     05  FILLER                    PIC X(13) VALUE 'Employee Name'.

 01  OUTPUT-LINE.
     05  FILLER                    PIC X(32) VALUE SPACES.
     05  DEPARTMENT-NO-OUT         PIC X(05).
     05  FILLER                    PIC X(17) VALUE SPACES.
     05  EMPLOYEE-NO-OUT           PIC X(05).
     05  FILLER                    PIC X(15) VALUE SPACES.
     05  EMPLOYEE-NAME-OUT         PIC X(20).
*************************************************************
 PROCEDURE DIVISION.
*************************************************************
*-----------------------------------------------------------*
 000-MAIN-CONTROL SECTION.
*-----------------------------------------------------------*
 000-START.
     PERFORM 100-INITIALIZATION.
     PERFORM 300-PROCESSING
         UNTIL FILE-STATUS = 'DONE'.
     PERFORM 500-TERMINATION.
     STOP RUN.
```

Figure 9.9 *Continued* Employee Report by Department [with SECTIONS]

```
         1   1   2   2   2   3   3   4   4   4   5   5   6   6   6   7
 4   8   2   6   0   4   8   2   6   0   4   8   2   6   0   4   8   2
-----------------------------------------------------------------------
 000-STOP.
     EXIT.
*-----------------------------------------------------------------*
 100-INITIALIZATION SECTION.
*-----------------------------------------------------------------*
 100-ENTRY.
     OPEN INPUT EMPLOYEE-FILE
          OUTPUT DEPARTMENT-REPORT.

 100-EXIT.
     EXIT.
*-----------------------------------------------------------------*
 300-PROCESSING SECTION.
*-----------------------------------------------------------------*
 300-ENTRY.
     READ EMPLOYEE-FILE
         AT END MOVE 'DONE' TO FILE-STATUS
                GO TO 300-EXIT.
     IF DEPARTMENT-NO-IN NOT EQUAL TO PREVIOUS-DEPARTMENT
         PERFORM 350-HEADINGS.
     MOVE DEPARTMENT-NO-IN      TO DEPARTMENT-NO-OUT.
     MOVE EMPLOYEE-NO-IN        TO EMPLOYEE-NO-OUT.
     MOVE EMPLOYEE-NAME-IN      TO EMPLOYEE-NAME-OUT.
     WRITE REPORT-LINE FROM OUTPUT-LINE
         AFTER ADVANCING 2 LINES.

 300-EXIT.
     EXIT.
*-----------------------------------------------------------------*
 350-HEADINGS SECTION.
*-----------------------------------------------------------------*
 350-ENTRY.
     MOVE DEPARTMENT-NO-IN      TO DEPARTMENT-HEADING-OUT,
                                   PREVIOUS-DEPARTMENT.
     WRITE REPORT-LINE FROM HEADING1-RECORD
         AFTER ADVANCING PAGE-TOP.
     WRITE REPORT-LINE FROM HEADING2-RECORD
         AFTER ADVANCING 1 LINES.
     WRITE REPORT-LINE FROM HEADING3-RECORD
         AFTER ADVANCING 3 LINES.

 350-EXIT.
     EXIT.
*-----------------------------------------------------------------*
 500-TERMINATION SECTION.
*-----------------------------------------------------------------*
 500-ENTRY.
     CLOSE EMPLOYEE-FILE,
           DEPARTMENT-REPORT.

 500-EXIT.
     EXIT.
```

Paragraphs Versus Sections

Previous program illustrations have shown some of the possible combinations of paragraphs, SECTIONs, PERFORM statements, and GO TO statements in the PROCEDURE DIVISION. However, not all combinations of these elements will work properly. Figure 9.10 illustrates five possible combinations of these elements. Case 1 employs a familiar arrangement of paragraphs and PERFORM statements. Although within the first procedure (assumed to be a paragraph in a control procedure), a PERFORM statement is executed for another paragraph (200-PROCESS). Since the PERFORM statement uses the UNTIL phrase, the paragraph is repeated until FILE-STATUS = 'DONE' is executed when the end-of-file is reached. At that point, the UNTIL condition is true and a return is issued to the statement immediately following the PERFORM statement.

In case 2 the PROCEDURE DIVISION code is similar to that in case 1, except that the READ statement has been moved to the top of the 200-PROCESS module, the AT END phase concludes with a GO TO 200-EXIT paragraph, and a 200-EXIT paragraph has been added. When the PERFORM/UNTIL statement is executed, 200-PROCESS is repeated until the end-of-file is reached. However, in this case FILE-STATUS = 'DONE' *and* a GO TO statement transfers control to the 200-EXIT paragraph. In this situation, since the 200-EXIT paragraph is totally *outside* (and independent of) the procedure being performed (200-PROCESS), the control of the PERFORM statement is interrupted and a fall-through occurs which causes the sequential execution of the remaining statements in the program. Furthermore, since no control is active when the last statement is executed, the computer will continue downward to what it expects to be the next statement, but there is none! The result is an addressing error. The computer ''loses its way,'' and you just fell off into the ''black hole'' from which there is no return. Thus, never, NEVER, NEVER use paragraphs, PERFORM statements, and GO TO statements together! You will invariably lose control in the execution of the procedure, and it is often difficult to locate where this loss of control occurred.

Case 3 is very similar to Case 1. The primary difference between these two cases is that SECTIONs are the major level used in the PROCEDURE DIVISION. Thus, when the PERFORM statement calls for the execution of 200-PROCESS, the UNTIL phrase continues to examine FILE-STATUS until its value is ''DONE.'' When the end-of-file is reached, the READ statement (at the bottom of the 200-ENTRY paragraph) causes the end-of-file variable to be set and a fall through occurs to the 200-EXIT paragraph. In this case, however, the fall-through remains in the same SECTION being performed. Thus, as soon as another SECTION name is encountered, a return to the statement immediately following the PERFORM statement is executed.

Case 4 looks very much like Case 2. Whereas Case 2 ended with an error, Case 4 will work correctly. Notice, again, that the code is written at the SECTION level, the READ statement is toward the top of the 200-PROCESS SECTION, and the 200-EXIT paragraph is present. In this case the 200-PROCESS SECTION is executed repeatedly until the end-of-file is reached. When this occurs, the end-of-file variable is set and a GO TO statement is executed which causes anunconditional branch to 200-EXIT. Note, however, that 200-EXIT is totally *within* the 200-PROCESS SECTION. Thus, the GO TO statement did not transfer control outside the procedure being executed. The fall-through that occurs finally reaches the end of the SECTION being performed and a return to the statement immediately following the PERFORM statement is executed.

Figure 9.10 Paragraphs, SECTIONs, PERFORM Statements and GO TO Statements

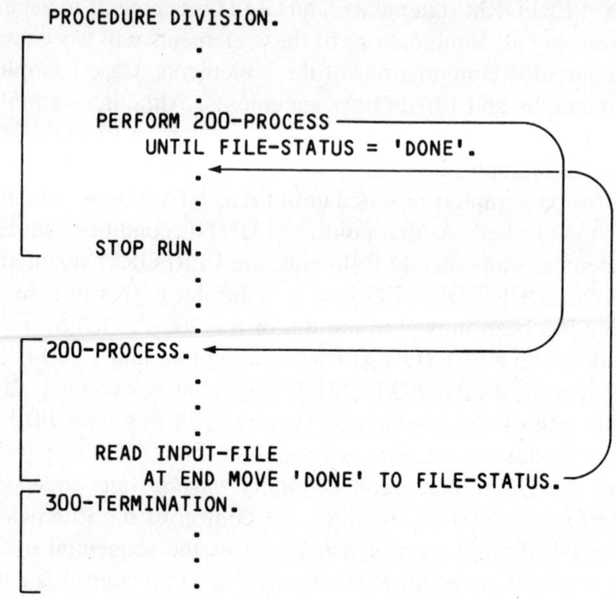
Case 1: Paragraphs and PERFORM Statements
PROCEDURE DIVISION.
PERFORM 200-PROCESS
UNTIL FILE-STATUS = 'DONE'.
STOP RUN.
200-PROCESS.
READ INPUT-FILE
AT END MOVE 'DONE' TO FILE-STATUS.
300-TERMINATION.

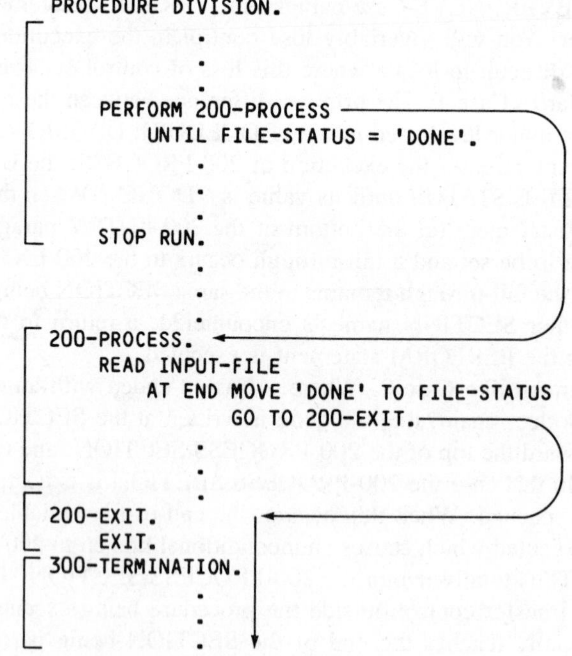
Case 2: Paragraphs, PERFORM Statements, and GO TO Statements
PROCEDURE DIVISION.
PERFORM 200-PROCESS
UNTIL FILE-STATUS = 'DONE'.
STOP RUN.
200-PROCESS.
READ INPUT-FILE
AT END MOVE 'DONE' TO FILE-STATUS
GO TO 200-EXIT.
200-EXIT.
EXIT.
300-TERMINATION.

Figure 9.10 *Continued* Paragraphs, SECTIONs, PERFORM Statements and GO TO Statements

Case 3: SECTIONs and PERFORM Statements

```
PROCEDURE DIVISION.
          .
          .
          .
    PERFORM 200-PROCESS
        UNTIL FILE-STATUS = 'DONE'.
          .
          .
          .
    STOP RUN.
          .
          .
          .
200-PROCESS SECTION.
200-ENTRY.
          .
          .
          .
    READ INPUT-FILE
        AT END MOVE 'DONE' TO FILE-STATUS.
200-EXIT.
    EXIT.
300-TERMINATION SECTION.
          .
          .
          .
```

Case 4: SECTIONs, PERFORM Statements, and GO TO Statements

```
PROCEDURE DIVISION.
          .
          .
          .
    PERFORM 200-PROCESS
        UNTIL FILE-STATUS = 'DONE'.
          .
          .
          .
    STOP RUN.
          .
          .
          .
200-PROCESS SECTION.
200-ENTRY.
    READ INPUT-FILE
        AT END MOVE 'DONE' TO FILE-STATUS
               GO TO 200-EXIT.
          .
          .
          .
200-EXIT.
    EXIT.
300-TERMINATION SECTION.
          .
          .
          .
```

Figure 9.10 *Continued* Paragraphs, SECTIONs, PERFORM Statements and GO TO Statements

```
Case 5:  SECTIONs, PERFORM Statements, and GO TO Statements

         PROCEDURE DIVISION.
                    .
                    .
                    .
            PERFORM 200-PROCESS
                UNTIL FILE-STATUS = 'DONE'.
                    .
                    .
                    .
            STOP RUN.
                    .
                    .
                    .
        200-PROCESS SECTION.
        200-ENTRY.
            READ INPUT-FILE
                AT END MOVE 'DONE' TO FILE-STATUS
                       GO TO 300-TERMINATION.
                    .
                    .
                    .
        200-EXIT.
            EXIT.
        300-TERMINATION SECTION.
                    .
                    .
                    .
```

Finally, Cases 2 and 5 share some similarities. Case 5 ends with a fall-through error caused by the same problem illustrated with Case 2. That is, the 200-PROCESS SECTION is performed. While repeating 200-PROCESS, the end-of-file is encountered, the end-of-file indicator is set, and an unconditional branch to the 300-TERMINATION SECTION is executed. Note that the GO TO statement passes control to a procedure at the same level as that being performed. As a result, the control of the PERFORM statement is interrupted and a sequential fall-through results.

To summarize, we should be aware of the possible pitfalls associated with combinations of paragraphs, SECTIONs, PERFORM statements, and GO TO statements. When coding the PROCEDURE DIVISION at the paragraph level, only PERFORM statements should be used to control the logical interrelationship between modules. GO TO statements should never be used when the PROCEDURE DIVISION is coded at the SECTION level, PERFORM statements should still supply the basic control of the logical interrelationships between modules. However, since paragraphs can exist within sections, GO TO statements *may* be used to transfer control to a paragraph within that SECTION. Under no circumstances should a GO TO statement reference a procedure-name at the same or a higher level in the PROCEDURE DIVISION when a PERFORM statement is active. Furthermore, it is not even a good idea to have the GO TO statement transfer control upward within a SECTION. This type of transfer may cause a continuous loop. Thus, do not attempt to thwart the control of a PERFORM statement. You are asking for trouble if you do.

Summary

In COBOL, most decision-oriented instructions take the form of IF statements. The relational conditions, discussed in this chapter, permit the comparison of two values based on greater than, equal to, or less than relationships. All IF statements provide for an imperative statement whether the specified condition is true or false; however, the false imperative statement may be omitted if no action is required. Furthermore, multiple actions may be executed in an imperative "statement."

IF statements use the logical operators AND and OR to create compound conditions. Where the subject of a compound condition is the source for several tests in a sequence, the subject may be implied after the first condition. If both the subject and the relational operator are the same for a series of conditions in a compound test, they may be implied.

Unlike the PERFORM statement, which permits the modular design of programs required of structured programming, the GO TO statement causes an interruption of the sequential execution of statements. In addition, because the GO TO statement is an *unconditional branch* instruction, another GO TO is needed to return to the original sequence of statements. This requirement opens the possibility of a *closed* or *continuous loop*.

Notes on Programming Style

Since the IF statement is very flexible, you should exercise caution and good judgment when constructing the code in which a series of decisions are to be made. You may be tempted to use nested IF statements under conditions that do not warrant their use. You might (eventually) get the structure to work properly, but have a little sympathy for those who have to "follow in your tracks." Remember that modification and maintenance of most programs used commercially is inevitable, so use the K-I-S-S principle (Keep It Simple Stupid) whenever possible. Who knows, you may have to modify *your own* program some day.

Because simplicity is the goal, the following design constraints should be followed whenever possible:

1. Do not use the logical relation NOT.
2. Use proper indention procedure, that is,

```
IF conditional expression
    true statement(s)
ELSE
    false statement(s).
```

3. Do not use nested IFs.
4. Do not use compound conditions.

The only one of these constraints that should always be used is the indention rule. Occasionally, the other rules will have to be broken because of the nature of the application. But, under all conditions, strive for the simplest possible expression of the decision.

Special Note. Even though it is theoretically possible to reference any COBOL statement in either the true or false imperative statements—even other IF statements—many compilers have difficulty properly translating an IF statement when an imperative statement includes a READ statement. Both the IF statement and the READ statement permit imperative statements, which could feasibly contain several instructions. The difficulty arises when the compiler tries to ''decide'' where one imperative statement ends and the other begins (or continues). For example, suppose a READ statement is to be executed when a specified condition is true. Assume a MOVE operation is also to be executed after the READ operation and only when the previously indicated condition is true. Where does the imperative statement for the READ operation end so that the MOVE statement is also a part of the IF statement's imperative statement? This seems like a problem with no solution, but these operations can be executed in the proper sequence by using two IF statements or by using the PERFORM statement in the IF's imperative statement to invoke the proper procedure (including a READ statement). Note the COBOL 85 uses the ENDIF ENDREAD, and ENDPERFORM to overcome these problems.

1985 COBOL Standards

Now, a few observations about the use of the PERFORM statement:

Although the PERFORM statement permits the use of the THRU option (procedure-name-1 THRU procedure-name-2), most programmers avoid its use. If a functional procedure is to be executed, the programmer should be able to structure the program so that only one procedure-name is necessary. When several procedures are to be executed, a lower level module (below the primary control procedure of the hierarchy chart) may constitute a sub-level control procedure. Suppose, for example, you found the following situation:

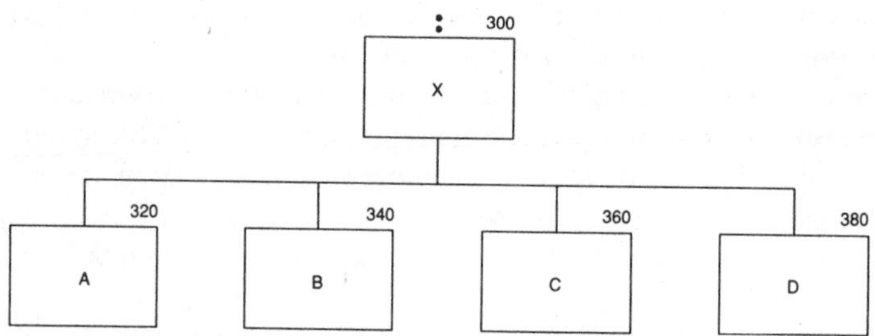

The module 300-X becomes a control module, but it does not control the entire program, only those elements that are subordinate to it. Thus, although we might be tempted to say ''PERFORM 320-A THRU 380-D'' in the 300-X module, an alternative to this would be

```
300-X.
    PERFORM 320-A.
    PERFORM 340-B.
    PERFORM 360-C.
    PERFORM 380-D.
```

```
300-X SECTION.              300-X SECTION.
300-Y. .                    300-Y.
       .                        PERFORM 320-A.
       .                        PERFORM 340-B.
320-A.                          PERFORM 360-C.
       .                        PERFORM 380-D.
       .                        GO TO 399-EXIT.
       .                    320-A.
```

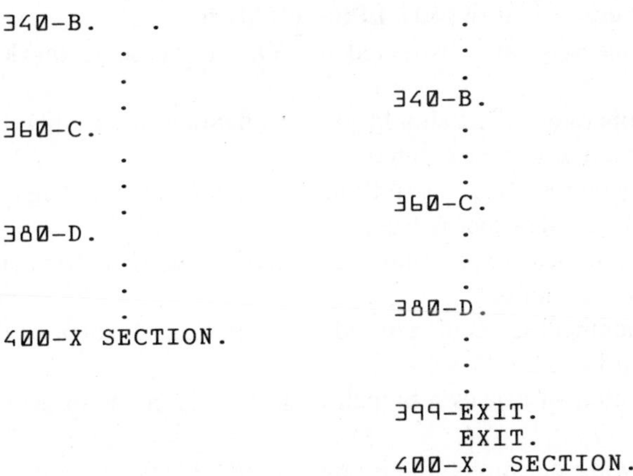

There are two advantages to this approach. First, only the specified procedures will be executed. If other procedures had been placed between two of these modules (by accident or otherwise), they would not be executed. This way, code may be placed in a program and not executed until other modules have been executed and fully tested. Second, if one of the executed procedures turns out to be executed only on a conditional basis, only a minor modification is necessary. Another way to avoid use of the THRU option is to design your program around SECTIONs, such as the first preceding example. Here the paragraph labeled "300-Y" becomes a control procedure, as paragraph 300-X was previously. We still have one small problem, however. To terminate the PERFORM of a SECTION, the end of the SECTION must be encountered serially (not under the control of a PERFORM from within the SECTION). We can do this with the sequence at the right in the preceding example. Without the GO TO statement in this structure, the procedure would encounter the end of the section by fall through, that is, the procedure 320-A through 380-D would be executed first by the PERFORM operation in paragraph 300-Y and then repeated by serial execution. Thus, the GO TO statement is used to "jump" to the bottom of the SECTION to avoid the unintentional reexecution of the procedures that follow.

We have now studied all the structure types that are fundamental to structured programming—the simple *sequence* (MOVE, READ, WRITE, and other statement types executed in a serial fashion), the *if-then-else* (IF statement), and the *do-until* (PERFORM/UNTIL statement).

Questions

Below, fill in the blank(s) with the appropriate word, words, or phrases.

1. IF statements appear in the _____ DIVISION.
2. COBOL permits _____ (number) different types of IF statements.
3. The _____ test is used to test the relationship between two values.
4. The _____ test is used to determine whether a numeric identifier is positive, zero, or negative.
5. The _____ test may be used to determine whether a value is numeric or alphabetic.

6. The relational equivalent to NOT LESS THAN is _____.

7. Compound tests may be constructed in COBOL by using the logical operators _____ and _____.

8. The logical operator _____ should join to relational tests when both tests must be true for the true branch to be executed.

9. The logical operator _____ should join two relational tests when the true branch is to be executed when either test is true.

10. In a complex logical expression _____ may be used to force the sequences of examination by the compiler.

11. A GO TO statement is often referred to as a(n) _____ statement.

12. A closed loop is _____.

13. A GO TO statement causes a branch to a(n) _____ name or a(n) _____ name.

Answer the following questions by circling either "T" for True or "F" for False.

T F 14. An IF statement may be used to determine the relationship between two numeric values.

T F 15. An IF statement may be used to determine the relationship between two alphanumeric values.

T F 16. A relational IF statement permits the comparison of a numeric literal to an arithmetic expression.

T F 17. A relational IF statement permits the comparison of an alphanumeric elementary-item to the figurative constant SPACES.

T F 18. When a testing operation requires no false branch, ELSE NEXT SENTENCE may be omitted from the IF statement.

T F 19. When a testing operation requires no true branch, ELSE NEXT SENTENCE may be omitted from the IF statement.

T F 20. The imperative statement of either a true or a false branch may contain multiple COBOL statements.

T F 21. The true branch is terminated in the IF statement by the occurrence of either a period or the reserved word ELSE.

T F 22. There is only one way to code true and false branches once the condition to be tested has been specified.

T F 23. Within complex logical expressions, the logical operator OR takes precedence over (is examined prior to) AND.

T F 24. When the same subject is used in two or more relational expressions of a compound test, only the subject for the first relationship need be stated.

T F 25. If the relational operator used in two adjacent relational tests is the same, the relational operator may be implied even though the subjects of the two tests may be different.

T F 26. Logical operators, when they are the same for several relational tests in a sequence, may be implied.

T F 27. When testing IF statements, the nested IF may appear in only the true branch of the parent IF statement.

T F 28. Types of conditions (e.g., relational and sign tests) may be combined in one logical expression by using AND or OR.

T F 29. Any COBOL statement may be used in the false branch of an IF statement.

T F 30. A GO TO statement may be used to alter the sequential execution of statements.

Exercises

1. Below is a series of IF statements. Indicate whether or not the statement has been coded in an acceptable form. If the form is correct, indicate which statement(s) constitute the "true" and "false" imperative statements. If the statement is in error, indicate the probable cause of the error.

a.
```
IF HOURS > 4          Ø
     MOVE 'OVERTIME WORKED' TO MESSAGE
ELSE
     MOVE 'NO OVERTIME' TO MESSAGE.
```
b.
```
IF PAY-AMOUNT IS NOT LESS THAN DEDUCTION-LIMIT
     NEXT SENTENCE
ELSE
     MOVE Ø TO DEDUCTION-AMOUNT.
```
c.
```
IF LAST-EMPLOYEE NOT EQUAL THIS-EMPLOYEE
     WRITE EMPLOYEE-RECORD AFTER ADVANCING 4 LINES.
```
d.
```
IF SPECIAL-PROVISION = 'EARNED INCOME CREDIT'
     PERFORM EIC-LOOKUP.
```
e.
```
IF HOSPITALIZATION = ZERO
     GO TO NO-HOSPITALIZATION;
     GO TO NEXT-OPERATION
ELSE
     GO TO DEDUCT-HOSPITALIZATION.
```
f.
```
IF FICA-YTD > FICA-LIMIT
ELSE
     PERFORM FICA-CALCULATION.
```

2. Write the COBOL IF statement(s) necessary to fulfill the following set of conditions. (IF any DATA DIVISION support is required, show that code also.)

a. When the cumulative salary for an employee exceeds $22,900 for the year, no (additional) FICA deduction is to be taken; otherwise a procedure is to be executed that calculates and deducts the FICA tax for the pay period.
b. When a W-5 form has been filed (a code value of 1 or 2), an Earned Income Credit (EIC) is to be calculated. When the form is filed by only one member of a family unit (a code value of 1), calculations are to be based on a single-filling party basis. When the code is 2, both husband and wife have (jointly) filed a W-5 form and calculations should be based on a two-party filing basis.
c. When (and if) the amount of net pay is less than or equal to zero or when it is greater than $5000.00, move the word "void" to an output message and write the output message; otherwise, move the amount of net pay to the output field and write the record.

Problems

9.1 You are to write a generalized mailing-label program capable of producing 1-up to 4-up labels and 3- or 4-line addresses. Two record types are to be used to accomplish this task. The first record is a control record (see the multiple-card layout form) and is composed of three fields:

1. Form used—1 digit and may contain the digits 1 through 4 to indicate the number of labels across the form (1-up to 4-up labels)

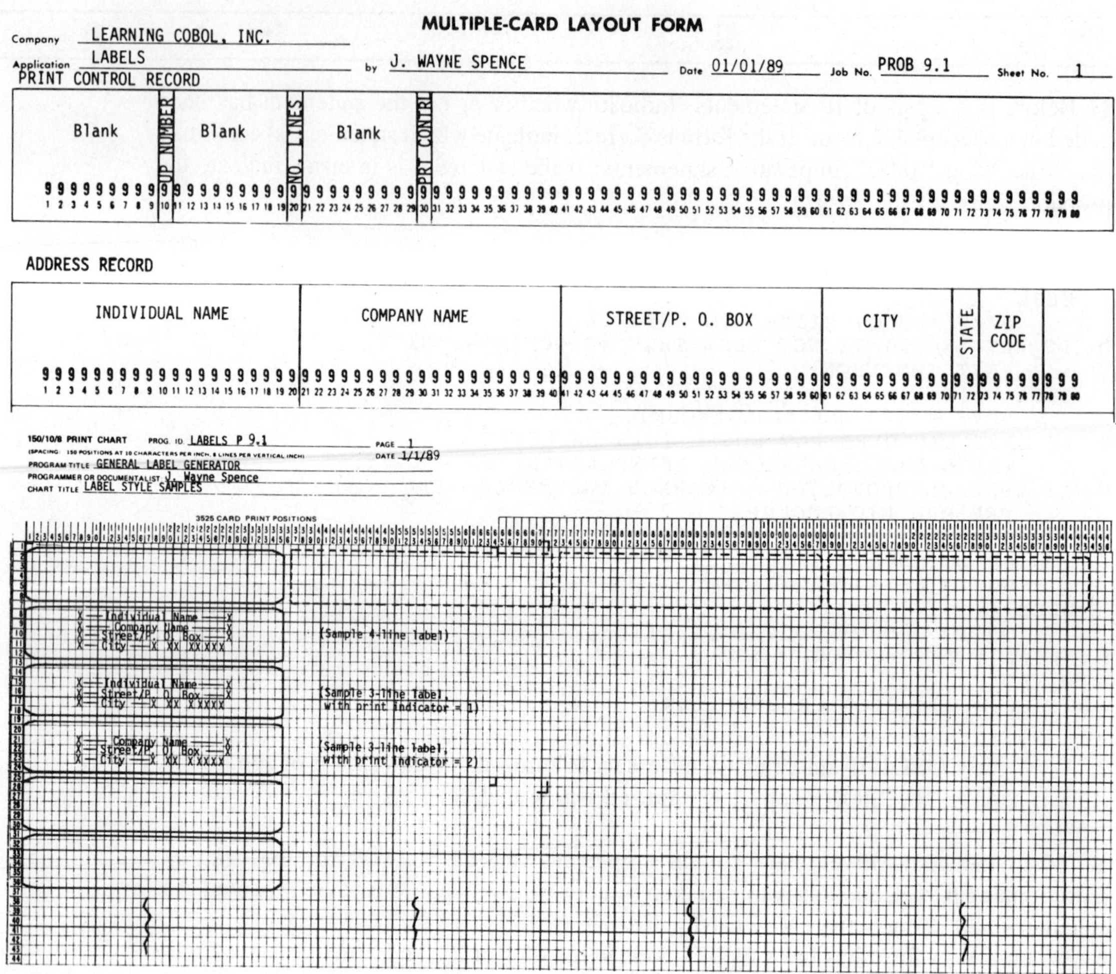
MULTIPLE-CARD LAYOUT FORM

Company LEARNING COBOL, INC.
Application LABELS by J. WAYNE SPENCE Date 01/01/89 Job No. PROB 9.1 Sheet No. 1

PRINT CONTROL RECORD

Blank	UP NUMBER	Blank	NO. LINES	Blank	PRT CONTRL	

ADDRESS RECORD

INDIVIDUAL NAME	COMPANY NAME	STREET/P. O. BOX	CITY	STATE	ZIP CODE	

150/10/8 PRINT CHART PROG. ID LABELS P 9.1 PAGE 1
PROGRAM TITLE GENERAL LABEL GENERATOR DATE 1/1/89
PROGRAMMER OR DOCUMENTALIST J. Wayne Spence
CHART TITLE LABEL STYLE SAMPLES

3525 CARD PRINT POSITIONS

X—Individual Name—X
X—Company Name—X
X—Street/P. O. Box—X
X—City—X XX XXXXX
(Sample 4-line label)

X—Individual Name—X
X—Street/P. O. Box—X
X—City—X XX XXXXX
(Sample 3-line label, with print indicator = 1)

X—Company Name—X
X—Street/P. O. Box—X
X—City—X XX XXXXX
(Sample 3-line label, with print indicator = 2)

2. Number of lines per label—1 digit and may contain either 3 or 4—to reflect 3- or 4-line labels. (On 4-line labels all data fields from the type-2 record are used.)
3. First-line print indicator—1 digit and may contain either 1 or 2.

The first-line print indicator is used only when 3-line labels are to be printed and is used to indicate whether the individual's name (indicator = 1) or the company's name (indicator = 2) is to be printed as the first line of the address. On 4-line labels, the individual's name should appear first, followed by the company name (line 2), street or P.O. Box (line 3), and the city-state-zip code (line 4).

The second record type contains the data to be printed and is represented by the following fields (see multiple-card layout form):

1. Individual name—20 characters
2. Company name—20 characters
3. Street or P.O. Box—20 characters

4. City—10 characters
5. State—2 characters (2-character state abbreviation)
6. Zip code—5 characters

The print chart demonstrates the possible variation in label printing. The elliptical shapes on the printer layout indicate the actual location and size of the mailing labels. *Note*: Multiple executions of the program will be required to demonstrate your program's capability to print 3- and 4-line labels with 1-, 2-, 3-, and 4-up labels.

9.2 Our corporate library contains a series of publication types, including books, government documents, magazines and other periodicals, pamphlets, manuals, and internal working papers. Each time one of these holdings is checked out of the library, the patron's name and the date are recorded. Periodically, we need to account for all publications. Obviously, a physical inventory of the library would indicate what materials are outstanding (have not been returned to the library). However, an examination of the "checkout" records would be faster. Unfortunately, the date of return has not been recorded on some of the records; thus, we cannot simply examine the records to see which do not have a return date. We must examine the checkout date (which is available for each record) to find the last user (most current checkout date). Once the last user is located, we examine the return date—if it is blank, the publication has not been returned, and the details of the record should be printed (as indicated on the print chart).

The data, described below and on the multiple-card layout form, has been organized by publication type (all books are first, followed by government documents, etc.) and

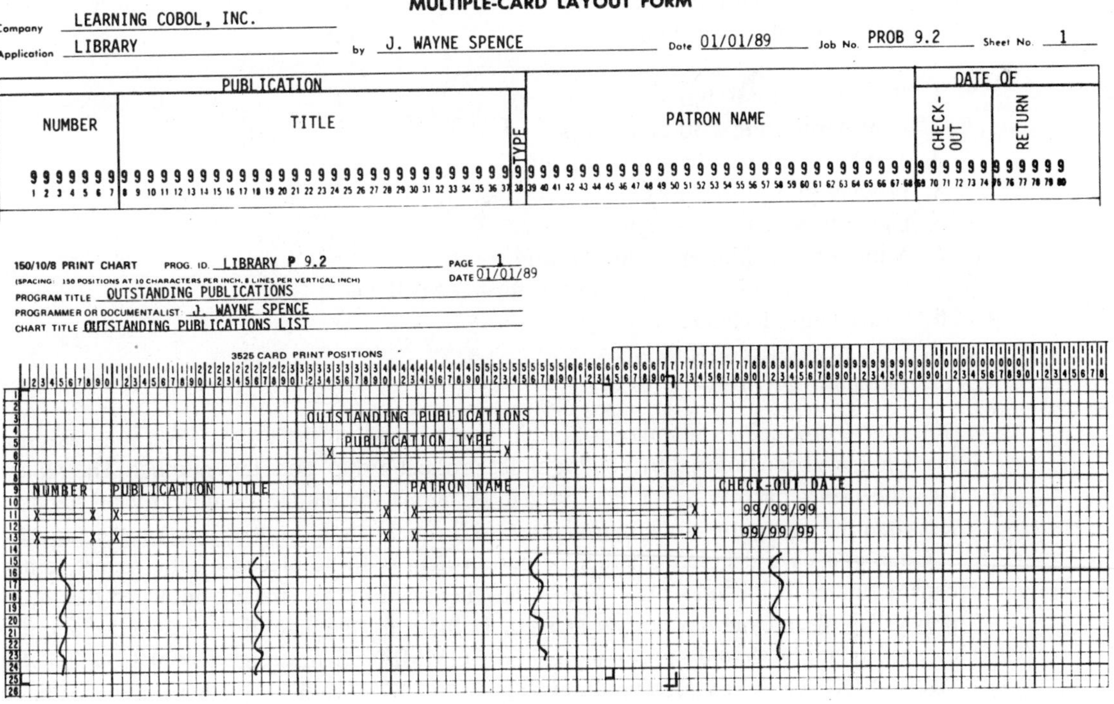

MULTIPLE-CARD LAYOUT FORM

Company LEARNING COBOL, INC.
Application LIBRARY by J. WAYNE SPENCE Date 01/01/89 Job No. PROB 9.2 Sheet No. 1

PUBLICATION				DATE OF	
NUMBER	TITLE	TYPE	PATRON NAME	CHECK-OUT	RETURN
1–7	8–37	38	39–68	69–74	75–80

150/10/8 PRINT CHART PROG. ID. LIBRARY P 9.2 PAGE 1
(SPACING: 150 POSITIONS AT 10 CHARACTERS PER INCH, 8 LINES PER VERTICAL INCH) DATE 01/01/89
PROGRAM TITLE OUTSTANDING PUBLICATIONS
PROGRAMMER OR DOCUMENTALIST: J. WAYNE SPENCE
CHART TITLE OUTSTANDING PUBLICATIONS LIST

3525 CARD PRINT POSITIONS

```
3                                OUTSTANDING PUBLICATIONS
5                                    PUBLICATION TYPE
6                                  X----------------X
9  NUMBER    PUBLICATION TITLE                     PATRON NAME                    CHECK-OUT DATE
11 X-----X   X-------------------------------X  X----------------------------X      99/99/99
13 X-----X   X-------------------------------X  X----------------------------X      99/99/99
```

by publication number, that is, all records for a given publication will be in one group. The fields of the checkout record are as follows:

1. Publication number—7 characters
2. Publication title—30 characters
3. Publication type—1 character
4. Patron name—30 characters
5. Checkout date—6 digits in the format MMDDYY
6. Return date—6 digits in the format MMDDYY

As previously noted, only the record of the most recent checkout is to be printed, and only if the return date for that record is blank. There are typically several checkout records for a single publication. The publication types are to be grouped—every time the publication type changes, a new heading is to be printed. The heading is to contain the name of the publication type according to the following list:

B—BOOK
G—GOVERNMENT DOCUMENT
M—MAGAZINE/PERIODICAL
P—PAMPHLET
N—MANUAL
W—WORKING PAPER

See the print chart for further details.

9.3 Inventory-status records have been created for the purchasing department to determine whether or not particular items should be ordered. Each of the inventory records consist of the following fields:

1. Item number—6 digits
2. Item description—30 characters
3. Vendor/supplier code—3 characters
4. Product group—3 digits
5. Quantity on hand—5 digits
6. Minimum stocking quantity—5 digits
7. Date of last order—6 digits in the format MMDDYY
8. Order flag—1 character
9. Quantity ordered—5 digits
10. Purchase-lot size—5 digits

You are to produce an inventory-reorder report based on these data. You may assume the data have been ordered by vendor code, product group, and item number. The report (see the print chart) is to include only those items for which the quantity on hand is less than the minimum stocking quantity. (All others should not appear on the report.)

Once you have decided whether or not an item is to be placed on the report, other considerations come into play. The order flag set to ''Y'' means an order has been previously placed and has not yet arrived. In this case the date of the last order and the ordered quantity should appear under the COMMENTS heading (99999 UNITS ORDERED ON XX/XX/XX). The order flag set to ''S'' means all further purchases have been suspended, and the message "PURCHASES SUSPENDED" should appear under the COMMENTS heading. If the order flag is blank or set to "N," a current order is not pending and a new order should be placed. In this case the message "BELOW MINIMUM STOCK LEVEL OF 99999—ORDER 99999 UNITS" should appear below the COMMENTS heading.

Other considerations are:

1. The reorder list should begin on a new page for each vendor code encountered.
2. A blank line should appear between each new product group, that is, product groups of different values.

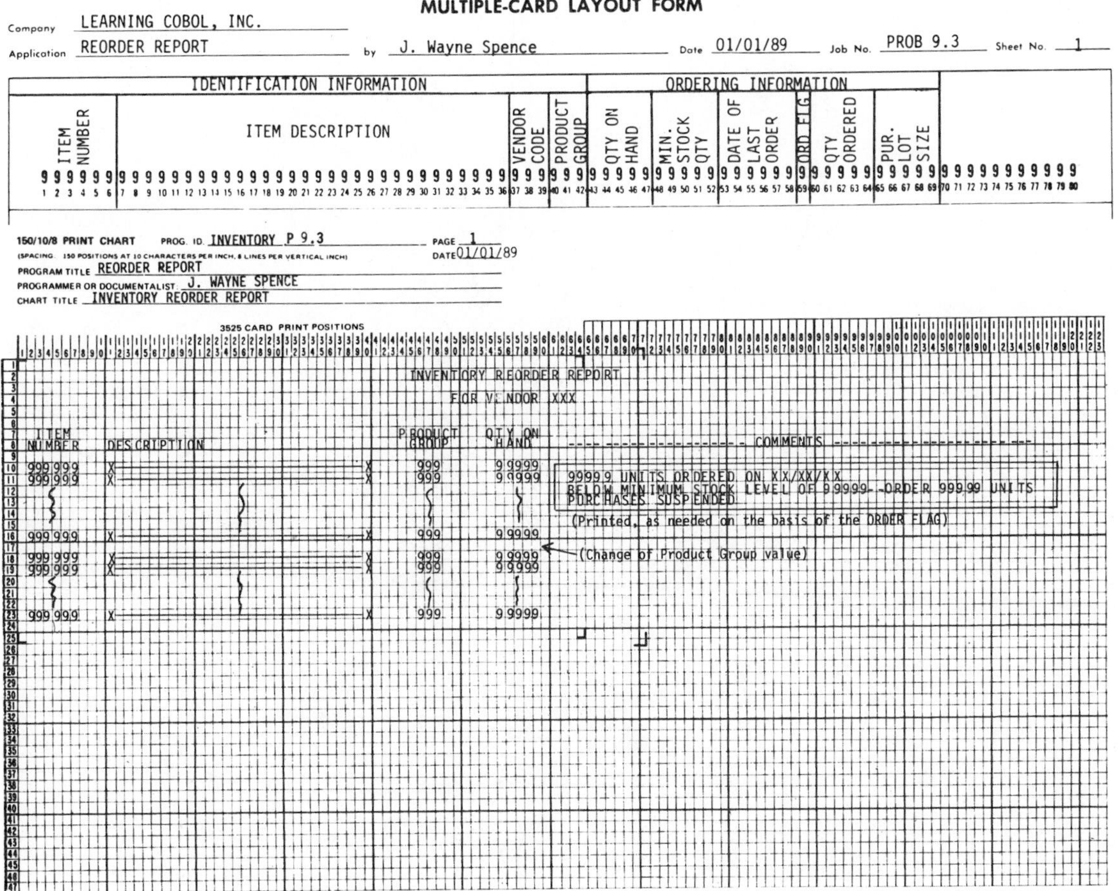

CHAPTER

10

Arithmetic Statements

COBOL is limited arithmetically to addition, subtraction, multiplication, division, and exponentiation (raising a number to a power). Other programming languages (e.g., PASCAL or BASIC) provide more arithmetical versatility, but COBOL's arithmetic capability is generally adequate for business data-processing applications.

There are five arithmetic statements in COBOL—ADD, SUBTRACT, MULTIPLY, DIVIDE, and COMPUTE. The first four of these statements (ADD, SUBTRACT, MULTIPLY, and DIVIDE) each perform a single arithmetic function. The COMPUTE statement can perform a variety of functions, including addition, subtraction, multiplication, division, and exponentiation.

The ADD Statement

The function of the ADD statement is to provide the sum of numeric items. There are two formats of the ADD statement, as presented in Figure 10.1. The first format of the ADD statement causes all identifiers and literals appearing before the required word TO to be added to the identifier(s) following the word TO. As an example, if the statement

```
ADD UNITS-PURCHASED, UNITS RETURNED, 10 TO UNITS-ON-HAND.
```

were to be executed, the values contained in UNITS-PURCHASED and UNITS-RETURNED and the value 10 (perhaps the number of "recovered" units) would be added to UNITS-ON-HAND. Thus, if UNITS-PURCHASED contains 5, UNITS-RETURNED contains 15, and UNITS-ON-HAND contains 30 before the execution of this statement, after the statement is executed, UNITS-PURCHASED and UNITS-RETURNED are unchanged, and UNITS-ON-HAND contains the results of the operation—the value 60. Thus, UNITS-ON-HAND both takes part in the addition operation *and* acts as the receiving field of the operation. If additional identifiers are listed after TO, they likewise take part in the addition operation and act as receiving fields for the results of the addition.

All identifiers in this form of the ADD statement must be nonedited, numeric data items. (Remember that a decimal point is an editing character.) All literals in the statement

Figure 10.1 Formats of the ADD Statement

```
Format 1:

     ⎧identifier-1⎫  ⎡identifier-2⎤
ADD  ⎨            ⎬  ⎢            ⎥  . . . TO identifier-m [ROUNDED]
     ⎩literal-1   ⎭  ⎣literal-2   ⎦

[ON SIZE ERROR imperative-statement-1]
[NOT ON SIZE ERROR imperative-statement-2]
[END-ADD]
```

```
Format-2:

     ⎧identifier-1⎫  ⎧identifier-2⎫        ⎡identifier-3⎤
ADD  ⎨            ⎬  ⎨            ⎬ [TO]   ⎢            ⎥  . . .
     ⎩literal-1   ⎭  ⎩literal-2   ⎭        ⎣literal-3   ⎦

GIVING identifiers-m [ROUNDED]
[ON SIZE ERROR imperative-statement-2]
[NOT ON SIZE ERROR imperative-statement-2]
[END-ADD]
```

must be numeric literals. The maximum size of each of the items in the ADD statement is set by the particular computer (but generally may be no more than 18 digits). The data items are decimal-point aligned before the addition takes place. Thus, overflow of the field to the left (high-order digits) or truncation to the right (after the decimal point) is possible.

Two optional clauses may be attached to the ADD statement. The ROUNDED option rounds the result in the receiving field to the field's PICTURE size. Thus, if the result of the addition operation has more positions following the decimal point than does the receiving field, the result is rounded to the size of the receiving field.

The SIZE ERROR option allows the programmer to specify the action to be taken in response to an addition-operation result that is too large for the receiving field, that is, when the number of high-order digits in the result exceeds the available space in the receiving field. If the ROUNDED option is also specified, rounding occurs before the SIZE ERROR is checked. The SIZE ERROR applies only to the final result of the computation and not to any intermediate results. If a SIZE ERROR occurs, the imperative statement is executed and the receiving field is not altered. If several identifiers are listed after TO, a SIZE ERROR applies to all identifiers. Identifiers listed *after* (and including) the identifier causing the SIZE ERROR are not changed by the execution of the ADD statement. All identifiers listed *before* the identifier causing the error will be altered by the ADD statement. New values are assigned to receiving fields from left to right.

1985 COBOL Standards 

In COBOL 85 two additional optional clauses may be included in the ADD statement. The NOT SIZE ERROR permits the programmer to specify the action to be taken in response to a successful addition operation. Both the SIZE ERROR and NOT SIZE ERROR options are permitted in the same ADD statement in COBOL 85. The END-ADD option is a *structured delimiter* use to mark the end of the ADD statement.

The remaining arithmetic statements also permit ROUNDED and SIZE ERROR options and the NOT SIZE ERROR and END-*arithmetic operation* in COBOL 85. The actions of these options are the same as those discussed earlier. However, when division is possible and there is an attempted division by zero, the SIZE ERROR option is also invoked. Thus, the SIZE ERROR option has an additional function for the DIVIDE and COMPUTE statements.

The second format of the ADD statement is the "ADD-GIVING" statement. It differs slightly from the first ADD statement. *Two* identifiers or literals are *required* before the word GIVING. *Only one* receiving field may be listed after the word GIVING (although this may vary by compiler). *TO does not appear in this format of the ADD.*

This ADD statement causes all the identifiers and literals before the word GIVING to be summed, and their sum is *placed* in the identifier following the word GIVING. The difference between the first ADD and this ADD is that the identifier following the word GIVING is a receiving field *only*—it does not take part in the addition operation.

As with the first ADD statement, all identifiers listed before the word GIVING must be numeric-nonedited elementary-items. Literals must be numeric literals. The identifier listed after the word GIVING (the receiving field) may be an *edited*-numeric field. And since it acts as a receiving field only, it need not contain a value prior to the execution of the ADD statement. *Initialization is a requirement for all other identifiers in both formats of the ADD.* The programmer should exercise caution in describing an edited-numeric field. If identifier-*m* is an edited-numeric field, it cannot be used as an operand in any other arithmetic operation, although it may appear again after the word GIVING. Thus, the value of the identifier is, for all intents and purposes, an end product. (Remember that the decimal point is an editing character.)

As an example of the ADD-GIVING statement, assume that PREVIOUS-SALES contains 123‸45 and CURRENT-SALES contains 945‸Ø2. If the statement

```
ADD PREVIOUS-SALES, CURRENT-SALES GIVING TOTAL-SALES.
```

is executed, the sum would be 1Ø68.47. However, if the PICTURE string of TOTAL-SALES is 999.9, the result stored in TOTAL-SALES will be Ø68.4 (regardless of the previous contents of TOTAL-SALES). The result placed in TOTAL-SALES has been truncated from both ends to fit the PICTURE string. (Most compilers provide a warning message indicating that high-order digits may be truncated, but no compiler warns that low-order digits will be truncated when the PICTURE string of the receiving field has as many digit positions before the decimal point as the items used to compute it.) IF the ROUNDED option is specified, that is,

```
ADD PREVIOUS-SALES, CURRENT-SALES GIVING TOTAL-SALES ROUNDED.
```

then the result placed in TOTAL-SALES would be Ø68.5—the digit(s) to be truncated from the rightmost position(s) is 5 or greater. However, there is still no indication that TOTAL-SALES has been truncated from the left. If the SIZE ERROR option is added to the statement; that is,

```
ADD PREVIOUS SALES, CURRENT-SALES
   GIVING TOTAL-SALES ROUNDED ON SIZE ERROR
   DISPLAY 'ERROR OCCURRED DURING ADDITION OF TOTAL SALES . . .
```

the value of TOTAL-SALES would be the value it contained before the ADD operation took place, and the message "ERROR OCCURRED DURING ADDITION OF TOTAL SALES" would appear on the output from the program. To complete the addition operation, you should enlarge the PICTURE string of TOTAL-SALES to at least 9999.9, if not larger. Remember that this PICTURE string is an edited-numeric field, so TOTAL-SALES can only be used as a receiving field in other arithmetic statements.

The SUBTRACT Statement

The SUBTRACT statement causes the subtraction (reduction or decrement) of an item (or items) from the value of one or more items. The two formats of the SUBTRACT statement appear in Figure 10.2.

Format 1 of the SUBTRACT statement causes the *algebraic* sum of the identifiers and literals preceding the word FROM to be subtracted from the identifier(s) listed after the word FROM. It is important to note that the algebraic sum is subtracted, because if the sum of the identifiers and literals is negative, the effect is to *add* the identifiers and literals before FROM to the identifier(s) after FROM. If a negative result is anticipated (or is possible), the receiving field's PICTURE string should contain an operational sign (S).

All identifiers in this format of the SUBTRACT statement must be nonedited-numeric fields and must contain values. Literals must be numeric literals.

Suppose that the statement

```
SUBTRACT APPROVED-OVERTIME-HOURS, 40 FROM TOTAL-HOURS.
```

was included in a program where APPROVED-OVERTIME-HOURS contains 30^8 and TOTAL-HOURS contains 086 and has a PICTURE of S999. The result stored in TOTAL-HOURS would be 015. Again, the fraction (.2) is truncated. If the PICTURE string of

Figure 10.2 Formats of the SUBTRACT Statement

```
Format 1:

         {identifier-1} [identifier-2]
SUBTRACT {              } [            ] . . . FROM identifier-m [ROUNDED]
         {literal-1   } [literal-2   ]
[identifier-n [ROUNDED]]...
[ON SIZE ERROR imperative-statement-1]
[NOT ON SIZE ERROR imperative-statement-2]
[END-SUBTRACT]
```

```
Format 2:

         {identifier-1} [identifier-2]            {identifier-m}
SUBTRACT {              } [            ] . . . FROM {              }
         {literal-1   } [literal-2   ]            {literal-m   }
GIVING identifier-n [ROUNDED]
[ON SIZE ERROR imperative-statement-1]
[NOT ON SIZE ERROR imperative-statement-2]
[END-SUBTRACT]
```

TOTAL-HOURS did not contain the operational sign (S) and the result of the subtraction is negative, the stored value would be unsigned (positive).

Format 2 of the SUBTRACT statement allows the algebraic sum of the identifiers and literals appearing before the word FROM to be subtracted from the identifier listed after the word FROM—the result being stored in the identifier shown after the word GIVING. As before, all identifiers listed before the word GIVING must be nonedited-numeric fields. The identifier after GIVING may be an edited-numeric field and does not have to contain a value before the execution of the statement.

Suppose the statement

```
SUBTRACT UNITS-SOLD FROM UNITS-ON-HAND GIVING UNITS-AVAILABLE
```

was contained in a program, where UNITS-SOLD contained 22‸6 and UNITS-ON-HAND contained 46‸8. The result of the execution of this statement would place 34‸2 in UNITS-AVAILABLE, regardless of its previous value. (The indicated value assumes the PICTURE clause of UNITS-AVAILABLE, is at least as large as 99.9) The values of UNITS-SOLD and UNITS-ON-HAND are unchanged after this operation.

The MULTIPLY Statement

The MULTIPLY statement performs the multiplication of only *two* data items (see Figure 10.3).

The first format of the MULTIPLY statement creates the product of the first identifier or numeric literal and the second identifier, and stores the result in the second identifier. The identifiers in this format of the MULTIPLY statement must be nonedited-numeric fields containing values.

Figure 10.3 Formats of the MULTIPLY Statement

```
Format 1:

          { identifier-1 }
MULTIPLY  {              }  BY identifier-2 [ROUNDED]
          { literal-1    }

[ON SIZE ERROR imperative-statement-1]
[NOT ON SIZE ERROR imperative-statement-2]
[END-MULTIPLY]
```

```
Format 2:

          { identifier-1 }        { identifier-2 }
MULTIPLY  {              }   BY   {              }
          { literal-1    }        { literal-2    }

GIVING identifier-3 [ROUNDED]
[ON SIZE ERROR imperative-statement-1]
[NOT ON SIZE ERROR imperative-statement-2]
[END-MULTIPLY]
```

For example, in the following statement,

```
MULTIPLY 12 BY DOZEN-ITEMS
```

if DOZEN-ITEMS contained the value 4 before the execution of the statement, it would contain 48 after the statement is executed. The numeric literal 12 can be used *only* in the location shown. An identifier *must* follow the word BY to serve as the receiving field for the calculation.

Format 2 of the MULTIPLY statement allows identifiers and literals to appear before and after the word BY. The identifiers must be nonedited-numeric fields; however, the field following the word GIVING may be an edited field that may or may not contain a value prior to the execution of the MULTIPLY statement. The result of the multiplication is stored in the identifier following the word GIVING.

If the statement

```
MULTIPLY UNIT-COST BY 1.15 GIVING MINIMUM-UNIT-PRICE.
```

is executed (with UNIT-COST containing 45 and MINIMUM-UNIT-PRICE having a PICTURE string of 999V99), the result stored in MINIMUM-UNIT-PRICE will be $051_{\wedge}75$.

The DIVIDE Statement

The DIVIDE statement produces a quotient when one data item is divided into another. As seen in Figure 10.4, the DIVIDE statement is similar to the MULTIPLY statement. In Format 1, identifier-1 (or literal-1) represents the divisor (or denominator), and identifier-2 represents the dividend (or numerator), that is,

$$\text{identifier-2} \div \frac{\text{identifier-1}}{\text{(or literal-1)}} \quad \text{or} \quad \frac{\text{identifier-2}}{\text{identifier-1 (or literal-1)}}.$$

The result of the division operation (the quotient) is placed in identifier-2 after the DIVIDE statement has been executed. In this form of the DIVIDE statement, the identifiers must be nonedited-numeric fields, and the literal must be a numeric literal. When an attempt is made to divide by zero, that is, when identifier-1 is zero, a SIZE ERROR occurs. If the SIZE ERROR option is not specified, an attempted division by zero will result in an ''ILLEGAL DECIMAL'' or ''DECIMAL DIVIDE EXCEPTION'' error.

Suppose the statement

```
DIVIDE LOT-SIZE INTO FULL-BOXES
```

was included in a program, where LOT-SIZE contained the value 12 and FULL-BOXES contained the value 54 before the execution of the statement. After the statement was executed, LOT-SIZE would be unchanged and FULL-BOXES would contain $4_{\wedge}5$ (provided the description of FULL-BOXES permitted for decimal positions).

In the second format of the DIVIDE statement, the result of the division operation is placed in the identifier following the word GIVING. With Format 2, the programmer has a choice of the reserved words BY or INTO. When the reserved word INTO is provided, the designation of divisor and dividend is the same as for Format 1. However, when the keyword BY is present, divisor and dividend are reversed (identifier-2 becomes the divisor, and identifier-1 becomes the dividend).

Figure 10.4 Formats of the DIVIDE Statement

```
Format 1:

DIVIDE { identifier-1 }  INTO identifier-2 [ROUNDED]
       { literal-1    }

[ON SIZE ERROR imperative-statement-1]
[NOT ON SIZE ERROR imperative-statement-2]
[END-DIVIDE]
```

```
Format 2:

DIVIDE { identifier-1 } { INTO } { identifier-2 } GIVING identifier-3 [ROUNDED]
       { literal-1    } { BY   } { literal-2    }

[REMAINDER identifier-4]
[ON SIZE ERROR imperative-statement-1]
[NOT ON SIZE ERROR imperative-statement-2]
[END-DIVIDE]
```

The Format 2 DIVIDE statement provides one option that does not appear in any other COBOL arithmetic statement—the reserved word REMAINDER. REMAINDER makes it possible to perform a division and retain the remainder—*modulo* division. Thus, the remainder is defined as being the dividend less the product of the quotient and the divisor.

Assume the statement

```
DIVIDE LOT-SIZE INTO INDIVIDUAL-UNITS GIVING FULL-BOXES.
```

is executed, where LOT-SIZE contains the value 12, INDIVIDUAL-UNITS contains the value 54, and FULL-BOXES has a PICTURE string of 99. The result of the division operation placed in FULL-BOXES would be Ø4. If the statement is modified to

```
    DIVIDE LOT-SIZE INTO INDIVIDUAL-UNITS GIVING FULL-BOXES
        REMAINDER PARTIAL-BOXES
```

and PARTIAL-BOXES has a PICTURE string of 99, the division operation would result in FULL-BOXES containing Ø4 and PARTIAL-BOXES containing Ø6 (the remainder). Finally, if the statement is further modified to

```
DIVIDE LOT-SIZE BY INDIVIDUAL-UNITS GIVING FULL-BOXES REMAINDER

    PARTIAL-BOXES
```

FULL-BOXES would contain ØØ and PARTIAL-BOXES would contain 54.

The COMPUTE Statement

The most versatile arithmetic statement is the COMPUTE statement. The COMPUTE statement permits the coding of a series of operations in algebraic form. The general format of the COMPUTE statement is presented in Figure 10.5. Identifier-1 is the

Figure 10.5 Format of the COMPUTE Statement

```
                                     ┌identifier-2           ┐
COMPUTE identifier-1 [ROUNDED] =    ┤literal-1              ├
                                     └arithmetic-expression  ┘

[ON SIZE ERROR imperative-statement-1]
[NOT on SIZE ERROR imperative-statement-2]
[END-COMPUTE]
```

receiving field, and like the other arithmetic statements with the GIVING phrase, the identifier may be an edited-numeric field not containing a value prior to the execution of the COMPUTE statement. This identifier is followed by an optional ROUNDED phrase (allowing the result of the computation to be rounded to the PICTURE size of identifier-1). The identifier is then followed by an equal symbol, the only required punctuation for the COMPUTE statement other than the normal period at the end of the statement.

All identifiers listed after the equal symbol must be nonedited-numeric fields, and all identifiers must contain a value. All literals must be numeric literals. In the format of the COMPUTE statement, the programmer has a choice of an identifier, a literal, or an arithmetic expression. If an identifier or a literal is chosen, it is assigned to the storage position identifier-1. This in no way affects the contents of identifier-2. In these cases, the compute statement is used much like the MOVE statement. However, if the programmer chooses to use them, the arithmetic capabilities of the COMPUTE statement are extensive.

An arithmetic expression in COBOL may be composed of arithmetic operators, identifiers, literals, and parentheses. The symbols used to represent arithmetic operators are

+ · · addition	/ · · division
− · · subtraction	** · · exponentiation
* · · multiplication	

Thus, the COMPUTE statement allows the same types of operations performed by the ADD, SUBTRACT, MULTIPLY, and DIVIDE statements plus exponentiation (raising a number to a power)—which is not easily done with the other arithmetic statements. The arithmetic operators should never appear adjacent to each other in an expression. When used, an operator should be preceded and followed by a space. And, in the absence of parentheses, exponentiation will be executed first; multiplication and division, second; and addition and subtraction, last. If multiple operations appear in an expression, and the operations are on the same ''level'' (as just described), the operations will be executed from left to right.

In some instances, the programmer may wish certain operations to be performed before others (e.g., an addition before a multiplication). To accomplish this, the programmer may specify the sequence of operations by placing parentheses around the operation to be executed first. That is, if parentheses are present in an arithmetic expression, the COBOL compiler proceeds by first eliminating (or resolving) sets of parentheses. If there are multiple sets of parentheses, the compiler resolves the parentheses from left to right. If the parentheses are ''nested'' (one set of parentheses within another),

Figure 10.6 Examples of the COMPUTE Statement

Formula*	COMPUTE Statement	Comments
$X = \frac{A}{B}$	COMPUTE X = A / B.	The same type of operation can be performed by the DIVIDE statement (e.g., DIVIDE A BY B GIVING X.)
$X = A + B - C$	COMPUTE X = A + B - C.	There is a direct translation between the formula and the COMPUTE statement. Addition is performed first, followed by subtraction, and then the assignment of the result to X.
$X = A + B^2$	COMPUTE X = A + B ** 2.	The representation B^2 in the formula is B ** 2 in the COMPUTE statement. This is called exponentiation. Note that the exponent (in this case 2) is placed after the double asterisk. Exponentiation occurs first, followed by addition.
$X = \frac{A + B}{C - D}$	COMPUTE X = (A + B) / (C - D).	Note that parentheses are required in both the numerator and denominator. This forces the operations to be done in the order (1) add A and B, (2) subtract D from C, and (3) divide the numerator by the denominator.
$X = \sqrt{\frac{AB}{C^2}}$	COMPUTE X = (A * B / C ** 2) ** .5.	Inside the square-root symbol (radical), the formula suggests that A and B should be multiplied (A * B), C squared (C ** 2), the numerator divided by the denominator (/), and the square root of the expression determined (** .5). Since the expression is enclosed in a set of parentheses, exponentiation, multiplication, and division take place in that order. Once the parentheses are resolved, the expression is "raised" to the .5 power—the square root.
$X = -B + \sqrt{\frac{B^2 - 4AC}{2A}}$	COMPUTE X = -B + ((B ** 2 - 4 * A * C) / (2 * A))** .5.	Notice that in this expression, there are "nested" parentheses. The entire expression under the radical is enclosed in the outermost set of parentheses, while the numerator and denominator are each enclosed in a separate set of parentheses.

*All identifiers are assumed to be a single character in length.

the compiler will begin the execution of the statement with the innermost set of parentheses. When parentheses are coded in an expression, a left (open) parenthesis should be preceded, but not followed by a space. The right (close) parenthesis should not be preceded by a space, but should be followed by a space or a period.

Figure 10.6 illustrates the COMPUTE statement as it relates to various types of formulas. Carefully read the comments associated with each of the examples.

The Electric Utility Company Program

The program illustrated in Figure 10.7 might be used by an electric utility company to determine electricity usage and the amount due the company based on that usage, plus any unpaid balance in the customer's account. To provide all necessary data, three types of input records are required. The first record type for each customer contains the customer history—the meter reading from the last month and the customer balance from previous periods. The second record type contains the customer payments to prior account balances. There may be none, one, or several payments for each customer. Assume that multiple payments are possible for multifamily dwellings. The total for all payments for a customer are not assumed to be exactly equal to the outstanding balance. The customer is issued a credit if he overpays his bill and is charged a finance charge for

Figure 10.7 Electric Utility Program (Hierarchy Chart)

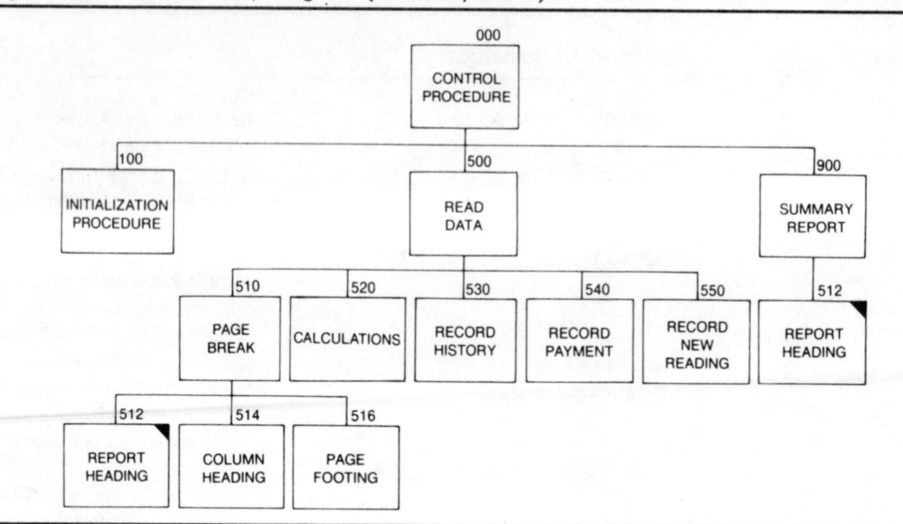

underpayment. The final record type contains a meter reading for the current month's usage of electricity. Furthermore, the programmer has been cautioned to guard against meter "roll over"—that is, where the meter exceeds its maximum reading and begins again from zero, like an automobile odometer. All these records are assumed to be ordered (sorted) by customer number and type of record.

Other requirements of the program are to (1) produce a report with one line for each customer, (2) produce a summary report containing the totals of all pertinent details, and (3) properly compute current charges based on the amount of electricity used. The current charges are based on the following: (1) a customer who uses less than 10 kilowatt hours (KWH) is charged a flat fee of $2.50; (2) a customer who uses 10 KWH to 5000 KWH is charged a rate of $0.0323 per KWH used; (3) the customer who uses over 5000 KWH is charged at the rate of $0.0255 per KWH. There is no charge for no usage.

The program CONTROL-PROCEDURE provides the overall control program. That is, the execution of the procedure is controlled by the CONTROL-PROCEDURE of the PROCEDURE DIVISION. In the program listing itself, each statement of the control section is a PERFORM statement that causes other paragraphs to be executed.

The process performed by the program is the creation of a report to be used within the electric utility company. The program is responsible for accepting input records that represent the past month's results (history) for each customer. In addition, each account may be updated to include payments received from the customer and new meter readings recorded. After all data for a particular account has been read, the program is to determine the amount of electricity (in kilowatt hours) used by the customer, the rate charged per kilowatt hour used, the base bill based on the kilowatt hours used, the remaining balance for the account after payments have been recorded, the finance charges for outstanding balances (if any), and the new balance the customer owes the utility company. After the program has processed all the accounts in this manner, a summary of all accounts is to be produced. The flowchart program listing and printed output of the program are provided in Figure 10.7.

Although this program appears to be much longer than many of the previous programs, try to determine the purpose of each of the paragraphs in the program. Some of them are different from others previously shown. For example, the INITIALIZATION-PROCEDURE reads two records from the input file. The first record contains a date, and the second record contains the initial customer record. However, if either of these records is not present in the input file, the program *aborts* (causes its own termination). This is a little unusual in that a procedure could have more than one exit, but given that the needed data are not present, it is an acceptable alternative to a continuation of the process (which would likely result in an error). The next major difference in the INITIALIZATION-PROCEDURE is the absence of a page-heading routine. Previous programs

Figure 10.7 *Continued* Electric Utility Program (Pseudocode)

```
START
     DO Initialization
     DO Read-data UNTIL eof
     DO Summary-report
     DO Termination
END

INITIALIZATION
     OPEN files
     MOVE initial values to page,
          line counters
     ACCEPT record date
     MOVE date to output
END

READ-DATA
    READ information
         IF eof
              SET eof indicator
              MOVE customer number
                   to last number
              DO Calculations
              DO Page break
              GOTO end
         ENDIF
    ENDREAD
    IF new page
         DO Page break
    ENDIF
    IF new customer
         DO Calculations
    ENDIF
    IF record type = 1
         DO Record history
    ENDIF
    IF record type = 2
         DO Record payment
    ENDIF
    IF record type = 3
         DO Record new reading
    ENDIF
    IF record type not 1,2,or 3
         DISPLAY error
END

RECORD HISTORY
    IF bottom of page
         MOVE customer to last number
    ENDIF
    MOVE input to working fields
    MOVE 0 to calculations
    ADD old balance to new balance
END

RECORD PAYMENT
    MOVE type to payment information
    ADD payment in to payments
    ADD 1 to payment count
END

RECORD NEW READING
    MOVE type to current information
    MOVE meter reading to calculation,
         output
END

PAGE BREAK
    IF bottom of page
         DO Page footing
    ENDIF
    IF eof
         DO Report heading
         DO Column heading
    ENDIF
    MOVE 0 to line counter
    MOVE customer number to 1st,
         hold number
END

REPORT HEADING
    ADD 1 to page numbers
    PRINT report headings
END

COLUMN HEADING
    WRITE column headings
END

PAGE FOOTING
    WRITE footings
END

CALCULATIONS
    SUBTRACT payments from balance
    IF balance > 0
         COMPUTE charge = balance * .015
    ENDIF
    COMPUTE kwatts
    IF kwatts < 0
         COMPUTE kwatts = current + 100000 - last
    ENDIF
    IF kwatts = 0
         MOVE 0 to bill
    ENDIF
    IF kwatts between 0 and 10
         MOVE 2.5 to bill
    ENDIF
    IF kwatts between 10 and 5001
         COMPUTE bill = .0255 * kwatts
    ENDIF
    IF kwatts > 5000
         COMPUTE bill = .0323 * kwatts
    ENDIF
    SUM total bill
    ADD customer totals
    MOVE calculations to output
    WRITE output
    ADD 1 to line counters
END

SUMMARY REPORT
    MOVE summary title to output
    DO Report heading
    MOVE summary data to output
    WRITE summary output
END

TERMINATION
    CLOSE files
END
```

Figure 10.7 *Continued* Electric Utility Program

```
          1   1   2   2   2   3   3   4   4   4   5   5   6   6   6   7
  4   8   2   6   0   4   8   2   6   0   4   8   2   6   0   4   8   2

*****************************************************************
 IDENTIFICATION DIVISION.
*****************************************************************
 PROGRAM-ID.    ELECTRIC-COMPANY.
 AUTHOR.        J. WAYNE SPENCE.
 DATE-WRITTEN.  JANUARY 1, 1989.
 DATE-COMPILED. JANUARY 1, 1989.
*    This program illustrates the use of multiple record types
*    in a data file, 01-levels in the WORKING-STORAGE SECTION
*    and a structured PROCEDURE DIVISION utilizing PERFORMs,
*    simple IF's and nested IF's.
*****************************************************************
 ENVIRONMENT DIVISION.
*****************************************************************
*---------------------------------------------------------------*
 CONFIGURATION SECTION.
*---------------------------------------------------------------*
 SOURCE-COMPUTER. IBM.
 OBJECT-COMPUTER. IBM.
 SPECIAL-NAMES.   C01 IS TOP-OF-PAGE.
*---------------------------------------------------------------*
 INPUT-OUTPUT SECTION.
*---------------------------------------------------------------*
 FILE-CONTROL.
     SELECT INFORMATION-FILE     ASSIGN TO UT-S-INPUT.
     SELECT ACTIVITY-REPORT-FILE ASSIGN TO UT-S-OUTPUT.
*****************************************************************
 DATA DIVISION.
*****************************************************************
*---------------------------------------------------------------*
 FILE SECTION.
*---------------------------------------------------------------*
 FD  INFORMATION-FILE LABEL RECORDS ARE OMITTED.
 01  HISTORY-RECORD.
     05 CUSTOMER-NUMBER-IN       PIC 9(06).
     05 FILLER                   PIC X(08).
     05 TYPE-INFORMATION-IN      PIC X(21).
     05 FILLER                   PIC X(44).
     05 RECORD-TYPE-IN           PIC 9(01).

 FD  ACTIVITY-REPORT-FILE LABEL RECORDS ARE OMITTED.
 01  REPORT-RECORD              PIC X(133).
*---------------------------------------------------------------*
 WORKING-STORAGE SECTION.
*---------------------------------------------------------------*
 01  WORKING-VARIABLES.
     05  FILE-STATUS             PIC X(04) VALUE SPACES.
     05  LINE-COUNT-WS           PIC S9(02) VALUE 0.
     05  CUSTOMER-ACCOUNT-WS     PIC S9(06) VALUE 0.
     05  LAST-METER-READING-WS   PIC S9(05).
     05  WORKING-BALANCE-WS      PIC S9(04)V9(02).
     05  PAYMENTS-WS             PIC S9(04)V9(02).
     05  NUMBER-OF-PAYMENTS-WS   PIC S9(02).
     05  CURRENT-METER-READING-WS PIC S9(05).
     05  KWATTS-USED-WS          PIC S9(06).
     05  FINANCE-CHARGE-WS       PIC S9(03)V9(02).
     05  AMOUNT-OF-BILL-WS       PIC S9(04)V9(02).
     05  BALANCE-BEFORE-PAYMENT-WS PIC S9(09)V9(02) VALUE 0.
     05  BALANCE-AFTER-PAYMENT-WS PIC S9(09)V9(02) VALUE 0.
     05  TOTAL-AMOUNT-WS         PIC S9(06)V9(02).
     05  TOTAL-NUMBER-OF-CUSTOMERS-WS PIC S9(06) VALUE 0.
     05  TOTAL-KWATTS-WS         PIC S9(09) VALUE 0.
     05  TOTAL-PAYMENTS-WS       PIC S9(09)V9(02) VALUE 0.
     05  TOTAL-NUMBER-OF-PAYMENTS-WS PIC S9(06) VALUE 0.
     05  TOTAL-AMOUNT-OF-BILL-WS PIC S9(09)V9(02) VALUE 0.
     05  TOTAL-FINANCE-CHARGE-WS PIC S9(09)V9(02) VALUE 0.
     05  TOTAL-AMOUNT-DUE-WS     PIC S9(09)V9(02) VALUE 0.
     05  HISTORY-INFORMATION-IN.
         10 LAST-METER-READING-IN PIC 9(05).
```

Figure 10.7 *Continued* Electric Utility Program

```
            1   1   2   2   2   3   3   4   4   4   5   5   6   6   6   7
   4   8    2   6   0   4   8   2   6   0   4   8   2   6   0   4   8   2

                10 FILLER             PIC X(10).
                10 PREVIOUS-BALANCE-IN PIC 9(04)V9(02).
            05  PAYMENT-INFORMATION-IN.
                10 FILLER             PIC X(15).
                10 PAYMENT-IN         PIC 9(04)V9(02).
            05  CURRENT-INFORMATION-IN.
                10 CURRENT-METER-READING-IN PIC 9(05).
            05  DATE-RECORD-IN.
                10 REPORT-YEAR-IN     PIC 9(02).
                10 REPORT-MONTH-IN    PIC 9(02).
                10 REPORT-DAY-IN      PIC 9(02).

        01  HEADING-1.
            05 FILLER                 PIC X(38) VALUE SPACES.
            05 HEAD-1                 PIC X(30) VALUE
                                      'Electric Power Utility Company'.

        01  HEADING-2.
            05 FILLER                 PIC X(37) VALUE SPACES.
            05 FILLER                 PIC X(32) VALUE
                                     'Customer Account Activity Report'.
            05 FILLER                 PIC X(30) VALUE SPACES.
            05 FILLER                 PIC X(05) VALUE 'Page'.
            05 PAGE-NUMBER-TOP        PIC 9(02).

        01  HEADING-3.
            05 FILLER                 PIC X(38) VALUE SPACES.
            05 FILLER                 PIC X(21) VALUE
                                      'For the Month Ending'.
            05 REPORT-DAY-OUT         PIC 9(02).
            05 FILLER                 PIC X(01) VALUE '/'.
            05 REPORT-MONTH-OUT       PIC 9(02).
            05 FILLER                 PIC X(01) VALUE '/'.
            05 REPORT-YEAR-OUT        PIC 9(02).

        01  LINE-ACROSS.
            05 FILLER                 PIC X(01) VALUE SPACES.
            05 FILLER                 PIC X(105) VALUE ALL '-'.

        01  HEADING-4.
            05 FILLER                 PIC X(132) VALUE
            ' ¦Customer¦    Meter Reading   ¦Kilowatt¦ Previous¦    Paym
      -     'ents    ¦Balance ¦ Base  ¦Finance¦   Total    ¦'.

        01  HEADING-5.
            05 FILLER                 PIC X(132) VALUE
            ' ¦ Account¦---------------------¦ Hours  ¦ Balance ¦--------
      -     '--------¦  After ¦ Bill  ¦Charges¦  Amount    ¦'.

        01  HEADING-6.
            05 FILLER                 PIC X(132) VALUE
            ' ¦ Number ¦Last Month¦This Month¦  Used  ¦         ¦  Amount
      -     ' ¦Number¦Payments¦       ¦        ¦    Due     ¦'.

        01  FOOTING-1.
            05 FILLER                 PIC X(30) VALUE
                                      ' Customer Numbers on this Page'.

        01  FOOTING-2.
            05 FILLER                 PIC X(07) VALUE SPACES.
            05 1ST-NUMBER-OUT         PIC 9(06).
            05 FILLER                 PIC X(04) VALUE ' to'.
            05 LAST-NUMBER-OUT        PIC 9(06).
            05 FILLER                 PIC X(76) VALUE SPACES.
            05 FILLER                 PIC X(05) VALUE 'Page'.
            05 PAGE-NUMBER-BOTTOM     PIC 9(02).

        01  DETAIL-RECORD.
            05 FILLER                 PIC X(03) VALUE SPACES.
```

Figure 10.7 *Continued* Electric Utility Program

```
            1   1   2   2   2   3   3   4   4   4   5   5   6   6   6   7
    4   8   2   6   0   4   8   2   6   0   4   8   2   6   0   4   8   2

           05 CUSTOMER-ACCOUNT-OUT        PIC 9(06).
           05 FILLER                      PIC X(06) VALUE SPACES.
           05 LAST-METER-READING-OUT      PIC ZZZZ9.
           05 FILLER                      PIC X(06) VALUE SPACES.
           05 CURRENT-METER-READING-OUT PIC ZZZZ9.
           05 FILLER                      PIC X(03) VALUE SPACES.
           05 KWATTS-USED-OUT             PIC ZZZZZ9.
           05 FILLER                      PIC X(02) VALUE SPACES.
           05 PREVIOUS-BALANCE-OUT        PIC $$,$$$.99.
           05 FILLER                      PIC X(01) VALUE SPACES.
           05 PAYMENT-AMOUNT-OUT          PIC $$,$$$.99.
           05 FILLER                      PIC X(03) VALUE SPACES.
           05 NUMBER-OF-PAYMENTS-OUT      PIC Z9.
           05 FILLER                      PIC X(03) VALUE SPACES.
           05 BALANCE-AFTER-PAYMENTS-OUT PIC $$$$.99-.
           05 FILLER                      PIC X(01) VALUE SPACES.
           05 AMOUNT-OF-BILL-OUT          PIC $$$$.99.
           05 FILLER                      PIC X(02) VALUE SPACES.
           05 FINANCE-CHARGE-OUT          PIC $$$.99.
           05 FILLER                      PIC X(01) VALUE SPACES.
           05 AMOUNT-DUE-OUT              PIC $$,$$$.99CR.
           05 FILLER                      PIC X(01) VALUE SPACES.

       01  SUMMARY-LINE.
           05 FILLER                      PIC X(23) VALUE SPACES.
           05 FILLER                      PIC X(06) VALUE 'Total'.
           05 DETAIL-SUMMARY              PIC X(53).

       01  SUMMARY-LINE-1.
           05 FILLER                      PIC X(31) VALUE
                                          'Number of Customers Processed'.
           05 TOTAL-NUMBER-OF-CUSTOMERS-OUT PIC ZZZ,ZZ9.

       01  SUMMARY-LINE-2.
           05 FILLER                      PIC X(21) VALUE
                                          'Kilowatt Hours Used'.
           05 TOTAL-KWATTS-OUT            PIC ZZZ,ZZZ,ZZ9.

       01  SUMMARY-LINE-3.
           05 FILLER                      PIC X(38) VALUE
                               'Outstanding Balances before Payments'.
           05 BALANCE-BEFORE-PAYMENTS-OUT PIC $$$$,$$$,$$$.99.

       01  SUMMARY-LINE-4.
           05 FILLER                      PIC X(17) VALUE
                                          'of All Payments'.
           05 TOTAL-PAYMENTS-OUT          PIC $$$$,$$$,$$$.99.

       01  SUMMARY-LINE-5.
           05 FILLER                      PIC X(29) VALUE
                                          'Number of Payments Received'.
           05 TOTAL-NUMBER-OF-PAYMENTS-OUT PIC ZZZ,ZZ9.

       01  SUMMARY-LINE-6.
           05 FILLER                      PIC X(37) VALUE
                                'Outstanding Balances after Payments'.
           05 TOTAL-BAL-AFTER-PAYMENTS-OUT PIC $$$$,$$$,$$$.99.

       01  SUMMARY-LINE-7.
           05 FILLER                      PIC X(19) VALUE
                                          'of All Base Bills'.
           05 TOTAL-AMOUNT-OF-BILL-OUT PIC $$$$,$$$,$$$.99.

       01  SUMMARY-LINE-8.
           05 FILLER                      PIC X(17) VALUE
                                          'Finance Charges'.
           05 TOTAL-FINANCE-CHARGE-OUT PIC $$$$,$$$,$$$.99.

       01  SUMMARY-LINE-9.
```

Figure 10.7 *Continued* Electric Utility Program

```
            1   1   2   2   2   3   3   4   4   4   5   5   6   6   6   7
   4   8    2   6   0   4   8   2   6   0   4   8   2   6   0   4   8   2

           05 FILLER                    PIC X(27) VALUE
                                        'Amount of All Receivables'.
           05 TOTAL-AMOUNT-DUE-OUT      PIC $$$$,$$$,$$$.99.
      ***************************************************************
       PROCEDURE DIVISION.
      ***************************************************************
      *-------------------------------------------------------------*
       000-CONTROL-PROCEDURE SECTION.
      *-------------------------------------------------------------*
           PERFORM 100-INITIALIZATION.
           PERFORM 500-READ-DATA
               UNTIL FILE-STATUS = 'DONE'.
           PERFORM 800-SUMMARY-REPORT.
           PERFORM 900-TERMINATION.
           STOP RUN.
      *-------------------------------------------------------------*
       100-INITIALIZATION SECTION.
      *-------------------------------------------------------------*
           OPEN INPUT INFORMATION-FILE, OUTPUT ACTIVITY-REPORT-FILE.
           MOVE 0                          TO PAGE-NUMBER-TOP
                                              PAGE-NUMBER-BOTTOM.
           MOVE 99                         TO LINE-COUNT-WS.
           ACCEPT DATE-RECORD-IN FROM DATE.
           MOVE REPORT-DAY-IN              TO REPORT-DAY-OUT.
           MOVE REPORT-MONTH-IN            TO REPORT-MONTH-OUT.
           MOVE REPORT-YEAR-IN             TO REPORT-YEAR-OUT.
      *-------------------------------------------------------------*
       500-READ-DATA SECTION.
      *-------------------------------------------------------------*
       500-ENTRY.
           READ INFORMATION-FILE AT END
               MOVE 'DONE' TO FILE-STATUS
               MOVE CUSTOMER-ACCOUNT-WS TO LAST-NUMBER-OUT
               PERFORM 520-CALCULATIONS
               PERFORM 510-PAGE-BREAK
               GO TO 500-EXIT.
           IF LINE-COUNT-WS GREATER THAN 19
               PERFORM 510-PAGE-BREAK.
           IF CUSTOMER-ACCOUNT-WS NOT EQUAL TO CUSTOMER-NUMBER-IN
               PERFORM 520-CALCULATIONS.
           IF RECORD-TYPE-IN = 1
               PERFORM 530-RECORD-HISTORY.
           IF RECORD-TYPE-IN = 2
               PERFORM 540-RECORD-PAYMENT.
           IF RECORD-TYPE-IN = 3
               PERFORM 550-RECORD-NEW-READING.
           IF RECORD-TYPE-IN < 1 OR > 3
               DISPLAY 'ERROR IN CODE'.
       500-EXIT.
           EXIT.
      *-------------------------------------------------------------*
       510-PAGE-BREAK SECTION.
      *-------------------------------------------------------------*
           IF LINE-COUNT-WS NOT = 99
               PERFORM 516-PAGE-FOOTING.
           IF FILE-STATUS NOT = 'DONE'
               PERFORM 512-REPORT-HEADING
               PERFORM 514-COLUMN-HEADING.
           MOVE 0                          TO LINE-COUNT-WS.
           MOVE CUSTOMER-NUMBER-IN         TO 1ST-NUMBER-OUT
                                              CUSTOMER-ACCOUNT-WS.
      *-------------------------------------------------------------*
       512-REPORT-HEADING SECTION.
      *-------------------------------------------------------------*
           ADD 1 TO PAGE-NUMBER-TOP, PAGE-NUMBER-BOTTOM.
           WRITE REPORT-RECORD FROM HEADING-1 AFTER TOP-OF-PAGE.
           MOVE SPACES                     TO HEAD-1.
           WRITE REPORT-RECORD FROM HEADING-2 AFTER 2 LINES.
           WRITE REPORT-RECORD FROM HEADING-3 AFTER 1 LINES.
```

Figure 10.7 *Continued* Electric Utility Program

```
           WRITE REPORT-RECORD FROM LINE-ACROSS AFTER 3 LINES.
      *-----------------------------------------------------------------*
       514-COLUMN-HEADING SECTION.
      *-----------------------------------------------------------------*
           WRITE REPORT-RECORD FROM HEADING-4 AFTER 1 LINES.
           WRITE REPORT-RECORD FROM HEADING-5 AFTER 1 LINES.
           WRITE REPORT-RECORD FROM HEADING-6 AFTER 1 LINES.
           WRITE REPORT-RECORD FROM LINE-ACROSS AFTER 1 LINES.
      *-----------------------------------------------------------------*
       516-PAGE-FOOTING SECTION.
      *-----------------------------------------------------------------*
           WRITE REPORT-RECORD FROM LINE-ACROSS AFTER 1 LINES.
           MOVE SPACES              TO REPORT-RECORD.
           WRITE REPORT-RECORD AFTER 2 LINES.
           WRITE REPORT-RECORD FROM FOOTING-1 AFTER 2 LINES.
           WRITE REPORT-RECORD FROM FOOTING-2 AFTER 1 LINES.
      *-----------------------------------------------------------------*
       520-CALCULATIONS SECTION.
      *-----------------------------------------------------------------*
           SUBTRACT PAYMENTS-WS FROM WORKING-BALANCE-WS.
           MOVE WORKING-BALANCE-WS  TO BALANCE-AFTER-PAYMENTS-OUT.
           MOVE PAYMENTS-WS         TO PAYMENT-AMOUNT-OUT.
           MOVE NUMBER-OF-PAYMENTS-WS TO NUMBER-OF-PAYMENTS-OUT.
           IF WORKING-BALANCE-WS GREATER THAN 0
               COMPUTE FINANCE-CHARGE-WS ROUNDED =
                 WORKING-BALANCE-WS * .015.
           MOVE FINANCE-CHARGE-WS   TO FINANCE-CHARGE-OUT.
           SUBTRACT LAST-METER-READING-WS FROM CURRENT-METER-READING-WS
               GIVING KWATTS-USED-WS.
           IF KWATTS-USED-WS LESS THAN 0
               COMPUTE KWATTS-USED-WS =
                 CURRENT-METER-READING-WS + 100000 -
                 LAST-METER-READING-WS.
           MOVE KWATTS-USED-WS      TO KWATTS-USED-OUT.
           IF KWATTS-USED-WS EQUAL TO 0
                 MOVE 0             TO AMOUNT-OF-BILL-WS.
           IF KWATTS-USED-WS > 0 AND < 10
                 MOVE 2.50          TO AMOUNT-OF-BILL-WS.
           IF KWATTS-USED-WS NOT < 10 AND < 5001
               MULTIPLY KWATTS-USED-WS BY .0255
                 GIVING AMOUNT-OF-BILL-WS ROUNDED.
           IF KWATTS-USED-WS > 5000
               MULTIPLY KWATTS-USED-WS BY .0323
                 GIVING AMOUNT-OF-BILL-WS ROUNDED.
           MOVE AMOUNT-OF-BILL-WS   TO AMOUNT-OF-BILL-OUT.
           ADD AMOUNT-OF-BILL-WS, WORKING-BALANCE-WS, FINANCE-CHARGE-WS
             GIVING TOTAL-AMOUNT-WS.
           MOVE TOTAL-AMOUNT-WS     TO AMOUNT-DUE-OUT.
           ADD 1 TO TOTAL-NUMBER-OF-CUSTOMERS-WS.
           ADD KWATTS-USED-WS TO TOTAL-KWATTS-WS.
           ADD WORKING-BALANCE-WS TO BALANCE-AFTER-PAYMENT-WS.
           ADD PAYMENTS-WS TO TOTAL-PAYMENTS-WS.
           ADD NUMBER-OF-PAYMENTS-WS TO TOTAL-NUMBER-OF-PAYMENTS-WS.
           ADD AMOUNT-OF-BILL-WS TO TOTAL-AMOUNT-OF-BILL-WS.
           ADD FINANCE-CHARGE-WS TO TOTAL-FINANCE-CHARGE-WS.
           ADD TOTAL-AMOUNT-WS TO TOTAL-AMOUNT-DUE-WS.
           WRITE REPORT-RECORD FROM DETAIL-RECORD AFTER 2 LINES.
           ADD 1 TO LINE-COUNT-WS.
      *-----------------------------------------------------------------*
       530-RECORD-HISTORY SECTION.
      *-----------------------------------------------------------------*
           MOVE TYPE-INFORMATION-IN TO HISTORY-INFORMATION-IN.
           MOVE CUSTOMER-NUMBER-IN  TO CUSTOMER-ACCOUNT-OUT
                                       CUSTOMER-ACCOUNT-WS.
           IF LINE-COUNT-WS = 19
               MOVE CUSTOMER-NUMBER-IN TO LAST-NUMBER-OUT.
           MOVE LAST-METER-READING-IN TO LAST-METER-READING-OUT
                                         LAST-METER-READING-WS
                                         CURRENT-METER-READING-OUT
```

Figure 10.7 *Continued* Electric Utility Program

```
            1   1   2   2   2   3   3   4   4   4   5   5   6   6   6   7
   4   8    2   6   0   4   8   2   6   0   4   8   2   6   0   4   8   2

                                          CURRENT-METER-READING-WS.
           MOVE PREVIOUS-BALANCE-IN TO PREVIOUS-BALANCE-OUT
                                       WORKING-BALANCE-WS.
           MOVE 0                   TO PAYMENTS-WS
                                       NUMBER-OF-PAYMENTS-WS
                                       FINANCE-CHARGE-WS
                                       KWATTS-USED-WS.
           ADD PREVIOUS-BALANCE-IN TO BALANCE-BEFORE-PAYMENT-WS.
      *---------------------------------------------------------------*
       540-RECORD-PAYMENT SECTION.
      *---------------------------------------------------------------*
           MOVE TYPE-INFORMATION-IN TO PAYMENT-INFORMATION-IN.
           ADD PAYMENT-IN TO PAYMENTS-WS.
           ADD 1 TO NUMBER-OF-PAYMENTS-WS.
      *---------------------------------------------------------------*
       550-RECORD-NEW-READING SECTION.
      *---------------------------------------------------------------*
           MOVE TYPE-INFORMATION-IN TO CURRENT-INFORMATION-IN.
           MOVE CURRENT-METER-READING-IN TO CURRENT-METER-READING-OUT
                                            CURRENT-METER-READING-WS.
      *---------------------------------------------------------------*
       800-SUMMARY-REPORT SECTION.
      *---------------------------------------------------------------*
           MOVE '          S U M M A R Y' TO HEAD-1.
           PERFORM 512-REPORT-HEADING.
           MOVE TOTAL-NUMBER-OF-CUSTOMERS-WS
             TO TOTAL-NUMBER-OF-CUSTOMERS-OUT.
           MOVE SUMMARY-LINE-1       TO DETAIL-SUMMARY.
           WRITE REPORT-RECORD FROM SUMMARY-LINE AFTER 2 LINES.
           MOVE TOTAL-KWATTS-WS      TO TOTAL-KWATTS-OUT.
           MOVE SUMMARY-LINE-2       TO DETAIL-SUMMARY.
           WRITE REPORT-RECORD FROM SUMMARY-LINE AFTER 2 LINES.
           MOVE BALANCE-BEFORE-PAYMENT-WS
             TO BALANCE-BEFORE-PAYMENTS-OUT.
           MOVE SUMMARY-LINE-3       TO DETAIL-SUMMARY.
           WRITE REPORT-RECORD FROM SUMMARY-LINE AFTER 2 LINES.
           MOVE TOTAL-PAYMENTS-WS    TO TOTAL-PAYMENTS-OUT.
           MOVE SUMMARY-LINE-4       TO DETAIL-SUMMARY.
           WRITE REPORT-RECORD FROM SUMMARY-LINE AFTER 2 LINES.
           MOVE TOTAL-NUMBER-OF-PAYMENTS-WS
             TO TOTAL-NUMBER-OF-PAYMENTS-OUT.
           MOVE SUMMARY-LINE-5       TO DETAIL-SUMMARY.
           WRITE REPORT-RECORD FROM SUMMARY-LINE AFTER 2 LINES.
           MOVE BALANCE-AFTER-PAYMENT-WS
                                     TO TOTAL-BAL-AFTER-PAYMENTS-OUT.
           MOVE SUMMARY-LINE-6       TO DETAIL-SUMMARY.
           WRITE REPORT-RECORD FROM SUMMARY-LINE AFTER 2 LINES.
           MOVE TOTAL-AMOUNT-OF-BILL-WS TO TOTAL-AMOUNT-OF-BILL-OUT.
           MOVE SUMMARY-LINE-7       TO DETAIL-SUMMARY.
           WRITE REPORT-RECORD FROM SUMMARY-LINE AFTER 2 LINES.
           MOVE TOTAL-FINANCE-CHARGE-WS TO TOTAL-FINANCE-CHARGE-OUT.
           MOVE SUMMARY-LINE-8       TO DETAIL-SUMMARY.
           WRITE REPORT-RECORD FROM SUMMARY-LINE AFTER 2 LINES.
           MOVE TOTAL-AMOUNT-DUE-WS TO TOTAL-AMOUNT-DUE-OUT.
           MOVE SUMMARY-LINE-9       TO DETAIL-SUMMARY.
           WRITE REPORT-RECORD FROM SUMMARY-LINE AFTER 2 LINES.
           WRITE REPORT-RECORD FROM LINE-ACROSS AFTER 2 LINES.
      *---------------------------------------------------------------*
       900-TERMINATION SECTION.
      *---------------------------------------------------------------*
           CLOSE INFORMATION-FILE
                 ACTIVITY-REPORT-FILE.
```

Figure 10.7 *Continued* Electric Utility Program (Data)

```
------------------------------------------------------------------------------------------
|      |         1         2         3         4         5         6         7         8|
|Record|12345678901234567890123456789012345678901234567890123456789012345678901234567890|
|----------------------------------------------------------------------------------------|
|     1|010185                                                                          |
|     2|110421        00598          043200                                            1|
|     3|110421                       040000                                            2|
|     4|110421        04325                                                            3|
|     5|111111        22222          123456                                            1|
|     6|111111                       123456                                            2|
|     7|111111        33333                                                            3|
|     8|114612        96182          003568                                            1|
|     9|114612                       003568                                            2|
|    10|114612        00013                                                            3|
|    11|118921        61984          005595                                            1|
|    12|118921        66418                                                            3|
|    13|121212        11111          001500                                            1|
|    14|121212                       001500                                            2|
|    15|121212        13425                                                            3|
|    16|176257        23925          007655                                            1|
|    17|176257                       076550                                            2|
|    18|176257        39876                                                            3|
|    19|185792        34128          012367                                            1|
|    20|185792                       012367                                            2|
|    21|185792        34134                                                            3|
|    22|185794        06195          147620                                            1|
|    23|185794                       147620                                            2|
|    24|185794                       014762                                            2|
|    25|185794        09195                                                            3|
|    26|195798        61622          014822                                            1|
|    27|195798                       014820                                            2|
|    28|195798        65984                                                            3|
|    29|199428        49462          004527                                            1|
|    30|234567        99827          012525                                            1|
|    31|234567                       012000                                            2|
|    32|235698        33982          014570                                            1|
|    33|235698        63419                                                            3|
|    34|237422        65922          205476                                            1|
|    35|237422                       200000                                            2|
|    36|237422        73155                                                            3|
|    37|241185        00002          026500                                            1|
|    38|241185                       025400                                            2|
|    39|241185                       001100                                            2|
|    40|241185        01496                                                            3|
|    41|244488        75320          054378                                            1|
|    42|244488                       030000                                            2|
|    43|244488                       005000                                            2|
|    44|244488        78793                                                            3|
|    45|245395        56218          052950                                            1|
|    46|245395                       030000                                            2|
|    47|245395        57315                                                            3|
|    48|251922        42417          000000                                            1|
|    49|252263        61538          057218                                            1|
|    50|252263                       057218                                            2|
------------------------------------------------------------------------------------------
```

Figure 10.7 *Continued* Electric Utility Program (Data)

```
-----------------------------------------------------------------------------------------
|      |         1         2         3         4         5         6         7         8|
|Record|12345678901234567890123456789012345678901234567890123456789012345678901234567890|
|--------------------------------------------------------------------------------------|
|    51|263477        04198          000650                                            1|
|    52|263477        07623                                                            3|
|    53|293647        98690          019250                                            1|
|    54|293647                       019250                                            2|
|    55|293647        00422                                                            3|
|    56|321619        70041          052150                                            1|
|    57|321619                       060000                                            2|
|    58|321619        76015                                                            3|
|    59|377619        19576          000000                                            1|
|    60|377619        20461                                                            3|
|    61|378906        98900          200000                                            1|
|    62|378906                       140000                                            2|
|    63|378906                       002000                                            2|
|    64|378906                       003000                                            2|
|    65|378906                       055000                                            2|
|    66|378906        01234                                                            3|
|    67|422442        45370          008915                                            1|
|    68|422442                       004000                                            2|
|    69|422442        47429                                                            3|
|    70|588883        00039          016000                                            1|
|    71|588883                       061000                                            2|
|    72|675782        07215          072575                                            1|
-----------------------------------------------------------------------------------------
```

have produced only a single page heading (on the first page only). Thus, if the output exceeded one page in length, no new heading would have been generated. In the electric utility program, it is anticipated that the printout will exceed one page. Placing a page heading in the INITIALIZATION-PROCEDURE would amount to a *special case.* All page headings, including the first one, are produced in the "body" procedure called READ-DATA. An additional discussion of multiple page headings follows shortly.

This particular program was selected for inclusion in the text because it *is* more complicated. The more complicated the program is, the more likely it is that you will attempt to incorporate a *second level of control* into the program. READ-DATA supplies this second level of control in the electric utility company procedure. Previously, a procedure in this position had contained a large portion of the operations executed by the program. In this case, however, if you tried to place all activities associated with updating the customer records and producing the report in one paragraph, the READ-DATA procedure would become (or at least appear to become) very complicated. Figure 10.7 illustrates that READ-DATA is, more or less, a control procedure. That is, READ-DATA controls other procedures that are subordinate to it. This has the effect of making READ-DATA easier to read and understand. Furthermore, by dividing the additional requirements of the program into individual modules, each of the remaining modules becomes more functionally oriented, and thereby easier to understand.

For some people it is difficult to make a transition to more complex problems when all the examples are simple. Although this program is longer and more complicated than those previously considered, you are encouraged to examine it in some detail. It comes much closer to representing the level of complexity required by programs used in industry than many of the others.

Figure 10.7 *Continued* Electric Utility Program (Output)

Electric Power Utility Company

Customer Account Activity Report
For the Month Ending 01/01/89

Page 01

Customer Account Number	Meter Reading Last Month	Meter Reading This Month	Kilowatt Hours Used	Previous Balance	Payments Amount	Payments Number	Balance After Payments	Base Bill	Finance Charges	Total Amount Due
110421	598	4325	3727	$432.00	$400.00	1	$32.00	$95.04	$.48	$127.52
111111	22222	33333	11111	$1,234.56	$1,234.56	1	$.00	$358.89	$.00	$358.89
114612	96182	13	3831	$35.68	$35.68	1	$.00	$97.69	$.00	$97.69
118921	61984	66418	4434	$55.95	$.00	0	$55.95	$113.07	$.84	$169.86
121212	11111	13425	2314	$15.00	$15.00	1	$.00	$59.01	$.00	$59.01
176257	23925	39876	15951	$76.55	$765.50	1	$688.95-	$515.22	$.00	$173.73CR
185792	34128	34134	6	$123.67	$123.67	1	$.00	$2.50	$.00	$2.50
185794	6195	9195	3000	$1,476.20	$1,623.82	2	$147.62-	$76.50	$.00	$71.12CR
195798	61622	65984	4362	$148.22	$148.20	1	$.02	$111.23	$.00	$111.25
199428	49462	49462	0	$45.27	$.00	0	$45.27	$.00	$.68	$45.95
234567	99827	99827	0	$125.25	$120.00	1	$5.25	$.00	$.08	$5.33
235698	33982	63419	29437	$145.70	$.00	0	$145.70	$950.82	$2.19	$1,098.71
237422	65922	73155	7233	$2,054.76	$2,000.00	1	$54.76	$233.63	$.82	$289.21
241185	2	1496	1494	$265.00	$265.00	2	$.00	$38.10	$.00	$38.10
244488	75320	78793	3473	$543.78	$350.00	2	$193.78	$88.56	$2.91	$285.25
245395	56218	57315	1097	$529.50	$300.00	1	$229.50	$27.97	$3.44	$260.91
251922	42417	42417	0	$.00	$.00	0	$.00	$.00	$.00	$.00
252263	61538	61538	0	$572.18	$572.18	1	$.00	$.00	$.00	$.00
263477	4198	7623	3425	$6.50	$.00	0	$6.50	$87.34	$.10	$93.94
293647	98690	422	1732	$192.50	$192.50	1	$.00	$44.17	$.00	$44.17

Customer Numbers on this Page
110421 to 293647

Page 01

Figure 10.7 *Continued* Electric Utility Program (Output)

Customer Account Activity Report
For the Month Ending 01/01/89

Page 02

Customer Account Number	Meter Reading Last Month	Meter Reading This Month	Kilowatt Hours Used	Previous Balance	Payments Amount	Payments Number	Balance After Payments	Base Bill	Finance Charges	Total Amount Due
321619	70041	76015	5974	$521.50	$600.00	1	$78.50-	$192.96	$.00	$114.46
377619	19576	20461	885	$.00	$.00	0	$.00	$22.57	$.00	$22.57
378906	98900	1234	2334	$2,000.00	$2,000.00	4	$.00	$59.52	$.00	$59.52
422442	45370	47429	2059	$89.15	$40.00	1	$49.15	$52.50	$.74	$102.39
588883	39	39	0	$160.00	$610.00	1	$450.00-	$.00	$.00	$450.00CR
675782	7215	7215	0	$725.75	$.00	0	$725.75	$.00	$10.89	$736.64

Customer Numbers on this Page
321619 to 675782

Page 02

Figure 10.7 *Continued* Electric Utility Program (Output)

```
                              S U M M A R Y

                     Customer Account Activity Report                        Page 03
                      For the Month Ending 01/01/89

----------------------------------------------------------------------------------------

          Total Number of Customers Processed         26

          Total Kilowatt Hours Used        107,879

          Total Outstanding Balances before Payments          $11,574.67

          Total of All Payments          $11,396.11

          Total Number of Payments Received          25

          Total Outstanding Balances after Payments            $178.56

          Total of All Base Bills          $3,227.29

          Total Finance Charges          $23.17

          Total Amount of All Receivables          $3,429.02

----------------------------------------------------------------------------------------
```

The Page Break

A relatively common programming concept is demonstrated in Figure 10.7—the page break. The page break is actually a specialized control break. (The control break was described in Chapter 9.) Unfortunately, few list-oriented print reports will fit neatly on one page. It is often desirable (if not necessary) to reproduce the heading at the top of *every* printed page. As a consequence, we need to know when a page is full. Such a mechanism is shown in lines 2440 and 2450. In the example, if 20 or more lines have been printed on a page (LINE-COUNT-WS IS GREATER THAN 19), a new page heading is to be printed (510-PAGE-BREAK is PERFORMed). The program keeps track of the lines printed with line 3340, which increments LINE-COUNT-WS by one each time the WRITE statement at 3330 is executed. When a page break occurs, this accumulator is reset to zero (or some minimal value) at line 2660.

Control breaks and page breaks are similar in nature—both require initial values to be set (line 480), and both check the content of at least one storage position. The difference is that the control break seeks any change in value, but the page break looks for a particular value. The control break variable changes each time a new value is available (in this example, from an input operation) and the page break variable (LINE-COUNT-WS) is typically controlled internally (e.g., by incrementing the variable each time a new line is printed).

Summary

This chapter has presented the arithmetic data-manipulation statements of COBOL. Numeric data may be manipulated in COBOL through the use of the ADD, SUBTRACT, MULTIPLY, DIVIDE, and COMPUTE statements. Generally, the ADD statement is capable of generating the algebraic sum of a series of identifiers and literals. The SUBTRACT statement calculates the algebraic sum of a series of data items that is deducted from another data value to achieve the result. The MULTIPLY statement is capable of producing the product of two data values. The DIVIDE statement generates the result of dividing one data value into (or by) another. Finally, the COMPUTE statement, through the creation of an arithmetic expression, may perform addition, subtraction, multiplication, division, and exponentiation (and combinations thereof).

Only numeric data, represented by identifiers or numeric literals, may be manipulated by these statement types. Furthermore, unless an identifier serves only as a receiving field for the calculation, all data items must be described as nonedited-numeric elementary-items. In addition, each of these identifiers must contain a data value prior to being used in an arithmetic operation.

1985 COBOL Standards

Three options are available with the arithmetic statement—ROUNDED, SIZE ERROR, and NOT SIZE ERROR. The ROUNDED option allows the result of a calculation to be rounded to the size of the PICTURE clause of the receiving field, thus avoiding low-order digit truncation. The SIZE ERROR option gives the programmer the means to perform special processing in the event that overflow of a receiving field occurs. In COBOL 85 the NOT SIZE ERROR gives the means to perform special processing in the event of no overflow occurring in the receiving field.

Notes on Programming Style

It is obvious that all computational capabilities of the ADD, SUBTRACT, MULTIPLY, and DIVIDE statements are present in the COMPUTE statement. Simple forms of the statements can also be expressed in the GIVING form of the same statement. For example, the statement

```
ADD 1 TO C
```

can be rewritten as

```
ADD 1, C GIVING C.
```

or

```
COMPUTE C = C + 1.
```

However, let me urge you to use the statements as they were intended to be used. When other arithmetic statements are used to replace the simple ADD statement, the code typically becomes less clear. If a computation is complex; that is, cannot be performed with a single ADD, SUBTRACT, MULTIPLY, or DIVIDE statement or a limited number of these statements in combination, the COMPUTE statement is a superior choice for the calculation from the standpoint of computer execution time. However, compared to the other arithmetic statements, COMPUTE statements generally require more time during compilation—since the COMPUTE statement could contain a number of different operations. The reason the COMPUTE statement generally solves complex problems faster than the corresponding ADD, SUBTRACT, MULTIPLY, and DIVIDE statements is that intermediate results are stored in the computer's storage (registers) and not placed directly into a programmer-supplied-name until the final result is achieved. This could eliminate a number of movements from (and to) ''working registers'' to (and from) programmer-accessible storage areas.

Finally, extreme care should be exercised when dealing with numeric data. It is more likely than not that your first execution-type error will be caused by numeric data that do not correspond to their PICTURE description. Suppose, for example, a particular data item is represented by the PICTURE clause 99V9. If any of the following values were placed (moved or read) into the data item, it would result in an error.

```
X42
7.3
45
```

The first value contains the letter "X"—not a numeric value (or character). The second value contains a decimal point—not a numeric value. The third value contains a blank—not a numeric value. Internal numeric variables (e.g., counters, accumulators, indicators, etc.) should always be initialized, either directly in the DATA DIVISION with a VALUE clause or in the initializing processes in the PROCEDURE DIVISION. Use *edited* fields in output (printer) record descriptions only. Their use in other locations invariably tends to cause problems for programmers.

Questions

Below fill in the blank(s) with the appropriate word, words, or phrases.

1. The COBOL verbs associated with arithmetic operations are _____ , _____ , _____ , _____ and _____ .
2. Only the _____ statement permits multiple types of arithmetic operations in one statement.
3. The _____ statement may be used to generate the sum of two numeric items.
4. The PICTURE description of all identifiers in the simple ADD statement must be _____ .
5. In the simple ADD statement, data values may be indicated before the reserved word TO by either _____ or _____ .
6. The optional phrases that may be associated with the simple ADD statement are _____ and _____ .
7. If the programmer wishes to identify situations in which receiving field overflow occurs, the _____ option should be used in arithmetic operations.
8. If the programmer wishes to identify situations in which division by zero has been attempted, the _____ option should be used.
9. In the simple ADD statement _____ (number) identifier(s) or literal(s) is/are required before the reserved word TO, whereas _____ (number) identifier(s) or literal(s), is/are required before the reserved word GIVING in the ADD-GIVING form of the statement.
10. The identifier following the reversed word GIVING in the ADD-GIVING statement may be a(n) _____ numeric field.
11. In the simple SUBTRACT statement, one or more _____ must follow the reserved word FROM.
12. The _____ statement causes the creation of the product of two data values.
13. A literal may appear after the reserved word BY only in the _____ form of the MULTIPLY statement.
14. The product of _____ (number) values is created by the MULTIPLY statement.
15. The SIZE ERROR option may be invoked in a DIVIDE statement when receiving field overflow occurs or when _____ is attempted.
16. When the REMAINDER option is provided in a DIVIDE statement, it is possible to perform _____ division.
17. When the reserved word BY appears in the DIVIDE-GIVING statement, identifier-1 is the _____ (divisor/dividend).

18. The only required punctuation in a COMPUTE statement (other than a period) is a(n) ____ .

19. An arithmetic expression in a COMPUTE statement may be composed of ____ , ____ , ____ , and ____ .

Answer the following questions by circling either "T" for True or "F" for False.

T F 20. COBOL is the most advanced programming language for performing computation.

T F 21. In the simple ADD statement, one or more identifiers may be added to another identifier.

T F 22. Only the identifier after the reserved word TO in the simple ADD statement is modified by the addition operation.

T F 23. It is possible to add to more than one identifier with the simple ADD statement.

T F 24. The identifier after the reserved word TO in a simple ADD statement does not necessarily have to contain a value prior to the addition operation.

T F 25. In the simple ADD statement it is permitted to record a literal after the reserved word TO.

T F 26. The ROUNDED option of the simple ADD statement causes rounding of the addition of the operation to an integer value.

T F 27. With the ADD statement it is possible to have receiving field overflow (high-order digit truncation) and underflow (low-order digit truncation).

T F 28. When a ROUNDED option is used in conjunction with an ADD statement, receiving field overflow will never occur.

T F 29. The reserved word TO appears in all forms of the ADD statement.

T F 30. Only one receiving field is permitted after the reserved word GIVING in the ADD-GIVING statement.

T F 31. All identifiers in the ADD-GIVING statement must contain a value.

T F 32. If an identifier in an ADD statement contained a negative value, the algebraic equivalent of subtraction could be achieved by the ADD statement.

T F 33. All identifiers in the simple SUBTRACT statement must be nonedited-numeric data items and contain a value.

T F 34. Both formats of the SUBTRACT statement require the reserved word FROM.

T F 35. In both formats of the SUBTRACT statement, the identifier following the reserved word FROM is modified by the subtraction operation.

T F 36. In both formats of the SUBTRACT statement, multiple identifiers could appear after the reserved word FROM.

T F 37. All identifiers used as receiving fields in both forms of the SUBTRACT statement must contain the operational-sign character(s) in their PICTURE string.

T F 38. Only two identifiers are permitted in the simple MULTIPLY, and both must be described as nonedited-numeric fields.

T F 39. The reserved word BY appears in both forms of the MULTIPLY statement.

T F 40. Multiple receiving fields are permitted in the simple form of the MULTIPLE statement.

T F 41. The reserved word BY is permitted in both forms of the DIVIDE statement.

T F 42. In the DIVIDE statement, the selection of the reserved words BY and INTO have no effect on the division operation of the DIVIDE-GIVING statement.

T F 43. The receiving field in the COMPUTE statement is the first identifier appearing in the statement.

T F **44.** Multiple receiving fields are permitted in a COMPUTE statement.
T F **45.** The receiving field of a COMPUTE statement may be an edited field.
T F **46.** There is no arithmetic operation that can be performed by the ADD, SUBTRACT, MULTIPLY, and DIVIDE statements that cannot also be performed by a COMPUTE statement.
T F **47.** In a COMPUTE statement, multiplication normally takes place before addition.
T F **48.** It is possible to have "nested" parentheses in a COMPUTE statement.

Exercises

1. Below is a series of ADD statements. Given the data-names, PICTURE clauses, and VALUE clauses indicated, determine the result of the execution of each ADD statement. (Consider each statement independently.)

```
01 FIELD-RECORD.
05 FIELD-1          PIC 99            VALUE 27.
05 FIELD-2          PIC 99            VALUE 62.
05 FIELD-3          PIC 999V99        VALUE 247.62.
05 FIELD-4          PIC 9(4)V99.
05 FIELD-5          PIC $$$$.$$.
```

a. ADD FIELD-1 TO FIELD-2.
b. ADD FIELD-1, FIELD-3 TO FIELD-2.
c. ADD FIELD-1, FIELD-3 GIVING FIELD-4.
d. ADD FIELD-1, FIELD-2, 40.5 GIVING FIELD-3.
e. ADD FIELD-1, 107.698, GIVING FIELD-4 ROUNDED.
f. ADD 10 TO FIELD-2.
g. ADD -40, FIELD-1 TO FIELD-2.
h. ADD -40, FIELD-1 GIVING FIELD-2 ROUNDED.
i. ADD -200, FIELD-3 GIVING FIELD-1 ROUNDED.
j. ADD 700, FIELD-1, FIELD-2 TO FIELD-3 ROUNDED
  ON SIZE ERROR
  MOVE 0 TO FIELD-3

2. Below is a series of SUBTRACT statements. Given the data-names, PICTURE clauses, and VALUE clauses indicated, determine the result of the execution of each SUBTRACT statement. (Consider each statement independently).

```
01 ITEM-RECORD.
05 ITEM-1           PIC 99            VALUE 75.
05 ITEM-2           PIC S999          VALUE -982.
05 ITEM-3           PIC S999V99       VALUE 44.73.
05 ITEM-4           PIC 9(4)          VALUE 64.
05 ITEM-5           PIC Z(4).99.
```

a. SUBTRACT 15 FROM ITEM-1.
b. SUBTRACT 25 FROM ITEM-2, ITEM-3.

c. SUBTRACT ITEM-2 FROM ITEM-4.
d. SUBTRACT ITEM-1, ITEM-4 FROM ITEM-3.
e. SUBTRACT ITEM-3, 40 FROM ITEM-1.
f. SUBTRACT ITEM-1 FROM ITEM-2 GIVING ITEM-3.
g. SUBTRACT ITEM-2 FROM ITEM-1 GIVING ITEM-4.
h. SUBTRACT ITEM-3 FROM ITEM-4 ROUNDED.
i. SUBTRACT ITEM-3 FROM ITEM-4 GIVING ITEM-5.
j. SUBTRACT ITEM-3 FROM ITEM-1 GIVING ITEM-2
   ON SIZE ERROR
   SUBTRACT ITEM-1 FROM ITEM-3 GIVING ITEM-2.

3. Below is a series of MULTIPLY statements. Given the data-names, PICTURE clauses, and VALUE clauses indicated, determine the result of the execution of each MULTIPLY statement. (Consider each statement independently.)

```
01 NUM-RECORD.
05 NUM-1          PIC 99              VALUE 10.
05 NUM-2          PIC S999            VALUE -25.
05 NUM-3          PIC 9(4)            VALUE 150.
05 NUM-4          PIC 99V99           VALUE 1.11.
05 NUM-5          PIC $$,$$$.$$
```

a. MULTIPLY 10 BY NUM-3.
b. MULTIPLY -1 BY NUM-2.
c. MULTIPLY NUM-1 BY NUM-4.
d. MULTIPLY NUM-3 BY NUM-1.
e. MULTIPLY -5 BY NUM-2.
f. MULTIPLY NUM-3 BY 10 GIVING NUM-5.
g. MULTIPLY NUM-2 BY NUM-4 GIVING NUM-3.
h. MULTIPLY .9 BY NUM-4 GIVING NUM-2 ROUNDED.
i. MULTIPLY NUM-2 BY NUM-4 GIVING NUM-5.
j. MULTIPLY NUM-1 BY NUM-2 GIVING NUM-3
   ON SIZE ERROR MOVE 0 to NUM-3.

4. Below is a series of DIVIDE statements. Given the data-names, PICTURE clauses, and VALUE clauses indicated, determine the result of the execution of each DIVIDE statement. (Consider each statement independently.)

```
01 DATA-RECORD.
05 DATA-1         PIC 999             VALUE 20
05 DATA-2         PIC S99V99          VALUE 9.25.
05 DATA-3         PIC 9(3)V99         VALUE 0
05 DATA-4         PIC V999            VALUE .01.
05 DATA-5         PIC +(4).++.
```

a. DIVIDE 10 INTO DATA-1.
b. DIVIDE .1 INTO DATA-1.
c. DIVIDE DATA-2 INTO DATA-1.
d. DIVIDE DATA-4 INTO DATA-4.
e. DIVIDE DATA-1 INTO DATA-2 ROUNDED.

f. DIVIDE DATA-4 BY DATA-2 GIVING DATA-3.
g. DIVIDE DATA-3 INTO DATA-2 GIVING DATA-3.
    ON SIZE ERROR MOVE 1 TO DATA-3
    DIVIDE DATA-3 INTO DATA-2 GIVING DATA-3.
h. DIVIDE DATA-2 BY .01 GIVING DATA-4 ROUNDED.
i. DIVIDE DATA-2 BY .1 GIVING DATA-1.
j. DIVIDE DATA-2 BY DATA-1 GIVING DATA-3.

5. Below is a series of COMPUTE statements. Given the data-names, PICTURE clauses, and VALUE clauses indicated, determine the result of the execution of each COMPUTE statement. (Consider each statement independently.)

```
01 VAL-RECORD.
   05 VAL-1          PIC 9(3)           VALUE 125.
   05 VAL-2          PIC 99V99          VALUE 5.
   05 VAL-3          PIC S9(4)V99       VALUE 25.
   05 VAL-4          PIC S9V999         VALUE 1.1.
   05 VAL-5          PIC Z(4).ZZ.
```

a. COMPUTE VAL-3 = VAL-1 / VAL-2 + 25.
b. COMPUTE VAL-2 = VAL-1 + VAL-3 − 100.
c. COMPUTE VAL-3 = VAL-2 − VAL-1 / 10.
d. COMPUTE VAL-2 = (VAL-1 + 500) ** .5.
e. COMPUTE VAL-4 = VAL-3 / VAL-2 / 10.
f. COMPUTE VAL-5 = VAL-3 **2.
g. COMPUTE VAL-1 ROUNDED = VAL-4 + (VAL-3 / VAL-2)*3.
h. COMPUTE VAL-3 = (VAL-3 − VAL-1) * .6.

Problems

10.1 Customer records have been prepared for processing to create an accounts receivable schedule. The accounts receivable schedule is to list all customer records and their outstanding balances (see the multiple-card layout form). The current balance is the amount (dollars and cents) a customer owes us from the last (current) billing period. The 30-day balance is the amount of money owed to us, which has been due over 30 days (1 month). The 60-day balance is the amount owed, which has been due 60 days (2 months). The 90-day balance is the amount owed us, which has been due 90 days or more (3 months or more). The 30-day balance is not included in the 60-day balance field or vice versa—they are independent of each other. The same relationship is true between the 60-day and 90-day balances.

MULTIPLE-CARD LAYOUT FORM

Company LEARNING COBOL, INC.
Application RECEIVABLES by J. WAYNE SPENCE Date 01/01/89 Job No. PROB 10.1 Sheet No. 1

CUSTOMER NUMBER	CUSTOMER NAME	OUTSTANDING BALANCES			
		CURRENT	30-DAY	60-DAY	90-DAY
9999999999	999999999999999999999999999999	99999999^99	99999999^99	99999999^99	99999999^99
1–10	11–40	41–50	51–60	61–70	71–80

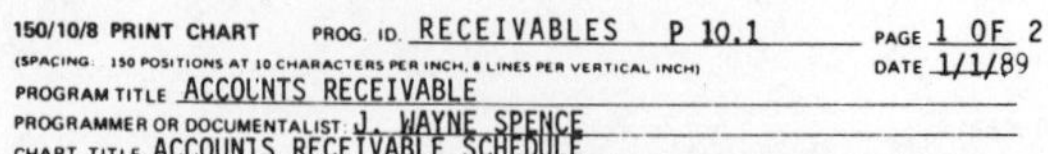

150/10/8 PRINT CHART PROG. ID. RECEIVABLES P 10.1 PAGE 1 OF 2
(SPACING: 150 POSITIONS AT 10 CHARACTERS PER INCH, 8 LINES PER VERTICAL INCH) DATE 1/1/89
PROGRAM TITLE ACCOUNTS RECEIVABLE
PROGRAMMER OR DOCUMENTALIST: J. WAYNE SPENCE
CHART TITLE ACCOUNTS RECEIVABLE SCHEDULE

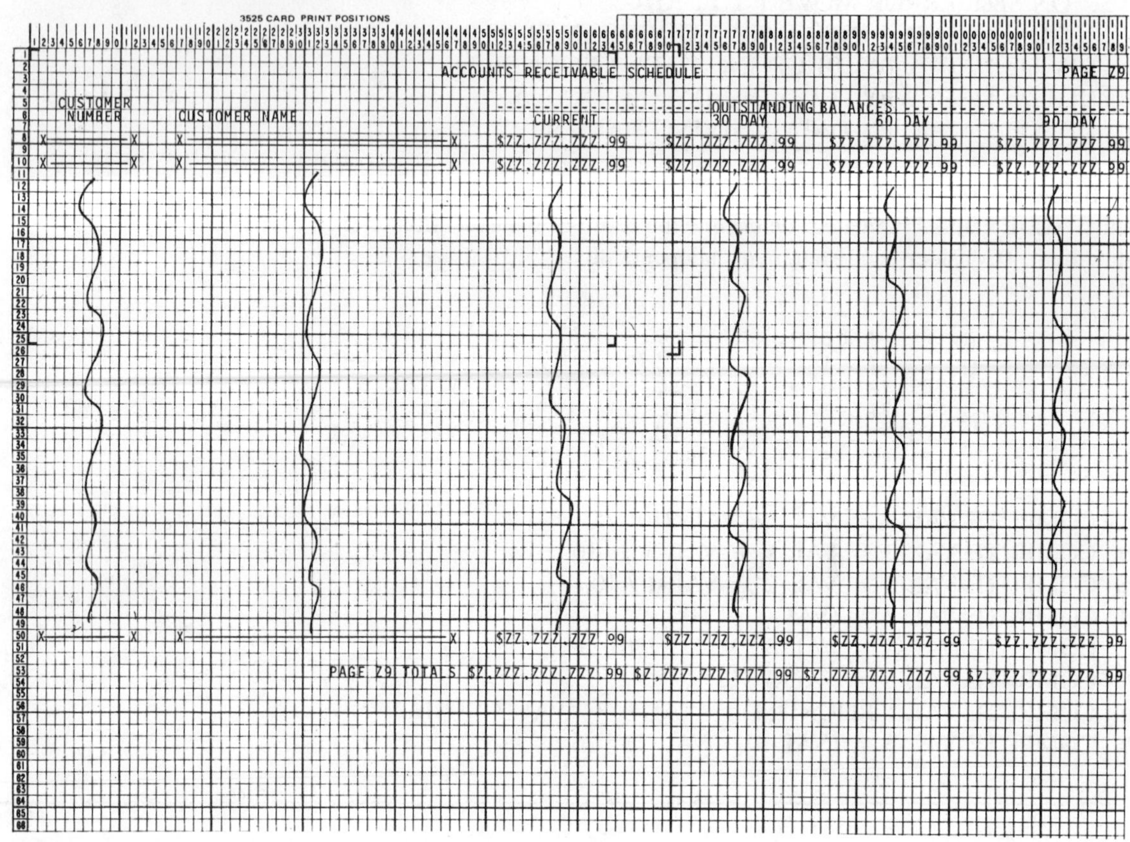

150/10/8 PRINT CHART PROG. ID. RECEIVABLES P 10.1 PAGE 2 OF 2
(SPACING: 150 POSITIONS AT 10 CHARACTERS PER INCH, 8 LINES PER VERTICAL INCH) DATE 1/1/89
PROGRAM TITLE ACCOUNTS RECEIVABLE
PROGRAMMER OR DOCUMENTALIST: J. WAYNE SPENCE
CHART TITLE ACCOUNTS RECEIVABLE SCHEDULE

3525 CARD PRINT POSITIONS

```
                          ACCOUNTS RECEIVABLE SCHEDULE                          PAGE Z9
                                  S U M M A R Y

                       -------TOTALS-------          ---CUMMULATIVE TOTALS---
      BALANCES               $               %                $              %
      CURRENT     $ZZ,ZZZ,ZZZ,ZZZ.99    ZZZ.ZZZ   $ZZ,ZZZ,ZZZ,ZZZ.99    ZZZ.ZZZ
      30 DAY      $ZZ,ZZZ,ZZZ,ZZZ.99    ZZZ.ZZZ   $ZZ,ZZZ,ZZZ,ZZZ.99    ZZZ.ZZZ
      60 DAY      $ZZ,ZZZ,ZZZ,ZZZ.99    ZZZ.ZZZ   $ZZ,ZZZ,ZZZ,ZZZ.99    ZZZ.ZZZ
      90 DAY      $ZZ,ZZZ,ZZZ,ZZZ.99    ZZZ.ZZZ   $ZZ,ZZZ,ZZZ,ZZZ.99    ZZZ.ZZZ

                 TOTAL ACCOUNTS RECEIVABLE $ZZZ,ZZZ,ZZZ,ZZZ.99
```

The report to be produced from these data is composed of two parts—a body, which contains a listing of all customer records, and a summary (see the print charts). The content of the body of the report is self-explanatory except that the pages are to be numbered, a heading is to appear on every page, and page totals are to be printed (the total of each monetary-amount column). Page totals reflect amounts appearing on that page only.

In the summary, several monetary values are presented. First, individual totals are to be printed for the current, 30-day, 60-day, and 90-day balances (along with the percentage each is of the grand total—total receivables). The second major group of data printed in the summary report is cumulative totals. In the order listed on the report, the cumulative current total is the same as the current total. The cumulative 30-day total is the 30-day total plus the current total, and so forth for the 60-day and 90-day cumulative totals. The cumulative percentages are again based on total receivables.

10.2 In an effort to reduce the amount of money invested in on-hand inventory, the inventory control manager has asked us to develop a planning model to evaluate three possible alternatives:

a. Do nothing—retain current inventory replenishment policies based on the reorder point (ROP).
b. Establish a new reorder point based on annual historical usage.
c. Establish a new reorder point based on annual historical usage, which does not include a safety stock margin.

To forecast product demand for each inventory item, we will assume that annual usage (demand) is constant—that is, demand does not fluctuate because of seasonal, cyclical, or trend influences.

To establish the average inventory cost for each alternative, we need to make the following computation:

The average number of units on-hand is equal to the reorder point (less safety stock, if any) divided by 2. (Again, a constant demand is assumed.) The safety stock, if any, is then added back, and the sum is multiplied by the cost per unit.

The cost of alternative (a)—using the current policy—is based on the existing reorder point value.

The reorder point value for alternative (b)—establish a new reorder point based on annual demand—is equal to the annual usage in units divided by the number of weeks' supply needed to cover the time lag between the placement of an order and the receipt of the order plus the safety stock. (Since there are 52 weeks in a year, the usage per week may be determined by dividing annual usage by 52. Then multiply the number of weeks between order and receipt to find the minimum quantity necessary to meet anticipated demand.) Now, with the new reorder point, proceed in the manner specified for alternative (a) to find the average cost of inventory.

For alternative (c), the computation is the same as for alternative (b) except that the safety stock level is assumed to be zero units.

On the basis of the preceding information, and after reviewing the graphic record layout, produce the report format specified on the print chart. Notice that the column INC/DEC ALT 1 has been added to the columns marked ALTERNATIVE 2 and ALTERNATIVE 3. This new column should reflect the increase or decrease in cost of the respective alternative with respect to ALTERNATIVE 1. Finally, totals are to be produced for each alternative.

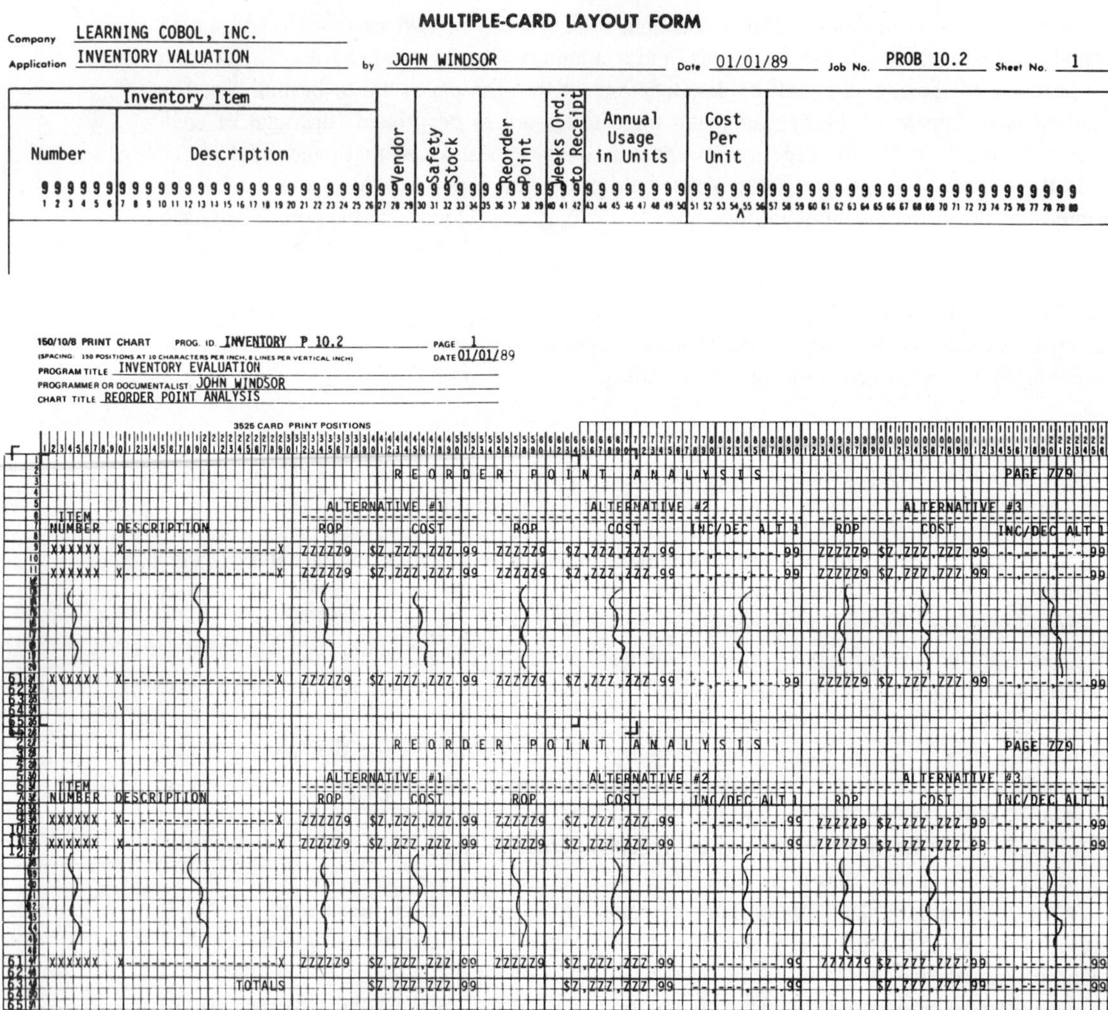

MULTIPLE-CARD LAYOUT FORM

Company LEARNING COBOL, INC.
Application INVENTORY VALUATION by JOHN WINDSOR Date 01/01/89 Job No. PROB 10.2 Sheet No. 1

Inventory Item								
Number	Description	Vendor	Safety Stock	Reorder Point	Weeks Ord. to Receipt	Annual Usage in Units	Cost Per Unit	
1–6	7–26	27–28	29–33	34–39	40–42	43–50	51–56	57–80

150/10/8 PRINT CHART PROG. ID INVENTORY P 10.2 PAGE 1
DATE 01/01/89
PROGRAM TITLE INVENTORY EVALUATION
PROGRAMMER OR DOCUMENTALIST JOHN WINDSOR
CHART TITLE REORDER POINT ANALYSIS

```
                                     R E O R D E R   P O I N T   A N A L Y S I S                          PAGE ZZ9

                               ALTERNATIVE #1              ALTERNATIVE #2                              ALTERNATIVE #3
 ITEM
 NUMBER  DESCRIPTION          ROP        COST            ROP        COST        INC/DEC ALT 1         ROP       COST        INC/DEC ALT 1
 XXXXXX  X----------------X  ZZZZZ9  $Z,ZZZ,ZZZ.99   ZZZZZ9  $Z,ZZZ,ZZZ.99  --,---,---.99   ZZZZZ9 $Z,ZZZ,ZZZ.99  --,---,---.99
 XXXXXX  X----------------X  ZZZZZ9  $Z,ZZZ,ZZZ.99   ZZZZZ9  $Z,ZZZ,ZZZ.99  --,---,---.99   ZZZZZ9 $Z,ZZZ,ZZZ.99  --,---,---.99

 XXXXXX  X----------------X  ZZZZZ9  $Z,ZZZ,ZZZ.99   ZZZZZ9  $Z,ZZZ,ZZZ.99  --,---,---.99   ZZZZZ9 $Z,ZZZ,ZZZ.99  --,---,---.99

                                     R E O R D E R   P O I N T   A N A L Y S I S                          PAGE ZZ9

                               ALTERNATIVE #1              ALTERNATIVE #2                              ALTERNATIVE #3
 ITEM
 NUMBER  DESCRIPTION          ROP        COST            ROP        COST        INC/DEC ALT 1         ROP       COST        INC/DEC ALT 1
 XXXXXX  X----------------X  ZZZZZ9  $Z,ZZZ,ZZZ.99   ZZZZZ9  $Z,ZZZ,ZZZ.99  --,---,---.99   ZZZZZ9 $Z,ZZZ,ZZZ.99  --,---,---.99
 XXXXXX  X----------------X  ZZZZZ9  $Z,ZZZ,ZZZ.99   ZZZZZ9  $Z,ZZZ,ZZZ.99  --,---,---.99   ZZZZZ9 $Z,ZZZ,ZZZ.99  --,---,---.99

 XXXXXX  X----------------X  ZZZZZ9  $Z,ZZZ,ZZZ.99   ZZZZZ9  $Z,ZZZ,ZZZ.99  --,---,---.99   ZZZZZ9 $Z,ZZZ,ZZZ.99  --,---,---.99
                     TOTALS          $Z,ZZZ,ZZZ.99          $Z,ZZZ,ZZZ.99  --,---,---.99          $Z,ZZZ,ZZZ.99  --,---,---.99
```

10.3 Your company has a fleet of automobiles used by both executives and sales personnel. The motor pool is responsible for maintaining the fleet and recording costs of vehicle operation. The fleet manager requests a report to assist in cost controls for the fleet as a whole and for individual vehicles. Each month the expense receipts are summarized and a record is developed (as indicated in the multiple-card layout form). The key elements of the record are the odometer readings at the beginning and end of each month, total receipts for gas and oil, receipts for repairs and other maintenance, average (historical) mileage per gallon for all past travel, and average (historical) cost per mile driven for all past travel.

The report the fleet manager requests contains the following features (see the print chart):

1. Number of miles driven during the month for each vehicle
2. Average miles per gallon for each vehicle during the month
3. Average cost per mile (which includes the cost for gas and repairs) during the month for each vehicle

4. A new historical average miles per gallon (which includes the current month and all past performance)
5. A new historical average cost per mile (which includes the current month and all past performance)
6. If the average miles per gallon or the cost per mile shows any more than a 10 percent deviation over the historical average, it is to be indicated
7. Any vehicle with a monthly mile per gallon of any value less than 10 mpg is to be indicated
8. Any vehicle that exceeds 35 cents per mile for operating cost during the month is to be indicated

For this report, the fleet manager requests no more than 30 vehicles to be listed per page and that the pages be numbered.

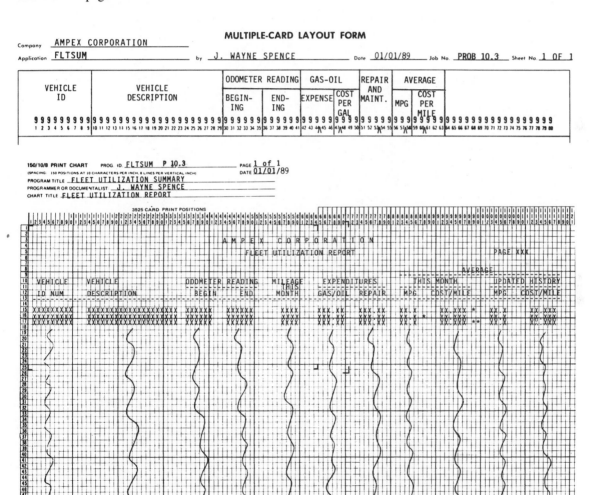

MULTIPLE-CARD LAYOUT FORM

Company AMPEX CORPORATION
Application FLTSUM by J. WAYNE SPENCE Date 01/01/89 Job No. PROB 10.3 Sheet No. 1 OF 1

VEHICLE ID	VEHICLE DESCRIPTION	ODOMETER READING		GAS-OIL		REPAIR AND MAINT.	AVERAGE		
		BEGIN-ING	END-ING	EXPENSE	COST PER GAL		MPG	COST PER MILE	
1–9	10–29	30–35	36–41	42–46	47–50	51–55	56–58	59–63	64–80

150/10/8 PRINT CHART PROG. ID. FLTSUM P 10.3 PAGE 1 of 1
(SPACING: 150 POSITIONS AT 10 CHARACTERS PER INCH, 8 LINES PER VERTICAL INCH) DATE 01/01/89
PROGRAM TITLE FLEET UTILIZATION SUMMARY
PROGRAMMER OR DOCUMENTALIST: J. WAYNE SPENCE
CHART TITLE FLEET UTILIZATION REPORT

3525 CARD PRINT POSITIONS

```
                                           A M P E X   C O R P O R A T I O N
                                                FLEET UTILIZATION REPORT                            PAGE XXX

                                                                                          AVERAGE
                                                                              ------------------------------------
 VEHICLE     VEHICLE                  ODOMETER READING   MILEAGE     EXPENDITURES       THIS MONTH         UPDATED HISTORY
                                      ----------------     THIS    ----------------  ----------------   ----------------
 ID NUM      DESCRIPTION                  BEGIN     END    MONTH    GAS/OIL  REPAIR   MPG   COST/MILE     MPG   COST/MILE
---------------------------------------------------------------------------------------------------------------------------
XXXXXXXXX   XXXXXXXXXXXXXXXXXXXXX  XXXXXX   XXXXXX    XXXX    XXX.XX   XXX.XX   XX.X    XX.XXX *     XX.X    XX.XXX
XXXXXXXXX   XXXXXXXXXXXXXXXXXXXXX  XXXXXX   XXXXXX    XXXX    XXX.XX   XXX.XX   XX.X *  XX.XXX       XX.X    XX.XXX
XXXXXXXXX   XXXXXXXXXXXXXXXXXXXXX  XXXXXX   XXXXXX    XXXX    XXX.XX   XXX.XX   XX.X    XX.XXX **    XX.X    XX.XXX

XXXXXXXXX   XXXXXXXXXXXXXXXXXXXXX  XXXXXX   XXXXXX    XXXX    XXX.XX   XXX.XX   XX.X    XX.XXX       XX.X    XX.XXX

 * EXCEEDS 10% INCREASE
** EXCEEDS 35 CENTS
```

CHAPTER

11

More on the IF Statements

In addition to the relational IF statement (discussed in Chapter 9) COBOL permits conditions to be stated in terms of a *sign test,* a *class test,* and a *condition-name test.* Many of the IF statement's properties described in Chapter 9 also apply to these new types of conditions.

The Sign Test

The sign test version of the IF statement (shown in Figure 11.1) provides the means for determining whether a numeric item is positive, negative, or zero. One difference between the sign test and the relational test is that the subject of a sign test may be an identifier or an arithmetic expression only. The test compares the sign of an item, so the identifier (or arithmetic expression) must be a numeric data item. A literal cannot be the subject of a sign test. The subject of the sign test is followed by one of three reserved words—POSITIVE, NEGATIVE, or ZERO. (Here the reserved word ZERO is not exactly the same as the figurative constant ZERO because the plural form of the word is not acceptable.) These reserved words are followed by true and false imperative statements (or NEXT SENTENCEs), as with the relational test.

The sign test does not possess a relational operator, as does the relational IF statement. Thus, the operator (POSITIVE, NEGATIVE, or ZERO) cannot be implied; however, logical operators may be used with the sign test. For example, it is permissible to have the statement

```
IF ACCOUNT-BALANCE IS POSITIVE OR
    ACCOUNT-BALANCE ZERO. . .
```

which uses the logical connective OR. (The programmer is cautioned against using the logical operator AND, since one value cannot be both positive *and* zero at the same time.) Because the subject of both conditions is ACCOUNT-BALANCE, the same statement could be written as

```
IF ACCOUNT-BALANCE IS POSITIVE OR ZERO . . .,
```

Figure 11.1 Format of the Sign Test

```
IF {identifier           } IS [NOT] {POSITIVE} [THEN] {imperative-statement-1}
   {arithmetic-expression}          {NEGATIVE}        {NEXT SENTENCE         }
                                    {ZERO    }

   [ELSE {imperative-statement-2}]
   [     {NEXT SENTENCE         }]

[END-IF]
```

Figure 11.2 Examples of the Sign Test

```
IF AVERAGE - 89.4 IS POSITIVE
    MOVE 'A' TO LETTER-GRADE
ELSE
    IF AVERAGE - 79.4 IS POSITIVE
        MOVE 'B' TO LETTER-GRADE
    ELSE
        IF AVERAGE - 69.4 IS POSITIVE
            MOVE 'C' TO LETTER-GRADE
        ELSE
            IF AVERAGE - 59.4 IS POSITIVE
                MOVE 'D' TO LETTER-GRADE
            ELSE
                MOVE 'F' TO LETTER-GRADE
```

in which case the subject (ACCOUNT-BALANCE) is implied. It is generally not necessary to use a compound sign test. In the preceding statements, the procedure is to be executed if ACCOUNT-BALANCE is either positive or zero. Another way of indicating the same condition is to say NOT NEGATIVE; that is,

```
IF ACCOUNT-BALANCE NOT NEGATIVE . . .
```

Like the relational test, the sign test also permits nesting; however, it is not generally necessary to nest sign tests that are examining the same data item. The sign test could be used to determine which letter grade should be assigned to a student on the basis of a numeric average. Figure 11.2 provides this somewhat artificial use of the sign test. Note that in the case of this program, short arithmetic expressions are necessary to "bracket" the numeric averages into letter-grade categories. Although the reserved word POSITIVE is used for each of these tests, it would be a simple matter to reverse the order of the tests; change the constants to 89.5, 79.5, and so on, and use the reversed word NOT NEGATIVE for each of the tests.

The Class Test

1985 COBOL Standards

The primary purpose of the class test is to determine whether an identifier is NUMERIC or ALPHABETIC. In COBOL 85 the class test can also be used to test for lower case alphabetic characters. The ALPHABETIC-UPPER class test is the same as the simple ALPHABETIC test. Note from Figure 11.3 that only an identifier is permitted to be the

Figure 11.3 Format of the Class Test

```
                       ⎧NUMERIC          ⎫          ⎧imperative-statement-1⎫
IF  identifier  IS [NOT] ⎨ALPHABETIC       ⎬ [THEN]  ⎨                      ⎬
                       ⎪ALPHABETIC-LOWER ⎪          ⎩NEXT SENTENCE         ⎭
                       ⎩ALPHABETIC-UPPER ⎭

  ⎡     ⎧imperative-statement-2⎫⎤
  ⎢ELSE ⎨                      ⎬⎥ [END-IF]
  ⎣     ⎩NEXT SENTENCE         ⎭⎦
```

subject of the class test and the identifier must be described in a form consistent with the type of test being made. That is, in a numeric class test, the description of the identifier in the DATA DIVISION *must not* be described (either implicitly or explicitly) as an alphabetic data item. The identifier will be classified as NUMERIC only if the contents of the identifier are numeric—composed only of digits and perhaps an operational sign. The converse of this is also true. If the class test specifies the reserved word ALPHABETIC, the true branch of this IF statement will be executed only if the content of the identifier consists of alphabetic characters and spaces.

The Condition-Name Test

The condition-name test is somewhat different from the other IF tests in that additional support for the test is required in the DATA DIVISION. The basic format for this statement is provided in Figure 11.4. Note the appearance of the statement. No relational operators or reserved words appear between the condition-name and the imperative statement (or NEXT SENTENCE) phrases of the statement. Thus, the test is made on the basis of the condition-name itself.

The condition-name is a special type of programmer-supplied-name in that it may be used only in conjunction with a condition-name test. While appearing to contain data values, condition-names cannot be used in place of data-names. Condition-names are specified in the DATA DIVISION of a COBOL program. Condition-names are *associated*

Figure 11.4 Format of the Condition-Name Test

```
                              ⎧imperative-statement-1⎫
IF  condition-name  [THEN]  ⎨                      ⎬
                              ⎩NEXT SENTENCE         ⎭

     ⎧imperative-statement-2⎫
ELSE ⎨                      ⎬ [END-IF]
     ⎩NEXT SENTENCE         ⎭
```

with preset values which may be contained in an elementary data item to which the condition-names are subordinate. Furthermore, a condition-name is always accompanied by a level-88 number. The format for the coding of condition-names is presented in Figure 11.5. A condition-name and a particular value or set of values of the elementary data item are associated by the use of a VALUE clause. As it is used here, the VALUE clause is slightly different from the VALUE clause presented in Chapter 5. The first major difference is that a condition-name may be associated with one literal, but it can also be associated with a series of literals. If more than one value is to be associated with a condition-name, the values should be listed in *ascending order* (with literal-1 receiving the smallest value in the sequence). Also, the literals must be consistent with the PICTURE type of the elementary data item. If the elementary-item is described as numeric, the literals should be numeric literals or figurative constants (e.g., ZERO). If the elementary-item is described as alphabetic or alphanumeric, the literals should be nonnumeric literals or figurative constants (e.g., SPACE). Finally, VALUE clauses connected with condition-names may appear in both the FILE SECTION and the WORKING-STORAGE SECTION.

An example of the creation of condition-names is in order. In the following illustration, condition-names are employed to distinguish between courses taught by different departments or colleges within a university system. Assuming the university is organized by colleges (e.g., colleges of arts and sciences, business, education, etc.), with each college having one or more course-prefix designations, it would be possible to determine which college teaches a particular course by the following condition-names and codes.

```
05 COURSE-DESCRIPTION-IN     PIC X(03).
   88  ARTS-AND SCIENCES-TEST
                             VALUES ARE 'ART', 'BIO', 'CHE',
                                        'COM', 'ECO', 'ENG',
                                        'GEO', 'GOV', 'HIS',
                                        'MAT', 'MUS', 'PE',
                                        'PHY', 'PSY',
   88  BUSINESS-TEST         VALUES ARE 'ACC', 'CSC', 'FIN',
                                        'MAN', 'MAR', 'OAD'.
   88  EDUCATION-TEST        VALUES ARE 'EED', 'SED'.
       .
       .
       .
```

If the following statements were placed in the PROCEDURE DIVISION, the first IF statement would be considered true if the COURSE-PREFIX contained any of the values ART, BIO, CHE, COM, ECO, ENG, GEO, GOV, HIS, MAT, MUS, PE, PHY, or PSY. The second IF statement would be true for COURSE-PREFIX values of ACC,

Figure 11.5 Format for the Creation of Condition-Names

```
level-number elementary-item-name {PICTURE} picture-string . . .
                                  {PIC    }

   88 condition-name-1 {VALUE IS  } literal-1  [THRU literal-2]
                       {VALUES ARE}

      [literal-3 [THRU literal-4]] . . .
```

CSC, FIN, MAN, MAR, or OAD. The third IF statement would be true for values of EED and SED, and so forth.

```
IF ARTS-AND-SCIENCES-TEST . . .
IF BUSINESS-TEST . . .
IF EDUCATION-TEST . . .
          .
          .
          .
```

To demonstrate further the use of the VALUE clause in the association of elementary-item values with condition-names, assume that college courses were numbered such that all 100s represent freshman courses; 200s, sophomore courses; 300s, junior courses; 400s, senior courses. The creation of condition-names under this situation might appear as

```
05  COURSE-SUFFIX-IN          PIC 9(03).
    88  FRESHMAN-LEVEL-TEST   VALUES ARE 100 THRU 199.
    88  SOPHOMORE-LEVEL-TEST  VALUES ARE 200 THRU 299.
    88  JUNIOR-LEVEL-TEST     VALUES ARE 300 THRU 399.
    88  SENIOR-LEVEL-TEST     VALUES ARE 400 THRU 499.
    88  GRADUATE-LEVEL-TEST   VALUES ARE 500 THRU 999.
        .
        .
        .
```

In the PROCEDURE DIVISION, the statements

```
IF FRESHMAN--LEVEL-TEST . . .
IF SOPHOMORE-LEVEL-TEST . . .
IF JUNIOR-LEVEL-TEST . . .
IF SENIOR-LEVEL-TEST . . .
IF GRADUATE-LEVEL-TEST . . .
          .
          .
          .
```

could be used to distinguish between different course levels.

The grade-assignment problem can also be constructed to utilize condition-name tests: Figure 11.6 demonstrates the procedure for incorporating condition-name tests into the problem for the determination of letter grades. First, to use the condition-name tests, the DATA DIVISION must be modified to create the condition-names. After the condition-names and their associated values have been provided, it is a very simple matter to modify the PROCEDURE DIVISION to use condition-name IF statements.

As you can see, programs may be written using a variety of IF statements. In some cases, types of IF statements can be interchanged, as in the grades problem. In other cases, only one of the IF statements will solve the problem.

An Inventory-Control Example

Figure 11.7 illustrates the use of condition-name tests in conjunction with the processing of records. In this illustration, data representing inventory records and transaction updates are read. The type of record is identified by the transaction-code value. Note that the data item TRANSACTION-CODE-IN is defined in line 480 of the input-record description. The meaning of possible code values is explained by the condition-names (lines 490-560). Data records in the inventory file are assumed to have been ordered such that all records

Figure 11.6 An Illustration of the Use of Condition-Name IF Statements

```
DATA DIVSION entries.

01  AVERAGE-OF-GRADES-WS.
    05  AVERAGE-WS                PIC 9(03)V9.
        88  GRADE-A-TEST          VALUES ARE 89.5 THRU 100.
        88  GRADE-B-TEST          VALUES ARE 79.5 THRU  89.4.
        88  GRADE-C-TEST          VALUES ARE 69.5 THRU  79.4.
        88  GRADE-D-TEST          VALUES ARE 59.5 THRU  69.4.
        88  GRADE-F-TEST          VALUES ARE  0   THRU  59.4.
                                  .
                                  .
                                  .
```

PROCEDURE DIVISION statements.

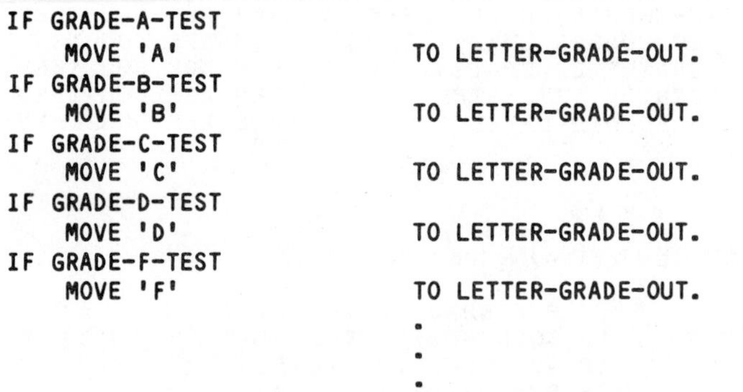

```
    IF GRADE-A-TEST
        MOVE 'A'                  TO LETTER-GRADE-OUT.
    IF GRADE-B-TEST
        MOVE 'B'                  TO LETTER-GRADE-OUT.
    IF GRADE-C-TEST
        MOVE 'C'                  TO LETTER-GRADE-OUT.
    IF GRADE-D-TEST
        MOVE 'D'                  TO LETTER-GRADE-OUT.
    IF GRADE-F-TEST
        MOVE 'F'                  TO LETTER-GRADE-OUT.
                                  .
                                  .
                                  .
```

Figure 11.7 Inventory Control Program (Hierarchy Chart)

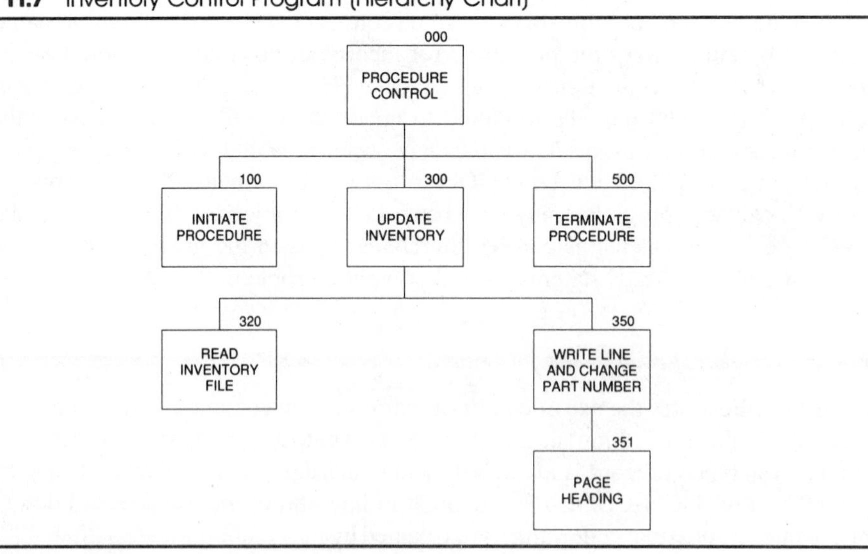

Figure 11.7 *Continued* Inventory Control Program (Pseudocode)

```
START
    DO Initiate procedure
    DO Update inventory
         UNTIL terminate or eof
    DO Terminate procedure
END

INITIATE PROCEDURE
    OPEN files
    SET file status
    DO Read inventroy
         MOVE part id to output
         SET balance to 0
         SET line counter
END

UPDATE INVENTORY
    IF old part not equal new part
         DO Write line change
    ENDIF
    IF beginning balance or units returned
       after sale or units recieved
         SET item status
         ADD volume input to balance
    ENDIF
    IF units sold or units returned after receipt
         SET item status
         SUBTRACT volume input from balance
    ENDIF
    IF transaction ommitted
         SET item status
         MOVE input to output
         WRITE ouput
    ENDIF
    IF not processed
         MOVE input to output
         WRITE output
    ENDIF
    DO Read inventroy
END

READ INVENTORY
    READ inventoy
         IF eof
              MOVE spaces to output
              SET messages
              SET file status
              WRITE output
         ENDIF
    ENDREAD
END

WRITE LINE CHANGE
    IF line counter greater than 40
         DO Page heading
    ENDIF
    MOVE balance to output
    ADD 2 to line counter
    IF balance less than 0
         SET message
    ENDIF
    WRITE detail line
         MOVE part id to output
         SET balance to 0
END

PAGE HEADING
    ADD 1 to page number
    SET line counter to 0
    Write headings
END

TERMINATE PROCEDURE
    CLOSE files
    DISPLAY end of job
END
```

with a particular PART-NUMBER-IN appear together. The procedure makes no assumption about the order of records within each group; however, it assumes that a beginning balance record (TRANSACTION-CODE-IN = 0) either has an initial amount on hand or is zero. The procedure is to be terminated on the basis of a specific value of TRANSACTION-CODE-IN (a value of 9) *or* on encountering the end-of-file (line 1000).

The predominant processing elements appear in the UPDATE-INVENTORY module (lines 1150-1410). This procedure determines whether the transaction volume is to be added to existing stock (conditions of BEGINNING-BALANCE, UNITS-RETURNED-AFTER-SALE, or UNITS-RECEIVED), subtracted from existing stock (conditions of UNITS-SOLD or UNITS-RETURNED-AFTER-RECEIPT), ignored altogether (condition of TRANSACTION-OMITTED), or identified as an error (ITEM-STATUS, line 590, does not contain the literal "PROCESSED"). The first decision of UPDATE-INVENTORY is to determine whether or not the current transaction record is for the *same* part number as that previously processed. This decision is necessary because only one line of output is produced for each part number, regardless of the number of transactions processed (i.e., unless a transaction is omitted or is in error).

Figure 11.7 *Continued* Inventory Control Program

```
            1   1   2   2   2   3   3   4   4   4   5   5   6   6   6   7
    4   8   2   6   0   4   8   2   6   0   4   8   2   6   0   4   8   2

      ***************************************************************
       IDENTIFICATION DIVISION.
      ***************************************************************
       PROGRAM-ID.     INVENTORY-CONTROL.
       AUTHOR.         JOHN WINDSOR.
       DATE-WRITTEN.   JANUARY 1, 1989.
       DATE-COMPILED.  JANUARY 1, 1989.
      ***************************************************************
       ENVIRONMENT DIVISION.
      ***************************************************************
      *-------------------------------------------------------------*
       CONFIGURATION SECTION.
      *-------------------------------------------------------------*
       SOURCE-COMPUTER. IBM.
       OBJECT-COMPUTER. IBM.
       SPECIAL-NAMES.    C01 IS NEXT-PAGE.
      *-------------------------------------------------------------*
       INPUT-OUTPUT SECTION.
      *-------------------------------------------------------------*
       FILE-CONTROL.
           SELECT INVENTORY-FILE ASSIGN TO UT-S-INPUT.
           SELECT REPORT-FILE    ASSIGN TO UT-S-OUTPUT.
      ***************************************************************
       DATA DIVISION.
      ***************************************************************
      *-------------------------------------------------------------*
       FILE SECTION.
      *-------------------------------------------------------------*
       FD  INVENTORY-FILE LABEL RECORDS ARE OMITTED.
       01  INVENTORY-RECORD                PIC X(80).

       FD  REPORT-FILE LABEL RECORDS ARE OMITTED.
       01  REPORT-RECORD                   PIC X(133).
      *-------------------------------------------------------------*
       WORKING-STORAGE SECTION.
      *-------------------------------------------------------------*
       01  WORKING-VARIABLES.
           05  LINE-COUNTER-WS             PIC 9(02).
           05  PAGE-NUMBER-WS              PIC 9(03) VALUE ZEROS.
           05  BALANCE-WS                  PIC S9(08).
           05  PART-NUMBER-WS              PIC 9(06) VALUE ZEROS.

       01  INVENTORY-INPUT.
           05 PART-NUMBER-IN               PIC 9(06).
           05 PART-DESCRIPTION-IN          PIC X(20).
           05 TRANSACTION-UNIT-VOLUME-IN PIC 9(06).
           05 FILLER                       PIC X(47).
           05 TRANSACTION-CODE-IN          PIC 9(01).
               88 BEGINNING-BALANCE                  VALUE 0.
               88 UNITS-SOLD                         VALUE 1.
               88 UNITS-RETURNED-AFTER-SALE          VALUE 2.
               88 UNITS-RECEIVED                     VALUE 3.
               88 UNITS-RETURNED-AFTER-RECEIPT       VALUE 4.
               88 TRANSACTION-OMITTED                VALUE 5.
               88 UNKNOWN-CODE                       VALUES 6 THRU 8.
               88 TERMINATE-PROCESSING               VALUE 9.

       01  STATUS-INDICATOR.
           05 FILE-STATUS                  PIC X(15).
               88 END-OF-FILE VALUE 'TERMINATE'.
           05 ITEM-STATUS                  PIC X(15).
               88 PROCESSED VALUE 'PROCESSED'.

       01  REPORT-TITLE.
           05 FILLER                       PIC X(54) VALUE SPACES.
           05 FILLER                       PIC X(24) VALUE
                                           'Inventory Control Report'.

       01  PAGE-NUMBER.
```

Figure 11.7 *Continued* Inventory Control Program (Data)

```
        1   1   2   2   2   3   3   4   4   4   5   5   6   6   6   7
4   8   2   6   0   4   8   2   6   0   4   8   2   6   0   4   8   2

           05 FILLER                      PIC X(115) VALUE SPACES.
           05 FILLER                      PIC X(05) VALUE 'Page'.
           05 PAGE-NUMBER-OUT             PIC ZZ9.

       01  HEADING-LINE.
           05 FILLER                      PIC X(33) VALUE SPACES.
           05 FILLER                      PIC X(16) VALUE 'Part Number'.
           05 FILLER                      PIC X(26) VALUE
                                          'Part Description'.
           05 FILLER                      PIC X(20) VALUE
                                          'Ending Balance'.
           05 FILLER                      PIC X(06) VALUE 'Notes:'.

       01  DETAIL-LINE.
           05 FILLER                      PIC X(35) VALUE SPACES.
           05 PART-NUMBER-OUT             PIC 9(06).
           05 FILLER                      PIC X(07) VALUE SPACES.
           05 PART-DESCRIPTION-OUT        PIC X(20).
           05 FILLER                      PIC X(08) VALUE SPACES.
           05 BALANCE-OUT                 PIC -Z(08).
           05 FILLER                      PIC X(10) VALUE SPACES.
           05 MESSAGE-OUT                 PIC X(35) VALUE SPACES.
      ************************************************************
       PROCEDURE DIVISION.
      ************************************************************
      *----------------------------------------------------------*
       000-PROCEDURE-CONTROL SECTION.
      *----------------------------------------------------------*
           PERFORM 100-INITIATE-PROCEDURE.
           PERFORM 300-UPDATE-INVENTORY
               UNTIL TERMINATE-PROCESSING OR END-OF-FILE.
           PERFORM 500-TERMINATE-PROCEDURE.
           STOP RUN.
      *----------------------------------------------------------*
       100-INITIATE-PROCEDURE SECTION.
      *----------------------------------------------------------*
           OPEN INPUT INVENTORY-FILE, OUTPUT REPORT-FILE.
           MOVE 'PROCESSING' TO FILE-STATUS.
           PERFORM 320-READ-INVENTORY-FILE.
           MOVE PART-NUMBER-IN       TO PART-NUMBER-WS
                                        PART-NUMBER-OUT.
           MOVE PART-DESCRIPTION-IN TO PART-DESCRIPTION-OUT.
           MOVE ZERO                 TO BALANCE-WS.
           MOVE 50                   TO LINE-COUNTER-WS.
      *----------------------------------------------------------*
       300-UPDATE-INVENTORY SECTION.
      *----------------------------------------------------------*
           IF PART-NUMBER-WS NOT EQUAL TO PART-NUMBER-IN
               PERFORM 350-WRITE-LINE-CHANGE-NUMBER.
           IF BEGINNING-BALANCE OR UNITS-RETURNED-AFTER-SALE
               OR UNITS-RECEIVED
               MOVE 'PROCESSED'      TO ITEM-STATUS
               ADD TRANSACTION-UNIT-VOLUME-IN TO BALANCE-WS.
           IF UNITS-SOLD OR UNITS-RETURNED-AFTER-RECEIPT
               MOVE 'PROCESSED'      TO ITEM-STATUS
               SUBTRACT TRANSACTION-UNIT-VOLUME-IN FROM BALANCE-WS.
           IF TRANSACTION-OMITTED
               MOVE 'PROCESSED'      TO ITEM-STATUS
               MOVE PART-NUMBER-IN   TO PART-NUMBER-OUT;
               MOVE TRANSACTION-UNIT-VOLUME-IN TO BALANCE-OUT;
               MOVE 'OMITTED'        TO MESSAGE-OUT;
               WRITE REPORT-RECORD FROM DETAIL-LINE AFTER 1 LINES;
               MOVE SPACES           TO MESSAGE-OUT;
               ADD 1 TO LINE-COUNTER-WS.
           IF NOT PROCESSED
               MOVE PART-NUMBER-IN   TO PART-NUMBER-OUT
               MOVE ZEROS            TO BALANCE-OUT
               MOVE 'ILLEGAL TRANSACTION' TO MESSAGE-OUT
               WRITE REPORT-RECORD FROM DETAIL-LINE AFTER 1 LINES
```

Figure 11.7 *Continued* Inventory Control Program (Output)

```
          1   1   2   2   2   3   3   4   4   4   5   5   6   6   6   7
   4   8  2   6   0   4   8   2   6   0   4   8   2   6   0   4   8   2

                 MOVE SPACES             TO MESSAGE-OUT
                 ADD 1 TO LINE-COUNTER-WS.
             PERFORM 320-READ-INVENTORY-FILE.
      *-----------------------------------------------------------*
       320-READ-INVENTORY-FILE SECTION.
      *-----------------------------------------------------------*
             READ INVENTORY-FILE INTO INVENTORY-INPUT AT END
                 MOVE 0                  TO PART-NUMBER-OUT
                                            BALANCE-OUT
                 MOVE SPACES             TO PART-DESCRIPTION-OUT
                 MOVE 'ILLEGAL TERMINATION' TO MESSAGE-OUT
                 WRITE REPORT-RECORD FROM DETAIL-LINE AFTER 3 LINES
                 MOVE 'TERMINATE'        TO FILE-STATUS.
      *-----------------------------------------------------------*
       350-WRITE-LINE-CHANGE-NUMBER SECTION.
      *-----------------------------------------------------------*
             IF LINE-COUNTER-WS GREATER THAN 40
                 PERFORM 351-PAGE-HEADING.
             MOVE BALANCE-WS             TO BALANCE-OUT.
             ADD 2 TO LINE-COUNTER-WS.
             IF BALANCE-WS LESS THAN 0
                 MOVE 'ACCOUNT BALANCE LESS THAN ZERO' TO MESSAGE-OUT.
             WRITE REPORT-RECORD FROM DETAIL-LINE AFTER 2 LINES.
             MOVE SPACES                 TO MESSAGE-OUT.
             MOVE PART-NUMBER-IN         TO PART-NUMBER-WS
                                            PART-NUMBER-OUT.
             MOVE PART-DESCRIPTION-IN TO PART-DESCRIPTION-OUT.
             MOVE ZERO                   TO BALANCE-WS.
      *-----------------------------------------------------------*
       351-PAGE-HEADING SECTION.
      *-----------------------------------------------------------*
             ADD 1 TO PAGE-NUMBER-WS.
             MOVE PAGE-NUMBER-WS         TO PAGE-NUMBER-OUT.
             MOVE 0                      TO LINE-COUNTER-WS.
             WRITE REPORT-RECORD FROM REPORT-TITLE AFTER NEXT-PAGE.
             WRITE REPORT-RECORD FROM PAGE-NUMBER AFTER 2 LINES.
             WRITE REPORT-RECORD FROM HEADING-LINE AFTER 2 LINES.
             MOVE SPACES                 TO REPORT-RECORD.
             WRITE REPORT-RECORD AFTER 1 LINES.
      *-----------------------------------------------------------*
       500-TERMINATE-PROCEDURE SECTION.
      *-----------------------------------------------------------*
             CLOSE INVENTORY-FILE, REPORT-FILE.
             DISPLAY 'END OF JOB'.
```

While creating output records, the procedure keeps track of the number of lines on a page and decides whether or not a new page heading is necessary. The output procedure also updates the saved part number (PART-NUMBER-WS) so that the next sequence through the UPDATE-INVENTORY procedure reflects the new item number. Other elements of the procedure are similar to those presented in previous illustrations.

Inventory Data Editing

Data editing, the process of examining data for accuracy (or at least reasonableness) is often necessary in commercial applications to ensure the proper execution of procedures. Most of the programs illustrated in this text assume the data are of the appropriate form (e.g., dates are legitimate, numeric fields contain numeric data, etc.). Unfortunately, data are frequently wrong, mostly because of keying errors. Data are often subjected

Figure 11.7 *Continued* Inventory Control Program (Data)

```
---------------------------------------------------------------------------------------
|      |         1         2         3         4         5         6         7         8|
|Record|12345678901234567890123456789012345678901234567890123456789012345678901234567890|
|--------------------------------------------------------------------------------------|
|     1|101100Light Brown Umbrella000025                                               0|
|     2|101100                    000030                                               2|
|     3|101100                    000015                                               2|
|     4|101100                    000045                                               6|
|     5|101100                    000006                                               3|
|     6|101100                    000150                                               1|
|     7|101100                    000050                                               1|
|     8|454550100 Watt Light Bulbs088500                                               0|
|     9|454550                    000100                                               5|
|    10|454550                    000050                                               3|
|    11|454550                    007000                                               1|
|    12|454550                    000045                                               7|
|    13|454550                    000300                                               4|
|    14|1249006 oz. Chocolate Bar 150000                                               0|
|    15|124900                    000820                                               6|
|    16|124900                    000760                                               1|
|    17|124900                    005000                                               1|
|    18|124900                    000050                                               1|
|    19|124900                    000100                                               2|
|    20|132240Yellow Comb         040000                                               0|
|    21|132240                    000460                                               5|
|    22|132240                    000790                                               4|
|    23|132240                    004000                                               1|
|    24|465465Green Comb          000431                                               0|
|    25|465465                    000200                                               3|
|    26|123450Laundry Soap        005900                                               0|
|    27|123450                    001000                                               1|
|    28|123450                    000030                                               2|
|    29|123450                    000020                                               3|
|    30|123450                    000040                                               4|
|    31|123450                    000010                                               5|
|    32|123450                    000100                                               1|
|    33|123450                    000040                                               1|
|    34|790000Mickey Mouse Watch  000010                                               0|
|    35|790000                    000100                                               7|
|    36|790000                    000075                                               1|
|    37|790000                    000400                                               2|
|    38|222200Headphones          033200                                               0|
|    39|222200                    000045                                               8|
|    40|222200                    000300                                               1|
|    41|222200                    000005                                               2|
|    42|222200                    000095                                               1|
|    43|222200                    000200                                               1|
|    44|222200                    000010                                               4|
|    45|152155Tub Margarine       000750                                               0|
|    46|152155                    000023                                               8|
|    47|152155                    000045                                               4|
|    48|152155                    000500                                               3|
|    49|457890Hula Hoop           002000                                               0|
|    50|457890                    000045                                               5|
|    51|457890                    000063                                               1|
---------------------------------------------------------------------------------------
```

Figure 11.7 *Continued* Inventory Control Program (Output)

```
                    Inventory Control Report
                                                              Page   1
Part Number      Part Description          Ending Balance    Notes:

  101100        Light Brown Umbrella              124        ACCOUNT BALANCE LESS THAN ZERO
  454550        100 Watt Light Bulbs              100        OMITTED

  454550        100 Watt Light Bulbs            81250

  124900        6 oz. Chocolate Bar            144290
  132240        Yellow Comb                       460        OMITTED

  132240        Yellow Comb                     35210

  465465        Green Comb                        631
  123450        Laundry Soap                       10        OMITTED

  123450        Laundry Soap                     4770

  790000        Mickey Mouse Watch                335

  222200        Headphones                      32600

  152155        Tub Margarine                    1205
  457890        Hula Hoop                          45        OMITTED

  457890        Hula Hoop                        2294

  123987        Red Food Coloring               94862
  302100        Aspirin                            30        OMITTED
```

to a number of tests before they are relied on for further processing to maintain some level of data accuracy. Figure 11.8 illustrates this process with an inventory data-editing problem.

The editing process often requires a series of tests for individual data fields. Editing of each field is performed in a separate module to permit easier procedure validation and to provide the opportunity to implement (and test) portions of the editing process while leaving other modules to be coded later. Furthermore, if editing requirements change, existing editing code for each field is easy to locate.

In Figure 11.8 a series of condition-names is provided in conjunction with the input-record description. The procedure assumes that a fixed number of vendor values are legitimate in the three categories of inventory items (general, lumber and paint, lines 390–410). It is assumed that the packaging unit and the vendor are related. That is, if we determine that an inventory item is purchased from a lumber vendor, we would expect the packaging unit to be in board-feet or linear-feet—condition-name values of "BF" and "LF." The condition-names specified in lines 480 through 520 establish the association between the vendor group and the packaging unit value. Finally, condition-names are used to indicate the status of individual inventory records (e.g., in line 630, "A" represents an active record; "I," an inactive record; "H," a record to be held; "D," a record to be deleted).

In the PROCEDURE DIVISION, the editing process begins in module 5000 (EDIT-INVENTORY-DATA). Beginning at line 2350, and for the next several lines, field-

Figure 11.8 Inventory Data-Editing (Hierarchy Chart)

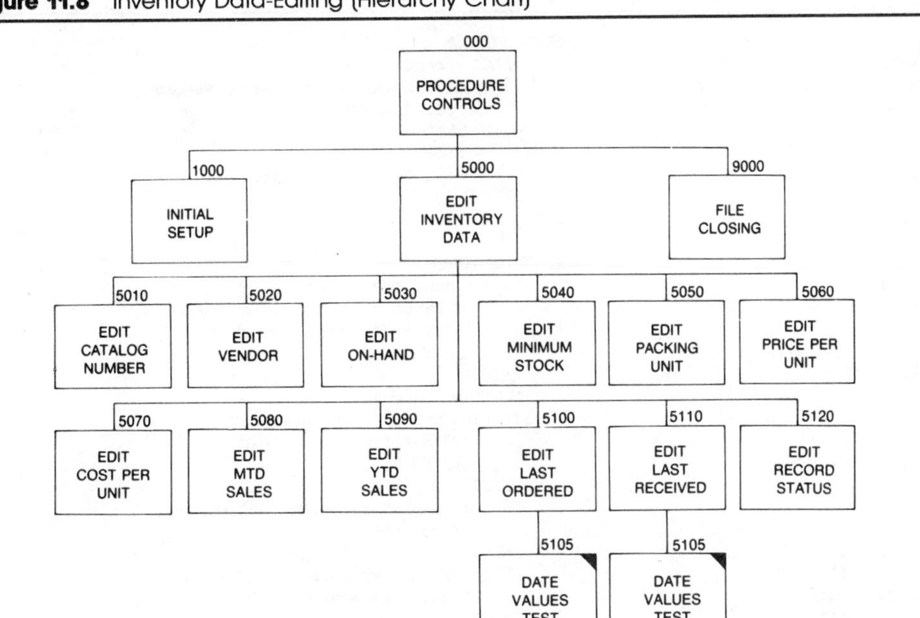

oriented edit modules are invoked, and the legitimacy of the field contents is established. In the several modules that follow, each type of IF statement is illustrated a number of times. The class test is demonstrated in line 2580 (CATALOG-NUMBER-TEST IS NOT NUMERIC). The condition-name test is illustrated in line 2630 (LUMBER-VENDOR AND NOT LUMBER-NUMBER). The sign test is illustrated in line 2840 (ON-HAND-TEST IS NEGATIVE). And the relational test is illustrated in line 3470 (COST-PER-UNIT-IN IS LESS THAN ZERO). In addition, the use of the logical operators AND and OR are illustrated in lines 2630 and 2720.

For each field to be edited, several field definitions are provided. Of course, the input-record description for each field is necessary. Each of the numeric fields are also provided with the alphanumeric counterpart in TEST-INVENTORY-RECORD (lines 650–750). Thus, when it is necessary to examine these numeric fields (e.g., catalog number), we are permitted to address the field using the data-name CATALOG-NUMBER-IN only if it contains numeric data. Otherwise, we must use CATALOG-NUMBER-TEST—an alphanumeric description of the same column positions of the input records. Thus, the initial test of the catalog number is "IF CATALOG-NUMBER-TEST IS NOT NUMERIC"—a test, which if passed, will ensure us that we are dealing with numeric data. In addition, it is necessary to establish two fields for each numeric output field. For example, CATALOG-NUMBER-OUT (line 820) is a numeric field to be used in the event that CATALOG-NUMBER-IN is numeric. CATALOG-NUMBER-DISP (line 1100) is used when CATALOG-NUMBER-TEST contains nonnumeric characters. (Although we could have declared CATALOG-NUMBER-OUT alphanumeric without any detrimental effect, we might have problems with fields such as PRICE-PER-UNIT-OUT.)

Figure 11.8 *Continued* Inventory Data-Editing (Pseudocode)

```
START
    DO Initial setup
    DO Edit inventory data UNTIL eof
    DO File closing
END

INITIAL SETUP
    OPEN files
    WRITE heading
END

EDIT INVENTORY DATA
    READ inventroy
         IF eof
               SET file status
               GO TO END
         ENDIF
    ENDREAD
    MOVE spaces to outputs
    MOVE input to output
    DO Catalog number
    DO Edit vendor
    DO Edit on hand
    DO Edit minimun stock
    DO Edit packing unit
    DO Edit price per unit
    DO Edit cost per unit
    DO Edit mtd sales
    DO Edit ytd sales
    DO Edit last ordered
    DO Edit last sold
    DO Edit record status
    WRITE output
    IF error not equal spaces
         WRITE error output
END

CATALOG NUMBER
    IF catalog number not numeric
         MOVE * to error field
         MOVE catalog number to error output
         GO TO END
    ENDIF
    MOVE catalog number to output
    IF lumber vendor and not lumber number
         move * to error field
    ENDIF
END

EDIT VENDOR
    MOVE vendor to output
    IF general vendor or lumber vendor
       or paint vendor
         THEN
         ELSE
              MOVE * to error field
    ENDIF
END

EDIT ON HAND
    IF on hand not numeric
         MOVE on hand to error output
         MOVE * to error field
         GO TO END
    ENDIF
    MOVE on hand to output
    IF on hand is negative
         MOVE * to error field
         GO TO END
    ENDIF
    IF minimum stock level not numeric
         GO TO END
    ENDIF
    IF on hand < minimum stock level
         MOVE * to error field
    ENDIF
END

EDIT MINIMUM STOCK
    IF minimum stock level not numeric
         MOVE minimum stock level to
           error output
         MOVE * to error field
         GO TO END
    ENDIF
    MOVE minimum stock level to output
    IF minimum stock level less than 0
         MOVE * to error field
    ENDIF
END

EDIT RECORD STATUS
    MOVE record status to output
    IF not valid status
         MOVE * to error field
    ENDIF
END
```

Figure 11.8 *Continued* Inventory Data-Editing (Pseudocode)

```
EDIT PACKING UNIT
    MOVE packaging unit to output
    IF general unit and general vendor
         GO TO END
    ENDIF
    IF lumber unit and lumber vendor
         GO TO END
    ENDIF
    IF paint unit and paint vendor
         GO TO END t
    ENDIF
    MOVE * to error field
END

EDIT PRICE PER UNIT
    IF price per unit not numeric
         MOVE price per unit to error output
         MOVE * to error field
         GO TO END
    ENDIF
    MOVE price per unit to output
    IF price per unit less than 0
         MOVE * to error field
         GO TO END
    ENDIF
    IF cost per unit not numeric
         GO TO END
    ENDIF
    IF price per unit < cost per unit
         MOVE * to error field
    ENDIF
END

EDIT COST PER UNIT
    IF cost per unit not numeric
         MOVE cost per unit to error output
         MOVE * to error field
         GO TO END
    ENDIF
    MOVE cost per unit to output
    IF cost per unit less than 0
         MOVE * to error field
    ENDIF
END

EDIT MTD SALES
    IF month to date sales not numeric
         MOVE month to date sales to error output
         MOVE * to error field
         GO TO END
    ENDIF
    MOVE month to date sales to output
    IF month to date sales < 0
         MOVE * to error field
    ENDIF
END

EDIT YTD SALES
    IF year to date sales not numeric
         MOVE year to date sales to error output
         MOVE * to error field
         GO TO END
    ENDIF
    MOVE year to date sales to output
    IF year to date sales is negative
         MOVE * to error field
         GO TO END
    ENDIF
    IF month to date sales not numeric
         GO TO END
    ENDIF
    IF year to date sales < month to date sales
         MOVE * to error field
    ENDIF
END

EDIT LAST ORDERED
    MOVE date last ordered to output
    IF date last ordered not numeric
         MOVE * to error field
         GO TO END
    ENDIF
    MOVE date last ordered to date test
    DO Date values test
         IF not valid month
              MOVE * to error field
         ENDIF
         IF not valid day
              MOVE * to error field
         ENDIF
         IF not valid year
              MOVE * to error field
         ENDIF
    ENDDO
    MOVE errors data to error output
END

EDIT LAST SOLD
    MOVE date last sold to output
    IF date last sold not numeric
         MOVE * to error field
         GO TO END
    ENDIF
    MOVE date last sold to date test
    DO date values test
    MOVE errors data to error output
END

FILE CLOSING
    CLOSE files
```

Figure 11.8 *Continued* Inventory Data-Editing

```
                1   1   2   2   2   3   3   4   4   4   5   5   6   6   6   7
    4   8   2   6   0   4   8   2   6   0   4   8   2   6   0   4   8   2
      *****************************************************************
       IDENTIFICATION DIVISION.
      *****************************************************************
       PROGRAM-ID.      INVENTORY-DATA-EDIT.
       AUTHOR.          J. WAYNE SPENCE.
       DATE-WRITTEN.    JANUARY 1, 1989.
       DATE-COMPILED.   JANUARY 1, 1989.
      *    This program illustrates the use of a variety of IF
      *    statements, which in combination serve to check the
      *    contents of data records for accuracy (or at least
      *    reasonableness).
      *****************************************************************
       ENVIRONMENT DIVISION.
      *****************************************************************
      *---------------------------------------------------------------*
       CONFIGURATION SECTION.
      *---------------------------------------------------------------*
       SOURCE-COMPUTER. IBM.
       OBJECT-COMPUTER. IBM.
       SPECIAL-NAMES.   C01 IS TO-TOP-OF-FORM.
      *---------------------------------------------------------------*
       INPUT-OUTPUT SECTION.
      *---------------------------------------------------------------*
       FILE-CONTROL.
           SELECT INVENTORY-FILE   ASSIGN TO UT-S-INPUT.
           SELECT EDIT-REPORT-FILE ASSIGN TO UT-S-OUTPUT.
      *****************************************************************
       DATA DIVISION.
      *****************************************************************
      *---------------------------------------------------------------*
       FILE SECTION.
      *---------------------------------------------------------------*
       FD  INVENTORY-FILE LABEL RECORDS ARE OMITTED.
       01  INVENTORY-RECORD.
           05 DESCRIPTIVE-DATA-IN.
              10 CATALOG-NUMBER-IN      PIC 9(10).
                   88 LUMBER-NUMBER      VALUES ARE 1000 THRU 1000000.
              10 VENDOR-IN              PIC X(03).
                   88 GENERAL-VENDOR     VALUE IS 'GEN'.
                   88 LUMBER-VENDOR      VALUES ARE 'WHR', 'UPA', 'IP '.
                   88 PAINT-VENDOR       VALUES ARE 'JMV', 'GLD', 'JB ',
                                                    'PIT', 'BM '.
              10 DESCRIPTION-IN         PIC X(20).
           05 UNIT-DATA-IN.
               10 ON-HAND-IN             PIC S9(05).
               10 MINIMUM-STOCK-LEVEL-IN PIC S9(05).
               10 PACKAGING-UNIT-IN      PIC X(02).
                   88 GENERAL-UNIT       VALUES ARE 'EA', 'X ', 'DZ',
                                                    'GR', 'C ', 'M ',
                                                    'OZ'.
                   88 LUMBER-UNIT        VALUES ARE 'BF', 'LF'.
                   88 PAINT-UNIT         VALUES ARE 'PT', 'QT', 'GA'.
           05 PRICE-COST-DATA-IN.
               10 PRICE-PER-UNIT-IN      PIC S9(03)V9(02).
               10 COST-PER-UNIT-IN       PIC S9(03)V9(02).
           05 SALES-DATA-IN.
               10 MONTH-TO-DATE-SALES-IN PIC S9(04)V9(02).
               10 YEAR-TO-DATE-SALES-IN PIC S9(04)V9(02).
           05 DATE-DATA-IN.
               10 DATE-LAST-ORDERED-IN PIC X(06).
               10 DATE-LAST-SOLD-IN      PIC X(06).
           05 RECORD-STATUS-IN           PIC X(01).
                   88 VALID-STATUS       VALUES ARE 'A', 'I', 'H', 'D'.

       01  TEST-INVENTORY-RECORD.
           05 CATALOG-NUMBER-TEST        PIC X(10).
           05 FILLER                     PIC X(23).
           05 ON-HAND-TEST               PIC X(05).
           05 MINIMUM-STOCK-LEVEL-TEST PIC X(05).
```

Figure 11.8 *Continued* Inventory Data-Editing

```
              1   1   2   2   2   3   3   4   4   4   5   5   6   6   6   7
   4   8   2   6   0   4   8   2   6   0   4   8   2   6   0   4   8   2

          05 FILLER                   PIC X(02).
          05 PRICE-PER-UNIT-TEST      PIC X(05).
          05 COST-PER-UNIT-TEST       PIC X(05).
          05 MONTH-TO-DATE-SALES-TEST PIC X(06).
          05 YEAR-TO-DATE-SALES-TEST  PIC X(06).
          05 FILLER                   PIC X(13).

      FD  EDIT-REPORT-FILE    LABEL RECORDS ARE OMITTED.
      01  OUTPUT-RECORD               PIC X(133).

      01  EDIT-RECORD.
          05 FILLER                   PIC X(01).
          05 CATALOG-NUMBER-OUT       PIC 9(10).
          05 FILLER                   PIC X(02).
          05 VENDOR-OUT               PIC X(03).
          05 FILLER                   PIC X(02).
          05 DESCRIPTION-OUT          PIC X(20).
          05 FILLER                   PIC X(02).
          05 ON-HAND-OUT              PIC 9(05).
          05 FILLER                   PIC X(02).
          05 MINIMUM-STOCK-LEVEL-OUT  PIC 9(05).
          05 FILLER                   PIC X(02).
          05 PACKAGING-UNIT-OUT       PIC X(02).
          05 FILLER                   PIC X(02).
          05 PRICE-PER-UNIT-OUT       PIC 9(03).9(02).
          05 FILLER                   PIC X(02).
          05 COST-PER-UNIT-OUT        PIC 9(03).9(02).
          05 FILLER                   PIC X(02).
          05 MONTH-TO-DATE-SALES-OUT  PIC 9(04).9(02).
          05 FILLER                   PIC X(02).
          05 YEAR-TO-DATE-SALES-OUT   PIC 9(04).9(02).
          05 FILLER                   PIC X(02).
          05 DATE-LAST-ORDERED-OUT    PIC XXBXXBXX.
          05 FILLER                   PIC X(02).
          05 DATE-LAST-SOLD-OUT       PIC XXBXXBXX.
          05 FILLER                   PIC X(02).
          05 RECORD-STATUS-OUT        PIC X(01).

      01  DISPLAY-RECORD.
          05 FILLER                   PIC X(01).
          05 CATALOG-NUMBER-DISP      PIC X(10).
          05 FILLER                   PIC X(29).
          05 ON-HAND-DISP             PIC X(05).
          05 FILLER                   PIC X(02).
          05 MINIMUM-STOCK-LEVEL-DISP PIC X(05).
          05 FILLER                   PIC X(02).
          05 PACKAGING-UNIT-DISP      PIC X(02).
          05 FILLER                   PIC X(02).
          05 PRICE-PER-UNIT-DISP      PIC X(06).
          05 FILLER                   PIC X(02).
          05 COST-PER-UNIT-DISP       PIC X(06).
          05 FILLER                   PIC X(02).
          05 MONTH-TO-DATE-SALES-DISP PIC X(07).
          05 FILLER                   PIC X(02).
          05 YEAR-TO-DATE-SALES-DISP  PIC X(07).
      *-----------------------------------------------------------*
       WORKING-STORAGE SECTION.
      *-----------------------------------------------------------*
      01  WORKING-VARIABLES.
          05 FILE-STATUS              PIC X(04) VALUE SPACES.

      01  HEADING-RECORD.
          05 FILLER                   PIC X(01) VALUE SPACE.
          05 CATALOG-NUMBER-HEAD      PIC X(10) VALUE 'Cat Number'.
          05 FILLER                   PIC X(02) VALUE SPACES.
          05 VENDOR-HEAD              PIC X(03) VALUE 'Ven'.
          05 FILLER                   PIC X(02) VALUE SPACES.
          05 DESCRIPTION-HEAD         PIC X(20) VALUE 'Description'.
          05 FILLER                   PIC X(02) VALUE SPACES.
```

Figure 11.8 *Continued* Inventory Data-Editing

```
              1   1   2   2   2   3   3   4   4   4   5   5   6   6   6   7
      4   8   2   6   0   4   8   2   6   0   4   8   2   6   0   4   8   2

               05 ON-HAND-HEAD               PIC X(05) VALUE 'Qty.'.
               05 FILLER                     PIC X(02) VALUE SPACES.
               05 MINIMUM-STOCK-LEVEL-HEAD   PIC X(05) VALUE 'Min.'.
               05 FILLER                     PIC X(02) VALUE SPACES.
               05 PACKAGING-UNIT-HEAD        PIC X(02) VALUE 'Pk'.
               05 FILLER                     PIC X(02) VALUE SPACES.
               05 PRICE-PER-UNIT-HEAD        PIC X(06) VALUE 'Price'.
               05 FILLER                     PIC X(02) VALUE SPACES.
               05 COST-PER-UNIT-HEAD         PIC X(06) VALUE ' Cost'.
               05 FILLER                     PIC X(02) VALUE SPACES.
               05 MONTH-TO-DATE-SALES-HEAD   PIC X(07) VALUE ' MTD $'.
               05 FILLER                     PIC X(02) VALUE SPACES.
               05 YEAR-TO-DATE-SALES-HEAD    PIC X(07) VALUE '  YTD $'.
               05 FILLER                     PIC X(02) VALUE SPACES.
               05 DATE-LAST-ORDERED-HEAD     PIC X(08) VALUE 'Last Ord'.
               05 FILLER                     PIC X(02) VALUE SPACES.
               05 DATE-LAST-SOLD-HEAD        PIC X(08) VALUE 'Last Sld'.
               05 FILLER                     PIC X(02) VALUE SPACES.
               05 RECORD-STATUS-HEAD         PIC X(02) VALUE 'St'.

           01  DATE-TEST-VALUES.
               05 TEST-MONTH                 PIC S9(02).
                   88 VALID-MONTH            VALUES ARE 1 THRU 12.
               05 TEST-DAY                   PIC S9(02).
                   88 VALID-DAY              VALUES ARE 1 THRU 31.
               05 TEST-YEAR                  PIC S9(02).
                   88 VALID-YEAR             VALUES ARE 77 THRU 81.
               05 DATE-ERROR.
                   10 MONTH-ERROR            PIC X(02).
                   10 DAY-ERROR              PIC X(02).
                   10 YEAR-ERROR             PIC X(02).

           01  ERROR-RECORD.
               05 FILLER                     PIC X(01).
               05 CATALOG-NUMBER-ERROR       PIC X(10).
               05 FILLER                     PIC X(02).
               05 VENDOR-ERROR               PIC X(03).
               05 FILLER                     PIC X(02).
               05 DESCRIPTION-ERROR          PIC X(20).
               05 FILLER                     PIC X(02).
               05 ON-HAND-ERROR              PIC X(05).
               05 FILLER                     PIC X(02).
               05 MINIMUM-STOCK-LEVEL-ERROR PIC X(05).
               05 FILLER                     PIC X(02).
               05 PACKAGING-UNIT-ERROR       PIC X(02).
               05 FILLER                     PIC X(02).
               05 PRICE-PER-UNIT-ERROR       PIC X(06).
               05 FILLER                     PIC X(02).
               05 COST-PER-UNIT-ERROR        PIC X(06).
               05 FILLER                     PIC X(02).
               05 MONTH-TO-DATE-SALES-ERROR PIC X(07).
               05 FILLER                     PIC X(02).
               05 YEAR-TO-DATE-SALES-ERROR   PIC X(07).
               05 FILLER                     PIC X(02).
               05 DATE-LAST-ORDERED-ERROR.
                   10 DO-MONTH-ERROR         PIC X(02).
                   10 FILLER                 PIC X(01).
                   10 DO-DAY-ERROR           PIC X(02).
                   10 FILLER                 PIC X(01).
                   10 DO-YEAR-ERROR          PIC X(02).
               05 FILLER                     PIC X(02).
               05 DATE-LAST-SOLD-ERROR.
                   10 DS-MONTH-ERROR         PIC X(02).
                   10 FILLER                 PIC X(01).
                   10 DS-DAY-ERROR           PIC X(02).
                   10 FILLER                 PIC X(01).
                   10 DS-YEAR-ERROR          PIC X(02).
               05 FILLER                     PIC X(02).
               05 RECORD-STATUS-ERROR        PIC X(01).
```

Figure 11.8 *Continued* Inventory Data-Editing

```
        1   1   2   2   2   3   3   4   4   4   5   5   6   6   6   7
4   8   2   6   0   4   8   2   6   0   4   8   2   6   0   4   8   2

      *****************************************************************
       PROCEDURE DIVISION.
      *****************************************************************
      *---------------------------------------------------------------*
       000-PROCEDURE-CONTROLS SECTION.
      *---------------------------------------------------------------*
           PERFORM 1000-INITIAL-SETUP.
           PERFORM 5000-EDIT-INVENTORY-DATA
               UNTIL FILE-STATUS = 'DONE'.
           PERFORM 9000-FILE-CLOSING.
           STOP RUN.
      *---------------------------------------------------------------*
       1000-INITIAL-SETUP SECTION.
      *---------------------------------------------------------------*
           OPEN INPUT INVENTORY-FILE, OUTPUT EDIT-REPORT-FILE.
           WRITE OUTPUT-RECORD FROM HEADING-RECORD AFTER
               ADVANCING TO-TOP-OF-FORM.
      *---------------------------------------------------------------*
       5000-EDIT-INVENTORY-DATA SECTION.
      *---------------------------------------------------------------*
           READ INVENTORY-FILE
               AT END MOVE 'DONE' TO FILE-STATUS
                      GO TO 5000-EXIT.
           MOVE SPACES                TO OUTPUT-RECORD
                                         ERROR-RECORD.
           MOVE DESCRIPTION-IN        TO DESCRIPTION-OUT.
           PERFORM 5010-CATALOG-NUMBER.
           PERFORM 5020-EDIT-VENDOR.
           PERFORM 5030-EDIT-ON-HAND.
           PERFORM 5040-EDIT-MINIMUM-STOCK.
           PERFORM 5050-EDIT-PACKING-UNIT.
           PERFORM 5060-EDIT-PRICE-PER-UNIT.
           PERFORM 5070-EDIT-COST-PER-UNIT.
           PERFORM 5080-EDIT-MTD-SALES.
           PERFORM 5090-EDIT-YTD-SALES.
           PERFORM 5100-EDIT-LAST-ORDERED.
           PERFORM 5110-EDIT-LAST-SOLD.
           PERFORM 5120-EDIT-RECORD-STATUS.
           WRITE OUTPUT-RECORD AFTER ADVANCING 2 LINES.
           IF ERROR-RECORD NOT EQUAL TO SPACES
               WRITE OUTPUT-RECORD FROM ERROR-RECORD AFTER
                 ADVANCING 1 LINES.

       5000-EXIT.
           EXIT.
      *---------------------------------------------------------------*
       5010-CATALOG-NUMBER SECTION.
      *---------------------------------------------------------------*
           IF CATALOG-NUMBER-TEST IS NOT NUMERIC
               MOVE ALL '*' TO CATALOG-NUMBER-ERROR
               MOVE CATALOG-NUMBER-TEST TO CATALOG-NUMBER-DISP
               GO TO 5010-EXIT.
           MOVE CATALOG-NUMBER-IN    TO CATALOG-NUMBER-OUT.
           IF LUMBER-VENDOR AND NOT LUMBER-NUMBER
               MOVE ALL '*' TO CATALOG-NUMBER-ERROR.

       5010-EXIT.
           EXIT.
      *---------------------------------------------------------------*
       5020-EDIT-VENDOR SECTION.
      *---------------------------------------------------------------*
           MOVE VENDOR-IN             TO VENDOR-OUT.
           IF GENERAL-VENDOR OR LUMBER-VENDOR OR PAINT-VENDOR
               NEXT SENTENCE
           ELSE
               MOVE ALL '*'           TO VENDOR-ERROR.
      *---------------------------------------------------------------*
       5030-EDIT-ON-HAND SECTION.
      *---------------------------------------------------------------*
```

Figure 11.8 *Continued* Inventory Data-Editing (Data)

```
            1   1   2   2   2   3   3   4   4   4   5   5   6   6   6   7
   4   8    2   6   0   4   8   2   6   0   4   8   2   6   0   4   8   2

           IF ON-HAND-TEST IS NOT NUMERIC
               MOVE ON-HAND-TEST      TO ON-HAND-DISP
               MOVE ALL '*'           TO ON-HAND-ERROR
               GO TO 5030-EXIT.
           MOVE ON-HAND-IN            TO ON-HAND-OUT.
           IF ON-HAND-IN IS NEGATIVE
               MOVE ALL '*'           TO ON-HAND-ERROR
               GO TO 5030-EXIT.
           IF MINIMUM-STOCK-LEVEL-TEST IS NOT NUMERIC
               GO TO 5030-EXIT.
           IF ON-HAND-IN IS LESS THAN MINIMUM-STOCK-LEVEL-IN
               MOVE ALL '*'           TO ON-HAND-ERROR.

       5030-EXIT.
           EXIT.
      *-----------------------------------------------------------*
       5040-EDIT-MINIMUM-STOCK SECTION.
      *-----------------------------------------------------------*
           IF MINIMUM-STOCK-LEVEL-TEST IS NOT NUMERIC
               MOVE MINIMUM-STOCK-LEVEL-TEST TO MINIMUM-STOCK-LEVEL-DISP
               MOVE ALL '*'           TO MINIMUM-STOCK-LEVEL-ERROR
               GO TO 5040-EXIT.
           MOVE MINIMUM-STOCK-LEVEL-IN TO MINIMUM-STOCK-LEVEL-OUT.
           IF MINIMUM-STOCK-LEVEL-IN IS LESS THAN ZERO
               MOVE ALL '*'           TO MINIMUM-STOCK-LEVEL-ERROR.

       5040-EXIT.
           EXIT.
      *-----------------------------------------------------------*
       5050-EDIT-PACKING-UNIT SECTION.
      *-----------------------------------------------------------*
           MOVE PACKAGING-UNIT-IN     TO PACKAGING-UNIT-OUT.
           IF GENERAL-UNIT AND GENERAL-VENDOR
               GO TO 5050-EXIT.
           IF LUMBER-UNIT AND LUMBER-VENDOR
               GO TO 5050-EXIT.
           IF PAINT-UNIT AND PAINT-VENDOR
               GO TO 5050-EXIT.
           MOVE ALL '*'               TO PACKAGING-UNIT-ERROR.

       5050-EXIT.
           EXIT.
      *-----------------------------------------------------------*
       5060-EDIT-PRICE-PER-UNIT SECTION.
      *-----------------------------------------------------------*
           IF PRICE-PER-UNIT-TEST IS NOT NUMERIC
               MOVE PRICE-PER-UNIT-TEST TO PRICE-PER-UNIT-DISP
               MOVE ALL '*'           TO PRICE-PER-UNIT-ERROR
               GO TO 5060-EXIT.
           MOVE PRICE-PER-UNIT-IN     TO PRICE-PER-UNIT-OUT.
           IF PRICE-PER-UNIT-IN IS LESS THAN ZERO
               MOVE ALL '*'           TO PRICE-PER-UNIT-ERROR
               GO TO 5060-EXIT.
           IF COST-PER-UNIT-TEST IS NOT NUMERIC
               GO TO 5060-EXIT.
           IF PRICE-PER-UNIT-IN < COST-PER-UNIT-IN
               MOVE ALL '*'           TO PRICE-PER-UNIT-ERROR.

       5060-EXIT.
           EXIT.
      *-----------------------------------------------------------*
       5070-EDIT-COST-PER-UNIT SECTION.
      *-----------------------------------------------------------*
           IF COST-PER-UNIT-TEST IS NOT NUMERIC
               MOVE COST-PER-UNIT-TEST TO COST-PER-UNIT-DISP
               MOVE ALL '*'           TO COST-PER-UNIT-ERROR
               GO TO 5070-EXIT.
           MOVE COST-PER-UNIT-IN      TO COST-PER-UNIT-OUT.
           IF COST-PER-UNIT-IN IS LESS THAN ZERO
```

Figure 11.8 *Continued* Inventory Data-Editing (Data)

```
          1   1   2   2   2   3   3   4   4   4   5   5   6   6   6   7
   4   8   2   6   0   4   8   2   6   0   4   8   2   6   0   4   8   2

               MOVE ALL '*'          TO COST-PER-UNIT-ERROR.

       5070-EXIT.
           EXIT.
      *-----------------------------------------------------------*
       5080-EDIT-MTD-SALES SECTION.
      *-----------------------------------------------------------*
           IF MONTH-TO-DATE-SALES-TEST IS NOT NUMERIC
               MOVE MONTH-TO-DATE-SALES-TEST TO MONTH-TO-DATE-SALES-DISP
               MOVE ALL '*'          TO MONTH-TO-DATE-SALES-ERROR
               GO TO 5080-EXIT.
           MOVE MONTH-TO-DATE-SALES-IN TO MONTH-TO-DATE-SALES-OUT.
           IF MONTH-TO-DATE-SALES-IN IS < ZERO
              MOVE ALL '*'          TO MONTH-TO-DATE-SALES-ERROR.

       5080-EXIT.
           EXIT.
      *-----------------------------------------------------------*
       5090-EDIT-YTD-SALES SECTION.
      *-----------------------------------------------------------*
       5090-ENTRY.
           IF YEAR-TO-DATE-SALES-TEST IS NOT NUMERIC
               MOVE YEAR-TO-DATE-SALES-TEST TO YEAR-TO-DATE-SALES-DISP
               MOVE ALL '*'          TO YEAR-TO-DATE-SALES-ERROR
               GO TO 5090-EXIT.
           MOVE YEAR-TO-DATE-SALES-IN TO YEAR-TO-DATE-SALES-OUT.
           IF YEAR-TO-DATE-SALES-IN IS NEGATIVE
               MOVE ALL '*'          TO YEAR-TO-DATE-SALES-ERROR
               GO TO 5090-EXIT.
           IF MONTH-TO-DATE-SALES-TEST IS NOT NUMERIC
               GO TO 5090-EXIT.
           IF YEAR-TO-DATE-SALES-IN < MONTH-TO-DATE-SALES-IN
               MOVE ALL '*'          TO YEAR-TO-DATE-SALES-ERROR.

       5090-EXIT.
           EXIT.
      *-----------------------------------------------------------*
       5100-EDIT-LAST-ORDERED SECTION.
      *-----------------------------------------------------------*
           MOVE DATE-LAST-ORDERED-IN TO DATE-LAST-ORDERED-OUT.
           MOVE SPACES               TO DATE-ERROR.
           IF DATE-LAST-ORDERED-IN IS NOT NUMERIC
               MOVE ALL '*'          TO DATE-LAST-ORDERED-ERROR
               GO TO 5100-EXIT.
           MOVE DATE-LAST-ORDERED-IN TO DATE-TEST-VALUES.
           PERFORM 5105-DATE-VALUES-TEST.
           MOVE MONTH-ERROR          TO DO-MONTH-ERROR.
           MOVE DAY-ERROR            TO DO-DAY-ERROR.
           MOVE YEAR-ERROR           TO DO-YEAR-ERROR.
           GO TO 5100-EXIT.

       5105-DATE-VALUES-TEST.
           IF NOT VALID-MONTH
               MOVE '**'             TO MONTH-ERROR.
           IF NOT VALID-DAY
               MOVE '**'             TO DAY-ERROR.
           IF NOT VALID-YEAR
               MOVE '**'             TO YEAR-ERROR.

       5100-EXIT.
           EXIT.
      *-----------------------------------------------------------*
       5110-EDIT-LAST-SOLD SECTION.
      *-----------------------------------------------------------*
           MOVE DATE-LAST-SOLD-IN    TO DATE-LAST-SOLD-OUT.
           MOVE SPACES               TO DATE-ERROR.
           IF DATE-LAST-SOLD-IN IS NOT NUMERIC
               MOVE ALL '*'          TO DATE-LAST-SOLD-ERROR
               GO TO 5110-EXIT.
```

Figure 11.8 *Continued* Inventory Data-Editing

```
       MOVE DATE-LAST-SOLD-IN      TO DATE-TEST-VALUES.
       PERFORM 5105-DATE-VALUES-TEST.
       MOVE MONTH-ERROR            TO DS-MONTH-ERROR.
       MOVE DAY-ERROR              TO DS-DAY-ERROR.
       MOVE YEAR-ERROR             TO DS-YEAR-ERROR.

   5110-EXIT.
       EXIT.
  *-----------------------------------------------------------*
   5120-EDIT-RECORD-STATUS SECTION.
  *-----------------------------------------------------------*
       MOVE RECORD-STATUS-IN       TO RECORD-STATUS-OUT.
       IF NOT VALID-STATUS
           MOVE ALL '*'            TO RECORD-STATUS-ERROR.
  *-----------------------------------------------------------*
   9000-FILE-CLOSING SECTION.
  *-----------------------------------------------------------*
       CLOSE INVENTORY-FILE, EDIT-REPORT-FILE.
```

Figure 11.8 *Continued* Inventory Data-Editing (Data)

```
      |         1         2         3         4         5         6         7         8
Record|12345678901234567890123456789012345678901234567890123456789012345678901234567890
     1|0000001000GEN4 Inch Nails            9000020000GR00500003000075000200001206800209 81H
     2|0000250500WHR4 X 4 Plywood           0050000200BF0070000450Fifty 075000May 80May 802
     3|0000385000PUAOak Planks              0010000200LF004000070004500002900007018007058 0A
     4|0004697000JMVSky-Blue Flat Paint     0006700020GA011000092507000007500011238002058 1A
     5|0000555550IP Maple Logs              Sixty00350LF030000220000500000750003298001168 0I
     6|0000709800GLDWhite Semi-Gloss        0805006500QT005500065000950000850002018102138 1D
     7|0000100000GEN10 ft. Ladder           0010000050EA015000105000600000750013128011118 0D
     8|0000330030PITTurpentine              0105001500PT000950004500091000151005208002177 9H
     9|0000000101WHR2 X 4 Redwood           0005000040EA022000250005250006050012058001258 1H
    10|0000600500IP Wood Panels             0025000300BF011000090000950001200012287801138 1U
    11|0000890200BM Yellow Exterior         0030600315DZtwelve11250075000050000870790630 80A
    12|0000224200GENNuts and Bolts          5000050000OZ000500000500012000015000207810205 82I
    13|0000985040JB Hot Pink Paint          00005 Two PT002000015000020000020009157904218 0H
    14|0000765090UPA4 X 6 Aspen             0054900500M 022000210001500001750004048106097 9D
    15|0000382110PITRed Interior            0015000200QT010000065000100000200001208012017 9D
    16|0001000000GENSmall Screwdriver       0080000500QT000950010000190000250010228010028 0E
    17|0000465470GLDAvocado-Kitchen         0009500075GA01250nine 00125000250004278004018 0R
    18|0000505020BM Golden Yellow Flat      0009500100GA014900135000280 0sixty 0303790303 79E
    19|0000610010JMVBurnt Orange Gloss      0005000075QT009250072000092500092502148102078 1I
    20|0000765050UPASheetrock               0100001000BF010000090000900000500011288002058 1A
```

Figure 11.8 *Continued* Inventory Data-Editing (Output)

```
Cat Number Ven  Description           Qty.  Min.  Pk  Price  Cost   MTD $    YTD $   Last Ord  Last Sld  St

0000001000 GEN  4 Inch Nails          90000 20000 GR  005.00 003.00 0075.00  0200.00 12 06 80  02 09 81  H

0000250500 WHR  4 X 4 Plywood         00500 00200 BF  007.00 004.50 Fifty    0750.00 Ma y  80  Ma y  80  2
                                                                    *******          ********  ********  *

0000385000 PUA  Oak Planks            00100 00200 LF  004.00 007.00 0450.00  0290.00 07 01 80  07 05 80  A
           ***                        *****       **  ******                 *******

0004697000 JMV  Sky-Blue Flat Paint   00067 00020 GA  011.00 009.25 0700.00  0750.00 11 23 80  02 05 81  A

0000555550 IP   Maple Logs            Sixty 00350 LF  030.00 022.00 0050.00  0075.00 03 29 80  01 16 80  I
                                      *****

0000709800 GLD  White Semi-Gloss      08050 06500 QT  005.50 006.50 0095.00  0085.00 02 01 81  02 13 81  D
                                                      ******                 *******

0000100000 GEN  10 ft. Ladder         00100 00050 EA  015.00 010.50 0060.00  0075.00 13 12 80  11 11 80  D
                                                                             **

0000330030 PIT  Turpentine            01050 01500 PT  000.95 000.45 0009.10  0015.10 05 20 80  02 17 79  H
                                      *****

0000000101 WHR  2 X 4 Redwood         00050 00040 EA  022.00 025.00 0525.00  0605.00 12 05 80  01 25 81  H
**********                                        **  ******

0000600500 IP   Wood Panels           00250 00300 BF  011.00 009.00 0095.00  0120.00 12 28 78  01 13 81  U
                                      *****                                                            *

0000890200 BM   Yellow Exterior       00306 00315 DZ  twelv  e1125  0075.00  0050.00 08 70 79  06 30 80  A
                                      *****       **  ****** ******          *******    **

0000224200 GEN  Nuts and Bolts        50000 50000 OZ  000.50 000.50 0012.00  0015.00 02 07 81  02 05 82  I
                                                                                             **

0000985040 JB   Hot Pink Paint        00005  Two  PT  002.00 001.50 0002.00  0002.00 09 15 79  04 21 80  H
                                            *****

0000765090 UPA  4 X 6 Aspen           00549 00500 M   022.00 021.00 0150.00  0175.00 04 04 81  06 09 79  D
                                                  **

0000382110 PIT  Red Interior          00150 00200 QT  010.00 006.50 0010.00  0020.00 01 20 80  12 01 79  D
                                      *****

0001000000 GEN  Small Screwdriver     00800 00500 QT  000.95 001.00 0019.00  0025.00 10 22 80  10 02 80  E
                                                  **  ******                                             *

0000465470 GLD  Avocado-Kitchen       00095 00075 GA  012.50 nine   0012.50  0025.00 04 27 80  04 01 80  R
                                                         ******                                          *

0000505020 BM   Golden Yellow Flat    00095 00100 GA  014.90 013.50 0028.00  sixty   03 03 79  03 03 79  E
                                      *****                                  *******                     *

0000610010 JMV  Burnt Orange Gloss    00050 00075 QT  009.25 007.20 0009.25  0009.25 02 14 81  02 07 81  I
                                      *****

0000765050 UPA  Sheetrock             01000 01000 BF  010.00 009.00 0090.00  0050.00 11 28 80  02 05 81  A
                                                                             *******
```

Summary

With the IF statement conditions presented in this chapter, all possible condition types available in standard COBOL have been discussed. Thus, the programmer may choose among IF statement conditions stated in terms of

1. A relational test
2. A sign test
3. A class test
4. A condition-name test

Conditions stated in the PERFORM/UNTIL can also be altered to use these condition types. And condition types may be joined in compound conditions (by using the logical operators AND or OR).

Notes on Programming Style

Although this chapter has introduced three new condition types, all the notes pertaining to IF statements presented in Chapter 9 still apply. You should select the condition type that makes your code the most readable and understandable. Some commercial installations have banned (or at least restricted) the use of the condition-name test. The rationale is that a person reading the code for the first time (e.g., a maintenance programmer) would be required to flip back and forth between the DATA DIVISION and the PROCEDURE DIVISION to determine the actual testing conditions each time a condition-name test is employed.

Questions

Below fill in the blank(s) with the appropriate word, words, or phrases.

1. If an identifier is used in a sign test, it must have a ____ PICTURE description.
2. The logical operator ____ may be used in a compound sign test, but the logical operator ____ results in an IF statement that will always be false.
3. The class test may be used to determine whether an identifier contains ____ or ____ data.
4. A condition-name is always associated with the level ____ number.
5. If a series of values are associated with a condition-name, they must be assigned in ____ order.
6. The values associated with a condition-name must be consistent with the ____ to which it is subordinate.

Answer the following questions by circling ''T'' for True or ''F'' for False.

T F 7. Literals may appear in a sign test.

T F 8. Both the subject and the sign test operator (e.g., ZERO) may be implied in a sign test.

T F 9. A class test in the NUMERIC test mode may be used to test the results of an arithmetic operation.

T F **10.** A condition-name has the same characteristics as any other data-name (e.g., it could be used for computational purposes).

T F **11.** A condition-name may be associated with a single value or a series of values.

T F **12.** Any condition stated in terms of a sign test could be restated in terms of a relational test.

T F **13.** Any condition stated in terms of a relational test could be restated in terms of a sign test.

Exercises

1. Below is a series of IF statements. Indicate whether or not each statement has been coded in acceptable form. If the form is correct, identify the condition in use and which statement(s) constitute the "true" and "false" imperative statements. If the statement is wrong, indicate the probable cause of the error.

a.
```
IF EXAM-TOTAL IS ZERO
    MOVE 'DIVISION ERROR-PROCEDURE ABORTED'
    TO OUTPUT-LINE
    WRITE OUTPUT-LINE AFTER ADVANCING 1 LINES
    STOP RUN.
```

b.
```
IF DEPENDENT-COUNT NUMERIC
    PERFORM DEPENDENT-DEDUCTIONS
ELSE
    NEXT SENTENCE.
```

c.
```
IF 1000 IS POSITIVE
    GO TO DEDUCT-STANDARD
ELSE
    GO TO DEDUCT-ITEMIZED.
```

d.
```
IF 'W2' IS ALPHABETIC
    MOVE 'W-2 FILED' TO EMPLOYEE-STATUS
ELSE
    MOVE 'NO W-2' TO EMPLOYEE-STATUS.
```

2. Below is a series of IF statements. Determine whether or not each statement is correct, and if so, indicate the type of condition(s) that is (are) used. If the statement is incorrect, indicate the probable cause of the error.

a.
```
IF EMPLOYEE-TYPE IS HOURLY AND
    HOURS-WORKED GREATER THAN 40
    PERFORM OVERTIME-CALCULATIONS
ELSE
    PERFORM STRAIGHT-TIME-CALCULATIONS.
```

b.
```
IF DAILY-HOURS IS GREATER THAN OR EQUAL TO 40
    PERFORM DAILY-OVERTIME.
```

c.
```
IF EXTRA-TAX-DEDUCTION IS POSITIVE AND NOT = 9999
    SUBTRACT EXTRA-TAX-DEDUCTION FROM NET-PAY.
```

d.
```
    05 MARITAL-STATUS            PIC X(01).
       88 SINGLE              VALUE 'S'.
       88 MARRIED             VALUE 'M'.
IF MARITAL-STATUS = MARRIED
    PERFORM MARRIED-TAX-TABLE
ELSE
    PERFORM SINGLE-TAX-TABLE
```

e.
```
    05 SHIFT-WORKED          PIC 9(01).
        88 1ST-SHIFT         VALUE 1.
        88 2ND-SHIFT         VALUE 2.
        88 3RD-SHIFT         VALUE 3.
IF 1ST-SHIFT
    MOVE 0 TO SHIFT-DIFFERENTIAL
ELSE
    IF 2ND-SHIFT
        MOVE PREMIUM-SECOND TO SHIFT-DIFFERENTIAL
    ELSE
        IF 3RD-SHIFT
            MOVE PREMIUM-THIRD TO SHIFT-DIFFERENTIAL
        ELSE
            MOVE 'SHIFT VALUE ERROR' TO MESSAGE-OUT
            WRITE PRINT-LINE AFTER ADVANCING 2 LINES.
```

f.
```
  04 DEPARTMENT-NUMBER               PIC 9(03).
     88 EXECUTIVE-STAFF              VALUE 100 THRU 150.
     88 ACCOUNTING-STAFF             VALUE 200 THRU 299.
     88 MARKETING-RESEARCH           VALUE 300.
     88 PRODUCTION-DEPARTMENT        VALUE 400 THRU 599.
     88 SHIPPING-DEPARTMENT          VALUE 600 THRU 610.
IF (EXECUTIVE-STAFF OR MARKETING RESEARCH) AND (PAY-TYPE =
    'H' OR 'X')
    MOVE 'PAY TYPE ERROR' TO MESSAGE
ELSE
    PERFORM PAY-CALCULATIONS.
```

3. In a payroll application, employees are often divided into at least four categories:

a. Salaried-exempt (salaried with no overtime pay)
b. Salaried-nonexempt (salaried with overtime pay possible)
c. Hourly-exempt (pay is based on rate per hour with no provision for overtime)
d. Hourly-nonexempt (pay is based on rate per hour with overtime pay when hours worked exceed the regular hourly limit)

Assume an input record contains a field called PAY-CODE. This field is a single character alphanumeric and should contain the following values:

VALUE	MEANING
S	Salaried-exempt
O	Salaried-nonexempt
X	Hourly exempt
H	Hourly nonexempt

Write the PROCEDURE DIVISION code necessary to distinguish between (among) the pay codes such that when PAY-CODE is S, the variable BASE contains "salary" and the variable OVERTIME contains "no." If an employee is nonexempt, OVERTIME should contain "yes." If an employee is paid on an hourly basis, BASE should contain "hours." Regardless of the values placed in BASE and OVERTIME, these values are to be written. Furthermore, do not assume that PAY-CODE contains only legitimate values. If PAY-CODE does not contain S, O, X, or H, both BASE and OVERTIME should contain "error."

Write this code using relational IF statements; then rewrite the code employing condition-name tests.

Problems

11.1 You are charged with checking all customer records for payment accuracy. Each customer has been sent a statement and has returned the statement along with a payment. Each record consists of the following (see multiple-card layout form):

1. Customer number—5 characters
2. Customer name—20 characters
3. Street address—20 characters
4. City—10 characters
5. State—2 characters (State-name abbreviations)
6. Zip code—5 digits
7. Amount of statement—5 digits including 2 decimal positions (dollars and cents)
8. Amount of payment—5 digits including 2 decimal positions (dollars and cents)
9. Date payment due— 4 digits in the format MMDD
10. Date of payment— 4 digits in the format MMDD

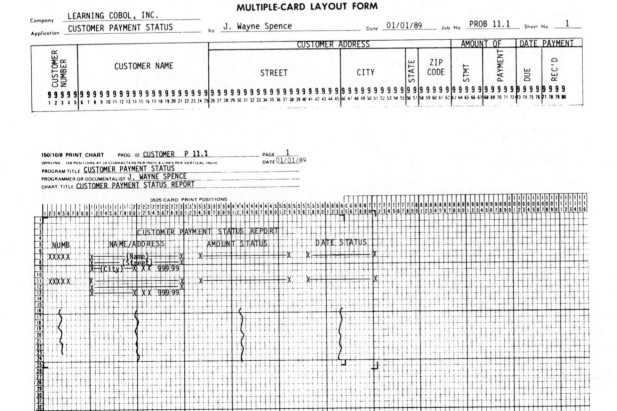

MULTIPLE-CARD LAYOUT FORM

Company LEARNING COBOL, INC.
Application CUSTOMER PAYMENT STATUS by J. Wayne Spence Date 01/01/89 Job No. PROB 11.1 Sheet No. 1

		CUSTOMER ADDRESS				AMOUNT OF		DATE PAYMENT	
CUSTOMER NUMBER	CUSTOMER NAME	STREET	CITY	STATE	ZIP CODE	STMT	PAYMENT	DUE	REC'D
9 9 9 9 9	9 9 9 9 9 9 9 9 9 9 9 9 9 9 9 9 9 9 9 9	9 9 9 9 9 9 9 9 9 9 9 9 9 9 9 9 9 9 9 9	9 9 9 9 9 9 9 9 9 9	9 9	9 9 9 9 9	9 9 9 9 9	9 9 9 9 9	9 9 9 9	9 9 9 9
1 2 3 4 5	6 7 8 9 10 11 12 13 14 15 16 17 18 19 20 21 22 23 24 25	26 27 28 29 30 31 32 33 34 35 36 37 38 39 40 41 42 43 44 45	46 47 48 49 50 51 52 53 54 55	56 57	58 59 60 61 62	63 64 65 66 67	68 69 70 71 72	73 74 75 76	77 78 79 80

150/10/8 PRINT CHART PROG. ID. CUSTOMER P 11.1 PAGE 1
(SPACING: 150 POSITIONS AT 10 CHARACTERS PER INCH, 8 LINES PER VERTICAL INCH) DATE 01/01/89
PROGRAM TITLE CUSTOMER PAYMENT STATUS
PROGRAMMER OR DOCUMENTALIST J. WAYNE SPENCE
CHART TITLE CUSTOMER PAYMENT STATUS REPORT

3525 CARD PRINT POSITIONS

```
3                      CUSTOMER PAYMENT STATUS REPORT
5   NUMB          NAME/ADDRESS              AMOUNT STATUS            DATE STATUS
7   XXXXX       X-----(Name)-----X     X------------------X     X---------------X
8               X-----(Street)---X
9               X-(City)-X XX 999 99
11  XXXXX       X----------------X     X------------------X     X---------------X
12              X----------------X
13              X--------X XX 999 99
```

Check the amount of the statement against the amount of payment, and print one of the following messages in the PAYMENT STATUS field:

1. "PAYMENT CORRECT"—amount of statement = payment
2. "PAYMENT INSUFFICIENT"—amount of statement greater than payment
3. "CREDIT DUE"—amount of statement less than payment

Then check the date the payment was due against the date the payment was received, and print one of the following messages in the DATE STATUS field:

1. "PAYMENT EARLY"—payment received prior to due date
2. "PAYMENT ON TIME"—payment received on due date
3. "PAYMENT LATE"—payment received after due date

See the print chart for additional details.

11.2 You are provided with a series of new employee records that are to be added to the Employee Data File. Before the records are added to the file, they should be edited for proper values. The new employee records have been ordered by department number, and the employee numbers should be in ascending order within each department.

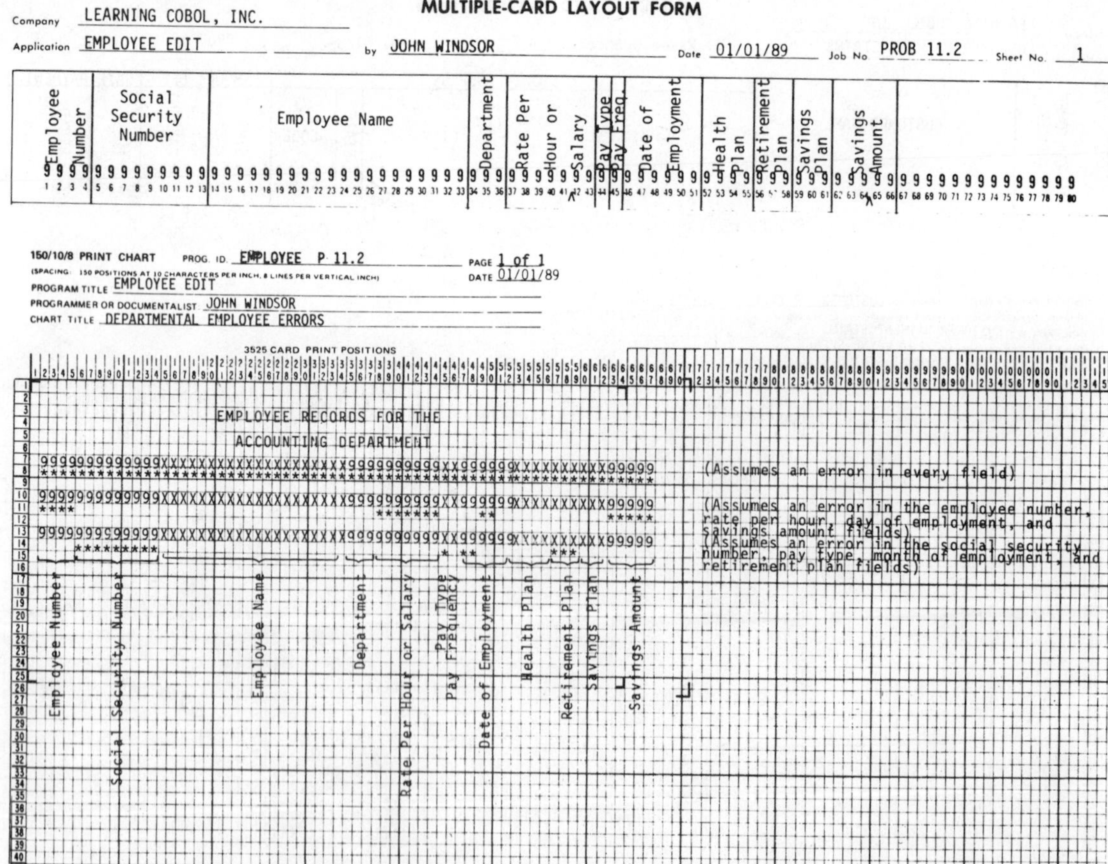

MULTIPLE-CARD LAYOUT FORM

Company LEARNING COBOL, INC.
Application EMPLOYEE EDIT by JOHN WINDSOR Date 01/01/89 Job No. PROB 11.2 Sheet No. 1

Card fields: Employee Number (1–4); Social Security Number (5–13); Employee Name (14–33); Department (34–36); Rate Per Hour or Salary (37–42); Pay Type (43); Pay Freq. (44); Date of Employment (45–51); Health Plan (52–55); Retirement Plan (56–58); Savings Plan (59–61); Savings Amount (62–66)

150/10/8 PRINT CHART PROG. ID. EMPLOYEE P 11.2 PAGE 1 of 1
(SPACING: 150 POSITIONS AT 10 CHARACTERS PER INCH, 8 LINES PER VERTICAL INCH) DATE 01/01/89
PROGRAM TITLE EMPLOYEE EDIT
PROGRAMMER OR DOCUMENTALIST JOHN WINDSOR
CHART TITLE DEPARTMENTAL EMPLOYEE ERRORS

EMPLOYEE RECORDS FOR THE
ACCOUNTING DEPARTMENT

999999999999XXXXXXXXXXXXXXXXXXXXX999999999XX99999XXXXXXXXX99999 (Assumes an error in every field)
999999999999XXXXXXXXXXXXXXXXXXXXX999999999XX99999XXXXXXXXX99999 (Assumes an error in the employee number, rate per hour, day of employment, and savings amount fields)
999999999999XXXXXXXXXXXXXXXXXXXXX999999999XX99999XXXXXXXXX99999 (Assumes an error in the social security number, pay type, month of employment, and retirement plan fields)

Employee Number, Social Security Number, Employee Name, Department, Rate Per Hour or Salary, Pay Type, Pay Frequency, Date of Employment, Health Plan, Retirement Plan, Savings Plan, Savings Amount

The following editing is to be performed on the fields of each new employee record (see multiple-column layout form):

1. The employee number should be numeric and in ascending order within a department.
2. The social security number should be numeric.
3. The employee name should not be blank.
4. The department number should be 100, 200, 300, 400, or 500 (and should be grouped together—that is, all 100s should be in a group, all 200s should be in a group, and so forth).
5. The pay type should be either H (hourly) or S (salaried).
6. The rate per hour or salary field should be numeric. If the pay type is H, the rate per hour should be in the range of $5 to $20. If the pay type is S, the salary should be between $200 and $800 if paid weekly, $400 to $1600 if paid biweekly, $500 to $2,000 if paid semimonthly, and $1000 to $4000 if paid monthly.
7. The pay frequency should be W (weekly), B (biweekly), S (semimonthly), or M (monthly).
8. The date of employment should be reasonable—the monthly value should be between 1 and 12, the daily value should be between 1 and 31, and the yearly value should be the current year.
9. The health plan should be "NONE" (no health plan), "HIGH" (health plan—high option), or "LOW" (health plan—low option).
10. The retirement plan should be either "YES" (enrolled in a retirement plan) or "NO" (not enrolled in a retirement plan).
11. The savings plan should be either "YES" (employee desires a savings deduction) or "NO" (employee does not desire a savings deduction).
12. The savings amount should either be numeric, if the savings plan code is "YES," or blank, if the savings plan code is "NO."

The printed edit-results report should mark (with asterisk) any field that does not conform to these editing standards. In the event that no errors are encountered, the employee record is not to be printed on the report—only those records with errors are to be printed. The output line for each employee record in error should be an exact duplicate of the input record. Each field in error should have asterisks located immediately below it. (See the print chart). Furthermore, each department should begin on a new page; "ACCOUNTING" should be printed in the heading if the department number is 100; "SALES," if 200; "MANUFACTURING," if 300; "PURCHASING," if 400; and "RECEIVING," if 500.

11.3 Presume another procedure has been executed to produce records to govern the printing of a balance sheet. (A *balance sheet* is a formal financial statement generally produced by the accounting department for purposes of determining a company's financial status.) The contents of each of these records is as follows (see the graphic record layout):

1. Account number—4 digits
2. Account title—30 characters
3. Monetary amount—8 digits (whole dollars)
4. Print control indicator—1 character

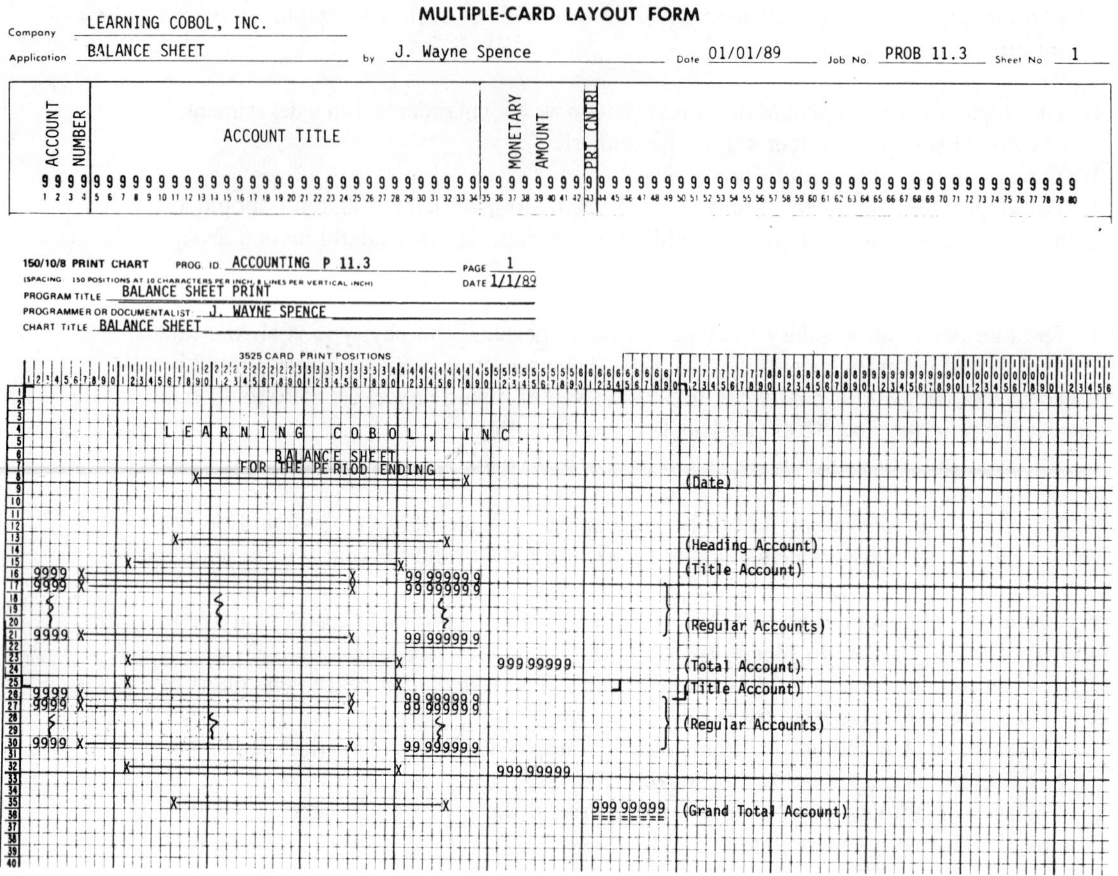

The print control indicator is used to distinguish between the different types of accounts and to determine what is to be printed and where. (See the print chart.) The print control indicator should be used as described here.

If the print control indicator is "1," the record contains a regular (money) account, and the account number, title, and monetary amount should be printed in the specified locations in a single-spaced format.

If the print control indicator is "2," the record contains a title account, and only the title is to be printed in the specified location, preceded by one blank line.

If the print control indicator is "3," the record contains a total account, and the account title and monetary amount should be printed in the specified locations preceded by one blank line. However, the preceding regular account record monetary-amount field should be underscored (use a row of hyphens on the next line if your printer does not permit underscoring).

If the print control indicator is "4," the record contains a heading-account record, and only the account title is to be printed in the specified location, preceded by four blank lines.

If the print control indicator is "5," the record contains a grand total amount, and the account title and monetary amount are to be printed in the specified locations preceded by two blank lines. The monetary-amount field should be double underscored (with a row of equal symbols) on the following line.

Special Options:

1. The *first* record in the data file contains the report date that is to appear in the heading. The date will appear in the account title field already formatted in the form needed for printing. (If this option is not used, the program due date should appear in the date field (as a literal).

2. The report heading is to be produced at the top of the page only when the first digit of the account number is 1 (assets) or 2 (liabilities) when a heading account record is processed. (If this option is not used, place the heading at the top of the first page only.)

CHAPTER

12

More on the PERFORM Statements

In Chapter 6, two PERFORM statements were discussed—the simple PERFORM and the PERFORM/UNTIL. The remaining PERFORM statements—the PERFORM/TIMES and the PERFORM/VARYING—are often controlled by counting operations.

The PERFORM/TIMES and PERFORM/VARYING statements, shown in Figures 12.1 and 12.3, are similar to the other PERFORM statements. The procedure-names specify the paragraphs or SECTIONs to be executed. If procedure-name-2 is specified with the THROUGH (THRU) option, it must be located below procedure-name-1 in the program. And when the procedure has been completed, program control returns to the statement that follows the PERFORM statement.

The PERFORM/TIMES Statement

The PERFORM/TIMES statement permits the programmer to execute a procedure a fixed number of times with one execution of the statement. Prior to the reserved word TIMES, the programmer specifies identifier-1 or integer-1. Identifier-1 must be described in the DATA DIVISION as an elementary data item with a numeric-nonedited description. Identifier-1 should contain a positive integer value prior to the execution of the PERFORM statement. Later, that value may be changed to zero or a negative if the PERFORM statement is to be bypassed during execution. Integer-1 must be a positive integer-value. Although the value of identifier-1 may be changed from one execution of the PERFORM statement to the next, each execution of the procedure will be repeated the number of times specified when the PERFORM *begins,* even if the value of the identifier is altered during execution of the procedure.

Figure 12.2 presents several illustrations of the PERFORM/TIMES statement. Each of the examples includes a list of the procedures executed.

In Figure 12.2a, a simple use of the PERFORM/TIMES statement is shown; HEADER-RECORD is executed two times. The paragraph is executed once when the procedure-name following HEADER-RECORD is encountered or when the end of the PROCEDURE DIVISION is reached. In Figure 12.2b, a set of procedures beginning with SETS-OF-LABELS and ending with LABEL-SUMMARY is executed three times. While

Figure 12.1 The PERFORM/TIMES Statement

```
Format 3: The PERFORM/TIMES Statement

PERFORM procedure-name-1 [{THROUGH | THRU} procedure-name-2]

[WITH TEST {BEFORE | AFTER}] {identifier-1 | integer-1} TIMES [[imperative-statement-1]

[END-PERFORM]]
```

Figure 12.2 Illustrations of the PERFORM/TIMES Statement

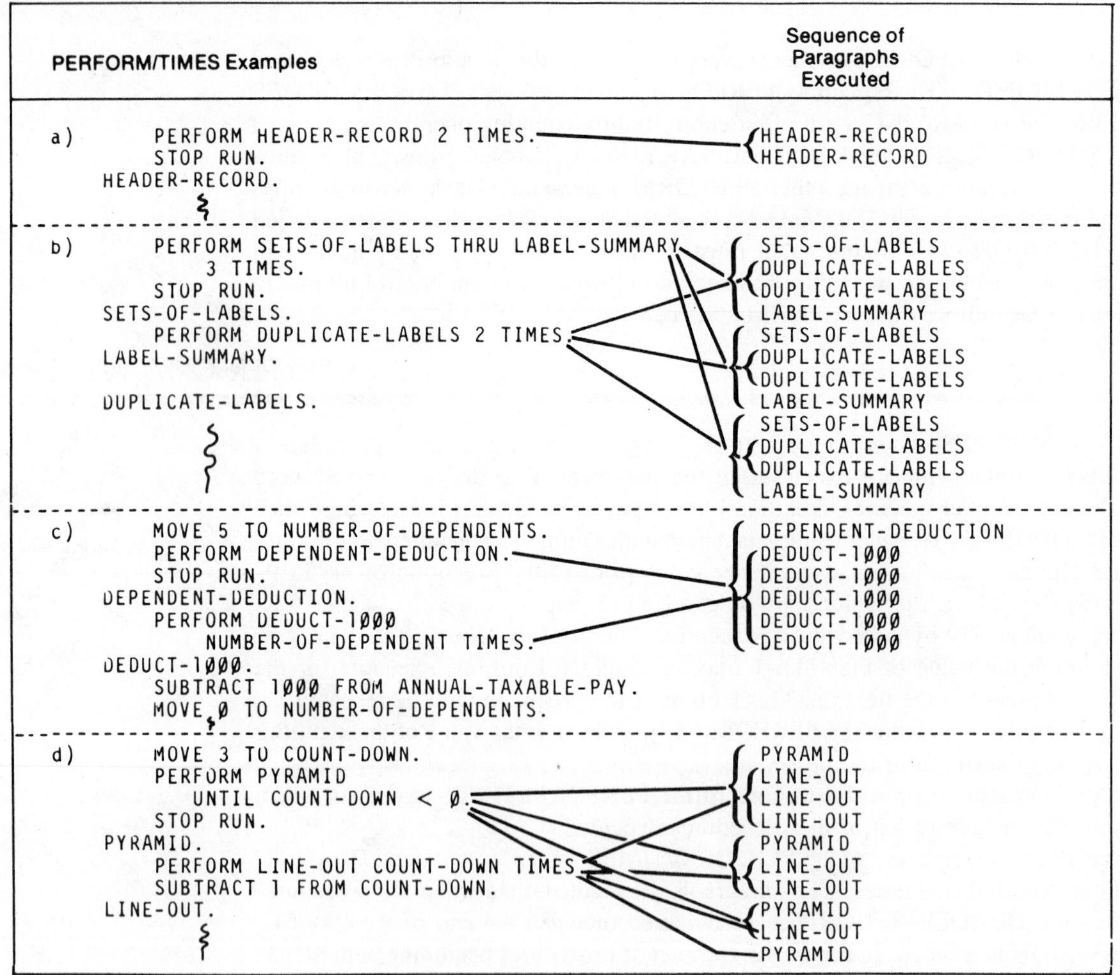

processing SETS-OF-LABELS the first time, another PERFORM/TIMES statement is encountered, causing DUPLICATE-LABELS to be executed twice. When the processing of DUPLICATE-LABELS has been completed, the execution sequence continues from the point where DUPLICATE-LABELS was originally invoked. LABEL-SUMMARY is then encountered in a "fall through" condition. When the end of LABEL-SUMMARY has been reached, the original PERFORM has completed one cycle. This cycle is completed two more times before the procedure is terminated.

In Figure 12.2c, a simple PERFORM statement is combined with a PERFORM/TIMES statement. In this example, the PERFORM/TIMES is based on the value of an identifier. Although the illustration shows the value of NUMBER-OF-DEPENDENTS being generated by a MOVE statement, the value could just as easily be derived from an input operation or through arithmetic manipulation. After the MOVE statement has been executed DEPENDENT-DEDUCTION is invoked. Within this paragraph, DEDUCT-1000 is invoked—to be repeated five times (the current value of NUMBER-OF-DEPENDENTS). Within the DEDUCT-1000 paragraph, NUMBER-OF-DEPENDENTS is set to zero, which has no effect on the number of times DEDUCT-1000 is executed in the illustrated procedure.

Figure 12.2d demonstrates a situation in which an identifier associated with a PERFORM/TIMES is modified, and the modification has an effect on the executed procedure. The illustration combines a PERFORM/UNTIL with a PERFORM/TIMES statement. The identifier COUNT-DOWN, used to control the activity of the procedure, is initialized to 3. Then a PERFORM/UNTIL is executed, to be terminated only when COUNT-DOWN is less than zero. While PYRAMID is being executed the first time, a PERFORM/TIMES statement is encountered, causing LINE-OUT to be executed COUNT-DOWN (3) times. When the execution of LINE-COUNT has been completed, COUNT-DOWN is decremented by one. The end of PYRAMID is encountered, but the current value of COUNT-DOWN (2) is not yet less than zero; thus, PYRAMID is repeated. With the reexecution of PYRAMID, the PERFORM/TIMES statement causes LINE-OUT to be executed twice. COUNT-DOWN is again decremented (to a value of one); COUNT-DOWN is still not less than zero. PYRAMID is reexecuted, and LINE-OUT is performed one time. Finally, COUNT-DOWN is decremented to zero, PYRAMID is repeated, LINE-COUNT is *not* performed, COUNT-DOWN is decremented to minus one, the UNTIL condition is true, and the procedure is terminated.

The PERFORM/VARYING Statement

The PERFORM/VARYING statement is most often (but not exclusively) used with the manipulation of tables in COBOL. (Table handling in COBOL is discussed in Chapters 13 and 14.) This type of PERFORM statement permits the modification of a data item (identifier-2) or data items (identifier-2, identifier-5, and identifier-8). (See Figure 12.3.) These data items may be either identifiers (numeric-nonedited elementary items) or *index-names*. Index-names are directly associated with table manipulations, and they will be discussed in detail in Chapter 14. This chapter is limited to the use of identifiers and/or literals in the PERFORM/VARYING statement.

During the execution of the PERFORM/VARYING statement, the value of the identifier following the reserved word VARYING will be altered as a result of other portions of the statement. Identifier-3 (identifier-6 and identifier-9), which follows the reserved word FROM, should be an elementary item containing a positive-integer value. Literal-1

Figure 12.3 The PERFORM/VARYING Statement

```
Format 4:  The PERFORM/VARYING Statement

                       [ {THROUGH}                    ]
PERFORM procedure-name-1 [ {THRU   }   procedure-name-2 ]

[            {BEFORE}]          {identifier-2}        {identifier-3}
[ WITH TEST  {      }] VARYING  {            } FROM   {index-name-2}
[            {AFTER }]          {index-name-1}        {literal-1   }

   {identifier-4}
BY {            } UNTIL  condition-1
   {literal-2   }

[       {identifier-5}        {identifier-6}      {identifier-7}
[ AFTER {            } FROM   {index-name-4}  BY  {            }
[       {index-name-3}        {literal-3   }      {literal-4   }

    UNTIL condition-2

        {identifier-8}        {identifier-9}      {identifier-10}
  AFTER {    FROM    }        {index-name-6}  BY  {             }
        {index-name-5}        {literal-3   }      {literal-6    }

    UNTIL condition-3                        ]
[                                            ]
[ imperative-statement-1 [END-PERFORM]       ]
```

(literal-3, and literal-5) should be a positive-integer numeric literal. This data item or value represents the initial value to be placed in identifier-2 (identifier-5 and identifier-8, respectively). Thus, the value indicated immediately after the reserved word FROM will be the value of the identifier when the PERFORM statement is executed initially.

The identifiers or literals immediately after the reserved word BY represent an incremental value—that is, these identifiers or literals are added to the value contained in the identifier(s) following the reserved words VARYING or AFTER. The identifier(s) following VARYING or AFTER will continue to be incremented until their respective conditions are found to be true. The incremental identifiers (identifier-4, identifier-7, and identifier-10) and literals (literal-2, literal-4, and literal-6) should be integers (but not necessarily positive) with the same restrictions for the initial values as for the identifier(s) being modified. The identifiers continue to be modified until the conditions associated with them are true. When a condition is true, the next step depends on the condition with which the identifier was associated. If only the VARYING phrase is specified, the execution of the PERFORM statement is terminated when condition-1 is true. If the first optional AFTER phrase is provided, and condition-2 is true, only that part of the PERFORM statement is terminated, identifier-2 is incremented, and condition-1 is tested. The same operation takes place for the second AFTER phrase. When condition-3 is true, that portion of the PERFORM statement is terminated, identifier-5 is incremented, and condition-2 is tested.

Figure 12.4 shows the inner workings of the PERFORM/VARYING statement. Figure 12.4a flowcharts the process executed by the PERFORM/VARYING statement. If the statement is written with only the VARYING phrase, the process begins by initializing the data item following the reserved word VARYING and testing the condition associated

Figure 12.4 Flowcharts of the PERFORM/VARING Statement

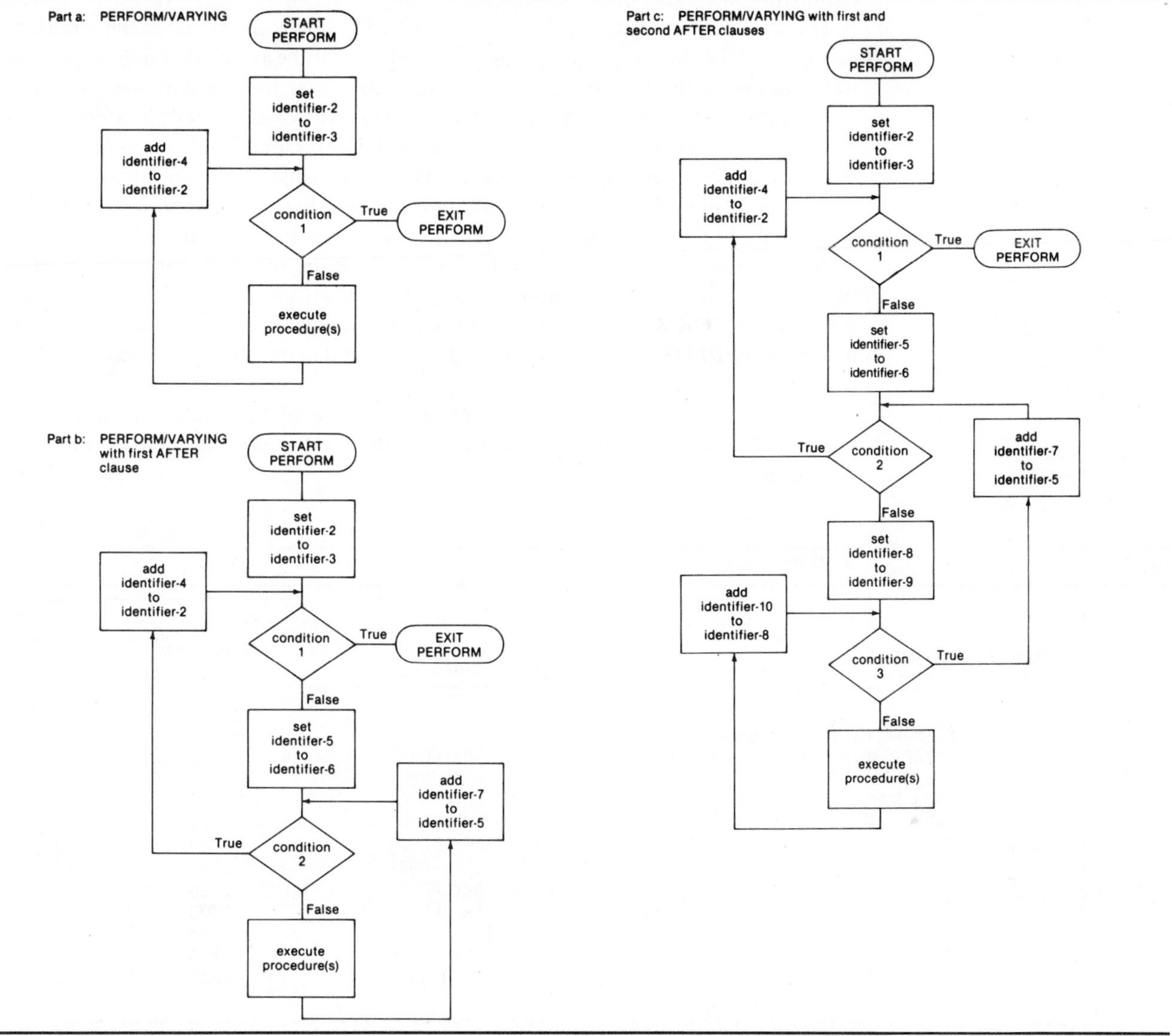

with the phrase. If the condition is false, the procedure or the indicated set of procedures is executed. After the procedure has been executed, the identifier is incremented, and the test of the condition is repeated. This process continues until the condition is true, at which time the PERFORM statement is terminated.

If the first optional AFTER phrase is added to the PERFORM/VARYING statement (Figure 12.4b), the function of the statement is the same as previously described up to the point when the procedure is executed. Prior to the execution of the procedure, the second identifier is initialized. The second condition is then tested. If the condition is false, the procedure is executed. After the procedure has been executed, the second identifier is incremented, and the second condition is retested. This process continues until condition-2 is true. Then, instead of the PERFORM statement being terminated, the first identifier is incremented, and condition-1 is retested. If condition-1 is false, the second identifier is reinitialized, and the process continues until condition-1 is true—terminating the PERFORM statement.

The final version of the PERFORM/VARYING statement calls for the addition of a second AFTER phrase (Figure 12.4c). As before, all the boxes that appear prior to the initialization of the third identifier are executed. After the second condition is tested (and found to be false), however, the third data item is initialized, and condition-3 is tested. If the condition is false, the procedure is executed, and the third identifier is incremented. If condition-3 is true, the path from the decision on condition-3 to increment the second identifier is executed. Condition-2 is retested, and if false the third identifier is reinitialized and the process is repeated. When condition-2 is true, the first identifier is incremented, condition-1 is retested, and if false the second identifier is reinitialized (which generally causes a reinitialization of the third identifier). When condition-1 is true, the PERFORM statement is terminated. Thus, regardless of the number of "levels" within the PERFORM statement, the only situation that terminates the statement is when condition-1 is true.

Figure 12.5 provides a series of examples. A list of the values of the identifier(s) modified by the statement and the names of the procedures executed are provided for each example.

Figure 12.5 Illustrations of the PERFORM/VARYING Statement

PERFORM/VARYING Examples	Sequence of Paragraphs Executed	Identifier(s) Values

a)

```
    PERFORM MILITARY-HOURS
        VARYING HOURS FROM 8ØØ BY 1ØØ
            UNTIL HOURS GREATER THAN 18ØØ.
    STOP RUN.
MILITARY-HOURS.
```

Sequence of Paragraphs Executed	HOURS
MILITARY-HOURS	800
MILITARY-HOURS	900
MILITARY-HOURS	1000
MILITARY-HOURS	1100
MILITARY-HOURS	1200
MILITARY-HOURS	1300
MILITARY-HOURS	1400
MILITARY-HOURS	1500
MILITARY-HOURS	1600
MILITARY-HOURS	1700
MILITARY-HOURS	1800
	1900

b)

```
    PERFORM INPUT-PROCEDURE
        VARYING RECORD-COUNT FROM 1 BY 1
            UNTIL FILE-STATUS = 'COMPLETE'.
    PERFORM AVERAGES.
    STOP RUN.
INPUT-PROCEDURE.
     READ EMPLOYEE-RECORDS
         AT END MOVE 'COMPLETE'
             TO FILE-STATUS.
     IF FILE-STATUS NOT = 'COMPLETE'
         PERFORM COMPUTE-AND-WRITE.
COMPUTE-AND-WRITE.

AVERAGES.
    SUBTRACT 1 FROM RECORD-COUNT.
```

Sequence of Paragraphs Executed	RECORD-COUNT
INPUT-PROCEDURE	1
COMPUTE-AND-WRITE	1
INPUT-PROCEDURE	2
COMPUTE-AND-WRITE	2
.	End-of-file
.	encountered on
.	EMPLOYEE-RECORDS
AVERAGES	

Figure 12.5a illustrates the simplest use of the PERFORM/VARYING statement. The "indexing" identifier is initialized to 800, and the condition is tested. Since HOURS is *not* greater than 1800, the paragraph MILITARY-HOURS is invoked. Once the end of the paragraph is reached, HOURS is incremented by 100 (to 900), and the condition is rechecked. Since the condition is not yet true, the paragraph is repeated. MILITARY-HOURS will continue to be repeated until HOURS is greater than 1800; that is, HOURS

Figure 12.5 *Continued* Illustrations of the PERFORM/VARYING Statements

PERFORM/VARYING Examples | **Sequence of Paragraphs Executed** | **Identifier(s) Values**

c)

```
        PERFORM CALENDAR
          VARYING YEAR FROM 1980 BY 1
            UNTIL YEAR > 1981
          AFTER MONTH FROM 1 BY 1
            UNTIL MONTH > 12.
        STOP RUN.
    CALENDAR.
```

Sequence of Paragraphs Executed	MONTH	YEAR
CALENDAR	1	1980
CALENDAR	2	1980
CALENDAR	3	1980
CALENDAR	4	1980
CALENDAR	5	1980
CALENDAR	6	1980
CALENDAR	7	1980
CALENDAR	8	1980
CALENDAR	9	1980
CALENDAR	10	1980
CALENDAR	11	1980
CALENDAR	12	1980
-	13	1980
CALENDAR	1	1981
CALENDAR	2	1981
.	.	.
.	.	.
.	.	.
CALENDAR	11	1981
CALENDAR	12	1981
-	13	1981
-	13	1982

d)

```
        MOVE 5 TO WORKDAYS.
        MOVE 3 TO MONTH-DURATION.
        PERFORM PROJECT-CYCLE
          VARYING MONTH FROM 1 BY 1
            UNTIL MONTH > MONTH-DURATION
          AFTER DAYS FROM 1 BY 1
            UNTIL DAYS > WORKDAYS.
          STOP RUN.
    PROJECT-CYCLE.
```

Sequence of Paragraphs Executed	DAYS	MONTH
PROJECT-CYCLE	1	1
PROJECT-CYCLE	2	1
PROJECT-CYCLE	3	1
PROJECT-CYCLE	4	1
PROJECT-CYCLE	5	1
-	6	1
PROJECT-CYCLE	1	2
PROJECT-CYCLE	2	2
PROJECT-CYCLE	3	2
PROJECT-CYCLE	4	2
PROJECT-CYCLE	5	2
-	6	2
PROJECT-CYCLE	1	3
PROJECT-CYCLE	2	3
PROJECT-CYCLE	3	3
PROJECT-CYCLE	4	3
PROJECT-CYCLE	5	3
-	6	3
-	6	4

Figure 12.5 Illustrations of the PERFORM/VARYING Statement

PERFORM/VARYING Examples	Sequence of Paragraphs Executed	Identifier(s) Values

e)

```
    MOVE 15 TO HOURS-INCREMENT.
    PERFORM TIME-SLOTS
      VARYING AM-PM FROM 1 BY 1
        UNTIL AM-PM > 2
      AFTER DAYS-OF-WEEK FROM 1 BY 1
        UNTIL DAYS-OF-WEEK > 7
      AFTER HOURS FROM Ø BY
        HOURS-INCREMENT
        UNTIL HOURS > 6Ø.
    STOP RUN.
TIME-SLOTS.
```

Sequence of Paragraphs Executed	HOURS	DAYS-OF-WEEK	AM-PM
TIME-SLOT	0	1	1
TIME-SLOT	15	1	1
TIME-SLOT	30	1	1
TIME-SLOT	60	1	1
-	75	1	1
TIME-SLOT	0	2	1
TIME-SLOT	15	2	1
TIME-SLOT	30	2	1
TIME-SLOT	60	2	1
-	75	2	1
TIME-SLOT	0	3	1
TIME-SLOT	15	3	1
...	...	...	...
TIME-SLOT	60	7	1
-	75	7	1
-	75	8	1
TIME-SLOT	0	1	2
...	...	...	...
TIME-SLOT	60	7	2
-	75	8	2
-	75	8	3

f)

```
    PERFORM INVERSION-SEQUENCE
      VARYING N FROM 1 BY 1
        UNTIL N > 4
      AFTER M FROM N BY 1
        UNTIL M > 4
      AFTER O FROM N BY -1
        UNTIL O < 1.
    STOP RUN
INVERSION-SEQUENCE.
```

Sequence of Paragraphs Executed	O	M	N
INVERSION-SEQUENCE	1	1	1
-	Ø	1	1
INVERSION-SEQUENCE	1	2	1
-	Ø	2	1
INVERSION-SEQUENCE	1	3	1
-	Ø	3	1
INVERSION-SEQUENCE	1	4	1
-	Ø	4	1
-	Ø	5	1
INVERSION-SEQUENCE	2	2	2
INVERSION-SEQUENCE	1	2	2
-	Ø	2	2
INVERSION-SEQUENCE	2	3	2
INVERSION-SEQUENCE	1	3	2
-	Ø	3	2
INVERSION-SEQUENCE	2	4	2
INVERSION-SEQUENCE	1	4	2
-	Ø	4	2
-	Ø	5	2
INVERSION-SEQUENCE	3	3	3
INVERSION-SEQUENCE	2	3	3
INVERSION-SEQUENCE	1	3	3
-	Ø	3	3
INVERSION-SEQUENCE	3	4	3
INVERSION-SEQUENCE	2	4	3
INVERSION-SEQUENCE	1	4	3
-	Ø	4	3
-	Ø	5	3
INVERSION-SEQUENCE	4	4	4
INVERSION-SEQUENCE	3	4	4
INVERSION-SEQUENCE	2	4	4
INVERSION-SEQUENCE	1	4	4
-	Ø	4	4
-	Ø	5	4
-	Ø	5	5

*"-" indicates the procedure is not executed; "..." means the repetition of a previously established pattern.

will be equal to 1900. At this point, the condition is true, the PERFORM is completed, and the procedure is terminated.

In Figure 12.5b, a PERFORM/VARYING statement is coupled with two simple PERFORM statements. In this example, however, the condition upon which the PERFORM/VARYING statement is terminated is *not* based on the data-name being changed by the statement. Rather, the statement is terminated upon encountering the end-of-file. The simple PERFORM statements are invoked on the conditions specified.

Figure 12.5c provides the first illustration of a PERFORM/VARYING statement with an AFTER option. Both MONTH and YEAR are initialized and modified (by increments of one). However, notice that MONTH will be incremented from 1 to 12 before YEAR is incremented. When YEAR is incremented, and provided its value is not greater than 1981, MONTH will proceed through the same sequence of values indicated for the first series of operations.

Figure 12.5d is different from Figure 12.5c in only two respects. First, the conditions used to terminate each phase of the PERFORM statement are based on a data-name rather than on a numeric literal. Second, the values of variables are different from the previous example to demonstrate that variables, rather than constants, may be used to control the activity of the PERFORM statement.

Figure 12.5e illustrates the maximum number of AFTER clauses that may be associated with a PERFORM/VARYING statement. In addition, a data-name is used to supply the incremental value of HOURS. As illustrated under the identifier values, HOURS is initialized to 0, along with DAYS-OF-WEEK and AM-PM (which are both set to 1). Further, notice that the full sequence of values to be associated with HOURS is generated before DAYS-OF-WEEK is incremented the first time. Eventually, enough sets of HOURS will be generated to cause DAYS-OF-WEEK to exceed 7. At that point, AM-PM is incremented the first time, and the entire process repeats itself. Thus, the last identifier associated with an AFTER option is the first identifier to be incremented and tested. When the conditions associated with the clause is true, then and only then are previously listed AFTER/VARYING-clause variables modified.

The final illustration, Figure 12.5f, demonstrates the possibility for interaction between the VARYING and AFTER clauses. Note from the illustration that the data-name N is being varied. In addition, N is used as the initial value of the two AFTER options. Finally, note that the values associated with the data-name O decline with each iteration. Decrementing is achieved, in this case, by using the numeric literal 1 as the incremental value of 0.

PERFORM/VARYING: An Example

One of the most commonly accepted principles used in the recovery of the cost of any major business asset (such as equipment) is depreciation. The Internal Revenue Service permits a tax "write-off" on the basis of the expected useful life of the asset, thereby permitting the business to recoup the cost of major investments (for possible later replacement). Although the intent of deducting depreciation from taxable income is a standard practice, the procedures for calculating the depreciation amount vary. The illustration in Figure 12.6 provides two different (but equally acceptable) ways of calculating depreciation.

In all cases, depreciation is based on the original value of the asset (less any salvage value after the expected useful life of the asset) spread over the useful life of the asset. In the straight-line depreciation method, the amount of depreciation is equal for all

Figure 12.6 Depreciation Schedules (Hierarchy Chart)

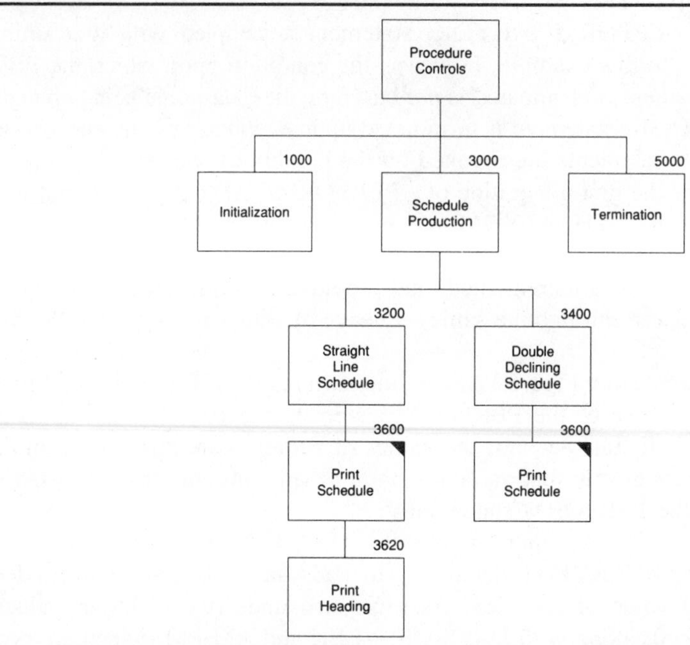

Figure 12.6 *Continued* Depreciation Schedules (Pseudocode)

```
START
    DO Initialization
    DO Schedule production UNTIL eof
    DO Termination
STOP

INITIALIZATION
    OPEN files
    MOVE 0 counters
END

SCHEDULE PRODUCTION
    READ input
         IF eof T END MOVE 'DONE'
              SET indicator
              GO TO END
         ENDIF
    SET schedule status
    SET page status
    MOVE input to output
    SUBTRACT salvage value from purchase value
         GIVING asset value
    IF straight line
         MOVE Straight Line to schedule title
         DO Straight line schedule
    ENDIF
    IF double declining balance
         MOVE Double Declining Balance
              to schedule title
         DO Double declining schedule
              VARYING depreciation period
               UNTIL schedule complete
         ENDDO
    ENDIF
    MOVE salvage value to output
    WRITE output
END

STRAIGHT LINE SCHEDULE
    COMPUTE depreciation =
            asset value * (1 / useful life)
    DO Print schedule
         VARYING depreciation period
         UNTIL schedule complete
    ENDDO
END

DOUBLE DECLINING SCHEDULE
    COMPUTE depreciation =
            asset value * (2 / useful life)
    DO Print schedule
END

PRINT SCHEDULE
    IF new page
         DO Print heading
    ENDIF
    SUBTRACT depreciation from asset value
         GIVING ending balance
    IF depreciation period = useful life
         SET schedule status
         ADD ending balance to depreciation
    ENDIF
    IF purchade month > 12
         MOVE 1 to purchase month
         ADD 1 to purchase year
         WRITE output
    ENDIF
    ADD depreciation to accumulation
    MOVE calculations to output
    WRITE output
    IF line count > 48
         SET page status
    ENDIF
    ADD 1 to purchase month
    MOVE ending balance to asset value
END

PRINT HEADING
    WRITE output
    ADD 1 to page count
    SET line counter
    SET page status
    WRITE output
    MOVE input to output
    WRITE heading output
    WRITE output
END

TERMINATION
    CLOSE files
END
```

Figure 12.6 *Continued* Depreciation Schedules

```
          1   1   2   2   2   3   3   4   4   4   5   5   6   6   6   7
   4   8   2   6   0   4   8   2   6   0   4   8   2   6   0   4   8   2

*****************************************************************
 IDENTIFICATION DIVISION.
*****************************************************************
 PROGRAM-ID.    DEPRECIATION-SCHEDULES.
 AUTHOR.        JOHN WINDSOR.
 DATE-WRITTEN.  JANUARY 1, 1989.
 DATE-COMPILED. JANUARY 1, 1989.
*****************************************************************
 ENVIRONMENT DIVISION.
*****************************************************************
*---------------------------------------------------------------*
 CONFIGURATION SECTION.
*---------------------------------------------------------------*
 SOURCE-COMPUTER.  IBM.
 OBJECT-COMPUTER.  IBM.
 SPECIAL-NAMES. C01 IS START-SCHEDULE.
*---------------------------------------------------------------*
 INPUT-OUTPUT SECTION.
*---------------------------------------------------------------*
 FILE-CONTROL.
     SELECT ASSET-FILE           ASSIGN TO UT-S-INPUT.
     SELECT SCHEDULE-REPORT-FILE ASSIGN TO UT-S-OUTPUT.
*****************************************************************
 DATA DIVISION.
*****************************************************************
*---------------------------------------------------------------*
 FILE SECTION.
*---------------------------------------------------------------*
 FD  ASSET-FILE LABEL RECORDS ARE OMITTED.
 01  ASSET-RECORD                PIC X(80).

 FD  SCHEDULE-REPORT-FILE LABEL RECORDS ARE OMITTED.
 01  SCHEDULE-RECORD             PIC X(133).
*---------------------------------------------------------------*
 WORKING-STORAGE SECTION.
*---------------------------------------------------------------*
 01  WORKING-STATUS-VARIABLES.
     05 FILE-STATUS              PIC X(04) VALUE SPACES.
     05 PAGE-STATUS-WS           PIC X(10).
        88 NEW-PAGE              VALUE 'PAGE'.
     05 SCHEDULE-STATUS-WS       PIC X(10).
        88 SCHEDULE-COMPLETE     VALUE 'COMPLETE'.
     05 PAGE-COUNT-WS            PIC 9(03).
     05 LINE-COUNT-WS            PIC 9(02).
     05 ASSET-VALUE-WS           PIC S9(07)V9(02).
     05 ENDING-BALANCE-WS        PIC S9(07)V9(02).
     05 DEPRECIATION-WS          PIC S9(07)V9(02).
     05 DEPRECIATION-PERIOD-WS   PIC 9(03).
     05 ACCUMULATED-DEPRECIATION-WS PIC S9(07)V9(02).

 01  ASSET-IN.
     05 ITEM-NUMBER-IN           PIC X(10).
     05 ITEM-DESCRIPTION-IN      PIC X(30).
     05 PURCHASE-VALUE-IN        PIC 9(07)V9(02).
     05 SALVAGE-VALUE-IN         PIC 9(07)V9(02).
     05 PURCHASE-DATE-IN.
        10 PURCHASE-MONTH-IN     PIC 9(02).
        10 PURCHASE-YEAR-IN      PIC 9(02).
     05 USEFUL-LIFE-IN           PIC 9(03).
     05 SCHEDULE-TYPE-IN         PIC 9(01).
        88 STRAIGHT-LINE         VALUE IS 1.
        88 DOUBLE-DECLINING-BALANCE VALUE IS 2.
        88 UNKNOWN-TYPE          VALUE IS 0, 3 THRU 9.

 01  SCHEDULE-HEADER.
     05 FILLER                   PIC X(05) VALUE SPACES.
     05 ITEM-NUMBER-OUT          PIC X(10).
     05 FILLER                   PIC X(05) VALUE SPACES.
     05 ITEM-DESCRIPTION-OUT     PIC X(30).
```

Figure 12.6 *Continued* Depreciation Schedules

```
          1   1   2   2   2   3   3   4   4   4   5   5   6   6   6   7
   4   8  2   6   0   4   8   2   6   0   4   8   2   6   0   4   8   2
-----------------------------------------------------------------------
           05 FILLER                      PIC X(05) VALUE SPACES.
           05 PURCHASE-VALUE-OUT          PIC -$$,$$$,$$$.$$.
           05 FILLER                      PIC X(05) VALUE SPACES.
           05 USEFUL-LIFE-OUT             PIC ZZ9.
           05 FILLER                      PIC X(05) VALUE SPACES.
           05 SCHEDULE-TITLE-OUT          PIC X(30).

       01  SCHEDULE-TEXT.
           05 FILLER                      PIC X(60) VALUE
           '      Item          Item Description'.
           05 FILLER                      PIC X(25) VALUE
           '  Balance      Life'.
           05 FILLER                      PIC X(10) VALUE SPACES.
           05 FILLER                      PIC X(05) VALUE 'Page '.
           05 PAGE-NUMBER-OUT             PIC ZZ9.

       01  DEPRECIATION-RECORD.
           05 FILLER                      PIC X(05) VALUE SPACES.
           05 PURCHASE-MONTH-OUT          PIC 9(02).
           05 FILLER                      PIC X(01) VALUE SPACES.
           05 PURCHASE-YEAR-OUT           PIC 9(02).
           05 FILLER                      PIC X(05) VALUE SPACES.
           05 BEGINNING-BALANCE-OUT       PIC -$$,$$$,$$$.$$.
           05 FILLER                      PIC X(05) VALUE SPACES.
           05 DEPRECIATION-OUT            PIC -$$,$$$,$$$.$$.
           05 FILLER                      PIC X(05) VALUE SPACES.
           05 ENDING-BALANCE-OUT          PIC -$$,$$$,$$$.$$.
           05 FILLER                      PIC X(05) VALUE SPACES.
           05 ACCUMULATED-DEPRECIATION-OUT PIC -$$,$$$,$$$.$$.

       01  COLUMN-HEADING.
           05 FILLER                      PIC X(55) VALUE
           ' Month Year     Beg. Balance              Depr'.
           05 FILLER                      PIC X(40) VALUE
           'End. Balance     Accum. Depreciation'.

       01  SALVAGE-RECORD.
           05 FILLER                      PIC X(52) VALUE
           '      Estimated Salvage Value After Depreciation'.
           05 SALVAGE-VALUE-OUT           PIC -$$$,$$$,$$$.99.

       01  CONTINUED-RECORD.
           05 FILLER                      PIC X(40).
      *****************************************************************
       PROCEDURE DIVISION.
      *****************************************************************
      *---------------------------------------------------------------*
       000-PROCEDURE-CONTROLS SECTION.
      *---------------------------------------------------------------*
           PERFORM 1000-INITIALIZATION.
           PERFORM 3000-SCHEDULE-PRODUCTION
               UNTIL FILE-STATUS = 'DONE'.
           PERFORM 5000-TERMINATION.
           STOP RUN.
      *---------------------------------------------------------------*
       1000-INITIALIZATION SECTION.
      *---------------------------------------------------------------*
           OPEN INPUT ASSET-FILE, OUTPUT SCHEDULE-REPORT-FILE.
           MOVE 0                    TO PAGE-COUNT-WS
                                        LINE-COUNT-WS.
      *---------------------------------------------------------------*
       3000-SCHEDULE-PRODUCTION SECTION.
      *---------------------------------------------------------------*
           READ ASSET-FILE INTO ASSET-IN
               AT END MOVE 'DONE'    TO FILE-STATUS
                      GO TO 3000-EXIT.
           MOVE 'PRODUCE'            TO SCHEDULE-STATUS-WS.
           MOVE SPACES               TO CONTINUED-RECORD.
           MOVE PURCHASE-MONTH-IN    TO PURCHASE-MONTH-OUT.
```

Figure 12.6 *Continued* Depreciation Schedules

```
            1   1   2   2   2   3   3   4   4   4   5   5   6   6   6   7
    4   8   2   6   0   4   8   2   6   0   4   8   2   6   0   4   8   2

           MOVE PURCHASE-YEAR-IN     TO PURCHASE-YEAR-OUT.
           MOVE 'PAGE'               TO PAGE-STATUS-WS.
           MOVE 0                    TO ACCUMULATED-DEPRECIATION-WS.
           SUBTRACT SALVAGE-VALUE-IN FROM PURCHASE-VALUE-IN
               GIVING ASSET-VALUE-WS.
           IF STRAIGHT-LINE
               MOVE 'Straight Line' TO SCHEDULE-TITLE-OUT
               PERFORM 3200-STRAIGHT-LINE-SCHEDULE.
           IF DOUBLE-DECLINING-BALANCE
               MOVE 'Double Declining Balance' TO SCHEDULE-TITLE-OUT
               PERFORM 3400-DOUBLE-DECLINING-SCHEDULE
                   VARYING DEPRECIATION-PERIOD-WS FROM 1 BY 1
                   UNTIL SCHEDULE-COMPLETE.
           MOVE SALVAGE-VALUE-IN     TO SALVAGE-VALUE-OUT.
           WRITE SCHEDULE-RECORD FROM SALVAGE-RECORD AFTER 2 LINES.

       3000-EXIT.
           EXIT.
      *-----------------------------------------------------------*
       3200-STRAIGHT-LINE-SCHEDULE SECTION.
      *-----------------------------------------------------------*
               COMPUTE DEPRECIATION-WS ROUNDED =
                   ASSET-VALUE-WS * (1 / USEFUL-LIFE-IN)
               PERFORM 3600-PRINT-SCHEDULE
                   VARYING DEPRECIATION-PERIOD-WS FROM 1 BY 1
                   UNTIL SCHEDULE-COMPLETE.
      *-----------------------------------------------------------*
       3400-DOUBLE-DECLINING-SCHEDULE SECTION.
      *-----------------------------------------------------------*
           COMPUTE DEPRECIATION-WS ROUNDED =
               ASSET-VALUE-WS * (2 / USEFUL-LIFE-IN).
           PERFORM 3250-PRINT-SCHEDULE.
      *-----------------------------------------------------------*
       3600-PRINT-SCHEDULE SECTION.
      *-----------------------------------------------------------*
           IF NEW-PAGE
               PERFORM 3620-PRINT-HEADING.
           SUBTRACT DEPRECIATION-WS FROM ASSET-VALUE-WS
               GIVING ENDING-BALANCE-WS.
           IF DEPRECIATION-PERIOD-WS = USEFUL-LIFE-IN
               MOVE 'COMPLETE'       TO SCHEDULE-STATUS-WS
               ADD ENDING-BALANCE-WS TO DEPRECIATION-WS
               MOVE 0                TO ENDING-BALANCE-WS.
           IF PURCHASE-MONTH-OUT > 12
               MOVE 1                TO PURCHASE-MONTH-OUT
               ADD 1 TO PURCHASE-YEAR-OUT
               MOVE SPACES           TO SCHEDULE-RECORD
               WRITE SCHEDULE-RECORD AFTER 1 LINES.
           MOVE ASSET-VALUE-WS       TO BEGINNING-BALANCE-OUT.
           MOVE DEPRECIATION-WS      TO DEPRECIATION-OUT.
           MOVE ENDING-BALANCE-WS    TO ENDING-BALANCE-OUT.
           ADD DEPRECIATION-WS       TO ACCUMULATED-DEPRECIATION-WS.
           MOVE ACCUMULATED-DEPRECIATION-WS
                                     TO ACCUMULATED-DEPRECIATION-OUT.
           WRITE SCHEDULE-RECORD FROM DEPRECIATION-RECORD
             AFTER ADVANCING 1 LINES.
           ADD 1 TO LINE-COUNT-WS.
           IF LINE-COUNT-WS > 48
               MOVE 'PAGE'           TO PAGE-STATUS-WS.
           ADD 1 TO PURCHASE-MONTH-OUT.
           MOVE ENDING-BALANCE-WS    TO ASSET-VALUE-WS.
      *-----------------------------------------------------------*
       3620-PRINT-HEADING SECTION.
      *-----------------------------------------------------------*
           WRITE SCHEDULE-RECORD FROM CONTINUED-RECORD AFTER 2 LINES.
           ADD 1 TO PAGE-COUNT-WS.
           MOVE 0                    TO LINE-COUNT-WS.
           MOVE PAGE-COUNT-WS        TO PAGE-NUMBER-OUT.
           MOVE 'NO PAGE'            TO PAGE-STATUS-WS.
```

Figure 12.6 *Continued* Depreciation Schedules

```
           WRITE SCHEDULE-RECORD FROM SCHEDULE-TEXT
               AFTER START-SCHEDULE.
           MOVE 0                     TO LINE-COUNT-WS.
           MOVE ITEM-NUMBER-IN        TO ITEM-NUMBER-OUT.
           MOVE ITEM-DESCRIPTION-IN TO ITEM-DESCRIPTION-OUT.
           MOVE PURCHASE-VALUE-IN     TO PURCHASE-VALUE-OUT.
           MOVE USEFUL-LIFE-IN        TO USEFUL-LIFE-OUT.
           WRITE SCHEDULE-RECORD FROM SCHEDULE-HEADER AFTER 1 LINES.
           WRITE SCHEDULE-RECORD FROM COLUMN-HEADING AFTER 2 LINES.
           MOVE SPACES                TO SCHEDULE-RECORD.
           WRITE SCHEDULE-RECORD AFTER ADVANCING 1 LINES.
           MOVE ' ***** Continued on Next Page *****'
                                      TO CONTINUED-RECORD.
      *-----------------------------------------------------------*
       5000-TERMINATION SECTION.
      *-----------------------------------------------------------*
           CLOSE ASSET-FILE, SCHEDULE-REPORT-FILE.
```

Figure 12.6 *Continued* Depreciation Schedules (Data)

```
|      |         1         2         3         4         5         6         7|
|Record|1234567890123456789012345678901234567890123456789012345678901234567890|
|------------------------------------------------------------------------------|
|     1|     12345Test Asset Desc                 0010000000000000001850121   |
|     2|ABCDE12345Test Asset Description          0002531290001000000484036 2  |
|     3|R2-X1147-3Milling Machine                 0047866900007000001083048 1  |
|     4|   T28-127Central Warehouse Building      0061300000000000000684060 2  |
```

Figure 12.6 *Continued* Depreciation Schedules (Output)

```
    Item            Item Description                    Balance      Life                Page   1
        12345       Test Asset Desc                   $10,000.00      12      Straight Line

Month Year        Beg. Balance            Depr       End. Balance     Accum. Depreciation

 01 85            $10,000.00            $830.00        $9,170.00           $830.00
 02 85             $9,170.00            $830.00        $8,340.00         $1,660.00
 03 85             $8,340.00            $830.00        $7,510.00         $2,490.00
 04 85             $7,510.00            $830.00        $6,680.00         $3,320.00
 05 85             $6,680.00            $830.00        $5,850.00         $4,150.00
 06 85             $5,850.00            $830.00        $5,020.00         $4,980.00
 07 85             $5,020.00            $830.00        $4,190.00         $5,810.00
 08 85             $4,190.00            $830.00        $3,360.00         $6,640.00
 09 85             $3,360.00            $830.00        $2,530.00         $7,470.00
 10 85             $2,530.00            $830.00        $1,700.00         $8,300.00
 11 85             $1,700.00            $830.00          $870.00         $9,130.00
 12 85               $870.00            $870.00                         $10,000.00

  Estimated Salvage Value After Depreciation               $.00
```

Figure 12.6 *Continued* Depreciation Schedules (Output)

```
   Item          Item Description                         Balance    Life                Page   2
 ABCDE12345      Test Asset Description                  $2,531.29    36        Double Declining Balance

Month Year     Beg. Balance            Depr           End. Balance     Accum. Depreciation

  04 84         $1,531.29              $84.22          $1,447.07            $84.22
  05 84         $1,447.07              $79.59          $1,367.48           $163.81
  06 84         $1,367.48              $75.21          $1,292.27           $239.02
  07 84         $1,292.27              $71.07          $1,221.20           $310.09
  08 84         $1,221.20              $67.17          $1,154.03           $377.26
  09 84         $1,154.03              $63.47          $1,090.56           $440.73
  10 84         $1,090.56              $59.98          $1,030.58           $500.71
  11 84         $1,030.58              $56.68            $973.90           $557.39
  12 84           $973.90              $53.56            $920.34           $610.95

  01 85           $920.34              $50.62            $869.72           $661.57
  02 85           $869.72              $47.83            $821.89           $709.40
  03 85           $821.89              $45.20            $776.69           $754.60
  04 85           $776.69              $42.72            $733.97           $797.32
  05 85           $733.97              $40.37            $693.60           $837.69
  06 85           $693.60              $38.15            $655.45           $875.84
  07 85           $655.45              $36.05            $619.40           $911.89
  08 85           $619.40              $34.07            $585.33           $945.96
  09 85           $585.33              $32.19            $553.14           $978.15
  10 85           $553.14              $30.42            $522.72         $1,008.57
  11 85           $522.72              $28.75            $493.97         $1,037.32
  12 85           $493.97              $27.17            $466.80         $1,064.49

  01 86           $466.80              $25.67            $441.13         $1,090.16
  02 86           $441.13              $24.26            $416.87         $1,114.42
  03 86           $416.87              $22.93            $393.94         $1,137.35
  04 86           $393.94              $21.67            $372.27         $1,159.02
  05 86           $372.27              $20.47            $351.80         $1,179.49
  06 86           $351.80              $19.35            $332.45         $1,198.84
  07 86           $332.45              $18.28            $314.17         $1,217.12
  08 86           $314.17              $17.28            $296.89         $1,234.40
  09 86           $296.89              $16.33            $280.56         $1,250.73
  10 86           $280.56              $15.43            $265.13         $1,266.16
  11 86           $265.13              $14.58            $250.55         $1,280.74
  12 86           $250.55              $13.78            $236.77         $1,294.52

  01 87           $236.77              $13.02            $223.75         $1,307.54
  02 87           $223.75              $12.31            $211.44         $1,319.85
  03 87           $211.44             $211.44                            $1,531.29

 Estimated Salvage Value After Depreciation             $1,000.00
```

periods. Thus, if an asset was expected to last for 6 months, one sixth of the original value of the asset would be depreciated each month.

The double-declining-balance depreciation method is an accelerated depreciation method. This procedure allows the depreciation to be calculated as 2 times the book value of the asset divided by the useful life. Thus, while the amount of depreciation allowed is greater during the earlier life of the asset, its value decreases at a corresponding rate.

Figure 12.6 *Continued* Depreciation Schedules (Output)

Item	Item Description	Balance	Life		Page 3
R2-X1147-3	Milling Machine	$47,866.90	48	Straight Line	

Month Year	Beg. Balance	Depr	End. Balance	Accum. Depreciation
10 83	$40,866.90	$817.34	$40,049.56	$817.34
11 83	$40,049.56	$817.34	$39,232.22	$1,634.68
12 83	$39,232.22	$817.34	$38,414.88	$2,452.02
01 84	$38,414.88	$817.34	$37,597.54	$3,269.36
02 84	$37,597.54	$817.34	$36,780.20	$4,086.70
03 84	$36,780.20	$817.34	$35,962.86	$4,904.04
04 84	$35,962.86	$817.34	$35,145.52	$5,721.38
05 84	$35,145.52	$817.34	$34,328.18	$6,538.72
06 84	$34,328.18	$817.34	$33,510.84	$7,356.06
07 84	$33,510.84	$817.34	$32,693.50	$8,173.40
08 84	$32,693.50	$817.34	$31,876.16	$8,990.74
09 84	$31,876.16	$817.34	$31,058.82	$9,808.08
10 84	$31,058.82	$817.34	$30,241.48	$10,625.42
11 84	$30,241.48	$817.34	$29,424.14	$11,442.76
12 84	$29,424.14	$817.34	$28,606.80	$12,260.10
01 85	$28,606.80	$817.34	$27,789.46	$13,077.44
02 85	$27,789.46	$817.34	$26,972.12	$13,894.78
03 85	$26,972.12	$817.34	$26,154.78	$14,712.12
04 85	$26,154.78	$817.34	$25,337.44	$15,529.46
05 85	$25,337.44	$817.34	$24,520.10	$16,346.80
06 85	$24,520.10	$817.34	$23,702.76	$17,164.14
07 85	$23,702.76	$817.34	$22,885.42	$17,981.48
08 85	$22,885.42	$817.34	$22,068.08	$18,798.82
09 85	$22,068.08	$817.34	$21,250.74	$19,616.16
10 85	$21,250.74	$817.34	$20,433.40	$20,433.50
11 85	$20,433.40	$817.34	$19,616.06	$21,250.84
12 85	$19,616.06	$817.34	$18,798.72	$22,068.18
01 86	$18,798.72	$817.34	$17,981.38	$22,885.52
02 86	$17,981.38	$817.34	$17,164.04	$23,702.86
03 86	$17,164.04	$817.34	$16,346.70	$24,520.20
04 86	$16,346.70	$817.34	$15,529.36	$25,337.54
05 86	$15,529.36	$817.34	$14,712.02	$26,154.88
06 86	$14,712.02	$817.34	$13,894.68	$26,972.22
07 86	$13,894.68	$817.34	$13,077.34	$27,789.56
08 86	$13,077.34	$817.34	$12,260.00	$28,606.90
09 86	$12,260.00	$817.34	$11,442.66	$29,424.24
10 86	$11,442.66	$817.34	$10,625.32	$30,241.58
11 86	$10,625.32	$817.34	$9,807.98	$31,058.92
12 86	$9,807.98	$817.34	$8,990.64	$31,876.26
01 87	$8,990.64	$817.34	$8,173.30	$32,693.60
02 87	$8,173.30	$817.34	$7,355.96	$33,510.94
03 87	$7,355.96	$817.34	$6,538.62	$34,328.28
04 87	$6,538.62	$817.34	$5,721.28	$35,145.62
05 87	$5,721.28	$817.34	$4,903.94	$35,962.96
06 87	$4,903.94	$817.34	$4,086.60	$36,780.30
07 87	$4,086.60	$817.34	$3,269.26	$37,597.64
08 87	$3,269.26	$817.34	$2,451.92	$38,414.98
09 87	$2,451.92	$2,451.92		$40,866.90
Estimated Salvage Value After Depreciation			$7,000.00	

Figure 12.6 *Continued* Depreciation Schedules (Output)

Item	Item Description	Balance	Life	Page 4
T28-127	Central Warehouse Building	$61,300.00	60	Double Declining Balance

Month Year	Beg. Balance	Depr	End. Balance	Accum. Depreciation
06 84	$61,300.00	$2,022.90	$59,277.10	$2,022.90
07 84	$59,277.10	$1,956.14	$57,320.96	$3,979.04
08 84	$57,320.96	$1,891.59	$55,429.37	$5,870.63
09 84	$55,429.37	$1,829.17	$53,600.20	$7,699.80
10 84	$53,600.20	$1,768.81	$51,831.39	$9,468.61
11 84	$51,831.39	$1,710.44	$50,120.95	$11,179.05
12 84	$50,120.95	$1,653.99	$48,466.96	$12,833.04
01 85	$48,466.96	$1,599.41	$46,867.55	$14,432.45
02 85	$46,867.55	$1,546.63	$45,320.92	$15,979.08
03 85	$45,320.92	$1,495.59	$43,825.33	$17,474.67
04 85	$43,825.33	$1,446.24	$42,379.09	$18,920.91
05 85	$42,379.09	$1,398.51	$40,980.58	$20,319.42
06 85	$40,980.58	$1,352.36	$39,628.22	$21,671.78
07 85	$39,628.22	$1,307.73	$38,320.49	$22,979.51
08 85	$38,320.49	$1,264.58	$37,055.91	$24,244.09
09 85	$37,055.91	$1,222.85	$35,833.06	$25,466.94
10 85	$35,833.06	$1,182.49	$34,650.57	$26,649.43
11 85	$34,650.57	$1,143.47	$33,507.10	$27,792.90
12 85	$33,507.10	$1,105.73	$32,401.37	$28,898.63
01 86	$32,401.37	$1,069.25	$31,332.12	$29,967.88
02 86	$31,332.12	$1,033.96	$30,298.16	$31,001.84
03 86	$30,298.16	$999.84	$29,298.32	$32,001.68
04 86	$29,298.32	$966.84	$28,331.48	$32,968.52
05 86	$28,331.48	$934.94	$27,396.54	$33,903.46
06 86	$27,396.54	$904.09	$26,492.45	$34,807.55
07 86	$26,492.45	$874.25	$25,618.20	$35,681.80
08 86	$25,618.20	$845.40	$24,772.80	$36,527.20
09 86	$24,772.80	$817.50	$23,955.30	$37,344.70
10 86	$23,955.30	$790.52	$23,164.78	$38,135.22
11 86	$23,164.78	$764.44	$22,400.34	$38,899.66
12 86	$22,400.34	$739.21	$21,661.13	$39,638.87
01 87	$21,661.13	$714.82	$20,946.31	$40,353.69
02 87	$20,946.31	$691.23	$20,255.08	$41,044.92
03 87	$20,255.08	$668.42	$19,586.66	$41,713.34
04 87	$19,586.66	$646.36	$18,940.30	$42,359.70
05 87	$18,940.30	$625.03	$18,315.27	$42,984.73
06 87	$18,315.27	$604.40	$17,710.87	$43,589.13
07 87	$17,710.87	$584.46	$17,126.41	$44,173.59
08 87	$17,126.41	$565.17	$16,561.24	$44,738.76
09 87	$16,561.24	$546.52	$16,014.72	$45,285.28
10 87	$16,014.72	$528.49	$15,486.23	$45,813.77
11 87	$15,486.23	$511.05	$14,975.18	$46,324.82
12 87	$14,975.18	$494.18	$14,481.00	$46,819.00
01 88	$14,481.00	$477.87	$14,003.13	$47,296.87
02 88	$14,003.13	$462.10	$13,541.03	$47,758.97
03 88	$13,541.03	$446.85	$13,094.18	$48,205.82
04 88	$13,094.18	$432.11	$12,662.07	$48,637.93
05 88	$12,662.07	$417.85	$12,244.22	$49,055.78
06 88	$12,244.22	$404.06	$11,840.16	$49,459.84

***** Continued on Next Page *****

Figure 12.6 *Continued* Depreciation Schedules (Output)

Item	Item Description	Balance	Life	Page 5
T28-127	Central Warehouse Building	$61,300.00	60	Double Declining Balance

Month Year	Beg. Balance	Depr	End. Balance	Accum. Depreciation
07 88	$11,840.16	$390.73	$11,449.43	$49,850.57
08 88	$11,449.43	$377.83	$11,071.60	$50,228.40
09 88	$11,071.60	$365.36	$10,706.24	$50,593.76
10 88	$10,706.24	$353.31	$10,352.93	$50,947.07
11 88	$10,352.93	$341.65	$10,011.28	$51,288.72
12 88	$10,011.28	$330.37	$9,680.91	$51,619.09
01 89	$9,680.91	$319.47	$9,361.44	$51,938.56
02 89	$9,361.44	$308.93	$9,052.51	$52,247.49
03 89	$9,052.51	$298.73	$8,753.78	$52,546.22
04 89	$8,753.78	$288.87	$8,464.91	$52,835.09
05 89	$8,464.91	$8,464.91		$61,300.00

Estimated Salvage Value After Depreciation $.00

Summary

In this chapter, the last two versions of the PERFORM statement have been discussed. Although the simple PERFORM and PERFORM/UNTIL statements are more often used in general structures in the PROCEDURE DIVISION, the PERFORM/TIMES and the PERFORM/VARYING are extremely useful when tackling certain types of problems (e.g., counting activities and table manipulation—to be discussed in Chapters 13 and 14).

The PERFORM/TIMES statement provides the programmer with the means to invoke a procedure (or set of procedures) a specified number of times. An identifier or a literal indicates the number of times the procedure is to be executed. If an identifier is modified during the execution of the procedure, the modification of the identifier in no way affects the number of times the procedure is executed.

The PERFORM/VARYING statement also provides the programmer with the means to invoke a procedure repetitively. Unlike the PERFORM/TIMES statement, however, the PERFORM/VARYING has a built-in "counting" feature. That is, the statement is capable of initializing, incrementing, and testing the value of an identifier. In addition, the condition associated with this statement does not necessarily have to reference the "index" identifier being initiated and incremented. The PERFORM/VARYING statement can also initialize, increment, and test an associated condition for up to three semi-independent identifiers in a "nested" arrangement.

Notes on Programming Style

Although the process involved in the PERFORM/VARYING and PERFORM/TIMES statements are similar to those of the simple PERFORM and PERFORM/UNTIL statements, you should be aware of several considerations in the use of these statements. First, the PERFORM/VARYING statement provides for the testing of conditions much like the PERFORM/UNTIL. One should be extremely careful in the construction of the condition to be tested in both these statements. It is conceivable, even likely, that you will construct a condition that will never be true. For example, the statement

```
        PERFORM PROCEDURE-1 VARYING I FROM 1 BY 2 UNTIL I = 10.
```

will never find a true condition; that is, I will equal 1, 3, 5, 7, 9, 11, 13, and so forth, but never 10. Thus, avoid testing for the equality of the varied identifier in a PERFORM/VARYING statement whenever possible. Also, the condition in the PERFORM/VARYING statement does not necessarily have anything to do with the varied identifier (although this is frequently the case). For example, the statement

```
  PERFORM READ-DATA
      VARYING ITEM-COUNT FROM 1 BY 1 UNTIL FILE-STATUS = 'DONE'.
```

could be used to perform two functions—execute a procedure until all data from a file have been processed *and* count the number of items read. (The count of the number of items will be off by one since ITEM-COUNT is incremented *before* the condition is tested during the execution of READ-DATA.) Finally, do not code yourself into a corner. That is, when structuring a PERFORM/VARYING statement, carefully examine the problem requirements. Do not automatically assume the initial value, incremental value, or perhaps termination condition will be based on a static (numeric literal) value. Because program generalization is typically preferable, these values are often not recorded as numeric literals, but rather, as identifiers, which may be modified in value.

Questions

Below fill in the blank(s) with the appropriate word, words, or phrases.

1. In total there are _____ (number) different forms of the PERFORM statement.
2. The version of the PERFORM statement that permits a specified repetition of a procedure is referred to as the _____ statement.
3. The number of times a procedure is to be executed may be specified in the PERFORM/TIMES statement by either a(n) _____ or a(n)_____ .
4. The PERFORM statement that includes a ''built-in'' counter is referred to as the _____ statement.
5. The PERFORM/VARYING permits the individual modification of _____ (number) identifiers.
6. After the procedure has been invoked in a PERFORM/VARYING statement, the identifier is incremented _____ (before/after) the specified condition is tested.
7. The statement that may be used to represent a common end point for several procedures is called the _____ statement.

Answer the following questions by circling either ''T'' for True or ''F'' for False.

T F **8.** COBOL does not permit the mixing of different forms of the PERFORM statement in a single procedure.
T F **9.** COBOL permits a PERFORM statement to invoke a procedure containing another PERFORM statement.
T F **10.** When an identifier is specified in the PERFORM/TIMES statement, it is possible to modify that identifier within the procedure being invoked.
T F **11.** When an identifier is specified in the PERFORM/TIMES statement, it is possible to modify that identifier within the procedure being invoked and thereby alter the number of times the procedure is executed.
T F **12.** When an identifier is specified in the PERFORM/TIMES statement and the value of the identifier is zero, the procedure is executed only once.
T F **13.** An identifier specified in the PERFORM/TIMES statement may not contain a negative value.
T F **14.** In the PERFORM/VARYING statement, an incremental value of one is always assumed.
T F **15.** In the PERFORM/VARYING statement the incremental value must always be positive.
T F **16.** In the PERFORM/VARYING statement, the condition used to terminate the perform activity must reference the identifier being incremented.
T F **17.** The condition specified in a PERFORM/VARYING must be a relational condition.
T F **18.** The same identifier may be incremented by both a VARYING phrase and an AFTER option in a PERFORM/VARYING statement.
T F **19.** When a PERFORM/VARYING statement contains an AFTER option, only one condition may be specified.

T F **20.** When a PERFORM/VARYING statement contains an AFTER option, the condition associated with the VARYING phrase is used to determine when the procedure has been completed.

T F **21.** Compound conditions may be associated with a PERFORM/VARYING statement.

T F **22.** If a relational condition is specified for the VARYING phrase of the PERFORM/VARYING statement, a relational condition must be specified for the first AFTER option, if used.

T F **23.** A PERFORM/VARYING statement may invoke a procedure that contains another PERFORM/VARYING statement.

T F **24.** A PERFORM/VARYING statement may invoke a procedure that contains another PERFORM/VARYING statement where both statements increment the same identifier.

T F **25.** The PERFORM/VARYING statement may use the reserved word AFTER as a substitute for the reserved word VARYING.

T F **26.** It is possible to encounter a PERFORM/VARYING statement and *not* execute the specified procedure.

T F **27.** The EXIT statement must be coded in a single-statement paragraph, if used.

Exercises

1. Below are several situations in which the PERFORM/TIMES statement is used. Record the paragraph names encountered during the execution of each procedure. If a paragraph is encountered by "fall through," record this situation adjacent to the paragraph name.

a.
```
        PERFORM PARA-1
        STOP RUN.
    PARA-1
        PERFORM PARA-2 5 TIMES.
    PARA-2.
```

b.
```
        PERFORM PARA-1 THRU PARA-2 3 TIMES
        STOP RUN.
    PARA-1.

    PARA-2.
        PERFORM PARA-3 2 TIMES.
    PARA-3.
```

c.
```
        MOVE 4 TO NO-OF.
        PERFORM PARA-1 NO-OF TIMES.
        PERFORM PARA-2 NO-OF TIMES.
        STOP RUN.
    PARA-1.
        MOVE 2 TO NO-OF.

    PARA-2.
```

d.
```
PARA-1.
     MOVE 0 TO MANY.
     PERFORM PARA-2 MANY TIMES.
     PERFORM PARA-3.
     STOP-RUN.
PARA-2.

PARA-3.
     PERFORM PARA-2 4 TIMES.
```

e.
```
     MOVE 1 TO MAX-NUM.
     PERFORM PARA-1 THRU PARA-3
         MAX-NUM TIMES.
     STOP RUN.
PARA-1.
     ADD 1 TO MAX-NUM.

PARA-2.
     IF MAX-NUM IS LESS THAN 5
         PERFORM PARA-1.

PARA-3.
     PERFORM PARA-4 MAX-NUM TIMES.
PARA-4.
```

2. Below are several situations in which the PERFORM/VARYING statement is used. Record the paragraph names encountered during the execution of each procedure. If a paragraph is encountered by "fall through," record this situation adjacent to the paragraph name. Furthermore, record the values of the PERFORM/VARYING index.

a.
```
     PERFORM PARA-1 VARYING I FROM 1
         BY 1 UNTIL I IS GREATER THAN 5.
     STOP RUN.
PARA-1.
```

b.
```
     PERFORM PARA-1 VARYING I FROM 1 BY 1
         UNTIL I IS GREATER THAN 3.
     STOP RUN.
PARA-1.
     PERFORM PARA-2 VARYING J FROM 1 BY 1
         UNTIL J IS GREATER THAN 2.

PARA-2.
```

c.
```
     PERFORM PARA-1
         VARYING I FROM 1 BY 1
             UNTIL I IS GREATER THAN 4
         AFTER J FROM 10 BY -2
             UNTIL J < 0.
     STOP RUN.
PARA-1.
```

d.

```
    MOVE 2 TO M, 0.
    MOVE 4 TO N, P.
    PERFORM PARA-1 THRU PARA-2
        VARYING I FROM M BY 1
            UNTIL I > N-1
        AFTER J FROM 1 BY 0
            UNTIL J > P
        AFTER K FROM M BY N
            UNTIL K > 10.
    STOP RUN.
PARA-1.

PARA-2.
    PERFORM PARA-3 3 TIMES.

PARA-3.
```

Problems

12.1 Records have been developed to indicate both the number of employees in departments within the company and employee names of individuals within each department. The data are organized in such a way that multiple sets (departments) are possible. That is, each set will be organized such that the first record indicates the number of employees in the department and the second record type (multiple records) contains the employees name. (See the multiple-card layout form.)

You are to design a procedure to decide, based on the number of employees in each department, the number of columns in which the employee roster should be printed. That is, some departments have as many as 200 employees, whereas other departments have as few as 10 members. Your departmental employee roster should fit on one page. Thus, for example, if a department has as few as 50 members, only one column should be printed. If the list is to contain up to 100 names, the list should be printed in two columns. Use three columns if the list contains up to 150 names and four columns for up to 200. The list, regardless of the number of employees, should appear centered on the page. Therefore, it will probably be desirable to have at least two output line formats—one when 1 or 3 columns are to be printed and one to be used if 2 or 4 columns are to be printed. (See the print chart on the next page.)

12.2 The Vice-President in Charge of Operations has received numerous complaints regarding the appointment and planning calendars purchased in bulk by the company. The current calendars are said to be difficult to use for at least two reasons. First, they do not provide an overview of the activities to be performed. Second, they do not provide sufficient space in which to record appointments and specifics of the subject of the appointment. The vice-president has decided to have a printer produce appointment and planning calendars in the future, but has decided a number of alternate designs might be desirable. He has asked us to make a series of possible calendar designs from a program.

One design that has been suggested is shown on the print chart. This design shows the time of the appointment across the top of the page and both the day of the week and the day of the month horizontally at the left margin of the page. Each appointment period is then marked off as a box. This calendar is to cover 1 month (regardless of the number of

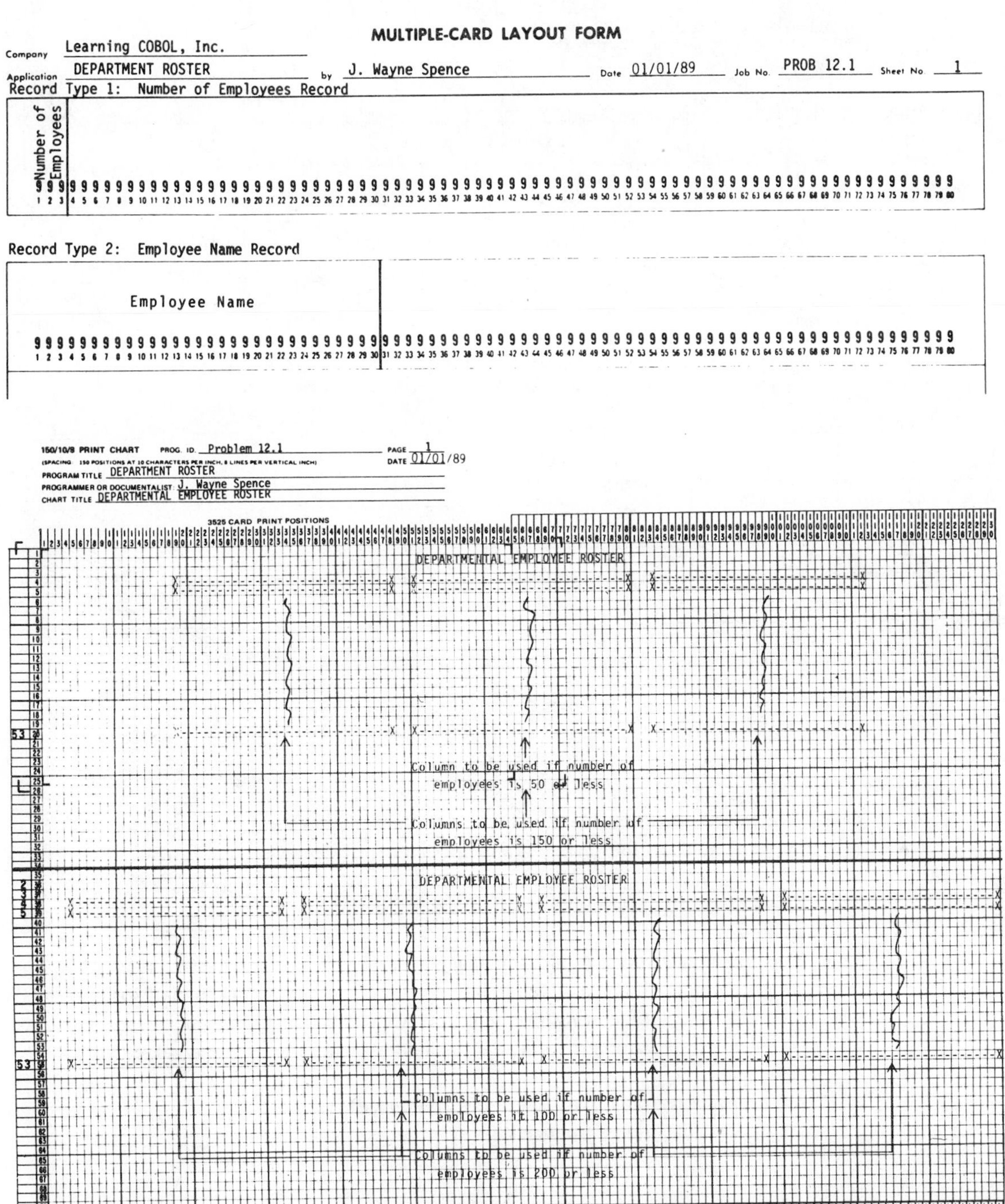

MULTIPLE-CARD LAYOUT FORM

Company Learning COBOL, Inc.
Application DEPARTMENT ROSTER by J. Wayne Spence Date 01/01/89 Job No. PROB 12.1 Sheet No. 1

Record Type 1: Number of Employees Record

Number of Employees (columns 1–3)

Record Type 2: Employee Name Record

Employee Name (columns 1–30)

150/10/8 PRINT CHART PROG. ID. Problem 12.1 PAGE 1
(SPACING: 150 POSITIONS AT 10 CHARACTERS PER INCH, 8 LINES PER VERTICAL INCH) DATE 01/01/89
PROGRAM TITLE DEPARTMENT ROSTER
PROGRAMMER OR DOCUMENTALIST J. Wayne Spence
CHART TITLE DEPARTMENTAL EMPLOYEE ROSTER

150/10/8 PRINT CHART PROG. ID. Problem 12.2 PAGE 1
(SPACING: 150 POSITIONS AT 10 CHARACTERS PER INCH, 8 LINES PER VERTICAL INCH) DATE 01/01/89
PROGRAM TITLE CALENDAR
PROGRAMMER OR DOCUMENTALIST: JOHN WINDSOR
CHART TITLE APPOINTMENT CALENDAR

3525 CARD PRINT POSITIONS

```
                                   A P P O I N T M E N T   C A L E N D A R

 DAY  OF
WEEK MONTH     8:00      9:00      10:00      11:00      12:00      1:00      2:00      3:00      4:00      5:00

  1      1
  2      2
  3      3
  4      4
  5      5
  6      6
  7      7
  1      8
  2      9
```

days in the month—assume 31). Finally, just to check the overall format, you are to produce two complete copies of the planning and appointment calendar in this format.

Note: This procedure does not require the use of input data.

12.3 When manufacturing a product, management often refers to a measurement known as the break-even point. The break-even point is that level of production (in units of a product) where the cost of manufacturing the item is exactly equal to the revenues received from selling the item. In its simplest form, the formula for determining the break-even point is:

a. (Fixed cost plus variable cost times units produced) less
(selling price times units produced) = 0

where

Fixed cost is the cost incurred as a result of maintaining a production capacity (such as the building in which the manufacturing plant is housed),
Variable cost is the cost directly associated with the production of units of an item (such as material and manpower costs), and
Selling price is the price at which we anticipate selling all units produced.

MULTIPLE-CARD LAYOUT FORM

Company LEARNING COBOL, INC.

Application BREAK-EVEN by J. Wayne Spence Date 01/01/89 Job No. PROB 12.3 Sheet No. 1

Product Name	Production Cost		Selling Price Per Unit	Production Lot Size	
	Fixed	Variable Per Unit			
1–30	31–40	41–48	49–56	57–61	62–80

150/10/8 PRINT CHART PROG. ID. Problem 12.3 PAGE 1

(SPACING: 150 POSITIONS AT 10 CHARACTERS PER INCH, 8 LINES PER VERTICAL INCH) DATE 01/01/89

PROGRAM TITLE BREAK-EVEN

PROGRAMMER OR DOCUMENTALIST J. Wayne Spence

CHART TITLE BREAK-EVEN POINT ANALYSIS

3525 CARD PRINT POSITIONS

```
                      B R E A K - E V E N   P O I N T   A N A L Y S I S                 PAGE ZZ9

PRODUCT NAME: X------------------------------X
FIXED COST: $ZZ,ZZZ,ZZZ.99                                         SELLING PRICE: $ZZ,ZZZ.99
VARIABLE COST PER UNIT: $ZZ,ZZZ.99                                 PRODUCTION LOT SIZE: ZZZZ9
                                 BREAK-EVEN POINT: ZZZZ9
-----------------------------------------------------------------------------------------
                                   PRODUCTION ANALYSIS

PRODUCTION
   LEVEL     FIXED COST   +  TOTAL VARIABLE COST  =  TOTAL COST        TOTAL REVENUE      PROFIT/LOSS
  ZZZZZ9   ZZ,ZZZ,ZZZ.99          ZZ,ZZZ,ZZZ.99    ZZ,ZZZ,ZZZ.99     ZZ,ZZZ,ZZZ.99     ---,---,---.99
  ZZZZZ9   ZZ,ZZZ,ZZZ.99          ZZ,ZZZ,ZZZ.99    ZZ,ZZZ,ZZZ.99     ZZ,ZZZ,ZZZ.99     ---,---,---.99

  ZZZZZ9   ZZ,ZZZ,ZZZ.99          ZZ,ZZZ,ZZZ.99    ZZ,ZZZ,ZZZ.99     ZZ,ZZZ,ZZZ.99     ---,---,---.99
```

To find the break-even point (in units), this formula may be factored to yield:

b. $$\text{Units produced} = \frac{\text{Fixed cost}}{\text{Sales price less variable cost}}$$

Thus, if fixed cost was $100; variable cost, $1 per unit; and selling price, $3 per unit, the company would have to produce 50 units to break even. Stated another way, the cost of manufacturing the item is exactly equal to the revenues received from selling the item when 50 units are produced.

You have two problems. Your company is anticipating the manufacture of several new products. Information concerning each of these products has been placed in a record (see the multiple-card layout form). You are to determine the break-even point (in units) for each product and then produce a schedule that illustrates all levels of production (in incremental levels of units) ranging from 90 percent to 110 percent of the break-even point (see the print chart). Note that the production level increment for an item may not be in single units. For example, although it might be practical to build one automobile at a time, it is hardly practical to produce paint one gallon at a time. Further note that a single schedule may be several pages long.

CHAPTER

13

Table Handling with Subscripts

In many programming applications, massive amounts of data must be stored within the computer's internal storage. Without the capability to store interrelated (or homogeneous) data within one area or block of computer storage, programming some types of problems would be inconvenient and other applications would be impractical or impossible. In COBOL, *tables* allow the programmer to store and reference bulk data easily without specifying an individual data-name for each location reserved for a data value.

A table is specified with the OCCURS clause in the DATA DIVISION. The OCCURS clause, pictured in Figure 13.1, specifies the number of storage positions to be associated with a single data-name. The OCCURS clause may be coded with data items at levels 02 through 49. The OCCURS clause cannot be used with data items at levels 01, 66, 77, or 88. Both groups and elementary-items may employ the OCCURS clause, making *multidimensional* tables possible. COBOL currently supports tables with a maximum of *three dimensions* by arranging COBOL clauses in subordinate relationships to one another. In COBOL 85 tables are supported up to a maximum of *seven dimensions*.

Single-Dimension Tables

As presented in Figure 13.1, the simple format of the OCCURS clause provides for the description of a table with static (nonvariable) dimensions. The size of the table described with this OCCURS clause does not change during the execution of a program. The programmer specifies the number of occurrences of a data-name within the table by providing a positive integer value for integer-2, which gives integer-2 storage positions that can be referenced using the data-name associated with the clause. If the OCCURS clause is specified for a group item, each subordinate data item will occur integer-2 times. A data item so described in COBOL is a *single-dimension table* or *vector*.

When a data item associated with an OCCURS clause is addressed in the PROCEDURE DIVISION, it must be written with a *subscript*. The values of the subscript indicate the occurrence to be referenced during execution. The subscript must be enclosed in parentheses with one space preceding the left parenthesis and a space or a punctuation character following the right parenthesis. The subscript value may be provided by either

Figure 13.1 Simple Format of the OCCURS Clause

```
Format 1 *

          OCCURS integer-2 TIMES
```

*Format, as written, is incomplete. Complete format provided in Chapter 14.

a data-name that describes integer fields containing a positive value or a positive integer value. In either case, the value of the subscript should be at least one, but no greater than, the number of occurrence positions in the table.

1985 COBOL Standards

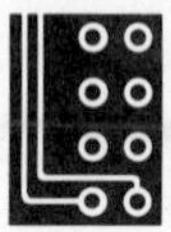

A subscripted table, in COBOL 85, allows the addressing of a table item through both *direct* and *relative* subscripts. Relative subscripts address a table position with a subscript identifier plus or minus an integer constant. For example, if TABLE-ITEM is a data name used to reference a one dimensional table that is subscripted by the identifier SUB, the table could be addressed by TABLE-ITEM (1), TABLE-ITEM(SUB), TABLE-ITEM(SUB + 2) or TABLE-ITEM (SUB-5). (The first pair of notations represents direct addressing; the second pair, relative addressing.

Figure 13.2 illustrates how a table is formed in COBOL. This illustration provides both the DATA DIVISION entries necessary to describe a table and the logical representation of the table in internal storage. In the figure, RATE-PER-HOUR-TABLE is a record-name that represents a subordinate table. When used in the PROCEDURE DIVISION, RATE-PER-HOUR-TABLE addresses all occurrences of the table subordinate to it (or 40 bytes of internal storage). RATE-PER-HOUR, since it is coded with a PICTURE clause, is an elementary data item. Since it is also coded with an OCCURS clause, RATE-PER-HOUR describes ten positions in internal storage, each of which is described by the PICTURE clause. Each appearance of the data-name RATE-PER-HOUR in the PROCEDURE DIVISION must be accompanied by a subscript within the range of 1 through 10, inclusive. Each occurrence of RATE-PER-HOUR addresses a four-digit number. Remember that RATE-PER-HOUR-TABLE is not subordinate to (or directly associated with) an OCCURS clause. Thus, when RATE-PER-HOUR-TABLE is referenced in the PROCEDURE DIVISION, it should *not* be written with a subscript.

Figure 13.2 A Simple One-dimension Table

```
Ø1  RATE-PER-HOUR-TABLE.
    Ø3 RATE-PER-HOUR OCCURS 1Ø TIME PICTURE 99V99.
```

RATE-PER-HOUR (1)	RATE-PER-HOUR-TABLE
RATE-PER-HOUR (2)	
RATE-PER-HOUR (3)	
RATE-PER-HOUR (4)	
RATE-PER-HOUR (5)	
RATE-PER-HOUR (6)	
RATE-PER-HOUR (7)	
RATE-PER-HOUR (8)	
RATE-PER-HOUR (9)	
RATE-PER-HOUR (1Ø)	

In Figure 13.3, a table that contains two types of data—a six-digit integer and a four-digit number with two decimal places—is described. The name of the entire table is EMPLOYEE-NUMBER-RATE-TABLE. EMPLOYEE-NUMBER-RATE-TABLE may be used in the PROCEDURE DIVISION to address all the subordinate data items (50 bytes of data—five occurrences of six bytes plus five occurrences of four bytes). Each subordinate data item is associated with an OCCURS clause. Since each OCCURS clause is independent of the other, the table is one-dimensional—only one subscript is necessary when addressing either EMPLOYEE-NUMBER or EMPLOYEE-RATE. Each of the elementary data items (EMPLOYEE-NUMBER and EMPLOYEE-RATE) OCCURS five times. Of course, it is not necessary that both EMPLOYEE-NUMBER and EMPLOYEE-RATE occur the same number of times. The important point is that since each OCCURS clause is independent of the other, the data are internally structured such that all occurrences of EMPLOYEE-NUMBER are *followed* by all occurrences of EMPLOYEE-RATE.

Figure 13.4 provides an additional method of describing single-dimension tables. (This form of table description is sometimes called a *pseudo-two-dimension table*). EMPLOYEE-NUMBER-RATE-TABLE still represents all the data subordinate to it (50 bytes); however, in this example, a group item (NUMBER-RATE-PAIRS) has been coded with an OCCURS clause. Any item subordinate to NUMBER-RATE-PAIRS will occur five times. Thus, there are five occurrences of EMPLOYEE-NUMBER and EMPLOYEE-RATE (as in the second example). In this case, however, the occurrences of the data items alternate. The first occurrence of EMPLOYEE-NUMBER is logically followed by the first occurrence of EMPLOYEE-RATE; the second occurrence of EMPLOYEE-NUMBER is followed by the second occurrence of EMPLOYEE-RATE, and so forth. EMPLOYEE-NUMBER and EMPLOYEE-RATE must still be referenced by a single subscript when addressed in the PROCEDURE DIVISION. A single occurrence of EMPLOYEE-NUMBER addresses six bytes, and EMPLOYEE-RATE addresses four bytes. Since a single occurrence of NUMBER-RATE-PAIRS addresses one occurrence of EMPLOYEE-NUMBER *and* EMPLOYEE-RATE, NUMBER-RATE-PAIRS must be accompanied by one subscript (within the range from 1 to 5) when referenced in the PROCEDURE DIVISION.

Figure 13.3 Two One-dimension Tables with Separate Occurrences

```
Ø1  EMPLOYEE-NUMBER-RATE-TABLE.
    Ø3 EMPLOYEE-NUMBER OCCURS 5 TIMES PICTURE 9(6).
    Ø3 EMPLOYEE-RATE OCCURS 5 TIMES PICTURE 99V99.

        EMPLOYEE-NUMBER (1)  ┐
        EMPLOYEE-NUMBER (2)  │
        EMPLOYEE-NUMBER (3)  │
        EMPLOYEE-NUMBER (4)  │
        EMPLOYEE-NUMBER (5)  │  EMPLOYEE-NUMBER-RATE-TABLE
         EMPLOYEE-RATE (1)   │
         EMPLOYEE-RATE (2)   │
         EMPLOYEE-RATE (3)   │
         EMPLOYEE-RATE (4)   │
         EMPLOYEE-RATE (5)   ┘
```

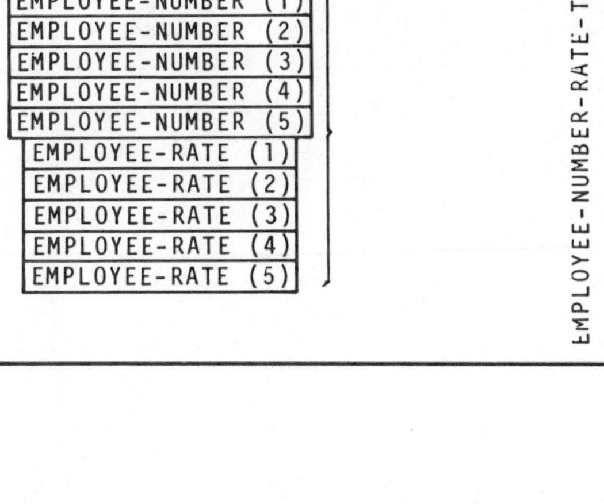

Figure 13.4 Two-Single-dimension Tables with Interleaved Occurrences

```
Ø1 EMPLOYEE-NUMBER-RATE-TABLE.
   Ø3 NUMBER-RATE-PAIRS OCCURS 5 TIMES.
      Ø5 EMPLOYEE-NUMBER PICTURE 9(6).
      Ø5 EMPLOYEE-RATE PICTURE 99V99.
```

EMPLOYEE-NUMBER (1)	EMPLOYEE-RATE (1)	NUMBER-RATE-PAIRS (1)
EMPLOYEE-NUMBER (2)	EMPLOYEE-RATE (2)	NUMBER-RATE-PAIRS (2)
EMPLOYEE-NUMBER (3)	EMPLOYEE-RATE (3)	NUMBER-RATE-PAIRS (3)
EMPLOYEE-NUMBER (4)	EMPLOYEE-RATE (4)	NUMBER-RATE-PAIRS (4)
EMPLOYEE-NUMBER (5)	EMPLOYEE-RATE (5)	NUMBER-RATE-PAIRS (5)

EMPLOYEE-NUMBER-RATE-TABLE

Inventory Control with A Table Lookup

In Chapter 11, we presented an inventory control program in which a series of input records were processed. In looking at this program previously, we needed an inventory record that was immediately followed by all transaction records. Now we have a tool, a single-dimension table, that permits us to arrange the data differently. Observe the layout of the data in Figure 13.5. Notice that all the inventory records are grouped together and appear before the first transaction record. In this example, we will read all the inventory records, store each in a table, and then determine which inventory record a transaction is supposed to update. Furthermore, it is not even necessary that the transaction records be grouped. The entire input process is completed before the first line of the inventory control report is printed.

Look at the program in Figure 13.5. Since two different types of records are to be read by the program, an INVENTORY-RECORD (lines 520–570) and a TRANSACTION-RECORD (lines 590–710) are placed in the WORKING-STORAGE SECTION. Next, a single-dimension table (INVENTORY-TABLE) is presented (lines 1020–1060).

Figure 13.5 Inventory Control [Single-dimension Table] (Hierarchy Chart)

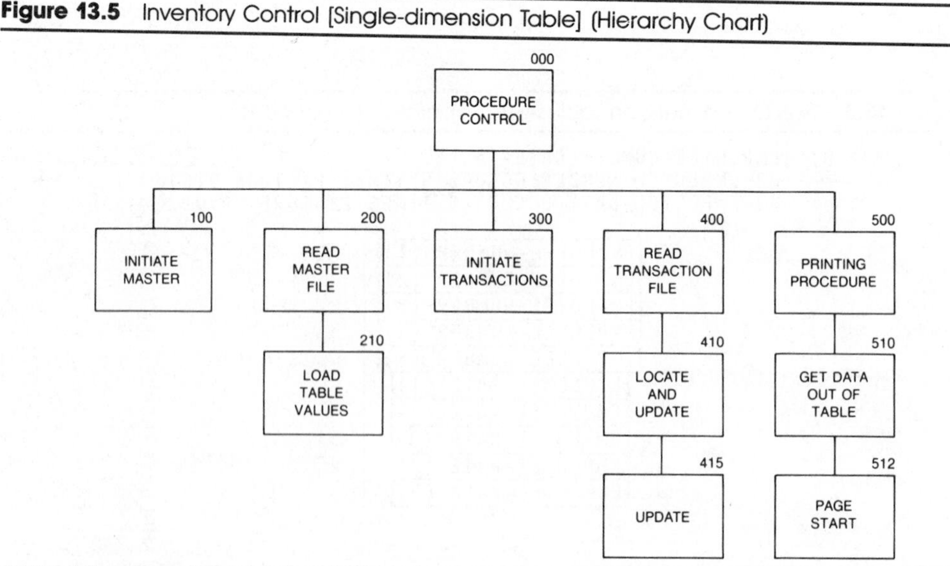

Figure 13.5 Inventory Control [Single-dimension Table] (Pseudocode)

```
START
    DO Initiate master
    DO Read master file UNTIL eof
    DO Initiate transactions
    DO Read transaction file UNTIL eof
    DO Printing procedure
END

INITIATE MASTER
    OPEN inventory master list
    READ input AT END DISPLAY message
         SET file status
         CLOSE file
    ENDREAD
END

READ MASTER FILE
    DO Load table values
    READ input AT END CLOSE file
         MOVE location to number
         DISPLAY message
         SET file status
    ENDREAD
END

LOAD TABLE VALUES
    ADD 1 to location
    MOVE input to table
END

INITIATE TRANSACTIONS
    OPEN inventory transaction file
    READ input AT END DISPLAY message
         SET file status
END

READ TRANSACTION FILE
    SET search status
    DO Locate and update
         VARYING location
         UNTIL end of table or found
    IF not found
         DISPLAY messge
    ENDIF
    READ input AT END DISPLAY message
         SET file status
END

LOCATE AND UPDATE
    IF table value EQUAL input value
         DO Update
         SET found
    ENDIF
END

UPDATE
    SET update status
    IF units returned after sale OR received
         SET update status
         ADD units TO table
    ENDIF
    IF units sold OR returned after receipt
         SET update status
         SUBTRACT units FROM table
    ENDIF
    IF transaction omitted
         SET update status
         DISPLAY message
    ENDIF
    IF terminate processing
         SET update status
    ENDIF
    IF update status = spaces
         DISPLAY message
    ENDIF
END

PRINTING PROCEDURE
    CLOSE input
    OPEN output
    SET line count
    DO Get data out of table
         VARYING location
         UNTIL end of table
    CLOSE output
END

GET DATA OUT OF TABLE
    IF line count > 40
         DO Page start
    MOVE table values to output
    IF table balance < 0
         MOVE message to output
    ENDIF
    WRITE output
END

PAGE START
    ADD 1 TO page count
    SET page count, line count
    WRITE output
END
```

This table is used first to collect inventory records as they are read and later to record the results of individual transactions.

Loading a Table with the READ Statement

Now turn to the PROCEDURE DIVISION. Note that the control structure (PROCEDURE CONTROL) is somewhat different from how it was used in earlier programs.

Figure 13.5 *Continued* Inventory Control [Single-dimension Table]

```
******************************************************************
 IDENTIFICATION DIVISION.
******************************************************************
 PROGRAM-ID.    INVENTORY-CONTROL-TABLE.
 AUTHOR.        JOHN WINDSOR.
 DATE-WRITTEN.  JANUARY 1, 1989.
 DATE-COMPILED. JANUARY 1, 1989.
*    This procedure uses a single-dimension table to save
*    inventory data.  Later, this data is used in an update
*    operation based on transaction records.  Using the table
*    in this mode is often called a "table lookup."
******************************************************************
 ENVIRONMENT DIVISION.
******************************************************************
*----------------------------------------------------------------*
 CONFIGURATION SECTION.
*----------------------------------------------------------------*
 SOURCE-COMPUTER. IBM.
 OBJECT-COMPUTER. IBM.
 SPECIAL-NAMES.   C01 IS NEXT-PAGE.
*----------------------------------------------------------------*
 INPUT-OUTPUT SECTION.
*----------------------------------------------------------------*
 FILE-CONTROL.
     SELECT INVENTORY-MASTER-LIST ASSIGN TO UT-S-MASTER.
     SELECT INVENTORY-TRANSACTION-FILE ASSIGN TO UT-S-INPUT.
     SELECT REPORT-FILE    ASSIGN TO UT-S-OUTPUT.
******************************************************************
 DATA DIVISION.
******************************************************************
 FILE SECTION.
 FD  INVENTORY-MASTER-LIST LABEL RECORDS ARE OMITTED.
 01  INVENTORY-MASTER-RECORD     PIC X(80).

 FD  INVENTORY-TRANSACTION-FILE LABEL RECORDS ARE OMITTED.
 01  INVENTORY-TRANSACTION-RECORD PIC X(80).

 FD  REPORT-FILE LABEL RECORDS ARE OMITTED.
 01  REPORT-RECORD               PIC X(133).
*----------------------------------------------------------------*
 WORKING-STORAGE SECTION.
*----------------------------------------------------------------*
 01  WORKING-RECORD.
     05  LINE-COUNT              PIC 9(02).
     05  PAGE-COUNT              PIC 9(03) VALUE ZEROS.
     05  LOCATION                PIC 9(03) VALUE ZEROS.
     05  NUMBER-OF-ITEMS         PIC 9(03) VALUE ZEROS.
     05  MASTER-STATUS           PIC X(10).
     05  SEARCH-STATUS           PIC X(10).
     05  UPDATE-STATUS           PIC X(10).

 01  INVENTORY-RECORD.
     05 PART-NUMBER-IR-IN        PIC 9(06).
     05 ITEM-DESCRIPTION-IR-IN   PIC X(20).
     05 TRANSACTION-UNIT-VOLUME-IR-IN PIC 9(06).
     05 FILLER                   PIC X(47).
     05 TRANSACTION-CODE-IR-IN   PIC 9(01).

 01  TRANSACTION-RECORD.
     05 PART-NUMBER-TR-IN        PIC 9(06).
     05 FILLER                   PIC X(20).
     05 TRANSACTION-UNIT-VOLUME-TR-IN PIC 9(06).
     05 FILLER                   PIC X(47).
     05 TRANSACTION-CODE-TR-IN   PIC 9(01).
         88 UNITS-SOLD                  VALUE 1.
         88 UNITS-RETURNED-AFTER-SALE   VALUE 2.
         88 UNITS-RECEIVED              VALUE 3.
         88 UNITS-RETURNED-AFTER-RECEIPT VALUE 4.
         88 TRANSACTION-OMITTED         VALUE 5.
```

Figure 13.5 *Continued* Inventory Control [Single-dimension Table]

```
        1   1   2   2   2   3   3   4   4   4   5   5   6   6   6   7
4   8   2   6   0   4   8   2   6   0   4   8   2   6   0   4   8   2

               88 UNKNOWN-CODE                   VALUES 0, 6 THRU 8.
               88 TERMINATE-PROCESSING           VALUE 9.

       01  REPORT-TITLE.
           05 FILLER                     PIC X(54) VALUE SPACES.
           05 FILLER                     PIC X(24) VALUE
                                         'Inventory Control Report'.

       01  PAGE-NUMBER-LINE.
           05 FILLER                     PIC X(115) VALUE SPACES.
           05 FILLER                     PIC X(05)  VALUE 'Page'.
           05 PAGE-NUMBER-OUT            PIC ZZ9.

       01  HEADING-LINE.
           05 FILLER                     PIC X(33) VALUE SPACES.
           05 FILLER                     PIC X(16) VALUE 'Part Number'.
           05 FILLER                     PIC X(26) VALUE
                                         'Part Description'.
           05 FILLER                     PIC X(18) VALUE
                                         'Ending Balance'.
           05 FILLER                     PIC X(06) VALUE 'Notes:'.

       01  DETAIL-LINE.
           05 FILLER                     PIC X(35) VALUE SPACES.
           05 PART-NUMBER-OUT            PIC 9(06).
           05 FILLER                     PIC X(07) VALUE SPACES.
           05 ITEM-DESCRIPTION-OUT       PIC X(20).
           05 FILLER                     PIC X(08) VALUE SPACES.
           05 BALANCE-OUT                PIC -Z(8).
           05 FILLER                     PIC X(10) VALUE SPACES.
           05 MESSAGE-OUT                PIC X(35) VALUE SPACES.

       01  INVENTORY-TABLE.
           05 ITEMS-T                    OCCURS 100 TIMES.
               10 PART-NUMBER-T          PIC 9(06).
               10 ITEM-DESCRIPTION-T     PIC X(20).
               10 BALANCE-T              PIC S9(08).
      ************************************************************
       PROCEDURE DIVISION.
      ************************************************************
      *----------------------------------------------------------*
       000-PROCEDURE-CONTROL SECTION.
      *----------------------------------------------------------*
           PERFORM 100-INITIATE-MASTER.
           PERFORM 200-READ-MASTER-FILE UNTIL
               MASTER-STATUS = 'ERROR' OR 'COMPLETE'.
           PERFORM 300-INITIATE-TRANSACTIONS.
           PERFORM 400-READ-TRANSACTION-FILE UNTIL
               MASTER-STATUS = 'ERROR' OR TERMINATE-PROCESSING.
           PERFORM 500-PRINTING-PROCEDURE.
           STOP RUN.
      *----------------------------------------------------------*
       100-INITIATE-MASTER SECTION.
      *----------------------------------------------------------*
           OPEN INPUT INVENTORY-MASTER-LIST.
           READ INVENTORY-MASTER-LIST INTO INVENTORY-RECORD
               AT END DISPLAY 'Error Occurred During Master File Input'
                      MOVE 'ERROR' TO MASTER-STATUS
                      CLOSE INVENTORY-MASTER-LIST.
      *----------------------------------------------------------*
       200-READ-MASTER-FILE SECTION.
      *----------------------------------------------------------*
           PERFORM 210-LOAD-TABLE-VALUES.
           READ INVENTORY-MASTER-LIST INTO INVENTORY-RECORD
               AT END CLOSE INVENTORY-TRANSACTION-FILE
               MOVE LOCATION TO NUMBER-OF-ITEMS
               DISPLAY 'Master File Input Complete'
               MOVE 'COMPLETE' TO MASTER-STATUS.
      *----------------------------------------------------------*
```

Figure 13.5 *Continued* Inventory Control [Single-dimension Table]

```
       1  1  2  2  2  3  3  4  4  4  5  5  6  6  6  7
 4  8  2  6  0  4  8  2  6  0  4  8  2  6  0  4  8  2

 210-LOAD-TABLE-VALUES SECTION.
*-------------------------------------------------------*
     ADD 1 TO LOCATION.
     MOVE PART-NUMBER-IR-IN   TO PART-NUMBER-T (LOCATION).
     MOVE ITEM-DESCRIPTION-IR-IN TO ITEM-DESCRIPTION-T (LOCATION).
     MOVE TRANSACTION-UNIT-VOLUME-IR-IN TO BALANCE-T (LOCATION).
*-------------------------------------------------------*
 300-INITIATE-TRANSACTIONS SECTION.
*-------------------------------------------------------*
     OPEN INPUT INVENTORY-TRANSACTION-FILE.
     READ INVENTORY-TRANSACTION-FILE INTO TRANSACTION-RECORD
         AT END DISPLAY 'Abnormal Termination of Update Procedure'
                MOVE 'ERROR' TO MASTER-STATUS.
*-------------------------------------------------------*
 400-READ-TRANSACTION-FILE SECTION.
*-------------------------------------------------------*
     MOVE 'SEARCHING' TO SEARCH-STATUS.
     PERFORM 410-LOCATE-AND-UPDATE
         VARYING LOCATION FROM 1 BY 1 UNTIL
         LOCATION > NUMBER-OF-ITEMS OR SEARCH-STATUS = 'FOUND'.
     IF SEARCH-STATUS NOT = 'FOUND'
         DISPLAY 'Part Number ', PART-NUMBER-TR-IN, ' Not Found'.
     READ INVENTORY-TRANSACTION-FILE INTO TRANSACTION-RECORD
         AT END DISPLAY 'Abnormal Termination of Update Procedure'
                MOVE 'ERROR' TO MASTER-STATUS.
*-------------------------------------------------------*
 410-LOCATE-AND-UPDATE SECTION.
*-------------------------------------------------------*
     IF PART-NUMBER-T (LOCATION) IS EQUAL TO PART-NUMBER-TR-IN
         PERFORM 415-UPDATE
         MOVE 'FOUND' TO SEARCH-STATUS.
*-------------------------------------------------------*
 415-UPDATE SECTION.
*-------------------------------------------------------*
     MOVE SPACES TO UPDATE-STATUS.
     IF UNITS-RETURNED-AFTER-SALE OR UNITS-RECEIVED
         MOVE 'UPDATED' TO UPDATE-STATUS
         ADD TRANSACTION-UNIT-VOLUME-TR-IN
                                 TO BALANCE-T (LOCATION).
     IF UNITS-SOLD OR UNITS-RETURNED-AFTER-RECEIPT
         MOVE 'UPDATED' TO UPDATE-STATUS
         SUBTRACT TRANSACTION-UNIT-VOLUME-TR-IN FROM
             BALANCE-T (LOCATION).
     IF TRANSACTION-OMITTED
         MOVE 'UPDATED' TO UPDATE-STATUS
         DISPLAY 'Transaction on Part Number ',
           PART-NUMBER-TR-IN, ' was Omitted'.
     IF TERMINATE-PROCESSING
         MOVE 'UPDATED' TO UPDATE-STATUS.
     IF UPDATE-STATUS = SPACES
         DISPLAY 'Illegal Transaction Encountered on Part Number '
           PART-NUMBER-TR-IN, '--Transaction Ignored'.
*-------------------------------------------------------*
 500-PRINTING-PROCEDURE SECTION.
*-------------------------------------------------------*
     CLOSE INVENTORY-TRANSACTION-FILE.
     OPEN OUTPUT REPORT-FILE.
     MOVE 99 TO LINE-COUNT.
     PERFORM 510-GET-DATA-OUT-OF-TABLE
         VARYING LOCATION FROM 1 BY 1
         UNTIL LOCATION > NUMBER-OF-ITEMS.
     CLOSE REPORT-FILE.
*-------------------------------------------------------*
 510-GET-DATA-OUT-OF-TABLE SECTION.
*-------------------------------------------------------*
     IF LINE-COUNT > 40
         PERFORM 512-PAGE-START.
     MOVE PART-NUMBER-T (LOCATION) TO PART-NUMBER-OUT.
     MOVE ITEM-DESCRIPTION-T (LOCATION) TO ITEM-DESCRIPTION-OUT.
```

Figure 13.5 *Continued* Inventory Control [Single-dimension Table]

```
           1   1   2   2   2   3   3   4   4   4   5   5   6   6   6   7
   4   8   2   6   0   4   8   2   6   0   4   8   2   6   0   4   8   2
------------------------------------------------------------------------
2080          MOVE BALANCE-T (LOCATION) TO BALANCE-OUT.
2090          IF BALANCE-T (LOCATION) < 0
2100              MOVE 'Account Balance Less Than Zero' TO MESSAGE-OUT.
2110          WRITE REPORT-RECORD  FROM DETAIL-LINE AFTER 2 LINES.
2120          MOVE SPACES               TO MESSAGE-OUT.
2130          ADD 2 TO LINE-COUNT.
2140      *-------------------------------------------------------------*
2150       512-PAGE-START SECTION.
2160      *-------------------------------------------------------------*
2170          ADD 1 TO PAGE-COUNT.
2180          MOVE PAGE-COUNT           TO PAGE-NUMBER-OUT.
2190          MOVE 0                    TO LINE-COUNT.
2200          WRITE REPORT-RECORD FROM REPORT-TITLE AFTER NEXT-PAGE.
2210          WRITE REPORT-RECORD FROM PAGE-NUMBER-LINE AFTER 2 LINES.
2220          WRITE REPORT-RECORD FROM HEADING-LINE AFTER 2 LINES.
2230          MOVE SPACES               TO REPORT-RECORD.
2240          WRITE REPORT-RECORD AFTER 1 LINES.
```

The procedures are to (1) initiate the program, (2) read all the inventory records and store them in a table, (3) initiate the transaction process, (4) update inventory records, and (5) print the inventory control report. Notice that the OPEN statement in line 1240 opens only one input file—the other files are not needed until later. Next, observe that all of the input operations (lines 1250 and 1330) place data into the INVENTORY-RECORD. The processing of the inventory records is completed with loading the INVENTORY-TABLE (lines 1410–1440). Note that in the 210-LOAD-TABLE-VALUES procedure, each time the procedure is executed, 1 is added to LOCATION. Thus, LOCATION keeps track of which occurrence position will be used by the inventory record data. Upon the first execution of the procedure, the part number, its description, and the number of units are placed into the appropriate fields in the INVENTORY-TABLE—which is the first occurrence position. With the second execution of the procedure, data are placed in the second occurrence position, and so on.

When the processing of transactions begins, a record is read (line 1490). Notice that this READ statement and the one in line 1610 place the input data into the TRANSACTION-RECORD. As we begin the update procedure (400-READ-TRANSACTION-FILE), we have a transaction for processing. However, we do not yet know which of the inventory records in the table will be affected. The purpose of the PERFORM statement in line 1560–1580 and the 410-LOCATE-AND-UPDATE procedure is to find which inventory record will be updated (based on a matching value of the part number from a transaction). Thus, the procedure looks for such a match in the first occurrence position of PART-NUMBER-T. If it is found at that point, the update proceeds. If not, the procedure is repeated and a match is sought in occurrence positions 2, 3, 4, and so on until either a match is found or all part numbers have been examined (in which case an error message is produced). Note that it does not matter which part number is indicated in the table—the procedure finds it. This process is known as a *table lookup*.

While processing the data a number of errors could be detected. Each of these possibilities is identified by a message that appears on a special portion of the printout (called *errors* in Figure 13.5). However, the intent of the program is ultimately to produce a printed report. The printing procedure begins with the execution of 500-PRINTING-PROCEDURE (line 1920). At this point, the input file is closed and the output file is opened. This should confirm that the entire report is produced from data

Figure 13.5 *Continued* Inventory Control [Single-dimension Table] (Transactions)

```
---------------------------------------------------------------------------------
|           1   1   2   2   2   3   3   4   4   4   5   5   6   6   6   7   7   8|
|   4   8   2   6   0   4   8   2   6   0   4   8   2   6   0   4   8   2   6   0|
|--------------------------------------------------------------------------------|
|                                                                                |
|454550                    000045                                               7|
|454550                    000300                                               4|
|124900                    000050                                               1|
|124900                    000100                                               2|
|132240                    000460                                               5|
|132240                    000790                                               4|
|132240                    004000                                               1|
|465465                    000200                                               3|
|123450                    001000                                               1|
|123987                    000462                                               4|
|123450                    000100                                               1|
|123450                    000030                                               2|
|123450                    000020                                               3|
|222200                    000005                                               2|
|222200                    000095                                               1|
|123450                    000040                                               4|
|124900                    000760                                               1|
|123450                    000010                                               5|
|123987                    000005                                               1|
|123450                    000040                                               1|
|790000                    000100                                               7|
|124900                    000820                                               6|
|124900                    005000                                               1|
|790000                    000075                                               1|
|790000                    000400                                               2|
|101100                    000030                                               2|
|101100                    000015                                               2|
|302100                    000200                                               6|
|101100                    000045                                               6|
|222200                    000045                                               8|
|302100                    002065                                               1|
|222200                    000300                                               1|
|457890                    000357                                               2|
|222200                    000200                                               1|
|302100                    000050                                               3|
|222200                    000010                                               4|
|152155                    000023                                               8|
|454550                    000100                                               5|
|302100                    000030                                               5|
|457890                    000045                                               5|
|302100                    000009                                               2|
|457890                    000063                                               1|
|302100                    000500                                               1|
|123987                    004631                                               1|
|302100                    000010                                               8|
|454550                    000050                                               3|
|302100                    000200                                               4|
|454550                    007000                                               1|
|152155                    000045                                               4|
|152155                    000500                                               3|
|123987                    000246                                               6|
|101100                    000006                                               3|
|101100                    000150                                               1|
|101100                    000050                                               1|
|123987                    000050                                               3|
|302100                    002045                                               1|
|302100                    000020                                               7|
|302100                    000046                                               2|
|302100                    000403                                               9|
|                                                                                |
|                                                                                |
|                                                                                |
|                                                                                |
|                                                                                |
|                                                                                |
|                                                                                |
|                                                                                |
|                                                                                |
|                                                                                |
|                                                                                |
---------------------------------------------------------------------------------
```

Figure 13.5 *Continued* Inventory Control [Single-dimension Table] (Master Data)

```
-------------------------------------------------------------------------------
|              1    1    2    2    2    3    3    4    4    4    5    5    6    6    6    7    7    8|
|    4    8    2    6    0    4    8    2    6    0    4    8    2    6    0    4    8    2    6    0|
|------------------------------------------------------------------------------|
|                                                                              |
|101100Light Brown Umbrella000025                                             0|
|454550100 Watt Light Bulbs088500                                             0|
|1249006 oz. Chocolate Bar 150000                                             0|
|132240Yellow Comb         040000                                             0|
|465465Green Comb          000431                                             0|
|123450Laundry Soap        005900                                             0|
|790000Mickey Mouse Watch  000010                                             0|
|222200Headphones          033200                                             0|
|152155Tub Margarine       000750                                             0|
|123987Red Food Coloring   099910                                             0|
|302100Aspirin             000100                                             0|
-------------------------------------------------------------------------------
```

Figure 13.5 *Continued* Inventory Control [Single-dimension Table] (Output)

```
Master File Input Complete
Illegal Transaction Encountered on Part Number 454550--Transaction Ignored
Transaction on Part Number 132240 was Omitted
Transaction on Part Number 123450 was Omitted
Illegal Transaction Encountered on Part Number 790000--Transaction Ignored
Illegal Transaction Encountered on Part Number 124900--Transaction Ignored
Illegal Transaction Encountered on Part Number 302100--Transaction Ignored
Illegal Transaction Encountered on Part Number 101100--Transaction Ignored
Illegal Transaction Encountered on Part Number 222200--Transaction Ignored
Part Number 457890 Not Found
Illegal Transaction Encountered on Part Number 152155--Transaction Ignored
Transaction on Part Number 454550 was Omitted
Transaction on Part Number 302100 was Omitted
Part Number 457890 Not Found
Part Number 457890 Not Found
Illegal Transaction Encountered on Part Number 302100--Transaction Ignored
Illegal Transaction Encountered on Part Number 123987--Transaction Ignored
Illegal Transaction Encountered on Part Number 302100--Transaction Ignored
```

Figure 13.5 *Continued* Inventory Control [Single-dimension Table] (Output)

```
                         Inventory Control Report
                                                                   Page   1
Part Number       Part Description          Ending Balance    Notes:

  101100         Light Brown Umbrella             124           Account Balance Less Than Zero
  454550         100 Watt Light Bulbs           81250
  124900         6 oz. Chocolate Bar           144290
  132240         Yellow Comb                    35210
  465465         Green Comb                       631
  123450         Laundry Soap                    4770
  790000         Mickey Mouse Watch               335
  222200         Headphones                     32600
  152155         Tub Margarine                   1205
  123987         Red Food Coloring              94862
  302100         Aspirin                         4605           Account Balance Less Than Zero
```

saved in the INVENTORY-TABLE. The PERFORM statement in line 1970 actually drives the production of the report. Each time the 510-GET-DATA-OUT-OF-TABLE procedure is executed, one occurrence position is addressed and one inventory record is retrieved from the table for printing.

Two-Dimension Tables

When a data-name associated with an OCCURS clause is subordinate to another OCCURS clause, the portion of the table described by the data-name is considered *two-dimensional*. That is, the data-name associated with one OCCURS clause that is subordinate to another may be logically thought of as having *rows* and *columns*—the data-name represents a *matrix*. In this representation, the integer value associated with the first OCCURS clause (from top to bottom) provides the number of *rows* of the table. The integer value associated with the second (subordinate) OCCURS provides the number of *columns* of the table. When a data item is described as being two-dimensional, *two* subscripts should be used to reference a single value from the table. As with single-dimension tables, the subscripts may be integer values or data-names that describe integer fields. Both subscript values should be enclosed in one set of parentheses and separated by a comma.

Figure 13.6 provides an example of a record description representing a two-dimension table. The record-name TRANSPORTATION-CHARGES may be used to address the entire table (360 bytes—ten rows by six columns by individual six-digit fields). As before, the table name may be referenced in the PROCEDURE DIVISION, but should *not* be written with a subscript. The first OCCURS clause is associated with WAREHOUSE-LOCATION. WAREHOUSE-LOCATION is a group-name even though it is jointly a single-dimension table. It references a complete row of the table. Thus, WAREHOUSE-LOCATION may be referenced in the PROCEDURE DIVISION and should be written with one subscript. The next data item in the description is REC-PT (receiving point), which is at the 10 level, and therefore is subordinate to WAREHOUSE-LO-

Figure 13.6 Two-dimension Table

```
01  TRANSPORTATION-CHARGES.
    05 WAREHOUSE-LOCATION OCCURS 10 TIMES.
       10 REC-PT          OCCURS 6 TIMES.
          15 CHARGE         PIC  9(4)V99.
```

WAREHOUSE-LOCATION (1)	CHARGE (1, 1) REC-PT (1, 1)	CHARGE (1, 2) REC-PT (1, 2)	CHARGE (1, 3) REC-PT (1, 3)	CHARGE (1, 4) REC-PT (1, 4)	CHARGE (1, 5) REC-PT (1, 5)	CHARGE (1, 6) REC-PT (1, 6)
WAREHOUSE-LOCATION (2)	CHARGE (2, 1) REC-PT (2, 1)	CHARGE (2, 2) REC-PT (2, 2)	CHARGE (2, 3) REC-PT (2, 3)	CHARGE (2, 4) REC-PT (2, 4)	CHARGE (2, 5) REC-PT (2, 5)	CHARGE (2, 6) REC-PT (2, 6)
WAREHOUSE-LOCATION (3)	CHARGE (3, 1) REC-PT (3, 1)	CHARGE (3, 2) REC-PT (3, 2)	CHARGE (3, 3) REC-PT (3, 3)	CHARGE (3, 4) REC-PT (3, 4)	CHARGE (3, 5) REC-PT (3, 5)	CHARGE (3, 6) REC-PT (3, 6)
WAREHOUSE-LOCATION (4)	CHARGE (4, 1) REC-PT (4, 1)	CHARGE (4, 2) REC-PT (4, 2)	CHARGE (4, 3) REC-PT (4, 3)	CHARGE (4, 4) REC-PT (4, 4)	CHARGE (4, 5) REC-PT (4, 5)	CHARGE (4, 6) REC-PT (4, 6)
WAREHOUSE-LOCATION (5)	CHARGE (5, 1) REC-PT (5, 1)	CHARGE (5, 2) REC-PT (5, 2)	CHARGE (5, 3) REC-PT (5, 3)	CHARGE (5, 4) REC-PT (5, 4)	CHARGE (5, 5) REC-PT (5, 5)	CHARGE (5, 6) REC-PT (5, 6)
WAREHOUSE-LOCATION (6)	CHARGE (6, 1) REC-PT (6, 1)	CHARGE (6, 2) REC-PT (6, 2)	CHARGE (6, 3) REC-PT (6, 3)	CHARGE (6, 4) REC-PT (6, 4)	CHARGE (6, 5) REC-PT (6, 5)	CHARGE (6, 6) REC-PT (6, 6)
WAREHOUSE-LOCATION (7)	CHARGE (7, 1) REC-PT (7, 1)	CHARGE (7, 2) REC-PT (7, 2)	CHARGE (7, 3) REC-PT (7, 3)	CHARGE (7, 4) REC-PT (7, 4)	CHARGE (7, 5) REC-PT (7, 5)	CHARGE (7, 6) REC-PT (7, 6)
WAREHOUSE-LOCATION (8)	CHARGE (8, 1) REC-PT (8, 1)	CHARGE (8, 2) REC-PT (8, 2)	CHARGE (8, 3) REC-PT (8, 3)	CHARGE (8, 4) REC-PT (8, 4)	CHARGE (8, 5) REC-PT (8, 5)	CHARGE (8, 6) REC-PT (8, 6)
WAREHOUSE-LOCATION (9)	CHARGE (9, 1) REC-PT (9, 1)	CHARGE (9, 2) REC-PT (9, 2)	CHARGE (9, 3) REC-PT (9, 3)	CHARGE (9, 4) REC-PT (9, 4)	CHARGE (9, 5) REC-PT (9, 5)	CHARGE (9, 6) REC-PT (9, 6)
WAREHOUSE-LOCATION (10)	CHARGE (10, 1) REC-PT (10, 1)	CHARGE (10, 2) REC-PT (10, 2)	CHARGE (10, 3) REC-PT (10, 3)	CHARGE (10, 4) REC-PT (10, 4)	CHARGE (10, 5) REC-PT (10, 5)	CHARGE (10, 6) REC-PT (10, 6)

TRANSPORTATION-CHARGES

Figure 13.7 Mixture of One- and Two-dimension Tables

```
Ø1  EMPLOYEE-RATE-AND-HOURS-TABLE.
    Ø3 RATE-AND-HOURS  OCCURS 5 TIMES.
       Ø5 RATE PICTURE 99V99.
       Ø5 HOURS OCCURS 7 TIMES PICTURE 99V9.
```

RATE (1)	HOURS (1,1)	HOURS (1,2)	HOURS (1,3)	HOURS (1,4)	HOURS (1,5)	HOURS (1,6)	HOURS (1,7)
RATE (2)	HOURS (2,1)	HOURS (2,2)	HOURS (2,3)	HOURS (2,4)	HOURS (2,5)	HOURS (2,6)	HOURS (2,7)
RATE (3)	HOURS (3,1)	HOURS (3,2)	HOURS (3,3)	HOURS (3,4)	HOURS (3,5)	HOURS (3,6)	HOURS (3,7)
RATE (4)	HOURS (4,1)	HOURS (4,2)	HOURS (4,3)	HOURS (4,4)	HOURS (4,5)	HOURS (4,6)	HOURS (4,7)
RATE (5)	HOURS (5,1)	HOURS (5,2)	HOURS (5,3)	HOURS (5,4)	HOURS (5,5)	HOURS (5,6)	HOURS (5,7)

EMPLOYEE-RATE-AND-HOURS-TABLE

RATE-AND-HOURS (5)
RATE-AND-HOURS (4)
RATE-AND-HOURS (3)
RATE-AND-HOURS (2)
RATE-AND-HOURS (1)

CATION. REC-PT OCCURS six times. For each occurence of WAREHOUSE-LOCATION, there are 6 data items known as REC-PT. WAREHOUSE-LOCATION OCCURS ten times, resulting in 60 data items in the entire table known as REC-PT. Each of these can be uniquely referenced by a particular set of subscripts. Each cell of the TRANSPORTATION-CHARGES table may be referenced by either the group-name REC-PT (an alphanumeric field) and a particular row-column pair or the data-name CHARGES, (a numeric-nonedited field) and a particular row-column pair.

Figure 13.7 illustrates a table composed of a mixture of tables. EMPLOYEE-RATE-AND-HOURS-TABLE, a record-name that describes all the subordinate data (125 bytes), should not be written with a subscript in the PROCEDURE DIVISION. RATES-AND-HOURS, a group name, is written with an OCCURS clause. RATES-AND-HOURS must be accompanied by one subscript when written in the PROCEDURE DIVISION; each occurrence addresses 25 bytes of internal storage. RATE is subordinate to the OCCURS clause associated with RATES-AND-HOURS. RATE occurs five times and must be written with one subscript in the PROCEDURE DIVISION; each occurrence addresses four bytes of storage. HOURS is subordinate to RATE-AND-HOURS and is written with an OCCURS clause, creating a two-dimensional table. HOURS is structured so that it logically appears to have five rows (from the OCCURS 5 TIMES associated with RATE-AND-HOURS) and seven columns (from the OCCURS 7 TIMES associated with HOURS), giving 35 distinct areas which can be referenced within HOURS. When HOURS is used in the PROCEDURE DIVISION, it must be written with two subscripts, with the first ranging from 1 to 5 and the second from 1 to 7. In the logical representation of the computer's storage, the first occurrence of RATE is followed by the first row of HOURS. The "row" as a group is represented by a single occurrence of RATE-AND-HOURS.

Sales Summary Report

Figure 13.8 illustrates how COBOL programs might utilize two-dimensional tables. In this illustration, it is assumed that a number of sales records exist, with the possibility of several records for each inventory item. The records represent dates of sale during a 12-month period. There might be either multiple records with the same item number, but with different month-of-sale values, or multiple records with the same item number and the same month-of-sale value, or there might be both. The objective of the procedure

Figure 13.8 Sales Summary Report [Two-dimension Table] (Hierarchy Chart)

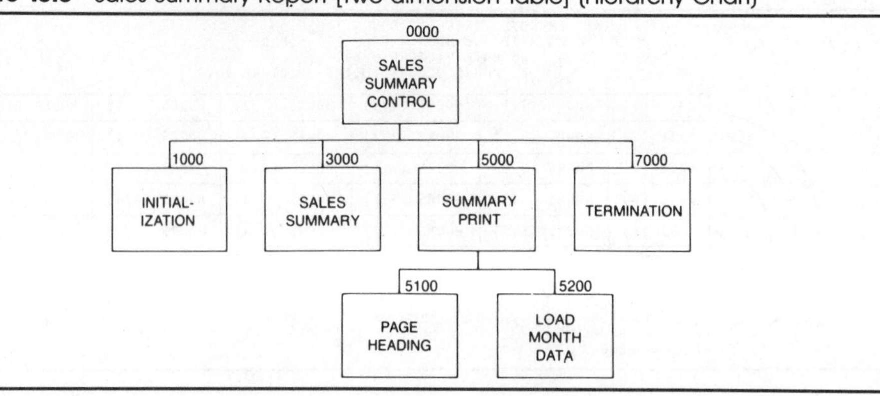

is to collect all the data for a single item (with summation if more than one sale occurred during a given month) and produce a "by-month" sales summary.

Now examine the code of Figure 13.8. Two data tables have been developed—an ITEM-TABLE (lines 620–650) and a SALES-BY-MONTH-TABLE (lines 670–700). The ITEM-TABLE is used to retain the values of ITEM-NUMBER-T and ITEM-DESCRIPTION-T as they are read from the SALES-FILE. Since we anticipate duplicate values for ITEM-NUMBER-T and ITEM-DESCRIPTION-T (multiple records for the same item representing different sales), we wish to retain only one "copy" of the data. The procedure can handle a *maximum* of 30 different items.

The SALES-BY-MONTH-TABLE is two-dimensional with 30 rows, corresponding to the 30 anticipated items, by 12 columns, corresponding to 12 months of a year. The application assumes that the value of the MONTH-OF-SALE-IN (line 400) corresponds to one of the columns. We may access all 12 months of sales data by using ITEMS-

Figure 13.8 *Continued* Sales Summary Report [Two-dimension Table] (Pseudocode)

```
START
    DO Initialization
    DO Sales summation UNTIL eof
    DO Summary print
         VARYING item UNTIL end of table
    DO Termination
END

INITIALIZATION
    OPEN input, output
    CLEAR tables
    READ SALES-FILE
         AT END SET file status
END

SALES SUMMATION
    IF item number NOT = last item
         MOVE item number TO last item
         ADD 1 TO item count
         MOVE input to table
    ENDIF
    ADD amount of sale TO table sales
    READ input
         AT END SET file status
END

SUMMARY PRINT
    DIVIDE line count BY 25
           GIVING page status
    IF page status = 0
         DO Page heading
    ENDIF
    MOVE table values to output
    DO Load month data
         VARYING month UNTIL > 12
    WRITE output
END

PAGE HEADING
    WRITE heading
    WRITE column heading
END

LOAD MONTH DATA
    MOVE work table to ouput table
END

TERMINATION
    CLOSE files
END
```

Figure 13.8 *Continued* Sales Summary Report [Two-dimension Table]

```
************************************************************
 IDENTIFICATION DIVISION.
************************************************************
 PROGRAM-ID.     SALES-SUMMARY.
 AUTHOR.         J. WAYNE SPENCE.
 DATE-WRITTEN.   JANUARY 1, 1989.
 DATE-COMPILED.  JANUARY 1, 1989.
*    Procedure to accumulate sales of items by month.
*    Procedure uses a one dimensional table to store the
*    item number and name and a two dimensional table to
*    record the monthly sales of each item.
************************************************************
 ENVIRONMENT DIVISION.
************************************************************
*----------------------------------------------------------*
 CONFIGURATION SECTION.
*----------------------------------------------------------*
 SOURCE-COMPUTER. IBM.
 OBJECT-COMPUTER. IBM.
 SPECIAL-NAMES.   C01 IS TOP-OF-PAGE.
*----------------------------------------------------------*
 INPUT-OUTPUT SECTION.
*----------------------------------------------------------*
 FILE-CONTROL.
     SELECT SALES-FILE  ASSIGN TO UT-S-INPUT.
     SELECT REPORT-FILE ASSIGN TO UT-S-OUTPUT.
************************************************************
 DATA DIVISION.
************************************************************
*----------------------------------------------------------*
 FILE SECTION.
*----------------------------------------------------------*
 FD  SALES-FILE
         LABEL RECORDS ARE OMITTED.
 01  SALES-RECORD.
     05  ITEM-NUMBER-IN          PIC 9(05).
     05  ITEM-DESCRIPTION-IN     PIC X(30).
     05  FILLER                  PIC X(01).
     05  DATE-OF-SALE-IN.
         10  MONTH-OF-SALE-IN    PIC 9(02).
         10  DAY-OF-SALE-IN      PIC 9(02).
         10  YEAR-OF-SALE-IN     PIC 9(02).
     05  FILLER                  PIC X(02).
     05  AMOUNT-OF-SALE-IN       PIC S9(3)V99.
     05  FILLER                  PIC X(31).

 FD  REPORT-FILE
         LABEL RECORDS ARE STANDARD.
 01  REPORT-RECORD                 PIC X(133).
*----------------------------------------------------------*
 WORKING-STORAGE SECTION.
*----------------------------------------------------------*
 01  WORKING-VARIABLES.
     05  FILE-STATUS             PIC X(10) VALUE SPACES.
     05  ITEM                    PIC 9(02) VALUE ZERO.
     05  MONTH                   PIC 9(02) VALUE ZERO.
     05  ITEM-COUNT              PIC 9(02) VALUE ZERO.
     05  LINE-COUNT              PIC 9(02) VALUE ZERO.
     05  PAGE-STATUS             PIC V999 VALUE ZERO.
     05  LAST-ITEM               PIC 9(05) VALUE ZERO.

 01  ITEM-TABLE.
     05  ITEM-ENTRY              OCCURS 30 TIMES.
         10  ITEM-NUMBER-T       PIC 9(5).
         10  ITEM-DESCRIPTION-T  PIC X(30).

 01  SALES-BY-MONTH-TABLE.
     05  ITEMS-SOLD              OCCURS 30 TIMES.
         10  MONTHLY-SALES       OCCURS 12 TIMES
```

Figure 13.8 *Continued* Sales Summary Report [Two-dimension Table]

```
           1   1   2   2   2   3   3   4   4   4   5   5   6   6   6   7
   4   8   2   6   0   4   8   2   6   0   4   8   2   6   0   4   8   2

                                       PIC S9(4)V99.

       01  PAGE-HEADING.
           05  FILLER                  PIC X(55) VALUE SPACES.
           05  FILLER                  PIC X(22) VALUE
                                       'Sales Summary by Month'.

       01  COLUMN-HEADING.
           05  FILLER                  PIC X(38) VALUE
                                       '   Item Description'.
           05  FILLER                  PIC X(92) VALUE
           'Jan.    Feb.    Mar.    Apr.    May     June    July    Aug.
      -    '    Sep.    Oct.    Nov.    Dec.'.

       01  DETAIL-LINE.
           05  FILLER                  PIC X(01) VALUE SPACES.
           05  ITEM-NUMBER-OUT         PIC 99B999.
           05  FILLER                  PIC X(01) VALUE SPACES.
           05  ITEM-DESCRIPTION-OUT    PIC X(25).
           05  FILLER                  PIC X(01) VALUE SPACES.
           05  MONTHLY-SALES-OUT       OCCURS 12 TIMES
                                       PIC ZZZZZ.99.
      *************************************************************
       PROCEDURE DIVISION.
      *************************************************************
      *-----------------------------------------------------------*
       0000-SALES-SUMMARY-CONTROL SECTION.
      *-----------------------------------------------------------*
           PERFORM 1000-INITIALIZATION.
           PERFORM 3000-SALES-SUMMATION
               UNTIL FILE-STATUS = 'DONE'.
           PERFORM 5000-SUMMARY-PRINT
               VARYING ITEM FROM 1 BY 1 UNTIL ITEM > ITEM-COUNT.
           PERFORM 7000-TERMINATION.
           STOP RUN.
      *-----------------------------------------------------------*
       1000-INITIALIZATION SECTION.
      *-----------------------------------------------------------*
           OPEN INPUT SALES-FILE
                OUTPUT REPORT-FILE.
           MOVE SPACES                TO ITEM-TABLE.
           MOVE ZEROS                 TO SALES-BY-MONTH-TABLE.
           READ SALES-FILE
               AT END MOVE 'DONE'     TO FILE-STATUS.
      *-----------------------------------------------------------*
       3000-SALES-SUMMATION SECTION.
      *-----------------------------------------------------------*
           IF ITEM-NUMBER-IN NOT = LAST-ITEM
               MOVE ITEM-NUMBER-IN    TO LAST-ITEM
               ADD 1 TO ITEM-COUNT
               MOVE ITEM-NUMBER-IN    TO ITEM-NUMBER-T (ITEM-COUNT)
               MOVE ITEM-DESCRIPTION-IN
                                      TO ITEM-DESCRIPTION-T (ITEM-COUNT).
           ADD AMOUNT-OF-SALE-IN TO
               MONTHLY-SALES (ITEM-COUNT, MONTH-OF-SALE-IN).
           READ SALES-FILE
               AT END MOVE 'DONE' TO FILE-STATUS.
      *-----------------------------------------------------------*
       5000-SUMMARY-PRINT SECTION.
      *-----------------------------------------------------------*
           DIVIDE LINE-COUNT BY 25 GIVING PAGE-STATUS.
           IF PAGE-STATUS = 0
               PERFORM 5100-PAGE-HEADING.
           MOVE ITEM-NUMBER-T (ITEM) TO ITEM-NUMBER-OUT.
           MOVE ITEM-DESCRIPTION-T (ITEM) TO ITEM-DESCRIPTION-OUT.
           PERFORM 5200-LOAD-MONTH-DATA
               VARYING MONTH FROM 1 BY 1 UNTIL MONTH > 12.
           WRITE REPORT-RECORD FROM DETAIL-LINE AFTER ADVANCING 2 LINES.
           ADD 2 TO LINE-COUNT.
```

Figure 13.8 *Continued* Sales Summary Report [Two-dimension Table]

```
            1   1   2   2   2   3   3   4   4   4   5   5   6   6   6   7
    4   8   2   6   0   4   8   2   6   0   4   8   2   6   0   4   8   2
--------------------------------------------------------------------------
1390     *-----------------------------------------------------------*
1400      5100-PAGE-HEADING SECTION.
1410     *-----------------------------------------------------------*
1420          WRITE REPORT-RECORD FROM PAGE-HEADING
1430              AFTER ADVANCING TOP-OF-PAGE.
1440          WRITE REPORT-RECORD FROM COLUMN-HEADING
1450              AFTER ADVANCING 2 LINES.
1460     *-----------------------------------------------------------*
1470      5200-LOAD-MONTH-DATA SECTION.
1480     *-----------------------------------------------------------*
1490          MOVE MONTHLY-SALES (ITEM, MONTH)
1500              TO MONTHLY-SALES-OUT (MONTH).
1510     *-----------------------------------------------------------*
1520      7000-TERMINATION SECTION.
1530     *-----------------------------------------------------------*
1540          CLOSE SALES-FILE
1550                REPORT-FILE.
```

SOLD-T (along with a single subscript); however, the elementary-item field is addressable only by MONTHLY-SALES-T (which must be recorded with two subscripts in the PROCEDURE DIVISION).

One other table, MONTHLY-SALES-OUT (a single-dimension table in lines 900 and 910), is used to prepare data for printed output.

In the PROCEDURE DIVISION, the process begins with an initialization sequence. In this sequence, both data tables are initialized. In line 1100 the ITEM-TABLE is initialized to spaces, and in line 1110 the SALES-BY-MONTH-TABLE is initialized to zeros. The initialization of the SALES-BY-MONTH-TABLE to zeros permit us to *add* AMOUNT-OF-SALES-IN (line 1230) to any applicable cell of the table without further initialization. In addition, any cell of MONTHLY-SALES-T that is not addressed will remain zero. (It if were not for this initialization procedure, MONTHLY-SALES-T could have simply been added to the bottom of the ITEM-TABLE definition to create a two-dimension table). In the SALES-SUMMATION module (3000), the procedure determines when a new item (ITEM-NUMBER-IN) is encountered. When this occurs, ITEM-COUNT is incremented, marking the location of the most recent item. (Until a new item is encountered, ITEM-COUNT will not be altered.) At the same time the current ITEM-NUMBER-IN and ITEM-DESCRIPTION-IN are moved into the indicated positions of ITEM-TABLE at the ITEM-COUNT location. The next step is to add the current AMOUNT-OF-SALES-IN for the record involved to MONTHLY-SALES-T. (The location is specified by ITEM-COUNT *and* MONTH-OF-SALE-T. Thus, one subscript is generated internally and the other is generated as a result of an input operation.)

The final procedure is to print all the collected data. Because we have counted the number of items placed in ITEM-TABLE (and MONTHLY-SALES-T), all that is necessary is to dump data in the tables from 1 to ITEM-COUNT. The PERFORM statement at lines 990 and 1000 loads the data from the ITEM-TABLE into the output line, and the procedure continues by loading individual MONTHLY-SALES-T entries into the appropriate output slot. This process is similar to extracting data from the ITEM-TABLE, except that the number of months in a year is known.

Figure 13.8 *Continued* Sales Summary Report [Two-dimension Table] (Data)

```
------------------------------------------------------------
|      |         1         2         3         4         5|
|Record|12345678901234567890123456789012345678901234567890|
|------------------------------------------------------------|
|     1|11232Ball Point Pen                011281  00198 |
|     2|11232Ball Point Pen                090181  00198 |
|     3|11232Ball Point Pen                090181  31522 |
|     4|11232Ball Point Pen                090181  00198 |
|     5|11232Ball Point Pen                090181  00198 |
|     6|11232Ball Point Pen                090181  06170 |
|     7|11232Ball Point Pen                021581  00225 |
|     8|11232Ball Point Pen                022281  00035 |
|     9|11232Ball Point Pen                022581  03300 |
|    10|11232Ball Point Pen                030581  00210 |
|    11|11232Ball Point Pen                031581  05115 |
|    12|11232Ball Point Pen                090181  00198 |
|    13|11232Ball Point Pen                053081  00550 |
|    14|11232Ball Point Pen                060681  02235 |
|    15|11232Ball Point Pen                042881  01422 |
|    16|11232Ball Point Pen                012281  05765 |
|    17|11232Ball Point Pen                121281  00098 |
|    18|11232Ball Point Pen                070781  00555 |
|    19|11232Ball Point Pen                111281  00450 |
|    20|11232Ball Point Pen                051581  00995 |
|    21|11232Ball Point Pen                101681  06100 |
|    22|11232Ball Point Pen                111181  04599 |
|    23|11232Ball Point Pen                010181  00155 |
|    24|11232Ball Point Pen                081581  00699 |
|    25|11232Ball Point Pen                040481  01555 |
|    26|11232Ball Point Pen                062381  29914 |
|    27|11232Ball Point Pen                092881  00814 |
|    28|11232Ball Point Pen                090181  00335 |
|    29|11232Ball Point Pen                030381  04125 |
|    30|11232Ball Point Pen                082281  39900 |
|    31|11232Ball Point Pen                060681  50000 |
|    32|11232Ball Point Pen                041881  00444 |
|    33|11232Ball Point Pen                022281  00245 |
|    34|11232Ball Point Pen                011281  00516 |
|    35|11232Ball Point Pen                081281  00198 |
|    36|11232Ball Point Pen                101181  31935 |
|    37|11232Ball Point Pen                053081  00485 |
|    38|11232Ball Point Pen                061781  08840 |
|    39|11232Ball Point Pen                112081  00198 |
|    40|11232Ball Point Pen                122081  04400 |
|    41|11232Ball Point Pen                090181  00198 |
|    42|11232Ball Point Pen                090181  00198 |
|    43|11232Ball Point Pen                050181  06170 |
|    44|11232Ball Point Pen                090181  08820 |
|    45|41127Typing Paper (Bond)           071381  01295 |
|    46|41127Typing Paper (Bond)           041381  41480 |
|    47|41127Typing Paper (Bond)           042281  81599 |
|    48|41127Typing Paper (Bond)           022081  02250 |
|    49|41127Typing Paper (Bond)           122081  12200 |
|    50|41127Typing Paper (Bond)           020181  01999 |
|    51|41127Typing Paper (Bond)           053081  05650 |
|    52|41127Typing Paper (Bond)           011681  09299 |
|    53|55237Copy Machine                  032281  35990 |
|    54|55237Copy Machine                  031581  71980 |
|    55|55237Copy Machine                  011581  35990 |
|    56|55237Copy Machine                  040181  71980 |
------------------------------------------------------------
```

Figure 13.8 *Continued* Sales Summary Report [Two-dimension Table] (Output)

Sales Summary by Month

Item Description	Jan.	Feb.	Mar.	Apr.	May	June	July	Aug.	Sep.	Oct.	Nov.	Dec.
11 232 Ball Point Pen	66.34	38.05	94.50	34.21	82.00	909.89	5.55	407.97	488.49	380.35	52.47	44.98
41 127 Typing Paper (Bond)	92.99	42.49	.00	1230.79	56.50	.00	12.95	.00	.00	.00	.00	122.00
55 237 Copy Machine	359.90	.00	1079.70	719.80	.00	.00	.00	.00	.00	.00	.00	.00

Three-Dimension Tables

When a data item associated with an OCCURS clause is subordinate to another OCCURS clause, which is itself subordinate to an OCCURS clause, the portion of the table addressed by the data item is considered *three-dimensional.* Logically a three-dimension table may be thought of as ''cubic,'' with data defined in rows (length), columns (width), and *ranks* (depth). To address data at the lowest level of this table requires three subscripts. The first references rows; the second, columns, the third, ranks. As before, these subscripts should be enclosed in parentheses and separated by commas.

Figure 13.9 illustrates a three-dimension table. In this example, FLIGHT-INFORMATION-TABLE references the entire table of 60 cells (360 bytes) and should not be subscripted when referred to in the PROCEDURE DIVISION. ORIGIN should be accompanied by one subscript. Each occurence of ORIGIN references 12 cells of the table. If ORIGIN(1) appeared in the PROCEDURE DIVISION, a reference would be made to all cells within the table having 1 as the first subscript value (the first ''layer''). DESTINATION provides for the four columns of the table since it OCCURS four times and is subordinate to ORIGIN. When referenced in the PROCEDURE DIVISION, DESTINATION should be accompanied by two subscripts. Each reference to DESTINATION in the PROCEDURE DIVISION addresses three cells of the table. For example, if DESTINATION (1, 1) appeared in the PROCEDURE DIVISION, CLASS (1, 1, 1), CLASS (1, 1, 2), AND CLASS (1, 1, 3) would be referenced. Finally, the elementary data item CLASS appears in the record description. Since CLASS appears with an OCCURS clause and is subordinate to both DESTINATION and ORIGIN, CLASS represents the third level of the table. All references to CLASS in the PROCEDURE DIVISION address a single cell of the table and should appear with three subscripts.

The final example, presented in Figure 13.10, provides a description of a three-dimension table associated with one-dimension tables. Suppose a company wanted to store 200 employee payroll records in one table. This information might be stored for an entire month, with an area reserved for each day of the month. In the description of this table, EMPLOYEE-MONTHLY-PAY-HISTORY is a record-name that addresses all 6,200 addressable cells of the table (20,800 bytes). NUMBER-OF-EMPLOYEES is associated with an OCCURS clause that provides for 200 employees (subordinate items). Each occurrence of NUMBER-OF-EMPLOYEES would logically reference one ''layer'' of the table. That is, the first occurrence of NUMBER-OF-EMPLOYEES would reference the first occurrence of NAME, ID-NUMBER, and RATE and HOURS from 1, 1, 1 to 1, 4, 7 (the top layer). Thus, each occurrence of NUMBER-OF-EMPLOYEES references 104 bytes of data. EMPLOYEE-IDENTIFICATION, which is subordinate to NUMBER-OF-EMPLOYEES, OCCURS 200 times. Each occurrence of EMPLOYEE-IDENTIFICATION provides a single occurence of NAME and ID-NUMBER. NAME

Figure 13.9 A Three-dimension Table

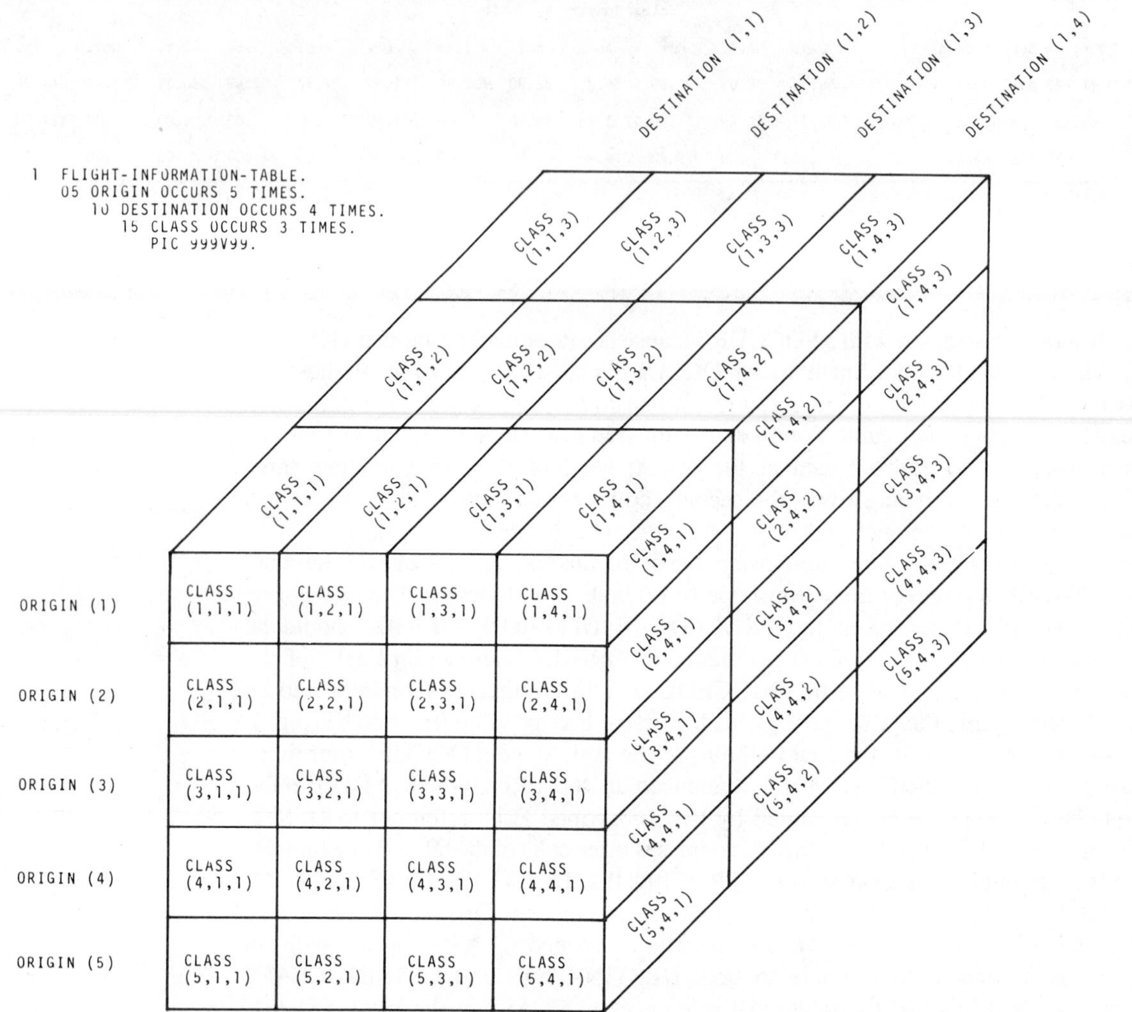

and ID NUMBER are subordinate to NUMBER-OF-EMPLOYEES and each OCCURS 200 times within the group-name EMPLOYEE-IDENTIFICATION. RATE, which is directly subordinate to NUMBER-OF-EMPLOYEES, OCCURS 200 times.

The next item that appears in the table is WEEK-OF-MONTH, which has an OCCURS clause that provides for four times for each occurrence of WEEK-OF-MONTH or any subordinate items. However, since WEEK-OF-MONTH is subordinate to NUMBER-OF-EMPLOYEES, it describes a two-dimension data item that represents 800 items (200 rows and 4 columns). Each occurrence of WEEK-OF-MONTH should be accompanied by two subscripts when referenced in the PROCEDURE DIVISION, and it would reference 12 bytes of internal storage. For example, WEEK-OF-MONTH (1, 1) would address HOURS (1, 1, 1) through HOURS (1, 1, 7). DAY-OF-WEEK, a group-name subordinate to WEEK-TO-MONTH, would address the same data as WEEK-OF-MONTH. Thus DAY-OF-WEEK (1, 1) is in every respect equivalent to WEEK-OF-MONTH (1, 1). The final entry in the table is HOURS. HOURS is an elementary data item

Figure 13.10 A Three-dimension Table with Appended One-dimension Table

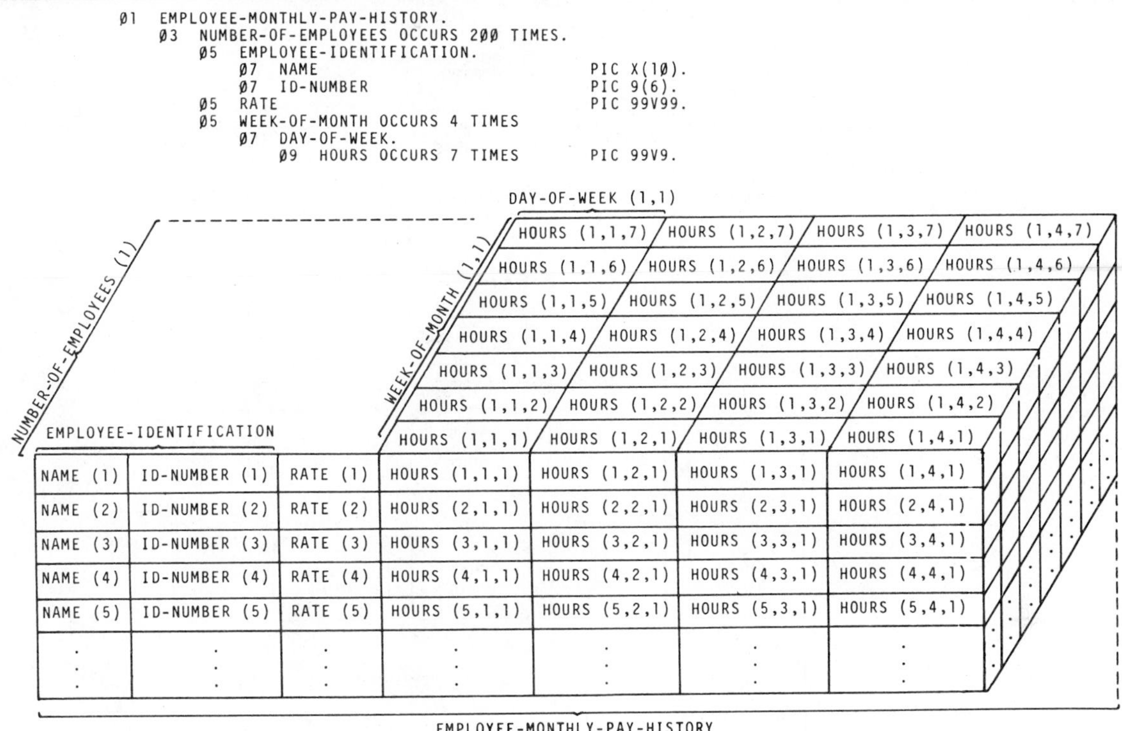

associated with an OCCURS clause. This OCCURS clause is subordinate to both previous OCCURS clauses, making HOURS a three-dimension table. Therefore, HOURS is represented by 200 rows, 4 columns, and 7 ranks, providing 5,600 separately addressable data items called HOURS. In the PROCEDURE DIVISION, a single occurrence of HOURS addresses three bytes of data, and HOURS should be written with three subscripts.

Character Processing with Tables

Although tables are frequently used to process numeric data, tables may also be used to perform operations known as *character processing*. This simply means that tables are used to manipulate individual characters (or groups of characters) rather than what we normally think of as a field. In the example in Figure 13.11, the program accepts a numeric field (representing a dollar value such as the amount of a check) and translates the digits of the field into the words that represent those digits. The problem requires the decomposition of the number into single-digit components and the translation of the digits (and their respective locations in the field) into the text that represents those digits. The textual data is stored in a table through a REDEFINE statement (redefinitions are discussed in Chapter 22) and ''looked-up'' each time the digit corresponding to the text is found. The program does this by examining each individual character of a field to determine the presence of blanks, which represents the end of the text for a particular numeric value.

Figure 13.11 A Text Process Program (Hierarchy Chart)

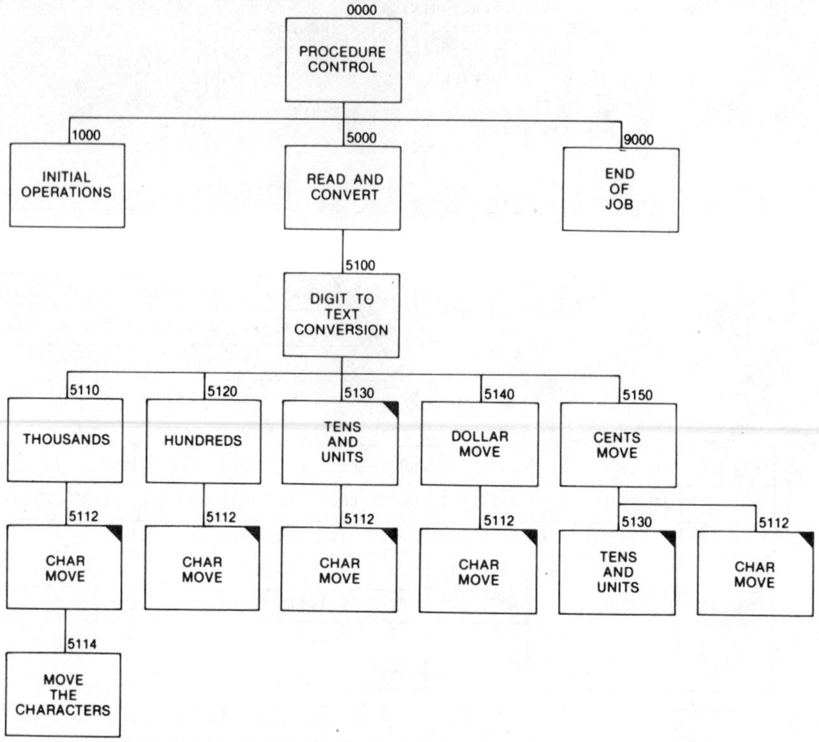

0000 PROCEDURE CONTROL

1000 INITIAL OPERATIONS

5000 READ AND CONVERT

9000 END OF JOB

5100 DIGIT TO TEXT CONVERSION

5110 THOUSANDS

5120 HUNDREDS

5130 TENS AND UNITS

5140 DOLLAR MOVE

5150 CENTS MOVE

5112 CHAR MOVE

5112 CHAR MOVE

5112 CHAR MOVE

5112 CHAR MOVE

5130 TENS AND UNITS

5112 CHAR MOVE

5114 MOVE THE CHARACTERS

Figure 13.11 *Continued* A Text Processing Program (Pseudocode)

```
START
    DO Initial operations
    DO Read and convert UNTIL eof
    DO End of job
END

INITIAL OPERATIONS
    OPEN files
END

READ AND CONVERT
    READ input AT END
         SET file status GO TO end
    DO Digit to text conversion
END

DIGIT TO TEXT CONVERSION
    SET location, lines
    MOVE input amount to amount
    DO Thousands
    DO Hundreds
    DO Tens and units
    DO Dollar move
    DO Cents move
END

THOUSANDS
    DIVIDE amount by 1000
         GIVING digit
    IF digit > 0
         MOVE table digit to line
         DO Char move
         MOVE digits (29) TO line
         DO Char move
    ENDIF
END

CHAR MOVE
    EXAMINE line TALLYING
         UNTIL space
    MOVE 0 to char location
    DO Move the characters
         tally times
    IF tally > 0
         ADD 1 to location
         MOVE '-' to table location
    ENDIF
END

MOVE THE CHARACTERS
    ADD 1 to locations
    MOVE chrs to chars
END

HUNDREDS
     COMPUTE amount = amount -
         digit * 1000
     DIVIDE amount by 100
         GIVING digit
     IF digit > 0
         MOVE table digit to line
         DO Char move
         MOVE digits (28) to line
         DO Char move
     ENDIF
     COMPUTE amount = amount -
         digit * 100
END

TENS AND UNITS
     IF amount > 0
         IF amount > 20
             DIVIDE amount by 10
                 GIVING digit
             ADD 18 to digit
             MOVE table digit to
             DO Char move
             SUBTRACT 18 from dig
             COMPUTE amount = amo
                 - digit * 10
             IF amount = 0
                 next sentence
             ENDIF
             DO Char move
         ELSE
             MOVE table digit to
             DO Char move
         ENDIF
     ENDIF
END

DOLLAR MOVE
     MOVE dollars to line
     Do Char move
END

CENTS MOVE
    MOVE and cents to line
    DO Char move
    MOVE input amount to line
    COMPUTE amount = (input amount -
        digit) * 100
    IF amount > 0
        DO Tens and units
        MOVE cents to line
        DO Char move
    ELSE
        MOVE no cents to line
        DO Char move
    ENDIF
    MOVE values to output
    WRITE output
END

END OF JOB
    CLOSE files
END
```

Figure 13.11 *Continued* A Text Processing Program

```
           1   1   2   2   2   3   3   4   4   4   5   5   6   6   6   7
   4   8   2   6   0   4   8   2   6   0   4   8   2   6   0   4   8   2

      *****************************************************************
       IDENTIFICATION DIVISION.
      *****************************************************************
       PROGRAM-ID.    CHECK-WRITER.
       AUTHOR.        JOHN WINDSOR.
       DATE-WRITTEN.  JANUARY 1, 1989.
       DATE-COMPILED. JANUARY 1, 1989.
      *    This program performs a number-to-text conversion
      *    on "amounts" as might appear on a check produced by a
      *    computer program.  Note that tables are used in the
      *    PROCEDURE DIVISION which have VALUEs assigned to them
      *    through a MOVE statement in the PROCEDURE DIVISION.
      *****************************************************************
       ENVIRONMENT DIVISION.
      *****************************************************************
      *---------------------------------------------------------------*
       CONFIGURATION SECTION.
      *---------------------------------------------------------------*
       SOURCE-COMPUTER. IBM.
       OBJECT-COMPUTER. IBM.
      *---------------------------------------------------------------*
       INPUT-OUTPUT SECTION.
      *---------------------------------------------------------------*
       FILE-CONTROL.
           SELECT PAY-FILE   ASSIGN TO UT-S-INPUT.
           SELECT CHECK-FILE ASSIGN TO UT-S-OUTPUT.
      *****************************************************************
       DATA DIVISION.
      *****************************************************************
      *---------------------------------------------------------------*
       FILE SECTION.
      *---------------------------------------------------------------*
       FD  PAY-FILE LABEL RECORDS ARE OMITTED.
       01  PAY-RECORD.
           05 AMOUNT-OF-CHECK-IN          PIC 9(04)V9(02).
           05 FILLER                      PIC X(74).

       FD  CHECK-FILE LABEL RECORDS ARE OMITTED.
       01  CHECK-RECORD                   PIC X(133).
      *---------------------------------------------------------------*
       WORKING-STORAGE SECTION.
      *---------------------------------------------------------------*
       01  WORKING-VARIABLES.
           05  FILE-STATUS                PIC X(04) VALUE SPACES.
           05  WHOLE-AMOUNT               PIC 9(04) VALUE ZERO.
           05  DIGIT-VALUE                PIC 9(04) VALUE ZERO.
           05  CHAR-LOCATION              PIC 9(01) VALUE ZERO.
           05  CHARACTER-LOCATION         PIC 9(02) VALUE ZERO.

       01  DOLLARS-AND-CENTS.
           05 DOLLARS                     PIC X(07) VALUE 'Dollars'.
           05 CENTS                       PIC X(05) VALUE 'Cents'.
           05 NO-CENTS                    PIC X(08) VALUE 'No-Cents'.
           05 AND-CENTS                   PIC X(03) VALUE 'and'.

       01  WRITTEN-AMOUNT-WS.
           05 CHARS                       OCCURS 75 TIMES
                                          PIC X(01).
       01  WORKING-LINE.
           05 CHRS     OCCURS 9 TIMES DEPENDING ON TALLY
                                          PIC X(01).
       01  LIST-OF-UNITS.
           05 FILLER                      PIC X(09) VALUE 'One'.
           05 FILLER                      PIC X(09) VALUE 'Two'.
           05 FILLER                      PIC X(09) VALUE 'Three'.
           05 FILLER                      PIC X(09) VALUE 'Four'.
           05 FILLER                      PIC X(09) VALUE 'Five'.
           05 FILLER                      PIC X(09) VALUE 'Six'.
           05 FILLER                      PIC X(09) VALUE 'Seven'.
```

Figure 13.11 *Continued* A Text Processing Program

```
       05 FILLER                    PIC X(09) VALUE 'Eight'.
       05 FILLER                    PIC X(09) VALUE 'Nine'.
       05 FILLER                    PIC X(09) VALUE 'Ten'.
       05 FILLER                    PIC X(09) VALUE 'Eleven'.
       05 FILLER                    PIC X(09) VALUE 'Twelve'.
       05 FILLER                    PIC X(09) VALUE 'Thirteen'.
       05 FILLER                    PIC X(09) VALUE 'Fourteen'.
       05 FILLER                    PIC X(09) VALUE 'Fifteen'.
       05 FILLER                    PIC X(09) VALUE 'Sixteen'.
       05 FILLER                    PIC X(09) VALUE 'Seventeen'.
       05 FILLER                    PIC X(09) VALUE 'Eighteen'.
       05 FILLER                    PIC X(09) VALUE 'Nineteen'.
       05 FILLER                    PIC X(09) VALUE 'Twenty'.
       05 FILLER                    PIC X(09) VALUE 'Thirty'.
       05 FILLER                    PIC X(09) VALUE 'Forth'.
       05 FILLER                    PIC X(09) VALUE 'Fifty'.
       05 FILLER                    PIC X(09) VALUE 'Sixty'.
       05 FILLER                    PIC X(09) VALUE 'Seventy'.
       05 FILLER                    PIC X(09) VALUE 'Eighty'.
       05 FILLER                    PIC X(09) VALUE 'Ninety'.
       05 FILLER                    PIC X(09) VALUE 'Hundred'.
       05 FILLER                    PIC X(09) VALUE 'Thousand'.

   01  DIGIT-TABLE REDEFINES LIST-OF-UNITS.
       05 DIGITS                    OCCURS 29 TIMES
                                    PIC X(09).
   01  AMOUNT-RECORD.
       05  FILLER                   PIC X(01).
       05  AMOUNT-OF-CHECK-OUT      PIC 9(04).9(02).
       05  FILLER                   PIC X(03) VALUE SPACES.
       05  WRITTEN-AMOUNT-OUT       PIC X(75).
  ***************************************************************
   PROCEDURE DIVISION.
  ***************************************************************
  *-------------------------------------------------------------*
   0000-PROCEDURE-CONTROL SECTION.
  *-------------------------------------------------------------*
       PERFORM 1000-INITIAL-OPERATIONS.
       PERFORM 5000-READ-AND-CONVERT
           UNTIL FILE-STATUS = 'DONE'.
       PERFORM 9000-END-OF-JOB.
       STOP RUN.
  *-------------------------------------------------------------*
   1000-INITIAL-OPERATIONS SECTION.
  *-------------------------------------------------------------*
       OPEN INPUT PAY-FILE, OUTPUT CHECK-FILE.
  *-------------------------------------------------------------*
   5000-READ-AND-CONVERT SECTION.
  *-------------------------------------------------------------*
   5000-ENTRY.
       READ PAY-FILE
           AT END MOVE 'DONE' TO FILE-STATUS
                  GO TO 5000-EXIT.
       PERFORM 5100-DIGIT-TO-TEXT-CONVERSION.

   5000-EXIT.
       EXIT.
  *-------------------------------------------------------------*
   5100-DIGIT-TO-TEXT-CONVERSION SECTION.
  *-------------------------------------------------------------*
       MOVE 0 TO CHARACTER-LOCATION.
       MOVE SPACES              TO WRITTEN-AMOUNT-WS
                                   WORKING-LINE.
       MOVE AMOUNT-OF-CHECK-IN  TO WHOLE-AMOUNT.
       PERFORM 5110-THOUSANDS.
       PERFORM 5120-HUNDREDS.
       PERFORM 5130-TENS-AND-UNITS.
       PERFORM 5140-DOLLAR-MOVE.
       PERFORM 5150-CENTS-MOVE.
```

Figure 13.11 *Continued* A Text Processing Program

```
        1   1   2   2   2   3   3   4   4   4   5   5   6   6   6   7
    4   8   2   6   0   4   8   2   6   0   4   8   2   6   0   4   8   2

      *-----------------------------------------------------------*
       5110-THOUSANDS SECTION.
      *-----------------------------------------------------------*
           DIVIDE WHOLE-AMOUNT BY 1000 GIVING DIGIT-VALUE.
           IF DIGIT-VALUE > 0
               MOVE DIGITS (DIGIT-VALUE) TO WORKING-LINE;
               PERFORM 5112-CHAR-MOVE;
               MOVE DIGITS (29)      TO WORKING-LINE;
               PERFORM 5112-CHAR-MOVE.
      *-----------------------------------------------------------*
       5112-CHAR-MOVE SECTION.
      *-----------------------------------------------------------*
      ***************************************************************
      *     The EXAMINE statement below is discussed in             *
      *     Chapter 23.                                             *
      *     The variable "TALLY" will contain the number of         *
      *     characters in a word as a result of this operation.     *
      *     The same operation could be achieved through the use    *
      *     of an IF statement within a PERFORM VARYING, however.   *
      ***************************************************************
      *
           EXAMINE WORKING-LINE TALLYING UNTIL FIRST SPACE.
           MOVE 0                       TO CHAR-LOCATION.
           PERFORM 5114-MOVE-THE-CHARACTERS TALLY TIMES.
           IF TALLY > 0
               ADD 1 TO CHARACTER-LOCATION;
               MOVE '-'                 TO CHARS (CHARACTER-LOCATION).
      *-----------------------------------------------------------*
       5114-MOVE-THE-CHARACTERS SECTION.
      *-----------------------------------------------------------*
           ADD 1 TO CHAR-LOCATION, CHARACTER-LOCATION.
           MOVE CHRS (CHAR-LOCATION) TO CHARS (CHARACTER-LOCATION).
      *-----------------------------------------------------------*
       5120-HUNDREDS SECTION.
      *-----------------------------------------------------------*
           COMPUTE WHOLE-AMOUNT = WHOLE-AMOUNT - DIGIT-VALUE * 1000.
           DIVIDE WHOLE-AMOUNT BY 100 GIVING DIGIT-VALUE.
           IF DIGIT-VALUE > 0
               MOVE DIGITS (DIGIT-VALUE) TO WORKING-LINE;
               PERFORM 5112-CHAR-MOVE;
               MOVE DIGITS (28)      TO WORKING-LINE;
               PERFORM 5112-CHAR-MOVE.
           COMPUTE WHOLE-AMOUNT = WHOLE-AMOUNT - DIGIT-VALUE * 100.
      *-----------------------------------------------------------*
       5130-TENS-AND-UNITS SECTION.
      *-----------------------------------------------------------*
           IF WHOLE-AMOUNT > 0
               IF WHOLE-AMOUNT > 20
                   DIVIDE WHOLE-AMOUNT BY 10 GIVING DIGIT-VALUE;
                   ADD 18 TO DIGIT-VALUE;
                   MOVE DIGITS (DIGIT-VALUE) TO WORKING-LINE;
                   PERFORM 5112-CHAR-MOVE
                   SUBTRACT 18 FROM DIGIT-VALUE
                   COMPUTE WHOLE-AMOUNT = WHOLE-AMOUNT -
                       DIGIT-VALUE * 10;
                   IF WHOLE-AMOUNT = 0
                       NEXT SENTENCE
                   ELSE
                       MOVE DIGITS (WHOLE-AMOUNT) TO WORKING-LINE;
                       PERFORM 5112-CHAR-MOVE
               ELSE
                   MOVE DIGITS (WHOLE-AMOUNT) TO WORKING-LINE;
                   PERFORM 5112-CHAR-MOVE.
      *-----------------------------------------------------------*
       5140-DOLLAR-MOVE SECTION.
      *-----------------------------------------------------------*
           MOVE DOLLARS                 TO WORKING-LINE.
           PERFORM 5112-CHAR-MOVE.
      *-----------------------------------------------------------*
```

Figure 13.11 *Continued* A Text Processing Program

```
            1   1   2   2   2   3   3   4   4   4   5   5   6   6   6   7
    4   8   2   6   0   4   8   2   6   0   4   8   2   6   0   4   8   2

       5150-CENTS-MOVE SECTION.
      *-----------------------------------------------------------*
           MOVE AND-CENTS              TO WORKING-LINE.
           PERFORM 5112-CHAR-MOVE.
           MOVE AMOUNT-OF-CHECK-IN   TO DIGIT-VALUE.
           COMPUTE WHOLE-AMOUNT = (AMOUNT-OF-CHECK-IN - DIGIT-VALUE)
               * 100.
           IF WHOLE-AMOUNT > 0
               PERFORM 5130-TENS-AND-UNITS;
               MOVE CENTS              TO WORKING-LINE;
               PERFORM 5112-CHAR-MOVE
           ELSE
               MOVE NO-CENTS           TO WORKING-LINE;
               PERFORM 5112-CHAR-MOVE.
           MOVE WRITTEN-AMOUNT-WS    TO WRITTEN-AMOUNT-OUT.
           MOVE AMOUNT-OF-CHECK-IN   TO AMOUNT-OF-CHECK-OUT.
           WRITE CHECK-RECORD FROM AMOUNT-RECORD AFTER 1 LINES.
      *-----------------------------------------------------------*
       9000-END-OF-JOB SECTION.
      *-----------------------------------------------------------*
           CLOSE PAY-FILE, CHECK-FILE.
```

Figure 13.11 *Continued* A Text Processing Program (Data)

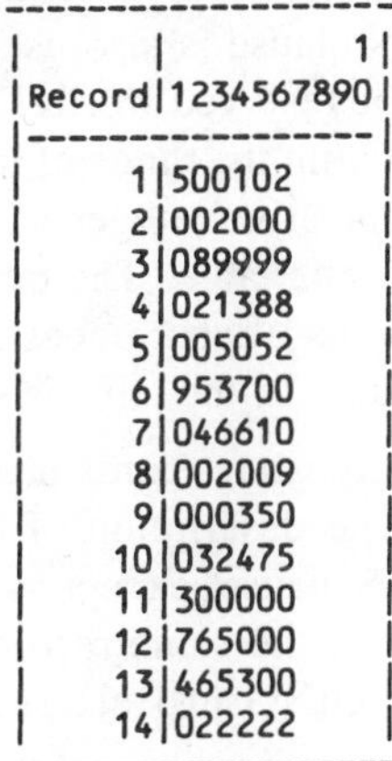

Record	1 1234567890
1	500102
2	002000
3	089999
4	021388
5	005052
6	953700
7	046610
8	002009
9	000350
10	032475
11	300000
12	765000
13	465300
14	022222

Figure 13.11 *Continued* A Text Processing Program (Output)

```
5001.02   Five-Thousand-One-Dollars-and-Two-Cents-
0020.00   Twenty-Dollars-and-No-Cents-
0899.99   Eight-Hundred-Ninety-Nine-Dollars-and-Ninety-Nine-Cents-
0213.88   Two-Hundred-Thirteen-Dollars-and-Eighty-Eight-Cents-
0050.52   Fifty-Dollars-and-Fifty-Two-Cents-
9537.00   Nine-Thousand-Five-Hundred-Thirty-Seven-Dollars-and-No-Cents-
0466.10   Four-Hundred-Sixty-Six-Dollars-and-Ten-Cents-
0020.09   Twenty-Dollars-and-Nine-Cents-
0003.50   Three-Dollars-and-Fifty-Cents-
0324.75   Three-Hundred-Twenty-Four-Dollars-and-Seventy-Five-Cents-
3000.00   Three-Thousand-Dollars-and-No-Cents-
7650.00   Seven-Thousand-Six-Hundred-Fifty-Dollars-and-No-Cents-
4653.00   Four-Thousand-Six-Hundred-Fifty-Three-Dollars-and-No-Cents-
0222.22   Two-Hundred-Twenty-Two-Dollars-and-Twenty-Two-Cents-
```

Figure 13.12 Format of the OCCURS/DEPENDING ON Clause

```
Format 2*

   OCCURS integer-1 TO integer-2 TIMES DEPENDING ON data-name-1
```

*Format, as written, is incomplete. Complete format provided in Chapter 14.

Variable-Length Tables

The second form of the OCCURS clause (Figure 13.12) permits the description of a *variable-length* table. A table is variable in length when its size may be changed during the execution of the program. This does *not* mean that COBOL can dynamically describe internal storage. A variable length table is considered to be static; for purposes of determining the amount of internal storage used, it is allocated the maximum number of occurrences.

In the Format 2 OCCURS clause, two integer values are specified. Integer-1 represents the minimum number of occurrences to be associated with a particular data-name. Integer-1 must be a non-negative integer value. Integer-2 provides for the maximum number of occurrences possible in the table. Integer-2 must be a positive integer value greater than integer-1. The DEPENDING ON clause is also used with the Format 2 OCCURS clause. Data-name-1, which follows the reserved words DEPENDING ON, specifies the actual number of usable occurrences within the range of integer-1 to integer-2. The table does not expand or contract with the positive integer value placed in data-name-1; the data-name indicates the *logical* size of the table. The table "appears" to contain data-name-1 occurrences, and only data-name-1 occurrences may be addressed with any reliability; however, the physical dimension of the table is specified by integer-2.

Data-name-1, as indicated previously, must contain a positive integer value within the range of integer-1 to integer-2. The description of data-name-1 must not be subordinate to or associated with OCCURS clause, except as presented in the DEPENDING ON option. Data-name-1 may appear in the same record description as a table that is described with the OCCURS DEPENDING ON clause, but only *before* the variable portion of the table.

Summary

1985 COBOL Standards

COBOL currently supports tables to a maximum of three dimensions (seven dimensions in COBOL 85). Tables are useful in solving problems that require the internal storage of massive quantities of data. In some cases these data may be homogeneous. In other cases the data are simply interrelated.

In COBOL, tables are created through the use of one or more OCCURS clauses. When a single OCCURS clause appears in a record description, the data item (and all subordinate data items) is classified as a single-dimension table (a vector or list). When referenced in the PROCEDURE DIVISION, this data item (and subordinate data items) must be accompanied by a single subscript indicating the occurrence position to be addressed.

A two-dimension table is created when one OCCURS clause of a record description is subordinate to another OCCURS clause. This data matrix requires both row and column subscripts when addressed at the lowest level. Finally, three-dimension tables, a data "cube," are created when a record contains three OCCURS clauses. However, each OCCURS clause must be coded so that no two are on the same level (recorded with the same level number). Each reference to an elementary-item of a three-dimension table requires row, column, and rank subscripts. Tables may be coded so that they appear to be variable in size (variable-length tables).

Notes on Programming Style

Internal tables, although useful, are not a "cure-all" nor should they be used in all circumstances where your first impression leads you to believe they are warranted. When using tables, look out for the following situations.

1. Having subscript values outside the bounds of the table
2. Attempting to read into a table when the table is larger than the logical record
3. Storing more detail in a table than the problem warrants
4. Assuming the table size you have decided upon is relevant to the problem.

One frequent problem for beginning programmers is inattention to the value of subscripts. Suppose, for example, you have defined a table to contain ten elements. The only valid values for a subscript that references this table are 1, 2, 3, 4, 5, 6, 7, 8, 9, and 10. Because most compilers do not protect you from providing a subscript value that is less than 1 or greater than 10, your program could address data that immediately precedes or follows the actual table definition.

COBOL is designed to deal with logical records (at least as far as the FD description is concerned). When reading data that is a table, it is frequently necessary to read only a portion of the table from the external source and then load that portion into an internal (WORKING-STORAGE) table definition. The entire table will ultimately be reconstructed internally by repeating this operation.

When designing a program to solve a particular problem that may require tables, programmers frequently rush into the solution without a thorough understanding of the requirements. If you are reading data that are to be stored in a table, ask yourself at least two questions: (1) Do you need all the fields presented in the record? Sometimes the answer is yes, and you may *also* find that additional fields are required. (2) Do you need the detail of every record? Again, sometimes the answer is yes; however, at least you will have studied the problem requirements and are not just blindly storing *all* data.

Beginning programmers also frequently make assumptions about the size of a table that are too narrow. When program development begins, ask yourself "What is the biggest this table could *ever* be?" You should know the maximum size for each table involved in the problem. Creating tables to their *maximum* dimension generalizes your solution to handle problems other than those in the original problem statement. After all, you do not want to redesign a program just because you were not farsighted enough to realize that the next time the program was used there were to be a few more items stored.

When generalizing the maximum table size, you should not assume that the table will always be full. If it is possible that the number of items may vary, *count them!*

Questions

Below fill in the blank(s) with the appropriate word, words, or phrases.

1. In COBOL, when it is necessary to store large amounts of data internally, ____ are often used.
2. In COBOL, a table is created through the use of a(n) ____ clause.
3. When the OCCURS clause is used in a record, it may appear anywhere from level ____ to level ____ .
4. COBOL supports tables to a maximum of ____ (number) dimensions.
5. A data item that is associated with only one OCCURS clause is referred to as a(n) ____ .
6. When a data item is written with an OCCURS clause, references to that data item in the PROCEDURE DIVISION must be accompanied by a(n) ____ .
7. An occurrence position within a table is specified through a(n) ____ .
8. When a data item OCCURS 20 TIMES, the valid occurrence positions within the table range from ____ (number) to ____ (number).
9. To create a two-dimension table (a table with rows and columns), a record must contain an OCCURS clause that is subordinate to a(n) ____ .
10. In a two-dimension table, the first OCCURS clause specifies the number of ____ (rows/columns) of the table, and the second clause indicates the number of ____ (rows/columns).
11. A two-dimension table may also be called a(n) ____ .
12. When a reference is made to a two-dimension table in the PROCEDURE DIVISION, ____ (number) subscripts must be used.
13. To construct a three-dimension table in COBOL, an OCCURS clause must be subordinate to an OCCURS clause that is subordinate to a(n) ____ .
14. The first subscript used to reference a three-dimension table represents the ____ (row, column, rank) position, the second, the ____ position, and the third, the ____ position.
15. In a variable-length table, the logically addressable positions (occurrences) of the table are specified by a(n) ____ .
16. In a variable-length table, the maximum physical size of the table is specified by ____ .

Answer the following questions by circling either "T" for True or "F" for False.

T F 17. An OCCURS clause may be associated with an independent elementary-item.

T F 18. The OCCURS clause may be written only at the elementary-item level.

T F 19. In the format of the OCCURS clause that provides for the description of static tables, an identifier may be used to indicate the number of occurrences of the table.

T F 20. If an OCCURS clause is used at the group level, all items subordinate to that group are tables.

T F 21. A data item that is subordinate to another data item written with an OCCURS clause must be subscripted when referenced in the PROCEDURE DIVISION.

T F **22.** A data item used as subscript may not be used for any other purpose in the PROCEDURE DIVISION.

T F **23.** When a table element is referenced with a subscript, the subscript must be enclosed in parentheses.

T F **24.** Only a data-name may be used as a subscript.

T F **25.** All records that contain two OCCURS clauses represent a two-dimension table.

T F **26.** When referencing a two-dimension table in the PROCEDURE DIVISION, the first subscript is a row reference.

T F **27.** In COBOL, a record could contain combinations of one- and two-dimension tables.

T F **28.** In a two-dimension table, the second OCCURS clause must be followed by a subordinate elementary-item.

T F **29.** In a two-dimension table, the second OCCURS clause is not permitted to have a subordinate elementary-item.

T F **30.** Only three OCCURS clauses are permitted within a single record in COBOL.

T F **31.** Variable-length tables in COBOL dynamically allocate internal storage.

Exercises

1. Complete a table with the indicated heading for each record description below. Each data-name in the record should be included in the table.

2. Below are a number of COBOL table descriptions. Sketch the logical appearance of each table, and indicate what portion of the table is addressed by each name.

a.
```
01 TABLE-1.
   02 LEVEL-1 OCCURS 10 TIMES          PIC 9(5).
```

b.
```
01 TABLE-2.
   02 LEVEL-1 OCCURS 3 TIMES.
      03 LEVEL-1A                      PIC 99.
      03 LEVEL 1-B                     PIC X(4).
```

c.
```
01 TABLE-3.
   02 LEVEL-1A OCCURS 5 TIMES          PIC 9(5).
   02 LEVEL-1B OCCURS 7 TIMES          PIC 9V99.
```

d.
```
01 TABLE-4.
   02 LEVEL-1 OCCURS 4 TIMES.
      03 LEVEL-2 OCCURS 6 TIMES        PIC XX.
```

e.
```
01 TABLE-5.
   02 LEVEL-1 OCCURS 2 TIMES.
      03 LEVEL-2 OCCURS 3 TIMES.
         04 LEVEL-2A                   PIC 9(4).
         04 LEVEL 2-B                  PIC XX.
```

	Table					
	Number of					
Data-Name	**Rows**	**Columns**	**Ranks**	**Size of a Single Item**	**Number of Items in Description**	**Total Bytes in Description**

a.
```
01 LIST-OF-CONTRIBUTORS.
   02 CONTRIBUTOR OCCURS 20 TIMES                        PIC X(20).
```

b.
```
01 SALESMAN-TABLE.
   02 SALESMAN-NAME OCCURS 50 TIMES.
      03 NAME                                            PIC X(30).
     03 ID-NUMBER                                        PIC 9(5).
     03 PHONE                                            PIC 9(7).
```

c.
```
01 COLLEGE-COURSES.
   02 DEPARTMENT OCCURS 30 TIMES                         PIC XXX.
 02 COURSE-NUMBER OCCURS 90 TIMES                        PIC 999.
```

d.
```
01 LEDGER-TABLE.
   02 ASSETS OCCURS 30 TIMES.
      03 ASSET-NO                                        PIC 9(5).
    03 ASSET-DESC                                        PIC X(25).
    03 ASSET-BALANCE                                     PIC S9(5)V99.
 02 LIABILITY OCCURS 10 TIMES.
    03 LIAB-NO                                           PIC 9(5).
    03 LIAB-DESC                                         PIC X(25).
    03 LIAB-BALANCE                                      PIC S9(5)V99.
```

e.
```
01 INTEREST-RATE-TABLE.
   02 INTEREST-RATE OCCURS 10 TIMES.
      03 YEARS-INVESTED OCCURS 20 TIMES.
         04 INTEREST                                     PIC 9(5)V9(5).
```

f.
```
01 STUDENT-INFORMATION-TABLE.
     02 STUDENT OCCURS 40 0 TIMES.
        03 NAME                                          PIC X(20).
      03 ID-NUMBER                                       PIC 9(9).
      03 CLASS                                           PIC XX
      03 COURSE OCCURS 50 TIMES.
         04 DEPT                                         PIC XXX.
         04 COURSE-NO                                    PIC 999.
         04 GRADE                                        PIC X.
```

g.
```
01 DEMOGRAPHIC-DATA.
   02 INCOME OCCURS 20 TIMES.
      03 AGE OCCURS 40 TIMES.
         04 SEX OCCURS 2 TIMES                           PIC X.
      04 MARITAL-STATUS OCCURS 2 TIMES.                  PIC X.
```

Problems

13.1 A series of records have been developed by the Personnel Department in preparation of the production of a company telephone book. The records contain the employees' names (last name first) and telephone numbers (see the multiple-card layout form).

The report (see the print chart) is to conform to a standard similar to that produced by telephone utility companies. That is, each page consists of two columns. Each column is composed of individuals' names and telephone numbers. (Since our company is geographically dispersed, the area code is to be included in the telephone number.) To assist the telephone

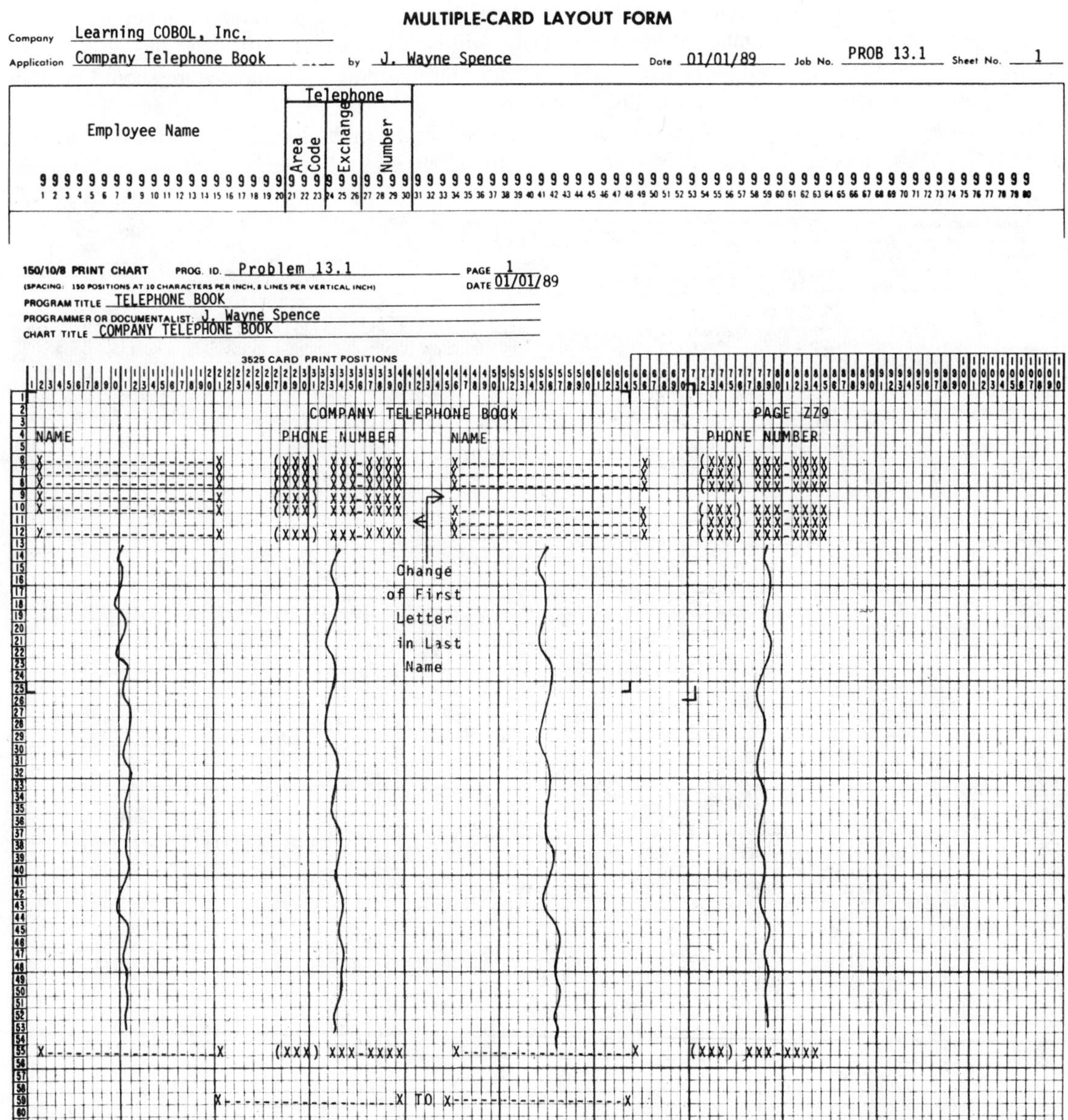

MULTIPLE-CARD LAYOUT FORM

Company Learning COBOL, Inc.
Application Company Telephone Book by J. Wayne Spence Date 01/01/89 Job No. PROB 13.1 Sheet No. 1

Employee Name | Telephone: Area Code, Exchange, Number

150/10/8 PRINT CHART PROG. ID. Problem 13.1 PAGE 1
(SPACING: 150 POSITIONS AT 10 CHARACTERS PER INCH, 8 LINES PER VERTICAL INCH) DATE 01/01/89
PROGRAM TITLE TELEPHONE BOOK
PROGRAMMER OR DOCUMENTALIST: J. Wayne Spence
CHART TITLE COMPANY TELEPHONE BOOK

3525 CARD PRINT POSITIONS

```
                                COMPANY TELEPHONE BOOK                          PAGE ZZ9
NAME                            PHONE NUMBER    NAME                            PHONE NUMBER

X-----------------------X       (XXX) XXX-XXXX  X-----------------------X       (XXX) XXX-XXXX
X-----------------------X       (XXX) XXX-XXXX  X-----------------------X       (XXX) XXX-XXXX
X-----------------------X       (XXX) XXX-XXXX  X-----------------------X       (XXX) XXX-XXXX
X-----------------------X       (XXX) XXX-XXXX
X-----------------------X       (XXX) XXX-XXXX  X-----------------------X       (XXX) XXX-XXXX
                                                X-----------------------X       (XXX) XXX-XXXX
X-----------------------X       (XXX) XXX-XXXX  X-----------------------X       (XXX) XXX-XXXX

                                         Change
                                         of First
                                         Letter
                                         in Last
                                         Name

X-----------------------X       (XXX) XXX-XXXX  X-----------------------X       (XXX) XXX-XXXX

                X-----------------------X TO X-----------------------X
```

book user, any time the first letter of an employee's name changes, a blank area should appear in the column. For example, when the employee name ''BACON, ALLEN D.'' is printed, his name should be preceded by a blank area (assuming of course that he is the first employee in the B's.) In addition, for quick-referencing purposes, the first and last employee names on the page are to be printed at the bottom of each page. The location of the quick-reference line should be in the same place on every page.

For purposes of this procedure, you may assume the data have been ordered by employee name.

13.2. An instructor has just given a true-false and multiple-choice exam to his class, and he wishes to have a program developed that will grade the exam. In addition, the instructor wants to use the same grading program for future exams and other classes. All questions will be equally weighted; however, each exam given (to separate classes) will not necessarily have the same number of questions. There will be a maximum of 50 questions on an exam and the maximum class size is 100 students. Furthermore, your procedure should be able to grade multiple classes in one execution.

We have devised the record formats presented in the multiple-card layout form to accomplish this task. Two record types will be used—the exam key record and student response

150/10/8 PRINT CHART PROG. ID. Problem 13.2 PAGE 1
(SPACING: 150 POSITIONS AT 10 CHARACTERS PER INCH, 8 LINES PER VERTICAL INCH) DATE 01/01/89
PROGRAM TITLE Exam Grading
PROGRAMMER OR DOCUMENTALIST: JOHN WINDSOR
CHART TITLE Student Grade Analysis

3525 CARD PRINT POSITIONS

EXAM: X-------------------------X
STUDENT GRADES PAGE ZZ9
STUDENT NAME ID. NUMBER GRADE
X------------------X X---------X ZZ9.9
X------------------X X---------X ZZ9.9
X------------------X X---------X ZZ9.9

EXAM: X-------------------------X
QUESTION ANALYSIS PAGE ZZ9
QUESTION NUMBER NUMBER INCORRECT
Z9 ZZ9
Z9 ZZ9
Z9 ZZ9

EXAM: X-------------------------X
SUMMARY PAGE ZZ9
A: ZZ9
B: ZZ9
C: ZZ9
D: ZZ9
F: ZZ9
HIGHEST: ZZ9.9
LOWEST: ZZ9.9
RANGE: ZZ9.9
AVERAGE: ZZ9.9

MULTIPLE-CARD LAYOUT FORM

Company: Learning COBOL, INC.
Application: Exam Grading by JOHN WINDSOR Date 01/01/89 Job No. PROB 13.2 Sheet No. 1

Key Record

KEY	Exam Identification	Correct Response to Question: 1	2	3	• • •	50

Student Response Record

Student: Identification Number	Name	Student Response to Question: 1	2	3	• • •	50

records. The exam key record will be constructed such that the first three characters of the record will contain the word "KEY," followed by the exam identification and the correct responses to individual questions 1 though n. The correct responses to each question will occupy one record column each. A blank column in the key record means that the question is not to be graded (or did not appear on the exam). Student response records follow a similar format, except that the first portion of the record contains the student identification number and the student's name.

Your procedure should determine (see the print chart):

1. The exam grade (score) for each student taking an exam
2. The number of incorrect responses to each exam question
3. The breakdown of student grades into A's, B's, C's, D's, and F's
4. The highest and lowest exam grade plus the grade range
5. The overall class average

13.3 Expense records have been provided to us for all departments within the company. Each expense record contains three fields (see the multiple-card layout form).

1. The department number of the department incurring an expense
2. The date on which the expense was paid (in a month-day-year format)
3. The amount of the expenditure

Corporate management wishes to see a summary of all expenditures of the company in two forms—by department and by the month in which the expense was incurred. As a consequence, the report designs shown on the print chart have been devised. Note that all department numbers (e.g., 100, 200, etc.) have been translated into the department name according to the following schedule.

Department Number(s)	Department Name
100–199	Accounting
200–239	Marketing-Sales
240–299	Marketing-Advertising & Research
300–399	Data Processing

600–699	Financial Controls & Budgets
700–799	Shipping & Receiving
800–819	Manufacturing-Fabrication
820–899	Manufacturing-Assembly & Packaging

You are to provide the name of the department in the departmental summary. Furthermore, you are to provide the name of the month (e.g., January, February, etc.) for the month number in the monthly summary.

MULTIPLE-CARD LAYOUT FORM

Company Learning COBOL, INC.

Application Expense Summary by J. Wayne Spence Date 01/01/89 Job No PROB 13.3 Sheet No. 1

Columns	Field
1–3	Dept. Number
4–9	Date of Expense
10–19 (decimal point marked ^ after column 17)	Expense Amount

150/10/8 PRINT CHART PROG. ID. Problem 13.3 PAGE 1

(SPACING: 150 POSITIONS AT 10 CHARACTERS PER INCH, 8 LINES PER VERTICAL INCH) DATE 01/01/88

PROGRAM TITLE EXPENSE SUMMARY

PROGRAMMER OR DOCUMENTALIST: J. WAYNE SPENCE

CHART TITLE DEPARTMENTAL AND MONTHLY EXPENSE SUMMARY

3525 CARD PRINT POSITIONS

```
                                    DEPARTMENTAL EXPENSE SUMMARY

                                    DEPARTMENT               AMOUNT
                                    ACCOUNTING         ZZZ,ZZZ,ZZZ.99

                               MARKETING--SALES        ZZZ,ZZZ,ZZZ.99
           MARKETING--ADVERTISING & RESEARCH           ZZZ,ZZZ,ZZZ.99
                                          {                 {

         MANUFACTURING--ASSEMBLY & PACKAGING           ZZZ,ZZZ,ZZZ.99
                                                       --------------
                                 TOTAL EXPENSES        ZZZ,ZZZ,ZZZ.99


                                    MONTHLY EXPENSE SUMMARY

                                          MONTH              AMOUNT
                                        JANUARY        ZZZ,ZZZ,ZZZ.99
                                       FEBRUARY        ZZZ,ZZZ,ZZZ.99
                                          MARCH        ZZZ,ZZZ,ZZZ.99
                                          {                 {

                                       DECEMBER        ZZZ,ZZZ,ZZZ.99

                                 TOTAL EXPENSES        ZZZ,ZZZ,ZZZ.99
```

CHAPTER

14

Table Handling with Indexes

Data in a table can be handled more efficiently when the table is *indexed* rather than subscripted. Indexes (locations within a table) are determined by the number of bytes (*displacement*) from the beginning of the table. An index value is based on the size of each of the items in the table. Thus, if the first item is to be addressed, the displacement (distance from the beginning of the table) would be zero bytes. If only the data name is present in the table and each occurrence of the item is five bytes in length, the location of the second item in the table would be five bytes from the beginning of the table, the third item would be ten bytes from the beginning, and so forth.

When a table is subscripted, rather than indexed, the location of an item is determined in much the same way; however, the computer must first determine the occurrence number and then determine the location of the item on the basis of the number of bytes from the beginning of the table, which requires extra processing.

The process of creating an indexed table is similar to creating a subscripted table. An indexed table also uses an OCCURS clause; but it also requires other clauses, as indicated in Figure 14.1.

The clause that distinguishes an indexed table from a subscripted table is the INDEXED BY clause, which causes the creation of an *index-name* that is used only in conjunction with the particular level of the table to which it is attached. So, the index-name may be used to reference only *that* level of *that* table. The INDEXED BY clause automatically defines the index-name as a full-word binary integer field, eliminating the need for any other reference to the index-name in the DATA DIVISION. The index-name is automatically ''synchronized'' (adjusted to an appropriate internal boundary), which assists in speeding table processing. With a subscripted table, the subscripts are user defined and could be DISPLAY data items, which the computer must translate into binary digits and adjust to the appropriate internal boundary before processing.

An indexed table allows the addressing of a table item through both *direct* and *relative indexing*. Relative indexing works exactly like relative subscripts discussed in Chapter 13, except that an index is used in place of the subscript.

Figure 14.1 Formats of the OCCURS Clause for Indexed Tables

```
FORMAT 1:

     OCCURS integer TIMES

        [{ASCENDING }                                          ]
        [{          }  KEY IS data-name-1  [data-name-2] ...   ] ...
        [{DESCENDING}                                          ]

        [INDEXED BY index-name-1  [index-name-2]  ...]
- - - - - - - - - - - - - - - - - - - - - - - - - - - - - - - - - - - -
FORMAT 2:

     OCCURS integer-1 TO integer-2 TIMES [DEPENDING ON data-name-3]

        [{ASCENDING }                                          ]
        [{          }  KEY IS data-name-1  [data-name-2] ...   ] ...
        [{DESCENDING}                                          ]

        [INDEXED BY index-name-1  [index-name-2] ...]
```

The PERFORM Statement

Although processing with indexed tables is more efficient, there are a number of restrictions on the modification of index-name values in the PROCEDURE DIVISION. When subscripts are used in conjunction with table processing, the programmer can use a wide range of statements to provide subscript values, such as the READ, ADD, SUBTRACT, MULTIPLY, DIVIDE, COMPUTE, MOVE, and PERFORM statements. Of these, *only* the PERFORM statement is permitted to modify the value associated with an index-name. The PERFORM/VARYING statement, often used in conjunction with the processing of subscripted tables, may also be used to process indexed tables. As mentioned in Chapter 12, the PERFORM/VARYING statement may be used to modify the value of either an identifier *or* an index-name. Thus, if the statement

```
PERFORM 100-SEARCH VARYING LCTN FROM 1 BY 1
                   UNTIL I = 100
```

appeared in a program, without examining the DATA DIVISION the programmer would be unable to determine whether LCTN represented a subscript or an index-name.

The SET Statement

Because index-name values are treated as byte displacements rather than as occurrence numbers, the MOVE, ADD, and SUBTRACT statements often used to create or modify the value of a subscript are not permitted to modify an index-name value. As a substitute, COBOL permits the SET statement to modify an index-name value in much the same way a MOVE, ADD, or SUBTRACT statement would modify a subscript.

The SET statement, shown in Figure 14.2, can be coded in two forms. The first format of the SET statement is a substitute for the MOVE statement; however, the order of the sending field and the receiving field(s) is the *reverse* of the MOVE statement. In

Figure 14.2 Formats of the SET Statement

```
Format 1:

        ⎧index-name-1⎫ ⎡index-name-2⎤             ⎧index-name-3⎫
    SET ⎨            ⎬ ⎢            ⎥ ...    TO   ⎨identifier-3⎬
        ⎩identifier-1⎭ ⎣identifier-2⎦             ⎩literal-1   ⎭
-----------------------------------------------------------------
Format 2:
                                          ⎧UP BY  ⎫ ⎧identifier-4⎫
    SET index-name-4 [index-name-5] ...   ⎨       ⎬ ⎨            ⎬
                                          ⎩DOWN BY⎭ ⎩literal-2   ⎭
```

other words, index-name-1 (or identifier-1) and index-name-2 (identifier-2) are *receiving* fields—their values are modified as a result of the execution of the SET statement. Index-name-3 (identifier-3 or literal-1) is the *sending* field. The index-names are implicitly described as integer fields. If identifiers are present, they must be described in the DATA DIVISION as integer fields, and literal-1 (if used) must be a positive integer. If index-name-3 is used as the sending field, no conversion is made (from occurrence position to byte displacement) when it is placed in the receiving field. That is, index-name-3 contains the byte displacement for the data item with which it is associated before the SET statement is executed, and that value (byte displacement) is placed in the receiving field.

If the receiving field is an identifier, the identifier should be described in the DATA DIVISION with a USAGE IS INDEX clause. When the USAGE IS INDEX clause is associated with a data item in the DATA DIVISION, the data item is automatically defined as a full-word, binary integer storage position—no PICTURE clause is needed. This data item (generally called an *index-data-name*) is often used in conjunction with the processing of indexed tables. For example, when it is necessary to *save* the value associated with a particular index-name, the value might be placed in an index-data-name—a field with the same characteristics as an index-name. However, an index-date-name is in no way directly connected with any table. Thus, an index-date-name could be used as a ''generalized'' storage position (e.g., the receiving field in the SET statement). In that case, when the sending field of a SET statement is an index-name, the value in index-name-3 (the sending field) is placed in index-data-name (the receiving field); that is, the byte displacement transfers directly.

When identifier-3 is used as the sending field, the transmitted value depends on the description of the identifier. If identifier-3 is not an index-data-name, the value in identifier-3 is converted to the byte displacement for that occurrence number of the table indexed by index-name-1 (or index-name-2); only index-names may appear as receiving fields. If identifier-3 is an index-data-name, the value in the sending field is placed in the receiving field(s) without conversion. The receiving fields can be either index-names or index-data-names.

When literal-1 is used, the receiving field must be an index-name. The value from the sending field is converted into the byte displacement for the table indexed by index-name-1 (or index-name-2).

Figure 14.3 shows results of different options of the SET statement. All entries in the DATA DIVISION appear in the WORKING-STORAGE SECTION. The first entry shows the creation of an index-data-name. Notice that IND-X is accompanied by a USAGE IS INDEX clause. NON-IND is a normal data-name. Following WORKING-RECORD, two tables are described. In the first description, the table is represented by ten occurrences of TABLE-1. When a reference is made to TABLE-1 in the PROCEDURE DIVISION, it should be made through the use of IND-1, the index-name. Each

Figure 14.3 Examples of the SET Statement (Relative to Table Size)

```
DATA DIVISION.

WORKING-STORAGE SECTION.
Ø1  WORKING-RECORD.
    Ø5 IND-X     USAGE IS INDEX.
    Ø5 NON-IND  PIC 99.
Ø1  FIRST-TABLE.
    Ø2 TABLE-1 OCCURS 1Ø TIMES
               INDEXED BY IND-1
               PIC 9(5).
Ø1  SECOND-TABLE.
    Ø2 TABLE-2 OCCURS 6 TIMES
               INDEXED BY IND-2
               PIC X(4).
```

TABLE-1

1	2	3	4	5	6	7	8	9	10	Occurrence Number

0 5 10 15 20 25 30 35 40 45 50 Byte Displacement

TABLE-2

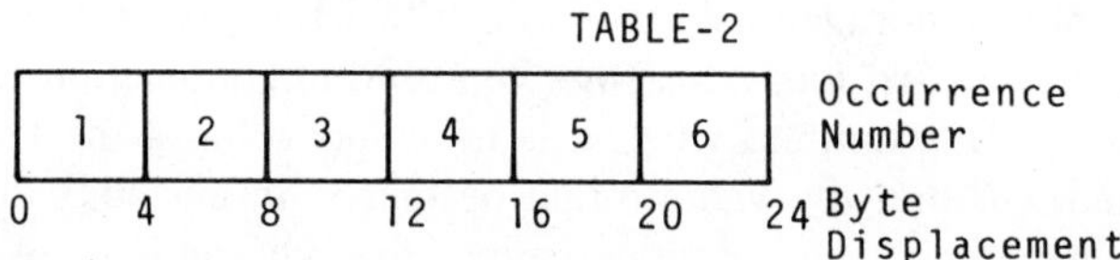

PROCEDURE DIVISION.	Values of IND-1	IND-2	IND-X
SET IND-1, IND-2 TO 1.	0	0	-
SET IND-1, IND-2 TO 5.	20	16	-
SET IND-1 TO 3.	10	16	-
SET IND-2, IND-X TO IND-1.	10	10	10
MOVE 6 TO NON-IND. SET IND-1, IND-2 TO NON-IND.	25	20	10
SET IND-1 TO IND-X	10	20	10
SET IND-2 TO 3.	10	8	10

occurrence of TABLE-1 consists of a five-digit number (five bytes). In the internal description of the table, which is provided below the DATA DIVISION entries, each occurrence number is associated with a byte displacement, which is used to reference each of the individual occurrence positions directly. So, a reference to occurrence-1 would be for a byte displacement of zero for a length of five bytes. If the second occurrence is addressed, the index value would be 5, for five bytes displacement from the beginning of the table.

The description of SECOND-TABLE is similar to FIRST-TABLE in that a one-dimension indexed table is created. There are six occurrences of TABLE-2, and each occurrence is 4 bytes long, for a total length of 24 bytes. The index-name could represent 0, 4, 8, 12, 16, or 20 bytes displacement from the beginning of the table.

In the SET statements that follow the internal organization of TABLE-1 and TABLE-2, remember that the index-names are directly associated with the tables with which they are coded. That is, TABLE-1 is indexed by IND-1, and TABLE-2 is indexed by IND-2. Thus, the determination of the index value is dependent on the characteristics of their respective tables. The first SET statement indicates that IND-1 and IND-2 are to be set to 1—the first occurrence positions of their respective tables. In each table, occurrence-1 begins at byte displacement 0. The second SET statement indicates that occurrence-5 is to be the value of IND-1 and IND-2. For TABLE-1, that is byte displacement 20, and for TABLE-2, byte displacement 16.

The third SET statement indicates that IND-1 is to be set to the third occurrence position. This would be byte displacement 10. The next SET statement places the value in IND-1 (10) into IND-2 and IND-X. Thus, IND-2 and IND-X will contain 10 (no conversion takes place). However, notice that a byte displacement of 10 for TABLE-2 would begin in the middle of occurrence-3. This is obviously an error.

The next series of statements causes 6 to be moved to NON-IND and the value of NON-IND to be used to SET IND-1 and IND-2. The value of NON-IND is converted before being placed into IND-1 and IND-2 to give these two index-names values that address the sixth occurrence of their respective tables. The next SET statement uses an index-data-name (IND-X) to set the value of an index-name (IND-1). Because the value of IND-X already represents a byte displacement value (not an occurrence number), no conversion takes place with this process. Thus, IND-1 would have a value of 10 after the execution of SET IND-1 TO IND-X. The final example of the SET statement illustrates the use of a literal to set the value of an index-name. When IND-2 is set to occurrence-3, the value 3 is translated to byte displacement 8.

The second format of the SET statement is a substitute for the ADD and SUBTRACT statements and is similar to their simple forms. (See Figure 14.2.) Index-name-4 (and index-name-5) must contain a value prior to execution. The programmer then has the option either to increment (UP BY) or decrement (DOWN BY) the index-name value. Identifier-4 (literal-2) is the amount by which the index-name value is to be modified. This amount is an occurrence number that is converted to a byte displacement amount before the index-name value is modified.

When this SET statement is executed, the index-name value is modified, allowing a programmer to "step through" a table by a specified displacement value. For example, if the statement

```
SET IND-1 UP BY 1
```

is placed in a program, each time the statement is executed, IND-1 is incremented by the number of bytes representing one occurrence. If the statement

```
SET IND-2 DOWN BY 3
```

is placed in a program, each time the statement is executed, IND-2 is reduced by the number of bytes representing three occurrences. Before the first execution of these statements, IND-1 and IND-2 must have values. Thereafter, the statements modify the index-name values when executed. If the literals 1 and 3 in the preceding examples were identifiers, a variable-stepping process would be possible.

Sales Summary Report With Indexed Tables

In Chapter 13, the Sales Summary Report procedure (Figure 13.8) was illustrated using subscripted tables. This procedure is repeated in Figure 14.4 using indexed tables. Although the two procedures produce the same result, a few differences are worth noting. First, a module called ZERO-ITEM (3200) has been added to initialize the MONTHLY-SALES items of the table because the ITEM-TABLE in Figure 14.4 includes MONTHLY-SALES. In Figure 13.8, MONTHLY-SALES was recorded as a separate table. All cells of the MONTHLY-SALES table were initialized by a MOVE statement in the INITIALIZATION module. In Figure 14.4, each ''row'' of the MONTHLY-SALES table is initialized as needed. Thus, only a part of the MONTHLY-SALES table includes legitimate numeric data—the part that is needed for processing purposes (see lines 1160–1170 and 1250–1270).

Of more direct concern is the definition of the ITEM-TABLE (lines 610–660). Notice that the clause INDEXED BY ITEM appears in conjunction with the first OCCURS clause at line 620. This transforms ITEM-TABLE from a subscripted table to an indexed table. Also, note that the data-name ITEM (the index-name) does not appear in the WORKING-VARIABLES record (as it did when it was used as a subscript in Figure 13.8). Next, note the INDEXED BY MONTH clause that appears at line 650. This clause completes the indexing operation. (Also notice that MONTH does not appear in WORKING-VARIABLES.) By virtue of these changes, only the index-names ITEM and MONTH may be used to address the ITEM-TABLE. ITEM is used to address ITEM-NUMBER-T and ITEM-DESCRIPTION-T in the PROCEDURE DIVISION. Both ITEM

Figure 14.4 A Sales Summary Report [Indexed Tables] (Hierarchy Chart)

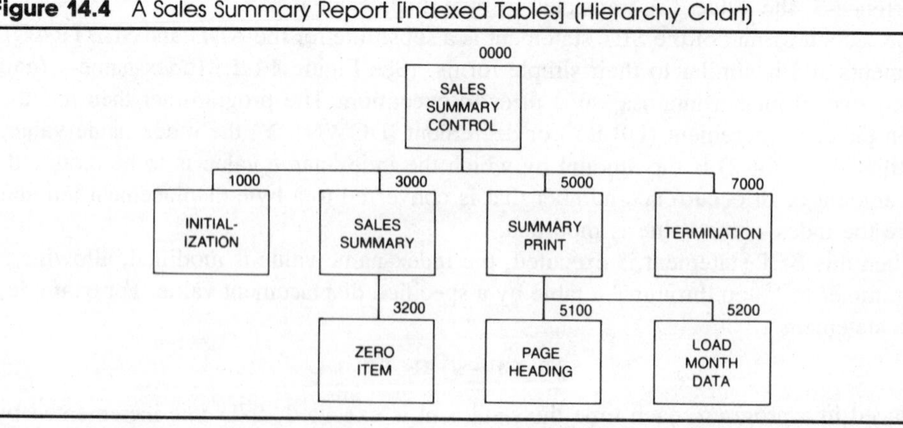

Figure 14.4 *Continued* A Sales Summary Report [Indexed Tables] (Pseudocode)

```
START
    DO Initialization
    DO Sales summation UNTIL eof
    DO Summary print
         VARYING item UNTIL end of table
    DO Termination
END

INITIALIZATION
    OPEN input, output
    CLEAR table
    READ SALES-FILE
         AT END SET file status
END

SALES SUMMATION
    IF item number NOT = last item
         MOVE item number TO last item
         ADD 1 TO item count
         SET item
         DO Zero item varying month
              until > 12
         MOVE input to table
    ENDIF
    SET month
    ADD amount of sale TO table sales
    READ input
         AT END SET file status
END

SUMMARY PRINT
    DIVIDE line count BY 25
          GIVING page status
    IF page status = 0
         DO Page heading
    ENDIF
    MOVE table values to output
    DO Load month data
         VARYING month UNTIL > 12
    WRITE output
END

PAGE HEADING
    WRITE heading
    WRITE column heading
END

LOAD MONTH DATA
    SET months
    MOVE work table to ouput table
END

ZERO ITEM
    MOVE 0 TO table
END

TERMINATION
    CLOSE files
END
```

and MONTH are used to address MONTHLY-SALES-T. These are the *only* data-names permitted to serve in an addressing capacity in conjunction with the ITEM-TABLE.

In the PROCEDURE DIVISION, ITEM is modified through a SET statement at line 1150. After this SET statement is executed, the value associated with ITEM will be the same as the value of ITEM-COUNT-WS. ITEM will not be the same *value,* but when ITEM-COUNT-WS is 1, ITEM will point to the first occurrence position of ITEM-TABLE. When ITEM-COUNT-WS is 2, ITEM will address the second occurrence position, and so on. The index-name MONTH receives a value by virtue of a SET statement at line 1200. Thus, the value associated with MONTH is generated from MONTH-OF-SALE-T.

Other manipulations of ITEM and MONTH occur during the SUMMARY-PRINT phase of the procedure. The PERFORM statement at line 970 generates values for ITEM such that ITEM will address the first, second, third, and so on, occurrence positions of ITEM-TABLE. The values for MONTH are produced through the PERFORM statement at line 1360. Thus, MONTH addresses the first through the twelfth positions of MONTHLY-SALES-T at a specified position of ITEM.

Finally, note the SET statement at line 1500. Since the values associated with MONTH are not 1 through 12, but rather, are the byte displacements represented by the first through the twelfth occurrence positions of MONTHLY-SALES-T, the statement will not accurately address the MONTHLY-SALES-OUT table (line 860); MONTH has to be converted first. To do this, an identifier (MONTH-NO-WS) is SET to the value of an index-name (MONTH). MONTH-NO-WS contains the values 1 through 12 (as a subscript value). This means that indexed and subscripted tables may be used in the *same* program.

Figure 14.4 *Continued* A Sales Summary Report [Indexed Tables]

```
                1   1   2   2   2   3   3   4   4   4   5   5   6   6   6   7
    4   8   2   6   0   4   8   2   6   0   4   8   2   6   0   4   8   2

      *****************************************************************
       IDENTIFICATION DIVISION.
      *****************************************************************
       PROGRAM-ID.    SALES-SUMMARY-INDEXED.
       AUTHOR.        J. WAYNE SPENCE.
       DATE-WRITTEN.  January 1, 1989.
       DATE-COMPILED. January 1, 1989.
      *     Procedure to accumulate sales of items by month.
      *     Procedrue uses a one dimensional table to store the
      *     item number and name and a two dimensional table to
      *     record the monthly sales of each item.
      *****************************************************************
       ENVIRONMENT DIVISION.
      *****************************************************************
      *---------------------------------------------------------------*
       CONFIGURATION SECTION.
      *---------------------------------------------------------------*
       SOURCE-COMPUTER. IBM.
       OBJECT-COMPUTER. IBM.
       SPECIAL-NAMES.   C01 IS TOP-OF-PAGE.
      *---------------------------------------------------------------*
       INPUT-OUTPUT SECTION.
      *---------------------------------------------------------------*
       FILE-CONTROL.
           SELECT SALES-FILE  ASSIGN TO UT-S-INPUT.
           SELECT REPORT-FILE ASSIGN TO UT-S-OUTPUT.
      *****************************************************************
       DATA DIVISION.
      *****************************************************************
      *---------------------------------------------------------------*
       FILE SECTION.
      *---------------------------------------------------------------*
       FD  SALES-FILE
               LABEL RECORDS ARE OMITTED.
       01  SALES-RECORD.
           05  ITEM-NUMBER-IN              PIC 9(05).
           05  ITEM-DESCRIPTION-IN         PIC X(30).
           05  FILLER                      PIC X(01).
           05  DATE-OF-SALE-IN.
               10  MONTH-OF-SALE-IN        PIC 9(02).
               10  DAY-OF-SALE-IN          PIC 9(02).
               10  YEAR-OF-SALE-IN         PIC 9(02).
           05  FILLER                      PIC X(02).
           05  AMOUNT-OF-SALE-IN           PIC S9(3)V99.
           05  FILLER                      PIC X(31).

       FD  REPORT-FILE
               LABEL RECORDS ARE STANDARD.
       01  REPORT-LINE                     PIC X(133).
      *---------------------------------------------------------------*
       WORKING-STORAGE SECTION.
      *---------------------------------------------------------------*
       01  WORKING-VARIABLES.
           05  FILE-STATUS                 PIC X(10).
           05  MONTH-NO-WS                 PIC 9(02) VALUE ZERO.
           05  ITEM-COUNT-WS               PIC 9(02) VALUE ZERO.
           05  LINE-COUNT-WS               PIC 9(02) VALUE ZERO.
           05  PAGE-STATUS-WS              PIC V999.
           05  LAST-ITEM-WS                PIC 9(05) VALUE ZERO.

       01  ITEM-TABLE.
           05  ITEM-ENTRY OCCURS 30 TIMES INDEXED BY ITEM.
               10  ITEM-NUMBER-T           PIC 9(5).
               10  ITEM-DESCRIPTION-T      PIC X(30).
               10  MONTHLY-SALES-T OCCURS 12 TIMES INDEXED BY MONTH
                                           PIC S9(4)V99.

       01  PAGE-HEADING.
           05  FILLER                      PIC X(55) VALUE SPACES.
```

Figure 14.4 *Continued* A Sales Summary Report [Indexed Tables]

```
                1   1   2   2   2   3   3   4   4   4   5   5   6   6   6   7
    4   8   2   6   0   4   8   2   6   0   4   8   2   6   0   4   8   2

           05  FILLER                    PIC X(22) VALUE
                                        'Sales Summary by Month'.

       01  COLUMN-HEADING.
           05  FILLER                    PIC X(38) VALUE
                                         '    Item Description'.
           05  FILLER                    PIC X(92) VALUE
           'Jan.    Feb.    Mar.    Apr.    May     June    July    Aug.
      -    '    Sep.    Oct.    Nov.    Dec.'.

       01  DETAIL-LINE.
           05  FILLER                    PIC X(01) VALUE SPACES.
           05  ITEM-NUMBER-OUT           PIC 99B999.
           05  FILLER                    PIC X(01) VALUE SPACES.
           05  ITEM-DESCRIPTION-OUT      PIC X(25).
           05  FILLER                    PIC X(01) VALUE SPACES.
           05  MONTHLY-SALES-T-OUT OCCURS 12 TIMES
                                         PIC ZZZZZ.99.
      *****************************************************************
       PROCEDURE DIVISION.
      *****************************************************************
      *---------------------------------------------------------------*
       000-SALES-SUMMARY-CONTROL SECTION.
      *---------------------------------------------------------------*
           PERFORM 1000-INITIALIZATION.
           PERFORM 3000-SALES-SUMMATION
               UNTIL FILE-STATUS = 'DONE'.
           PERFORM 5000-SUMMARY-PRINT
               VARYING ITEM FROM 1 BY 1 UNTIL ITEM > ITEM-COUNT-WS.
           PERFORM 7000-TERMINATION.
           STOP RUN.
      *---------------------------------------------------------------*
       1000-INITIALIZATION SECTION.
      *---------------------------------------------------------------*
           OPEN INPUT SALES-FILE
                OUTPUT REPORT-FILE.
           MOVE SPACES TO ITEM-TABLE.
           READ SALES-FILE
                AT END MOVE 'DONE' TO FILE-STATUS.
      *---------------------------------------------------------------*
       3000-SALES-SUMMATION SECTION.
      *---------------------------------------------------------------*
           IF ITEM-NUMBER-IN NOT = LAST-ITEM-WS
               MOVE ITEM-NUMBER-IN TO LAST-ITEM-WS
               ADD 1 TO ITEM-COUNT-WS
               SET ITEM TO ITEM-COUNT-WS
               PERFORM 3200-ZERO-ITEM
                   VARYING MONTH FROM 1 BY 1 UNTIL MONTH > 12
               MOVE ITEM-NUMBER-IN TO ITEM-NUMBER-T (ITEM)
               MOVE ITEM-DESCRIPTION-IN TO ITEM-DESCRIPTION-T (ITEM).
           SET MONTH TO MONTH-OF-SALE-IN.
           ADD AMOUNT-OF-SALE-IN TO MONTHLY-SALES-T (ITEM, MONTH).
           READ SALES-FILE
               AT END MOVE 'DONE' TO FILE-STATUS.
      *---------------------------------------------------------------*
       3200-ZERO-ITEM SECTION.
      *---------------------------------------------------------------*
           MOVE ZERO TO MONTHLY-SALES-T (ITEM, MONTH).
      *---------------------------------------------------------------*
       5000-SUMMARY-PRINT SECTION.
      *---------------------------------------------------------------*
           DIVIDE LINE-COUNT-WS BY 25 GIVING PAGE-STATUS-WS.
           IF PAGE-STATUS-WS = 0
               PERFORM 5100-PAGE-HEADING.
           MOVE ITEM-NUMBER-T (ITEM) TO ITEM-NUMBER-OUT.
           MOVE ITEM-DESCRIPTION-T (ITEM) TO ITEM-DESCRIPTION-OUT.
           PERFORM 5200-LOAD-MONTH-DATA
               VARYING MONTH FROM 1 BY 1 UNTIL MONTH > 12.
           WRITE REPORT-LINE FROM DETAIL-LINE AFTER ADVANCING 2 LINES.
```

Figure 14.4 *Continued* A Sales Summary Report [Indexed Tables]

```
           ADD 2 TO LINE-COUNT-WS.
       *-------------------------------------------------------*
       5100-PAGE-HEADING SECTION.
       *-------------------------------------------------------*
           WRITE REPORT-LINE FROM PAGE-HEADING
               AFTER ADVANCING TOP-OF-PAGE.
           WRITE REPORT-LINE FROM COLUMN-HEADING
               AFTER ADVANCING 2 LINES.
       *-------------------------------------------------------*
       5200-LOAD-MONTH-DATA SECTION.
       *-------------------------------------------------------*
           SET MONTH-NO-WS TO MONTH.
           MOVE MONTHLY-SALES-T (ITEM, MONTH) TO
               MONTHLY-SALES-T-OUT (MONTH-NO-WS).
       *-------------------------------------------------------*
       7000-TERMINATION SECTION.
       *-------------------------------------------------------*
           CLOSE SALES-FILE
                 REPORT-FILE.
```

The SEARCH Statement

With an indexed table, COBOL also permits use of the SEARCH statement. The SEARCH allows the programmer to ''look through'' items in a table for an occurrence that meets certain conditions.

The SEARCH statement causes the COBOL compiler to generate the code necessary to conduct a *linear* (or sequential) SEARCH of a table. The table is examined one occurrence at a time, beginning with the last index-name setting, until a specified condition is encountered or the end of the table is reached. Figure 14.5 shows the format of the SEARCH statement. Identifier-1 must be a data-name representing an indexed table. The identifier itself cannot be subordinate to an OCCURS clause, but rather, should be directly associated with the first OCCURS clause (using an INDEXED BY clause) in the record description. For example, suppose the following description of an indexed table is presented in the DATA DIVISION.

Figure 14.5 Format of the SEARCH Statement

```
SEARCH identifier-1 [VARYING {index-name-1 | identifier-2}] [AT END imperative-statement-1]

    WHEN condition-1 {imperative-statement-2 | NEXT SENTENCE}

   [WHEN condition-1 {imperative-statement-3 | NEXT SENTENCE}]

[END-SEARCH]
```

```
01 TABLE-NAME.
   02 TABLE-OCCURRENCES OCCURS
         25 TIMES INDEXED BY NUM.
      03 ITEM-A        PIC 9(05).
      03 ITEM-B        PIC X(03).
```

The only data-name in this description that could be used as identifier-1 is TABLE-OCCURRENCES. TABLE-OCCURRENCES would normally be written with an index (position) reference, but in the SEARCH statement only the data-name should be used.

The next clause that may appear in the SEARCH statement is the VARYING clause, which automatically modifies an index-name or an identifier. *This index-name or identifier should not be the index-name associated with the table being searched.* For example, the SEARCH statement will automatically increment the index-name NUM associated with TABLE-NAME regardless of the presence or absence of the VARYING clause. The intent of the VARYING clause is to modify the index-name value of another table (or perhaps a subscript, though identifier-2, of another table). If an index-name is specified in the VARYING clause, the value of the index-name will be the same value as the index-name associated with the table being searched. That is, since index-name NUM is being modified by the SEARCH statement (in terms of byte displacement values), the value of index-name-1 would be modified by the same amount. (NUM and index-name-1 would have the same value only if set to the same value prior to the execution of the SEARCH statement.) If the VARYING clause is written with identifier-2, identifier-2 will be incremented by 1 every time the index-name of the table is incremented by one occurrence. (If identifier-2 is an index-data-name, the increment will be in byte displacement values rather than increments of 1.)

Another optional clause provided with the SEARCH statement is the AT END clause. This clause allows the programmer to specify the operations to take place if the end of the table is reached without any of the WHEN conditions being satisfied. The imperative statement is executed after the last occurrence of the table has been reached and no item in the table satisfies any of the specified conditions. If the AT END clause has not been specified (or the imperative statement does not perform an unconditional branch) when the end of the table is reached, the SEARCH statement is terminated, and execution continues with the statement immediately following the SEARCH statement.

It is important to note that the SEARCH statement will proceed through the table until the last occurrence is reached. This is true even if the table is not completely filled with data. When searching a partially filled (static) table, the programmer should provide for the termination of the SEARCH through one of the WHEN clauses. Otherwise, the programmer is forced to make the table a variable-length table (through the DEPENDING ON clause) or run the risk of encountering a position in the table that does not contain data.

Following the optional VARYING and AT END clauses, the programmer must specify one or more WHEN clauses. Each WHEN clause is written with a condition and an action to be taken (imperative statement or NEXT SENTENCE) when the condition is true. The WHEN clauses are roughly equivalent to an IF statement with only a true branch. (The false branch would be the next WHEN clause or the end of the SEARCH statement.) Thus, the reserved word IF is replaced with the reserved word WHEN, and the clause takes on the form of a conditional statement. The condition may be a relational test, a sign test, a class test, or a condition-name test. Furthermore, the logical operators NOT, AND, and OR may be used in each condition to create compound tests.

Each of the WHEN clauses is tested, in the order in which it appears, for each increment of the index associated with the table being searched. If none of the conditions is true, the index is incremented to the next occurrence position, and the tests are repeated. The process continues until the end of the table is reached or one of the conditions is found to be true. In either case the SEARCH statement is terminated. If the imperative statement does not cause an unconditional branch when the imperative statement is executed, the SEARCH statement is terminated, and execution continues with the statement immediately following the SEARCH statement.

Two additional issues should be mentioned. First, prior to the execution of the SEARCH statement, the index-name associated with the table must be initialized. Under most circumstances, the programmer desires to search the entire table rather than a portion of it. In this case, prior to the initial execution of the SEARCH statement, the index-name should be set to the first occurrence position. Otherwise, the operation begins with the last index setting for the table and continues a linear search from that point. If the index setting is for the last occurrence position in the table, the SEARCH will terminate immediately after examining the WHEN clause(s).

Second, only one index-name is modified by the SEARCH statement—the index-name associated with the lowest level of the table. Thus, if it is desirable to search a multidimension table, the SEARCH statement will increment only the last index of the table. The programmer must increment other index-names associated with the table and reexecute the SEARCH statement.

Figure 14.6 illustrates the searching of a table. In the first example, EMPLOYEE-TABLE describes a one-dimension table indexed by NUM. The desired process is to search the entire table (assuming it contains 100 entries) and locate the entries for employees who have worked more than 40 hours during the week. In the PROCEDURE DIVISION, NUM is SET to 1. Thus the search begins with the first occurrence of EMPLOYEE-TABLE. At the first occurrence position, NUMBER-OF-HOURS is checked to determine whether or not it exceeds 40. If it does not, NUM is incremented by 1 until the condition is true or the end of the table is reached. When the condition is true, the name of the employee and his location in the table are displayed. Execution of the true phrase normally would cause the termination of the SEARCH statement, but in this example the index is SET UP BY 1, and the SEARCH statement is restarted. Thus, the search begins again, immediately after the last NUMBER-OF-HOURS that was greater than 40. Thus, these statements search the entire table even if the condition is true one or more times. The operation is terminated only when the end of the table is reached and the perform indicator is set to "COMPLETE."

In the second example, RATE-TABLE describes a two-dimension table. The procedure checks the occurrence positions of the table to determine whether or not any occurrence in a particular column contains a RATE that is not positive. The table is organized such that the index-name ROWS addresses rows of the table. As previously mentioned, the SEARCH statement only modifies the lowest level of the table—that is, the part of the table indexed by COLS. Thus, in the PROCEDURE DIVISION, a PERFORM statement is used to modify ROWS. In the TABLE-SEARCH paragraph, COLS is set to 1, indicating that each column of the table should be searched, beginning with the first occurrence. The SEARCH statement starts searching the first column (since ROWS initially has a value of 1) until the first nonpositive RATE is found or until the end of the column has been encountered. When the SEARCH statement is terminated by the WHEN condition, the amount of RATE is displayed. There may be other nonpositive values below the location of the first, but they are not displayed.

When the end of the TABLE-SEARCH paragraph is encountered, the PERFORM statement increments ROWS by 1. This will cause a search of the second (third, fourth,

Figure 14.6 Illustrations of the SEARCH Statement

```
Example 1:

    DATA DIVISION.
              .
              .

    WORKING-STORAGE SECTION.
    Ø1  WORKING-RECORD.
        Ø5 NO-OF-EMPLOYEES          PIC 999 VALUE ZERO.
        Ø5 SEARCH-PROCESS           PIC X(1Ø).
    Ø1  EMPLOYEE-TABLE.
        Ø2 EMPLOYEE OCCURS 100 TIMES INDEXED BY NUM.
           Ø3 ID-NUMBER             PIC 9(6).
           Ø3 EMPLOYEE-NAME         PIC X(2Ø).
           Ø3 RATE-PER-HOUR         PIC 99V99.
           Ø3 NUMBER-OF-HOURS       PIC 99V9.
              .
              .
    PROCEDURE DIVISION.
              .
              .
        SET NUM TO 1.
        PERFORM SEARCH-ENTIRE-TABLE UNTIL SEARCH-PROCESS = 'COMPLETE'.
        PERFORM NEXT-PROCESS.
        STOP RUN.
    SEARCH-ENTIRE-TABLE.
        SEARCH EMPLOYEE       VARYING NO-OF-EMPLOYEES
            AT END MOVE 'COMPLETE' TO SEARCH-PROCESS.
            WHEN NUMBER-OF-HOURS (NUM) GREATER THAN 4Ø
                DISPLAY 'IN TABLE POSITION', NO-OF-EMPLOYEE, ' ',
                   EMPLOYEE (NUM), 'WORKED MORE THAN 4Ø HOURS';
                SET NUM UP BY 1.
    NEXT-PROCESS.
              .
              .
              .
```

```
Example 2:

    DATA DIVISION.
              .
              .
    WORKING-STORAGE SECTION.
    Ø1  RATE-TABLE.
        Ø2 ORIGINS OCCURS 3Ø TIMES INDEXED BY ROWS.
           Ø3 DESTINATIONS OCCURS 5Ø TIMES INDEXED BY COLS.
              Ø4 RATE                  PIC 9999V99.
              .
              .
    PROCEDURE DIVISION.
              .
              .
        PERFORM TABLE-SEARCH VARYING ROWS FROM 1 BY 1 UNTIL ROWS GREATER THAN 4Ø.
        PERFORM NEXT-PROCESS.
        STOP RUN.
    TABLE-SEARCH.
        SET COLS TO 1.
        SEARCH ORGINS
            WHEN RATE (ROWS, COLS) IS ZERO OR NEGATIVE
                DISPLAY RATE (ROWS, COLS).
    NEXT-PROCESS.
              .
              .
              .
```

Figure 14.7 Format of the SEARCH ALL Statement

```
SEARCH ALL identifier-1  [AT END imperative-statement-1]

                     { imperative-statement-2 }
    WHEN  condition-1 {                        }
                     { NEXT SENTENCE          }

   [                  { imperative-statement-3 } ]
   [ AND  condition-1 {                        } ]
   [                  { NEXT SENTENCE          } ]

[END-SEARCH]
```

etc.) column of the table. The operation is halted when the PERFORM has incremented ROWS past 30. NEXT-PROCESS is then performed.

The second form of the SEARCH statement, shown in Figure 14.7, is referred to as the SEARCH ALL statement. A SEARCH ALL may be conducted only for indexed tables that are *keyed*. The discussion of the ASCENDING/DESCENDING KEY clause, shown in Figure 14.1, has been delayed because the clause is necessary only when a SEARCH ALL statement is to be used. To refresh your memory, this clause (associated with the OCCURS clause) is written as

```
[{ASCENDING }     KEY IS data-name-2     [data-name-3] ...] ...
 {DESCENDING}
```

The clause is used to direct the operation of the SEARCH ALL statement. That is, when the SEARCH ALL statement is executed, the data items in the table should be sequenced on (sorted by) data-name-2 (data-name-3, etc.).

When ASCENDING is specified, the data in the table should be arranged by the programmer in ascending order (from the smallest value to the largest value) by the data-name(s) listed in the key(s) *before* the SEARCH ALL is executed. DESCENDING is an indication of ordering of data values from largest to smallest. (Note that the data do not have to be in the specified order when initially placed in the table. However, before the execution of the SEARCH ALL statement, the data should be organized in the indicated sequence.)

When the ASCENDING/DESCENDING KEY clause is specified, the keys (data-name-2, etc.) are listed in decreasing order of significance; that is, data-name-2 is a *major key,* with data-name-3, and so on representing *minor keys*. There may be a maximum of 12 keys listed, but they must not exceed 256 bytes in length. The KEY data-name(s) must be subordinate to the table being searched, but must not be written with an OCCURS clause or be subordinate to a level of a table other than that being searched.

The SEARCH ALL statement conducts a *binary* search of table items based on the keys described in the table. For larger tables, binary searching is more efficient than linear searching. Figure 14.8 illustrates this point. As demonstrated by the illustration, the first value examined is at the middle of the table. When the search for key 691 is

Figure 14.8 Demonstration of a Binary Search

Comparisons: Binary Search for 691	Comparisons: Binary Search for 459	Table Position	Ascending Key	Contents of Record
		1	295	
		2	321	
		3	442	
	2nd	4	454	
	4th	5	515	
	3rd	6	542	
		7	631	
1st	1st	8	644	
		9	677	
3rd		10	691	
		11	827	
2nd		12	859	
		13	921	
		14	945	
		15	986	

being performed, a comparison of 691 and the value in the middle of the table (644) results in the sought item being a larger value. By the process of elimination, the top half of the table is ''disregarded'' from the search—the solution, if it exists, cannot be in the top half of the table (since the table is ordered). Of the remaining items, the middle item is examined (position 12 of table). In this case 691 is smaller than the table value (827). Again, by the process of elimination, the solution cannot be from position 12 to the end of the table. The key at the midpoint of the remaining items is inspected. The search is terminated with the location of item 691. As indicated in the illustration, a conclusion of the search is reached after three comparisons—a comparison of each key from position 1 to position 10 of the table.

The second column of the table is a representation of what happens when a sought item does not exist in the table. The same process (dividing the remaining positions in half with every inspection) is followed. However, after the fourth inspection, all possible positions in the table have been exhausted without finding the item. Consequently, the search is terminated without a solution. For the illustrated table, four comparisons (the maximum) were required, whereas a linear search would take a minimum of five comparisons. (A SEARCH would inspect all 15 key values of the table before reaching the conclusion that 459 did not exist because the data do not necessarily have to be in ascending (or descending) order for the SEARCH statement.)

In the SEARCH ALL statement, identifier-1 is the name of a table that is *indexed and keyed*. As with the SEARCH statement, the identifier should be a data-name associated with the first OCCURS clause in the table description. The optional AT END clause operates in the same manner for the SEARCH ALL as it did for the SEARCH statement; however, the AT END is not invoked upon encountering the end of the table. Rather, the imperative statement is executed when the search has reached a *logical* conclusion without finding a match on a keyed item. (The ''end'' could be at any position in the table.)

The SEARCH ALL statement *does not* contain the VARYING clause, and only *one* WHEN clause is permitted. Furthermore, the condition is allowed to test only for equality, using the relational operations IS = OR IS EQUAL TO. In addition, a compound condition is allowed only with the use of the logical operator AND. The imperative statement may take the same form as with the SEARCH statement. Termination of the SEARCH ALL statement is caused by the same conditions as for the SEARCH statement—by executing the WHEN clause imperative statement or the AT END imperative statement. When the AT END is omitted or the imperative statement connected to the WHEN clause does not perform an unconditional branch, the statement immediately following the SEARCH ALL statement will be executed.

The Sales Analysis Program with SEARCH Statements

The Sales Analysis procedure illustrated in Figure 14.9 also uses indexed tables. Although the Sales Summary Report procedure and the Sales Analysis procedure are similar in design, the number, type, and use of tables are different. The first table used in the Sales Analysis procedure is defined in lines 740–850. It is defined as an indexed table by the INDEXED BY clause at line 760. The purpose of the SALESMAN-DATA-TABLE is similar to that of the ITEM-TABLE from the previous example—to retain and accumulate data. This table is also a variable-length table by virtue of the DEPENDING ON SALESMAN-COUNT clause in line 760. Using a variable-length table, has two advantages. First, it is not necessary to initialize the table. Secondly, the SEARCH for corresponding salesman identification entries does not have to test to determine whether the end of the table has been encountered (see lines 1900–1990).

Figure 14.9 Sales Analysis [SEARCH Statement] (Hierarchy Chart)

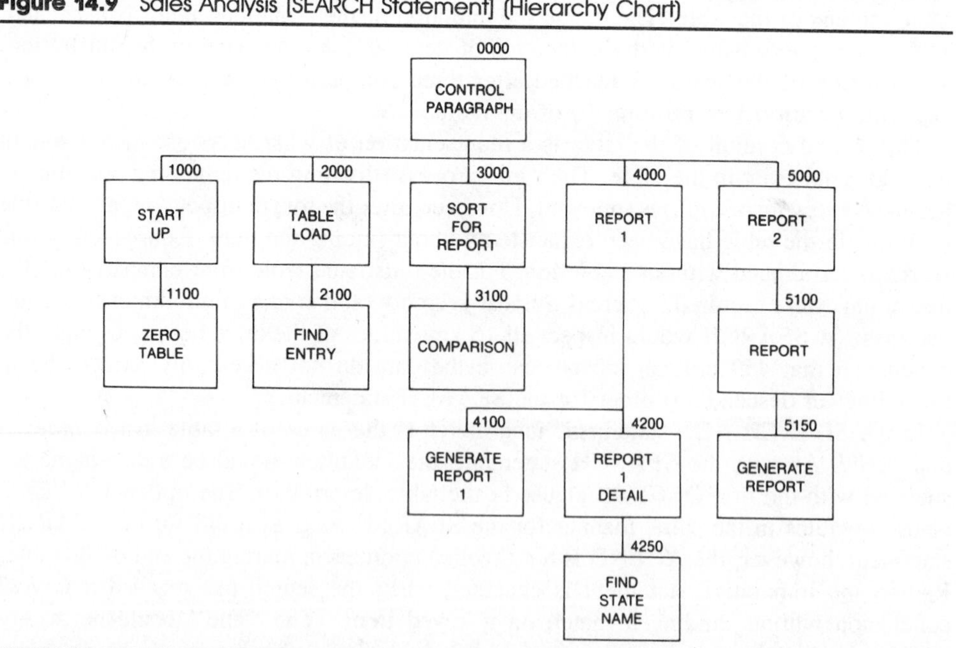

Figure 14.9 *Continued* Sales Analysis [SEARCH Statement] (Pseudocode)

```
START
    DO Start up
    DO Table load UNTIL eof
    DO Sort for report UNTIL sorted
    DO Report 1
    DO Report 2
    CLOSE files
END

START UP
    OPEN files
    SET file status, state, lctn
    READ input at end
         SET file status
END

TABLE LOAD
    MOVE input to work
    DO Find entry
    READ input at end
         SET file status
END

FIND ENTRY
    SEARCH sales table
    AT END ADD 1 to count, sorted
           SET lctn to count
           MOVE work to table
    WHEN table id = id
              ADD amount to table
    ENDSEARCH
END

SORT FOR REPORT
    SET sort status
    DO Comparison varying lctn until = items
    IF not sorted SUBTRACT 1 from items
END

COMPARISON
    IF table id > table id +1
         MOVE row to work
         MOVE row +1 to row
         MOVE work to row +1
         SET sort status
    ENDIF
END

REPORT 1
    MOVE values to titles
    SET lctn
    WRITE output
    DO Generate report 1 varying lctn
         UNTIL > count
    DO Reprot 1 detail
END

GENERATE REPORT 1
    IF table district not equal district
         DO Report 1 detail
    ELSE
         ADD table amount to district
    ENDIF
END

REPORT 1 DETAIL
    MOVE values to output
    DO Find state name
    MOVE state name to output
    WRITE output
    MOVE table values to work
END

FIND STATE NAME
    SEARCH ALL state codes
         WHEN table state = district
              MOVE table name to work
    ENDSEARCH
END

REPORT 2
    MOVE title to output
    DO Report
END

REPORT
    WRITE heading
    DO Generate report varying lctn > count
    SET items, sort status
END

GENERATE REPORT
    IF table district not = district
         MOVE table district to district
         DO Find state name
         MOVE state name to output
         MOVE table district to output
    ENDIF
    MOVE table values to output
    WRITE output
END
```

Instead, the SEARCH statement simply *adds* a new item to the bottom of the existing table when no match on ID-INFORMATION is found.

The second table in Figure 14.9 is the STATE-CODE-TABLE (lines 1040–1090), which is used for internal purposes only; that is, when it becomes necessary to translate a district number from a numeric value to its corresponding state name, the STATE-CODE-TABLE will be employed. Notice, however, that the table definition not only indicates the table is indexed (INDEXED BY STATE), but that it is (or is capable of being) keyed (ASCENDING KEY IS STATE-CODE-T). The STATE-CODE-TABLE is

Figure 14.9 *Continued* Sales Analysis [SEARCH Statement]

```
           1   1   2   2   2   3   3   4   4   4   5   5   6   6   6   7
   4   8   2   6   0   4   8   2   6   0   4   8   2   6   0   4   8   2
      ***************************************************************
       IDENTIFICATION DIVISION.
      ***************************************************************
       PROGRAM-ID.       SALES-ANALYSIS.
       AUTHOR.           J. WAYNE SPENCE.
       DATE-WRITTEN.     JANUARY 1, 1989.
       DATE-COMPILED.    JANUARY 1, 1989.
      *     This program illustrates the use of indexed TABLES.
      *     It defines the tables and, in some instances, provides
      *     the initial values to be placed in the table.  In the
      *     PROCEDURE DIVISION, the indexed tables are processed
      *     and a "bubble" sort is applied to rearrange the data
      *     internally.  In conjunction witht eh tables, SET;
      *     SEARCH; SEARCH ALL; and index-names are used.
      ***************************************************************
       ENVIRONMENT DIVISION.
      ***************************************************************
      *-------------------------------------------------------------*
       CONFIGURATION SECTION.
      *-------------------------------------------------------------*
       SOURCE-COMPUTER. IBM.
       OBJECT-COMPUTER. IBM.
       SPECIAL-NAMES.    C01 IS PAGE-TOP.
      *-------------------------------------------------------------*
       INPUT-OUTPUT SECTION.
      *-------------------------------------------------------------*
       FILE-CONTROL.
           SELECT SALES-FILE  ASSIGN TO UT-S-INPUT.
           SELECT REPORT-FILE ASSIGN TO UT-S-OUTPUT.
      ***************************************************************
       DATA DIVISION.
      ***************************************************************
      *-------------------------------------------------------------*
       FILE SECTION.
      *-------------------------------------------------------------*
       FD  SALES-FILE LABEL RECORDS ARE OMITTED.
       01  SALES-RECORD.
           05 SALESMAN-NAME-IN.
               10 LAST-NAME-IN              PIC X(20).
               10 FIRST-NAME-IN             PIC X(20).
               10 MIDDLE-INITIAL-IN         PIC X(01).
           05 FILLER                        PIC X(08).
           05 ID-INFORMATION-IN.
               10 SALESMAN-ID-IN            PIC 9(05).
               10 FILLER                    PIC X(05).
               10 DISTRICT-NUMBER-IN        PIC 9(02).
           05 FILLER                        PIC X(08).
           05 AMOUNT-OF-SALE-IN             PIC 9(05)V9(02).
           05 FILLER                        PIC X(04).

       FD  REPORT-FILE LABEL RECORDS ARE OMITTED.
       01  OUTPUT-LINE                      PIC X(133).
      *-------------------------------------------------------------*
       WORKING-STORAGE SECTION.
      *-------------------------------------------------------------*
       01  WORKING-VARIABLES.
           05  FILE-STATUS                  PIC X(15).
           05  SORT-INDICATOR-WS            PIC X(15).
           05  DISTRICT-TOTAL-WS            PIC 9(07)V9(02).
           05  ITEMS-TO-BE-SORTED-WS        PIC 9(03) VALUE ZERO.
           05  STATE-NAME-WS                PIC X(12).
           05  SALESMAN-COUNT-WS            PIC 9(03) VALUE ZERO.

       01  SAVE-REORGANIZE-RECORD.
           05 ID-INFORMATION.
               10 DISTRICT-NUMBER-WS        PIC 9(02).
               10 SALESMAN-ID-WS            PIC 9(05).
           05 AMOUNT-OF-SALE-WS             PIC 9(06)V9(02).
           05 SALESMAN-NAME-WS.
```

Figure 14.9 *Continued* Sales Analysis [SEARCH Statement]

```
            1   1   2   2   2   3   3   4   4   4   5   5   6   6   6   7
    4   8   2   6   0   4   8   2   6   0   4   8   2   6   0   4   8   2
               10 LAST-NAME-WS             PIC X(20).
               10 FIRST-NAME-WS            PIC X(20).
               10 MIDDLE-INITIAL-WS        PIC X(01).
       01  SALESMAN-DATA-TABLE.
           05 SALESMAN-ENTRY-T OCCURS 0 TO 100 TIMES
                  DEPENDING ON SALESMAN-COUNT-WS
                  INDEXED BY LCTN.
               10 ID-INFORMATION-T.
                   15 DISTRICT-NUMBER-T PIC 9(02).
                   15 SALESMAN-ID-T     PIC 9(05).
               10 AMOUNT-OF-SALE-T     PIC 9(06)V9(02).
               10 SALESMAN-NAME-T.
                   15 LAST-NAME-T       PIC X(20).
                   15 FIRST-NAME-T      PIC X(20).
                   15 MIDDLE-INITIAL-T  PIC X(01).
       01  CODE-STATE-LIST.
           05 FILLER                       PIC X(14) VALUE '01Alabama'.
           05 FILLER                       PIC X(14) VALUE '04Arkansas'.
           05 FILLER                       PIC X(14) VALUE '09Florida'.
           05 FILLER                       PIC X(14) VALUE '10Georgia'.
           05 FILLER                       PIC X(14) VALUE '15Iowa'.
           05 FILLER                       PIC X(14) VALUE '25Missouri'.
           05 FILLER                       PIC X(14) VALUE '30New Jersey'.
           05 FILLER                       PIC X(14) VALUE '34North Dakota'.
           05 FILLER                       PIC X(14) VALUE '35Ohio'.
           05 FILLER                       PIC X(14) VALUE '36Oklahoma'.
           05 FILLER                       PIC X(14) VALUE '42Tennessee'.
           05 FILLER                       PIC X(14) VALUE '43Texas'.
           05 FILLER                       PIC X(14) VALUE '46Virginia'.
           05 FILLER                       PIC X(14) VALUE '49Wisconsin'.
           05 FILLER                       PIC X(14) VALUE '50Wyoming'.
       01  STATE-CODE-TABLE REDEFINES CODE-STATE-LIST.
           05 STATE-CODE-ENTRIES-T OCCURS 15 TIMES
              ASCENDING KEY IS STATE-CODE-T
              INDEXED BY STATE.
               10 STATE-CODE-T             PIC 9(02).
               10 STATE-NAME-T             PIC X(12).
       01  REPORT-HEADING.
           05 FILLER                       PIC X(40) VALUE SPACES.
           05 FILLER                       PIC X(23) VALUE
                                           'Salesman Weekly Report'.
           05 TITLE-OUT                    PIC X(40).
       01  DISTRICT-DETAIL.
           05 FILLER                       PIC X(38) VALUE SPACES.
           05 DISTRICT-NUMBER-DD-OUT       PIC Z9.
           05 FILLER                       PIC X(05) VALUE SPACES.
           05 STATE-NAME-DD-OUT            PIC X(12).
           05 FILLER                       PIC X(05) VALUE SPACES.
           05 DISTRICT-TOTAL-DD-OUT        PIC $$,$$$,$$$.99.
       01  SALESMAN-DETAIL.
           05 FILLER                       PIC X(21) VALUE SPACES.
           05 SALESMAN-NAME-SD-OUT         PIC X(41).
           05 FILLER                       PIC X(05) VALUE SPACES.
           05 SALESMAN-NUMBER-SD-OUT       PIC ZZZZZ9.
           05 FILLER                       PIC X(05) VALUE SPACES.
           05 DISTRICT-NUMBER-SD-OUT       PIC Z9(01).
           05 FILLER                       PIC X(05) VALUE SPACES.
           05 STATE-NAME-SD-OUT            PIC X(12).
           05 FILLER                       PIC X(05) VALUE SPACES.
           05 AMOUNT-OF-SALE-SD-OUT        PIC $$$$,$$$.9(02).
      ***************************************************************
       PROCEDURE DIVISION.
      ***************************************************************
```

Figure 14.9 *Continued* Sales Analysis [SEARCH Statement]

```
       1   1   2   2   2   3   3   4   4   4   5   5   6   6   6   7
   4   8   2   6   0   4   8   2   6   0   4   8   2   6   0   4   8   2

 *-----------------------------------------------------------*
  0000-CONTROL-PARAGRAPH SECTION.
 *-----------------------------------------------------------*
      PERFORM 1000-START-UP.
      PERFORM 2000-TABLE-LOAD UNTIL FILE-STATUS = 'FILE COMPLETE'.
      PERFORM 3000-SORT-FOR-REPORT
          UNTIL SORT-INDICATOR-WS = 'SORT COMPLETE'.
      PERFORM 4000-REPORT-1.
      PERFORM 5000-REPORT-2.
      CLOSE SALES-FILE, REPORT-FILE.
      STOP RUN.
 *-----------------------------------------------------------*
  1000-START-UP SECTION.
 *-----------------------------------------------------------*
      OPEN INPUT SALES-FILE OUTPUT REPORT-FILE.
      MOVE 'READING FILE'          TO FILE-STATUS.
      MOVE SPACES                  TO OUTPUT-LINE.
      SET STATE, LCTN TO 1.
      READ SALES-FILE AT END
          MOVE 'FILE COMPLETE' TO FILE-STATUS.
 *-----------------------------------------------------------*
  2000-TABLE-LOAD SECTION.
 *-----------------------------------------------------------*
      MOVE SALESMAN-NAME-IN      TO SALESMAN-NAME-WS.
      MOVE SALESMAN-ID-IN        TO SALESMAN-ID-WS.
      MOVE DISTRICT-NUMBER-IN    TO DISTRICT-NUMBER-WS.
      MOVE AMOUNT-OF-SALE-IN     TO AMOUNT-OF-SALE-WS.
      PERFORM 2100-FIND-ENTRY.
      READ SALES-FILE AT END
          MOVE 'FILE COMPLETE' TO FILE-STATUS.
 *-----------------------------------------------------------*
  2100-FIND-ENTRY SECTION.
 *-----------------------------------------------------------*
      SET LCTN TO 1.
      SEARCH SALESMAN-ENTRY-T
          AT END
              ADD 1 TO SALESMAN-COUNT-WS, ITEMS-TO-BE-SORTED-WS;
              SET LCTN TO SALESMAN-COUNT-WS;
              MOVE SAVE-REORGANIZE-RECORD
                   TO SALESMAN-ENTRY-T (LCTN)
          WHEN ID-INFORMATION-T (LCTN) = ID-INFORMATION
              ADD AMOUNT-OF-SALE-WS TO AMOUNT-OF-SALE-T (LCTN).
 *-----------------------------------------------------------*
  3000-SORT-FOR-REPORT SECTION.
 *-----------------------------------------------------------*
      MOVE 'SORT COMPLETE'      TO SORT-INDICATOR-WS.
      PERFORM 3100-COMPARISON VARYING LCTN FROM 1 BY 1
          UNTIL LCTN IS EQUAL TO ITEMS-TO-BE-SORTED-WS.
      IF SORT-INDICATOR-WS NOT EQUAL TO 'SORT COMPLETE'
              SUBTRACT 1 FROM ITEMS-TO-BE-SORTED-WS.
 *-----------------------------------------------------------*
  3100-COMPARISON SECTION.
 *-----------------------------------------------------------*
      IF SALESMAN-ID-T (LCTN) IS GREATER THAN
        SALESMAN-ID-T (LCTN + 1)
          MOVE SALESMAN-ENTRY-T (LCTN) TO SAVE-REORGANIZE-RECORD
          MOVE SALESMAN-ENTRY-T (LCTN + 1)
                               TO SALESMAN-ENTRY-T (LCTN)
          MOVE SAVE-REORGANIZE-RECORD
                               TO SALESMAN-ENTRY-T (LCTN + 1)
          MOVE 'ITEM SWITCHED' TO SORT-INDICATOR-WS.
 *-----------------------------------------------------------*
  4000-REPORT-1 SECTION.
 *-----------------------------------------------------------*
      MOVE 'by District'        TO TITLE-OUT.
      SET LCTN TO 1.
      WRITE OUTPUT-LINE FROM REPORT-HEADING AFTER PAGE-TOP.
      MOVE AMOUNT-OF-SALE-T (LCTN) TO DISTRICT-TOTAL-WS.
      MOVE DISTRICT-NUMBER-T (LCTN) TO DISTRICT-NUMBER-WS.
```

Figure 14.9 *Continued* Sales Analysis [SEARCH Statement]

```
             1   1   2   2   2   3   3   4   4   4   5   5   6   6   6   7
     4   8   2   6   0   4   8   2   6   0   4   8   2   6   0   4   8   2
2080         PERFORM 4100-GENERATE-REPORT-1 VARYING LCTN FROM 2 BY 1
2090             UNTIL LCTN IS GREATER THAN SALESMAN-COUNT-WS.
2100         PERFORM 4200-REPORT-1-DETAIL.
2110    *-------------------------------------------------------------*
2120     4100-GENERATE-REPORT-1 SECTION.
2130    *-------------------------------------------------------------*
2140         IF DISTRICT-NUMBER-T (LCTN) IS NOT EQUAL TO
2150            DISTRICT-NUMBER-WS
2160             PERFORM 4200-REPORT-1-DETAIL
2170         ELSE
2180             ADD AMOUNT-OF-SALE-T (LCTN) TO DISTRICT-TOTAL-WS.
2190    *-------------------------------------------------------------*
2200     4200-REPORT-1-DETAIL SECTION.
2210    *-------------------------------------------------------------*
2220         MOVE DISTRICT-NUMBER-WS  TO DISTRICT-NUMBER-DD-OUT.
2230         MOVE DISTRICT-TOTAL-WS   TO DISTRICT-TOTAL-DD-OUT.
2240         PERFORM 4250-FIND-STATE-NAME.
2250         MOVE STATE-NAME-WS           TO STATE-NAME-DD-OUT.
2260         WRITE OUTPUT-LINE FROM DISTRICT-DETAIL AFTER 2 LINES.
2270         MOVE DISTRICT-NUMBER-T (LCTN) TO DISTRICT-NUMBER-WS.
2280         MOVE AMOUNT-OF-SALE-T (LCTN) TO DISTRICT-TOTAL-WS.
2290    *-------------------------------------------------------------*
2300     4250-FIND-STATE-NAME SECTION.
2310    *-------------------------------------------------------------*
2320         SET STATE TO 1.
2330         SEARCH ALL STATE-CODE-ENTRIES-T WHEN STATE-CODE-T (STATE) IS
2340           EQUAL TO DISTRICT-NUMBER-WS
2350             MOVE STATE-NAME-T (STATE) TO STATE-NAME-WS.
2360    *-------------------------------------------------------------*
2370     5000-REPORT-2 SECTION.
2380    *-------------------------------------------------------------*
2390         MOVE 'by Salesman Number within District' TO TITLE-OUT.
2400         PERFORM 5100-REPORT.
2410    *-------------------------------------------------------------*
2420     5100-REPORT SECTION.
2430    *-------------------------------------------------------------*
2440         WRITE OUTPUT-LINE FROM REPORT-HEADING AFTER PAGE-TOP.
2450         MOVE 0                   TO DISTRICT-NUMBER-WS.
2460         PERFORM 5150-GENERATE-REPORT VARYING LCTN FROM 1 BY 1
2470             UNTIL LCTN IS GREATER THAN SALESMAN-COUNT-WS.
2480         MOVE SALESMAN-COUNT-WS   TO ITEMS-TO-BE-SORTED-WS.
2490         MOVE 'RESTART'           TO SORT-INDICATOR-WS.
2500    *-------------------------------------------------------------*
2510     5150-GENERATE-REPORT SECTION.
2520    *-------------------------------------------------------------*
2530           IF DISTRICT-NUMBER-T (LCTN) IS NOT EQUAL TO
2540            DISTRICT-NUMBER-WS
2550              MOVE DISTRICT-NUMBER-T (LCTN) TO DISTRICT-NUMBER-WS;
2560              PERFORM 4250-FIND-STATE-NAME;
2570              MOVE STATE-NAME-WS      TO STATE-NAME-SD-OUT;
2580              MOVE DISTRICT-NUMBER-T (LCTN) TO DISTRICT-NUMBER-SD-OUT.
2590         MOVE SALESMAN-NAME-T (LCTN) TO SALESMAN-NAME-SD-OUT.
2600         MOVE AMOUNT-OF-SALE-T (LCTN) TO AMOUNT-OF-SALE-SD-OUT.
2610         MOVE SALESMAN-ID-T (LCTN) TO SALESMAN-NUMBER-SD-OUT.
2620         WRITE OUTPUT-LINE FROM SALESMAN-DETAIL AFTER 2 LINES.
```

loaded with the values in CODE-STATE-LIST with the REDEFINES statement (line 1040). The CODE-STATE-LIST contains a two-digit number (01 through 50, nonconsecutive) in the first two bytes of each value, thus when these values are placed in the STATE-CODE-TABLE, the two-digit numbers are loaded into STATE-CODE-T (line 1080), and the state names fall into STATE-NAME (line 1090). As a result, the STATE-CODE-T values are ascending.

In the PROCEDURE DIVISION, several new variations of the use of indexes and indexed tables are presented. First, the index-names STATE and LCTN are initialized

Figure 14.9 *Continued* Sales Analysis [SEARCH Statement] (Data)

```
------------------------------------------------------------------------------------------
|      |         1         2         3         4         5         6         7         8|
|Record|12345678901234567890123456789012345678901234567890123456789012345678901234567890|
|-----------------------------------------------------------------------------------------
|     1|Anderson            Heather             D        14250     43        0001995     |
|     2|Miller              Herman              T        20200     10        0002999     |
|     3|Johnson             Susan               A        54220     25        0001500     |
|     4|Baker               Willard             V        12770     50        0004966     |
|     5|Bruce               Fayette             S        55500     49        0002245     |
|     6|Griffin             Amy                 D        78980     30        0007599     |
|     7|Tuddle              Jackie              F        69632     36        0008565     |
|     8|Griffin             Amy                 D        78980     30        0002552     |
|     9|Miller              Herman              T        20200     10        0035050     |
|    10|Martin              Diane               C        33358     42        0014995     |
|    11|Martin              Diane               C        33358     42        0004554     |
|    12|Martin              Diane               C        33358     42        0002543     |
|    13|Schwartz            Monica              B        64632     46        0000995     |
|    14|Johnson             Susan               A        54220     25        0002988     |
|    15|Griffin             Amy                 D        78980     30        0004875     |
|    16|Fellman             Robert              R        99604     42        0000774     |
|    17|Anderson            Heather             D        14250     43        0002550     |
|    18|Baker               Willard             V        12770     50        0009595     |
|    19|Whitman             Claudette           E        10100     34        0001995     |
|    20|Bradford            Michael             D        45002     04        0003525     |
|    21|Kline               Tracey              L        42130     01        0003449     |
|    22|Griffin             Amy                 D        78980     30        0002995     |
|    23|Mayes               David               M        22250     15        0019595     |
|    24|Martin              Diane               C        33358     42        0001435     |
|    25|Martin              Diane               C        33358     42        0000950     |
|    26|Tuddle              Jackie              F        69632     36        0000299     |
|    27|Tuddle              Jackie              F        69632     36        0025621     |
|    28|Schwartz            Monica              B        64632     46        0002995     |
|    29|Smith               Mary                A        33320     35        0001525     |
|    30|Smith               Mary                A        33320     35        0025000     |
|    31|Miller              Herman              T        20200     10        0012500     |
|    32|Schwartz            Monica              B        64632     46        0006423     |
|    33|Kline               Tracey              L        42130     01        0002286     |
|    34|Griffin             Amy                 D        78980     30        0025350     |
|    35|Johnson             Susan               A        54220     25        0000999     |
|    36|Baker               Willard             V        12770     50        0025099     |
|    37|Mayes               David               M        22250     15        0002195     |
|    38|Douglas             Richard             J        25600     09        0001139     |
|    39|Whitman             Claudette           E        10100     34        0052796     |
|    40|Mayes               David               M        22250     15        0000965     |
|    41|Tuddle              Jackie              F        69632     36        0007329     |
|    42|Mayes               David               M        22250     15        0000559     |
|    43|Bradford            Michael             D        45002     04        0002589     |
|    44|Bradford            Michael             D        45002     04        0001775     |
|    45|Bradford            Michael             D        45002     04        0019995     |
|    46|Kline               Tracey              L        42130     01        0009995     |
|    47|Fellman             Robert              R        99604     42        0001875     |
|    48|Fellman             Robert              R        99604     42        0039999     |
|    49|Bradford            Michael             D        45002     04        0001295     |
|    50|Kline               Tracey              L        42130     01        0008990     |
|    51|Mayes               David               M        22250     15        0003529     |
------------------------------------------------------------------------------------------
```

Figure 14.9 *Continued* Sales Analysis [SEARCH Statement] (Output)

Salesman Weekly Report by Salesman Number within District

Kline	Tracey	L	42130	1	Alabama	$323.62
Bradford	Michael	D	45002	4	Arkansas	$291.79
Douglas	Richard	J	25600	9	Florida	$611.34
Miller	Herman	T	20200	10	Georgia	$505.49
Mayes	David	M	22250	15	Iowa	$303.71
Johnson	Susan	A	54220	25	Missouri	$134.82
Griffin	Amy	D	78980	30	New Jersey	$459.57
Whitman	Claudette	E	10100	34	North Dakota	$547.91
Smith	Mary	A	33320	35	Ohio	$320.14
Tuddle	Jackie	F	69632	36	Oklahoma	$438.09
Martin	Diane	C	33358	42	Tennessee	$244.77
Fellman	Robert	R	99604	42	Tennessee	$426.48
Anderson	Heather	D	14250	43	Texas	$45.45
Schwartz	Monica	B	64632	46	Virginia	$104.13
Bruce	Fayette	S	55500	49	Wisconsin	$92.14
Baker	Willard	V	12770	50	Wyoming	$396.60

(to the first occurrence position) by a SET statement in line 1560. The FIND-ENTRY module (lines 1700–1810) represents the first use of a SEARCH statement, which is to determine whether or not a particular salesman's record has been previously placed in the table. (A salesman is identified through the SALES-MAN-ID-T and DISTRICT-NUMBER-T fields.) Unlike the Sales Summary Report procedure (Figure 14.4), the Sales Analysis procedure does not assume any particular order for the data in the SALES-FILE. When the SEARCH statement is invoked (via the PERFORM statement at line 1660), LCTN is set to the first occurrence position (to make sure the complete table is searched if necessary). When a table entry containing zeros is found (before finding the sought salesman identification), it is assumed that the salesman's record is not present in the table. Thus, information contained in the salesman's record is *added* to the table. The movement of SAVE-REORGANIZE-RECORD to SALESMAN-ENTRY-T places data in all fields of the SALESMAN-DATA-TABLE at the LCTN position. If, however, a match is found between the identifying fields in the SALES-RECORD and ID-INFORMATION-T (a table group) in the SALESMAN-DATA-TABLE, the AMOUNT-OF-SALE-T is simply added to the existing value of AMOUNT-OF-SALE-T in the table.

After all data have been loaded into the SALESMAN-DATA-TABLE, the data in the table are sorted. In this particular procedure, an *internal* sorting operation is performed.

The sorting procedure selected (and illustrated in the SORT-FOR-REPORT and COMPARISON modules (lines 1820–1990) is generally known as the "bubble" or "triangular-method" sort. The procedure compares the ID-INFORMATION-T field for two *adjacent* occurrence positions; if the value associated with ID-INFORMATION-T of the first item is the larger of the two, the data are interchanged or swapped. (See lines 1940–1980.) This movement of data involves the first use of relative addressing—the use of LCTN + 1 as an address reference. The procedure continues through all positions of the SALESMAN-DATA-TABLE comparing adjacent items and swapping occurrence positions as necessary. This is called "raising the bubble," even though the value is actually sinking like a rock. After one pass through the data, the data-name SORT-INDICATOR-WS is tested, if no items have been swapped, the data have been ordered, and the sort is complete. If, however, even one pair of items has been swapped, the procedure is repeated.

The final use of an indexed table in the procedure is in conjunction with the SEARCH ALL statement in the FIND-STATE-NAME module. The SEARCH ALL statement "looks for" a match between the STATE-CODE-T value in the STATE-CODE-TABLE and the DISTRICT-NUMBER-WS (which was loaded into the SAVE-REORGANIZE-RECORD from DISTRICT-NUMBER-T of the SALESMAN-DATA-TABLE). Once a match is found, the STATE-NAME-T in the corresponding table position is retained to be placed in the output record for printing.

Summary

Although there is little difference in outward appearance between subscripted and indexed tables, the internal means of addressing a particular table position is considerably different. Subscripts are occurrence positions that must be translated into an internal storage address, whereas indexes are references to a byte displacement value from the beginning of the table—much more nearly the value used to address an internal position.

Indexed tables are created through the combination of the OCCURS and INDEXED BY clauses; however, an index is a different type of storage position from a subscript, and therefore, only a selected set of statements is permitted to modify the value of an index. As with a subscripted table, a PERFORM statement is permitted to modify an index. Where MOVE, ADD, and SUBTRACT statements may be used to alter the value of a subscript, a SET statement may be used to alter an index. Two forms of the SEARCH statement are also capable of altering the value of an index.

The SEARCH statement provides the programmer with the means of "automatically" conducting a linear search through an indexed table. In addition, the SEARCH ALL statement may be employed to conduct a binary search operation.

Notes on Programming Style

Even though we have been discussing indexed tables, their treatment in a program is governed by the same set of general rules laid out in the programming style notes in Chapter 13. Most systems scrutinize the value associated with an index more closely than the value of a subscript; however it is still possible to address erroneous data. Of course, the other concerns relating to tables should be examined for indexed tables—reading directly into a table, storing more detail than is necessary, and determining a rationale for the size of tables.

Questions

Below fill in the blank(s) with the appropriate word, words or phrases.

1. When a table reference position is determined, subscripted tables internally utilize _____ , whereas indexed tables utilize _____ .

2. A displacement value for an indexed table is measured in _____ and represents _____ .

3. The clause that distinguishes an indexed from a subscripted table is the _____ clause.

4. Unlike a subscript, a(n) _____ is directly associated with a given level of a given table.

5. A subscripted table must use direct (subscript) addressing, whereas indexed tables are permitted to use both direct and _____ addressing.

6. If ITEM was the name of an indexed table (vector), the reference ITEM (LCTN) is an example of _____ addressing, whereas ITEM (LCTN + 4) is an example of _____ addressing.

7. The only statements permitted to create or modify an index-name are _____ , _____ , and _____ .

8. An index-data-name may be created only through the use of a(n) _____ clause.

9. The identifier referred to in a simple SET statement is generally a(n) _____ .

10. Although the MOVE statement is similar to the simple SET statement, the _____ statement, used in conjunction with indexed tables, is similar to both the ADD and SUBTRACT statements.

11. In the SET UP/DOWN BY statement, the value to be added to/subtracted from an index-name must be a(n) _____ or a(n) _____ .

12. The SEARCH statement may be used only in conjunction with a(n) _____ (subscripted/indexed) table.

13. The SEARCH statement performs a(n) _____ searching process through a table, whereas a SEARCH ALL statement performs a _____ searching operation.

14. The identifier that specifies the table to be examined through a SEARCH statement is the identifier in a table description that _____ .

15. The VARYING option of the SEARCH statement is used to modify _____ .

16. The AT END option of the SEARCH statement is executed when _____ .

17. A SEARCH statement is terminated when _____ or when _____ .

18. A SEARCH ALL statement may be used on an indexed table only if the table description includes a(n) _____ clause.

19. In an ASCENDING/DESCENDING KEY clause, the keys are listed in _____ (increasing/decreasing) order of importance.

20. Before a SEARCH ALL statement is executed on a table, the table must be _____ .

21. The conditions associated with the WHEN phrase of the SEARCH statement may be _____ (condition type(s)), whereas only a _____ (condition type) may be stated in the SEARCH ALL WHEN phrase.

Answer the following questions by circling either "T" for True or "F" for False.

T F **22.** Indexed tables are more efficient than subscripted tables.

T F **23.** An index-name, which appears in an INDEXED BY clause, requires no further reference in the DATA DIVISION.

T F **24.** Both subscripted and indexed tables may be addressed by both direct and relative means.

T F **25.** The statements that might be used to create or modify a subscript may also create or modify an index-name.

T F **26.** An index-name is the same thing as an index-data-name.

T F **27.** An index-name never requires a PICTURE clause.

T F **28.** An index-data-name never requires a PICTURE clause.

T F **29.** An index-data-name, like an index-name, is directly associated with a particular indexed table.

T F **30.** When an index-name is the receiving field of a SET statement, the value in the sending field is always converted to byte displacement mode prior to being placed in the index-name.

T F **31.** When an index-data-name is the receiving field of a SET statement and the sending field is an index-name, conversion never takes place.

T F **32.** When the sending field in a SET statement is a literal, the value is always converted before being placed in the receiving field.

T F **33.** In the simple SET statement, the receiving field must contain a value prior to the execution of the statement.

T F **34.** In the SET UP/DOWN BY statement, the receiving field must contain a value prior to the execution of the statement.

T F **35.** In a SET UP/DOWN BY statement, the value to be added to/subtracted from the index-name is always converted to byte displacement mode prior to the incrementing/decrementing process.

T F **36.** The ASCENDING/DESCENDING KEY clause must be used in the description of an indexed table to permit the use of the SEARCH statement in the PROCEDURE DIVISION.

T F **37.** The VARYING option of the SEARCH statement is used to vary the index-name of the table being searched.

T F **38.** The VARYING option may be used on either the SEARCH or SEARCH ALL statement.

T F **39.** The AT END phrase may be used in both the SEARCH and SEARCH ALL statements.

T F **40.** When an indexed table is accompanied by an ASCENDING/DESCENDING KEY clause, data must be placed in the table in the order specified by the key clause.

T F **41.** Only one key may be specified in an ASCENDING/DESCENDING KEY clause.

Exercises

1. Below are a series of indexed tables. Diagram each table, and jointly indicate occurrence positions and beginning byte displacements of each cell of the tables.

a.
```
01 CODE-TO-RATE-CONVERSION.
   02 RATE OCCURS 8 TIMES
      INDEXED BY CODE        PIC 99V99.
```

b.
```
01 FEDERAL-TAX-TABLE.
   02 TAX-BRACKET OCCURS 7 TIMES
      INDEXED BY INCOME.
      03 LOWER-LIMIT          PIC 9(5)V99.
      03 UPPER-LIMIT          PIC 9(5)V99.
      03 BASE-TAX             PIC 9(4)V99.
      03 PERCENT-TAX          PIC V99.
```

c.
```
01 RATE-PREMIUM-CONVERSION.
   02 PAY-SCALE OCCURS 5 TIMES
      INDEXED BY PAY-CODE.
      03 SHIFT OCCURS 3 TIMES
         INDEXED BY SHIFT-CODE.
         04 ADJUSTMENT        PIC 9V999.
```

2. Given the DATA DIVISION entries below, determine the actual value of the index-name or identifier in each SET statement.

```
WORKING-STORAGE SECTION.
01 WORKING-RECORD.
   05 IND-ALT           USAGE IS INDEX.
   05 LCTN              PIC 999.
01 DATA-TABLE.
   02 DATA-ITEM OCCURS 15 TIMES
      INDEXED BY IND-1
      PIC 999.
01 ITEM-TABLE.
   02 ITEM OCCURS 7 TIMES
      INDEXED BY IND-2
      PIC 9(5).
```

Result.

a. `SET IND-1 TO 3.`

b. `SET IND-2 TO 5.`

c.
```
MOVE 5 TO LCTN.
SET IND-1 TO LCTN.
```

d.
```
SET IND-1 TO 2.
SET IND-ALT TO IND-1.
SET IND-2 TO IND-ALT.
```

e.
```
SET IND-2 TO 4.
SET IND-ALT TO IND-2.
SET IND-2 TO IND-ALT.
```

3. In each of the following situations, write the SEARCH statement (and supporting code) necessary to fulfill the searching situation. Assume the presence of the indicated table below, as appropriate.

```
01 INVENTORY-TABLE.
   02 INVENTORY-ITEM OCCURS 300 TIMES
      INDEXED BY ITEM.
      03 ITEM-NUMBER          PIC 9(5).
      03 VENDOR-CODE          PIC XXX.
      03 UNITS-ON-HAND        PIC 9(5).
      03 PRICE                PIC 9(5)V99.
      03 COST                 PIC 9(5)V99.
      03 MINIMUM-LEVEL        PIC 999.
01 VENDOR-TABLE.
   02 VENDOR-SUPPLIER OCCURS 30 TIMES
      INDEXED BY VEND.
      03 VENDOR-NUMBER        PIC 9(7).
```

```
03 VEND-CODE              PIC XXX.
03 VENDOR-NAME            PIC X(30).
03 TERMS                  PIC 9(4).
```

a. Find the inventory item that carries the number "14728," and print all the values in the table for that item. If it is not found in the table, print an error message.
b. Find and print *all* inventory item numbers where the minimum level is greater than or equal to the units on hand.
c. Find the vendor code "RXT" and print the vendor's name. If that particular vendor is not in the table, add it to the end of the table, move "NEW VENDOR" to the vendor's name, assign the vendor number of the previous last vendor + 1 as the new vendor number, and put zeros in the numeric fields. All unused positions in the vendor table show blank in the vendor code.
d. Find *all* inventory items with a vendor code of "SRV" and print the vendor code, item number, and units on hand.
e. Print *all* items in the inventory table where the investment is greater than $10,000 (e.g., units on hand times the price per unit is greater than $10,000).
f. Print all records in the inventory table vendor code and print the name of each vendor along with the inventory item information.

4. In the following situations write the code necessary to conduct a binary search as indicated. Use the table definitions in exercise 3, and modify them accordingly. You may assume the data are ordered in the table in any order you wish, so long as you state the assumed order. You may also assume you know the number of positions in the table that actually contain data. (This value, if used, may be assumed in a data-name called ACTIVE.)

a. Find the inventory item number "04782" and print the vendor code for that record. If not found, write an error message.
b. Verify that each vendor code that appears in the inventory table coexists in the vendor table. If the code does not exist, write an error message, otherwise do nothing.
c. Determine whether or not the vendor number "147" is associated with vendor code "RCB" in the vendor table.

Problems

14.1 A list of purchase order records have been prepared representing the purchase of individual line items of inventory. Each record (see the multiple-card layout form) contains the inventory item number purchased, the vendor code (which follows), the date of purchase MMDDYY), the purchased quantity, and the total dollar cost to purchase the items. You are to produce a breakdown of these purchase order records by

a. The vendor—such that we may determine the total dollar cost of all items purchased from a single vendor
b. An exceptions list containing all individual inventory items to be purchased, provided the dollar cost of purchasing the item is $10,000 or more. (See the print chart.)

MULTIPLE-CARD LAYOUT FORM

Company LEARNING COBOL, INC.
Application Vendor Summary by J. Wayne Spence Date 01/01/89 Job No. PROB 14.1 Sheet No 1

Item Number	Vendor Code	Date of Sale	Purchased Quantity	Dollar Cost	
1–6	7–9	10–15	16–20	21–30	31–80

150/10/8 PRINT CHART PROG. ID. Vendor Summary P 14.1 PAGE 1
(SPACING: 150 POSITIONS AT 10 CHARACTERS PER INCH, 8 LINES PER VERTICAL INCH) DATE 01/01/89
PROGRAM TITLE Vendor Summary and Exception Listing
PROGRAMMER OR DOCUMENTALIST J. Wayne Spence
CHART TITLE Vendor Summary/Exception List

3525 CARD PRINT POSITIONS

```
                    VENDOR SUMMARY
                                          VENDOR       TOTAL
 VENDOR NAME                               CODE      PURCHASED
 X------------------------------X          XXX    $ZZ,ZZZ,ZZZ.ZZ
 X------------------------------X          XXX    $ZZ,ZZZ,ZZZ.ZZ

 X------------------------------X          XXX    $ZZ,ZZZ,ZZZ.ZZ

                    EXCEPTION LIST
   ITEM    VENDOR    DATE OF    QUANTITY   TOTAL DOLLARS
 NUMBER     CODE    PURCHASE   PURCHASED     PURCHASED
 XXXXXX     XXX     XX-XX-XX     ZZZZ9    $ZZ,ZZZ,ZZZ.ZZ
 XXXXXX     XXX     XX-XX-XX     ZZZZ9    $ZZ,ZZZ,ZZZ.ZZ

 XXXXXX     XXX     XX-XX-XX     ZZZZ9    $ZZ,ZZZ,ZZZ.ZZ
```

When the vendor summary is produced, the vendor code should be accompanied by the vendor's name. The permitted (legal acceptable) vendor codes and names are

Vendor Code	Vendor Name
AMC	Apex Manufacturing Company
ASM	Adams and Sons Manufacturing
BBB	Biltmore Breaker Boxes
CH	Clinton-Hall
ECE	East Coast Electrical Supply
LLF	Lincoln Lighting and Fixtures
NL	Northern Lights
RTC	Reynolds Terminal Connectors
SWI	South Wire Incorporated
WGE	West Gate Electric Company

These names are to be stored in a table (internally, without any data being read) and utilized when the vendor summary is printed.

14.2 You are provided with a set of historical sales records for different products. The historical sales records are composed of a product number, a product name, a date of sale (MMYY), and the sales volume in units for the month (see multiple-card layout form). You will receive the past 12 monthly records (not necessarily a calendar year) in no particular order, as a group. You are to graph the sales performance of each product in the form demonstrated on the print chart.

Note: Since several products are to be displayed in this manner, you should consider (1) scaling the data over the range of sales specified in the monthly records (since there are limited printing positions that may be used to reflect magnitude), (2) the possibility that the origin does not represent zero units sold (thus providing greater dispersion of values on the graph), and (3) the monthly sequence (e.g., July to June) may not be the same for all products (e.g., January to December). The month numbers are to be translated into month names.

MULTIPLE-CARD LAYOUT FORM

Company LEARNING COBOL, INC.

Application SALES PERFORMANCE by JOHN WINDSOR Date 01/01/89 Job No. PROB 14.2 Sheet No. 1

Product		Sales		
Number	Name	Date	Volume (Units)	
1–7	8–36	37–40	41–45	46–80

150/10/8 PRINT CHART PROG. ID. Problem 14.2 PAGE 1
(SPACING: 150 POSITIONS AT 10 CHARACTERS PER INCH, 8 LINES PER VERTICAL INCH) DATE 01/01/89
PROGRAM TITLE SALES PERFORMANCE ANALYSIS
PROGRAMMER OR DOCUMENTALIST: JOHN WINDSOR
CHART TITLE SALES PERFORMANCE (GRAPHIC)

3525 CARD PRINT POSITIONS

```
PRODUCT NUMBER: XXXXXXX   PRODUCT NAME: X-------------------------X      SALES

      MAY 1980                                                           ZZZZ9
     JUNE 1980                                                           ZZZZ9
     JULY 1980                                                           ZZZZ9
   AUGUST 1980                                                           ZZZZ9
SEPTEMBER 1980                                                           ZZZZ9
  OCTOBER 1980                                                           ZZZZ9
 NOVEMBER 1980                                                           ZZZZ9
 DECEMBER 1980                                                           ZZZZ9
  JANUARY 1981                                                           ZZZZ9
 FEBRUARY 1981                                                           ZZZZ9
    MARCH 1981                                                           ZZZZ9
    APRIL 1981                                                           ZZZZ9
          ZZZZ9  ZZZZ9  ZZZZ9  ZZZZ9  ZZZZ9  ZZZZ9  ZZZZ9  ZZZZ9  ZZZZ9  ZZZZ9  ZZZZ9
     PERIOD:  MAY 1980 TO  APRIL 1981  SCALE: ZZZZ9  RANGE: ZZZZ9  MINIMUM: ZZZZ9  MAXIMUM: ZZZZ9
```

14.3 You are to create a limited Bill Of Materials Processing (BOMP) system. A bill of materials is simply a list of all the materials (and their quantities) necessary to create a particular product. For example, if you were going to manufacture a single lawnmower, you would need

Item	Quantity
Mower deck	1
Engine	1
Wheels	4
Mower blade	1
Wheel nut	4
Cotter pin	4
Medium washer	8
Heavy duty bolt	3
Blade safety nut	1
Heavy duty washer	2
Handle assembly	2
Handle grip	2
Throttle assembly	1

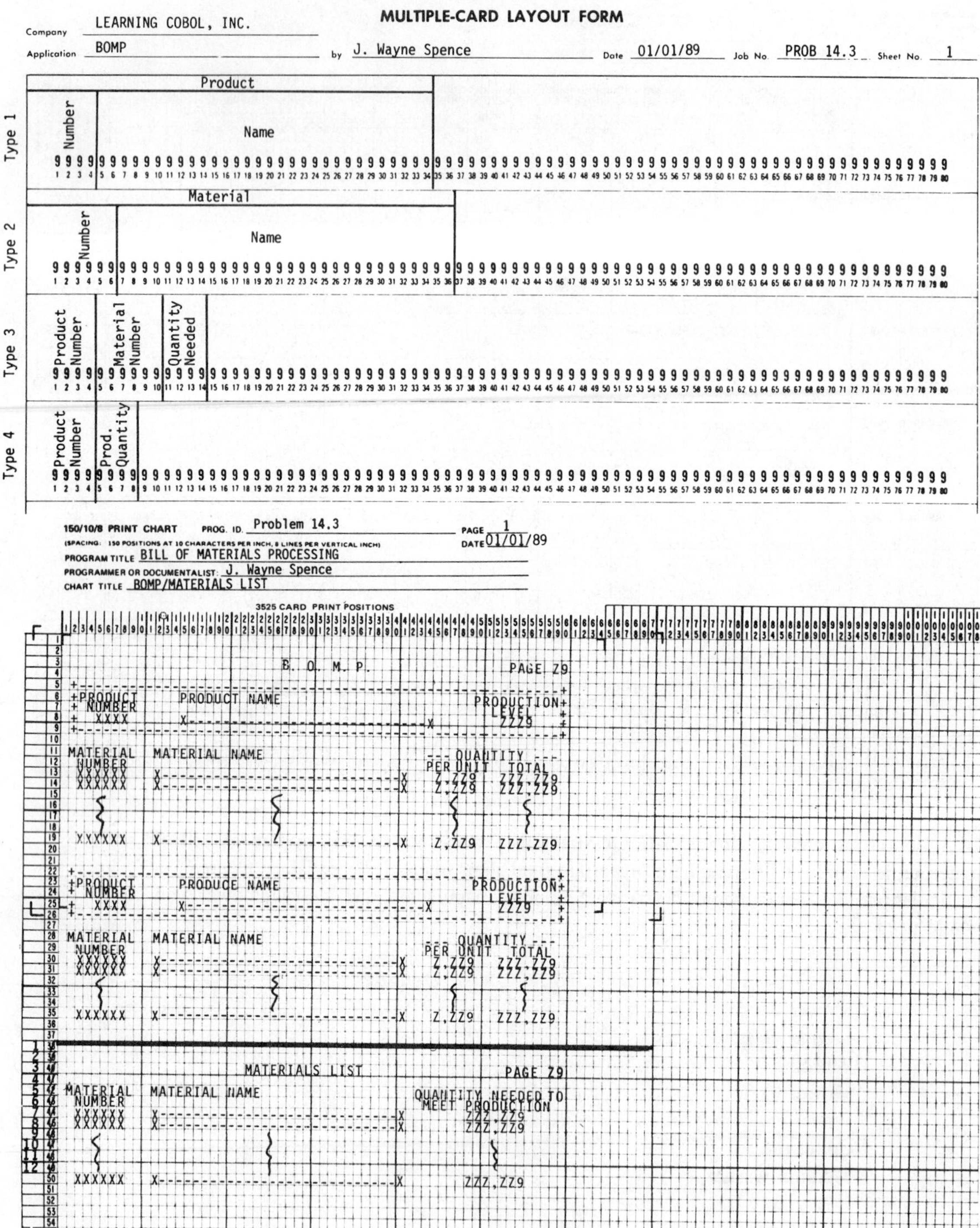
MULTIPLE-CARD LAYOUT FORM

Company: LEARNING COBOL, INC.
Application: BOMP by J. Wayne Spence Date 01/01/89 Job No. PROB 14.3 Sheet No. 1

Type 1: Product — Number (1–4), Name (5–34)
Type 2: Material — Number (1–6), Name (7–36)
Type 3: Product Number (1–4), Material Number (5–10), Quantity Needed (11–14)
Type 4: Product Number (1–4), Prod. Quantity (5–8)

150/10/8 PRINT CHART PROG. ID. Problem 14.3 PAGE 1
(SPACING: 150 POSITIONS AT 10 CHARACTERS PER INCH, 8 LINES PER VERTICAL INCH) DATE 01/01/89
PROGRAM TITLE BILL OF MATERIALS PROCESSING
PROGRAMMER OR DOCUMENTALIST: J. Wayne Spence
CHART TITLE BOMP/MATERIALS LIST

```
                                 B. O. M. P.                  PAGE Z9
+------------------------------------------------------------------+
+PRODUCT     PRODUCT NAME                           PRODUCTION+
+ NUMBER                                               LEVEL   +
+  XXXX     X------------------------------X           ZZZ9   +
+------------------------------------------------------------------+

MATERIAL   MATERIAL NAME                        --- QUANTITY ---
 NUMBER                                         PER UNIT   TOTAL
XXXXXX     X------------------------------X      Z,ZZ9   ZZZ,ZZ9
XXXXXX     X------------------------------X      Z,ZZ9   ZZZ,ZZ9

 XXXXXX    X------------------------------X      Z,ZZ9   ZZZ,ZZ9

+------------------------------------------------------------------+
+PRODUCT     PRODUCE NAME                           PRODUCTION+
+ NUMBER                                               LEVEL   +
+  XXXX     X------------------------------X           ZZZ9   +
+------------------------------------------------------------------+
MATERIAL   MATERIAL NAME                        --- QUANTITY ---
 NUMBER                                         PER UNIT   TOTAL
XXXXXX     X------------------------------X      Z,ZZ9   ZZZ,ZZ9
XXXXXX     X------------------------------X      Z,ZZ9   ZZZ,ZZ9

 XXXXXX    X------------------------------X      Z,ZZ9   ZZZ,ZZ9
```

```
                           MATERIALS LIST                  PAGE Z9

MATERIAL   MATERIAL NAME                     QUANTITY NEEDED TO
 NUMBER                                        MEET PRODUCTION
XXXXXX     X------------------------------X      ZZZ,ZZ9
XXXXXX     X------------------------------X      ZZZ,ZZ9

 XXXXXX    X------------------------------X      ZZZ,ZZ9
```

Presuming this is a complete list of materials necessary to build one basic lawnmower, we should find it a simple task to determine the number of parts necessary to build 500 lawnmowers. As a result, we may easily determine if we have enough parts on hand to build that number of lawnmowers.

Now assume that we also make two different versions of the lawnmower—a basic model and a self-propelled unit. We would not necessarily have a completely different list of materials to make both products. Perhaps the only difference between the two models is a different mower deck type, a wheel driving assembly, and a mechanism to engage the wheel driving assembly. Of course, we could add garden tillers and other related home and garden implements. Soon we would find that certain materials appear in more than one product (e.g., an engine), but not necessarily in the same numbers (e.g., the garden tiller has only two wheels) or perhaps not at all (e.g., the garden tiller blades are hardly interchangeable with lawnmower blades). However, it is possible to determine what materials are necessary to produce 500 basic lawnmowers, 125 self-propelled lawnmowers, and 30 garden tillers.

Now, suppose that we manufacture 20 different product lines and each line will require no more than 10 different materials (i.e., product 1 may require 10 materials, and product 2 may require 10 materials—some of which may be the same as used in product 1). Now examine the multiple-card layout form. To perform the BOMP activities, we will use four record types. The first record type will contain a product number and the product name. After all product number-name records, a blank record will be inserted (as a delimiter). These records are to be read and stored for future reference. The second type of record contains material names and numbers. These names and numbers are also to be stored in a table for later use. These records will also be followed by a blank record. The third record type will contain a single product number, a single material number, and the quantity of the material needed to produce one unit of the product. In other words, several type-3 records (in no particular order) will be necessary to construct a complete bill of materials for an individual product. Of course the same would be true to complete the bill of materials of all other products involved. After all the product number-material number-quantity records, a blank record will appear. Finally, the fourth record type will contain a product number and the quantity to be produced.

Processing requirements call for the determination of the number of units of each material necessary to produce the indicated quantity of the product (see the multiple-card layout form) and a summary list indicating the materials and the amounts that should be on hand to meet the indicated production levels.

PART III

FUNDAMENTAL FILE PROCESSING CONCEPTS

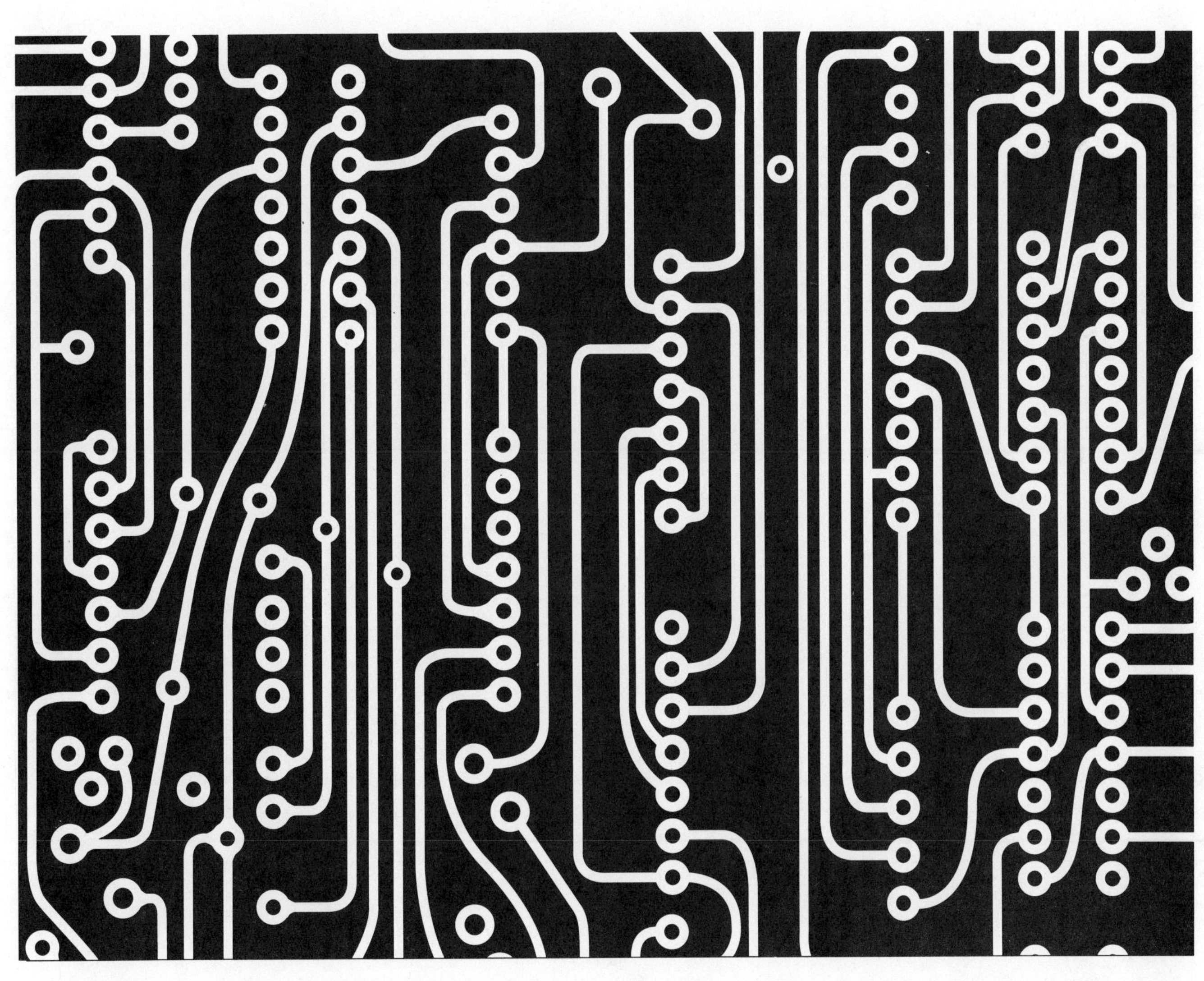

CHAPTER

15

Report Writer

Up to this point, the primary purpose of most programs has been to produce a printed report. The *printed report* is the primary means in most programs to communicate information to the ultimate user. Thus, we as programmers are frequently faced with the task of producing hard-copy to satisfy a particular user need.

As previously noted, printed reports produced by conventional means often require WRITE statements to generate the individual lines of the report, IF statements to determine when control breaks are necessary, IF statements, line counters, and page counters for page break purposes, accumulators for totals, and so on. When all these functions are incorporated into a single program, the logic of that program can become very complex. When other requirements of the program are added to this complexity, a single program can become very complex.

The report writer feature of COBOL is specifically designed to facilitate the easy development of printed reports. As such, the report writer significantly reduces the complexity of PROCEDURE DIVISION programming in support of printed reports.

Report Writer: The Advantages

Since the report writer feature is used to support the programmer in his or her role of providing printed reports, the report writer must present some substantial benefits over the conventional means of producing printed reports. Among these advantages are:

1. Automatic generation of headings
2. Automatic counting of pages and lines per page
3. Automatic movement of data values to output items
4. Easily implemented control breaks (on several levels)
5. Easily implemented summation operations
6. Simple PROCEDURE DIVISION coding
7. Simple placement of printed items (both vertically and horizontally)

Report Writer: The Disadvantages

Although the report writer feature does provide a number of advantages, it also has a number of extremely important disadvantages. The most significant is that the report writer feature is not supported as a standard part of COBOL. However, even though it is not a part of ANS COBOL, its characteristics are relatively consistent in those systems on which it is implemented.

The second major limitation is that the report writer is not universally supported. It is typically available on most larger (mainframe) computers; however, it is generally unavailable on most minicomputers. Furthermore, we know of no microcomputer on which the report writer has been implemented.

Third, the report writer is not particularly efficient. When the report writer is used, the actual machine instructions generated are typically less efficient than those produced by conventional means.

Fourth, utilization of the report writer creates substantial overhead for a program. Although all features of the report writer may not be used on every report generated, they are typically incorporated into the machine instructions generated. Thus, the report writer is frequently referred to as a ''memory hog''—it utilizes a substantial amount of internal storage space.

The fifth limitation is that the report writer feature generates printed reports automatically. This is an advantage in one sense, but it is a disadvantage in another. The report writer automatically produces all elements of a report. If exceptional circumstances exist during the printing of that report, it is sometimes difficult to instruct the report writer to handle them. Much of the control of printing the report is taken away from the programmer. Thus, the report writer may assume that one particular sequence of printed items is required, whereas the actual requirements may be somewhat different. The result is twofold. The report writer is not intended to support all types of printed reports. In fact, you will find that many report formats are much easier to produce by conventional means. In addition, programming around those features the report writer does automatically is sometimes difficult. Finally, interweaving output generated by the report writer and that produced by conventional means is not advisable. Although it is typically possible to use WRITE statements that generate printed output within a program generating output via the report writer, controlling this output so that the desired printed report form is achieved is frequently very difficult.

The Anatomy of a Printed Report

If we were to examine the characteristics of printed reports in general, we would find that many reports have a great deal in common. An examination of Figure 15.1 reveals that a single printed page may contain elements called a page heading, a body, and a page footing. The *page heading* may actually contain several identifiable items, such as the name of the report, the date on which the report was produced, a page number, and column headings that appear above each column of information printed in the body. However, regardless of the characteristics of the information produced at the top of each page, these items would be known collectively as a page heading.

The *body* of the report may also be composed of several identifiable items. In the most simple situation, the body is composed of a series of printed lines reflecting specific data values related to the data (records) being processed. These lines are frequently

Figure 15.1 The Anatomy of a Printed Report

General Appearance	Examples of Report Items	Report Writer Designation
Page Heading	Report date, page number, column heading	PAGE HEADING
Body	Individual data records,	DETAIL
	control break - heading	CONTROL HEADING
	- footing	CONTROL FOOTING
Page Footing	Page totals, page numbers, page references	PAGE FOOTING

referred to as *detail lines,* since they reflect the most detailed (specific) level of data. As the body of a report becomes more complicated, the report may also include control breaks. For example, if we were producing a report containing employee data, we might want some special treatment between sets of employees in different departments. If the data are organized by department, perhaps we might want the name (or number) of the department printed at the beginning of that department's set of records and printed again when the department value changes. This operation is known as a control break that produces an internal heading—a *control heading*. In a similar fashion, perhaps we want to produce summary statistics regarding the employees in each department. This information would typically follow all the employees within that department. Thus, we may wish to print the number of employees within the department, the total of hours worked by individuals within the department, and so on. This operation is known as a control break that produces an internal footing (ending)—a *control footing*.

Finally, a given page may be ''summarized'' in some way. That is, perhaps we wish to place a page number at the bottom of the page. Furthermore, we may want to include other items, such as totals for the page, reference values indicating other characteristics of the data printed on the page, and so on. Thus, these details would appear at the bottom of each page—a *page footing*.

Although not specifically identified in Figure 15.1, two other items may be produced in a printed report. The first is a *report heading,* a printed item produced only once at the beginning of a report. This item may identify the name of the company or some other printed material that needs to be specified, but not on every page. Therefore, a report heading is generated only on the first page of a printed report, whereas a page heading is produced at the top of every page of the report. The second item is a *report footing;* this is produced only once, and only at the end of the report. The most likely candidate for this item is a summary report, or ''recap'', that immediately follows a detailed report. Thus, it is similar to a page footing in that a report footing would appear at the end, but different because it prints only once—not on each page.

Obviously, not all reports contain all these elements. The programmer typically chooses those needed for a particular report format. The point here is that the report writer feature supports each of the seven identifiable elements of a report, summarized as follows.

Report Element	Frequency Per Report
1. Report heading	Once per report, at the beginning
2. Page heading	Multiple per report, one per page
3. Control heading	Multiple per page, possible
4. Detail	Multiple per page
5. Control footing	Multiple per page, possible
6. Page footing	Multiple per report, one per page
7. Report footing	Once per report, at the end

Figure 15.2 illustrates the relationship between the report writer elements and elements of a printed report. Line 1 of the first page of the output contains ''ABC Manufacturing Company.'' Since this line is not repeated on the second page, it is considered to be a report heading. Lines 2–6 appear exactly the same at the top of both pages 1 and 2. Thus, these lines represent a page heading. Lines 7–9 and lines 17–19 on page 1 and lines 7–9 on page 2 are control headings. They are printed when the product group value changes. (Line 7 is placed in the control heading part of the report since there is evidence—line 17 on page 1—that a blank line is produced both before and after the ''Product Group'' heading.) Lines 10–14 and lines 20–24 on page 1 and lines 10–14 on page 2 are detail lines—they contain detail information. Although they are specified by line number on this illustration, there actually may be varying numbers of lines in each group. Lines 15–16 and lines 25–26 on page 1 and lines 15–16 and 20–21 on page 2 are identified as control footings. They are produced at the end of each group. Lines 27–28 on page 1 and lines 22–23 on page 2 represent page footings. Even though these lines are in different positions in the illustration, they would normally appear in consistent line positions on a printed page—much the same as headings normally occupy a fixed position at the top of a page. Finally, the report ends with lines 24–25 of page 2. This item is a report footing since it is the only time it appears in the report.

FILE SECTION Entries

Although the report writer feature has a dramatic impact on the DATA DIVISION as a whole, very little of that impact is noticed in the FILE SECTION. Figure 15.3 illustrates the only report writer related entry in this section. Notice the output FD is very similar to what has been used before, except that the REPORT clause is also included. The file to which the REPORT clause is attached must be consistent with a output-oriented device. That is, the FD must be associated with a printer (ASSIGNed to this file in the ENVIRONMENT DIVISION) or to some other device capable of supporting print-oriented output.

The REPORT clause establishes all the reports which will be generated via this particular file. At least one report-name must be provided, although several reports may be generated through one file. Normally, several reports cannot be produced simultaneously through one file without formatting difficulties.

Figure 15.2 An Example Report Format

```
                                                                          Report Writer
Line                                                                         Element
---------------------------------------------------------------------------------------------
  1|                  ABC Manufacturing Company                         | Report Heading
  2|                   Sales Performance Report                         | Page Heading
  3|                       As of 01/01/85                       Page  1| Page Heading
  4|                                                                    | Page Heading
  5| Item                                       Price     Units     Net  | Page Heading
  6|Number  Product Description                Per Unit    Sold   Proceeds| Page Heading
  7|                                                                    | Control Heading
  8|Product Group: xxxxxx                                               | Control Heading
  9|                                                                    | Control Heading
 10|xxxxxx  xxxxxxxxxxxxxxxxxxxxxxxxxxxxxx  xxxxx.xx  xxxxxx  xxxxxxx.xx| Detail
 11|  .                 .                      .        .         .    | Detail
 12|  .                 .                      .        .         .    | Detail
 13|  .                 .                      .        .         .    | Detail
 14|xxxxxx  xxxxxxxxxxxxxxxxxxxxxxxxxxxxxx  xxxxx.xx  xxxxxx  xxxxxxx.xx| Detail
 15|                                                                    | Control Footing
 16|                                      Total Net Proceeds xxxxxxx.xx| Control Footing
 17|                                                                    | Control Heading
 18|Product Group: xxxxxx                                               | Control Heading
 19|                                                                    | Control Heading
 20|xxxxxx  xxxxxxxxxxxxxxxxxxxxxxxxxxxxxx  xxxxx.xx  xxxxxx  xxxxxxx.xx| Detail
 21|  .                 .                      .        .         .    | Detail
 22|  .                 .                      .        .         .    | Detail
 23|  .                 .                      .        .         .    | Detail
 24|xxxxxx  xxxxxxxxxxxxxxxxxxxxxxxxxxxxxx  xxxxx.xx  xxxxxx  xxxxxxx.xx| Detail
 25|                                                                    | Control Footing
 26|                                      Total Net Proceeds xxxxxxx.xx| Control Footing
 27|                                                                    | Page Footing
 28|Product Groups: xxxxxx to xxxxxx                                    | Page Footing
---------------------------------------------------------------------------------------------
  1|                                                                    | blank
  2|                   Sales Performance Report                         | Page Heading
  3|                       As of 01/01/85                       Page  2| Page Heading
  4|                                                                    | Page Heading
  5| Item                                       Price     Units     Net  | Page Heading
  6|Number  Product Description                Per Unit    Sold   Proceeds| Page Heading
  7|                                                                    | Control Heading
  8|Product Group: xxxxxx                                               | Control Heading
  9|                                                                    | Control Heading
 10|xxxxxx  xxxxxxxxxxxxxxxxxxxxxxxxxxxxxx  xxxxx.xx  xxxxxx  xxxxxxx.xx| Detail
 11|  .                 .                      .        .         .    | Detail
 12|  .                 .                      .        .         .    | Detail
 13|  .                 .                      .        .         .    | Detail
 14|xxxxxx  xxxxxxxxxxxxxxxxxxxxxxxxxxxxxx  xxxxx.xx  xxxxxx  xxxxxxx.xx| Detail
 15|                                                                    | Control Footing
 16|                                      Total Net Proceeds xxxxxxx.xx| Control Footing
 17|  .                 .                      .        .         .    | repetition
 18|  .                 .                      .        .         .    | repetition
 19|  .                 .                      .        .         .    | repetition
 20|                                                                    | Control Footing
 21|                                      Total Net Proceeds xxxxxxx.xx| Control Footing
 22|                                                                    | Page Footing
 23|Product Groups: xxxxxx to xxxxxx                                    | Page Footing
 24|                                                                    | Report Footing
 25|                                             Grand Total xxxxxxx.xx| Report Footing
---------------------------------------------------------------------------------------------
```

Figure 15.3 Format of the FILE SECTION Entries

```
DATA DIVISION.
FILE SECTION.
FD print-file-name

        { RECORD IS    }
  LABEL {              } OMITTED
        { RECORDS ARE  }

[{ REPORT IS   }
 {             }  report-name-1 [,report-name-2] . . . ]
 { REPORTS ARE }
[01 record-description-entries.]
```

One final comment concerning the FD entry for the report writer: notice that the record description is optional. The report writer will automatically generate an output record description based on information provided elsewhere in the DATA DIVISION. However, you are permitted to provide your own record description, if you wish. One word of caution is worth mentioning. While the report writer automatically keeps track of lines of output it produces, lines produced via WRITE statements (using the record name associated with the report FD) are not counted. They are the programmer's responsibility.

The REPORT SECTION

The REPORT SECTION holds the majority of the entries related to the report writer. The REPORT SECTION is a part of the DATA DIVISION and should appear after the WORKING-STORAGE SECTION. The structure of the REPORT SECTION is similar to that of the FILE SECTION. That is, although the FILE SECTION is divided into one or more FD (file description) entries, the REPORT SECTION is divided into one or more RD (report description) entries, as illustrated in Figure 15.4. Note that the report-names specified in the REPORTS ARE clause in the FILE SECTION must be associated with an RD in the REPORT SECTION.

Figure 15.4 General Form of the REPORT SECTION

```
[REPORT SECTION.
  RD report-name-1
     report description entries.
  [RD report-name-2
     report description entries... ]]
```

Describing the General Appearance of a Printed Page

In the FILE SECTION, each FD entry may be supported by a number of additional clauses (e.g., the LABEL RECORDS clause) which provide more general information about a file. Likewise, each RD used to describe the format of a report may be supported by a series of additional clauses, as shown in Figure 15.5. As illustrated, the RD must begin with a report-name. This is one of only two data-names required in the entire report format—including the record descriptions that follow. The second data-name is associated with the detail-line record description, which is described later.

Following the report-name, a series of entries is provided that helps the programmer logically "draw" the overall format of a printed page to be produced by the report writer. Of these clauses, only the PAGE LIMIT clause is required. PAGE LIMIT establishes the length, or number of lines, on a printed page. Integer-1 specifies the number of lines per page and must be a positive integer value.

Another important element of the report writer is connected to the PAGE LIMIT clause. When the report writer is used, it automatically creates a *special register* called LINE-COUNTER. As lines of output are produced by the report writer, LINE-COUNTER is automatically incremented to reflect those lines of output. Finally, when the value of LINE-COUNTER reaches the value of the integer number associated with PAGE LIMIT, a page eject is automatically generated. Thus, when LINE-COUNTER is equal to PAGE LIMIT, a new page is started. However, only lines generated by the report writer cause LINE-COUNTER to be incremented.

Another special register associated with this process is PAGE-COUNTER. Whereas LINE-COUNTER keeps track of the number of lines per page, PAGE-COUNTER keeps track of the page number. It is automatically initialized to 1 and incremented by 1 each time a page break occurs. Even though these are special registers, they may be addressed in both the REPORT SECTION of the DATA DIVISION and the PROCEDURE DIVISION. Their implied description is equivalent to a data item with a PICTURE clause of a five-digit integer in packed decimal (COMP-3) form. (See Chapter 23 for more

Figure 15.5 General Form of an RD Entry

```
RD  report-name

         ┌ LIMIT IS  ┐             ┌ LINE  ┐
    PAGE │           │  integer-1  │       │
         └ LIMITS ARE┘             └ LINES ┘

    [HEADING integer-2]

    [FIRST DETAIL integer-3]

    [LAST DETAIL integer-4]

    [FOOTING integer-5]

 ┌ ┌ CONTROL IS   ┐ ┌ FINAL                                          ┐ ┐
 │ │              │ │ identifier-1 [, identifier-2] . . .            │ │
 └ └ CONTROLS ARE ┘ └ FINAL, identifier-1 [, identifier-2] . . .     ┘ ┘
```

details concerning packed decimal representation.) Remember, both LINE-COUNTER and PAGE-COUNTER are special registers, and as such, are reserved words. Any attempt to define them in the DATA DIVISION will result in a compiler error.

The remaining clauses are optional. However, the next four clauses (HEADING, FIRST DETAIL, LAST DETAIL, and FOOTING) may be used to establish bands of line numbers within which certain elements of the report must be produced. The integers associated with each must be positive integer values, limited in some cases by the values assigned to one of the other clauses. In no case can the value of any of these integers be greater than the value of PAGE LIMIT. The relationship between these integer values is best represented by the illustration in Figure 15.6. Note that integer-1 (PAGE LIMIT) establishes the overall length of a printed page. Integer-2 (HEADING) establishes the location for the beginning of each page. Thus, no printed output may be produced before integer-2. The lines between integer-2 and integer-1 may be used for either a report heading or a report footing, if specified. Integer-3 (FIRST DETAIL) identifies the beginning location of the first detail line. Furthermore, it indicates where a page heading must end. If a page heading is used, it must be completed before integer-3. Integer-4 (LAST DETAIL) specifies the last line on a page that may contain a detail line. Thus, the lines between and including integer-3 and integer-4 may be used for detail lines and control headings, if cited. Integer-5 (FOOTING) specifies the line number at which a page footing may begin. Control footings are bounded by integer-3 and integer-5. Therefore, a control footing may be printed in an area that lies between integer-4 and integer-5. A page footing, if present, must be produced between the line numbers represented by integer-5 and integer-1.

Because of the relationship between these integer values, the programmer must adhere to certain limitations. For example, none of the other integer values may be greater than integer-

Figure 15.6 Relationship Between Integer Values in the RD Entry

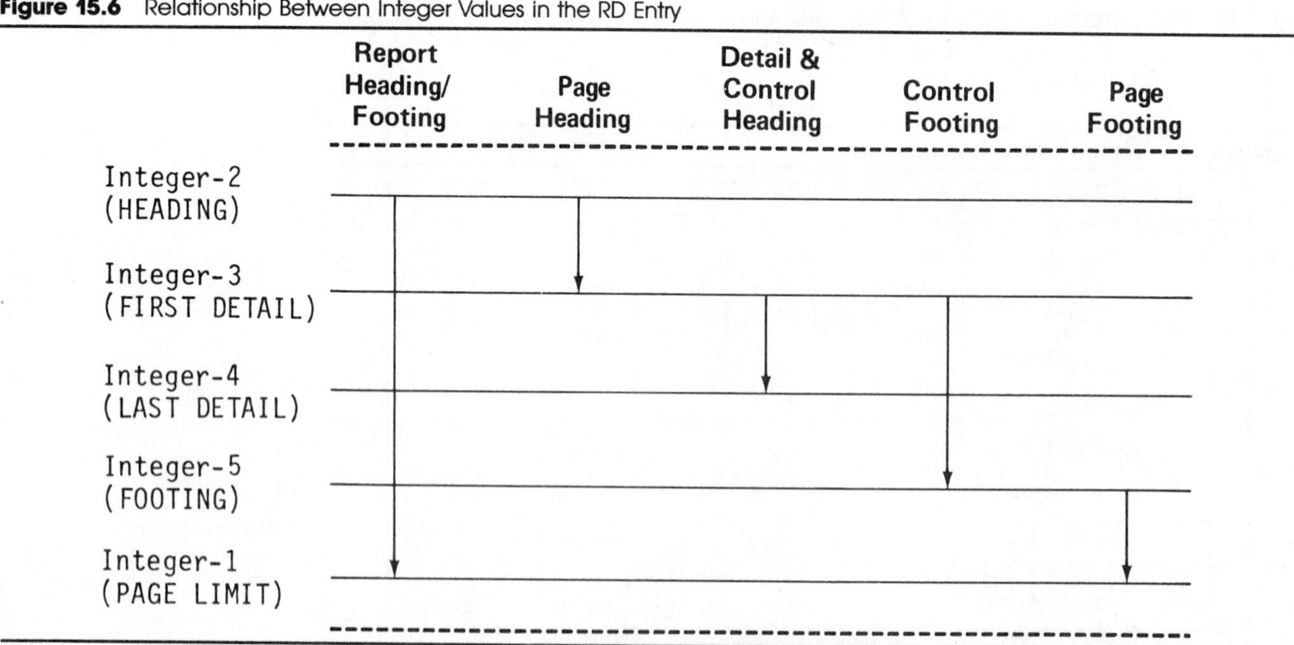

Figure 15.7 An Example of an RD Entry

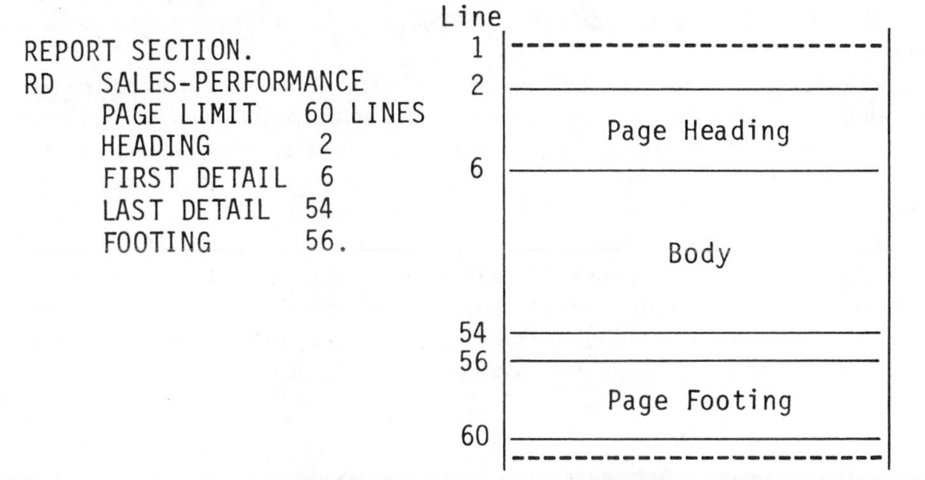

1. Integer-4 must be greater than integer-3, integer-5 must be greater than integer-4, and so on.

Perhaps an illustration of the relationship between these items would be helpful. Examine Figure 15.7. In the illustration, the REPORT SECTION begins with a description of the page characteristics of a report called SALES-PERFORMANCE. The length of a printed page is 60 lines (even though the physical number of lines on a typical page is 66). The first printable line is on line 2, one line below the perforation between pages. Page headings may begin on this line and continue through line 5. Beginning on line 6, detail lines may be produced and continue through line 54. (Control headings are bounded by the same line numbers. Control footings may continue to line 56.) Beginning at line 56, page footings may begin, so long as they are completed by line 60.

So much for when all entries are included. What about the situation in which some of the options are eliminated? For example, if the FOOTING clause were eliminated, a totally blank area would exist between lines 56 and 60, except for that used by control footings. If both the FOOTING and LAST DETAIL clauses were omitted, detail lines could be printed down to line 60. If the HEADING clause is left out, printing may begin on line 1. If the FIRST DETAIL clause is omitted, the first detail line could be printed on the first available line after the page heading, provided a page heading is specified. Thus, depending on the characteristics of the report to be printed, you are permitted to pick and choose those clauses that help support the design of the report.

The CONTROL clause, shown in Figure 15.5, is used in conjunction with control headings and footings. The description of its use is addressed in conjunction with the discussion of control headings and control footings later in the chapter.

Record Definitions within the REPORT SECTION

As is the case in other sections within the DATA DIVISION, the fundamental structure of the REPORT SECTION is based on record descriptions. Records within the REPORT

SECTION, as in other sections, may be composed of groups and elementary-items. However, as illustrated in Figure 15.8, record, group, and elementary-item descriptions may be somewhat more complex in the REPORT SECTION than is typical of the other sections.

Carefully observe the characteristics of each element of a report writer record description. Note that, as with other records, each entry begins with a level number. However, although a data-name (record-name, group-name, or elementary-item-name) normally follows the level number in a typical record description, data-names are optional within the report writer records. At the record level, once the level number and optional record-name have been supplied, the only required clause is the TYPE clause. As illustrated in Figure 15.9, the TYPE clause identifies each record within a report as a particular element within the report format. Note that each record type may be spelled out (e.g., REPORT HEADING), or may be represented by the appropriate abbreviation (e.g., RH). More details about each record type will be discussed later.

The LINE Clause

The next clause, the LINE clause, may appear at any level within a REPORT SECTION record description. It is used to control vertical line spacing *before* a line of output is produced. Thus, it causes line spacing that is similar to that achieved by a WRITE statement with an AFTER ADVANCING option. The format of this clause is presented in Figure 15.10. The LINE clause is used in conjunction with RD clauses (e.g., HEADING, FIRST DETAIL, etc.) to establish the appropriate vertical position for a particular line of output. It is required for all output lines. For each element of a record description that produces a physically separate line of output, a LINE clause must be specified. This also means that a single record description could represent several lines of output. For example, page headings typically occupy more than one line of output. With the assistance of the LINE clause, all print lines of the heading would be within one record description. This usually means that the LINE clause would be at either the group or elementary-item level. If a series of elementary-items is used to represent a line of output and the LINE clause does not appear at either the record or group level, the LINE clause must be associated with the first element of the set of elementary-items. All elementary-items that are either directly associated with a LINE clause or appear before the next LINE clause are assumed to be on the same line of output.

When the ''LINE NUMBER IS integer-1'' clause is used, integer-1 must be a positive integer value, and specify an absolute line number on the page. If the clause LINE NUMBER IS 6 was used in a record description, that element would always be printed on line 6 of the printout. Such fixed-line numbers are frequently used in report elements such as page headings and page footings. Thus, absolute line numbers are used when you want the output to appear in a fixed position on a printed page. However, you should be aware of any previous limitations you have placed on elements, such as page headings, in the RD description. Absolute line numbers should be consistent with what has been previously specified.

When the ''LINE NUMBER IS PLUS integer-2'' clause is used, integer-2 must be a positive integer value, and it specifies a line position relative to previously printed output. If the clause LINE NUMBER PLUS 2 was used, that element would appear two lines below any previously printed output in that area of the report. Relative line numbers are frequently employed for detail-line descriptions (and control headings and

Figure 15.8 General Format for Records in the REPORT SECTION

```
Record Definitions:
------------------------------------------------------------
01 [record-name]
     TYPE clause
     [LINE clause]
     [NEXT GROUP clause]
     [USAGE clause]
------------------------------------------------------------
Group Definitions:
------------------------------------------------------------
     level-number [group-name]
          [LINE clause]
          [USAGE clause]
------------------------------------------------------------
Elementary-item Definitions:
------------------------------------------------------------
     level-number [data-name]
          [LINE clause]
          [COLUMN clause]
           PICTURE clause
          { SOURCE }
          { SUM    }  clause
          { VALUE  }
          [RESET clause]
          [GROUP clause]
          [USAGE clause]
          [BLANK WHEN ZERO clause]
          [JUSTIFIED clause]
```

Figure 15.9 The TYPE Clause

```
           { {REPORT HEADING}                                  }
           { {RH            }                                  }
           { {PAGE HEADING}                                    }
           { {PH          }                                    }
           { {CONTROL HEADING}    {identifier-n}               }
           { {CH             }    {FINAL       }               }
TYPE IS    { {DETAIL}                                          }
           { {DE    }                                          }
           { {CONTROL FOOTING}    {identifier-n}               }
           { {CF             }    {FINAL       }               }
           { {PAGE FOOTING}                                    }
           { {PF          }                                    }
           { {REPORT FOOTING}                                  }
           { {RF            }                                  }
```

Figure 15.10 The LINE Clause

```
                       ⎧ integer-1      ⎫
LINE NUMBER IS         ⎨ PLUS integer-2 ⎬
                       ⎩ NEXT PAGE      ⎭
```

footings) because their placement on the page depends on whether they follow other detail lines on that same page. If the report item is the first to be produced in a group, the relative line number is ignored. For example, suppose a detail-line description contains the clause LINE PLUS 2. If the clause FIRST DETAIL 10 is specified in the RD and this is the first detail line on the page, it will be printed on line 10. All subsequent detail lines on that page would be double-spaced from any previously printed line. Finally, within a record description consisting of several lines of output, a relative line reference may not be followed by an absolute line reference.

When the "LINE NUMBER IS NEXT PAGE" clause is specified, the report item will not be printed until after a page eject has occurred. Thus, if you wish to stop printing on the current page and continue printing on the next page, you may do so by specifying LINE NEXT PAGE. For example, suppose you wanted to print a control heading (maybe a subtitle) for a group of detail lines and do not need other information (with the possible exception of a page heading) preceding it on the same page. This can be accomplished by simply indicating LINE NEXT PAGE with the control heading record description.

The LINE clause also has an influence on the special register LINE-COUNTER. When the "LINE NUMBER IS integer-1" clause is used, LINE-COUNTER is initialized to integer-1. When the "LINE NUMBER IS PLUS integer-2" clause is used, LINE-COUNTER is incremented by integer-2. When the "LINE NUMBER IS NEXT PAGE" clause is used, LINE-COUNTER is set to the maximum value for that report item. That is, if LINE NEXT PAGE is used with a control footing, LINE-COUNTER would be set either to the value of FOOTING or to PAGE LIMIT, in the absence of FOOTING.

The NEXT GROUP Clause

The NEXT GROUP clause may be specified only at the record level. Its function is similar to the LINE clause, except that it controls the vertical location of items printed *after* the completion of the current report-item. Thus, if you wanted to make sure that a particular line spacing follows the current report item, the NEXT GROUP clause may be used to achieve this objective (see Figure 15.11).

Figure 15.11 The NEXT GROUP Clause

```
                       ⎧ integer-1      ⎫
NEXT GROUP IS          ⎨ PLUS integer-2 ⎬
                       ⎩ NEXT PAGE      ⎭
```

Other than the before-versus-after difference, the LINE clause and NEXT GROUP clause function in the same way. For example, if you were working on a page heading that could be followed by a control heading and wanted to make sure the control heading did not begin before line 10, you could specify NEXT GROUP 10 in the page heading description. To make certain the next report item following a control footing was three lines below it, you could specify NEXT GROUP PLUS 3. To ensure a particular control footing (maybe a subtotal) was the last item on a page, you could specify NEXT GROUP NEXT PAGE.

The NEXT GROUP clause also has the same type of impact on the LINE-COUNTER special register as the LINE clause does.

The COLUMN Clause

The COLUMN clause, as the name implies, is used to indicate the horizontal position of a report item on a print line. The general form of this clause is given in Figure 15.12. The column position is specified by integer-1, which must be a positive integer value. Furthermore, the value of integer-1 should not exceed the length of a printable line (generally 133 characters). The position indicated by integer-1 is the leftmost column of an elementary-item field, based on its PICTURE clause.

The COLUMN clause may be used only in conjunction with an elementary-item. The COLUMN clauses associated with a series of elementary-items to be printed on the same line should be organized on a left-to-right basis. That is, within that group of elementary-items, the values of integer-1 must be in ascending order. Finally, if an elementary-item is not accompanied by a COLUMN clause, although all other elements of the elementary-item description are in place, the item will not appear on the printout. In other words, if the COLUMN clause is omitted, the printing of that elementary-item is suppressed.

The SOURCE, VALUE, and SUM Clauses

Although the PICTURE clause is the next clause in sequence for an elementary-item in Figure 15.8, the PICTURE strings associated with the reporter writer elementary-items are fundamentally no different from those that may be associated within any typical print-oriented field. More important, how are data values placed into these fields? This operation is accomplished by the use of the SOURCE, VALUE, and SUM clauses.

The form of the SOURCE clause, as shown in Figure 15.13, is very simple. Effectively, the SOURCE clause acts as a MOVE statement. The identifier specified in the SOURCE clause is moved into the field associated with it. This operation is performed at the point during the production of the report when the report element is to be printed. Thus, only the most current value of identifier-1 is moved into the PICTURE field. Since the operation is equivalent to a MOVE statement, all the rules that apply to the MOVE statement apply. For example, if the PICTURE string of a report element is

Figure 15.12 The COLUMN Clause

```
COLUMN NUMBER IS integer-1
```

Figure 15.13 The SOURCE, SUM, and VALUE Clauses

```
SOURCE IS identifier-1
-------------------------------------------------------------
VALUE IS literal-1
-------------------------------------------------------------
SUM identifier-2 [, identifier-3] . . . [UPON data-name]
```

numeric, you are not permitted to use as its SOURCE an alphanumeric data item that would normally contain alphanumeric data. (If you are unfamiliar with the rules governing the movement of data between sending field and receiving field, you should review the discussion of PICTURE strings and MOVE statements, found in Chapters 6 and 8.)

The simplest means of placing a data value into a PICTURE string is by means of the VALUE clause. The VALUE clause, as used in the REPORT SECTION, has the same characteristics as does the VALUE clause used in the WORKING-STORAGE SECTION. Thus, numeric literals, nonnumeric literals, and figurative constants may be used with the VALUE clause. (For more information on the use of the VALUE clause, see Chapter 6.) As is usually the case with printed reports, the VALUE clause is predominantly used to provide the text for report elements such as page headings and column headings. This use of the VALUE clause is the same within the report writer.

The SUM clause is another means by which a data value may be placed into a PICTURE string. The SUM clause causes automatic accumulation (summation) of a numeric data item. As indicated in Figure 15.13, the accumulation operation may involve one or more identifiers. In any case, these identifiers must be explicitly defined as nonedited numeric elementary-items if they are defined outside the REPORT SECTION. The elementary-items must be either implicitly or explicitly defined as nonedited numeric elementary-items if they appear within the REPORT SECTION. In addition, the PICTURE clause with which the SUM clause is associated can be a numeric edited field. Thus, within the REPORT SECTION, a SUM clause identifier may appear to have an edited numeric appearance. For the purposes of the SUM operation, the report writer automatically generates a nonedited numeric holding field in which the actual accumulation is performed. This holding field will have the same characteristics as the PICTURE string with which the SUM clause is associated. For example, if the PICTURE string is $$$,$$$.$$ the holding field would be equivalent to 9(05)V99.

The SUM clause is permitted *only in a control footing* record description. The actual accumulation activity is performed when the SUM identifier(s) is presented for printing. Thus, if you wished to sum the value of an identifier that appeared in a particular detail-line definition, the summation activity would occur immediately upon the printing of that identifier. Furthermore, the report writer permits the programmer to perform summation on any numeric elementary-item that may be referenced by a data-name (including the results of other SUM clauses.) The UPON clause is used for selective summation of the indicated identifier(s). Thus, if identifier-2 (and so on) appears in more than one detail-line definition, the UPON clause may be used to indicate which detail line (by its data-name) should be used for purposes of accumulation.

Figure 15.14 The RESET Clause

```
            { identifier-1 }
RESET ON    {              }
            { FINAL        }
```

The RESET Clause

The RESET clause, as shown in Figure 15.14, is sometimes used in conjunction with the SUM clause to specify the frequency at which the accumulation process is reinitialized to zero. Normally, the value of the accumulator is reset to zero when the value of that accumulator is printed. That is, as soon as the control footing containing the SUM clause is printed, the summation field is reset to zero. If the RESET clause is used, the reinitialization process depends on the change in the specified data-name. Thus, the accumulator is reset to zero when the value of the data-name changes. This may be more or less frequently than when the SUM value is printed.

For example, suppose the Sales Performance Report required both a total of particular product groups *and* a total across groups that had the same group prefix. This would require two SUM clauses—one for the product group and one for the group prefix. Both totals would usually be printed when the product group changes (for a CONTROL FOOTING) and both accumulation fields would be reset to zero. However, if we were to indicate that the summation activity for group prefixes should be RESET only when the group prefix changes, this accumulator would be reset only when that identifier changes. In this example, we might presume that the prefix change is less frequent than changes in product group values. The summation of sales controlled by a RESET on the group prefix would be a larger value upon the second, third, and subsequent printing of the total for that group of items than the values associated with the product group only. Thus, a summation activity controlled by product groups might represent a first-level subtotal and that controlled by a RESET on group prefix values might be a second-level subtotal.

If FINAL is specified for a RESET clause, the accumulator is not reset to zero until the complete report has been produced; a SUM clause associated with a RESET ON FINAL clause may be used to create a grand total.

The GROUP INDICATE Clause

The GROUP INDICATE clause, shown in Figure 15.15, is used to suppress the printing of what would otherwise be redundant output. If used, it must appear in conjunction with an elementary-item within a detail-line description. For example, if you were dealing

Figure 15.15 The GROUP INDICATE Clause

```
GROUP INDICATE
```

with a set of records representing sales data, and the sales data were grouped according to a salesman's name or identification number, consecutive lines of a printed report representing these records would contain the same name or identification number. However, if the GROUP INDICATE clause is attached to this field, the value of the name or number would be printed only on the first line of output. It would, thereafter, be suppressed until the value of the field changes or the consecutive set of print lines is interrupted by a control break or page break. When interrupted, the next detail line produced would contain the value of the name or number, and thereafter would be suppressed again.

Other Clauses

The remaining clauses that are listed in Figure 15.8 (USAGE, BLANK WHEN ZERO, and JUSTIFIED) are generally elsewhere within the DATA DIVISION (e.g., in the WORKING-STORAGE SECTION). A description of these clauses may be found in Chapter 23.

Creation of Report Writer Record Types

Before we begin an examination of each of the record types that may be created with the report writer, perhaps a summary of the clauses presented thus far and the limitations on their use would be helpful. As shown in Table 15.1, not all clauses may be used with all record types, and some clauses are limited by the record type. For example, special attention should be given to the LINE and NEXT GROUP clauses because only limited forms of these clauses may be used in all record types. The COLUMN, PICTURE, SOURCE, and VALUE clauses may be used with all record types, the SUM

Table 15.1 Record Description Clauses and Limitations by Record TYPE

	Record TYPE						
Clause	**REPORT HEADING RH**	**PAGE HEADING PH**	**CONTROL HEADING CH**	**DETAIL DE**	**CONTROL FOOTING CF**	**PAGE FOOTING PF**	**REPORT FOOTING RF**
LINE integer	X	X	X*	X*	X*	X	X
LINE PLUS integer	X	X	X	X	X	X	X
LINE NEXT PAGE	—	—	X*	X*	X*	X*	X
NEXT GROUP integer	X	—	X*	X*	X*	—	—
NEXT GROUP PLUS integer	X	—	X	X	X	—	—
NEXT GROUP NEXT PAGE	X	—	X*	X*	X*	—	—
COLUMN integer	X	X	X	X	X	X	X
PICTURE string	X	X	X	X	X	X	X
SOURCE identifier	X	X	X	X	X	X	X
SUM identifier	—	—	—	—	X	—	—
VALUE identifier	X	X	X	X	X	X	X
RESET indentifier	—	—	—	—	X	—	—
GROUP INDICATE	—	—	—	X	—	—	—

*Only certain elements of the clause may be used or the clause may be used only when multiple records of this type are present.

and RESET clauses, with control footings, and the GROUP INDICATE clause, in a detail-line description.

Many of the following examples, based on the example report layout presented in Figure 15.2, may assist you to understand more completely the relationships between a report layout and the record descriptions with the REPORT SECTION.

The REPORT HEADING (RH) Record Type

The REPORT HEADING record type is primarily used to provide a report title, such as a company name or other descriptive information, that is not required on each page of the report. You are permitted only one such record type within a single RD. To illustrate the structure of the REPORT HEADING record type, suppose the following code was placed in the REPORT SECTION.

```
01  TYPE IS REPORT HEADING.
    05  LINE NUMBER IS 1.
        10 COLUMN 54         PIC X (25) VALUE
                             'ABC Manufacturing Company'.
```

As soon as the report is initiated, the literal 'ABC Manufacturing Company' would be printed such that it appears approximately in the middle of a 133-character print line. As a slightly more elaborate example, suppose you choose to provide code in the REPORT SECTION, such as

```
01  TYPE RH NEXT GROUP NEXT PAGE.
    05  LINE 3.
        10  COLUMN 100       PIC X(04) VALUE 'Page'.
        10  COLUMN 105       PIC Z(03) SOURCE PAGE-COUNTER.
    05  LINE 30.
        10  COLUMN 54        PIC X(25) VALUE
                             'ABC Manufacturing Company'.
    05  LINE PLUS 2.
        10  COLUMN 59        PIC X(24) VALUE
                             'Sales Performance Report'.
    05  LINE PLUS 2.
        10  COLUMN 59        PIC X(05) VALUE
                             'As of'.
        10  COLUMN 65        PIC X(08) SOURCE CURRENT-DATE.
```

Although this description is also a REPORT HEADING (RH), it is more detailed than the previous example. First, by virtue of the NEXT GROUP clause, the report heading will be the only information to appear on the first page of the report. All information that follows is forced to begin on the NEXT (second) PAGE. On the right end of the third line of the first page, the text "Page 1" will be printed. Notice that both a VALUE and a SOURCE clause are used and the special register PAGE-COUNTER is identified as the SOURCE of the page number. Then, beginning on line 30 and double-spaced thereafter, the text

```
ABC Manufacturing Company
 Sales Performance Report
      As of 01/01/85
```

will be printed. These lines are both centered on a left-to-right basis (assuming a 133-character line) and from top to bottom (assuming a 66-line page). Again, both VALUE and SOURCE clauses are used, and, in the case of the SOURCE clause, the special register CURRENT-DATE (available on IBM computers) is used to provide the report date.

The PAGE HEADING (PH) Record Type

The PAGE HEADING record type is a report item that will appear at the top of each page of output. Like the REPORT HEADING, only one record type of PAGE HEADING is allowed per RD. Its primary use is to provide title information, such as the report-name, report date, page numbers, and column headings. To illustrate the structure of the PAGE HEADING record type, suppose the following code was placed in the REPORT SECTION.

```
01  TYPE PH.
    05  LINE 2.
        10  COLUMN 55          PIC X(24) VALUE
                               'Sales Performance Report'.
    05  LINE 3.
        10  COLUMN 59          PIC X(05) VALUE 'As of'.
        10  COLUMN 65          PIC X(08) SOURCE CURRENT-DATE.
        10  COLUMN 100         PIC X(04) VALUE 'Page'.
        10  COLUMN 100         PIC Z(03) SOURCE PAGE-COUNTER.
    05  LINE 5.
        10  COLUMN 2           PIC X(04) VALUE 'Item'.
        10  COLUMN 51          PIC X(05) VALUE 'Price'.
        10  COLUMN 70          PIC X(05) VALUE 'Units'.
        10  COLUMN 92          PIC X(03) VALUE 'Net'.
    05  LINE 6.
        10  COLUMN 1           PIC X(06) VALUE 'Number'.
        10  COLUMN 10          PIC X(19) VALUE
                               'Product Description'.
        10  COLUMN 50          PIC X(08) VALUE 'Per Unit'.
        10  COLUMN 71          PIC X(04) VALUE 'Sold'.
        10  COLUMN 90          PIC X(03) VALUE 'Proceeds'.
```

The information provided in this record description would be printed on every page of the report. Thus, lines 2 and 3 would always contain

```
                     Sales Performance Report
                          As of 01/01/85              Page nnn
```

where "nnn" is the page number. Lines 5 and 6 would contain descriptive column headings such that those headings produced in line 6 are approximately under (on a left-to-right basis) those produced in line 5. Thus, these headings would appear as

```
 Item                                 Price    Units     Net
Number  Product Description         Per Unit   Sold   Proceeds
```

Finally, note that no reference was made to line 4. Thus, line 4 will be blank on each page.

DETAIL (DE) Record Types

DETAIL record types, of which there may be more than one within a single RD, contain the most specific information in a report. Since there may be more than one DETAIL-line description, all record types of DETAIL must be accompanied by a data-name. A single DETAIL-line description is likely to be produced several times per page. To illustrate the structure of a DETAIL record type, suppose the following code was placed in the REPORT SECTION.

```
01  ITEM-RECORD TYPE DETAIL LINE PLUS 1.
    05  COLUMN 1       PIC X(06) SOURCE ITEM-NUMBER.
    05  COLUMN 10      PIC X(30) SOURCE
                       PRODUCT-DESCRIPTION.
    05  COLUMN 50      PIC Z(05).99 SOURCE
                       PRICE-PER-UNIT.
    05  COLUMN 69      PIC Z(06) SOURCE UNITS-SOLD.
    05  COLUMN 88      PIC Z(07).99 SOURCE
                       NET-PROCEEDS.
```

This DETAIL line named ITEM-RECORD will cause the output produced by the report writer to be single-spaced (LINE PLUS 1) between DETAIL lines. The values placed into the report fields are all provided by the SOURCE clause. Note that both nonedited alphanumeric and edited numeric fields are presented by the PICTURE clauses. Finally, by comparing the column locations in the DETAIL line with those provided in the PAGE HEADING, you should be able to determine that the data values printed will appear below the appropriate column headings.

Suppose you are designing a report containing two different types of DETAIL-line descriptions. To do this, two different record descriptions would have to be provided in the REPORT SECTION for the same RD. To illustrate this point, assume the following code was used.

```
01  DEBIT-RECORD TYPE DETAIL.
    05  LINE PLUS 1.
        10  COLUMN 1       PIC 9(05)B9              SOURCE
                           CUSTOMER-NUMBER.
        10  COLUMN 10      PIC X(30)                SOURCE
                           CUSTOMER-NAME.                  .
        10  COLUMN 50      PIC $$$$,$$$.99DB        SOURCE
                           DEBIT-AMOUNT.
        10  COLUMN 70      PIC X(08)                SOURCE
                           TRANSACTION-DATE         GROUP INDICATE.
        10  COLUMN 90      PIC X(05)                VALUE 'Debit'.
                           01  CREDIT-RECORD TYPE DETAIL.
    05  LINE PLUS 1.
        10  COLUMN 1       PIC 9(05)B9              SOURCE
                           CUSTOMER-NUMBER.
        10                 PIC X(30)                SOURCE
                           CUSTOMER-NAME.
        10  COLUMN 50      PIC $$$$,$$$.99CR        SOURCE
                           CREDIT-AMOUNT.
        10  COLUMN 70      PIC X(08)                SOURCE
                           TRANSACTION-DATE         GROUP INDICATE.
        10  COLUMN 90      PIC X(06)                VALUE 'Credit'.
        10  COLUMN 100      PIC X(03)               SOURCE
                           AUTHORIZATION-CODE.
```

The two records, DEBIT-RECORD and CREDIT-RECORD, have similar characteristics. Although similar characteristics are not essential when creating multiple DETAIL lines within a report, for this illustration similarity is reasonable. The first two report fields are the same (CUSTOMER-NUMBER and CUSTOMER-NAME) in both records. However, the CUSTOMER-NAME field of the CREDIT-NAME) in both records. However, the CUSTOMER-NAME field of the CREDIT-RECORD is a ''hidden'' or nonprinting field since it does not have a COLUMN clause. (You should also note the

PICTURE string for CUSTOMER-NUMBER.) Also, the fourth field (TRANSACTION-DATE) is the same. Note that this field is accompanied by a GROUP clause, meaning that the field is printed only if the value in the field has changed since it was last printed. (You should be aware of the fact that the GROUP clause for the DEBIT-RECORD is independent of the GROUP clause in the CREDIT-RECORD.)

All other fields are somewhat different. For example, the DEBIT-AMOUNT field uses a floating dollar sign editing character followed by the DB fixed insertion characters. The CREDIT-AMOUNT field used the CR symbol. The field following the TRANSACTION-DATE contains a VALUE of "Debit" for the DEBIT-RECORD and "Credit" for the CREDIT-RECORD. Thus, the programmer should be able to identify explicitly which record was produced on the printout. (Also, this is the only illustration in this text of a VALUE clause used in a DETAIL-line record description.) Finally, the CREDIT-RECORD contains an extra field, AUTHORIZATION-CODE, that is not found in the DEBIT-RECORD.

The PAGE FOOTING (PF) Record Type

The PAGE FOOTING record type is a report item that will appear at the end of each page of output. Like the PAGE HEADING, only one record type of PAGE FOOTING is allowed per RD. Its primary use is to provide summary or "recap" information such as page totals, index references, and page numbers. To illustrate the structure of the PAGE FOOTING record type, suppose the following code was placed in the REPORT SECTION.

```
01  TYPE PAGE FOOTING LINE 56.
    05  COLUMN 1    PIC X(15)               VALUE
                    'Product Groups:'.
    05  COLUMN 17   PIC X(06)               SOURCE
                    FIRST-PRODUCT-GROUP.
    05  COLUMN 23   PIC X(02)               VALUE 'to'.
    05  COLUMN 26   PIC X(06)               SOURCE
                    LAST-PRODUCT-GROUP.
```

This PAGE FOOTING will appear on line 56 of each printed page of the report. It will contain indexing information that should assist anyone wishing to thumb through a multipage report containing the output indicated in the other record types. The form of this output will be

```
Product Groups: xxxxxx to xxxxxx
```

where the first field should be the first product group value on the page and the second field should be the last product group value on the page. (This arrangement requires that the programmer know when a page break is about to occur, and during the process of printing a page, save the first and last product group values. This technique is illustrated later in Figure 15.17.)

As an alternative to the indexing information, suppose you wanted to provide subtotals of all the information provided on the page. You might provide a code that appears similar to the following.

```
01  TYPE PF.
    05  LINE PLUS 2.
        10  COLUMN 60     PIC X(12)           VALUE
                          'Total Debits'.
```

```
10   COLUMN 74     PIC $ZZZ,ZZZ.99      SOURCE
                   TOTAL-DEBITS.
10   COLUMN 90     PIC X(13)            VALUE
                   'Total Credits'.
10   COLUMN 105    PIC $ZZZ,ZZZ.99      SOURCE
                   TOTAL-CREDITS.
10   COLUMN 120    PIC X(04)            VALUE
                   'Page'.
10   COLUMN 125    PIC Z9               SOURCE
                   PAGE-COUNTER.
```

The output from this record would begin in column 60 and appear as

```
Total Debts $xxx,xxx.xx Total Credits $xxx,xxx.xx Page
xx
```

Note that both VALUE and SOURCE clauses are used. Also, remember that SUM clauses are permitted only in CONTROL FOOTINGs. Thus, it is the programmers responsibility to somehow create the values of TOTAL-DEBITS and TOTAL-CREDITS. Finally, note that the special register PAGE-COUNTER may be used in PAGE FOOTINGs. PAGE-COUNTER will retain the current page number until after the PAGE-FOOTING has been produced.

The REPORT FOOTING (RF) Record Type

The REPORT FOOTING record type is primarily used to provide summary information, which is not required on each page of the report. You are permitted only one REPORT FOOTING record type within a single RD, and it is produced after all other printout has been generated. To illustrate the structure of the REPORT FOOTING record type, suppose the following code was placed in the REPORT SECTION.

```
01   TYPE REPORT FOOTING LINE 58.
     05   COLUMN 76       PIC X(11)          VALUE
                          'Grand Total'.
     05   COLUMN 88       PIC Z(07).99       SOURCE
                          GRAND-TOTAL.
```

This report item would be produced on line 58 of the last page of the printout. It would begin in column 76 and appear as

```
Grand Total xxxxxxx.xx
```

where the value of GRAND-TOTAL would have to be produced by the programmer, since a SUM clause is not permitted in a REPORT FOOTING.

A more elaborate illustration of a REPORT FOOTING might appear as follows.

```
01   TYPE RF LINE NEXT PAGE.
     05   LINE 3.
          10   COLUMN 100      PIC X(04) VALUE 'Page'.
          10   COLUMN 105      PIC Z(03) SOURCE PAGE-COUNTER.
     05   LINE 30.
          10   COLUMN 54       PIC X(25) VALUE
                               'ABC Manufacturing Company'.
     05   LINE PLUS 2.
          10   COLUMN 51       PIC X(32) VALUE
                               'Sales Performance Summary Report'.
     05   LINE PLUS 2.
          10   COLUMN 59       PIC X(05) VALUE 'As of'.
          05   COLUMN 65       PIC X(08) SOURCE CURRENT-DATE.
```

```
05  LINE PLUS 2.
    10  COLUMN 55          PIC X(11)            VALUE
                           'Grand Total'.
    10  COLUMN 66          PIC Z(07).99         SOURCE
                           GRAND-TOTAL.
```

The LINE clause in this record description means that the REPORT FOOTING will appear on a page by itself. On the third line of this page, the page number is produced using the special register PAGE-COUNTER. Then, approximately in the middle of the page, on both left-to-right and top-to-bottom bases, the following text will be printed.

```
         ABC Manufacturing Company
     Sales Performance Summary Report
              AS of 01/01/85
          Grand Total xxxxxxx.xx
```

Although this seems quite simple, one problem exists. Because we have referenced a new page, the report writer will attempt to produce a PAGE HEADING on this page. Since we would not normally want a print item such as column headings above this summary, we must find a way to suppress printing the PAGE HEADING. A discussion of how to suppress, or override, a process normally executed by the report writer will be discussed shortly.

The CONTROLS Clause and its Relationship with CONTROL HEADINGs and CONTROL FOOTINGs

The CONTROLS clause, CONTROL HEADINGs, and CONTROL FOOTINGs are used together to create control breaks, perhaps on several levels. The CONTROLS clause, presented in Figure 15.5 appeared as

```
[ { CONTROL IS   }  { FINAL                                          } ]
  {              }  { identifier-1 [, identifier-2] . . .            }
  { CONTROLS ARE }  { FINAL, identifier-1 [, identifier-2] . . .     }
```

This clause is used to establish both the order of control breaks and the identifier(s) on which control breaks are to be executed. In the case of the report writer, control breaks are executed when a change in the indicated identifier(s) occurs. Furthermore, the reserved word FINAL may be used in the CONTROLS clause. FINAL is a global control break triggered at the beginning of the report for CONTROL HEADINGs and at the end of the report for CONTROL FOOTINGs. Thus, a CONTROL HEADING triggered by FINAL will be produced immediately after the PAGE HEADING on the first page only. A CONTROL FOOTING associated with FINAL will be printed at the end of the report, immediately prior to the PAGE FOOTING on the last page of the report.

The other identifiers, if used, establish a hierarchy or sequence of execution for CONTROL HEADINGs or CONTROL FOOTINGs. That is, the first identifier specified acts as a major control break, whereas the last identifier is the most minor control break. Normally, minor control breaks will occur more frequently than major control breaks.

To illustrate the control break sequence of a particular CONTROLS clause, assume we have a data file containing sales information. Each record in the file might contain data related to the salesman, the district in which that salesman works, the amount of the transaction, and the date of the transaction. Furthermore, assume the data have been organized by the district, salesman, and transaction date such that all sales from one district are together, and within that grouping, salesmen are ordered. Finally, suppose that for each salesman the records are organized by the transaction date. Now assume the following CONTROLS clause appears in the RD description of a report.

```
CONTROLS ARE FINAL, DISTRICT, SALESMAN, TRANSACTION-DATE.
```

The usual control break sequence for this report would be (based on changes in the identifiers specified in the CONTROLS clause)

1. CONTROL HEADING based on FINAL (one per report)
2. CONTROL HEADING based on DISTRICT (several per report)
3. CONTROL HEADING based on SALESMAN (several per DISTRICT)
4. CONTROL HEADING based on TRANSACTION-DATE (several per SALESMAN)
5. Detail lines
6. CONTROL FOOTING based on TRANSACTION-DATE (several per SALESMAN),
7. CONTROL FOOTING based on SALESMAN (several per DISTRICT)
8. CONTROL FOOTING based on DISTRICT (several per report)
9. CONTROL FOOTING based on FINAL (one per report)

Thus, for example, each time the value of TRANSACTION-DATE changes, the following would occur.

- Last detail line printed for previous group (before change)
- Change in TRANSACTION-DATE value for the next detail line
- CONTROL FOOTING for TRANSACTION-DATE printed
- CONTROL HEADING for TRANSACTION-DATE printed
- First detail line printed for present group.

Furthermore, a change in the next higher level control break item (SALESMAN) would cause the following sequence to be generated.

- Last detail line printed for previous group (before change)
- Change in SALESMAN for the next detail line
- CONTROL FOOTING for TRANSACTION-DATE printed
- CONTROL FOOTING for SALESMAN printed
- CONTROL HEADING for SALESMAN printed
- CONTROL HEADING for TRANSACTION-DATE printed
- First detail line printed for present group

Note that this sequence is produced regardless of whether the value of TRANSACTION-DATE changes. Thus, a change in a major control break item implies a change in all subsequent (minor) control break items.

When a control break on FINAL is detected, the following is generated (preceded only by the REPORT HEADING and the first PAGE HEADING).

- CONTROL HEADING on FINAL
- CONTROL HEADING on DISTRICT

- CONTROL HEADING on SALESMAN
- CONTROL HEADING on TRANSACTION-DATE
- First detail line

at the beginning of the report and

- Last detail line
- CONTROL FOOTING on TRANSACTION-DATE
- CONTROL FOOTING on SALESMAN
- CONTROL FOOTING on DISTRICT
- CONTROL FOOTING on FINAL

at the end of the report. A PAGE FOOTING would follow this sequence, and finally, a REPORT FOOTING would be produced.

As previously indicated, a CONTROL HEADING, a CONTROL FOOTING, or perhaps both are usually associated with each control break item. That is, you may choose to code both a CONTROL HEADING and a CONTROL FOOTING for each identifier, or a CONTROL HEADING for some items and CONTROL FOOTINGs for others. Thus, CONTROL HEADINGs and CONTROL FOOTINGs are independent of each other from the standpoint of coding—one may be coded for a particular report without the necessity of coding the other. (Note that you are not required to specify either a CONTROL HEADING or a CONTROL FOOTING for an identifier specified in the CONTROLS clause.)

The general form of CONTROL HEADINGs and CONTROL FOOTINGs, as illustrated in Figure 15.9, was

```
           { { CONTROL HEADING }   { identifier-n } }
           { { CH              }   { FINAL        } }
TYPE IS    {                                        }
           { { CONTROL FOOTING }   { identifier-n } }
           { { CF              }   { FINAL        } }
```

Notice that for each CONTROL HEADING or CONTROL FOOTING record description, you are required to specify an identifier or the reserved word FINAL. You may only specify those identifiers (and FINAL) indicated in the CONTROLS clause for the report. Furthermore, only one CONTROL HEADING and CONTROL FOOTING may be specified for each identifier (or FINAL). However, because several identifiers may be listed in the CONTROLS clause, it should be obvious that you are permitted to have multiple records within one report description that have a TYPE of CONTROL HEADING or CONTROL FOOTING.

To illustrate the structure of a control break operation, suppose the following code was placed in the REPORT SECTION.

```
RD
 .
 .
 .
```

```
       CONTROL IS PRODUCT-GROUP.
    01 TYPE CONTROL HEADING PRODUCT-GROUP
       LINE PLUS 2
       NEXT GROUP PLUS 2.
       05 COLUMN 1      PIC X(14)                VALUE
                        'Product Group:'.
       05 COLUMN 16     PIC X(06)                SOURCE
                        PRODUCT-GROUP.
    01 TYPE IS CONTROL  FOOTING PRODUCT-GROUP
       LINE PLUS 1.
       05 COLUMN 69     PIC X(18)                VALUE
                        'Total Net Proceeds'.
       05 COLUMN 88     PIC Z(07).99             SUM
                        NET-PROCEEDS.
```

Each time the value of PRODUCT-GROUP changes, the following is produced.

```
Product Group: xxxxxx
                     Total Net Proceeds xxxxxxx.xx
```

The CONTROL HEADING/FOOTING sequence is triggered by a change in PRODUCT-GROUP. In the illustrated output, the CONTROL FOOTING would be followed immediately by the next CONTROL HEADING, unless a page break is also necessary. The CONTROL HEADING is double-spaced below any previously produced output. After the CONTROL HEADING is printed, another double space occurs to avoid the next line appearing immediately below this text. The structure of the CONTROL HEADING is somewhat typical of other record types in that both VALUE and SOURCE clauses are used. Although PRODUCT-GROUP is the only identifier to appear in a SOURCE clause in this example, other identifiers could appear in this description. Furthermore, PRODUCT-GROUP does not have to appear in the CONTROL HEADING record description as an elementary-item.

The CONTROL FOOTING record description is rather typical, except that the SUM clause is used to accumulate the value of NET-PROCEEDS. That is, each time NET PROCEEDS is printed in the detail-line description, its value is added to the CONTROL FOOTING accumulator. Once the CONTROL FOOTING, with the accumulated value of NET-PROCEEDS, is printed, the accumulator is reset to zero. Thus, this control break will provide a subtotal of NET-PROCEEDS for each PRODUCT-GROUP. To illustrate further the use of the SUM clause in CONTROL FOOTINGs, examine the following code.

```
01   TYPE CF TRANSACTION-DATE LINE PLUS 2.
     05  DATE-TOTAL COLUMN 70             PIC $ZZZ,ZZZ.99 SUM
                                          SALES-AMOUNT.
     05  COLUMN 100                       PIC $ZZZ,ZZZ.99 SUM
                                          SALES-AMOUNT
                                          RESET ON FINAL.
01   TYPE CF SALESMAN LINE PLUS 2.
     05  SALESMAN-TOTAL COLUMN 70        PIC $ZZZ,ZZZ.99 SUM
                                         DATE-TOTAL.
01   TYPE CF DISTRICT LINE PLUS 2.
     05  DISTRICT-TOTAL COLUMN 70        PIC $ZZZ,ZZZ.99 SUM
                                         SALESMAN-TOTAL.
01   TYPE CF FINAL LINE PLUS 2.
     05  COLUMN 70                       PIC $ZZZ,ZZZ.99 SUM
                                         DISTRICT-TOTAL.
```

Assuming these CONTROL FOOTINGs are listed in the REPORT SECTION by their frequency of occurrence, the first CONTROL FOOTING would produce two totals—a total of SALES-AMOUNT for a group of records having the same TRANSACTION-DATE (to be reset to zero each time the footing is printed) and a cumulative total of SALES-AMOUNT (which is not reset to zero each time the footing is printed, but, rather, is reset on FINAL—the end of the report). In addition, the first total field is accompanied by the data-name DATE-TOTAL. An examination of the second CONTROL FOOTING indicates that the summation operation is performed on DATE-TOTAL, not SALES-AMOUNT. That is, the subtotal for the SALESMAN control break is created by adding the intermediate totals that are produced for each TRANSACTION-DATE control break. Notice that the same type of operation is performed in the CONTROL FOOTINGs for DISTRICT and FINAL. Furthermore, the cumulative total created through the first control break and the total created by the CONTROL FOOTING on FINAL should be the same value at the end of the report. Creating these values by alternate means may be used as a cross check on the accuracy of the report writer program. Short of the accuracy check, the value of cumulative total could be used as a SOURCE for the FINAL CONTROL FOOTING, provided it is named. You may ask, why go to all the trouble of using intermediate totals to create higher level totals or grand totals? The answer lies in the fact that the operation is more efficient.

The PROCEDURE DIVISION

As stated earlier in this chapter, one of the objectives of the report writer is to reduce coding complexity in the PROCEDURE DIVISION. This means that most of the procedures usually included in the PROCEDURE DIVISION that are directly related to the production of printed reports are eliminated. These procedures are replaced by three rather simple statements as shown in Figure 15.16.

The first statement in the PROCEDURE DIVISION associated with the report writer is the INITIATE statement. This statement, although it does not produce any printed output of its own, is responsible for all initialization operations for the specified report. Among the functions performed by the INITIATE statements are:

1. Initializing the PAGE-COUNTER special register to 1
2. Initializing the LINE-COUNTER special register to 0
3. Initializing all accumulators associated with SUM clauses to 0
4. Establishing the appropriate control break sequences
5. Setting the initial sequence of CONTROL HEADINGS to the ''on'' mode

Figure 15.16 The PROCEDURE DIVISION Statements

```
INITIATE   report-name-1 [,report-name-2] . . .
-------------------------------------------------------
GENERATE   detail-line-name
-------------------------------------------------------
TERMINATE  report-name-1 [,report-name-2] . . .
```

Note that one of the functions not performed by the INITIATE statement is a file opening operation. The output file must still be OPENed, as was previously the case. Furthermore, the output file must be OPENed prior to the execution of the INITIATE statement.

As indicated by the form of the INITIATE statement, one or more report-names may be identified in the INITIATE statement. These report-names must be associated with a REPORTS clause in the FILE SECTION and an RD in the REPORT SECTION. Once a report has been INITIATEd, it cannot be reinitiated until the execution of a TERMINATE statement.

The GENERATE statement is solely responsible for the generation of a report. As noted in the general form of the statement, one and only one DETAIL-line-name must be specified for each GENERATE statement. Recall that all DETAIL record descriptions must be accompanied by a record-name. Thus, the programmer has the option, given multiple DETAIL-line definitions, to select the particular DETAIL-line format that meets the needs of the program. This means that multiple GENERATE statements are permitted within a single program. Furthermore, the same DETAIL-line-name may be specified in more than one GENERATE statement.

Among the functions associated with the GENERATE statement are:

1. Produce DETAIL lines, as indicated
2. Increment and test the LINE-COUNTER for page break conditions and produce PAGE FOOTINGS, as necessary
3. Increment PAGE-COUNTER when page breaks occur and produce PAGE HEADINGs
4. Test for conditions that warrant the production of CONTROL HEADINGs and CONTROL FOOTINGs
5. Accumulate SUM fields and reinitialize these fields to zero, as warranted
6. Produce REPORT HEADINGs and REPORT FOOTINGs, as needed
7. React to specialized processing requirements, as indicated by the USE statement. (Details of the USE statement are discussed later in this chapter.)

The TERMINATE statement performs all concluding activities. At the end to the processing operations that may involve reading input data, there are a series of report items that need to be produced. Thus, the function of the TERMINATE statement is to produce

1. The final set of CONTROL FOOTINGs, including the CONTROL FOOTING based on FINAL, if present
2. The final PAGE FOOTING
3. The REPORT FOOTING

During the closing processes, the TERMINATE statement will also check for the end of page condition and, if necessary, produce a final PAGE HEADING.

Logically, the TERMINATE statement should be located toward the end of the procedure. However, since the TERMINATE does not close the output file, it should be located prior to the CLOSE statement for the output file. Like the INITIATE statement, once a report has been TERMINATEd, it cannot be terminated again until INITIATEd. Finally, the generation of the first DETAIL line enables the activity of the TERMINATE statement. That is, if the TERMINATE statement is encountered before a DETAIL line has been produced, the output from the TERMINATE statement will be suppressed.

To illustrate how these statements would appear in a procedure and their placement relative to other statements, examine the following code.

```
PROCEDURE DIVISION.
000-MAIN-CONTROL SECTION
000-MAIN-CONTROL-ENTRY.
    PERFORM 100-INITIALIZATION.
    PERFORM 200-PRODUCE-REPORT
        UNTIL FILE-STATUS = 'DONE'.
    PERFORM 300-TERMINATION.
    STOP RUN.
000-MAIN-CONTROL-EXIT.
    EXIT.
100-INITIALIZATION SECTION.
100-INITIALIZATION-ENTRY.
    OPEN INPUT input-file-name
         OUTPUT output-file-name.
   INITIATE SALES-PERFORMANCE.
100-INITIALIZATION-EXIT.
   EXIT.
200-PRODUCE-REPORT SECTION.
200-PRODUCE-REPORT-ENTRY.
    READ input-file-name
       AT END MOVE 'DONE' to FILE-STATUS
       GO TO 200-PRODUCE-REPORT-EXIT.
    MULTIPLY PRICE-PER-UNIT BY UNITS-SOLD
       GIVING NET-PROCEEDS.
    GENERATE ITEM-RECORD.
200-PRODUCE-REPORT-EXIT.
     EXIT.
300-TERMINATION SECTION.
300-TERMINATION-ENTRY.
    TERMINATE SALES-PERFORMANCE.
    CLOSE input-file-name, output-file-name.
```

As indicated, the INITIATE statement would naturally appear in the INITIALIZATION sequence. However, note that its placement after the OPEN statement is not accidental. In the body of the procedure (PRODUCE-REPORT), the GENERATE statement produces individual DETAIL lines. It should be obvious that the value of all data-items used in the DETAIL line should be established before the GENERATE statement is executed. The READ statement should provide a majority of these values. However, a MULTIPLY statement is used to provide the value of NET-PROCEEDS. Finally, the TERMINATE statement appears in the TERMINATION procedure, preceding the CLOSE statement.

A Report Writer Program

Output produced by the report writer is very tightly controlled by the report processor. One of the disadvantages is that this control is sometimes constraining; that is, it is difficult to achieve what you want printed. In other cases, the report writer produces a particular sequence of output items not desired. Finally, the report writer has limitations on the use of items such as the SUM clause. The program presented in Figure 15.17 is provided to help you understand some of the means by which the programmer can circumvent what the report writer normally wants to do.

The program in Figure 15.17 is a repetition of one of the most involved procedures presented in the text—Figure 10.7—the Electric Utility Company program. This particular program was selected for a number of reasons. First, because the program is

Figure 15.17 Electric Utility Company (Hierarchy Chart)

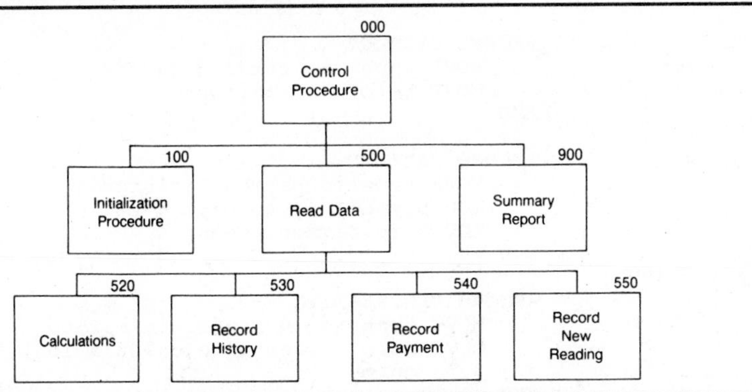

somewhat complicated, it lends itself to a solution by the report writer. Solving the report format problems by the report writer, the programmer can concentrate more on input and computational complexities of the problem. Second, the report obviously calls for a report heading, page headings, and page footings. Therefore, more of the elements of the report writer may be employed. Finally, the procedure requires a report footing involving obvious summations. This is a twofold problem—we must find a way both to perform summations that may be utilized by the report footing and to eliminate the page heading normally produced, since the report footing is on a page by itself.

An examination of Figure 15.17 demonstrates the report-name is to be BILLING-INFORMATION (lines 440 and 830). The WORKING-STORAGE SECTION (lines 460–790) still needs a number of intermediate computational, control, and input record layout entries. However, as compared to Figure 10.7, the number of fields used for this purpose is somewhat less than previously required. Furthermore, all report format items have been eliminated.

The REPORT SECTION begins in line 810. The page characteristics employed for the BILLING-INFORMATION report are somewhat more detailed, since a page footing is to be produced. Also, note two data items (FINAL and ON-FIVE) have been identified in the CONTROLS ARE clause. (These items will be more fully discussed shortly). Following the general layout of the report are definitions of the REPORT HEADING (lines 910–940), which is produced on line 1 of only the first page of the printed report, a multiline PAGE HEADING (lines 960–1300), which provides for a report-name, report date, and column headings on each page of the report beginning on line 2. Two important items need to be identified. First, note the use of the special register PAGE-COUNTER in line 1030, used to provide page numbers. Second, the PAGE HEADING is a named record called PAGE-HEADING. This piece of information will become useful in a later discussion.

The DETAIL line, named BILLING-LINE, is defined in lines 1320–1560. Several important differences exist in this definition relative to that previously demonstrated. First, the initial field in this record contains no COLUMN clause. As a result, this item will never appear on the printed report. The data item CUSTOMER-COUNT is the SOURCE for this field. Its original definition appears in line 500 of the WORKING-STORAGE SECTION and is valued at 1. The reason for its use will become apparent later, but for now simply acknowledge its presence and note its value is never modified in the PROCEDURE DIVISION—it is always 1 (and is not printed). Second, note that

Figure 15.17 *Continued* Electric Utility Company (Pseudocode)

```
START
     DECLARE Page heading process
     DO Initialization
     DO Read-data UNTIL eof
     DO Summary-report
     DO Termination
END

PAGE HEADING PROCESS
     USE before report
     MOVE first customer to footing
     IF eof
          MOVE 1 to print switch
END

INITIALIZATION
     OPEN files
     READ information into work
          IF eof
               DISPLAY message
               CLOSE files
               STOP
          ENDIF
     ENDREAD
     READ information
          IF eof
               DISPLAY message
               CLOSE files
               STOP
          ENDIF
     ENDREAD
     MOVE date to output
     INITIATE report
END

READ-DATA
    IF new customer
         DO Calculations
    ENDIF
    IF record type = 1
         DO Record history
    ENDIF
    IF record type = 2
         DO Record payment
    ENDIF
    IF record type = 3
         DO Record new reading
    ENDIF
    IF record type not 1,2,or 3
         DISPLAY error
    READ information
         IF eof
              SET eof indicator
              MOVE customer number
                   to last number
              DO Calculations
         ENDIF
    ENDREAD
END

RECORD HISTORY
    MOVE input to working fields
    MOVE 0 to calculations
END

RECORD PAYMENT
    MOVE type to payment information
    ADD payment in to payments
    ADD 1 to payment count
END

RECORD NEW READING
    MOVE type to current information
    MOVE meter reading to calculation,
         output
END

CALCULATIONS
    SUBTRACT payments from balance
    IF balance > 0
         COMPUTE charge = balance * .015
    ENDIF
    COMPUTE kwatts = old - current
    IF kwatts < 0
         COMPUTE kwatts = current + 100000 - old
    ENDIF
    IF kwatts = 0
         MOVE 0 to bill
    ENDIF
    IF kwatts between 0 and 10
         MOVE 2.5 to bill
    ENDIF
    IF kwatts between 10 and 5001
         COMPUTE bill = .0255 * kwatts
    ENDIF
    IF kwatts > 5000
         COMPUTE bill = .0323 * kwatts
    ENDIF
    SUM total bill
    COMPUTE decimal = (line - 8)/5
    COMPUTE integer = (line - 8)/5
    IF decimal = integer
         ADD 1 to on five
    ENDIF
    GENERATE output
END

TERMINATION
    TERMINATE report
    CLOSE files
END
```

Figure 15.17 *Continued* Electric Utility Company [by Report Writer]

```
        1   1   2   2   2   3   3   4   4   4   5   5   6   6   6   7
4   8   2   6   0   4   8   2   6   0   4   8   2   6   0   4   8   2

      ***************************************************************
       IDENTIFICATION DIVISION.
      ***************************************************************
       PROGRAM-ID.          ELECTRIC-COMPANY-REPORT.
       AUTHOR.              J. WAYNE SPENCE.
       DATE-WRITTEN.        JANUARY 1, 1989.
       DATE-COMPILED.       JANUARY 1, 1989.
      *    This program illustrates the use of the Report Writer
      *    feature.  It involves the use of SOURCE, VALUE and SUM
      *    clauses, page footings, and control breaks at several
      *    levels.  This program is a repeat of one presented in
      *    Chapter 10.
      ***************************************************************
       ENVIRONMENT DIVISION.
      ***************************************************************
      *-------------------------------------------------------------*
       CONFIGURATION SECTION.
      *-------------------------------------------------------------*
       SOURCE-COMPUTER.  IBM.
       OBJECT-COMPUTER.  IBM.
      *-------------------------------------------------------------*
       INPUT-OUTPUT SECTION.
      *-------------------------------------------------------------*
       FILE-CONTROL.
           SELECT INFORMATION-FILE ASSIGN TO UT-S-INPUT.
           SELECT ACTIVITY-REPORT  ASSIGN TO UT-S-OUTPUT.
      ***************************************************************
       DATA DIVISION.
      ***************************************************************
      *-------------------------------------------------------------*
       FILE SECTION.
      *-------------------------------------------------------------*
       FD  INFORMATION-FILE
               LABEL RECORDS ARE OMITTED.
       01  HISTORY-RECORD.
           05  CUSTOMER-NUMBER-IN       PIC 9(06).
           05  FILLER                   PIC X(08).
           05  TYPE-INFORMATION-IN      PIC X(21).
           05  FILLER                   PIC X(44).
           05  RECORD-TYPE-IN           PIC 9(01).

       FD  ACTIVITY-REPORT
               LABEL RECORDS ARE OMITTED
               REPORT IS BILLING-INFORMATION.
      *-------------------------------------------------------------*
       WORKING-STORAGE SECTION.
      *-------------------------------------------------------------*
       01  WORKING-VARIABLES.
           05  FILE-STATUS              PIC X(15)           VALUE SPACES.
           05  CUSTOMER-COUNT           PIC 9(01)           VALUE 1.
           05  CUSTOMER-NUMBER-SAVE     PIC 9(06)           VALUE 0.
           05  FIRST-CUSTOMER-NUMBER    PIC 9(06)           VALUE 0.
           05  LAST-CUSTOMER-NUMBER     PIC 9(06)           VALUE 0.
           05  OLD-READING              PIC 9(05)           VALUE 0.
           05  OLD-BALANCE              PIC S9(04)V9(02)    VALUE 0.
           05  PAYMENTS                 PIC S9(04)V9(02)    VALUE 0.
           05  NUMBER-OF-PAYMENTS       PIC 9(02)           VALUE 0.
           05  THIS-READING             PIC 9(05)           VALUE 0.
           05  KWATTS-USED              PIC S9(06)          VALUE 0.
           05  FINANCE-CHARGE           PIC S9(03)V9(02)    VALUE 0.
           05  AMOUNT-OF-BILL           PIC S9(04)V9(02)    VALUE 0.
           05  TOTAL-AMOUNT-OF-BILL     PIC S9(04)V9(02)    VALUE 0.
           05  ON-FIVE                  PIC 9(01)           VALUE 0.
           05  DECIMAL-DIVIDE           PIC 9(02)V9         VALUE 0.
           05  INTEGER-DIVIDE           PIC 9(02)           VALUE 0.
           05  HISTORY-INFORMATION.
               10  LAST-METER-READING   PIC 9(05)           VALUE 0.
               10  FILLER               PIC X(10)           VALUE SPACES.
               10  PREVIOUS-BALANCE     PIC 9(04)V9(02)     VALUE 0.
```

Figure 15.17 *Continued* Electric Utility Company [by Report Writer]

```
        1   1   2   2   2   3   3   4   4   4   5   5   6   6   6   7
4   8   2   6   0   4   8   2   6   0   4   8   2   6   0   4   8   2
-----------------------------------------------------------------------
           05  PAYMENT-INFORMATION.
               10  FILLER                 PIC X(15)          VALUE SPACES.
               10  PAYMENT                PIC 9(04)V9(02)    VALUE 0.
           05  CURRENT-INFORMATION.
               10  CURRENT-METER-READING PIC 9(05)           VALUE 0.

       01  DATE-RECORD.
           05  REPORT-DAY                 PIC 9(02)          VALUE 0.
           05  REPORT-MONTH               PIC 9(02)          VALUE 0.
           05  REPORT-YEAR                PIC 9(02)          VALUE 0.
      *---------------------------------------------------------------*
       REPORT SECTION.
      *---------------------------------------------------------------*
       RD  BILLING-INFORMATION
             PAGE LIMIT   45 LINES
             HEADING       1
             FIRST DETAIL 10
             LAST DETAIL  39
             FOOTING      40
             CONTROLS ARE FINAL, ON-FIVE.

       01  TYPE IS REPORT HEADING.
           05  LINE 1.
               10  COLUMN 39              PIC X(30)          VALUE
                                          'Electric Power Utility Company'.

       01  PAGE-HEADING TYPE IS PAGE HEADING.
           05  LINE 2.
               10  COLUMN 38              PIC X(32)          VALUE
                                        'Customer Account Activity Report'.
               10  COLUMN 101             PIC X(04)          VALUE
                                          'Page'.
               10  COLUMN 107             PIC Z9             SOURCE
                                          PAGE-COUNTER.
           05  LINE 3.
               10  COLUMN 39              PIC X(30)          VALUE
                                          'For the Month Ending'.
               10  COLUMN 60              PIC 9(02)          SOURCE
                                          REPORT-DAY.
               10  COLUMN 62              PIC X(01)          VALUE '/'.
               10  COLUMN 63              PIC 9(02)          SOURCE
                                          REPORT-MONTH.
               10  COLUMN 65              PIC X(01)          VALUE '/'.
               10  COLUMN 66              PIC 9(02)          SOURCE
                                          REPORT-YEAR.
           05  LINE 4.
               10  COLUMN 2               PIC X(105)       VALUE ALL '-'.
           05  LINE 5.
               10  COLUMN 1               PIC X(132)         VALUE
           ' |Customer|     Meter Reading    |Kilowatt| Previous|      Paym
      -    'ents    |Balance | Base   |Finance|   Total    |'.
           05  LINE 6.
               10  COLUMN 1               PIC X(132)         VALUE
           ' | Account|----------------------| Hours  | Balance |--------
      -    '--------|  After | Bill   |Charges|  Amount    |'.
           05  LINE 7.
               10  COLUMN 1               PIC X(132)         VALUE
           ' | Number |Last Month|This Month|  Used  |         |   Amount
      -    ' |Number|Payment  |        |       |    Due     |'.
           05  LINE 8.
               10 COLUMN 2                PIC X(105)       VALUE ALL '-'.

       01  BILLING-LINE   TYPE IS DETAIL.
           05  LINE PLUS 1.
               10                         PIC 9(01)          SOURCE
                                          CUSTOMER-COUNT.
               10  COLUMN 4               PIC 9(06)          SOURCE
                                          CUSTOMER-NUMBER-SAVE.
               10  COLUMN 16              PIC ZZZZ9          SOURCE
```

Figure 15.17 *Continued* Electric Utility Company [by Report Writer]

```
         1   1   2   2   2   3   3   4   4   4   5   5   6   6   6   7
 4   8   2   6   0   4   8   2   6   0   4   8   2   6   0   4   8   2

                                        LAST-METER-READING.
            10  COLUMN 27               PIC ZZZZ9           SOURCE
                                        CURRENT-METER-READING.
            10  COLUMN 35               PIC ZZZZZ9          SOURCE
                                        KWATTS-USED.
            10  COLUMN 43               PIC $$,$$$.99       SOURCE
                                        PREVIOUS-BALANCE.
            10  COLUMN 53               PIC $$,$$$.99       SOURCE
                                        PAYMENTS.
            10  COLUMN 65               PIC Z9              SOURCE
                                        NUMBER-OF-PAYMENTS.
            10  COLUMN 70               PIC $$$$.99-        SOURCE
                                        OLD-BALANCE.
            10  COLUMN 79               PIC $$$$.99         SOURCE
                                        AMOUNT-OF-BILL.
            10  COLUMN 88               PIC $$$.99          SOURCE
                                        FINANCE-CHARGE.
            10  COLUMN 95               PIC $$,$$$.99CR     SOURCE
                                        TOTAL-AMOUNT-OF-BILL.

    01  TYPE IS CONTROL FOOTING  ON-FIVE.
        05  LINE PLUS 1.

    01  SUMMATIONS TYPE CONTROL FOOTING  FINAL.
        05  TOTAL-NUMBER-OF-CUSTOMERS PIC 9(06)             SUM
                                        CUSTOMER-COUNT.
        05  TOTAL-KWH                   PIC 9(09)           SUM
                                        KWATTS-USED.
        05  TOTAL-BAL-BEFORE-PAYMENT PIC 9(09)V99           SUM
                                        PREVIOUS-BALANCE.
        05  TOTAL-PAYMENTS              PIC 9(09)V99        SUM
                                        PAYMENTS.
        05  TOTAL-NUMBER-OF-PAYMENTS PIC 9(06)              SUM
                                        NUMBER-OF-PAYMENTS.
        05  TOTAL-BAL-AFTER-PAYMENT PIC 9(09)V99            SUM
                                        OLD-BALANCE.
        05  TOTAL-AMOUNT-OF-BILLS       PIC 9(09)V99        SUM
                                        AMOUNT-OF-BILL.
        05  TOTAL-FINANCE-CHARGE        PIC 9(09)V99        SUM
                                        FINANCE-CHARGE.
        05  TOTAL-AMOUNT                PIC 9(09)V99        SUM
                                        TOTAL-AMOUNT-OF-BILL.

    01  TYPE PAGE FOOTING.
        05  LINE PLUS 1.
            10  COLUMN 2                PIC X(105) VALUE ALL '-'.
        05  LINE PLUS 1.
            10  COLUMN 2                PIC X(30)  VALUE
                                        'Customer Numbers on this Page'.
        05  LINE PLUS 1.
            10  COLUMN 8                PIC 9(06)           SOURCE
                                        FIRST-CUSTOMER-NUMBER.
            10  COLUMN 16               PIC X(02)           VALUE 'to'.
            10  COLUMN 19               PIC 9(06)           SOURCE
                                        LAST-CUSTOMER-NUMBER.
            10  COLUMN 101              PIC X(04)           VALUE
                                        'Page'.
            10  COLUMN 107              PIC Z9              SOURCE
                                        PAGE-COUNTER.

    01  TYPE IS REPORT FOOTING.
        05  LINE 10.
            10  COLUMN 44               PIC X(30)           VALUE
                                        ' S  u  m  m  a  r  y'.
        05  LINE 12.
            10  COLUMN 38               PIC X(32)           VALUE
                                      'Customer Account Activity Report'.
            10  COLUMN 101              PIC X(04)           VALUE
                                        'Page'.
```

Figure 15.17 *Continued* Electric Utility Company [by Report Writer]

```
              10  COLUMN 107            PIC Z9              SOURCE
                                        PAGE-COUNTER.
          05  LINE 13.
              10  COLUMN 39             PIC X(20)           VALUE
                                        'For the Month Ending'.
              10  COLUMN 60             PIC 9(02)           SOURCE
                                        REPORT-DAY.
              10  COLUMN 62             PIC X(01)           VALUE '/'.
              10  COLUMN 63             PIC 9(02)           SOURCE
                                        REPORT-MONTH.
              10  COLUMN 65             PIC X(01)           VALUE '/'.
              10  COLUMN 66             PIC 9(02)           SOURCE
                                        REPORT-YEAR.
          05  LINE 14.
              10  COLUMN 2              PIC X(105)        VALUE ALL '-'.
          05  LINE 16.
              10  COLUMN 24             PIC X(35)           VALUE
                               'Total Number of Customers Processed'.
              10  COLUMN 73             PIC ZZZ,ZZ9         SOURCE
                                        TOTAL-NUMBER-OF-CUSTOMERS.
          05  LINE 18.
              10  COLUMN 24             PIC X(25)           VALUE
                                        'Total Kilowatt Hours Used'.
              10  COLUMN 69             PIC ZZZ,ZZZ,ZZ9     SOURCE
                                        TOTAL-KWH.
          05  LINE 20.
              10  COLUMN 24             PIC X(42)           VALUE
                  'Total Outstanding Balances before Payments'.
              10  COLUMN 68             PIC $$$$,$$$,$$$.99 SOURCE
                                        TOTAL-BAL-BEFORE-PAYMENT.
          05  LINE 22.
              10  COLUMN 24             PIC X(21)           VALUE
                                        'Total of All Payments'.
              10  COLUMN 68             PIC $$$$,$$$,$$$.99 SOURCE
                                        TOTAL-PAYMENTS.
          05  LINE 24.
              10  COLUMN 24             PIC X(33)           VALUE
                                   'Total Number of Payments Received'.
              10  COLUMN 73             PIC ZZZ,ZZ9         SOURCE
                                        TOTAL-NUMBER-OF-PAYMENTS.
          05  LINE 26.
              10  COLUMN 24             PIC X(41)           VALUE
                  'Total Outstanding Balances after Payments'.
              10  COLUMN 68             PIC $$$$,$$$,$$$.99 SOURCE
                                        TOTAL-BAL-AFTER-PAYMENT.
          05  LINE 28.
              10  COLUMN 24             PIC X(23)           VALUE
                                        'Total of All Base Bills'.
              10  COLUMN 68             PIC $$$$,$$$,$$$.99 SOURCE
                                        TOTAL-AMOUNT-OF-BILLS.
          05  LINE 30.
              10  COLUMN 24             PIC X(21)           VALUE
                                        'Total Finance Charges'.
              10  COLUMN 68             PIC $$$$,$$$,$$$.99 SOURCE
                                        TOTAL-FINANCE-CHARGE.
          05  LINE 32.
              10  COLUMN 24             PIC X(31)           VALUE
                                       'Total Amount of All Receivables'.
              10  COLUMN 68             PIC $$$$,$$$,$$$.99 SOURCE
                                        TOTAL-AMOUNT.
          05  LINE 34.
              10  COLUMN 2              PIC X(105)        VALUE ALL '-'.
      *****************************************************************
       PROCEDURE DIVISION.
      *****************************************************************
       DECLARATIVES.
      *---------------------------------------------------------------*
       PAGE-HEADING-PROCESS SECTION.
      *---------------------------------------------------------------*
```

Figure 15.17 *Continued* Electric Utility Company [by Report Writer]

```
        1   1   2   2   2   3   3   4   4   4   5   5   6   6   6   7
4   8   2   6   0   4   8   2   6   0   4   8   2   6   0   4   8   2

     USE BEFORE REPORTING PAGE-HEADING.

 PAGE-HEADING-PROCESS-1.
     MOVE CUSTOMER-NUMBER-SAVE TO FIRST-CUSTOMER-NUMBER.

 PAGE-HEADING-PROCESS-2.
     IF FILE-STATUS = 'DONE'
         MOVE 1                   TO PRINT-SWITCH.

 END DECLARATIVES.
*------------------------------------------------------------*
 000-CONTROL-PROCEDURE SECTION.
*------------------------------------------------------------*
     PERFORM 100-INITIALIZATION-PROCEDURE.
     PERFORM 500-READ-DATA
         UNTIL FILE-STATUS = 'DONE'.
     PERFORM 900-SUMMARY-REPORT.
     STOP RUN.
*------------------------------------------------------------*
 100-INITIALIZATION-PROCEDURE SECTION.
*------------------------------------------------------------*
     OPEN INPUT INFORMATION-FILE
         OUTPUT ACTIVITY-REPORT.
     READ INFORMATION-FILE INTO DATE-RECORD
         AT END DISPLAY 'No Data in File'
                CLOSE INFORMATION-FILE, ACTIVITY-REPORT
                STOP RUN.
     READ INFORMATION-FILE
         AT END DISPLAY 'No Data in File'
                CLOSE INFORMATION-FILE, ACTIVITY-REPORT
                STOP RUN.
     MOVE CUSTOMER-NUMBER-IN  TO CUSTOMER-NUMBER-SAVE.
     INITIATE BILLING-INFORMATION.
*------------------------------------------------------------*
 500-READ-DATA SECTION.
*------------------------------------------------------------*
     IF CUSTOMER-NUMBER-SAVE NOT EQUAL TO CUSTOMER-NUMBER-IN
         PERFORM 520-CALCULATIONS.
     IF RECORD-TYPE-IN = 1
         PERFORM 530-RECORD-HISTORY.
     IF RECORD-TYPE-IN = 2
         PERFORM 540-RECORD-PAYMENT.
     IF RECORD-TYPE-IN = 3
         PERFORM 550-RECORD-NEW-READING.
     IF RECORD-TYPE-IN < 1 OR > 3
         DISPLAY 'Error in Code'.
     READ INFORMATION-FILE
         AT END MOVE 'DONE'   TO FILE-STATUS
                MOVE CUSTOMER-NUMBER-IN TO LAST-CUSTOMER-NUMBER
                PERFORM 520-CALCULATIONS.
*------------------------------------------------------------*
 520-CALCULATIONS SECTION.
*------------------------------------------------------------*
     SUBTRACT PAYMENTS FROM OLD-BALANCE.
     IF OLD-BALANCE GREATER THAN 0
         COMPUTE FINANCE-CHARGE ROUNDED = OLD-BALANCE * .015.
     SUBTRACT OLD-READING FROM THIS-READING GIVING KWATTS-USED.
     IF KWATTS-USED LESS THAN 0
         COMPUTE KWATTS-USED =
           THIS-READING + 100000 - OLD-READING.
     IF KWATTS-USED EQUAL TO 0
         MOVE 0                   TO AMOUNT-OF-BILL.
     IF KWATTS-USED > 0 AND < 10
         MOVE 2.50                TO AMOUNT-OF-BILL.
     IF KWATTS-USED NOT < 10 AND < 5001
         MULTIPLY KWATTS-USED BY .0255
           GIVING AMOUNT-OF-BILL ROUNDED.
     IF KWATTS-USED > 5000
         MULTIPLY KWATTS-USED BY .0323
```

Figure 15.17 *Continued* Electric Utility Company [by Report Writer]

```
             1   1   2   2   2   3   3   4   4   4   5   5   6   6   6   7
     4   8   2   6   0   4   8   2   6   0   4   8   2   6   0   4   8   2
--------------------------------------------------------------------------
3460                GIVING AMOUNT-OF-BILL ROUNDED.
3470          ADD AMOUNT-OF-BILL, OLD-BALANCE, FINANCE-CHARGE
3480            GIVING TOTAL-AMOUNT-OF-BILL.
3490          COMPUTE DECIMAL-DIVIDE = (LINE-COUNTER - 8) / 5.
3500          COMPUTE INTEGER-DIVIDE = (LINE-COUNTER - 8) / 5.
3510          IF DECIMAL-DIVIDE = INTEGER-DIVIDE
3520              ADD 1 TO ON-FIVE.
3530          GENERATE BILLING-LINE.
3540      *-------------------------------------------------------------*
3550       530-RECORD-HISTORY SECTION.
3560      *-------------------------------------------------------------*
3570          MOVE TYPE-INFORMATION-IN TO HISTORY-INFORMATION.
3580          MOVE CUSTOMER-NUMBER-SAVE TO LAST-CUSTOMER-NUMBER.
3590          MOVE CUSTOMER-NUMBER-IN  TO CUSTOMER-NUMBER-SAVE.
3600          MOVE LAST-METER-READING  TO OLD-READING,
3610                                      THIS-READING.
3620          MOVE PREVIOUS-BALANCE    TO OLD-BALANCE.
3630          MOVE 0                   TO PAYMENTS,
3640                                      NUMBER-OF-PAYMENTS,
3650                                      FINANCE-CHARGE,
3660                                      KWATTS-USED.
3670      *-------------------------------------------------------------*
3680       540-RECORD-PAYMENT SECTION.
3690      *-------------------------------------------------------------*
3700          MOVE TYPE-INFORMATION-IN TO PAYMENT-INFORMATION.
3710          ADD PAYMENT TO PAYMENTS.
3720          ADD 1 TO NUMBER-OF-PAYMENTS.
3730      *-------------------------------------------------------------*
3740       550-RECORD-NEW-READING SECTION.
3750      *-------------------------------------------------------------*
3760          MOVE TYPE-INFORMATION-IN TO CURRENT-INFORMATION.
3770          MOVE CURRENT-METER-READING TO THIS-READING.
3780      *-------------------------------------------------------------*
3790       900-SUMMARY-REPORT SECTION.
3800      *-------------------------------------------------------------*
3810          CLOSE INFORMATION-FILE.
3820          TERMINATE BILLING-INFORMATION.
3830          CLOSE ACTIVITY-REPORT.
```

both VALUE and SOURCE clauses appear in the detail-line definition. Finally, notice that among the identifiers used with the SOURCE clause, some come (either directly or indirectly) from an input record, whereas others are the result of computations that take place in the PROCEDURE DIVISION. Therefore, your only limitation on the use of data items employed in a SOURCE clause for a DETAIL line is that the value of the data item be available before the detail line is generated.

The next record description is that of a CONTROL FOOTING (lines 1590–1600). Note that this footing is controlled by a variable called ON-FIVE. Each time the value of ON-FIVE changes, this footing is produced on the line immediately following the previous detail line. The line is used for nothing more than visual spacing—no data are produced. As we shall see in the PROCEDURE DIVISION, this control heading is triggered after each set of five detail lines, thereby providing a visual break.

Among the most peculiar record descriptions in this report is that of the SUMMATIONS CONTROL FOOTING (lines 1620–1790). Several fields are shown in the definition, yet not one is accompanied by a COLUMN clause. As a result, this particular record does not produce a single line of output (at least directly). This CONTROL FOOTING is based on FINAL, meaning the output generated by this line would not be triggered until the end of the report. Next, examine the individual elementary-items.

Figure 15.17 *Continued* Electric Utility Company [by Report Writer] (Data)

```
-----------------------------------------------------------------------------------------
|      |         1         2         3         4         5         6         7         8|
|Record|12345678901234567890123456789012345678901234567890123456789012345678901234567890|
|---------------------------------------------------------------------------------------
|     1|010185                                                                          |
|     2|110421        00598          043200                                            1|
|     3|110421                       040000                                            2|
|     4|110421        04325                                                            3|
|     5|111111        22222          123456                                            1|
|     6|111111                       123456                                            2|
|     7|111111        33333                                                            3|
|     8|114612        96182          003568                                            1|
|     9|114612                       003568                                            2|
|    10|114612        00013                                                            3|
|    11|118921        61984          005595                                            1|
|    12|118921        66418                                                            3|
|    13|121212        11111          001500                                            1|
|    14|121212                       001500                                            2|
|    15|121212        13425                                                            3|
|    16|176257        23925          007655                                            1|
|    17|176257                       076550                                            2|
|    18|176257        39876                                                            3|
|    19|185792        34128          012367                                            1|
|    20|185792                       012367                                            2|
|    21|185792        34134                                                            3|
|    22|185794        06195          147620                                            1|
|    23|185794                       147620                                            2|
|    24|185794                       014762                                            2|
|    25|185794        09195                                                            3|
|    26|195798        61622          014822                                            1|
|    27|195798                       014820                                            2|
|    28|195798        65984                                                            3|
|    29|199428        49462          004527                                            1|
|    30|234567        99827          012525                                            1|
|    31|234567                       012000                                            2|
|    32|235698        33982          014570                                            1|
|    33|235698        63419                                                            3|
|    34|237422        65922          205476                                            1|
|    35|237422                       200000                                            2|
|    36|237422        73155                                                            3|
|    37|241185        00002          026500                                            1|
|    38|241185                       025400                                            2|
|    39|241185                       001100                                            2|
|    40|241185        01496                                                            3|
|    41|244488        75320          054378                                            1|
|    42|244488                       030000                                            2|
|    43|244488                       005000                                            2|
|    44|244488        78793                                                            3|
|    45|245395        56218          052950                                            1|
|    46|245395                       030000                                            2|
|    47|245395        57315                                                            3|
|    48|251922        42417          000000                                            1|
|    49|252263        61538          057218                                            1|
|    50|252263                       057218                                            2|
-----------------------------------------------------------------------------------------
```

Figure 15.17 *Continued* Electric Utility Company [by Report Writer] (Data)

```
-----------------------------------------------------------------------------------------
|      |         1         2         3         4         5         6         7         8|
|Record|12345678901234567890123456789012345678901234567890123456789012345678901234567890|
|-----------------------------------------------------------------------------------------
|    51|263477        04198          000650                                             1|
|    52|263477        07623                                                             3|
|    53|293647        98690          019250                                             1|
|    54|293647                       019250                                             2|
|    55|293647        00422                                                             3|
|    56|321619        70041          052150                                             1|
|    57|321619                       060000                                             2|
|    58|321619        76015                                                             3|
|    59|377619        19576          000000                                             1|
|    60|377619        20461                                                             3|
|    61|378906        98900          200000                                             1|
|    62|378906                       140000                                             2|
|    63|378906                       002000                                             2|
|    64|378906                       003000                                             2|
|    65|378906                       055000                                             2|
|    66|378906        01234                                                             3|
|    67|422442        45370          008915                                             1|
|    68|422442                       004000                                             2|
|    69|422442        47429                                                             3|
|    70|588883        00039          016000                                             1|
|    71|588883                       061000                                             2|
|    72|675782        07215          072575                                             1|
-----------------------------------------------------------------------------------------
```

Figure 15.17 *Continued* Electric Utility Company [by Report Writer] (Output)

```
                                 Electric Power Utility Company
                                Customer Account Activity Report                         Page   1
                                 For the Month Ending 01/01/85
-----------------------------------------------------------------------------------------------
!Customer!      Meter Reading     !Kilowatt! Previous!     Payments      !Balance ! Base   !Finance!   Total    !
! Account!------------------------! Hours  ! Balance !------------------!  After ! Bill   !Charges!  Amount    !
! Number !Last Month!This Month!   Used   !         !   Amount  !Number!Payment  !        !       !    Due     !
-----------------------------------------------------------------------------------------------

  110421        598       4325      3727    $432.00    $400.00    1     $32.00    $95.04    $.48    $127.52
  111111      22222      33333     11111  $1,234.56  $1,234.56    1       $.00   $358.89    $.00    $358.89
  114612      96182         13      3831     $35.68     $35.68    1       $.00    $97.69    $.00     $97.69
  118921      61984      66418      4434     $55.95       $.00    0     $55.95   $113.07    $.84    $169.86

  121212      11111      13425      2314     $15.00     $15.00    1       $.00    $59.01    $.00     $59.01
  176257      23925      39876     15951     $76.55    $765.50    1   $688.95-   $515.22    $.00    $173.73CR
  185792      34128      34134         6    $123.67    $123.67    1       $.00     $2.50    $.00      $2.50
  185794       6195       9195      3000  $1,476.20  $1,623.82    2   $147.62-    $76.50    $.00     $71.12CR

  195798      61622      65984      4362    $148.22    $148.20    1       $.02   $111.23    $.00    $111.25
  199428      49462      65984         0     $45.27       $.00    0     $45.27      $.00    $.68     $45.95
  234567      99827      65984         0    $125.25    $120.00    1      $5.25      $.00    $.08      $5.33
  235698      33982      63419     29437    $145.70       $.00    0    $145.70   $950.82   $2.19  $1,098.71

  237422      65922      73155      7233  $2,054.76  $2,000.00    1     $54.76   $233.63    $.82    $289.21
  241185          2       1496      1494    $265.00    $265.00    2       $.00    $38.10    $.00     $38.10
  244488      75320      78793      3473    $543.78    $350.00    2    $193.78    $88.56   $2.91    $285.25
  245395      56218      57315      1097    $529.50    $300.00    1    $229.50    $27.97   $3.44    $260.91

  251922      42417      57315         0       $.00       $.00    0       $.00      $.00    $.00       $.00
  252263      61538      57315         0    $572.18    $572.18    1       $.00      $.00    $.00       $.00
  263477       4198       7623      3425      $6.50       $.00    0      $6.50    $87.34    $.10     $93.94
  293647      98690        422      1732    $192.50    $192.50    1       $.00    $44.17    $.00     $44.17

  321619      70041      76015      5974    $521.50    $600.00    1    $78.50-   $192.96    $.00    $114.46
  377619      19576      20461       885       $.00       $.00    0       $.00    $22.57    $.00     $22.57
  378906      98900       1234      2334  $2,000.00  $2,000.00    4       $.00    $59.52    $.00     $59.52
  422442      45370      47429      2059     $89.15     $40.00    1     $49.15    $52.50    $.74    $102.39


-----------------------------------------------------------------------------------------------
Customer Numbers on this Page
      110421  to 422442                                                                  Page   1
```

Figure 15.17 *Continued* Electric Utility Company [by Report Writer] (Output)

```
                              Customer Account Activity Report                           Page   2
                               For the Month Ending 01/01/85
-------------------------------------------------------------------------------------------------
!Customer!     Meter Reading    !Kilowatt! Previous!     Payments      !Balance ! Base  !Finance!   Total   !
! Account!----------------------! Hours  ! Balance !-----------------! After  ! Bill  !Charges!  Amount   !
! Number !Last Month!This Month!  Used  !         !  Amount !Number!Payment !       !       !    Due    !
-------------------------------------------------------------------------------------------------

  588883        39       47429        0     $160.00   $610.00     1   $450.00-     $.00     $.00   $450.00CR
  675782      7215       47429        0     $725.75      $.00     0   $725.75      $.00   $10.89   $736.64


-------------------------------------------------------------------------------------------------
Customer Numbers on this Page
     588883  to 675782                                                                    Page   2
```

Figure 15.17 *Continued* Electric Utility Company [by Report Writer] (Output)

```
                                      S u m m a r y

                              Customer Account Activity Report                           Page   3
                               For the Month Ending 01/01/85
-------------------------------------------------------------------------------------------------
                    Total Number of Customers Processed                26

                    Total Kilowatt Hours Used                      107,879

                    Total Outstanding Balances before Payments  $11,574.67

                    Total of All Payments                       $11,396.11

                    Total Number of Payments Received                  25

                    Total Outstanding Balances after Payments      $178.56

                    Total of All Base Bills                      $3,227.29

                    Total Finance Charges                           $23.17

                    Total Amount of All Receivables              $3,429.02

-------------------------------------------------------------------------------------------------
```

Although none of the items are accompanied by a COLUMN clause (each has its printing suppressed), each is named and may be used by other elements of the report. Finally, each is assigned its value by a SUM clause which causes an accumulation of the indicated identifier every time that identifier is produced as output (either literally as a printed field or figuratively, as is the case with the first field—a suppressed field in the detail-line definition). Since each of these fields is in the detail-line definition, their value is added to the indicated accumulation field every time the detail line is printed. Since the value of CUSTOMER-COUNT is 1, each time the detail line is generated the customer is counted. All the other fields are simply summed. Finally, since this CONTROL FOOTING is controlled by FINAL, these accumulators will not be automatically reset until the end of the report.

Lines 1820–1920 provide a PAGE FOOTING on each page of the report. That is, every time a detail line is produced on line 39, the PAGE FOOTING is triggered. The individual lines in the page footing are relatively simple in design—providing a row of asterisks across the bottom of each page, an identification of the first and last customer numbers on the page (previously saved data values), and a page number. This type of information on a long report will make the user's job easier, since the report can be "thumbed" and the information at the bottom of the page will be visible without completely opening the pages.

The final definition in the REPORT SECTION is that of the REPORT FOOTING (lines 1900–2690). By virtue of the line numbers used (e.g., LINE 10 shown in line 2000 of the listing), the REPORT FOOTING will be on a new page—the page that follows the one containing the last set of detail lines. The report footing begins with preliminary heading information (report title, page number, data, etc.), followed by a vertical list of summary information, each containing a title (via a VALUE clause) and a numeric value (via a SOURCE clause). Because these items are of a similar nature, only one needs to be discussed. Examine lines 2230–2270. Note that a specific line number (16) is referenced. Then the text "Total Number of Customers Processed" is produced. Finally, a field called TOTAL-NUMBER-OF-CUSTOMERS is used in a SOURCE clause. TOTAL-NUMBER-OF-CUSTOMERS (as are the other fields employed in SOURCE clauses in this description) is defined in the SUMMATIONS CONTROL FOOTING. Thus, the SUMMATIONS footing is used to calculate, retain, and act as a series of SOURCE fields for the REPORT FOOTING. We have, therefore, obviously circumvented the problem of not being able to utilize SUM clauses in other than CONTROL FOOTINGs. We simply name the wanted fields in a CONTROL FOOTING, suppress its printing (if need be), and use the SOURCE clause (which identifies that item) in the record description in which it is needed.

The USE BEFORE REPORTING Statement

As you begin to examine the PROCEDURE DIVISION, you will notice an initial structure that is slightly out of the ordinary. The DECLARATIVES area of the program (lines 2730–2860) is also used for exceptional processing, but on a somewhat selective basis. (The structural setup of the DECLARATIVES section is described in the USE FOR DEBUGGING statement discussion in Appendix E. It is recommended you review this discussion before proceeding.) As indicated in Figure 15.18, the USE BEFORE REPORTING statement is relatively simple. The only requirement for its use is that the identifier specify a record-name in the REPORT SECTION. When the statement is included in the DECLARATIVES section, it causes the execution of the associated procedure prior to the production of the specified report item.

Figure 15.18 Format of the USE BEFORE REPORTING Statement

```
USE BEFORE REPORTING record-name
```

As indicated in Figure 15.17, the USE statement indicates a particular procedure is to be executed prior to the printing of PAGE-HEADING, the record-name attached to the PAGE HEADING report item. The associated procedure accomplishes two tasks. First, the current customer is identified as the first customer number on the page (line 2800) so that it may be correctly printed in the page footing. Second, a decision is made to determine whether or not the last record has been processed. If so (FILE-STATUS = 'DONE'), all detail lines and appropriate footings have been produced, and it only remains to generate the REPORT FOOTING. The problem is that the report footing is on a page by itself. Since a page eject is sure to occur, the report writer would attempt to generate a PAGE HEADING on that page—a page heading we do not want. Thus, the instruction "MOVE 1 TO PRINT-SWITCH" in line 2840 is used to suppress printing the normally produced page heading. PRINT-SWITCH is a special register attached to the report writer in IBM systems. When PRINT-SWITCH contains a value of 1 prior to printing a report item, the report item is suppressed. Otherwise, the report item is printed. In addition, PRINT-SWITCH is automatically reset to 0—the print setting—each time a report item is produced. Other systems support the same type of feature, although the special register may be identified by some other name (e.g., SUPPRESS-PRINT) and may be manipulated differently. Consult with your instructor about the means your compiler uses to suppress printing the report writer items.

The PROCEDURE DIVISION of Figure 15.17 is otherwise structurally similar to that in Figure 10.7. Note the location of the INITIATE statement (line 3090). Remember that, prior to the production of a page heading, the current customer number must be saved for use in the page footing. Thus, the placement of the INITIATE statement must be after that of the first READ statement that accepts a customer record. The GENERATE statement is located in line 3530. Generally speaking, the GENERATE statement produces the bulk of the report.

Immediately above the GENERATE statement (lines 3490–3520) there are statements that cause the CONTROL FOOTING triggered by ON-FIVE to work properly. The definitions of DECIMAL-DIVIDE and INTEGER-DIVIDE (lines 640 and 650) are the key to this process. Note that one of the fields is described as a whole number (integer) field, whereas the other is permitted to have one decimal digit. Now, consider what happens in this sequence during the production of the report. The special register LINE-COUNTER is automatically incremented each time a line of output is produced. Thus, it will contain integer values between 1 and 40 (e.g., 1, 2, 3, . . . , 40). (The offset by 8 is to accommodate headings on the same page.) After these values are divided by 5, DECIMAL-DIVIDE and INTEGER-DIVIDE will only be equal under particular circumstances—when the value is a multiple of 5 (e.g., 5, 10, 15, etc.) Thus, the extra line produced by the CONTROL FOOTING triggered by ON-FIVE is only printed once every five lines of output.

Finally, the TERMINATE statement is located at line 3820. Notice it is flanked by a CLOSE statement for the input file and a CLOSE statement for the output file. The TERMINATE statement must be executed prior to the CLOSE for the output file.

Summary

In this chapter, we have examined a new means by which a printed report can be produced. Although the report writer has some rather serious limitations, in some cases these limitations are offset by its overwhelming advantages. We have seen that the anatomy of a report may be divided into seven items, identified as

- Report heading
- Page headings
- Control headings
- Detail lines
- Control footings
- Page footings
- Report footing

Furthermore, we have examined how each of these items may be defined and produced by the report writer. In addition, we have described both horizontal (COLUMN clause) and vertical (LINE and NEXT GROUP clauses) spacing and how data may be placed into a field (VALUE, SOURCE, and SUM clauses).

Finally, we discussed several of the techniques by which some features of the report writer may be overriden. We examined suppressing fields and alternate means of producing summations, as well as the complete suppression of a report item with the USE BEFORE REPORTING statement in a new area of the PROCEDURE DIVISION called DECLARATIVES.

Notes on Programming Style

The first note should be one of caution against relying totally on the report writer to produce printed reports. As indicated in the disadvantages section of this chapter, the report writer is a nonstandard element of COBOL. It has not been incorporated into all compilers. Furthermore, even when it is implemented, all implementations have not been standardized. Next, some companies prohibit their programmers from using the report writer. It consumes excessive resources and tends to tie the company to one particular use of COBOL compilers, making it difficult in the long run to go from one machine to another. Finally, although the report writer seems to be exceedingly flexible, some report formats are much more easily implemented by not using the report writer. Thus, you should never abandon the skills necessary to produce a printed report by conventional means. There are simply too many unknowns to start limiting yourself at this point in your career.

The programs presented in this chapter can serve as a guide for programming style. Since a majority of the report writer coding is in the DATA DIVISION, you should continue to maintain appropriate indentation standards. However, you now must consider indentation of items such as the COLUMN clause. Like PICTURE clauses, you will find it much easier to determine where each item is located on a print line if all the COLUMN clauses are aligned. Second, by aligning VALUE, SOURCE, and SUM clauses, you should be able to determine more simply how a field derives its value. Third, if a report item consists of multiple lines, it is recommended that the LINE clauses be set off from other clauses by placing them at the group level within the record description. This provides a useful visual break, making it easier to determine which report items are grouped together (on the same report line). Finally, you are encouraged to name report items, even though only a limited number of these names are required by the report writer itself. Frequently, additional data-names are helpful in more completely documenting the purpose of each report item.

Questions

Below fill in the blank(s) with the appropriate word, words, or phrases.

1. A report item that appears at the top of every page of a printed report is called a(n) _____ .

2. A report item that is an internal heading and is produced only when certain data values change is called a(n) _____ .

3. A report item that appears only on the first page of a printed report is called a(n) _____ .

4. A report item that appears at the bottom of each page of a printed report is called a(n) _____ .

5. A report footing is produced _____ (number) per printed report.

6. The first evidence that a printed report is to be produced by the report writer is the appearance of the _____ clause in the FILE SECTION.

7. The report writer feature may be used only in conjunction with _____ -oriented files or devices.

8. Each report-name identified in the REPORTS clause should be identified by a(n) _____ in the _____ SECTION.

9. Of the clauses associated with each RD, only the _____ clause is required.

10. The HEADING clause of the RD establishes where report and page headings _____ (begin/end).

11. The FIRST DETAIL clause of the RD establishes where detail lines of the report _____ (begin/end).

12. The report writer record types that may be produced between the lines established for FIRST DETAIL and LAST DETAIL include _____ , _____ , and _____ .

13. When both LAST DETAIL and FOOTING are specified for a report, the only record type that may be printed between these lines is a(n) _____ .

14. As the report writer is producing a report, it keeps track of the number of lines on a printed page in the special register called _____ .

15. The number, order, and frequency of control breaks is established in a report by the _____ clause in the RD.

16. Page footings for a printed report would be produced between the lines established by the _____ clause and the _____ clause.

17. Only two data-names are required in the definition of a report in the report writer. These names are _____ and _____ .

18. The general characteristics of a record within the report writer that determines when it will be produced is established by the _____ clause, which is required in every record description.

19. Vertical spacing before a line is produced within a report is controlled by the _____ clause.

20. Horizontal spacing on a given line of a report is established by the _____ clause.

21. Whereas the LINE clause controls vertical spacing before an item is produced, the _____ clause may be used to control vertical spacing after a line is produced.

22. The value to be associated with a particular field within the report writer may be established by using the ____ , the ____ , or the ____ clause.
23. The clause that creates a value for a printing field that is highly similar to a MOVE statement is the ____ clause.
24. The clause that creates a value for a printing field by an accumulation activity is the ____ clause.
25. The SUM clause may only appear in the ____ record type.
26. The field associated with the ____ is automatically reinitialized to zero when a CONTROL FOOTING containing the field is printed.
27. If you wish to hasten or retard the reinitialization of the accumulation field associated with a SUM clause relative to its normal reinitialization, you may do so by employing the ____ clause.
28. If you wish to suppress the printing of a field, you may do so by omitting the ____ clause.
29. If you wish to suppress the printing of a field only when the content of the field is the same as that of the previous content of the field, you may do so by employing the ____ clause.
30. The record type of REPORT HEADING may also be specified by using its abbreviation of ____ .
31. When either a CONTROL HEADING or a CONTROL FOOTING is specified, the definition must be accompanied by the controlling identifier or the reserved word ____ .
32. Only ____ (number) records of the PAGE FOOTING type may be specified for a single report.
33. When the clause LINE NUMBER IS 20 is specified for a report item, it will always be printed on line ____ (number) of a report page.
34. When the clause LINE NUMBER PLUS 2 is specified for a report item, repetitive production of the item will result in a printed page that is ____ (single-, double-, etc.) spaced.
35. In general, relative line numbers (e.g., LINE NUMBER PLUS n) should always be used in the definition of ____ record types.
36. The identifiers listed in the CONTROLS clause are shown in order from ____ (most/least) frequently changed to ____ (most/least) frequently changed.
37. A count of the number of printed pages produced with the report writer is placed in a special register called ____ .
38. In the PROCEDURE DIVISION, the ____ statement and the ____ statement are generally executed only once for a given report.
39. The ____ -name is identified in an INITIATE statement, whereas a ____ -name is identified in a GENERATE statement.
40. The report is "setup," and items such as counter variables are established and initialized by the ____ statement.
41. The bulk of a printed report is normally produced by the ____ statement.
42. The final set of control footings, the last page footing, and the report footing are generally produced by the ____ statement.
43. If a report description contains the definition of a CONTROL HEADING, DETAIL line, and a CONTROL FOOTING, the first of these items to be printed when the control identifier changes is the ____ item.
44. Sometimes it is possible to override the output normally produced by the report writer by employing the USE ____ statement.

45. The USE statement should appear in a special area of the PROCEDURE DIVISION called _____ .

Answer the following questions by circling either "T" for true or "F" for false.

T F **46.** The report writer feature is a part of ANS COBOL.

T F **47.** The report writer feature includes the capability to produce control breaks "automatically."

T F **48.** A single program is permitted to produce one or more reports at the same time, that is, within the same program.

T F **49.** Using the report writer frequently simplifies coding the PROCEDURE DIVISION.

T F **50.** The report writer is frequently implemented on microcomputers.

T F **51.** The report writer feature is generally very efficient and requires little extra internal storage space.

T F **52.** All report formats may easily be produced by using the report writer feature.

T F **53.** If a page heading is described for a report, unless suppressed, it will always appear before the first detail line.

T F **54.** Generally, the report writer record types of DETAIL, CONTROL HEADING, and CONTROL FOOTING may occupy the same area (body) of a printed report.

T F **55.** If specified, a CONTROL FOOTING will always be produced on every page of a printed report.

T F **56.** It is possible to have a multiple CONTROL HEADINGs produced on the same page of a printed report.

T F **57.** The REPORTS clause may identify several reports that are attached to the same print file.

T F **58.** The REPORT SECTION may be composed of one or more RD entries.

T F **59.** When coding the RD for a report, when FIRST DETAIL is specified, LAST DETAIL must also be specified.

T F **60.** The only required clause in the RD for a report is the CONTROLS clause.

T F **61.** When the CONTROLS clause specifies ITEM-1, ITEM-2, and ITEM-3, in that order, ITEM-3 would cause the most frequently occurring control break.

T F **62.** When the clause FOOTING 50 is specified for a report, the last line on a printed page would be line 50.

T F **63.** Every definition of a report is required to have a PAGE HEADING record type.

T F **64.** The only required name within a report is the report-name.

T F **65.** The clause LINE IS NEXT PAGE would frequently be used for a PAGE HEADING record type.

T F **66.** An individual record may not contain both the LINE clause and the NEXT GROUP clause.

T F **67.** The TYPE clause is required in all record descriptions within the REPORT SECTION.

T F **68.** In the REPORT SECTION, a group item is permitted to have a VALUE clause.

T F **69.** The SOURCE clause may be used in conjunction with an elementary-item description in the REPORT SECTION within a PAGE FOOTING definition.

T F **70.** The VALUE clause may be used in conjunction with an elementary-item description in the REPORT SECTION within a PAGE FOOTING definition.

T F **71.** The SUM clause may be used in conjunction with an elementary-item description in the REPORT SECTION within a PAGE FOOTING definition.

T F **72.** When used to represent a single line of output, COLUMN clauses within a single record description must be listed in ascending column-value order.

T F **73.** When a DETAIL record TYPE is defined, the record must be named.

T F **74.** The reserved word FILLER is frequently used within record descriptions in the REPORT SECTION.

T F **75.** A single report is permitted to have multiple records of the DETAIL type.

T F **76.** Relative line numbers (e.g., LINE PLUS 1) are frequently used in the description of a DETAIL record type.

T F **77.** When the SUM clause is specified for a field in a CONTROL FOOTING, the programmer is required to initialize the field and reset the field to zero. The report writer will not perform this function under any circumstance.

T F **78.** Multiple identifiers may be specified for a single SUM clause.

T F **79.** The GROUP INDICATE clause is frequently used to provide control headings or footings within a report.

T F **80.** The INITIATE statement performs an open operation for the output file.

T F **81.** It is possible to have more than one GENERATE statement in a program producing a single report.

T F **82.** One record type within the report writer may generate several lines of output.

T F **83.** The USE BEFORE REPORTING statement is frequently used by the report writer to cause a top-of-form advance before the next output line is generated.

T F **84.** A single GENERATE statement may identify several DETAIL records at the same time.

T F **85.** The special register LINE-COUNTER may be accessed within the PROCEDURE DIVISION.

Exercises

Below is an illustration of a printed report that is to be generated via the report writer feature of COBOL. The information in lowercase in the report layout is either an indication of a PICTURE field (as "n") or the frequency at which an item is printed. Uppercase entries are generally headings, which may be produced in either upper- or lowercase. This report is to be produced from records with the following layout.

Record layout:

```
01  INVOICE-RECORD.
    05  INVOICE-NUMBER-IN    PIC 9(05).
    05  CUSTOMER-NUMBER-IN   PIC X(05).
    05  AMOUNT-IN            PIC 9(05)V99.
```

These data are ordered by the customer number and invoice number. Report layout:

```
First page only         CUSTOMER PURCHASES

                                                                PAGE nn
Top of each page    CUSTOMER       INVOICE       INVOICE
                     NUMBER         NUMBER        AMOUNT

For each record      nnnnn          nnnnn      nn,nnn.nn
Customer number                     nnnnn      nn,nnn.nn
 suppressed                         nnnnn      nn,nnn.nn
For each customer   TOTAL SALES:              nnn,nnn.nn
```

```
                   nnnnn          nnnnn    nn,nnn.nn
                                  nnnnn    nn,nnn.nn
                                  nnnnn    nn,nnn.nn
                  TOTAL SALES:            nnn,nnn.nn
Top of each page  CUSTOMER       INVOICE     INVOICE
                   NUMBER         NUMBER      AMOUNT

                   nnnnn          nnnnn    nn,nnn.nn
                                  nnnnn    nn,nnn.nn
                                  nnnnn    nn,nnn.nn
                  TOTAL SALES:            nnn,nnn.nn

                   nnnnn          nnnnn    nn,nnn.nn
                                  nnnnn    nn,nnn.nn
                                  nnnnn    nn,nnn.nn
                  TOTAL SALES:            nnn,nnn.nn

End of report     COMPANY SALES:     nnn,nnn,nnn.nn
```

1. Write the RD entries necessary to describe this report. The report-name should be CUSTOMER-PURCHASES.

2. Write the record necessary to describe the report heading.

3. Write the record(s) necessary to describe the control footings. Assume the COMPANY SALES total is produced as a control footing.

4. Write the record necessary to describe the detail line. (*Note:* Only one detail line should be specified.)

5. Assuming COMPANY SALES is a report footing, write the record necessary to describe the report footing.

6. Given that the following clauses are present in a report description, provide all the information possible about the general appearance of a printed page.

```
PAGE LIMIT     50 LINES
   HEADING       4
   FIRST DETAIL  8
   LAST DETAIL  46
   FOOTING      48.
```

7. Given the following CONTROLS clause and the assumption that control headings and footings are recorded in a report description for each (where applicable), record the sequence of headings and footings produced given the indicated data-name change.

```
CONTROLS ARE FINAL, INVOICE-NUMBER, CUSTOMER-NUMBER,
DATE-OF-SALE.
a. DATE-OF-SALE
b. CUSTOMER-NUMBER
c. INVOICE-NUMBER
d. end of report (FINAL)
```

Below is a description of a report that could be produced by the report writer feature of COBOL. Answer the following questions based on the report layout and the data information provided.

Data Name	Type of Data Represented
ITEM-NUMBER-IN	Numeric value of an item number
ITEM-DESCRIPTION-IN	Alphanumeric value of the item description
BALANCE-IN	Numeric dollars and cents value of the initial balance of an item

DEPR-METHOD-IN	Alphanumeric value of the depreciation method
DEPR-MO-IN	Numeric value of the month in which depreciation occurred
DEPR-YR-IN	Numeric value of the year in which depreciation occurred
BEG-BAL-IN	Numeric dollars and cents value of an item at the beginning of a depreciation period
DEPR-IN	Numeric dollars and cents value of the depreciation for a given period
END-BAL-IN	Numeric dollars and cents value of an item at the end of a depreciation period

Report format:

```
                                     DEPRECIATION REPORT                                       PAGE Z9
ITEM NUMBER        ITEM DESCRIPTION        BALANCE      USEFUL LIFE nn
   nnnnn        XXXXXXXXXXXXXXXXXXXX    $$$$,$$$.$$  XXXXXXXXXXXXXXX
                                                      (Depr-Method-In)
MONTH YEAR        BEG. BALANCE           DEPRECIATION          END. BALANCE

   nn nn           $$$$,$$$.$$            $$$$,$$$.$$            $$$$,$$$.$$
   nn              $$$$,$$$.$$            $$$$,$$$.$$            $$$$,$$$.$$
   nn              $$$$,$$$.$$            $$$$,$$$.$$            $$$$,$$$.$$
   nn              $$$$,$$$.$$            $$$$,$$$.$$            $$$$,$$$,$$
   nn              $$$$,$$$.$$            $$$$,$$$.$$            $$$$,$$$,$$

       TOTAL ANNUAL DEPRECIATION        $$$$,$$$.$$

MONTH YEAR        BEG. BALANCE           DEPRECIATION          END. BALANCE

   nn nn           $$$$,$$$.$$            $$$$,$$$.$$            $$$$,$$$.$$
   nn              $$$$,$$$.$$            $$$$,$$$.$$            $$$$,$$$.$$
   nn              $$$$,$$$.$$            $$$$,$$$.$$            $$$$,$$$,$$
   nn              $$$$,$$$.$$            $$$$,$$$.$$            $$$$,$$$,$$
    .                 .                      .                      .
    .                 .                      .                      .
    .                 .                      .                      .
```

8. Write the code necessary to describe the RD for DEPRECIATION-REPORT.
9. Write the code necessary to describe the page heading.
10. Write the code necessary to describe the detail line.
11. Write the code necessary to describe the control footing. (*Note:* the control break occurs on the change of year value.)

Problems

15.1 Solve problem 8.3 using the report writer feature to produce the printed report.
15.2 Solve problem 10.1 using the report writer feature, where possible, to produce the printed report.
15.3 Solve problem 14.3 using the report writer feature to produce the printed report.

CHAPTER

16

The SORT Statement

In some commercial installations, as much as 60 to 80 percent of the computer's time is spent sorting data. *Sorting* simply means the arrangement of data into a specified sequence. Many problems require data to be in a particular sequence. With others, the process is greatly simplified (or more efficient) if data are in a known sequence. As a consequence, sorting is often a necessary first step toward solving a problem.

The Sorting Process

The only problem presented thus far in the text that rearranged (sorted) data was the Sales Analysis problem in Chapter 14, in which an *internal* sort was coded into the program. Unfortunately, all internal sorts suffer the same difficulty—all the data to be sorted must be placed into the computer's internal storage at the same time. The problem presented in Figure 14.9 could accommodate up to 100 individual salesman entries in a table, but what would happen if we were required to sort 1,000 records, or 10,000 records, or 100,000 records? The internal sort would require sufficient internal storage to retain all the data, in addition to which, the sorting time might be prohibitive.

The procedure provided through the SORT statement is an *external* sort. This procedure requires only enough computer memory to store the actual program code and a segment of the data to be sorted; most of the data are temporarily stored on an external medium (e.g., magnetic tape or disk) until needed. The procedure is known as a *sort-merge* procedure. In this procedure, a limited amount of data is sorted internally and then stored on an external medium. This ''sorting and writing'' process is repeated until all the data have been accepted. Then, the groups of sorted data are *merged*.

Consider for a moment a deck of regular playing cards. Suppose you wished to order all the playing cards into a specified sequence. Because it is more difficult with all 52 cards, you divide the deck into four equal stacks, each containing 13 cards. You then proceed to order the playing cards in each stack into the appropriate order. After the four stacks have been ordered, you start merging the stacks. You examine stacks 1 and 2. After looking at the first card in each stack, you decide which is higher and place this card in a new stack. You then compare the two cards that now appear on the top

Figure 16.1 The SORT Statement

```
SORT sort-file-name ON {ASCENDING } KEY identifier-1 [identifier-2] ...
                       {DESCENDING}

[ON {ASCENDING } KEY identifier-m [identifier-n] ...] ...
    {DESCENDING}

[WITH DUPLICATES IN ORDER]

{USING file-name-1 . . .                                         }
{INPUT PROCEDURE IS section-name-1 [THRU section-name-2]         }

{GIVING file-name-2 . . .                                        }
{OUTPUT PROCEDURE IS section-name-3 [THRU section-name-4]        }
```

of each stack and select the higher card, adding it to the new stack. The process continues until you have "merged" the two smaller stacks into one stack containing 26 cards. You then repeat the process for stacks 3 and 4 to build another stack of 26 cards in the appropriate order. Finally, you perform the merging process on the two stacks of 26 cards, building a single stack of 52 cards. The result is an ordered deck of playing cards. The procedure performed by the SORT statement is very similar. The biggest difference is that, rather than laying stacks of playing cards on a table, the SORT statement records these groups of ordered data on a magnetic medium for later recall.

The form of the SORT statement is presented in Figure 16.1. The statement has four distinct phases—the identification of the sort file, the specification of sort keys, a description of the input process, and an indication of the output process. Each of these phases will be discussed in turn.

The SORT File

The statement begins with the required reserved word SORT, followed by a "sort-file-name." All previous descriptions of files in COBOL have simply identified a "file-name." As is the case with other files, the sort-file-name must appear in a SELECT clause in the FILE-CONTROL paragraph of the ENVIRONMENT DIVISION. The sort-file must be assigned (via an ASSIGN clause) to a device consistent with the use of magnetic media. Because ASSIGN clause requirements are different from installation to installation, check with your computer center to determine the specific requirements for a sort-file.

All files used in a COBOL program must be described in the FILE SECTION of the DATA DIVISION. The sort-file is no exception; however, the sort-file is described with an SD entry instead of an FD entry. Figure 16.2 illustrates a "typical" file and a sort-file. Note that both an INVOICE-FILE and an INVOICE-SORT-FILE are selected in the FILE-CONTROL paragraph. An FD description is presented in the FILE SECTION for the INVOICE-FILE. Following the description of the INVOICE-FILE, the SD for the INVOICE-SORT-FILE is provided.

Figure 16.2 An Illustration of a Sort-File SD

```
ENVIRONMENT DIVISION.
CONFIGURATION SECTION.
SOURCE-COMPUTER.   IBM-370.
OBJECT-COMPUTER.   IBM-370.
INPUT-OUTPUT SECTION.
FILE-CONTROL.
    SELECT INVOICE-FILE ASSIGN TO UT-S-INPUT.
    SELECT INVOICE-SORT-FILE ASSIGN TO UT-S-SORTWK01,
                                          SORTWK02,
                                          SORTWK03.
DATA DIVISION.
FILE SECTION.
FD  INVOICE-FILE
        LABEL RECORDS ARE OMITTED.
01  INVOICE-RECORD.
    05 INVOICE-NUMBER              PIC 9(05).
    05 CUSTOMER-NUMBER             PIC X(10).
    05 DATE-OF-PURCHASE.
       10 MONTH-PUR                PIC 9(02).
       10 DAY-PUR                  PIC 9(02).
       10 YEAR-PUR                 PIC 9(02).
    05 PURCHASE-AMOUNT             PIC 9(05)V99.
    05 DISCOUNT-AMOUNT             PIC 9(03)V99.
    05 TAX-AMOUNT                  PIC 9(03)V99.
    05 FILLER                      PIC X(42).
SD  INVOICE-SORT-FILE.
01  INVOICE-RECORD-SORT.
    05 INVOICE-NUMBER-SORT         PIC 9(05).
    05 CUSTOMER-NUMBER-SORT        PIC X(10).
    05 DATE-OF-PURCHASE-SORT.
       10 MONTH-PUR-SORT           PIC 9(02).
       10 DAY-PUR-SORT             PIC 9(02).
       10 YEAR-PUR-SORT            PIC 9(02).
    05 PURCHASE-AMOUNT-SORT        PIC 9(05)V99.
    05 DISCOUNT-AMOUNT-SORT        PIC 9(03)V99.
    05 TAX-AMOUNT-SORT             PIC 9(03)V99.
```

The Specification of Sort Keys

Immediately following the identification of the sort-file in Figure 16.1, the SORT statement specifies the keys on which the data are to be sorted. Keys are specified as either ASCENDING (from lowest to highest value) or DESCENDING (from highest to lowest value) according to the *collating sequence* of the computer you are using, EBCDIC or ASCII. These collating sequences are repeated in Table 16.1. To illustrate the importance of the collating sequence, assume that you wished to sort a customer address field in ASCENDING order. If you were using an EBCDIC machine (e.g., IBM), you would expect P.O. Box addresses to appear before street addresses—street addresses begin with digits. In other words, letters have a lower value on the EBCDIC collating sequence than do digits. Conversely, if you performed the same sort on an ASCII machine (e.g., Honeywell), you would expect the street addresses to appear before P.O. Box addresses—digits are lower in value in the ASCII collating sequence than are letters.

Table 16.1 The COBOL Character Sets
(in Collating Sequence Order from Lowest Value to Highest Value)

EBCDIC		ASCII	
	space		space
.	period or decimal point	"	quote symbol
<	less than symbol	$	currency symbol
(	left parenthesis	'	apostrophe
+	plus symbol	(	left parenthesis
$	currency symbol	)	right parenthesis
*	asterisk	*	asterisk
)	right parenthesis	+	plus symbol
;	semicolon	,	comma
–	hyphen or minus symbol	–	hyphen or minus symbol
/	slash	.	period or decimal point
,	comma	/	slash
>	greater than symbol	0–9	numeric characters (digits)
'	apostrophe	;	semicolon
=	equal symbol	<	less than symbol
"	quote symbol	=	equal symbol
A–Z	alphabetic characters (letters)	>	greater than symbol
0–9	numeric characters (digits)	A–Z	alphabetic characters (letters)

The ordering of sort keys is also important. In Figure 16.1, notice that several identifiers (identifier-1, identifier-2, etc.) may be listed after the words ASCENDING or DESCENDING. The identifiers are listed in the order of their importance. Identifier-1 is the *major* sort key. Only when values of identifier-1 are equal will identifier-2 have any effect on the sequence of sorted data. When more than one sort record has the same value for identifier-1, they will be ordered by identifier-2. Figure 16.3 illustrates this. In part A, a single key (INVOICE-NUMBER-SORT) is specified in an ASCENDING order. Compare the order of the data before and after the sorting operation. The data have been ordered on an ASCENDING sequence based on INVOICE-NUMBER-SORT. In part B, multiple ASCENDING keys are specified—CUSTOMER-NUMBER-SORT, YEAR-PUR-SORT, MONTH-PUR-SORT, and DAY-PUR-SORT. Again, compare the sequence of the data before and after the sorting operation. The CUSTOMER-NUMBER-SORT has been ordered in an ascending sequence; however, the last two records contain the same customer number. Thus, during the sorting process, the values of YEAR-PUR-SORT were compared (80 versus 81). If more than one record had contained the same year, then the sorting procedure would have compared the values of MONTH-PUR-SORT to determine the appropriate sequence. If more than one record contained the same customer number, year, and month, DAY-PUR-SORT would have been examined.

In part C, a DESCENDING key of PURCHASE-AMOUNT-SORT has been specified, and the purchase amount field has been ordered from the *largest* to the *smallest* value. In part D, both the ASCENDING and DESCENDING phrases are specified in the same sorting operation. Examining the results of this process indicates the data have been ordered by year and month (ASCENDING). In the final two records of the result, the year and month values are the same. Thus, the invoice number of these two items are

Figure 16.3 Illustrations of the ASCENDING/DESCENDING KEY Clause

A)...ASCENDING KEY INVOICE-NUMBER-SORT...

Data BEFORE Sorting

		DATE OF PURCHASE SORT					
INVOICE NUMBER SORT	CUSTOMER NUMBER SORT	MONTH PUR SORT	DAY PUR SORT	YEAR PUR SORT	PURCHASE AMOUNT SORT	DISCOUNT AMOUNT SORT	TAX AMOUNT SORT
44193	113R397ƀƀƀ	Ø4	15	81	ØØØ24∧65	ØØØ∧24	ØØ1∧33
31962	227A5Ø3ƀƀƀ	Ø4	22	81	ØØ221∧33	ØØ2∧21	Ø11∧Ø7
631ØØ	Ø89U846ƀƀƀ	Ø3	1Ø	81	Ø335Ø∧ØØ	Ø33∧5Ø	167∧5Ø
Ø1862	227A5Ø3ƀƀƀ	12	15	8Ø	ØØ792∧15	ØØ7∧92	Ø39∧61

Data AFTER Sorting

		DATE OF PURCHASE SORT					
INVOICE NUMBER SORT	CUSTOMER NUMBER SORT	MONTH PUR SORT	DAY PUR SORT	YEAR PUR SORT	PURCHASE AMOUNT SORT	DISCOUNT AMOUNT SORT	TAX AMOUNT SORT
Ø1862	227A5Ø3ƀƀƀ	12	15	8Ø	ØØ792∧15	ØØ7∧92	Ø39∧61
31962	227A5Ø3ƀƀƀ	Ø4	22	81	ØØ221∧33	ØØ2∧21	Ø11∧Ø7
44193	113R397ƀƀƀ	Ø4	15	81	ØØØ24∧65	ØØØ∧24	ØØ1∧33
631ØØ	Ø89U846ƀƀƀ	Ø3	1Ø	81	Ø335Ø∧ØØ	Ø33∧5Ø	167∧5Ø

B)...ASCENDING KEY CUSTOMER-NUMBER-SORT, YEAR-PUR-SORT
MONTH-PUR-SORT, DAY-PUR-SORT ...

Data BEFORE Sorting

		DATE OF PURCHASE SORT					
INVOICE NUMBER SORT	CUSTOMER NUMBER SORT	MONTH PUR SORT	DAY PUR SORT	YEAR PUR SORT	PURCHASE AMOUNT SORT	DISCOUNT AMOUNT SORT	TAX AMOUNT SORT
44193	113R397ƀƀƀ	Ø4	15	81	ØØØ24∧65	ØØØ∧24	ØØ1∧33
31962	227A5Ø3ƀƀƀ	Ø4	22	81	ØØ221∧33	ØØ2∧21	Ø11∧Ø7
631ØØ	Ø89U846ƀƀƀ	Ø3	1Ø	81	Ø335Ø∧ØØ	Ø33∧5Ø	167∧5Ø
Ø1862	227A5Ø3ƀƀƀ	12	15	8Ø	ØØ792∧15	ØØ7∧92	Ø39∧61

Data AFTER Sorting

		DATE OF PURCHASE SORT					
INVOICE NUMBER SORT	CUSTOMER NUMBER SORT	MONTH PUR SORT	DAY PUR SORT	YEAR PUR SORT	PURCHASE AMOUNT SORT	DISCOUNT AMOUNT SORT	TAX AMOUNT SORT
631ØØ	Ø89U846ƀƀƀ	Ø3	1Ø	81	Ø335Ø∧ØØ	Ø33∧5Ø	167∧5Ø
44193	113R397ƀƀƀ	Ø4	15	81	ØØØ24∧65	ØØØ∧24	ØØ1∧33
Ø1862	227A5Ø3ƀƀƀ	12	15	8Ø	ØØ792∧15	ØØ7∧92	Ø39∧61
31962	227A5Ø3ƀƀƀ	Ø4	22	81	ØØ221∧33	ØØ2∧21	Ø11∧Ø7

C)...DESCENDING KEY PURCHASE-AMOUNT-SORT...

Data BEFORE Sorting

		DATE OF PURCHASE SORT					
INVOICE NUMBER SORT	CUSTOMER NUMBER SORT	MONTH PUR SORT	DAY PUR SORT	YEAR PUR SORT	PURCHASE AMOUNT SORT	DISCOUNT AMOUNT SORT	TAX AMOUNT SORT
44193	113R397ƀƀƀ	Ø4	15	81	ØØØ24∧65	ØØØ∧24	ØØ1∧33
31962	227A5Ø3ƀƀƀ	Ø4	22	81	ØØ221∧33	ØØ2∧21	Ø11∧Ø7
631ØØ	Ø89U846ƀƀƀ	Ø3	1Ø	81	Ø335Ø∧ØØ	Ø33∧5Ø	167∧5Ø
Ø1862	227A5Ø3ƀƀƀ	12	15	8Ø	ØØ792∧15	ØØ7∧15	Ø39∧61

compared and the larger of the two values is recorded first (since the key sequence for INVOICE-NUMBER-SORT is DESCENDING).

All sort key fields *must* be recorded in the sort-record description; that is, they must be subordinate to an SD. The number and maximum length of all keys combined may be restricted. For example, IBM compilers permit a maximum of 12 keys, the total length of which may not exceed 256 bytes. If multiple record descriptions are provided with the SD, the key must be the same displacement from the beginning of the record (location) in all descriptions. Also, the programmer is not limited with regard to the type of data definition used in conjunction with a sort key. Sort keys may be either numeric or alphanumeric. In addition, the sort key could be a group-name or an elementary-item described as numeric-edited, binary, packed decimal, alphabetic, and so forth. (Binary and packed-decimal data types are described in Chapter 23.)

1985 COBOL Standards 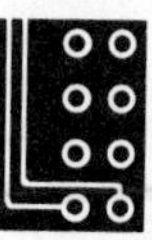

In COBOL 85 the programmer is given the option of specifying how records with the same value in the sort key are to be handled. In earlier versions records with duplicate keys would appear in any order. However, the WITH DUPLICATES IN ORDER option forces the records having duplicate keys to appear in the same order they are released to the sort file.

Figure 16.3 *Continued* Illustrations of the ASCENDING/DESCENDING KEY Clause

Data AFTER Sorting

INVOICE NUMBER SORT	CUSTOMER NUMBER SORT	DATE OF PURCHASE SORT: MONTH PUR SORT	DAY PUR SORT	YEAR PUR SORT	PURCHASE AMOUNT SORT	DISCOUNT AMOUNT SORT	TAX AMOUNT SORT
631ØØ	Ø89U846ƀƀƀ	Ø3	1Ø	81	Ø335Ø∧ØØ	Ø33∧5Ø	167∧5Ø
Ø1862	227A5Ø3ƀƀƀ	12	15	8Ø	ØØ792∧15	ØØ7∧92	Ø39∧61
31962	227A5Ø3ƀƀƀ	Ø4	22	81	ØØ221∧33	ØØ2∧21	Ø11∧Ø7
44193	113R397ƀƀƀ	Ø4	15	81	ØØØ24∧65	ØØØ∧24	ØØ1∧33

D)...ASCENDING KEY YEAR-PUR-SORT, MONTH-PUR-SORT
DESCENDING KEY INVOICE-NUMBER-SORT...

Data BEFORE Sorting

INVOICE NUMBER SORT	CUSTOMER NUMBER SORT	DATE OF PURCHASE SORT: MONTH PUR SORT	DAY PUR SORT	YEAR PUR SORT	PURCHASE AMOUNT SORT	DISCOUNT AMOUNT SORT	TAX AMOUNT SORT
44193	113R397ƀƀƀ	Ø4	15	81	ØØØ24∧65	ØØØ∧24	ØØ1∧33
31962	227A5Ø3ƀƀƀ	Ø4	22	81	ØØ221∧33	ØØ2∧21	Ø11∧Ø7
631ØØ	Ø89U846ƀƀƀ	Ø3	1Ø	81	Ø335Ø∧5Ø	Ø33∧5Ø	167∧5Ø
Ø1862	227A5Ø3ƀƀƀ	12	15	8Ø	ØØ792∧15	ØØ7∧92	Ø39∧61

Data AFTER Sorting

INVOICE NUMBER SORT	CUSTOMER NUMBER SORT	DATE OF PURCHASE SORT: MONTH PUR SORT	DAY PUR SORT	YEAR PUR SORT	PURCHASE AMOUNT SORT	DISCOUNT AMOUNT SORT	TAX AMOUNT SORT
Ø1862	227A5Ø3ƀƀƀ	12	15	8Ø	ØØ792∧15	ØØ7∧92	Ø39∧61
631ØØ	Ø89U846ƀƀƀ	Ø3	1Ø	81	Ø335Ø∧ØØ	Ø33∧5Ø	167∧5Ø
44193	113R397ƀƀƀ	Ø4	15	81	ØØØ24∧65	ØØØ∧24	ØØ1∧33
31962	227A5Ø3ƀƀƀ	Ø4	22	81	ØØ221∧33	ØØ2∧21	Ø11∧Ø7

The Input Process

Figure 16.1 shows that the programmer has a choice of two phrases designed to accommodate the input of data into the sorting process—USING and INPUT PROCEDURE. The programmer selects one of these two options depending on the requirements of the problems. The first option, USING file-name-1, indicates that data are to be extracted from file-name-1 and transmitted to the sorting process. That is, the SORT statement with the USING phrase causes file-name-1 to be OPENed in the INPUT mode, data from file-name-1 to be READ into internal storage, the content of the input record to be MOVEd to the sort-record description, the sort-record to be written to the sort-file and, when all records from file-name-1 have been processed, file-name-1 is CLOSEd. For the USING phrase to be employed, file-name-1 must exist, it must be a standard sequential file, and the length of the input record must be the same as the sort record.

Figure 16.4 illustrates the USING phrase. Notice that the record description in Figure 16.4 is a general record description—PIC X(80). The programmer will not be using the fields of the input file in the PROCEDURE DIVISION. Rather, the field-names in the sort record will be used after the sorting has been completed. Also, notice that the record lengths of INVOICE-RECORD and INVOICE-SORT-RECORD are exactly the same. Finally, note it is not necessary that the first field of the sort record description be used as the sort key.

The second alternative available to the programmer for input processing is the INPUT PROCEDURE. As indicated in Figure 16.1, the identification of the INPUT PROCEDURE is specified by a SECTION name (or perhaps a range of sections, as is permitted with the PERFORM statements using the THRU option). In COBOL 85 the input procedure may be a SECTION or a PARAGRAPH (or a range of SECTIONs or PARAGRAPHs). With this option, it is the programmer's responsibility to provide all the COBOL code necessary to accept input data and send data to the sort procedure. There are a number of situations when the USING phrase cannot be used and the INPUT PROCEDURE is required. If the input file is not a sequential file, and USING phrase cannot be used. If the programmer wishes to lengthen the sort-record by adding more fields or shorten the record by eliminating fields that are not needed in the output phase, the INPUT PROCEDURE must be used. The same is true if the programmer wishes to eliminate some records from being sorted or if data must be joined from two or more files in the sort-file. Likewise, if the programmer wanted to select particular records or edit the records before sorting, an INPUT PROCEDURE must be used. Of course there are other reasons for using an INPUT PROCEDURE, but those identified earlier provide sufficient cause for *not* always employing the USING phrase.

Since the programmer is responsible for providing code to satisfy the input phase of the sort when the INPUT PROCEDURE is used, the programmer must OPEN the input file, READ the records from the file, MOVE the data to the sort-record description, write the sort-record to the sort-file, and CLOSE the input file. However, since the sort-file is a special file (notice that opening and closing the sort-file has *not* been mentioned), the programmer is not permitted to use a WRITE statement to transmit data to the sort-file. Instead, the programmer uses a RELEASE statement, as illustrated in Figure 16.5. The function (and appearance) of the RELEASE statement is highly similar to the WRITE statement. In fact, if the ADVANCING clause were to be dropped from the WRITE statement and the word *WRITE* were replaced with the word *RELEASE,* the two would

Figure 16.4 An Illustration of the USING Phrase

```
ENVIRONMENT DIVISION.
CONFIGURATION SECTION.
SOURCE-COMPUTER.  IBM.
OBJECT-COMPUTER.  IBM.
INPUT-OUTPUT SECTION.
FILE-CONTROL.
    SELECT INVOICE-FILE ASSIGN TO UT-S-INPUT.
    SELECT INVOICE-SORT-FILE ASSIGN TO UT-S-SORTWKØ1,
                                       UT-S-SORTWKØ2,
                                       UT-S-SORTWKØ3.
    .
    .
    .
DATA DIVISION.
FILE SECTION.
FD  INVOICE-FILE
    LABEL RECORDS ARE OMITTED.
Ø1  INVOICE-RECORD                    PIC X(8Ø).
SD  INVOICE-SORT-FILE.
Ø1  INVOICE-SORT-RECORD.
    Ø5 INVOICE-NUMBER-SORT            PIC 9(Ø5).
    Ø5 CUSTOMER-NUMBER-SORT           PIC X(1Ø).
    Ø5 DATE-OF-PURCHASE-SORT.
       1Ø MONTH-PUR-SORT              PIC 9(Ø2).
       1Ø DAY-PUR-SORT                PIC 9(Ø2).
       1Ø YEAR-PUR-SORT               PIC 9(Ø2).
    Ø5 PURCHASE-AMOUNT-SORT           PIC 9(Ø5)V99.
    Ø5 DISCOUNT-AMOUNT-SORT           PIC 9(Ø3)V99.
    Ø5 TAX-AMOUNT-SORT                PIC 9(Ø3)V99.
    Ø5 FILLER                         PIC X(42).
       .
       .
       .
PROCEDURE DIVISION.
SORT-CONTROL SECTION.
    SORT INVOICE-SORT-FILE
        ASCENDING KEY PURCHASE-AMOUNT-SORT
        USING INVOICE-FILE . . .
        .
        .
        .
```

Figure 16.5 The RELEASE Statement

```
RELEASE sort-record-name [FROM identifier]
```

be identical. Thus, the statement causes data in the sort-file (under the sort-record description) to be transmitted to the sorting process. If an INPUT PROCEDURE is used, the SECTION(s) identifying the COBOL code *must* contain a RELEASE statement—otherwise no data are transmitted to the sorting process. In COBOL 85, this is not a requirement.

Figure 16.6 illustrates one possible use of the INPUT PROCEDURE. Note the change in PICTURE descriptions of INVOICE-NUMBER and PURCHASE-AMOUNT of INVOICE-RECORD from that in previous illustrations. The procedure is to check the invoice number to ensure it is numeric and to verify the purchase amount is positive. In addition, notice the record lengths of INVOICE-RECORD and INVOICE-SORT-RECORD are not the same. Only those fields necessary for the output process have been included in the sort-record description. In the PROCEDURE DIVISION, the SORT statement identifies the INPUT PROCEDURE as 300-CHECK-INVOICES—a SECTION. Upon entering 300-CHECK-INVOICES, a series of procedures are performed; however, notice each of the procedures PERFORMed is also SECTIONs. Thus, when 300-CHECK-INVOICES is finished, another SECTION is encountered—causing a return to the output phase of the SORT statement. As the procedure continues, the input file is opened (320-INITIALIZE-INPUT SECTION) and an iterative process begins (340-EDIT-INVOICES SECTION), which verifies the accuracy of the input data. If the input data are correct, within the guidelines previously established, the desired data are moved to the sort-record, and the sort-record is RELEASEd to the sort process. This procedure continues until an end-of-file is encountered on the INVOICE-FILE—which causes an unconditional branch to 349-EXIT—terminating the 340-EDIT-INVOICES SECTION. Finally, 360-TERMINATE-INPUT is executed. After the termination sequence has been completed, the INPUT PROCEDURE is finished, causing a return to the SORT statement.

The Output Process

Like the input phase, the output phase of the SORT statement provides two options—GIVING and OUTPUT PROCEDURE. These options mirror the options provided in the input phase. The GIVING phrase allows the programmer to create an output file from the sorted data. Like the USING phrase, with the GIVING phrase, the output file must be a standard sequential file, and the record lengths of the sort-file and the output file must be the same. The GIVING phrase creates file-name-2.

The OUTPUT PROCEDURE allows the programmer to access individual records as they are returned from the sort-file. Again, since the programmer is to provide the code to accomplish the output task, the procedure must OPEN the output file, read records from the sort-file, MOVE data from the sort record to the output record, WRITE the output record, and, after all data have been read from the sort-file, CLOSE the output file. However, since the sort-file is a specialized file, the programmer is not permitted to READ the sort-file. Figure 16.7 illustrates the RETURN statement, which provides the programmer with the tool by which records may be retrieved from the sort-file. The

Figure 16.6 An Illustration of the INPUT PROCEDURE

```
ENVIRONMENT DIVISION.
CONFIGURATION SECTION.
SOURCE-COMPUTER.  IBM.
OBJECT-COMPUTER.  IBM.
INPUT-OUTPUT SECTION.
FILE-CONTROL.
    SELECT INVOICE-FILE       ASSIGN TO UT-S-INPUT.
    SELECT INVOICE-SORT-FILE  ASSIGN TO UT-S-SORTWK01,
                                          SORTWK02,
                                          SORTWK03.
       .
       .
       .
DATA DIVISION.
FILE SECTION.
FD  INVOICE-FILE
    LABEL RECORDS ARE OMITTED.
01  INVOICE-RECORD.
    05  INVOICE-NUMBER-IN          PIC X(05).
    05  CUSTOMER-NUMBER-IN         PIC X(10).
    05  DATE-OF-PURCHASE-IN        PIC 9(06).
    05  PURCHASE-AMOUNT-IN         PIC S9(05)V99.
    05  DISCOUNT-AMOUNT-IN         PIC 9(03)V99.
    05  TAX-AMOUNT-IN              PIC 9(03)V99.
    05  FILLER                     PIC X(43).
SD  INVOICE-SORT-FILE.
01  INVOICE-SORT-RECORD.
    05  INVOICE-NUMBER-SORT        PIC 9(05).
    05  DATE-OF-PURCHASE-SORT      PIC 9(06).
    05  PURCHASE-AMOUNT-SORT       PIC S9(05)V99.
       .
       .
       .
WORKING-STORAGE SECTION.
01  WORKING-RECORD.
    05  FILE-STATUS                PIC X(05).
    05  SORT-STATUS                PIC X(10).
       .
       .
       .
PROCEDURE DIVISION.
000-SORT-CONTROL SECTION.
    SORT INVOICE-SORT-FILE
        ASCENDING KEY INVOICE-NUMBER-SORT
        INPUT PROCEDURE 300-CHECK-INVOICES . . .
       .                                  MUST BE A SECTION
       .
       .
300-CHECK-INVOICES SECTION.
    PERFORM 320-INITIALIZE-INPUT.
    PERFORM 340-EDIT-INVOICES
        UNTIL FILE-STATUS = 'DONE'.
    PERFORM 360-TERMINATE-INPUT.
320-INITIALIZE-INPUT SECTION.
    OPEN INPUT INVOICE-FILE.
340-EDIT-INVOICES SECTION.
    READ INVOICE-FILE
        AT END MOVE 'DONE' TO FILE-STATUS
               GO TO 340-EXIT.
    MOVE 'RELEASE' TO SORT-STATUS.
```

Figure 16.6 *Continued* An Illustration of the INPUT PROCEDURE

```
        IF INVOICE-NUMBER-IN NOT NUMERIC
            MOVE 'NO RELEASE' TO SORT-STATUS.
        IF PURCHASE-AMOUNT-IN NOT POSITIVE
            MOVE 'NO RELEASE' TO SORT-STATUS.
        IF SORT-STATUS = 'RELEASE'
            MOVE INVOICE-NUMBER-IN TO INVOICE-NUMBER-SORT
            MOVE DATE-OF-PURCHASE-IN TO DATE-OF-PURCHASE-SORT
            MOVE PURCHASE-AMOUNT-IN TO PURCHASE-AMOUNT-SORT
            RELEASE INVOICE-SORT-RECORD.
    340-EXIT.
        EXIT.
    360-TERMINATE-INPUT SECTION.
        CLOSE INVOICE-FILE.
            .
            .
            .
```

Figure 16.7 The RETURN Statement

```
RETURN sort-file-name [INTO identifier]
       [AT END imperative-statement-1]
       [NOT AT END imperative-statement-2]
       [END-RETURN]
```

only difference between the READ statement for a sequential file and the RETURN statement is that the word *READ* has been replaced with the word *RETURN*.

The Inventory Sort Problem

Figure 16.8 illustrates the use of a SORT statement in the context of a complete program. This procedure utilizes a SORT statement with INPUT PROCEDURE and OUTPUT PROCEDURE options (see lines 1120–1150). The record descriptions in the FILE SECTION are all of different lengths. In the PROCEDURE DIVISION, the INPUT PROCEDURE is a section; the remaining parts of the INPUT PROCEDURE are coded at the paragraph level. To terminate the INPUT PROCEDURE, the programmer must execute an unconditional branch to the end of the SECTION (190-INPUT-TERMINATION). The processing sequence involves an examination of each input record to determine whether or not the quantity ON-HAND is below the MIN-STOCK-LEVEL. If insufficient stock is ON-HAND, the record is transmitted to the sort process via 165-MOVE-AND-RELEASE.

After the INPUT PROCEDURE has been completed, the OUTPUT PROCEDURE proceeds to print a report based on the sorted data. Thus, records are RETURNed from the sort-file at lines 1660 and 1820. Note the similarity between the OUTPUT PROCEDURE of this problem and that in problems that did not use the SORT statement. If the RETURN statements were replaced by READ statements, the OUTPUT

Figure 16.8 Inventory Sort (Hierarchy Chart)

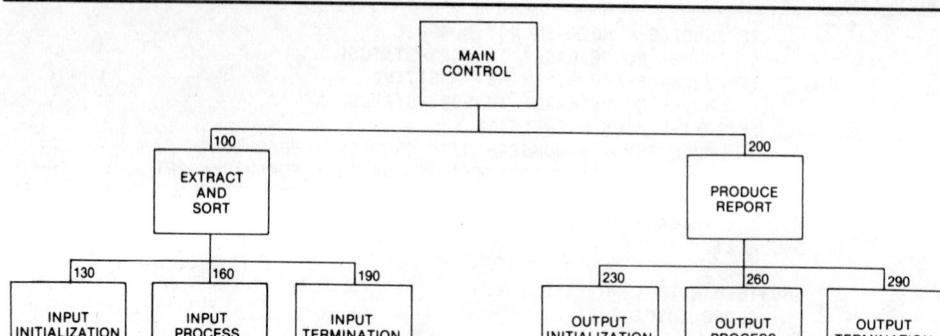

Figure 16.8 *Continued* Inventory Sort (Pseudocode)

```
START
     SORT Inventory file
          ASCENDING vendor, item
          INPUT Extract and sort
          OUTPUT produce report
     ENDSORT
END

EXTRACT AND SORT
     DO Input initialization
     DO Input process UNTIL eof
     GOTO Input termination
END

INPUT INITIALIZATION
     OPEN input file
     READ input file
          IF eof
               SET file status
          ENDIF
     ENDREAD
END

INPUT PROCESS
     IF on hand < min stock level
          DO Move and release
     ENDIF
     READ input file
          IF eof
               SET file status
          ENDIF
     ENDREAD
END

MOVE AND RELEASE
     MOVE input to sort file
     RELEASE sort record
END

INPUT TERMINATION
     CLOSE input file
END

PRODUCE REPORT
     DO Output initialization
     DO Output process UNTIL eof
     GOTO Output termination
END

OUTPUT INITIALIZATION
     OPEN output file
     SET file status
     SET line count
     RETURN sort file
     IF eof
          SET file status
     ENDIF
END

OUTPUT PROCESS
     IF line count > 40
          DO Headings
     ENDIF
     MOVE sort to output
     WRITE output AFTER 2 lines
     ADD 2 to line count
     RETURN sort file
     IF eof
          SET file status
     ENDIF
END

HEADINGS
     MOVE 0 to line count
     WRITE heading
END

OUTPUT TERMINATION
     CLOSE output file
```

Figure 16.8 *Continued* Inventory Sort

```
        1   1   2   2   2   3   3   4   4   4   5   5   6   6   6   7
    4   8   2   6   0   4   8   2   6   0   4   8   2   6   0   4   8   2

*****************************************************************
 IDENTIFICATION DIVISION.
*****************************************************************
 PROGRAM-ID.     INVENTORY-SORT.
 AUTHOR.         J. WAYNE SPENCE.
 DATE-WRITTEN.   JANUARY 1, 1989.
 DATE-COMPILED.  JANUARY 1, 1989.
*****************************************************************
 ENVIRONMENT DIVISION.
*****************************************************************
*---------------------------------------------------------------*
 CONFIGURATION SECTION.
*---------------------------------------------------------------*
 SOURCE-COMPUTER.  IBM.
 OBJECT-COMPUTER.  IBM.
 SPECIAL-NAMES.
                   C01 IS PAGE-TOP.
*---------------------------------------------------------------*
 INPUT-OUTPUT SECTION.
*---------------------------------------------------------------*
 FILE-CONTROL.
     SELECT INVENTORY-FILE      ASSIGN TO UT-S-INPUT.
     SELECT OUTPUT-FILE         ASSIGN TO UT-S-OUTPUT.
     SELECT INVENTORY-SORT-FILE ASSIGN TO UT-S-SORTWK01.
*****************************************************************
 DATA DIVISION.
*****************************************************************
*---------------------------------------------------------------*
 FILE SECTION.
*---------------------------------------------------------------*
 FD  INVENTORY-FILE
     LABEL RECORDS ARE OMITTED.
 01  INVENTORY-RECORD.
     05  ITEM-IN                     PIC X(06).
     05  DESCRIPTION-IN              PIC X(30).
     05  VENDOR-IN                   PIC X(03).
     05  ON-HAND-IN                  PIC X(05).
     05  MIN-STOCK-LEVEL-IN          PIC X(05).
     05  UNIT-COST-IN                PIC 9(05)V99.
     05  UNIT-PRICE-IN               PIC 9(05)V99.
     05  YTD-SALES-IN                PIC 9(12).
     05  FILLER                      PIC X(05).

 FD  OUTPUT-FILE
     LABEL RECORDS ARE OMITTED
     RECORD CONTAINS 133 CHARACTERS.
 01  OUTPUT-RECORD                   PIC X(133).

 SD  INVENTORY-SORT-FILE.
 01  SORT-RECORD.
     05  ITEM-SORT                   PIC X(06).
     05  DESCRIPTION-SORT            PIC X(30).
     05  VENDOR-SORT                 PIC X(03).
     05  ON-HAND-SORT                PIC X(05).
     05  MIN-STOCK-LEVEL-SORT        PIC X(05).
     05  UNIT-COST-SORT              PIC 9(05)V99.
     05  YTD-SALES-SORT              PIC 9(12).
*---------------------------------------------------------------*
 WORKING-STORAGE SECTION.
*---------------------------------------------------------------*
 01  WORKING-VARIABLES.
     05  FILE-STATUS                 PIC X(05)  VALUE 'START'.
     05  LINE-COUNT                  PIC 9(02)  VALUE ZERO.

 01  HEADING1.
     05  FILLER                      PIC X(55)  VALUE SPACES.
     05  FILLER                      PIC X(20)  VALUE
                                     'Learning COBOL, Inc.'.
     05  FILLER                      PIC X(58)  VALUE SPACES.
```

Figure 16.8 *Continued* Inventory Sort

```
                1   1   2   2   2   3   3   4   4   4   5   5   6   6   6   7
    4   8   2   6   0   4   8   2   6   0   4   8   2   6   0   4   8   2

       01  HEADING2.
           05  FILLER                      PIC X(08)  VALUE SPACES.
           05  FILLER                      PIC X(04)  VALUE 'Item'.
           05  FILLER                      PIC X(16)  VALUE SPACES.
           05  FILLER                      PIC X(11)  VALUE 'Description'.
           05  FILLER                      PIC X(19)  VALUE SPACES.
           05  FILLER                      PIC X(06)  VALUE 'Vendor'.
           05  FILLER                      PIC X(05)  VALUE SPACES.
           05  FILLER                      PIC X(07)  VALUE 'On Hand'.
           05  FILLER                      PIC X(06)  VALUE SPACES.
           05  FILLER                      PIC X(07)  VALUE 'Minimum'.
           05  FILLER                      PIC X(08)  VALUE SPACES.
           05  FILLER                      PIC X(04)  VALUE 'Cost'.
           05  FILLER                      PIC X(11)  VALUE SPACES.
           05  FILLER                      PIC X(09)  VALUE 'YTD Sales'.
           05  FILLER                      PIC X(12)  VALUE SPACES.

       01  REPORT-LINE.
           05  FILLER                      PIC X(08)  VALUE SPACES.
           05  ITEM-OUT                    PIC X(06)  VALUE SPACES.
           05  FILLER                      PIC X(08)  VALUE SPACES.
           05  DESCRIPTION-OUT             PIC X(30)  VALUE SPACES.
           05  FILLER                      PIC X(08)  VALUE SPACES.
           05  VENDOR-OUT                  PIC X(03)  VALUE SPACES.
           05  FILLER                      PIC X(05)  VALUE SPACES.
           05  ON-HAND-OUT                 PIC Z(04)9  VALUE ZERO.
           05  FILLER                      PIC X(08)  VALUE SPACES.
           05  MIN-STOCK-LEVEL-OUT         PIC Z(04)9  VALUE ZERO.
           05  FILLER                      PIC X(07)  VALUE SPACES.
           05  UNIT-COST-OUT               PIC $$,$$$.99  VALUE ZERO.
           05  FILLER                      PIC X(04)  VALUE SPACES.
           05  YTD-SALES-OUT               PIC Z(11)9  VALUE ZERO.
           05  FILLER                      PIC X(15)  VALUE SPACES.
      *****************************************************************
       PROCEDURE DIVISION.
      *****************************************************************
      *---------------------------------------------------------------*
       000-MAIN-CONTROL SECTION.
      *---------------------------------------------------------------*
       000-ENTRY.
           MOVE 50000                  TO SORT-CORE-SIZE.
           SORT INVENTORY-SORT-FILE
               ASCENDING KEY VENDOR-SORT, ITEM-SORT
               INPUT PROCEDURE 100-EXTRACT-AND-SORT
               OUTPUT PROCEDURE 200-PRODUCE-REPORT.
           STOP RUN.

       000-EXIT.
           EXIT.
      *---------------------------------------------------------------*
       100-EXTRACT-AND-SORT SECTION.
      *---------------------------------------------------------------*
           PERFORM 130-INPUT-INITIALIZATION.
           PERFORM 160-INPUT-PROCESS
               UNTIL FILE-STATUS = 'DONE'.
           GO TO 190-INPUT-TERMINATION.

       130-INPUT-INITIALIZATION.
           OPEN INPUT INVENTORY-FILE.
           READ INVENTORY-FILE
               AT END MOVE 'DONE' TO FILE-STATUS.

       160-INPUT-PROCESS.
           IF ON-HAND-IN < MIN-STOCK-LEVEL-IN
               PERFORM 165-MOVE-AND-RELEASE.
           READ INVENTORY-FILE
               AT END MOVE 'DONE' TO FILE-STATUS.
```

Figure 16.8 *Continued* Inventory Sort

```
165-MOVE-AND-RELEASE.
    MOVE ITEM-IN                TO ITEM-SORT.
    MOVE DESCRIPTION-IN         TO DESCRIPTION-SORT.
    MOVE VENDOR-IN              TO VENDOR-SORT.
    MOVE ON-HAND-IN             TO ON-HAND-SORT.
    MOVE MIN-STOCK-LEVEL-IN     TO MIN-STOCK-LEVEL-SORT.
    MOVE UNIT-COST-IN           TO UNIT-COST-SORT.
    MOVE YTD-SALES-IN           TO YTD-SALES-SORT.
    RELEASE SORT-RECORD.

190-INPUT-TERMINATION.
    CLOSE INVENTORY-FILE.

199-EXTRACT-AND-SORT-EXIT.
    EXIT.
*-----------------------------------------------------------*
200-PRODUCE-REPORT SECTION.
*-----------------------------------------------------------*
    PERFORM 230-OUTPUT-INITIALIZATION.
    PERFORM 260-OUTPUT-PROCESS
        UNTIL FILE-STATUS = 'DONE'.
    GO TO 290-OUTPUT-TERMINATION.

230-OUTPUT-INITIALIZATION.
    OPEN OUTPUT OUTPUT-FILE.
    MOVE 'START '               TO FILE-STATUS.
    MOVE 45                     TO LINE-COUNT.
    RETURN INVENTORY-SORT-FILE
        AT END MOVE 'DONE' TO FILE-STATUS.

260-OUTPUT-PROCESS.
    IF LINE-COUNT > 40
        PERFORM 265-HEADINGS.
    MOVE ITEM-SORT              TO ITEM-OUT.
    MOVE DESCRIPTION-SORT       TO DESCRIPTION-OUT.
    MOVE VENDOR-SORT            TO VENDOR-OUT.
    MOVE ON-HAND-SORT           TO ON-HAND-OUT.
    MOVE MIN-STOCK-LEVEL-SORT TO MIN-STOCK-LEVEL-OUT.
    MOVE UNIT-COST-SORT         TO UNIT-COST-OUT.
    MOVE YTD-SALES-SORT         TO YTD-SALES-OUT.
    WRITE OUTPUT-RECORD FROM REPORT-LINE
        AFTER ADVANCING 2 LINES.
    ADD 2 TO LINE-COUNT.
    RETURN INVENTORY-SORT-FILE
        AT END MOVE 'DONE' TO FILE-STATUS.

265-HEADINGS.
    MOVE 0                      TO LINE-COUNT.
    WRITE OUTPUT-RECORD FROM HEADING1
        AFTER ADVANCING PAGE-TOP.
    WRITE OUTPUT-RECORD FROM HEADING2
        AFTER ADVANCING 3 LINES.

290-OUTPUT-TERMINATION.
    CLOSE OUTPUT-FILE.

299-PRODUCE-REPORT-EXIT.
    EXIT.
```

Figure 16.8 *Continued* Inventory Sort (Data)

```
-------------------------------------------------------------------------------------------
|      |         1         2         3         4         5         6         7         8|
|Record|12345678901234567890123456789012345678901234567890123456789012345678901234567890|
|------------------------------------------------------------------------------------------
|     1|Album Thriller--Michael Jackson     32500051000500000990000250000000000250      |
|     2|Video Don't Stand So Close--Police  10700091000800000499000989000000000400      |
|     3|Video What's Love--Tina Turner      10700004181100000549000899000000000545      |
|     4|Album Footloose--Kenny Loggins      14300081001000000499000899000000000490      |
|     5|Video Beat It--Michael Jackson      32500072000750000429000899000000000375      |
|     6|CassetBorn in the USA--B Springstein14300082000750000399000699000000000370      |
|     7|CassetFootloose--Kenny Loggins      14300069000500000349000659000000000240      |
|     8|Video Infatuation--Rod Stewart      39900029000250000399000799000000000120      |
|     9|Album 1984--Van Halen               28700088000900000449000799000000000440      |
|    10|Album Talk Show--Go Go's            21900062000500000425000789000000000240      |
|    11|Album Can't Slow Down--L. Richie    21900071000850000499000899000000000420      |
|    12|CassetTalk Show--Go Go's            21900042000600000429000729000000000285      |
|    13|CassetCan't Slow Down--L. Richie    21900077000800000399000699000000000390      |
|    14|Video Ghost Busters--R. Parker, Jr. 10700092001000000529000979000000000495      |
|    15|Video When Doves Cry--Prince        28700041000350000599001129000000000175      |
|    16|Album Pyromania--Def Leppard        28700052000550000659000997000000000260      |
|    17|Video Reflex--Duran Duran           10700094000950000429000899000000000455      |
|    18|CassetRoll on--Alabama              14300040000550000429000799000000000265      |
|    19|Video In My Arms Again--P. Bryson   14300075000700000529000999000000000340      |
|    20|Album Born in the USA--B Springstein14300060000650000529000699000000000320      |
|    21|Album Greatest Hits--Air Supply     10700022000250000495000699000000000103      |
|    22|Video Heart of R & R--Huey Lewis    10700275002000000590000899000000000550      |
|    23|Video Girls/have Fun--Cindy Lopper  14300149001500000499000829000000000428      |
|    24|Video Thriller--Michael Jackson     32500120001000000529000899000000000520      |
|    25|Casset1984--Van Halen               28700095001000000499000729000000000515      |
|    26|Video Night Ranger--Sister Christian39900075001500000599000999000000000685      |
|    27|Album Caught in the Act--Styx       21900092001000000599000899000000000497      |
|    28|Album Roll on--Alabama              14300029000500000599000899000000000235      |
|    29|CassetGreatest Hits--Air Supply     10700150001250000399000699000000000520      |
|    30|CassetThe Wild Heart--Stevie Nicks  14300087000800000419000688000000000325      |
|    31|CassetCaught in the Act--Styx       21900059000750000399000699000000000310      |
|    32|Video Billy Jean--Michael Jackson   32500102001450000549000999000000000650      |
|    33|Video Oh, Sherry--Steve Perry       39900079000750000499000949000000000300      |
|    34|Album The Wild Heart--Stevie Nicks  14300091001000000488000695000000000515      |
|    35|Album Synchronicity--Police         10700127001500000550000850000000000690      |
|    36|Album American Summer--Beach Boys   10700089001100000599000899000000000550      |
|    37|Video Stuck on You--Lionel Richie   21900105001550000549000997000000000580      |
|    38|CassetAmerican Summer--Beach Boys   10700072000707777699001249000000000330      |
|    39|CassetPyromania--Def Leppard        28700120001250000429000729000000000400      |
|    40|CassetFlashdance (Sound Track)      39900092001000000452000749000000000500      |
|    41|Album Eyes See in the Dark--K Rogers32500062000750000549000895000000000325      |
|    42|Album What's New--Linda Ronstadt    14300059000500000550000899000000000260      |
|    43|CassetSynchronicity--Police         10700072000700000449000999000000000320      |
|    44|Video Stay the Night--Chicago       14300064000750000529000998000000000375      |
|    45|CassetInto the Gap--Thompson Twins  28700061000600000599000899000000000305      |
|    46|Album Best of Willie--Willie Nelson 32500103001000000475000799000000000515      |
|    47|CassetBest of Willie--Willie Nelson 32500098001000000489000799000000000520      |
|    48|Video Hello--Lionel Richie          21900144001500000542000998000000000750      |
|    49|CassetWhat's New--Linda Ronstadt    14300112001250000519000699000000000700      |
|    50|CassetThriller--Michael Jackson     32500115001000000499000698000000000520      |
|    51|Video State of Shock--Jackson/Jagger39900101001250000529000998000000000535      |
|    52|Album Into the Gap--Thompson Twins  28700090000750000450000899000000000400      |
-------------------------------------------------------------------------------------------
```

Figure 16.8 *Continued* Inventory Sort (Output)

Learning COBOL, Inc.

Item	Description	Vendor	On Hand	Minimum	Cost	YTD Sales
Album	Greatest Hits--Air Supply	107	22	25	$4.95	103
Album	Synchronicity--Police	107	127	150	$5.50	690
Album	American Summer--Beach Boys	107	89	110	$5.99	550
Video	What's Love--Tina Turner	107	4	18110	$5.49	545
Video	Ghost Busters--R. Parker, Jr.	107	92	100	$5.29	495
Video	Reflex--Duran Duran	107	94	95	$4.29	455
Album	Footloose--Kenny Loggins	143	81	100	$4.99	490
Album	Born in the USA--B Springstein	143	60	65	$5.29	320
Album	Roll on--Alabama	143	29	50	$5.99	235
Album	The Wild Heart--Stevie Nicks	143	91	100	$4.88	515
Casset	Roll on--Alabama	143	40	55	$4.29	265
Casset	What's New--Linda Ronstadt	143	112	125	$5.19	700
Video	Girls/have Fun--Cindy Lopper	143	149	150	$4.99	428
Video	Stay the Night--Chicago	143	64	75	$5.29	375
Album	Can't Slow Down--L. Richie	219	71	85	$4.99	420
Album	Caught in the Act--Styx	219	92	100	$5.99	497
Casset	Talk Show--Go Go's	219	42	60	$4.29	285
Casset	Can't Slow Down--L. Richie	219	77	80	$3.99	390
Casset	Caught in the Act--Styx	219	59	75	$3.99	310
Video	Stuck on You--Lionel Richie	219	105	155	$5.49	580
Video	Hello--Lionel Richie	219	144	150	$5.42	750
Album	1984--Van Halen	287	88	90	$4.49	440
Album	Pyromania--Def Leppard	287	52	55	$6.59	260
Casset	1984--Van Halen	287	95	100	$4.99	515
Casset	Pyromania--Def Leppard	287	120	125	$4.29	400
Album	Eyes See in the Dark--K Rogers	325	62	75	$5.49	325
Casset	Best of Willie--Willie Nelson	325	98	100	$4.89	520
Video	Beat It--Michael Jackson	325	72	75	$4.29	375
Video	Billy Jean--Michael Jackson	325	102	145	$5.49	650
Casset	Flashdance (Sound Track)	399	92	100	$4.52	500
Video	Night Ranger--Sister Christian	399	75	150	$5.99	685
Video	State of Shock--Jackson/Jagger	399	101	125	$5.29	535

PROCEDURE could be a stand-alone program. After the OUTPUT PROCEDURE is terminated (by the unconditional branch to 290-OUTPUT-TERMINATION), control passes back to the sort statement and the sorting process is completed and the STOP RUN statement is encountered.

General Limitations

Although not previously noted, there are a few general limitations on using the SORT statement. First, COBOL does not permit two SORT statements to be active *at the same time;* however, multiple SORT statements can still appear in the same program. Second, although COBOL will permit procedures in an OUTPUT PROCEDURE to be accessed (possibly by a PERFORM statement) from the INPUT PROCEDURE, a RETURN statement must not be encountered while in the OUTPUT PROCEDURE. If in the OUTPUT PROCEDURE, procedure-names in the INPUT PROCEDURE are invoked, a RELEASE statement must not be encountered. Third, magnetic media, that is, magnetic tape or disk, must be available on the system to permit the use of the SORT statement. Recall that sort-work files are necessary. Finally, the SORT statement requires at least some limited amount of internal storage in which to order sets of records. Some COBOL compilers (e.g., IBM) provide a special register called SORT-CORE-SIZE to provide the programmer with the option of indicating the amount of internal storage to be allocated to the internal sorting process. Figure 16.8 illustrates the use of this special register in line 1110. The MOVE statement causes 50,000 bytes of internal storage to be set aside for the internal sorting process. Thus, a rather significant number of records could be ordered in storage before being transmitted to a tape or disk work file.

Summary

In this chapter, the SORT statement has been described. The sorting process performed by the SORT statement may be viewed as being a ''sort-merge'' process with four distinct phases:

1. Identification of the sort-file
2. Specification of sort keys and sequence for sorting
3. Reference to the input phase
4. Reference to the output phase

The statement permits multiple sort keys, which may be specified in ASCENDING or DESCENDING sequences. The programmer has a choice of a USING or an INPUT PROCEDURE phrase for the input phase and a GIVING or an OUTPUT PROCEDURE phrase for the output phase.

Notes on Programming Style

The SORT statement is a powerful statement that can manipulate large data files into a desired sequence. Although the programmer may have any combination of phrases in the input and output phases of the process, a USING/GIVING set would not usually be chosen. Although COBOL places no restrictions on the combination of these phrases, the USING/GIVING combination is typically not an effective use of either machine or programmer time. A USING/GIVING set causes a sequential file to be read and sorted and the results written to an output sequential file. Fortunately, sort *utilities* are generally available at most installations. These utilities perform exactly the same process and typically require very little code. For example, a complete COBOL program could be replaced by four or five records. Furthermore, sort utilities are typically more efficient than a COBOL program.

Questions

Below fill in the blank(s) with the appropriate word, words or phrases.

1. The overall function of the SORT statement is to ____ .
2. When the programmer supplies the code to order data within a program (e.g., a bubble sort), the procedure is known as a(n) ____ sort, whereas the SORT statement is generally known as a(n) ____ sort.
3. The SORT statement is capable of ordering large data sets because only groups of data are sequenced internally in what is referred to as the ____ phase, then those groups are joined during a process known as the ____ phase.
4. The reserved words in a SORT statement that indicate the direction of ordering data are ____ and ____ .
5. The record length of the sort-record and the input record must be the same when ____ is used for the input phase.
6. If the INPUT PROCEDURE is specified, a(n) ____ statement must appear in the procedure.
7. If an INPUT PROCEDURE is specified, code in the PROCEDURE DIVISION that identifies the input process must be coded at the ____ level.
8. When a GIVING phrase is specified, the input file must be organized as a(n) ____ file type.
9. The output phase of a SORT statement is specified by the ____ and ____ phrases.
10. Each OUTPUT PROCEDURE must contain at least one ____ statement.

Answer the following questions by circling either "T" for True or "F" for False.

T F **11.** A sort-file name must appear in a SELECT clause.
T F **12.** In the DATA DIVISION, a sort-file is described with an FD entry.
T F **13.** Record descriptions for records in the sort-file are essentially the same as records in a typical file.
T F **14.** It is possible for a sort-record description to be shorter than the record description of an input file to be sorted.
T F **15.** It is possible for a sort-record description to be longer than the record description of an input file to be sorted.
T F **16.** It is possible to sort records from two files into the same sort-file.
T F **17.** If the USING phrase is specified in the SORT statement, the same sort statement may also use the INPUT PROCEDURE phrase.
T F **18.** Sort keys must be numeric.
T F **19.** Only one sort key may be specified for a single SORT statement.
T F **20.** The SORT statement is only capable of sorting data from the largest to the smallest value.

T F **21.** Both ASCENDING and DESCENDING keys may be specified in one SORT statement.

T F **22.** If an INPUT PROCEDURE is specified for the input phase, an OUTPUT PROCEDURE must be specified for the output phase.

T F **23.** If an input file contains 100 records, it is always necessary to sort all 100 records.

T F **24.** Two SORT statements could appear in the same program.

T F **25.** The SORT statements always require both an input and output phase.

Exercises

1. Below are a series of situations in which a SORT statement is used. Given the FILE SECTION entries below, identify all possible errors related to the correct usage of the SORT statements.

```
FILE SECTION.
FD   INPUT-FILE
     LABEL RECORDS OMITTED.
01 INPUT-RECORD.
     05 IN-FIELD-1                 PIC X(10).
     05 IN-FIELD-2                 PIC 9(03).
     05 IN-GROUP-1.
        10 IN-FIELD-3              PIC 99V99.
        10 IN-FIELD-4              PIC X(05).
FD      OUTPUT-FILE LABEL RECORDS OMITTED.
01   OUTPUT-RECORD                 PIC X(90).
SD   SORT-FILE.
01   SORT-RECORD.
       02 SORT-FIELD-1             PIC X(05).
       02 SORT-GROUP-1.
          04 SORT-FIELD-2          PIC X(10).
          04 SORT-FIELD-3          PIC 9(07).
```

a.
```
SORT SORT-FILE
     ASCENDING KEY SORT-FIELD-1
     USING INPUT-FILE
     OUTPUT PROCEDURE 200-REPORT.
        .
        .
        .
200-REPORT SECTION
```

b.
```
SORT SORT-FILE
     ASCENDING KEY IN-FIELD-1
     DESCENDING KEY IN-FIELD-4
     USING INPUT-FILE.
     GIVING OUTPUT-FILE.
```

c.
```
SORT INPUT-FILE
     ASCENDING KEY SORT-GROUP-1
     INPUT PROCEDURE 100-TEST.
        .
        .
        .
100-TEST.
```

d.
```
SORT SORT-FILE
     DESCENDING SORT-RECORD
```

```
            INPUT INPUT-FILE
            OUTPUT PROCEDURE 500-DUMP-REC.
                 .
                 .
                 .
    500-DUMP-REC SECTION.
```

e.
```
    SORT SORT-FILE
         ON DESCENDING SORT-FIELD-2
         INPUT PROCEDURE 200-SUM-VALUES
         GIVING OUTPUT-FILE.
              .
              .
              .
    200-SUM-VALUES SECTION.
```

f.
```
    SORT SORT-FILE.
         DESCENDING KEY IS SORT-FIELD-1.
         INPUT PROCEDURE 200-FIRST.
         OUTPUT PROCEDURE 300-LAST.
              .
              .
              .
    200-FIRST SECTION.
              .
              .
              .
        RETURN SORT-FILE
           AT END GO TO 300-LAST.
              .
              .
              .
    300-LAST SECTION.
              .
              .
              .
        RELEASE SORT-FILE.
              .
              .
              .
        SORT SORT-FILE DESCENDING TEST-1
            USING INPUT-FILE GIVING
            OUTPUT-FILE.
```

2. Below is a set of data that are to be sorted. For each of the following, indicate the sequence in which the data would appear after it was sorted with the specified key phrases.

Check Number	Payee Number	Check Amount	Check Date	Check Year	Voucher Number	Cleared by	Control Number
1129	JOHN PHILLIPS	033∧45	04–15	81	395	RLS	44193
1039	MARK ANDERSON	062∧15	04–02	81	287	BBR	83642
1427	JAMES HARRIS	731∧44	05–05	81	528	JWS	83953
1319	MARK ANDERSON	005∧95	04–19	81	407	JWS	41294
1220	JOHN JONES	062∧88	04–20	81	401	RLS	79830
0921	MARK ANDERSON	314∧14	03–26	81	263	BBR	97541
1006	ANDREW SMITH	842∧15	03–30	81	270	DCD	06272

a. `...ASCENDING CHECK-NUMBER...`

b. `...ASCENDING PAYEE-NAME, CHECK-NUMBER...`

c. `...DESCENDING CHECK-AMOUNT...`

d.
```
...DESCENDING CLEARED-BY
   ASCENDING CHECK-AMOUNT...
```

e. `...DESCENDING CONTROL-NUMBER...`

f. `...ASCENDING CHECK-YEAR, CHECK-DATE, CHECK-NUMBER....`

g.
```
...ASCENDING PAYEE-NAME
   DESCENDING VOUCHER-NUMBER...
```

h.
```
...ASCENDING CLEARED-BY
   DESCENDING PAYEE-NAME
   ASCENDING CHECK-YEAR, CHECK-DATE...
```

Problems

16.1. To update the customer file without processing errors or undue overhead in the updating procedure, we have been asked to edit invoice records to ensure that they are legitimate (or at least reasonable). The invoice records contain a number of fields, each of which is subject to one or more errors. The fields, listed with possible errors, are specified as follows:

Field	Possible Error
Invoice number	Duplicated Missing, i.e., nonconsecutive Nonnumeric
Customer number	Blank (Other checks would be made if we were to access the customer file)
Data of invoice	Month error (not within the legitimate range of month values) Day error (not within the legitimate range of day values) Year error (not the same year as other invoice records)
Amount of invoice	Nonnumeric
Amount of tax	Nonnumeric Tax not 0, 4, 5, or 6 percent of invoice amount
Amount of discount	Discount not 0, 5, 10, or 15 percent of invoice amount Nonnumeric
Amount of cost	Nonnumeric Cost greater than invoice amount

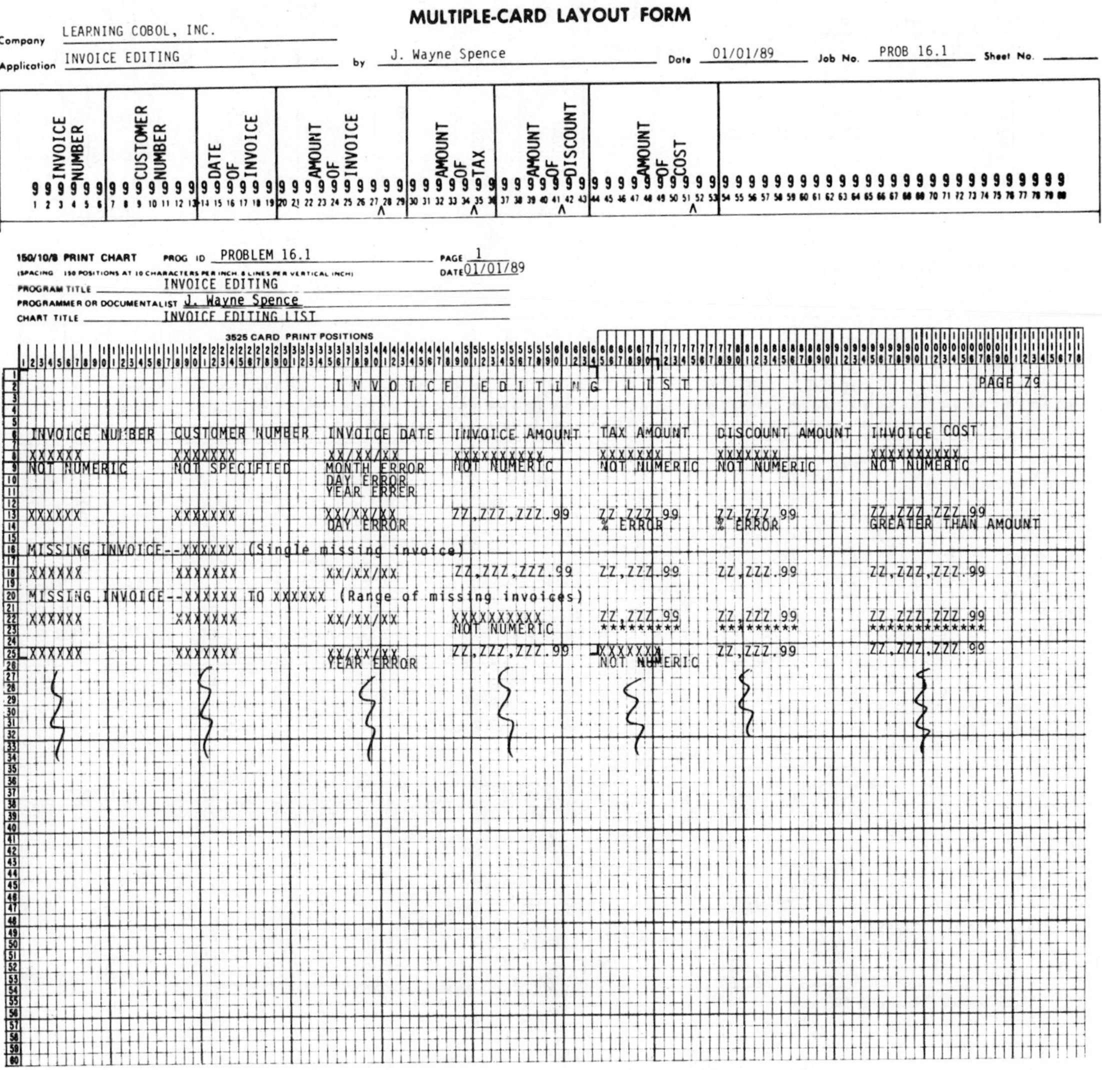

MULTIPLE-CARD LAYOUT FORM

Company LEARNING COBOL, INC.

Application INVOICE EDITING by J. Wayne Spence Date 01/01/89 Job No. PROB 16.1 Sheet No.

INVOICE NUMBER	CUSTOMER NUMBER	DATE OF INVOICE	AMOUNT OF INVOICE	AMOUNT OF TAX	AMOUNT OF DISCOUNT	AMOUNT OF COST	
1–6	7–13	14–19	20–29	30–36	37–43	44–53	54–80

150/10/8 PRINT CHART PROG ID PROBLEM 16.1 PAGE 1

(SPACING 150 POSITIONS AT 10 CHARACTERS PER INCH, 8 LINES PER VERTICAL INCH) DATE 01/01/89

PROGRAM TITLE INVOICE EDITING

PROGRAMMER OR DOCUMENTALIST J. Wayne Spence

CHART TITLE INVOICE EDITING LIST

3525 CARD PRINT POSITIONS

```
                        I N V O I C E   E D I T I N G   L I S T                                    PAGE Z9

INVOICE NUMBER  CUSTOMER NUMBER  INVOICE DATE  INVOICE AMOUNT  TAX AMOUNT    DISCOUNT AMOUNT  INVOICE COST

XXXXXX          XXXXXXX          XX/XX/XX      XXXXXXXXXX      XXXXXXX       XXXXXXX          XXXXXXXXXX
NOT NUMERIC     NOT SPECIFIED    MONTH ERROR   NOT NUMERIC     NOT NUMERIC   NOT NUMERIC      NOT NUMERIC
                                 DAY ERROR
                                 YEAR ERRER

XXXXXX          XXXXXXX          XX/XX/XX      ZZ,ZZZ,ZZZ.99   ZZ,ZZZ.99     ZZ,ZZZ.99        ZZ,ZZZ,ZZZ.99
                                 DAY ERROR                     % ERROR       % ERROR          GREATER THAN AMOUNT

MISSING INVOICE--XXXXXX (Single missing invoice)

XXXXXX          XXXXXXX          XX/XX/XX      ZZ,ZZZ,ZZZ.99   ZZ,ZZZ.99     ZZ,ZZZ.99        ZZ,ZZZ,ZZZ.99

MISSING INVOICE--XXXXXX TO XXXXXX (Range of missing invoices)

XXXXXX          XXXXXXX          XX/XX/XX      XXXXXXXXXX      ZZ,ZZZ.99     ZZ,ZZZ.99        ZZ,ZZZ,ZZZ.99
                                               NOT NUMERIC     *********     *********        *************

XXXXXX          XXXXXXX          XX/XX/XX      ZZ,ZZZ,ZZZ.99   XXXXXXX       ZZ,ZZZ.99        ZZ,ZZZ,ZZZ.99
                                 YEAR ERROR                    NOT NUMERIC
```

Many of these checks may (and should) be made before the data are ordered (for purposes of checking for duplicate/missing invoices). However, only invoices that indicate nonnumeric invoice numbers are to be excluded from the sorting procedure.

The report format presented in the print chart should be used for this procedure.

16.2. The inventory control manager is interested in developing a profit profile for all items in inventory. The profit profile is to be produced by outlet number. Within each outlet, inventory records are to be listed by vendor code. Finally, within each vendor group, items are to be listed by item number.

MULTIPLE-CARD LAYOUT FORM

Company: LEARNING COBOL, INC.

Application: PROFIT PROFILE | by J. Wayne Spence Date 01/01/89 Job No. PROB 16.2 & 3 Sheet No. 1

Field	Columns
ITEM NUMBER	1–6
VENDOR CODE	7–9
ITEM DESCRIPTION	10–39
PRODUCT GROUP	40–44
OUTLET NUMBER	45–49
UNITS ON HAND	50–55
MINIMUM STOCK LEVEL	56–61
PRICE PER UNIT	62–69
COST PER UNIT	70–77
MEASURE.	78–79
	80

(Record Continued--Bytes 81-160)

Field	Columns
DATE OF LAST PURCHASE	1–5
DATE LAST PURCHASE RECEIVED	6–11
LAST PURCHASE QUANTITY	12–17
DATE OF LAST SALE	18–23
YTD SALES (UNITS)	24–33
YTD SALES (DOLLARS)	34–45
YTD COST (DOLLARS)	46–57
MTD SALES (UNITS)	58–67
MTD SALES (DOLLARS)	68–79
	80

(Record Continued--Bytes 161-171)

Field	Columns
MTD COST (DOLLARS)	1–11
	12–80

150/10/8 PRINT CHART PROG ID Problem 16.2 PAGE 1

DATE 01/01/89

PROGRAM TITLE PROFIT PROFILE

PROGRAMMER OR DOCUMENTALIST J. Wayne Spence

CHART TITLE PROFIT PROFILE REPORT

```
                                          PROFIT PROFILE REPORT                                   PAGE ZZ9
OUTLET GROUP: 99999
          VENDOR GROUP: XXX
ITEM
NUMBER   ITEM DESCRIPTION                    YTD SALES          YTD COST         YTD PROFIT

 XXXXX   XXXXXXXXXXXXXXXXXXXXXXXXXXXXXX   Z,ZZZ,ZZZ,ZZZ.99   Z,ZZZ,ZZZ,ZZZ.99   Z,ZZZ,ZZZ,ZZZ.99
 XXXXX   XXXXXXXXXXXXXXXXXXXXXXXXXXXXXX   Z,ZZZ,ZZZ,ZZZ.99   Z,ZZZ,ZZZ,ZZZ.99   Z,ZZZ,ZZZ,ZZZ.99

 XXXXX   XXXXXXXXXXXXXXXXXXXXXXXXXXXXXX   Z,ZZZ,ZZZ,ZZZ.99   Z,ZZZ,ZZZ,ZZZ.99   Z,ZZZ,ZZZ,ZZZ.99

          VENDOR GROUP XXX TOTAL PROFIT
                                                                           ZZZ,ZZZ,ZZZ,ZZZ.99
          VENDOR GROUP: XXX

ITEM
NUMBER   ITEM DESCRIPTION                    YTD SALES          YTD COST         YTD PROFIT

 XXXXX   XXXXXXXXXXXXXXXXXXXXXXXXXXXXXX   Z,ZZZ,ZZZ,ZZZ.99   Z,ZZZ,ZZZ,ZZZ.99   Z,ZZZ,ZZZ,ZZZ.99
 XXXXX   XXXXXXXXXXXXXXXXXXXXXXXXXXXXXX   Z,ZZZ,ZZZ,ZZZ.99   Z,ZZZ,ZZZ,ZZZ.99   Z,ZZZ,ZZZ,ZZZ.99

 XXXXX   XXXXXXXXXXXXXXXXXXXXXXXXXXXXXX   Z,ZZZ,ZZZ,ZZZ.99   Z,ZZZ,ZZZ,ZZZ.99   Z,ZZZ,ZZZ,ZZZ.99
          VENDOR GROUP XXX TOTAL PROFIT                                    ZZZ,ZZZ,ZZZ,ZZZ.99
OUTLET GROUP 99999 TOTAL PROFIT                                                  ZZZ,ZZZ,ZZZ,ZZZ.99

OUTLET GROUP: 99999
                                                                                                  PAGE ZZ9

                                          PROFIT PROFILE REPORT                                   PAGE ZZ9
OUTLET GROUP: 99999
          VENDOR GROUP: XXX
ITEM
NUMBER   ITEM DESCRIPTION                    YTD SALES          YTD COST         YTD PROFIT
 XXXXX   XXXXXXXXXXXXXXXXXXXXXXXXXXXXXX   Z,ZZZ,ZZZ,ZZZ.99   Z,ZZZ,ZZZ,ZZZ.99   Z,ZZZ,ZZZ,ZZZ.99

          VENDOR GROUP XXX TOTAL PROFIT                                    ZZZ,ZZZ,ZZZ,ZZZ.99
OUTLET GROUP 99999 TOTAL PROFIT                                                  ZZZ,ZZZ,ZZZ,ZZZ.99
***** COMPANY TOTAL *****                                                              ZZZ,ZZZ,ZZZ,ZZZ.99
```

The report (illustrated in the printer spacing chart) is to be printed such that it adheres to the following guidelines:

a. All pages should be numbered at the right margin on both the top and bottom of each page.
b. Each outlet is to begin on a new page, and the outlet number should appear both in the heading and at the lower left margin of each page.
c. A heading should appear each time the vendor group changes and should be preceded and followed by two blank lines.
d. Group subtotals should be produced for each vendor group, as indicated.
e. Subtotals should be printed for each outlet.
f. Grand totals should be printed for each company.

Note: Gross profit is calculated as year-to-date sales less year-to-date cost.

16.3. The inventory control manager wishes to receive an analysis of inventory movement. The particular analysis requested is referred to as the "A-B-C Analysis." The inventory data to be used are in the same format as illustrated for Problem 16.2.

A-B-C Analysis is an examination of the inventory on the basis of the level of investment in each inventory item. The level of investment is based on the total cost of units on hand (that is, the on-hand quantity multiplied by cost per unit). The A-B-C breakdown should be as follows:

Class A—The top 10 percent of the inventory items based on the level of investment
Class B—The next 20 percent of the inventory items
Class C—The remaining 70 percent of the inventory items

For each inventory item, the reorder report should contain the item number, vendor, description, reorder point, amount on hand, cost, level of investment, cumulative level of investment for all items (including the current item) within the class, and cumulative level of investment of all items without regard to class.

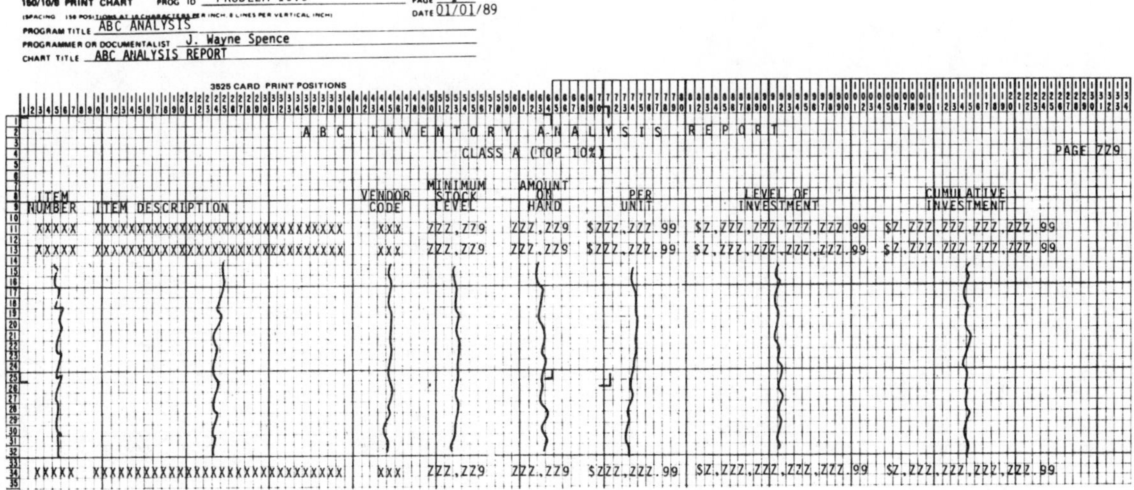

150/10/8 PRINT CHART PROG ID PROBLEM 16.3 PAGE 1
DATE 01/01/89
PROGRAM TITLE ABC ANALYSIS
PROGRAMMER OR DOCUMENTALIST J. Wayne Spence
CHART TITLE ABC ANALYSIS REPORT

```
                              A B C   I N V E N T O R Y   A N A L Y S I S   R E P O R T
                                                   CLASS A (TOP 10%)                                                  PAGE ZZ9

ITEM                                 VENDOR  MINIMUM    AMOUNT      PER              LEVEL OF                 CUMULATIVE
NUMBER  ITEM DESCRIPTION              CODE   STOCK      ON          UNIT             INVESTMENT               INVESTMENT
                                             LEVEL      HAND
 XXXXX  XXXXXXXXXXXXXXXXXXXXXXXXXXXXXX  XXX   ZZZ,ZZ9   ZZZ,ZZ9  $ZZZ,ZZZ.99  $Z,ZZZ,ZZZ,ZZZ,ZZZ.99  $Z,ZZZ,ZZZ,ZZZ,ZZZ.99
 XXXXX  XXXXXXXXXXXXXXXXXXXXXXXXXXXXXX  XXX   ZZZ,ZZ9   ZZZ,ZZ9  $ZZZ,ZZZ.99  $Z,ZZZ,ZZZ,ZZZ,ZZZ.99  $Z,ZZZ,ZZZ,ZZZ,ZZZ.99

 XXXXX  XXXXXXXXXXXXXXXXXXXXXXXXXXXXXX  XXX   ZZZ,ZZ9   ZZZ,ZZ9  $ZZZ,ZZZ.99  $Z,ZZZ,ZZZ,ZZZ,ZZZ.99  $Z,ZZZ,ZZZ,ZZZ,ZZZ.99
```

Each class should be clearly labeled on the printout (i.e., A, B, or C) with page breaks between classes. Pages should be numbered and have appropriate headings. Each column should have appropriate column headings. If the level of investment for two or more items is equivalent, the items of equivalent value should be listed in vendor-code order. If the level of investment of two or more items is equivalent for the same vendor, the items should be listed in item-number order.

CHAPTER

17

Sequential File Processing

Most of this text has been devoted to processing files based on a sequential input medium and a print-oriented output medium. Computer installations use a variety of media for the retention and manipulation of data. Among the most common media types are magnetic tape and magnetic disk. Magnetic media provide a number of very important advantages over card image and printed paper.

The first advantage is that magnetic media are reusable. Data may be erased and new data recorded, making data modification possible. It is not possible to modify data on such media as punched cards. Once holes have been punched into cards the medium is expended.

Second, once data have been written to a magnetic medium, it can also be read. Thus, a mass amount of data may be stored for future reference.

Third, records on a magnetic medium are as long (or as short) as necessary to record the needed data. To retain 35 characters (bytes) of data, the record need only be 35 bytes long. To retain 300 bytes of data, the record may be 300 bytes long. Both the punched cards and printed media are fixed length media. Card images are 80 columns long, whether or not all 80 columns contain data. Printed lines are typically 133 columns, whether or not all 133 columns contain printing.

Fourth, data stored on magnetic media may be written to much more rapidly than writing output to a printer.

Fifth, data stored on magnetic media are much more compact than data stored in either a printed or card image form. A typical magnetic tape could contain 48 million characters or more, and a magnetic disk could contain 200 million characters or more. To record 48 million characters on card image records would require approximately 600,000 lines or approximately 5500 printed pages.

Finally, the magnetic media allow more flexibility in dealing with both *logical* and *physical* records. A logical record is application-oriented, that is, the record the programmer views when writing a program. In COBOL, a logical record is coded for each FD in the FILE SECTION. A physical record is composed of *one or more* logical records. A physical record is read or written by a device (e.g., card reader, tape drive, or disk drive). The programmer may decide the number of logical records in a physical record for magnetic media.

Why is the distinction between logical and physical records important? There are two reasons—space conservation and speed. As shown in Figure 17.1, magnetic media require that a space (called an *inter-record gap*-IRG) be present between each physical record. On a magnetic tape, this space is typically expressed in inches, and may require 0.5 to 0.75 inches of tape. On a magnetic disk, this space is usually expressed in bytes of recording surface, and may need as much as 150 bytes of recording surface. Note the recording of data in sequential form on tape requires the data to be spread down the length of the tape, whereas on disk the data are recorded in concentric rings called *tracks*.

When data are recorded on a magnetic medium in an unblocked (one logical record per physical record) form, an inter-record gap is placed between each record. Suppose we were recording data on a magnetic tape with a *recording density* of 1600 bytes per inch (BPI), logical record lengths of 200 bytes, and an inter-record gap of 0.5 inch. To record 1000 records would require 625 inches (approximately 52 feet) of tape (200 / 1600 x 1000 + .5 x 1000 = 625). In this case the data occupy 0.125 inch of tape per record, and the gap is 0.5 inch—more of the tape is gap than data. If, however, a *blocking*

Figure 17.1 Physical Versus Logical Records

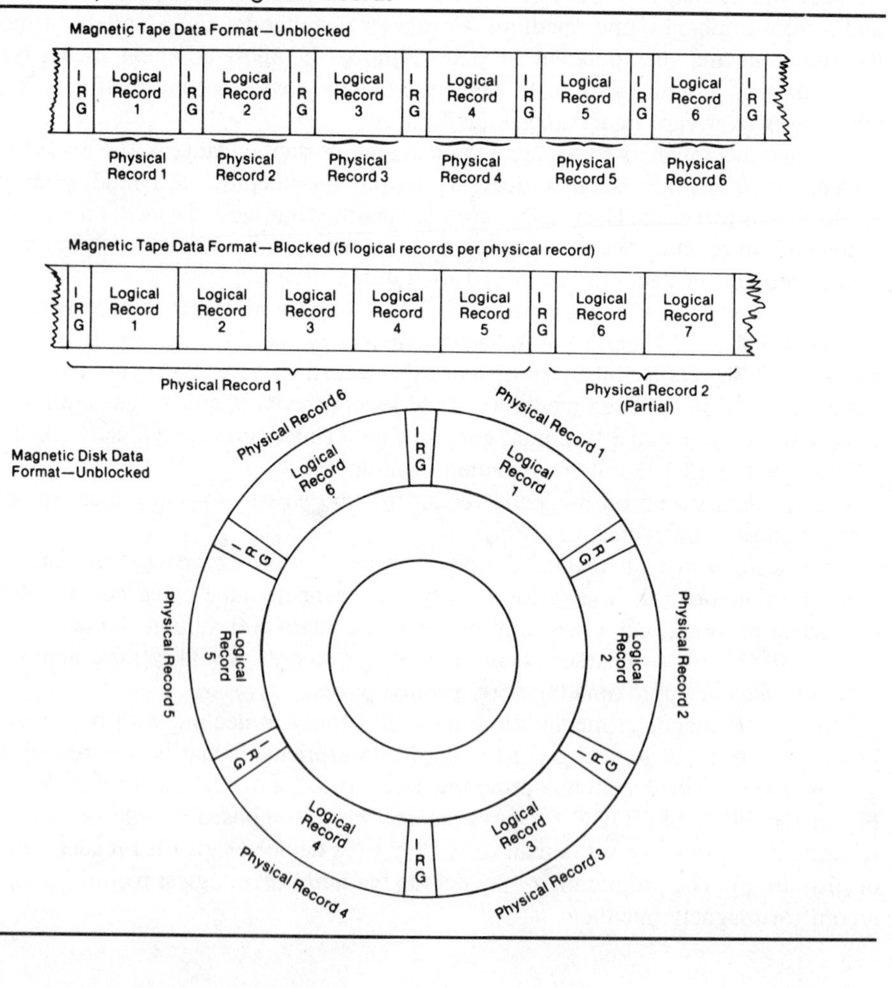

Figure 17.1 *Continued* Physical Versus Logical Records

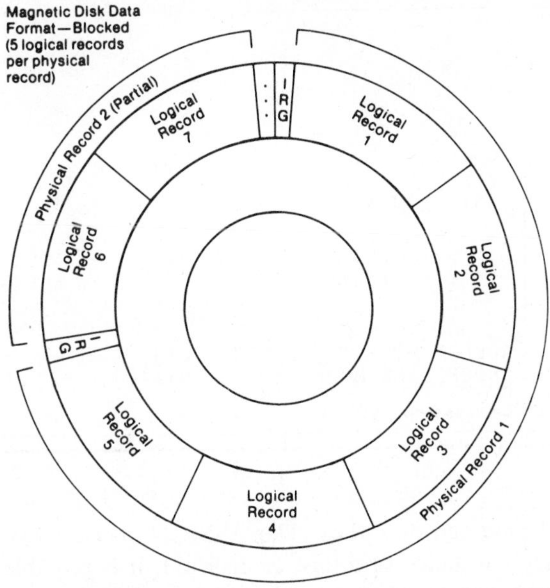

factor of 5 (5 logical records per physical record) is used, the amount of tape used falls to 225 inches (approximately 19 feet)! That is, 200 physical records times 1000/1600 inches per physical record plus 0.5 inch per *block*. This not only amounts to a substantial savings of media, but also results in improved input-output performance for the data file.

How does input-output performance improve? The answer is simple. When we request data from the file (e.g., by a READ statement), two blocks are retrieved—5 logical records are placed in each of two input *buffers* (a total of ten logical records at one time). Buffers are described more fully shortly. As a result, our program will only have to communicate to the device once for every ten logical READs in the procedure. When the CPU has to "converse" with a device, an *input-output interrupt* is generated by the operating system, which, in effect, causes the CPU to *wait* for the device either to transmit data to the CPU or the CPU to transmit data to the device. This is often called an *I-O wait state*. Thus, our program only has to "slow down" to device speed every ten READs in our program, rather than every two. Therefore, the more logical records we can transmit to the CPU at one time, the fewer the wait states and the faster a procedure can perform I-O operations.

The procedure would be the same for magnetic disk. The major difference between tape and disk in handling sequential files is that tape is read and written serially down the length of the tape. The same process on a magnetic disk drive might require re-positioning read-write heads to jump from track to track.

ENVIRONMENT DIVISION Considerations

To utilize magnetic tape and disk files in COBOL may require a few alterations in the ENVIRONMENT DIVISION. The basic format of the FILE-CONTROL paragraph (see Chapter 5) is expanded in Figure 17.2. The ASSIGN clause is the only change necessary

Figure 17.2 The Format of the INPUT-OUTPUT SECTION

```
  .
  .
  .
[INPUT-OUTPUT SECTION.
 FILE-CONTROL.
      SELECT file-name
      ASSIGN TO system-name
     ┌                                          ┐
     │ RESERVE {NO     } ALTERNATE      [AREA ] │
     │         {integer}                [AREAS] │
     └                                          ┘
     [ACCESS MODE IS SEQUENTIAL*]
     [PROCESSING MODE IS SEQUENTIAL]. . . .]
```

*The paragraph, as shown, is incomplete.

to process sequential tape and disk files. The ASSIGN clause must reflect a system-name that designates your choice of a tape or disk file. It is possible to have multiple tape and disk files within one program, which Figure 17.3 illustrates. In this figure, four files are assigned in the form necessary for an IBM system using the OS operating system. Notice the file-names are similar to those appearing in previous programs; however, the assignment sequence is somewhat different. All file assignments are still prefixed by ''UT-S'' (utility-sequential), but a new series of programmer-selected names (OLDMAST, NEWMAST, and TRANS) have been supplied to complete the system-name. These programmer selected names are referred to as *ddnames* and used to interface the program to JCL statements which provide additional information about the file. (Additional JCL is frequently necessary when using tape and disk files.)

Figure 17.3 Data File ASSIGNments

```
          .
          .
          .
ENVIRONMENT DIVISION.
CONFIGURATION SECTION.
SOURCE-COMPUTER.  IBM.
OBJECT-COMPUTER.  IBM.
SPECIAL-NAMES.  CØ1 IS TOP-OF-PAGE.
INPUT-OUTPUT SECTION.
FILE-CONTROL.
    SELECT INVOICE-FILE ASSIGN TO UT-S-OLDMAST.
    SELECT NEW-INVOICE-FILE ASSIGN TO UT-S-NEWMAST.
    SELECT REPORT-FILE ASSIGN TO UT-S-OUTPUT.
    SELECT SALES-FILE ASSIGN TO UT-S-TRANS.
          .
          .
          .
```

Other FILE CONTROL Paragraph Clauses

Although only the SELECT and ASSIGN clauses are required to indicate the presence of input and output files, other clauses may be used to improve input or output speed or to improve documentation. These clauses must have a period only after the *last* clause for the file (although other types of punctuation are permitted).

The only other clause that has a functional effect on files is the RESERVE clause. The RESERVE clause, which is optional, is used to manipulate the number of input and output buffers. A *buffer* is simply an area of internal storage set aside to store physical input and output records. It has no logical impact on the programming of a problem, but it is simply used to reduce the numbers of physical input and output operations the computer must perform. Thus, although every input statement *appears* to cause a single logical record to be introduced from an external medium, not every such statement causes the computer to interact with the input device. Some input statements physically cause several records to be read; others cause no physical input operation.

An illustration of a buffered input operation is given in Figure 17.4. When the computer executes the first READ statement for the first time, the computer reacts by reading the first *three* records from the input file; in one physical read operation all assigned buffers will be filled. Each time the buffers are filled, the operating system automatically sets a *pointer* that *addresses* the first buffer, which is the area addressed by the execution of the first logical input statement. Data are now available for processing.

Figure 17.4 Illustration of the Input of a Buffered File (Three Buffers Assumed)

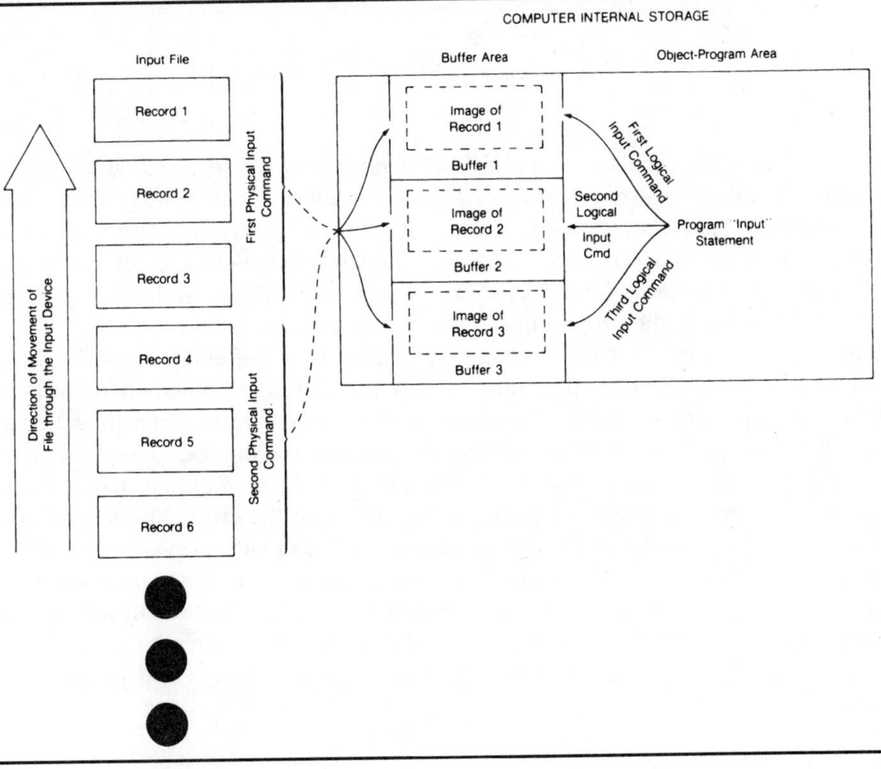

Upon encountering the second logical input statement, the pointer is simply repositioned to address the second input buffer, and, consequently, the image of the second data record, so no physical input takes place. When the third logical input statement is executed, the pointer is repositioned again to the buffer assigned.

With the attempted access to the fourth buffer by execution of the fourth logical input statement, no more buffers are found. As a result, the operating system responds by refilling the three assigned buffers with the next three input records. Thus, record 4 is placed in the first buffer, record 5 is placed in the second buffer, record 6 is recorded in the third buffer, and the addressing pointer is repositioned to the first buffer. This cyclic execution of three logical input statements to one physical input operation continues throughout the execution of the program. The same process is used for all files. For example, if a printed output file were assigned three buffers, three logical output commands would have to be executed before the program ''dumps'' output to the line printer. That is, output physically occurs only when the output buffers are full or upon termination of the program.

This process seems unnecessary, but since no currently available input or output device operates as fast as the computer, it is possible to improve the total input and output speed (efficiency) of a program by increasing the number of input and output buffers. Of course, there must be enough internal storage space available for the buffers, since physical records will be placed in internal storage. This is important for most business applications since they generally use many input-output operations. Again, the use of additional input or output buffers has *no* logical impact on a program; buffers simply improve speed by the use of more internal storage.

The format of the RESERVE clause is

```
RESERVE { NO      }  ALTERNATE [ AREA  ]
        { integer }            [ AREAS ]
```

The programmer may choose to specify NO if *no additional input* or output areas are required. This allows *one-physical-record-at-a-time* either to enter or exit the computer. The programmer may also choose to indicate an integer (generally between a minimum of 1 and maximum of 254), which allocates enough internal storage for the necessary single buffer plus the additional ''integer'' number of buffers. And, of course, since the clause is optional, the programmer may choose to leave it out.

One note of caution: All COBOL compilers do not treat buffers in the same way. For example, IBM DOS allows a maximum of only two buffers (the default when the RESERVE clause is omitted). In addition, many operating systems do not print the contents of output buffers until all buffers are full or the program is complete. The difficulty here is that if a program terminates abnormally, one or more lines of output may not appear. This sometimes makes it difficult to locate the source of the error. You should consult with your installation to determine the maximum number of buffers available to a file and the disposition of the contents of output buffers in cases of abnormal termination.

The remaining clauses, ACCESS MODE and PROCESSING MODE as shown, are documentation clauses. When using sequential devices, only sequential access and processing are possible. If the clauses are omitted, sequential access and processing will be assumed.

Figure 17.5 Example of an Enhanced ENVIRONMENT DIVISION.

```
ENVIRONMENT DIVISION.
CONFIGURATION SECTION.
SOURCE-COMPUTER.  IBM.
OBJECT-COMPUTER.  IBM.
SPECIAL-NAMES.    C01 IS TOP-OF-PAGE.
INPUT-OUTPUT SECTION.
FILE-CONTROL.
    SELECT MASTER-FILE
        ASSIGN TO UT-S-INPUT
        RESERVE 15 ALTERNATE AREAS
        ACCESS MODE IS SEQUENTIAL
        PROCESSING MODE IS SEQUENTIAL.
    SELECT EXCEPTION-REPORT
        ASSIGN TO UT-S-OUTPUT
        RESERVE NO ALTERNATE AREAS.
```

Now examine Figure 17.5. This illustration of an ENVIRONMENT DIVISION is somewhat more complete that previously presented. Although the CONFIGURATION SECTION is rather typical, the INPUT-OUTPUT SECTION utilizes the newly presented clauses. The description of the MASTER-FILE includes all these clauses. The SELECT and ASSIGN clauses look very normal. However, the RESERVE clause indicates that 15 alternate areas have been assigned to the file. That is, MASTER-FILE has 16 buffers (15 alternate buffers plus the one required buffer). Each physical input operation will cause 16 physical records to be read. The next clause indicates that the ACCESS MODE is to be SEQUENTIAL. Again, this clause is not required since the default ACCESS MODE is SEQUENTIAL. Finally, the PROCESSING MODE for the MASTER-FILE is SEQUENTIAL. (This clause is a comment only.)

The EXCEPTION-REPORT file is a description of a print-oriented file. In addition to the SELECT and ASSIGN clauses, the RESERVE clause is used. When NO is specified in the RESERVE clause, the file is allocated one buffer (rather than the default of two buffers). Remember that a file must have at least one buffer in order to communicate with the assigned device. (The ACCESS MODE is SEQUENTIAL by default.)

System Flowcharts

Because we may now be faced with several input files and several output files, a new type of flowchart, the system *flowchart,* is often necessary to describe the types, number, and usage of different files. It provides a logical flow pattern for data entering and exiting a procedure. Specifying media types and relations to a procedure requires a new series of symbols, as shown in Figure 17.6. Each symbol shown in this figure identifies a particular type of medium (or procedure) and its possible uses in a system flowchart.

Figure 17.7 illustrates the relationship of the system flowchart to a procedure, using the file assignments in Figure 17.3. The system flowchart assumes that the INVOICE-FILE and the SALES-FILE are input files to the procedure and NEW-INVOICE-FILE and REPORT-FILE are produced as output files.

Figure 17.6 System Flowcharting Symbols

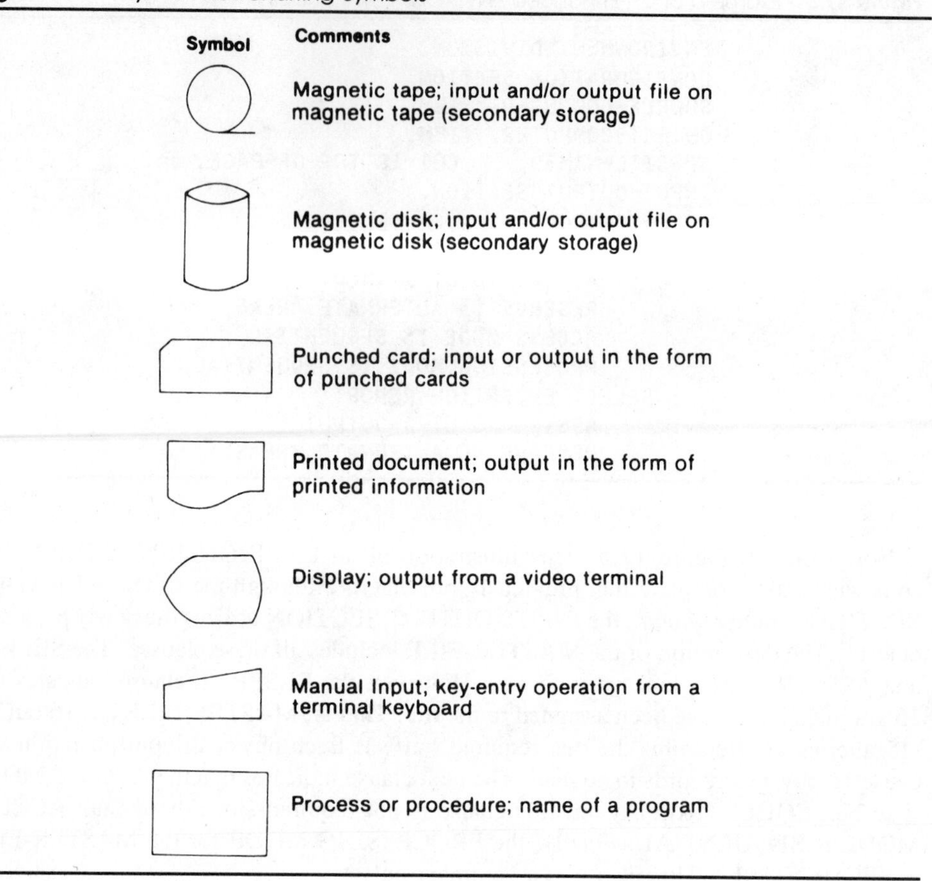

Symbol	Comments
	Magnetic tape; input and/or output file on magnetic tape (secondary storage)
	Magnetic disk; input and/or output file on magnetic disk (secondary storage)
	Punched card; input or output in the form of punched cards
	Printed document; output in the form of printed information
	Display; output from a video terminal
	Manual Input; key-entry operation from a terminal keyboard
	Process or procedure; name of a program

Figure 17.7 A System Flowchart Illustration

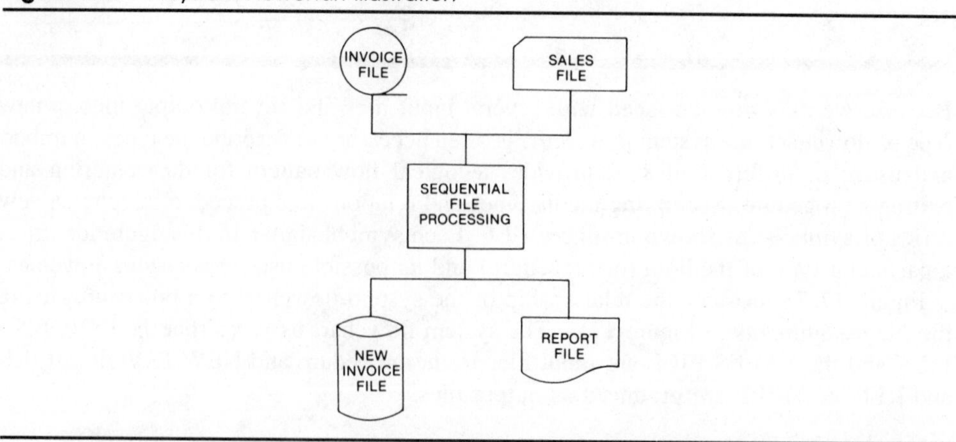

DATA DIVISION Considerations

As in previous programs, it is necessary to describe each file SELECTed with an FD in the FILE SECTION of the DATA DIVISION. For a sequential file FD a number of new clauses are needed (see Figure 17.8). The first new clause is the BLOCK CONTAINS clause, which indicates the blocking factor for records recorded on a magnetic medium. (A punched-card file and a printer file must be unblocked.) Integer-2 must be a non-negative integer number. It specifies either the number of characters in a physical record (block) or the number of logical records in a physical record. For example, if the clause was written as

```
BLOCK CONTAINS 500 CHARACTERS
```

COBOL would assume that the physical record was 500 bytes in length. The (logical) record description for this file should be a multiple of 100 (e.g., five 100-byte records). If the clause was written as

```
BLOCK CONTAINS 5 RECORDS
```

COBOL would assume the physical record length to be five times the (logical) record length. (Note that IBM COBOL permits integer-2 to be zero—indicating that the blocking factor is to be defaulted to that specified in the JCL.) If integer-1 is specified, integer-1 must be a positive integer number that represents the minimum length of a physical record. Then, integer-2 becomes the maximum record length (and must be greater in value than integer-1). This option permits the specification of *variable-length* blocks in COBOL; that is, all physical records do not necessarily have to be the same length. If the BLOCK CONTAINS clause is omitted, the file is unblocked.

The RECORD CONTAINS clause may be used to specify the logical record length. As in the BLOCK CONTAINS clause, integer-2 represents the maximum length of a

Figure 17.8 Sequential File FDs

```
 DATA DIVISION.
[FILE SECTION.
 FD  file-name

    [                                               { CHARACTERS } ]
    [ BLOCK CONTAINS  [integer-1 TO] integer-2      {            } ]
    [                                               { RECORDS    } ]

    [         { CONTAINS [integer-3 TO] integer-4 CHARACTERS          } ]
    [ RECORD  { IS VARYING IN SIZE                                    } ]
    [         {    [ [FROM integer-5] [TO integer-6] CHARACTERS]      } ]
    [         {    [DEPENDING ON data-name-1]                         } ]

           { RECORD IS  }   { OMITTED  }
    LABEL  {            }   {          }
           { RECORD ARE }   { STANDARD }

           { RECORD IS  }
   [DATA   {            }        data-name-2 [data-name-3] . . .] .]
           { RECORD ARE }
```

1985 COBOL Standards

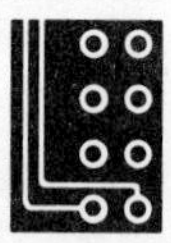

(logical) record. COBOL checks the length specified against the cumulative total of the PICTURE clauses to determine whether or not the record description's total length has been accurately stated. Cobol 85 allows the specification of a data-name that contains the size of a variable-length record through the use of the IS VARYING IN SIZE DEPENDING ON clause. The LABEL RECORDS clause has been previously discussed; however, Figure 17.8 shows that a file may either possess no label (OMITTED) or a STANDARD label. Data files recorded on magnetic media generally are recorded with STANDARD, system-generated labels.

Finally, the DATA RECORDS clause allows the programmer to identify the record-names (data-name-1, data-name-2, etc.) that are written in conjunction with each file description. The DATA RECORDS clause is treated as a comment.

Figure 17.9 illustrates the relationship of SELECTed files to the description of the files in the FILE SECTION. The INVOICE-FILE is a standard sequential (tape) file, thus the LABEL RECORDS clause is set to STANDARD. The logical record for this file is 100 bytes, and 50 logical records compose each physical record. The NEW-INVOICE-FILE is also standard sequential—perhaps a disk file and has 100-byte logical records. The BLOCK CONTAINS clause indicates, however, that the physical record length is 5000 bytes (50 times 100). The REPORT-FILE is a print-oriented file; thus, the LABEL RECORDS ARE OMITTED, the record length is 133 bytes, and the file is unblocked (no BLOCK CONTAINS clause). In addition, the DATA RECORDS clause indicates that the record-names PRINT-LINE and MESSAGE-LINE are to appear in conjunction with the FD. Finally, the FD for SALES-FILE is provided. SALES-FILE is assumed to be a punched-card file. LABEL RECORDS ARE OMITTED and the logical record length is 80 bytes. However, in the FILE-CONTROL paragraph, 16 buffers (15 ALTERNATE AREAS) are indicated, providing the capability to read 16 cards at a time.

Processing Sequential Files—New Statement Options

Figure 17.10 provides a new look at the OPEN statement. New options are provided in this statement because of the media involved. Note that an INPUT file may be opened REVERSED. That is, a standard sequential file may be opened such that it is positioned at the end of the file and read *backward!* This option applies primarily to magnetic tape, allowing the programmer to read (or reread) a file without rewinding it. The NO REWIND option of the OPEN statement is treated as a comment. And a new option is added to the OPEN statement. A file may be opened in an INPUT, OUTPUT, or I-O mode. That is, in the I-O mode, both reading and writing activity may take place in conjunction with a file in one processing sequence. However, to be opened in an I-O mode, the file must previously exist and the file must be on a mass storage device (e.g., magnetic disk).

As with the OPEN statement, the CLOSE statement has new options when used in conjunction with standard sequential files (see Figure 17.11). Both the REEL and NO REWIND options apply to sequential files on magnetic tape. The optional reserved word REEL may be used for documentation purposes to make explicit the use of a magnetic tape. The NO REWIND option, if present, forces the operating system to leave the magnetic tape at the end-of-file when it is CLOSEd. In the absence of the NO REWIND option, the file is rewound (repositioned for magnetic disk) to the beginning of the file. The LOCK option specifies that after the file has been rewound further operations on

Figure 17.9 Illustrations of Sequential File FDs

```
           .
           .
           .
       FILE-CONTROL.
           SELECT INVOICE-FILE
               ASSIGN TO UT-S-OLDMAST.
           SELECT NEW-INVOICE-FILE.
               ASSIGN TO UT-S-NEWMAST.
           SELECT REPORT-FILE
               ASSIGN TO UT-S-OUTPUT.
           SELECT SALES-FILE
               ASSIGN TO UT-S-INPUT
               RESERVE 15 ALTERNATE AREAS.
       DATA DIVISION.
       FILE SECTION.
       FD  INVOICE-FILE
               LABEL RECORDS ARE STANDARD
               BLOCK CONTAINS 5Ø RECORDS
               RECORD CONTAINS 1ØØ CHARACTERS.
       Ø1  INVOICE-RECORD                PIC X(1ØØ).
       FD  NEW-INVOICE-FILE
               LABEL RECORDS ARE STANDARD
               BLOCK CONTAINS 5ØØØ CHARACTERS
               RECORD CONTAINS 1ØØ CHARACTERS.
       Ø1  NEW-INVOICE-RECORD.
           Ø5  INVOICE-NUMBER            PIC 9(Ø6).
           Ø5  CUSTOMER-NUMBER           PIC X(1Ø).
           Ø5  FILLER                    PIC X(Ø6).
           Ø5  PURCHASE-AMOUNT           PIC S9(Ø6)V99.
           Ø5  FILLER                    PIC X(67).
       FD  REPORT-FILE
               LABEL RECORDS ARE OMITTED
               RECORD CONTAINS 133 CHARACTERS
               DATA RECORDS ARE PRINT-LINE, MESSAGE-LINE.
       Ø1  PRINT-LINE                    PIC X(133).
       Ø1  MESSAGE-LINE.
           Ø5  FILLER                    PIC X(83).
           Ø5  MESSAGE-OUT               PIC X(5Ø).
       FD  SALES-FILE
               LABEL RECORDS ARE OMITTED
               RECORD CONTAINS 8Ø CHARACTERS.
       Ø1  SALES-RECORD                  PIC X(8Ø).
```

Figure 17.10 Sequential File OPEN Statement

```
OPEN  [INPUT   file-name    [REVERSED       ]     . . .]
                            [WITH NO REWIND ]

      [OUTPUT  file-name    [WITH NO REWIND]   . . .]

      [I-O   file-name   . . .]
```

Figure 17.11 Sequential File CLOSE Statement

```
CLOSE file-name  [REEL]     [WITH  {NO REWIND} ]
                 [UNIT]            {LOCK     }
      [file-name [REEL]     [WITH  {NO REWIND} ]]. . .
                 [UNIT]            {LOCK     }
```

Figure 17.12 Sequential File WRITE Statement

```
WRITE record-name [FROM identifier]

[END-WRITE]
```

the file are to be inhibited for the remainder of the program. Without this option, the file could be reopened and processed again. The LOCK option can be used with tape or disk. Finally, the UNIT reserved word may be used to identify a mass storage medium type and, like the REEL option, is treated as a comment.

The WRITE statement is also modified (Figure 17.12) when creating a standard sequential file. The BEFORE/AFTER ADVANCING option, previously presented in conjunction with output to a printer, has been dropped. That is, top-of-form, single-space, and so on, have no meaning to a magnetic tape or disk. (In addition, it should be mentioned that the READ statement, previously described in conjunction with simple input files, is not altered when dealing with standard sequential files.)

Building a Sequential File

To be considered a standard sequential file, the file must have one record sequentially following another. For file-processing purposes, however, many files are ordered on the basis of a particular field to permit efficient manipulation of the file. For example, compare the file sequences provided in Figure 17.13. Both illustrations represent sequential files; however, the second file would be somewhat easier to manipulate—customer number 400 is preceded by customer number 380 and followed by 405. On the other hand, suppose we are "looking" for a record not in the file, a record identified by customer number 305. To determine that this record does not exist in the first file, we would have to read the entire file. When processing the second file, since it is

Figure 17.13 Unordered Versus Ordered Sequential Files

```
File 1:  Unordered

                                        FIELD
CUSTOMER
 NUMBER      REMAINDER OF RECORD

  320        ~~~~~~~~~~~~~~~~~~~~~~~~~~~~~~~~~~~~~~~~
  405        ~~~~~~~~~~~~~~~~~~~~~~~~~~~~~~~~~~~~~~~~
  180        ~~~~~~~~~~~~~~~~~~~~~~~~~~~~~~~~~~~~~~~~
  310        ~~~~~~~~~~~~~~~~~~~~~~~~~~~~~~~~~~~~~~~~
  400        ~~~~~~~~~~~~~~~~~~~~~~~~~~~~~~~~~~~~~~~~
  570        ~~~~~~~~~~~~~~~~~~~~~~~~~~~~~~~~~~~~~~~~
  260        ~~~~~~~~~~~~~~~~~~~~~~~~~~~~~~~~~~~~~~~~
  380        ~~~~~~~~~~~~~~~~~~~~~~~~~~~~~~~~~~~~~~~~
  605        ~~~~~~~~~~~~~~~~~~~~~~~~~~~~~~~~~~~~~~~~
  410        ~~~~~~~~~~~~~~~~~~~~~~~~~~~~~~~~~~~~~~~~

File 2:  Ordered by Customer Number

                                        FIELD
CUSTOMER
 NUMBER      REMAINDER OF RECORD

  180        ~~~~~~~~~~~~~~~~~~~~~~~~~~~~~~~~~~~~~~~~
  260        ~~~~~~~~~~~~~~~~~~~~~~~~~~~~~~~~~~~~~~~~
  310        ~~~~~~~~~~~~~~~~~~~~~~~~~~~~~~~~~~~~~~~~
  320        ~~~~~~~~~~~~~~~~~~~~~~~~~~~~~~~~~~~~~~~~
  380        ~~~~~~~~~~~~~~~~~~~~~~~~~~~~~~~~~~~~~~~~
  400        ~~~~~~~~~~~~~~~~~~~~~~~~~~~~~~~~~~~~~~~~
  405        ~~~~~~~~~~~~~~~~~~~~~~~~~~~~~~~~~~~~~~~~
  410        ~~~~~~~~~~~~~~~~~~~~~~~~~~~~~~~~~~~~~~~~
  570        ~~~~~~~~~~~~~~~~~~~~~~~~~~~~~~~~~~~~~~~~
  605        ~~~~~~~~~~~~~~~~~~~~~~~~~~~~~~~~~~~~~~~~
```

sequenced on the customer number field, encountering customer number 310 (without having previously encountered 305) would mean that customer number 305 is not present in the file. Thus, standard sequential files are frequently ordered on some identifying field to simplify file-processing requirements.

Now turn to Figure 17.14. This program is responsible for building a standard sequential CUSTOMER-IN-FILE. For this type of file, customer numbers should be unique. The procedure specifies that the CUSTOMER-IN-FILE is presumed to be an unordered file. Thus, the PROCEDURE DIVISION begins with a SORT statement (with a USING phrase—see Chapter 16). When the OUTPUT PROCEDURE begins, the data have been ordered, and any duplicate CUSTOMER-NUMBERs will be adjacent to each other (CUSTOMER-NUMBER-SORT is the sort key). As records are returned from the CUSTOMER-SORT-FILE (lines 1260 and 1380), they are checked to determine whether or not they are the same as those of the previous record (line 1330). If the customer number is a duplicate, the duplication is noted on the EXCEPTION-REPORT, and the record is omitted from the output file. If the customer number is not a duplicate, the customer record (from the sort file) is placed in the newly created output file (CUSTOMER-OUT-FILE), with the WRITE statement in line 1630. Thus, a new file has been created (sequenced on the customer number field) and retained for further processing.

Figure 17.14 Building a Sequential File (System Flowchart)

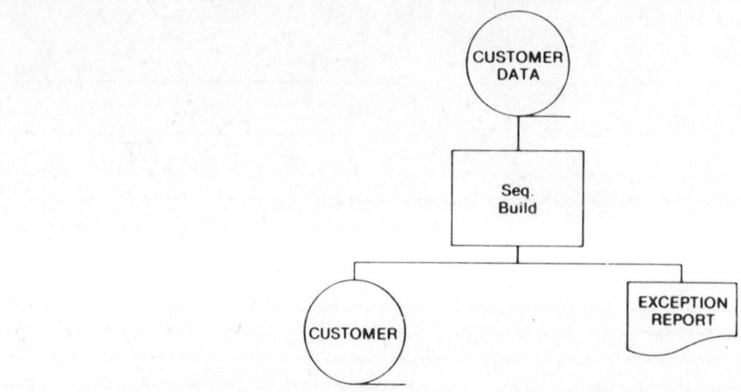

Figure 17.14 *Continued* Building a Sequential File (Hierarchy Chart)

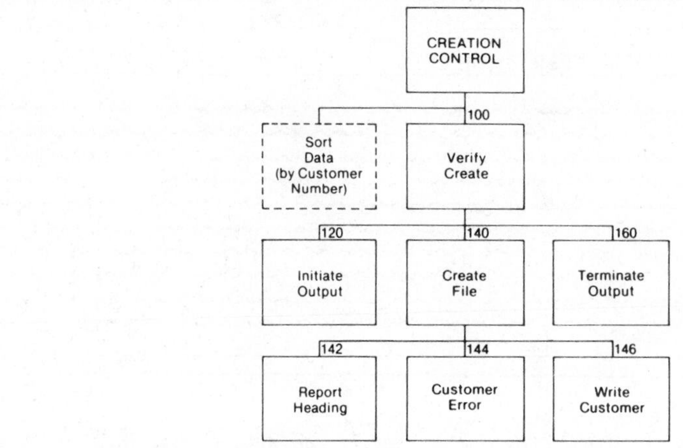

Figure 17.14 *Continued* Building a Sequential File (Pseudocode)

```
START
    SORT customer file
        ASCENDING customer number
        OUTPUT Verify Create
    ENDSORT
END

VERIFY CREATE
    DO Initiate output
    DO Create file UNTIL eof
    DO Terminate output
END

INITIATE OUTPUT
    OPEN output files
    RETURN customer file
        IF eof
            SET file status
        ENDIF
END

CREATE FILE
    IF line number > 40
        DO Report heading
    ENDIF
    IF customer number = last customer number
        DO Customer error
    ELSE
        DO Write customer
    ENDIF
    MOVE customer number to last customer number
    RETURN customer file
        IF eof
            SET file status
        ENDIF
END

REPORT HEADING
    ADD 1 to page number
    WRITE headings
    MOVE 0 to line number
END

CUSTOMER ERROR
    ADD 1 to error count
    MOVE customer number to output
    WRITE error
    ADD 1 to line number
END

WRITE CUSTOMER
    ADD 1 to customer count
    WRITE output
END

TERMINATE OUTPUT
    MOVE counts to output
    WRITE output summary
    CLOSE files
END
```

Figure 17.14 *Continued* Building a Sequential File

```
        1   1   2   2   2   3   3   4   4   4   5   5   6   6   6   7
4   8   2   6   0   4   8   2   6   0   4   8   2   6   0   4   8   2

 ******************************************************************
  IDENTIFICATION DIVISION.
 ******************************************************************
  PROGRAM-ID.     SEQUENTIAL-BUILD.
  AUTHOR.         JOHN WINDOSR.
  DATE-WRITTEN.   JANUARY 1, 1989.
  DATE-COMPILED.  JANUARY 1, 1989.
 *    The purpose of this procedure is to produce a sequential
 *    data file based on customer records.  The file is to be
 *    ordered on the customer number field.
 ******************************************************************
  ENVIRONMENT DIVISION.
 ******************************************************************
 *---------------------------------------------------------------*
  CONFIGURATION SECTION.
 *---------------------------------------------------------------*
  SOURCE-COMPUTER. IBM.
  OBJECT-COMPUTER. IBM.
  SPECIAL-NAMES.
                 C01 IS TOP-OF-PAGE.
 *---------------------------------------------------------------*
  INPUT-OUTPUT SECTION.
 *---------------------------------------------------------------*
  FILE-CONTROL.
      SELECT CUSTOMER-IN-FILE       ASSIGN TO UT-S-INPUT.
      SELECT CUSTOMER-OUT-FILE      ASSIGN TO UT-S-OUTPUT2.
      SELECT CUSTOMER-SORT-FILE     ASSIGN TO UT-S-SORTWK01.
      SELECT EXCEPTION-REPORT-FILE ASSIGN TO UT-S-OUTPUT.
 ******************************************************************
  DATA DIVISION.
 ******************************************************************
 *---------------------------------------------------------------*
  FILE SECTION.
 *---------------------------------------------------------------*
  FD  CUSTOMER-IN-FILE
      LABEL RECORDS ARE STANDARD
      RECORD CONTAINS 124 CHARACTERS
      BLOCK CONTAINS 0 RECORDS.
  01  CUSTOMER-RECORD-IN                PIC X(124).

  FD  CUSTOMER-OUT-FILE
      LABEL RECORDS ARE STANDARD
      RECORD CONTAINS 124 CHARACTERS
      BLOCK CONTAINS 0 RECORDS.
  01  CUSTOMER-RECORD-OUT.
      05  CUSTOMER-NUMBER-OUT      PIC X(10).
      05  CUSTOMER-NAME-OUT        PIC X(30).
      05  CUSTOMER-ADDRESS-OUT     PIC X(30).
      05  CUSTOMER-CITY-OUT        PIC X(20).
      05  CUSTOMER-STATE-OUT       PIC X(02).
      05  CUSTOMER-ZIP-OUT         PIC X(10).
      05  OUTSTANDING-BALANCE-OUT  PIC S9(9)V99.
      05  CREDIT-LIMIT-OUT         PIC S9(9)V99.

  SD  CUSTOMER-SORT-FILE.
  01  CUSTOMER-RECORD-SORT.
      05  CUSTOMER-NUMBER-SORT     PIC X(10).
      05  FILLER                   PIC X(114).

  FD  EXCEPTION-REPORT-FILE
      LABEL RECORDS ARE OMITTED.
  01  REPORT-RECORD                PIC X(133).
 *---------------------------------------------------------------*
  WORKING-STORAGE SECTION.
 *---------------------------------------------------------------*
  01  WORKING-VARIABLES.
      05  FILE-STATUS              PIC X(04) VALUE SPACES.
      05  CUSTOMER-NUMBER-LAST     PIC X(10) VALUE SPACES.
      05  LINE-NUMBER-WS           PIC 9(02) VALUE 99.
```

Figure 17.14 *Continued* Building a Sequential File

```
                1   1   2   2   2   3   3   4   4   4   5   5   6   6   6   7
    4   8   2   6   0   4   8   2   6   0   4   8   2   6   0   4   8   2
           05  PAGE-NUMBER-WS           PIC 9(02) VALUE ZERO.
           05  ERROR-COUNT-WS           PIC 9(04) VALUE ZERO.
           05  CUSTOMER-COUNT-WS        PIC 9(04) VALUE ZERO.
       01  HEADING-1.
           05  FILLER                   PIC X(32) VALUE SPACES.
           05  FILLER                   PIC X(16) VALUE
                                        'Exception Report'.
           05  FILLER                   PIC X(25) VALUE SPACES.
           05  FILLER                   PIC X(05) VALUE 'Page'.
           05  PAGE-NUMBER-OUT          PIC Z9.
       01  HEADING-2.
           05  FILLER                   PIC X(20) VALUE
                                        ' Customer Number'.
           05  FILLER                   PIC X(20) VALUE
                                        'Comments'.
       01  HEADING-3.
           05  FILLER                   PIC X(01) VALUE SPACES.
           05  FILLER                   PIC X(80) VALUE ALL '-'.
       01  ERROR-LINE.
           05  FILLER                   PIC X(02) VALUE SPACES.
           05  CUSTOMER-NUMBER-ERROR    PIC X(10).
           05  FILLER                   PIC X(08) VALUE SPACES.
           05  FILLER                   PIC X(50) VALUE
               'Customer Number Duplicate Encountered--ELIMINATED'.
       01  SUMMARY-LINE.
           05  FILLER                   PIC X(01) VALUE SPACES.
           05  CUSTOMER-COUNT-OUT       PIC *,**9.
           05  FILLER                   PIC X(27) VALUE
                                        ' Customer Records Written--'.
           05  ERROR-COUNT-OUT          PIC *,**9.
           05  FILLER                   PIC X(25) VALUE
                                        ' Duplicates Encountered'.
      *****************************************************************
       PROCEDURE DIVISION.
      *****************************************************************
      *---------------------------------------------------------------*
       000-CREATION-CONTROL SECTION.
      *---------------------------------------------------------------*
           SORT CUSTOMER-SORT-FILE
               ASCENDING KEY CUSTOMER-NUMBER-SORT
               USING CUSTOMER-IN-FILE
               OUTPUT PROCEDURE 100-VERIFY-CREATE.
           STOP RUN.
      *---------------------------------------------------------------*
       100-VERIFY-CREATE SECTION.
      *---------------------------------------------------------------*
       100-ENTRY.
           PERFORM 120-INITIATE-OUTPUT.
           PERFORM 140-CREATE-FILE
               UNTIL FILE-STATUS = 'DONE'.
           PERFORM 160-TERMINATE-OUTPUT.
      *---------------------------------------------------------------*
       120-INITIATE-OUTPUT SECTION.
      *---------------------------------------------------------------*
           OPEN OUTPUT CUSTOMER-OUT-FILE
                       EXCEPTION-REPORT-FILE.
           RETURN CUSTOMER-SORT-FILE INTO CUSTOMER-RECORD-OUT
               AT END MOVE 'DONE' TO FILE-STATUS.
      *---------------------------------------------------------------*
       140-CREATE-FILE SECTION.
      *---------------------------------------------------------------*
           IF LINE-NUMBER-WS IS GREATER THAN 40
               PERFORM 142-REPORT-HEADING.
           IF CUSTOMER-NUMBER-SORT = CUSTOMER-NUMBER-LAST
               PERFORM 144-CUSTOMER-ERROR
           ELSE
               PERFORM 146-WRITE-CUSTOMER.
           MOVE CUSTOMER-NUMBER-SORT TO CUSTOMER-NUMBER-LAST.
           RETURN CUSTOMER-SORT-FILE INTO CUSTOMER-RECORD-OUT
```

Figure 17.14 *Continued* Building a Sequential File

```
             1   1   2   2   2   3   3   4   4   4   5   5   6   6   6   7
   4   8   2   6   0   4   8   2   6   0   4   8   2   6   0   4   8   2
-----------------------------------------------------------------------
               AT END MOVE 'DONE' TO FILE-STATUS.
       *-----------------------------------------------------------*
        142-REPORT-HEADING SECTION.
       *-----------------------------------------------------------*
           ADD 1 TO PAGE-NUMBER-WS.
           MOVE PAGE-NUMBER-WS          TO PAGE-NUMBER-OUT.
           WRITE REPORT-RECORD FROM HEADING-1
               AFTER ADVANCING TOP-OF-PAGE.
           WRITE REPORT-RECORD FROM HEADING-2 AFTER ADVANCING 3 LINES.
           WRITE REPORT-RECORD FROM HEADING-3 AFTER ADVANCING 1 LINES.
           MOVE SPACES                  TO REPORT-RECORD.
           WRITE REPORT-RECORD AFTER ADVANCING 1 LINES.
           MOVE 0                       TO LINE-NUMBER-WS.
       *-----------------------------------------------------------*
        144-CUSTOMER-ERROR SECTION.
       *-----------------------------------------------------------*
           ADD 1 TO ERROR-COUNT-WS.
           MOVE CUSTOMER-NUMBER-OUT TO CUSTOMER-NUMBER-ERROR.
           WRITE REPORT-RECORD FROM ERROR-LINE AFTER ADVANCING 1 LINES.
           ADD 1 TO LINE-NUMBER-WS.
       *-----------------------------------------------------------*
        146-WRITE-CUSTOMER SECTION.
       *-----------------------------------------------------------*
           ADD 1 TO CUSTOMER-COUNT-WS.
           WRITE CUSTOMER-RECORD-OUT.
       *-----------------------------------------------------------*
        160-TERMINATE-OUTPUT SECTION.
       *-----------------------------------------------------------*
           MOVE ERROR-COUNT-WS          TO ERROR-COUNT-OUT.
           MOVE CUSTOMER-COUNT-WS       TO CUSTOMER-COUNT-OUT.
           WRITE REPORT-RECORD FROM SUMMARY-LINE
               AFTER ADVANCING 2 LINES.
           CLOSE EXCEPTION-REPORT-FILE
                 CUSTOMER-OUT-FILE.
```

Figure 17.14 *Continued* Building a Sequential File [CUSTOMER-IN] (Data)

```
      |                                                                                                   1         1         1
      |         1         2         3         4         5         6         7         8         9         0         1         2
Record|123456789012345678901234567890123456789012345678901234567890123456789012345678901234567890123456789012345678901234
---------------------------------------------------------------------------------------------------------------------------
     1|4412X47390Marshall Silverman                2219 West 7th Street          Cleveland          OH30119   0000000000000000500000
     2|3199127X33James Thompkins                   44339 South Wacker Drive      Chicago            IL60606   0000002291800000500000
     3|1141944103Edwin Williams                    2139 South Colgate Street     Perryton           TX79070   0000033193300035000000
     4|6213937661Jason Madison                     8831 Cedar Drive N.W.         Norwich            CN00218   0000041452300003000000
     5|5270215827Charles Everest                   8821 Ocean Parkway            Miami              FL51332   0000000000000000500000
     6|3333333333Julia Harriston                   6132 Mill Road Avenue         Shreveport         LA63341   0000035134300005000000
     7|3498966451Jacob R. Sullivan                 6134 Malibu Drive             Los Angeles        CA96512   0000000000000004400000
     8|1RX14219-3John P. Villiman                  8887 Peach Tree Lane          Dallas             TX75002   0000000314300000500000
     9|6427633-94Mark U. Lemon                     P. O. Box 51244               New York           NY03158   0000000000000000005000
    10|773194221BHelen B. Overstreet               3153 Yellow Brick Road        Yellow Stone Park  MT41229   0000001284200000000000
    11|9XO-334RDSAnthony P. Jones                  Executive Office Building     Washington         DC00000   0000000000000000000000
    12|3333333333Raymond J. Taylor                 912 Dusty Road                Plains             GA39100   0000052353600010000000
```

Figure 17.14 *Continued* Building a Sequential File [CUSTOMER-OUT] (Data)

```
-----------------------------------------------------------------------------------------------------------------------------------
|                                                                                                             1         1         1   |
|      |         1         2         3         4         5         6         7         8         9         0         1         2   |
|Record|1234567890123456789012345678901234567890123456789012345678901234567890123456789012345678901234567890123456789012345678901234|
|-----------------------------------------------------------------------------------------------------------------------------------
|     1|1RX14219-3John P. Villiman                8887 Peach Tree Lane         Dallas              TX75002    0000000314300000500000|
|     2|1141944103Edwin Williams                  2139 South Colgate Street    Perryton            TX79070    0000033193300035000000|
|     3|3199127X33James Thompkins                 44339 South Wacker Drive     Chicago             IL60606    0000002291800000500000|
|     4|3333333333Julia Harriston                 6132 Mill Road Avenue        Shreveport          LA63341    0000035134300005000000|
|     5|3498966451Jacob R. Sullivan               6134 Malibu Drive            Los Angeles         CA96512    0000000000000004400000|
|     6|4412X47390Marshall Silverman              2219 West 7th Street         Cleveland           OH30119    0000000000000000500000|
|     7|5270215827Charles Everest                 8821 Ocean Parkway           Miami               FL51332    0000000000000000500000|
|     8|6213937661Jason Madison                   8831 Cedar Drive N.W.        Norwich             CT00218    0000041452300003000000|
|     9|6427633-94Mark U. Lemon                   P. O. Box 51244              New York            NY03158    0000000000000000005000|
|    10|773194221BHelen B. Overstreet             3153 Yellow Brick Road       Yellow Stone Park   MT41229    0000001284200000000000|
|    11|9X0-334RDSAnthony P. Jones                Executive Office Building    Washington          DC00000    0000000000000000000000|
-----------------------------------------------------------------------------------------------------------------------------------
```

Figure 17.14 *Continued* Building a Sequential File (Output)

```
                                 Exception Report                                  Page  1

Customer Number    Comments
---------------------------------------------------------------------------------------

 3333333333        Customer Number Duplicate Encountered--ELIMINATED

***11 Customer Records Written--****1 Duplicates Encountered
```

One final note about building sequential files: The building process is typically required only *once*. That is, after the data have been examined for correctness, and the sequence has been established, all further processing works from this sequence.

Updating a Sequential File

Unlike the building process, file updating is typically a repetitive process. That is, periodically a file may be modified to reflect more current information. For example, the customer file may be updated by altering the customer's address, modifying the credit limit, or incrementing (decrementing) the outstanding balance to reflect sales (and payments). Updating a record in a file properly requires that both the record be updated and the update itself (for a particular record) be processed at the same time. Figure 17.15 illustrates the logic of this process. Note that the CUSTOMER FILE (sometimes referred to as a *MASTER* file) and the SALES FILE (sometimes referred to as a *TRANSACTION* file) are both sequenced on the customer number. Further, notice that for a particular customer number in the CUSTOMER FILE there may be no corresponding record in the SALES FILE. In other cases, however, one or more records in the SALES FILE could have a corresponding customer number. Finally, there may be customer numbers in the SALES FILE that do not exist in the CUSTOMER FILE—a probable error.

How do we determine what to do with each customer record in the CUSTOMER FILE and when to do it? To simplify the update logic, the programmer only has to be concerned with three basic relationships between the customer number of the CUSTOMER FILE and the customer number of the SALES FILE, as illustrated in Figure 17.16. Of course, we anticipate finding situations in which the customer number from the two files are equal (e.g., 260, 320, and 410 appear in both files). However, there may be circumstances under which a customer record is not updated (e.g., customer numbers 180, 310, 380, 400, 405, 570, and 605 of the CUSTOMER FILE). Finally, there may be customer numbers in the transaction file that do not have corresponding numbers in the CUSTOMER FILE (e.g., 350 in the SALES FILE).

Now examine Figure 17.16. First, we read one record from each file, that is, 180 from the CUSTOMER FILE and 260 from the SALES FILE. Since 180 is less than 260, we write customer record 180 to a new file and read the next customer record — 260—from the CUSTOMER FILE. Customer number 180 was not updated in this case, but the same logic will be used to write a record after *all* transactions have been processed. Now, the two customer numbers match, the affected fields are modified, and the next record from the SALES FILE is read—320. The customer number from the CUSTOMER FILE is again less than that from the SALES FILE (260 is less than 320). The *changed*

Figure 17.15 Master Files and Transaction Files

CUSTOMER FILE (Master File)

CUSTOMER NUMBER	REMAINDER OF RECORD
180	~~~~~~~~
260	~~~~~~~~
310	~~~~~~~~
320	~~~~~~~~
380	~~~~~~~~
400	~~~~~~~~
405	~~~~~~~~
410	~~~~~~~~
570	~~~~~~~~
605	~~~~~~~~

SALES FILE (Transaction File)

CUSTOMER NUMBER	CONTENT OF UPDATE
260	~~~~~~~~
320	~~~~~~~~
320	~~~~~~~~
350	~~~~~~~~
410	~~~~~~~~
410	~~~~~~~~
410	~~~~~~~~
410	~~~~~~~~

customer record is written to a new file and the next customer record from the CUSTOMER FILE (310) is read. The customer number from the CUSTOMER FILE is still less than that from the SALES FILE. The customer record is written (copied), as was done with 180, and the next record (320) is read from the CUSTOMER FILE. The customer numbers are again equal, the affected field in the customer record is changed, and the next SALES RECORD (320) is read. The customer numbers are still equal, so another change is made to the customer record, and another record (350) is read from the SALES FILE. The customer number from the CUSTOMER FILE is now less than the customer number from the SALES FILE (320 is less than 350), the changed customer record is written to the new CUSTOMER FILE, and a new customer record (380) is read from the old CUSTOMER FILE. The current value of the customer number from the CUSTOMER FILE is *greater than* that from the SALES FILE (350)—a condition that can exist only if 350 is not present in the CUSTOMER FILE. Therefore, we declare 350 to be an error—if it had existed in the CUSTOMER FILE we would have read it prior to 380. An error message is written, and a new record (410) is read from the SALES FILE. After this, records 380, 400, and 405 will be copied to the new CUSTOMER FILE; CUSTOMER FILE record 410 will be updated four times; and CUSTOMER FILE records 410, 570, and 605 will be written to the new CUSTOMER FILE. Thus, a complete file update has been performed.

The program presented in Figure 17.17 performs such an update. One problem not addressed with Figures 17.15 and 17.16 was the end-of-file process for the two files. By examining the PERFORM statement in lines 1320 through 1340, the programmer can establish the condition under which 1400-UPDATE-FILE is terminated—both the CUSTOMER-NUMBER-OUTFILE and CUSTOMER-NUMBER-SORT (associated with the sorted sales records) are HIGH-VALUES. It is unlikely that a customer would be HIGH-VALUES (the highest value in the computer's collating sequence); thus, this value is generated by some other means. Now, turn to the procedures responsible for getting input data from the sort file (the RETURN statement in line 1980) and the customer file (the READ statement in line 2140). Note that the end-of-file condition for each

Figure 17.16 Sequential File Update Logic (No duplicate master-file keys assumed)

UPDATE LOGIC

(Modification of fields in existing records in an old master file based on data found in a transaction file)

Key Relationship	Procedure
Master = Transaction	Change the indicated field(s), as appropriate, in the old master-file record, and read a new transaction record. (Procedure will accommodate one or more transactions per master record.)
Master < Transaction	Write a new record into the new master file from the old master file, and read another record from the old master file. (Create a new, updated record in the new master file or copy a nonupdated record from the old master file to the new master file.)
Master > Transaction	Error–no old master record contains the key specified in the transaction record. Write an error message and read a new transaction record.

Figure 17.17 Updating a Sequential File (System Flowchart)

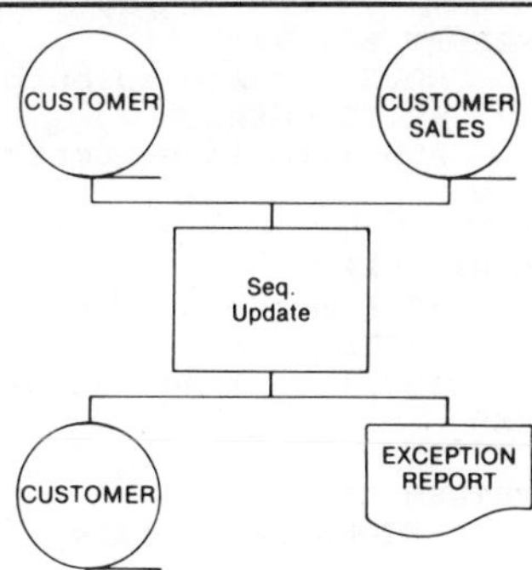

statement causes HIGH-VALUES to be moved to their respective key fields. Therefore, if we were to encounter the end of the sort file first, CUSTOMER-NUMBER-OUTFILE would be *less than* CUSTOMER-NUMBER-SORT, forcing the remainder of the records in the CUSTOMER-IN-FILE to be copied to the new CUSTOMER-OUT-FILE. On the other hand, if the end of the CUSTOMER-IN-FILE is encountered first, HIGH-VALUES is moved to CUSTOMER-NUMBER-OUTFILE. From this point forward, the CUSTOMER-NUMBER-OUTFILE would be *greater than* CUSTOMER-NUMBER-SORT—all remaining sales records would be identified as an error. Thus, no exceptional processing is required to handle end-of-file processing.

Figure 17.17 *Continued* Updating a Sequential File (Hierarchy Chart)

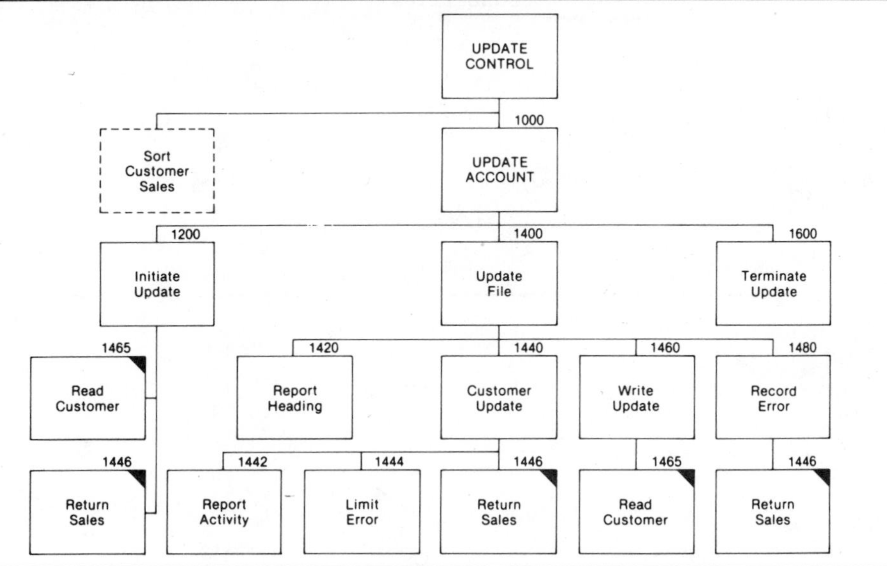

Figure 17.17 *Continued* Updating a Sequential File (Pseudocode)

```
START
    SORT sales file
         ASCENDING customer number
         OUTPUT Update Account
    ENDSORT
END

UPDATE ACCOUNT
    DO Initiate update
    DO Update file
         UNTIL customer number out = high values
         AND customer number sort = high values
    DO Terminate update
END

INITIATE UPDATE
    OPEN files
    DO Read customer
    DO Return sales
END

UPDATE FILE
    IF line number > 40
         DO Reprot heading
    ENDIF
    IF customer number out = customer number sort
         DO Customer update
         GOTO end
    ENDIF
    IF customer number out < customer number sort
         DO Write update
         GOTO end
    ENDIF
    IF customer number out > customer number sort
         DO Record error
         GOTO end
    ENDIF
END

REPORT HEADING
    ADD 1 to page number
    MOVE 0 to line number
    WRITE headings
END

CUSTOMER UPDATE
    IF balance + purchase > credit limit
         DO Limit error
    ELSE
         ADD purchase to balance
         DO Report activity
    ENDIF
    DO Return sales
END

REPORT ACTIVITY
    MOVE message to output
    WRITE output
    ADD 1 to line number
END

LIMIT ERROR
    MOVE message to output
    WRITE output
    ADD 1 to line number
END

RETURN SALES
    RETURN sales file
    IF eof
         MOVE high values to customer number sort
    ENDIF
    IF customer number sort not high values
         MOVE sort to output
    ENDIF
END

WRITE UPDATE
    WRITE output
    DO Read customer
END

READ CUSTOMER
    READ customer file
    IF eof
         MOVE high values to customer number out
    ENDIF
END

RECORD ERROR
    WRITE error output
    ADD 5 to line number
    DO Return sales
END

TERMINATE UPDATE
    CLOSE files
END
```

Figure 17.17 *Continued* Updating a Sequential File

```
            1   1   2   2   2   3   3   4   4   4   5   5   6   6   6   7
    4   8   2   6   0   4   8   2   6   0   4   8   2   6   0   4   8   2

      ***************************************************************
       IDENTIFICATION DIVISION.
      ***************************************************************
       PROGRAM-ID.     SEQUENTIAL-UPDATE.
       AUTHOR.         JOHN WINDSOR.
       DATE-WRITTEN.   JANUARY 1, 1989.
       DATE-COMPILED.  JANUARY 1, 1989.
      *     The purpose of this procedure is to update an existing
      *     sequential (customer) file on the basis of information
      *     contained in a sales file.  Multiple updates per customer
      *     record are permitted and customer updates (sales records)
      *     without a corresponding customer record are identified.
      ***************************************************************
       ENVIRONMENT DIVISION.
      ***************************************************************
      *-------------------------------------------------------------*
       CONFIGURATION SECTION.
      *-------------------------------------------------------------*
       SOURCE-COMPUTER. IBM.
       OBJECT-COMPUTER. IBM.
       SPECIAL-NAMES.
                        C01 IS TOP-OF-PAGE.
      *-------------------------------------------------------------*
       INPUT-OUTPUT SECTION.
      *-------------------------------------------------------------*
       FILE-CONTROL.
           SELECT CUSTOMER-IN-FILE      ASSIGN TO UT-S-INPUT.
           SELECT CUSTOMER-OUT-FILE     ASSIGN TO UT-S-OUTPUT2.
           SELECT SALES-IN-FILE         ASSIGN TO UT-S-INPUT2.
           SELECT SALES-SORT-FILE       ASSIGN TO UT-S-SORTWK01.
           SELECT EXCEPTION-REPORT-FILE ASSIGN TO UT-S-OUTPUT.
      ***************************************************************
       DATA DIVISION.
      ***************************************************************
      *-------------------------------------------------------------*
       FILE SECTION.
      *-------------------------------------------------------------*
       FD  CUSTOMER-IN-FILE
           LABEL RECORDS ARE STANDARD
           RECORD CONTAINS 124 CHARACTERS
           BLOCK CONTAINS 0 RECORDS.
       01  CUSTOMER-RECORD-IN          PIC X(124).

       FD  CUSTOMER-OUT-FILE
           LABEL RECORDS ARE STANDARD
           RECORD CONTAINS 124 CHARACTERS
           BLOCK CONTAINS 0 RECORDS.
       01  CUSTOMER-RECORD-OUT.
           05  CUSTOMER-NUMBER-OUTFILE PIC X(10).
           05  CUSTOMER-NAME-OUTFILE   PIC X(30).
           05  CUSTOMER-ADDRESS-OUTFILE PIC X(30).
           05  CUSTOMER-CITY-OUTFILE   PIC X(20).
           05  CUSTOMER-STATE-OUTFILE  PIC X(02).
           05  CUSTOMER-ZIP-OUTFILE    PIC X(10).
           05  CUSTOMER-BALANCE-OUTFILE PIC S9(9)V99.
           05  CUSTOMER-CREDIT-LIMIT-OUTFILE PIC S9(9)V99.

       FD  SALES-IN-FILE
           LABEL RECORDS ARE STANDARD
           RECORD CONTAINS 80 CHARACTERS
           BLOCK CONTAINS 0 RECORDS.
       01  CUSTOMER-SALES-RECORD       PIC X(80).

       SD  SALES-SORT-FILE.
       01  SALES-RECORD-SORT.
           05  CUSTOMER-NUMBER-SORT    PIC X(10).
           05  DATE-OF-PURCHASE-SORT.
               10  PURCHASE-MONTH-SORT PIC X(02).
               10  PURCHASE-DAY-SORT   PIC X(02).
```

Figure 17.17 *Continued* Updating a Sequential File

```
       1   1   2   2   2   3   3   4   4   4   5   5   6   6   7
   4   8   2   6   0   4   8   2   6   0   4   8   2   6   0   4   8   2

         10 PURCHASE-YEAR-SORT  PIC X(02).
    05  PURCHASE-ITEM-SORT      PIC X(10).
    05  PURCHASE-AMOUNT-SORT    PIC S9(09)V99.
    05  FILLER                  PIC X(43).

FD  EXCEPTION-REPORT-FILE
    LABEL RECORDS ARE OMITTED.
01  REPORT-RECORD                 PIC X(133).
*------------------------------------------------------------*
WORKING-STORAGE SECTION.
*------------------------------------------------------------*
01  WORKING-VARIABLES.
    05  LINE-NUMBER-WS          PIC 9(02) VALUE 99.
    05  PAGE-NUMBER-WS          PIC 9(02) VALUE ZERO.

01  HEADING-1.
    05  FILLER                  PIC X(32) VALUE SPACES.
    05  FILLER                  PIC X(16) VALUE
                                'Exception Report'.
    05  FILLER                  PIC X(25) VALUE SPACES.
    05  FILLER                  PIC X(05) VALUE 'Page'.
    05  PAGE-NUMBER-OUT         PIC Z9.

01  HEADING-2.
    05  FILLER                  PIC X(20) VALUE
                                ' Customer Number'.
    05  FILLER                  PIC X(50) VALUE
        '  Date      Purchase Amount      Comments'+

01  HEADING-3.
    05  FILLER                  PIC X(01) VALUE SPACES.
    05  FILLER                  PIC X(80) VALUE ALL '-'.

01  ERROR-LINE.
    05  FILLER                  PIC X(02) VALUE SPACES.
    05  CUSTOMER-NUMBER-OUT     PIC X(10).
    05  FILLER                  PIC X(08) VALUE SPACES.
    05  PURCHASE-MONTH-OUT      PIC X(02).
    05  FILLER                  PIC X(01) VALUE '/'.
    05  PURCHASE-DAY-OUT        PIC X(02).
    05  FILLER                  PIC X(01) VALUE '/'.
    05  PURCHASE-YEAR-OUT       PIC X(02).
    05  FILLER                  PIC X(05) VALUE SPACES.
    05  PURCHASE-AMOUNT-OUT     PIC ZZZ,ZZZ,ZZZ.ZZ.
    05  FILLER                  PIC X(05) VALUE SPACES.
    05  MESSAGE-OUT             PIC X(50) VALUE SPACES.
**************************************************************
PROCEDURE DIVISION.
**************************************************************
*------------------------------------------------------------*
0000-UPDATE-CONTROL SECTION.
*------------------------------------------------------------*
    MOVE 50000 TO SORT-CORE-SIZE.
    SORT SALES-SORT-FILE
        ASCENDING KEY CUSTOMER-NUMBER-SORT
        USING SALES-IN-FILE
        OUTPUT PROCEDURE 1000-UPDATE-ACCOUNT.
    STOP RUN.
*------------------------------------------------------------*
1000-UPDATE-ACCOUNT SECTION.
*------------------------------------------------------------*
    PERFORM 1200-INITIATE-UPDATE.
    PERFORM 1400-UPDATE-FILE
        UNTIL CUSTOMER-NUMBER-OUTFILE = HIGH-VALUES
          AND CUSTOMER-NUMBER-SORT    = HIGH-VALUES.
    PERFORM 1600-TERMINATE-UPDATE.
*------------------------------------------------------------*
1200-INITIATE-UPDATE SECTION.
*------------------------------------------------------------*
```

Figure 17.17 *Continued* Updating a Sequential File

```
           OPEN INPUT CUSTOMER-IN-FILE
                OUTPUT EXCEPTION-REPORT-FILE
                       CUSTOMER-OUT-FILE.
           PERFORM 1465-READ-CUSTOMER.
           PERFORM 1446-RETURN-SALES.
      *----------------------------------------------------------*
       1400-UPDATE-FILE SECTION.
      *----------------------------------------------------------*
           IF LINE-NUMBER-WS IS GREATER THAN 40
               PERFORM 1420-REPORT-HEADING.
           IF CUSTOMER-NUMBER-OUTFILE = CUSTOMER-NUMBER-SORT
               PERFORM 1440-CUSTOMER-UPDATE
               GO TO 1499-EXIT.
           IF CUSTOMER-NUMBER-OUTFILE < CUSTOMER-NUMBER-SORT
               PERFORM 1460-WRITE-UPDATE
               GO TO 1499-EXIT.
           IF CUSTOMER-NUMBER-OUTFILE > CUSTOMER-NUMBER-SORT
               PERFORM 1480-RECORD-ERROR
               GO TO 1499-EXIT.

       1499-EXIT.
           EXIT.
      *----------------------------------------------------------*
       1420-REPORT-HEADING SECTION.
      *----------------------------------------------------------*
           ADD 1 TO PAGE-NUMBER-WS.
           MOVE PAGE-NUMBER-WS        TO PAGE-NUMBER-OUT.
           MOVE 0                     TO LINE-NUMBER-WS.
           WRITE REPORT-RECORD FROM HEADING-1
               AFTER ADVANCING TOP-OF-PAGE.
           WRITE REPORT-RECORD FROM HEADING-2 AFTER ADVANCING 2 LINES.
           WRITE REPORT-RECORD FROM HEADING-3 AFTER ADVANCING 1 LINES.
           MOVE SPACES                TO REPORT-RECORD.
           WRITE REPORT-RECORD AFTER ADVANCING 1 LINES.
      *----------------------------------------------------------*
       1440-CUSTOMER-UPDATE SECTION.
      *----------------------------------------------------------*
           IF CUSTOMER-BALANCE-OUTFILE + PURCHASE-AMOUNT-SORT >
             CUSTOMER-CREDIT-LIMIT-OUTFILE
               PERFORM 1444-LIMIT-ERROR
           ELSE
               ADD PURCHASE-AMOUNT-SORT TO CUSTOMER-BALANCE-OUTFILE
               PERFORM 1442-REPORT-ACTIVITY.
           PERFORM 1446-RETURN-SALES.
      *----------------------------------------------------------*
       1442-REPORT-ACTIVITY SECTION.
      *----------------------------------------------------------*
           MOVE 'Customer Record Updated' TO MESSAGE-OUT.
           WRITE REPORT-RECORD FROM ERROR-LINE AFTER ADVANCING 1 LINES.
           ADD 1 TO LINE-NUMBER-WS.
      *----------------------------------------------------------*
       1444-LIMIT-ERROR SECTION.
      *----------------------------------------------------------*
           MOVE 'Credit Limit Exceeded' TO MESSAGE-OUT.
           WRITE REPORT-RECORD FROM ERROR-LINE AFTER ADVANCING 1 LINES.
           ADD 1 TO LINE-NUMBER-WS.
      *----------------------------------------------------------*
       1446-RETURN-SALES SECTION.
      *----------------------------------------------------------*
           RETURN SALES-SORT-FILE
               AT END MOVE HIGH-VALUES TO CUSTOMER-NUMBER-SORT.
           IF CUSTOMER-NUMBER-SORT NOT = HIGH-VALUES
               MOVE CUSTOMER-NUMBER-SORT TO CUSTOMER-NUMBER-OUT
               MOVE PURCHASE-MONTH-SORT  TO PURCHASE-MONTH-OUT
               MOVE PURCHASE-DAY-SORT    TO PURCHASE-DAY-OUT
               MOVE PURCHASE-YEAR-SORT   TO PURCHASE-YEAR-OUT
               MOVE PURCHASE-AMOUNT-SORT TO PURCHASE-AMOUNT-OUT.
      *----------------------------------------------------------*
       1460-WRITE-UPDATE SECTION.
```

Figure 17.17 *Continued* Updating a Sequential File

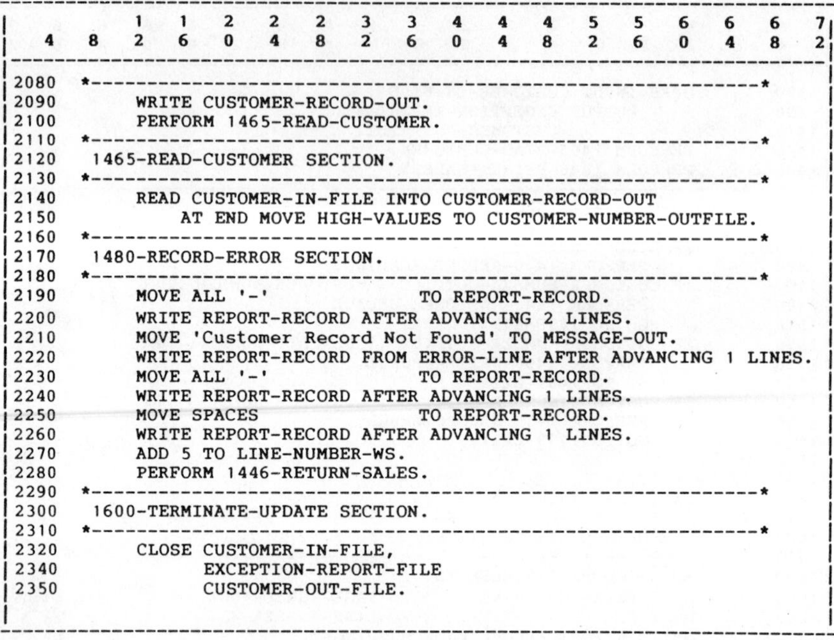

```
         1   1   2   2   2   3   3   4   4   4   5   5   6   6   6   7
 4   8   2   6   0   4   8   2   6   0   4   8   2   6   0   4   8   2

      *-----------------------------------------------------------*
           WRITE CUSTOMER-RECORD-OUT.
           PERFORM 1465-READ-CUSTOMER.
      *-----------------------------------------------------------*
       1465-READ-CUSTOMER SECTION.
      *-----------------------------------------------------------*
           READ CUSTOMER-IN-FILE INTO CUSTOMER-RECORD-OUT
               AT END MOVE HIGH-VALUES TO CUSTOMER-NUMBER-OUTFILE.
      *-----------------------------------------------------------*
       1480-RECORD-ERROR SECTION.
      *-----------------------------------------------------------*
           MOVE ALL '-'                TO REPORT-RECORD.
           WRITE REPORT-RECORD AFTER ADVANCING 2 LINES.
           MOVE 'Customer Record Not Found' TO MESSAGE-OUT.
           WRITE REPORT-RECORD FROM ERROR-LINE AFTER ADVANCING 1 LINES.
           MOVE ALL '-'                TO REPORT-RECORD.
           WRITE REPORT-RECORD AFTER ADVANCING 1 LINES.
           MOVE SPACES                 TO REPORT-RECORD.
           WRITE REPORT-RECORD AFTER ADVANCING 1 LINES.
           ADD 5 TO LINE-NUMBER-WS.
           PERFORM 1446-RETURN-SALES.
      *-----------------------------------------------------------*
       1600-TERMINATE-UPDATE SECTION.
      *-----------------------------------------------------------*
           CLOSE CUSTOMER-IN-FILE,
                 EXCEPTION-REPORT-FILE
                 CUSTOMER-OUT-FILE.
```

Figure 17.17 *Continued* Updating a Sequential File [CUSTOMER-SALES] (Data)

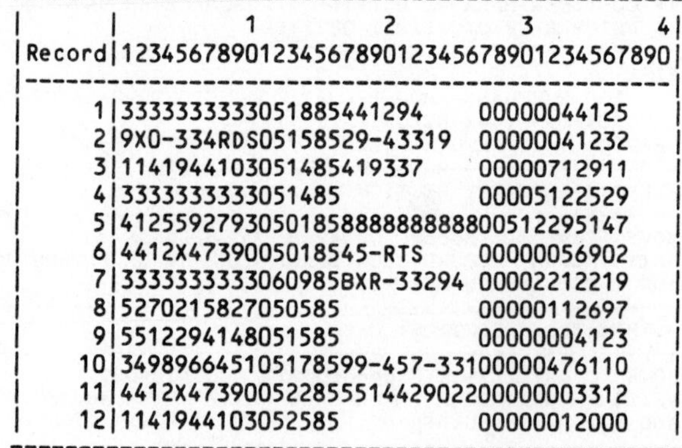

```
-------------------------------------------------
|      |         1         2         3         4|
|Record|1234567890123456789012345678901234567890|
|-----------------------------------------------|
|     1|3333333333051885441294      00000044125 |
|     2|9X0-334RDS05158529-43319    00000041232 |
|     3|1141944103051485419337      00000712911 |
|     4|3333333333051485            00005122529 |
|     5|41255927930501858888888888800512295147 |
|     6|4412X4739005018545-RTS      00000056902 |
|     7|3333333333060985BXR-33294   00002212219 |
|     8|5270215827050585            00000112697 |
|     9|5512294148051585            00000004123 |
|    10|349896645105178599-457-33100000476110 |
|    11|4412X473900522855514429022000000003312 |
|    12|1141944103052585            00000012000 |
-------------------------------------------------
```

Figure 17.17 *Continued* Updating a Sequential File [CUSTOMER-SALES] (Data)

```
------------------------------------------------------------------------------------------------------------------------------------
|                                                                                                              1         1         1   |
|      |         1         2         3         4         5         6         7         8         9         0         1         2   |
|Record|1234567890123456789012345678901234567890123456789012345678901234567890123456789012345678901234567890123456789012345678901234|
|------------------------------------------------------------------------------------------------------------------------------------
|     1|1RX14219-3John P. Villiman                        8887 Peach Tree Lane          Dallas            TX75002     00000003143000000500000|
|     2|1141944103Edwin Williams                          2139 South Colgate Street     Perryton          TX79070     0000105684D00035000000|
|     3|3199127X33James Thompkins                         44339 South Wacker Drive      Chicago           IL60606     00000022918000000500000|
|     4|3333333333Julia Harriston                         6132 Mill Road Avenue         Shreveport        LA63341     0000260768G00005000000|
|     5|3498966451Jacob R. Sullivan                       6134 Malibu Drive             Los Angeles       CA96512     000047611 00004400000|
|     6|4412X47390Marshall Silverman                      2219 West 7th Street          Cleveland         OH30119     0000006021D00000500000|
|     7|5270215827Charles Everest                         8821 Ocean Parkway            Miami             FL51332     0000011269G00000500000|
|     8|6213937661Jason Madison                           8831 Cedar Drive N.W.         Norwich   *       CT00218     00000414523000003000000|
|     9|6427633-94Mark U. Lemon                           P. O. Box 51244               New York          NY03158     0000000000000000000005000|
|    10|773194221BHelen B. Overstreet                     3153 Yellow Brick Road        Yellow Stone Park MT41229     00000012842000000000000|
|    11|9X0-334RDSAnthony P. Jones                        Executive Office Building     Washington        DC00000     000000000000000000000000|
------------------------------------------------------------------------------------------------------------------------------------
```

Figure 17.17 *Continued* Updating a Sequential File (Output)

```
                                Exception Report                        Page  1

    Customer Number     Date       Purchase Amount    Comments
    ---------------------------------------------------------------------------------

      1141944103       05/14/85           7,129.11     Customer Record Updated
      1141944103       05/25/85             120.00     Customer Record Updated
      3333333333       05/18/85             441.25     Customer Record Updated
      3333333333       05/14/85          51,225.29     Credit Limit Exceeded
      3333333333       06/09/85          22,122.19     Customer Record Updated
      3498966451       05/17/85           4,761.10     Customer Record Updated

     --------------------------------------------------------------------------------


      4125592793       05/01/85       5,122,951.47     Customer Record Not Found
     --------------------------------------------------------------------------------


      4412X47390       05/01/85             569.02     Customer Record Updated
      4412X47390       05/22/85              33.12     Customer Record Updated
      5270215827       05/05/85           1,126.97     Customer Record Updated

     --------------------------------------------------------------------------------


      5512294148       05/15/85              41.23     Customer Record Not Found
     --------------------------------------------------------------------------------
```

Figure 17.18 Sequential File Addition Logic

ADDITION LOGIC

(Addition of new records to an old master file based on records in a transaction file)

Key Relationship	Procedure
Master = Transaction	DUPLICATE RECORD: If no duplicates are to be allowed in the master file, write an error message indicating the attempt to add a duplicate, and read another record from the transaction file. If duplicates are to be allowed and the old master record is to appear first in the new master file, write the old record to the new master file, and read another record from the old master file. If duplicates are to be allowed and the transaction record is to appear first in the new master file, write the transaction record to the new master file, and read another transaction.
Master > Transaction	Write the transaction record to the new master file, and read another transaction record.
Master < Transaction	Write the old record to the new master file, and read another record from the old master file.

Adding to a Sequential File

Unfortunately, files like the CUSTOMER file do not usually remain static—they are subject to changes in addition to the update process described in the previous section. For example, suppose a new customer (or series of new customers) is to be added to the file. Usually, the new customer records are interspersed with existing customer records.

As with the update process, three relationships are possible between a master CUSTOMER FILE and a transaction ADDITION FILE. These three relationships, along with probable responses, are shown in Figure 17.18. If a customer number from the CUSTOMER FILE is equal to a customer number from the ADDITION file, a duplicate record exists. If the customer number from the CUSTOMER FILE is greater than that from the ADDITION FILE, the location of the record to be added has been found and the ADDITION FILE record is written. If the customer number from the CUSTOMER FILE is less than that from the ADDITION FILE, the existing customer record must be copied before proceeding by writing it to the new master file.

The program illustrated in Figure 17.19 performs the addition process. As explained in Figure 17.18, each of the three possible relationships between keys is provided in 1400-ADD-RECORDS SECTION (lines 1400-1480). The end-of-file process is handled exactly the same as explained in Figure 17.17.

Figure 17.19 Adding to a Sequential File (System Flowchart)

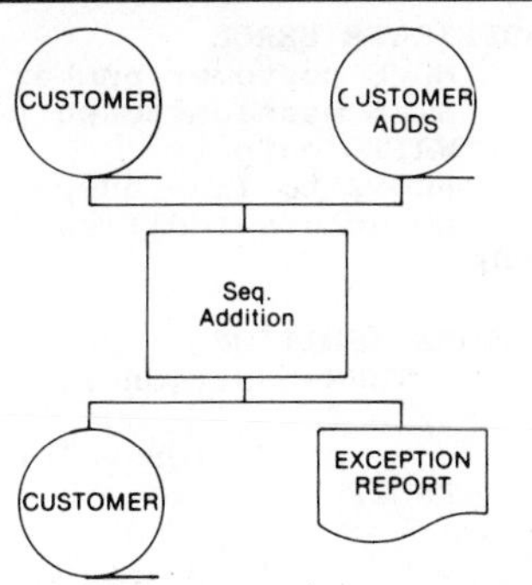

Figure 17.19 *Continued* Adding to a Sequential File (Hierarchy Chart)

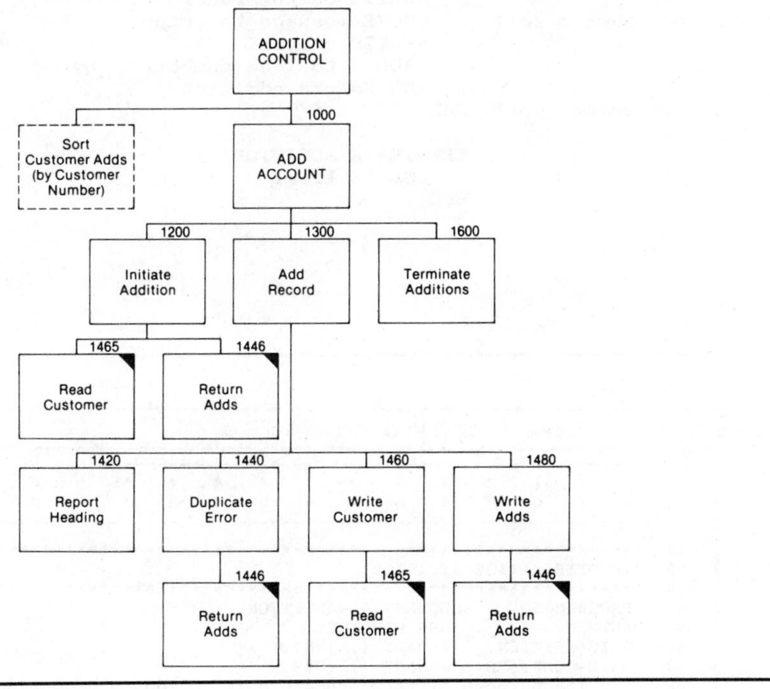

Figure 17.19 *Continued* Adding to a Sequential File (Pseudocode)

```
START
    SORT addition file
         ASCENDING customer number
         OUTPUT Update account
    ENDSORT
END

UPDATE ACCOUNT
    DO Initiate addition
    DO Add records
         UNTIL customer number in = high values
         AND customer number sort = high values
    DO Terminate addition
END

INITIATE ADDITION
    OPEN files
    DO Read customer
    DO Return addition
END

ADD RECORDS
    IF line number > 40
         DO Report heading
    ENDIF
    IF customer number in = customer number sort
         DO Duplicate error
         GOTO end
    ENDIF
    IF customer number in < customer number sort
         DO Write customer
         GOTO end
    ENDIF
    IF customer number in > customer number sort
         DO Write addition
         GOTO end
    ENDIF
END

REPORT HEADING
    ADD 1 to page number
    MOVE 0 to line number
    WRITE headings
END

DUPLICATE ERROR
    MOVE customer number to output
    MOVE message to output
    WRITE output
    ADD 2 to line number
    DO Return addition
END

RETURN ADDITION
    RETURN addition file
    IF eof
         MOVE high values to customer number sort
    ENDIF
END

WRITE CUSTOMER
    WRITE customer output
    DO Read customer
END

READ CUSTOMER
    READ customer file
    IF eof
         MOVE high values to customer number in
    ENDIF
END

WRITE ADDITION
    WRITE output record
    MOVE message to output
    WRITE output
    ADD 2 to line number
    DO Return addition
END

TERMINATE ADDITION
    CLOSE files
END
```

Figure 17.19 *Continued* Adding to a Sequential File

```
           1   1   2   2   2   3   3   4   4   4   5   5   6   6   6   7
   4   8   2   6   0   4   8   2   6   0   4   8   2   6   0   4   8   2

      ****************************************************************
       IDENTIFICATION DIVISION.
      ****************************************************************
       PROGRAM-ID.    SEQUENTIAL-ADDITION.
       AUTHOR.        JOHN WINDSOR.
       DATE-WRITTEN.  JANUARY 1, 1989.
       DATE-COMPILED. JANUARY 1, 1989.
      *    The purpose of this procedure is to add records (new customers)
      *    to an existing sequential (customer) file.  The procedure
      *    prohibits duplicate customer records with the same customer
      *    number.
      ****************************************************************
       ENVIRONMENT DIVISION.
      ****************************************************************
```

Figure 17.19 *Continued* Adding to a Sequential File

```
         1   1   2   2   2   3   3   4   4   4   5   5   6   6   6   7
 4   8   2   6   0   4   8   2   6   0   4   8   2   6   0   4   8   2

      *-----------------------------------------------------------*
       CONFIGURATION SECTION.
      *-----------------------------------------------------------*
       SOURCE-COMPUTER. IBM.
       OBJECT-COMPUTER. IBM.
       SPECIAL-NAMES.
                        C01 IS TOP-OF-PAGE.
      *-----------------------------------------------------------*
       INPUT-OUTPUT SECTION.
      *-----------------------------------------------------------*
       FILE-CONTROL.
           SELECT CUSTOMER-IN-FILE       ASSIGN TO UT-S-INPUT.
           SELECT CUSTOMER-OUT-FILE      ASSIGN TO UT-S-OUTPUT2.
           SELECT CUSTOMER-ADDITION-FILE ASSIGN TO UT-S-INPUT2.
           SELECT ADDITION-SORT-FILE     ASSIGN TO UT-S-SORTWK01.
           SELECT EXCEPTION-REPORT-FILE  ASSIGN TO UT-S-OUTPUT.
      *************************************************************
       DATA DIVISION.
      *************************************************************
      *-----------------------------------------------------------*
       FILE SECTION.
      *-----------------------------------------------------------*
       FD  CUSTOMER-IN-FILE
           LABEL RECORDS ARE STANDARD
           RECORD CONTAINS 124 CHARACTERS
           BLOCK CONTAINS 0 RECORDS.
       01  CUSTOMER-RECORD.
           05  CUSTOMER-NUMBER-IN        PIC X(10).
           05  FILLER                    PIC X(114).

       FD  CUSTOMER-OUT-FILE
           LABEL RECORDS ARE STANDARD
           RECORD CONTAINS 124 CHARACTERS
           BLOCK CONTAINS 0 RECORDS.
       01  CUSTOMER-RECORD-OUT           PIC X(124).

       FD  CUSTOMER-ADDITION-FILE
           LABEL RECORDS ARE STANDARD
           RECORD CONTAINS 124 CHARACTERS
           BLOCK CONTAINS 0 RECORDS.
       01  CUSTOMER-ADDITION-RECORD      PIC X(124).

       SD  ADDITION-SORT-FILE.
       01  ADDITION-RECORD-SORT.
           05  CUSTOMER-NUMBER-SORT      PIC X(10).
           05  FILLER                    PIC X(114).

       FD  EXCEPTION-REPORT-FILE
           LABEL RECORDS ARE OMITTED.
       01  REPORT-RECORD                 PIC X(133).
      *-----------------------------------------------------------*
       WORKING-STORAGE SECTION.
      *-----------------------------------------------------------*
       01  WORKING-VARIABLES.
           05  LINE-NUMBER-WS            PIC 9(02) VALUE 99.
           05  PAGE-NUMBER-WS            PIC 9(02) VALUE ZERO.

       01  HEADING-1.
           05  FILLER                    PIC X(32) VALUE SPACES.
           05  FILLER                    PIC X(16) VALUE
                                         'Exception Report'.
           05  FILLER                    PIC X(25) VALUE SPACES.
           05  FILLER                    PIC X(05) VALUE 'Page'.
           05  PAGE-OUT                  PIC Z9.

       01  HEADING-2.
           05  FILLER                    PIC X(20) VALUE
                                         ' Customer Number'.
           05  FILLER                    PIC X(50) VALUE
                                         'Comments'.

       01  HEADING-3.
           05  FILLER                    PIC X(01) VALUE SPACES.
           05  FILLER                    PIC X(80) VALUE ALL '-'.
```

Figure 17.19 *Continued* Adding to a Sequential Statement

```
                        1   1   2   2   2   3   3   4   4   4   5   5   6   6   6   7
        4       8       2   6   0   4   8   2   6   0   4   8   2   6   0   4   8   2

       01  ERROR-LINE.
           05  FILLER                       PIC X(02) VALUE SPACES.
           05  CUSTOMER-NUMBER-OUT          PIC X(10).
           05  FILLER                       PIC X(08) VALUE SPACES.
           05  MESSAGE-OUT                  PIC X(50) VALUE SPACES.
      *****************************************************************
       PROCEDURE DIVISION.
      *****************************************************************
      *---------------------------------------------------------------*
       0000-ADDITION-CONTROL SECTION.
      *---------------------------------------------------------------*
           MOVE 50000                  TO SORT-CORE-SIZE.
           SORT ADDITION-SORT-FILE
               ASCENDING KEY CUSTOMER-NUMBER-SORT
               USING CUSTOMER-ADDITION-FILE
               OUTPUT PROCEDURE 1000-UPDATE-ACCOUNT.
           STOP RUN.
      *---------------------------------------------------------------*
       1000-UPDATE-ACCOUNT SECTION.
      *---------------------------------------------------------------*
           PERFORM 1200-INITIATE-ADDITION.
           PERFORM 1400-ADD-RECORDS
               UNTIL CUSTOMER-NUMBER-IN   = HIGH-VALUES
                   AND CUSTOMER-NUMBER-SORT = HIGH-VALUES.
           PERFORM 1600-TERMINATE-ADDITION.
      *---------------------------------------------------------------*
       1200-INITIATE-ADDITION SECTION.
      *---------------------------------------------------------------*
           OPEN INPUT CUSTOMER-IN-FILE
                OUTPUT EXCEPTION-REPORT-FILE
                       CUSTOMER-OUT-FILE.
           PERFORM 1465-READ-CUSTOMER.
           PERFORM 1446-RETURN-ADDITION.
      *---------------------------------------------------------------*
       1400-ADD-RECORDS SECTION.
      *---------------------------------------------------------------*
           IF LINE-NUMBER-WS IS GREATER THAN 40
               PERFORM 1420-REPORT-HEADING.
           IF CUSTOMER-NUMBER-IN = CUSTOMER-NUMBER-SORT
               PERFORM 1440-DUPLICATE-ERROR
               GO TO 1499-EXIT.
           IF CUSTOMER-NUMBER-IN < CUSTOMER-NUMBER-SORT
               PERFORM 1460-WRITE-CUSTOMER
               GO TO 1499-EXIT.
           IF CUSTOMER-NUMBER-IN > CUSTOMER-NUMBER-SORT
               PERFORM 1480-WRITE-ADDITION
               GO TO 1499-EXIT.

       1499-EXIT.
           EXIT.
      *---------------------------------------------------------------*
       1420-REPORT-HEADING SECTION.
      *---------------------------------------------------------------*
           ADD 1 TO PAGE-NUMBER-WS.
           MOVE PAGE-NUMBER-WS          TO PAGE-OUT.
           MOVE 0                       TO LINE-NUMBER-WS.
           WRITE REPORT-RECORD FROM HEADING-1
               AFTER ADVANCING TOP-OF-PAGE.
           WRITE REPORT-RECORD FROM HEADING-2 AFTER ADVANCING 2 LINES.
           WRITE REPORT-RECORD FROM HEADING-3 AFTER ADVANCING 1 LINES.
           MOVE SPACES                  TO REPORT-RECORD.
           WRITE REPORT-RECORD AFTER ADVANCING 1 LINES.
      *---------------------------------------------------------------*
       1440-DUPLICATE-ERROR SECTION.
      *---------------------------------------------------------------*
           MOVE CUSTOMER-NUMBER-SORT TO CUSTOMER-NUMBER-OUT.
           MOVE 'Attempt to Add a Duplicate Record' TO MESSAGE-OUT.
           WRITE REPORT-RECORD FROM ERROR-LINE AFTER 2.
           ADD 2 TO LINE-NUMBER-WS.
           PERFORM 1446-RETURN-ADDITION.
```

Figure 17.19 *Continued* Adding to a Sequential File

```
         1   1   2   2   2   3   3   4   4   4   5   5   6   6   6   7
 4   8   2   6   0   4   8   2   6   0   4   8   2   6   0   4   8   2
 *-----------------------------------------------------------*
  1446-RETURN-ADDITION SECTION.
 *-----------------------------------------------------------*
      RETURN ADDITION-SORT-FILE
          AT END MOVE HIGH-VALUES TO CUSTOMER-NUMBER-SORT.
 *-----------------------------------------------------------*
  1460-WRITE-CUSTOMER SECTION.
 *-----------------------------------------------------------*
      WRITE CUSTOMER-RECORD-OUT FROM CUSTOMER-RECORD.
      PERFORM 1465-READ-CUSTOMER.
 *-----------------------------------------------------------*
  1465-READ-CUSTOMER SECTION.
 *-----------------------------------------------------------*
      READ CUSTOMER-IN-FILE
          AT END MOVE HIGH-VALUES TO CUSTOMER-NUMBER-IN.
 *-----------------------------------------------------------*
  1480-WRITE-ADDITION SECTION.
 *-----------------------------------------------------------*
      WRITE CUSTOMER-RECORD-OUT FROM ADDITION-RECORD-SORT.
      MOVE CUSTOMER-NUMBER-SORT TO CUSTOMER-NUMBER-OUT.
      MOVE 'Customer Record Added' TO MESSAGE-OUT.
      WRITE REPORT-RECORD FROM ERROR-LINE AFTER ADVANCING 2 LINES.
      ADD 2 TO LINE-NUMBER-WS.
      PERFORM 1446-RETURN-ADDITION.
 *-----------------------------------------------------------*
  1600-TERMINATE-ADDITION SECTION.
 *-----------------------------------------------------------*
      CLOSE CUSTOMER-IN-FILE,
            EXCEPTION-REPORT-FILE
            CUSTOMER-OUT-FILE.
```

Figure 17.19 *Continued* Adding to a Sequential File [CUSTOMER-ADDITION] (Data)

```
                                                                                                            1         1         1
      |         1         2         3         4         5         6         7         8         9         0         1         2
Record|1234567890123456789012345678901234567890123456789012345678901234567890123456789012345678901234567890123456789012345678901234
     1|3333333333George P. Martin              Las Vegas Hilton         Las Vegas          NV81222         9999999999900000000000
     2|2199428878Stewart A. Alexander          5112 Hamilton Parkway    Minneapolis        MN21132         0000062239000001000000
     3|5122314151Mark R. White                 55123 War Memorial Drive Cleveland          OH41229         0000004123300000050000
     4|X14339-278Rober P. Evans                1422 N. W. Classen Blvd. Oklahoma City      OK65124         0000000000000000300000
```

Figure 17.19 *Continued* Adding to a Sequential File [CUSTOMER-ADDITION] (Data)

```
                                                                                                            1         1         1
      |         1         2         3         4         5         6         7         8         9         0         1         2
Record|1234567890123456789012345678901234567890123456789012345678901234567890123456789012345678901234567890123456789012345678901234
     1|X14339-278Robert P. Evans               1422 N. W. Classen Blvd.   Oklahoma City      OK65124         0000000000000000300000
     2|1RX14219-3John P. Villiman              8887 Peach Tree Lane       Dallas             TX75002         0000000314300000500000
     3|1141944103Edwin Williams                2139 South Colgate Street  Perryton           TX79070         0000105684D00035000000
     4|2199428878Stewart A. Alexander          5112 Hamilton Parkway      Minneapolis        MN21132         0000062239000001000000
     5|3199127X33James Thompkins               44339 South Wacker Drive   Chicago            IL60606         0000002291800000500000
     6|3333333333Julia Harriston               6132 Mill Road Avenue      Shreveport         LA63341         0000260768G00005000000
     7|3498966451Jacob R. Sullivan             6134 Malibu Drive          Los Angeles        CA96512         0000047611 00004400000
     8|4412X47390Marshall Silverman            2219 West 7th Street       Cleveland          OH30119         0000006021D00000500000
     9|5122314151Mark R. White                 55123 War Memorial Drive   Cleveland          OH41229         0000004123300000050000
    10|5270215827Charles Everest               8821 Ocean Parkway         Miami              FL51332         0000011269G00000500000
    11|6213937661Jason Madison                 8831 Cedar Drive N.W.      Norwich            CT00218         0000041452300003000000
    12|6427633-94Mark U. Lemon                 P. O. Box 51244            New York           NY03158         0000000000000000005000
    13|773194221BHelen B. Overstreet           3153 Yellow Brick Road     Yellow Stone Park  MT41229         0000001284200000000000
    14|9XO-334RDSAnthony P. Jones              Executive Office Building  Washington         DC00000         0000000000000000000000
```

Figure 17.19 *Continued* Adding to a Sequential File (Output)

```
                              Exception Report                              Page  1

Customer Number    Comments
------------------------------------------------------------------------------------


 X14339-278          Customer Record Added

 2199428878          Customer Record Added

 3333333333          Attempt to Add a Duplicate Record

 5122314151          Customer Record Added
```

Deleting from a Sequential File

Often, we will also have to delete existing records. For example, customers may go out of business, choose not to do business with us, or move away. In any case, if we continually add to a file without periodically eliminating unneeded records, our file would grow until it became unmanageable. Figure 17.20 illustrates the deletion process based, again, on the three primary relationships between keys. If the customer number from the CUSTOMER FILE is equal to the customer number of the DELETE FILE, we have located the record to be deleted. Deletion is accomplished by *not writing* the record to the new CUSTOMER FILE. Since both records, in effect have been dealt with, it is necessary to read a record from both the old CUSTOMER FILE *and* the DELETE FILE. If the customer number of the CUSTOMER FILE is greater than that of the DELETE FILE, that customer is not in the CUSTOMER FILE. Then, an error message is written and a new record from the DELETE FILE is read. If the customer number of the CUSTOMER FILE is less than that of the DELETE FILE, the customer

Figure 17.20 Sequential File Deletion Logic

DELETION LOGIC

(Delete an existing record from the master file based on the key of a transaction file record)

Key Relationship	Procedure
Master = Transaction	If duplicates *do not* exist in the master file, read a new transaction record *and* another record from the old master file. If duplicates *do* exist in the master file and all records with a specified key are to be deleted, read the next record from the old master file and indicate the transaction has been employed.
Master > Transaction	If duplicates do not exist in the master file, write an error (the transaction key value was not found), and read another transaction record. If duplicates exist and were to be deleted from the master file, check to determine whether or not the transaction key has been employed. If the transaction key was not used, execute the same sequence and perform the operations as defined for files without duplicates. If the transaction key has been used, read the next transaction record.
Master < Transaction	Write the old master record to the new master file and read the next record from the old master file.

Figure 17.21 The REWRITE Statement (for Sequential Files)

```
REWRITE record-name [FROM identifier]

[END-REWRITE]
```

record is copied to the new CUSTOMER FILE, and another record from the old CUSTOMER FILE is read.

The process just described causes the *physical deletion* of a record; however, it might be desired to suspend or *logically delete* a record. In that case, the deletion process is the same as the update process. The update would cause an alteration of an existing field (the customer name field might be replaced with the word DELETE). Thus, the record would still be in the file. A much more likely circumstance is that a special field representing record status would be added to the record description during the initial development of the customer records system. Thus, the customer record might be 125 bytes or more. The extra space would be used to record the status of individual customers. However, since the record would still be present in the file, it would be read along with other records. Therefore, the programmer's code would have to be modified to reflect that deleted records should be read and bypassed, if found.

Sequential File Processing with Magnetic Disk

All of the processes previously described may be performed on either magnetic tape or disk. However, we have additional latitude with magnetic disk. Recall from the first part of this chapter that a mass storage device (e.g., magnetic disk) can be OPENed in an *I-O* mode. That is, records may be read or written in one procedure (without virtue of multiple open and close statements). This additional capability only impacts the update (and perhaps logical deletion) process. File building, adding new records, and physically deleting records remains the same.

When a disk file is opened I-O, it is assumed updates will be placed in the existing master file; that is, records will be read from the master file, changed, and rewritten. Most systems require a special statement to perform this rewriting (or *overwriting*) process. The REWRITE statement, as illustrated in Figure 17.21, performs this function. (Check your compiler to determine which statement causes the rewriting function.) The function of the REWRITE statement, like the WRITE statement, is to cause data to be written to a device. In the case of a REWRITE statement, the device is magnetic disk or other mass storage medium. However, whereas the WRITE statement directs the *next* record to be written to a file, the REWRITE statement for a file causes the *last record READ* to be overwritten. Consequently, during the update process, it would no longer be necessary to write a record if it were not changed, eliminating the "copying" operation. Therefore, the logic of the update process would require that a status field be updated each time a record is changed. Then, when the master file key is less than the transaction file key, it would be necessary to determine whether or not the status field showed a change for the existing record. If not, the next master record is read. If the status field indicated a change, the existing record would be rewritten, the status field would be changed for the new record, and the next master record would be read. All other operations would remain the same.

Summary

In this chapter, the COBOL statements and the logic necessary to perform sequential file processing on magnetic tape or disk have been illustrated. Modifications to the OPEN, CLOSE, and WRITE statements may become useful to accomplish certain tasks related to sequential file processing. Furthermore, the characteristics of the ENVIRONMENT and DATA DIVISIONs may be slightly altered to handle data more efficiently. An example of the more efficient manipulation of data from sequential files is the use of the BLOCK CONTAINS clause to record multiple logical records per physical record. Finally, the logic and procedure necessary to build, update, add records, and delete records in a sequential file were presented.

Notes on Programming Style

The structure presented in this chapter can be improved upon in a couple of ways. For example, the end-of-file processing illustrated in the programs in this chapter could be handled more efficiently by a specialized routine to copy records, identify errors, or add records. Specialized routines would be more efficient because a decision on the relationship of keys would not have to be established.

A second modification of the procedures illustrated might be a change to the paragraph level for the decision-making (key comparison) process. It would be possible to have a single paragraph perform the same function that a SECTION performed and eliminate the GO TO statements causing an unconditional branch to the exit. One word of caution is necessary. If you choose to use a ''fall through'' procedure (checking the next decision in the key relationship sequence regardless of whether or not a previous decision was true), the equality relationship should be the first test. Otherwise, it is possible to have both the master key and the transaction key assigned HIGH-VALUES, and therefore the test would presume a valid relationship for illegal data—an error!

Questions

Below, fill in the blank(s) with the appropriate word, words, or phrases.

1. Data that are recorded on _____ can be erased.
2. Relative to punched card and printed output devices, data are transmitted at a ___ rate than when compared to the transmission rate of magnetic media.
3. In terms of storage space, data stored on magnetic media require _____ than the equivalent data stored on punched cards.
4. One _____ record may contain one or more _____ records.
5. Relative to the length of a physical record, one buffer is (longer than, the same size as, shorter than) _____ a buffer.
6. Two reasons for blocking a data file are _____ and _____ .
7. An unblocked file means _____ (number) logical record per physical record.
8. On a magnetic medium, a(n) _____ separates two physical records.
9. Data stored on magnetic disk are recorded around concentric rings called _____ .
10. An input-output interrupt is generated each time the CPU interfaces with a(n) _____ .

11. A diagram that illustrates the types of devices (or media) to be interfaced to a procedure (program) is called a(n) ____ .

12. The ____ clause of the DATA DIVISION is used to control the number of logical records per physical record; the ____ clause of the ENVIRONMENT DIVISION is used to control the number of buffers per file.

13. A disk can be opened in the ____, ____, or ____ mode.

14. Before a file can be read, it must first be opened in the ____ mode and written.

15. If a magnetic media file is closed, without the use of any special options, the file is ____ .

16. Under the strictest definition of a sequential file, the records in the file must be ____ related to each other.

17. For processing purposes, a sequential file is generally ____ before file manipulation begins.

18. The statement that causes records to be placed in a file is the ____ statement.

19. A process known as ____ results in the modification or change in the existing records of a sequential file.

20. The three relationships that should be tested between a master key and a transaction key to determine the appropriate process are ____, ____, and ____.

21. The process of incorporating new records into an existing file is often referred to as ____

22. The process of eliminating existing records from a file that are no longer needed is referred to as ____.

23. A ____ statement is capable of overwriting existing data in a magnetic disk file.

Answer the following questions by circling either "T" for True or "F" for False.

T F **24.** A punched card record is 80 bytes long even if only 50 columns are used.

T F **25.** A logical record on magnetic tape must be less than 500 bytes in length.

T F **26.** A block can contain more than one physical record.

T F **27.** A block can contain more than one logical record.

T F **28.** Physical records on magnetic disk are separated by an area called an inter-record gap.

T F **29.** A buffer may contain one or more physical records.

T F **30.** Data may be transmitted to the CPU from magnetic tape faster than the CPU is capable of handling it.

T F **31.** A logical record is the same as a physical record.

T F **32.** Magnetic tape is a more compact medium than are punched cards.

T F **33.** The ACCESS MODE clause is required in the ENVIRONMENT DIVISION for sequential files.

T F **34.** More than two files may be ASSIGNed in one program.

T F **35.** A program flowchart and a system flowchart serve the same purpose.

T F **36.** The number of logical records per physical record is controlled by the REVERSE clause.

T F **37.** The number of logical records per physical record is controlled by the RECORD CONTAINS clause.

T F **38.** The DATA RECORDS clause is required when two or more record descriptions are recorded for a single file.

T F **39.** The LABEL RECORDS clause is required for sequential files.

T F **40.** When a file is LOCKed on the CLOSE statement, it means the file may not be used again in the same program.

T F **41.** A WRITE statement that transmits data to a magnetic disk file would normally have a BEFORE / AFTER ADVANCING clause.

T F **42.** A file may be opened in an I-O mode before it has been created.

T F **43.** The READ statement used to get data from a sequential tape file uses the same format as the READ statement used to get data from a punched card file.

T F **44.** To update a file means to change some characteristic of an existing record or series of records.

T F **45.** A file that is referred to as a MASTER file is the same as a TRANSACTION file.

T F **46.** To be processed correctly for an update process, the master file must be ordered on an ascending basis.

T F **47.** If, during the addition process, the master key and the transaction key are the same value, it means that a duplicate record is about to be added to the master file.

T F **48.** A record is physically deleted from a sequential file by not writing it to the new file.

T F **49.** Logically deleted records are the same as physically deleted records.

T F **50.** Record addition for a magnetic tape file is fundamentally different from the addition process for a magnetic disk file.

Problems

17.1 We are requested to develop a system capable of processing inventory records. The system is to be limited to four procedures:

a. Building an inventory file from data
b. Adding to an existing inventory file
c. Updating an inventory file from sales records
d. Producing an inventory reorder report

The relationships among these processes is presented in the system flowchart for inventory processing.

Part A. Building an Inventory File

The system flowchart indicates that an inventory file (for processing purposes) is to be developed. An inventory data file is to be provided as input to the process. (See the multiple-card layout form of an inventory record. The same record format will be used for all procedures, except that the record is to be expanded to 200 bytes—a FILLER at the end of the record—to accommodate future applications using the inventory file.) The procedure is to order the data by item number, vendor, and outlet. Individual item numbers, vendors, and outlets will not necessarily be unique; however, if coupled together an item number-vendor-outlet set should be unique. If a particular item number-vendor-outlet set is not unique, it is a duplicate record, and only the first such record should be placed in the inventory file. The creation report should reflect all duplicates. Only the item number, vendor, and outlet number need appear on the report. In addition, the number of records placed in

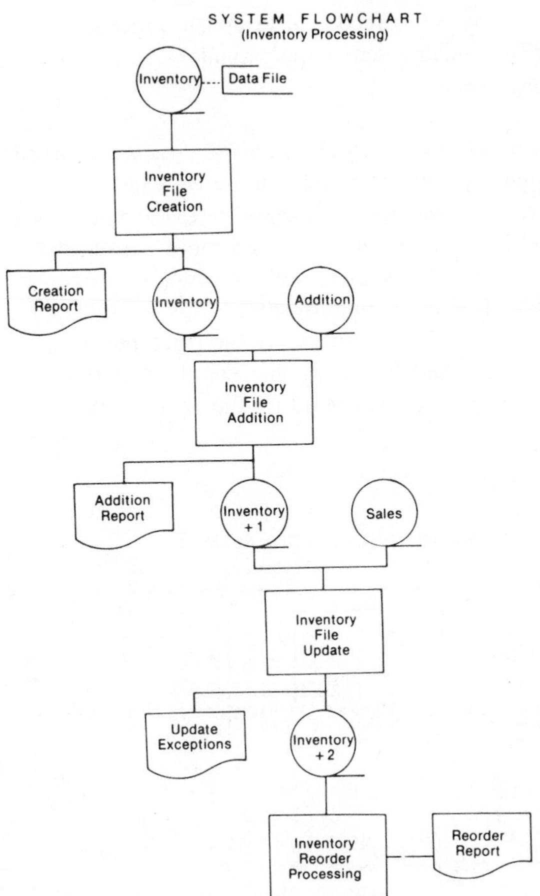

the file should appear on the report. Use your judgment in the design of the report from the standpoint of headings, page numbers, and so on.

Part B. Adding to the Inventory File

The second procedure illustrated in the system flowchart is to perform an addition operation. The records in the addition file are in the same format as those in the inventory data file. The process should cause new records to be placed in the inventory file in their appropriate position (relative to item number-vendor-outlet number keys). The data file is not ordered on any particular basis. The addition report is to reflect any attempt to add a duplicate record to the file. Like the creation report, it is only necessary to identify the duplicate records by item number, vendor, and outlet number fields. Duplicate records should not be added to the file.

Part C. Updating the Inventory File

The third procedure is to perform an update operation on the basis of data found in the sales file. (See the record format of a sales record. The data in this file are not ordered in any particular way.) Multiple updates for a single inventory record are possible as well as no update for a particular inventory record. The update procedure should accommodate the following operations (if matching item number-vendor-outlet number keys are found in both the inventory and sales files):

a. *Provided the on-hand amount of the inventory record is not less than the quanity sold*, subtract the quantity sold from the amount on hand.
b. Record the date of (last) sale from the sales file to the date of last sale in the inventory file. The date should be changed only if it is a more current date.
c. Add the quantity sold to the year-to-date and month-to-date sales in units field.
d. Adjust the year-to-date and month-to-date sales in dollars fields. The amount of adjustment is the quantity sold multiplied by the price per unit.
e. Adjust the year-to-date and month-to-date cost in dollars fields. The amount of the adjustment is the quantity sold multiplied by the cost per unit.

MULTIPLE-CARD LAYOUT FORM

Company LEARNING COBOL, INC.
Application INVENTORY PROCESSING by J. Wayne Spence Date 01/01/89 Job No. PROB 17.1 Sheet No. 1

Inventory Record

ITEM NUMBER	VENDOR CODE	ITEM DESCRIPTION	PRODUCT GROUP	OUTLET NUMBER	UNITS ON HAND	MINIMUM STOCK LEVEL	PRICE PER UNIT	COST PER UNIT	MEASURE.	
1–6	7–9	10–39	40–44	45–49	50–55	56–61	62–69 (^ after 67)	70–77 (^ after 75)	78–79	80

(Inventory Record Continued--Bytes 81 - 160)

DATE LAST PURCHASE	DATE LAST RECEIVED	PURCHASE QUANTITY	DATE LAST SOLD	YTD SALES (UNITS)	YTD SALES (DOLLARS)	YTD COST (DOLLARS)	MTD SALES (UNITS)	MTD SALES (DOLLARS)	
1–5	6–11	12–17	18–23	24–33	34–45 (^ after 43)	46–57 (^ after 55)	58–67	68–79 (^ after 77)	80

(Inventory Record Continued--Bytes 161 - 171)

MTD COST (DOLLARS)	
1–11 (^ after 9)	12–80

MULTIPLE-CARD LAYOUT FORM

Company LEARNING COBOL, INC.
Application INVENTORY PROCESSING by J. Wayne Spence Date 01/01/89 Job No. PROB 17.1 Sheet No. 1

Sales Record

CUSTOMER NUMBER	SALESMAN CODE	ITEM NUMBER	VENDOR CODE	OUTLET NUMBER	QUANTITY SOLD	DATE OF SALE	
1–6	7–9	10–15	16–18	19–23	24–29	30–35	36–80

```
150/10/8 PRINT CHART     PROG ID PROBLEM 17.1                PAGE 1
(SPACING  150 POSITIONS AT 10 CHARACTERS PER INCH, 8 LINES PER VERTICAL INCH)   DATE 01/01/89
PROGRAM TITLE INVENTORY FILE UPDATE
PROGRAMMER OR DOCUMENTALIST J. Wayne Spence
CHART TITLE INVENTORY UPDATE REPORT
3525 CARD PRINT POSITIONS

                                               INVENTORY UPDATE REPORT
                                                         M O N T H   T O   D A T E                      DATE OF
 ITEM     VENDOR   OUTLET   QUANTITY   QUANTITY                                                            LAST
 NUMBER    CODE    NUMBER    ON HAND     SOLD    SALES (UNITS)    SALES (DOLLARS)       COST (DOLLARS)     SALE
 XXXXXX    XXX     99,999    ZZZ,ZZ9             Z,ZZZ,ZZZ,ZZZ   $Z,ZZZ,ZZZ,ZZZ.99   $Z,ZZZ,ZZZ,ZZZ.99   XX/XX/XX
                                       ZZZ,ZZ9
                                       ZZZ,ZZ9
                                       ZZZ,ZZ9
                             ZZZ,ZZ9             Z,ZZZ,ZZZ,ZZZ   $Z,ZZZ,ZZZ,ZZZ.99   $Z,ZZZ,ZZZ,ZZZ.99   XX/XX/XX
 XXXXXX    XXX     99,999    ZZZ,ZZ9             Z,ZZZ,ZZZ,ZZZ   $Z,ZZZ,ZZZ,ZZZ.99   $Z,ZZZ,ZZZ,ZZZ.99   XX/XX/XX
                                       ZZZ,ZZ9
                                       ZZZ,ZZ9 CAUSES ON HAND TO BECOME NEGATIVE--UPDATE FOR CUSTOMER XXXXXXX ABORTED
                                       ZZZ,ZZ9
                                       ZZZ,ZZ9
                                       ZZZ,ZZ9
                                       ZZZ,ZZ9
                             ZZZ,ZZ9             Z,ZZZ,ZZZ,ZZZ   $Z,ZZZ,ZZZ,ZZZ.99   $Z,ZZZ,ZZZ,ZZZ.99   XX/XX/XX
 XXXXXX    XXX     99,999                        INVENTORY RECORD NOT FOUND
 XXXXXX    XXX     99,999    ZZZ,ZZ9             Z,ZZZ,ZZZ,ZZZ   $Z,ZZZ,ZZZ,ZZZ.99   $Z,ZZZ,ZZZ,ZZZ.99   XX/XX/XX
                                       ZZZ,ZZ9
                             ZZZ,ZZ9             Z,ZZZ,ZZZ,ZZZ   $Z,ZZZ,ZZZ,ZZZ.99   $Z,ZZZ,ZZZ,ZZZ.99   XX/XX/XX
```

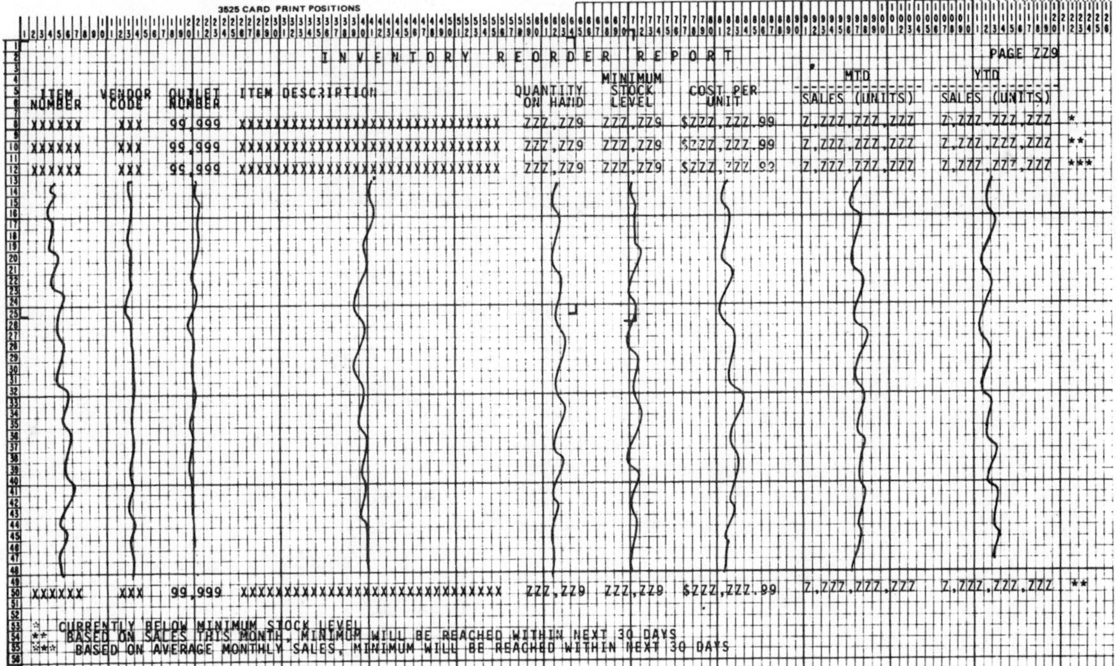

```
150/10/8 PRINT CHART     PROG ID PROBLEM 17.1                PAGE 1
(SPACING  150 POSITIONS AT 10 CHARACTERS PER INCH, 8 LINES PER VERTICAL INCH)   DATE 01/01/89
PROGRAM TITLE INVENTORY REORDER PROCESSING
PROGRAMMER OR DOCUMENTALIST J. Wayne Spence
CHART TITLE INVENTORY REORDER REPORT
3525 CARD PRINT POSITIONS

                                  I N V E N T O R Y   R E O R D E R   R E P O R T                                 PAGE ZZ9
                                                                       MINIMUM                     MTD               YTD
 ITEM    VENDOR  OUTLET  ITEM DESCRIPTION                    QUANTITY   STOCK     COST PER   ---------------   ---------------
 NUMBER   CODE   NUMBER                                       ON HAND   LEVEL       UNIT     SALES (UNITS)     SALES (UNITS)
 XXXXXX   XXX    99,999  XXXXXXXXXXXXXXXXXXXXXXXXXXXXXXXXXX   ZZZ,ZZ9  ZZZ,ZZ9  $ZZZ,ZZZ.99  Z,ZZZ,ZZZ,ZZZ     Z,ZZZ,ZZZ,ZZZ  *
 XXXXXX   XXX    99,999  XXXXXXXXXXXXXXXXXXXXXXXXXXXXXXXXXX   ZZZ,ZZ9  ZZZ,ZZ9  $ZZZ,ZZZ.99  Z,ZZZ,ZZZ,ZZZ     Z,ZZZ,ZZZ,ZZZ  **
 XXXXXX   XXX    99,999  XXXXXXXXXXXXXXXXXXXXXXXXXXXXXXXXXX   ZZZ,ZZ9  ZZZ,ZZ9  $ZZZ,ZZZ.99  Z,ZZZ,ZZZ,ZZZ     Z,ZZZ,ZZZ,ZZZ  ***

 XXXXXX   XXX    99,999  XXXXXXXXXXXXXXXXXXXXXXXXXXXXXXXXXX   ZZZ,ZZ9  ZZZ,ZZ9  $ZZZ,ZZZ.99  Z,ZZZ,ZZZ,ZZZ     Z,ZZZ,ZZZ,ZZZ  **

 *   CURRENTLY BELOW MINIMUM STOCK LEVEL
 **  BASED ON SALES THIS MONTH, MINIMUM WILL BE REACHED WITHIN NEXT 30 DAYS
 *** BASED ON AVERAGE MONTHLY SALES, MINIMUM WILL BE REACHED WITHIN NEXT 30 DAYS
```

If the quantity sold is greater than the on-hand amount, *no update is to be performed.* That is, all fields of the record should be exactly the same both before and after processing the sales record. Examine the report layout to determine the requirements of this procedure from the standpoint of printed output.

Part D. Producing a Reorder Report

The final procedure in the system is to produce a report indicating those inventory items for which the on-hand amount is either equal to or less than the minimum stock level (reorder point). The data printed on this report should be ordered by vendor, item number, and outlet. Each vendor should begin on a separate page. See the report layout form for additional details of the reorder report.

17.2 You are to create a system including all the properties illustrated in the attached system flowchart for customer processing. This processing consists of four parts:

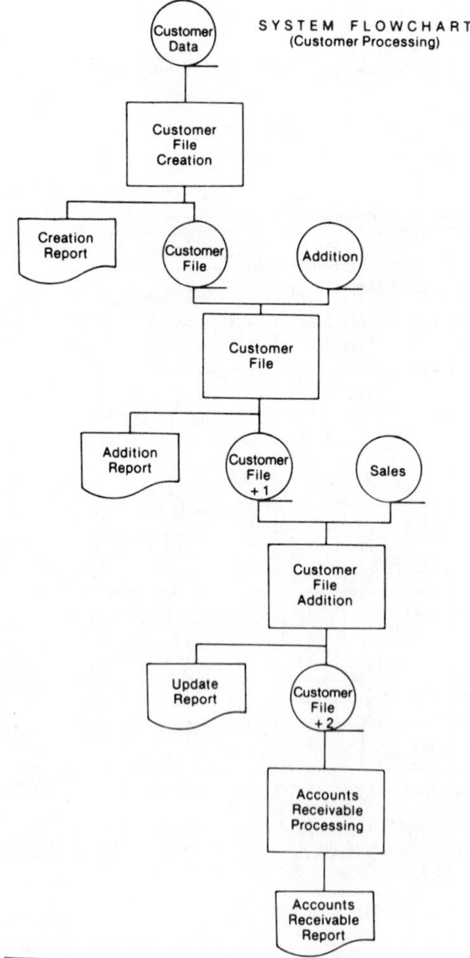

MULTIPLE-CARD LAYOUT FORM

Company LEARNING COBOL, INC.

Application CUSTOMER PROCESS by JOHN WINDSOR Date 01/01/89 Job No. PROB 17.2 Sheet No. 1

Customer Record

CUSTOMER NUMBER	LAST NAME	FIRST NAME	MIDDLE NAME	STREET ADDRESS/P O BOX
1–6	7–21	22–36	37–51	52–80

(Customer Record Continued--Bytes 81 - 160)

	CITY	STATE	ZIP CODE	CURRENT BALANCE	30-DAY BALANCE	60-DAY BALANCE	90-DAY BALANCE	DATE LAST STMT	
1	2–21	22–23	24–33	34–43	44–53	54–63	64–73	74–79	80

(Customer Record Continued--Bytes 161 - 171)

DATE LAST PAYMENT	DATE LAST PURCHASE	
1–5	6–11	12–80

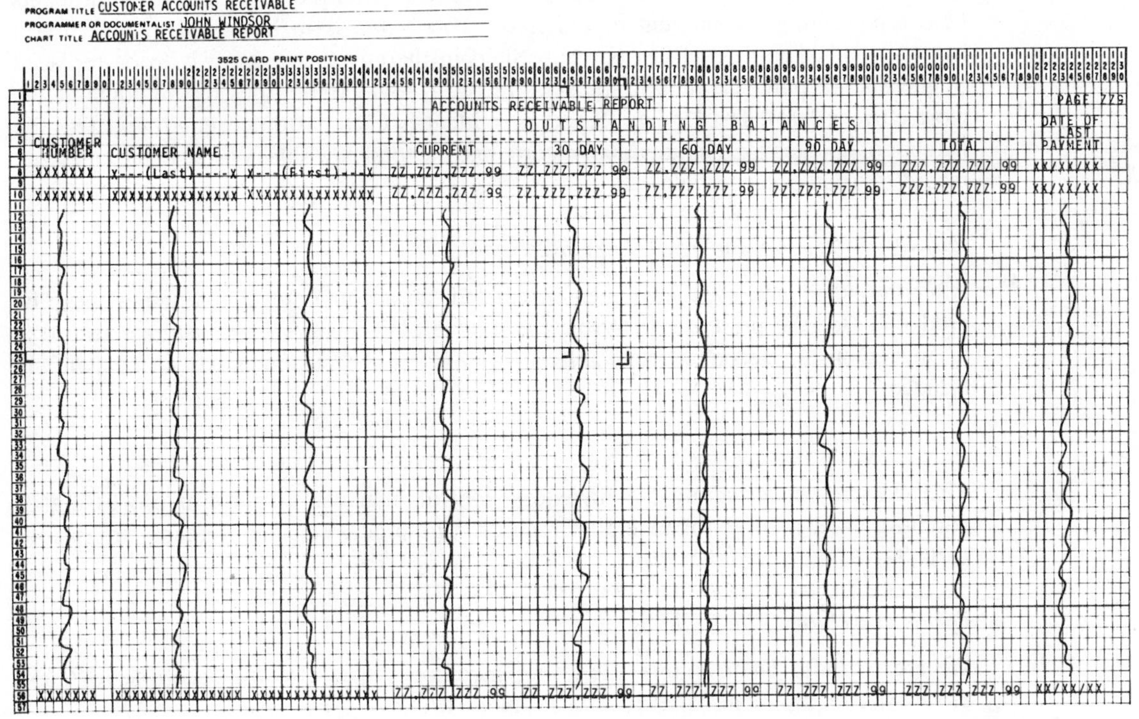

150/10/8 PRINT CHART PROG ID PROBLEM 17.2 PAGE 1
DATE 01/01/89
PROGRAM TITLE CUSTOMER ACCOUNTS RECEIVABLE
PROGRAMMER OR DOCUMENTALIST JOHN WINDSOR
CHART TITLE ACCOUNTS RECEIVABLE REPORT

```
                                                       ACCOUNTS RECEIVABLE REPORT                                              PAGE ZZ9
                                                                 O U T S T A N D I N G   B A L A N C E S                      DATE OF
CUSTOMER                                                                                                                         LAST
 NUMBER   CUSTOMER NAME                              CURRENT          30 DAY           60 DAY           90 DAY           TOTAL          PAYMENT

XXXXXXX   X---(Last)----X X---(First)---X    ZZ,ZZZ,ZZZ.99    ZZ,ZZZ,ZZZ.99    ZZ,ZZZ,ZZZ.99    ZZ,ZZZ,ZZZ.99    ZZZ,ZZZ,ZZZ.99   XX/XX/XX

XXXXXXX   XXXXXXXXXXXXXXX XXXXXXXXXXXXXXX    ZZ,ZZZ,ZZZ.99    ZZ,ZZZ,ZZZ.99    ZZ,ZZZ,ZZZ.99    ZZ,ZZZ,ZZZ.99    ZZZ,ZZZ,ZZZ.99   XX/XX/XX

XXXXXXX   XXXXXXXXXXXXXXX XXXXXXXXXXXXXXX    ZZ,ZZZ,ZZZ.99    ZZ,ZZZ,ZZZ.99    ZZ,ZZZ,ZZZ.99    ZZ,ZZZ,ZZZ.99    ZZZ,ZZZ,ZZZ.99   XX/XX/XX
```

Part A: Build the Customer File

The record layout of the data in this file is shown in the multiple-card layout form. The data should be ordered by customer number to create the customer file. The format of the customer file should be the same as shown in the multiple-card layout form. The creation report should be generated in customer number order. The report should identify duplicate customer numbers, and duplicates should be eliminated from the file. In addition, any customer record for which the past due balance is greater than zero should be printed on the report, along with the values of the outstanding balance. (The outstanding balance is the sum of 30-day, 60-day, and 90-day balances.)

Part B: Add Records to the Customer File

The addition file contains records in the same format as the customer file. The records in the addition file should be added in the appropriate location in the customer file with respect to the customer number field. The addition file is in no particular order. The addition report should identify all attempts to add a duplicate record. When all additions have been attempted, the addition report should indicate the number of records that were in the original customer file, the number of records added to the new customer file, the number of duplicate records rejected, and the total number of records in the new customer file.

Part C: Update the Customer File

The customer file is to be updated using a series of sales records. The graphic record layout of records that are in the sales file is given in Problem 17.1. The fields in the customer record to be updated are in current balance and date of last purchase. The QUANTITY SOLD field of the sales record is to be interpreted as a dollars and cents field representing the amount of purchase. This value is to be added to the current balance field. The date-of-last-purchase field in the customer record is to be replaced by the date-of-purchase field in the sales record (provided the sales record contains the more current date). The Update Report is to identify each customer record updated, the number of updates for the individual record, and the total new sales posted to the customer record (current balance field).

Part D: Process Customer Accounts Receivable

After the other processes have been completed, an accounts receivable report is to be produced (see the print chart) by the total value of receivables. A customer record is to appear on the accounts receivable report only if the customer has an outstanding balance.

17.3 We are requested by the inventory control manager to perform processing of purchase order records for inventory records. The processing requirements are in four parts.

Part A: Inventory File Building

We are to build an inventory file using inventory data. Use the record layout and processing requirements of Part A in Problem 17.1.

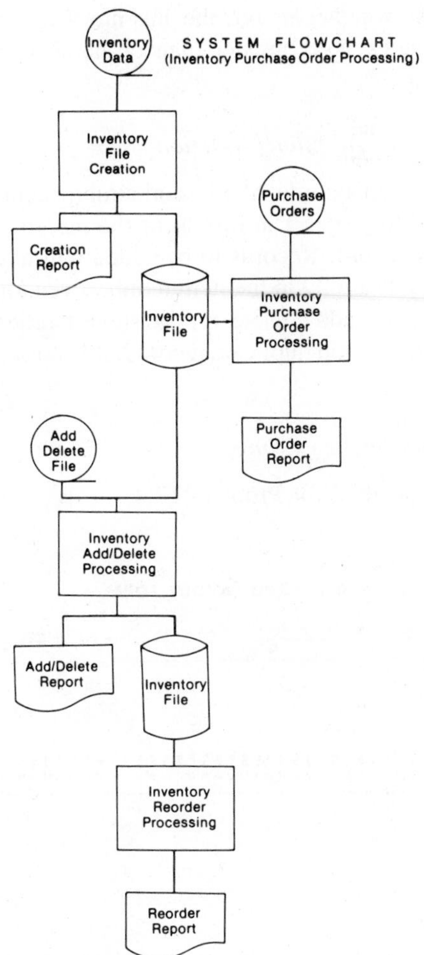

Part B: Purchase Order Processing

We are to update the inventory records to reflect the receipt of purchased inventory items. That is, we have ordered from our vendors to replenish quantities on hand. The records in the purchase-order file are in no particular order. When we find a matching inventory item (by item number, vendor, and outlet number), we are to perform the following update sequence:

a. Add the quantity in the purchase order record to the on-hand field of the inventory record.
b. Replace the date last purchased of the inventory record with the date of purchase of the purchase order record (provided the purchase order date is more current than the existing date of last purchase).

The purchase order report is to reflect the update activity. That is, the purchase order report should indicate all inventory records updated, the change in the on-hand amount, and any purchase orders for which an inventory record cannot be located. Finally, the report should indicate whether or not the inventory record still falls into the reorder category (minimum stock level greater than on-hand quantity) after all updates have been completed.

Part C: Inventory Record Addition / Deletion

The add / delete file is an unordered file containing records to be either added to or deleted from the inventory file. The format of the records in the add / delete file is the same as the inventory record. Records to be added will have data in all fields. Records to be deleted will have data only in the item number, vendor, and outlet fields—all other fields will be blank. The add / delete report should reflect the consequence of each add / delete record. Do-not-add duplicate records. It is possible that a record to be deleted may not exist.

Part D: Inventory Reorder Processing

Complete Part D as specified for Problem 17.1.

MULTIPLE-CARD LAYOUT FORM

Company LEARNING COBOL, INC.

Application PURCHASE ORDER PROCESS by J. Wayne Spence Date 01/01/89 Job No. PROB 17.3 Sheet No. 1

Purchase Order Record

VENDOR CODE	ITEM NUMBER	OUTLET NUMBER	QUANTITY PURCHASED	DATE OF PURCHASE	
1–3	4–9	10–14	15–20	21–26	27–80

CHAPTER

18

Indexed File Processing

An indexed (or keyed) data file allows each record in the file to be uniquely addressed. In a sequential file the programmer's only access option is to get the *next* sequential record. This accessing procedure *may* be used with an indexed or keyed file, but the programmer may also supply an index or key to allow retrieval of *specific* records. That is, records in an indexed file may be retrieved at *random,* without consideration for the present location in the file.

Figure 18.1 shows how an indexed file may be accessed randomly. Of course, random access is not truly random, but rather, is based on a value typically provided from a transaction file. Thus, when it is necessary to move from one area of the file to another, all that is needed is to provide the appropriate key value, and the operating system takes care of the file positioning.

Although most systems provide some type of indexed or keyed file, the implementation of the file type varies from one manufacturer to another. The basis for this chapter is the indexed sequential access method (ISAM), as implemented by IBM.

ENVIRONMENT DIVISION Considerations

Although the INPUT-OUTPUT SECTION of the ENVIRONMENTAL DIVISION (see Figure 18.2) is similar to that presented in Chapter 17, three clauses are either new or modified. The first is the ACCESS MODE clause, which had previously specified only SEQUENTIAL access. Since sequential access is assumed if the clause is absent from the FILE-CONTROL paragraph, all previous files were sequential. However, indexed sequential files may be accessed in *either* SEQUENTIAL or RANDOM mode.

The second change in the INPUT-OUTPUT SECTION is the addition of the RECORD KEY clause. The RECORD KEY clause *must always be present* in the file definition of an indexed sequential file (whether the access is sequential or random). Identifier-1 must be a field in the indexed sequential file record description. The limitations on identifier-1 are that its total length must not exceed 256 bytes and, if record delete codes are to be used or the file is unblocked, identifier-1 must not start in the first byte of the

Figure 18.1 An Illustration of Random Access

INDEXED FILE (MASTER): File keyed on CUSTOMER NUMBER

RECORD NUMBER	CUSTOMER NUMBER	REMAINDER OF RECORD
1.	180	~~~
2.	210	~~~
3.	250	~~~
4.	300	~~~
5.	305	~~~
6.	310	~~~
7.	370	~~~
8.	400	~~~
9.	420	~~~
10.	500	~~~
11.	670	~~~

TRANSACTION FILE: Sequential File Type

CUSTOMER NUMBER	REMAINDER OF RECORD	COMMENTS
305	~~~	Jump to record 5
500	~~~	Jump from record 5 to record 10
210	~~~	Jump from record 10 to record 2
400	~~~	Jump from record 2 to record 8
305	~~~	Jump from record 8 to record 5
300	~~~	Jump from record 5 to record 4
670	~~~	Jump from record 4 to record 11
210	~~~	Jump from record 11 to record 2

Figure 18.2 INPUT-OUTPUT SECTION for IBM Indexed-Sequential-File Organization

```
ENVIRONMENT DIVISION.
        .
        .
        .
[INPUT-OUTPUT SECTION.
 FILE-CONTROL.
     SELECT file-name
     ASSIGN TO system-name

    [RESERVE {NO     }   ALTERNATE   [AREA ]]
             {integer}               [AREAS]

    [ACCESS MODE IS {SEQUENTIAL}  ]
                    {RANDOM    }
    [PROCESSING MODE IS SEQUENTIAL ]
    [RECORD KEY IS identifier-1]
    [NOMINAL KEY IS identifier-2].   . . .]
```

indexed-sequential-file record description. (Delete codes are discussed more fully in the DATA DIVISION considerations.)

The final change in the INPUT-OUTPUT SECTION is the addition of the NOMINAL KEY clause (an IBM extension). The NOMINAL KEY clause is only necessary when records are to be accessed in a RANDOM mode. Identifier-2 must be defined in the WORKING-STORAGE SECTION, it must be a fixed displacement from the beginning of a record (it must not be subsequent to an OCCURS/DEPENDING ON), it may not exceed 256 bytes in length, and the definition of the item should be consistent with the definition of the RECORD KEY identifier. That is, since the identifer specified as the NOMINAL KEY will be used to ''find'' records in the indexed sequential file, it must match the value of the RECORD KEY identifier exactly. Thus, if the RECORD KEY identifier was described in the indexed sequential record as a PICTURE 9(05) and the NOMINAL KEY identifier's description in WORKING STORAGE was PICTURE X(10), the values in these two identifiers would never be the same. (THE WORKING-STORAGE item is longer, and, at a minimum, would contain blanks if loaded with the same value as was placed in the RECORD KEY identifier.)

The file described as an indexed sequential file *must be recorded on a mass storage device* (e.g., magnetic disk). The file type is no longer purely sequential—requiring a change to the IBM system-name. Thus, the prefix of ''DA-I'' before a ddname indicates that the file will be placed on a direct access (DA) device and the file type is indexed (I). Indexed sequential files must be recorded on magnetic disk in *cylinders*. A cylinder is the same track number on all recording surfaces (platters) of a disk pack. Although this requirement does not necessarily have any direct impact on COBOL code, JCL modifications will be necessary. Consult your installation guide for information concerning the allocation requirements for indexed sequential files.

Figure 18.3 illustrates the appearance of the ENVIRONMENT DIVISION in a program using an indexed sequential file. Note from the illustration that CUSTOMER-FILE is ASSIGNed to the system-name DA-I-MASTER, which specifically indicates that an indexed sequential file is being used. Next, the ACCESS MODE clause is specified, indicating RANDOM access. The RECORD KEY clause, always required for an indexed sequential file, indicates the field that identifies individual records is called CUSTOMER-NUMBER. The NOMINAL KEY clause (required when the ACCESS MODE is RANDOM) identifies the data-name LOCATE-CUSTOMER as the field to be used when it is necessary to locate a particular indexed sequential record *Note:* When the access to an indexed sequential file is sequential, neither the ACCESS MODE nor the NOMINAL KEY clause is required.

Figure 18.3 An Illustration of the ENVIRONMENT DIVISION for an Indexed Sequential File

```
ENVIRONMENT DIVISION.
CONFIGURATION SECTION.
SOURCE-COMPUTER. IBM.
OBJECT-COMPUTER. IBM.
INPUT-OUTPUT SECTION.
FILE-CONTROL
    SELECT CUSTOMER-FILE
        ASSIGN TO DA-I-MASTER
        ACCESS MODE IS RANDOM
        RECORD KEY IS CUSTOMER-NUMBER
        NOMINAL KEY IS LOCATE-CUSTOMER.
```

DATA DIVISION Considerations

The options for using the LABEL RECORDS, BLOCK CONTAINS, RECORD CONTAINS, and DATA RECORDS clauses are the same for indexed sequential files as they are for sequential files. There may be differences in the record description of the same file between standard sequential files and indexed sequential files, however. The identifier specified as the RECORD KEY in the FILE-CONTROL paragraph of the ENVIRONMENT DIVISION *must* appear in the indexed sequential file record and may be located in other than the first bytes of the record. The RECORD KEY could be a group-item or an elementary-item; however, the *contents of the field must be unique among all the records in the file*. Records with duplicate RECORD KEY values are not permitted in an indexed sequential file.

The second possible modification of the indexed-sequential-file record deals with the possible deletion of records in the file. The first byte (character) position of an indexed-sequential-file record is a special byte. If this position in the record contains HIGH-VALUES, the record is assumed to be a deleted record. It will be treated as if it had been physically deleted (e.g., READ statements will bypass the record), even though the record may still be physically present in the file. If the first byte contains any other value, the record is assumed to be a valid record for processing purposes. Thus, the first byte of an indexed-sequential-file record is often called a ''delete byte.''

PROCEDURE DIVISION Considerations

All the processing described in Chapter 17 related to updating, adding, and deleting records on a magnetic disk medium apply equally to an indexed sequential file. So long as a RECORD KEY has been assigned for a file, an indexed sequential file may be READ in exactly the same manner as used for a standard sequential file. But, because the file is a ''keyed'' file and may be addressed in either SEQUENTIAL or RANDOM mode, some statements may be slightly modified.

The READ statement, shown in Figure 18.4, is given an INVALID KEY phrase in the same area occupied by the AT END phrase. If the ACCESS MODE is SEQUENTIAL, the programmer must supply the RECORD KEY in the FILE-CONTROL paragraph for the indexed sequential file, and the READ statement will employ the AT END phrase. The AT END imperative statement is executed when the end of file is encountered. If the programmer has selected ACCESS MODE IS RANDOM, both the RECORD KEY

Figure 18.4 Indexed Sequential File READ Statement

```
READ file-name RECORD [INTO identifier]

     [{AT END imperative-statement-1}      ]
     [{INVALID KEY imperative-statemenr-2} ]

     [{NOT AT END imperative-statement-3}       ]
     [{NOT INVALID KEY imperative-statement-4}  ]

[END-READ]
```

Figure 18.5 Indexed Sequential File WRITE Statement

```
WRITE file-name RECORD [FROM identifier]
     [INVALID KEY imperative-statemenr-2]
     [NOT INVALID KEY imperative-statement-4]
[END-WRITE]
```

and NOMINAL KEY must be supplied in the FILE-CONTROL paragraph, the NOMINAL KEY must be loaded with a value equal to that of the RECORD KEY of the record to be located and read, and the READ statement must employ the INVALID KEY phrase. The INVALID KEY imperative statement is executed in the event that (1) the specified NOMINAL KEY value cannot be located in the file, (2) an attempt is made to read past the end-of-file, or (3) a device error occurs. In other words, if the specified record is *not found* for whatever reason, the imperative statement is executed. The NOT INVALID KEY imperative statement, available in COBOL 85, will be executed in all other cases.

The WRITE statement, Figure 18.5, is also modified to include an INVALID KEY phrase. For indexed sequential files, the WRITE statement is used to build a file or to add records to an existing file—it is not always necessary to create a new file when it is necessary to add records. The INVALID KEY imperative statement is executed in the event that (1) an attempt is made to place a record with a *duplicate* RECORD KEY value in the file (either during the building or adding process), (2) file space has been exhausted, or (3) a device error occurs. The NOT INVALID KEY imperative statement, available in COBOL 85, will be executed in all other cases. During the file-building process, the ACCESS MODE should be SEQUENTIAL, and a RECORD KEY clause must appear in the FILE-CONTROL paragraph. If records are to be added to a file, the ACCESS MODE could be either SEQUENTIAL or RANDOM. The RECORD KEY and NOMINAL KEY clause should be provided, and the NOMINAL KEY should be loaded with the RECORD KEY value of the record to be added. Thus, if the value of the NOMINAL KEY is found in the file, the INVALID KEY (for a duplicate RECORD KEY) is executed.

For purposes of updating an indexed sequential file, the REWRITE statement, Figure 18.6, is used. Like the REWRITE statement for updating sequential files on mass storage

Figure 18.6 Indexed Sequential File REWRITE Statement

```
REWRITE file-name RECORD [FROM identifier]
     [INVALID KEY imperative-statemenr-2]
     [NOT INVALID KEY imperative-statement-4]
[END-REWRITE]
```

devices (as illustrated in Chapter 17), the REWRITE statement for an indexed sequential file causes an existing record to be overwritten—replacing old data with new. Like the sequential REWRITE operation, the rewritten data are placed in the same location as the data last READ by the procedure. Thus, a READ statement should always precede a REWRITE statement in the PROCEDURE DIVISION; however, a REWRITE should *not follow* a READ statement that has encountered the end-of-file. The INVALID KEY clause is included for consistency and is never executed for a REWRITE on an indexed sequential file—the READ activity would encounter an INVALID KEY prior to the execution of the REWRITE statement!

The START statement, illustrated in 18.7, is the only new statement type included for use with indexed sequential files. The START statement is used when the programmer wishes to process an indexed sequential file in a sequential manner (i.e., ACCESS MODE is SEQUENTIAL), but wishes to initiate the process at a record location other than the first (next) record in the file. In other words, the START statement permits the programmer to "jump ahead" in the file to the position of the *next* record to be processed. The START statement, if used, must be executed prior to the execution of a READ statement.

In the Format 1 version of the START statement, the value placed in the NOMINAL KEY field is used to locate the (next) record. Therefore, the NOMINAL KEY clause is required when this format is used, and the NOMINAL KEY identifier must contain the value of the record to be located prior to the execution of the START statement. The INVALID KEY imperative statement is executed in the event the specified NOMINAL KEY value cannot be located in the file.

Figure 18.7 The START Statement

```
START file-name
      [INVALID KEY imperative-statemenr-2]
      [NOT INVALID KEY imperative-statement-4]
[END-START]
```

```
START file-name
                                   ⎧ IS EQUAL TO                     ⎫
                                   ⎪ IS =                            ⎪
                                   ⎪ IS GREATER THAN                 ⎪
                                   ⎪ IS >                            ⎪
      USING KEY identifier-1       ⎨ IS NOT LESS THAN                ⎬ identifier-2
                                   ⎪ IS NOT <                        ⎪
                                   ⎪ IS GREATER THAN OR EQUAL TO     ⎪
                                   ⎩ IS >=                           ⎭
      [INVALID KEY imperative-statemenr-2]
      [NOT INVALID KEY imperative-statement-4]
[END-START]
```

When the Format 2 version of the START statement is used, the NOMINAL KEY clause is not *required.* Identifier-1 must be the RECORD KEY identifier. Identifier-2 is referred to as a *generic key.* That is, identifier-2 is defined in the DATA DIVISION, but is in no way associated with any key clause in the FILE-CONTROL paragraph of the ENVIRONMENT DIVISION. Identifier-2 may be less than or equal to the length of the RECORD KEY identifier and should not be a part of the indexed-sequential-file record. Upon execution of the Format 2 START statement, the system searches for the first RECORD KEY value that matches the value of the generic key. Thus, if the definition of the generic key is shorter than the RECORD KEY identifier, this START statement may be used to find the first record in an indexed sequential file that begins with the generic key ''prefix.'' That is, if the generic key is three characters long and the RECORD KEY identifier is eight characters long (and perhaps contains a series of values prefixed with the same first three characters), the START statement will locate the first occurrence of this ''prefix'' in the indexed sequential file.

Building an Indexed Sequential File

The building or development of an indexed sequential file follows many of the characteristics of building a standard sequential file. As illustrated in the system flowchart of Figure 18.8, a sequential file (perhaps on magnetic tape) is processed into an output file (which must be on a mass storage device) in an indexed sequential form. The same basic procedure illustrated in Chapter 17 is provided in the procedure of Figure 18.8. First, turn to the definition of the file in the ENVIRONMENT DIVISION. Note that the CUSTOMER-OUT-FILE is assigned to a direct access (DA) device, and the RECORD KEY is CUSTOMER-NUMBER-OUT. The ACCESS MODE is specifically identified as SEQUENTIAL, although sequential access would be assumed in the absence of the clause. Next, examine the record description of the indexed sequential file (lines 460–550). As indicated by the RECORD CONTAINS clause, the output record contains 125 characters (as opposed to the 124-byte input record). Note that the first field of the output record is DELETE-BYTE-OUT—a one-byte field to be used to delete records, if necessary. The next field of the output record is CUSTOMER-NUMBER-OUT—the RECORD KEY field.

Figure 18.8 Building an Indexed Sequential File (System Flowchart)

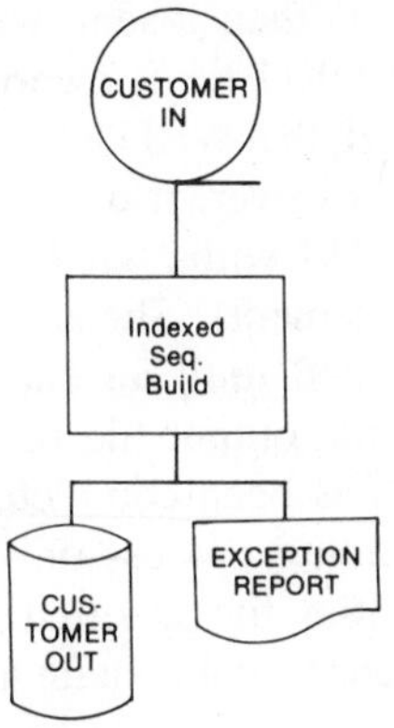

Figure 18.8 *Continued* Building an Indexed Sequential File (Hierarchy Chart)

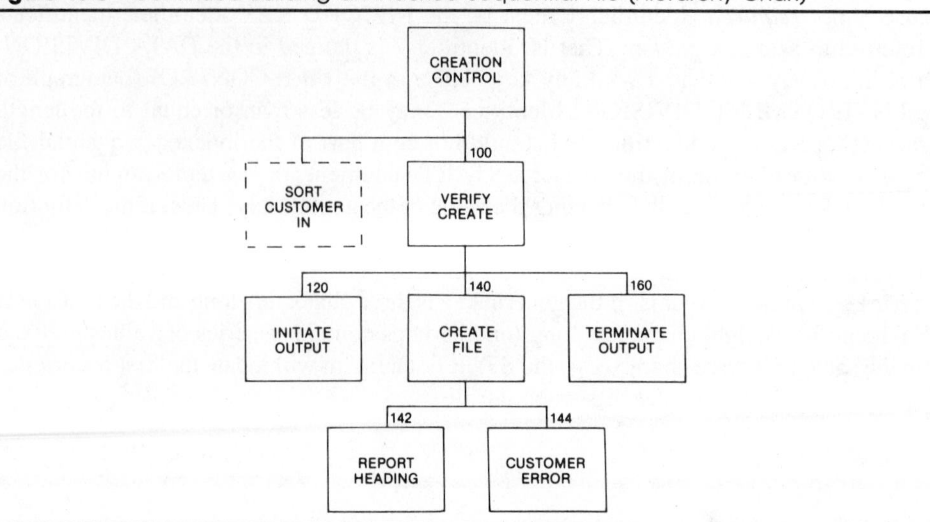

Turning to the PROCEDURE DIVISION, notice that the input file is to be sorted on the CUSTOMER-NUMBER-SORT field. To create an indexed sequential file, the data placed in the RECORD KEY field (CUSTOMER-NUMBER-OUT) must be ordered on an *ascending* basis. In the OUTPUT PROCEDURE, during the process initialization phase, the output file (CUSTOMER-OUT-FILE) is opened in an OUTPUT mode. Thus, in this procedure, only output data will be accepted by the file. As the process progresses, data are RETURNed from the CUSTOMER-SORT-FILE in preparation for writing the first record. Notice that both this RETURN statement and the second RETURN statement in line 1490 place the data from the sort file into RECORD-CONTENTS (line 770). Further examination of the DATA DIVISION in the area of RECORDS-CONTENTS show the field is preceded by a one-byte field, which will contain a space. This one-byte field will ultimately be placed in the DELETE-BYTE-OUT position of the CUSTOMER-OUT-FILE record. In 140-CREATE-FILE (a repetitive procedure), the status variable OUTPUT-STATUS is loaded with a value of "RECORDED"—in anticipation of writing a record to the indexed sequential file. The CUSTOMER-RECORD-OUT is then loaded with the data of INPUT-OUTPUT-RECORD (at which time the RECORD KEY receives its value). An attempt is then made to WRITE the new record. If the WRITE operation works, a record is placed in the indexed sequential file. If, however, it does not, the INVALID KEY phrase is executed—loading OUTPUT-STATUS with "DUPLICATE" (the assumed reason for the execution of the imperative statement). Shortly thereafter, the next record is RETURNed, and the process is repeated until an end-of-file has been encountered for CUSTOMER-SORT-FILE. When the output file (CUSTOMER-OUT-FILE) is closed in line 1780, the creation process has been completed.

As with sequential files, the building process only occurs once. However, unlike a sequential file, an indexed sequential file is often copied or rebuilt periodically to restructure the file and eliminate records that contain a HIGH-VALUE delete-byte value.

Figure 18.8 *Continued* Building an Indexed Sequential File (Pseudocode)

```
START
    SORT customer file
         ASCENDING customer number
         OUTPUT Verify Create
    ENDSORT
END

VERIFY CREATE
    DO Initiate output
    DO Create file UNTIL eof
    DO Terminate output
END

INITIATE OUTPUT
    OPEN output files
    RETURN customer file
         IF eof
              SET file status
         ENDIF
END

CREATE FILE
    IF line number > 40
         DO Report heading
    ENDIF
    SET output status
    WRITE output record
         IF invalid key
              DO Customer error
              SET output status
         ENDIF
    ENDWRITE
    IF output status = recorded
         ADD 1 to customer count
    ENDIF
    RETURN customer file
         IF eof
              SET file status
         ENDIF
END

REPORT HEADING
    ADD 1 to page number
    WRITE headings
    MOVE 0 to line number
END

CUSTOMER ERROR
    ADD 1 to error count
    MOVE customer number to output
    WRITE error
    ADD 1 to line number
END

TERMINATE OUTPUT
    MOVE counts to output
    WRITE output summary
    CLOSE files
END
```

Figure 18.8 *Continued* Building an Indexed Sequential File

```
           1   1   2   2   2   3   3   4   4   4   5   5   6   6   6   7
   4   8   2   6   0   4   8   2   6   0   4   8   2   6   0   4   8   2

      ***************************************************************
       IDENTIFICATION DIVISION.
      ***************************************************************
       PROGRAM-ID.    INDEXED-SEQUENTIAL-BUILD.
       AUTHOR.        J. WAYNE SPENCE.
       DATE-WRITTEN.  JANUARY 1, 1989.
       DATE-COMPILED. JANUARY 1, 1989.
      *    The purpose of this procedure is to produce an indexed
      *    sequential data file based on customer records.  The file
      *    is to be keyed on the customer number field.
      ***************************************************************
       ENVIRONMENT DIVISION.
      ***************************************************************
      *-------------------------------------------------------------*
       CONFIGURATION SECTION.
      *-------------------------------------------------------------*
       SOURCE-COMPUTER. IBM.
       OBJECT-COMPUTER. IBM.
       SPECIAL-NAMES.
                           C01 IS TOP-OF-PAGE.
```

Figure 18.8 *Continued* Building an Indexed Sequential File

```
            1   1   2   2   2   3   3   4   4   4   5   5   6   6   6   7
    4   8   2   6   0   4   8   2   6   0   4   8   2   6   0   4   8   2

      *-----------------------------------------------------------------*
       INPUT-OUTPUT SECTION.
      *-----------------------------------------------------------------*
       FILE-CONTROL.
           SELECT CUSTOMER-IN-FILE ASSIGN TO UT-S-INPUT.
           SELECT CUSTOMER-OUT-FILE ASSIGN TO DA-I-OUTPUT2
               RECORD KEY IS CUSTOMER-NUMBER-OUT
               ACCESS IS SEQUENTIAL.
           SELECT CUSTOMER-SORT-FILE ASSIGN TO UT-S-SORTWK01.
           SELECT EXCEPTION-REPORT-FILE ASSIGN TO UT-S-OUTPUT.
      *******************************************************************
       DATA DIVISION.
      *******************************************************************
      *-----------------------------------------------------------------*
       FILE SECTION.
      *-----------------------------------------------------------------*
       FD  CUSTOMER-IN-FILE
           LABEL RECORDS ARE STANDARD
           RECORD CONTAINS 124 CHARACTERS
           BLOCK CONTAINS 0 RECORDS.
       01  CUSTOMER-RECORD-IN            PIC X(124).

       FD  CUSTOMER-OUT-FILE
           LABEL RECORDS ARE STANDARD
           RECORD CONTAINS 125 CHARACTERS.
       01  CUSTOMER-RECORD-OUT.
           05  DELETE-BYTE-OUT           PIC X(01).
           05  CUSTOMER-NUMBER-OUT       PIC X(10).
           05  CUSTOMER-NAME-OUT         PIC X(30).
           05  CUSTOMER-ADDRESS-OUT      PIC X(30).
           05  CUSTOMER-CITY-OUT         PIC X(20).
           05  CUSTOMER-STATE-OUT        PIC X(02).
           05  CUSTOMER-ZIP-OUT          PIC X(10).
           05  CUSTOMER-BALANCE-OUT      PIC S9(09)V99.
           05  CUSTOMER-CREDIT-LIMIT-OUT PIC S9(09)V99.

       SD  CUSTOMER-SORT-FILE.
       01  CUSTOMER-RECORD-SORT.
           05  CUSTOMER-NUMBER-SORT      PIC X(10).
           05  FILLER                    PIC X(114).

       FD  EXCEPTION-REPORT-FILE
           LABEL RECORDS ARE OMITTED.
       01  REPORT-RECORD                     PIC X(133).
      *-----------------------------------------------------------------*
       WORKING-STORAGE SECTION.
      *-----------------------------------------------------------------*
       01  WORKING-VARIABLES.
           05  FILE-STATUS               PIC X(04) VALUE SPACES.
           05  OUTPUT-STATUS             PIC X(10) VALUE SPACES.
           05  LINE-NUMBER-WS            PIC 9(02) VALUE 99.
           05  PAGE-NUMBER-WS            PIC 9(02) VALUE ZERO.
           05  ERROR-COUNT-WS            PIC 9(04) VALUE ZERO.
           05  CUSTOMER-COUNT-WS         PIC 9(04) VALUE ZERO.
           05  INPUT-OUTPUT-RECORD.
               10  FILLER                PIC X(01) VALUE SPACES.
               10  RECORD-CONTENTS       PIC X(124).

       01  HEADING-1.
           05  FILLER                    PIC X(32) VALUE SPACES.
           05  FILLER                    PIC X(16) VALUE
                                         'Exception Report'.
           05  FILLER                    PIC X(25) VALUE SPACES.
           05  FILLER                    PIC X(05) VALUE 'Page'.
           05  PAGE-NUMBER-OUT           PIC Z9.

       01  HEADING-2.
           05  FILLER                    PIC X(20) VALUE
                                         ' Customer Number'.
           05  FILLER                    PIC X(20) VALUE
                                         'Comments'.
```

Figure 18.8 *Continued* Building an Indexed Sequential File

```
            1   1   2   2   2   3   3   4   4   4   5   5   6   6   6   7
    4   8   2   6   0   4   8   2   6   0   4   8   2   6   0   4   8   2
--------------------------------------------------------------------------
        01  HEADING-3.
            05  FILLER                      PIC X(01) VALUE SPACES.
            05  FILLER                      PIC X(80) VALUE ALL '-'.

        01  ERROR-LINE.
            05  FILLER                      PIC X(02) VALUE SPACES.
            05  CUSTOMER-NUMBER-ERROR       PIC X(10).
            05  FILLER                      PIC X(08) VALUE SPACES.
            05  FILLER                      PIC X(50) VALUE
                'Customer Number Duplicate Encountered--ELIMINATED'.

        01  SUMMARY-LINE.
            05  FILLER                      PIC X(01) VALUE SPACES.
            05  CUSTOMER-COUNT-OUT          PIC *,**9.
            05  FILLER                      PIC X(27) VALUE
                                            ' Customer Records Written--'.
            05  ERROR-COUNT-OUT             PIC *,**9.
            05  FILLER                      PIC X(25) VALUE
                                            ' Duplicates Encountered'.
      *************************************************************
       PROCEDURE DIVISION.
      *************************************************************
      *-----------------------------------------------------------*
       000-CREATION-CONTROL SECTION.
      *-----------------------------------------------------------*
           MOVE 45000               TO SORT-CORE-SIZE.
           SORT CUSTOMER-SORT-FILE
               ASCENDING KEY CUSTOMER-NUMBER-SORT
               USING CUSTOMER-IN-FILE
               OUTPUT PROCEDURE 100-VERIFY-CREATE.
           STOP RUN.
      *-----------------------------------------------------------*
       100-VERIFY-CREATE SECTION.
      *-----------------------------------------------------------*
           PERFORM 120-INITIATE-OUTPUT.
           PERFORM 140-CREATE-FILE
               UNTIL FILE-STATUS = 'DONE'.
           PERFORM 160-TERMINATE-OUTPUT.
      *-----------------------------------------------------------*
       120-INITIATE-OUTPUT SECTION.
      *-----------------------------------------------------------*
           OPEN OUTPUT CUSTOMER-OUT-FILE
                       EXCEPTION-REPORT-FILE.
           RETURN CUSTOMER-SORT-FILE INTO RECORD-CONTENTS
               AT END MOVE 'DONE' TO FILE-STATUS.
      *-----------------------------------------------------------*
       140-CREATE-FILE SECTION.
      *-----------------------------------------------------------*
           IF LINE-NUMBER-WS IS GREATER THAN 40
               PERFORM 142-REPORT-HEADING.
           MOVE 'RECORDED'           TO OUTPUT-STATUS.
           WRITE CUSTOMER-RECORD-OUT FROM INPUT-OUTPUT-RECORD
               INVALID KEY PERFORM 144-CUSTOMER-ERROR
                         MOVE 'DUPLICATE' TO OUTPUT-STATUS.
           IF OUTPUT-STATUS = 'RECORDED'
               ADD 1 TO CUSTOMER-COUNT-WS.
           RETURN CUSTOMER-SORT-FILE INTO RECORD-CONTENTS
               AT END MOVE 'DONE' TO FILE-STATUS.
      *-----------------------------------------------------------*
       142-REPORT-HEADING SECTION.
      *-----------------------------------------------------------*
           ADD 1 TO PAGE-NUMBER-WS.
           MOVE PAGE-NUMBER-WS       TO PAGE-NUMBER-OUT.
           WRITE REPORT-RECORD FROM HEADING-1
               AFTER ADVANCING TOP-OF-PAGE.
           WRITE REPORT-RECORD FROM HEADING-2 AFTER ADVANCING 3 LINES.
           WRITE REPORT-RECORD FROM HEADING-3 AFTER ADVANCING 1 LINES.
           MOVE SPACES               TO REPORT-RECORD.
           WRITE REPORT-RECORD AFTER ADVANCING 1 LINES.
           MOVE 0                    TO LINE-NUMBER-WS.
```

Figure 18.8 *Continued* Building an Indexed Sequential File

```
       *-----------------------------------------------------------*
        144-CUSTOMER-ERROR SECTION.
       *-----------------------------------------------------------*
            ADD 1 TO ERROR-COUNT-WS.
            MOVE CUSTOMER-NUMBER-OUT TO CUSTOMER-NUMBER-ERROR.
            WRITE REPORT-RECORD FROM ERROR-LINE AFTER ADVANCING 1 LINES.
            ADD 1 TO LINE-NUMBER-WS.
       *-----------------------------------------------------------*
        160-TERMINATE-OUTPUT SECTION.
       *-----------------------------------------------------------*
            MOVE ERROR-COUNT-WS      TO ERROR-COUNT-OUT.
            MOVE CUSTOMER-COUNT-WS   TO CUSTOMER-COUNT-OUT.
            WRITE REPORT-RECORD FROM SUMMARY-LINE
                AFTER ADVANCING 2 LINES.
            CLOSE EXCEPTION-REPORT-FILE
                  CUSTOMER-OUT-FILE.
```

Figure 18.8 *Continued* Building an Indexed Sequential File [CUSTOMER-IN] (Data)

```
                                                                                                 1         1         1
      |         1         2         3         4         5         6         7         8         9         0         1         2
Record|1234567890123456789012345678901234567890123456789012345678901234567890123456789012345678901234567890123456789012345678901234
------------------------------------------------------------------------------------------------------------------------------------
     1|4412X47390Marshall Silverman            2219 West 7th Street          Cleveland           OH30119    000000000000000500000
     2|3199127X33James Thompkins               44339 South Wacker Drive      Chicago             IL60606    000000229180000500000
     3|1141944103Edwin Williams                2139 South Colgate Street     Perryton            TX79070    000003319330035000000
     4|6213937661Jason Madison                 8831 Cedar Drive N.W.         Norwich             CN00218    000004145230003000000
     5|5270215827Charles Everest               8821 Ocean Parkway            Miami               FL51332    000000000000000500000
     6|3333333333Julia Harriston               6132 Mill Road Avenue         Shreveport          LA63341    000003513430005000000
     7|3498966451Jacob R. Sullivan             6134 Malibu Drive             Los Angeles         CA96512    000000000000004400000
     8|1RX14219-3John P. Villiman              8887 Peach Tree Lane          Dallas              TX75002    000000031430000500000
     9|6427633-94Mark U. Lemon                 P. O. Box 51244               New York            NY03158    000000000000000005000
    10|773194221BHelen B. Overstreet           3153 Yellow Brick Road        Yellow Stone Park   MT41229    000000128420000000000
    11|9X0-334RDSAnthony P. Jones              Executive Office Building     Washington          DC00000    000000000000000000000
    12|3333333333Raymond J. Taylor             912 Dusty Road                Plains              GA39100    000005235360001000000
```

Figure 18.8 *Continued* Building an Indexed Sequential File [CUSTOMER-OUT] (Data)

```
                                                                                                 1         1         1
      |         1         2         3         4         5         6         7         8         9         0         1         2
Record|12345678901234567890123456789012345678901234567890123456789012345678901234567890123456789012345678901234567890123456789012345
-------------------------------------------------------------------------------------------------------------------------------------
     1| 1RX14219-3John P. Villiman             8887 Peach Tree Lane          Dallas              TX75002    000000031430000500000
     2| 1141944103Edwin Williams               2139 South Colgate Street     Perryton            TX79070    000003319330035000000
     3| 3199127X33James Thompkins              44339 South Wacker Drive      Chicago             IL60606    000000229180000500000
     4| 3333333333Julia Harriston              6132 Mill Road Avenue         Shreveport          LA63341    000003513430005000000
     5| 3498966451Jacob R. Sullivan            6134 Malibu Drive             Los Angeles         CA96512    000000000000004400000
     6| 4412X47390Marshall Silverman           2219 West 7th Street          Cleveland           OH30119    000000000000000500000
     7| 5270215827Charles Everest              8821 Ocean Parkway            Miami               FL51332    000000000000000500000
     8| 6213937661Jason Madison                8831 Cedar Drive N.W.         Norwich             CT00218    000004145230003000000
     9| 6427633-94Mark U. Lemon                P. O. Box 51244               New York            NY03158    000000000000000005000
    10| 773194221BHelen B. Overstreet          3153 Yellow Brick Road        Yellow Stone Park   MT41229    000000128420000000000
    11| 9X0-334RDSAnthony P. Jones             Executive Office Building     Washington          DC00000    000000000000000000000
```

Figure 18.8 *Continued* Building an Indexed Sequential File (Output)

```
                              Exception Report                         Page  1

    Customer Number    Comments
    ---------------------------------------------------------------------------
     3333333333        Customer Number Duplicate Encountered--ELIMINATED
```

Updating an Indexed Sequential File

Although the building process for sequential and indexed sequential files is similar, the updating process may be considerably different. Recall from the sequential-file-update process in Chapter 17 that it was necessary to establish a greater than, equal to, or less than relationship between the CUSTOMER (master) file and the SALES (transaction) file. Unless a mass storage device was employed for the master file, a new file had to be created that contained the updated data. In addition, the transaction file had to be ordered in the same sequence as the master file.

If the programmer selects the random mode (ACCESS MODE IS RANDOM) to update an indexed sequential file, none of these conditions are specifically required. Turn to Figure 18.9—a random update of the CUSTOMER file. In the system flowchart, the CUSTOMER-IO-FILE is used both for input and output purposes, as indicated by the two-way arrow. In the ENVIRONMENT DIVISION, the specification of the file indicates that, again, the CUSTOMER-IO-FILE is assigned to a mass storage device (DA), and CUSTOMER-NUMBER-IO is the RECORD KEY. In addition, a NOMINAL KEY variable of CUSTOMER-NUMBER-FIND-WS (defined in line 750) and ACCESS MODE IS RANDOM are provided.

The PROCEDURE DIVISION is initiated (without a SORT statement), and in the 1400-INITIATE-UPDATE SECTION, the CUSTOMER-IO-FILE is opened in an I-O mode—both reading and writing operations are permitted. During the actual updating procedure (lines 1280–1520), a record is READ from the CUSTOMER-SALES-FILE, the NOMINAL KEY value is established via the MOVE statement in line 1350, an INPUT-STATUS indicator is set (presuming a record will be successfully read), and an attempt is made to READ the record to be updated. If the indicated record is successfully read, that is, the value placed in the NOMINAL KEY variable matches one of the RECORD KEY values, the 1440-CUSTOMER-UPDATE procedure is invoked. Otherwise, the INPUT-STATUS indicator is set to ''NOT FOUND'' by the INVALID KEY

Figure 18.9 Updating an Indexed Sequential File (System Flowchart)

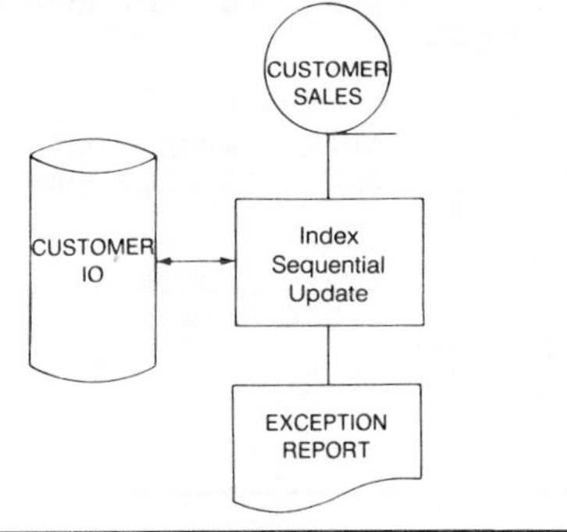

Figure 18.9 *Continued* Updating an Indexed Sequential File (Hierarchy Chart)

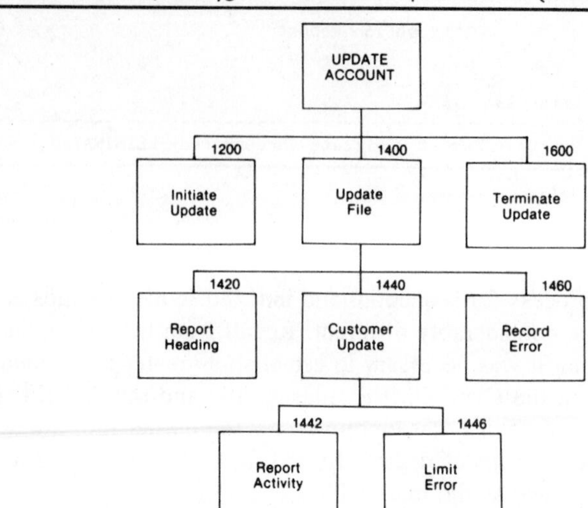

Figure 18.9 *Continued* Updating an Indexed Sequential File (Pseudocode)

```
START
    DO Initiate update
    DO Update file UNTIL eof
    DO Terminate update
END

INITIATE UPDATE
    OPEN files
END

UPDATE FILE
    IF line number > 40
         DO Reprot heading
    ENDIF
    READ customer sales
    IF eof
         SET file status
         GOTO end
    ENDIF
    MOVE input to output
    SET input status
    READ customer file
    IF invalid key
         SET input status
    ENDIF
    IF input status = found
         DO Customer update
    ELSE
         DO Record error
    ENDIF
END

REPORT HEADING
    ADD 1 to page number
    MOVE 0 to line number
    WRITE headings
END

CUSTOMER UPDATE
    IF balance + purchase > credit limit
         DO Limit error
    ELSE
         ADD purchase to balance
         DO Report activity
    ENDIF
END

REPORT ACTIVITY
    MOVE message to output
    REWRITE output
    IF invalid key
         MOVE message to output
    ENDIF
    WRITE message
    ADD 1 to line number
END

LIMIT ERROR
    MOVE message to output
    WRITE output
    ADD 1 to line number
END

RECORD ERROR
    WRITE error output
    ADD 5 to line number
END

TERMINATE UPDATE
    CLOSE files
END
```

Figure 18.9 *Continued* Updating an Indexed Sequential File

```
                          1   1   2   2   2   3   3   4   4   4   5   5   6   6   6   7
   4   8   2   6   0   4   8   2   6   0   4   8   2   6   0   4   8   2

 *****************************************************************
  IDENTIFICATION DIVISION.
 *****************************************************************
  PROGRAM-ID.     INDEX-SEQUENTIAL-UPDATE.
  AUTHOR.         J. WAYNE SPENCE.
  DATE-WRITTEN.  JANUARY 1, 1989.
  DATE-COMPILED. JANUARY 1, 1989.
 *    The purpose of this procedure is to update an existing
 *    indexed sequential file (CUSTOMER) on the basis of informatio
 *    contained in a sales file.  Mulitple updates per customer
 *    records are permitted (in random order) and customer updates
 *    (sales records) without a corresponding customer record are
 *    identified.
 *****************************************************************
  ENVIRONMENT DIVISION.
 *****************************************************************
 *---------------------------------------------------------------*
  CONFIGURATION SECTION.
 *---------------------------------------------------------------*
  SOURCE-COMPUTER. IBM.
  OBJECT-COMPUTER. IBM.
  SPECIAL-NAMES.
                  C01 IS TOP-OF-PAGE.
 *---------------------------------------------------------------*
  INPUT-OUTPUT SECTION.
 *---------------------------------------------------------------*
  FILE-CONTROL.
      SELECT CUSTOMER-IO-FILE       ASSIGN TO DA-I-INOUT
          RECORD  KEY IS CUSTOMER-NUMBER-IO
          NOMINAL KEY IS CUSTOMER-NUMBER-FIND-WS
          ACCESS IS RANDOM.
      SELECT CUSTOMER-SALES-FILE    ASSIGN TO UT-S-INPUT.
      SELECT EXCEPTION-REPORT-FILE ASSIGN TO UT-S-OUTPUT.
 *****************************************************************
  DATA DIVISION.
 *****************************************************************
  FILE SECTION.
  FD  CUSTOMER-IO-FILE
      LABEL RECORDS ARE STANDARD
      RECORD CONTAINS 125 CHARACTERS.
  01  CUSTOMER-RECORD.
      05  DELETE-BYTE-IO            PIC X(01).
      05  CUSTOMER-NUMBER-IO        PIC X(10).
      05  CUSTOMER-NAME-IO          PIC X(30).
      05  CUSTOMER-ADDRESS-IO       PIC X(30).
      05  CUSTOMER-CITY-IO          PIC X(20).
      05  CUSTOMER-STATE-IO         PIC X(02).
      05  CUSTOMER-ZIP-IO           PIC X(10).
      05  CUSTOMER-BALANCE-IO       PIC S9(09)V99.
      05  CUSTOMER-CREDIT-LIMIT-IO PIC S9(09)V99.

  FD  CUSTOMER-SALES-FILE
      LABEL RECORDS ARE STANDARD
      RECORD CONTAINS 80 CHARACTERS
      BLOCK CONTAINS 0 RECORDS.
  01  SALES-RECORD.
      05  CUSTOMER-NUMBER-SALES     PIC X(10).
      05  DATE-OF-PURCHASE-SALES.
          10  PURCHASE-MONTH-SALES PIC X(02).
          10  PURCHASE-DAY-SALES   PIC X(02).
          10  PURCHASE-YEAR-SALES  PIC X(02).
      05  PURCHASE-ITEM-SALES       PIC X(10).
      05  PURCHASE-AMOUNT-SALES     PIC S9(09)V99.
      05  FILLER                    PIC X(43).

  FD  EXCEPTION-REPORT-FILE
      LABEL RECORDS ARE OMITTED.
  01  REPORT-RECORD                     PIC X(133).
 *---------------------------------------------------------------*
```

Figure 18.9 *Continued* Updating an Indexed Sequential File

```
                    1   1   2   2   2   3   3   4   4   4   5   5   6   6   6   7
    4   8   2   6   0   4   8   2   6   0   4   8   2   6   0   4   8   2

 WORKING-STORAGE SECTION.
*-----------------------------------------------------------------*
 01  WORKING-VARIABLES.
     05  FILE-STATUS                PIC X(04) VALUE SPACES.
     05  INPUT-STATUS               PIC X(10) VALUE SPACES.
     05  CUSTOMER-NUMBER-FIND-WS    PIC X(10).
     05  LINE-NUMBER-WS             PIC 9(02) VALUE 99.
     05  PAGE-NUMBER-WS             PIC 9(02) VALUE ZERO.

 01  HEADING-1.
     05  FILLER                     PIC X(32) VALUE SPACES.
     05  FILLER                     PIC X(16) VALUE
                                    'Exception Report'.
     05  FILLER                     PIC X(25) VALUE SPACES.
     05  FILLER                     PIC X(05) VALUE 'Page'.
     05  PAGE-NUMBER-OUT            PIC Z9.

 01  HEADING-2.
     05  FILLER                     PIC X(20) VALUE
                                    ' Customer Number'.
     05  FILLER                     PIC X(50) VALUE
           '  Date      Purchase Amount     Comments'.

 01  HEADING-3.
     05  FILLER                     PIC X(01) VALUE SPACES.
     05  FILLER                     PIC X(80) VALUE ALL '-'.

 01  ERROR-LINE.
     05  FILLER                     PIC X(02) VALUE SPACES.
     05  CUSTOMER-NUMBER-OUT        PIC X(10).
     05  FILLER                     PIC X(08) VALUE SPACES.
     05  PURCHASE-MONTH-OUT         PIC X(02).
     05  FILLER                     PIC X(01) VALUE '/'.
     05  PURCHASE-DAY-OUT           PIC X(02).
     05  FILLER                     PIC X(01) VALUE '/'.
     05  PURCHASE-YEAR-OUT          PIC X(02).
     05  FILLER                     PIC X(05) VALUE SPACES.
     05  PURCHASE-AMOUNT-OUT        PIC ZZZ,ZZZ,ZZZ.ZZ.
     05  FILLER                     PIC X(05) VALUE SPACES.
     05  MESSAGE-OUT                PIC X(50) VALUE SPACES.
******************************************************************
 PROCEDURE DIVISION.
******************************************************************
*-----------------------------------------------------------------*
 1000-UPDATE-ACCOUNT SECTION.
*-----------------------------------------------------------------*
     PERFORM 1200-INITIATE-UPDATE.
     PERFORM 1400-UPDATE-FILE
         UNTIL FILE-STATUS = 'DONE'.
     PERFORM 1600-TERMINATE-UPDATE.
     STOP RUN.
*-----------------------------------------------------------------*
 1200-INITIATE-UPDATE SECTION.
*-----------------------------------------------------------------*
     OPEN I-O CUSTOMER-IO-FILE
          INPUT CUSTOMER-SALES-FILE
          OUTPUT EXCEPTION-REPORT-FILE.
*-----------------------------------------------------------------*
 1400-UPDATE-FILE SECTION.
*-----------------------------------------------------------------*
     IF LINE-NUMBER-WS IS GREATER THAN 40
        PERFORM 1420-REPORT-HEADING.
     READ CUSTOMER-SALES-FILE
         AT END MOVE 'DONE' TO FILE-STATUS
                GO TO 1499-EXIT.
     MOVE CUSTOMER-NUMBER-SALES TO CUSTOMER-NUMBER-OUT
                                   CUSTOMER-NUMBER-FIND-WS.
     MOVE PURCHASE-MONTH-SALES TO PURCHASE-MONTH-OUT.
     MOVE PURCHASE-DAY-SALES  TO PURCHASE-DAY-OUT.
```

Figure 18.9 *Continued* Building an Indexed Sequential File

```
       1   1   2   2   2   3   3   4   4   4   5   5   6   6   6   7
   4   8   2   6   0   4   8   2   6   0   4   8   2   6   0   4   8   2

           MOVE PURCHASE-YEAR-SALES TO PURCHASE-YEAR-OUT.
           MOVE PURCHASE-AMOUNT-SALES TO PURCHASE-AMOUNT-OUT.
           MOVE 'FOUND'                  TO INPUT-STATUS.
           READ CUSTOMER-IO-FILE
               INVALID KEY MOVE 'NOT FOUND' TO INPUT-STATUS.
           IF INPUT-STATUS = 'FOUND'
               PERFORM 1440-CUSTOMER-UPDATE
           ELSE
               PERFORM 1460-RECORD-ERROR.

       1499-EXIT.
           EXIT.
      *-----------------------------------------------------------*
       1420-REPORT-HEADING SECTION.
      *-----------------------------------------------------------*
           ADD 1 TO PAGE-NUMBER-WS.
           MOVE PAGE-NUMBER-WS          TO PAGE-NUMBER-OUT.
           MOVE 0                       TO LINE-NUMBER-WS.
           WRITE REPORT-RECORD FROM HEADING-1
               AFTER ADVANCING TOP-OF-PAGE.
           WRITE REPORT-RECORD FROM HEADING-2 AFTER ADVANCING 2 LINES.
           WRITE REPORT-RECORD FROM HEADING-3 AFTER ADVANCING 1 LINES.
           MOVE SPACES                  TO REPORT-RECORD.
           WRITE REPORT-RECORD AFTER ADVANCING 1 LINES.
      *-----------------------------------------------------------*
       1440-CUSTOMER-UPDATE SECTION.
      *-----------------------------------------------------------*
           IF CUSTOMER-BALANCE-IO + PURCHASE-AMOUNT-SALES >
             CUSTOMER-CREDIT-LIMIT-IO
               PERFORM 1444-LIMIT-ERROR
           ELSE
               ADD PURCHASE-AMOUNT-SALES TO CUSTOMER-BALANCE-IO
               PERFORM 1442-REPORT-ACTIVITY.
      *-----------------------------------------------------------*
       1442-REPORT-ACTIVITY SECTION.
      *-----------------------------------------------------------*
           MOVE 'Customer Record Updated' TO MESSAGE-OUT.
           REWRITE CUSTOMER-RECORD
               INVALID KEY MOVE 'Error--Record Not Updated' TO
                              MESSAGE-OUT.
           WRITE REPORT-RECORD FROM ERROR-LINE AFTER ADVANCING 1 LINES.
           ADD 1 TO LINE-NUMBER-WS.
      *-----------------------------------------------------------*
       1444-LIMIT-ERROR SECTION.
      *-----------------------------------------------------------*
           MOVE 'Credit Limit Exceeded' TO MESSAGE-OUT.
           WRITE REPORT-RECORD FROM ERROR-LINE AFTER ADVANCING 1 LINES.
           ADD 1 TO LINE-NUMBER-WS.
      *-----------------------------------------------------------*
       1460-RECORD-ERROR SECTION.
      *-----------------------------------------------------------*
           MOVE ALL '-'                 TO REPORT-RECORD.
           WRITE REPORT-RECORD AFTER ADVANCING 2 LINES.
           MOVE 'Customer Record Not Found' TO MESSAGE-OUT.
           WRITE REPORT-RECORD FROM ERROR-LINE AFTER ADVANCING 1 LINES.
           MOVE ALL '-'                 TO REPORT-RECORD.
           WRITE REPORT-RECORD AFTER ADVANCING 1 LINES.
           MOVE SPACES                  TO REPORT-RECORD.
           WRITE REPORT-RECORD AFTER ADVANCING 1 LINES.
           ADD 5 TO LINE-NUMBER-WS.
      *-----------------------------------------------------------*
       1600-TERMINATE-UPDATE SECTION.
      *-----------------------------------------------------------*
           CLOSE CUSTOMER-IO-FILE,
                 CUSTOMER-SALES-FILE
                 EXCEPTION-REPORT-FILE.
```

Figure 18.9 *Continued* Updating an Indexed Sequential File [CUSTOMER-SALES] (Data)

```
-------------------------------------------------
|      |         1         2         3         4|
|Record|1234567890123456789012345678901234567890|
|-----------------------------------------------|
|     1|33333333333051885441294     00000044125 |
|     2|9X0-334RDS05158529-43319    00000041232 |
|     3|11419441030514854193 37     00000712911 |
|     4|3333333333051485            00005122529 |
|     5|412559279305018588888888880051229 5147 |
|     6|4412X4739005018545-RTS      00000056902 |
|     7|3333333333060985BXR-33294   00002212219 |
|     8|5270215827050585            00000112697 |
|     9|5512294148051585            00000004123 |
|    10|349896645105178599-457-3310000476110    |
|    11|4412X473900522855514429022000000 03312  |
|    12|1141944103052585            00000012000 |
-------------------------------------------------
```

Figure 18.9 *Continued* Updating an Indexed Sequential File [CUSTOMER-SALES] (Data)

```
--------------------------------------------------------------------------------------------------------------------------------------
|                                                                                                          1         1         1    |
|      |         1         2         3         4         5         6         7         8         9         0         1         2    |
|Record|12345678901234567890123456789012345678901234567890123456789012345678901234567890123456789012345678901234567890123456789012345|
|-------------------------------------------------------------------------------------------------------------------------------------
|     1| 1RX14219-3John P. Villiman              8887 Peach Tree Lane          Dallas               TX75002      0000000314300000500000|
|     2| 1141944103Edwin Williams                2139 South Colgate Street     Perryton             TX79070      0000105684D00035000000|
|     3| 3199127X33James Thompkins               44339 South Wacker Drive      Chicago              IL60606      0000002291800000500000|
|     4| 3333333333Julia Harriston               6132 Mill Road Avenue         Shreveport           LA63341      0000260768G00005000000|
|     5| 3498966451Jacob R. Sullivan             6134 Malibu Drive             Los Angeles          CA96512      0000047611 00004400000|
|     6| 4412X47390Marshall Silverman            2219 West 7th Street          Cleveland            OH30119      0000006021D00000500000|
|     7| 5270215827Charles Everest               8821 Ocean Parkway            Miami                FL51332      0000011269G00000500000|
|     8| 6213937661Jason Madison                 8831 Cedar Drive N.W.         Norwich              CT00218      0000041452300003000000|
|     9| 6427633-94Mark U. Lemon                 P. O. Box 51244               New York             NY03158      0000000000000000005000|
|    10| 773194221BHelen B. Overstreet           3153 Yellow Brick Road        Yellow Stone Park    MT41229      0000001284200000000000|
|    11| 9X0-334RDSAnthony P. Jones              Executive Office Building     Washington           DC00000      0000000000000000000000|
--------------------------------------------------------------------------------------------------------------------------------------
```

phrase of the READ statement (the NOMINAL KEY and any RECORD KEY value did not match exactly), and an error routine (1460-RECORD-ERROR) is invoked.

During the update sequence (lines 1640–1710), if the transaction contains a legitimate change (the credit limit is not exceeded), the CUSTOMER-BALANCE-IO field is modified, and the record is rewritten to the indexed sequential file (line 1760). Otherwise, a limit error is printed (1444-LIMIT-ERROR). Notice that if the record is not modified—if a limit error is encountered—the record from the indexed sequential file does not have to be rewritten. Since nothing in the record was modified, rewriting the record would be pointless—the file contains the data currently in internal storage. Finally, notice that the update sequence from the transaction file is in no particular order. Examine either the output in the EXCEPTION-RECORD or the data in the CUSTOMER-SALES-FILE. Notice that only the contents of the record in the CUSTOMER-IO-FILE have been modified—the sequence of the records in the indexed sequential file has not been affected.

Figure 18.9 *Continued* Updating an Indexed Sequential File (Output)

```
                              Exception Report                        Page  1

  Customer Number        Date       Purchase Amount      Comments
 -------------------------------------------------------------------------------

  3333333333           05/18/85             441.25       Customer Record Updated
  9XO-334RDS           05/15/85             412.32       Credit Limit Exceeded
  1141944103           05/14/85           7,129.11       Customer Record Updated
  3333333333           05/14/85          51,225.29       Credit Limit Exceeded
 -------------------------------------------------------------------------------

  4125592793           05/01/85       5,122,951.47       Customer Record Not Found
 -------------------------------------------------------------------------------

  4412X47390           05/01/85             569.02       Customer Record Updated
  3333333333           06/09/85          22,122.19       Customer Record Updated
  5270215827           05/05/85           1,126.97       Customer Record Updated
 -------------------------------------------------------------------------------

  5512294148           05/15/85              41.23       Customer Record Not Found
 -------------------------------------------------------------------------------

  3498966451           05/17/85           4,761.10       Customer Record Updated
  4412X47390           05/22/85              33.12       Customer Record Updated
```

Adding to an Indexed Sequential File

Recall from Chapter 17 that the addition process for a sequential file requires a new file be created. In the system flowchart in Figure 18.10, note only one CUSTOMER file is required to perform additions for an indexed sequential file. Whether a standard sequential file is recorded on magnetic tape or a mass storage medium, it must be rewritten to add records to any position of the file except at its end. In the indexed sequential file illustrated in Figure 18.10, records are added at the beginning of the file and interspersed with existing records in the file.

Figure 18.10 Adding to an Indexed Sequential File (System Flowchart)

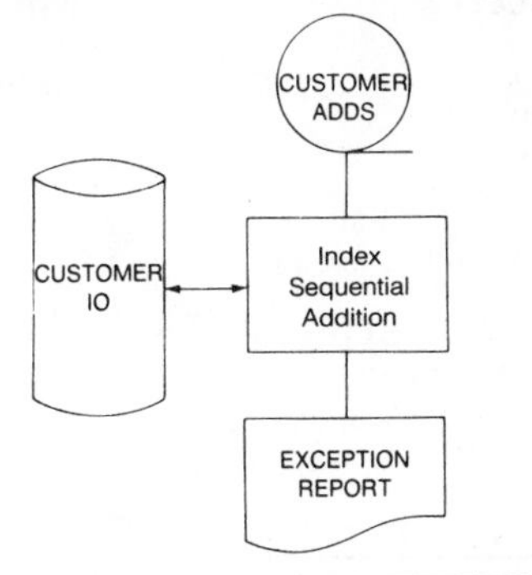

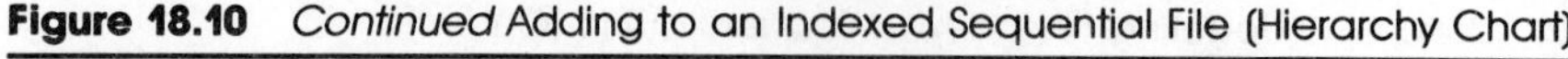

Figure 18.10 *Continued* Adding to an Indexed Sequential File (Hierarchy Chart)

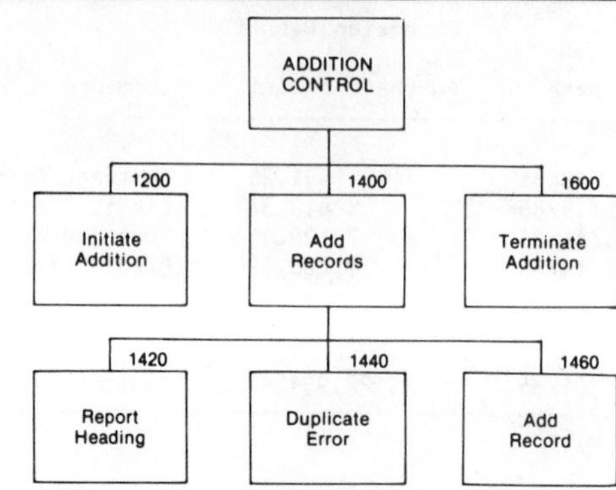

In the ENVIRONMENT DIVISION, the RANDOM access mode has been selected; thus both the RECORD KEY and the NOMINAL KEY are required. In the PROCEDURE DIVISION, the CUSTOMER-IO file is opened in an I-O mode. In the repetitive procedure of the 1400-ADD-RECORDS SECTION, a record is read from the CUSTOMER-ADDITION-FILE and the NOMINAL KEY variable is initialized with the MOVE statement at line 1180.

Figure 18.10 *Continued* Adding to an Indexed Sequential File (Pseudocode)

```
START
    DO Initiate addition
    DO Add records UNTIL eof
    DO Terminate addition
END

INITIATE ADDITION
    OPEN files
END

ADD RECORDS
    IF line number > 40
         DO Report heading
    ENDIF
    READ input file
    IF eof
         SET file status
         GOTO end
    ENDIF
    MOVE input to output
    SET output status
    WRITE output record
         IF invalid key
              SET output status
         ENDIF
    IF output status = duplicate
         DO Duplicate error
    ELSE
         DO Write record
    ENDIF
END
```

```
REPORT HEADING
    ADD 1 to page number
    MOVE 0 to line number
    WRITE headings
END

DUPLICATE ERROR
    MOVE message to output
    WRITE output
    ADD 2 to line number
END

WRITE RECORD
    MOVE message to output
    WRITE customer output
    ADD 2 to line number
END

TERMINATE ADDITION
    CLOSE files
END
```

Figure 18.10 *Continued* Adding to an Indexed Sequential File

```
        1   1   2   2   2   3   3   4   4   4   5   5   6   6   6   7
4   8   2   6   0   4   8   2   6   0   4   8   2   6   0   4   8   2

 ************************************************************
  IDENTIFICATION DIVISION.
 ************************************************************
  PROGRAM-ID.     INDEX-SEQUENTIAL-ADDITION.
  AUTHOR.         J. WAYNE SPENCE.
  DATE-WRITTEN.   JANUARY 1, 1989.
  DATE-COMPILED.  JANUARY 1, 1989.
 *    The purpose of this procedure is to add records (new customer
 *    to an existing indexed sequential (CUSTOMER) file.  The proce
 *    prohibits duplicate customer records with the same customer
 *    number.
 ************************************************************
  ENVIRONMENT DIVISION.
 ************************************************************
 *----------------------------------------------------------*
  CONFIGURATION SECTION.
 *----------------------------------------------------------*
  SOURCE-COMPUTER. IBM.
  OBJECT-COMPUTER. IBM.
  SPECIAL-NAMES.
                   C01 IS TOP-OF-PAGE.
 *----------------------------------------------------------*
  INPUT-OUTPUT SECTION.
 *----------------------------------------------------------*
  FILE-CONTROL.
      SELECT CUSTOMER-IO              ASSIGN TO DA-I-INPUT
          RECORD KEY IS CUSTOMER-NUMBER-IO
          NOMINAL KEY IS CUSTOMER-NUMBER-FIND-WS
          ACCESS IS RANDOM.
      SELECT CUSTOMER-ADDITION-FILE ASSIGN TO UT-S-INPUT2.
      SELECT EXCEPTION-REPORT-FILE  ASSIGN TO UT-S-OUTPUT.
 ************************************************************
  DATA DIVISION.
 ************************************************************
 *----------------------------------------------------------*
  FILE SECTION.
 *----------------------------------------------------------*
  FD  CUSTOMER-IO
      LABEL RECORDS ARE STANDARD
      RECORD CONTAINS 125 CHARACTERS.
  01  CUSTOMER-REC.
      05  DELETE-CODE-IO           PIC X(01).
      05  CUSTOMER-NUMBER-IO       PIC X(10).
      05  FILLER                   PIC X(114).

  FD  CUSTOMER-ADDITION-FILE
      LABEL RECORDS ARE STANDARD
      RECORD CONTAINS 124 CHARACTERS
      BLOCK CONTAINS 0 RECORDS.
  01  CUSTOMER-ADDITION-RECORD.
      05  CUSTOMER-NUMBER-ADDS     PIC X(10).
      05  FILLER                   PIC X(114).

  FD  EXCEPTION-REPORT-FILE
      LABEL RECORDS ARE OMITTED.
  01  REPORT-RECORD                PIC X(133).
 *----------------------------------------------------------*
  WORKING-STORAGE SECTION.
 *----------------------------------------------------------*
  01  PROGRAM-CONTROL-VARIABLES.
      05  FILE-STATUS              PIC X(04) VALUE SPACES.
      05  OUTPUT-STATUS            PIC X(15).
      05  CUSTOMER-NUMBER-FIND-WS  PIC X(10).
      05  LINE-NUMBER-WS           PIC 9(02) VALUE 99.
      05  PAGE-NUMBER-WS           PIC 9(02) VALUE ZERO.
      05  INPUT-OUTPUT-RECORD.
          10  FIRST-BYTE           PIC X(01) VALUE SPACES.
          10  RECORD-CONTENTS      PIC X(124).
```

Figure 18.10 *Continued* Adding to an Indexed Sequential File [CUSTOMER—IN] (Data)

```
           1   1   2   2   2   3   3   4   4   4   5   5   6   6   6   7
   4   8   2   6   0   4   8   2   6   0   4   8   2   6   0   4   8   2
------------------------------------------------------------------------
       01  HEADING-1.
           05  FILLER                        PIC X(32) VALUE SPACES.
           05  FILLER                        PIC X(16) VALUE
                                             'Exception Report'.
           05  FILLER                        PIC X(25) VALUE SPACES.
           05  FILLER                        PIC X(05) VALUE 'Page'.
           05  PAGE-NUMBER-OUT               PIC Z9.

       01  HEADING-2.
           05  FILLER                        PIC X(20) VALUE
                                             ' Customer Number'.
           05  FILLER                        PIC X(50) VALUE
                                             'Comments'.

       01  HEADING-3.
           05  FILLER                        PIC X(01) VALUE SPACES.
           05  FILLER                        PIC X(80) VALUE ALL '-'.

       01  ERROR-LINE.
           05  FILLER                        PIC X(02) VALUE SPACES.
           05  CUSTOMER-NUMBER-OUT           PIC X(10).
           05  FILLER                        PIC X(08) VALUE SPACES.
           05  MESSAGE-OUT                   PIC X(50) VALUE SPACES.
      ***************************************************************
       PROCEDURE DIVISION.
      ***************************************************************
      *-------------------------------------------------------------*
       1000-ADDITION-CONTROL SECTION.
      *-------------------------------------------------------------*
           PERFORM 1200-INITIATE-ADDITION.
           PERFORM 1400-ADD-RECORDS
               UNTIL FILE-STATUS = 'DONE'.
           PERFORM 1600-TERMINATE-ADDITION.
           STOP RUN.
      *-------------------------------------------------------------*
       1200-INITIATE-ADDITION SECTION.
      *-------------------------------------------------------------*
           OPEN I-O CUSTOMER-IO
                INPUT CUSTOMER-ADDITION-FILE
                OUTPUT EXCEPTION-REPORT-FILE.
      *-------------------------------------------------------------*
       1400-ADD-RECORDS SECTION.
      *-------------------------------------------------------------*
           IF LINE-NUMBER-WS IS GREATER THAN 40
               PERFORM 1420-REPORT-HEADING.
           READ CUSTOMER-ADDITION-FILE INTO RECORD-CONTENTS
               AT END MOVE 'DONE' TO FILE-STATUS
                      GO TO 1499-EXIT.
           MOVE CUSTOMER-NUMBER-ADDS TO CUSTOMER-NUMBER-OUT
                                        CUSTOMER-NUMBER-FIND-WS.
           MOVE 'NO DUPLICATE'       TO OUTPUT-STATUS.
           WRITE CUSTOMER-REC FROM INPUT-OUTPUT-RECORD
               INVALID KEY MOVE 'DUPLICATE' TO OUTPUT-STATUS.
           IF OUTPUT-STATUS = 'DUPLICATE'
               PERFORM 1440-DUPLICATE-ERROR
           ELSE
               PERFORM 1460-WRITE-RECORD.

       1499-EXIT.
           EXIT.
      *-------------------------------------------------------------*
       1420-REPORT-HEADING SECTION.
      *-------------------------------------------------------------*
           ADD 1 TO PAGE-NUMBER-WS.
           MOVE PAGE-NUMBER-WS          TO PAGE-NUMBER-OUT.
           MOVE 0                       TO LINE-NUMBER-WS.
           WRITE REPORT-RECORD FROM HEADING-1
               AFTER ADVANCING TOP-OF-PAGE.
           WRITE REPORT-RECORD FROM HEADING-2 AFTER ADVANCING 2 LINES.
```

Figure 18.10 *Continued* Adding to an Indexed Sequential File

```
           WRITE REPORT-RECORD FROM HEADING-3 AFTER ADVANCING 1 LINES.
           MOVE SPACES                TO REPORT-RECORD.
           WRITE REPORT-RECORD AFTER ADVANCING 1 LINES.
      *--------------------------------------------------------------*
       1440-DUPLICATE-ERROR SECTION.
      *--------------------------------------------------------------*
           MOVE 'Attempt to Add a Duplicate Record' TO MESSAGE-OUT.
           WRITE REPORT-RECORD FROM ERROR-LINE AFTER 2.
           ADD 2 TO LINE-NUMBER-WS.
      *--------------------------------------------------------------*
       1460-WRITE-RECORD SECTION.
      *--------------------------------------------------------------*
           MOVE 'Record Added'        TO MESSAGE-OUT.
           WRITE REPORT-RECORD FROM ERROR-LINE AFTER 2.
           ADD 2 TO LINE-NUMBER-WS.
      *--------------------------------------------------------------*
       1600-TERMINATE-ADDITION SECTION.
      *--------------------------------------------------------------*
           CLOSE CUSTOMER-IO,
                 EXCEPTION-REPORT-FILE
                 CUSTOMER-ADDITION-FILE.
```

Figure 18.10 *Continued* Adding to an Indexed Sequential File [CUSTOMER—IN] (Data)

```
      |         1         2         3         4         5         6         7         8         9         1         1         1
      |                                                                                                   0         1         2
Record|123456789012345678901234567890123456789012345678901234567890123456789012345678901234567890123456789012345678901234567890123456789012345
     1| X14339-278Robert P. Evans                   1422 N. W. Classen Blvd.   Oklahoma City         OK65124     0000000000000000300000
     2| 1RX14219-3John P. Villiman                  8887 Peach Tree Lane       Dallas                TX75002     0000000314300000500000
     3| 1141944103Edwin Williams                    2139 South Colgate Street  Perryton              TX79070     000010568400003500000
     4| 2199428878Stewart A. Alexander              5112 Hamilton Parkway      Minneapolis           MN21132     0000062239000001000000
     5| 3199127X33James Thompkins                   44339 South Wacker Drive   Chicago               IL60606     0000002291800000500000
     6| 3333333333Julia Harriston                   6132 Mill Road Avenue      Shreveport            LA63341     0000260768G00005000000
     7| 3498966451Jacob R. Sullivan                 6134 Malibu Drive          Los Angeles           CA96512     0000047611 00004400000
     8| 4412X47390Marshall Silverman                2219 West 7th Street       Cleveland             OH30119     0000006021D00000500000
     9| 5122314151Mark R. White                     55123 War Memorial Drive   Cleveland             OH41229     0000004123300000050000
    10| 5270215827Charles Everest                   8821 Ocean Parkway         Miami                 FL51332     0000011269G00000500000
    11| 6213937661Jason Madison                     8831 Cedar Drive N.W.      Norwich               CT00218     0000041452300003000000
    12| 6427633-94Mark U. Lemon                     P. O. Box 51244            New York              NY03158     0000000000000000005000
    13| 773194221BHelen B. Overstreet               3153 Yellow Brick Road     Yellow Stone Park     MT41229     0000001284200000000000
    14| 9X0-334RDSAnthony P. Jones                  Executive Office Building  Washington            DC00000     0000000000000000000000
```

The process varies somewhat from the update process at this point. Instead of setting a status variable and *reading* a record from the indexed sequential file, the process sets the status variable and *writes* a (new) record to the indexed sequential file. Provided the WRITE operation is successful, an output routine is invoked to print a message reflecting the addition of the record. However, if an INVALID KEY is caused by the WRITE operation, the attempt to place the new record in the file causes a duplication of an existing RECORD KEY—the record is not placed in the file and a message indicating the situation is printed. Of course, if a large number of records have been added to the file, the "DUPLICATE" message might be in error. Existing file space *could* have been exhausted.

Figure 18.10 *Continued* Adding to an Indexed Sequential File [CUSTOMER—ADDITION] (Data)

```
                                                                                                                 1         1         1    |
       |         1         2         3         4         5         6         7         8         9         0         1         2    |
Record|1234567890123456789012345678901234567890123456789012345678901234567890123456789012345678901234567890123456789012345678901234|
------------------------------------------------------------------------------------------------------------------------------------
     1|3333333333George P. Martin              Las Vegas Hilton              Las Vegas           NV81222      999999999990000000000|
     2|2199428878Stewart A. Alexander          5112 Hamilton Parkway         Minneapolis         MN21132      000006223900000100000|
     3|5122314151Mark R. White                 55123 War Memorial Drive      Cleveland           OH41229      000000412330000005000|
     4|X14339-278Rober P. Evans                1422 N. W. Classen Blvd.      Oklahoma City       OK65124      000000000000000030000|
------------------------------------------------------------------------------------------------------------------------------------
```

Figure 18.10 *Continued* Adding to an Indexed Sequential File (Output)

```
                              Exception Report                               Page  1

     Customer Number    Comments
     --------------------------------------------------------------------------------

     3333333333         Attempt to Add a Duplicate Record
     2199428878         Record Added
     5122314151         Record Added
```

Summary

In this chapter, the process of building, updating, and adding records to an indexed sequential file has been illustrated. Files of this type may be read or written either sequentially or randomly. Records may be updated, added, or deleted without rewriting the file. If the records in the file are to be updated randomly, only those records affected by the update would be accessed. Other records in the file would not be either read or written. Records may be added to the file at the beginning or the end of the file, or interspersed throughout, provided sufficient space for the records remains in the file. Records may be logically deleted (such that they are transparent to the programmer) by simply moving HIGH-VALUES in the first byte of the record. Sequential file processing may be improved through the use of a specific or generic key in the START statement—permitting sequential access and processing of an indexed sequential file at other than the first (next) serial record.

Notes on Programming Style

Although it might seem that no one in his or her right mind would select a sequential file organization for a master file (over an indexed sequential file), there are a number of excellent reasons for using other file types. First, indexed sequential files require more media space than does a sequential file. RECORD KEYs occupy additional space in the indexed sequential file. ''Deleted'' records may also occupy needed space. Other disadvantages are the manner in which records are added to the file, and the retention and manipulation of indexes (also stored in the file). As you progress through Chapter 19, you will become aware of other choices that should provide a more complete picture of data access arrangements in today's commercial environment.

Questions

Below, answer each question by supplying the appropriate word, words, or phrase.

1. Another term that indicates a file is indexed is that it is ____ .
2. An indexed file may be accessed either ____or ____ .
3. For an indexed sequential file the ____ KEY clause is always required.
4. An index sequential file must be recorded on a ____ medium.
5. When an indexed sequential file is to be accessed in a RANDOM mode, the ____ clause is required.
6. An indexed sequential file that is READ sequentially should use a(n) ____ phrase prior to the imperative statement.
7. An indexed sequential file that is READ randomly use use a(n) ____ clause prior to the imperative statement.
8. The identifier used as the RECORD KEY must appear in the ____ record description.
9. The identifier used as the NOMINAL KEY must appear as a field in the ____ SECTION.
10 A(n) ____ statement is used to build or add records to an indexed sequential file, whereas a(n) ____ statement is used to update the file.
11. The space on a magnetic disk must be allocated by ____ for an indexed sequential file.
12. If records are to be deleted from an indexed sequential file using the delete byte, the value ____ must be moved to the ____ byte of the record description.
13. When an indexed sequential file is built, the values in the RECORD KEY variable must be ____ and must be arranged in a(n) ____ order.
14. The most likely reason for the execution of an imperative statement of a READ statement using the INVALID KEY phrase is that ____.
15. The most likely reason for the execution of an imperative statement of the WRITE statement is that ____.
16. If an indexed sequential file is to be read sequentially, the first record accessed may be other than the first physical record if the ____ statement is employed.
17. The only condition under which an item may be addressed using a value other than an exact match of the RECORD KEY in an operation designed to locate existing records is when a(n) ____ key is used in a(n) ____ statement.

For the question below, answer by circling "T" for True and "F" for False.

T F 18. Records may be added to an indexed sequential file with a REWRITE statement.

T F 19. The identifier specified as a RECORD KEY must appear in the record description of the indexed sequential file.

T F 20. For an indexed sequential file, the RECORD KEY must be specified only under certain conditions.

T F 21. The description of a RECORD KEY must be numeric.

T F 22. The description of the RECORD KEY must be the same as the NOMINAL KEY identifier.

T F 23. An indexed sequential file must not be blocked.

T F **24.** An indexed sequential file must be recorded on a direct access type of storage device.

T F **25.** Media space on a magnetic disk for an indexed sequential file may be specific in either tracks or cylinders.

T F **26.** The description of the NOMINAL KEY variable, depending on the application, may appear in the FILE SECTION.

T F **27.** An INVALID KEY imperative statement for an indexed-sequential-file reading operation may be caused by the location of a duplicate record in the file.

T F **28.** A REWRITE statement should always be logically preceded by a READ statement.

T F **29.** A NOMINAL KEY clause must be supplied whenever a START statement is used.

T F **30.** A generic key for the START statement may have a description that is shorter than the RECORD KEY description.

T F **31.** It is always necessary that prior to the actual update of an indexed sequential file, the transaction records must be ordered in the same sequence as the indexed sequential file.

Problems

18.1 Complete Problem 17.1. Alter the file type of the inventory file to indexed sequential. Alter the requirements of the update exceptions report so that updated records are printed after each record from the sales file has been processed. In other words, do not reorder the sales file to conform to the order of the inventory file. Finally, some reorganization of the inventory record may be required to create a single ''field'' that represents the key for the record.

18.2 Complete Problem 17.2. Alter the file type of the customer file to indexed sequential. Order the sales file data such that all updates for a single customer record may be handled at one time.

18.3 Complete Problem 17.3. Alter the file type of the inventory file to indexed sequential. The purchase orders are to be handled in the sequence they appear in the purchase order file. Some reorganization of the inventory record may be required to create a single ''field'' that represents the key for the record. In addition, the length of the record may be altered to accommodate record deletions.

CHAPTER

19

Relative and Virtual Files

Historically, COBOL has supported three versions of file organization: sequential, indexed, and relative. In the previous two chapters, you were introduced to sequential and indexed files. This chapter concludes the introduction to file types with a discussion of relative files (the last of the historical file types) and virtual files (the most recent type of file organization introduced to COBOL).

An Introduction To Relative Files

Relative files, sometimes called *direct access* files, share some similarity with the direct access mode of retrieving data from an indexed file. First, both file organizations must be recorded on a direct access device (e.g., magnetic disk). Second, when an indexed file is accessed in direct mode, it appears as though a record is retrieved directly from the file without regard to its location (or association with other records in the file). More specifically, when a record is retrieved in this manner from an indexed file, the computer uses the key of the record to ''look up'' the record location by using a series of indexes.

When a record is retrieved from a relative file, no record key is used. Rather, the record is retrieved directly on the basis of its *location*. That is, the programmer must determine which record location to retrieve and then instruct the computer to read a record from that position in the file. This type of access is called *relative* since the record location is derived on the basis of its relative position from the beginning of the file. Thus, an indexed file retrieves a record on the basis of the value of its record key, whereas a relative file retrieves a record on the basis of its location or *relative address*.

To illustrate how a relative file is organized, examine Figure 19.1. The concentric rings in this figure represent adjacent disk tracks (although a relative file could just as easily be arranged on the basis of tracks in the one or more cylinders). As you examine the outer track, notice each record location is assigned a consecutive number from 1 through 8 (assuming no more than eight records may occupy a single track). The second track begins with the next consecutive number, and the record locations are identified as 9 through 16. For a larger file, the next track would also contain eight records bearing the record locations 17 through 24, and so on. (This numbering system is used here for

Figure 19.1 Structure of a Relative File

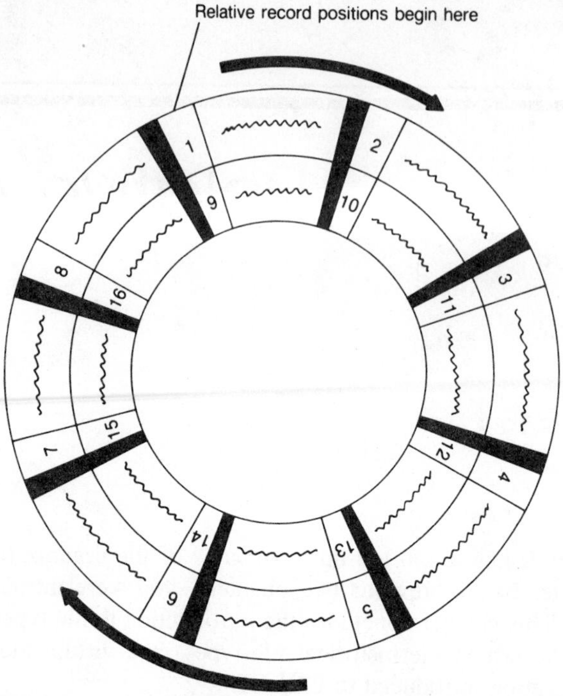

convenience. Most relative file numbering systems for record locations begin with record location 0.) Do not confuse records with record locations. Some record locations will not contain data, as you will see shortly.

By using this technique, you assign each possible record location in the file its own unique address. Thus, to place a record in the file or retrieve an existing record, you need only supply its record location. Furthermore, since there is no requirement that the records be accessed in any particular order, accessing any sequence of available record locations is permitted.

Advantages and Disadvantages

Among the advantages of a relative file over other file types is its ability to retrieve individual records rapidly from a file. When comparing retrieval speeds of a relative file against any of the other file types presented in this text, you will find a relative file is typically the fastest (frequently by a substantial margin). The second advantage of relative files is that an individual record's location in the file may be independent of any of its logical properties. When either a sequential or an indexed file is built, the records are generally ordered on an ascending sequence based on some field within the record itself. The location of a record within a relative file is not necessarily based on any field within the record.

The disadvantages of relative files are numerous. First, since each record is totally independent of the others, the file will require more physical space than any other file organization. The primary reason for this is that relative files are unblocked; that is, a logical record and a physical record are the same. In addition, a programmer usually allocates extra space to the file to accommodate later additions to the file. Finally, since the location of the record is not of necessity based on anything within the record, it is the programmer's responsibility to determine a record's location. This problem will be discussed more fully later.

Based on these advantages and disadvantages, one factor becomes very clear. A programmer chooses to employ a relative file *only* when rapid retrieval of individual records is a primary concern.

ENVIRONMENT DIVISION Considerations

An examination of Figure 19.2 reveals the ENVIRONMENT DIVISION entries for a relative file are somewhat similar to those for an indexed file. As is required for all files, the SELECT and ASSIGN clauses are specified. However, as shown in Figure 19.3, the ASSIGN clause must specify a direct access device is to be used (DA) and that the file organization is relative (R).

Although there are similarities in the appearance of the ENVIRONMENT DIVISION entries between an indexed and a relative file, notice there are several notable absences. First, the RESERVE clause is omitted. Thus, regardless of whether a relative file is being accessed in either a.sequential or random access manner, only a single physical record is retrieved from the file at one time. Second, the RECORD KEY clause is omitted. That is, there is no field within a relative record that necessarily specifies the record's location within the file.

Among the other ENVIRONMENT DIVISION similarities between an indexed and a relative file are the presence of the ACCESS MODE, PROCESSING MODE, and NOMINAL KEY clauses. The ACCESS MODE clause indicates whether the file is to be accessed in s SEQUENTIAL or RANDOM (direct access) manner. Case 1 of Figure 19.3 specifies that the ACCESS MODE IS SEQUENTIAL. When SEQUENTIAL access is indicated, the file is either being created (or space is being preallocated) or sequentially read. If the file is being created (or space is being preallocated), the NOMINAL KEY clause is required. If the file is being read sequentially, the NOMINAL KEY clause may

Figure 19.2 INPUT-OUTPUT SECTION for a Relative File Organization

```
ENVIRONMENT DIVISION.
        .
        .
        .
[INPUT-OUTPUT SECTION.
 FILE-CONTROL.
     SELECT file-name
     ASSIGN TO system-name
                      {SEQUENTIAL}
    [ACCESS MODE IS   {          }      ]
                      {RANDOM    }
    [PROCESSING MODE IS SEQUENTIAL]
    [NOMINAL KEY IS identifier-1]
```

Figure 19.3 Illustrations of the ENVIRONMENT DIVISION for a Relative File

```
Case 1:

          ENVIRONMENT DIVISION.
          CONFIGURATION SECTION.
          SOURCE-COMPUTER. IBM.
          OBJECT-COMPUTER. IBM.
          INPUT-OUTPUT SECTION.
              SELECT CUSTOMER-FILE
                  ASSIGN TO DA-R-MASTER
                  ACCESS MODE IS SEQUENTIAL.

Case 2:

          ENVIRONMENT DIVISION.
          CONFIGURATION SECTION.
          SOURCE-COMPUTER. IBM.
          OBJECT-COMPUTER. IBM.
          INPUT-OUTPUT SECTION.
              SELECT CUSTOMER-FILE
                  ASSIGN TO DA-R-MASTER
                  NOMINAL KEY IS RECORD-LOCATION-WS
                  ACCESS MODE IS RANDOM.
```

be omitted. In case 2 of Figure 19.3, ACCESS MODE IS RANDOM. In the RANDOM mode, the NOMINAL KEY clause is always required. The PROCESSING MODE clause, as was the case with previous files, acts only as a comment entry and (if present,) is ignored.

The NOMINAL KEY clause is used to specify a record's relative location from the beginning of the file. The identifier associated with the clause must be specified in the WORKING-STORAGE SECTION. Furthermore, the identifier must be described as a numeric, eight-digit, integer, binary (COMPUTATIONAL) data item. (COMPUTATIONAL data types are described in Chapter 23.) In addition, the value placed in this identifier must be nonnegative and not greater than 15,728,640. Finally, the identifier must not be subordinate to an OCCURS DEPENDING ON clause. (See Chapter 13.)

DATA DIVISION Considerations

The FILE SECTION entries for a relative file are somewhat restrictive. The LABEL RECORDS clause must be included and should indicate STANDARD labels are used. The DATA RECORDS clause may be specified for all file types in the FD entry, but is treated as a comment. The RECORD CONTAINS clause may be specified, but may only specify a fixed length record. Finally, the BLOCK CONTAINS clause should be omitted. Thus, records within a relative file must be both fixed length and unblocked. Furthermore, since the RESERVE clause is not specified, only one physical record is retrieved from the file at a time. Therefore, when only one physical record is retrieved at a time and the file is unblocked, only a single *logical* record is retrieved at a time.

PROCEDURE DIVISION Considerations

No new statement types are required to process a relative file beyond those presented in Chapters 17 and 18. However, to refresh your memory, examine Table 19.1. This table presents the allowable statements and options based on how the file is to be accessed.

The first case illustrated in Table 19.1 is for the sequential retrieval of records from a relative file. The OPEN statement using an INPUT mode and a READ statement with the AT END phrase are employed to retrieve relative records sequentially. However, the programmer should realize the data contained in the file are not in any particular order. Furthermore, there may be "blank" or unused areas of the file that do not contain records.

The second case is the first to utilize the NOMINAL KEY clause. The value of the NOMINAL KEY identifier specifies the relative record location into which a record is to be placed. This brings us to a major difficulty associated with relative files. It is the programmer's responsibility to specify the record location into which a record is to be placed. This frequently calls for the development of what is known as a *data-to-address transformation, mapping,* or *hashing* function; the programmer must determine a method by which records are to be placed in (and later received from) the file.

To illustrate this problem, recall that relative record locations are sequentially numbered from 0 to some maximum value (based on the anticipated number of records in the file). Assume that you wish to create a relative file containing a record for each member of your class. If the class contains 73 members, you would have to allocate at least 73 record positions in the file. However, if other members were later added to your class, 73 record positions would not be sufficient. Thus, you might wish to reserve

Table 19.1 Relative File Statement Options and Uses

Type of Operation	ACCESS MODE	NOMINAL KEY Required	OPEN Statement	Input/Output Statement(s)
Sequential Record Retrieval	[SEQUENTIAL]	No	INPUT	READ [INTO] AT END
Random Record Retrieval	RANDOM	Yes	INPUT	READ [INTO] INVALID KEY
Creation or Record Addition	[SEQUENTIAL]	Yes	OUTPUT	WRITE [FROM] INVALID KEY
Record Update	RANDOM	Yes	I-O	READ [INTO] REWRITE [FROM] INVALID KEY WRITE [FROM] INVALID KEY

another ten record positions in anticipation of adding more records later. Now you would need 83 record positions. Finally, since you cannot be absolutely sure that your data-to-address transformation function will produce unique record locations for each record, you may allocate some amount of excess space. It is often recommended that an additional 20 percent be added to the allocated space to overcome this problem. Now you need approximately 100 record positions (83 + 83(.2) = 99.6).

Once you have decided how many record positions are required, you can proceed to develop the data-to-address transformation function. Suppose you wished to use a class member's social security number to identify his or her record. Suppose the lowest value for a social security number in the class is 234–00–0000 and the highest is 567–00–0000. If you treated the social security numbers as numeric fields (without hyphens) and subtracted them (to determine the range of social security numbers), you would have 333,000,000. Unfortunately, you cannot use a range of 333,000,000 as relative record addresses. You have allocated only 100 record positions. Furthermore, there is no guarantee that a new class member might not have a social security number smaller than 234–00–0000 or larger than 567–00–0000. Thus, you need to establish some other procedure that would accept not only current social security numbers, but would also accept anticipated numbers as well, and convert them into the range of 0 to 100.

One approach frequently employed to develop data-to-address transformation function is to use *modulus division.* Modulus division involves retaining the remainder after a division operation takes place. (See the DIVIDE statement in Chapter 10.) The remainder then becomes a record position. For our problem, this might amount to a data-to-address transformation function such as

```
DIVIDE SOCIAL-SECURITY-NUMBER BY 97 GIVING WHOLE-NUMBER
                    REMAINDER RECORD-LOCATION.
```

The remainders generated by this function will be 0 to 96—very close to the 0 to 100 range sought. The numeric literal 97 was chosen because it is a *prime number;* that is, it can only be evenly divided by itself and 1. A prime number is selected to reduce the number of *synonyms* produced by the data-to-address transformation function. In the illustration, a synonym would be produced if two or more social security numbers produced the same record location. For example, both 234–56–7890 and 456–78–9070, when divided by 97, result in a remainder of 65—the same record position based on the previous data-to-address transformation function (234,567,890/97 = 2,418,225, remainder = 65 and 456,789,070/97 = 4,709,165, remainder = 65).

When synonyms are produced, it is the programmer's responsibility (1) to determine that a synonym has been produced and (2) to resolve the synonym problem by an alternate means of identifying record locations. One common procedure for providing alternate locations is simply to add 1 to the record location until an available position is found.

Of course, there are many other possible data-to-address transformation functions in addition to modulus division, including *truncation* (only using a portion of the digits available), *folding* (breaking the value into two or more parts and adding the parts), and *digit manipulation* (selecting particular digits from the value and performing some type of manipulation on them), to name just a few. Generating a data-to-address transformation function often requires an examination of the data values to be used in the function in order that a successful function may be derived. However, such an examination is beyond the scope of this text.

Figure 19.4 Relative File Priming Operation (System Flowchart)

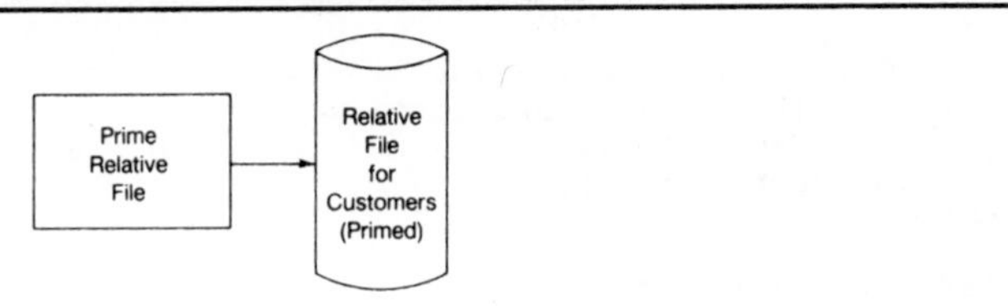

Preparing a Relative File for Use

When space (a number of record positions) is allocated for a relative file, the space does not contain any known data value. The fact that record locations initially contain no data frequently causes the programmer to preallocate the space and place some known data values in each record position. This operation is sometimes called ***priming*** the data space. (Priming operations are not always required. Check with your installation to determine whether it is necessary.)

The program presented in Figure 19.4 illustrates how the priming operation might be accomplished. The first notable difference between this and previous programs appears in line 250. Notice that the prefix "DA-R" appears in the ASSIGN clause, which designates a direct access device and a relative file type. In subsequent lines (260 and 270), the NOMINAL KEY is established and SEQUENTIAL access is specified. An examination of the WORKING-STORAGE SECTION reveals that NOMINAL KEY identifier (CUSTOMER-RECORD-LOCATION) is specified as a numeric data item described as a binary (COMP) field—a requirement for the NOMINAL KEY identifier for a relative file.

In the PROCEDURE DIVISION, several operations need to be noted. First, the CUSTOMER-OUT-FILE is opened in an OUTPUT mode. Second, spaces are moved to the CUSTOMER-RECORD-OUT. Since no further mention is made of this record (or subordinate fields), the record remains blank throughout the operation. Third, the record locations are generated by the PERFORM statement in lines 600–620. Based on this statement and the WRITE statement (line 730), record locations 1 through 60 are addressed and a blank record is placed in each. Thus, the operation "initializes" the record positions in the file and places spaces (a known value) in each of the record positions. Finally, the relative file is closed (Line 770).

Figure 19.4 *Continued* Relative File Priming Operation (Hierarchy Chart)

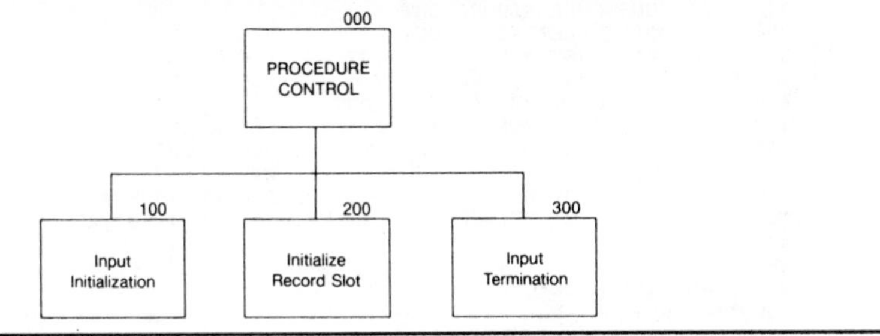

Figure 19.4 *Continued* Relative File Priming Operation (Pseudocode)

```
START
    DO Input Initialization
    DO Initialize record slots
        VARYING customer location UNTIL > 60
    DO Input termination
END

INPUT INITIALIZATION
    OPEN output file
    MOVE spaces to output
END

INITIALIZE RECORD SLOTS
    WRITE output
END

INPUT TERMINATION
    CLOSE file
END
```

Figure 19.4 *Continued* Relative File Priming Operation

```
           1   1   2   2   2   3   3   4   4   4   5   5   6   6   6   7
   4   8   2   6   0   4   8   2   6   0   4   8   2   6   0   4   8   2

      ***************************************************************
       IDENTIFICATION DIVISION.
      ***************************************************************
       PROGRAM-ID.    RELATIVE-ACCESS-PRIME.
       AUTHOR.        JOHN WINDSOR.
       DATE-WRITTEN.  JANUARY 1, 1989.
       DATE-COMPILED. JANUARY 1, 1989.
      *    The purpose of this procedure is to pre-allocate space
      *    for a relative file.  60 record slots are made available
      *    and filled with spaces.
      ***************************************************************
       ENVIRONMENT DIVISION.
      ***************************************************************
      *-------------------------------------------------------------*
       CONFIGURATION SECTION.
      *-------------------------------------------------------------*
       SOURCE-COMPUTER. IBM.
       OBJECT-COMPUTER. IBM.
       SPECIAL-NAMES.
                        C01 IS TOP-OF-PAGE.
      *-------------------------------------------------------------*
       INPUT-OUTPUT SECTION.
      *-------------------------------------------------------------*
       FILE-CONTROL.
           SELECT CUSTOMER-OUT-FILE ASSIGN TO DA-R-OUTPUT
               NOMINAL KEY IS CUSTOMER-DATA-SEQUENCE
               ACCESS IS SEQUENTIAL.
      ***************************************************************
       DATA DIVISION.
      ***************************************************************
      *-------------------------------------------------------------*
       FILE SECTION.
      *-------------------------------------------------------------*
       FD  CUSTOMER-OUT-FILE
           LABEL RECORDS ARE STANDARD
           RECORD CONTAINS 125 CHARACTERS.
       01  CUSTOMER-RECORD-OUT.
           05  DELETE-BYTE-OUT            PIC X(01).
           05  CUSTOMER-NUMBER-OUT        PIC X(10).
           05  CUSTOMER-NAME-OUT          PIC X(30).
           05  CUSTOMER-ADDRESS-OUT       PIC X(30).
           05  CUSTOMER-CITY-OUT          PIC X(20).
           05  CUSTOMER-STATE-OUT         PIC X(02).
           05  CUSTOMER-ZIP-OUT           PIC X(10).
           05  CUSTOMER-BALANCE-OUT       PIC S9(09)V99.
           05  CUSTOMER-CREDIT-LIMIT-OUT PIC S9(09)V99.

      *-------------------------------------------------------------*
       WORKING-STORAGE SECTION.
      *-------------------------------------------------------------*
```

Figure 19.4 *Continued* Relative File Priming Operation

```
            1   1   2   2   2   3   3   4   4   4   5   5   6   6   6   7
    4   8   2   6   0   4   8   2   6   0   4   8   2   6   0   4   8   2

        01  WORKING-VARIABLES.
            05  CUSTOMER-RECORD-LOCATION PIC 9(08) COMP.
       *****************************************************************
        PROCEDURE DIVISION.
       *****************************************************************
       *---------------------------------------------------------------*
        000-CREATION-CONTROL SECTION.
       *---------------------------------------------------------------*
            PERFORM 100-INPUT-INITIALIZATION.
            PERFORM 200-INITIALIZE-RECORD-SLOTS
               VARYING CUSTOMER-RECORD-LOCATION FROM 1 BY 1
                UNTIL CUSTOMER-RECORD-LOCATION > 60.
            PERFORM 160-INPUT-TERMINATION.
            STOP RUN.
       *---------------------------------------------------------------*
        100-INPUT-INITIALIZATION SECTION.
       *---------------------------------------------------------------*
            OPEN OUTPUT CUSTOMER-OUT-FILE.
            MOVE SPACES TO CUSTOMER-RECORD-OUT.
       *---------------------------------------------------------------*
        200-INITIALIZE-RECORD-SLOTS SECTION.
       *---------------------------------------------------------------*
            WRITE CUSTOMER-RECORD-OUT.
       *---------------------------------------------------------------*
        160-INPUT-TERMINATION SECTION.
       *---------------------------------------------------------------*
            CLOSE CUSTOMER-OUT-FILE.
```

Building a Relative File

Once the relative file has been primed, the programmer may proceed to place records in the file. In Figure 19.5, the relative file is called CUSTOMER-OUT-FILE (line 260). Notice the NOMINAL KEY identifier is CUSTOMER-RECORD-LOCATION and that ACCESS IS RANDOM for this file. Thus records will be placed in this file in a random order based on the value of CUSTOMER-RECORD-LOCATION.

Figure 19.5 Relative File Building and Addition Operation (System Flowchart)

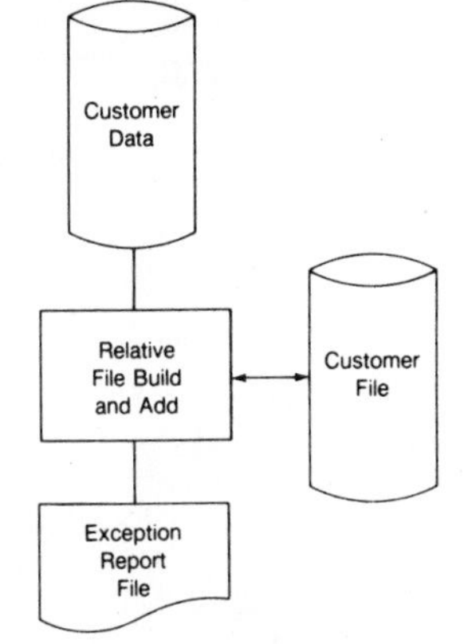

Based on the data in the CUSTOMER-IN-FILE, there is one minor problem: No single numeric field uniquely identifies a record. In previous illustrations of the use of this file, the customer number was used to address individual records, and it contains alphanumeric data. However, relative files require the use of a numeric field to identify record locations.

To overcome this problem, you must ''play a trick'' on the computer. First, notice that CUSTOMER-RECORD-LOCATION is a binary, numeric data item and is subordinate to CUSTOMER-NUMBER-GROUP (lines 740–750). Next, notice that a MOVE statement (line 0000) places the value of CUSTOMER-NUMBER-IN into CUSTOMER-NUMBER-GROUP. Since CUSTOMER-RECORD-LOCATION is subordinate to CUSTOMER-NUMBER-GROUP, it also receives the same data value. The next operation (the DIVIDE statement in line 1460 of the PROCEDURE DIVISION) would, on first glance, cause an error. That is, the MOVE statement caused alphanumeric data to be placed into CUSTOMER-RECORD-LOCATION. However, an examination of the output from this procedure indicates the program obviously works. What has happened is that the data placed with CUSTOMER-RECORD-LOCATION are viewed as binary. All data, including alphanumeric data, exist within internal storage as a binary pattern. Thus, the MOVE statement effectively ''converts'' the alphanumeric

Figure 19.5 *Continued* Relative File Building and Addition Operation (Hierarchy Chart)

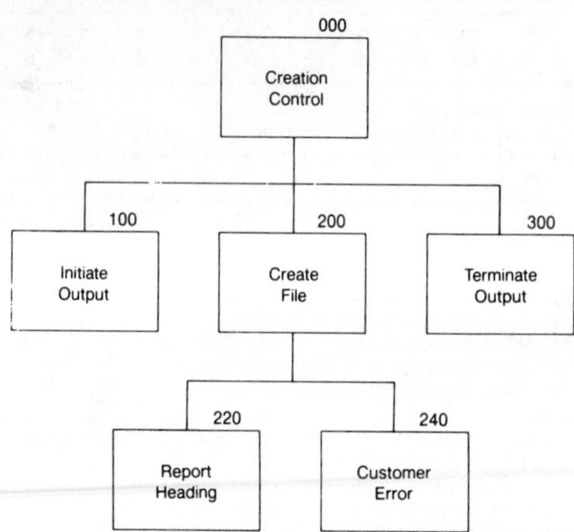

Figure 19.5 *Continued* Relative File Building and Addition Operation (Pseudocode)

```
START
    DO Initiate output
    DO Create file UNTIL eof
    DO Terminate output
END

INITIATE OUTPUT
    OPEN files
    SET file status
    MOVE 99 to record location
    READ Customer in
    IF eof
         SET file status
    ENDIF
END

CREATE FILE
    IF line number > 40
         DO Report heading
    ENDIF
    MOVE customer number to customer group
    DIVIDE customer sequence by 53
         GIVING digits
         REMAINDER record location
    MOVE record location to customer sequence
    READ customre out
    IF invalid key
         SET io status
    ENDIF
    IF customer number out not = spaces
         DO Customer error
    ELSE
         ADD 1 to customer count
         REWRITE output
    ENDIF
    READ customer in
    IF eof
         SET file status
    ENDIF
END

REPORT HEADING
    ADD 1 to page number
    WRITE output
    MOVE 0 to line number
END

CUSTOMER ERROR
    ADD 1 to error count
    MOVE input to output
    WRITE output
    ADD 1 to line number
END

TERMINATE OUTPUT
    MOVE counts to output
    WRITE output summary
    CLOSE files
END
```

Figure 19.5 *Continued* Relative File Building and Addition Operation

```
        1   1   2   2   2   3   3   4   4   4   5   5   6   6   6   7
4   8   2   6   0   4   8   2   6   0   4   8   2   6   0   4   8   2
-------------------------------------------------------------------------
*****************************************************************
 IDENTIFICATION DIVISION.
*****************************************************************
 PROGRAM-ID.     RELATIVE-ACCESS-BUILD-ADD.
 AUTHOR.         JOHN WINDSOR.
 DATE-WRITTEN.   JANUARY 1, 1989.
 DATE-COMPILED.  JANUARY 1, 1989.
*    The purpose of this procedure is to place customer
*    records into a relative file in a random sequence and to
*    determine whether or not the output operation is
*    successful, i.e. if the record location is vacant.
*****************************************************************
 ENVIRONMENT DIVISION.
*****************************************************************
*---------------------------------------------------------------*
 CONFIGURATION SECTION.
*---------------------------------------------------------------*
 SOURCE-COMPUTER. IBM.
 OBJECT-COMPUTER. IBM.
 SPECIAL-NAMES.    C01 IS TOP-OF-PAGE.
*---------------------------------------------------------------*
 INPUT-OUTPUT SECTION.
*---------------------------------------------------------------*
 FILE-CONTROL.
     SELECT CUSTOMER-IN-FILE      ASSIGN TO UT-S-INPUT.
     SELECT CUSTOMER-OUT-FILE     ASSIGN TO DA-R-OUTPUT2
         NOMINAL KEY IS CUSTOMER-RECORD-LOCATION
         ACCESS IS RANDOM.
     SELECT EXCEPTION-REPORT-FILE ASSIGN TO UT-S-OUTPUT.
*****************************************************************
 DATA DIVISION.
*****************************************************************
*---------------------------------------------------------------*
 FILE SECTION.
*---------------------------------------------------------------*
 FD  CUSTOMER-IN-FILE
     LABEL RECORDS ARE STANDARD
     RECORD CONTAINS 124 CHARACTERS
     BLOCK CONTAINS 0 RECORDS.
 01  CUSTOMER-RECORD-IN.
     05  CUSTOMER-NUMBER-IN        PIC X(10).
     05  FILLER                    PIC X(114).

 FD  CUSTOMER-OUT-FILE
     LABEL RECORDS ARE STANDARD
     RECORD CONTAINS 125 CHARACTERS.
 01  CUSTOMER-RECORD-OUT.
     05  DELETE-BYTE-OUT           PIC X(01).
     05  CUSTOMER-NUMBER-OUT       PIC X(10).
     05  CUSTOMER-NAME-OUT         PIC X(30).
     05  CUSTOMER-ADDRESS-OUT      PIC X(30).
     05  CUSTOMER-CITY-OUT         PIC X(20).
     05  CUSTOMER-STATE-OUT        PIC X(02).
     05  CUSTOMER-ZIP-OUT          PIC X(10).
     05  CUSTOMER-BALANCE-OUT      PIC S9(09)V99.
     05  CUSTOMER-CREDIT-LIMIT-OUT PIC S9(09)V99.

 FD  EXCEPTION-REPORT-FILE
     LABEL RECORDS ARE OMITTED.
 01  REPORT-RECORD                     PIC X(133).
*---------------------------------------------------------------*
 WORKING-STORAGE SECTION.
*---------------------------------------------------------------*
 01  WORKING-VARIABLES.
     05  FILE-STATUS               PIC X(04) VALUE SPACES.
     05  IO-STATUS                 PIC X(20) VALUE SPACES.
     05  LINE-NUMBER-WS            PIC 9(02) VALUE 99.
     05  PAGE-NUMBER-WS            PIC 9(02) VALUE ZERO.
     05  ERROR-COUNT-WS            PIC 9(04) VALUE ZERO.
```

Figure 19.5 *Continued* Relative File Building and Addition Operation

```
       1   1   2   2   2   3   3   4   4   4   5   5   6   6   6   7
4  8   2   6   0   4   8   2   6   0   4   8   2   6   0   4   8   2
-------------------------------------------------------------------
           05  CUSTOMER-COUNT-WS         PIC 9(04) VALUE ZERO.
           05  INPUT-OUTPUT-RECORD.
               10  FILLER                PIC X(01) VALUE SPACES.
               10  RECORD-CONTENTS       PIC X(124).
           05  CUSTOMER-NUMBER-GROUP.
               10  CUSTOMER-DATA-SEQUENCE PIC 9(08) COMP.
           05  RECORD-LOCATION          PIC 9(02).
           05  UNWANTED-DIGITS          PIC 9(08).
       01  HEADING-1.
           05  FILLER                    PIC X(32) VALUE SPACES.
           05  FILLER                    PIC X(16) VALUE
                                         'Exception Report'.
           05  FILLER                    PIC X(64) VALUE SPACES.
           05  FILLER                    PIC X(05) VALUE 'Page'.
           05  PAGE-NUMBER-OUT           PIC Z9.
       01  HEADING-2.
           05  FILLER                    PIC X(20) VALUE
                                         ' Customer Number'.
           05  FILLER                    PIC X(20) VALUE
                                         'Comments'.
       01  HEADING-3.
           05  FILLER                    PIC X(01) VALUE SPACES.
           05  FILLER                    PIC X(120) VALUE ALL '-'.
       01  ERROR-LINE.
           05  FILLER                    PIC X(02) VALUE SPACES.
           05  CUSTOMER-NUMBER-ERROR     PIC X(10).
           05  FILLER                    PIC X(08) VALUE SPACES.
           05  FILLER                    PIC X(50) VALUE
               'Location Duplicate Encountered--Record ELIMINATED'.
           05  FILLER                    PIC X(05) VALUE SPACES.
           05  FILLER                    PIC X(19) VALUE
                                         'Location Reference'.
           05  RECORD-LOCATION-OUT       PIC Z9.
           05  FILLER                    PIC X(10) VALUE
                                         ' Contains'.
           05  CUSTOMER-NUMBER-GOOD      PIC 9(10).
       01  SUMMARY-LINE.
           05  FILLER                    PIC X(01) VALUE SPACES.
           05  CUSTOMER-COUNT-OUT        PIC *,**9.
           05  FILLER                    PIC X(27) VALUE
                                         ' Customer Records Written--'.
           05  ERROR-COUNT-OUT           PIC *,**9.
           05  FILLER                    PIC X(25) VALUE
                                         ' Duplicates Encountered'.
      ****************************************************************
       PROCEDURE DIVISION.
      ****************************************************************
      *--------------------------------------------------------------*
       000-CREATION-CONTROL SECTION.
      *--------------------------------------------------------------*
           PERFORM 100-INITIATE-OUTPUT.
           PERFORM 200-CREATE-FILE
               UNTIL FILE-STATUS = 'DONE'.
           PERFORM 300-TERMINATE-OUTPUT.
           STOP RUN.
      *--------------------------------------------------------------*
       100-INITIATE-OUTPUT SECTION.
      *--------------------------------------------------------------*
           OPEN INPUT  CUSTOMER-IN-FILE
                I-O    CUSTOMER-OUT-FILE
                OUTPUT EXCEPTION-REPORT-FILE.
           MOVE SPACES         TO FILE-STATUS.
           MOVE 99             TO RECORD-LOCATION.
           READ CUSTOMER-IN-FILE INTO RECORD-CONTENTS
```

Figure 19.5 *Continued* Relative File Building and Addition Operation

```
           AT END MOVE 'DONE' TO FILE-STATUS.
      *-----------------------------------------------------------*
       200-CREATE-FILE SECTION.
      *-----------------------------------------------------------*
           IF LINE-NUMBER-WS IS GREATER THAN 40
               PERFORM 220-REPORT-HEADING.
           MOVE CUSTOMER-NUMBER-IN TO CUSTOMER-NUMBER-GROUP.
           DIVIDE CUSTOMER-DATA-SEQUENCE BY 53
               GIVING UNWANTED-DIGITS
               REMAINDER RECORD-LOCATION.
           MOVE RECORD-LOCATION TO CUSTOMER-DATA-SEQUENCE.
           READ CUSTOMER-OUT-FILE
               INVALID KEY MOVE 'Invalid I/O Attempt' TO IO-STATUS.
           IF CUSTOMER-NUMBER-OUT NOT = SPACES
               PERFORM 240-CUSTOMER-ERROR
           ELSE
               ADD 1 TO CUSTOMER-COUNT-WS
               REWRITE CUSTOMER-RECORD-OUT FROM INPUT-OUTPUT-RECORD.
           READ CUSTOMER-IN-FILE INTO RECORD-CONTENTS
               AT END MOVE 'DONE' TO FILE-STATUS.
      *-----------------------------------------------------------*
       220-REPORT-HEADING SECTION.
      *-----------------------------------------------------------*
           ADD 1 TO PAGE-NUMBER-WS.
           MOVE PAGE-NUMBER-WS      TO PAGE-NUMBER-OUT.
           WRITE REPORT-RECORD FROM HEADING-1
               AFTER ADVANCING TOP-OF-PAGE.
           WRITE REPORT-RECORD FROM HEADING-2 AFTER ADVANCING 3 LINES.
           WRITE REPORT-RECORD FROM HEADING-3 AFTER ADVANCING 1 LINES.
           MOVE SPACES              TO REPORT-RECORD.
           WRITE REPORT-RECORD AFTER ADVANCING 1 LINES.
           MOVE 0                   TO LINE-NUMBER-WS.
      *-----------------------------------------------------------*
       240-CUSTOMER-ERROR SECTION.
      *-----------------------------------------------------------*
           ADD 1 TO ERROR-COUNT-WS.
           MOVE CUSTOMER-NUMBER-IN TO CUSTOMER-NUMBER-ERROR.
           MOVE CUSTOMER-NUMBER-OUT TO CUSTOMER-NUMBER-GOOD.
           MOVE RECORD-LOCATION TO RECORD-LOCATION-OUT.
           WRITE REPORT-RECORD FROM ERROR-LINE AFTER ADVANCING 1 LINES.
           ADD 1 TO LINE-NUMBER-WS.
      *-----------------------------------------------------------*
       300-TERMINATE-OUTPUT SECTION.
      *-----------------------------------------------------------*
           MOVE ERROR-COUNT-WS      TO ERROR-COUNT-OUT.
           MOVE CUSTOMER-COUNT-WS   TO CUSTOMER-COUNT-OUT.
           WRITE REPORT-RECORD FROM SUMMARY-LINE
               AFTER ADVANCING 2 LINES.
           CLOSE EXCEPTION-REPORT-FILE
                 CUSTOMER-OUT-FILE
                 CUSTOMER-IN-FILE.
```

Figure 19.5 *Continued* Relative File Building and Addition Operations [Customer-IN] (Data)

```
                                                                                                 1         1         1 |
      |         1         2         3         4         5         6         7         8         9         0         1         2 |
Record|12345678901234567890123456789012345678901234567890123456789012345678901234567890123456789012345678901234567890123456789012345|
-------------------------------------------------------------------------------------------------------------------------------------
     1|4412X47390Marshall Silverman          2219 West 7th Street     Cleveland          OH30119   0000000000000000500000|
     2|3199127X33James Thompkins             44339 South Wacker Drive Chicago            IL60606   0000002291800000500000|
     3|1141944103Edwin Williams              2139 South Colgate Street Perryton          TX79070   0000033193300035000000|
     4|6213937661Jason Madison               8831 Cedar Drive N.W.    Norwich            CN00218   0000041452300003000000|
     5|5270215827Charles Everest             8821 Ocean Parkway       Miami              FL51332   0000000000000000500000|
     6|3333333333Julia Harriston             6132 Mill Road Avenue    Shreveport         LA63341   0000035134300005000000|
     7|3498966451Jacob R. Sullivan           6134 Malibu Drive        Los Angeles        CA96512   0000000000000004400000|
     8|1RX14219-3John P. Villiman            8887 Peach Tree Lane     Dallas             TX75002   0000000314300000500000|
     9|6427633-94Mark U. Lemon               P. O. Box 51244          New York           NY03158   0000000000000000005000|
    10|773194221BHelen B. Overstreet        3153 Yellow Brick Road   Yellow Stone Park  MT41229   0000001284200000000000|
    11|9XO-334RDSAnthony P. Jones            Executive Office Building Washington        DC00000   0000000000000000000000|
    12|3333333333Raymond J. Taylor           912 Dusty Road           Plains             GA39100   0000052353600010000000|
```

Figure 19.5 *Continued* Relative File Building and Addition Operation [Customer-OUT] (Data)

```
-------------------------------------------------------------------------------------------------------------------------------------
|      |                                                                                                   1         1         1     |
|      |         1         2         3         4         5         6         7         8         9         0         1         2     |
|Record|12345678901234567890123456789012345678901234567890123456789012345678901234567890123456789012345678901234567890123456789012345|
|-----------------------------------------------------------------------------------------------------------------------------------|
|     1|                                                                                                                             |
|     2|                                                                                                                             |
|     3|                                                                                                                             |
|     4|                                                                                                                             |
|     5|                                                                                                                             |
|     6|                                                                                                                             |
|     7|                                                                                                                             |
|     8|                                                                                                                             |
|     9|                                                                                                                             |
|    10|                                                                                                                             |
|    11|                                                                                                                             |
|    12|                                                                                                                             |
|    13|                                                                                                                             |
|    14|1141944103Edwin Williams                2139 South Colgate Street     Perryton            TX79070     000003319330003500000|
|    15|5270215827Charles Everest               8821 Ocean Parkway            Miami               FL51332     000000000000000500000|
|    16|                                                                                                                             |
|    17|                                                                                                                             |
|    18|                                                                                                                             |
|    19|                                                                                                                             |
|    20|                                                                                                                             |
|    21|                                                                                                                             |
|    22|4412X47390Marshall Silverman            2219 West 7th Street          Cleveland           OH30119     000000000000000500000|
|    23|                                                                                                                             |
|    24|773194221BHelen B. Overstreet           3153 Yellow Brick Road        Yellow Stone Park   MT41229     000000128420000000000|
|    25|3199127X33James Thompkins               44339 South Wacker Drive      Chicago             IL60606     000000229180000500000|
|    26|                                                                                                                             |
|    27|3333333333Julia Harriston               6132 Mill Road Avenue         Shreveport          LA63341     000003513430000500000|
|    28|                                                                                                                             |
|    29|                                                                                                                             |
|    30|                                                                                                                             |
|    31|                                                                                                                             |
|    32|                                                                                                                             |
|    33|                                                                                                                             |
|    34|9XO-334RDSAnthony P. Jones              Executive Office Building     Washington          DC00000     000000000000000000000|
|    35|                                                                                                                             |
|    36|                                                                                                                             |
|    37|                                                                                                                             |
|    38|                                                                                                                             |
|    39|1RX14219-3John P. Villiman              8887 Peach Tree Lane          Dallas              TX75002     000000031430000500000|
|    40|                                                                                                                             |
|    41|                                                                                                                             |
|    42|                                                                                                                             |
|    43|                                                                                                                             |
|    44|                                                                                                                             |
|    45|                                                                                                                             |
|    46|                                                                                                                             |
|    47|                                                                                                                             |
|    48|3498966451Jacob R. Sullivan             6134 Malibu Drive             Los Angeles         CA96512     000000000000000440000|
|    49|                                                                                                                             |
|    50|                                                                                                                             |
|    51|6213937661Jason Madison                 8831 Cedar Drive N.W.         Norwich             CN00218     000004145230000300000|
|    52|                                                                                                                             |
|    53|6427633-94Mark U. Lemon                 P. O. Box 51244               New York            NY03158     000000000000000005000|
-------------------------------------------------------------------------------------------------------------------------------------
```

data in CUSTOMER-NUMBER-IN into a numeric value when addressed as CUSTOMER-RECORD-LOCATION. One word of caution. A numeric field that is described as a eight-digit binary data item is only four bytes in length. Thus, it is necessary for the first four characters of the customer number to identify the record uniquely. Also, alphanumeric data placed into a binary field will result in a negative value. Since CUSTOMER-RECORD-LOCATION is unsigned, all data referenced by this identifier are assumed to be positive. See Chapter 23 for further details.

Figure 19.5 *Continued* Relative File Building and Addition Operation (Output)

```
                                   Exception Report                                                     Page  1

Customer Number    Comments
----------------------------------------------------------------------------------------------------------------

 3333333333          Location Duplicate Encountered--Record ELIMINATED       Location Reference 26 Contains 3333333333

***11 Customer Records Written--****1 Duplicates Encountered
```

Now, examine the logic of the building process. First, it should be noticed that the CUSTOMER-OUT-FILE is opened in an input-output mode. Thus, the program may both read from and write to the CUSTOMER-OUT-FILE. This is important because the program must first check a record location to determine whether or not it is currently in use. That is, when a record location is identified, the program reads the record in that location. If the location contains blanks, it is considered available for use. Otherwise, a record already exists in that location. Within the 200-CREATE-FILE procedure (lines 1410–1580), the record location is determined (lines 1450–1480). Notice that the DIVIDE statement employs the numeric literal 53 in the data-to-address transformation function. This value was selected because larger prime numbers between 53 and 60 tend to produce a greater number of synonyms based on the data used. Once the record location has been determined, the record at that address is read (line 1500). Provided a record is retrieved (e.g., the data-to-address transformation function has not generated a value less than zero or greater than 60), the record at that position is examined for spaces. If the customer number is blank, the record position is currently unused and the new record is written to that position (line 1520). Otherwise, the record position is currently in use and an error message is produced. Finally, the next record from the customer input file is read and the process is repeated until the end of the input file is reached.

It should be noted that on the basis of the number of records actually placed in the file, the file space is somewhat sparsely populated with customer records. This should allow a rather large number of additions at a later time. However, if you are sequentially reading the file, provisions should be made to bypass any record that contains blanks.

Updating a Relative File

A random update of a relative file is logically no different from the random update of an indexed file. Thus, records are read from the input file (CUSTOMER-SALES-FILE) and, based on the customer number in the transaction, the appropriate customer record is retrieved from the CUSTOMER-IO-FILE. Notice that in Figure 19.6 the NOMINAL KEY is defined as before (line 280 and lines 750–760) and ACCESS IS RANDOM (line 290). In the PROCEDURE DIVISION, the customer master file is opened in an input-output mode (line 1280) and the transaction is read (lines 1360–1380). The customer number from the transaction is moved to CUSTOMER-NUMBER-GROUP, as in the building operation. Once some preliminary operations have been completed to set up the printed output record, the record location is calculated (lines 1700–1760). It is vital to understand that *once a data-to-address transformation function has been specified,*

Figure 19.6 Relative File Update Operation (System Flowchart)

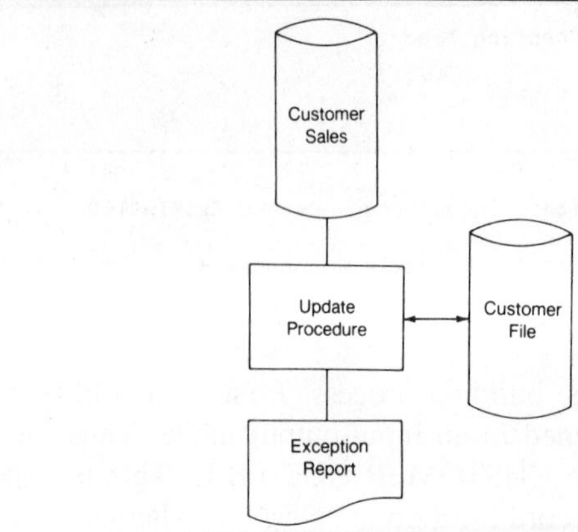

such as in the building program, *all other programs that retrieve data from the same relative file in a random access mode must utilize the same data-to-address transformation function*. That is, once a procedure has been established to place records into a relative file, the same procedure must be used to retrieve records from that file. Otherwise, ''finding'' the desired record will be an extremely difficult process.

Once the record location has been determined, a READ statement (lines 1470–1480) retrieves a record from the file. However, there is no guarantee the record retrieved from that location is the correct record. Thus, it is necessary to determine whether the customer numbers match (line 1500) before proceeding with the update activity. If a

Figure 19.6 *Continued* Relative File Update Operation (Hierarchy Chart)

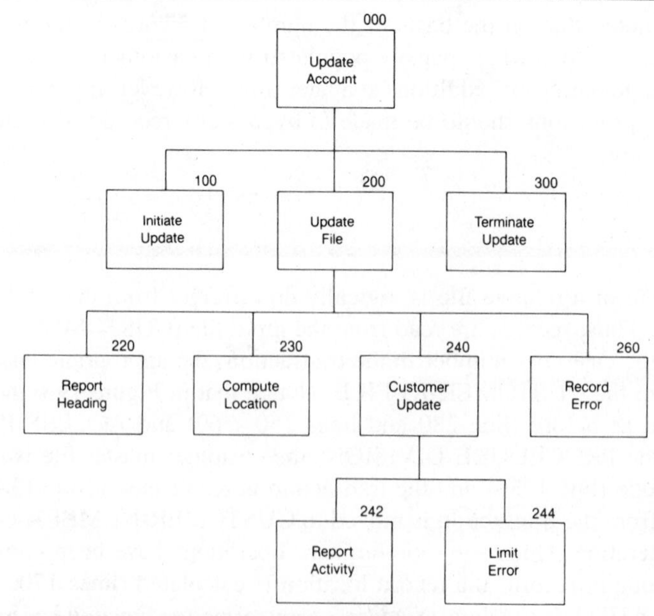

Figure 19.6 *Continued* Relative File Update Operation (Pseudocode)

```
START
    DO Initiate update
    DO Update file UNTIL eof
    DO Terminate update
END

INITIATE UPDATE
    OPEN files
END

UPDATE FILE
    IF line number > 40
         DO Report heading
    ENDIF
    READ customer sales
    IF eof
         SET file status
         GOTO end
    ENDIF
    MOVE input to output
    SET input status
    DO Compute location
    READ Customer file
    IF invalid key
         SET input status
    ENDIF
    IF input status = found and
       customer numbers are equal
         DO Customer update
    ELSE
         DO Record error
    ENDIF
END

REPORT HEADING
    ADD 1 to page number
    MOVE 0 to line number
    WRITE headings
END

COMPUTE LOCATION
    SET output status
    DIVIDE record location by 53 giving
      digits REMAINDER location
    MOVE location to customer location
END

CUSTOMER UPDATE
    IF balance + purchase > credit limit
         DO Limit error
    ELSE
         ADD purchase to balance
         DO Report activity
END

REPORT ACTIVITY
    MOVE message to output
    REWRITE customer
    IF invalid key
      MOVE message to output
    ENDIF
    WRITE output
    ADD 1 to line number
END

LIMIT ERROR
    MOVE message to output
    WRITE output
    ADD 1 to line number
END

RECORD ERROR
    MOVE message to output
    WRITE error lines
    ADD 5 to line number
END

TERMINATE UPDATE
    CLOSE files
END
```

Figure 19.6 *Continued* Relative File Update Operation

```
*****************************************************************
 IDENTIFICATION DIVISION.
*****************************************************************
 PROGRAM-ID.     RELATIVE-ACCESS-UPDATE.
 AUTHOR.         J. WAYNE SPENCE.
 DATE-WRITTEN.   JANUARY 1, 1989.
 DATE-COMPILED.  JANUARY 1, 1989.
*     The purpose of this procedure is to update an existing
*     relative file (CUSTOMER) on the basis of information
*     contained in a sales file.  Mulitple updates per customer
*     records are permitted (in random order) and customer updates
*     (sales records) without a corresponding customer record are
*     identified.
*****************************************************************
 ENVIRONMENT DIVISION.
*****************************************************************
*---------------------------------------------------------------*
 CONFIGURATION SECTION.
*---------------------------------------------------------------*
```

Figure 19.6 *Continued* Relative File Update Operation

```
           1   1   2   2   2   3   3   4   4   4   5   5   6   6   6   7
   4   8   2   6   0   4   8   2   6   0   4   8   2   6   0   4   8   2

        SOURCE-COMPUTER. IBM.
        OBJECT-COMPUTER. IBM.
        SPECIAL-NAMES.   C01 IS TOP-OF-PAGE.
       *------------------------------------------------------------*
        INPUT-OUTPUT SECTION.
       *------------------------------------------------------------*
        FILE-CONTROL.
            SELECT CUSTOMER-IO-FILE      ASSIGN TO DA-R-INOUT
                NOMINAL KEY IS CUSTOMER-LOCATION-WS
                ACCESS IS RANDOM.
            SELECT CUSTOMER-SALES-FILE   ASSIGN TO UT-S-INPUT.
            SELECT EXCEPTION-REPORT-FILE ASSIGN TO UT-S-OUTPUT.
       **************************************************************
        DATA DIVISION.
       **************************************************************
       *------------------------------------------------------------*
        FILE SECTION.
       *------------------------------------------------------------*
        FD  CUSTOMER-IO-FILE
            LABEL RECORDS ARE STANDARD
            RECORD CONTAINS 125 CHARACTERS.
        01  CUSTOMER-RECORD.
            05  DELETE-CODE                PIC X(01).
            05  CUSTOMER-NUMBER-IO         PIC X(10).
            05  CUSTOMER-NAME-IO           PIC X(30).
            05  CUSTOMER-ADDRESS-IO        PIC X(30).
            05  CUSTOMER-CITY-IO           PIC X(20).
            05  CUSTOMER-STATE-IO          PIC X(02).
            05  CUSTOMER-ZIP-IO            PIC X(10).
            05  CUSTOMER-BALANCE-IO        PIC S9(09)V99.
            05  CUSTOMER-CREDIT-LIMIT-IO PIC S9(09)V99.

        FD  CUSTOMER-SALES-FILE
            LABEL RECORDS ARE STANDARD
            RECORD CONTAINS 80 CHARACTERS
            BLOCK CONTAINS 0 RECORDS.
        01  SALES-RECORD.
            05  CUSTOMER-NUMBER-SALES      PIC X(10).
            05  DATE-OF-PURCHASE-SALES.
                10  PURCHASE-MONTH-SALES PIC X(02).
                10  PURCHASE-DAY-SALES   PIC X(02).
                10  PURCHASE-YEAR-SALES  PIC X(02).
            05  PURCHASE-ITEM-SALES        PIC X(10).
            05  PURCHASE-AMOUNT-SALES      PIC S9(09)V99.
            05  FILLER                     PIC X(43).

        FD  EXCEPTION-REPORT-FILE
            LABEL RECORDS ARE OMITTED.
        01  REPORT-RECORD                    PIC X(133).
       *------------------------------------------------------------*
        WORKING-STORAGE SECTION.
       *------------------------------------------------------------*
        01  WORKING-VARIABLES.
            05  FILE-STATUS                PIC X(04) VALUE SPACES.
            05  INPUT-STATUS               PIC X(10) VALUE SPACES.
            05  CUSTOMER-NUMBER-WS.
                10  CUSTOMER-LOCATION-WS  PIC 9(08) COMP.
            05  RECORD-LOCATION-WS         PIC 9(09).
            05  UNWANTED-DIGITS-WS         PIC 9(09).
            05  OUTPUT-STATUS              PIC X(10).
            05  LINE-NUMBER-WS             PIC 9(02) VALUE 99.
            05  PAGE-NUMBER-WS             PIC 9(02) VALUE ZERO.

        01  HEADING-1.
            05  FILLER                     PIC X(32) VALUE SPACES.
            05  FILLER                     PIC X(16) VALUE
                                           'Exception Report'.
            05  FILLER                     PIC X(25) VALUE SPACES.
            05  FILLER                     PIC X(05) VALUE 'Page'.
            05  PAGE-NUMBER-OUT            PIC Z9.
```

Figure 19.6 *Continued* Relative File Update Operation

```
            1   1   2   2   2   3   3   4   4   4   5   5   6   6   6   7
    4   8   2   6   0   4   8   2   6   0   4   8   2   6   0   4   8   2
-----------------------------------------------------------------------------

 01  HEADING-2.
     05  FILLER                  PIC X(20) VALUE
                                 ' Customer Number'.
     05  FILLER                  PIC X(50) VALUE
         '  Date      Purchase Amount     Comments'.

 01  HEADING-3.
     05  FILLER                  PIC X(01) VALUE SPACES.
     05  FILLER                  PIC X(80) VALUE ALL '-'.

 01  ERROR-LINE.
     05  FILLER                  PIC X(02) VALUE SPACES.
     05  CUSTOMER-NUMBER-OUT     PIC X(10).
     05  FILLER                  PIC X(08) VALUE SPACES.
     05  PURCHASE-MONTH-OUT      PIC X(02).
     05  FILLER                  PIC X(01) VALUE '/'.
     05  PURCHASE-DAY-OUT        PIC X(02).
     05  FILLER                  PIC X(01) VALUE '/'.
     05  PURCHASE-YEAR-OUT       PIC X(02).
     05  FILLER                  PIC X(05) VALUE SPACES.
     05  PURCHASE-AMOUNT-OUT     PIC ZZZ,ZZZ,ZZZ.ZZ.
     05  FILLER                  PIC X(05) VALUE SPACES.
     05  MESSAGE-OUT             PIC X(50) VALUE SPACES.
*****************************************************************
 PROCEDURE DIVISION.
*****************************************************************
*---------------------------------------------------------------*
 000-UPDATE-ACCOUNT SECTION.
*---------------------------------------------------------------*
     PERFORM 100-INITIATE-UPDATE.
     PERFORM 200-UPDATE-FILE
         UNTIL FILE-STATUS = 'DONE'.
     PERFORM 300-TERMINATE-UPDATE.
     STOP RUN.
*---------------------------------------------------------------*
 100-INITIATE-UPDATE SECTION.
*---------------------------------------------------------------*
     OPEN I-O CUSTOMER-IO-FILE
          INPUT CUSTOMER-SALES-FILE
          OUTPUT EXCEPTION-REPORT-FILE.
*---------------------------------------------------------------*
 200-UPDATE-FILE SECTION.
*---------------------------------------------------------------*
     IF LINE-NUMBER-WS IS GREATER THAN 40
        PERFORM 220-REPORT-HEADING.
     READ CUSTOMER-SALES-FILE
         AT END MOVE 'DONE' TO FILE-STATUS
                GO TO 299-EXIT.
     MOVE CUSTOMER-NUMBER-SALES TO CUSTOMER-NUMBER-OUT
                                   CUSTOMER-NUMBER-WS.
     MOVE PURCHASE-MONTH-SALES TO PURCHASE-MONTH-OUT.
     MOVE PURCHASE-DAY-SALES  TO PURCHASE-DAY-OUT.
     MOVE PURCHASE-YEAR-SALES TO PURCHASE-YEAR-OUT.
     MOVE PURCHASE-AMOUNT-SALES TO PURCHASE-AMOUNT-OUT.
     MOVE 'FOUND'             TO INPUT-STATUS.
     PERFORM 230-COMPUTE-LOCATION.
     READ CUSTOMER-IO-FILE
         INVALID KEY MOVE 'NOT FOUND' TO INPUT-STATUS.
     IF INPUT-STATUS = 'FOUND'
       AND CUSTOMER-NUMBER-SALES = CUSTOMER-NUMBER-IO
         PERFORM 240-CUSTOMER-UPDATE
     ELSE
         PERFORM 260-RECORD-ERROR.

 299-EXIT.
     EXIT.
```

Figure 19.6 *Continued* Relative File Update Operation (Pseudocode)

```
               1   1   2   2   2   3   3   4   4   4   5   5   6   6   6   7
   4   8   2   6   0   4   8   2   6   0   4   8   2   6   0   4   8   2
      *----------------------------------------------------------------*
       220-REPORT-HEADING SECTION.
      *----------------------------------------------------------------*
           ADD 1 TO PAGE-NUMBER-WS.
           MOVE PAGE-NUMBER-WS          TO PAGE-NUMBER-OUT.
           MOVE 0                       TO LINE-NUMBER-WS.
           WRITE REPORT-RECORD FROM HEADING-1
               AFTER ADVANCING TOP-OF-PAGE.
           WRITE REPORT-RECORD FROM HEADING-2 AFTER ADVANCING 2 LINES.
           WRITE REPORT-RECORD FROM HEADING-3 AFTER ADVANCING 1 LINES.
           MOVE SPACES                  TO REPORT-RECORD.
           WRITE REPORT-RECORD AFTER ADVANCING 1 LINES.
      *----------------------------------------------------------------*
       230-COMPUTE-LOCATION SECTION.
      *----------------------------------------------------------------*
           MOVE 'RECORDED'              TO OUTPUT-STATUS.
           DIVIDE CUSTOMER-RECORD-LOCATION BY 53
               GIVING UNWANTED-DIGITS-WS
               REMAINDER RECORD-LOCATION-WS.
           MOVE RECORD-LOCATION-WS TO CUSTOMER-LOCATION-WS.
      *----------------------------------------------------------------*
       240-CUSTOMER-UPDATE SECTION.
      *----------------------------------------------------------------*
           IF CUSTOMER-BALANCE-IO + PURCHASE-AMOUNT-SALES >
             CUSTOMER-CREDIT-LIMIT-IO
               PERFORM 244-LIMIT-ERROR
           ELSE
               ADD PURCHASE-AMOUNT-SALES TO CUSTOMER-BALANCE-IO
               PERFORM 242-REPORT-ACTIVITY.
      *----------------------------------------------------------------*
       242-REPORT-ACTIVITY SECTION.
      *----------------------------------------------------------------*
           MOVE 'Customer Record Updated' TO MESSAGE-OUT.
           REWRITE CUSTOMER-RECORD
               INVALID KEY MOVE 'Error--Record Not Updated' TO
                               MESSAGE-OUT.
           WRITE REPORT-RECORD FROM ERROR-LINE AFTER ADVANCING 1 LINES.
           ADD 1 TO LINE-NUMBER-WS.
      *----------------------------------------------------------------*
       244-LIMIT-ERROR SECTION.
      *----------------------------------------------------------------*
           MOVE 'Credit Limit Exceeded' TO MESSAGE-OUT.
           WRITE REPORT-RECORD FROM ERROR-LINE AFTER ADVANCING 1 LINES.
           ADD 1 TO LINE-NUMBER-WS.
      *----------------------------------------------------------------*
       260-RECORD-ERROR SECTION.
      *----------------------------------------------------------------*
           MOVE ALL '-'                 TO REPORT-RECORD.
           WRITE REPORT-RECORD AFTER ADVANCING 2 LINES.
           MOVE 'Customer Record Not Found' TO MESSAGE-OUT.
           WRITE REPORT-RECORD FROM ERROR-LINE AFTER ADVANCING 1 LINES.
           MOVE ALL '-'                 TO REPORT-RECORD.
           WRITE REPORT-RECORD AFTER ADVANCING 1 LINES.
           MOVE SPACES                  TO REPORT-RECORD.
           WRITE REPORT-RECORD AFTER ADVANCING 1 LINES.
           ADD 5 TO LINE-NUMBER-WS.
      *----------------------------------------------------------------*
       300-TERMINATE-UPDATE SECTION.
      *----------------------------------------------------------------*
           CLOSE CUSTOMER-IO-FILE,
                 CUSTOMER-SALES-FILE
                 EXCEPTION-REPORT-FILE.
```

Figure 19.6 *Continued* Relative File Update Operation [CUSTOMER-SALES] (Data)

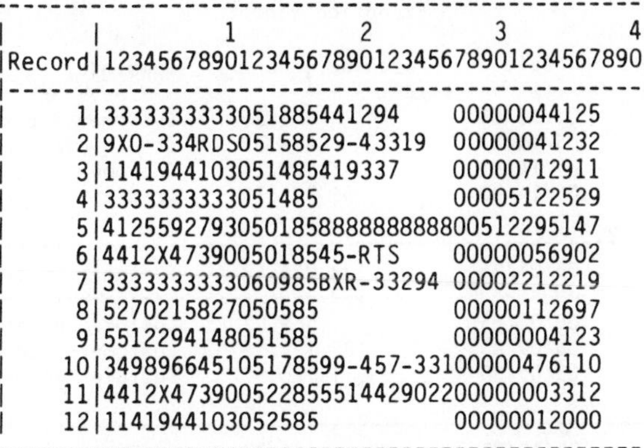

```
-------------------------------------------------
|      |         1         2         3         4|
|Record|1234567890123456789012345678901234567890|
|-----------------------------------------------|
|     1|33333333333051885441294     00000044125 |
|     2|9X0-334RDS05158529-43319    00000041232 |
|     3|11419441030514854l9337      00000712911 |
|     4|3333333333051485            00005122529 |
|     5|41255927930501858888888888800512295147  |
|     6|4412X4739005018545-RTS      00000056902 |
|     7|333333333306098 5BXR-33294  00002212219 |
|     8|5270215827050585            00000112697 |
|     9|5512294148051585            00000004123 |
|    10|349896645105178599-457-33100000476110   |
|    11|4412X4739005228555144290220000000 3312  |
|    12|1141944103052585            00000012000 |
-------------------------------------------------
```

Figure 19.6 *Continued* Relative File Update Operation [CUSTOMER-IO] (Data)

```
-----------------------------------------------------------------------------------------------------------------------------------
|                                                                                                       1         1         1     |
|      |         1         2         3         4         5         6         7         8         9         0         1         2     |
|Record|12345678901234567890123456789012345678901234567890123456789012345678901234567890123456789012345678901234567890123456789012345|
|---------------------------------------------------------------------------------------------------------------------------------|
|     1|                                                                                                                            |
|     2|                                                                                                                            |
|     3|                                                                                                                            |
|     4|                                                                                                                            |
|     5|                                                                                                                            |
|     6|                                                                                                                            |
|     7|                                                                                                                            |
|     8|                                                                                                                            |
|     9|                                                                                                                            |
|    10|                                                                                                                            |
|    11|                                                                                                                            |
|    12|                                                                                                                            |
|    13|                                                                                                                            |
|    14| 1141944103Edwin Williams               2139 South Colgate Street    Perryton            TX79070    0000105684D00035000000|
|    15| 5270215827Charles Everest              8821 Ocean Parkway           Miami               FL51332    0000011269G00000500000|
|    16|                                                                                                                            |
|    17|                                                                                                                            |
|    18|                                                                                                                            |
|    19|                                                                                                                            |
|    20|                                                                                                                            |
|    21|                                                                                                                            |
|    22| 4412X47390Marshall Silverman           2219 West 7th Street         Cleveland           OH30119    0000006021D00000500000|
|    23|                                                                                                                            |
|    24| 773194221BHelen B. Overstreet          3153 Yellow Brick Road       Yellow Stone Park   MT41229    0000001284200000000000|
|    25| 3199127X33James Thompkins              44339 South Wacker Drive     Chicago             IL60606    0000002291800000500000|
|    26|                                                                                                                            |
|    27| 3333333333Julia Harriston              6132 Mill Road Avenue        Shreveport          LA63341    0000260768G00005000000|
|    28|                                                                                                                            |
|    29|                                                                                                                            |
|    30|                                                                                                                            |
|    31|                                                                                                                            |
|    32|                                                                                                                            |
|    33|                                                                                                                            |
|    34| 9X0-334RDSAnthony P. Jones             Executive Office Building    Washington          DC00000    0000000000000000000000|
|    35|                                                                                                                            |
|    36|                                                                                                                            |
|    37|                                                                                                                            |
|    38|                                                                                                                            |
|    39| 1RX14219-3John P. Villiman             8887 Peach Tree Lane         Dallas              TX75002    0000000314300000500000|
|    40|                                                                                                                            |
|    41|                                                                                                                            |
|    42|                                                                                                                            |
|    43|                                                                                                                            |
|    44|                                                                                                                            |
|    45|                                                                                                                            |
|    46|                                                                                                                            |
|    47|                                                                                                                            |
|    48| 3498966451Jacob R. Sullivan            6134 Malibu Drive            Los Angeles         CA96512    0000047611 00004400000|
|    49|                                                                                                                            |
|    50|                                                                                                                            |
|    51| 6213937661Jason Madison                8831 Cedar Drive N.W.        Norwich             CT00218    0000041452300003000000|
|    52|                                                                                                                            |
|    53| 6427633-94Mark U. Lemon                P. O. Box 51244              New York            NY03158    0000000000000000005000|
-----------------------------------------------------------------------------------------------------------------------------------
```

Figure 19.6 *Continued* Relative File Update (Output)

Exception Report — Page 1

Customer Number	Date	Purchase Amount	Comments
3333333333	05/18/85	441.25	Customer Record Updated
9X0-334RDS	05/15/85	412.32	Credit Limit Exceeded
1141944103	05/14/85	7,129.11	Customer Record Updated
3333333333	05/14/85	51,225.29	Credit Limit Exceeded
4125592793	05/01/85	5,122,951.47	Customer Record Not Found
4412X47390	05/01/85	569.02	Customer Record Updated
3333333333	06/09/85	22,122.19	Customer Record Updated
5270215827	05/05/85	1,126.97	Customer Record Updated
5512294148	05/15/85	41.23	Customer Record Not Found
3498966451	05/17/85	4,761.10	Customer Record Updated
4412X47390	05/22/85	33.12	Customer Record Updated
1141944103	05/25/85	120.00	Customer Record Updated

record is retrieved and the customer numbers match, the update is performed (lines 1780–1850) and the record is (possibly) rewritten (line 1900). Otherwise, an error message is produced. Thus, although there are some procedural differences between a random update of an indexed file and the random update of a relative file, the sequence of (1) setting up the key value or location reference, (2) reading an existing record, and (3) rewriting the record are logically the same.

Adding Records to a Relative File

Based on the procedure used to create the relative file in Figures 19.4 and 19.5, the program presented in Figure 19.5 may also be used to add records to a relative file. The results shown in Figure 19.7 are produced by reexecuting the program shown in Figure 19.5 after the relative file has been built and updated. Thus, the program presented in Figure 19.5 may be viewed as a multipurpose procedure for building and adding records to a relative file.

Figure 19.7 Adding to a Relative File [CUSTOMER-ADDITION] (Data)

```
-----------------------------------------------------------------------------------------------------------------------------------
|                                                                                                             1         1         1 |
|      |        1         2         3         4         5         6         7         8         9         0         1         2 |
|Record|1234567890123456789012345678901234567890123456789012345678901234567890123456789012345678901234567890123456789012345678901234|
|----------------------------------------------------------------------------------------------------------------------------------|
|     1|3333333333George P. Martin              Las Vegas Hilton              Las Vegas          NV81222    99999999999000000000000|
|     2|2199428878Stewart A. Alexander          5112 Hamilton Parkway         Minneapolis        MN21132    00000622390000010000000|
|     3|5122314151Mark R. White                 55123 War Memorial Drive      Cleveland          OH41229    00000041233000000500000|
|     4|X14339-278Rober P. Evans                1422 N. W. Classen Blvd.      Oklahoma City      OK65124    00000000000000003000000|
-----------------------------------------------------------------------------------------------------------------------------------
```

Figure 19.7 *Continued* Adding to a Relative File [CUSTOMER-OUT] (Data)

```
--------------------------------------------------------------------------------------------------------------------------------------------
|      |                                                                                                   1         1         1  |
|      |         1         2         3         4         5         6         7         8         9         0         1         2  |
|Record|123456789012345678901234567890123456789012345678901234567890123456789012345678901234567890123456789012345678901234567890123456789012345|
|-------------------------------------------------------------------------------------------------------------------------------------------|
|     1|                                                                                                                            |
|     2|                                                                                                                            |
|     3|                                                                                                                            |
|     4|                                                                                                                            |
|     5|                                                                                                                            |
|     6|                                                                                                                            |
|     7|                                                                                                                            |
|     8|                                                                                                                            |
|     9|                                                                                                                            |
|    10|                                                                                                                            |
|    11|                                                                                                                            |
|    12|                                                                                                                            |
|    13|                                                                                                                            |
|    14| 1141944103Edwin Williams              2139 South Colgate Street    Perryton          TX79070     0000105684D000035000000|
|    15| 5270215827Charles Everest             8821 Ocean Parkway           Miami             FL51332     0000011269G00000500000|
|    16|                                                                                                                            |
|    17|                                                                                                                            |
|    18|                                                                                                                            |
|    19|                                                                                                                            |
|    20|                                                                                                                            |
|    21|                                                                                                                            |
|    22| 4412X47390Marshall Silverman          2219 West 7th Street         Cleveland         OH30119     0000006021D000005000000|
|    23|                                                                                                                            |
|    24| 773194221BHelen B. Overstreet         3153 Yellow Brick Road       Yellow Stone Park MT41229     0000001284200000000000|
|    25| 3199127X33James Thompkins             44339 South Wacker Drive     Chicago           IL60606     0000002291800000500000|
|    26|                                                                                                                            |
|    27| 3333333333Julia Harriston             6132 Mill Road Avenue        Shreveport        LA63341     0000260768G00005000000|
|    28|                                                                                                                            |
|    29|                                                                                                                            |
|    30|                                                                                                                            |
|    31|                                                                                                                            |
|    32|                                                                                                                            |
|    33|                                                                                                                            |
|    34| 9X0-334RDSAnthony P. Jones            Executive Office Building    Washington        DC00000     0000000000000000000000|
|    35|                                                                                                                            |
|    36| X14339-278Robert P. Evans             1422 N. W. Classen Blvd.     Oklahoma City     OK65124     0000000000000000300000|
|    37|                                                                                                                            |
|    38| 2199428878Stewart A. Alexander        5112 Hamilton Parkway        Minneapolis       MN21132     0000062239000001000000|
|    39| 1RX14219-3John P. Villiman            8887 Peach Tree Lane         Dallas            TX75002     0000000314300000500000|
|    40|                                                                                                                            |
|    41|                                                                                                                            |
|    42|                                                                                                                            |
|    43|                                                                                                                            |
|    44|                                                                                                                            |
|    45|                                                                                                                            |
|    46|                                                                                                                            |
|    47|                                                                                                                            |
|    48| 3498966451Jacob R. Sullivan           6134 Malibu Drive            Los Angeles       CA96512     0000047611 00004400000|
|    49| 5122314151Mark R. White               55123 War Memorial Drive     Cleveland         OH41229     0000004123300000050000|
|    50|                                                                                                                            |
|    51| 6213937661Jason Madison               8831 Cedar Drive N.W.        Norwich           CT00218     0000041452300003000000|
|    52|                                                                                                                            |
|    53| 6427633-94Mark U. Lemon               P. O. Box 51244              New York          NY03158     0000000000000000005000|
--------------------------------------------------------------------------------------------------------------------------------------------
```

Figure 19.7 *Continued* Adding to a Relative File (Output)

```
                              Exception Report                                                          Page  1


Customer Number    Comments
---------------------------------------------------------------------------------------------------------------
 3333333333        Location Duplicate Encountered--Record ELIMINATED      Location Reference 26 Contains 3333333333
```

Other Considerations for Relative Files

You may have noticed that a DELETE-BYTE was included in the record description of the relative file. The procedure for deleting records from a relative file is one developed by the programmer. Thus, whereas there is a specific procedure for deleting records from a sequential file and an indexed sequential file, no such procedure exists for a relative file. In the preceding illustrations, the delete byte could be used to "mark" the records that are no longer desired. Thus, if the DELETE-BYTE is blank, the record could be viewed as an active record. If the DELETE-BYTE contains some other character (say, an "X"), it could be viewed as a deleted record that could be replaced by another record.

The "delete code" approach is generally preferred to moving spaces to a deleted record, especially when an alternate procedure is specified to resolve synonyms. The point of using a delete code is to indicate that the record position was in use at one time. Since the record position would remain "occupied," any procedure that attempts to retrieve the record would indicate the presence of a record rather than an "empty" space. Many record retrieval procedures utilize a "searching" process if the record is not located on the first attempt. Most of these procedures terminate with a "not found" condition when an empty space is located. Thus, knowing that a record position was once occupied is as important under these conditions as knowing the record position is currently occupied.

Virtual Files

During the 1970s, computers began to be manufactured that provided *virtual storage*. Virtual storage is essentially a means by which internal storage seems to be expanded virtually to infinity. Although internal storage is not expanded infinitely, virtual operating systems (e.g., IBM's VS1, VS2, MVS, etc.) utilize a specialized disk storage space area as an extension of internal storage. Thus, infinity is measured by the amount of such disk storage space available.

Along with these improvements in operating systems and computer architecture, which for the most part operate behind the scenes, it became desirable to take advantage of virtual storage from a COBOL program. Thus, during the later 1970s the *VSAM (Virtual Storage Access Method)* was introduced by IBM. Today, VSAM represents the most recent addition to file types available to the programmer. However, to be able to utilize VSAM, your installation must be utilizing one of IBM's virtual operating systems and must have one of the more recent (since 1974) COBOL compilers.

To be accurate, VASM represents a family of file types. These file types include an *entry-sequenced data set (ESDS file), a key-sequenced data set (KSDS file)* and a *relative record data set (RRDS file)*. Essentially, ESDS files are the same as sequential files, presented in Chapter 17. KSDS files were included as a replacement for ISAM files, presented in Chapter 18, and are generally superior in performance. KSDS files are the most frequently used of the file types within VSAM and will be addressed in some detail in the remainder of this chapter. Earlier in this chapter relative files were discussed. RRDS files are essentially the same as relative files.

The VSAM Structure

Among the many disadvantages of an ISAM file is its inability to satisfactorily handle record additions and deletions. That is, as an ISAM file grows, dramatic performance drops occur, and decreased response times may only be achieved by recreating the file. VSAM files are structurally much different, in order to handle performance problems of this nature.

VSAM files exist within what is known as a *DATA space.* As illustrated in Figure 19.8, a data space cluster can be considered a collection or a group of several files, some of which are VSAM files and perhaps others that are non-VSAM files. A data space is really a generic (or *cataloged*) name for a group of files and may be created through the use of the *Access Method Services (AMS)* utility program called *IDCAMS.* (Both AMS and IDCAMS are beyond the scope of this text. Consult your local installation guide or the IBM AMS manual for additional material related to the creation of data space.) Within a data space, the programmer may request a cluster. A cluster is essentially

Figure 19.8 The Structure of a VSAM Data Space

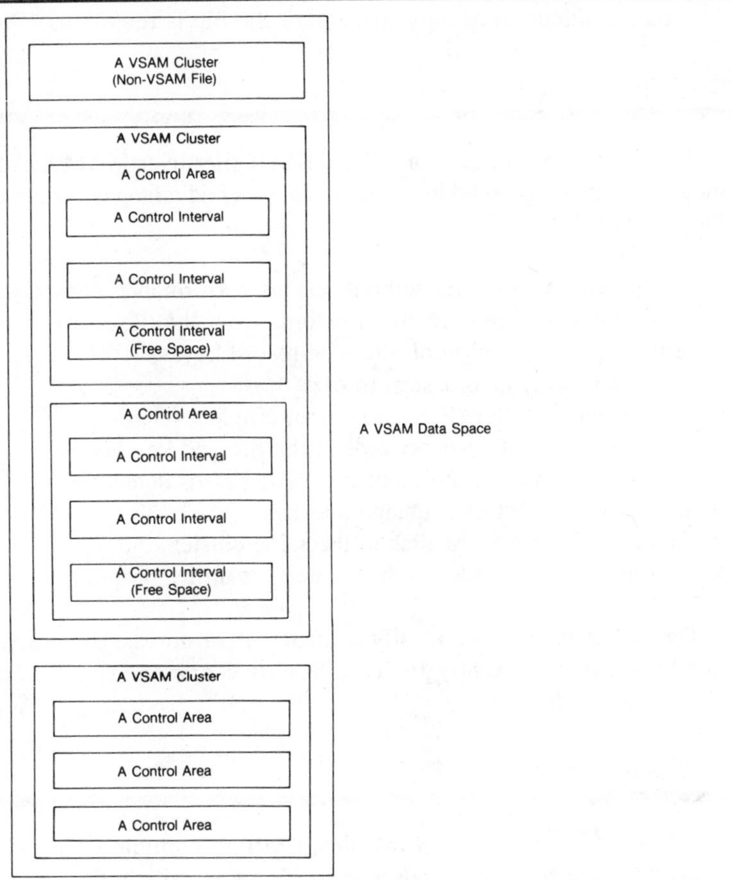

the same as a file. The cluster is then composed of *control areas* that are similar to large chunks of a file. Each control area may contain either data or a set of indexes that point to data in another control area. Finally, a control area is composed of multiple *control intervals*. For VSAM files, a control interval is the replacement unit for a block of records. That is, when a VSAM file is being processed, complete control intervals are physically read or written at one time.

Within a control area, some control intervals are typically empty or referred to as *free space*. This empty space is used when records are added to the file. When a record is added to the file, VSAM maintains the records in a physical sequence. Thus, existing records within a control interval are moved around to accommodate new records. When a control interval is full and a record is added, a *control interval split* occurs whereby a portion of the records are placed in adjacent free space control intervals. If an attempt is made to perform a control interval split and all free space has been consumed within a control area, a *control area split* occurs whereby free space that exists is spread between adjacent control areas. It should be obvious that eventually all free space could be consumed and the file would have to be recreated. However, before all free space is consumed, retrieval speeds are slowed only slightly (in comparison to an ISAM file). Furthermore, when records are deleted from a VSAM file, they are physically removed and their space is returned to free space. When records are "deleted" from an ISAM file, they continue to occupy space until the file is rewritten.

Advantages and Disadvantages

Although some advantages of VSAM KSDS files over ISAM files have been mentioned, they bear repeating. In addition, there are other advantages. When compared to an ISAM file, VSAM files

- Accept record additions without serious performance consequences
- Physically delete (and remove) records from the file
- Permit the specification of alternate record keys
- Permit duplicate record keys to exist
- Automatically "block" records to an efficient length
- Process authorization passwords at the file and key levels
- Provide extended input-output processing error detection
- Minimize job control language interfaces
- Can accept non-VSAM files in the same cluster
- Can process ISAM files with an interface utility program

The disadvantages are mostly a matter of resources. To process VSAM files, your installation must currently be using a virtual operating system and must have a VS-COBOL compiler.

ENVIRONMENT DIVISION Considerations

With the introduction of VSAM files, COBOL compilers have changed rather dramatically with respect to the clauses available to describe a file. An examination of Figure 19.9 reveals a number of these changes. First, as illustrated in Figure 19.10, the only requirement of the system-name is an indication of the external name. The device class

Figure 19.9 INPUT-OUTPUT SECTION for VSAM File Organizations

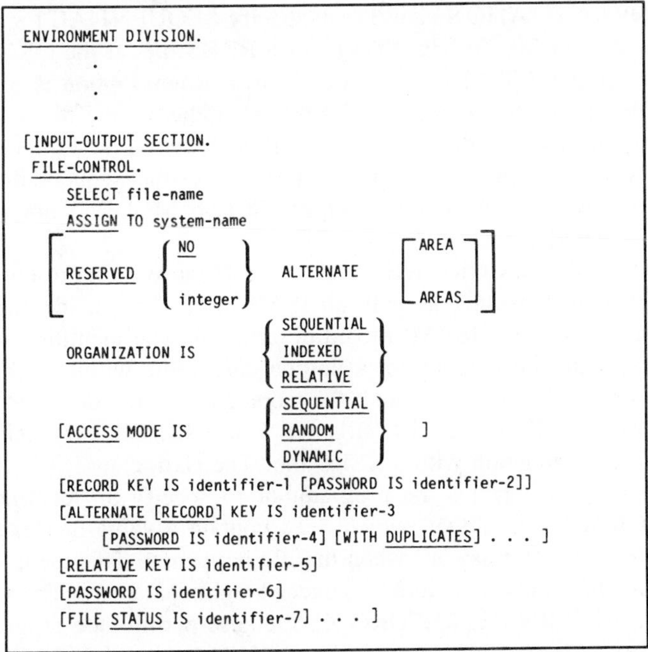
```
ENVIRONMENT DIVISION.
      .
      .
      .
[INPUT-OUTPUT SECTION.
 FILE-CONTROL.
     SELECT file-name
     ASSIGN TO system-name
   [              { NO      }                 [ AREA  ] ]
   [ RESERVED     {         }   ALTERNATE     [       ] ]
   [              { integer }                 [ AREAS ] ]
                             { SEQUENTIAL }
     ORGANIZATION IS         { INDEXED    }
                             { RELATIVE   }
                             { SEQUENTIAL }
    [ACCESS MODE IS          { RANDOM     }       ]
                             { DYNAMIC    }
    [RECORD KEY IS identifier-1 [PASSWORD IS identifier-2]]
    [ALTERNATE [RECORD] KEY IS identifier-3
         [PASSWORD IS identifier-4] [WITH DUPLICATES] . . . ]
    [RELATIVE KEY IS identifier-5]
    [PASSWORD IS identifier-6]
    [FILE STATUS IS identifier-7] . . . ]
```

Figure 19.10 Illustrations of the ENVIRONMENT DIVISION for a VSAM KSDS File

Case 1:

```
ENVIRONMENT DIVISION.
CONFIGURATION SECTION.
SOURCE-COMPUTER.  IBM.
OBJECT-COMPUTER.  IBM.
INPUT-OUTPUT SECTION.
    SELECT CUSTOMER-FILE
        ASSIGN TO MASTER
        ORGANIZATION IS INDEXED
        ACCESS MODE IS RANDOM
        RECORD KEY IS CUSTOMER-NUMBER
        FILE STATUS IS FILE-STATUS.
```

Case 2:

```
ENVIRONMENT DIVISION.
CONFIGURATION SECTION.
SOURCE-COMPUTER.  IBM.
OBJECT-COMPUTER.  IBM.
INPUT-OUTPUT SECTION.
    SELECT CUSTOMER-FILE
        ASSIGN TO MASTER
        ORGANIZATION IS INDEXED
        ACCESS IS DYNAMIC
        RECORD KEY IS CUSTOMER-NUMBER
        ALTERNATE KEY IS CUSTOMER-NAME WITH DUPLICATES
        FILE STATUS IS FILE-STATUS.
```

(which must be a direct access storage device) and the file type are both optional. Second, the RESERVE clause is again permitted. Third, an entirely new clause is included. The ORGANIZATION clause may specify SEQUENTIAL for an ESDS file, INDEXED for a KSDS file, or RELATIVE for a RRDS file. If the ORGANIZATION is not specified, SEQUENTIAL is assumed. Fourth, a new option is provided in the ACCESS MODE clause. As before, SEQUENTIAL indicates the file will be accessed sequentially and RANDOM indicates the file will be accessed on a direct access basis. However, DYNAMIC indicates the file may be processed either sequentially or randomly within the same procedure. As before, if the ACCESS MODE is not specified, SEQUENTIAL is assumed.

The fifth clause is the RECORD KEY clause. This clause, first presented in Chapter 18, is used in the same manner as with an ISAM file. That is, identifier-1 must be present within the VSAM (or ISAM) record description. The identifier may be of any definable data type and must represent a unique data value within each record. Furthermore, when the VSAM file is created, the records must be ordered on an ascending basis by this identifier. Both the RECORD KEY and ALTERNATE RECORD KEY clauses are used in conjunction with a KSDS file. The sixth clause, PASSWORD, is a new clause. This clause enables the programmer to specify an identifier within the WORKING-STORAGE SECTION, which must contain a value that exactly matches that contained in the file's password when the file is opened. This identifier should be represented by an alphanumeric field not to exceed eight characters. The seventh clause is also new. The ALTERNATE RECORD KEY clause permits the programmer to establish one or more additional identifiers within the VSAM record description. The other characteristics of a RECORD KEY also apply, except that the value of the identifier does not necessarily have to be unique if WITH DUPLICATES is specified.

The eighth clause is the RELATIVE KEY clause. This clause is used in conjunction with a RRDS file. Identifier-5 must be described as an unsigned integer data item outside the record definition for the relative record itself. Unlike traditional relative files, this identifier need not be a binary description and is not limited to eight digits. The ninth clause is a repeat of the PASSWORD clause. However, the intent of this repetition is to convey that both SEQUENTIAL and RELATIVE files are permitted to contain a password data item. All other characteristics of the PASSWORD clause are the same as previously described.

Finally, the FILE STATUS clause has been added to provide more complete user diagnostics in conjunction with file operations. If the clause is used, identifier-7 must represent a two-character field described within the DATA DIVISION. This data item may not be described in either the FILE SECTION or REPORT SECTION. As a result of any file manipulation of the associated file, the identifier will be modified to contain a two-digit value. The possible values and their related causes are presented in Table 19.2

DATA DIVISION Considerations

Other than those previously mentioned, there are no new requirements for describing VSAM files. To reiterate, the RECORD KEY (and ALTERNATE RECORD KEY) identifiers must be present within the VSAM record description for a KSDS file. The RECORD KEY (and ALTERNATE RECORD KEY) may be of any definable data type. The RECORD KEY (and ALTERNATE RECORD KEY if WITH DUPLICATES is omitted) must be unique for each record. The RELATIVE KEY identifier must be

Table 19.2 Possible Values of the FILE STATUS Identifier

First Digit	Second Digit	Input-Output Status or Condition
0	0	Successful operation
0	2	Duplicate keys and DUPLICATES specified
1	0	End of file encountered
2	0	Invalid key, no further information
2	1	Invalid key, data out of sequence
2	2	Invalid key, duplicate key found and duplicate key is not permitted
2	3	Invalid key, no record found
2	4	Invalid key, boundary violation
3	0	Permanent I-0 error, cause unknown
3	4	Permanent I-0 error, boundary violation for a sequential file
9	0	Other error, no further information
9	1	Password failed
9	2	Logic error
9	3	Device or resource not available
9	4	Sequential record not available
9	5	File information invalid or incomplete
9	6	JCL error

described outside the relative file description for a RRDS file. PASSWORD and FILE STATUS identifiers must be described in the DATA DIVISION (outside the FILE SECTION), and the FILE STATUS identifier must be two-bytes in length.

There are, on the other hand, additional differences from the files previously described in the text. VSAM files and traditional relative files share the common restriction that the BLOCK CONTAINS clause should not be specified for these file types. The data set management routine for VSAM handles the efficient allocation of logical records to the direct access device. If the BLOCK CONTAINS clause is specified, it is treated as a comment. In previous descriptions of ISAM records, a delete byte is included as the first byte of the record if records are to be deleted. As shown shortly, VSAM files have no such requirement.

PROCEDURE DIVISION Considerations

For the most part, the types of statements needed to process VSAM files have been presented in previous chapters. However, to summarize the types of statements and their association with types of access to a VSAM file, examine Table 19.3.

The first set of entries in Table 19.3 describe the types of options available for an ESDS file. As previously noted, an ESDS file is essentially a sequential file. Thus, on examining the table entries associated with an ESDS file, we find they are fundamentally no different from those presented in Chapter 17. The first difference noted in this table is that the imperative statement associated with the READ statement is optional. The AT END phrase is optional and would, if used, perform the same operations as in the past. However, with the addition of the FILE STATUS identifier, an end-of-file condition may be determined by alternate means; that is, the FILE STATUS identifier contains the value 10 at the end-of-file, as shown in Table 19.2. Another difference is related to the OPEN statement. Although the file would normally be OPENed in an OUTPUT mode for creation, a VSAM ESDS file may be OPENed as an OUTPUT or EXTENDED

Table 19.3 VSAM File Statement Options and Uses

Type of Operation	ORGANIZATION	ACCESS MODE*	KEY Required	OPEN Statement	Input/Output Statement(s)
		Entry Sequence Data Sets (ESDS)			
Sequential Record Retrieval (ESDS)	[SEQUENTIAL]	[SEQUENTIAL]	No	INPUT I-O	READ [INTO] [AT END]
Creation or Record Addition (ESDS)	[SEQUENTIAL]	[SEQUENTIAL]	No	OUTPUT EXTENDED	WRITE [FROM]
Sequential Record Update (ESDS)	[SEQUENTIAL]	[SEQUENTIAL]	No	I-O	READ [INTO] [AT END] REWRITE [FROM]
		Key Sequence Data Sets (KSDS)			
Sequential Record Retrieval (KSDS)	INDEXED	[SEQUENTIAL]	RECORD [ALTERNATE]	INPUT	READ [INTO] [AT END] START [KEY] [INVALID KEY]
Creation or Record Addition (KSDS)	INDEXED	[SEQUENTIAL]	RECORD [ALTERNATE]	OUTPUT EXTENDED	WRITE [FROM] [INVALID KEY]
Sequential Record Update (KSDS)	INDEXED	[SEQUENTIAL]	RECORD [ALTERNATE]	I-O	READ [INTO] [AT END] START [KEY] [INVALID KEY] REWRITE [FROM] [INVALID KEY] DELETE
Random Record Retrieval (KSDS)	INDEXED	RANDOM	RECORD [ALTERNATE]	INPUT	READ [INTO] [INVALID KEY]
Random Record Addition (KSDS)	INDEXED	RANDOM	RECORD [ALTERNATE]	OUTPUT	WRITE [FROM] [INVALID KEY]

Table 19.3 *Continued* VSAM File Statement Options and Uses

Type of Operation	ORGANIZATION	ACCESS MODE*	KEY Required	OPEN Statement	Input/Output Statement
		Relative Record Data Sets (RRDS)			
Random Update (KSDS)	INDEXED	RANDOM	RECORD [ALTERNATE]	I-O	READ [INTO] [INVALID KEY] REWIRTE [FROM] [INVALID KEY] DELETE [INVALID KEY] WRITE [FROM] [INVALID KEY]
Sequential Record Retrieval (RRDS)	RELATIVE	[SEQUENTIAL]	[RELATIVE]	INPUT	READ [INTO] [AT END] START [KEY] [INVALID KEY]
Creation and Record Addition (RRDS)	RELATIVE	[SEQUENTIAL]	RELATIVE	OUTPUT	WRITE [FROM] [INVALID KEY]
Sequential Record Update (RRDS)	RELATIVE	[SEQUENTIAL]	[RELATIVE]	I-O	READ [INTO] [AT END] REWRITE [FROM] [INVALID KEY] START [KEY] [INVALID KEY] DELETE
Random Record Retrieval (RRDS)	RELATIVE	RANDOM	RELATIVE	INPUT	READ [INTO] [INVALID KEY]
Random Record Addition (RRDS)	RELATIVE	RANDOM	RELATIVE	OUTPUT	WRITE [FROM] [INVALID KEY]
Random Record Update (RRDS)	RELATIVE	RANDOM	RELATIVE	I-O	READ [INTO] [INVALID KEY] WRITE [FROM] [INVALID KEY] REWRITE [FROM] [INVALID KEY] DELETE

*For DYNAMIC access of KSDS and RRDS files, combinations of SEQUENTIAL and RANDOM access entries and statements may be used.

file. The EXTENDED option specifies that new records are to be physically placed at the end of the file, that is, after the current last record. However, if the programmer wishes to maintain a record sequence based on some identifier within the record, it is still necessary to rewrite the file and insert new records in their appropriate physical locations.

When the programmer defines a KSDS file, the ORGANIZATION IS INDEXED clause and the RECORD KEY clause must always be specified. However, the ACCESS MODE clause is needed only when the file is to be accessed in a RANDOM (or DYNAMIC) mode. When a KSDS file is opened in the sequential INPUT mode, both the sequential READ and START statements are permitted. Recall from Chapter 18 (Figure 18.7) that a START statement may be used when an ISAM file is to be processed sequentially in a mode that permits a ''jump ahead'' operation. The same option is available for a VSAM KSDS file being accessed sequentially in either the INPUT or I-O modes. The creation of a KSDS file is also very similar to that for an ISAM file. Note that the file must be OPENed in the OUTPUT (or EXTENDED) mode and that a WRITE statement is used to place records into the file. Finally, in the sequential access mode, a KSDS file may be updated.

Although most of the statements that are permitted for this activity have been previously discussed, a new statement type is permitted. The DELETE statement, illustrated in Figure 19.11, is used to physically remove a record from a VSAM KSDS file or RRDS file. The deletion operation for VSAM files is fundamentally different from that for traditional files in that the identified record is physically, rather than logically, removed from the file. Furthermore, whereas ISAM files require a special delete byte at the beginning of the record for deletion purposes, no such field is required for a VSAM file. The operation is performed in much the same way that an update is performed. That is, the record is first read and then ''replaced'' by a DELETE statement rather than by a REWRITE statement.

When the access to a KSDS file is RANDOM, the types of operations and statements appear to be very similar to those used for randomly accessing an ISAM file. Thus, when a KSDS file is OPENed in the INPUT mode, a READ statement with an optional INVALID KEY clause is used to retrieve the data. When OPENed in the OUTPUT mode, a WRITE statement with an optional INVALID KEY clause is used to place new records into the file. When records are to be updated, the file is OPENed in the I-O mode and records are retrieved by a READ statement and replaced by a REWRITE statement. Of course, the ''replacement'' may be performed by a DELETE statement, which removes the record from the file and returns the area used by the record to free space.

The last type of file that may be manipulated by VSAM is a RRDS file. Since a RRDS file is very similar to a traditional relative file, you would expect the operations and statements to be very similar. In fact, once ORGANIZATION IS RELATIVE is

Figure 19.11 Format of the DELETE Statement

```
DELETE file-name RECORD
    [INVALID KEY imperative-statement]
```

specified for a file, and the RELATIVE KEY clause replaces the NOMINAL KEY clause, most of the activities associated with the file would be the same as for a relative file. The obvious exceptions include optional AT END and INVALID KEY clauses, the capability of using a START statement when the file is being accessed sequentially, and the use of DELETE statement to physically remove a record from the file. These options and statements operate the same as previously discussed in conjunction with an ESDS file and a KSDS file.

Building a VSAM KSDS File

As previously mentioned, a VSAM KSDS file possesses properties similar to those of an ISAM file. Although the building of a VSAM KSDS file is not exactly the same as building an ISAM file, the program presented in Figure 19.12 demonstrates relatively few differences. In previous illustrations of the building process, the system-name used for the CUSTOMER-OUT-FILE was slightly more detailed. (Also, see line 470.) The ASSIGN clause (line 250) indicates that only the external name need be specified. That is, the "UT-S" or other prefixes are unnecessary for all VSAM files. The second difference the programmer would notice is the use of the ORGANIZATION IS INDEXED clause, which specifies the file type to be a KSDS file. (SEQUENTIAL would be used for an ESDS file and RELATIVE would be used for a RRDS file). Next, the RECORD KEY indicates that CUSTOMER-NUMBER-OUT is to be the key field. This is no different from that previously demonstrated for an ISAM file. Then, ACCESS MODE IS SEQUENTIAL is explicitly stated. Of course, the default access is sequential. Finally, the FILE STATUS clause is included, along with its description (line 740).

In conjunction with the FD entries for the CUSTOMER-OUT-FILE, no apparent difference exists. However, you should notice that the BLOCK CONTAINS clause has

Figure 19.12 Building a VSAM KSDS File (System Flowchart)

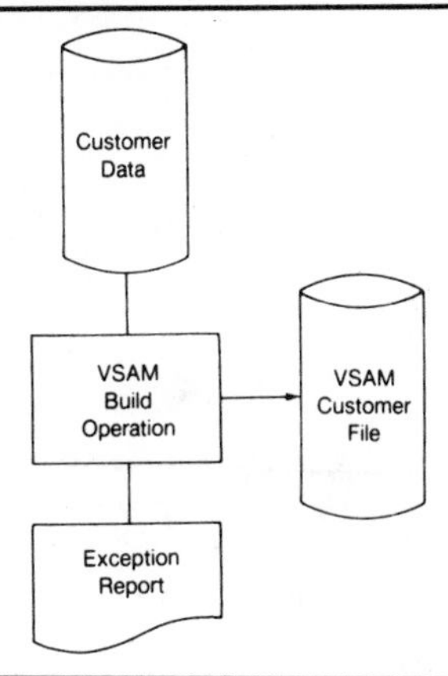

Figure 19.12 *Continued* Building a VSAM KSDS File (Hierarchy Chart)

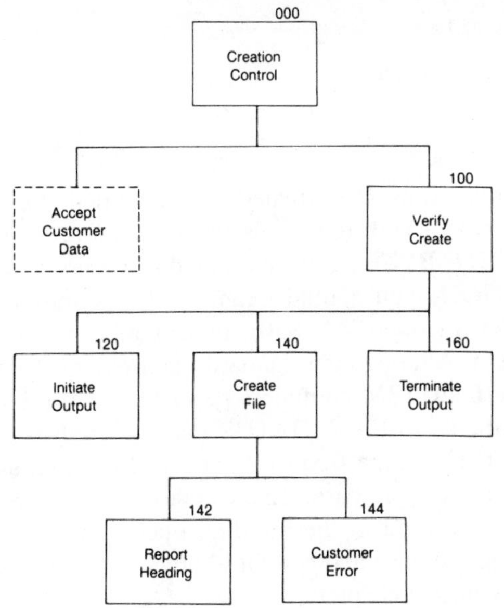

Figure 19.12 *Continued* Building a VSAM KSDS File (Pseudocode)

```
START
    SORT customer file
         ASCENDING customer number
         OUTPUT Verify Create
    ENDSORT
END

VERIFY CREATE
    DO Initiate output
    DO Create file UNTIL eof
    DO Terminate output
END

INITIATE OUTPUT
    OPEN output files
    RETURN customer file
         IF eof
              SET file status
         ENDIF
END

CREATE FILE
    IF line number > 40
         DO Report heading
    ENDIF
    WRITE output record
    MOVE message to output
    IF out of sequence
         MOVE message to output
    ENDIF
    IF duplicate key
         MOVE message to output
    ENDIF
    IF out of space
         MOVE message to output
    ENDIF
    IF successful
         ADD 1 to customer count
    ELSE
         DO Customer error
    ENDIF
    RETURN customer file
         IF eof
              SET file status
         ENDIF
END

REPORT HEADING
    ADD 1 to page number
    WRITE headings
    MOVE 0 to line number
END

CUSTOMER ERROR
    ADD 1 to error count
    MOVE customer number to output
    WRITE error
    ADD 1 to line number
END

TERMINATE OUTPUT
    MOVE counts to output
    WRITE output summary
    CLOSE files
END
```

been intentionally omitted since it is treated as a comment for all VSAM files. The record description associated with the file is the same as previously indicated for the ISAM file, except DELETE-BYTE has been omitted and is not necessary. In the WORKING-STORAGE SECTION, you should examine the definition and condition-name support for FILE-STATUS (Lines 740–830). First, notice the FILE-STATUS field definition is a two-digit field. Although the standard requirements for this variable is a two-character alphanumeric field, IBM compilers permit the definition to be numeric. The condition-names subordinate to FILE-STATUS may be used in place of AT END and INVALID KEY phrases, which are frequently attached to input and output statements. The condition-name definitions are based on the codes presented in Table 19.2. Although all these codes will not be used in the building operation, you may find it easier to develop this coding structure once and copy it to other programs as needed, as has been done for later programs in this chapter.

Figure 19.12 *Continued* Building a VSAM KSDS File

```
          1   1   2   2   2   3   3   4   4   4   5   5   6   6   6   7
  4   8   2   6   0   4   8   2   6   0   4   8   2   6   0   4   8   2

      ****************************************************************
       IDENTIFICATION DIVISION.
      ****************************************************************
       PROGRAM-ID.     VSAM-KSDS-BUILD.
       AUTHOR.         JOHN WINDSOR.
       DATE-WRITTEN.   JANUARY 1, 1989.
       DATE-COMPILED.  JANUARY 1, 1989.
      *     The purpose of this procedure is to produce a VSAM keyed
      *     sequential data set (KSDS) based on customer records.
      *     The file is to be keyed on the customer number field.
      ****************************************************************
       ENVIRONMENT DIVISION.
      ****************************************************************
      *--------------------------------------------------------------*
       CONFIGURATION SECTION.
      *--------------------------------------------------------------*
       SOURCE-COMPUTER. IBM.
       OBJECT-COMPUTER. IBM.
       SPECIAL-NAMES.    C01 IS TOP-OF-PAGE.
      *--------------------------------------------------------------*
       INPUT-OUTPUT SECTION.
      *--------------------------------------------------------------*
       FILE-CONTROL.
           SELECT CUSTOMER-IN-FILE ASSIGN TO UT-S-INPUT.
           SELECT CUSTOMER-OUT-FILE ASSIGN TO OUTPUT2
               ORGANIZATION IS INDEXED
               RECORD KEY IS CUSTOMER-NUMBER-OUT
               ACCESS IS SEQUENTIAL
               FILE STATUS IS FILE-STATUS.
           SELECT CUSTOMER-SORT-FILE ASSIGN TO UT-S-SORTWK01.
           SELECT EXCEPTION-REPORT-FILE ASSIGN TO UT-S-OUTPUT.
      ****************************************************************
       DATA DIVISION.
      ****************************************************************
      *--------------------------------------------------------------*
       FILE SECTION.
      *--------------------------------------------------------------*
       FD  CUSTOMER-IN-FILE
           LABEL RECORDS ARE STANDARD
           RECORD CONTAINS 124 CHARACTERS.
       01  CUSTOMER-RECORD-IN            PIC X(124).

       FD  CUSTOMER-OUT-FILE
           LABEL RECORDS ARE STANDARD
           RECORD CONTAINS 124 CHARACTERS.
       01  CUSTOMER-RECORD-OUT.
           05  CUSTOMER-NUMBER-OUT       PIC X(10).
           05  CUSTOMER-NAME-OUT         PIC X(30).
           05  CUSTOMER-ADDRESS-OUT      PIC X(30).
           05  CUSTOMER-CITY-OUT         PIC X(20).
           05  CUSTOMER-STATE-OUT        PIC X(02).
           05  CUSTOMER-ZIP-OUT          PIC X(10).
           05  CUSTOMER-BALANCE-OUT      PIC S9(09)V99.
           05  CUSTOMER-CREDIT-LIMIT-OUT PIC S9(09)V99.

       SD  CUSTOMER-SORT-FILE.
       01  CUSTOMER-RECORD-SORT.
           05  CUSTOMER-NUMBER-SORT      PIC X(10).
           05  FILLER                    PIC X(114).

       FD  EXCEPTION-REPORT-FILE
           LABEL RECORDS ARE OMITTED.
       01  REPORT-RECORD                   PIC X(133).
      *--------------------------------------------------------------*
       WORKING-STORAGE SECTION.
      *--------------------------------------------------------------*
       01  WORKING-VARIABLES.
           05  SORT-STATUS               PIC X(04) VALUE SPACES.
           05  LINE-NUMBER-WS            PIC 9(02) VALUE 99.
```

Figure 19.12 *Continued* Building a VSAM KSDS File

```
                 1   1   2   2   2   3   3   4   4   4   5   5   6   6   6   7
    4    8       2   6   0   4   8   2   6   0   4   8   2   6   0   4   8   2
           05  PAGE-NUMBER-WS              PIC 9(02) VALUE ZERO.
           05  ERROR-COUNT-WS              PIC 9(04) VALUE ZERO.
           05  CUSTOMER-COUNT-WS           PIC 9(04) VALUE ZERO.

       01  VSAM-FILE-STATUS.
           05  FILE-STATUS                 PIC 9(02).
               88  SUCCESSFUL-IO                     VALUE 0.
               88  EOF                               VALUE 10.
               88  OUT-OF-SEQUENCE                   VALUE 21.
               88  DUPLICATE-KEY                     VALUE 22.
               88  NOT-FOUND                         VALUE 23.
               88  OUT-OF-SPACE                      VALUE 24.
               88  IO-ERROR                          VALUE 30.
               88  LOGIC-ERROR                       VALUE 90 THRU 97.

       01  HEADING-1.
           05  FILLER                      PIC X(32) VALUE SPACES.
           05  FILLER                      PIC X(16) VALUE
                                           'Exception Report'.
           05  FILLER                      PIC X(25) VALUE SPACES.
           05  FILLER                      PIC X(05) VALUE 'Page'.
           05  PAGE-NUMBER-OUT             PIC Z9.

       01  HEADING-2.
           05  FILLER                      PIC X(20) VALUE
                                           ' Customer Number'.
           05  FILLER                      PIC X(20) VALUE
                                           'Comments'.

       01  HEADING-3.
           05  FILLER                      PIC X(01) VALUE SPACES.
           05  FILLER                      PIC X(80) VALUE ALL '-'.

       01  ERROR-LINE.
           05  FILLER                      PIC X(02) VALUE SPACES.
           05  CUSTOMER-NUMBER-ERROR       PIC X(10).
           05  FILLER                      PIC X(08) VALUE SPACES.
           05  ERROR-MESSAGE-OUT           PIC X(50) VALUE SPACES.

       01  SUMMARY-LINE.
           05  FILLER                      PIC X(01) VALUE SPACES.
           05  CUSTOMER-COUNT-OUT          PIC *,**9.
           05  FILLER                      PIC X(27) VALUE
                                           ' Customer Records Written--'.
           05  ERROR-COUNT-OUT             PIC *,**9.
           05  FILLER                      PIC X(25) VALUE
                                           ' Duplicates Encountered'.
      ***************************************************************
       PROCEDURE DIVISION.
      ***************************************************************
      *-------------------------------------------------------------*
       000-CREATION-CONTROL SECTION.
      *-------------------------------------------------------------*
           MOVE 45000              TO SORT-CORE-SIZE.
           SORT CUSTOMER-SORT-FILE
               ASCENDING KEY CUSTOMER-NUMBER-SORT
               USING CUSTOMER-IN-FILE
               OUTPUT PROCEDURE 100-VERIFY-CREATE.
           STOP RUN.
      *-------------------------------------------------------------*
       100-VERIFY-CREATE SECTION.
      *-------------------------------------------------------------*
           PERFORM 120-INITIATE-OUTPUT.
           PERFORM 140-CREATE-FILE
               UNTIL SORT-STATUS = 'DONE'.
           PERFORM 160-TERMINATE-OUTPUT.
      *-------------------------------------------------------------*
       120-INITIATE-OUTPUT SECTION
      *-------------------------------------------------------------*
```

Figure 19.12 *Continued* Building a VSAM KSDS File

```
----------------------------------------------------------------------------------------
|               1   1   2   2   2   3   3   4   4   4   5   5   6   6   6   7|
|   4   8   2   6   0   4   8   2   6   0   4   8   2   6   0   4   8   2|
|---------------------------------------------------------------------------------------
|
|1390          OPEN OUTPUT CUSTOMER-OUT-FILE
|1400                      EXCEPTION-REPORT-FILE.
|1410          RETURN CUSTOMER-SORT-FILE INTO CUSTOMER-RECORD-OUT
|1420              AT END MOVE 'DONE' TO SORT-STATUS.
|1430      *-----------------------------------------------------------*
|1440       140-CREATE-FILE SECTION.
|1450      *-----------------------------------------------------------*
|1460          IF LINE-NUMBER-WS IS GREATER THAN 40
|1470              PERFORM 142-REPORT-HEADING.
|1480          WRITE CUSTOMER-RECORD-OUT.
|1490          MOVE 'Unknown Error'       TO ERROR-MESSAGE-OUT.
|1500          IF OUT-OF-SEQUENCE
|1510              MOVE 'Record Out of Sequence' TO ERROR-MESSAGE-OUT.
|1520          IF DUPLICATE-KEY
|1530              MOVE 'Customer Number Duplicate Encountered--ELIMINATED'
|1540                                     TO ERROR-MESSAGE-OUT.
|1550          IF OUT-OF-SPACE
|1560              MOVE 'File Space Exhausted' TO ERROR-MESSAGE-OUT.
|1570          IF SUCCESSFUL-IO
|1580              ADD 1 TO CUSTOMER-COUNT-WS
|1590          ELSE
|1600              PERFORM 144-CUSTOMER-ERROR.
|1610          RETURN CUSTOMER-SORT-FILE INTO CUSTOMER-RECORD-OUT
|1620              AT END MOVE 'DONE' TO SORT-STATUS.
|1630      *-----------------------------------------------------------*
|1640       142-REPORT-HEADING SECTION.
|1650      *-----------------------------------------------------------*
|1660          ADD 1 TO PAGE-NUMBER-WS.
|1670          MOVE PAGE-NUMBER-WS        TO PAGE-NUMBER-OUT.
|1680          WRITE REPORT-RECORD FROM HEADING-1
|1690              AFTER ADVANCING TOP-OF-PAGE.
|1700          WRITE REPORT-RECORD FROM HEADING-2 AFTER ADVANCING 3 LINES.
|1710          WRITE REPORT-RECORD FROM HEADING-3 AFTER ADVANCING 1 LINES.
|1720          MOVE SPACES                TO REPORT-RECORD.
|1730          WRITE REPORT-RECORD AFTER ADVANCING 1 LINES.
|1740          MOVE 0                     TO LINE-NUMBER-WS.
|1750      *-----------------------------------------------------------*
|1760       144-CUSTOMER-ERROR SECTION.
|1770      *-----------------------------------------------------------*
|1780          ADD 1 TO ERROR-COUNT-WS.
|1790          MOVE CUSTOMER-NUMBER-OUT TO CUSTOMER-NUMBER-ERROR.
|1800          WRITE REPORT-RECORD FROM ERROR-LINE AFTER ADVANCING 1 LINES.
|1810          ADD 1 TO LINE-NUMBER-WS.
|1820      *-----------------------------------------------------------*
|1830       160-TERMINATE-OUTPUT SECTION.
|1840      *-----------------------------------------------------------*
|1850          MOVE ERROR-COUNT-WS        TO ERROR-COUNT-OUT.
|1860          MOVE CUSTOMER-COUNT-WS     TO CUSTOMER-COUNT-OUT.
|1870          WRITE REPORT-RECORD FROM SUMMARY-LINE
|1880              AFTER ADVANCING 2 LINES.
|1890          CLOSE EXCEPTION-REPORT-FILE
|1900                CUSTOMER-OUT-FILE.
|
----------------------------------------------------------------------------------------
```

The first operation that appears in the PROCEDURE DIVISION is sorting customer records. However, from the standpoint of examining the VSAM file, the first file operation is to OPEN the CUSTOMER-OUT-FILE in OUTPUT mode (line 1390). Neither the opening or closing operation is any different for the VSAM file as those expressed for the building of the ISAM file. The file creation process is performed by a WRITE statement (line 1480). Although the WRITE statement is permitted to present an INVALID KEY clause, output error-checking is more explicitly performed by the series of IF statements (lines 1500–1600). Note that each of these statements utilizes one of the condition-names associated with the FILE-STATUS variable. Thus, the programmer should be able to establish more easily the cause of errors that occur during the creation of the file.

Figure 19.12 *Continued* Building a VSAM KSDS File [CUSTOMER-IN] (Data)

```
----------------------------------------------------------------------------------------------------------------------------------
|                                                                                                           1         1         1 |
|      |         1         2         3         4         5         6         7         8         9         0         1         2 |
|Record|1234567890123456789012345678901234567890123456789012345678901234567890123456789012345678901234567890123456789012345678901234|
|-----------------------------------------------------------------------------------------------------------------------------------|
|     1|4412X47390Marshall Silverman          2219 West 7th Street          Cleveland          OH30119     000000000000000000500000|
|     2|3199127X33James Thompkins             44339 South Wacker Drive      Chicago            IL60606     000000229180000050000 0|
|     3|1141944103Edwin Williams              2139 South Colgate Street     Perryton           TX79070     000003319330003500000 0|
|     4|6213937661Jason Madison               8831 Cedar Drive N.W.         Norwich            CN00218     000004145230000300000 0|
|     5|5270215827Charles Everest             8821 Ocean Parkway            Miami              FL51332     000000000000000000500000|
|     6|3333333333Julia Harriston             6132 Mill Road Avenue         Shreveport         LA63341     000003513430000500000 0|
|     7|3498966451Jacob R. Sullivan           6134 Malibu Drive             Los Angeles        CA96512     000000000000000044000 00|
|     8|1RX14219-3John P. Villiman            8887 Peach Tree Lane          Dallas             TX75002     000000031430000050000 0|
|     9|6427633-94Mark U. Lemon               P. O. Box 51244               New York           NY03158     000000000000000000050000|
|    10|773194221BHelen B. Overstreet         3153 Yellow Brick Road        Yellow Stone Park  MT41229     000000128420000000000 0|
|    11|9X0-334RDSAnthony P. Jones            Executive Office Building     Washington         DC00000     000000000000000000000000|
|    12|3333333333Raymond J. Taylor           912 Dusty Road                Plains             GA39100     000005235360001000000 0|
----------------------------------------------------------------------------------------------------------------------------------
```

Figure 19.12 *Continued* Building a VSAM KSDS File [CUSTOMER-OUT] (Data)

```
----------------------------------------------------------------------------------------------------------------------------------
|                                                                                                           1         1         1 |
|      |         1         2         3         4         5         6         7         8         9         0         1         2 |
|Record|1234567890123456789012345678901234567890123456789012345678901234567890123456789012345678901234567890123456789012345678901234|
|-----------------------------------------------------------------------------------------------------------------------------------|
|     1|1RX14219-3John P. Villiman            8887 Peach Tree Lane          Dallas             TX75002     000000031430000050000 0|
|     2|1141944103Edwin Williams              2139 South Colgate Street     Perryton           TX79070     0000105684D0003500000 0|
|     3|3199127X33James Thompkins             44339 South Wacker Drive      Chicago            IL60606     000000229180000050000 0|
|     4|3333333333Julia Harriston             6132 Mill Road Avenue         Shreveport         LA63341     0000260768G0000500000 0|
|     5|3498966451Jacob R. Sullivan           6134 Malibu Drive             Los Angeles        CA96512     0000047611 00004400000|
|     6|4412X47390Marshall Silverman          2219 West 7th Street          Cleveland          OH30119     0000006021D0000050000 0|
|     7|5270215827Charles Everest             8821 Ocean Parkway            Miami              FL51332     0000011269G0000050000 0|
|     8|6213937661Jason Madison               8831 Cedar Drive N.W.         Norwich            CT00218     000004145230000300000 0|
|     9|6427633-94Mark U. Lemon               P. O. Box 51244               New York           NY03158     000000000000000000050000|
|    10|773194221BHelen B. Overstreet         3153 Yellow Brick Road        Yellow Stone Park  MT41229     000000128420000000000 0|
|    11|9X0-334RDSAnthony P. Jones            Executive Office Building     Washington         DC00000     000000000000000000000000|
----------------------------------------------------------------------------------------------------------------------------------
```

Figure 19.12 *Continued* Building a VSAM KSDS File (Output)

```
                                  Exception Report                          Page  1
      Customer Number    Comments
      ---------------------------------------------------------------------------
       3333333333        Record Out of Sequence

      ***11 Customer Records Written--****1 Duplicates Encountered
```

Updating a VSAM KSDS File

Like the building process, the update process for a VSAM KSDS file is very similar to that for an ISAM file. Figure 19.13 demonstrates a procedure that updates the CUSTOMER-IO-FILE. The initial description of the file (lines 270–310) indicates the file is INDEXED and is accessed in a RANDOM manner. The other characteristics are the same as those mentioned in conjunction with the building process. Furthermore, there is no substantial difference in the DATA DIVISION relative to the VSAM building process or ISAM update process.

Figure 19.13 Updating a VSAM KSDS File (System Flowchart)

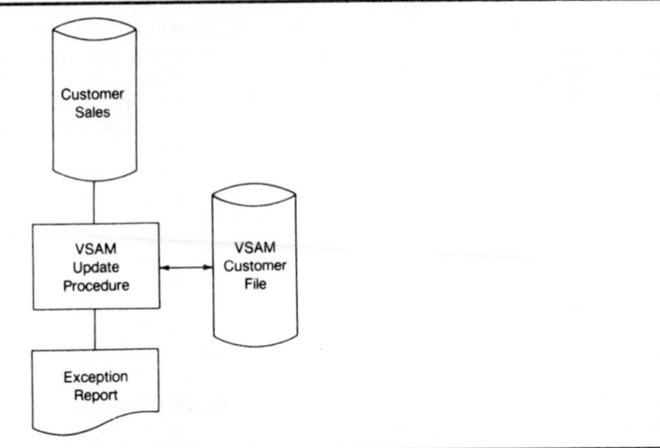

Figure 19.13 *Continued* Updating a VSAM KSDS File (Hierarchy Chart)

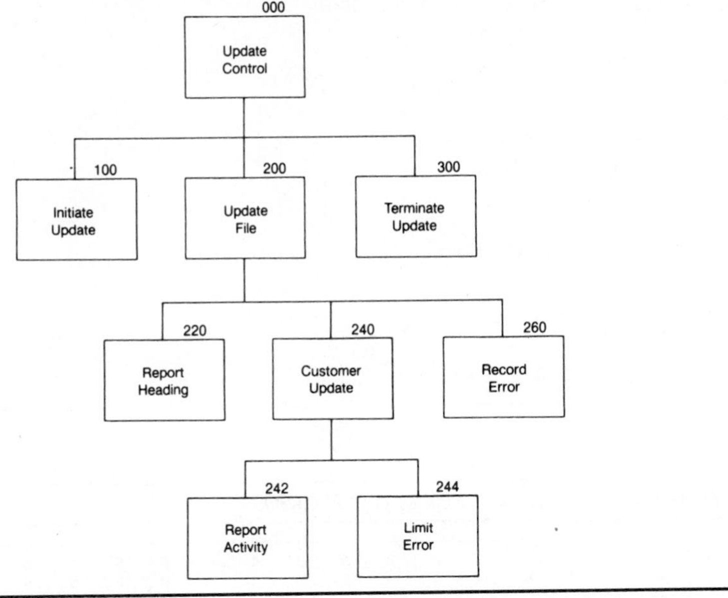

In the PROCEDURE DIVISION, the CUSTOMER-IO-FILE is opened in an I-O mode (line 1320). Thus, the programmer is permitted both to read from and write to the CUSTOMER-IO-FILE. In the 200-UPDATE-FILE procedure, a record is retrieved from the CUSTOMER-SALE-FILE, and the value associated with the key field is moved to the RECORD KEY identifier (lines 1430–1440). Then, after some preliminary moves to set up the printed output record, the indicated record is read from the CUSTOMER-IO-FILE (line 1490). Provided the input operation is successful, the update routine is performed (lines 1700–1780). Once the record has been updated, the record is placed back into the file with a REWRITE statement (line 1820). Finally, if this output activity is not successful, an error is reported before an attempt is made to process the next record.

Figure 19.13 *Continued* Updating a VSAM KSDS File (Pseudocode)

```
START
    DO Initiate update
    DO Update file UNTIL eof
    DO Terminate update
END

INITIATE UPDATE
    OPEN files
END

UPDATE FILE
    IF line number > 40
         DO Reprot heading
    ENDIF
    READ customer sales
    IF eof
         SET file status
         GOTO end
    ENDIF
    MOVE input to output
    READ customer file
    IF successful
         DO Customer update
    ELSE
         DO Record error
    ENDIF
END

REPORT HEADING
    ADD 1 to page number
    MOVE 0 to line number
    WRITE headings
END

CUSTOMER UPDATE
    IF balance + purchase > credit limit
         DO Limit error
    ELSE
         ADD purchase to balance
         DO Report activity
    ENDIF
END

REPORT ACTIVITY
    MOVE message to output
    REWRITE output
    IF not successful
         MOVE message to output
    ENDIF
    WRITE message
    ADD 1 to line number
END

LIMIT ERROR
    MOVE message to output
    WRITE output
    ADD 1 to line number
END

RECORD ERROR
    MOVE messge to output
    WRITE error output
    ADD 5 to line number
END

TERMINATE UPDATE
    CLOSE files
END
```

Figure 19.13 *Continued* Updating a VSAM KSDS File

```
             1   1   2   2   2   3   3   4   4   4   5   5   6   6   6   7
   4   8     2   6   0   4   8   2   6   0   4   8   2   6   0   4   8   2

      ****************************************************************
       IDENTIFICATION DIVISION.
      ****************************************************************
       PROGRAM-ID.    VSAM-KSDS-RANDOM-UPDATE.
       AUTHOR.        JOHN WINDSOR.
       DATE-WRITTEN.  JANUARY 1, 1989.
       DATE-COMPILED. JANUARY 1, 1989.
      *    The purpose of this procedure is to update an existing
      *    VSAM keyed sequential data set (KSDS) (CUSTOMER) on the
      *    basis of information contained in a sales file.  Mulitple
      *    updates per customer records are permitted (in random order)
      *    and customer updates (sales records) without a corresponding
      *    customer record are identified.
      ****************************************************************
       ENVIRONMENT DIVISION.
      ****************************************************************
```

Figure 19.13 *Continued* Updating a VSAM KSDS File

```
         1   1   2   2   2   3   3   4   4   4   5   5   6   6   6   7
 4   8   2   6   0   4   8   2   6   0   4   8   2   6   0   4   8   2

*-----------------------------------------------------------*
 CONFIGURATION SECTION.
*-----------------------------------------------------------*
 SOURCE-COMPUTER. IBM.
 OBJECT-COMPUTER. IBM.
 SPECIAL-NAMES.   C01 IS TOP-OF-PAGE.
*-----------------------------------------------------------*
 INPUT-OUTPUT SECTION.
*-----------------------------------------------------------*
 FILE-CONTROL.
     SELECT CUSTOMER-IO-FILE      ASSIGN TO INOUT
         ORGANIZATION IS INDEXED
         RECORD KEY IS CUSTOMER-NUMBER-IO
         ACCESS IS RANDOM
         FILE STATUS IS FILE-STATUS.
     SELECT CUSTOMER-SALES-FILE   ASSIGN TO UT-S-INPUT.
     SELECT EXCEPTION-REPORT-FILE ASSIGN TO UT-S-OUTPUT.
*************************************************************
 DATA DIVISION.
*************************************************************
 FILE SECTION.
 FD  CUSTOMER-IO-FILE
     LABEL RECORDS ARE STANDARD
     RECORD CONTAINS 124 CHARACTERS.
 01  CUSTOMER-RECORD.
     05  CUSTOMER-NUMBER-IO      PIC X(10).
     05  CUSTOMER-NAME-IO        PIC X(30).
     05  CUSTOMER-ADDRESS-IO     PIC X(30).
     05  CUSTOMER-CITY-IO        PIC X(20).
     05  CUSTOMER-STATE-IO       PIC X(02).
     05  CUSTOMER-ZIP-IO         PIC X(10).
     05  CUSTOMER-BALANCE-IO     PIC S9(09)V99.
     05  CUSTOMER-CREDIT-LIMIT-IO PIC S9(09)V99.

 FD  CUSTOMER-SALES-FILE
     LABEL RECORDS ARE STANDARD
     RECORD CONTAINS 80 CHARACTERS
     BLOCK CONTAINS 0 RECORDS.
 01  SALES-RECORD.
     05  CUSTOMER-NUMBER-SALES   PIC X(10).
     05  DATE-OF-PURCHASE-SALES.
         10  PURCHASE-MONTH-SALES PIC X(02).
         10  PURCHASE-DAY-SALES  PIC X(02).
         10  PURCHASE-YEAR-SALES PIC X(02).
     05  PURCHASE-ITEM-SALES     PIC X(10).
     05  PURCHASE-AMOUNT-SALES   PIC S9(09)V99.
     05  FILLER                  PIC X(43).

 FD  EXCEPTION-REPORT-FILE
     LABEL RECORDS ARE OMITTED.
 01  REPORT-RECORD                  PIC X(133).
*-----------------------------------------------------------*
 WORKING-STORAGE SECTION.
*-----------------------------------------------------------*
 01  WORKING-VARIABLES.
     05  SALES-STATUS            PIC X(04) VALUE SPACES.
     05  LINE-NUMBER-WS          PIC 9(02) VALUE 99.
     05  PAGE-NUMBER-WS          PIC 9(02) VALUE ZERO.

 01  VSAM-FILE-STATUS.
     05  FILE-STATUS             PIC 9(02).
         88  SUCCESSFUL-IO                 VALUE 0.
         88  EOF                           VALUE 10.
         88  OUT-OF-SEQUENCE               VALUE 21.
         88  DUPLICATE-KEY                 VALUE 22.
         88  NOT-FOUND                     VALUE 23.
         88  OUT-OF-SPACE                  VALUE 24.
         88  IO-ERROR                      VALUE 30.
         88  LOGIC-ERROR                   VALUE 90 THRU 97.

 01  HEADING-1.
     05  FILLER                  PIC X(32) VALUE SPACES.
     05  FILLER                  PIC X(16) VALUE
```

Figure 19.13 *Continued* Updating a VSAM KSDS File

```
               1   1   2   2   2   3   3   4   4   4   5   5   6   6   6   7
   4   8   2   6   0   4   8   2   6   0   4   8   2   6   0   4   8   2

                                'Exception Report'.
    05  FILLER                  PIC X(25) VALUE SPACES.
    05  FILLER                  PIC X(05) VALUE 'Page'.
    05  PAGE-NUMBER-OUT         PIC Z9.

01  HEADING-2.
    05  FILLER                  PIC X(20) VALUE
                                ' Customer Number'.
    05  FILLER                  PIC X(50) VALUE
        '  Date      Purchase Amount     Comments'.

01  HEADING-3.
    05  FILLER                  PIC X(01) VALUE SPACES.
    05  FILLER                  PIC X(80) VALUE ALL '-'.

01  ERROR-LINE.
    05  FILLER                  PIC X(02) VALUE SPACES.
    05  CUSTOMER-NUMBER-OUT     PIC X(10).
    05  FILLER                  PIC X(08) VALUE SPACES.
    05  PURCHASE-MONTH-OUT      PIC X(02).
    05  FILLER                  PIC X(01) VALUE '/'.
    05  PURCHASE-DAY-OUT        PIC X(02).
    05  FILLER                  PIC X(01) VALUE '/'.
    05  PURCHASE-YEAR-OUT       PIC X(02).
    05  FILLER                  PIC X(05) VALUE SPACES.
    05  PURCHASE-AMOUNT-OUT     PIC ZZZ,ZZZ,ZZZ.ZZ.
    05  FILLER                  PIC X(05) VALUE SPACES.
    05  MESSAGE-OUT             PIC X(50) VALUE SPACES.
***************************************************************
 PROCEDURE DIVISION.
***************************************************************
*------------------------------------------------------------*
 1000-UPDATE-ACCOUNT SECTION.
*------------------------------------------------------------*
     PERFORM 1200-INITIATE-UPDATE.
     PERFORM 1400-UPDATE-FILE
           UNTIL SALES-STATUS = 'DONE'.
     PERFORM 1600-TERMINATE-UPDATE.
     STOP RUN.
*------------------------------------------------------------*
 1200-INITIATE-UPDATE SECTION.
*------------------------------------------------------------*
     OPEN I-O CUSTOMER-IO-FILE
          INPUT CUSTOMER-SALES-FILE
          OUTPUT EXCEPTION-REPORT-FILE.
*------------------------------------------------------------*
 1400-UPDATE-FILE SECTION.
*------------------------------------------------------------*
     IF LINE-NUMBER-WS IS GREATER THAN 40
        PERFORM 1420-REPORT-HEADING.
     READ CUSTOMER-SALES-FILE
         AT END MOVE 'DONE' TO SALES-STATUS
                GO TO 1499-EXIT.
     MOVE CUSTOMER-NUMBER-SALES TO CUSTOMER-NUMBER-OUT
                                   CUSTOMER-NUMBER-IO.
     MOVE PURCHASE-MONTH-SALES TO PURCHASE-MONTH-OUT.
     MOVE PURCHASE-DAY-SALES  TO PURCHASE-DAY-OUT.
     MOVE PURCHASE-YEAR-SALES TO PURCHASE-YEAR-OUT.
     MOVE PURCHASE-AMOUNT-SALES TO PURCHASE-AMOUNT-OUT.
     READ CUSTOMER-IO-FILE.
     IF SUCCESSFUL-IO
         PERFORM 1440-CUSTOMER-UPDATE
     ELSE
         PERFORM 1460-RECORD-ERROR.

 1499-EXIT.
     EXIT.
*------------------------------------------------------------*
 1420-REPORT-HEADING SECTION.
*------------------------------------------------------------*
```

Figure 19.13 *Continued* Updating a VSAM KSDS File

```
                1   1   2   2   2   3   3   4   4   4   5   5   6   6   6   7
    4   8   2   6   0   4   8   2   6   0   4   8   2   6   0   4   8   2

           ADD 1 TO PAGE-NUMBER-WS.
           MOVE PAGE-NUMBER-WS        TO PAGE-NUMBER-OUT.
           MOVE 0                     TO LINE-NUMBER-WS.
           WRITE REPORT-RECORD FROM HEADING-1
               AFTER ADVANCING TOP-OF-PAGE.
           WRITE REPORT-RECORD FROM HEADING-2 AFTER ADVANCING 2 LINES.
           WRITE REPORT-RECORD FROM HEADING-3 AFTER ADVANCING 1 LINES.
           MOVE SPACES                TO REPORT-RECORD.
           WRITE REPORT-RECORD AFTER ADVANCING 1 LINES.
      *-----------------------------------------------------------*
       1440-CUSTOMER-UPDATE SECTION.
      *-----------------------------------------------------------*
           IF CUSTOMER-BALANCE-IO + PURCHASE-AMOUNT-SALES >
             CUSTOMER-CREDIT-LIMIT-IO
               PERFORM 1444-LIMIT-ERROR
           ELSE
               ADD PURCHASE-AMOUNT-SALES TO CUSTOMER-BALANCE-IO
               PERFORM 1442-REPORT-ACTIVITY.
      *-----------------------------------------------------------*
       1442-REPORT-ACTIVITY SECTION.
      *-----------------------------------------------------------*
           MOVE 'Customer Record Updated' TO MESSAGE-OUT.
           REWRITE CUSTOMER-RECORD.
           IF NOT SUCCESSFUL-IO
                MOVE 'Rewrite Error--Record Not Updated' TO MESSAGE-OUT.
           WRITE REPORT-RECORD FROM ERROR-LINE AFTER ADVANCING 1 LINES.
           ADD 1 TO LINE-NUMBER-WS.
      *-----------------------------------------------------------*
       1444-LIMIT-ERROR SECTION.
      *-----------------------------------------------------------*
           MOVE 'Credit Limit Exceeded' TO MESSAGE-OUT.
           WRITE REPORT-RECORD FROM ERROR-LINE AFTER ADVANCING 1 LINES.
           ADD 1 TO LINE-NUMBER-WS.
      *-----------------------------------------------------------*
       1460-RECORD-ERROR SECTION,
      *-----------------------------------------------------------*
           MOVE ALL '-'               TO REPORT-RECORD.
           WRITE REPORT-RECORD AFTER ADVANCING 2 LINES.
           MOVE 'Unknown Error'       TO MESSAGE-OUT.
           IF NOT-FOUND
               MOVE 'Customer Record Not Found' TO MESSAGE-OUT.
           WRITE REPORT-RECORD FROM ERROR-LINE AFTER ADVANCING 1 LINES.
           MOVE ALL '-'               TO REPORT-RECORD.
           WRITE REPORT-RECORD AFTER ADVANCING 1 LINES.
           MOVE SPACES                TO REPORT-RECORD.
           WRITE REPORT-RECORD AFTER ADVANCING 1 LINES.
           ADD 5 TO LINE-NUMBER-WS.
      *-----------------------------------------------------------*
       1600-TERMINATE-UPDATE SECTION.
      *-----------------------------------------------------------*
           CLOSE CUSTOMER-IO-FILE,
                 CUSTOMER-SALES-FILE
                 EXCEPTION-REPORT-FILE.
```

Figure 19.13 *Continued* Updating a VSAM KSDS File [CUSTOMER-SALES] (Data)

```
-----------------------------------------------
|      |         1         2         3         4|
|Record|1234567890123456789012345678901234567890|
|----------------------------------------------|
|     1|3333333333051885441294    00000044125   |
|     2|9X0-334RDS05158529-43319  00000041232   |
|     3|1141944103051485419337    00000712911   |
|     4|3333333333051485          00005122529   |
|     5|4125592793050185888888888800512295147   |
|     6|4412X47390050185 45-RTS   00000056902   |
|     7|3333333333060985BXR-33294 00002212219   |
|     8|5270215827050585          00000112697   |
|     9|5512294148051585          00000004123   |
|    10|349896645105178599-457-3310000476110   |
|    11|4412X473900522855514429022000000003312   |
|    12|1141944103052585          00000012000   |
-----------------------------------------------
```

Figure 19.13 *Continued* Updating a VSAM KSDS File [CUSTOMER IO] (Data)

```
-------------------------------------------------------------------------------------------------------------------------------------
|
|      |                                                                                                   1         1         1 |
|      |         1         2         3         4         5         6         7         8         9         0         1         2 |
|Record|1234567890123456789012345678901234567890123456789012345678901234567890123456789012345678901234567890123456789012345678901234|
|-----------------------------------------------------------------------------------------------------------------------------------|
|     1|1RX14219-3John P. Villiman              8887 Peach Tree Lane          Dallas              TX75002     0000000314300000500000|
|     2|1141944103Edwin Williams                2139 South Colgate Street     Perryton            TX79070     0000033193300035000000|
|     3|3199127X33James Thompkins               44339 South Wacker Drive      Chicago             IL60606     0000002291800000500000|
|     4|3333333333Julia Harriston               6132 Mill Road Avenue         Shreveport          LA63341     0000035134300005000000|
|     5|3498966451Jacob R. Sullivan             6134 Malibu Drive             Los Angeles         CA96512     0000000000000004400000|
|     6|4412X47390Marshall Silverman            2219 West 7th Street          Cleveland           OH30119     0000000000000000500000|
|     7|5270215827Charles Everest               8821 Ocean Parkway            Miami               FL51332     0000000000000000500000|
|     8|6213937661Jason Madison                 8831 Cedar Drive N.W.         Norwich             CT00218     0000041452300003000000|
|     9|6427633-94Mark U. Lemon                 P. O. Box 51244               New York            NY03158     0000000000000000005000|
|    10|773194221BHelen B. Overstreet           3153 Yellow Brick Road        Yellow Stone Park   MT41229     0000001284200000000000|
|    11|9X0-334RDSAnthony P. Jones              Executive Office Building     Washington          DC00000     0000000000000000000000|
-------------------------------------------------------------------------------------------------------------------------------------
```

Figure 19.13 *Continued* Updating a VSAM KSDS File (Output)

```
                                     Exception Report                           Page  1

Customer Number      Date          Purchase Amount        Comments
-----------------------------------------------------------------------------------------
3333333333           05/18/85               441.25        Customer Record Updated
9X0-334RDS           05/15/85               412.32        Credit Limit Exceeded
1141944103           05/14/85             7,129.11        Customer Record Updated
3333333333           05/14/85            51,225.29        Credit Limit Exceeded

-----------------------------------------------------------------------------------------
4125592793           05/01/85         5,122,951.47        Customer Record Not Found
-----------------------------------------------------------------------------------------
4412X47390           05/01/85               569.02        Customer Record Updated
3333333333           06/09/85            22,122.19        Customer Record Updated
5270215827           05/05/85             1,126.97        Customer Record Updated

-----------------------------------------------------------------------------------------
5512294148           05/15/85                41.23        Customer Record Not Found
-----------------------------------------------------------------------------------------
3498966451           05/17/85             4,761.10        Customer Record Updated
4412X47390           05/22/85                33.12        Customer Record Updated
1141944103           05/25/85               120.00        Customer Record Updated
```

Adding to a VSAM KSDS File

The last process demonstrated for all previously discussed files is record addition. As shown in Figure 19.14, adding records to a VSAM KSDS file is essentially the same as record addition for an ISAM file. However, you should recall VSAM handles record addition (and deletion) much more efficiently than ISAM. The ENVIRONMENT DIVISION and DATA DIVISION entries for the VSAM file for the addition operation are the same as for update operation. In the PROCEDURE DIVISION, the CUSTOMER-IO-FILE is again opened in an I-O mode. In the 1400-ADD-RECORDS procedure, a new record is read (line 1200) and its contents are placed directly into the CUSTOMER-REC. (line 410). Thus, both the data and the key value for the new record are established. Then the record is written to the customer file (line 1250). If the output operation is successful, the addition of the record to the file is indicated on a printed report. Otherwise an error is recorded.

Figure 19.14 Adding to a VSAM KSDS File (System Flowchart)

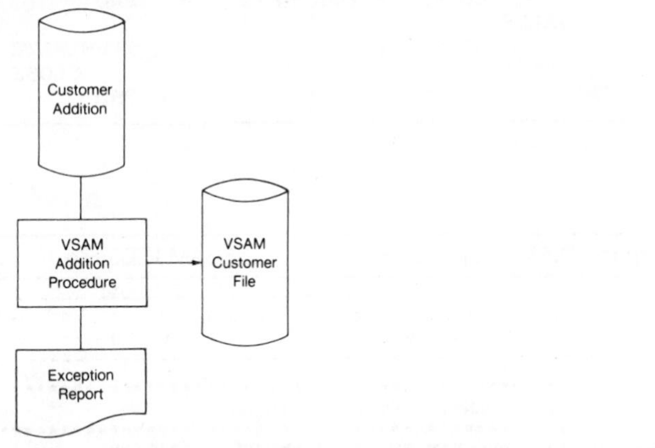

Figure 19.14 *Continued* Adding to a VSAM KSDS File (Hierarchy Chart)

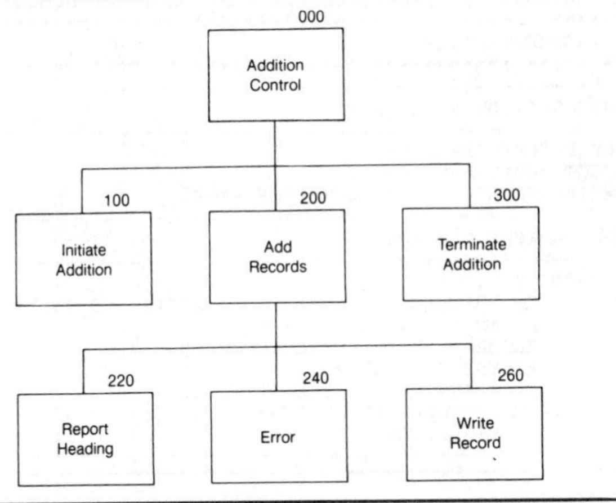

Figure 19.14 *Continued* Adding to a VSAM KSDS File (Pseudocode)

```
START
    DO Initiate addition
    DO Add records UNTIL eof
    DO Terminate addition
END

INITIATE ADDITION
    OPEN files
END

ADD RECORDS
    IF line number > 40
         DO Report heading
    ENDIF
    READ input file
    IF eof
         SET addition status
         GOTO end
    ENDIF
    MOVE input to output
    WRITE output record
    IF successful
         DO Write record
    ELSE
         DO Error
    ENDIF
END

REPORT HEADING
    ADD 1 to page number
    MOVE 0 to line number
    WRITE headings
END

ERROR
    MOVE message to output
    IF duplicate key
         MOVE message to output
    ENDIF
    IF out of space
         MOVE message to output
    ENDIF
    WRITE output
    ADD 2 to line number
END

WRITE RECORD
    MOVE message to output
    WRITE customer output
    ADD 2 to line number
END

TERMINATE ADDITION
    CLOSE files
END
```

Figure 19.14 *Continued* Adding to a VSAM KSDS File

```
           1   1   2   2   2   3   3   4   4   4   5   5   6   6   6   7
   4   8   2   6   0   4   8   2   6   0   4   8   2   6   0   4   8   2

 ************************************************************
  IDENTIFICATION DIVISION.
 ************************************************************
  PROGRAM-ID.     VSAM-KSDS-ADDITION.
  AUTHOR.         JOHN WINDSOR.
  DATE-WRITTEN.  JANUARY 1, 1989.
  DATE-COMPILED. JANUARY 1, 1989.
 *     The purpose of this procedure is to add records (new
 *     customers) to an existing VSAM keyed sequential data set
 *     (KSDS) (CUSTOMER) file.  The procedure prohibits duplicate
 *     customer records with the same customer number.
 ************************************************************
  ENVIRONMENT DIVISION.
 ************************************************************
 *----------------------------------------------------------*
  CONFIGURATION SECTION.
 *----------------------------------------------------------*
  SOURCE-COMPUTER. IBM.
  OBJECT-COMPUTER. IBM.
  SPECIAL-NAMES.    C01 IS TOP-OF-PAGE.
 *----------------------------------------------------------*
  INPUT-OUTPUT SECTION.
 *----------------------------------------------------------*
  FILE-CONTROL.
      SELECT CUSTOMER-IO             ASSIGN TO INOUT
          ORGANIZATION IS INDEXED
          RECORD KEY IS CUSTOMER-NUMBER-IO
          ACCESS IS RANDOM
          FILE STATUS IS FILE-STATUS.
      SELECT CUSTOMER-ADDITION-FILE ASSIGN TO UT-S-INPUT2.
      SELECT EXCEPTION-REPORT-FILE  ASSIGN TO UT-S-OUTPUT.
```

Figure 19.14 *Continued* Adding to a VSAM KSDS File

```
*****************************************************************
 DATA DIVISION.
*****************************************************************
*---------------------------------------------------------------*
 FILE SECTION.
*---------------------------------------------------------------*
 FD  CUSTOMER-IO
     LABEL RECORDS ARE STANDARD
     RECORD CONTAINS 124 CHARACTERS.
 01  CUSTOMER-REC.
     05  CUSTOMER-NUMBER-IO       PIC X(10).
     05  FILLER                   PIC X(114).

 FD  CUSTOMER-ADDITION-FILE
     LABEL RECORDS ARE STANDARD
     RECORD CONTAINS 124 CHARACTERS
     BLOCK CONTAINS 0 RECORDS.
 01  CUSTOMER-ADDITION-RECORD.
     05  CUSTOMER-NUMBER-ADDS     PIC X(10).
     05  FILLER                   PIC X(114).

 FD  EXCEPTION-REPORT-FILE
     LABEL RECORDS ARE OMITTED.
 01  REPORT-RECORD                PIC X(133).
*---------------------------------------------------------------*
 WORKING-STORAGE SECTION.
*---------------------------------------------------------------*
 01  PROGRAM-CONTROL-VARIABLES.
     05  ADDITION-STATUS          PIC X(04) VALUE SPACES.
     05  LINE-NUMBER-WS           PIC 9(02) VALUE 99.
     05  PAGE-NUMBER-WS           PIC 9(02) VALUE ZERO.

 01  VSAM-FILE-STATUS.
     05  FILE-STATUS              PIC 9(02).
         88  SUCCESSFUL-IO                  VALUE 0.
         88  EOF                            VALUE 10.
         88  OUT-OF-SEQUENCE                VALUE 21.
         88  DUPLICATE-KEY                  VALUE 22.
         88  NOT-FOUND                      VALUE 23.
         88  OUT-OF-SPACE                   VALUE 24.
         88  IO-ERROR                       VALUE 30.
         88  LOGIC-ERROR                    VALUE 90 THRU 97.

 01  HEADING-1.
     05  FILLER                   PIC X(32) VALUE SPACES.
     05  FILLER                   PIC X(16) VALUE
                                  'Exception Report'.
     05  FILLER                   PIC X(25) VALUE SPACES.
     05  FILLER                   PIC X(05) VALUE 'Page'.
     05  PAGE-NUMBER-OUT          PIC Z9.

 01  HEADING-2.
     05  FILLER                   PIC X(20) VALUE
                                  ' Customer Number'.
     05  FILLER                   PIC X(50) VALUE
                                  'Comments'.

 01  HEADING-3.
     05  FILLER                   PIC X(01) VALUE SPACES.
     05  FILLER                   PIC X(80) VALUE ALL '-'.

 01  ERROR-LINE.
     05  FILLER                   PIC X(02) VALUE SPACES.
     05  CUSTOMER-NUMBER-OUT      PIC X(10).
     05  FILLER                   PIC X(08) VALUE SPACES.
     05  MESSAGE-OUT              PIC X(50) VALUE SPACES.
*****************************************************************
 PROCEDURE DIVISION.
*****************************************************************
*---------------------------------------------------------------*
 1000-ADDITION-CONTROL SECTION.
*---------------------------------------------------------------*
```

Figure 19.14 *Continued* Adding to a VSAM KSDS File

```
               1   1   2   2   2   3   3   4   4   4   5   5   6   6   6   7
       4   8   2   6   0   4   8   2   6   0   4   8   2   6   0   4   8   2

           PERFORM 1200-INITIATE-ADDITION.
           PERFORM 1400-ADD-RECORDS
               UNTIL ADDITION-STATUS = 'DONE'.
           PERFORM 1600-TERMINATE-ADDITION.
           STOP RUN.
      *----------------------------------------------------------------*
       1200-INITIATE-ADDITION SECTION.
      *----------------------------------------------------------------*
           OPEN I-O CUSTOMER-IO
                INPUT CUSTOMER-ADDITION-FILE
                OUTPUT EXCEPTION-REPORT-FILE.
      *----------------------------------------------------------------*
       1400-ADD-RECORDS SECTION.
      *----------------------------------------------------------------*
           IF LINE-NUMBER-WS IS GREATER THAN 40
               PERFORM 1420-REPORT-HEADING.
           READ CUSTOMER-ADDITION-FILE INTO CUSTOMER-REC
               AT END MOVE 'DONE' TO ADDITION-STATUS
                      GO TO 1499-EXIT.
           MOVE CUSTOMER-NUMBER-ADDS TO CUSTOMER-NUMBER-OUT.
           WRITE CUSTOMER-REC.
           IF SUCCESSFUL-IO
               PERFORM 1460-WRITE-RECORD
           ELSE
               PERFORM 1440-ERROR.

       1499-EXIT.
           EXIT.
      *----------------------------------------------------------------*
       1420-REPORT-HEADING SECTION.
      *----------------------------------------------------------------*
           ADD 1 TO PAGE-NUMBER-WS.
           MOVE PAGE-NUMBER-WS         TO PAGE-NUMBER-OUT.
           MOVE 0                      TO LINE-NUMBER-WS.
           WRITE REPORT-RECORD FROM HEADING-1
               AFTER ADVANCING TOP-OF-PAGE.
           WRITE REPORT-RECORD FROM HEADING-2 AFTER ADVANCING 2 LINES.
           WRITE REPORT-RECORD FROM HEADING-3 AFTER ADVANCING 1 LINES.
           MOVE SPACES                 TO REPORT-RECORD.
           WRITE REPORT-RECORD AFTER ADVANCING 1 LINES.
      *----------------------------------------------------------------*
       1440-ERROR SECTION.
      *----------------------------------------------------------------*
           MOVE 'Unknown Error'        TO MESSAGE-OUT.
           IF DUPLICATE-KEY
               MOVE 'Attempt to Add a Duplicate Record' TO MESSAGE-OUT.
           IF OUT-OF-SPACE
               MOVE 'File Space is Exhausted' TO MESSAGE-OUT.
           WRITE REPORT-RECORD FROM ERROR-LINE AFTER 2.
           ADD 2 TO LINE-NUMBER-WS.
      *----------------------------------------------------------------*
       1460-WRITE-RECORD SECTION.
      *----------------------------------------------------------------*
           MOVE 'Record Added'         TO MESSAGE-OUT.
           WRITE REPORT-RECORD FROM ERROR-LINE AFTER 2.
           ADD 2 TO LINE-NUMBER-WS.
      *----------------------------------------------------------------*
       1600-TERMINATE-ADDITION SECTION.
      *----------------------------------------------------------------*
           CLOSE CUSTOMER-IO,
                 EXCEPTION-REPORT-FILE
                 CUSTOMER-ADDITION-FILE.
```

Figure 19.14 *Continued* Adding to a VSAM KSDS File [CUSTOMER-ADDITION] (Data)

```
------------------------------------------------------------------------------------------------------------------------------------
|                                                                                                             1         1         1 |
|      |         1         2         3         4         5         6         7         8         9         0         1         2 |
|Record|12345678901234567890123456789012345678901234567890123456789012345678901234567890123456789012345678901234567890123456789012345|
|-----------------------------------------------------------------------------------------------------------------------------------|
|     1|3333333333George P. Martin              Las Vegas Hilton              Las Vegas           NV81222     9999999999900000000000|
|     2|2199428878Stewart A. Alexander          5112 Hamilton Parkway         Minneapolis         MN21132     0000062239000001000000|
|     3|5122314151Mark R. White                 55123 War Memorial Drive      Cleveland           OH41229     0000004123300000050000|
|     4|X14339-278Rober P. Evans                1422 N. W. Classen Blvd.      Oklahoma City       OK65124     0000000000000000300000|
------------------------------------------------------------------------------------------------------------------------------------
```

Figure 19.14 *Continued* Adding to a VSAM KSDS File [CUSTOMER-IO] (Data)

```
------------------------------------------------------------------------------------------------------------------------------------
|                                                                                                             1         1         1 |
|      |         1         2         3         4         5         6         7         8         9         0         1         2 |
|Record|12345678901234567890123456789012345678901234567890123456789012345678901234567890123456789012345678901234567890123456789012345|
|-----------------------------------------------------------------------------------------------------------------------------------|
|     1|X14339-278Robert P. Evans               1422 N. W. Classen Blvd.      Oklahoma City       OK65124     0000000000000000300000|
|     2|1RX14219-3John P. Villiman              8887 Peach Tree Lane          Dallas              TX75002     0000000314300000500000|
|     3|1141944103Edwin Williams                2139 South Colgate Street     Perryton            TX79070     0000105684D00035000000|
|     4|2199428878Stewart A. Alexander          5112 Hamilton Parkway         Minneapolis         MN21132     0000062239000001000000|
|     5|3199127X33James Thompkins               44339 South Wacker Drive      Chicago             IL60606     0000002291800000500000|
|     6|3333333333Julia Harriston               6132 Mill Road Avenue         Shreveport          LA63341     0000260768G00005000000|
|     7|3498966451Jacob R. Sullivan             6134 Malibu Drive             Los Angeles         CA96512     0000047611 00004400000|
|     8|4412X47390Marshall Silverman            2219 West 7th Street          Cleveland           OH30119     0000006021D00000500000|
|     9|5122314151Mark R. White                 55123 War Memorial Drive      Cleveland           OH41229     0000004123300000050000|
|    10|5270215827Charles Everest               8821 Ocean Parkway            Miami               FL51332     0000011269G00000500000|
|    11|6213937661Jason Madison                 8831 Cedar Drive N.W.         Norwich             CT00218     0000041452300003000000|
|    12|6427633-94Mark U. Lemon                 P. O. Box 51244               New York            NY03158     0000000000000000005000|
|    13|773194221BHelen B. Overstreet           3153 Yellow Brick Road        Yellow Stone Park   MT41229     0000001284200000000000|
|    14|9XO-334RDSAnthony P. Jones              Executive Office Building     Washington          DC00000     0000000000000000000000|
------------------------------------------------------------------------------------------------------------------------------------
```

Figure 19.14 *Continued* Adding to a VSAM KSDS File (Output)

```
                                        Exception Report                        Page  1

          Customer Number    Comments
          ------------------------------------------------------------------------------

          X14339-278         Record Added

          2199428878         Record Added

          3333333333         Attempt to Add a Duplicate Record

          5122314151         Record Added
```

Summary

In this chapter, the third type of traditional file—the relative file—has been presented. As indicated, a relative file is fundamentally different from either a sequential or an indexed file. Each record placed in a relative file is recorded in a relative record location, based on a data-to-address transformation function and is physically independent of any other record in the file. Furthermore, it has been demonstrated that rapid retrieval of individual records is the fundamental advantage of relative files, whereas space and possible complexity of the data-to-address transformation function are among the disadvantages.

This chapter also provided an introduction to a family of file organizations known as VSAM. VSAM supports three different file types, including

An entry sequence data set (ESDS file), which is highly similar to a sequential file
A key sequence data set (KSDS file), which is highly similar to an ISAM file
A relative record data set (RRDS file), which is highly similar to a relative file
The relative strengths and flexibility of VSAM over traditional file organizations were also demonstrated.

Notes on Programming Style

First, it should be noted that relative files are used relatively infrequently. Because of the limitations of relative files, the programmer should not try to force a file to fit into a relative file mode. Normally, there would have to be substantial and compelling reasons for using a relative file. A decision to use this type of file should not be made casually.

Second, you are encouraged to utilize VSAM files whenever possible. They tend to be much more flexible than traditional files. That is, it is a relatively simple process to go from one type of file organization to another. Furthermore, existing non-VSAM files can be converted into VSAM format or referenced directly (through a processing interface) as though they were VSAM files.

Finally, you should employ the FILE STATUS identifier whenever possible. The INVALID KEY phrase, which is attached to many input or output statements for VSAM files, does not provide the same level of detail or error diagnostics as is possible with the FILE STATUS identifier. Develop a common convention for using this identifier, such as illustrated in this chapter, and use it religiously. After all, knowing more about a problem, especially when it is related to a file, is always better than knowing less and having to guess at the solution.

Questions

Below, fill in the blank(s) with the appropriate word, words, or phrases.

1. Among the traditional file types are file organizations known as sequential, indexed, and _____ .

2. Although records may be accessed by keys with an indexed file, records are normally accessed by _____ _____ with a relative file.

3. Relative files are sometimes also called _____ _____ files.

4. A record location or position may also be called a(n) _____ .

5. Record locations in a relative file are normally consecutively numbered, beginning with location _____ (number).

6. The primary advantage of using a relative file is _____ .

7. Generally, a relative file would use _____ (more/less) disk space than a sequential file containing the same number of records.

8. Relative files are unblocked files. This means that a logical record is the same as a _____ record.

9. Relative files are somewhat similar to indexed files in that both require the use of a _____ KEY clause.
10. The NOMINAL KEY identifier for a relative file must be defined in the _____ SECTION.
11. The NOMINAL KEY identifier for a relative file must be described as a _____ data item.
12. The _____ clause is not permitted in the FD description of a relative file.
13. To read a relative file sequentially, the programmer should define the file with an ACCESS MODE IS _____ clause, and the READ statement should use the _____ phrase.
14. To read a relative file randomly, the programmer must define the file with an ACCESS MODE IS _____ clause, and the READ statement should use the _____ phrase.
15. One of the problems associated with using a relative file is the development of a _____ function.
16. One common approach to deriving a data-to-address transformation function is to use _____ division.
17. A _____ number is a number that may only be divided evenly by itself and by 1.
18. A _____ is the result when a data-to-address transformation function produces the same record location for two or more unique data values.
19. When a data-to-address transformation function produces a synonym, it is the programmer's responsibility to determine that a synonym has been produced and _____ .
20. _____ is an operation that is frequently performed during the initial development of a relative file whereby disk space is preallocated and initialized to some known data value.
21. When randomly retrieving a record from a relative file, the programmer needs to (a) determine the record location, (b) read the specified location, and (c) _____ .
22. VSAM files are permitted only on computers using _____ operating systems.
23. The VSAM file type that most closely resembles a sequential file is a(n) _____ .
24. The VSAM file type that most closely resembles an indexed file is a(n) _____ .
25. The VSAM file type that most closely resembles a relative file is a(n) _____ .
26. A VSAM KSDS file is superior to an ISAM file because it handles record _____ and _____ more efficiently.
27. A group of VSAM files is known as a _____ .
28. Within the VSAM structure, the element that most closely approximates a file is the _____ .
29. A VSAM file is subdivided into _____ , which are divided into _____ .
30. A VSAM file often contains empty areas known as _____ .
31. As records are added to a VSAM file, a control interval _____ may result.
32. A utility program called _____ , which is part of Access Method Services, may be used to manipulate VSAM files.
33. Within the FILE-CONTROL paragraph, the VSAM file type is specified through the _____ clause.
34. The RECORD KEY clause must always be specified for a(n) _____ file.
35. The RELATIVE KEY clause is generally specified for a(n) _____ file.
36. To determine the cause of file processing errors, the programmer may use an identifier associated with the _____ clause.
37. RECORD KEY values for an ALTERNATE KEY clause do not have to be unique for a KSDS file if the _____ clause is specified.

38. If a KSDS file or a RRDS file is to be accessed randomly, the ____ clause must be specified.

39. For a VSAM file, the ____ clause of the FD is treated as a comment since the physical record allocations are handled by VSAM.

40. The ____ and ____ clauses are optional for input-output statements for VSAM files.

41. The only statement that may be used only in conjunction with a VSAM file (as opposed to traditional files) is the ____ statement.

Answer the following questions by circling either "T" for True or "F" for False.

T F **42.** Each record location within a relative file would normally contain data.

T F **43.** The NOMINAL KEY for a relative file must be defined as an eight-digit integer binary data item.

T F **44.** The data item on which a record location is based must be numeric.

T F **45.** A relative file may be allocated disk space in either tracks or cylinders.

T F **46.** One of the advantages of a relative file is the minimal amount of disk space used by the file (in comparison to other file types).

T F **47.** A relative file may not be read sequentially.

T F **48.** Within a relative file, logical records and physical records are the same.

T F **49.** Normally, records are placed into a relative file based on an ascending sequence of values of some data item within the relative file record description.

T F **50.** The NOMINAL KEY identifier for a relative file must appear within the relative file record description.

T F **51.** Modulus division is the only method by which a data-to-address transformation function may be developed.

T F **52.** Hashing and mapping functions are the same as data-to-address transformation functions.

T F **53.** When synonyms are produced by a data-to-address transformation function, two or more records are recorded in the same record location.

T F **54.** After a data-to-address transformation function has been used to create a file, it may be extensively modified for record retrieval purposes.

T F **55.** There are essentially no extra hardware or software requirements for using VSAM files.

T F **56.** RRDS files are the most frequently used VSAM file type.

T F **57.** ESDS files may be accessed randomly.

T F **58.** The RELATIVE KEY clause for a RRDS file has the same internal requirements as a NOMINAL KEY for a relative file.

T F **59.** The RELATIVE KEY clause for a RRDS file is not required when the file is read sequentially.

T F **60.** A KSDS file may be processed either sequentially or randomly.

T F **61.** When a file is identified with an ACCESS IS DYNAMIC clause, the file may be processed sequentially, randomly, or both within the same program.

T F **62.** Records that are deleted from a VSAM file are no longer accessible, but they continue to occupy space.

T F **63.** One advantage of VSAM files over other file types is the capability of the user to specify a file password.

T F **64.** A VSAM file description in the FILE-CONTROL paragraph must be accompanied by a FILE STATUS clause.

T F **65.** If the value of the FILE STATUS identifier is 10, an end-of-file condition has been detected.

T F **66.** Some non-VSAM files may be accessed as though they were VSAM files.

T F **67.** When a VSAM file is OPENed in the EXTENDED mode, records may be added to the file at any desired position within the file.

T F **68.** The DELETE statement is not permitted for an ESDS file.

T F **69.** VSAM files are historically older than relative files.

T F **70.** A delete byte is generally required at the beginning of every VSAM record description.

Problems

19.1 Complete Problem 17.1. Alter the file type of the inventory file to a relative file. Alter the requirements of the update exceptions report so that updated records are printed after each record from the sales file has been processed. In other words, do not reorder the sales file to conform to the order of the inventory file. Finally, some reorganization of the inventory record may be required to create a single field that uniquely identifies the record.

19.2 Complete Problem 17.2. Alter the file type of the customer file to a relative file. Order the sales file data such that all updates for a single customer may be handled at one time.

19.3 Complete Problem 17.3. Alter the file type of the inventory file to a relative file. The purchase orders are to be handled in the sequence they appear in the purchase order file. Some reorganization of the inventory record may be required to establish a single field that uniquely identifies the record. In addition, the length of the record may be altered to accommodate record deletions.

19.4 Complete Problem 17.1. Alter the file type of the inventory file to a VSAM KSDS file. Alter the requirements of the update exceptions report so that updated records are printed after each record from the sales file has been processed. In other words, do not reorder the sales file to conform to the order of the inventory file.

19.5 Complete Problem 17.2. Alter the file type of the customer file to a VSAM KSDS file. Order the sales file data such that all updates for a single customer may be handled at one time.

19.6 Complete Problem 17.3. Alter the file type of the inventory file to a VSAM KSDS file. The purchase orders are to be handled in the sequence they appear in the purchase order file.

PART

IV

SPECIAL USAGE COBOL CONCEPTS

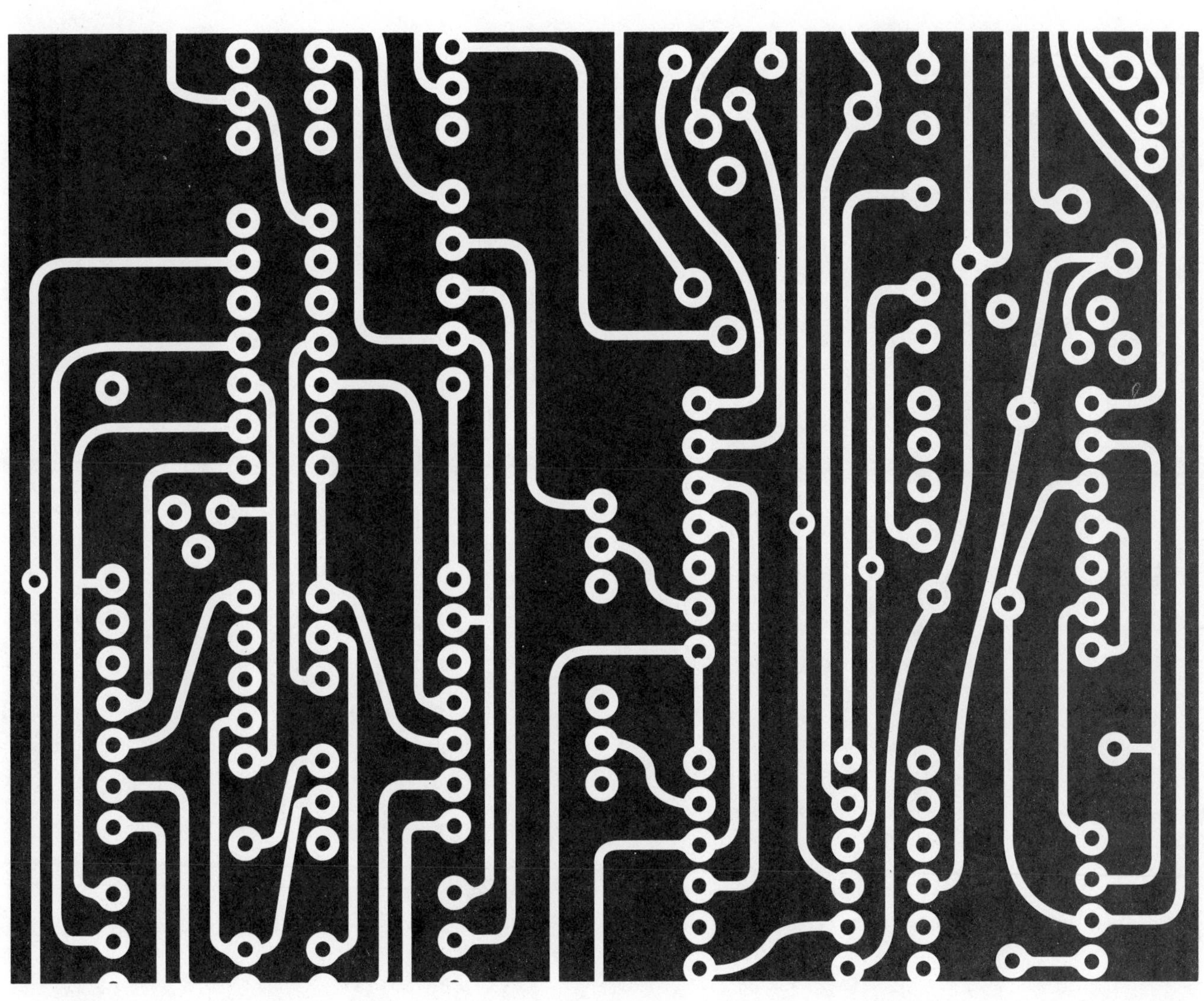

CHAPTER

20

The COPY Verb and Subprograms

Programmers are sometimes faced with situations in which the complexity of a programming task calls for more expertise than the programmer has. In other situations, a programmer may wish to use code that had previously been used in conjunction with another program to avoid rewriting it or to eliminate the chance for errors. It is sometimes desirable to incorporate instructions written by someone else into your program or to reuse code that you have written earlier. Both of these activities are supported by the COPY verb and subprograms.

There is a fundamental difference between what happens when a COPY statement is placed in a program when compared with the results of a linkage to a subprogram. When a COPY statement is executed, the result is new source code "inserted" into an existing program. When a subprogram is used, an existing program passes control to another separate, complete, and independently compiled program.

The COPY Statement

The COPY statement, as already indicated, is used to "insert" portions of a program (e.g., record descriptions or parts of the PROCEDURE DIVISION) from a file that is external to the program itself. Suppose a common record description is to be used in several programs. One approach that may be used to make sure the record is consistent among all programs is to create the record description only once and place it in a file. Several programs could then COPY the contents of the file when needed. This approach ensures that all the programs would have the same record description, as well as consistent record descriptions.

In the PROCEDURE DIVISION, suppose a relatively complicated piece of code is required by several programs. One experienced person could be assigned the responsibility of writing this code and other less proficient programmers could simply copy it into the programs they are developing. Thus, with this approach, the expertise of one programmer could be shared with several other programmers. The result would be more quickly developed programs and programs with fewer errors.

The format of the COPY statement is shown in Figure 20.1. Note that in its simplest form the statement might appear as

```
COPY file-name
```

Therefore, the complete contents of the file-name would be inserted at the location of the program where the COPY statement appears. To illustrate this point, assume you have developed a file-name called COMMON-SALES-RECORD (a sales record), which contains the following.

```
01 DUMMY-RECORD.
   05 ITEM-PURCHASED           PIC X(06).
   05 QUANTITY-PURCHASED       PIC 9(06).
   05 DATE-PURCHASED.
      10 DP-MONTH              PIC X(02).
      10 DP-DAY                PIC X(02).
      10 DP-YEAR               PIC X(02).
```

This file would be available to any program that contained the statement

```
COPY COMMON-SALES-RECORD.
```

Thus, if we produce the code

```
.
.
.
DATA DIVISION.
FILE SECTION.
FD SALES-FILE
   LABEL RECORDS ARE STANDARD.
01 SALES-RECORD COPY COMMON-SALES-RECORD.
.
.
.
```

as the program is being compiled, the COMMON-SALES-RECORD file would be inserted in the program at the point of the COPY statement. This would result in code, which would be presented to the COBOL compiler (as reflected by a later source program listing) as

```
.
.
.
DATA DIVISION.
FILE SECTION.
```

Figure 20.1 Format of the COPY Statement

```
COPY file-name

    [REPLACING { identifier-1 }  BY  { identifier-2 }
               { literal-1    }      { literal-2    }
               { word-1       }      { word-2       }

               { identifier-3 }  BY  { identifier-4 }  ] . . . ]
               { literal-3    }      { literal-4    }
               { word-3       }      { word-4       }
```

```
FD SALES-FILE
   LABEL RECORDS ARE STANDARD.
01 SALES-RECORD.
   05 ITEM-PURCHASED             PIC X(06).
   05 QUANTITY-PURCHASED         PIC 9(06).
   05 DATE-PURCHASED.
      10 DP-MONTH                PIC X(02).
      10 DP-DAY                  PIC X(02).
      10 DP-YEAR                 PIC X(02).
.
.
.
```

Note that in the example, the record-name (SALES-RECORD) is retained from the current program, and the record-name (DUMMY-RECORD) from the copied file is eliminated.

The COPY statement may appear in the ENVIRONMENT DIVISION, DATA DIVISION, and PROCEDURE DIVISION, as illustrated in Table 20.1. As indicated, the

Table 20.1 Uses of the COPY Statement

```
ENVIRONMENT DIVISION.
CONFIGURATION SECTION.
SOURCE-COMPUTER.  COPY statement.
OBJECT-COMPUTER.  COPY statement.
SPECIAL-NAMES.    COPY statement.

INPUT-OUTPUT SECTION.
FILE-CONTROL  COPY statement.
    SELECT file-name COPY statement.

DATA DIVISION.
FILE SECTION.
FD  file-name COPY statement.
01  record-name COPY statement.

SD  sort-file-name COPY statement.
01  sort-record-name COPY statement.

WORKING-STORAGE SECTION.
01  record-name COPY statement.
01  record-name-1 REDEFINES record-name-2 COPY statement.

REPORT SECTION.
RD  report-name COPY statement.
01  [record-name] COPY statement.

LINKAGE SECTION. (Described later in this chapter)
01  record-name COPY statement.
01  record-name-1 REDEFINES record-name-2 COPY statement.

PROCEDURE DIVISION.
section-name SECTION.
    COPY statement.
paragraph-name.
    COPY statement.
```

COPY statement may be used after a paragraph name in the CONFIGURATION SECTION and INPUT-OUTPUT SECTION. Furthermore, the COPY statement may be used as a replacement for the ASSIGN clause in the FILE-CONTROL paragraph. In the DATA DIVISION, the COPY statement may be used in the FILE SECTION, WORKING-STORAGE SECTION, and REPORT SECTION. In the FILE SECTION, the COPY statement may follow a file-name (supplying all other entries for either an FD or SD that describe that file) or after a record-name (describing all the fields associated with that record). In the WORKING-STORAGE SECTION, the COPY statement may follow a record-name. In the REPORT SECTION, a COPY statement may follow a report-name. Finally, in the PROCEDURE DIVISION, the COPY statement may appear after either a SECTION or paragraph name. However, a COPY statement cannot appear in a file that itself is a COPY file.

The REPLACING option is not a standard option for the COPY statement, but it is available in a number of COBOL compilers, including those produced by IBM. The REPLACING option may be used to perform limited editing on the code copied from a COPY file. With the REPLACING option, the text copied from the file is examined for all occurrences of word-1 (and word-3). Each time the specified word is found in the copied text, it is replaced by the specified word, literal, or value of the indicated identifier (which should be implicitly or explicitly defined as an alphanumeric data item). Thus, each program that uses a COPY file may ''customize'' the copied text so that it is more integrated with the current program. However, the contents of the COPY file itself remains unchanged. To illustrate this point, suppose the following code is placed in a program.

```
.
.
.
DATA DIVISION.
FILE SECTION.
FD SALES-FILE
   LABEL RECORDS ARE STANDARD.
01 SALES-RECORD
   COPY COMMON-SALES-RECORD
   REPLACING DATE-PURCHASED BY DATE-ACQUIRED.
.
.
.
```

The result of this operation would be

```
.
.
.
DATA DIVISION.
FILE SECTION.
FD SALES-FILE
   LABEL RECORDS ARE STANDARD.
01 SALES-RECORD.
   05 ITEM-PURCHASED                    PIC X(06).
   05 QUANTITY-PURCHASED                PIC 9(06).
   05 DATE-ACQUIRED.
      10 DP-MONTH                       PIC X(02).
      10 DP-DAY                         PIC X(02).
      10 DP-YEAR                        PIC X(02).
.
.
.
```

Therefore, due to the action of the REPLACING clause, DATE-PURCHASED is replaced by DATE-ACQUIRED. Finally, the REPLACING option applies only to the copied text. It has no impact on any other code that exists elsewhere within the program.

An Example of Using the COPY Verb

Now, we should examine what it might mean to use a COPY statement in a program. Suppose an instructor wanted to develop a program that examined numeric student grades to determine the appropriate letter grade for a course. Normally, an instructor teaches a number of courses, and perhaps the format of records is different for each course. How do you resolve this problem without writing an individual program for each situation (different record formats)? Furthermore, suppose the instructor decided to use different letter grade breakpoints for individual classes. Does this means a program would have to be written for each record type *and* each type of procedure for determining letter grades?

With the COPY statement, solving these problems is quite simple. A cursory examination of the problem indicates that only two areas of the program will change based on the preceding situation—the input record formats and the determination of grades. Thus, it is only necessary to create the individual record descriptions and grade determination procedures separately from the program.

An examination of the ''original code'' portion of Figure 20.2 reveals the approach. All of the general code is present. However, the input record description has been omitted and replaced by a COPY statement (line 340). Next, the grade determination procedure is omitted from the PROCEDURE DIVISION, but is replaced by two elements. First, a PERFORM statement (line 1200) is utilized to execute the grade determination procedure. The procedure (399-COPY-PROCEDURE) reveals the presence of another COPY statement (line 1340). Thus, neither of these elements is actually present in the original code. They will be inserted (from the specified files) when the program is compiled.

The COPY files are also shown in Figure 20.2. The record description is placed in a COPY file called STREC. This record description may be changed separately from the original code. Next, the COPY file DETGRD contains the grade determination procedure. Since it is also apart from the original code, it can be separately changed whenever necessary.

The final portion of Figure 20.2 illustrates the result of the COPY statement after the program has been compiled. Notice that in the particular system used, the COPY statement from the original code is retained (lines 340 and 1420). However, immediately following the COPY statement, the contents of the indicated files are inserted—the record description (lines 350–420) and the grade determination procedure (lines 1430–1520). Some compilers also mark the copied lines to easily determine which lines are a result of the original code and which lines have been copied. You should check with your installation to determine whether or not any JCL support is needed to perform COPY operations.

Subprograms

Although the COPY statement may be used to merge portions of programs into a current program, a COBOL program is also capable of accessing subprograms. Subprograms,

Figure 20.2 Using the COPY Verb [Original Code]

```
         1   1   2   2   2   3   3   4   4   4   5   5   6   6   6   7
 4   8   2   6   0   4   8   2   6   0   4   8   2   6   0   4   8   2

 *****************************************************************
  IDENTIFICATION DIVISION.
 *****************************************************************
  PROGRAM-ID.     GRADES-ANALYSIS-COPY.
  AUTHOR.         J. WAYNE SPENCE.
  DATE-WRITTEN.   JANUARY 1, 1989.
  DATE-COMPILED.  JANUARY 1, 1989.
 *     This program illustrates the use of the COPY statement
 *     One example of the COPY verb is used to insert a record
 *     description in the FILE SECTION.  The other copies
 *     statements for a paragraph in the PROCEDURE DIVISION.
 *****************************************************************
  ENVIRONMENT DIVISION.
 *****************************************************************
 *---------------------------------------------------------------*
  CONFIGURATION SECTION.
 *---------------------------------------------------------------*
  SOURCE-COMPUTER. IBM.
  OBJECT-COMPUTER. IBM.
  SPECIAL-NAMES.   C01 IS HEAD-OF-PAGE.
 *---------------------------------------------------------------*
  INPUT-OUTPUT SECTION.
 *---------------------------------------------------------------*
  FILE-CONTROL.
      SELECT STUDENT-FILE      ASSIGN TO UT-S-INPUT.
      SELECT GRADE-REPORT-FILE ASSIGN TO UT-S-OUTPUT.
 *****************************************************************
  DATA DIVISION.
 *****************************************************************
 *---------------------------------------------------------------*
  FILE SECTION.
 *---------------------------------------------------------------*
  FD  STUDENT-FILE LABEL RECORDS ARE OMITTED.
  01  INPUT-RECORD         COPY STREC.

  FD  GRADE-REPORT-FILE LABEL RECORDS ARE OMITTED.
  01  GRADE-REPORT-RECORD              PIC X(133).
 *---------------------------------------------------------------*
  WORKING-STORAGE SECTION.
 *---------------------------------------------------------------*
  01  WORKING-VARIABLES.
      05  FILE-STATUS                  PIC X(05)      VALUE 'START'.
      05  EXAM-COUNTER-WS              PIC 9(03)      VALUE ZERO.
      05  EXAM-1-TOTAL-WS              PIC 9(05)      VALUE ZERO.
      05  EXAM-2-TOTAL-WS              PIC 9(05)      VALUE ZERO.
      05  EXAM-3-TOTAL-WS              PIC 9(05)      VALUE ZERO.
      05  GRAND-TOTAL-WS               PIC 9(06)      VALUE ZERO.
      05  AVERAGE-WS                   PIC 9(03)V9(01).

  01  TITLE-LINE.
      05 FILLER                        PIC X(55) VALUE SPACES.
      05 FILLER                        PIC X(22) VALUE
                                       'Student Grade Averages'.
      05 FILLER                        PIC X(56) VALUE SPACES.

  01  COLUMN-HEADINGS.
      05 FILLER                        PIC X(41) VALUE SPACES.
      05 FILLER                        PIC X(12) VALUE
                                       'Student Name'.
      05 FILLER                        PIC X(10) VALUE SPACES.
      05 FILLER                        PIC X(07) VALUE 'Average'.
      05 FILLER                        PIC X(10) VALUE SPACES.
      05 FILLER                        PIC X(12) VALUE 'Letter Grade'.

  01  ASTER-ROW.
      05 FILLER                        PIC X(41) VALUE SPACES.
      05 FILLER                        PIC X(51) VALUE ALL '*'.

  01  OUTPUT-RECORD.
```

Figure 20.2 *Continued* Using the COPY Verb [Original Code]

```
         1   1   2   2   2   3   3   4   4   4   5   5   6   6   6   7
 4   8   2   6   0   4   8   2   6   0   4   8   2   6   0   4   8   2
-------------------------------------------------------------------------
           05 FILLER                   PIC X(41) VALUE SPACES.
           05 STUDENT-NAME-OUT         PIC X(20).
           05 FILLER                   PIC X(03) VALUE SPACES.
           05 AVERAGE-GRADE-OUT        PIC ZZ9.9.
           05 FILLER                   PIC X(16) VALUE SPACES.
           05 LETTER-GRADE-OUT         PIC X(01).

       01  STATISTICS.
           05 FILLER                   PIC X(27) VALUE SPACES.
           05 FILLER                   PIC X(24) VALUE
                                       'Summary Class Statistics'.
           05 FILLER                   PIC X(05) VALUE SPACES.
           05 EXAM-1-AVERAGE-OUT       PIC ZZ9.9.
           05 FILLER                   PIC X(05) VALUE SPACES.
           05 EXAM-2-AVERAGE-OUT       PIC ZZ9.9.
           05 FILLER                   PIC X(05) VALUE SPACES.
           05 EXAM-3-AVERAGE-OUT       PIC ZZ9.9.
           05 FILLER                   PIC X(05) VALUE SPACES.
           05 OVERALL-AVERAGE-OUT      PIC ZZ9.9.
      ***************************************************************
       PROCEDURE DIVISION.
      ***************************************************************
      *-------------------------------------------------------------*
       000-PROCEDURE-CONTROL SECTION.
      *-------------------------------------------------------------*
           PERFORM 100-INITIAL-OPERATIONS.
           PERFORM 300-DETERMINE-GRADES
               UNTIL FILE-STATUS = 'DONE'.
           PERFORM 500-OVERALL-STATS.
           PERFORM 700-CLOSE-FILES.
           STOP RUN.
      *-------------------------------------------------------------*
       100-INITIAL-OPERATIONS SECTION.
      *-------------------------------------------------------------*
           OPEN INPUT STUDENT-FILE, OUTPUT GRADE-REPORT-FILE.
           WRITE GRADE-REPORT-RECORD FROM TITLE-LINE AFTER HEAD-OF-PAGE.
           WRITE GRADE-REPORT-RECORD FROM COLUMN-HEADINGS AFTER 1 LINES.
           WRITE GRADE-REPORT-RECORD FROM ASTER-ROW AFTER 1 LINES.
           READ STUDENT-FILE
               AT END MOVE 'DONE' TO FILE-STATUS.
      *-------------------------------------------------------------*
       300-DETERMINE-GRADES SECTION.
      *-------------------------------------------------------------*
           COMPUTE AVERAGE-WS ROUNDED =
             (EXAM-1-IN + EXAM-2-IN + EXAM-3-IN) / 3.
           ADD EXAM-1-IN TO EXAM-1-TOTAL-WS, GRAND-TOTAL-WS.
           ADD EXAM-2-IN TO EXAM-2-TOTAL-WS, GRAND-TOTAL-WS.
           ADD EXAM-3-IN TO EXAM-3-TOTAL-WS, GRAND-TOTAL-WS.
           ADD 1 TO EXAM-COUNTER-WS.

           PERFORM 399-COPY-PROCEDURE.

           PERFORM 350-PRINT-OUTPUT-LINE.
           READ STUDENT-FILE
               AT END MOVE 'DONE' TO FILE-STATUS.
      *-------------------------------------------------------------*
       350-PRINT-OUTPUT-LINE SECTION.
      *-------------------------------------------------------------*
           MOVE STUDENT-NAME-IN     TO STUDENT-NAME-OUT.
           MOVE AVERAGE-WS          TO AVERAGE-GRADE-OUT.
           WRITE GRADE-REPORT-RECORD FROM OUTPUT-RECORD AFTER 2 LINES.
      *-------------------------------------------------------------*
       399-COPY-PROCEDURE SECTION.
      *-------------------------------------------------------------*
           COPY DETGRD.
      *-------------------------------------------------------------*
       500-OVERALL-STATS SECTION.
      *-------------------------------------------------------------*
           WRITE GRADE-REPORT-RECORD FROM ASTER-ROW AFTER 2 LINES.
```

Figure 20.2 *Continued* Using the COPY Verb [Original Code]

```
               1   1   2   2   2   3   3   4   4   4   5   5   6   6   6   7
   4   8   2   6   0   4   8   2   6   0   4   8   2   6   0   4   8   2
-------------------------------------------------------------------------------
               DIVIDE EXAM-1-TOTAL-WS BY EXAM-COUNTER-WS
                 GIVING EXAM-1-AVERAGE-OUT ROUNDED.
               DIVIDE EXAM-2-TOTAL-WS BY EXAM-COUNTER-WS
                 GIVING EXAM-2-AVERAGE-OUT ROUNDED.
               DIVIDE EXAM-3-TOTAL-WS BY EXAM-COUNTER-WS
                 GIVING EXAM-3-AVERAGE-OUT ROUNDED.
               COMPUTE OVERALL-AVERAGE-OUT ROUNDED = GRAND-TOTAL-WS /
                 (EXAM-COUNTER-WS * 3).
               WRITE GRADE-REPORT-RECORD AFTER ADVANCING 2 LINES.
               WRITE GRADE-REPORT-RECORD FROM STATISTICS AFTER 2 LINES.
       *-----------------------------------------------------------*
        700-CLOSE-FILES SECTION.
       *-----------------------------------------------------------*
               CLOSE STUDENT-FILE, GRADE-REPORT-FILE.
```

Figure 20.2 *Continued* Using the COPY Verb [The STREC COPY File]

```
               1   1   2   2   2   3   3   4   4   4   5   5   6   6   6   7
   4   8   2   6   0   4   8   2   6   0   4   8   2   6   0   4   8   2
-------------------------------------------------------------------------------
        01  STUDENT-RECORD.
            05 STUDENT-NAME-IN              PIC X(20).
            05 FILLER                       PIC X(10).
            05 GRADES-IN.
                10 EXAM-1-IN                PIC 9(03).
                10 EXAM-2-IN                PIC 9(03).
                10 EXAM-3-IN                PIC 9(03).
            05 FILLER                       PIC X(41).
```

Figure 20.2 *Continued* Using the COPY Verb [The DTRGD COPY File]

```
               1   1   2   2   2   3   3   4   4   4   5   5   6   6   6   7
   4   8   2   6   0   4   8   2   6   0   4   8   2   6   0   4   8   2
-------------------------------------------------------------------------------
            IF AVERAGE-WS IS GREATER THAN 89.4
                MOVE 'A' TO LETTER-GRADE-OUT.
            IF AVERAGE-WS IS GREATER THAN 79.4 AND LESS THAN 89.5
                MOVE 'B' TO LETTER-GRADE-OUT.
            IF AVERAGE-WS IS GREATER THAN 69.4 AND LESS THAN 79.5
                MOVE 'C' TO LETTER-GRADE-OUT.
            IF AVERAGE-WS IS GREATER THAN 59.4 AND LESS THAN 69.5
                MOVE 'D' TO LETTER-GRADE-OUT.
            IF AVERAGE-WS IS LESS THAN 59.5
                MOVE 'F' TO LETTER-GRADE-OUT.
```

Figure 20.2 *Continued* Using the COPY Verb [Original Code after Copy]

```
       1   1   2   2   2   3   3   4   4   4   5   5   6   6   6   7
4  8   2   6   0   4   8   2   6   0   4   8   2   6   0   4   8   2

 ***************************************************************
  IDENTIFICATION DIVISION.
 ***************************************************************
  PROGRAM-ID.      GRADES-ANALYSIS-COPY.
  AUTHOR.          J. WAYNE SPENCE.
  DATE-WRITTEN.    JANUARY 1, 1989.
  DATE-COMPILED.   JANUARY 1, 1989.
 *    This program illustrates the use of the COPY statement.
 *    One example of the COPY verb is used to insert a record
 *    description in the FILE SECTION.  The other copies
 *    statements for a paragraph in the PROCEDURE DIVISION.
 ***************************************************************
  ENVIRONMENT DIVISION.
 ***************************************************************
 *-------------------------------------------------------------*
  CONFIGURATION SECTION.
 *-------------------------------------------------------------*
  SOURCE-COMPUTER. IBM.
  OBJECT-COMPUTER. IBM.
  SPECIAL-NAMES.    C01 IS HEAD-OF-PAGE.
 *-------------------------------------------------------------*
  INPUT-OUTPUT SECTION.
 *-------------------------------------------------------------*
  FILE-CONTROL.
      SELECT STUDENT-FILE      ASSIGN TO UT-S-INPUT.
      SELECT GRADE-REPORT-FILE ASSIGN TO UT-S-OUTPUT.
 ***************************************************************
  DATA DIVISION.
 ***************************************************************
 *-------------------------------------------------------------*
  FILE SECTION.
 *-------------------------------------------------------------*
  FD  STUDENT-FILE LABEL RECORDS ARE OMITTED.
  01  INPUT-RECORD      COPY STREC.
  01  STUDENT-RECORD.
      05 STUDENT-NAME-IN           PIC X(20).
      05 FILLER                    PIC X(10).
      05 GRADES-IN.
          10 EXAM-1-IN             PIC 9(03).
          10 EXAM-2-IN             PIC 9(03).
          10 EXAM-3-IN             PIC 9(03).
      05 FILLER                    PIC X(41).

  FD  GRADE-REPORT-FILE LABEL RECORDS ARE OMITTED.
  01  GRADE-REPORT-RECORD          PIC X(133).
 *-------------------------------------------------------------*
  WORKING-STORAGE SECTION.
 *-------------------------------------------------------------*
  01  WORKING-VARIABLES.
      05  FILE-STATUS              PIC X(05)      VALUE 'START'.
      05  EXAM-COUNTER-WS          PIC 9(03)      VALUE ZERO.
      05  EXAM-1-TOTAL-WS          PIC 9(05)      VALUE ZERO.
      05  EXAM-2-TOTAL-WS          PIC 9(05)      VALUE ZERO.
      05  EXAM-3-TOTAL-WS          PIC 9(05)      VALUE ZERO.
      05  GRAND-TOTAL-WS           PIC 9(06)      VALUE ZERO.
      05  AVERAGE-WS               PIC 9(03)V9(01).

  01  TITLE-LINE.
      05 FILLER                    PIC X(55) VALUE SPACES.
      05 FILLER                    PIC X(22) VALUE
                                   'Student Grade Averages'.
      05 FILLER                    PIC X(56) VALUE SPACES.

  01  COLUMN-HEADINGS.
      05 FILLER                    PIC X(41) VALUE SPACES.
      05 FILLER                    PIC X(12) VALUE
                                   'Student Name'.
      05 FILLER                    PIC X(10) VALUE SPACES.
      05 FILLER                    PIC X(07) VALUE 'Average'.
```

Figure 20.2 *Continued* Using the COPY Verb [Original Code after Copy]

```
                1   1   2   2   2   3   3   4   4   4   5   5   6   6   6   7
    4   8   2   6   0   4   8   2   6   0   4   8   2   6   0   4   8   2

           05 FILLER                       PIC X(10) VALUE SPACES.
           05 FILLER                       PIC X(12) VALUE 'Letter Grade'.

       01  ASTER-ROW.
           05 FILLER                       PIC X(41) VALUE SPACES.
           05 FILLER                       PIC X(51) VALUE ALL '*'.

       01  OUTPUT-RECORD.
           05 FILLER                       PIC X(41) VALUE SPACES.
           05 STUDENT-NAME-OUT             PIC X(20).
           05 FILLER                       PIC X(03) VALUE SPACES.
           05 AVERAGE-GRADE-OUT            PIC ZZ9.9.
           05 FILLER                       PIC X(16) VALUE SPACES.
           05 LETTER-GRADE-OUT             PIC X(01).

       01  STATISTICS.
           05 FILLER                       PIC X(27) VALUE SPACES.
           05 FILLER                       PIC X(24) VALUE
                                           'Summary Class Statistics'.
           05 FILLER                       PIC X(05) VALUE SPACES.
           05 EXAM-1-AVERAGE-OUT           PIC ZZ9.9.
           05 FILLER                       PIC X(05) VALUE SPACES.
           05 EXAM-2-AVERAGE-OUT           PIC ZZ9.9.
           05 FILLER                       PIC X(05) VALUE SPACES.
           05 EXAM-3-AVERAGE-OUT           PIC ZZ9.9.
           05 FILLER                       PIC X(05) VALUE SPACES.
           05 OVERALL-AVERAGE-OUT          PIC ZZ9.9.
      ****************************************************************
       PROCEDURE DIVISION.
      ****************************************************************
      *--------------------------------------------------------------*
       000-PROCEDURE-CONTROL SECTION.
      *--------------------------------------------------------------*
           PERFORM 100-INITIAL-OPERATIONS.
           PERFORM 300-DETERMINE-GRADES
               UNTIL FILE-STATUS = 'DONE'.
           PERFORM 500-OVERALL-STATS.
           PERFORM 700-CLOSE-FILES.
           STOP RUN.
      *--------------------------------------------------------------*
       100-INITIAL-OPERATIONS SECTION.
      *--------------------------------------------------------------*
           OPEN INPUT STUDENT-FILE, OUTPUT GRADE-REPORT-FILE.
           WRITE GRADE-REPORT-RECORD FROM TITLE-LINE AFTER HEAD-OF-PAGE.
           WRITE GRADE-REPORT-RECORD FROM COLUMN-HEADINGS AFTER 1 LINES.
           WRITE GRADE-REPORT-RECORD FROM ASTER-ROW AFTER 1 LINES.
           READ STUDENT-FILE
               AT END MOVE 'DONE' TO FILE-STATUS.
      *--------------------------------------------------------------*
       300-DETERMINE-GRADES SECTION.
      *--------------------------------------------------------------*
           COMPUTE AVERAGE-WS ROUNDED =
             (EXAM-1-IN + EXAM-2-IN + EXAM-3-IN) / 3.
           ADD EXAM-1-IN TO EXAM-1-TOTAL-WS, GRAND-TOTAL-WS.
           ADD EXAM-2-IN TO EXAM-2-TOTAL-WS, GRAND-TOTAL-WS.
           ADD EXAM-3-IN TO EXAM-3-TOTAL-WS, GRAND-TOTAL-WS.
           ADD 1 TO EXAM-COUNTER-WS.

           PERFORM 399-COPY-PROCEDURE.

           PERFORM 350-PRINT-OUTPUT-LINE.
           READ STUDENT-FILE
               AT END MOVE 'DONE' TO FILE-STATUS.
      *--------------------------------------------------------------*
       350-PRINT-OUTPUT-LINE SECTION.
      *--------------------------------------------------------------*
           MOVE STUDENT-NAME-IN     TO STUDENT-NAME-OUT.
           MOVE AVERAGE-WS          TO AVERAGE-GRADE-OUT.
           WRITE GRADE-REPORT-RECORD FROM OUTPUT-RECORD AFTER 2 LINES.
```

Figure 20.2 *Continued* Using the COPY Verb [Original Code after Copy]

```
        1   1   2   2   2   3   3   4   4   4   5   5   6   6   6   7
4   8   2   6   0   4   8   2   6   0   4   8   2   6   0   4   8   2

      *-----------------------------------------------------------*
       399-COPY-PROCEDURE SECTION.
      *-----------------------------------------------------------*
           COPY DETGRD.
           IF AVERAGE-WS IS GREATER THAN 89.4
               MOVE 'A' TO LETTER-GRADE-OUT.
           IF AVERAGE-WS IS GREATER THAN 79.4 AND LESS THAN 89.5
               MOVE 'B' TO LETTER-GRADE-OUT.
           IF AVERAGE-WS IS GREATER THAN 69.4 AND LESS THAN 79.5
               MOVE 'C' TO LETTER-GRADE-OUT.
           IF AVERAGE-WS IS GREATER THAN 59.4 AND LESS THAN 69.5
               MOVE 'D' TO LETTER-GRADE-OUT.
           IF AVERAGE-WS IS LESS THAN 59.5
               MOVE 'F' TO LETTER-GRADE-OUT.
      *-----------------------------------------------------------*
       500-OVERALL-STATS SECTION.
      *-----------------------------------------------------------*
           WRITE GRADE-REPORT-RECORD FROM ASTER-ROW AFTER 2 LINES.
           DIVIDE EXAM-1-TOTAL-WS BY EXAM-COUNTER-WS
             GIVING EXAM-1-AVERAGE-OUT ROUNDED.
           DIVIDE EXAM-2-TOTAL-WS BY EXAM-COUNTER-WS
             GIVING EXAM-2-AVERAGE-OUT ROUNDED.
           DIVIDE EXAM-3-TOTAL-WS BY EXAM-COUNTER-WS
             GIVING EXAM-3-AVERAGE-OUT ROUNDED.
           COMPUTE OVERALL-AVERAGE-OUT ROUNDED = GRAND-TOTAL-WS
             (EXAM-COUNTER-WS * 3).
           WRITE GRADE-REPORT-RECORD AFTER ADVANCING 2 LINES.
           WRITE GRADE-REPORT-RECORD FROM STATISTICS AFTER 2 LINES.
      *-----------------------------------------------------------*
       700-CLOSE-FILES SECTION.
      *-----------------------------------------------------------*
           CLOSE STUDENT-FILE, GRADE-REPORT-FILE.
```

sometimes referred to as ***subroutines,*** may actually be what would otherwise be called complete programs. Among the uses of subprograms are:

- To link together programs written by several programmers
- To break-up programs that would otherwise be too cumbersome to work with or that would require excessive amounts of internal storage
- To eliminate the repetition of redundant or frequently used code
- To access specialized procedures to perform certain functions that would typically be outside the expertise range of an average programmer
- To access specialized functions that could be more easily produced in a programming language other than COBOL.

When a totally separate subprogram is executed from an initial program (often called a main program), it is said that the subprogram has been *invoked* or *accessed*. However, the term *called* is generally more specific, since most programming languages use a CALL statement to invoke a subprogram.

When a subprogram is called, COBOL reacts as though a PERFORM statement has been executed that somehow causes the execution of another program. Furthermore, unless instructed to the contrary, when the execution of a subprogram is completed, control returns to the initial (main) program at the location following the CALL statement in the main program. Figure 20.3 illustrates this procedure. Furthermore, since a COBOL subprogram has a structure that is generally similar to any typical COBOL program, it

Figure 20.3 The Logic of Calling a Subprogram

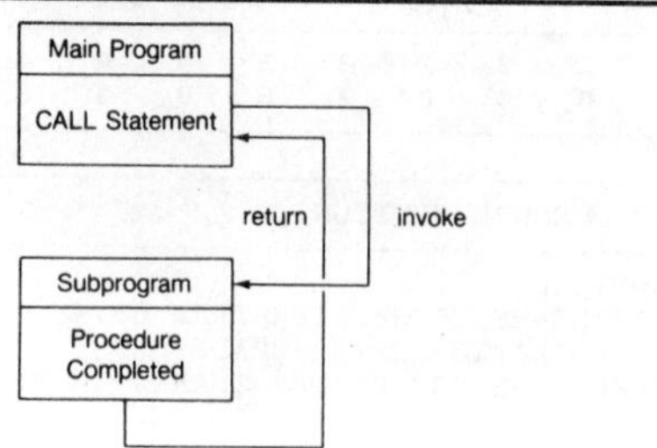

is possible for a subprogram to call yet another subprogram. (This also means that a main program can call several subprograms.) Thus, unless a STOP RUN command is executed from a called subprogram, control is returned in a fashion similar to that which would occur if a PERFORM statement caused the execution of a procedure containing another PERFORM statement. Control is passed from the main program to the first subprogram, from the first subprogram to the second, and so on. The return sequence is from the second subprogram to the first and from the first subprogram to the main program.

The CALL Statement

In COBOL, the statement that causes the execution of a subprogram (whether from a main program or another subprogram) is the CALL statement, as illustrated in Figure 20.4. As shown in the general format of the CALL statement, the subprogram name may be specified as either literal-1 (in format 1) or identifier-2 (in format 2). If an identifier-2 is used, the identifier must be explicitly defined as alphanumeric. The subprogram name is identified as the PROGRAM-ID name in the subprogram. If the optional list of identifiers is omitted, the data of the main program are completely isolated from the subprogram. Each program works independently of the other with respect to data values placed into internal storage.

The fact that the two programs are independent means that one program is only vaguely aware of the other's existence. If the same data-name appears in both programs,

Figure 20.4 Formats of the CALL Statement

```
Format 1:

CALL literal-1 [USING identifier-1 [identifier-2] . . . ]

[END-CALL]
```

```
Format 2:

CALL identifier-2 [USING identifier-2 [identifier-3] . . . ]

[END-CALL]
```

neither affects the data that might have been stored by the other program. This is one of the reasons that linking programs written by two different programmers is possible. Since neither program ''knows'' the structure of the other, both may be linked together without fear of having duplicate data-names, procedure-names, and so on.

The GOBACK and EXIT PROGRAM Statements

Although the typical program is terminated by a STOP RUN statement, if this statement appears in a subprogram, all procedures are terminated (whether the STOP RUN statement is placed in the main program, the first subprogram, or a subprogram that has been called by another subprogram). To effect the return of control to the calling program (whether the procedure was invoked by a CALL from the main program or by one of several subprograms), special statements are utilized. The format of these statements, as shown in Figure 20.5, is extremely simple. In a subprogram, a GOBACK or an EXIT PROGRAM statement normally would be used in place of a STOP RUN statement. The difference between using the GOBACK and EXIT PROGRAM statements is relatively easy. The GOBACK statement is an extension of COBOL and may be employed as a direct substitute for the STOP RUN statement. A GOBACK statement may appear at the end of a series of imperative statements, rather than in a procedure by itself (as is required by the EXIT PROGRAM statement). Furthermore, a GOBACK statement may appear in either a subprogram or a main program. If the GOBACK statement is executed and no CALL statements are active, the procedure is terminated. Otherwise, a return is executed to the calling program. As illustrated, the EXIT PROGRAM statement is structurally similar to the EXIT statement used in conjunction with the PERFORM statement because the EXIT statement must appear in a paragraph by itself. It should appear only in subprograms. If a CALL statement is active, a return is executed to the calling program. Otherwise, the EXIT statement is ignored and the next sequential statement is executed. Regardless of which you choose, execution of either the GOBACK or EXIT PROGRAM statement typically causes control to be passed back to the calling (main) program.

Linking Data Values

In many cases, it is desirable to be able to pass data back and forth between a main program and a subprogram (or between two subprograms). If this capability is desired,

Figure 20.5a Format of the GOBACK Statement

```
GOBACK
```

Figure 20.5b Format of the EXIT PROGRAM Statement

```
paragraph-name.  EXIT PROGRAM.
```

Figure 20.6 Format of the PROCEDURE DIVISION Heading for Subprograms

```
PROCEDURE DIVISION [USING identifier-1 [identifier-2] . . . ]
```

the calling program may use what is generally referred to as an *arguments list,* which is really only a list of identifiers that share data values (in "common" storage locations) between a main program and a subprogram.

For two programs to share data, the CALL statement would include a list of identifiers. The value of these, and *only* these, identifiers are shared between the main program and a subprogram. Thus, the form of the CALL statement might be similar to the following statement for a main program designed to process payroll information, where the actual computation of net pay was performed by a subprogram.

```
CALL 'COMPANY' USING RATE-PER-HOUR-IN, HOURS-WORKED-IN.
```

Although this CALL statement will pass the values for RATE-PER-HOUR-IN and HOURS-WORKED-IN to the subprogram, the subprogram itself must be able to access these values. Therefore, in order that the appropriate linkage of data values is performed between a main program and a subprogram, a modified PROCEDURE DIVISION heading, as shown in Figure 20.6, would appear in the subprogram.

Thus, the identifiers that are specified in a CALL statement in a main program (or subprogram) will be "mapped" to the identifiers specified in the PROCEDURE DIVISION heading of the indicated subprogram. The idea of mapping involves the position of an identifier in the arguments listed. For example, if the calling program used the CALL statement previously illustrated, and the PROCEDURE DIVISION of a subprogram utilizes the following characteristics

```
PROCEDURE DIVISION USING RATE, HOURS.
```

then RATE-PER-HOUR-IN of the CALL statement would correspond to RATE in the PROCEDURE DIVISION heading and HOURS-WORKED-IN would correspond to HOURS. Furthermore, the DATA DIVISION description of RATE-PER-HOUR-IN in the calling program must match that of RATE in the called program The same requirements also exist for the relationship between HOURS-WORKED-IN and HOURS. Finally, the number and type of arguments in the CALL statement of a calling program must exactly match those present in the PROCEDURE DIVISION heading of the called program.

The LINKAGE SECTION

The definition of the arguments in the calling program (e.g. main program) may appear anywhere within the DATA DIVISION (except the REPORT SECTION); however, data passed to a subprogram is treated in a special manner. In a subprogram, all data values passed via arguments must appear in a new section of the DATA DIVISION called the LINKAGE SECTION. In the preceding illustration, RATE-PER-HOUR-IN and HOURS-WORKED-IN might be defined in either the FILE SECTION or the WORKING-STORAGE SECTION of the main program. However, RATE and HOURS, which are used in a subprogram, must be defined in the LINKAGE SECTION. The structure of the

Figure 20.7 Format of the LINKAGE SECTION

```
[LINKAGE SECTION.
[77  elementary-item-description] . . .
[01  record-description] . . . ]
```

LINKAGE SECTION is similar to the typical WORKING-STORAGE SECTION, as shown in Figure 20.7. Both 77-level and record-level data-items are permitted. As with the WORKING-STORAGE SECTION, 77-level items must appear before the first record description. The *LINKAGE SECTION must appear after the WORKING-STORAGE SECTION of a subprogram,* if the WORKING-STORAGE SECTION is necessary. If data types other than a USAGE of DISPLAY (e.g., COMPUTATIONAL or COMP-3) are passed as an argument, it is up to the programmer to ensure proper internal data alignment. (See Chapter 23 for further details.) Thus, in our earlier example, the LINKAGE SECTION of the subprogram might appear as

```
LINKAGE SECTION.
01  SHARED-DATA.
    05 RATE            PIC 9(05)V99.
    05 HOURS           PIC 9(02)V9.
```

This also means that the description of RATE-PER-HOUR-IN in the calling program must be 9(05)V99, whereas HOURS-WORKED-IN must be 9(02)V9. Finally, VALUE clauses may not be used in the LINKAGE SECTION, except in conjunction with condition-names (88 level data items).

A COBOL Main and Subprogram

In the preceding illustration, we concentrated on elementary-item descriptions. However, if several data values are to be passed between a main program and a subprogram, it may be worthwhile to create a record description of all shared items in the WORKING-STORAGE SECTION of the main program and a similar record description, possibly with different data-names, in the LINKAGE SECTION of the subprogram.

The program presented in Figure 20.8 (a main program) and that in Figure 20.9 (a subprogram) show how records may be shared. The purpose of this program (which is

Figure 20.8 A COBOL Main Program (Hierarchy Chart)

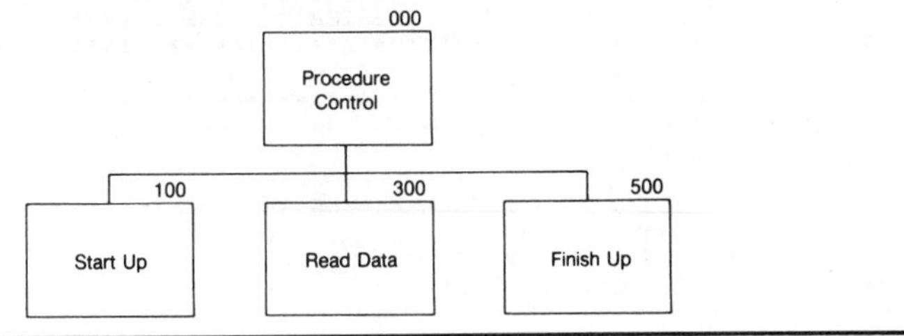

Figure 20.8 *Continued* A COBOL Main Program (Pseudocode)

```
START
    DO Start up
    DO Read data UNTIL eof
    DO Finish up
END

START UP
    OPEN files
    WRITE headings
END

READ DATA
    READ input
    IF eof
        SET file status
        GO TO end
    ENDIF
    MOVE sales in TO sales sub
    CALL subroutine USING variables
    MOVE values to output
    ADD sales sub, tax GIVING total
    ADD sales sub to cum sales
    ADD tax to cum tax
    ADD 1 to count
    WRITE output
END

FINISH UP
    ADD cum tax, cum sales GIVING cum total
    WRITE summary heading
    MOVE values to output
    WRITE output
    CLOSE files
END
```

Figure 20.8 *Continued* A COBOL Main Program

```
       1   1   2   2   2   3   3   4   4   4   5   5   6   6   6   7
   4   8   2   6   0   4   8   2   6   0   4   8   2   6   0   4   8   2

      ******************************************************************
       IDENTIFICATION  DIVISION.
      ******************************************************************
       PROGRAM-ID.     COBMAIN.
       AUTHOR.         JOHN WINDSOR.
       DATE-WRITTEN.   JANUARY 1, 1989.
       DATE-COMPILED.  JANUARY 1, 1989.
      *   This program illustrates the use of a subprogram CALL.
      ******************************************************************
       ENVIRONMENT DIVISION.
      ******************************************************************
      *----------------------------------------------------------------*
       CONFIGURATION SECTION.
      *----------------------------------------------------------------*
       SOURCE-COMPUTER.  IBM.
       OBJECT-COMPUTER.  IBM.
       SPECIAL-NAMES.    C01 IS TOP-OF-PAGE.
      *----------------------------------------------------------------*
       INPUT-OUTPUT SECTION.
      *----------------------------------------------------------------*
       FILE-CONTROL.
           SELECT CUSTOMER-FILE ASSIGN TO UT-S-INPUT.
           SELECT REPORT-FILE   ASSIGN TO UT-S-OUTPUT.
      ******************************************************************
       DATA DIVISION.
      ******************************************************************
      *----------------------------------------------------------------*
       FILE SECTION.
      *----------------------------------------------------------------*
       FD  CUSTOMER-FILE LABEL RECORDS ARE OMITTED.
       01  CUSTOMER-RECORD.
           05 CUSTOMER-NUMBER-IN          PIC 9(05).
           05 CUSTOMER-NAME-IN            PIC X(20).
```

Figure 20.8 *Continued* A COBOL Main Program

```
          1   1   2   2   2   3   3   4   4   4   5   5   6   6   6   7
  4   8   2   6   0   4   8   2   6   0   4   8   2   6   0   4   8   2

            05 SALES-AMOUNT-IN          PIC 9(04)V9(02).
            05 FILLER                   PIC X(49).

        FD  REPORT-FILE LABEL RECORDS ARE OMITTED.
        01  REPORT-RECORD.
            05 FILLER                   PIC X(35).
            05 CUSTOMER-NAME-OUT        PIC X(20).
            05 FILLER                   PIC X(05).
            05 CUSTOMER-NUMBER-OUT      PIC Z(4)9.
            05 FILLER                   PIC X(05).
            05 SALES-AMOUNT-OUT         PIC $(5).99.
            05 FILLER                   PIC X(05).
            05 SALES-TAX-OUT            PIC $$$$.99.
            05 FILLER                   PIC X(05).
            05 TOTAL-AMOUNT-OUT         PIC $$$,$$$.99.
            05 FILLER                   PIC X(28).
      *------------------------------------------------------------*
        WORKING-STORAGE SECTION.
      *------------------------------------------------------------*
        01  WORKING-VARIABLES.
            05  FILE-STATUS             PIC X(04)       VALUE SPACES.
            05  TRANSACTION-COUNT-WS    PIC 9(04)       VALUE ZERO.
            05  CUM-SALES-AMOUNT-WS     PIC 9(10)V9(02) VALUE ZERO.
            05  CUM-TAX-WS              PIC 9(10)V9(02) VALUE ZERO.

        01  SUBROUTINE-VARIABLES.
            05  SALES-AMOUNT-SV         PIC 9(04)V9(02).
            05  TAX-SV                  PIC 9(03)V9(02) VALUE ZERO.

        01  REPORT-HEADING.
            05 FILLER                   PIC X(60) VALUE SPACES.
            05 FILLER                   PIC X(06) VALUE 'Sales'.
            05 TYPE-OF-HEADING-OUT      PIC X(07) VALUE 'Detail'.

        01  SUMMARY-RECORD.
            05 FILLER                   PIC X(31) VALUE SPACES.
            05 TRANSACTION-COUNT-SR     PIC ZZZ9.
            05 FILLER                   PIC X(05) VALUE SPACES.
            05 CUM-SALES-AMOUNT-SR      PIC $$,$$$,$$$,$$$.99.
            05 FILLER                   PIC X(05) VALUE SPACES.
            05 CUM-TAX-SR               PIC $$,$$$,$$$,$$$.99.
            05 FILLER                   PIC X(05) VALUE SPACES.
            05 CUM-TOTAL-AMOUNT-SR      PIC $$,$$$,$$$,$$$.99.
      **************************************************************
        PROCEDURE DIVISION.
      **************************************************************
      *------------------------------------------------------------*
        000-PROCEDURE-CONTROL SECTION.
      *------------------------------------------------------------*
            PERFORM 100-START-UP.
            PERFORM 300-READ-DATA
                UNTIL FILE-STATUS = 'DONE'.
            PERFORM 500-FINISH-UP.
            STOP RUN.
      *------------------------------------------------------------*
        100-START-UP SECTION.
      *------------------------------------------------------------*
            OPEN INPUT CUSTOMER-FILE, OUTPUT REPORT-FILE.
            WRITE REPORT-RECORD FROM REPORT-HEADING AFTER TOP-OF-PAGE.
            MOVE SPACES             TO REPORT-RECORD.
            WRITE REPORT-RECORD AFTER ADVANCING 1 LINES.
      *------------------------------------------------------------*
        300-READ-DATA SECTION.
      *------------------------------------------------------------*
            READ CUSTOMER-FILE
                AT END MOVE 'DONE'   TO FILE-STATUS
                       GO TO 300-EXIT.
            MOVE SALES-AMOUNT-IN     TO SALES-AMOUNT-SV.

            CALL 'COBSUB' USING SUBROUTINE-VARIABLES.
```

Figure 20.8 *Continued* A COBOL Main Program (Pseudocode)

```
        1   1   2   2   2   3   3   4   4   4   5   5   6   6   6   7
4   8   2   6   0   4   8   2   6   0   4   8   2   6   0   4   8   2
1060
1070           MOVE CUSTOMER-NUMBER-IN  TO CUSTOMER-NUMBER-OUT.
1080           MOVE CUSTOMER-NAME-IN    TO CUSTOMER-NAME-OUT.
1090           MOVE SALES-AMOUNT-SV     TO SALES-AMOUNT-OUT.
1100           MOVE TAX-SV              TO SALES-TAX-OUT.
1110           ADD SALES-AMOUNT-SV, TAX-SV GIVING TOTAL-AMOUNT-OUT.
1120           ADD SALES-AMOUNT-SV TO CUM-SALES-AMOUNT-WS.
1130           ADD TAX-SV TO CUM-TAX-WS.
1140           ADD 1 TO TRANSACTION-COUNT-WS.
1150           WRITE REPORT-RECORD AFTER ADVANCING 1 LINES.
1160
1170       300-EXIT.
1180           EXIT.
1190      *-------------------------------------------------------*
1200       500-FINISH-UP SECTION.
1210      *-------------------------------------------------------*
1220           ADD CUM-TAX-WS, CUM-SALES-AMOUNT-WS GIVING
1230               CUM-TOTAL-AMOUNT-SR.
1240           MOVE 'Summary'           TO TYPE-OF-HEADING-OUT.
1250           WRITE REPORT-RECORD FROM REPORT-HEADING AFTER TOP-OF-PAGE.
1260           MOVE CUM-TAX-WS          TO CUM-TAX-SR.
1270           MOVE TRANSACTION-COUNT-WS TO TRANSACTION-COUNT-SR.
1280           MOVE CUM-SALES-AMOUNT-WS TO CUM-SALES-AMOUNT-SR.
1290           WRITE REPORT-RECORD FROM SUMMARY-RECORD AFTER 2 LINES.
1300           CLOSE CUSTOMER-FILE, REPORT-FILE.
```

basically a repeat of the program presented in Figure 10.7) is to compute sales tax based on the sales amount. In the illustration, it is assumed that the tax computation warrants the creation of a subprogram, to be called by the main program that processes the remainder of the data. The data to be passed from the main program (COBMAIN) to the subprogram (COBSUB) are identified in the SUBROUTINE-VARIABLES record description (lines 590–610). Then in the PROCEDURE DIVISION of the main program, the tax subprogram is invoked with the statement

```
CALL 'COBSUB' USING SUBROUTINES-VARIABLES.
```

in line 1020. After the subprogram has completed its operation, a new value for TAX-WS would be available to the main program.

In the subprogram, execution begins with the PROCEDURE DIVISION heading, which appears as

```
PROCEDURE DIVISION USING WORKING-RECORD.
```

Further examination of the subprogram indicates that WORKING-RECORD (lines 250–270) is defined in the LINKAGE SECTION. Thus, the data identified as SALES-

Figure 20.9 A COBOL Subprogram (Pseudocode)

```
START
    MULTIPLY sales by .04
          GIVING tax
END
```

Figure 20.9 *Continued* A COBOL Subprogram

```
       1   1   2   2   2   3   3   4   4   4   5   5   6   6   6   7
   4   8   2   6   0   4   8   2   6   0   4   8   2   6   0   4   8   2

      ****************************************************************
       IDENTIFICATION  DIVISION.
      ****************************************************************
       PROGRAM-ID.      COBSUB.
       AUTHOR.          JOHN WINDSOR.
       DATE-WRITTEN.    JANUARY 1, 1989.
       DATE-COMPILED.   JANUARY 1, 1989.
      *    This procedure is a COBOL subprogram.  Note the use of
      *    the LINKAGE SECTION in the DATA DIVISION and the
      *    modification of the PROCEDURE DIVISION heading.
      ****************************************************************
       ENVIRONMENT DIVISION.
      ****************************************************************
      *--------------------------------------------------------------*
       CONFIGURATION SECTION.
      *--------------------------------------------------------------*
       SOURCE-COMPUTER.  IBM.
       OBJECT-COMPUTER.  IBM.
      ****************************************************************
       DATA DIVISION.
      ****************************************************************
      *--------------------------------------------------------------*
       LINKAGE SECTION.
      *--------------------------------------------------------------*
       01  WORKING-RECORD.
           05  AMOUNT-OF-SALES              PIC 9(04)V99.
           05  COMPUTED-TAX                 PIC 9(03)V99.
      ****************************************************************
       PROCEDURE DIVISION USING WORKING-RECORD.
      ****************************************************************
      *--------------------------------------------------------------*
       000-TAX-COMPUTATION SECTION.
      *--------------------------------------------------------------*
           MULTIPLY AMOUNT-OF-SALES BY .04 GIVING COMPUTED-TAX ROUNDED.
           GOBACK.
```

AMOUNT-WS in the main program are the same as AMOUNT-OF-SALES in the subprogram. Also, TAX-WS in the main program is the same as COMPUTED-TAX in the subprogram. As a result of calling COBSUB, the amount of sale, derived in the main program from an input record, is passed to the subprogram. The subprogram uses these data in the computation of the sales tax value, which is passed back to the main program for presentation on a printed line.

Summary

In this chapter, we have examined two means by which a programmer may access coding that is not a part of the original program. Whereas the COPY statement is used to insert new code into the present program, the CALL statement is used to pass control of the procedure from one program to another.

Notes on Programming Style

Although both the COPY and CALL statements tend to be employed more frequently in more "sophisticated" programming environments, they are extremely useful in programming the solution to simple problems. Generally, the use of the REPLACING option should be avoided—especially when the intent of the COPY operation is to maintain consistency between (among) programs. Using the REPLACING option negates this consistency by "customizing" the COPY file. Thus, if the program is subject to examination (e.g., modification or maintenance) by a person other than the original coder, learning the new names for data items becomes more difficult—at least it takes fractionally more time.

When using the CALL statement and subprograms, the programmer should follow the hierarchical structure that has been utilized throughout this text. The main program may be viewed as a "driving module" and the subroutines as "subordinate modules." Therefore, control of a procedure should always return to the main program in a manner similar to the completion of a PERFORM statement. Finally, you should never attempt to have a subprogram call *itself* or call another subprogram that has already called the current subprogram. These two situations could cause a continuous loop in much the same manner as a PERFORM statement either causing the execution of the procedure it is in or executing the procedure that executed it. Both are a result of poor design (or a design error) and should be avoided.

Questions

Below fill in the blank(s) with the appropriate word, words, or phrases.

1. Two means by which additional code may be "added" to the "original code you write are by using the _____ and _____.

2. COPY statement allows you to _____ code into an original set of code during the compilation process.

3. At a minimum, the COPY statement must specify a _____ name.

4. When a file is being copied via the COPY statement, the contents of that file may be altered by the _____ option.

5. The only DIVISION of a COBOL program not permitted to use the COPY statement is the _____ DIVISION.

6. In the PROCEDURE DIVISION, the COPY statement must be used at the _____ or _____ level.

7. Linkage to a subprogram is made during the _____ phase of running a program.

8. Whereas parts of programs may be "merged" with a program using COPY statements, subprograms are more like _____programs.

9. When a subprogram is to be executed, a _____ statement is used.

10. When control has been passed to a subprogram, it may be returned to a main program by the _____ or _____ statements.

11. When data are to be shared between a main program and a subprogram, both the CALL statement of the main program and the PROCEDURE DIVISION heading of the subprogram must contain the _____ option.

12. When data are to be shared between a main program and a subprogram, the subprogram should contain a _____ SECTION.

13. Linkage is established between a main program and a subprogram through a CALL statement that identifies the _____ name of the subprogram.

14. When a subprogram causes the execution of another subprogram, the first subprogram must contain a _____ statement.

Answer the following questions by circling either "T" for true or "F" for false.

T F 15. A single program is permitted to use multiple COPY statements.

T F 16. The contents of a COPY file are added to the original source code during the execution of the program.

T F 17. The COPY statement indicates where it is to be placed in the original code by a line number reference.

T F 18. It is possible to COPY the same file into two different locations of the same program.

T F 19. COPY statements are permitted in both the DATA and PROCEDURE DIVISIONs of a COBOL program.

T F 20. A COBOL main program is permitted to call one or more subprograms.

T F 21. A COBOL subprogram is permitted to call the main program.

T F 22. A COBOL subprogram is permitted to call another subprogram.

T F 23. A COBOL subprogram is permitted to call itself.

T F 24. When a CALL statement that specifies five arguments is used in a program, the PROCEDURE DIVISION heading of the subprogram must also specify five arguments.

T F 25. When the length of the arguments in a CALL statement is 50 bytes, the length of the arguments in the PROCEDURE DIVISION heading of the subprogram must also be 50 bytes.

CHAPTER

21

GO TO/DEPENDING ON and EVALUATE Statements

In Chapter 9, a simple unconditional GO TO statement was presented for the purpose of illustrating the looping process—a series of statements that are repeated due to the action of the GO TO statement. Another form of the GO TO statement is available in the COBOL language—the GO TO/DEPENDING ON. This statement is useful under very limited sets of circumstances; however, under those circumstances, programming using the GO TO/DEPENDING ON statement is greatly simplified.

The GO TO/DEPENDING ON Statement

The GO TO/DEPENDING ON statement, illustrated in Figure 21.1, provides the capability of branching on the basis of the value of a particular data item. From a single point in a program, one of several paths may be taken, depending on the value contained by the identifier in Figure 21.1. The identifier must be defined in the DATA DIVISION as being a numeric-elementary data item and must contain an integer value. The PICTURE string for this data item must be four digits or less.

Upon execution of the GO TO/DEPENDING ON statement, the value of the identifier is examined. If the value of the identifier is 1, a branch to procedure-name-1 is executed. If the value of the identifier is 2, a branch to procedure-name-2 is executed, and so forth. If the value of the identifier is either less than 1 or greater than the maximum number of the procedure-names provided in the statement, the GO TO/DEPENDING ON statement is ignored. In this case, the program execution continues with the next statement.

Figure 21.2 demonstrates the use of the GO TO/DEPENDING ON statement. In Chapters 9 and 11, programs were presented that changed the logic sequence of state-

Figure 21.1 Format of the GO TO/DEPENDING ON Statement

```
GO TO procedure-name-1 [procedure-name-2] . . .DEPENDING ON identifier
```

ments executed depending on the value found in some field. The process was accomplished in a number of different ways by using various forms of the IF statement. In the program shown in Figure 21.2, the letter grade assignment problem presented in Chapter 20, the same process is accomplished through the use of a GO TO/DEPENDING ON statement. However, since exam averages do not generally begin with the value 1 (with increments of 1), it is necessary to ''scale'' the averages so that a grade of 59.4 or less receives a value of 1 (or less); 59.5 to 69.4 is scaled to a value of 2; 69.5 to 79.4, a value of 3; and so forth. The only changes needed in the procedure from that shown in Figure 10.8 are the DETERMINE GRADE module and paragraph of the program.

A COMPUTE statement in the program provides a value for data-name BRANCH-WS and is responsible for the scaling of the average scores. Note that 40 is subtracted from the AVERAGE-WS. By doing this, most averages will then fall into a 60 to 0 range. (Subtracting 40 will also cause some averages to become negative, but if the value of the identifier (BRANCH-WS) is less than 1, the GO TO/DEPENDING ON statement is ignored—causing execution of the next sequential statement. In the program any average that would result in a negative number after subtracting 40 would normally receive the letter grade F. Notice that if the GO TO/DEPENDING ON statement is ignored, the next statement moves F to LETTER-GRADE-OUT.) However, subtracting 40 from 59.5 and then dividing the result by 10 would cause the value of BRANCH-WS to be 1 (because BRANCH-WS is an integer field). Thus, .5 is added to the result of the subtraction, causing any fraction of .5 or more to be ''rounded up'' after the division takes place. As a result, averages between 49.5 and 59.4 would be recoded to 1; 59.5 to 69.4 would cause BRANCH-WS to receive a value of 2; 69.5 to 79.4, the value 3; 79.5 to 89.4, the value 4; and 89.5 to 99.4 would result in BRANCH-WS receiving the value 5. One minor problem is that values over 99.4 will be recoded to 6; however, this value also represents an average that should receive the letter grade A, thus the extra GRADE-A paragraph name. Without this extra paragraph name, anyone having an average score between 99.5 and 100 would receive the letter grade F—a major program error.

Figure 21.2 An Illustration of the GO TO/DEPENDING ON Statement (Hierarchy Chart)

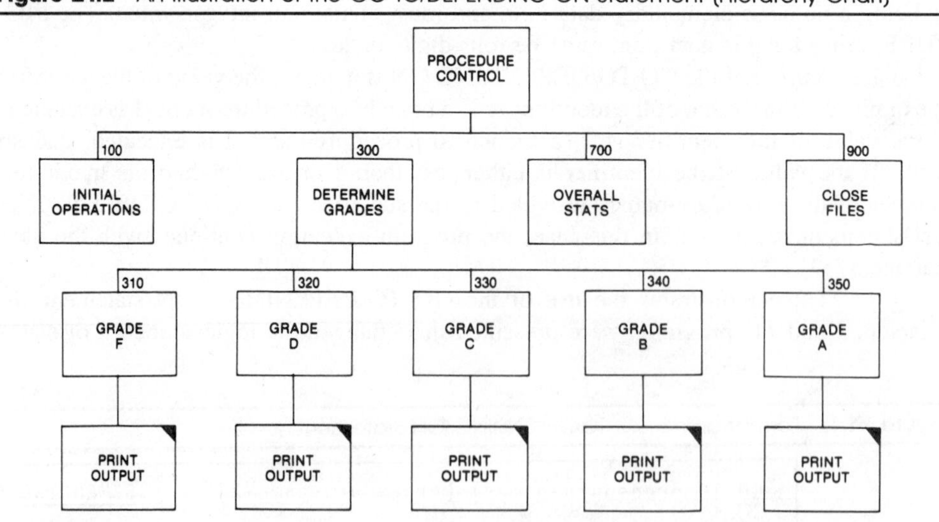

Figure 21.2 *Continued* An Illustration of the GO TO/DEPENDING Statement (Pseudocode)

```
START
    DO Initial operations
    DO Determine grades UNTIL eof
    DO Overall stats
    DO Close files
END

INITIAL OPERATIONS
    OPEN files
    WRITE heading
    SET file status
    READ input
         AT END set file status
END

DETERMINE GRADES
    COMPUTE average =
         (exam1 + exan2 + exam3)/3
    ADD exam1 to exam1 total, grand total
    ADD exam2 to exam2 total, grand total
    ADD exam3 to exam3 total, grand total
    ADD 1 to counter
    COMPUTE branch = (average - 40 + .5)/10
    GO TO grade f, grade d, grade c, grade b,
         grade a, grade a
         DEPENDING on branch
    END-GOTO
END

GRADE F
    MOVE F to grade
    DO Print output line
END

GRADE D
    MOVE D to grade
    DO Print output line
END

GRADE C
    MOVE C to grade
    DO Print output line
END

GRADE B
    MOVE B to grade
    DO Print output line
END

GRADE A
    MOVE A to grade
    DO Print output line
END

PRINT OUTPUT LINE
    MOVE values to output
    WRITE output
    READ input
         AT END set file status
END

OVERALL STATS
    DIVIDE exam1 total by counter
         GIVING exam1 average
    DIVIDE exam2 total by counter
         GIVING exam2 average
    DIVIDE exam3 total by counter
         GIVING exam3 average
    COMPUTE total average = grand total/counter*3
    WRITE output
END

CLOSE FILES
    CLOSE files
END
```

Figure 21.2 *Continued* An Illustration of the GO TO/DEPENDING ON Statement

```
              1   1   2   2   2   3   3   4   4   4   5   5   6   6   6   7
      4   8   2   6   0   4   8   2   6   0   4   8   2   6   0   4   8   2

    ***************************************************************
     IDENTIFICATION DIVISION.
    ***************************************************************
     PROGRAM-ID.    GRADES-ANALYSIS.
     AUTHOR.        J. WAYNE SPENCE.
     DATE-WRITTEN.  JANUARY 1, 1989.
     DATE-COMPILED. JANUARY 1, 1989.
    *    This program illustrates the use of the GO TO/
    *    DEPENDING ON statement.  In addition, arithmetic
    *    statements, accumulators, exam-counters, edited output
    *    and VALUE clauses are used.
    ***************************************************************
     ENVIRONMENT DIVISION.
    ***************************************************************
    *-------------------------------------------------------------*
     CONFIGURATION SECTION.
    *-------------------------------------------------------------*
     SOURCE-COMPUTER.  IBM.
     OBJECT-COMPUTER.  IBM.
     SPECIAL-NAMES.    C01 IS HEAD-OF-PAGE.
```

Figure 21.2 *Continued* An Illustration of the GO TO/DEPENDING Statement

```
              1   1   2   2   2   3   3   4   4   4   5   5   6   6   6   7
   4      8   2   6   0   4   8   2   6   0   4   8   2   6   0   4   8   2

210    *-----------------------------------------------------------*
220     INPUT-OUTPUT SECTION.
230    *-----------------------------------------------------------*
240     FILE-CONTROL.
250         SELECT STUDENT-FILE ASSIGN TO UT-S-INPUT.
260         SELECT REPORT-FILE  ASSIGN TO UT-S-OUTPUT.
270    *************************************************************
280     DATA DIVISION.
290    *************************************************************
300    *-----------------------------------------------------------*
310     FILE SECTION.
320    *-----------------------------------------------------------*
330     FD  STUDENT-FILE LABEL RECORDS ARE OMITTED.
340     01  STUDENT-RECORD.
350         05 STUDENT-NAME-IN            PIC X(20).
360         05 FILLER                     PIC X(10).
370         05 GRADES-IN.
380             10 EXAM-1-IN              PIC 9(03).
390             10 EXAM-2-IN              PIC 9(03).
400             10 EXAM-3-IN              PIC 9(03).
410         05 FILLER                     PIC X(41).
420
430     FD  REPORT-FILE LABEL RECORDS ARE OMITTED.
440     01  REPORT-RECORD                 PIC X(133).
450    *-----------------------------------------------------------*
460     WORKING-STORAGE SECTION.
470    *-----------------------------------------------------------*
480     01  WORKING-VARIABLES.
490         05  FILE-STATUS               PIC X(08).
500         05  EXAM-COUNTER-WS           PIC 9(03) VALUE ZERO.
510         05  EXAM-1-TOTAL-WS           PIC 9(05) VALUE ZERO.
520         05  EXAM-2-TOTAL-WS           PIC 9(05) VALUE ZERO.
530         05  EXAM-3-TOTAL-WS           PIC 9(05) VALUE ZERO.
540         05  GRAND-TOTAL-WS            PIC 9(06) VALUE ZERO.
550         05  AVERAGE-WS                PIC 9(03)V9(01).
560         05  BRANCH-WS                 PIC 9(01).
570
580     01  TITLE-RECORD.
590         05 FILLER                     PIC X(55) VALUE SPACES.
600         05 FILLER                     PIC X(22) VALUE
610                                       'Student Grade Averages'.
620         05 FILLER                     PIC X(56) VALUE SPACES.
630
640     01  HEADING-RECORD.
650         05 FILLER                     PIC X(41) VALUE SPACES.
660         05 FILLER                     PIC X(12) VALUE
670                                       'Student Name'.
680         05 FILLER                     PIC X(10) VALUE SPACES.
690         05 FILLER                     PIC X(07) VALUE 'Average'.
700         05 FILLER                     PIC X(10) VALUE SPACES.
710         05 FILLER                     PIC X(12) VALUE 'Letter Grade'.
720
730     01  ASTERISK-RECORD.
740         05 FILLER                     PIC X(41) VALUE SPACES.
750         05 FILLER                     PIC X(51) VALUE ALL '*'.
760
770     01  STUDENT-OUT-RECORD.
780         05 FILLER                     PIC X(41) VALUE SPACES.
790         05 STUDENT-NAME-OUT           PIC X(20).
800         05 FILLER                     PIC X(03) VALUE SPACES.
810         05 AVERAGE-OUT                PIC ZZ9.9.
820         05 FILLER                     PIC X(16) VALUE SPACES.
830         05 LETTER-GRADE-OUT           PIC X(01).
840
850     01  STATISTICS-RECORD.
860         05 FILLER                     PIC X(27) VALUE SPACES.
870         05 FILLER                     PIC X(24) VALUE
880                                       'Summary Class Statistics'.
890         05 FILLER                     PIC X(05) VALUE SPACES.
900         05 EXAM-1-AVERAGE-OUT         PIC ZZ9.9.
910         05 FILLER                     PIC X(05) VALUE SPACES.
```

Figure 21.2 *Continued* An Illustration of the GO TO/DEPENDING ON Statement

```
          1   1   2   2   2   3   3   4   4   4   5   5   6   6   6   7
   4   8  2   6   0   4   8   2   6   0   4   8   2   6   0   4   8   2

           05 EXAM-2-AVERAGE-OUT        PIC ZZ9.9.
           05 FILLER                    PIC X(05) VALUE SPACES.
           05 EXAM-3-AVERAGE-OUT        PIC ZZ9.9.
           05 FILLER                    PIC X(05) VALUE SPACES.
           05 OVERALL-AVERAGE-OUT       PIC ZZ9.9.
      *************************************************************
       PROCEDURE DIVISION.
      *************************************************************
      *-----------------------------------------------------------*
       000-PROCEDURE-CONTROL SECTION.
      *-----------------------------------------------------------*
           PERFORM 100-INITIAL-OPERATIONS.
           PERFORM 300-DETERMINE-GRADES
               UNTIL FILE-STATUS = 'DONE'.
           PERFORM 700-OVERALL-STATS.
           PERFORM 900-CLOSE-FILES.
           STOP RUN.
      *-----------------------------------------------------------*
       100-INITIAL-OPERATIONS SECTION.
      *-----------------------------------------------------------*
           OPEN INPUT STUDENT-FILE, OUTPUT REPORT-FILE.
           WRITE REPORT-RECORD FROM TITLE-RECORD AFTER HEAD-OF-PAGE.
           WRITE REPORT-RECORD FROM HEADING-RECORD AFTER 1 LINES.
           WRITE REPORT-RECORD FROM ASTERISK-RECORD AFTER 1 LINES.
           MOVE 'START'            TO FILE-STATUS.
           READ STUDENT-FILE
               AT END MOVE 'DONE' TO FILE-STATUS.
      *-----------------------------------------------------------*
       300-DETERMINE-GRADES SECTION.
      *-----------------------------------------------------------*
           COMPUTE AVERAGE-WS ROUNDED =
               (EXAM-1-IN + EXAM-2-IN + EXAM-3-IN) / 3.
           ADD EXAM-1-IN TO EXAM-1-TOTAL-WS, GRAND-TOTAL-WS.
           ADD EXAM-2-IN TO EXAM-2-TOTAL-WS, GRAND-TOTAL-WS.
           ADD EXAM-3-IN TO EXAM-3-TOTAL-WS, GRAND-TOTAL-WS.
           ADD 1 TO EXAM-COUNTER-WS.
           COMPUTE BRANCH-WS = (AVERAGE-WS - 40 + .5) / 10.
           GO TO 310-GRADE-F
                 320-GRADE-D
                 330-GRADE-C
                 340-GRADE-B
                 350-GRADE-A
                 350-GRADE-A
                 DEPENDING ON BRANCH-WS.
      *-----------------------------------------------------------*
       310-GRADE-F SECTION.
      *-----------------------------------------------------------*
           MOVE 'F'                TO LETTER-GRADE-OUT.
           PERFORM 315-PRINT-OUTPUT-LINE.
      *-----------------------------------------------------------*
       320-GRADE-D SECTION.
      *-----------------------------------------------------------*
           MOVE 'D'                TO LETTER-GRADE-OUT.
           PERFORM 315-PRINT-OUTPUT-LINE.
      *-----------------------------------------------------------*
       330-GRADE-C SECTION.
      *-----------------------------------------------------------*
           MOVE 'C'                TO LETTER-GRADE-OUT.
           PERFORM 315-PRINT-OUTPUT-LINE.
      *-----------------------------------------------------------*
       340-GRADE-B SECTION.
      *-----------------------------------------------------------*
           MOVE 'B'                TO LETTER-GRADE-OUT.
           PERFORM 315-PRINT-OUTPUT-LINE.
      *-----------------------------------------------------------*
       350-GRADE-A SECTION.
      *-----------------------------------------------------------*
           MOVE 'A'                TO LETTER-GRADE-OUT.
           PERFORM 315-PRINT-OUTPUT-LINE.
      *-----------------------------------------------------------*
       315-PRINT-OUTPUT-LINE SECTION.
      *-----------------------------------------------------------*
```

Figure 21.2 *Continued* An Illustration of the GO TO/DEPENDING ON Statement

```
            1   1   2   2   2   3   3   4   4   4   5   5   6   6   6   7
    4   8   2   6   0   4   8   2   6   0   4   8   2   6   0   4   8   2

           MOVE STUDENT-NAME-IN      TO STUDENT-NAME-OUT.
           MOVE AVERAGE-WS           TO AVERAGE-OUT.
           WRITE REPORT-RECORD FROM STUDENT-OUT-RECORD AFTER 2 LINES.
           READ STUDENT-FILE
               AT END MOVE 'DONE' TO FILE-STATUS.
       *--------------------------------------------------------------*
        700-OVERALL-STATS SECTION.
       *--------------------------------------------------------------*
           WRITE REPORT-RECORD FROM ASTERISK-RECORD AFTER 2 LINES.
           DIVIDE EXAM-1-TOTAL-WS BY EXAM-COUNTER-WS
               GIVING EXAM-1-AVERAGE-OUT ROUNDED.
           DIVIDE EXAM-2-TOTAL-WS BY EXAM-COUNTER-WS
               GIVING EXAM-2-AVERAGE-OUT ROUNDED.
           DIVIDE EXAM-3-TOTAL-WS BY EXAM-COUNTER-WS
               GIVING EXAM-3-AVERAGE-OUT ROUNDED.
           COMPUTE OVERALL-AVERAGE-OUT ROUNDED = GRAND-TOTAL-WS /
               (EXAM-COUNTER-WS * 3).
           WRITE REPORT-RECORD AFTER ADVANCING 2 LINES.
           WRITE REPORT-RECORD FROM STATISTICS-RECORD AFTER 2 LINES.
       *--------------------------------------------------------------*
        900-CLOSE-FILES SECTION.
       *--------------------------------------------------------------*
           CLOSE STUDENT-FILE, REPORT-FILE.
```

Figure 21.2 *Continued* An Illustration of the GO TO/DEPENDING ON Statement (Data)

```
      |         1         2         3         4
Record|1234567890123456789012345678901234567890
------|----------------------------------------
     1|Adams, Forest                  053051051
     2|Balles, William                070075072
     3|Bond, George                   090096090
     4|Broadus, Cathy                 086080081
     5|Cesario, Winnie                068051058
     6|Clement, Debora                094093085
     7|Decker, Lawrence               044045050
     8|Edmiston, Gary                 079071074
     9|Elliott, Jose                  081080084
    10|Ford, James                    086084061
    11|Gapinski, Maureen              054057051
    12|Haffey, Ernest                 093090094
    13|Healton, Tim                   084095098
    14|Hill, Robert                   077070071
    15|Hooson, Kim                    076075076
    16|Kaskadden, Nancy               081086080
    17|Keyes, Andy                    063054080
    18|Klavon, Kevin                  084088085
    19|Kos, Janie                     100099099
    20|Lorenz, Linda                  082087081
    21|Meyer, Robert                  099092095
    22|Miller, Mark                   071069068
    23|MYers, Audrey                  072075070
    24|Roehl, Marty                   081093095
    25|Senger, Marvin                 053053055
    26|Shogren, Marcus                091094089
    27|Smith, Dennis                  025072028
    28|Swanson, Jeff                  100100100
    29|Tidwell, Jane                  065066067
```

Figure 21.2 *Continued* An Illustration of the GO TO/DEPENDING ON Statement (Output)

```
                    Student Grade Averages
Student Name             Average         Letter Grade
*************************************************
Adams, Forest              51.7               F
Balles, William            72.3               C
Bond, George               92.0               A
Broadus, Cathy             82.3               B
Cesario, Winnie            59.0               F
Clement, Debora            90.7               A
Decker, Lawrence           46.3               F
Edmiston, Gary             74.7               C
Elliott, Jose              81.7               B
Ford, James                77.0               C
Gapinski, Maureen          54.0               F
Haffey, Ernest             92.3               A
Healton, Tim               92.3               A
Hill, Robert               72.7               C
Hooson, Kim                75.7               C
Kaskadden, Nancy           82.3               B
Keyes, Andy                65.7               D
Klavon, Kevin              85.7               B
Kos, Janie                 99.3               A
Lorenz, Linda              83.3               B
Meyer, Robert              95.3               A
Miller, Mark               69.3               D
Myers, Audrey              72.3               C
Roehl, Marty               89.7               A
Senger, Marvin             53.7               F
Shogren, Marcus            91.3               A
Smith, Dennis              41.7               F
Swanson, Jeff             100.0               A
Tidwell, Jane              66.0               D
*************************************************
*************************************************
Summary Class Statistics     75.9      77.3      75.4      76.2
```

The EVALUATE Statement

1985 COBOL Standards

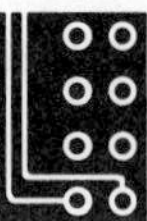

Under the COBOL 85 standards, the same type of case structure can be implemented with the use of the EVALUATE statement. The general format for this statement is presented in Figure 21.3, and is capable of handling very complex logical structures. One of the dangers of the EVALUATE statement is that you can create code that is extremely difficult to understand. For this reason, our recommendation is that the statement be used only when it simplifies the code.

The EVALUATE statement can be used in place of a set of *linear* IF statements or the GO TO/DEPENDING ON structure. If the EVALUATE statement is used in place of the GO TO/DEPENDING ON structure in the grade assignment program presented in Figure 21.2, lines 1290–1610 would be replaced with the following code.

```
EVALUATE BRANCH-WS
    WHEN 1              MOVE "F' TO LETTER-GRADE-OUT
    WHEN 2              MOVE "D' TO LETTER-GRADE-OUT
    WHEN 3              MOVE "C' TO LETTER-GRADE-OUT
    WHEN 4              MOVE "B' TO LETTER-GRADE-OUT
    WHEN 5 THRU 6       MOVE "A' TO LETTER-GRADE-OUT
END-EVALUATE.
PERFORM 315-PRINT-OUTPUT-LINE.
```

Figure 21.3 Format of the EVALUATE Statement

```
           { identifier-1 }            { identifier-2 }
           { literal-1    }            { literal-2    }
EVALUATE   { expression-1 }     ALSO   { expression-2 }
           { TRUE         }            { TRUE         }
           { FALES        }            { FALSE        }

{{WHEN
   { ANY                                                                      }
   { condition-1                                                              }
   { TRUE                                                                     }
   { FALSE                                                                    }
   { [NOT] {{identifier-3 }} [{THROUGH} {identifier-4 }]                      }
   {       {{literal-3    }} [{THRU   } {literal-4    }]                      }
   {       {{expression-3 }} [          {expression-4 }]                      }
[ALSO
   { ANY                                                                      }
   { condition-1                                                              }
   { TRUE                                                                     }
   { FALSE                                                                    }
   { [NOT] {{identifier-3 }} [{THROUGH} {identifier-4 }]                      }
   {       {{literal-3    }} [{THRU   } {literal-4    }]                      }
   {       {{expression-3 }} [          {expression-4 }]                      }
   imperative-statement-1} . . .

[WHEN OTHER imperative-statement-2]

[END-EVALUATE]
```

Summary

In this chapter, an additional form of the GO TO statement has been presented. The GO TO/DEPENDING ON statement is capable of executing an unconditional branch to a procedure name by "selecting" a particular procedure-name from a list of procedures. This selection is used on a correspondence between the value of an identifier associated with the GO TO/DEPENDING ON statement and the location (first, second, third, etc.) of a procedure in the list of procedures. The EVALUATE statement was also presented as a COBOL 85 alternative to the GO TO/DEPENDING ON statement and a set of *linear* IF statements.

Notes on Programming Style

The case structure is probably best approximated in COBOL through the use of the GO TO/DEPENDING ON statement. However, do not get yourself trapped when designing code to use this statement, you will frequently find it necessary to use the SECTION level in the PROCEDURE DIVISION. Otherwise, you will have to cancel a PERFORM statement that is probably controlling the overall procedure. You will be calling for help from your favorite deity if that happens.

Carlisle Graphics/2530 Kerper Blvd./Dubuque, IA 52001 G 3 JOB5 16239$2101

Questions

Fill in the following blank(s) with the appropriate word, words, or phrase.

1. In total, there are ____ (number) formats of the GO TO statement.
2. The types of GO TO statements provided in COBOL include the ____ and ____ statements.
3. The simple GO TO statement provides for a single, unconditional branch; the GO TO/DEPENDING ON statement provides for ____.

Answer the following questions by circling "T" for True or "F" for False.

T F **4.** The identifier associated with the GO TO/DEPENDING ON statement must be defined as an integer field.
T F **5.** The identifier associated with the GO TO/DEPENDING ON statement could contain zero.
T F **6.** If the identifier associated with a GO TO/DEPENDING ON statement contained a negative value, the GO TO/DEPENDING ON statement is executed.

Summary

CHAPTER

22

Multiple Record Descriptions, Redefinitions, and Renaming of Data Items

Some problems require that the definitions of records, groups of items, or elementary-items describe the same space in the computer's internal storage. Two benefits are derived from this technique. First, by describing two or more data items (records, groups, or elementary-items) to occupy the same place, the programmer can conserve the computer's internal storage. Second, alternate descriptions (with varied field sizes and characteristics) for the same area of the computer's storage are provided.

Multiple Record Descriptions

Under some circumstances, the input data for a program have varied formats (i.e., all the input records have different field designations or sizes and characteristics). If it were not possible to have multiple record descriptions for these records, it would be difficult to accept these data and interpret their meanings. Multiple record descriptions can be placed in the FILE SECTION to be associated with one file or FD. If a problem requires the input (or output) of two or more records with differing characteristics and if the programmer codes these records in one FD record, the program can accommodate those variations.

As an illustration of this process, assume a program must handle three different types of records from the same file (see Figure 22.1). If the programmer incorporates multiple record descriptions in the file description for this file, all of these records can be read into the computer's internal storage. The record descriptions for these three records are also shown in Figure 22.1. Note that each of these descriptions begins with the level number 01—the COBOL notation for records—and that the fields and their characteristics are different from one record to another. Also, some fields in the same columns of the respective records use different labels (data-names). When data are needed in the PROCEDURE DIVISION, the programmer must determine which of the record descriptions contains the correct interpretation of the record last read. This is often done by placing a code field in one of the columns of the record. In the example, the programmer could use the code in column 80 of each record to determine which record description to use in the PROCEDURE DIVISION. (If the code is 1, the first record description should

Figure 22.1 Multiple Record Layouts

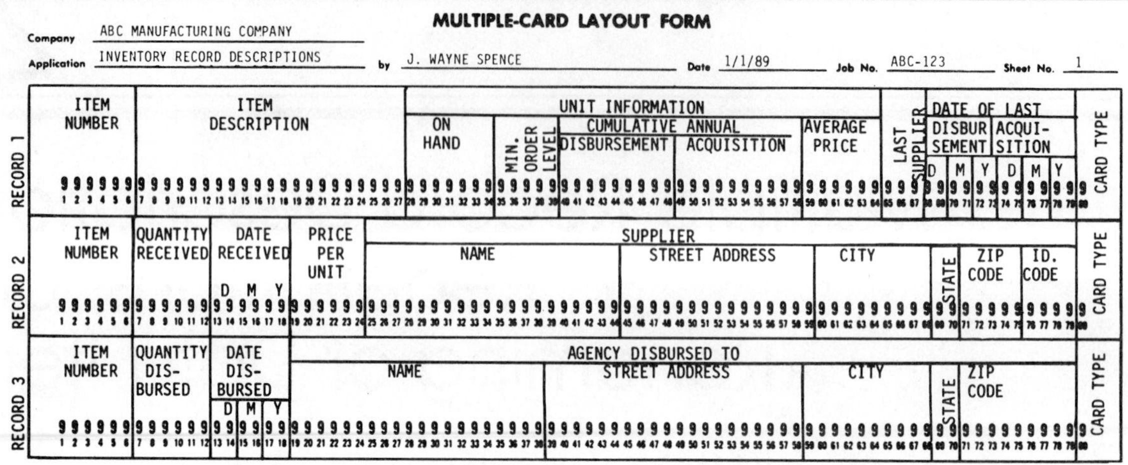

MULTIPLE-CARD LAYOUT FORM

Company ABC MANUFACTURING COMPANY
Application INVENTORY RECORD DESCRIPTIONS by J. WAYNE SPENCE Date 1/1/89 Job No. ABC-123 Sheet No. 1

RECORD 1: ITEM NUMBER | ITEM DESCRIPTION | UNIT INFORMATION: ON HAND | MIN. ORDER LEVEL | CUMULATIVE ANNUAL DISBURSEMENT | CUMULATIVE ANNUAL ACQUISITION | AVERAGE PRICE | LAST SUPPLIER | DATE OF LAST DISBURSEMENT (D M Y) | DATE OF LAST ACQUISITION (D M Y) | CARD TYPE

RECORD 2: ITEM NUMBER | QUANTITY RECEIVED | DATE RECEIVED (D M Y) | PRICE PER UNIT | SUPPLIER: NAME | STREET ADDRESS | CITY | STATE | ZIP CODE | ID. CODE | CARD TYPE

RECORD 3: ITEM NUMBER | QUANTITY DIS-BURSED | DATE DIS-BURSED (D M Y) | AGENCY DISBURSED TO: NAME | STREET ADDRESS | CITY | STATE | ZIP CODE | CARD TYPE

be used; if the code is 2, the second record description should be used; and so forth.)

The COBOL compiler assumes that the three record descriptions in the FILE SECTION of Figure 22.2 describe the same space in the computer's internal storage. The compiler makes no such assumption about records described in the WORKING-STORAGE SECTION. These three record descriptions occupy 80 characters of computer storage if located in the FILE SECTION, but 240 characters of storage (three independent records) if in the WORKING-STORAGE SECTION.

The records illustrated in Figure 22.1 are different in many respects, including different field names (e.g., ITEM DESCRIPTION in record 1 versus QUANTITY DISBURSED in record 2) and different field characteristics (e.g., ITEM DESCRIPTION of record 1 is an alphanumeric field; QUANTITY RECEIVED and QUANTITY DISBURSED of records 2 and 3 are numeric fields). Even though the records are different, they may be read into the same buffer. Recall from Chapters 4, 6 and 17 that the FILE SECTION of the DATA DIVISION represents internal storage employed for input and output buffers. The program can accept any type of data in the input buffer.It is only when data are to be accessed in the PROCEDURE DIVISION that they must be referenced with an appropriate PICTURE string. To *utilize* data in an input buffer, they must be matched with a data item description. Then, data can be read; otherwise, a fatal error may result.

After data have been read into an input buffer, the programmer must use the appropriate data-names to access the data. The approach used in Figure 22.2 is a code (CARD-TYPE), which indicates the difference between the formats. If the CARD-TYPE contained the value 1, the programmer could interpret this to mean that a MASTER-RECORD has entered the buffer. The value 2 could be used for RECEIPT-RECORD identification, and the value 3 could represent a DISBURSEMENT-RECORD. However, this is not the only means to distinguish among records. For example, to distinguish between a MASTER-RECORD and a RECEIPT-RECORD, the STATE field of the RECEIPT-RECORD could be examined to determine whether its contents was alphabetic. (If the statement IF STATE OF RECEIPT-RECORD IS ALPHABETIC was placed in the program, a false result would indicate that a MASTER-RECORD was in the input buffer—assuming the DATE-OF-LAST-DISBURSEMENT was recorded as a number.)

Figure 22.2 Multiple Record Descriptions in the FILE SECTION

```
DATA DIVISION.
FILE SECTION.
FD  INVENTORY-FILE
       LABEL RECORDS ARE OMITTED.
01  MASTER-RECORD.
    05  INVENTORY-NUMBER-IN          PIC 9(06).
    05  ITEM-DESCRIPTION-IN          PIC X(21).
    05  UNIT-INFORMATION-IN.
        10  ON-HAND-IN               PIC 9(07).
        10  MIN-ORDER-LEVEL-IN       PIC 9(04).
        10  CUMULATIVE-ANNUAL-IN.
            15  DISBURSEMENTS-IN     PIC 9(10).
            15  ACQUISITIONS-IN      PIC 9(10).
        10  AVERAGE-PRICE-IN         PIC 9(04)V99.
    05  LAST-SUPPLIER-IN             PIC 9(03).
    05  DATE-OF-LAST-IN.
        10  DISBURSEMENT-DATE-IN.
            15  DAY-DISBURSE-IN      PIC 9(02).
            15  MONTH-DISBURSE-IN    PIC 9(02).
            15  YEAR-DISBURSE-IN     PIC 9(02).
        10  ACQUIRE-DATE-IN.
            15  DAY-ACQUIRE-IN       PIC 9(02).
            15  MONTH-ACQUIRE-IN     PIC 9(02).
            15  YEAR-ACQUIRE-IN      PIC 9(02).
    05  CARD-TYPE-IN                 PIC 9(01).

01  RECEIPT-RECORD.
    05  ITEM-NUMBER-IN               PIC 9(06).
    05  QUANTITY-RECEIVED-IN         PIC 9(06).
    05  DATE-RECEIVED-IN.
        10  DAY-RECEIVED-IN          PIC 9(02).
        10  MONTH-RECEIVED-IN        PIC 9(02).
        10  YEAR-RECEIVED-IN         PIC 9(02).
    05  PRICE-PER-UNIT-IN            PIC 9(04)V99.
    05  SUPPLIER-IN.
        10  SUPPLIER-NAME-IN         PIC X(20).
        10  SUPPLIER-STREET-IN       PIC X(15).
        10  SUPPLIER-CITY-IN         PIC X(09).
        10  SUPPLIER-STATE-IN        PIC X(20).
        10  SUPPLIER-ZIP-IN          PIC 9(05).
    05  SUPPLIER-ID-CODE-IN          PIC 9(04).
    05  CARD-TYPE-IN                 PIC 9(01).

01  DISBURSEMENT-RECORD.
    05  ITEM-NUMBER-IN               PIC 9(06).
    05  QUANTITY-DISBURSED-IN        PIC 9(06).
    05  DATE-DISBURSED-IN.
        10  DAY-DISBURSED-IN         PIC 9(02).
        10  MONTH-DISBURSED-IN       PIC 9(02).
        10  YEAR-DISBURSED-IN        PIC 9(02).
    05  AGENCY-DISBURSED-TO-IN.
        10  AGENCY-NAME-IN           PIC X(20).
        10  AGENCY-STREET-IN         PIC X(20).
        10  AGENCY-CITY-IN           PIC X(10).
        10  AGENCY-STATE-IN          PIC X(02).
        10  AGENCY-ZIP-IN            PIC 9(05).
    05  FILLER                       PIC X(04).
    05  CARD-TYPE-IN                 PIC 9(01).
```

05 Card-type-in pic 9
88 ADD-REC value 1
88 change-rec value 2
88 delete-rec value 3

IF Add Rec THEN PERFORM

To distinguish between a RECEIPT-RECORD and a DISBURSEMENT-RECORD, the ID-CODE of RECEIPT-RECORD could be examined to determine whether its contents was a number (the appropriate contents for an ID-CODE) or spaces (the normal contents of FILLER). Thus, the programmer does not have to rely totally on the foresight of those responsible for designing input records.

The REDEFINES Clause

In some cases, the records to be read by a program have highly similar characteristics. For example, the input-record descriptions presented in Figure 22.2 include an ITEM-NUMBER in the first six columns of each record. Each of the records presents a CARD-TYPE code in column 80.

By using the REDEFINES clause in the description of records, the programmer does not have to recode any fields that are present in one or more records (or groups). Only the different portions of the records (in size or characteristics) need be coded. In addition, one WORKING-STORAGE SECTION record description may be *overlaid* on another by using the REDEFINES clause. Fields (or groups) may be overlaid in *either* the FILE SECTION or the WORKING-STORAGE SECTION. By placing one record (or a portion of a record) in the same internal storage location as another, space in the WORKING-STORAGE SECTION may be conserved. The format of the REDEFINES clause is presented in Figure 22.3.

Data-name-1, as specified in Figure 22.3, must not be the name of a record in the FILE SECTION. As seen in the discussion of multiple records in the FILE SECTION, a redefinition of these records at level-Ø1 is redundant—the records are already *implicitly* redefined. Data-name-1 also must not be a level-66 or 88 data item. Level-66 is used with the RENAMES clause, which is discussed later in this chapter. Level-88 is used with condition-names as described in Chapter 11. Both data-name-1 and data-name-2 may represent a table (a data item that is accompanied by an OCCURS clause—see Chapter 13). Neither data-name-1 nor data-name-2 may be a variable-length table. Data-name-2 may not be written with or subordinate to an OCCURS clause, but it may have an OCCURS clause with one of *its* subordinate items.

The level number associated with the REDEFINES clause is the key to understanding the redefinition process. Data-name-2 must appear in a description of data prior to the redefinition itself. The level number associated with data-name-2 must be the same level number as the redefinition. For example, if data-name-2 is coded a level-Ø5, the redefinition must be at level-Ø5. If data-name-2 is an elementary data item, the redefinition must immediately follow the data-name-2 entry. If data-name-2 is a group (or record), the redefinition must follow data-name-2 at the programmer's first opportunity to enter a level number equivalent to that of data-name-2. For example, if data-name-2 is coded at level-Ø5, the redifinition must begin before the next level-Ø5 which would normally appear in the record description.

Figure 22.3 Format of the REDEFINES Clause

```
level-number data-name-1 REDEFINES data-name-2
```

The redefinition is terminated by the occurrence of a level that is higher than or equal to that of the redefinition. If the redefinition begins with level-05, the redefinition is terminated with the next occurrence of level-01, 02, 03, 04, or 05. The redefinition should be exactly the same length as the original definition of the data being redefined. If the original description of the data (in or subordinate to data-name-2) is 30 characters or digits, the redefinition should also represent 30 characters or digits. If multiple redefinitions of the same data fields are necessary, each redefinition should use the name (data-name-2) of the original data description. (Some compilers—for example, IBM—permit a redefinition *of* a redefinition.) It is also possible to have a redefinition *within* a redefinition. COBOL allows the programmer to redefine a portion of a record description that is associated with a REDEFINES clause.

Figure 22.4 shows how the REDEFINES clause is used. This illustration provides an alternative to the FILE SECTION entries in Figure 22.2, using the same description of data presented in Figure 22.1. However, this description is somewhat shorter and does not require PROCEDURE DIVISION qualification of the data-names ITEM-NUMBER and CARD-TYPE.

Redefinition of Tables

It is often useful to have a table constructed in the computer's internal storage that is provided with data prior to program execution. During the creation of the table, the table is ''loaded'' with data. This may be done with the REDEFINES clause. Recall that the REDEFINES clause may be used with OCCURS clauses to provide alternate descriptions of the same area of the internal storage. The programmer should also remember that a VALUE clause cannot be written with or subordinate to an OCCURS

Figure 22.4 An Illustration of the REDEFINES Clause

```
DATA DIVISION.
FILE SECTION.
FD  INVENTORY-FILE
        LABEL RECORDS ARE OMITTED.
01  INVENTORY-RECORDS.
    05  INVENTORY-NUMBER-IN                     PIC 9(06).
    05  BODY-OF-RECORD-IN.
        10  ITEM-DESCRIPTION-IN                 PIC X(21).
        10  UNIT-INFORMATION-IN.
            15  ON-HAND-IN                      PIC 9(07).
            15  MIN-ORDER-LEVEL-IN              PIC 9(04).
            15  CUMULATIVE-ANNUAL-IN.
                20  DISBURSEMENTS-IN            PIC 9(10).
                20  ACQUISITIONS-IN             PIC 9(10).
            15  AVERAGE-PRICE-IN                PIC 9(04)V99.
        10  LAST-SUPPLIER-IN                    PIC 9(03).
        10  DATE-OF-LAST-IN.
            15  DISBURSEMENT-DATE-IN.
                20  DAY-DISBURSE-IN             PIC 9(02).
                20  MONTH-DISBURSE-IN           PIC 9(02).
                20  YEAR-DISBURSE-IN            PIC 9(02).
            15  ACQUIRE-DATE-IN.
                20  DAY-ACQUIRE-IN              PIC 9(02).
                20  MONTH-ACQUIRE-IN            PIC 9(02).
                20  YEAR-ACQUIRE-IN             PIC 9(02).
```

Figure 22.4 continued on next page

Figure 22.4 *Continued* An Illustration of the REDEFINES Clause

```
05  RECEIPT-DISBURSEMENT-RECORD-IN
       REDEFINES BODY-OF-RECORD-IN.
    10  QUANTITY-RECEIVED-DISBURSED-IN     PIC 9(06).
    10  DATE-RECEIVED-DISBURSED-IN.
        15  DAY-RECEIVED-DISBURSED-IN      PIC 9(02).
        15  MONTH-RECEIVED-DISBURSED-IN    PIC 9(02).
        15  YEAR-RECEIVED-DISBURSED-IN     PIC 9(02).
    10  RECEIPT-INFORMATION-IN.
        15  PRICE-PER-UNIT-IN              PIC 9(04)V99.
        15  SUPPLIER-IN.
            20  SUPPLIER-NAME-IN           PIC X(20).
            20  SUPPLIER-STREET-IN         PIC X(15).
            20  SUPPLIER-CITY-IN           PIC X(09).
            20  SUPPLIER-STATE-IN          PIC X(20).
            20  SUPPLIER-ZIP-IN            PIC 9(05).
            20  SUPPLIER-ID-CODE-IN        PIC 9(04).

05  DISBURSEMENT-INFORMATION-IN
      REDEFINES RECEIPT-INFORMATION-IN.
    10  AGENCY-DISBURSED-TO-IN.
        15  AGENCY-NAME-IN                 PIC X(20).
        15  AGENCY-STREET-IN               PIC X(20).
        15  AGENCY-CITY-IN                 PIC X(10).
        15  AGENCY-STATE-IN                PIC X(02).
        15  AGENCY-ZIP-IN                  PIC 9(05).
        15  FILLER                         PIC X(04).
05  CARD-TYPE-IN                           PIC 9(01).
```

clause, except as might be used with condition-names. Thus, unless the programmer plans to MOVE data into a table during the execution of the PROCEDURE DIVISION, the only alternative to loading a table with data values prior to program execution is to utilize the REDEFINES clause.

Figure 22.5 provides an example of how the REDEFINES clause is used to provide initial values for table items. (It is assumed that the code of Figure 22.5 is in the WORKING-STORAGE SECTION, since the VALUE clause is being employed.) Notice that it is first necessary to construct a ''dummy'' record containing the data values to be placed in the table. DATA-RECORD is such a record. The sole purpose of DATA-RECORD is to provide values to be placed in certain positions with NAMES-OF-STATES. VALUE clauses may be used with the FILLER items of DATA-RECORD, but they could not be used with any item associated with NAMES-OF-STATES. The programmer must be careful when providing data values to be placed in a table. The description of the data must be consistent with the description of the table. In Figure 22.5, STATE-ABBREVIATION and STATE (each of which OCCURS 12 times) alternate in internal storage. (The alternating process was described in Chapter 13.) Thus, the description of the data values to be placed in the table must alternate.

Figure 22.6 illustrates the same type of data arrangement as in Figure 22.5; however, in this illustration, the table is described in such a way that all occurrences of STATE-ABBREVIATION appear before the first occurrence of STATE. Thus, the data placed into DATA-RECORD must be organized so that all values for STATE-ABBREVIATION are provided before the value to be placed in the first occurrence of STATE.

Figure 22.5 An Example of Table Initialization

```
01  DATA-RECORD.
    05  FILLER                   PIC X(12)    VALUE 'LALouisanna'.
    05  FILLER                   PIC X(12)    VALUE 'TXTexas'.
    05  FILLER                   PIC X(12)    VALUE 'NMNew Mexico'.
    05  FILLER                   PIC X(12)    VALUE 'AZArizona'.
    05  FILLER                   PIC X(12)    VALUE 'NVNevada'.
    05  FILLER                   PIC X(12)    VALUE 'UTUtah'.
    05  FILLER                   PIC X(12)    VALUE 'COColorado'.
    05  FILLER                   PIC X(12)    VALUE 'OKOklahoma'.
    05  FILLER                   PIC X(12)    VALUE 'ARArkansas'.
    05  FILLER                   PIC X(12)    VALUE 'MOMissouri'.
    05  FILLER                   PIC X(12)    VALUE 'KSKansas'.
    05  FILLER                   PIC X(12)    VALUE 'NENebraska'.

01  NAMES-OF-STATES REDEFINES DATA-RECORD.
    05  STATE-PAIR                OCCURS 12 TIMES.
        10  STATE-ABBREVIATION    PIC X(02).
        10  STATE                 PIC X(10).
```

NAME-OF-STATES

STATE-ABBREVIATION (1)	LA	Lousianna	STATE (1)
STATE-ABBREVIATION (2)	TX	Texas	STATE (2)
STATE-ABBREVIATION (3)	NM	New Mexico	STATE (3)
STATE-ABBREVIATION (4)	AZ	Arizona	STATE (4)
STATE-ABBREVIATION (5)	NV	Nevada	STATE (5)
STATE-ABBREVIATION (6)	UT	Utah	STATE (6)
STATE-ABBREVIATION (7)	CO	Colorado	STATE (7)
STATE-ABBREVIATION (8)	OK	Oklahoma	STATE (8)
STATE-ABBREVIATION (9)	AR	Arkansas	STATE (9)
STATE-ABBREVIATION (10)	MO	Missouri	STATE (10)
STATE-ABBREVIATION (11)	KS	Kansas	STATE (11)
STATE-ABBREVIATION (12)	NE	Nebraska	STATE (12)

Figure 22.6 A Second Illustration of Table Initialization

```
01  DATA-RECORD.
    05  FILLER                        PIC X(24)    VALUE
                                      'LATXNMAZNVUTCOOKARMOKSNE'.
    05  FILLER                        PIC X(120)   VALUE
    'Louisanna Texas     New MexicoArizona   Nevada    Utah
-   'Colorado  Oklahoma  Arkansas  Missouri  Kansas    Nebraska'.

01  NAMES-OF-STATES REDEFINES DATA-RECORD.
    05  STATE-ABBREVIATION            OCCURS 12 TIMES
                                      PIC X(02).
    05  STATE                         OCCURS 12 TIMES
                                      PIC X(10).
```

Figure 22.6 continued on next page

Figure 22.6 *Continued* A Second Illustration of Table Initialization

STATE-ABBREVIATION (1)	LA
STATE-ABBREVIATION (2)	TX
STATE-ABBREVIATION (3)	NM
STATE-ABBREVIATION (4)	AZ
STATE-ABBREVIATION (5)	NV
STATE-ABBREVIATION (6)	UT
STATE-ABBREVIATION (7)	CO
STATE-ABBREVIATION (8)	OK
STATE-ABBREVIATION (9)	AR
STATE-ABBREVIATION (10)	MO
STATE-ABBREVIATION (12)	KS
STATE-ABBREVIATION (12)	NE
STATE (1)	Louisanna
STATE (2)	Texas
STATE (3)	New Mexico
STATE (4)	Arizona
STATE (5)	Nevada
STATE (6)	Utah
STATE (7)	Colorado
STATE (8)	Oklahoma
STATE (9)	Arkansas
STATE (10)	Missouri
STATE (11)	Kansas
STATE (12)	Nebraska

The RENAMES Clause

The final clause to be discussed in this chapter is the RENAMES clause. This clause allows the programmer to change the names of data items or groups or create a totally new groupings of data items. The RENAMES clause is different from the REDEFINES clause in a number of respects. As the format of the RENAMES clause in Figure 22.7 indicates, it is always accompanied by a level-66 number. This level number should be coded in Area A of a COBOL entry. The RENAMES clause should appear immediately *after* a record description—not within the record description, as with the REDEFINES clause. In addition, the REDEFINES clause may be accompanied by a PICTURE clause or have subordinate data items that modify the original characteristics of the same data area. The RENAMES clause may not be written with a PICTURE clause. It may only be used to provide an alternate name for data already described. In addition, there may not be data items subordinate to a RENAMES clause. Thus, the RENAMES clause cannot change the characteristics of a data area. Finally, the RENAMES clause cannot be used to provide alternate data-names for other items accompanied by level number Ø1, 66, 77, or 88.

In Figure 22.7, data-name-1 represents a new data-name which acts as an alternate to data-name-2 (which should appear in the preceding record). In the PROCEDURE DIVISION, data-name-1 and data-name-2 may be used interchangeably—both represent the same data. If data-name-2 is an elementary data item, data-name-1 is assumed to be an elementary data item with the same characteristics. If data-name-2 is a group item, data-name-1 is also considered to be a group item. The only difference between data-name-1 and data-name-2 is that data-name-1 may not be used in the qualification of a data-name that is subordinate to data-name-2.

Figure 22.7 Format of the RENAMES Clause

```
66 data-name-1 RENAMES data-name-2 [THRU data-name-3]
```

When both data-name-2 and data-name-3 are used, data-name-1 is considered to be a group item. Data-name-2 and data-name-3 should not be the same name. Data-name-3 should physically follow data-name-2 in the record description, but data-name-3 should not be subordinate to data-name-2. When the RENAMES is complete, data-name-1 is considered to be a group item that includes all data items between data-name-2 and data-name-3 (and if data-name-3 is a group name, data-name-1 includes all data items subordinate to data-name-3). Data-name-2 and data-name-3 may be either elementary data items or group names.

The RENAMES clause may be used in the description of the inventory records presented in Figures 22.2 and 22.4. Figure 22.8 presents the use of multiple records, REDEFINES clauses, and RENAMES clauses. This illustration provides a description of the MASTER-RECORD and a RECEIPT-DISBURSEMENT-RECORD, which is used jointly by both receipts and disbursements. Note that in the RECEIPT-DISBURSEMENT-RECORD the redefinition is slightly different from the redefinition in Figure 22.4. Only the different portions of the receipt and disbursement records are included in the redefined area. Thus, STATE and ZIP CODE, being in the same columns in both records, are not redefined. Immediately following the RECEIPT-DISBURSEMENT-RECORD are a series of RENAMES clauses. The first RENAMES clause is used to provide an alternate name for QUANTITY-RECEIVED. In the PROCEDURE DIVISION, columns 7 through 12 of the input record could be represented by either QUANTITY-RECEIVED or QUANTITY-DISBURSED (i.e., they are both numeric elementary data items). The second RENAMES clause is used to provide an alternate name for DATA-RECEIVED—a group name. Thus, DATA-DISBURSED could be used in the PROCEDURE DIVISION as a group representation for DAY, MONTH, and YEAR.

The third RENAMES clause is used to regroup data items separated during the redefinition process. In the receipt record, the PRICE-PER-UNIT, NAME, ADDRESS, CITY, STATE, ZIP-CODE, and ID-CODE are placed in a group called SUPPLIER-INFORMATION. (Note that with the RENAMES clause, PRICE-PER-UNIT could be replaced by SUPPLIER-SPECIFIC-INFORMATION or RECEIPT-DISBURSEMENT-INFORMATION with the same result). The last-RENAMES clause presented in the illustration is used to regroup items that would normally be associated with a disbursement. Thus, NAME, ADDRESS, CITY (all of which are part of a redefinition), STATE, and ZIP-CODE are grouped together to form a group known as AGENCY-DISBURSED-TO. (Note that PRICE-PER-UNIT could be replaced with either DISBURSE-SPECIFIC-INFORMATION, NAME OF DISBURSE-SPECIFIC-INFORMATION, or either of the two identifiers mentioned with the previous renaming process with the same result.)

Figure 22.9 provides multiple records used in the context of a program. (The completed program appears in Chapter 10). The purpose of the program is to compute a summary of the information that would be produced on a customer bill by an electric utility company. The input to the program consists of four types of records. The first record is a previous history record containing the customer account number, electricity usage

Figure 22.8 An Illustration of Multiple Record Descriptions, REDEFINES Clauses, and RENAMES Clauses

```
DATA DIVISION.
FILE SECTION.
FD  INVENTORY-FILE
        LABEL RECORDS ARE OMITTED.
01  MASTER-RECORD.
    05  INVENTORY-NUMBER-IN                     PIC 9(06).
    05  ITEM-DESCRIPTION-IN                     PIC X(21).
    05  UNIT-INFORMATION-IN.
        10  ON-HAND-IN                          PIC 9(07).
        10  MIN-ORDER-LEVEL-IN                  PIC 9(04).
        10  CUMULATIVE-ANNUAL-IN.
            15  DISBURSEMENTS-IN                PIC 9(10).
            15  ACQUISITIONS-IN                 PIC 9(10).
        10  AVERAGE-PRICE-IN                    PIC 9(04)V99.
    05  LAST-SUPPLIER-IN                        PIC 9(03).
    05  DATE-OF-LAST-IN.
        10  DISBURSEMENT-DATE-IN.
            15  DAY-DISBURSE-IN                 PIC 9(02).
            15  MONTH-DISBURSE-IN               PIC 9(02).
            15  YEAR-DISBURSE-IN                PIC 9(02).
        10  ACQUIRE-DATE-IN.
            15  DAY-ACQUIRE-IN                  PIC 9(02).
            15  MONTH-ACQUIRE-IN                PIC 9(02).
            15  YEAR-ACQUIRE-IN                 PIC 9(02).
    05  CARD-TYPE-IN                            PIC 9(01).

01  RECEIPT-DISBURSEMENT-RECORD.
    05  ITEM-NUMBER-IN                          PIC 9(06).
    05  QUANTITY-RECEIVED-IN                    PIC 9(06).
    05  DATE-RECEIVED-IN.
        10  DAY-RECEIVED-IN                     PIC 9(02).
        10  MONTH-RECEIVED-IN                   PIC 9(02).
        10  YEAR-RECEIVED-IN                    PIC 9(02).
    05  RECEIPT-DISBURSEMENT-INFORMATION-IN.
        10  SUPPLIER-SPECIFIC-INFORMATION.
            15  PRICE-PER-UNIT-IN               PIC 9(04)V99.
            15  SUPPLIER-IN.
                20  SUPPLIER-NAME-IN            PIC X(20).
                20  SUPPLIER-STREET-IN          PIC X(15).
                20  SUPPLIER-CITY-IN            PIC X(09).
                20  SUPPLIER-STATE-IN           PIC X(20).
                20  SUPPLIER-ZIP-IN             PIC 9(05).
        10  DISBURSE-SPECIFIC-INFORMATION
              REDEFINES SUPPLIER-SPECIFIC-INFORMATION.
            15  AGENCY-DISBURSED-TO-IN.
                20  AGENCY-NAME-IN              PIC X(20).
                20  AGENCY-STREET-IN            PIC X(20).
                20  AGENCY-CITY-IN              PIC X(10).
                20  AGENCY-STATE-IN             PIC X(02).
                20  AGENCY-ZIP-IN               PIC 9(05).
    05  SUPPLIER-ID-CODE-IN                     PIC 9(04).
    05  CARD-TYPE-IN                            PIC 9(01).
    66  QUANTITY-DISBURSED-IN           RENAMES QUANTITY-RECEIVED-IN.
    66  DATE-DISBURSED-IN               RENAMES DATE-RECEIVED-IN.
    66  SUPPLIER-INFORMATION-IN         RENAMES PRICE-PER-UNIT-IN
                                           THRU SUPPLIER-ID-CODE-IN.
    66  AGENCY-DISBURSED-TO-IN          RENAMES PRICE-PER-UNIT-IN
                                           THRU SUPPLIER-ZIP-IN.
```

Figure 22.9 A Program Illustration (Record Layouts)

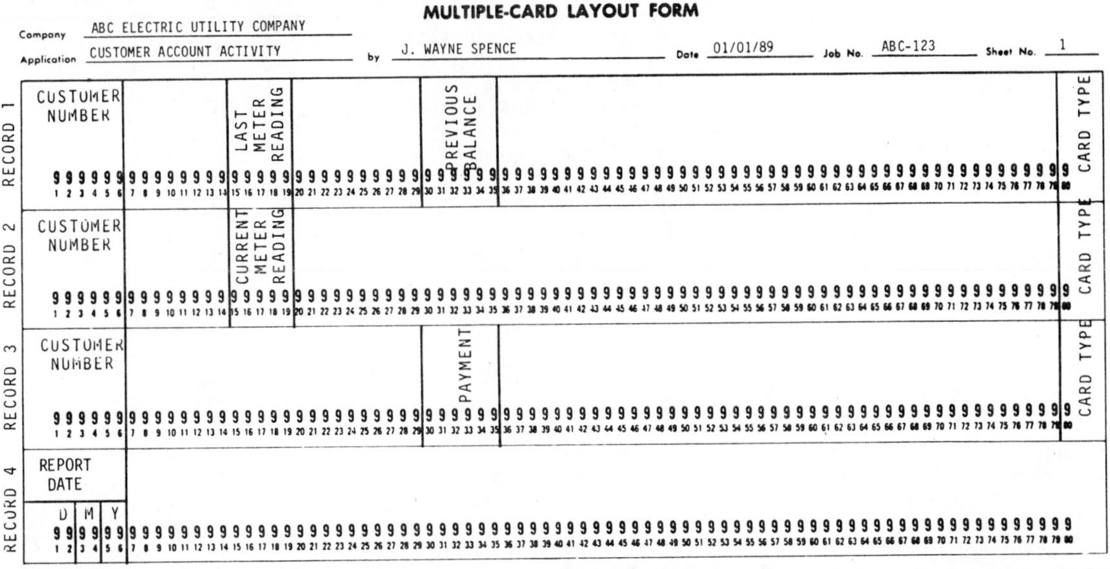

MULTIPLE-CARD LAYOUT FORM

Company: ABC ELECTRIC UTILITY COMPANY
Application: CUSTOMER ACCOUNT ACTIVITY
by: J. WAYNE SPENCE
Date: 01/01/89
Job No.: ABC-123
Sheet No.: 1

RECORD 1: CUSTOMER NUMBER (columns 1–6); LAST METER READING (columns 15–19); PREVIOUS BALANCE (columns 30–35); CARD TYPE (column 80)
RECORD 2: CUSTOMER NUMBER (columns 1–6); CURRENT METER READING (columns 15–19); CARD TYPE (column 80)
RECORD 3: CUSTOMER NUMBER (columns 1–6); PAYMENT (columns 30–35); CARD TYPE (column 80)
RECORD 4: REPORT DATE — D (columns 1–2), M (columns 3–4), Y (columns 5–6)

meter reading from the past month, and any customer account balance carried forward from the previous month's bill. The second record is an account payment record. It contains the customer's account number and an amount of payment. The third record format is the electricity usage during the current month. Each of the records contains a code number in column 80 to allow the programmer to distinguish between the records. (Note that redefinitions are used in this program. However, these redefinitions could be replaced by RENAMES clauses since all meter readings and amounts appear in the same input record columns.) The last record to be used by this program is a record containing the current date. (Note that some compilers have special registers that allow the transmission of the current date to the programmer's work area. For example, a programmer using an IBM computer may reference the special register CURRENT-DATE to receive the data entered into the computer at the beginning of the day's operation.)

Figure 22.10 provides three separate examples of how the records presented in Figure 22.9 might be incorporated into such a program. Example 1 demonstrates the use of multiple record descriptions. Example 2 uses a single record description into which redefinitions have been introduced. Example 3 uses a single record description, redefinitions, and renaming of data items.

Figure 22.11 illustrates the use of redefinitions to "load" a table with initial values. The code shown in Example 1 was originally presented in Chapter 14. In that problem, it was necessary to MOVE CODE-STATE-LIST TO STATE-CODE-TABLE in the PROCEDURE DIVISION. If the code in Example 1 were used as a replacement (with STATE-CODE-TABLE REDEFINES CODE-STATE-LIST included), the MOVE statement could be eliminated. In the second example, the program code comes from a problem (CHECK-WRITER) in Chapter 13. Again, a redefinition is used to initialize DIGIT-TABLE so that it contains the various words necessary to perform the digit-to-text conversion.

Figure 22.10 Program Illustration of Multiple Record Descriptions, REDEFINES Clauses, and RENAMES Clauses

```
Example 1:  Multiple Record Descriptions

       FD  INFORMATION-FILE
               LABEL RECORDS ARE OMITTED.
       01  HISTORY-RECORD.
           05  CUSTOMER-NUMBER-IN                    PIC 9(06).
           05  FILLER                                PIC X(08).
           05  LAST-METER-READING-IN                 PIC 9(05).
           05  FILLER                                PIC X(10).
           05  PREVIOUS-BALANCE-IN                   PIC 9(04)V99.
           05  FILLER                                PIC X(44).
           05  CARD-TYPE-IN                          PIC 9(01).
               88  HISTORY                                     VALUE 1.

       01  PAYMENT-RECORD.
           05  FILLER                                PIC X(29).
           05  PAYMENT-IN                            PIC 9(04)V99.
           05  FILLER                                PIC X(44).
           05  CARD-TYPE-IN                          PIC 9(01).
               88  ACCOUNT-PAYMENT                             VALUE 2.

       01  METER-READING-RECORD.
           05  FILLER                                PIC X(14).
           05  CURRENT-METER-READING-IN              PIC 9(05).
           05  FILLER                                PIC X(60).
           05  CARD-TYPE-IN                          PIC 9(01).
               88  CURRENT-INFORMATION                         VALUE 3.

       01  DATE-RECORD.
           05  REPORT-DAY-IN                         PIC 9(02).
           05  REPORT-MONTH-IN                       PIC 9(02).
           05  REPORT-YEAR-IN                        PIC 9(02).
           05  FILLER                                PIC X(74).

Example 2:  REDEFINES Clause

       FD  INFORMATION-FILE
               LABEL RECORDS ARE OMITTED.
       01  LAYOUT-RECORDS.
           05  CUSTOMER-NUMBER-IN                    PIC 9(06).
           05  DATE-RECORD-IN              REDEFINES CUSTOMER-NUMBER-IN.
               10  REPORT-DAY-IN                     PIC 9(02).
               10  REPORT-MONTH-IN                   PIC 9(02).
               10  REPORT-YEAR-IN                    PIC 9(02).
           05  FILLER                                PIC X(08).
           05  HISTORY-INFORMATION-IN.
               10  LAST-METER-READING-IN             PIC 9(05).
               10  FILLER                            PIC X(10).
               10  PREVIOUS-BALANCE-IN               PIC 9(04)V99.
           05  PAYMENT-INFORMATION-IN    REDEFINES HISTORY-INFORMATION-IN.
               10  FILLER                            PIC X(15).
               10  PAYMENT-IN                        PIC 9(04)V99.
           05  CURRENT-INFORMATION-IN    REDEFINES HISTORY-INFORMATION-IN.
               10  CURRENT-METER-READING-IN          PIC 9(05).
               10  FILLER                            PIC X(15).
           05  FILLER                                PIC X(44).
           05  CARD-TYPE-IN.
               88  HISTORY                                     VALUE 1.
               88  ACCOUNT-PAYMENT                             VALUE 2.
               88  CURRENT-INFORMATION                         VALUE 3.
```

Figure 22.10 *Continued* Program Illustration of Multiple Record Descriptions, REDEFINES Clauses, and RENAMES Clauses

```
Example 3:  RENAMES Clauses

        FD  INFORMATION-FILE
                LABEL RECORDS ARE OMITTED.
        01  LAYOUT-RECORDS.
            05  CUSTOMER-NUMBER-IN                PIC 9(06).
            05  DATE-RECORD-IN          REDEFINES CUSTOMER-NUMBER-IN.
                10  REPORT-DAY-IN                 PIC 9(02).
                10  REPORT-MONTH-IN               PIC 9(02).
                10  REPORT-YEAR-IN                PIC 9(02).
            05  FILLER                            PIC X(08).
            05  LAST-METER-READING-IN             PIC 9(05).
            05  FILLER                            PIC X(10).
            05  PREVIOUS-BALANCE-IN               PIC 9(04)V99.
            05  FILLER                            PIC X(44).
            05  CARD-TYPE-IN                      PIC 9(01).
                88  HISTORY                                 VALUE 1.
                88  ACCOUNT-PAYMENT                         VALUE 2.
                88  CURRENT-INFORMATION                     VALUE 3.
            66  CURRENT-METER-READING-IN    RENAMES LAST-METER-READING-IN.
            66  PAYMENT-IN                  RENAMES PREVIOUS-BALANCE-IN.
```

Figure 22.11 Table Initialization through Redefinition

```
Example 1:

        01  CODE-STATE-LIST.
            05  FILLER              PIC X(14) VALUE '01Alabama'.
            05  FILLER              PIC X(14) VALUE '04Arkansas'.
            05  FILLER              PIC X(14) VALUE '09Florida'.
            05  FILLER              PIC X(14) VALUE '10Georgia'.
            05  FILLER              PIC X(14) VALUE '15Iowa'.
            05  FILLER              PIC X(14) VALUE '25Missouri'.
            05  FILLER              PIC X(14) VALUE '30New Jersey'.
            05  FILLER              PIC X(14) VALUE '34North Carolina'.
            05  FILLER              PIC X(14) VALUE '35Ohio'.
            05  FILLER              PIC X(14) VALUE '36Oklahoma'.
            05  FILLER              PIC X(14) VALUE '42Tennessee'.
            05  FILLER              PIC X(14) VALUE '43Texas'.
            05  FILLER              PIC X(14) VALUE '46West Virginia'.
            05  FILLER              PIC X(14) VALUE '49Wisconsin'.
            05  FILLER              PIC X(14) VALUE '50Wyoming'.

        01  STATE-CODE-TABLE        REDEFINES CODE-STATE-LIST.
            05  STATE-CODE-ENTRY-T  OCCURS 15 TIMES.
                ASCENDING KEY IS STATE-CODE-T
                INDEXED BY STATE.
                15  STATE-CODE-T    PIC 9(02).
                15  STATE-NAME-T    PIC X(12).
```

Figure 22.11 *Continued* Table Initialization through Redefinition

```
Example 2:

       01  LIST-OF-UNITS.
           05  FILLER                       PIC X(09) VALUE 'One'.
           05  FILLER                       PIC X(09) VALUE 'Two'.
           05  FILLER                       PIC X(09) VALUE 'Three'.
           05  FILLER                       PIC X(09) VALUE 'Four'.
           05  FILLER                       PIC X(09) VALUE 'Five'.
           05  FILLER                       PIC X(09) VALUE 'Six'.
           05  FILLER                       PIC X(09) VALUE 'Seven'.
           05  FILLER                       PIC X(09) VALUE 'Eight'.
           05  FILLER                       PIC X(09) VALUE 'Nine'.
           05  FILLER                       PIC X(09) VALUE 'Ten'.
           05  FILLER                       PIC X(09) VALUE 'Eleven'.
           05  FILLER                       PIC X(09) VALUE 'Twelve'.
           05  FILLER                       PIC X(09) VALUE 'Thirteen'.
           05  FILLER                       PIC X(09) VALUE 'Fourteen'.
           05  FILLER                       PIC X(09) VALUE 'Fifteen'.
           05  FILLER                       PIC X(09) VALUE 'Sixteen'.
           05  FILLER                       PIC X(09) VALUE 'Seventeen'.
           05  FILLER                       PIC X(09) VALUE 'Eighteen'.
           05  FILLER                       PIC X(09) VALUE 'Nineteen'.
           05  FILLER                       PIC X(09) VALUE 'Twenty'.
           05  FILLER                       PIC X(09) VALUE 'Thirty'.
           05  FILLER                       PIC X(09) VALUE 'Forty'.
           05  FILLER                       PIC X(09) VALUE 'Fifty'.
           05  FILLER                       PIC X(09) VALUE 'Sixty'.
           05  FILLER                       PIC X(09) VALUE 'Seventy'.
           05  FILLER                       PIC X(09) VALUE 'Eighty'.
           05  FILLER                       PIC X(09) VALUE 'Ninety'.
           05  FILLER                       PIC X(09) VALUE 'Hundred'.
           05  FILLER                       PIC X(09) VALUE 'Thousand'.

       01  DIGIT-TABLE                      REDEFINES LIST-OF-UNITS.
           05  DIGIT-T                      OCCURS 29 TIMES
                                            PIC X(09).
```

Summary

This chapter has compared three interrelated facets of the DATA DIVISION—multiple record descriptions in the FILE SECTION, the REDEFINES clause, and the RENAMES clause. Each of these alternatives in the DATA DIVISION has an impact on the ease of coding the PROCEDURE DIVISION and the amount of internal storage used. In the FILE SECTION, multiple record descriptions can be provided in one FD. When several types of input records are anticipated from a single file, the programmer has only to write the record descriptions for each anticipated record type. Data do not have to match the field types recorded in the input-record description when a record is read. However, the programmer is responsible for ensuring the data match the field description when the data-name is referenced.

The REDEFINES clause is *not* limited only to the FILE SECTION. It may also be used in the WORKING-STORAGE SECTION. Furthermore, redefinitions may be used at the record, group, or elementary-item level. Although the length of a redefinition must generally be the same as the original data description, field characteristics may be changed.

Finally, the RENAMES clause may appear in both the FILE and WORKING-STORAGE SECTIONs. The purpose of the RENAMES clause is to provide alternate names for identifiers. In addition, the clause may be used to form alternate groupings of data items.

Notes on Programming Style

Most commercial programming standards reduce the use (if not totally eliminate) of the RENAMES clause. The rationale is that the initial data item should have been named properly or that data should be explicitly moved to the data item. By avoiding the use of the RENAMES clause, the programmer should never get confused about how a particular data item received its value.

Current opinions regarding the use of the REDEFINES clause range from "its the best thing to come along since sliced bread" to "don't let me catch you using that again." There are several positive arguments for the use of the REDEFINES clause, including the concise presentation of a wide variety of data representations for a single area of internal storage. Most of these representations, however, could be separately coded and the data moved into them. Check the coding standards in your shop before using the REDEFINES clause.

Questions

Below, fill in the blank(s) with the appropriate word, words, or phrases.

1. The advantages of having two or more data-names address the same internal storage locations are ____ and ____ .

2. If four 80-byte record descriptions are provided under one FD in the FILE SECTION, the minimum amount of internal storage used would be ____ bytes.

3. The REDEFINES clause may be used at the ____ or ____ level in the FILE SECTION.

4. The REDEFINES clause may be used at the ____ , ____ , or ____ level in the WORKING-STORAGE SECTION.

5. Both the original description of data and its redefinition must be coded at the ____ level number.

6. If a programmer wishes to redefine an elementary-item, the redefinition must ____ .

7. The redefinition of a group item is assumed to be terminated when ____ .

8. If a data area of ten bytes is to be redefined, the redefinition should be ____ (number) bytes in length.

9. When multiple redefinition of the same area is required, each subsequent redefinition should reference (as data-name-2) ____ .

10. Level-66 is always associated with the ____ clause.

11. Level-66 items used in conjunction with a particular record must be located ____ the record.

12. The purpose of the RENAMES clause is to ____ or ____ .

13. When the THRU option of the RENAMES clause is used, the newly created data item is assumed to represent a ____ level item.

Answer the following questions by circling either "T" for True or "F" for False.

T F **14.** It is possible for two data-names to address the same positions in the computer's internal storage.

T F **15.** Only one record description is permitted within one FD in the FILE SECTION.

T F **16.** It is possible to have an internal storage address with two different characteristics (e.g., accessed as a number in one case and as an alphanumeric field in the second).

T F **17.** Regardless of the number of records associated with a single FD, no more space is consumed than for a single record description.

T F **18.** Each record description in the WORKING-STORAGE SECTION, unless redefined utilizes additional storage.

T F **19.** The REDEFINES clause may be used in both the FILE SECTION and WORKING-STORAGE SECTION.

T F **20.** Records can be REDEFINED in the FILE SECTION.

T F **21.** Records can be REDEFINED in the WORKING-STORAGE SECTION.

T F **22.** A REDEFINES clause can be used to place two table descriptions in the same location in internal storage.

T F **23.** A redefinition may be longer (in bytes) than the original description of the data.

T F **24.** A redefinition can always be redefined by additional code.

T F **25.** A redefinition can include a redefinition.

T F **26.** A redefinition can physically precede the description of the data to be redefined in the program code.

T F **27.** It is possible to alter an elementary-item's PICTURE description with a REDEFINES clause.

T F **28.** It is possible to alter an elementary-item's PICTURE description with a RENAMES clause.

T F **29.** An elementary-item may be subordinate to a level-66.

T F **30.** A level-66 item may rename an elementary-item.

T F **31.** A level-66 item may rename a group item.

T F **32.** The new name created through a RENAMES clause may be qualified.

T F **33.** It is possible to create a totally new grouping of data (a grouping not indicated in the prior record description) with the RENAMES clause.

CHAPTER

23

Noncharacter-oriented Data Storage

Up to this point, the discussion of data storage has revolved around a type of data representation called DISPLAY. When PICTURE clauses were presented in the DATA DIVISION (Chapter 6), each elementary-item was assumed to have a USAGE IS DISPLAY clause attached. The DISPLAY usage is a representation of data in a ''character'' form.Each 9, A, or X in a PICTURE clause requires one character position (or byte) of computer storage. DISPLAY usage is required when the input medium is punched cards and the output medium is printed paper. However, within the computer's storage (or on nonunit record media) it is possible to store numeric data in a more compact form than one digit per byte.

A *byte* is generally the smallest unit of the computer's storage that can be directly addressed as a data-storage position in COBOL. A byte is normally six or eight bits. A *bit* is the smallest unit of the computer's storage. (''Bit'' is an acronym for *binary digit.* A *binary digit* is a digit value of either 0 or 1 in the binary numbering system.) The internal storage capacity of most computers is specified by the number of bytes or ''words'' that the computer can store at one time. The size of each *word* of storage is often stated in terms of the number of bits or bytes it contains. For example, one type of computer may be characterized as a 60-bit word machine (e.g., CDC); others may be classified as a 32-bit word or 4-byte word machine (e.g., IBM), and still another machine may be based on a 16-bit word (e.g., PDP-11). For the sake of simplicity the examples in this chapter are based on a 32-bit word computer (using four 8-bit bytes). The coding scheme used by an IBM computer—EBCDIC—will be used when necessary. (Remember, the other coding scheme is ASCII.) If you want more information about the internal architecture of your computer, consult with the computer personnel at your installation.

As previously indicated, there are alternative ways in which numeric data may be described. (Numeric data, in this context, means a nonedited numeric field associated with an elementary data item.) The types of internal representation provided by all computers (with the use of a COBOL compiler) are DISPLAY (also called *external decimal* or *character* data) and COMPUTATIONAL (also called *binary* data). In addition, many computers offer data representations in COMPUTATIONAL-1 (known as ''short''

Figure 23.1 Format of the USAGE Clause

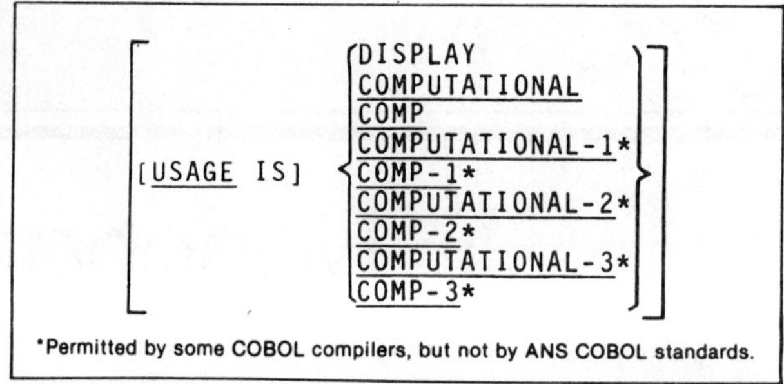

floating-point data), COMPUTATIONAL-2 (''long'' floating-point data), and COMPUTATIONAL-3 (*packed-decimal*). Most of the internal data representations used in COBOL are DISPLAY, COMPUTATIONAL or COMPUTATIONAL-3.

The format of the USAGE clause is provided in Figure 23.1. The clause is optional; when the USAGE clause is omitted, USAGE IS DISPLAY is assumed. (Any other USAGE for a nonnumeric or edited-numeric field will result in an error.)

DISPLAY Data Items

When an elementary data item is coded with a USAGE IS DISPLAY clause or without a USAGE clause, the data described by the item is recorded in external decimal (or character form). Figure 23.2 presents a number of examples of data storage where the USAGE IS DISPLAY clause accompanies a PICTURE clause. For every 9 that appears in a numeric PICTURE clause, one byte of internal storage is allocated. For example, the first illustration of Figure 23.2 assumes that the elementary data item is described with a PICTURE 9(02) USAGE IS DISPLAY entry. The stored result (internal representation) requires two bytes of internal storage. Each byte of the field is composed of high-order and low-order half-bytes (four-bits each in the example). For an unsigned

Figure 23.2 Illustrations of Numeric Data Stored with a DISPLAY Usage

Data Value Placed in the Field	Picture Clause Described with a Usage is Display	Internal Representation*
27	9(02)	F:2 | F:7
−27	9(02)	F:2 | F:7
−27	S9(02)	F:2 | D:7
12473	S9(05)	F:1 | F:2 | F:4 | F:7 | F:3
−6418	S9(05)	F:0 | F:6 | F:4 | F:1 | D:8
+1738	S9(04)	F:1 | F:7 | F:3 | C:8

*Internal representation based on a machine using a 32-bit word, 8-bit byte and an EBCDIC coding scheme. Each box represents one byte.

field, each of the high-order half-bytes contains the hexadecimal number F. The low-order half-bytes contain the digit value placed in the field. Thus, the value 27, when placed in a data field described by PICTURE 9(02) USAGE IS DISPLAY entry, is recorded internally as F2F7.

The other illustrations in Figure 23.2 follow a similar pattern except some of the data values and PICTURE clauses result in signed data being stored. The sign for a DISPLAY data item is recorded in the high-order half-byte of the last full byte of the field. The sign position contains the hexadecimal value F if the number is unsigned (as in the first example), the value C if the number is positive, and D if the number is negative. However, remember that both the data and the PICTURE clause must be combined for a sign to be stored. If the data contains a sign, but the PICTURE clause does not permit a sign, the resulting data value will be unsigned. In addition, if the PICTURE clause permits a sign, but the data values are unsigned the store value is assumed to be positive.

Binary Data Items

The second form of the USAGE clause is for a COMPUTATIONAL data item. The reserved word COMPUTATIONAL (or its abbreviation COMP) indicates that a numeric data item is to be stored in a binary form. Storing data in binary form has two basic advantages. First, data stored in binary can be manipulated faster by a computer than data stored in DISPLAY form. DISPLAY data must be translated into its binary equivalent before an arithmetic manipulation may be made, and once the manipulation is complete, data being stored in a DISPLAY field must be converted from binary back to ''character'' form. Second, data stored in binary form may require less internal storage than the same data stored in a DISPLAY form.

Although COMPUTATIONAL usage is permitted under ANS COBOL, the COMPUTATIONAL data item is described differently by the programmer depending on the computer. Some COBOL compilers (e.g., IBM) require that COMPUTATIONAL data items be accompanied by a PICTURE clause. With this type of compiler, a PICTURE clause of a single digit (9) to four digits (9(04)) will require a half-word (2 bytes) of internal storage. A PICTURE clause that contains five digits (9(05)) to nine digits (9(09)) uses a full word of computer storage. PICTURE clauses containing 10 digits (9(10)) to 18 digits (9(18)) require two words of internal storage. A COMPUTATIONAL data item may contain an operational sign and an implied decimal point. (Any unsigned COMPUTATIONAL field is assumed to contain only positive values.) Other computers (e.g., Honeywell) do not permit PICTURE clauses in conjunction with a COMPUTATIONAL data item. In this situation, the COBOL compiler assumes the data field to be one full word in size; it can contain up to a nine-digit, signed, integer number.

Figure 23.3 illustrates the internal representation of data stored in a COMPUTATIONAL field. Each of the elementary-items in this example must be accompanied by a USAGE IS COMPUTATIONAL or a USAGE is COMP clause. The sign in a COMPUTATIONAL data item is stored in the high-order (leftmost) *bit* in the field. For a positive number the sign bit is zero. For a negative number the sign bit is one. Also notice that negative numbers are stored in *''two's complement'' form* so that the first bit of the field is the binary digit 1.

For those compilers that *do not* permit a PICTURE clause to be associated with a COMPUTATIONAL data item, the amount of internal storage used for a field is a full word. For a computer using a 32-bit word, the amount of storage would be the same

Figure 23.3 Illustrations of Numeric Data Stored with a COMPUTATIONAL Usage

Data Value Placed in the Field	Picture Clause Described with a Usage is Computational	Internal Representation*
27	9(02) COMPUTATIONAL	0000:0000 | 0001:1011
−27	S9(04) COMP	1111:1111 | 1110:0101
+5729	S9(04) COMP	0001:0110 | 0110:0001
−7982	S9(04) COMPUTATIONAL	1110:0000 | 1101:0001
462985	S9(09) COMPUTATIONAL	0000:0000 | 0000:0111 | 0001:0000 | 1000:1001

*Internal representation based on a computer using a 32-bit word, 8-bit byte, and a COBOL compiler permitting the use of a PICTURE clause with a COMPUTATIONAL data item. Each box represents one byte.

as for the last example in Figure 23.3. Thus, if any of the first four data values presented in Figure 23.3 were to be stored in a computer that did not permit a PICTURE clause, the COMPUTATIONAL field would be twice as large as the internal representation in the examples. If any of the examples had contained an implied decimal point, there would be no equivalent storage in a COMPUTATIONAL field.

Packed-Decimal Data Items

Another type of data storage often available with COBOL compilers is COMPUTATIONAL-3. A COMPUTATIONAL-3 data item is often referred to as a *packed-decimal* data item. In other words, the data are internally stored in a form similar to DISPLAY. However, in DISPLAY almost half the data storage area is wasted. In a DISPLAY field, most of the high-order half-bytes (sometimes called *zone-bits*) are filled with a character code for a number (a hexadecimal F). Although these character codes are useful in the recording of alphabetic and special characters, they serve no useful purpose in a numeric field. Thus, in a COMPUTATIONAL-3 data field each of the unnecessary character codes (zone codes) is eliminated—leaving only the digits and a code for the sign of the data.

Figure 23.4 illustrates data stored in a COMPUTATIONAL-3 field. Notice from the examples that each field is recorded in terms of full bytes (i.e., half-byte addressing in COBOL is not permitted). One character (zone) code is retained (the zone code for the

Figure 23.4 Illustrations of Numeric Data Stored with a COMPUTATIONAL-3 Usage

Data Value Placed in the Field	Picture Clause Described with a Usage is Computational-3	Internal Representation*
27	9(02) COMPUTATIONAL-3	0:2 | 7:F
−684	S9(03) COMPUTATIONAL-3	6:8 | 4:D
+6295	S9(04) COMP-3	0:6 | 2:9 | 5:C
−93874	9(05) COMP-3	9:3 | 8:7 | 4:F

*Internal representation based on a computer using a 32-bit word, 8-bit byte, and an EBCDIC coding scheme. Each box represents one byte.

sign of the number); however, this code is placed in the low-order half-byte of each field. (As with DISPLAY data fields, the hexadecimal digit F represents an unsigned data value, C represents a positive value, and D indicates a negative value.) Comparing the amount of internal storage required for a packed-decimal field to what is required when the data are in DISPLAY form, we find about one-half the internal storage is used. (The amount of internal storage used would be exactly half the number of digits in the PICTURE clause if it were not necessary to store the sign of the data value.)

Floating-Point Data Items

The final two types of data storage are called COMPUTATIONAL-1 (COMP-1) and COMPUTATIONAL-2 (COMP-2). These two internal representations of data are not part of ANS COBOL and are available with a limited number of compilers. Both COMPUTATIONAL-1 and COMPUTATIONAL-2 are often referred to as internal floating-point data storage. The term *floating-point* is frequently used in conjunction with data stored within the computer's storage in exponential form. Neither a COMPUTATIONAL-1 nor a COMPUTATIONAL-2 data description is written with a PICTURE clause. When USAGE IS COMPUTATIONAL-1 is declared for an elementary-item, one full word of computer storage is allocated to the field. When USAGE IS COMPUTATIONAL-2 is specified, two full words of internal storage are used. For this reason, and because of the resulting capability to store more significant digits, COMPUTATIONAL-1 is referred to as *short* floating-point; COMPUTATIONAL-2 is called *long* floating-point. The format of a data item stored in COMPUTATIONAL-1 or COMPUTATIONAL-2 is presented in Figure 23.5.

With both COMPUTATIONAL-1 and COMPUTATIONAL-2 the internal formats of the data represented are basically the same. Bit 0 of either a 32-bit word or a 64-bit double word contains the sign of the data value. The next 7 bits (bits 1 through 7) are used to store the *exponent* of the data value (i.e., the exponent represents the power of 10 to be multiplied by the *mantissa* or fraction). The function of the exponent is to move the location of the assumed decimal point in the data value either to the left or to the right a specified number of positions, depending on the positive or negative value stored in bits 1 through 7. The mantissa or fraction (bits 8 through 31 for COMPUTATIONAL-1 and bits 8 through 63 for COMPUTATIONAL-2) is a decimal fraction containing the significant digits of the data value itself. (COMPUTATIONAL-1 provides sufficient space for a value that can be represented by approximately 7 significant decimal digits; COMPUTATIONAL-2 permits a value equivalent to approximately 16 significant digits.) These field types provide the capability to store a number of extremely large or

Figure 23.5 Internal Formats of COMPUTATIONAL-1 and COMPUTATIONAL-2 Data Items

Format of a COMPUTATIONAL-1 Data Item

S	EXPONENT	MANTISSA (FRACTION)
0	1 7	8 31

Format of a COMPUTATIONAL-2 Data Item

S	EXPONENT	MANTISSA (FRACTION) //
0	1 7	8 63

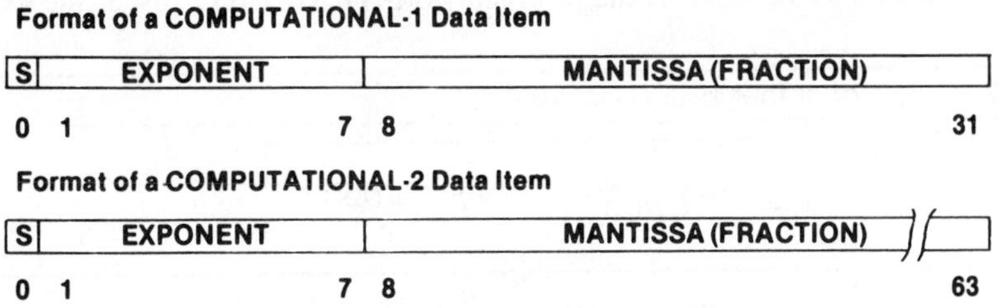

extremely small magnitude. Values that can be stored in COMPUTATIONAL-1 and COMPUTATIONAL-2 fields range from a minimum magnitude of $\pm 5.4 \times 10^{-79}$ to a maximum magnitude of $\pm 7.2 \times 10^{75}$.

Other Clauses Related to the Descriptions of Data

Figure 23.6 Format of the BLANK WHEN ZERO Clause

```
[BLANK WHEN ZERO]
```

Four other clauses are permitted in the DATA DIVISION of an ANS COBOL program. Each of these clauses permits a specialized treatment of the data itself in the location of that data within the computer's storage. These clauses are BLANK WHEN ZERO, JUSTIFIED, SIGN, and SYNCHRONIZED.

The BLANK WHEN ZERO clause (Figure 23.6) may be used in conjunction with a numeric (DISPLAY) or a numeric-edited field. When the clause accompanies a numeric field, the field is treated as a numeric-edited field. The purpose of the BLANK WHEN ZERO clause is to cause the entire numeric field to be replaced with spaces when the value placed in the field is zero. This action is taken regardless of the PICTURE characters used to describe the numeric field. The clause may not be used in conjunction with a level-66 or 88 data items.

The JUSTIFIED clause (Figure 23.7) is used to alter the normal alignment of data placed in an alphabetic or alphanumeric field. Normally, when data are placed in an alphabetic or alphanumeric field, the data are left-justified (i.e., the data begins at the leftmost position within the field and are either truncated or blank-filled to the right as necessary). The JUSTIFIED (JUST) clause reverses the normal alignment so that the data are right-justified. The clause causes the last character of the data to be placed in the right-most position of the field. If the field is larger than the data, blanks will be inserted to the left until the field is filled. If the field is smaller than the length of the data being supplied, characters are truncated from the left until the data exactly fill the field. The JUSTIFIED clause may be specified only for an elementary data item, and it may not be used in conjunction with a level-66 or 88 data item.

The SIGN clause, presented in Figure 23.8, is used to modify the location of the operational sign of a numeric field. When the clause is used, it may only be used in conjunction with a numeric (DISPLAY) data item (although if coded at the group level, it pertains to all subordinate numeric fields). As noted in Figure 23.2, when numeric data are placed in a DISPLAY data item, the sign of the number is placed in the high-order half-byte of the *last* byte of the field—the normal location of the operational sign. The location of the sign would not be changed if the clause SIGN IS TRAILING was added to the description of the data item. However, if the clause SIGN IS LEADING was specified, the sign of the number would be in the high-order half-byte of the *first* byte of the field. In either case, the operational sign character (S) does not cause any additional space to be added to the field.

When the phrase SEPARATE CHARACTER is added to the SIGN clause, an additional byte is added to the field. If the reserved word TRAILING is used, the extra byte

Figure 23.7 Format of the JUSTIFIED Clause

```
[ {JUSTIFIED}  RIGHT]
  {JUST     }
```

Figure 23.8 Format of the SIGN Clause

```
[[SIGN IS] {LEADING }  [SEPARATE CHARACTER]]
           {TRAILING}
```

is added to the end of the field and the sign is placed in this byte. If LEADING is specified, the extra byte is added before the first byte that would normally be in the field, and the sign is placed in this byte. Thus, the sign is placed in a SEPARATE CHARACTER position. When the SEPARATE CHARACTER phrase is employed, the data *must* contain an operational sign. The character "+" should be used for a positive operational sign, and the character "−" should be used for a negative operational sign. Since the compiler expects one of these two characters to be present, the absence of one of them will cause a fatal error, and the program will be terminated. When the data item is used in the PROCEDURE DIVISION, any conversion of the sign necessary for manipulation, computation, or comparison automatically takes place prior to the operation.

The format of the SYNCHRONIZED clause is presented in Figure 23.9. The clause causes the COBOL compiler to generate extra instructions for a data alignment appropriate to the particular type of data item being described. Data alignment internally shifts a data field so that it is located on the proper boundaries within internal storage. This improves overall operating efficiency when the data are being used for arithmetic manipulation. By aligning fields properly within internal storage, the programmer reduces the amount of time required to locate data, process them, and if necessary, return them to the field. This shifting of data items within internal storage often uses additional storage.

The key reserved word in the clause is SYNCHRONIZED, or its abbreviation SYNC. The clause may appear only in conjunction with an elementary data item. Following the reserved word SYNCHRONIZED, the programmer may specify the reserved words LEFT or RIGHT; however, under most circumstances LEFT and RIGHT are treated as comments. As was the case with noncharacter data storage presented earlier in this chapter, the function or the SYNCHRONIZED clause varies with particular COBOL compilers. For example, Honeywell COBOL compilers automatically "synchronize" COMPUTATIONAL (as well as COMPUTATIIONAL-1, COMPUTATIONAL-2, and COMPUTATIONAL-3) data items. Then,the SYNCHRONIZED clause is treated as a comment. Often compilers do not automatically synchronize or align the data on the natural internal boundaries of internal storage. For an IBM COBOL program (as well as others), it may be necessary to use the SYNCHRONIZED clause to indicate to the COBOL compiler that proper data alignment is desired.

Figure 23.10 illustrates the action taken by a COBOL compiler to align data on an appropriate internal boundary. In this illustration, the same record is coded without SYNCHRONIZED clauses and with SYNCHRONIZED clauses. In the first record de-

Figure 23.9 Format of the SYNCHRONIZED Clause

```
[ {SYNCHRONIZED}  [LEFT ] ]
  {SYNC        }  [RIGHT]
```

scription, the data are placed in one byte after another without regard for the natural internal boundaries used by the computer. The only natural boundary sought by the compiler in placing the record into internal storage is a double-word boundary. In this example (assumed to be for an IBM computer), each record is aligned on a double-word boundary, and the bytes described by the record are allocated beginning with this boundary.

In the second record description, a boundary alignment is sought for each of the elementary data items coded with a SYNCHRONIZED clause. For data described (either implicitly or explicitly) as DISPLAY, the SYNCHRONIZED clause is ignored. For COMPUTATIONAL data items the alignment depends on the size of the field. If a COMPUTATIONAL data item contains from 1 to 4 digits, it requires one-half word (2 bytes) of computer storage. These data are aligned on a half-word internal boundary. For COMPUTATIONAL data items of 5 to 18 digits, the alignment is on a full-word boundary (not necessarily a double word). COMPUTATIONAL-1 data items are placed on a full-word boundary, and COMPUTATIONAL-2 data items are aligned on a double-word boundary. If a data field does not fall on the proper internal boundary by default, extra bytes (often called *"slack bytes"*) are added to the field so that the data are placed on the appropriate boundary. Notice from the second record description and its internal

Figure 23.10 Illustrations of Internal Mappings of Record Descriptions

```
01  DATA-RECORD-1.
    05  FIELD-1  PIC  X(06).
    05  FIELD-2  PIC  9(05)V99 COMP.
    05  FIELD-3  PIC  9(01).
    05  FIELD-4  PIC S9(02)V99 COMP.
    05  FIELD-5  PIC  X(10).
    05  FIELD-6  PIC S9(12)V99 COMP.
    05  FIELD-7  PIC  X(01).
    05  FIELD-8  PIC S9(06)V99 COMP.
    05  FIELD-9  PIC  X(14).
    05  FIELD-10 PIC S9(07)     COMP.
    05  FIELD-11 PIC  9(04)     COMP.
```

```
01  DATA-RECORD-2.
    05  FIELD-1  PIC  X(06).
    05  FIELD-2  PIC  9(05)V99 COMP SYNC.
    05  FIELD-3  PIC  9(01).
    05  FIELD-4  PIC S9(02)V99 COMP SYNC.
    05  FIELD-5  PIC  X(10).
    05  FIELD-6  PIC S9(12)V99 COMP SYNC.
    05  FIELD-7  PIC  X(01).
    05  FIELD-8  PIC S9(06)V99 COMP SYNC.
    05  FIELD-9  PIC  X(14).
    05  FIELD-10 PIC S9(07)     COMP SYNC.
    05  FIELD-11 PIC  9(04)     COMP SYNC.
```

Internal Mappings of Records*

DATA-RECORD-1

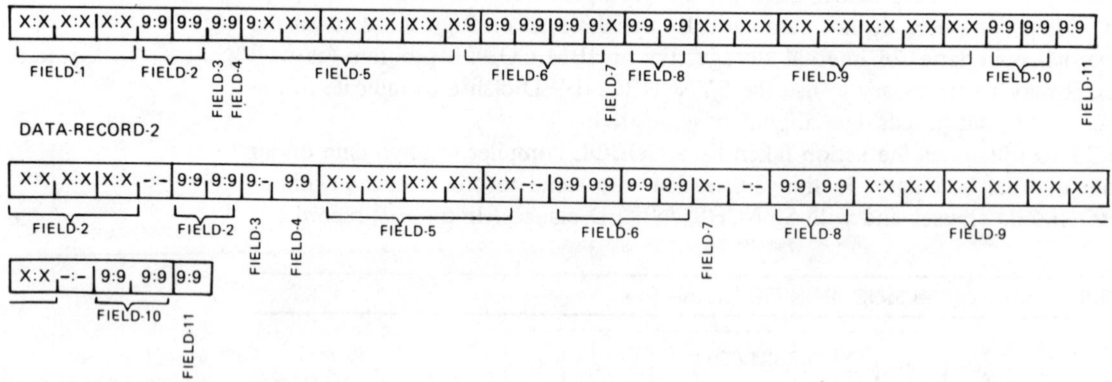

*—Indicates the location of intra-record slack bytes.

mapping that extra bytes have been inserted between some data items so that proper alignment is maintained.

SYNCHRONIZED data items also require careful handling. Since data items can be redefined (with a REDEFINES clause), the original data description may be SYNCHRONIZED without the redefinition being SYNCHRONIZED. This is only important for the redefinition because the numeric data items in the redefined area do not necessarily fall on the same natural boundaries as the original data items. Furthermore, since extra bytes may be used in the internal alignment of the original data items, the original record may be longer than the PICTURE strings of the elementary-items indicate. If the redefinition contains SYNCHRONIZED clauses and the original data description does not contain SYNCHRONIZED clauses,it is the programmer's responsibility to align the original data items so that the SYNCHRONIZED redefined items fall on the appropriate boundaries.

Noncharacter-oriented Data, Tables, and the SYNCHRONIZED Clause

Although the majority of this text has assumed data to be in character form, it is possible to describe elementary-items (or groups of items) more efficiently as binary or packed-decimal numeric fields as already noted. This is extremely important in the description of data items that are included in tables. With very little effort on the part of the programmer, mass areas of storage may be allocated through the OCCURS clause. This mass of data area may be somewhat reduced in size and processed more efficiently if the programmer carefully studies the organization of the table, the characteristics of the data items in the table, and the expected amount of use of each of the data items.

Figure 23.11 illustrates this point. The first table is described using character-oriented (DISPLAY) data fields. The second table provides the same capability to store numeric data values, but the numeric data items have all been declared to be COMPUTATIONAL (except for the alphanumeric field—FIELD-3). (Note that the COMPUTATIONAL data items are presumed to allow PICTURE clauses.) The third table is a representation of each numeric data item if coded with a COMPUTATIONAL-3 usage. Again, the table requires less space (COMPUTATIONAL-3 is *not* always shorter than COMPUTATIONAL.) The final alternative is a table coded with the type of USAGE that would result in the least amount of space being used for each data item. When the number of bytes is totaled, the fourth record description takes the most advantage of the internal storage of the computer.

Suppose that for efficiency an entire record is classified as COMPUTATIONAL. To make table processing more efficient, each of the COMPUTATIONAL items should also be SYNCHRONIZED. The record might then be described as presented in Figure 23.12. The synchronization of the COMPUTATIONAL items results in slack bytes being inserted, as indicated in the storage layout that appears below the record. Each occurrence of the data items occupies 50 bytes, although only 46 bytes of data are described. In physical layout, slack bytes (sometimes referred to as *intraoccurrence* slack bytes) have been added so that the COMPUTATIONAL data fall on the appropriate internal boundaries. In addition, 2 bytes are not used at the end of each occurrence in the table. These extra bytes (called *interoccurrence* slack bytes) are added so that each occurrence of the table requires 52 bytes, and the entire table will use 5200 bytes of internal storage.

Figure 23.11 Illustrations of Table Descriptions with Various Usages

```
a) Ø1  TABLE-RECORD.
       Ø5  TABLE-ITEM OCCURS 1ØØ TIMES.
           1Ø  FIELD-1         PIC 9(Ø1).
           1Ø  FIELD-2         PIC 9(Ø6).
           1Ø  FIELD-3         PIC X(2Ø).
           1Ø  FIELD-4         PIC 9(Ø9).
           1Ø  FIELD-5         PIC 9(Ø2).
           1Ø  FIELD-6         PIC 9(12).
           1Ø  FIELD-7         PIC 9(Ø3)V99.
           1Ø  FIELD-8         PIC 9(Ø3).

   Length per Occurrence--58 bytes
   Total Length of Table--5,800 bytes

b) Ø1  TABLE-RECORD.
       Ø5  TABLE-ITEM OCCURS 1ØØ TIMES.
           1Ø  FIELD-1         PIC 9(Ø1) COMP.
           1Ø  FIELD-2         PIC 9(Ø6) COMP.
           1Ø  FIELD-3         PIC X(2Ø).
           1Ø  FIELD-4         PIC 9(Ø9) COMP.
           1Ø  FIELD-5         PIC 9(Ø2) COMP.
           1Ø  FIELD-6         PIC 9(12) COMP.
           1Ø  FIELD-7         PIC 9(Ø3)V99 COMP.
           1Ø  FIELD-8         PIC 9(Ø3) COMP.

   Length per Occurrence--46 bytes
   Total Length of Table--4,600 bytes

c) Ø1  TABLE-RECORD.
       Ø5  TABLE-ITEM OCCURS 1ØØ TIMES.
           1Ø  FIELD-1         PIC 9(Ø1) COMP-3.
           1Ø  FIELD-2         PIC 9(Ø6) COMP-3.
           1Ø  FIELD-3         PIC X(2Ø).
           1Ø  FIELD-4         PIC 9(Ø9) COMP-3.
           1Ø  FIELD-5         PIC 9(Ø2) COMP-3.
           1Ø  FIELD-6         PIC 9(12) COMP-3.
           1Ø  FIELD-7         PIC 9(Ø3)V99 COMP-3.
           1Ø  FIELD-8         PIC 9(Ø3) COMP-3.

   Length per Occurrence--47 bytes
   Total Length of Table--4,700 bytes

d) Ø1  TABLE-RECORD.
       Ø5  TABLE-ITEM OCCURS 1ØØ TIMES.
           1Ø  FIELD-1         PIC 9(Ø1). (or COMP-3)
           1Ø  FIELD-2         PIC 9(Ø6) COMP. (or COMP-3)
           1Ø  FIELD-3         PIC X(2Ø).
           1Ø  FIELD-4         PIC 9(Ø9) COMP.
           1Ø  FIELD-5         PIC 9(Ø2) COMP. (or COMP-3)
           1Ø  FIELD-6         PIC 9(12) COMP-3.
           1Ø  FIELD-7         PIC 9(Ø3)V99 COMP-3.
           1Ø  FIELD-8         PIC 9(Ø3) COMP. (or COMP-3)

       Length per Occurrence--43 bytes
       Total Length of Table--4,300 bytes
```

Figure 23.12 An Illustration of COMPUTATIONAL and SYNCHRONIZED Table Items (Slack Bytes Added)

```
01  TABLE-RECORD.
    05  TABLE-ITEM                  OCCURS 100 TIMES.
        10  FIELD-1                 PIC 9(01)      COMP SYNC.
        10  FIELD-2                 PIC 9(06)      COMP SYNC.
        10  FIELD-3                 PIC X(20).
        10  FIELD-4                 PIC 9(09)      COMP SYNC.
        10  FIELD-5                 PIC 9(02)      COMP SYNC.
        10  FIELD-6                 PIC 9(12)      COMP SYNC.
        10  FIELD-7                 PIC 9(03)V99 COMP SYNC.
        10  FIELD-8                 PIC 9(03)      COMP SYNC.
```

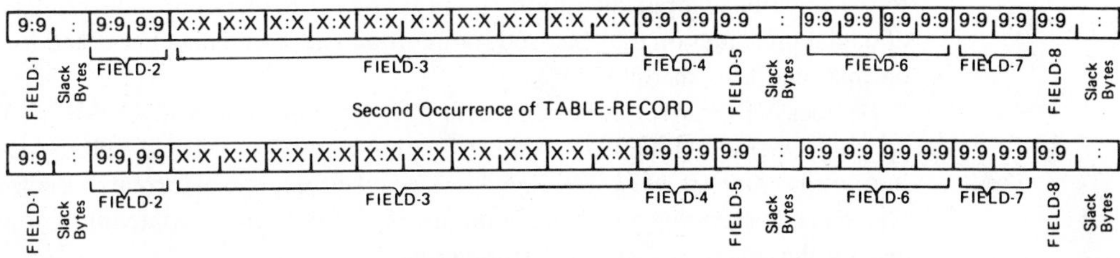

Now compare this record description to the record description in Figure 23.13. If the programmer has the latitude to arrange the table, he or she might reorganize the data items in the table to conserve internal storage while maintaining processing efficiency.

Figure 23.13 An Illustration of COMPUTATIONAL and SYNCHRONIZED Table Items (Slack Bytes Eliminated)

```
01  TABLE-RECORD.
    05  TABLE-ITEM                  OCCURS 100 TIMES.
        10  FIELD-1                 PIC 9(01)      COMP SYNC.
        10  FIELD-5                 PIC 9(02)      COMP SYNC.
        10  FIELD-2                 PIC 9(06)      COMP SYNC.
        10  FIELD-3                 PIC X(20).
        10  FIELD-4                 PIC 9(09)      COMP SYNC.
        10  FIELD-6                 PIC 9(12)      COMP SYNC.
        10  FIELD-7                 PIC 9(03)V99 COMP SYNC.
        10  FIELD-8                 PIC 9(03)      COMP SYNC.
```

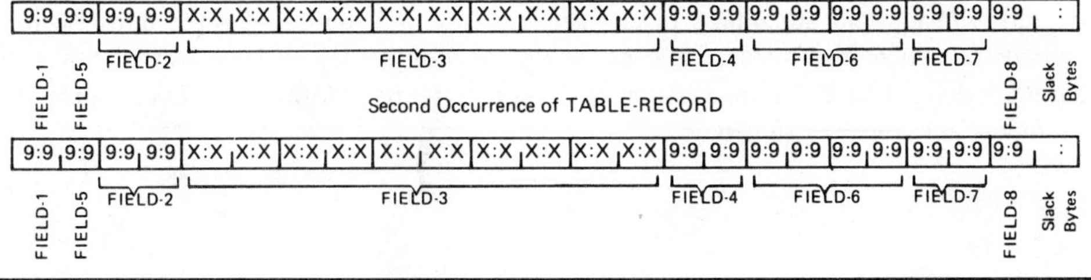

The tables created in Figures 23.12 and 23.13 both describe the same amount of data. However, a single occurrence of the table in Figure 23.13 requires only 46 bytes for data and 2 bytes for interoccurrence slack bytes. The new table uses 48 bytes per occurrence. The table requires 4800 bytes in total. This amounts to a savings of 800 bytes in the description of this rather small table.

Summary

In this chapter, various means of describing numeric data have been discussed. Normally, numeric data are described in DISPLAY mode; however, the USAGE clause may be added to the description of nonedited-numeric data items to achieve alternate forms of internal data storage. Although data must be described in DISPLAY mode (character form) for input-output operations involving card readers and line printers, other forms of data representation may be used for internally accessed data items and for data recorded on disk and tape media.

Besides DISPLAY data items, data may be represented in COMPUTATIONAL (binary), COMPUTATIONAL-1 (short floating-point), COMPUTATIONAL-2 (long floating-point), and COMPUTATIONAL-3 (packed-decimal) formats. Each of these data types has its own impact on the computer's ability to manipulate numeric values quickly and on the amount of internal storage used.

Table 23.1 presents the completed table of allowable movements of data for COBOL that provides for the USAGE clauses discussed in this chapter. In addition, other clauses may be added to the description of data items either to enhance the programmer's capability to manipulate data values or to improve the computer's access to data values in storage. They are the BLANK WHEN ZERO, JUSTIFIED, SIGN, and SYNCHRONIZED clauses.

Notes on Programming Style

The use of noncharacter data representations within a program seems to follow a similar line to many of the other special usage items described in Part 4 of this text. Almost every shop would like to use the most efficient form of data representation available for every data item. The question again arises—''What will the negative impact be if we employ this type of code?'' Unfortunately, many companies have been forced to use DISPLAY representation exclusively because of the lack of sophistication of many of their entry-level programmers. This lack of familiarity with noncharacter representations, coupled with a slight advantage in program debugging (you can see the numeric representations when displayed), have caused many companies to stay away from noncharacter data. Thus, ''human efficiency'' seems to be winning out over ''program efficiency'' or ''space efficiency.''

Table 23.1 The Complete Table of Allowable Moves in COBOL

Sending Field	Receiving Field								
	Group	Alphabetic	Alphanumeric	Alphanumeric-edited	Numeric (DISPLAY)	Numeric-edited	Binary (COMP)	Floating-point (COMP-1/COMP-2)	Packed-decimal (COMP-3)
Group	Y	Y	Y	Y[1]	Y[1]	Y[1]	Y[1]	Y[1]	Y[1]
Alphabetic (A)	Y	Y	Y	Y	N	N	N	N	N
Alphanumeric (X)	Y	Y	Y	Y	Y[4]	Y[4]	Y[4]	Y[4]	Y[4]
Alphanumeric-edited	Y	Y	Y	Y	N	N	N	N	N
Numeric (DISPLAY)(9)	Y[1]	N	Y[2]	Y[2]	Y	Y	Y	Y	Y
Numeric-edited	Y	N	Y	Y	N	N	N	N	N
Binary (COMP)	Y[1]	N	Y[2]	Y[2]	Y	Y	Y	Y	Y
Floating-point (COMP-1/COMP-2)	Y[1]	N	N	N	Y	Y	Y	Y	Y
Packed-decimal (COMP-3)	Y[1]	N	Y[2]	Y[2]	Y	Y	Y	Y	Y
Figurative Constants ZEROS	Y	N	Y	Y	Y[3]	Y[3]	Y[3]	Y[3]	Y[3]
SPACES	Y	Y	Y	Y	N	N	N	N	N
HIGH-VALUE LOW-VALUE QUOTE	Y	N	Y	Y	N	N	N	N	N
ALL literal	Y	Y	Y	Y	Y[5]	Y[5]	Y[5]	N	Y[5]
Numeric literal	Y[1]	N	Y[2]	Y[2]	Y	Y	Y	Y	Y
Nonnumeric literal	Y	Y	Y	Y	Y[5]	Y[5]	Y[5]	N	Y[5]

LEGEND: Y = yes; N = no.
[1]Move treated like an alphanumeric to alphanumeric move—no data conversion is made.
[2]Decimal point must be to the right of the least significant digit treated as a numeric move.
[3]Treated as a numeric move.
[4]Alphanumeric field treated as an integer numeric (DISPLAY) field.
[5]Literal treated as an integer numeric (DISPLAY) field and may contain only numeric characters.

Questions

Below fill in the blank(s) with the appropriate word, words, or phrases.

T F 1. When a USAGE clause is not specified for a data item, the assumed usage is _____ .

T F 2. In a DISPLAY mode, each 9 in a PICTURE string requires one _____ of internal storage.

T F 3. When data are being read from a punched-card device, all data fields must be described in _____ mode.

T F 4. The smallest unit of internal storage generally addressable in COBOL is the _____ .

T F 5. Bit is an acronym for _____ _____ .

T F 6. A byte is a combination of _____ .

T F 7. Most computer internal storage capacity is stated in terms of _____ or _____ .

T F 8. The two most frequently used internal coding schemes are _____ and _____ .

T F 9. Another term that means the same as DISPLAY-mode data is _____ .

T F 10. Data that are stored in COMPUTATIONAL-mode are stored in _____ form.

T F 11. Data that are stored in COMPUTATIONAL-3 mode are stored in _____ form.

T F 12. The sign of numeric DISPLAY data is recorded in the _____ .

T F 13. For an unsigned, numeric DISPLAY data value,the high-order half-byte for each digit position contains the hexadecimal digit _____ .

T F 14. The two advantages that COMPUTATIONAL data have over DISPLAY data are that COMPUTATIONAL data _____ and_____ .

T F 15. The sign of a COMPUTATIONAL data item is stored in the _____ .

T F 16. Provided a PICTURE clause is permitted in conjunction with a COMPUTATIONAL data item, the PICTURE characters that may be used to describe the field include _____ , _____ , and _____ .

T F 17. The sign bit of passive COMPUTATIONAL data contains a binary value of _____ .

T F 18. Negative binary data are stored in _____ form.

T F 19. Packed-decimal data may be described by using the USAGE IS _____ clause.

T F 20. Another term for ''high-order'' bits is _____ bits.

T F 21. In a packed-decimal format, each byte of internal storage may contain up to _____ (number) digits.

T F 22. Where data are described as being in COMP-3 mode, the sign is recorded in the _____ .

T F 23. Both COMP-1 and COMP-2 provide for internal data representation in _____ form.

T F 24. COMP-1 requires _____ of internal storage, and COMP-2 requires _____ .

T F 25. The sign bit of a COMP-1 field is in the same location and has the same representation as data stored in the _____ mode.

T F 26. The BLANK WHEN ZERO clause may be used only in conjunction with fields declared to be in _____ mode.

T F 27. When the JUSTIFIED RIGHT clause is attached to an alphanumeric field description, data placed in the field is _____-justified.

T F 28. When the SIGN IS TRAILING clause is added to the description of a data item, the sign is located in the _____ .

T F **29.** When the SEPARATE CHARACTER phrase is added to the SIGN clause, the length of the data field is _____ .

T F **30.** The SYNCHRONIZED clause is used to ensure _____ of numeric data.

T F **31.** To achieve the proper internal alignment, SYNCHRONIZED fields often cause _____ to be added to the internal representation of the data, if necessary.

T F **32.** If SYNCHRONIZED clauses are used in conjunction with a table, _____ and _____ may be generated to achieve proper internal boundary alignment.

Answer the following questions by circling either "T" for True or "F" for False.

T F **33.** The internal architecture of all computers is the same.

T F **34.** Only numeric data may be described in non-DISPLAY form.

T F **35.** The only forms in which data may be stored in COBOL are external-decimal, binary, and packed-decimal.

T F **36.** It is possible to mix data types (e.g., DISPLAY and COMP) in one program.

T F **37.** Regardless of the type of computer used, DISPLAY data items always require a PICTURE clause.

T F **38.** Regardless of the type of computer used, COMPUTATIONAL data items always require a PICTURE clause.

T F **39.** Regardless of the type of computer used, COMPUTATIONAL data items are always integers (whole numbers).

T F **40.** Data stored in COMP-1 mode is recorded in an exponential format.

T F **41.** COMP-1 and COMP-2 fields require PICTURE clauses with their descriptions.

T F **42.** It is possible to store a fractional value in a COMP-1 field.

T F **43.** A new type of PICTURE string character is available when data are stored in COMP-3 form.

T F **44.** HIGH-VALUES may be moved to a COMPUTATIONAL field.

T F **45.** The BLANK WHEN ZERO clause, when properly used, causes a field to contain blanks regardless of the PICTURE description when the data value of zero is placed in the field.

T F **46.** Normally, data in an alphanumeric field are left-justified.

T F **47.** The SIGN clause may be used only in conjunction with numeric data fields in the COMP mode.

T F **48.** When the SIGN IS SEPARATE clause is used, the data description (PICTURE string) must include the operational sign character.

T F **49.** When the SIGN IS SEPARATE clause is used, the data must contain a sign.

T F **50.** Data that are SYNCHRONIZED may be manipulated by the computer more quickly than nonsynchronized data.

T F **51.** Data that are SYNCHRONIZED requires less internal storage than do nonsynchronized data.

CHAPTER

24

Character-oriented Data Processing

Numeric data are not the only data that can be manipulated by a program. For example, it is possible to manipulate a string of characters in a person's name or item-description. The STRING and UNSTRING statements are useful to manipulate character strings. The STRING statement's function is *concatenation*—to take data values in two or more fields and place these values together in a single field. The UNSTRING statement performs a *parsing* operation—taking data in one field and separating it into two or more fields. The STRING and UNSTRING statements were added to ANS COBOL in 1974. For this reason, unless your installation is using a current ANS COBOL compiler, these statements may not be available. Other statement types, including INSPECT, EXAMINE, TRANSFORM, and INITIALIZE are also available for field examination and manipulation. These statements, however, are not uniformly available in COBOL compilers.

The STRING Statement

The format of the STRING statement is provided in Figure 24.1. In this statement, identifier-1 (literal-1), identifier-2 (literal-2), identifier-4 (literal-4), identifier-5 (literal-5) represent sending fields. Each of these identifiers must be implicitly or explicitly described with the USAGE IS DISPLAY clause. None of these identifiers may use the character P in a PICTURE string. Identifier-7 must be a nonedited-alphanumeric elementary data item. All literals must be nonnumeric literals or figurative constants other than ALL.

The effect of the STRING statement is to copy one character at a time (from left to right) from the sending field into the receiving field (from left to right). This process is completed for identifier-1 before the examination and transmission of any characters from subsequent fields.

Two optional clauses may be used with the STRING statement. The POINTER clause may be used to indicate a count of the number of characters placed in the receiving field. Each character placed in the receiving field will cause identifier-8 to be incremented by 1. Identifier-8 must be described as a nonedited-numeric integer data item. It should

Figure 24.1 Format of the STRING Statement

```
STRING {{identifier-1} {idnetifier-2}   DELIMITED BY {identifier-3}}
        {literal-1   } {literal-2   }                {literal-3   }
                                                     {SIZE        }
       {{identifier-4} {idnetifier-5}   DELIMITED BY {identifier-6}}
        {literal-4   } {literal-5   }                {literal-6   }
                                                     {SIZE        }
   INTO identifier-7 [WITH POINTER identifier-8]
  [ON OVERFLOW imperative-statement]
  [NOT ON OVERFLOW imperative-statement]
  [END-STRING]
```

be capable of storing a value equal to the maximum number of characters in the receiving field (identifier-7) plus one digit. The programmer is responsible for initializing identifier-8 prior to each execution of the STRING statement. The initial value of the identifier must be a positive integer. The programmer may also use this identifier in other statements of his or her program.

The OVERFLOW clause allows the programmer to specify execution of the imperative statement when an attempt is made to place more characters in a receiving field than it is capable of holding. Any receiving field that appears after the identifier causing the overflow will not have its value altered. The NOT OVERFLOW clause allows the programmer to specify execution of the imperative statement when no error occurs in the execution of the STRING statement.

1985 COBOL Standards

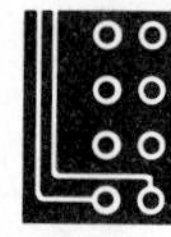

Figure 24.2 presents several examples of the STRING statement. Ordinarily, data would not be placed in the sending fields by MOVE statements immediately preceding the STRING statement. However, suppose that ALPHA-1, ALPHA-2, and ALPHA-3 (in the first two examples) are 15-character alphanumeric fields. In the first example, the blanks after the character C of ALPHA-1 are eliminated in the receiving field due to the DELIMITED BY clause. The data are placed in ALPHA-3, left-justified, and blank filled. In the second example, the character E of ALPHA-2 is not transmitted to ALPHA-3. Also, notice that a literal may be used as a sending field.

The third example is used to demonstrate a way of compressing data values that represent name fields to produce a field that is more normal in appearance for an individual's name. Each of the sending fields, except MIDDLE-INITIAL, might be ten or more characters in length. Thus, the STRING statement is used to ''squeeze'' unnecessary blanks from the data fields as characters are placed in a receiving field.

The last two examples demonstrate the use of the optional clauses. With the fourth example, the POINTER clause is used to count the number of characters placed in the receiving field. The example assumes that ZIP is described as a five-digit integer field. Notice that CHAR-COUNT is initialized to 1 prior to the execution of the statement. If the value of CHAR-COUNT was not changed prior to the execution of the statement, CHAR-COUNT would be incremented from the last value it contained.

The last example employs the OVERFLOW clause. Assuming the field size for STREET-ADDRESS is 20 characters, we find an overflow would exist for this statement

Figure 24.2 Examples of the STRING Statement

```
Example 1:
          MOVE 'ABC' TO ALPHA-1.
          MOVE 'DEF' TO ALPHA-2.
          STRING ALPHA-1, ALPHA-2 DELIMITED BY SPACE INTO ALPHA-3.
                 (ALPHA-3 = ABCDEF)
```

```
Example 2:
          MOVE 'ABCDEFGHIJ' TO ALPHA-1.
          MOVE 'NOPE' TO ALPHA-2.
          STRING ALPHA-1, 'KLM' DELIMITED BY SIZE
                 ALPHA-2 DELIMITED BY 'E' INTO ALPHA-3.
                 (ALPHA-3 = ABCDEFGHIJKLMNOP)
```

```
Example 3:
          MOVE 'JEFFERSON' TO LAST-NAME.
          MOVE 'ANDREW' TO FIRST-NAME.
          MOVE 'R' TO MIDDLE-INITIAL.
          STRING FIRST-NAME DELIMITED BY SPACE
                 ' ', MIDDLE-INITIAL, '. ' DELIMITED BY SIZE
                 LAST-NAME DELIMITED BY SPACE INTO NAME-FIELD.
                 (NAME-FIELD = ANDREW R. JEFFERSON)
```

```
Example 4:
          MOVE 1 TO CHAR-COUNT.
          MOVE 'CHICAGO' TO CITY.
          MOVE 'ILLINOIS' TO STATE.
          MOVE 60606 TO ZIP.
          STRING CITY DELIMITED BY SPACE ', ' DELIMITED BY SIZE
                 STATE DELIMITED BY SPACE ' ', ZIP DELIMITED BY SIZE
                 INTO ADDRESS WITH POINTER CHAR-COUNT.
                 (ADDRESS = CHICAGO, ILLINOIS 60606)
                 (CHAR-COUNT = 23)
```

```
Example 5:
          MOVE '12345' TO STREET-NUMBER.
          MOVE 'MOCKINGBIRD' TO STREET-NAME.
          MOVE 'BOULEVARD' TO ST-AVE-ETC.
          STRING STREET-NUMBER DELIMITED BY SPACE ' ' DELIMITED BY SIZE
                 STREET-NAME DELIMITED BY SPACE ' ' DELIMITED BY SIZE
                 ST-AVE-ETC DELIMITED BY SPACE INTO STREET-ADDRESS
                 ON OVERFLOW DISPLAY STREET-NUMBER, STREET-NAME, ST-AVE-ETC.
                 (STREET-ADDRESS = 12345 MOCKINGBIRD BO)
```

and the value in STREET-NUMBER, STREET-NAME and ST-AVE-ETC would be displayed. Note that data would be placed in the receiving field, even though an overflow condition exists.

Using the STRING Statement

In Chapter 13 a program was presented that accepted a dollar amount as input and translated the digits into the text representing those digits. The text-processing program is repeated in Figure 24.3. However, in this illustration, the STRING statement is used to concatenate the words that represent the digits. The STRING statement greatly simplifies the program.

Figure 24.3 A Text-processing Program (Hierarchy Chart)

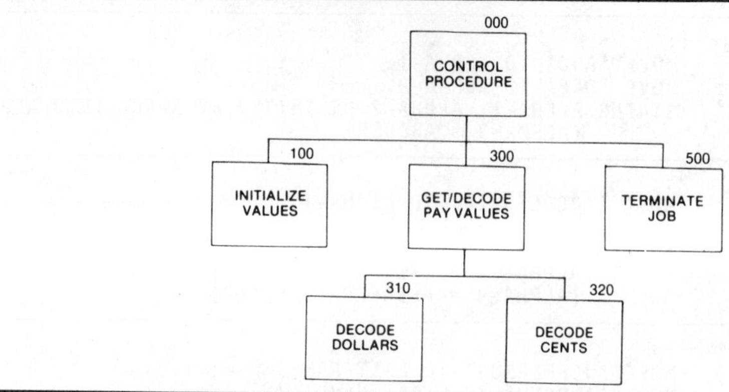

Figure 24.3 *Continued* A Text-processing Program (Pseudocode)

```
START
     DO Initialize values
     DO Get decode pay values UNTIL eof
     DO Terminate job
END

INITIALIZE VALUES
     OPEN files
     SET file status
     READ input
          AT END set file status
END

GET DECODE PAY VALUES
     MOVE amount to output
     DO Decode dollars
     DO Decode cents
     STRING text amount
          DELIMITED by space into amount out
     WRITE output
     READ input
          AT END set file status
END

DECODE DOLLARS
     IF digit (1) > 0
          MOVE value to thousands
     ELSE
          MOVE spaces to thousands
     ENDIF
     IF digit (2) > 0
          MOVE value to hundreds
     ELSE
          MOVE spaces to hundreds
     ENDIF
     IF digit (3) = 1
          MOVE value to tens
     ENDIF
     IF digit (3) > 1
          MOVE value to tens
     ENDIF
     IF digit (4) > 0 AND digit (3) NOT = 1
          MOVE value to ones
     ELSE
          MOVE spaces to ones
     ENDIF
     IF amount in < 1
          MOVE 'No-'to ones
     ENDIF
END

DECODE CENTS
     IF digit (5) = 1
          MOVE value to tens of cents
     ENDIF
     IF digit (5) > 1
          MOVE value to tens of cents
     ENDIF
     IF digit (6) > 0 AND digit (5) NOT = 1
          MOVE value to cents
     ENDIF
     IF digit (6) > 0 AND digit (5) NOT = 1
          MOVE value to cents
     ENDIF
     IF digit (5) = 0 AND digit (6) = 0
          MOVE 'No-' to cents
     ENDIF
END

TERMINATE JOB
     CLOSE files
END
```

Figure 24.3 *Continued* A Text-processing Program

```
          1   1   2   2   2   3   3   4   4   4   5   5   6   6   6   7
   4   8  2   6   0   4   8   2   6   0   4   8   2   6   0   4   8   2
-------------------------------------------------------------------------
      *****************************************************************
       IDENTIFICATION DIVISION.
      *****************************************************************
       PROGRAM-ID.      CHECK-WRITER.
       AUTHOR.          J. WAYNE SPENCE.
       DATE-WRITTEN.    JANUARY 1, 1989.
       DATE-COMPILED.   JANUARY 1, 1989.
      *    This program performs a number to text conversion on
      *    "amounts" as might appear on a check produced by a
      *    computer program.  Note that tables are used in the
      *    PROCEDURE DIVISION which have values assigned to them
      *    in the DATA DIVISION through a redefinition.  The amount
      *    to text conversion is done by the STRING statement.
      *****************************************************************
       ENVIRONMENT DIVISION.
      *****************************************************************
      *---------------------------------------------------------------*
       CONFIGURATION SECTION.
      *---------------------------------------------------------------*
       SOURCE-COMPUTER. IBM.
       OBJECT-COMPUTER. IBM.
      *---------------------------------------------------------------*
       INPUT-OUTPUT SECTION.
      *---------------------------------------------------------------*
       FILE-CONTROL.
           SELECT PAY-FILE   ASSIGN TO UT-S-INPUT.
           SELECT CHECK-FILE ASSIGN TO UT-S-OUTPUT.
      *****************************************************************
       DATA DIVISION.
      *****************************************************************
      *---------------------------------------------------------------*
       FILE SECTION.
      *---------------------------------------------------------------*
       FD  PAY-FILE LABEL RECORDS ARE OMITTED.
       01  PAY-RECORD.
           05 AMOUNT-OF-CHECK-IN          PIC 9(04)V9(02).
           05 AMOUNT-T-IN REDEFINES AMOUNT-OF-CHECK-IN.
               10 DIGIT-T OCCURS 6 TIMES PIC 9(01).
           05 FILLER                      PIC X(74).

       FD  CHECK-FILE LABEL RECORDS ARE OMITTED.
       01  CHECK-RECORD                   PIC X(133).
      *---------------------------------------------------------------*
       WORKING-STORAGE SECTION.
      *---------------------------------------------------------------*
       01  WORKING-VARIABLES.
           05  FILE-STATUS                PIC X(15).
           05  THOUSANDS                  PIC X(10).
           05  HUNDREDS                   PIC X(10).
           05  TENS                       PIC X(10).
           05  ONES                       PIC X(10).
           05  TENS-OF-CENTS              PIC X(10).
           05  SINGLE-CENTS               PIC X(10).
           05  THOUSAND-WS                PIC X(10).
           05  HUNDRED-WS                 PIC X(10).
           05  BODY                       PIC 9(02).

       01  DOLLARS-AND-CENTS.
           05 DOLLARS-AND                 PIC X(12) VALUE
                                          'Dollars-and-'.
           05 CENTS                       PIC X(05) VALUE 'Cents'.

       01  LIST-OF-UNITS.
           05 FILLER                      PIC X(10) VALUE 'One-'.
           05 FILLER                      PIC X(10) VALUE 'Two-'.
           05 FILLER                      PIC X(10) VALUE 'Three-'.
           05 FILLER                      PIC X(10) VALUE 'Four-'.
           05 FILLER                      PIC X(10) VALUE 'Five-'.
           05 FILLER                      PIC X(10) VALUE 'Six-'.
```

Figure 24.3 *Continued* A Text-processing Program

```
           05 FILLER                      PIC X(10) VALUE 'Seven-'.
           05 FILLER                      PIC X(10) VALUE 'Eight-'.
           05 FILLER                      PIC X(10) VALUE 'Nine-'.
           05 FILLER                      PIC X(10) VALUE 'Ten-'.
           05 FILLER                      PIC X(10) VALUE 'Eleven-'.
           05 FILLER                      PIC X(10) VALUE 'Twelve-'.
           05 FILLER                      PIC X(10) VALUE 'Thirteen-'.
           05 FILLER                      PIC X(10) VALUE 'Fourteen-'.
           05 FILLER                      PIC X(10) VALUE 'Fifteen-'.
           05 FILLER                      PIC X(10) VALUE 'Sixteen-'.
           05 FILLER                      PIC X(10) VALUE 'Seventeen-'.
           05 FILLER                      PIC X(10) VALUE 'Eighteen-'.
           05 FILLER                      PIC X(10) VALUE 'Nineteen-'.
           05 FILLER                      PIC X(10) VALUE 'Twenty-'.
           05 FILLER                      PIC X(10) VALUE 'Thirty-'.
           05 FILLER                      PIC X(10) VALUE 'Forty-'.
           05 FILLER                      PIC X(10) VALUE 'Fifty-'.
           05 FILLER                      PIC X(10) VALUE 'Sixty-'.
           05 FILLER                      PIC X(10) VALUE 'Seventy-'.
           05 FILLER                      PIC X(10) VALUE 'Eighty-'.
           05 FILLER                      PIC X(10) VALUE 'Ninety-'.
           05 FILLER                      PIC X(10) VALUE 'Hundred-'.
           05 FILLER                      PIC X(10) VALUE 'Thousand-'.

       01  DIGIT-TABLE REDEFINES LIST-OF-UNITS.
           05 LETTER-T OCCURS 29 TIMES PIC X(10).

       01  AMOUNT-RECORD.
           05  FILLER                     PIC X(01).
           05  AMOUNT-OF-CHECK-OUT        PIC 9(04).9(02).
           05  FILLER                     PIC X(03) VALUE SPACES.
           05  WRITTEN-AMOUNT-OUT         PIC X(72).
      ****************************************************************
       PROCEDURE DIVISION.
      ****************************************************************
      *--------------------------------------------------------------*
       000-CONTROL-PROCEDURE SECTION.
      *--------------------------------------------------------------*
           PERFORM 100-INITIALIZE-VALUES.
           PERFORM 300-GET-DECODE-PAY-VALUES
               UNTIL FILE-STATUS = 'DONE'.
           PERFORM 500-TERMINATE-JOB.
           STOP RUN.
      *--------------------------------------------------------------*
       100-INITIALIZE-VALUES SECTION.
      *--------------------------------------------------------------*
           OPEN INPUT PAY-FILE, OUTPUT CHECK-FILE.
           MOVE 'START'             TO FILE-STATUS.
           READ PAY-FILE
                AT END MOVE 'DONE' TO FILE-STATUS.
      *--------------------------------------------------------------*
       300-GET-DECODE-PAY-VALUES SECTION.
      *--------------------------------------------------------------*
           MOVE AMOUNT-OF-CHECK-IN  TO AMOUNT-OF-CHECK-OUT.
           MOVE SPACES              TO WRITTEN-AMOUNT-OUT.
           PERFORM 310-DECODE-DOLLARS.
           PERFORM 320-DECODE-CENTS.
           STRING THOUSANDS, THOUSAND-WS, HUNDREDS, HUNDRED-WS, TENS,
               ONES, DOLLARS-AND, TENS-OF-CENTS, SINGLE-CENTS, CENTS
                DELIMITED BY SPACE INTO WRITTEN-AMOUNT-OUT.
           WRITE CHECK-RECORD FROM AMOUNT-RECORD AFTER ADVANCING 1 LINES
           READ PAY-FILE
                AT END MOVE 'DONE' TO FILE-STATUS.
      *--------------------------------------------------------------*
       310-DECODE-DOLLARS SECTION.
      *--------------------------------------------------------------*
           IF DIGIT-T (1) > 0
                MOVE DIGIT-T (1)      TO BODY
                MOVE LETTER-T (BODY) TO THOUSANDS
```

Figure 24.3 *Continued* A Text-processing Program

```
          1   1   2   2   2   3   3   4   4   4   5   5   6   6   6   7
  4   8   2   6   0   4   8   2   6   0   4   8   2   6   0   4   8   2
---------------------------------------------------------------------------
               MOVE LETTER-T (29)      TO THOUSAND-WS
           ELSE
               MOVE SPACES             TO THOUSANDS, THOUSAND-WS.
           IF DIGIT-T (2) > 0
               MOVE DIGIT-T (2)        TO BODY
               MOVE LETTER-T (BODY) TO HUNDREDS
               MOVE LETTER-T (28)      TO HUNDRED-WS
           ELSE
               MOVE SPACES             TO HUNDREDS, HUNDRED-WS.
           MOVE SPACES                 TO TENS.
           IF DIGIT-T (3) = 1
               ADD 10, DIGIT-T (4) GIVING BODY
               MOVE LETTER-T (BODY) TO TENS
               MOVE SPACES             TO ONES.
           IF DIGIT-T (3) > 1
               ADD 18, DIGIT-T (3) GIVING BODY
               MOVE LETTER-T (BODY) TO TENS.
           IF DIGIT-T (4) > 0 AND DIGIT-T (3) NOT = 1
               MOVE DIGIT-T (4)        TO BODY
               MOVE LETTER-T (BODY) TO ONES
           ELSE
               MOVE SPACES             TO ONES.
           IF AMOUNT-OF-CHECK-IN < 1
               MOVE 'No-'              TO ONES.
       *-------------------------------------------------------------*
        320-DECODE-CENTS SECTION.
       *-------------------------------------------------------------*
           MOVE SPACES                 TO TENS-OF-CENTS.
           IF DIGIT-T (5) = 1
               ADD 10, DIGIT-T (6) GIVING BODY
               MOVE LETTER-T (BODY) TO TENS-OF-CENTS
               MOVE SPACES             TO SINGLE-CENTS.
           IF DIGIT-T (5) > 1
               ADD 18, DIGIT-T (5) GIVING BODY
               MOVE LETTER-T (BODY) TO TENS-OF-CENTS.
           IF DIGIT-T (6) > 0 AND DIGIT-T (5) NOT = 1
               MOVE DIGIT-T (6)        TO BODY
               MOVE LETTER-T (BODY) TO SINGLE-CENTS.
           MOVE SPACES                 TO SINGLE-CENTS.
           IF DIGIT-T (6) > 0 AND DIGIT-T (5) NOT = 1
               MOVE DIGIT-T (6)        TO BODY
               MOVE LETTER-T (BODY) TO SINGLE-CENTS.
           IF DIGIT-T (5) = 0 AND DIGIT-T (6) = 0
               MOVE 'No-'              TO SINGLE-CENTS.
       *-------------------------------------------------------------*
        500-TERMINATE-JOB SECTION.
       *-------------------------------------------------------------*
           CLOSE PAY-FILE, CHECK-FILE.
---------------------------------------------------------------------------
```

Figure 24.3 *Continued* A Text-processing Program (Data)

Record	1234567890
1	500102
2	002000
3	089999
4	021388
5	005052
6	953700
7	046610
8	002009
9	000350
10	032475
11	300000
12	765000
13	465300
14	022222

Figure 24.3 *Continued* A Text-processing Program (Output)

```
5001.02  Five-Thousand-One-Dollars-and-Two-Cents
0020.00  Twenty-Dollars-and-No-Cents
0899.99  Eight-Hundred-Ninety-Nine-Dollars-and-Ninety-Nine-Cents
0213.88  Two-Hundred-Thirteen-Dollars-and-Eighty-Eight-Cents
0050.52  Fifty-Dollars-and-Fifty-Two-Cents
9537.00  Nine-Thousand-Five-Hundred-Thirty-Seven-Dollars-and-No-Cents
0466.10  Four-Hundred-Sixty-Six-Dollars-and-Ten-Cents
0020.09  Twenty-Dollars-and-Nine-Cents
0003.50  Three-Dollars-and-Fifty-Cents
0324.75  Three-Hundred-Twenty-Four-Dollars-and-Seventy-Five-Cents
3000.00  Three-Thousand-Dollars-and-No-Cents
7650.00  Seven-Thousand-Six-Hundred-Fifty-Dollars-and-No-Cents
4653.00  Four-Thousand-Six-Hundred-Fifty-Three-Dollars-and-No-Cents
```

The UNSTRING Statement

The UNSTRING statement is the logical complement of the STRING statement. It separates data from one field into several fields.

The format of the UNSTRING statement is shown in Figure 24.4. In this statement identifier-1 is the sending field and identifier-4 (identifier-7, etc.) is the receiving field. Identifier-1 must be described as an alphanumeric field. Identifier-4 (identifier-7, etc.) must be described as a nonedited-alphanumeric field, implicitly or explicitly described as a DISPLAY field.

When the UNSTRING statement is executed, the sending field is examined, one character at a time from left to right. The characters are placed in the first receiving field (identifier-4) until the character specified in the DELIMITED BY clause is encountered. Identifier-2 (identifier-3, etc.) of the DELIMITED BY clause must be an alphanumeric data item. Literal-1 (literal-2, etc.) must be a nonnumeric literal or a figurative constant other than ALL. Thus, when this character is encountered in the sending field, the movement of characters from the sending field to the first receiving field is terminated. If a second (third, etc.) receiving field is specified, movement of data continues, as before, with the character immediately following the character that caused the termination of the previous movement of data.

When the DELIMITED BY clause is specified, the DELIMITER IN and the COUNT IN clause may be listed for the receiving field(s). Unless the DELIMITER IN clause is specified, the character that caused the termination of the movement of data from the sending field will be lost. Since the DELIMITED BY clause could cause the termination of character movement on the basis of several characters, the DELIMITER IN clause may be used to retain the delimiter for further reference. The location of the delimiter character will be identifier-5 (identifier-8, etc.). This identifier must be a nonedited-alphanumeric field.

The COUNT IN clause may be used to count the number of characters placed in a receiving field. This count does not include an increment for the delimiter character. Identifier-6 (identifier-9, etc.) must be a nonedited-numeric field without the PICTURE

Figure 24.4 Format of the UNSTRING Statement

```
UNSTRING  identifier-1

   [DELIMITED BY [ALL] {identifier-2} [OR [ALL] {identifier-3}] ...]
                       {literal-1   }            {literal-2   }

    INTO identifier-4 [DELIMITER IN identifier-5][COUNT IN identifier-6]

        [identifier-7 [DELIMITER IN identifier-8][COUNT IN identifier-9]

   [WITH POINTER identifier-10] [TALLYING IN identifier-11]

   [ON OVERFLOW imperative-statement]

   [NOT ON OVERFLOW imperative-statement]

   [END-STRING]
```

character P. These identifiers will be initialized to zero and incremented by one for each character moved into the receiving field. If two successive delimiting characters are encountered, the count will remain zero for that receiving field. (The receiving field will be blank.)

Three optional clauses accompany the UNSTRING statement—the POINTER clause, the TALLYING clause, and the OVERFLOW clause. As with the STRING statement, the POINTER clause is used to keep track of the character being examined in the sending field of the UNSTRING statement. Identifier-10 must be a nonedited-numeric elementary-item that cannot contain the character P in the PICTURE string. The UNSTRING statement increments the identifier by one for each character examined; the programmer is responsible for initializing the identifier to some nonnegative value prior to each execution of the statement. The TALLYING option follows the same basic form as the POINTER phrase. The characteristics of identifier-11 are the same as those for identifier-10; however, identifier-11 contains a count of the number of receiving fields that have received data from the sending field.

An OVERFLOW condition is caused by either of two situations: (1) when the POINTER identifier contains a value less than 1 or (2) when all receiving fields have received data and characters remain unexamined in identifier-1. When either of these conditions occurs, the UNSTRING statement is terminated and the OVERFLOW imperative statement is executed.

Now look at Figure 24.5. This illustration provides several examples of the use of UNSTRING statements. The first example illustrates how to extract the ''prefix'' from a character string. Data are placed in FEDERAL-ID-GROUP until a hyphen is encountered (e.g., to extract hyphens from a social security number). In the second example, a portion of the sending field (the first six characters) is to be bypassed such that the parsing operation begins at the seventh character of the field. The third example illustrates more of the full potential of the UNSTRING statement. In this example, data from one

Figure 24.5 Examples of the UNSTRING Statement

Example 1:

```
MOVE '75-1234567' TO FEDERAL-ID-NUMBER.
UNSTRING FEDERAL-ID-NUMBER DELIMITED BY '-'
    INTO FEDERAL-ID-GROUP.
    (FEDERAL-ID-GROUP = 75)
```

Example 2:

```
MOVE 7 TO JUMP-PAST-AREA-CODE.
MOVE '(214) 382-8671' TO PHONE-NUMBER.
UNSTRING PHONE-NUMBER DELIMITED BY '-'
    INTO EXCHANGE
    WITH POINTER JUMP-PAST-AREA-CODE.
    (EXCHANGE = 382)
```

Figure 24.5 *Continued* Examples of the UNSTRING Statement

Example 3:

```
MOVE '$5,277.Ø8' TO DOLLAR-CHARACTERS.
UNSTRING DOLLAR-CHARACTERS
    DELIMITED BY '$' INTO LEADING-BLANKS
        DELIMITER IN DOLLAR-SIGN
    DELIMITED BY ',' INTO THOUSANDS
        DELIMITER IN COMMA-CHARACTER
    DELIMITED BY '.' HUNDREDS-TENS-ONES
        DELIMITER IN DECIMAL-POINT
    DELIMTED BY SPACE INTO CENTS.
    (LEADING-BLANKS = NO DATA
    DOLLAR-SIGN = $
    THOUSANDS = 5
    COMMA-CHARACTER = ,
    HUNDREDS-TENS-ONES = 277
    DECIMAL-POINT = .
    CENTS = Ø8)
```

Example 4:

```
MOVE 'JULY 4, 1947' TO DATE-OF-BIRTH.
UNSTRING DATE-OF-BIRTH
    DELIMITED BY SPACE INTO DOB-MONTH
    DELIMITED BY ',' INTO DOB-DAY
    DELIMITED BY '9' OR '8' INTO UNNEEDED-DATA
    DELIMITED BY SPACE INTO DOB-YEAR.
    (DOB-MONTH = JULY
    DOB-DAY = 4
    UNNEEDED-DATA = 19
    DOB-YEAR = 47
    DELIMITERS NOT SAVED)
```

Figure 24.5 *Continued* Examples of the UNSTRING Statement

Example 5:

```
    MOVE 0 TO WORD-COUNT.
    MOVE 1 TO BEGIN-AT.
    MOVE 'THE QUICK BROWN FOX JUMPED
       OVER THE LAZY DOG.' TO TEXT-STRING
    PERFORM PARSE-TEXT VARYING I FROM
       1 BY 1 UNTIL INDICATOR = 'STOP'.
       .
       .
       .
PARSE-TEXT
    MOVE 0 TO WORD-LENGTH (I).
    UNSTRING TEXT-STRING
        DELIMITED BY SPACE INTO TEXT-WORD (I)
        DELIMITER IN SPACE-BETWEEN
        COUNT IN WORD-LENGTH (I)
        WITH POINTER BEGIN-AT
        TALLYING IN WORD-COUNT
        ON OVERFLOW MOVE 'STOP' TO INDICATOR.
    ADD 1, WORD-LENGTH (I) TO BEGIN-AT.
```

```
(TEXT-WORD (1) = THE    ; WORD-LENGTH (1) = 3
     "     (2) = QUICK        "       (2) = 5
     "     (3) = BROWN        "       (3) = 5
     "     (4) = FOX          "       (4) = 3
     "     (5) = JUMPED       "       (5) = 6
     "     (6) = OVER         "       (6) = 4
     "     (7) = THE          "       (7) = 3
     "     (8) = LAZY         "       (8) = 4
     "     (9) = DOG          "       (9) = 3
WORD-COUNT = 9)
```

field are divided into several receiving fields, and each delimiter is retained for data reference. The fourth example is similar to the third example, but the delimiters are not retained.

The final example demonstrates how other PROCEDURE DIVISION statements are used so that the UNSTRING statement is executed until all the data from the sending field have been examined. The UNSTRING statement must avoid beginning at the first character position of the sending field each time the statement is executed, thus the POINTER phrase is employed. The data that are parsed with each execution of the UNSTRING statement is placed in a table along with its length.

Key Word in Context

The process known as ''key word in context'' scans a specified text for one or more occurrences of a specified word or phrase. The process is illustrated in Figure 24.6. The problem can be divided into three distinct phases: (1) reading the text to be searched (the READ-TEXT procedure—3200), (2) writing the text that has been read (the WRITE-TEXT procedure—3400), and (3) searching for one or more key words or phrases (the PROCESS-KEYWORDS procedure—3600).

The procedure, as designed, utilizes an UNSTRING statement within the key word searching segment. After the text has been read and a key word is available, the identifier TEXT-TABLE is searched. TEXT-TABLE contains all of the text. The delimiter sought in the searching sequence is the key word. To ensure that only the key word (without trailing blanks) is sought, the programmer places the key word in KEY-WORD-TABLE. The DELIMITER IN phrase is used to determine whether or not a key word was found.

Figure 24.6 Key Word in Context (Hierarchy Chart)

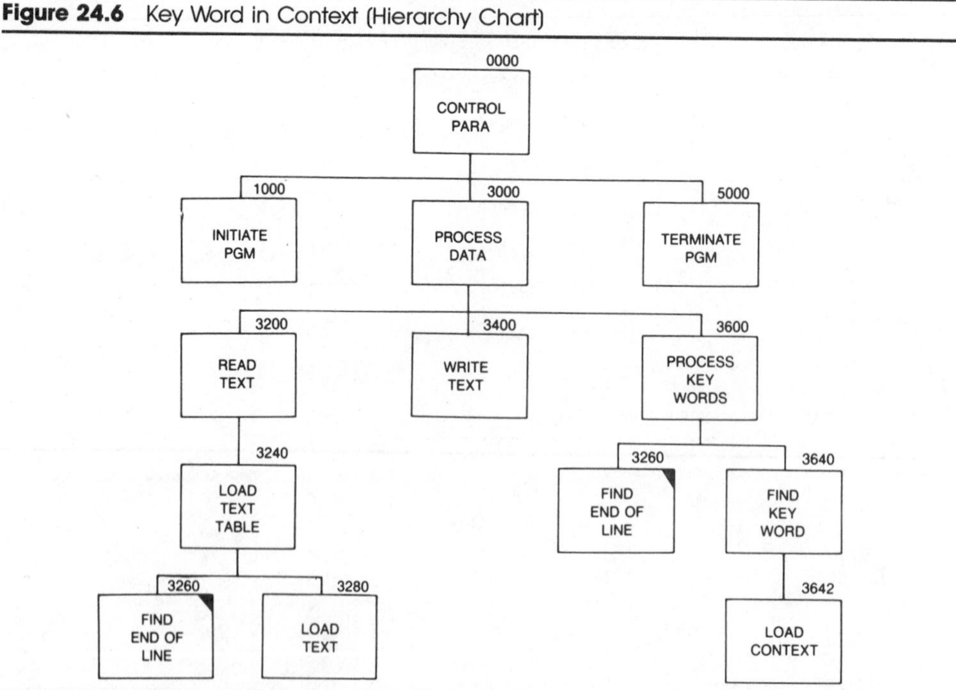

Figure 24.6 *Continued* Key Word in Context (Pseudocode)

```
START
    DO Initiate program
    DO Process data UNTIL eof
    DO Terminate program
END

INITIATE PROGRAM
    OPEN files
    MOVE spaces to tables
    READ input
         AT END set file status
                move * to text
END

PROCESS DATA
    DO Read text UNTIL text = *
    MOVE 0 to orig
    WRITE output
    DO Write text VARYING lctn UNTIL > bload
    IF output table NOT = spaces
         MOVE output table to output
         WRITE output
    ENDIF
    READ input
         AT END set file status
    DO Process key words
         UNTIL text = * OR eof
END
READ TEXT
    DO Load test table
    READ input
         AT END set file status
                move * to text
END

LOAD TEXT TABLE
    SET search status
    DO Find end of line VARYING lctn
         FROM 80 UNTIL lctn < 1
         OR search status = found
    ADD lctn, 1 to load
    MOVE 0 to orig
    DO Text load VARYING lctn
         FROM bload UNTIL lctn > eload
         OR 2500
    ADD 1 to eload
    ADD eload, 1 GIVING bload
END

FIND END OF LINE
    IF input character (lctn) NOT = space
         SET search status
    ENDIF
END

TEXT LOAD
    ADD 1 to orig
    MOVE input character (orig) TO text character (lctn)
END
```

Figure 24.6 *Continued* Key Word in Context (Pseudocode)

```
WRITE TEXT
    IF orig > 80 AND text character (lctn) = space
         MOVE output table to output
         WRITE output
         MOVE 0 to orig
    ENDIF
    ADD 1 to orig
    MOVE text character (lctn) to output character (orig)
END

PROCESS KEY WORDS
    MOVE 1 to bpoint
    MOVE 0 slength, word
    SET search status
    DO Find end of line VARYING lctn
         FROM 80 UNTIL < 1 OR search status = found
    ADD lctn, 1 GIVING wlength
    MOVE key word to table, output
    WRITE output
    DO Find key word UNTIL bpoint > 2500
    SUBTRACT 1 FROM word GIVING words out
    WRITE output
    READ input AT END set file status
END
FIND KEY WORD
    MOVE ? to wcheck
    UNSTRING text table
         DELIMITED by key word table
         INTO output table
         DELIMITER in wcheck
         COUNT in slength
         WITH POINTER bpoint
         TALLYING in word
    MOVE 0 to orig
    MOVE spaces to text, output
    SUBTRACT 40 from bpoint GIVING bload
    ADD bload, 82, wlength GIVING eload
    DO Load context VARYING lctn
         FROM bload UNTIL lctn > eload OR 2500
    MOVE values to output
    IF wcheck NOT = ?
         WRITE output
    ENDIF
    ADD wlength to bpoint
END

LOAD CONTEXT
    ADD 1 to orig
    IF lctn > 0
         MOVE text character (lctn) to output character (orig)
    ELSE
         MOVE space to output character (orig)
    ENDIF
END

TERMINATE PROGRAM
    CLOSE files
END
```

Figure 24.6 *Continued* Key Word in Context

```
        1   1   2   2   2   3   3   4   4   4   5   5   6   6   6   7
4   8   2   6   0   4   8   2   6   0   4   8   2   6   0   4   8   2
***************************************************************
 IDENTIFICATION DIVISION.
***************************************************************
 PROGRAM-ID.    KWIC.
 AUTHOR.        JOHN WINDSOR.
 DATE-WRITTEN.  JANUARY 1, 1989.
 DATE-COMPILED. JANUARY 1, 1989.
***************************************************************
 ENVIRONMENT DIVISION.
***************************************************************
*-------------------------------------------------------------*
 CONFIGURATION SECTION.
*-------------------------------------------------------------*
 SOURCE-COMPUTER.  IBM.
 OBJECT-COMPUTER.  IBM.
 SPECIAL-NAMES.    C01 IS TOP-OF-PAGE.
*-------------------------------------------------------------*
 INPUT-OUTPUT SECTION.
*-------------------------------------------------------------*
 FILE-CONTROL.
     SELECT KEY-WORD-FILE ASSIGN TO UT-S-INPUT.
     SELECT OUTPUT-FILE   ASSIGN TO UT-S-OUTPUT.
***************************************************************
 DATA DIVISION.
***************************************************************
*-------------------------------------------------------------*
 FILE SECTION.
*-------------------------------------------------------------*
 FD  KEY-WORD-FILE LABEL RECORDS ARE OMITTED.
 01  TEXT-RECORD.
     05 INPUT-CHARACTER OCCURS 80 TIMES PIC X(01).
 01  KEY-WORD-RECORD.
     05 KEY-WORD-IN                PIC X(80).
 FD  OUTPUT-FILE LABEL RECORDS ARE OMITTED.
 01  OUTPUT-RECORD.
     05 FILLER                     PIC X(01).
     05 OUTPUT-LINE                PIC X(132).
*-------------------------------------------------------------*
 WORKING-STORAGE SECTION.
*-------------------------------------------------------------*
 01  WORKING-STATUS-VARIABLES.
     05 FILE-STATUS                PIC X(10).
     05 SEARCH-STATUS              PIC X(10).
     05 BEGIN-LOAD                 PIC S9(04) VALUE 1.
     05 END-LOAD                   PIC 9(04)  VALUE 0.
     05 LCTN                       PIC 9(04).
     05 ORIG                       PIC 9(04).
     05 WORDS-FOUND-WS             PIC 9(02).
     05 WORD-CHECK-WS              PIC X(01).
     05 BEGIN-POINT-WS             PIC 9(04).
     05 STRING-LENGTH-WS           PIC 9(04).
     05 WORD-LENGTH-WS             PIC 9(02).
 01  TEXT-TABLE.
     05 TEXT-CHARACTER OCCURS 2500 TIMES PIC X(01).
 01  OUTPUT-TABLE.
     05 OUTPUT-CHARACTER OCCURS 2500 TIMES PIC X(01).
 01  KEY-WORD-TABLE.
     05 KEY-WORD-CHARACTER OCCURS 1 TO 80 TIMES
         DEPENDING ON WORD-LENGTH-WS PIC X(01).
 01  KEY-WORD-LINE.
     05 FILLER                     PIC X(01) VALUE SPACES.
     05 FILLER                     PIC X(22) VALUE
                                   'Search for Key Word:'.
     05 KEY-WORD-OUT               PIC X(80).
```

Figure 24.6 *Continued* Key Word in Context

```
           1   1   2   2   2   3   3   4   4   4   5   5   6   6   6   7
   4   8   2   6   0   4   8   2   6   0   4   8   2   6   0   4   8   2

 01  COUNT-LINE.
     05 FILLER                         PIC X(01) VALUE SPACES.
     05 FILLER                         PIC X(28) VALUE
                                       'Number of Key Words Found:'.
     05 WORDS-FOUND-OUT                     PIC Z9.
*****************************************************************
 PROCEDURE DIVISION.
*****************************************************************
*---------------------------------------------------------------*
 0000-CONTROL SECTION.
*---------------------------------------------------------------*
     PERFORM 1000-INITIATE-PROGRAM.
     PERFORM 3000-PROCESS-DATA
         UNTIL FILE-STATUS = 'DONE'.
     PERFORM 5000-TERMINATE-PROGRAM.
     STOP RUN.
*---------------------------------------------------------------*
 1000-INITIATE-PROGRAM SECTION.
*---------------------------------------------------------------*
     OPEN INPUT KEY-WORD-FILE, OUTPUT OUTPUT-FILE.
     MOVE SPACES                    TO TEXT-TABLE
                                       OUTPUT-TABLE
                                       OUTPUT-RECORD.
     READ KEY-WORD-FILE
         AT END MOVE 'DONE'         TO FILE-STATUS;
             MOVE ALL '*'           TO TEXT-RECORD.
*---------------------------------------------------------------*
 3000-PROCESS-DATA SECTION.
*---------------------------------------------------------------*
     PERFORM 3200-READ-TEXT
         UNTIL TEXT-RECORD = ALL '*'.
     MOVE 0 TO ORIG.
     MOVE 'Text as Read:'           TO OUTPUT-LINE.
     WRITE OUTPUT-RECORD AFTER ADVANCING TOP-OF-PAGE.
     MOVE SPACES                    TO OUTPUT-LINE.
     WRITE OUTPUT-RECORD AFTER ADVANCING 2 LINES.
     PERFORM 3400-WRITE-TEXT
         VARYING LCTN FROM 1 BY 1 UNTIL LCTN > BEGIN-LOAD.
     IF OUTPUT-TABLE NOT = SPACES
         MOVE OUTPUT-TABLE          TO OUTPUT-LINE
         WRITE OUTPUT-RECORD AFTER 1 LINES.
     READ KEY-WORD-FILE
         AT END MOVE 'DONE'         TO FILE-STATUS.
     PERFORM 3600-PROCESS-KEY-WORDS
         UNTIL TEXT-RECORD = ALL '*' OR FILE-STATUS = 'DONE'.
*---------------------------------------------------------------*
 3200-READ-TEXT SECTION.
*---------------------------------------------------------------*
     PERFORM 3240-LOAD-TEXT-TABLE.
     READ KEY-WORD-FILE
         AT END MOVE 'DONE'         TO FILE-STATUS;
             MOVE ALL '*'           TO TEXT-RECORD.
*---------------------------------------------------------------*
 3240-LOAD-TEXT-TABLE SECTION.
*---------------------------------------------------------------*
     MOVE 'LOOKING'                 TO SEARCH-STATUS.
     PERFORM 3260-FIND-END-OF-LINE
         VARYING LCTN FROM 80 BY -1 UNTIL LCTN < 1
         OR SEARCH-STATUS = 'FOUND'.
     ADD LCTN, 1 TO END-LOAD.
     MOVE 0                         TO ORIG.
     PERFORM 3280-TEXT-LOAD
         VARYING LCTN FROM BEGIN-LOAD BY 1 UNTIL LCTN > END-LOAD
         OR 2500.
     ADD 1 TO END-LOAD.
     ADD END-LOAD 1 GIVING BEGIN-LOAD.
*---------------------------------------------------------------*
 3260-FIND-END-OF-LINE SECTION.
*---------------------------------------------------------------*
     IF INPUT-CHARACTER (LCTN) NOT = SPACE
         MOVE 'FOUND'               TO SEARCH-STATUS.
```

Figure 24.6 *Continued* Key Word in Context

```
        1   1   2   2   2   3   3   4   4   4   5   5   6   6   6   7
    4   8   2   6   0   4   8   2   6   0   4   8   2   6   0   4   8   2
-------------------------------------------------------------------------
*---------------------------------------------------------------*
 3280-TEXT-LOAD SECTION.
*---------------------------------------------------------------*
     ADD 1 TO ORIG.
     MOVE INPUT-CHARACTER (ORIG) TO TEXT-CHARACTER (LCTN).
*---------------------------------------------------------------*
 3400-WRITE-TEXT SECTION.
*---------------------------------------------------------------*
     IF ORIG > 80 AND TEXT-CHARACTER (LCTN) = SPACE
         MOVE OUTPUT-TABLE       TO OUTPUT-LINE
         WRITE OUTPUT-RECORD AFTER 1 LINES
         MOVE SPACES             TO OUTPUT-TABLE
         MOVE 0                  TO ORIG.
     ADD 1 TO ORIG.
     MOVE TEXT-CHARACTER (LCTN) TO OUTPUT-CHARACTER (ORIG).
*---------------------------------------------------------------*
 3600-PROCESS-KEY-WORDS SECTION.
*---------------------------------------------------------------*
     MOVE 1                      TO BEGIN-POINT-WS.
     MOVE 0                      TO STRING-LENGTH-WS
                                    WORDS-FOUND-WS.
     MOVE 'SEARCH'               TO SEARCH-STATUS.
     PERFORM 3260-FIND-END-OF-LINE
         VARYING LCTN FROM 80 BY -1 UNTIL
           SEARCH-STATUS = 'FOUND' OR LCTN < 1.
     ADD LCTN, 1 GIVING WORD-LENGTH-WS.
     MOVE KEY-WORD-IN            TO KEY-WORD-TABLE
                                    KEY-WORD-OUT.
     WRITE OUTPUT-RECORD FROM KEY-WORD-LINE
         AFTER ADVANCING TOP-OF-PAGE.
     MOVE SPACES                 TO OUTPUT-LINE.
     WRITE OUTPUT-RECORD AFTER ADVANCING 2 LINES.
     PERFORM 3640-FIND-KEY-WORD
         UNTIL BEGIN-POINT-WS > 2500.
     SUBTRACT 1 FROM WORDS-FOUND-WS GIVING WORDS-FOUND-OUT.
     WRITE OUTPUT-RECORD FROM COUNT-LINE AFTER 4 LINES.
     READ KEY-WORD-FILE
         AT END MOVE 'DONE' TO FILE-STATUS.
*---------------------------------------------------------------*
 3640-FIND-KEY-WORD SECTION.
*---------------------------------------------------------------*
     MOVE '?'                    TO WORD-CHECK-WS.
     UNSTRING TEXT-TABLE
         DELIMITED BY KEY-WORD-TABLE
         INTO OUTPUT-TABLE
         DELIMITER IN WORD-CHECK-WS
         COUNT IN STRING-LENGTH-WS
         WITH POINTER BEGIN-POINT-WS
         TALLYING IN WORDS-FOUND-WS.
     MOVE 0                      TO ORIG.
     MOVE SPACES                 TO TEXT-RECORD
                                    OUTPUT-TABLE.
     SUBTRACT 40 FROM BEGIN-POINT-WS GIVING BEGIN-LOAD.
     ADD BEGIN-LOAD, 82, WORD-LENGTH-WS GIVING END-LOAD.
     PERFORM 3642-LOAD-CONTEXT
         VARYING LCTN FROM BEGIN-LOAD BY 1
         UNTIL LCTN > END-LOAD OR 2500.
     MOVE OUTPUT-TABLE           TO OUTPUT-LINE.
     IF WORD-CHECK-WS NOT = '?'
         WRITE OUTPUT-RECORD AFTER ADVANCING 2 LINES.
     ADD WORD-LENGTH-WS TO BEGIN-POINT-WS.
*---------------------------------------------------------------*
 3642-LOAD-CONTEXT SECTION.
*---------------------------------------------------------------*
     ADD 1 TO ORIG.
     IF LCTN > 0
         MOVE TEXT-CHARACTER (LCTN) TO OUTPUT-CHARACTER (ORIG)
     ELSE
         MOVE SPACE              TO OUTPUT-CHARACTER (ORIG).
*---------------------------------------------------------------*
 5000-TERMINATE-PROGRAM SECTION.
*---------------------------------------------------------------*
     CLOSE KEY-WORD-FILE, OUTPUT-FILE.
```

Figure 24.6 *Continued* Key Word in Context (Data)

```
-------------------------------------------------------------------------------------------
|      |         1         2         3         4         5         6         7         8|
|Record|12345678901234567890123456789012345678901234567890123456789012345678901234567890|
|-----------------------------------------------------------------------------------------|
|     1|"Any organization interested in reproducing the COBOL report and specifications |
|     2|in whole or in part, using ideas taken from this report as a basis for an       |
|     3|instruction manual or for any other purpose is free to do so.  However, all     |
|     4|such organizations are requested to reproduce this section as part of the       |
|     5|introduction to the document.  Those using a short passage, as in a book review,|
|     6|are requested to mention 'COBOL' in acknowledgement of the source, but need not |
|     7|quote this entire section.  COBOL is an industry language and is not the        |
|     8|property of any company or group of companies, or of any organization or group  |
|     9|of organizations.  No warranty, expressed or implied, is made by any contributor|
|    10|or by the COBOL committee as to the accuracy and functioning of the programming |
|    11|system and language.  Moreover, no responsibility is assumed by any contributor,|
|    12|or by the committee, in connection therewith.  Procedures have been established |
|    13|for the maintenance of COBOL.  Inquiries concerning the procedures for proposed |
|    14|changes should be directed to the executive committee of the Conference on Data |
|    15|System Languages.                                                               |
|    16|********************************************************************************|
|    17|COBOL                                                                           |
|    18|report                                                                          |
|    19|procedures                                                                      |
|    20|committee                                                                       |
|    21|language                                                                        |
-------------------------------------------------------------------------------------------
```

Figure 24.6 *Continued* Key Word in Context (Output)

```
"Any organization interested in reproducing the COBOL report and specifications in
 whole or in part, using ideas taken from this report as a basis for an instruction
 manual or for any other purpose is free to do so.  However, all such organizations
 are requested to reproduce this section as part of the introduction to the document.
  Those using a short passage, as in a book review, are requested to mention 'COBOL'
 in acknowledgement of the source, but need not quote this entire section.  COBOL
 is an industry language and is not the property of any company or group of companies,
 or of any organization or group of organizations.  No warranty, expressed or implied,
 is made by any contributor or by the COBOL committee as to the accuracy and functioning
 of the programming system and language.  Moreover, no responsibility is assumed by
 any contributor, or by the committee, in connection therewith.  Procedures have been
 established for the maintenance of COBOL.  Inquiries concerning the procedures for
 proposed changes should be directed to the executive committee of the Conference
 on Data System Languages.
```

Figure 24.6 *Continued* Key Word in Context (Output)

```
tion interested in reproducing the COBOL report and specifications in whole or in part,

 review, are requested to mention 'COBOL' in acknowledgement of the source, but need not

ed not quote this entire section.  COBOL is an industry language and is not the property

 made by any contributor or by the COBOL committee as to the accuracy and functioning of

established for the maintenance of COBOL.  Inquiries concerning the procedures for propo



Number of Key Words Found:   5
```

Figure 24.6 *Continued* Key Word in Context (Output)

```
Search for Key Word:  report


terested in reproducing the COBOL report and specifications in whole or in part, using id

part, using ideas taken from this report as a basis for an instruction manual or for any



Number of Key Words Found:   2
```

Figure 24.6 *Continued* Key Word in Context (Output)

```
Search for Key Word:  procedures


OL.  Inquiries concerning the procedures for proposed changes should be directed to the execu



Number of Key Words Found:   1
```

Figure 24.6 *Continued* Key Word in Context (Output)

```
Search for Key Word:  committee


ny contributor or by the COBOL committee as to the accuracy and functioning of the programmi

 by any contributor, or by the committee, in connection therewith.  Procedures have been est

d be directed to the executive committee of the Conference on Data System Languages.



Number of Key Words Found:   3
```

Figure 24.6 *Continued* Key Word in Context (Output)

```
Search for Key Word:  language


 section.  COBOL is an industry language and is not the property of any company or group of

g of the programming system and language.  Moreover, no responsibility is assumed by any co



Number of Key Words Found:   2
```

When WORD-CHECK-WS contains the question mark symbol after searching, a key word *has not* been found. The STRING-LENGTH-WS identifier is used to determine the number of characters that precede the key word, and the BEGIN-POINT-WS identifier establishes where searching is to begin. (If BEGIN-POINT-WS were not used, searching would always begin at the beginning of the string—the first character—and the same key word would repetitively be found.) The number of times the key word is found is determined by using the TALLYING phrase to increment WORDS-FOUND-WS each time the UNSTRING activity is attempted.

The INSPECT Statement

The INSPECT statement allows the programmer to scrutinize the contents of a data item with the possible aim of counting the number of occurrences of specific characters, replacing occurrences of certain characters with other characters, or both. The purpose of the INSPECT statement is to interrogate the contents of a data field.

The formats of the INSPECT statement, shown in Figure 24.7, are among the most complex in the COBOL language because of the number of options available to the

Figure 24.7 Formats of the INSPECT Statement

```
Format 1:

    INSPECT identifier-1 TALLYING

        {identifier-2 FOR {{{ALL    } {identifier-3}}
                           { {LEADING} {literal-1   }}
                           { CHARACTERS              }

            [{BEFORE} INITIAL {identifier-4}]} . . . } . . .
            [{AFTER }         {literal-2   }]

Format 2:

    INSPECT identifier-1 REPLACING

        { CHARACTERS BY {identifier-6} [{BEFORE} INITIAL {identifier-7}]
        {               {literal-4   } [{AFTER }         {literal-5   }]
        {
        {    {ALL    } {{identifier-5} BY {identifier-6}
        {    {LEADING} {{literal-3   }    {literal-4   }
        {    {FIRST  }
                                                           } . . . } . . .
            [{BEFORE} INITIAL {identifier-7}]}
            [{AFTER }         {literal-5   }]}

Format 3:

    INSPECT identifier-1 TALLYING

        {identifier-2 FOR {{{ALL    } {identifier-3}}
                           { {LEADING} {literal-1   }}
                           { CHARACTERS              }

            [{BEFORE} INITIAL {identifier-4}]} . . . } . . .
            [{AFTER }         {literal-2   }]

    REPLACING

        { CHARACTERS BY {identifier-6} [{BEFORE} INITIAL {identifier-4}]
        {               {literal-4   } [{AFTER }         {literal-2   }]
        { {
        { {  {ALL    } {{identifier-5} BY {identifier-6}
        { {  {LEADING} {{literal-3   }    {literal-4   }
        { {  {FIRST  }

            [{BEFORE} INITIAL {identifier-7}]}   . . . } . . . }
            [{AFTER }         {literal-5   }]}

Format 4:
INSPECT identifier-1 CONVERTING {identifier-2} TO {identifier-3}
                                {identifier-1}    {identifier-2}

  [{BEFORE} INITIAL {identifier-4}]  . . .
  [{AFTER }         {identifier-3}]
```

programmer. The three forms of the INSPECT statement are INSPECT TALLYING, INSPECT REPLACING, and INSPECT TALLYING/REPLACING. The function of the TALLYING option is to count the occurrences of specific types of characters in a data item (identifier-1). Identifier-1 in all three options of the INSPECT statement must be either an elementary-item or a group-name that appears in DISPLAY (USAGE IS DISPLAY) form. Identifier-2 (of formats 1 and 2) contains a count of the number of characters for which the tally is to be taken. The identifier must be defined as a numeric elementary-item. Identifier-2 is not initialized by the INSPECT statement; it is the programmer's responsibility to provide the initial value for identifier-2. All remaining identifiers (and literals) in the INSPECT statement (format 1) must be single-character fields (or single-character nonnumeric literals or figurative constants except ALL). The identifiers must be elementary data items.

The format 1 INSPECT statement permits the programmer to select between two types of tallying operations. The first option provides for the tallying of either ALL or LEADING occurrences of the character indicated by identifier-3 (literal-1). Using the reserved word ALL, the programmer counts all of the characters within the specified portion of identifier-1. When LEADING is indicated, only the leading characters within the specified portion of identifier-1 are tallied. (If either ALL or LEADING is specified, identifier-3 or literal-1 must be specified.) When using the second option by selecting the reserved word CHARACTERS in this position, *any* character that falls within the specified portion of identifier-1 is counted. The count is performed by examining the characters contained in identifier-1 one at a time. If the specified character is located, the counter (identifier-2) is incremented by one.

The final option of the format 1 INSPECT statement allows the programmer to indicate the character position within identifier-1 at which the inspection is to begin. For example, the programmer may specify that scanning of identifier-1 is to end BEFORE the first occurrence of identifier-4 (literal-2). If the BEFORE/AFTER option is omitted, the entire field is examined for the character indicated in the ALL/LEADING or CHARACTERS option.

Format 2 of the INSPECT statement is the REPLACING option. Its primary function is to locate specific characters in identifier-1 and replace them with characters indicated by one of the options. With the CHARACTERS BY option, the INSPECT statement will replace any character that appears in identifier-1 (within the specified range) with identifier-6 (literal-4). As with the TALLYING option of the INSPECT statement, all identifiers (except identifier-1) must be single-character elementary data items. Literals must be single-character nonnumeric literal or figurative constants (except ALL). The REPLACING option is also similar to the TALLYING option in that the programmer can specify a beginning or ending point for scanning by indicating the BEFORE or AFTER option. An alternative to the CHARACTERS BY option allows the programmer to select a specific character for replacement using the reserved word ALL, LEADING, or FIRST. As with the TALLYING option, the reserved word ALL causes the replacement of all the identifier-5 (literal-3) character *BY* identifier-6 (literal-4) characters. The reserved word LEADING has the same connotation as in the TALLYING option; namely, that the specified characters are replaced and not counted. The optional BEFORE/AFTER phrase, used to indicate beginning or ending points of the scanning operations, is also available with this form of the REPLACING option.

Format 2 of the INSPECT statement is simply a combination of formats 1 and 2. Format 3 permits a programmer both to count and replace specific characters in identifier-1. The rules that apply to the identifiers specified in formats 1 and 2 also apply to the format 3 INSPECT statement. It is possible to count characters of one type while replacing other characters. The final format of the INSPECT statement is designed to handle a special case of format 2. If the programmer wants to replace a string of characters, the REPLACE clause would have to be repeated for each character to be replaced. The CONVERT clause allows the programmer to replace a string of characters with another string. The rules that apply to the identifiers in format 2 also apply to the format 4 INSPECT statement.

1985 COBOL Standards

Using the INSPECT Statement

Examples of the three versions of the INSPECT statement are presented in Figure 24.8.

The INSPECT statement is especially useful because it allows the programmer to interrogate data fields that might cause an error. Recall from Chapter 10 that a numeric data item is not permitted to contain blanks. If the processing of this data item had included an arithmetic manipulation, the program would have encountered a fatal error resulting in an abnormal termination. However, if the programmer suspects that one or more of the numeric data fields may contain blanks, he or she can resolve the problem by inspecting those fields and replacing all occurrences of blanks with zeros. Figure 24.9 illustrates the procedure for STUDENT-ID-IN. When the STUDENT-ID-IN for Rose Franklin is encountered, the INSPECT statement will encounter blanks and will convert blanks to zeros.

Figure 24.8 Examples of the INSPECT Statement

INSPECT Statement Illustration	Contents of TEST-FIELD* Before	Contents of TEST-FIELD* After	Result in CHAR-COUNT**
INSPECT TEST-FIELD TALLYING CHAR-COUNT FOR ALL SPACES.	P.ƀ0.ƀBOXƀ	P.ƀ0.ƀBOXƀ	3
INSPECT TEST-FIELD TALLYING CHAR-COUNT FOR LEADING ZEROS.	ØØ14Ø37ØØ	ØØ14Ø37ØØ	2
INSPECT TEST-FIELD TALLYING CHAR-COUNT FOR ALL 'X' AFTER SPACE.	AXBXƀNXXDX	AXBXƀNXXDX	3
INSPECT TEST-FIELD TALLYING CHAR-COUNT FOR LEADING SPACES BEFORE 'X'	1ƀ3ƀ3ƀXƀ4ƀ	1ƀ3ƀ3ƀXƀ4ƀ	1
INSPECT TEST-FIELD TALLYING CHAR-COUNT FOR CHARACTERS.	P.ƀ0.ƀBOXƀ	P.ƀ0.ƀBOXƀ	7
INSPECT TEST-FIELD REPLACING CHARACTERS BY ZERO.	1ƀ3ƀ3ƀXƀ4ƀ	1ƀ3ƀ3ƀØƀ4ƀ	-
INSPECT TEST-FIELD REPLACING CHARACTERS BY 'X' AFTER SPACE.	P.ƀ0.ƀBOXƀ	P.ƀXXƀXXXƀ	-
INSPECT TEST-FIELD REPLACING ALL SPACES BY ZERO.	ƀƀ14Ø37ƀƀ	ØØ14Ø37ØØ	-
INSPECT TEST-FIELD REPLACING LEADING 'A' BY 'B'.	AAAABBBAA	BBBBBBBAA	-
INSPECT TEST-FIELD REPLACING FIRST '1' BY 'X'.	ƀ5Aƀ115	ƀ5AƀX15	-
INSPECT TEST-FIELD REPLACING ALL SPACES BY 'Ø' AFTER 'X'.	Pƀ0ƀBOXƀ5ƀ	Pƀ0ƀBOXØ5Ø	-
INSPECT TEST-FIELD TALLYING CHAR-COUNT FOR ALL SPACES REPLACING CHARACTERS BY ZERO.	ƀƀ14Ø37Øƀƀ	ƀƀØØØØØØƀƀ	4
INSPECT TEST-FIELD TALLYING CHAR-COUNT FOR LEADING ZEROS REPLACING LEADING ZEROS BY SPACES.	ØØØ12Ø34Ø	ƀƀƀ12Ø34Ø	3
INSPECT TEST-FIELD TALLYING CHAR-COUNT FOR CHARACTERS REPLACING ALL 'A' BY 'B' LEADING SPACES BY ZERO AFTER 'B'.	ƀƀAABBAAƀ	ƀƀBBBBBBØ	6

* The character ƀ indicates the location of blanks in the TEST-FIELD data item contents.
**CHAR-COUNT is assumed to be initialized to zero before the execution of each INSPECT Statement.

Figure 24.9 An Illustration of the INSPECT Statement

```
            1   1   2   2   2   3   3   4   4   4   5   5   6   6   6   7
    4   8   2   6   0   4   8   2   6   0   4   8   2   6   0   4   8   2

      *****************************************************************
       IDENTIFICATION DIVISION.
      *****************************************************************
       PROGRAM-ID.     EXAMPLE-INSPECT.
       AUTHOR.         CARI DIANE SPENCE.
       DATE-WRITTEN.  JANUARY 1, 1989.
       DATE-COMPILED. JANUARY 1, 1989.
      *    This program demonstrates the use of an INSPECT
      *    statement to modify incorrectly coded numeric data.
      *****************************************************************
       ENVIRONMENT DIVISION.
      *****************************************************************
      *---------------------------------------------------------------*
       CONFIGURATION SECTION.
      *---------------------------------------------------------------*
       SOURCE-COMPUTER. IBM.
       OBJECT-COMPUTER. IBM.
       SPECIAL-NAMES.   C01 IS TOP-OF-NEXT-PAGE.
      *---------------------------------------------------------------*
       INPUT-OUTPUT SECTION.
      *---------------------------------------------------------------*
       FILE-CONTROL.
           SELECT STUDENT-FILE ASSIGN TO UT-S-INPUT.
           SELECT REPORT-FILE  ASSIGN TO UT-S-OUTPUT.
      *****************************************************************
       DATA DIVISION.
      *****************************************************************
      *---------------------------------------------------------------*
       FILE SECTION.
      *---------------------------------------------------------------*
       FD  STUDENT-FILE LABEL RECORDS ARE OMITTED.
       01  STUDENT-RECORD.
           05 STUDENT-IDENTIFICATION-IN.
               10 LAST-NAME-IN               PIC X(10).
               10 FIRST-NAME-IN              PIC X(10).
               10 MIDDLE-INITIAL-IN          PIC X(01).
               10 STUDENT-ID-IN              PIC 9(09).
           05 FILLER                         PIC X(05).
           05 ENROLLMENT-INFO-IN.
               10 CLASSIFICATION-IN          PIC X(02).
               10 TOTAL-HOURS-IN             PIC 9(03).
               10 HOURS-THIS-SEM-IN          PIC 9(02).
               10 MAJOR-IN                   PIC X(03).
           05  FILLER                        PIC X(35).

       FD  REPORT-FILE LABEL RECORDS ARE OMITTED.
       01  REPORT-RECORD                     PIC X(133).
      *---------------------------------------------------------------*
       WORKING-STORAGE SECTION.
      *---------------------------------------------------------------*
       01  WORKING-VARIABLES.
           05  FILE-STATUS                   PIC X(04).

       01  OUTPUT-RECORD.
           05 FILLER                         PIC X(03) VALUE ' *'.
           05 FIRST-NAME-OUT                 PIC X(11).
           05 MIDDLE-INITIAL-OUT             PIC X(01).
           05 FILLER                         PIC X(02) VALUE '.'.
           05 LAST-NAME-OUT                  PIC X(10).
           05 FILLER                         PIC X(04) VALUE ' *'.
           05 STUDENT-ID-OUT                 PIC 9(09).
           05 FILLER                         PIC X(05) VALUE '  *'.
           05 CLASSIFICATION-OUT             PIC X(02).
           05 FILLER                         PIC X(06) VALUE '   *'.
           05 MAJOR-OUT                      PIC X(03).
           05 FILLER                         PIC X(08) VALUE '  *'.
           05 HOURS-THIS-SEM-OUT             PIC 9(02).
           05 FILLER                         PIC X(08) VALUE '     *'.
           05 TOTAL-HOURS-OUT                PIC 9(03).
```

Figure 24.9 An Illustration of the INSPECT Statement

```
-------------------------------------------------------------------------------
|             1    1    2    2    2    3    3    4    4    4    5    5    6    6    6    7|
|   4    8    2    6    0    4    8    2    6    0    4    8    2    6    0    4    8    2|
|-------------------------------------------------------------------------------|
| 700        05 FILLER                       PIC X(03) VALUE '  *'.                      |
| 710  ***************************************************************                  |
| 720   PROCEDURE DIVISION.                                                              |
| 730  ***************************************************************                  |
| 740  *-------------------------------------------------------------*                  |
| 750   000-CONTROL-PROCEDURE SECTION.                                                   |
| 760  *-------------------------------------------------------------*                  |
| 770       PERFORM 100-INITIALIZATION.                                                  |
| 780       PERFORM 300-READ-RECORDS-PRINT-DETAILS                                       |
| 790           UNTIL FILE-STATUS = 'DONE'.                                              |
| 800       PERFORM 500-TERMINATION.                                                     |
| 810       STOP RUN.                                                                   |
| 820  *-------------------------------------------------------------*                  |
| 830   100-INITIALIZATION SECTION.                                                      |
| 840  *-------------------------------------------------------------*                  |
| 850       MOVE 'START'                 TO FILE-STATUS.                                 |
| 860       OPEN INPUT STUDENT-FILE, OUTPUT REPORT-FILE.                                 |
| 870       READ STUDENT-FILE                                                           |
| 880           AT END MOVE 'DONE'       TO FILE-STATUS.                                 |
| 890  *-------------------------------------------------------------*                  |
| 900   300-READ-RECORDS-PRINT-DETAILS SECTION.                                          |
| 910  *-------------------------------------------------------------*                  |
| 920       INSPECT STUDENT-ID-IN REPLACING ALL ' ' BY '0'.                              |
| 930                                                                                   |
| 940       MOVE STUDENT-ID-IN           TO STUDENT-ID-OUT.                              |
| 950       MOVE LAST-NAME-IN            TO LAST-NAME-OUT.                               |
| 960       MOVE FIRST-NAME-IN           TO FIRST-NAME-OUT.                              |
| 970       MOVE MIDDLE-INITIAL-IN       TO MIDDLE-INITIAL-OUT.                          |
| 980       MOVE CLASSIFICATION-IN       TO CLASSIFICATION-OUT.                          |
| 990       MOVE TOTAL-HOURS-IN          TO TOTAL-HOURS-OUT.                             |
|1000       MOVE HOURS-THIS-SEM-IN       TO HOURS-THIS-SEM-OUT.                          |
|1010       MOVE MAJOR-IN                TO MAJOR-OUT.                                   |
|1020       WRITE REPORT-RECORD FROM OUTPUT-RECORD AFTER 2 LINES.                        |
|1030       READ STUDENT-FILE                                                           |
|1040           AT END MOVE 'DONE'       TO FILE-STATUS.                                 |
|1050  *-------------------------------------------------------------*                  |
|1060   500-TERMINATION SECTION.                                                         |
|1070  *-------------------------------------------------------------*                  |
|1080       CLOSE STUDENT-FILE, REPORT-FILE.                                             |
-------------------------------------------------------------------------------
```

Figure 24.9 *Continued* An Illustration of the EXAMINE Statement (Data)

```
------------------------------------------------------------
|      |         1         2         3         4         5|
|Record|12345678901234567890123456789012345678901234567890|
|----------------------------------------------------------|
|     1|Anderson  Jimmy     Q343564321     Gr21900Csc      |
|     2|Booker    John      A555667777     Fr03515Mgt      |
|     3|Carter    Matt      N456789012     Jr09408Mgt      |
|     4|Davidson  Anthony   R353492761     Sr13816Eco      |
|     5|Eldridge  David     Q376495268     So04712Fin      |
|     6|Franklin  Rose      V        1     Gr18912Gbu      |
|     7|Garrison  Kenneth   A537903251     So02816Mgt      |
|     8|Hamilton  Mark      C486762389     Jr09618Csc      |
|     9|Issacs    Matt      H474653790     Sr12018Eco      |
|    10|Jefferson Harold    Q502326955     Fr01818Mkt      |
|    11|Kennedy   Floyd     R476329092     Jr06012Mkt      |
|    12|Lincoln   Steven    0442648942     So04515Mkt      |
|    13|Monroe    Jeff      V546677219     Sr09918Csc      |
------------------------------------------------------------
```

Figure 24.9 An Illustration of the INSPECT Statement (Output)

```
| Jimmy     Q. Anderson  | 343564321 | Gr | Csc |   00   | 219 |
| John      A. Booker    | 555667777 | Fr | Mgt |   15   | 035 |
| Matt      N. Carter    | 456789012 | Jr | Mgt |   08   | 094 |
| Anthony   R. Davidson  | 353492761 | Sr | Eco |   16   | 138 |
| David     Q. Eldridge  | 376495268 | So | Fin |   12   | 047 |
| Rose      V. Franklin  | 000000001 | Gr | Gbu |   12   | 189 |
| Kenneth   A. Garrison  | 537903251 | So | Mgt |   16   | 028 |
| Mark      C. Hamilton  | 486762389 | Jr | Csc |   18   | 096 |
| Matt      H. Issacs    | 474653790 | Sr | Eco |   18   | 120 |
| Harold    Q. Jefferson | 502326955 | Fr | Mkt |   18   | 018 |
| Floyd     R. Kennedy   | 476329092 | Jr | Mkt |   12   | 060 |
| Steven    O. Lincoln   | 442648942 | So | Mkt |   15   | 045 |
```

The EXAMINE, TRANSFORM and INITIALIZE Statements

Some computer manufacturers do not include the INSPECT statement in their ANS COBOL compilers. Those compilers that do not contain the INSPECT statement often support the EXAMINE or the TRANSFORM statement. Older versions of IBM COBOL compilers do not contain the INSPECT statement, but they do contain both the EXAMINE and the TRANSFORM statements. (A few compilers, including newer IBM compilers, that contain the INSPECT statement also permit the use of the EXAMINE statement.)

Both statements are intended as a substitute for the INSPECT statement. The EXAMINE statement, shown in Figure 24.10, has two formats. The first format is similar to the format 3 INSPECT statement—it is capable of both TALLYING and REPLACING characters that appear in an identifier. As with the INSPECT statement, the identifier that appears immediately after the reserved word EXAMINE must be described as a DISPLAY elementary-item or group. No other identifiers appear in the formats of the EXAMINE statement. The first format of the statement can count the occurrences of the specified character (literal-1). Compilers that support the EXAMINE statement provide a *special register* called TALLY. TALLY is implicitly defined by the compiler as being a numeric data item that may contain up to a five-digit integer number. When the TALLYING form of the EXAMINE statement is used, the value of TALLY is automatically set to zero before each execution of the statement. The character count contained in TALLY may then be used as an internal data-name in other COBOL statements.

The EXAMINE statement is also similar to the INSPECT statement in that it permits an inspection of a data field as dictated by the reserved words ALL and LEADING, and a procedure for scanning the data field is provided with the reserved words UNTIL FIRST. As with the INSPECT statement, when ALL is specified, every occurrence of literal-1 is counted (in TALLY) and replaced with the character specified by literal-2.

Figure 24.10 Formats of the EXAMINE Statement (Non-ANS Standard)

```
Format 1:

                                      {UNTIL FIRST}
     EXAMINE identifier TALLYING      {ALL        }   literal-1
                                      {LEADING    }

          [REPLACING BY literal-2]

- - - - - - - - - - - - - - - - - - - - - - - - - - - - - - - - - -
Format 2:

                                      {ALL        }
                                      {LEADING    }
     EXAMINE identifier REPLACING     {FIRST      }  literal-1 BY literal-2
                                      {UNTIL FIRST}
```

(Both literal-1 and literal-2 must be single-character nonnumeric literals or a figurative constant, except ALL.) When LEADING is chosen, the leading characters are indicated as an uninterrupted string of the literal-1 character, beginning with the leftmost character in the field. The first nonliteral-1 character found in the data field terminates the EXAMINE statement. With UNTIL FIRST, the character string to be inspected by the EXAMINE statement is that string of characters (from left to right) which is terminated by the first occurrence of the literal-1 character.

Format 2 of the EXAMINE statement is similar to the format 2 INSPECT statement. The purpose of this form is to locate the occurrence(s) of literal-1 and replace it (them) with the literal-2 character. Like format 1 of the EXAMINE statement, format 2 utilizes the reserved words ALL, LEADING, and UNTIL FIRST to control the character scanning operation. These words have the same meaning in format 2 as they have in format 1. However, like format 2 of the INSPECT statement, format 2 of the EXAMINE statement also permits the use of the reserved word FIRST. The use of FIRST allows only a single replacement of literal-1 *BY* literal-2. That is, only the first occurrence of literal-1 in the identifier is replaced by literal-2.

Another non-ANS COBOL statement, the TRANSFORM statement, performs some of the same functions as the INSPECT statement. The format of the TRANSFORM statement is presented in Figure 24.11. As with the identifier being INSPECTed or EXAMINEd, identifier-3 of the TRANSFORM statement must be an elementary data

Figure 24.11 Format of the TRANSFORM Statement (Non-ANS Standard)

```
                                                {figurative-constant-1 }
     TRANSFORM identifier-3 CHARACTERS FROM     {non-numeric-literal-1 }
                                                {identifier-1          }
                {figurative-constant-2}
          TO    {non-numeric-literal-2}
                {identifier-2         }
```

item or a group-name that is described in DISPLAY form. The essence of the TRANSFORM statement is like that of the INSPECT REPLACING or the EXAMINE REPLACING. The character(s) represented by figurative-constant-1, nonnumeric-literal-1, or identifier-1 are replaced by the character(s) represented by figurative-constant-2, nonnumeric-literal-2, or identifier-2. However there is a major difference in the description of identifier-1 (literal-1) and identifier-2 (literal-2). These identifiers (and literals) may be composed of one *or more* characters. The identifier must still be described as an elementary data item in DISPLAY form.

When identifier-1 (or literal-1) is used, identifier-2 (or literal-2) must be the same length as identifier-1 (or literal-1) or a single character. Figurative constants in either position are treated as a single character. In this case, every occurrence of the first item in the characters of identifier-3 is replaced by the second item. If the first item is longer than one character and the second item is a single character, any character that appears in both identifier-3 and the first item is replaced by the second item (character). When the first item and second item are both longer than one character, both items (regardless of their type) must be the same length. During the inspection of identifier-3, any occurrence of the first character of the first item is replaced by the first character of the second item; the second character in the first item is replaced by the second character of the second item, and so forth. Thus, the replacement of characters is performed character by character (or character *for* character) for the first item and the second item.

Figure 24.12 illustrates both the EXAMINE statement and the TRANSFORM statement. Many of the examples presented in the illustration are similar to those included in Figure 24.10 (examples of the INSPECT Statement).

Figure 24.12 Examples of the EXAMINE and TRANSFORM Statements

EXAMINE and TRANSFORM Statement Illustrations	Contents of TEST-FIELD*		Results in TALLY**
	Before	After	
EXAMINE TEST-FIELD TALLYING ALL SPACES.	P.ƀ0.ƀBOXƀ	P.ƀ0.ƀBOXƀ	3
EXAMINE TEST-FIELD TALLYING LEADING ZEROS.	ØØ14Ø37ØØ	ØØ14Ø37ØØ	2
EXAMINE TEST-FIELD TALLYING ALL 'X'.	AXBXƀNXXDX	AXBXƀNXXDX	5
EXAMINE TEST-FIELD TALLYING UNTIL FIRST 'X'.	P.ƀ0.ƀBOXƀ	P.ƀ0.ƀBOXƀ	8
EXAMINE TEST-FIELD REPLACING ALL SPACES BY ZERO. or TRANSFORM TEST-FIELD FROM SPACES TO ZERO.	ƀƀ14Ø37ƀƀ	ØØ14Ø37ØØ	-
EXAMINE TEST-FIELD REPLACING LEADING 'A' BY 'B'.	AAAABBBAA	BBBBBBBAA	-
EXAMINE TEST-FIELD REPLACING FIRST '1' BY 'X'.	ƀ5Aƀ115	ƀ5AƀX15	-
EXAMINE TEST-FIELD REPLACING UNTIL FIRST 'X' BY 'Ø'.	P.ƀ0.ƀBOXƀ	ØØØØØØØØXƀ	-
EXAMINE TEST-FIELD TALLYING ALL SPACES REPLACING BY ZERO.	ƀƀ14Ø37Øƀƀ	ØØ14Ø37ØØØ	4
EXAMINE TEST-FIELD TALLYING LEADING ZEROS REPLACING BY SPACES.	ØØØ12Ø34Ø	ƀƀƀ12Ø34Ø	3
TRANSFORM TEST-FIELD FROM 'X' TO 'Ø'.	AXBXƀNXXDX	AØBØƀNØØDØ	-
TRANSFORM TEST-FIELD FROM 'ABC' TO '123'.	AABACADABA	112131D121	-
TRANSFORM TEST-FIELD FROM 'ABC' TO 'BCD'.	AABACADABA	DDDDDDDDDD	-
TRANSFORM TEST-FIELD FROM 'Ø123456789' TO SPACE.	ƀƀ14Ø37Øƀƀ	ƀƀƀƀƀƀƀƀƀƀ	-

* The character ƀ indicates the location of blanks in the contents of TEST-FIELD.
**TALLY is automatically initialized to zero before the execution of each EXAMINE statement.

Using the EXAMINE Statement

Figure 24.13 illustrates the use of an EXAMINE statement. Recall that in Figure 24.9, an INSPECT statement was used to scan the characters in STUDENT-ID-IN and replace any occurrence of a blank with a zero. Line 920 of Figure 24.13 performs the same conversion process, except an EXAMINE statement has been substituted for the INSPECT statement. In Chapter 6 the DATA DIVISION was introduced. At that time it was recommended that fields identified in the WORKING-STORAGE SECTION be initialized using the VALUE clause. If this does not match the standards for your installation, COBOL 85 provides the INITIALIZE statement. The general form of the INITIALIZE statement is presented in Figure 24.14. In its simplest form, without the REPLACING clause, numeric items will be initialized at zero, and nonnumeric items will be initialized with spaces. The REPLACING clause allows the programmer to specify the type of field to be initialized and the value (identifier-2 or literal) to be used for initialization. Under this option the field being initialized and identifier-2 must be the same size. Finally, the INITIALIZE clause may be used to initialize any or all elementary items within a group.

1985 COBOL Standards

Figure 24.13 An Illustration of the EXAMINE Statement

```
              1   1   2   2   2   3   3   4   4   4   5   5   6   6   6   7
      4   8   2   6   0   4   8   2   6   0   4   8   2   6   0   4   8   2

  10    ******************************************************************
  20     IDENTIFICATION DIVISION.
  30    ******************************************************************
  40     PROGRAM-ID.      EXAMPLE-EXAMINE.
  50     AUTHOR.          LAURA WINDSOR.
  60     DATE-WRITTEN.    JANUARY 1, 1989.
  70     DATE-COMPILED.   JANUARY 1, 1989.
  80    *     This program demonstrates the use of an EXAMINE
  90    *     statement to modify incorrectly coded numeric data.
 100    ******************************************************************
 110     ENVIRONMENT DIVISION.
 120    ******************************************************************
 130    *----------------------------------------------------------------*
 140     CONFIGURATION SECTION.
 150    *----------------------------------------------------------------*
 160     SOURCE-COMPUTER. IBM.
 170     OBJECT-COMPUTER. IBM.
 180     SPECIAL-NAMES.   C01 IS TOP-OF-NEXT-PAGE.
 190    *----------------------------------------------------------------*
 200     INPUT-OUTPUT SECTION.
 210    *----------------------------------------------------------------*
 220     FILE-CONTROL.
 230         SELECT STUDENT-FILE ASSIGN TO UT-S-INPUT.
 240         SELECT REPORT-FILE  ASSIGN TO UT-S-OUTPUT.
 250    ******************************************************************
 260     DATA DIVISION.
 270    ******************************************************************
 280    *----------------------------------------------------------------*
 290     FILE SECTION.
 300    *----------------------------------------------------------------*
 310     FD  STUDENT-FILE LABEL RECORDS ARE OMITTED.
 320     01  STUDENT-RECORD.
 330         05 STUDENT-IDENTIFICATION-IN.
 340             10 LAST-NAME-IN          PIC X(10).
 350             10 FIRST-NAME-IN         PIC X(10).
 360             10 MIDDLE-INITIAL-IN     PIC X(01).
 370             10 STUDENT-ID-IN         PIC X(09).
 380         05 FILLER                    PIC X(05).
 390         05 ENROLLMENT-INFO-IN.
 400             10 CLASSIFICATION-IN     PIC X(02).
 410             10 TOTAL-HOURS-IN        PIC 9(03).
```

Figure 24.13 *Continued* An Illustration of the EXAMINE Statement

```
        10 HOURS-THIS-SEM-IN        PIC 9(02).
        10 MAJOR-IN                 PIC X(03).
     05 FILLER                      PIC X(35).

FD  REPORT-FILE LABEL RECORDS ARE OMITTED.
01  REPORT-RECORD                   PIC X(133).
*-------------------------------------------------------------*
WORKING-STORAGE SECTION.
*-------------------------------------------------------------*
01  WORKING-VARIABLES.
    05  FILE-STATUS                 PIC X(04).

01  OUTPUT-RECORD.
    05 FILLER                       PIC X(03) VALUE ' *'.
    05 FIRST-NAME-OUT               PIC X(11).
    05 MIDDLE-INITIAL-OUT           PIC X(01).
    05 FILLER                       PIC X(02) VALUE '.'.
    05 LAST-NAME-OUT                PIC X(10).
    05 FILLER                       PIC X(04) VALUE ' *'.
    05 STUDENT-ID-OUT               PIC 9(09).
    05 FILLER                       PIC X(05) VALUE '  *'.
    05 CLASSIFICATION-OUT           PIC X(02).
    05 FILLER                       PIC X(06) VALUE '   *'.
    05 MAJOR-OUT                    PIC X(03).
    05 FILLER                       PIC X(08) VALUE '  *'.
    05 HOURS-THIS-SEM-OUT           PIC 9(02).
    05 FILLER                       PIC X(08) VALUE '     *'.
    05 TOTAL-HOURS-OUT              PIC 9(03).
    05 FILLER                       PIC X(03) VALUE ' *'.
***************************************************************
PROCEDURE DIVISION.
***************************************************************
*-------------------------------------------------------------*
000-CONTROL-PROCEDURE SECTION.
*-------------------------------------------------------------*
    PERFORM 100-INITIALIZATION.
    PERFORM 300-READ-RECORDS-PRINT-DETAILS
        UNTIL FILE-STATUS = 'DONE'.
    PERFORM 500-TERMINATION.
    STOP RUN.
*-------------------------------------------------------------*
100-INITIALIZATION SECTION.
*-------------------------------------------------------------*
    MOVE 'START'                TO FILE-STATUS.
    OPEN INPUT STUDENT-FILE, OUTPUT REPORT-FILE.
    READ STUDENT-FILE
        AT END MOVE 'DONE'      TO FILE-STATUS.
*-------------------------------------------------------------*
300-READ-RECORDS-PRINT-DETAILS SECTION.
*-------------------------------------------------------------*
    EXAMINE STUDENT-ID-IN REPLACING ALL ' ' BY '0'.

    MOVE STUDENT-ID-IN          TO STUDENT-ID-OUT.
    MOVE LAST-NAME-IN           TO LAST-NAME-OUT.
    MOVE FIRST-NAME-IN          TO FIRST-NAME-OUT.
    MOVE MIDDLE-INITIAL-IN      TO MIDDLE-INITIAL-OUT.
    MOVE CLASSIFICATION-IN      TO CLASSIFICATION-OUT.
    MOVE TOTAL-HOURS-IN         TO TOTAL-HOURS-OUT.
    MOVE HOURS-THIS-SEM-IN      TO HOURS-THIS-SEM-OUT.
    MOVE MAJOR-IN               TO MAJOR-OUT.
    WRITE REPORT-RECORD FROM OUTPUT-RECORD AFTER 2 LINES.
    READ STUDENT-FILE
        AT END MOVE 'DONE'      TO FILE-STATUS.
*-------------------------------------------------------------*
500-TERMINATION SECTION.
*-------------------------------------------------------------*
    CLOSE STUDENT-FILE, REPORT-FILE.
```

Figure 24.13 *Continued* An Illustration of the EXAMINE Statement (Output)

```
| Jimmy     Q. Anderson  | 343564321 | Gr | Csc |  00  | 219 |
| John      A. Booker    | 555667777 | Fr | Mgt |  15  | 035 |
| Matt      N. Carter    | 456789012 | Jr | Mgt |  08  | 094 |
| Anthony   R. Davidson  | 353492761 | Sr | Eco |  16  | 138 |
| David     Q. Eldridge  | 376495268 | So | Fin |  12  | 047 |
| Rose      V. Franklin  | 000000001 | Gr | Gbu |  12  | 189 |
| Kenneth   A. Garrison  | 537903251 | So | Mgt |  16  | 028 |
| Mark      C. Hamilton  | 486762389 | Jr | Csc |  18  | 096 |
| Matt      H. Issacs    | 474653790 | Sr | Eco |  18  | 120 |
| Harold    Q. Jefferson | 502326955 | Fr | Mkt |  18  | 018 |
| Floyd     R. Kennedy   | 476329092 | Jr | Mkt |  12  | 060 |
| Steven    O. Lincoln   | 442648942 | So | Mkt |  15  | 045 |
```

Figure 24.14 Format of the INITIALIZE Statement

```
INITIALIZE identifier-1 . . .

             ⎧⎧ALPHABETIC          ⎫                ⎫
             ⎪⎪ALPHANUMERIC        ⎪         ⎧identifier-2⎫⎪
   REPLACING ⎨⎨NUMERIC             ⎬ DATA BY ⎨            ⎬⎬
             ⎪⎪ALPHANUMERIC-EDITED ⎪         ⎩literal     ⎭⎪
             ⎩⎩NUMERIC-EDITED      ⎭                ⎭
```

Summary

This chapter has presented statements specifically designed to manipulate character data. The STRING statement may be used to copy data from two or more fields into one receiving field. With the use of optional clauses, the STRING statement may count the characters placed in the receiving field and indicate the procedure to be executed in the event that the data to be strung together overflow the receiving field.

The UNSTRING statement, on the other hand, allows the programmer to extract data from one field and have the result placed in multiple receiving fields. In addition, the UNSTRING statement provides options that permit the programmer to count the number of characters moved to each receiving field, initialize UNSTRING operations in a location other than the first character of the sending field, count the number of receiving fields, and indicate the procedure to be executed in the event that all receiving fields did not receive data as a consequence of the unstringing operation.

The INSPECT, EXAMINE, TRANSFORM, and INITIALIZE statements serve a slightly different function in that they are capable of manipulating existing data in a single field. In addition, the INSPECT and EXAMINE statements are also capable of performing a counting function.

Notes on Programming Style

The STRING and UNSTRING statements have been examined last in this text because these statements represent the direction in which COBOL is moving. The STRING and UNSTRING statements were not included in the ANS COBOL standard instruction set until 1974. These statements obviously have very specialized uses, as will be the case when other statements or type representations are added to the language in the future.

Future programming will require better communication with the user. An operator sitting at a CRT terminal may request certain operations to be performed in the form of a sentence or phrase, and it will be the program's task to determine from the sentence or phrase what is being requested. Furthermore, responses to the operator may be more textual than they are today. Thus, it may be the program's responsibility to *construct* meaningful sentences or phrases to respond to user requests. Both these functions would obviously be much easier to handle with the availability of statements like STRING and UNSTRING. The next version of COBOL will likely include more string-oriented operations than the current versions.

One word of caution about the EXAMINE and TRANSFORM statements. Since these are not ANS standard COBOL statements, the possibility exists that the manufacturers that support these statements may choose to withdraw that support at any time. Therefore, many installations choose not to use these statements to avoid incompatibility with future compilers, and so that switching to other computers is more easily accomplished.

Questions

Below fill in the blank(s) with the appropriate word, words, or phrases.

1. The STRING and the UNSTRING statement are used in the manipulation of ____ .

2. The STRING statement provides the programmer with the function of ____ .

3. The UNSTRING statement provides the programmer with the function of ____ .

4. The STRING statement causes data to be copied from the sending field into the receiving field until the situation or value specified in the ____ phrase is encountered.

5. In a STRING operation, the programmer is provided the capability of counting the number of characters moved through the ____ option.

6. When the operation of the STRING statement attempts to place more characters in the receiving field than it is capable of retaining, the ____ option is invoked, if present.

7. The movement of data from the sending field to the first receiving field in the UNSTRING statement is terminated by ____ .

8. Statement types that may be used to manipulate the contents of existing fields include ____ , ____ , and ____ .

9. If one wished to count the number of occurrences of a particular character in a field, one might use the ____ or ____ statement.

Answer the following questions by circling either "T" for True or "F" for False.

T F **10.** Concatenation means to place two or more items together.

T F **11.** Parsing means to segment one item into two or more items.

T F **12.** The receiving field of a STRING statement must be an alphanumeric field.

T F 13. The identifier used in the POINTER option of the STRING statement is automatically initialized by the execution of the STRING statement.

T F 14. In the STRING statement no more than one receiving field may be employed.

T F 15. In the UNSTRING statement no more than one receiving field may be employed.

T F 16. Data must be described in DISPLAY form to be used in either the STRING or UNSTRING statement.

T F 17. In the STRING statement, no more than one sending field may be employed.

T F 18. In the UNSTRING statement, no more than one sending field may be employed.

T F 19. In the STRING statement, one sending field may be employed.

T F 20. In the UNSTRING statement, one receiving field may be employed.

APPENDIXES

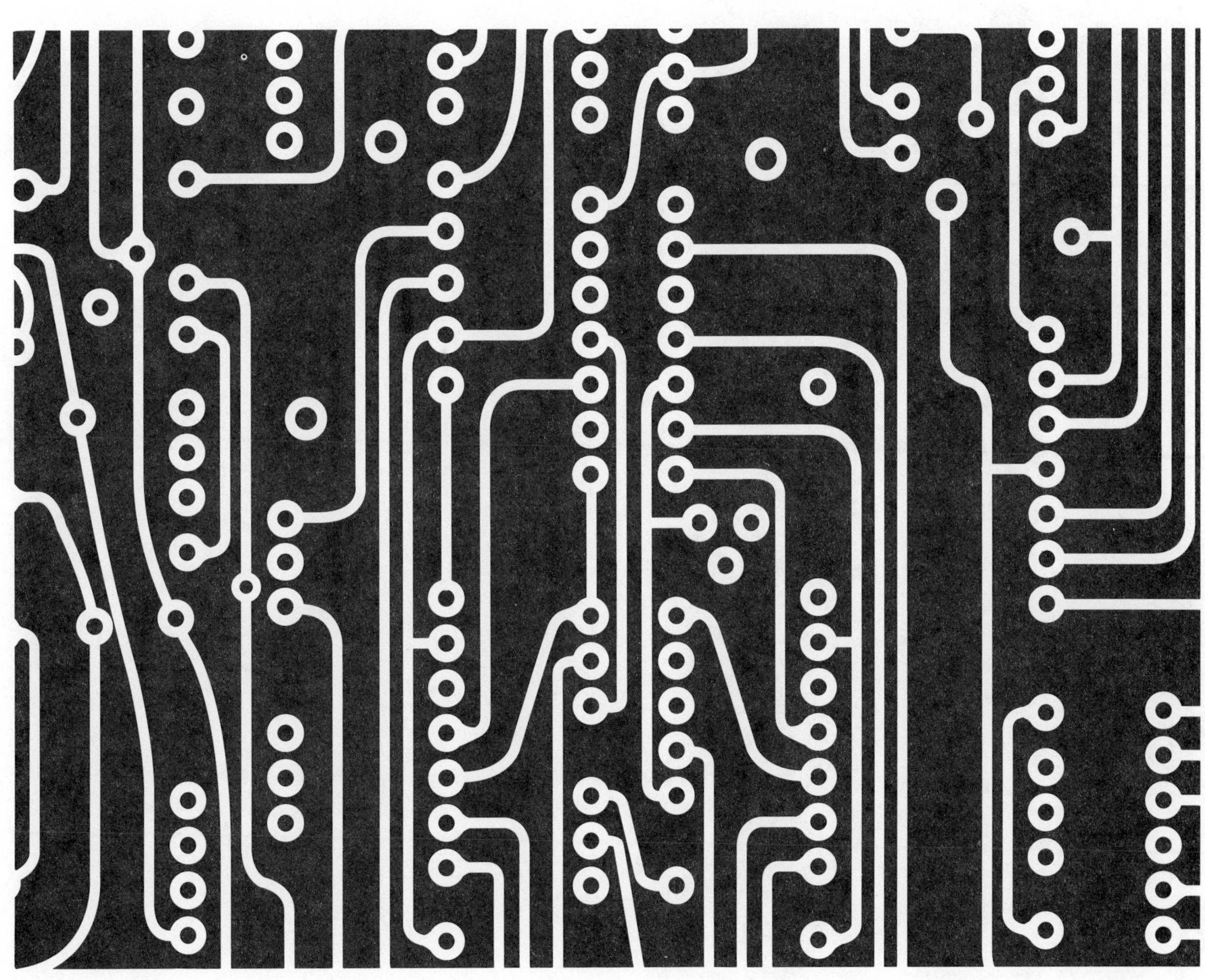

APPENDIX

List of Reserved Words

ACCEPT
ACCESS
\+ ACTIVE
* ACTUAL
ADD
* ADDRESS
ADVANCING
AFTER
ALL
ALPHABETIC
ALPHABETIC-LOWER
ALPHABETIC-UPPER
\# ALPHANUMERIC
\# ALPHANUMERIC-EDITED
ALTER
ALTERNATE
\+ AN
AND
ANY
* APPLY
ARE
AREA
AREAS
ASCENDING

@ ASCII
\+ ASM
ASSIGN
AT
AUTHOR

\# BASIS
BEFORE
* BEGINNING
@ BINARY
BLANK
BLOCK
BOTTOM
BY

CALL
CANCEL
* CARD-PUNCH
* CARD-READER
\# CBL
CD
CF
\+ CFH
CH

* CHANGED
@ CHANNEL
CHARACTER
CHARACTERS
CLOCK-UNITS
CLOSE
COBOL
CODE
CODE-SET
COLLATING
COLUMN
\# COM-REG
COMMA
* COMMON-STORAGE
COMMUNICATION
COMP
* COMP-1
* COMP-2
* COMP-3
* COMP-4
\+ COMPACT
COMPUTATIONAL
* COMPUTATIONAL-1
* COMPUTATIONAL-2

* Adopted by multiple manufacturers
@ Digital Equipment Corporation
\# IBM (VS, OS, DOS)
& Honeywell/Xerox
\+ Univac
COBOL 85 New Standard

* COMPUTATIONAL-3
* COMPUTATIONAL-4
COMPUTE
CONFIGURATION
* CONSOLE
# CONSTANT
CONTAINS
CONTINUE
CONTROL
CONTROLS
CONVERTING
COPY
* CORE-INDEX
CORR
CORRESPONDING
COUNT
+ CREATION-DATE
# CSP
CURRENCY
CURRENT-DATE
+ CYCLES
# CYL-INDEX
# CYL-OVERFLOW
# C01
# C02

DATA
DATE
DATE-COMPILED
DATE-WRITTEN
+ DATE-TIME
DAY
DAY-OF-WEEK
DE
DEBUG-CONTENTS
DEBUG-ITEM
DEBUG-LINE
DEBUG-NAME
DEBUG-SUB-1
DEBUG-SUB-2
DEBUG-SUB-3
DEBUGGING
DECIMAL-POINT
DECLARATIVES
@ DEFERRED
DELETE
DELIMITED
DELIMITER
@ DENSITY
DEPENDING
* DEPTH
DESCENDING
DESTINATION
DETAIL
+ DIRECT
DISABLE
* DISP
DISPLAY
DISPLAY-ST
* DISPLAY-n
DIVISION
DOWN
DUPLICATES
DYNAMIC

@ EBCDIC
EGI
# EJECT
ELSE
EMI
ENABLE
END
END-ADD
END-CALL
END-COMPUTE
END-DELETE
END-DIVIDE
END-EVALUATE
END-IF
END-MULTIPLY
END-PERFORM
END-READ
END-RETURN
END-REWRITE
END-SEARCH
END-START
END-SUBTRACT
END-UNSTRING
END-WRITE
END-OF-PAGE
* ENDING
ENTER
* ENTRY
ENVIRONMENT
+ EOF
EOP
EQUAL
* EUQLAS
ERROR
ESI
* ETI
EVALUATE
+ EVEN
EVERY
* EXAMINE
* EXCEEDS
EXCEPTION
* EXHIBIT
+ EXREF
EXIT
EXTEND
EXTENDED-SEARCH

FALSE
FD
FILE
+ FILE-ACCESS
FILE-CONTROL
+ FILE-ID
* FILE-LIMIT
* FILE-LIMITS
+ FILE-QUALIFIER
FILLER
FINAL
FIRST
FOOTING
FOR
+ FORMnn
+ FORM-REQUEST

* Adopted by multiple manufacturers
@ Digital Equipment Corporation
# IBM (VS, OS, DOS)
& Honeywell/Xerox
+ Univac
COBOL 85 New Standard

FOR
* FORTRAN
@ FORTRAN IV
+ FREE
FROM

GENERATE
GIVING
GO
* GOBACK
GREATER
GROUP

HEADING
HIGH-VALUE
HIGH-VALUES
* HOLD

I-O
I-O CONTROL
* ID
IDENTIFICATION
IF
IN
+ INACTIVE
& INCLUDE
INDEX
INDEX-n
INITIAL
INITIALIZE
INITIATE
+ INLINE
INPUT
INPUT-OUTPUT
INSERT
INSPECT
INSTALLATION
+ INTER-LOCK
+ INTERNAL
INTO
INVALID
IS

JUST
JUSTIFIED

KEY
* KEYS

LABEL
LABEL-RETURN
LAST
LEADING
LEAVE
LEFT
LENGTH
LESS
LIBRARY
LIMIT
LIMITS
LINAGE
LINAGE-COUNTER
LINE
LINE-COUNTER
@ LINE-PRINTER
LINES
LINKAGE
+ LION
+ LOCATION
LOCK
LOW-VALUE
LOW-VALUES
* LOWER-BOUND
* LOWER-BOUNDS

@ MACRO
@ MAP 4
@ MAP 5
@ MAP 6
@ MAP 7
@ MAP 8
+ MASS-STORAGE
# MASTER-INDEX
+ MCFLAG
MEMORY
MERGE
MESSAGE
MODE
MODULES
+ MONITOR
# MORE-LABELS
MOVE
MULTIPLE
MULTIPLY

* NAMED
NATIVE
NEGATIVE
NEXT
NO
NOMINAL
NOT
* NOTE
# NSTD-REELS
NUMBER
NUMERIC
NUMERIC-EDITED

OBJECT-COMPUTER
OBJECT- PROGRAM
OCCURS
@ ODD
OF
OFF
OH
OMITTED
ON
OPEN
OPTIONAL
OR
ORGANIZATION
* OTHERWISE
OUTPUT
OV
OVERFLOW

PACKED DECIMAL.
PAGE
PAGE-COUNTER

* Adopted by multiple manufacturers
@ Digital Equipment Corporation
# IBM (VS, OS, DOS)
& Honeywell/Xerox
+ Univac
COBOL 85 New Standard

@ PAPER-TAPE-PUNCH
@ PAPER-TAPE-READER
@ PARITY
# PASSWORD
PERFORM
PF
PH
PIC
PICTURE
+ PLACE
+ PLACES
PLUS
+ POINT
POINTER
+ POINTS
POSITION
POSITIONING
POSITIVE
PREPARED
* PRINTER
PRINTING
@ PRINT-CONTROL
# PRINT-SWITCH
# PRIORITY
PROCEDURE
PROCEDURES
PROCEED
PROCESS
* PROCESSING
PROGRAM
PROGRAM-ID
+ PROTECT
+ PURGE-DATE

QUEUE
QUOTE
QUOTES

RANDOM
RANGE
READ
@ READ-AHEAD
READY
RECEIVE
RECORD
RECORD-OVERFLOW
* RECORDING
RECORDS
REDEFINES
REEL
REFERENCES
RELATIVE
RELEASE
RELOAD
REMAINDER
* REMARKS
REMOVAL
RENAMES
& RENAMING
# REORG-CRITERIA
REPLACING
REPORT
REPORTING
REPORTS
REREAD
RERUN
RESERVE
RESET
RETURN
RETURN-CODE
REVERSED
REWIND
REWRITE
RF
RH
RIGHT
ROUNDED
RUN

SA
SAME
SD
SEARCH
SECTION
SECURITY
* SEEK
SEGMENT
SEGMENT-LIMIT
SELECT
SELECTED
SEND
SENTENCE
SEPARATE
SEQUENCE
SEQUENTIAL
SERVICE
SET
+ SET-ID
SIGN
SIZE
SKIP 1
SKIP 2
SKIP 3
SORT
SORT-CORE-SIZE
SORT-FILE-SIZE
SORT-MERGE
SORT-MESSAGE
SORT-MODE-SIZE
SORT-OPTION
SORT-RETURN
SOURCE
SOURCE-COMPUTER
SPACE
SPACES
SPECIAL-NAMES
STANDARD
STANDARD-1
START
STATUS
STOP
STRING
SUB-QUEUE-1
SUB-QUEUE-2
SUB-QUEUE-3
SUBTRACT
SUM
SUPERVISOR
SUPPRESS

* Adopted by multiple manufacturers
@ Digital Equipment Corporation
# IBM (VS, OS, DOS)
& Honeywell/Xerox
+ Univac
COBOL 85 New Standard

SUSPEND
* SWITCH
SYMBOLIC
SYNC
SYNCHRONIZED
SYSIN
SYSIPT
SYSLST
SYSOUT
SYSPLH
SYSPUNCH
S01
S02

TABLE
* TALLY
TALLYING
TAPE
TERMINAL
TERMINATE
TEST
TEXT
THAN
THEN
THROUGH
THRU
TIME
TIME-OF-DAY
TIMES
TO

@ TODAY
TOP
TOTALED
TOTALING
* TRACE
# TRACK
# TRACK-AREA
# TRACK-LIMIT
# TRACKS
TRAILING
* TRANSFORM
TRUE
TYPE

UNEQUAL
UNIT
+ UNISERVO
+ UNSERVOS
+ UNLOCK
UNSTRING
UNTIL
UP
* UPPER-BOUND
* UPPER-BOUNDS
UPON
UPSI 0
UPSI 1
UPSI 2

UPSI 3
UPSI 4
UPSI 5
UPSI 6
UPSI 7
USAGE
USE
@ USER-NUMBER
USING

VALUE
VALUES
VARYING

WHEN
WHEN-COMPILED
WITH
+ WORD
WORDS
WORKING-STORAGE
WRITE
@ WRITE-BEHIND
* WRITE-ONLY
# WRITE-VERIFY

ZERO
ZEROES
ZEROS

* Adopted by multiple manufacturers
@ Digital Equipment Corporation
# IBM (VS, OS, DOS)
& Honeywell/Xerox
+ Univac
COBOL 85 New Standard

APPENDIX

B

General Forms of COBOL Statements

The following are the general formats for all COBOL statements used in this text

General Format for Identification Division

CHAPTER 4

```
 IDENTIFICATION DIVISION.
 PROGRAM-ID. program-name.
[AUTHOR. [comment-entry] ...]
[INSTALLATION. [comment-entry] ...]
[DATE-WRITTEN. [comment-entry] ...]
[DATE-COMPILED. [comment-entry] ...]
[SECURITY. [comment-entry] ...]
```

General Format for Environment Division

CHAPTER 5

```
ENVIRONMENT DIVISION.
CONFIGURATION SECTION.
```

APPENDIX E

```
SOURCE-COMPUTER. computer-name [WITH DEBUGGING MODE]
OBJECT-COMPUTER. computer-name
```

CHAPTER

```
[SPECIAL-NAMES. system-name IS mnemonic-name.]
[INPUT-OUTPUT SECTION.
 FILE-CONTROL.
[SELECT [OPTIONAL] file-name
 ASSIGN TO implementor-name-1 [, implementor-name-2]
```

CHAPTER 17

```
[; RESERVE {NO        } ALTERNATE [AREA ]]
           {integer-1}            [AREAS]

[; ORGANIZATION IS SEQUENTIAL]
[; ACCESS MODE IS SEQUENTIAL]
```

CHAPTER 18

```
[SELECT file-name
    ASSIGN TO implementor-name-1
          [, implementor-name-2] ...
    [; RESERVE {NO        } ALTERNATE [AREA ]]
               {integer-1}            [AREAS]

     ; ORGANIZATION IS INDEXED
```

```
[; ACCESS MODE IS {SEQUENTIAL}]
                  {RANDOM    }

 ; RECORD KEY IS data-name-1

[, NOMINAL KEY IS data-name-2]
```

General Format for Data Division

CHAPTER 6

```
 DATA DIVISION.
[FILE SECTION.
[FD file-name
```

CHAPTER 17, 18, 19

```
[BLOCK CONTAINS [integer-1 TO] integer-2 {CHARACTERS}]
                                         {RECORDS   }

[         {CONTAINS [integer-3 TO] integer-4 CHARACTERS      }]
[RECORD   {IS VARYING IN SIZE                                }]
[         {   [ [FROM integer-5] [TO integer-6] CHARACTERS]  }]
[         {   [ DEPENDING ON data-name-1]]                   }]

       {RECORD IS }  {OMITTED }
 LABEL {          }  {        }
       {RECORD ARE}  {STANDARD}

       {RECORD IS }
[DATA  {          } data-name-2 [data-name-3] ...] .]
       {RECORD ARE}
```

CHAPTER 15

```
       {REPORT IS  }
     ; {           } report-name-1 [, report-name-2] ...
       {REPORTS ARE}

[record-description-entry] ...   ...
```

CHAPTER 16

```
[SD file-name
     [; RECORD CONTAINS [integer-1 TO] integer-2 CHARACTERS]
[        {RECORD  IS }                                        ]
[ ; DATA {           }     data-name-1 [, data-name-2] ...   ] .
[        {RECORDS ARE}                                        ]
    {record-description-entry} ... ] ...]
    [WORKING-STORAGE SECTION.
    [77-level-description-entry]     ]
    [record-description-entry  ] ... ]
```

General Format for Data Description Entry

CHAPTER 6

```
FORMAT 1:
level-number {data-name-1}
             {FILLER     }
```

CHAPTER 22

```
[; REDEFINES data-name-2]
```

CHAPTERS 6, 8, 23

```
[; {PICTURE} IS character-string]
   {PIC    }
```

CHAPTER 23

```
[ ; [USAGE IS] { COMPUTATIONAL } ]
               { COMP          }
               { DISPLAY       }
               { INDEX         }
```

CHAPTER 23

```
[ ; [SIGN IS] { LEADING  } [SEPARATE CHARACTER] ]
              { TRAILING }
```

CHAPTER 13, 14

```
[ ; OCCURS { integer-1 TO integer-2 TIMES DEPENDING } ]
           { integer-2 TIMES          ON data-name-3 }
```

CHAPTER 14

```
[ { ASCENDING  } KEY IS data-name-4 [, data-name-5] ... ] ...
  { DESCENDING }
```

CHAPTER 14

```
          [INDEXED BY index-name-1 [, index-name-2] ...] ]
```

CHAPTER 23

```
[ ; { SYNCHRONIZED } { LEFT  } ]
    { SYNC         } { RIGHT }
```

CHAPTER 23

```
[ ; { JUSTIFIED } RIGHT ]
    { JUST      }
```

CHAPTER 23

```
[; BLANK WHEN ZERO]
```

CHAPTER 6

```
[; VALUE IS literal]
FORMAT 2:
```

CHAPTER 22

```
66 data-name-1; RENAMES data-name-2 [ { THROUGH } data-name-3 ]
                                      { THRU    }
```

CHAPTER 11

```
FORMAT 3:

88 condition-name; { VALUE IS   } literal-1 [ { THROUGH } literal-2 ]
                   { VALUES ARE }             { THRU    }
   [, literal-3 [ { THROUGH } literal-4    ... . ] ]
                  { THRU    }
```

CHAPTER 15

```
REPORT SECTION.
RD report-name

PAGE [ LIMIT IS   ] integer-1 { LINE  }
     [ LIMITS ARE ]           { LINES }
[HEADING integer-2]
[FIRST DETAIL integer-3]
[LAST DETAIL integer-4]
[FOOTING integer-5]
[ { CONTROL IS   }  { FINAL                                     } ]
[ {              }  { identifier-1 [, identifier-2] ...         } ]
[ { CONTROLS ARE }  { FINAL, identifier-1 [, identifier-2]      } ]
```

CHAPTER 15

```
level-number [data-name]
```

CHAPTER 23

```
[BLANK WHEN ZERO clause]
```

CHAPTER 15

```
[COLUMN NUMBER IS integer-1]
```

CHAPTER 15 [GROUP INDICATE]

CHAPTER 23 [JUSTIFIED clause]

CHAPTER 15
```
[                  {integer-1      }]
[LINE NUMBER IS    {PLUS integer-2 }]
[                  {NEXT PAGE      }]
```

CHAPTER 15
```
[                  {integer-1      }]
[NEXT GROUP IS     {PLUS integer-2 }]
[                  {NEXT PAGE      }]
```

CHAPTER 15
```
[RESET ON {identifier-1}]
[         {FINAL       }]
```

CHAPTER 15 SOURCE IS identifier-1

CHAPTER 15 SUM identifier-2 [, identifier-3] ... [UPON data-name]

CHAPTER 15
```
          {{REPORT HEADING }                    }
          {{RH             }                    }
          {{PAGE HEADING   }                    }
          {{PH             }                    }
          {{CONTROL HEADING} {identifier-n}     }
          {{CH             } {FINAL       }     }
TYPE IS   {{DETAIL         }                    }
          {{DE             }                    }
          {{CONTROL FOOTING} {identifier-n}     }
          {{CF             } {FINAL       }     }
          {{PAGE FOOTING   }                    }
          {{PF             }                    }
          {{REPORT FOOTING }                    }
          {{RF             }                    }
```

CHAPTER 6, 15 VALUE IS literal-1

CHAPTER 23 [USAGE clause]

CHAPTER 20
```
[LINKAGE SECTION.
[77 elementary-item-description] ...
[01 record-description] ...]
```

General Format for Procedure Division

CHAPTER 7, 2 PROCEDURE DIVISION.

CHAPTER 20 PROCEDURE DIVISION [USING identifier-1 [identifier-2]...]

APPENDIX E
```
[DECLARATIVES.
{section-name SECTION. declarative-sentence.
[paragraph-name. [sentence] ...] ... } ...
 END DECLARATIVES.]
{section-name SECTION
[paragraph-name. [sentence] ...] ... } ...
```

General Format for Verbs

CHAPTER 7

```
ACCEPT identifier [FROM mnemonic-name]
```

CHAPTER 7

```
                               DATE
ACCEPT identifier-2 FROM     { DAY         }
                               TIME
                               DAY-OF-WEEK
```

CHAPTER 7

```
ACCEPT
 ({ LIN {+} integer-1 } , { COL {+} integer-3 } )
 {      {-}           }   {     {-}           }
 { integer-2          }   { integer-4         }
 identifier-1
 [WITH [{SPACE-FILL}] [{LEFT-JUSTIFY }]
        {ZERO-FILL }    {RIGHT-JUSTIFY}
 [TRAILING-SIGN] [PROMPT] [UPDATE]
 [LENGTH-CHECK] [AUTO-SKIP] [BEEP] ...]
```

CHAPTER 7

```
ACCEPT identifier-1 [UNIT {identifier-2}
                          {literal-1   }

LINE {identifier-3} POSITION {identifier-4}
     {literal-2   }          {literal-3   }

[SIZE {identifier-5}]   [PROMPT [literal-5]]
      {literal-4   }

[ECHO] [CONVERT] [TAB] [ERASE] [NO BEEP]
[OFF] [{HIGH}] [BLINK] [REVERSE]
       {LOW }
[ON EXCEPTION identifier-6 imperative-statement)} ...
```

CHAPTER 10

```
FORMAT 1:
ADD {identifier-1} [identifier-2] ...TO identifier-m [ROUNDED]
    {literal-1   } [literal-2   ]

[ON SIZE ERROR imperative-statement-1]
[NOT ON SIZE ERROR imperative-statement-2]
[END-END]
```

CHAPTER 10

```
FORMAT 2:
ADD {identifier-1} {identifier-2} [TO] [identifier-3] ...
    {literal-1   } {literal-2   }      [literal-3   ]

GIVING identifiers-m [ROUNDED]
[ON SIZE ERROR imperative-statement-1]
[NOT ON SIZE ERROR imperative-statement-2]
[END-END]
```

CHAPTER 20

```
FORMAT 1:
CALL literal-1 [USING identifier-1 [identifier-2]...]
FORMAT 2:
CALL identifier-1 [USING identifier-2 [identifier-3]...]
```

CHAPTERS 7, 17, 18, 19

```
                     [{REEL} [WITH NO REWIND]]
CLOSE file-name-1    [{UNIT} [FOR REMOVAL   ]]
                     [                       ]
                     [ WITH {NO REWIND}      ]
                     [      {LOCK     }      ]
```

```
[                  [{REEL} [WITH NO REWIND]]]
[ ,file-name-2     [{UNIT} [FOR REMOVAL   ]]]...
[                  [WITH {NO REWIND}       ]]
[                  [     {LOCK     }       ]]
```

CHAPTERS 7, 17, 18, 19

```
CLOSE file-name-1 [WITH LOCK] [, file-name-2

        [WITH LOCK]] ...
```

CHAPTER 10

```
                                  {identifier-2          }
COMPUTE identifier-1 [ROUNDED] =  {literal-1             }
                                  {arithmetic-expression }

[ON SIZE ERROR imperative-statement-1]
[NOT ON SIZE ERROR imperative-statement-2]
[END-COMPUTE]
```

CHAPTER 20

```
COPY file-name
                            {word-2      }
[REPLACING word-1 BY        {literal-1   }
                            {identifier-1}

                            {word-4      }
          [word-3 BY        {literal-2   } ]...[
                            {identifier-2}
```

CHAPTER 19

```
DELETE record-name
  [INVALID key imperative-statement]
```

CHAPTER 7s, Appendix E

```
DISPLAY {identifier-1} [, identifier-2]
        {literal-1   } [, literal-2   ]...
        [UPON mnemonic-name]
```

CHAPTER 7s

```
DISPLAY

{(LIN {+} integer-1}     {COL {+} integer-3}
{     {-}          }  ,  {    {-}          }  )
{ integer-2        }     {integer-4        }

{identifier-1}
{literal-1   } ...
{ERASE       }

[UPON mnemonic-name]
```

CHAPTER 7s

```
DISPLAY {identifier-1} [UNIT  {identifier-2}]
        {literal-1   } [      {literal-2   }]

LINE    {identifier-3} POSITION {identifier-4}
        {literal-3   }          {literal-4   }
[SIZE   {identifier-5}]
[       {literal-5   }]

[BEEP]  [{HIGH}]  [BLINK] [REVERSE] [ERASE]
        [{LOW }]
```

CHAPTER 10 Format 1:

```
DIVIDE {identifier-1} INTO identifier-2 [ROUNDED]
       {literal-1   }

[ON SIZE ERROR imperative-statement-1]
[NOT ON SIZE ERROR imperative-statement-2]
[END-DIVIDE]
```

CHAPTER 10 Format-2:

```
DIVIDE {identifier-1} {INTO} {identifier-2} GIVING identifier-3 [ROUNDED]
       {literal-1   } {BY  } {literal-2   }

[REMAINDER identifier-4]
[ON SIZE ERROR imperative-statement-1]
[NOT ON SIZE ERROR imperative-statement-2]
[END-DIVIDE]
```

CHAPTER 21

```
         {identifier-1}        {identifier-2}
         {literal-1   }        {literal-2   }
EVALUATE {expression-1}  ALSO  {expression-2}
         {TRUE        }        {TRUE        }
         {FALSE       }        {FALSE       }
{{WHEN
    {ANY                                                                   }
    {condition-1                                                           }
    {TRUE                                                                  }
    {FALSE                                                                 }
    {                {{identifier-3}} [{THROUGH} {identifier-4}]}          }
    {[NOT]          {{literal-3   }} [{THRU   } {literal-4   }]}           }
    {                {{expression-3}} [          {expression-4}]}          }

[ALSO
    {ANY                                                                   }
    {condition-1                                                           }
    {TRUE                                                                  }
    {FALSE                                                                 }
    {                {{identifier-3}} [{THROUGH} {identifier-4}]}          }
    {[NOT]          {{literal-3   }} [{THRU   } {literal-4   }]}           }
    {                {{expression-3}} [          {expression-4}]}          }

     imperative-statement-1]  ...

[WHEN OTHER imperative-statement-2]

[END EVALUATE]
```

CHAPTER 9 EXIT.

CHAPTER 20 EXIT PROGRAM

CHAPTER 15 GENERATE detail-line-name

CHAPTER 20 GOBACK

CHAPTER 9 GO TO procedure-name.

CHAPTER 21

```
GO TO procedure-name-1 [, procedure-name-2] ...
    , procedure-name-n
    DEPENDING ON identifier
```

CHAPTER 9, 11

```
IF condition; [THEN] {statement-1    } {; ELSE statement-2    }
                     {NEXT SENTENCE  } {; ELSE NEXT SENTENCE  }
[END-IF]
```

CHAPTER 24

```
INITIALIZE identifier-1 ...
[           {{ALPHABETIC            }                            }]
[           {{ALPHANUMERIC          }              {identifier-2}}]
[ REPLACING {{NUMERIC               } DATA-BY      {            }}]
[           {{ALPHANUMERIC-EDITED   }              {literal     }}]
[           {{NUMERIC-EDITED        }                            }]
```

CHAPTER 15

```
INITIATE report-name-1 [, report-name-2] ...
```

CHAPTER 24

```
INSPECT identifier-1 TALLYING
  {                      {   {{ALL    }  {identifier-3}}
  {, identifier-2 FOR    {,  {{LEADING}  {literal-1   }}
  {                      {   {CHARACTERS               }
  [{BEFORE}  INITIAL {identifier-4}]  }     }
  [{AFTER }          {literal-2   }]  } ... } ...
```

CHAPTER 24

```
INSPECT identifier-1 REPLACING
{CHARACTERS BY {identifier-6} [{BEFORE}   INITIAL {identifier-7}]
{              {literal-4   } [{AFTER }           {literal-5   }]
{ {  {ALL    }    {  {identifier-5}    BY   {identifier-6}
{ {, {LEADING}    {, {literal-3   }         {literal-4   }
{ {  {FIRST  }
    [{BEFORE}  INITIAL  {identifier-7}]  }     }     }
    [{AFTER }           {literal-5   }]  } ... } ... }
```

CHAPTER 24

```
INSPECT identifier-1 TALLYING
{                   { {{ALL    } {identifier-3}}
{, identifer-2 FOR  {,{{LEADING} {literal-1   }}
{                   { {CHARACTERS              }
  [{BEFORE}   INITIAL{identifier-4}]}     }
  [{AFTER }          {literal-2   }]}  ...} ...
REPLACING
{CHARACTERS BY  {identifier-6}[{BEFORE} INITIAL {identifier-7}]
{               {literal-4   }[{AFTER }         {literal-5   }]
{ {  {ALL    } {  {identifier-5}  BY  {identifier-6}
{ {, {LEADING} {, {             }     {             }
{ {  {FIRST  } {  {literal-3    }     {literal-4    }
    {BEFORE} INITIAL {identifier-7}
    {AFTER }         {literal-5   } ...} ...}
```

CHAPTER 24 Format 4:

```
INSPECT identifier-1 CONVERTING {identifier-2} TO {identifier-3}
                                {literal-1   }    {literal-2   }

    [{BEFORE} INITIAL {identifier-4}] ...
     {AFTER }         {literal-3   }
```

CHAPTERS 7, 8, 23

```
MOVE {identifier-1} TO identifier-2 [, identifier-3] ....
     {literal     }
```

CHAPTER 10 Format 1:

```
MULTIPLY {identifier-1} BY identifier-2 [ROUNDED]
         {literal-1   }

[ON SIZE ERROR imperative-statement-1]
[NOT ON SIZE ERROR imperative-statement-2]
[END-MULTIPLY]
```

Format 2:

```
MULTIPLY {identifier-1} BY {identifier-2}
         {literal-2   }    {literal-2   }

GIVING identifier-3 [ROUNDED]
[ON SIZE ERROR imperative-statement-1]
[NOT ON SIZE ERROR imperative-statement-2]
[END-MULTIPLY]
```

CHAPTERS 17, 18, 19

```
  [, identifier-4 [ROUNDED] ...
        [; ON SIZE ERROR imperative-statement]
      {INPUT file-name-1 [REVERSED         ]                 }
      {                  [WITH NO REWIND   ]                 }
OPEN  {[, file-name-2    [REVERSED         ]] ...            } ...
      {                  [WITH NO REWIND   ]                 }
      {OUTPUT file-name-3 [WITH NO REWIND]                   }
      { [, file-name-4 [WITH NO REWIND] ] ...                }
      {I-O file-name-5 [, file-name-6] ...                   }
```

CHAPTERS 7, 17, 18, 19

```
OPEN [INPUT file-name-1 [, file-name-2] ...  ] ...
     [OUTPUT file-name-3 [, file-name-4] ... ]
     [I-O file-name-5 [, file-name-6] ...    ]
```

CHAPTER 7

```
PERFORM [procedure-name-1] [{THROUGH} procedure-name-2]
                            {THRU   }

      [imperative-statement
      END-PERFORM]
```

CHAPTER 12 Format 3: The PERFORM/TIMES Statement

```
PERFORM  procedure-name-1 [{THROUGH}  procedure-name-2]
                           {THRU   }

[WITH TEST {BEFORE}]  {identifier-1} TIMES [imperative-statement-1]
           {AFTER }   {integer-1   }
[END-PERFORM]
```

CHAPTER 7

```
PERFORM [procedure-name-1] [{THROUGH} procedure-name-2]
                            {THRU   }

[WITH TEST {BEFORE}] [UNTIL condition]
           {AFTER }

[imperative-statement
END-PERFORM]
```

CHAPTER 12

```
Format 4:  The PERFORM/VARYING Statement
PERFORM [procedure-name-1] {THROUGH} procedure-name-2
                           {THRU   }

[WITH TEST {BEFORE}] VARYING {identifier-2} FROM {identifier-3}
           {AFTER }          {index-name-1}      {index-name-2}
                                                 {literal-1   }

 BY {identifier-4} UNTIL condition-1
    {literal-2   }

[AFTER {identifier-5} FROM {identifier-6} BY {identifier-7}
       {index-name-3}      {index-name-4}    {literal-4   }
                           {literal-3   }

    UNTIL condition-2

[AFTER {identifier-8} FROM {identifier-9} BY {identifier-10}
       {index-name-5}      {index-name-5}    {literal-6    }
                           {literal-5   }

    UNTIL condition-3]]
[imperative-statement-1 [END-PERFORM]]
```

CHAPTER 7, 17, 18, 19

```
READ file-name RECORD [INTO identifier]
       [AT END imperative-statement]
       [NOT AT END imperative-statement]
[END-READ]
```

CHAPTER 18, 19

```
READ file-name RECORD [INTO identifier]
    [ INVALID KEY imperative-statement]
    [ NOT INVALID KEY imperative-statement]
[END-READ]
```

CHAPTER 16

```
RELEASE record-name [FROM identifier]
```

CHAPTER 16

```
RETURN sort-file-name [INTO identifier]
     [AT END imperative-statement-1]
[NOT AT END imperative-statement-2]
[END-RETURN]
```

CHAPTER 17

```
REWRITE record-name [FROM identifier]
[END-REWRITE]
```

CHAPTER 18, 19

```
;REWRITE Record-name [FROM identifier]
    [INVALID KEY imperative-statement]
    [NOT INVALID KEY imperative-statement]
[END-REWRITE]
```

CHAPTER 14

```
SEARCH identifier-1 [VARYING {identifier-2 } [END-REWRITE]]
                             {index-name-1 }

    [; AT END imperative-statement-1]

   ; WHEN condition-1 {imperative-statement-2}
                      {NEXT SENTENCE         }

[; WHEN condition-2 {imperative-statement-3}]
[                   {NEXT SENTENCE         }]

[END-SEARCH]
```

CHAPTER 14

```
 SEARCH ALL identifier-1 [; AT END imperative-statement-1]
 ; WHEN {data-name-1 {IS EQUAL TO} {identifier-3              }}
        {            {IS =        } {literal-1                 }}
        {condition-name-1           {arithmetic-expression-1   }}

[AND {data-name-2 {IS EQUAL TO} {identifier-4             }}]...
[    {            {IS =       } {literal-2                }}]
[    {condition-name-2          {arithmetic-expression-2  }}]

{imperative-statement-2}
{NEXT SENTENCE         }
[END-SEARCH]
```

CHAPTER 14

```
SET {identifier-1 [, identifier-2]} ...    TO {identifier-3 }
    {index-name-1 [index-name-2]  } ...       {index-name-3 }
                                              {integer-1    }
```

CHAPTER 14

```
SET index-name-4 [, index-name-5] ...{ UP BY   }
                                     { DOWN BY }
{identifier-4}
{integer-2   }
```

CHAPTER 16

```
SORT file-name-1 ON {ASCENDING }
                    {DESCENDING}

    KEY data-name-1 [, data-name-2] ...
 [ON {ASCENDING } KEY data-name-3 [, data-name-4] ...] ...
 [   {DESCENDING}                                    ]
[WITH DUPLICATES IN ORDER]
{INPUT PROCEDURE IS section-name-1 [THROUGH] section-name-2}
{                                  [THRU   ]               }
{USING file-name-2 [, file-name-3] ...                     }
{OUTPUT PROCEDURE IS section-name-3[ {THROUGH} section-name-4 }
{                                    {THRU   }                }
{GIVING file-name-4                                           }
```

CHAPTER 18

```
START file-name
    ┌                     ┌ IS EQUAL TO                      ┐           ┐
    │                     │ IS =                             │           │
    │                     │ IS GREATER THAN                  │           │
    │ USING KEY identifier-1 ┤ IS >                          ├identifier-2 │
    │                     │ IS NOT LESS THAN                 │           │
    │                     │ IS NOT <                         │           │
    │                     │ IS GREATER THAN OR EQUAL TO      │           │
    └                     └ IS >=                            ┘           ┘
    [INVALID KEY imperative-statement-2]
    [NOT INVALID KEY imperative-statement-4]
[END-START]
```

CHAPTER 7

```
STOP {RUN    }
     {literal}
```

CHAPTER 24

```
STRING {identifier-1} [, identifier-2] ...
       {literal-1   } [, literal-2   ]
    DELIMITED BY {identifier-3}
                 {literal-3   }
                 {SIZE        }
    [, {identifier-4} [, identifier-5] ...
       {literal-4   } [, literal-5   ]
    DELIMITED BY {identifier-6}  ] ...
                 {literal-6   }
                 {SIZE        }
    INTO identifier-7 [WITH POINTER identifier-8
    [ON OVERFLOW imperative-statement]
    [NOT ON OVERFLOW imperative-statement]
    [END-STRING]
```

CHAPTER 10 Format 1:

```
SUBTRACT {identifier-1} [identifier-2] ...FROM identifier-m [ROUNDED]
         {literal-1   } [literal-2   ]
 [dentifier-n [ROUNDED]]...
[ON SIZE ERROR imperative-statement-1]
[NOT ON SIZE ERROR imperative-statement-2]
[END-SUBTRACT]
```

CHAPTER 10 Format 2:

```
SUBTRACT {identifier-1} [identifier-2] ...FROM {identifier-m}
         {literal-1   } [literal-2   ]         {literal-m   }
GIVING identifier-n [ROUNDED]
[ON SIZE ERROR imperative-statement-1]
[NOT ON SIZE ERROR imperative-statement-2]
[END-SUBTRACT]
```

CHAPTER 15

```
TERMINATE report-name-1 [, report-name-2] ...
```

CHAPTER 24

```
UNSTRING identifier-1
   [DELIMITED BY [ALL] {identifier-2}
                       {literal-1   }
          [, OR [ALL] {identifier-3}  ] ...]
                      {literal-2   }
     INTO identifier-4 [, DELIMITER IN identifier-5]
   [, COUNT IN identifier-6]
    [, identifier-7 [, DELIMITER IN identifier-8]
    [, COUNT IN identifier-9]] ...
[WITH POINTER identifier-10] [TALLYING IN identifier-11]
[, ON OVERFLOW imperative-statement]
[NOT ON OVERFLOW imperative-statement]
[END-STRING]
```

APPENDIX E

```
                        {[ALL REFERENCES OF] identifier-1}
USE FOR DEBUGGING ON    {file-name-1                     }
                        {procedure-name-1                }
                        {ALL PROCEDURES                  }

[  {[ALL REFERENCES OF] identifier-2}]
[, {file-name-2                     }] ... .
[  {procedure-name-2                }]
[  {ALL PROCEDURES                  }]
```

CHAPTER 15

```
USE BEFORE REPORTING record-name
```

CHAPTER 7, 17

```
WRITE record-name [FROM identifier-1]
[                       {identifier-2} [LINE ] ]
[ {BEFORE}  ADVANCING   {integer     } [LINES] ]
[ {AFTER }              {mnemonic-name}        ]
[                       {PAGE         }        ]
[   ; AT {END-OF-PAGE} imperative-statement]
         {EOP        }
[END-WRITE]
```

CHAPTER 18, 19

```
WRITE record-name [FROM identifier]
    [INVALID KEY imperative-statement]
    [NOT INVALID KEY imperative-statement]
[END-WRITE]
```

General Format for Conditions

CHAPTER 9

```
RELATION CONDITION:
                                  {IS [NOT] GREATER THAN}
{identifier-1            }        {IS [NOT] LESS THAN   }
{literal-1               }        {IS [NOT EQUAL TO     }
{arithmetic-expression-1 }        {IS [NOT >            }
{index-name-1            }        {IS [NOT <            }
                                  {IS [NOT =            }
```

```
{identifier-2              }
{literal-2                 }
{arithmetic-expression-2   }
{index-name-2              }
```

CHAPTER 11 CLASS CONDITION:

```
identifier IS [NOT] {NUMERIC   }
                    {ALPHABETIC}
```

CHAPTER 11 SIGN CONDITION:

```
                                   {POSITIVE}
arithmetic-expression is [NOT]     {NEGATIVE}
                                   {ZERO    }
```

CHAPTER 11 CONDITION-NAME CONDITION:

```
condition-name
```

CHAPTER 9 NEGATED SIMPLE CONDITION:

```
NOT simple-condition
```

CHAPTER 9 COMBINED CONDITION:

```
condition { {AND} condition } ...
          { {OR } condition }
```

CHAPTER 8 ABBREVIATED COMBINED RELATION CONDITION:

```
relation-condition
   {{AND}                                         }
   {{   } [NOT] [relational-operator]             } object ...
   {{OR }                                         }
```

Miscellaneous Formats

CHAPTER 13

SUBSCRIPTING:

```
{data-name     }
{condition-name}
  (subscript-1 [, subscript-2 [, subscript-3]])
```

CHAPTER 14 INDEXING:

```
{data-name     } ( {index-name-1 [{±} literal-2]}
{condition-name}   {literal-1                   }
 [, {index-name-2 [{±} literal-4]}
 [  {literal-3                   }
    [, {index-name-3 [{±} literal-6]}]  ]  )
    [  {literal-5                   }]  ]
```

CHAPTER 13 IDENTIFIER: FORMAT 2:

```
data-name-1 [ {OF} data-name-2 ] ... [(subscript-1
              {IN}
[, subscript-2 [, subscript-3]])]
```

CHAPTER 14 IDENTIFIER: FORMAT 2:

```
data-name-1 [ {OF} data-name-2 ] ...
              {IN}
  [ ( {index-name-1 [{±} literal-2]}
  [   {literal-1                   }
  [ , {index-name-2 [{±} literal-4]}
  [   {literal-3                   }
  [ , {index-name-3 [{±} literal-6]} ]] ) ]
  [   {literal-5                   } ]]   ]
```

APPENDIX

C

Table of Allowable Data Movements

Sending Field	Receiving Field								
	Group	Alphabetic	Alphanumeric	Alphanumeric-edited	Numeric (DISPLAY)	Numeric-edited	Binariy (COMP)	Floating-point (COMP-1/COMP-2)	Packed-decimal (COMP-3)
Group	Y	Y	Y	Y[1]	Y[1]	Y[1]	Y[1]	Y[1]	Y[1]
Alphabetic (A)	Y	Y	Y	Y	N	N	N	N	N
Alphanumeric (X)	Y	Y	Y	Y	Y[4]	Y[4]	Y[4]	Y[4]	Y[4]
Alphanumeric-edited	Y	Y	Y	Y	N	N	N	N	N
Numeric (DISPLAY) (9)	Y[1]	N	Y[2]	Y[2]	Y	Y	Y	Y	Y
Numeric-edited	Y	N	Y	Y	N[6]	N[6]	N	N	N
Binary (COMP)	Y[1]	N	Y[2]	Y[2]	Y	Y	Y	Y	Y
Floating-point (COMP-1/COMP-2)	Y[1]	N	N	N	Y	Y	Y	Y	Y
Packed-decimal (COMP-3)	Y[1]	N	Y[2]	Y[2]	Y	Y	Y	Y	Y
Figurative Constants ZEROS	Y	N	Y	Y	Y[3]	Y[3]	Y[3]	Y[3]	Y[3]
SPACES	Y	Y	Y	Y	N	N	N	N	N
HIGH-VALUE LOW-VALUE QUOTE	Y	N	Y	Y	N	N	N	N	N
All literal	Y	Y	Y	Y	Y[5]	Y[5]	Y[5]	N	Y[5]
Numeric literal	Y[1]	N	Y[2]	Y[2]	Y	Y	Y	Y	Y
Nonnumeric literal	Y	Y	Y	Y	Y[5]	Y[5]	Y[5]	N	Y[5]

LEGEND: Y = yes; N = no

[1]Move treated like an alphanumeric to alphanumeric move—no data conversion is made.

[2]Decimal point must be to the right of the least significant digit treated as a numeric move.

[3]Treated as a numeric move.

[4]Alphanumeric field treated an integer numeric (DISPLAY) field.

[5]Literal treated as an integer numeric (DISPLAY) field and may contain only numeric characters.

[6]COBOL 85 will un-edit an edited field.

APPENDIX

D

Answers to Selected Questions and Exercises

Chapter 1

Answers to Questions

1. COmmon Business-Oriented Language
3. commercial/business-oriented
5. Committee On Data System Languages
7. U.S. government (Defense Department); universities (educators); computer manufacturers; computer uses
9. American National Standards Institute
11. COBOL
13. disciplined
15. central processing unit (CPU), tape and/or disk units
17. software
19. operating system
21. object
23. application
25. Job Control Language (JCL)
27. data
29. **a.** not a highly mathematical language
b. wordy-lengthy
c. not the easiest language to learn
d. not the best language for structured design
31. Compile
Link
Go

Chapter 2

Answers to Questions

1. analysis
3. bugs
5. flowchart
7. arrowheads
9. functionally
11. **a.** simple sequence
b. if-then-else
c. do-while
13. **a.** larger, more complex problems may be approached on the basis of smaller, less complex subproblems
b. time required to develop a program is reduced
c. errors may be located and eliminated more quickly
d. the program may be developed in sections
e. standardization is promoted
15. tree; stair step
17. indicator
19. control module
21. case
23. F—normally repetitive debugging operations follow the first attempted execution of a program
25. F—one block may be used to represent a series of similar operations (e.g., a series of MOVEs)
27. T
29. F—only when an error exit is desired should a module have multiple exit points
31. T
33. T

Chapter 3

Answers to Questions

1. DIVISION
3. SECTIONs: paragraphs
5. IDENTIFICATION; PROCEDURE
7. PROCEDURE
9. identify the resources (computers and devices) needed by the program
11. DATA
13. PROCEDURE
15. hyphen; seven
17. A
19. numeric; alphabetic; special characters
21. period
23. reserved words; programmer-supplied-names
25. DATA

27. constants
29. 120
31. reserved
33. F—IDENTIFICATION DIVISION does not
35. F—statement
37. F—only in the PROCEDURE DIVISION
39. F—only when reserved words, data-names, or constants are borken
41. T
43. T
45. F—but this is desirable from a coding standpoint
47. F—period
49. F—e.g., procedure-names
51. T
53. F—they are reserved words
55. F—not with a decimal point

Answers to Exercises

1. **a.** legal
3. **b.** illegal—$ is a special character
   c. legal
   d. legal for a procedure-name only
   e. legal
   f. illegal—must be a continuous character string (use hyphens)
   g. illegal—exceeds 30 characters
   h. illegal—decimal point/period is an illegal character
   i. illegal—a reserved word
   j. legal

Chapter 4

Answers to Questions

1. IDENTIFICATION
3. SECTION
5. A
7. DATE-COMPILED
9. period
11. F—the specified order must be maintained
13. F—the PROGRAM-ID paragraph must be first
15. T
17. T—and a space must follow the period
19. F—these entries must fall wholly within columns 12 through 72

Answers to Exercises

1. **a.** period after division heading
   b. PROGRAM-ID omitted

c. period after author's name is missing
d. DATE-COMPILED précedes DATE-WRITTEN
e. DATE-COMPILED must be hyphenated
f. DATE-WRITTEN is misspelled
g. a period must immediately follow SECURITY paragraph name
h. "PART II. . ." should begin in Area B—columns 12 through 72

3. IDENTIFICATION DIVISION.
PROGRAM-ID. DFCM214.

Chapter 5

Answers to Questions

1. the resources necessary to execute the program
3. SOURCE-COMPUTER; OBJECT-COMPUTER
5. top of form—the top of the printer page
7. INPUT-OUTPUT
9. ASSIGN
11. F—the ENVIRONMENT DIVISION is system sensitive
13. T
15. F—the entires may be used to interface special system functions to a COBOL program
17. F
19. F—not necessarily

Answers to Exercises

1. a. ENVIRONMENT is misspelled
b. CONFIGURATION SECTION is not hyphenated
c. OBJECT-COMPUTER is hyphenated
d. SPECIAL-NAMES not "TERMS"
e. CØ1 should be a continuous string
f. period should appear after NEXT-PAGE
g. INPUT-OUTPUT should be followed by the reserved word SECTION
h. FILE-CONTROL paragraph is missing
i. period after MY-INPUT-FILE should be omitted
j. SELECT MY-PRINT-FILE should begin in Area B
k. ALTERNATIVE should be ALTERNATE

Chapter 6

Answers to Questions

1. FILE; WORKING-STORAGE
3. WORKING-STORAGE
5. eighty (80)
7. groups; elementary-items
9. Ø1
11. PICTURE (PIC)
13. alphabetic; alphanumeric; numeric
15. Sign character (S); first (leftmost); minus sign overpunched; last (rightmost)

17. replication factor in parentheses
19. eighty (80); 160
21. T
23. T
25. T
27. F—level numbers are Ø1 through 49
29. T
31. T—unless multiple lines are necessary (two cannot appear on the same line)
33. T—this is also true for record-names
35. F—it may not be the rightmost character
37. T—it must be described as an alphanumeric field
39. T
41. T—level-77 data items must immediately follow the WORKING-STORAGE SECTION heading
43. f—SPACE(S) is an illegal value for a numeric data item
45. T

Answers to Exercises

1. Record Description

Data-Name	Group or Elementary-Item	Length	Columns or Positions
INVOICE-RECORD	Group	75	1–75
DESCRIPTIVE-INFORMATION	Group	70	1–70
INVOICE-NUMBER	Elementary-Item	5	1–5
CUSTOMER-NUMBER	Group	9	6–14
CUSTOMER-GROUP	Elementary-Item	2	6–7
CUSTOMER-SUFFIX	Elementary-Item	7	8–14
ITEM-INFORMATION	Group	56	15–70
ITEM-NUMBER	Elementary-Item	10	15–24
ITEM-DESCRIPTION	Elementary-Item	30	25–54
QUANTITY-PURCHASED	Elementary-Item	5	55–59
PRICE-PER-UNIT	Elementary-Item	5	60–64
COST-PER-UNIT	Elementary-Item	5	65–69
UNIT-MEASUREMENT	Elementary-Item	1	70
FILLER	Elementary-Item	5	71–75

3. a)
```
01 NAME-ADDRESS-LABEL
   02 CONTACT-NAME          PIC X(20).
   02 BUSINESS-NAME         PIC X(19).
   02 STREET-ADDRESS        PIC X(20).
   02 CITY                  PIC A(14).
   02 STATE                 PIC XX.
   02 ZIP-CODE              PIC X(5).
```

b)
```
01 INVENTORY-RECORD.
   02 IDENTIFICATION-INFORMATION.
      03 ITEM-NUMBER        PIC 9(9).
      03 ITEM-DESCRIPTION   PIC X(30).
   02 CURRENT-INFORMATION.
      03 PRICE-GROUP        PIC 9(5).
      03 UNIT-PRICE         PIC 9(4)V99.
```

```
        03 UNIT-COST            PIC 9(4)V99.
        03 ON-HAND              PIC 9(6).
     2 STATISTICAL-INFORMATION.
        3 MTD-SALES             PIC 9(8).
        3 YTD-SALES             PIC 9(8).
     2 FILLER                   PIC XX.
```

c)
```
   01 STUDENT-GRADE-RECORD.
      02 STUDENT-NAME          PIC X(20).
      02 STUDENT-ID-NUMBER     PIC 9(9).
      02 EXAM-GRADES.
         03 EXAM-1             PIC 999V9.
         03 EXAM-2             PIC 999V9.
         03 EXAM-3             PIC 999V9.
         03 EXAM-4             PIC 999V9.
      2 COURSE-DATE.
         03 PREFIX             PIC XXXX.
         03 NUMBER             PIC 9999.
         03 COURSE-TITLE       PIC X(27).
```

5.
```
WORKING-STORAGE SECTION.
01 HEADING-1.
   02 FILLER           PIC X(23) VALUE SPACES.
   02 FILLER           PIC X(22) VALUE
                             'INVENTORY USAGE REPORT'.
01 HEADING-2.
   02 FILLER           PIC X(24) VALUE SPACES.
   02 FILLER           PIC X(12) VALUE 'REPORT DATE'.
   02 MONTH            PIC 99.
   02 FILLER           PIC X VALUE '/'.
   02 DAY              PIC 99.
   02 FILLER           PIC X VALUE '/'.
   02 YEAR             PIC 99.
   02 FILLER           PIC X(15) VALUE SPACES.
   02 PAGE-NO          PIC 99.
01 HEADING-3.
   02 FILLER           PIC X(14) VALUE ' ITEM'.
   02 FILLER           PIC X(22) VALUE 'ITEM'.
   02 FILLER           PIC X(14) VALUE 'UNITS ON'.
   02 FILLER           PIC X(8) VALUE 'MONTH TO'.
01 HEADING-4.
   02 FILLER           PIC X VALUE SPACES.
   02 FILLER           PIC X(59) VALUE
   'NUMBER   DESCRIPTION        HAND DATE USAGE'.
01 HEADING-5.
   02 FILLER           PIC X(60) VALUE All '*'.
```

Chapter 7

Answers to Questions

1. sentence; statement
3. DATA; PROCEDURE; PROCEDURE
5. SELECT; FD
7. CLOSE
9. PHYSICAL
11. SENTENCE
13. one(1)
15. FROM

17. integer; identifier; mnemonic-name
19. SPECIAL-NAMES; ENVIRONMENT
21. sending
23. right; left
25. the statement immediately following the PERFORM statement
27. one (1)
29. zero (Ø)
31. T
33. T—BEFORE reverses the operation
35. F—but the programmer is responsible for the result
37. F–truncation or blank (zero) filling takes place
39. F—the PROCEDURE DIVISION is always last
41. F—all SECTIONs and/or paragraphs are programmer supplied
43. T
45. F—although the word OUTPUT may appear
47. T—but a file which has been opened may not be re-opened until it is closed
49. F—not is a single program
51. F—closing operations require no key word indicating how the file was being used
53. T
55. T—even when the INTO option is present
57. T—after the branch has been executed there is no way to access it
59. F—the procedure may be either above or below the PERFORM
61. F—a range of procedures may be executed with the THRU option
63. F—either paragraphs or SECTIONs
65. F—individual PERFORM statements are independent of each other
67. T
69. F—all condition types are permitted

1. Answers to Exercises

Data-Name	Value from First Read	Value from Second Read
POLICY NUMBER	AX-14293-4	R42219-Cbb
CLIENT-NUMBER	ØØ5Ø2148	1Ø8521Ø2
POLICY-ANNIVERSARY-DATE*	Ø415	Ø831
ANNIVERSARY-MONTH	Ø4	Ø8
ANNIVERSARY-DAY	15	31
POLICY-EXPIRATION-DATE*	Ø22682	1Ø2881
EXPIRATION-MONTH	Ø2	1Ø
EXPIRATION-DAY	26	28
EXPIRATION-YEAR	82	81
PREMIUM-AMOUNT	ØØ723∧88	Ø1911∧76
COMMISSION-AMOUNT	Ø86∧9Ø	116∧62
SALESMAN-CODE	JWS	DEW
STATE-CODE	TX	IL

*Group-names—the record-name references all the data

Chapter 8

Answers to Questions

1. Fixed insertion
3. Minus (−) insertion
5. floating
7. Ø and B
9. * and Z
11. F—e.g., +, −, and $ are both fixed- and floating-insertion characters
13. F—it may also appear on the right side of the PICTURE clause
15. F—., ,, Ø, B, CR, and DB are only fixed-insertion characters
17. T
19. F—combinations may be used (e.g., $999,999.99-)
21. F—only one character per PICTURE string may be either a floating or replacement character
23. T
25. T—e.g., in the PICTURE string $$$,$$$.$$ a $ will replace the comma when the value placed in the field is less than 1,000
27. T—e.g., as illustrated in the answer to question #25
29. F
31. T—e.g., ZZZ,ZZZ when the value in the field is less than 1,000, the comma is replaced with a blank

Answers to Questions

1. Result* / Length

	Result*	Length
a.	69,274	6
b.	Ø3,192.88	9
c.	−ØØ24.76	8
d.	−627.ØØ	7
e.	+27	3
f.	667.44ƀƀ	8
g.	$7,621.88ƀ-	11
h.	ƀ$4,562.89	10
i.	ƀƀƀ$.Ø1	7
j.	$855.97	7
k.	−ƀ$9,884.6Ø	11
l.	ƀƀƀƀƀƀƀ	7
m.	+$**462.88	10
n.	12ƀ86ƀØØ	8
o.	HELPƀƀME	8

*ƀ represents the location of the blank character

Chapter 9

Answers to Questions

1. PROCEDURE
3. relational

5. class
7. AND; OR
9. OR
11. unconditional branch
13. paragraph; SECTION
15. T
17. T
19. F—ELSE causes a syntax error and NEXT SENTENCE must be stated
21. T
23. F—only parentheses may be used to alter the sequence
25. F—the relation cannot be implied without implying the same subject
27. F—it may also appear in the false branch
29. T

Answers to Exercises

1. **a.** correct; True: MOVE 'OVERTIME WORKED' TO MESSAGE
   False: MOVE 'NO OVERTIME' TO MESSAGE
   b. correct; True: NEXT SENTENCE
   False: MOVE 0 TO DEDUCTION-AMOUNT
   c. incorrect; relations should be NOT EQUAL TO
   d. correct; True: PERFORM EIC-LOOKUP
   False: nonestated
   e. incorrect; GO TO NEXT-OPERATION can never be executed because it is preceded by another GO TO statement
   f. incorrect; no true statement has been provided—NEXT SENTENCE should be supplied
3. **a.** A-PART
   B-PART
   b. 1ST-PARA
   2ND-PARA will continue to be executed infinitely
   1ST-PARA
   c. PARA-A
   PARA-B
   PARA-C
   PARA-B
   d. PART-1
   PART-2
   PART-1—fall through
   PART-2
   PART-2—fall through
   PART-3—fall through
   e. DO-1ST
   DO-2ND
   DO-3RD
   DO-2ND
   DO-LAST
   DO-2ND
   DO-2ND—fall through
   DO-3RD—fall through
   DO-2ND

DO-LAST
DO-2ND
DO-LAST—fall through
DO-2ND

Chapter 10

Answers to Questions

1. ADD; SUBTRACT; MULTIPLY; DIVIDE; COMPUTE
3. ADD or COMPUTE
5. data items; numeric literals
7. ON SIZE ERROR
9. one (1); two (2)
11. data items
13. GIVING
15. division by zero
17. dividend
19. numeric data items, numeric literals, operators (+, −, *, /, **); parentheses
21. T
23. T—e.g., ADD 1 TO A,B.
25. F—only identifiers may appear as receiving fields
27. T
29. F—i.e., ADD A, B GIVING C—the GIVING form of the statement does not contain the reserved word TO
31. F—the receiving field (data-name following GIVING) does not have to contain a value prior to the execution of the statement.
33. T
35. F—only in a simple SUBTRACT statement
37. F—although generally desirable, neither form of the SUBTRACT statement requires an operational sign (S) on the receiving field
39. T
41. F—BY is permitted only in the GIVING form of the DIVIDE statement
43. T
45. T—since it only acts as a receiving field
47. T—this sequence can only be altered by the use of parentheses

Answers to Exercises

1. **a.** FIELD-2 = 89
b. FIELD-2 = 36 (both overflow and underflow occurs)
c. FIELD-4 = Ø274.62
d. FIELD-3 = 129.5Ø
e. FIELD-4 = Ø134.7Ø (rounding occurs)
f. FIELD-2 = 72
g. FIELD-2 = 49
h. FIELD-2 = 13 (a positive value since FIELD-2 does not contain an operational sign)
i. FIELD-1 = 48 (rounding occurs)

j. FIELD-3 = 0 (ON SIZE ERROR option executed since the result will cause an overflow of the receiving field)

3. a. NUM-3 = 1500
   b. NUM-2 = 025 (a positive value)
   c. NUM-4 = 11.10
   d. NUM-1 = 00 (overflow occurs)
   e. NUM-2 = 125
   f. NUM-5 = $1,500.00
   g. NUM-3 = 27 (no operational sign; thus the value is positive, and the fractional part of the result is truncated)
   h. NUM-2 = 001 (.999 is rounded to 1)
   i. NUM-5 = bbb$27.75 (no sign option, thus the negative sign is dropped)
   j. NUM-3 = 0250 (ON SIZE ERROR option is not invoked by the dropping of the sign)

5. a. VAL-1 = 0050.00
   b. VAL-2 = 50.00
   c. VAL-3 = 0017.50
   d. VAL-2 = 25.00
   e. VAL-4 = 0.500
   f. VAL-5 = b625.00
   g. VAL-1 = 016
   h. VAL-3 = −0060.00

Chapter 11

Answers to Questions

1. numeric
3. NUMERIC; ALPHABETIC
5. ascending
7. F—not by themselves, but may be used when in an arithmetic expression
9. F—only an identifier may be tested in the condition
11. T
13. F—for example, testing a field for contents of a nonnumeric literal may be performed in a relational test

Answers to Exercises

1. a. correct; sign; true
   MOVE 'DIVISION ERROR—PROCEDURE ABORTED' TO OUTPUT-LINE
   WRITE OUTPUT-LINE AFTER ADVANCING 1 LINES
   STOP RUN
   b. correct; class; true: PERFORM DEPENDENT-DEDUCTIONS
   false: NEXT SENTENCE (redundant)
   c. incorrect; a numeric literal may not be tested by itself in a sign test
   d. correct; class; true: MOVE 'W-2 FILED' TO EMPLOYEE-STATUS
   false: MOVE 'NO W-2' TO EMPLOYEE-STATUS

3. Relational Tests:

```
MOVE SPACES TO BASE, OVERTIME.
IF PAY-CODE = 'S'
   MOVE 'SALARY' TO BASE
   MOVE 'NO' TO OVERTIME.
IF PAY-CODE = 'X'
   MOVE 'HOURLY' TO BASE
   MOVE 'NO' TO OVERTIME.
IF PAY-CODE = 'H'
   MOVE 'HOURLY' TO BASE
   MOVE 'YES' TO OVERTIME.
IF BASE = SPACES OR OVERTIME = SPACES
   MOVE 'ERROR' TO BASE, OVERTIME.
IF PAY-CODE = 'O'
   MOVE 'SALARY' TO BASE
   MOVE 'YES' TO OVERTIME.
   MOVE 'ERROR' TO BASE, OVERTIME.
IF PAY-CODE = 'S' OR 'O'
   MOVE 'SALARY' TO BASE.
IF PAY-CODE = 'X' or 'H'
   MOVE 'HOURLY' TO BASE.
IF PAY-CODE = 'S' OR 'X'
   MOVE 'NO' TO OVERTIME.
IF PAY-CODE = 'O' OR 'H'
   MOVE 'YES' TO OVERTIME.
```

Condition-name Test:

```
005 PAY-CODE                   PIC X.
       88 SALARIED-EXEMPT      VALUE 'S'.
       88 SALARIED-NON-EXEMPT  VALUE 'O'.
       88 HOURLY-EXEMPT        VALUE 'X'.
       88 HOURLY-NON-EXEMPT    VALUE 'H'.
MOVE 'ERROR' TO BASE, OVERTIME.
IF SALARIED-EXEMPT OR SALARIED-NON-EXEMPT
   MOVE 'SALARY' TO BASE.
IF HOURLY-EXEMPT OR HOURLY-NON-EXEMPT
   MOVE 'HOURLY' TO BASE.
IF SALARIED-EXEMPT OR HOURLY-EXEMPT
   MOVE 'NO' TO OVERTIME.
IF SALARIED-NON-EXEMPT OR HOURLY-NON-EXEMPT
   MOVE 'YES' TO OVERTIME.
```

Chapter 12

Answers to Questions

1. four (4)
3. numeric identifier or numeric literal
5. three (3)
7. EXIT
9. T
11. F—altering the identifier has no impact on the number of times the procedure is repeated
13. F—it may contain a negative value, but the procedure will not be executed
15. F—the increment may be negative
17. F—it may be any of the condition types, including compound conditions
19. F—one condition must be stated with the VARYING phrase and one condition must be specified for each AFTER option used

21. T
23. T
25. F—syntax requirements dictate the location of these reserved words
27. T—the EXIT statement must be the only statement in the paragraph

Answers to Exercises

1. a. PARA-1
PARA-2
PARA-2
PARA-2
PARA-2
PARA-2

b. PARA-1
PARA-2
PARA-3
PARA-3
PARA-1
PARA-1
PARA-2
PARA-1
PARA-2
PARA-3
PARA-3
PARA-1
PARA-2
PARA-3
PARA-3

c. PARA-1
PARA-1
PARA-1

d. PARA-1
PARA-3
PARA-2
PARA-2
PARA-2

e. PARA-1
PARA-2 (fall through)
PARA-1
PARA-3 (fall through)
PARA-4
PARA-4
PARA-4

Chapter 13

Answers to Questions

1. tables
3. Ø2; 49
5. single-dimension table (list, vector)
7. subscript
9. OCCURS clause
11. matrix
13. OCCURS clause
15. identifier
17. F—tables may be defined only within record descriptions
19. F—the identifier is used only for variable-length tables
21. T
23. T
25. F—only if one OCCURS clause is subordinate to another OCCURS clause
27. T
29. F—the subordinate description may be used to describe one, two, or more inter-related tables.

Answers to Exercises

Data-name	Number of			Length of a Single Item	# of Items in Descrip.	Total Bytes in Descrip.
	Rows	Cols	Ranks			
1. a. LIST-OF-CONTRIBUTORS	—	—	—	400	1	400
CONTRIBUTOR	20	—	—	20	20	400
b. SALESMAN—TABLE	—	—	—	2010	1	2010
SALESMAN-NAME	50	—	—	42	50	2010
NAME	50	—	—	30	50	1500
ID-NUMBER	50	—	—	5	50	250
PHONE	50	—	—	7	50	350
c. COLLEGE-COURSE	—	—	—	360	1	360
DEPARTMENT	30	—	—	3	30	90
COURSE-NUMBER	90	—	—	3	90	270
d. LEDGER-TABLE	—	—	—	1480	1	1480
ASSETS	30	—	—	37	30	1110
ASSET-NO	30	—	—	5	30	150
ASSET-DESC	30	—	—	25	30	750
ASSET-BALANCE	30	—	—	7	30	210
LIABILITY	10	—	—	37	10	370
LIAB-NO	10	—	—	5	10	50
LIAB-DESC	10	—	—	25	10	250
LIAB-BALANCE	10	—	—	7	10	70
e. INTEREST-RATE-TABLE	—	—	—	2000	10	2000
INTEREST-RATE	10	—	—	200	10	2000
YEARS-INVESTED	10	20	—	10	200	2000
INTEREST	10	20	—	10	200	2000
f. STUDENT-INFORMATION-TABLE	—	—	—	26400	1	26400
STUDENT	400	—	—	31	400	12400
NAME	400	—	—	20	400	8000
ID-NUMBER	400	—	—	9	400	3600
CLASS	400	—	—	2	400	800
COURSE	400	50	—	7	2000	14000
DEPT	400	50	—	3	2000	6000
COURSE-NO	400	50	—	3	2000	6000
GRADE	400	50	—	1	2000	2000
g. DEMOGRAPHIC-DATA	—	—	—	3200	1	3200
INCOME	20	—	—	160	20	3200
AGE	20	40	—	4	800	3200
SEX	20	40	2	1	1600	1600
MARITAL-STATUS	20	40	2	1	1600	1600

Chapter 14

Answers to Questions

1. occurrence positions; byte displacement
3. INDEXED BY
5. relative
7. PERFORM; SET; SEARCH
9. index-name
11. numeric literal; identifier
13. linear; binary
15. the index-name of another table
17. the specified condition is found to be true; the logical end of the searching process has been encountered
19. decreasing
21. relational, sign, class, or condition-name conditions; relational condition
23. T—the identifier is implicitly defined as a full-word, binary, integer storage position
25. F—of the statements generally used to modify a subscript, only the PERFORM statement is permitted to modify an index
27. T—it is implicitly defined by its appearance in an INDEXED BY clause
29. F—an index-data-name is not directly related to a table—it may be used in conjunction with the processing of several tables
31. T—the actual byte displacement value is placed in the index-data-name
33. F—the receiving fields in the SET statement are treated similarly to those used as the receiving fields of MOVE statements
35. T
37. F—it is used to vary the index of another, perhaps related table
39. T—but the logic behind the execution of each is different
41. F—several keys, in decreasing order of importance, may be stated

Answers to Exercises

1. a.

CODE-TO-RATE CONVERSION	Byte Displacement Begins	Ends
RATE (1)	0	3
RATE (2)	4	7
RATE (3)	8	11
RATE (4)	12	15
RATE (5)	16	19
RATE (6)	20	23
RATE (7)	24	27
RATE (8)	28	31

b.

FEDERAL-TAX-TABLE

TAX-BRACKET (1) (0–21)	LOWER-LIMIT (1) (0–6)	UPPER-LIMIT (1) (7–13)	BASE-TAX (1) (14–19)	PERCENT-TAX (1) (20–21)
TAX-BRACKET (2) (22–43)	LOWER-LIMIT (2) (22–28)	UPPER-LIMIT (2) (29-35)	BASE-TAX (2) (36–41)	PERCENT-TAX (2) (42–43)
TAX-BRACKET (3) (44–65)	LOWER-LIMIT (3) (44–50)	UPPER-LIMIT (3) (51–57)	BASE-TAX (3) (58–63)	PERCENT-TAX (3) (64–65)
TAX-BRACKET (4) (66–87)	LOWER-LIMIT (4) (66–72)	UPPER-LIMIT (4) (73–79)	BASE-TAX (4) (80–85)	PERCENT-TAX (4) (86–87)
TAX-BRACKET (5) (88–109)	LOWER-LIMIT (5) (88–94)	UPPER-LIMIT (5) (95–101)	BASE-TAX (5) (102–107)	PERCENT-TAX (5) (108–109)
TAX-BRACKET (6) (110–116)	LOWER-LIMIT (6) (110–116)	UPPER-LIMIT (6) (117–123)	BASE-TAX (6) (124–129)	PERCENT-TAX (6) (130–131)
TAX-BRACKET (7) (132–153)	LOWER-LIMIT (7) (132–138)	UPPER-LIMIT (7) (139–145)	BASE-TAX (7) (146–151)	PERCENT-TAX (7) (152–153)

c.

RATE-PREMIUM-CONVERSION

PAY-SCALE (1) (0–11)	SHIFT (1,1) ADJUSTMENT (1,1) (0–3)	SHIFT (1,2) ADJUSTMENT (1,2) (4–7)	SHIFT (1,3) ADJUSTMENT (1,3) (8–11)
PAY-SCALE (2) (12–23)	SHIFT (2,1) ADJUSTMENT (2,1) (12–15)	SHIFT (2,2) ADJUSTMENT (2,2) (16–19)	SHIFT (2,3) ADJUSTMENT (2,3) (20–23)
PAY-SCALE (3) (24–35)	SHIFT (3,1) ADJUSTMENT (3,1) (24–27)	SHIFT (3,2) ADJUSTMENT (3,2) (28–31)	SHIFT (3,3) ADJUSTMENT (3,3) (32–35)
PAY-SCALE (4) (36–47)	SHIFT (4,1) ADJUSTMENT (4,1) (36–39)	SHIFT (4,2) ADJUSTMENT (4,2) (40–43)	SHIFT (4,3) ADJUSTMENT (4,3) (44–47)
PAY-SCALE (5) (48–59)	SHIFT (5,1) ADJUSTMENT (5,1) (48–51)	SHIFT (5,2) ADJUSTMENT (5,2) (52–55)	SHIFT (5,3) ADJUSTMENT (5,3) (56–59)

3. d.

```
        SET ITEM TO 1.
        MOVE 'BEGIN' TO SEARCH-STATUS.
        PERFORM SEARCH-ITEMS
            UNTIL SEARCH-STATUS = 'COMPLETE'.
        STOP RUN.
    SEARCH-ITEMS.
        SEARCH INVENTORY-ITEMS
            AT END
                MOVE 'COMPLETE' TO SEARCH-STATUS
           WHEN VENDOR-CODE (ITEM) = 'SRV'
                DISPLAY 'ITEM', ITEM-NUMBER (ITEM),
                        'VENDOR', VENDOR-CODE (ITEM),
                        'UNITS', UNITS-ON-HAND (ITEM).
```

e.

```
        SET ITEM TO 1.
        MOVE 'BEGIN' TO SEARCH-STATUS.
```

```
    PERFORM SEARCH-ITEMS
        UNTIL SEARCH-STATUS = 'COMPLETE'.
    STOP RUN.
SEARCH-ITEMS.
    SEARCH INVENTORY-ITEMS
        AT END
            MOVE 'COMPLETE' TO SEARCH-STATUS
        WHEN
        PRICE (ITEM) * UNITS-ON-HAND (ITEM)
            GREATER THAN 10000
            DISPLAY ITEM-NUMBER (ITEM).
```

f.

```
    PERFORM OUTPUT-INVENTORY
        VARYING ITEM FROM 1 BY 1 UNTIL ITEM GREATER
        THAN 300.
    STOP RUN.
OUTPUT-INVENTORY.
    SET VEND TO 1.
    MOVE ITEM-NUMBER (ITEM) TO ITEM-OUT.
    MOVE VENDOR-CODE (ITEM) TO VENDOR-OUT.
    SEARCH VENDOR-SUPPLIER
        AT END MOVE 'NOT FOUND' TO VENDOR-NAME-OUT
        WHEN VENDOR-CODE (ITEM) = VEND-CODE (VEND)
            MOVE VENDOR-NAME (VEND) TO
            VENDOR-NAME-OUT.
    WRITE OUTPUT-LINE AFTER ADVANCING 1 LINES.
```

4. a.

```
01 INVENTORY-TABLE.
   02 INVENTORY-ITEM
        OCCURS 0 TO 300 TIMES DEPENDING ON ACTIVE
        ASCENDING KEY IS ITEM-NUMBER
        INDEXED BY ITEM.
            .
            .
            .
(assume ITEM has previously been set to some legitimate
value)
   SEARCH ALL INVENTORY-ITEM
       AT END DISPLAY 'ITEM NOT FOUND'
       WHEN ITEM-NUMBER (ITEM) = 4782
           DISPLAY 'ITEM', ITEM-NUMBER (ITEM),
                   'VENDOR', VENDOR-CODE (ITEM).
```

Chapter 15

Answers to Questions

1. page heading
3. report heading
5. 1 (once)
7. print
9. PAGE LIMIT
11. begin
13. control footing
15. CONTROL(S) IS (ARE) clause
17. report-name, detail-line-name
19. LINE
21. NEXT GROUP
23. SOURCE

25. CONTROL FOOTING (CF)
27. RESET
29. GROUP INDICATE
31. FINAL
33. 20th
35. DETAIL (DE)
37. PAGE-COUNTER
39. report, detail-line
41. GENERATE
43. CONTROL FOOTING
45. DECLARATIVES
47. T
49. T
51. F—it typically uses a rather large amount of resources
53. T
55. F—it is printed only when the control variable changes which may not occur for several pages
57. T
59. F—the clauses are independent
61. T
63. F—although it is rather normal
65. F—it appears at the top of a page anyway
67. T
69. T
71. F—the SUM clause may only be used in control footings
73. T
75. T
77. F—this function is automatic
79. F—it has nothing to do with control headings or footings
81. T
83. F—its purpose is for exception processing
85. T

Answers to Exercises

1.
```
RD  CUSTOMER-PURCHASES
    PAGE LIMIT 50
    CONTROLS ARE FINAL, CUSTOMER-NUMBER-IN.
```

3.
```
01  TYPE CONTROL FOOTING CUSTOMER-NUMBER-IN
    NEXT GROUP PLUS 1.
    05 LINE PLUS 1.
        10 COLUMN 2  PIC X(12) VALUE
                     'Total Sales:'.
       10 COLUMN 24 PIC ZZZ,ZZZ.99 SUM AMOUNT-IN.
01  TYPE CONTROL FOOTING FINAL.
    05 LINE PLUS 1.
       10 COLUMN 2   PIC X(14) VALUE
                     'Company Sales:'.
       10 COLUMN 20  PIC ZZZ,ZZZ, ZZZ.99 SUM AMOUNT-IN.
```

5.
```
01  TYPE REPORT FOOTING.
    05 LINE PLUS 1.
```

```
        10 COLUMN 2     PIC X(14) VALUE
                        'Company Sales:'.
        10 COLUMN 20    PIC ZZZ,ZZZ,ZZZ.99 SOURCE
                        AMOUNT-TOTAL.
```

(AMOUNT-TOTAL would have to be developed within the procedure.)

7. a. control footing for DATE-OF-SALE, control heading for DATE-OF-SALE

b. control footing for DATE-OF-SALE, control footing for CUSTOMER-NUMBER, control heading for CUSTOMER-NUMBER, control heading for DATE-OF-SALE

c. control footing for DATE-OF-SALE, control footing for CUSTOMER-NUMBER, control footing for INVOICE-NUMBER, control footing for INVOICE-NUMBER, control heading for CUSTOMER-NUMBER, control heading for DATE-OF-SALE

d. control footing for DATE-OF-SALE, control footing for CUSTOMER-NUMBER, control footing for INVOICE-NUMBER, control footing for FINAL

9.
```
01 TYPE IS PAGE HEADING.
    05 LINE PLUS 1.
        10 COLUMN 26    PIC X(19) VALUE
                        'Depreciation Report'.
        10 COLUMN 62    PIC X(04) VALUE 'Page'.
        10 COLUMN 67    PIC Z9     SOURCE PAGE-COUNTER.
    05 LINE PLUS 2.
        10 COLUMN 1     PIC X(11) VALUE
                        'Item Number'.
        10 COLUMN 16    PIC X(16) VALUE
                        'Item Description'.
        10 COLUMN 39    PIC X(07) VALUE
                        'Balance'.
        10 COLUMN 52    PIC X(11) VALUE
                        'Useful Life'.
        10 COLUMN 64    PIC Z9     SOURCE USEFUL-LIFE.
    05 LINE PLUS 1.
        10 COLUMN 4     PIC 9(05) SOURCE ITEM-NUMBER-IN.
        10 COLUMN 14    PIC X(20) SOURCE
                        ITEM-DESCRIPTION-IN.
        10 COLUMN 37    PIC $$$$,$$$.$$ SOURCE
                        BALANCE-IN
        10 COLUMN 52    PIC X(15) SOURCE DEPR-METHOD-IN.
```

11.
```
01 TYPE CONTROL FOOTING DEPR-YR-IN
    NEXT GROUP PLUS 1.
    05 LINE PLUS 2.
        10 COLUMN 8     PIC X(25) VALUE
                        'Total Annual Depreciation'.
        10 COLUMN 36    PIC $$$$,$$$.$$ SUM DEPR-IN.
```

Chapter 16

Answers to Questions

1. to order data into a specified sequence
3. sort; merge
5. USING
7. SECTION
9. GIVING; OUTPUT PROCEDURE
11. T

13. T
15. T—providing the USING phrase is not employed
17. F—only one of the two phrases may be employed
19. F—multiple keys may be specified (up to a maximum of 12)
21. T
23. F—the desired records may be selected for RELEASE in the INPUT PROCEDURE
25. T

Answers to Exercises

1. **a.** correct; provided 200-REPORT contains a RETURN statement
   b. incorrect; record length of OUTPUT-FILE is longer than the SORT-FILE
   incorrect; IN-FIELD-1 and IN-FIELD-2 are not in the SORT-RECORD description
   c. incorrect; no output phrase is specified
   incorrect; 100-TEST is a paragraph name
   incorrect; INPUT-FILE is not a sort-file-name
   d. incorrect; required reserved word PROCEDURE omitted from input phrase
   e. incorrect; OUTPUT-FILE not the same length as SORT-FILE
   f. incorrect; DESCENDING misspelled
   incorrect; RETURN statement must not appear in an INPUT PROCEDURE
   incorrect; RELEASE statement must not appear in an OUTPUT PROCEDURE
   incorrect; SORT statement must not appear in an OUTPUT PROCEDURE
   incorrect; TEST-1 not defined as a sort key
   incorrect; OUTPUT-FILE not the same length as SORT-FILE
   incorrect; GO TO 300-LAST causes execution of an OUTPUT PROCEDURE without a return to the SORT statement

Chapter 17

Answers to Questions

1. magnetic medium
3. less space
5. the same size as
7. one (1)
9. tracks
11. system flowchart
13. INPUT, OUTPUT, I-O
15. rewound
17. sorted or ordered
19. updating
21. addition
23. REWRITE
25. F—the limitation is different from system to system, but none restrict the user to 500 bytes or less
27. T
29. F—a buffer is exactly one physical record in length
31. F—only when a file is unblocked; then they are the same in length but different in meaning

33. F—the access mode is assumed to be sequential if omitted
35. F—a system flowchart is global in nature, while a program flowchart concentrates solely on the procedure
37. F—it is controlled by the BLOCK CONTAINS clause
39. T—it is required for all files (except a SORT file)
41. F—a disk, for example, does not know what the top of page means
43. T
45. F—a master file is more permanent in nature and typically retains historical data
47. T—provided the procedure is capable of adding a duplicate
49. F—logically deleted records appear in the file; physically deleted records do not

Chapter 18

Answers to Questions

1. keyed
3. RECORD
5. NOMINAL KEY
7. INVALID KEY
9. WORKING-STORAGE
11. cylinders
13. unique; ascending
15. a duplicate RECORD KEY value already exists in the file
17. generic; START
19. T
21. F—the description could be alphanumeric, for example
23. F—it may be blocked at the programmer's discretion
25. F—only cylinder allocation is permitted
27. F—duplicate records are only identified by WRITE statements
29. F—the second form of the START statement does not require the NOMINAL KEY clause
31. F—since the records may be accessed randomly, ordering the transaction records may be pointless

Chapter 19

Answers to Questions

1. relative
3. direct access
5. 0 (zero)
7. more
9. NOMINAL
11. numeric binary (COMPUTATIONAL) integer
13. SEQUENTIAL, AT END
15. data-to-address transformation
17. prime
19. determine an alternate location for the record
21. determine whether the record in that position is a match

23. entry sequence data set (ESDS)
25. relative record data set (RRDS)
27. cluster
29. control areas, control intervals
31. split
33. ORGANIZATION
35. relative record data set (RRDS)
37. DUPLICATES
39. BLOCK CONTAINS
41. DELETE
43. T
45. T
47. F
49. F—the location of a record is independent of any sequence
51. F—for example, folding or digit manipulation are other methods
53. F—only one record may be recorded in a given position
55. F—a virtual machine, operating system, and a VS-COBOL compiler are required
57. F
59. T
61. T
63. T
65. T
67. F—records are added to the end of the file only
69. F—VSAM files are newer

Chapter 20

Answers to Questions

1. COPY statements, subprogram CALL statements
3. file
5. IDENTIFICATION
7. execution
9. CALL
11. USING
13. PROGRAM-ID
15. T
17. F—by its location in the program
19. T
21. F
23. F
25. T

Chapter 21

Answers to Questions

1. two (2)
3. multiple branches from a single location
5. T

Chapter 22

Answers to Questions

1. memory usage is conserved; alternate (more descriptive) naming of data items is possible
3. WORKING-STORAGE SECTION; group (not record) level (or below)
5. same
7. a level number equivalent (or higher) to that at the beginning of the redefinition is encountered
9. the original definition of the data item
11. immediately after
13. group
15. F—as many as needed may appear in one FD, and they are assumed to be implicit redefinitions of each other
17. T—the length of the longest record if all are not the same length
19. T—but only at the group or elementary-item level in the FILE SECTION
21. T
23. F—most compilers require the redefinition to be the same length as the original description; none will permit the redefinition to be shorter
25. T—but it cannot redefine the entire redefinition
27. T—although if only an elementary-item is being redefined, it still must be the same length
29. F—66-levels do not have subordinate definition
31. T
33. T

Chapter 23

Answers to Questions

1. DISPLAY (zone decimal or external decimal)
3. DISPLAY
5. *b*inary digi*ts*
7. bytes; words
9. zone decimal (external decimal)
11. packed decimal
13. F
15. first bit
17. zero (0)
19. COMPUTATIONAL-3 (COMP-3)
21. two (2)
23. floating point
25. COMPUTATIONAL-2 (COMP-2)
27. right
29. increased by one byte
31. slack bytes
33. F

35. F—COMP-1 and COMP—2 (short and long floating point) are permitted by some compilers
37. T
39. F—this is true only when a PICTURE clause is not permitted
41. F
43. F
45. F—may only be used in conjunction with DISPLAY fields
47. F—DISPLAY mode only
49. T
51. F—at least the same (and more if slack bytes must be inserted)

Chapter 24

Answers to Questions

1. character data
3. parsing
5. POINTER
7. DELIMITED BY
9. INSPECT, EXAMINE
11. T
13. F—the programmer must initialize the pointer variable
15. F
17. F
19. T

APPENDIX

E

Debugging COBOL Programs

Unfortunately, programmers are human and humans are not perfect. As a consequence, programs written by humans are prone to have *bugs*. The word "bug" is a data processing term meaning error. There are two broad categories of errors related to programming—*compilation errors* and *execution errors*.

Compilation errors are errors discovered by the compiler in an attempt to translate a source-language program (e.g., a COBOL program) into an object-language program. These errors are generally caused by a violation of the *syntax* (e.g., format or grammar) rules specified for a particular programming language, such as the incorrect spelling of a reserved word in COBOL. Such an error would cause a message to be printed by the compiler. These *diagnostics* assist the programmer in eliminating syntax errors.

Not all errors identified by the compiler will terminate a program before it begins execution. Most compilers generate at least two levels of error messages. The first category of compiler-detected errors is *fatal errors*. These terminate the program before execution begins. The second category is *warning errors*. The messages produced by a compiler in this category are intended to bring the programmer's attention to a potential problem. In most cases, warnings will not cause program termination. One additional note with regard to compilation errors—certain violations of syntax rules will cause the compiler to generate several error messages. In many cases, the compiler will provide alternative explanations for the cause of the error. Also, many compilers are prone to provide error messages because of a condition previously found in the program. For this reason, the programmer should concentrate initial corrections on the top portion of the program and proceed from top to bottom.

Execution errors are those errors detected by the computer while acting on the instructions within a program. In some cases, these errors are caused by the interaction of data with the program instructions. In other situations, these errors may be due to incorrect program logic. Both kinds may be difficult to trace because of the possibility that they are caused by interacting conditions or may occur at many locations within the program code. Although both data errors and logic errors are frustrating, logic errors are generally more difficult to eliminate because of the varied conditions that may cause them and because the logical requirements of a program vary from one program to another. Thus, there may be no standard pattern for the elimination of logic errors. However, structured design (discussed in Chapter 2) is often helpful in the elimination of these errors.

Errors produced by the interaction of data with the program code are generally caused by a discrepancy between the description of the data item and the actual contents of the data item. The problem could be that the description of the data item is inconsistent with the allowed use of that type of data item (e.g., using an edited-numeric data item in a position intended for a nonedited item) or the contents of the data item are not consistent with the PICTURE string (e.g., numeric field that contains nonnumeric data). Under these circumstances, the computer may produce a message like DATA EXCEPTION or ILLEGAL DECIMAL. These messages are designed to indicate to the programmer that one of the two preceding conditions exists. In most cases, the computer may not indicate *where* the problem arose. If the computer indicates the location (address) of the error, it may be a location that has meaning to the computers, but not necessarily to the programmer. Thus, it is often left up to the programmer to employ his or her own devices to locate and correct the error.

All compilers can produce what is called a "*core dump.*" A core dump is a printed listing of the contents of the computer's internal storage. The only problem with analyzing a core dump is that the organization and content of the printout is different for computers manufactured by different companies (and in some cases, different within the same company). It is often difficult to read (or analyze) a core dump unless the programmer is familiar with the computer being used, its internal architecture (structure), and its assembly language.

To make debugging more manageable, most computer systems can provide more limited (and to the novice, more useful) information regarding the source of an error. This type of diagnostic assistance varies from computer to computer; however, generally available diagnostic aids such as a DATA DIVISION mapping and a condensed listing of the verbs present in the PROCEDURE DIVISION (e.g., an IBM COBOL CLIST) are often useful in debugging. The information contained in these diagnostics is not so detailed as a core dump, but they require knowledge of the hexadecimal or octal numbering systems (depending on the computer) and how to subtract in these numbering systems. In most cases, a simple subtraction will provide the address of the COBOL statement that caused the error. (The operation usually requires subtracting the address of the program *load point*—where the program was located in internal storage—from the address of the instruction causing the error.) This address is a computer storage address, and it is necessary to translate this number to find the COBOL statement that caused the error. (A CLIST or PROCEDURE DIVISION mapping will often provide this type of information. For further details on the availability and use of computer generated diagnostics mentioned earlier, consult with your computer installation.)

The DISPLAY Statement

After locating the statement that produced the error, the cause of the error may not be apparent. Other diagnostic aids may be necessary to isolate the problem further. One of these diagnostic aids is the DISPLAY statement, presented in Figure E.1, first mentioned in the supplement to Chapter 7. It is capable of producing textual types of information (nonnumeric literals) and the contents of storage positions (identifiers). Both identifiers and literals (except the figurative constant ALL) or combinations of identifiers and literals may appear in the DISPLAY statement, which makes it useful in the detection of both data and logical errors.

Figure E.1 Format of the DISPLAY Statement

```
DISPLAY {literal-1   } [literal-2   ] . . . [UPON {system-name  } ]
        {identifier-1} [identifier-2]             {mnemonic-name}
```

By using a combination of identifiers (and possibly literals), the programmer can use the DISPLAY statement to print the contents of data items. These items (noted as identifiers in the format) may be elementary-items, groups, or records. If the data are in an unreadable form—not in DISPLAY form—it will be converted. (Non-DISPLAY descriptions of data items are presented in Chapter 23.)

The size of these items is sometimes limited. The product of the DISPLAY statement is produced on the system output device designated in the UPON clause. The UPON clause is optional and may provide a system-name known by the COBOL compiler or a mnemonic-name which was presented in the SPECIAL-NAMES paragraph of the ENVIRONMENT DIVISION. If the clause is omitted, the default system output device will be used. This device may be a line printer or the computer operator console. Before employing the DISPLAY statement, check with your compiler installation to determine which device is used by default.

Figure E.2 provides an illustration of how the DISPLAY statement might be used to locate a data value that is causing an error. The statement DISPLAY Student ID. Number', STUDENT-ID-IN causes the printing of each value of STUDENT-ID-IN as it appears on the input record along with a message prior to the execution of the WRITE statement.

The DISPLAY statement can also be employed for the detection of logical error. DISPLAY statements could be placed in suspect procedures to determine whether the correct logical sequence of procedures is being executed. Under many circumstances, the DISPLAY of data items is not necessary. Thus, specific messages (nonnumeric literals) would be included in the DISPLAY statement so the programmer could determine whether the correct logical sequence is being properly executed. This procedure might be called a logical tracing of the execution of a program.

DISPLAY statements are very useful for debugging programs, but some programmers use them for other purposes (e.g., instead of WRITE statements in the production of output). The programmer should be cautioned against such practices. WRITE statements are more efficient (faster) in the production of output than DISPLAY statements. (WRITE statements utilize output buffers; DISPLAY statements do not.) Therefore, DISPLAY statements should be used sparingly, if at all, in the final version of a program.

The USE FOR DEBUGGING Statement

One ANS COBOL statement is specifically designed for the purpose of debugging programs. The USE FOR DEBUGGING statement, though not available on all compilers (including older IBM compilers), is very useful as a diagnostic tool. To activate the procedure the programmer must modify the SOURCE-COMPUTER paragraph of the ENVIRONMENT DIVISION by adding the phrase WITH DEBUGGING MODE after the SOURCE-COMPUTER computer-name. The error-checking process specified in the

Figure E.2 An Illustration of the DISPLAY Statement

```
       1   1   2   2   2   3   3   4   4   4   5   5   6   6   6   7
4   8  2   6   0   4   8   2   6   0   4   8   2   6   0   4   8   2

************************************************************
 IDENTIFICATION DIVISION.
************************************************************
 PROGRAM-ID.     EXAMPLE-DISPLAY.
 AUTHOR.         PATRICK THOMAS SPENCE.
 DATE-WRITTEN.   JANUARY 1, 1989.
 DATE-COMPILED.  JANUARY 1, 1989.
*    This program illustrates the use of the DISPLAY
*    statement used for the purpose of determining the
*    contents of an identifier which seems to be producing
*    a problem.
************************************************************
 ENVIRONMENT DIVISION.
************************************************************
*----------------------------------------------------------*
 CONFIGURATION SECTION.
*----------------------------------------------------------*
 SOURCE-COMPUTER. IBM.
 OBJECT-COMPUTER. IBM.
 SPECIAL-NAMES.   C01 IS TOP-OF-NEXT-PAGE.
*----------------------------------------------------------*
 INPUT-OUTPUT SECTION.
*----------------------------------------------------------*
 FILE-CONTROL.
     SELECT STUDENT-FILE ASSIGN TO UT-S-INPUT.
     SELECT REPORT-FILE  ASSIGN TO UT-S-OUTPUT.
************************************************************
 DATA DIVISION.
************************************************************
*----------------------------------------------------------*
 FILE SECTION.
*----------------------------------------------------------*
 FD  STUDENT-FILE LABEL RECORDS ARE OMITTED.
 01  STUDENT-RECORD.
     05 STUDENT-IDENTIFICATION-IN.
         10 LAST-NAME-IN         PIC X(10).
         10 FIRST-NAME-IN        PIC X(10).
         10 MIDDLE-INITIAL-IN    PIC X(01).
         10 STUDENT-ID-IN        PIC 9(09).
     05 FILLER                   PIC X(05).
     05 ENROLLMENT-INFO-IN.
         10 CLASSIFICATION-IN    PIC X(02).
         10 TOTAL-HOURS-IN       PIC 9(03).
         10 HOURS-THIS-SEM-IN    PIC 9(02).
         10 MAJOR-IN             PIC X(03).
     05   FILLER                 PIC X(35).

 FD  REPORT-FILE LABEL RECORDS ARE OMITTED.
 01  REPORT-RECORD               PIC X(133).
*----------------------------------------------------------*
 WORKING-STORAGE SECTION.
*----------------------------------------------------------*
 01  WORKING-VARIABLES.
     05   FILE-STATUS            PIC X(04).

 01  OUTPUT-RECORD.
     05 FILLER                   PIC X(03) VALUE ' *'.
     05 FIRST-NAME-OUT           PIC X(11).
     05 MIDDLE-INITIAL-OUT       PIC X(01).
     05 FILLER                   PIC X(02) VALUE '.'.
     05 LAST-NAME-OUT            PIC X(10).
     05 FILLER                   PIC X(04) VALUE ' *'.
     05 STUDENT-ID-OUT           PIC 9(09).
     05 FILLER                   PIC X(05) VALUE '  *'.
     05 CLASSIFICATION-OUT       PIC X(02).
     05 FILLER                   PIC X(06) VALUE '   *'.
     05 MAJOR-OUT                PIC X(03).
     05 FILLER                   PIC X(08) VALUE '  *'.
     05 HOURS-THIS-SEM-OUT       PIC 9(02).
```

Figure E.2 *Continued* An Illustration of the DISPLAY Statement

```
           1   1   2   2   2   3   3   4   4   4   5   5   6   6   6   7
   4   8   2   6   0   4   8   2   6   0   4   8   2   6   0   4   8   2
-----------------------------------------------------------------------
           05 FILLER                        PIC X(08) VALUE '      *'.
           05 TOTAL-HOURS-OUT               PIC 9(03).
           05 FILLER                        PIC X(03) VALUE '  *'.
      *****************************************************************
       PROCEDURE DIVISION.
      *****************************************************************
      *---------------------------------------------------------------*
       000-CONTROL-PROCEDURE SECTION.
      *---------------------------------------------------------------*
           PERFORM 100-INITIALIZATION.
           PERFORM 300-READ-RECORDS-PRINT-DETAILS
               UNTIL FILE-STATUS = 'DONE'.
           PERFORM 500-TERMINATION.
           STOP RUN.
      *---------------------------------------------------------------*
       100-INITIALIZATION SECTION.
      *---------------------------------------------------------------*
           MOVE 'START'               TO FILE-STATUS.
           OPEN INPUT STUDENT-FILE, OUTPUT REPORT-FILE.
           READ STUDENT-FILE
               AT END MOVE 'DONE'     TO FILE-STATUS.
      *---------------------------------------------------------------*
       300-READ-RECORDS-PRINT-DETAILS SECTION.
      *---------------------------------------------------------------*
           DISPLAY 'Student ID Number ', STUDENT-ID-IN.
           MOVE STUDENT-ID-IN         TO STUDENT-ID-OUT.
           MOVE LAST-NAME-IN          TO LAST-NAME-OUT.
           MOVE FIRST-NAME-IN         TO FIRST-NAME-OUT.
           MOVE MIDDLE-INITIAL-IN     TO MIDDLE-INITIAL-OUT.
           MOVE CLASSIFICATION-IN     TO CLASSIFICATION-OUT.
           MOVE TOTAL-HOURS-IN        TO TOTAL-HOURS-OUT.
           MOVE HOURS-THIS-SEM-IN     TO HOURS-THIS-SEM-OUT.
           MOVE MAJOR-IN              TO MAJOR-OUT.
           WRITE REPORT-RECORD FROM OUTPUT-RECORD AFTER 2 LINES.
           READ STUDENT-FILE
               AT END MOVE 'DONE'     TO FILE-STATUS.
      *---------------------------------------------------------------*
       500-TERMINATION SECTION.
      *---------------------------------------------------------------*
           CLOSE STUDENT-FILE, REPORT-FILE.
```

Figure E.2 *Continued* An Illustration of the DISPLAY Statement (Data)

```
      |         1         2         3         4         5|
Record|12345678901234567890123456789012345678901234567890|
------------------------------------------------------------
     1|Anderson  Jimmy     Q343564321      Gr21900Csc
     2|Booker    John      A555667777      Fr03515Mgt
     3|Carter    Matt      N456789012      Jr09408Mgt
     4|Davidson  Anthony   R353492761      Sr13816Eco
     5|Eldridge  David     Q376495268      So04712Fin
     6|Franklin  Rose      V000000001      Gr18912Gbu
     7|Garrison  Kenneth   A537903251      So02816Mgt
     8|Hamilton  Mark      C486762389      Jr09618Csc
     9|Issacs    Matt      H474653790      Sr12018Eco
    10|Jefferson Harold    Q502326955      Fr01818Mkt
    11|Kennedy   Floyd     R476329092      Jr06012Mkt
    12|Lincoln   Steven    0442648942      So04515Mkt
    13|Monroe    Jeff      V546677219      Sr09918Csc
```

Figure E.2 *Continued* An Illustration of the DISPLAY Statement (Output)

a. Displayed Results:

```
Student ID Number 343564321
Student ID Number 555667777
Student ID Number 456789012
Student ID Number 353492761
Student ID Number 376495268
Student ID Number 000000001
Student ID Number 537903251
Student ID Number 486762389
Student ID Number 474653790
Student ID Number 502326955
Student ID Number 476329092
Student ID Number 442648942
```

b. Printed (Written) Results:

```
| Jimmy     Q. Anderson  | 343564321 | Gr | Csc | 00 | 219 |

| John      A. Booker    | 555667777 | Fr | Mgt | 15 | 035 |

| Matt      N. Carter    | 456789012 | Jr | Mgt | 08 | 094 |

| Anthony   R. Davidson  | 353492761 | Sr | Eco | 16 | 138 |

| David     Q. Eldridge  | 376495268 | So | Fin | 12 | 047 |

| Rose      V. Franklin  | 000000001 | Gr | Gbu | 12 | 189 |

| Kenneth   A. Garrison  | 537903251 | So | Mgt | 16 | 028 |

| Mark      C. Hamilton  | 486762389 | Jr | Csc | 18 | 096 |

| Matt      H. Issacs    | 474653790 | Sr | Eco | 18 | 120 |

| Harold    Q. Jefferson | 502326955 | Fr | Mkt | 18 | 018 |

| Floyd     R. Kennedy   | 476329092 | Jr | Mkt | 12 | 060 |

| Steven    O. Lincoln   | 442648942 | So | Mkt | 15 | 045 |
```

PROCEDURE is activated by this phrase, allowing a variety of diagnostic messages to be produced. (The words DEBUGGING and MODE are required; WITH is optional.) The format of the USE FOR DEBUGGING statement appears in Figure E.3.

A number of alternative USE FOR DEBUGGING statements can be used to debug a program. The programmer may produce his or her own diagnostics or procedures using *interrupts* based on (1) a particular data-name (identifier), (2) a particular file-name, (3) a particular procedure (paragraph or SECTION name), or (4) all procedures in the PROCEDURE DIVISION. On encountering any of the identifiers, files, or procedures listed in the USE FOR DEBUGGING statement, the programmer temporarily interrupts the execution of the body of the PROCEDURE DIVISION until the procedure accompanying the USE FOR DEBUGGING statement is executed. After the USE FOR DEBUGGING procedure is completed, execution of the body of the PROCEDURE DIVISION continues from the point where the interrupt occurred.

An identifier, file-name, or procedure-name that appears in one USE FOR DEBUGGING statement cannot appear in any other USE FOR DEBUGGING statement.

When identifier-1 (or identifier-2, etc.) is specified in the USE FOR DEBUGGING statement, *any* occurrence of that identifier in the PROCEDURE DIVISION will cause

Figure E.3 Format of the USE FOR DEBUGGING Statement

```
                           ⎧[ALL REFERENCES OF] identifier-1⎫
USE FOR DEBUGGING ON       ⎨file-name-1                     ⎬
                           ⎪PROCEDURE procedure-name-1      ⎪
                           ⎩ALL PROCEDURES                  ⎭

                          ⎡⎧[ALL REFERENCES OF] identifier-2⎫⎤
                          ⎢⎨file-name-2                     ⎬⎥  . . .
                          ⎢⎪PROCEDURE procedure-name-2      ⎪⎥
                          ⎣⎩ALL PROCEDURES                  ⎭⎦
```

the programmer-supplied procedure associated with the USE FOR DEBUGGING statement to be executed. The identifier must not be a data item described in the REPORT SECTION of a program. However, the data item may be a table or a part of a table (a data item subordinate to an OCCURS clause—as discussed in Chapter 13). However, when a table name is used, the table name should appear in the USE FOR DEBUGGING statement without subscripts or indexes.

When a file-name is specified, the programmer-supplied procedure is executed after the execution of any OPEN, CLOSE, WRITE, REWRITE, or READ statement that does not cause the AT END imperative statement to be executed. If the procedure-name (a paragraph or SECTION name) is specified, the programmer-supplied procedure associated with the USE FOR DEBUGGING is executed upon encountering the procedure-name during the execution of the program. When ALL PROCEDURES is specified, the programmer-supplied procedure is executed for every paragraph or SECTION encountered during the execution of the program, except those paragraphs or SECTIONs that appear in DECLARATIVES.

Although it is not often necessary (or desirable) to execute portions of the programmer-supplied procedure associated with the USE FOR DEBUGGING statement from the normal code of a program, within a limited set of circumstances, the programmer is allowed to access instructions that appear in DECLARATIVES. However, procedures connected with the USE FOR DEBUGGING statements cannot be executed directly from the normal code. Within DECLARATIVES, the procedure specified for one USE FOR DEBUGGING statement may be PERFORMed by the procedure associated with another USE FOR DEBUGGING statement. (The PERFORM statement is discussed in Chapter 7.) Other than this one exception, USE FOR DEBUGGING statements and their procedures cannot be connected to each other or to the remaining code of the program.

The USE FOR DEBUGGING statement and the accompanying procedure must be located in the PROCEDURE DIVISION immediately after a DECLARATIVES heading. (The DECLARATIVES area of a program is often used for special purpose operations including, but not limited to, the debugging for a program.) The location of the DECLARATIVES heading relative to other parts of a program is shown in Figure E.4.

The USE FOR DEBUGGING statement and its accompanying procedure must appear within a SECTION. In the program PGM-DEBUG SECTION is a programmer-supplied SECTION name. The USE FOR DEBUGGING statement should immediately follow

Figure E.4 An Illustration of the USE FOR DEBUGGING Statement

```
                1   1   2   2   2   3   3   4   4   4   5   5   6   6   6   7
    4   8   2   6   0   4   8   2   6   0   4   8   2   6   0   4   8   2
-------------------------------------------------------------------------------
      ************************************************************
       IDENTIFICATION DIVISION.
      ************************************************************
       PROGRAM-ID.      EXAMPLE-DEBUG1.
       AUTHOR.          RACHEL WINDSOR.
       DATE-WRITTEN.    JANUARY 1, 1989.
       DATE-COMPILED.   JANUARY 1, 1989.
      *     This program illustrates the use of the DEBUGGING
      *     facility available in most ANS COBOL compilers.
      *     The "USE FOR DEBUGGING" statement appears in the
      *     DECLARATIVES and DEBUG-ITEM (a special record) is
      *     DISPLAYed.  (Viewing a data item.)
      ************************************************************
       ENVIRONMENT DIVISION.
      ************************************************************
      *----------------------------------------------------------*
       CONFIGURATION SECTION.
      *----------------------------------------------------------*
       SOURCE-COMPUTER. IBM WITH DEBUGGING MODE.
       OBJECT-COMPUTER. IBM.
       SPECIAL-NAMES.   C01 IS TOP-OF-NEXT-PAGE.
      *----------------------------------------------------------*
       INPUT-OUTPUT SECTION.
      *----------------------------------------------------------*
       FILE-CONTROL.
           SELECT STUDENT-FILE ASSIGN TO UT-S-INPUT.
           SELECT REPORT-FILE  ASSIGN TO UT-S-OUTPUT.
      ************************************************************
       DATA DIVISION.
      ************************************************************
      *----------------------------------------------------------*
       FILE SECTION.
      *----------------------------------------------------------*
       FD  STUDENT-FILE LABEL RECORDS ARE OMITTED.
       01  STUDENT-RECORD.
           05 STUDENT-IDENTIFICATION-IN.
               10 LAST-NAME-IN          PIC X(10).
               10 FIRST-NAME-IN         PIC X(10).
               10 MIDDLE-INITIAL-IN     PIC X(01).
               10 STUDENT-ID-IN         PIC 9(09).
           05 FILLER                    PIC X(05).
           05 ENROLLMENT-INFO-IN.
               10 CLASSIFICATION-IN     PIC X(02).
               10 TOTAL-HOURS-IN        PIC 9(03).
               10 HOURS-THIS-SEM-IN     PIC 9(02).
               10 MAJOR-IN              PIC X(03).
           05  FILLER                   PIC X(35).

       FD  REPORT-FILE LABEL RECORDS ARE OMITTED.
       01  REPORT-RECORD                PIC X(133).
      *----------------------------------------------------------*
       WORKING-STORAGE SECTION.
      *----------------------------------------------------------*
       01  WORKING-VARIABLES.
           05  FILE-STATUS              PIC X(04).

       01  OUTPUT-RECORD.
           05 FILLER                    PIC X(03) VALUE ' *'.
           05 FIRST-NAME-OUT            PIC X(11).
           05 MIDDLE-INITIAL-OUT        PIC X(01).
           05 FILLER                    PIC X(02) VALUE '.'.
           05 LAST-NAME-OUT             PIC X(10).
           05 FILLER                    PIC X(04) VALUE ' *'.
           05 STUDENT-ID-OUT            PIC 9(09).
           05 FILLER                    PIC X(05) VALUE '   *'.
           05 CLASSIFICATION-OUT        PIC X(02).
           05 FILLER                    PIC X(06) VALUE '    *'.
           05 MAJOR-OUT                 PIC X(03).
           05 FILLER                    PIC X(08) VALUE '   *'.
```

Figure E.4 *Continued* An Illustration of the USE FOR DEBUGGING Statement

```
           1   1   2   2   2   3   3   4   4   4   5   5   6   6   6   7
   4   8   2   6   0   4   8   2   6   0   4   8   2   6   0   4   8   2
---------------------------------------------------------------------------
               05 HOURS-THIS-SEM-OUT        PIC 9(02).
               05 FILLER                    PIC X(08) VALUE '      *'.
               05 TOTAL-HOURS-OUT           PIC 9(03).
               05 FILLER                    PIC X(03) VALUE '  *'.
      *************************************************************
       PROCEDURE DIVISION.
      *************************************************************
       DECLARATIVES.
      *-----------------------------------------------------------*
       PGM-DEBUG SECTION.
      *-----------------------------------------------------------*
           USE FOR DEBUGGING ON ALL REFERENCES OF STUDENT-ID-IN.

       DISPLAY-PARA.
           DISPLAY DEBUG-ITEM.

       END DECLARATIVES.
      *-----------------------------------------------------------*
       000-CONTROL-PROCEDURE SECTION.
      *-----------------------------------------------------------*
           PERFORM 100-INITIALIZATION.
           PERFORM 300-READ-RECORDS-PRINT-DETAILS
               UNTIL FILE-STATUS = 'DONE'.
           PERFORM 500-TERMINATION.
           STOP RUN.
      *-----------------------------------------------------------*
       100-INITIALIZATION SECTION.
      *-----------------------------------------------------------*
           MOVE 'START'                TO FILE-STATUS.
           OPEN INPUT STUDENT-FILE, OUTPUT REPORT-FILE.
           READ STUDENT-FILE
               AT END MOVE 'DONE'      TO FILE-STATUS.
      *-----------------------------------------------------------*
       300-READ-RECORDS-PRINT-DETAILS SECTION.
      *-----------------------------------------------------------*
           MOVE STUDENT-ID-IN          TO STUDENT-ID-OUT.
           MOVE LAST-NAME-IN           TO LAST-NAME-OUT.
           MOVE FIRST-NAME-IN          TO FIRST-NAME-OUT.
           MOVE MIDDLE-INITIAL-IN      TO MIDDLE-INITIAL-OUT.
           MOVE CLASSIFICATION-IN      TO CLASSIFICATION-OUT.
           MOVE TOTAL-HOURS-IN         TO TOTAL-HOURS-OUT.
           MOVE HOURS-THIS-SEM-IN      TO HOURS-THIS-SEM-OUT.
           MOVE MAJOR-IN               TO MAJOR-OUT.
           WRITE REPORT-RECORD FROM OUTPUT-RECORD AFTER 2 LINES.
           READ STUDENT-FILE
               AT END MOVE 'DONE'      TO FILE-STATUS.
      *-----------------------------------------------------------*
       500-TERMINATION SECTION.
      *-----------------------------------------------------------*
           CLOSE STUDENT-FILE, REPORT-FILE.
---------------------------------------------------------------------------
```

this SECTION name. The procedure that accompanies the USE FOR DEBUGGING statement must appear in a paragraph immediately following the USE FOR DEBUGGING statement. In the example program, DISPLAY-PARA indicates the procedure to be executed when the USE FOR DEBUGGING statement is invoked. DISPLAY statements are used in the example, but any set of COBOL statements (except another USE FOR DEBUGGING statement) may appear in this paragraph. The code is not limited to a single paragraph. The procedure associated with a particular USE FOR DEBUGGING is terminated with the appearance of another SECTION name in the DECLARATIVES or the END DECLARATIVES heading. In the example, END DECLARATIVES terminates the procedure. Thus, if multiple USE FOR DEBUGGING statements were required within a program, each such set of statements would be placed within a SEC-

Figure E.4 *Continued* An Illustration of the USE FOR DEBUGGING Statement (Output)

a. Displayed Results:

```
000105 STUDENT-ID-IN                                    343564321
000105 STUDENT-ID-IN                                    555667777
000105 STUDENT-ID-IN                                    456789012
000105 STUDENT-ID-IN                                    353492761
000105 STUDENT-ID-IN                                    376495268
000105 STUDENT-ID-IN                                    000000001
000105 STUDENT-ID-IN                                    537903251
000105 STUDENT-ID-IN                                    486762389
000105 STUDENT-ID-IN                                    474653790
000105 STUDENT-ID-IN                                    502326955
000105 STUDENT-ID-IN                                    476329092
000105 STUDENT-ID-IN                                    442648942
```

b. Printed (Written) Results:

```
| Jimmy     Q. Anderson  | 343564321 | Gr | Csc |   00   | 219 |

| John      A. Booker    | 555667777 | Fr | Mgt |   15   | 035 |

| Matt      N. Carter    | 456789012 | Jr | Mgt |   08   | 094 |

| Anthony   R. Davidson  | 353492761 | Sr | Eco |   16   | 138 |

| David     Q. Eldridge  | 376495268 | So | Fin |   12   | 047 |

| Rose      V. Franklin  | 000000001 | Gr | Gbu |   12   | 189 |

| Kenneth   A. Garrison  | 537903251 | So | Mgt |   16   | 028 |

| Mark      C. Hamilton  | 486762389 | Jr | Csc |   18   | 096 |

| Matt      H. Issacs    | 474653790 | Sr | Eco |   18   | 120 |

| Harold    Q. Jefferson | 502326955 | Fr | Mkt |   18   | 018 |

| Floyd     R. Kennedy   | 476329092 | Jr | Mkt |   12   | 060 |

| Steven    O. Lincoln   | 442648942 | So | Mkt |   15   | 045 |
```

TION, isolating it within that SECTION from other USE FOR DEBUGGING statements or other statements.

The DECLARATIVES area of a program is terminated by the END DECLARATIVES marker. Under usual conditions, the program should not begin with the DECLARATIVES portion of a program. Execution of the program should begin with the first executable statement following the END DECLARATIVES marker. In the example program, the first executable statement is the PERFORM statement in the 000-CONTROL-PROCEDURE paragraph. However, most systems require a SECTION name to follow the END DECLARATIVES. The PGM-CODE SECTION was added to the program to satisfy this requirement. (This makes the paragraph name 000-CONTROL-PROCEDURE unnecessary in some systems, but it is retained as a reference point.)

As the program in Figure E.4 is executed, the program checks for an occurrence of the data item STUDENT-ID-IN. (The statement USE FOR DEBUGGING ON ALL REFERENCES OF STUDENT-ID-IN causes this action.) When STUDENT-ID-IN is found during program execution, the statements in DISPLAY-PARA (a DISPLAY statements) are executed. The statement reads DISPLAY DEBUG-ITEM. Upon examining the entire program, the programmer will notice that there is no description of DEBUG-

ITEM in the DATA DIVISION. When the USE FOR DEBUGGING statement appears in a program, the COBOL compiler automatically inserts the description of DEBUG-ITEM. Thus, DEBUG-ITEM is a special record. Its description is as follows.

```
01  DEBUG-ITEM.
    05  DEBUG-LINE              PIC X(06).
    05  FILLER                  PIC X(01) VALUE SPACE.
    05  DEBUG-NAME              PIC X(30).
    05  FILLER                  PIC X(01) VALUE SPACE.
    05  DEBUG-SUB-1             PIC 9(04).
    05  FILLER                  PIC X(01) VALUE SPACE.
    05  DEBUG-SUB-2             PIC 9(04).
    05  FILLER                  PIC X(01) VALUE SPACE.
    05  DEBUG-SUB-3             PIC 9(04).
    05  FILLER                  PIC X(01) VALUE SPACE.
    05  DEBUG-CONTENTS          PIC X(nn).
```

DEBUG-ITEM is an implicit record description that does not appear in the program code. Each of the elementary-items in this record description is often referred to as a *special* COBOL *register.* Depending on the particular option specified in the USE FOR DEBUGGING statement, the appropriate information will be placed in these special registers. Table E.1 presents a summary of the types of information to be placed in these special registers.

Descriptions of DEBUG-LINE, DEBUG-NAME, and DEBUG-CONTENTS are presented in Table E.1, but DEBUG-SUB-1, DEBUG-SUB-2, and DEBUG-SUB-3 are not mentioned. These special registers contain information only when the identifier indicated in the USE FOR DEBUGGING statement is a table. (Tables are discussed in Chapters 13 and 14.) The content of these special registers is the subscript (or index) value of the identifier (table). If an identifier is not used in the statement or the identifier is not a table (or part of a table), these special registers contain spaces.

Figure E.5 further illustrates the USE FOR DEBUGGING statement. This program is similar to the program presented in Figure E.4; however, here the USE FOR DE-

Table E.1 The Contents of DEBUG-ITEM on the Execution of a USE FOR DEBUGGING Statement

	USE FOR DEBUGGING ON			
			procedure-name-1 when	
Field	**identifier-1**	**file-name-1**	**encountered by branching**	**encountered sequentially**
DEBUG-LINE	Identifies the source statement containing identifier-1 (The statement line number.)	Identifies the source statement referencing file-name-1	Identifies the source statement that causes the branch to take place.	Identifies the source statement immediately prior to the procedure-name
DEBUG-NAME	The data name of the identifier	File-name-1	Procedure-name-1	Procedure-name 1
DEBUG-CONTENTS	The data value contained in identifier-1 after the statement containing the identifier is executed	Spaces for OPEN and CLOSE statements; the contents of the input record for READ statements	Spaces (except when an ALTER statement has caused the branch. In this case, procedure-name-2 of the ALTER statement is produced.)	The nonnumeric literal FALL THROUGH

Figure E.5 A Second Illustration of the USE FOR DEBUGGING Statement

```
         1   1   2   2   2   3   3   4   4   4   5   5   6   6   6   7
 4   8   2   6   0   4   8   2   6   0   4   8   2   6   0   4   8   2
-----------------------------------------------------------------------

      *****************************************************************
       IDENTIFICATION DIVISION.
      *****************************************************************
       PROGRAM-ID.      EXAMPLE-DEBUG2.
       AUTHOR.          LAURA WINDSOR.
       DATE-WRITTEN.    JANUARY 1, 1989.
       DATE-COMPILED.   JANUARY 1, 1989.
      *     This program illustrates the use of the DEBUGGING
      *     facility available in most ANS COBOL compilers.
      *     The "USE FOR DEBUGGING" statement appears in the
      *     DECLARATIVES and DEBUG-ITEM (a special record) is
      *     DISPLAYed.  (Tracing a procedure.)
      *****************************************************************
       ENVIRONMENT DIVISION.
      *****************************************************************
      *---------------------------------------------------------------*
       CONFIGURATION SECTION.
      *---------------------------------------------------------------*
       SOURCE-COMPUTER. IBM WITH DEBUGGING MODE.
       OBJECT-COMPUTER. IBM.
       SPECIAL-NAMES.    C01 IS TOP-OF-NEXT-PAGE.
      *---------------------------------------------------------------*
       INPUT-OUTPUT SECTION.
      *---------------------------------------------------------------*
       FILE-CONTROL.
           SELECT STUDENT-FILE ASSIGN TO UT-S-INPUT.
           SELECT REPORT-FILE  ASSIGN TO UT-S-OUTPUT.
      *****************************************************************
       DATA DIVISION.
      *****************************************************************
      *---------------------------------------------------------------*
       FILE SECTION.
      *---------------------------------------------------------------*
       FD  STUDENT-FILE LABEL RECORDS ARE OMITTED.
       01  STUDENT-RECORD.
           05 STUDENT-IDENTIFICATION-IN.
               10 LAST-NAME-IN             PIC X(10).
               10 FIRST-NAME-IN            PIC X(10).
               10 MIDDLE-INITIAL-IN        PIC X(01).
               10 STUDENT-ID-IN            PIC 9(09).
           05 FILLER                       PIC X(05).
           05 ENROLLMENT-INFO-IN.
               10 CLASSIFICATION-IN        PIC X(02).
               10 TOTAL-HOURS-IN           PIC 9(03).
               10 HOURS-THIS-SEM-IN        PIC 9(02).
               10 MAJOR-IN                 PIC X(03).
           05  FILLER                      PIC X(35).

       FD  REPORT-FILE LABEL RECORDS ARE OMITTED.
       01  REPORT-RECORD                   PIC X(133).
      *---------------------------------------------------------------*
       WORKING-STORAGE SECTION.
      *---------------------------------------------------------------*
       01  WORKING-VARIABLES.
           05  FILE-STATUS                 PIC X(04).

       01  OUTPUT-RECORD.
           05 FILLER                       PIC X(03) VALUE ' *'.
           05 FIRST-NAME-OUT               PIC X(11).
           05 MIDDLE-INITIAL-OUT           PIC X(01).
           05 FILLER                       PIC X(02) VALUE '.'.
           05 LAST-NAME-OUT                PIC X(10).
           05 FILLER                       PIC X(04) VALUE ' *'.
           05 STUDENT-ID-OUT               PIC 9(09).
           05 FILLER                       PIC X(05) VALUE '  *'.
           05 CLASSIFICATION-OUT           PIC X(02).
           05 FILLER                       PIC X(06) VALUE '    *'.
           05 MAJOR-OUT                    PIC X(03).
           05 FILLER                       PIC X(08) VALUE '  *'.
```

Figure E.5 *Continued* A Second Illustration of the USE FOR DEBUGGING Statement

```
       1   1   2   2   2   3   3   4   4   4   5   5   6   6   6   7
   4   8   2   6   0   4   8   2   6   0   4   8   2   6   0   4   8   2

 700        05 HOURS-THIS-SEM-OUT         PIC 9(02).
 710        05 FILLER                     PIC X(08) VALUE '      *'.
 720        05 TOTAL-HOURS-OUT            PIC 9(03).
 730        05 FILLER                     PIC X(03) VALUE '  *'.
 740    *************************************************************
 750     PROCEDURE DIVISION.
 760    *************************************************************
 770     DECLARATIVES.
 780
 790    *-----------------------------------------------------------*
 800     PGM-DEBUG SECTION.
 810    *-----------------------------------------------------------*
 820         USE FOR DEBUGGING ON
 830              ALL PROCEDURES.
 840
 850     DISPLAY-PARA.
 860         DISPLAY DEBUG-ITEM.
 870
 880     END DECLARATIVES.
 890    *-----------------------------------------------------------*
 900     000-CONTROL-PROCEDURE SECTION.
 910    *-----------------------------------------------------------*
 920         PERFORM 100-INITIALIZATION.
 930         PERFORM 300-READ-RECORDS-PRINT-DETAILS
 940             UNTIL FILE-STATUS = 'DONE'.
 950         PERFORM 500-TERMINATION.
 960         STOP RUN.
 970    *-----------------------------------------------------------*
 980     100-INITIALIZATION SECTION.
 990    *-----------------------------------------------------------*
1000         MOVE 'START'              TO FILE-STATUS.
1010         OPEN INPUT STUDENT-FILE,  OUTPUT REPORT-FILE.
1020         READ STUDENT-FILE
1030             AT END MOVE 'DONE'    TO FILE-STATUS.
1040    *-----------------------------------------------------------*
1050     300-READ-RECORDS-PRINT-DETAILS SECTION.
1060    *-----------------------------------------------------------*
1070         MOVE STUDENT-ID-IN        TO STUDENT-ID-OUT.
1080         MOVE LAST-NAME-IN         TO LAST-NAME-OUT.
1090         MOVE FIRST-NAME-IN        TO FIRST-NAME-OUT.
1100         MOVE MIDDLE-INITIAL-IN    TO MIDDLE-INITIAL-OUT.
1110         MOVE CLASSIFICATION-IN    TO CLASSIFICATION-OUT.
1120         MOVE TOTAL-HOURS-IN       TO TOTAL-HOURS-OUT.
1130         MOVE HOURS-THIS-SEM-IN    TO HOURS-THIS-SEM-OUT.
1140         MOVE MAJOR-IN             TO MAJOR-OUT.
1150         WRITE REPORT-RECORD FROM OUTPUT-RECORD AFTER 2 LINES.
1160         READ STUDENT-FILE
1170             AT END MOVE 'DONE'    TO FILE-STATUS.
1180    *-----------------------------------------------------------*
1190     500-TERMINATION SECTION.
1200    *-----------------------------------------------------------*
1210         CLOSE STUDENT-FILE, REPORT-FILE.
```

BUGGING statement references ALL PROCEDURES. In all other respects the programs are the same.

In the output produced by the execution of this program, the DISPLAY of DEBUG-ITEM presents the first procedure name of the program (PGM-CODE) which lies outside the DECLARATIVES area. This line also indicates the program line number (92) and the reason the line was displayed (START-PROGRAM). Next, the output indicates that 000-CONTROL-PROGRAM was reached by FALL THROUGH. (Line 89 references the PROCEDURE DIVISION heading which was the direct cause of the FALL THROUGH.) Then the output indicates that 100-INITIALIZATION was executed by virtue of a PERFORM LOOP (a PERFORM statement) located at line 92. Finally, the

Figure E.5 *Continued* A Second Illustration of the USE FOR DEBUGGING Statement (Output)

a. Displayed Results:

```
000092 PGM-CODE                                              START PROGRAM
000089 000-CONTROL-PROCEDURE                                 FALL THROUGH
000092 100-INITIALIZATION                                    PERFORM LOOP
000093 300-READ-RECORDS-PRINT-DETAILS                        PERFORM LOOP
000093 300-READ-RECORDS-PRINT-DETAILS                        PERFORM LOOP
000093 300-READ-RECORDS-PRINT-DETAILS                        PERFORM LOOP
000093 300-READ-RECORDS-PRINT-DETAILS                        PERFORM LOOP
000093 300-READ-RECORDS-PRINT-DETAILS                        PERFORM LOOP
000093 300-READ-RECORDS-PRINT-DETAILS                        PERFORM LOOP
000093 300-READ-RECORDS-PRINT-DETAILS                        PERFORM LOOP
000093 300-READ-RECORDS-PRINT-DETAILS                        PERFORM LOOP
000093 300-READ-RECORDS-PRINT-DETAILS                        PERFORM LOOP
000093 300-READ-RECORDS-PRINT-DETAILS                        PERFORM LOOP
000093 300-READ-RECORDS-PRINT-DETAILS                        PERFORM LOOP
000093 300-READ-RECORDS-PRINT-DETAILS                        PERFORM LOOP
000093 300-READ-RECORDS-PRINT-DETAILS                        PERFORM LOOP
```

b. Printed (Written) Results:

```
| Jimmy      Q. Anderson  | 343564321 | Gr | Csc |   00   | 219 |

| John       A. Booker    | 555667777 | Fr | Mgt |   15   | 035 |

| Matt       N. Carter    | 456789012 | Jr | Mgt |   08   | 094 |

| Anthony    R. Davidson  | 353492761 | Sr | Eco |   16   | 138 |

| David      Q. Eldridge  | 376495268 | So | Fin |   12   | 047 |

| Rose       V. Franklin  | 000000001 | Gr | Gbu |   12   | 189 |

| Kenneth    A. Garrison  | 537903251 | So | Mgt |   16   | 028 |

| Mark       C. Hamilton  | 486762389 | Jr | Csc |   18   | 096 |

| Matt       H. Issacs    | 474653790 | Sr | Eco |   18   | 120 |

| Harold     Q. Jefferson | 502326955 | Fr | Mkt |   18   | 018 |

| Floyd      R. Kennedy   | 476329092 | Jr | Mkt |   12   | 060 |

| Steven     O. Lincoln   | 442648942 | So | Mkt |   15   | 045 |
```

output indicates that 300-READ-RECORD-PRINT-DETAILS was executed repetitively by a PERFORM LOOP (resulting from the PERFORM statement at line 93).

The EXHIBIT Statement

Although the USE FOR DEBUGGING statement is an ANS COBOL statement, COBOL compilers produced by some computer manufacturers do not include the statement. However, the compilers that do not contain the USE FOR DEBUGGING statement often support other nonstandard statements that perform some of the same debugging functions. For example, IBM COBOL compilers support the EXHIBIT statement.

The format of the EXHIBIT statement, shown in Figure E.6, is similar to the DISPLAY statement. The function of the EXHIBIT statement is to produce on the system output device (usually a line printer) values associated with one or more identifiers. Unlike the

Figure E.6 Format of the EXHIBIT Statement (Non-ANS Standard)

```
         ⎧NAMED        ⎫ ⎧identifier-1              ⎫ ⎡identifier-2              ⎤
EXHIBIT  ⎨CHANGED NAMED⎬ ⎨                          ⎬ ⎢                          ⎥ . . .
         ⎩CHANGED      ⎭ ⎩non-numeric-literal-1     ⎭ ⎣non-numeric-literal-2     ⎦
```

DISPLAY statement, however, the EXHIBIT statement may produce other helpful information (and in some cases, it does not produce the information that is not essential).

The three reserved words that follow the word EXHIBIT are used to control the output produced by the statement. If the reserved word NAMED is specified in the EXHIBIT statement, both the data-name and the contents of the data-name are produced for each identifier shown in the statement. Thus, if the statement

```
EXHIBIT NAMED STUDENT-ID-IN, LAST-NAME-IN
```

were placed in a program, when the statement is executed the identifier-name (i.e., STUDENT-ID-IN and LAST-NAME-IN) would be written along with the current value stored in those storage positions. If the statement contains a nonnumeric literal, the literal is displayed along with the data item names and values.

When the CHANGED NAME option of the EXHIBIT statements is used, the identifiers and their values are displayed only if the values have been altered since the last execution of the EXHIBIT statement. The EXHIBIT automatically produces all values and data item names when initially encountered in the program, thereafter the output of the statement depends on the values of the identifiers. If the value of an identifier changes, the value and name of the identifier is displayed; otherwise, no output is generated. Nonnumeric literals are produced by this statement, if present, in the same manner as with the NAMED option.

The last option of the EXHIBIT statement includes the reserved word CHANGED. It is similar to the CHANGED NAMED option because output is produced only if the value of an identifier has changed from one execution of the statement to the next encounter with the EXHIBIT statement. Unlike the CHANGED NAMED (or the NAMED) option, however, the identifier-name is *not* displayed with the value of the identifier with the CHANGED option. For this reason, the output produced by this form of the EXHIBIT statement is in a fixed columnar format. This allows the programmer to determine more easily which identifier value has been changed. With either the CHANGED NAMED or the CHANGED options, if no values are changed from one execution of the EXHIBIT statement to another, a blank will be produced on the output.

Figure E.7 illustrates the use of an EXHIBIT statement in a program. At line 920, an EXHIBIT is used to display the values of STUDENT-ID-IN and MAJOR-IN along with the data-names themselves, when their data values change. In the output from this program, STUDENT-ID-IN changes for every record, and the data-name and value are printed every time. However, an examination of MAJOR-IN demonstrates instances where the value of the data item did not change. For example, between the records for Harold Q. Jefferson and Floyd R. Kennedy a blank area is printed. An examination of the output indicates that both individuals are ''MKT'' students. As a consequence, the value for MAJOR-IN is not printed. (Also notice that Steven O. Lincoln is a marketing student.)

Figure E.7 An Illustration of the EXHIBIT Statement

```
           1   1   2   2   2   3   3   4   4   4   5   5   6   6   6   7
   4   8   2   6   0   4   8   2   6   0   4   8   2   6   0   4   8   2
-----------------------------------------------------------------------
    10 ************************************************************
    20  IDENTIFICATION DIVISION.
    30 ************************************************************
    40  PROGRAM-ID.     EXHIBIT-STATEMENT.
    50  AUTHOR.         J. WAYNE SPENCE.
    60  DATE-WRITTEN.   JANUARY 1, 1989.
    70  DATE-COMPILED.  JANUARY 1, 1989.
    80 *    This program illustrates the use of the EXHIBIT statement
    90 *    to trace the values placed in identifiers.
   100 ************************************************************
   110  ENVIRONMENT DIVISION.
   120 ************************************************************
   130 *----------------------------------------------------------*
   140  CONFIGURATION SECTION.
   150 *----------------------------------------------------------*
   160  SOURCE-COMPUTER. IBM.
   170  OBJECT-COMPUTER. IBM.
   180  SPECIAL-NAMES.   C01 IS TOP-OF-NEXT-PAGE.
   190 *----------------------------------------------------------*
   200  INPUT-OUTPUT SECTION.
   210 *----------------------------------------------------------*
   220  FILE-CONTROL.
   230      SELECT STUDENT-FILE ASSIGN TO UT-S-INPUT.
   240      SELECT REPORT-FILE  ASSIGN TO UT-S-OUTPUT.
   250 ************************************************************
   260  DATA DIVISION.
   270 ************************************************************
   280 *----------------------------------------------------------*
   290  FILE SECTION.
   300 *----------------------------------------------------------*
   310  FD  STUDENT-FILE LABEL RECORDS ARE OMITTED.
   320  01  STUDENT-RECORD.
   330      05 STUDENT-IDENTIFICATION-IN.
   340         10 LAST-NAME-IN          PIC X(10).
   350         10 FIRST-NAME-IN         PIC X(10).
   360         10 MIDDLE-INITIAL-IN     PIC X(01).
   370         10 STUDENT-ID-IN         PIC 9(09).
   380      05 FILLER                   PIC X(05).
   390      05 ENROLLMENT-INFO-IN.
   400         10 CLASSIFICATION-IN     PIC X(02).
   410         10 TOTAL-HOURS-IN        PIC 9(03).
   420         10 HOURS-THIS-SEM-IN     PIC 9(02).
   430         10 MAJOR-IN              PIC X(03).
   440      05  FILLER                  PIC X(35).
   450
   460  FD  REPORT-FILE LABEL RECORDS ARE OMITTED.
   470  01  REPORT-RECORD               PIC X(133).
   480 *----------------------------------------------------------*
   490  WORKING-STORAGE SECTION.
   500 *----------------------------------------------------------*
   510  01  WORKING-VARIABLES.
   520      05  FILE-STATUS             PIC X(04).
   530
   540  01  OUTPUT-RECORD.
   550      05 FILLER                   PIC X(03) VALUE ' *'.
   560      05 FIRST-NAME-OUT           PIC X(11).
   570      05 MIDDLE-INITIAL-OUT       PIC X(01).
   580      05 FILLER                   PIC X(02) VALUE '.'.
   590      05 LAST-NAME-OUT            PIC X(10).
   600      05 FILLER                   PIC X(04) VALUE ' *'.
   610      05 STUDENT-ID-OUT           PIC 9(09).
   620      05 FILLER                   PIC X(05) VALUE '   *'.
   630      05 CLASSIFICATION-OUT       PIC X(02).
   640      05 FILLER                   PIC X(06) VALUE '    *'.
   650      05 MAJOR-OUT                PIC X(03).
   660      05 FILLER                   PIC X(08) VALUE ' *'.
   670      05 HOURS-THIS-SEM-OUT       PIC 9(02).
   680      05 FILLER                   PIC X(08) VALUE '     *'.
   690      05 TOTAL-HOURS-OUT          PIC 9(03).
```

Figure E.7 *Continued* An Illustration of the EXHIBIT Statement

```
               1   1   2   2   2   3   3   4   4   4   5   5   6   6   6   7
       4   8   2   6   0   4   8   2   6   0   4   8   2   6   0   4   8   2

           05 FILLER                        PIC X(03) VALUE '  *'.
      ******************************************************************
       PROCEDURE DIVISION.
      ******************************************************************
      *----------------------------------------------------------------*
       000-CONTROL-PROCEDURE SECTION.
      *----------------------------------------------------------------*
           PERFORM 100-INITIALIZATION.
           PERFORM 300-READ-RECORDS-PRINT-DETAILS
               UNTIL FILE-STATUS = 'DONE'.
           PERFORM 500-TERMINATION.
           STOP RUN.
      *----------------------------------------------------------------*
       100-INITIALIZATION SECTION.
      *----------------------------------------------------------------*
           MOVE 'START'                TO FILE-STATUS.
           OPEN INPUT STUDENT-FILE, OUTPUT REPORT-FILE.
           READ STUDENT-FILE
               AT END MOVE 'DONE'      TO FILE-STATUS.
      *----------------------------------------------------------------*
       300-READ-RECORDS-PRINT-DETAILS SECTION.
      *----------------------------------------------------------------*
           EXHIBIT CHANGED NAMED STUDENT-ID-IN, MAJOR-IN.
           MOVE STUDENT-ID-IN          TO STUDENT-ID-OUT.
           MOVE LAST-NAME-IN           TO LAST-NAME-OUT.
           MOVE FIRST-NAME-IN          TO FIRST-NAME-OUT.
           MOVE MIDDLE-INITIAL-IN      TO MIDDLE-INITIAL-OUT.
           MOVE CLASSIFICATION-IN      TO CLASSIFICATION-OUT.
           MOVE TOTAL-HOURS-IN         TO TOTAL-HOURS-OUT.
           MOVE HOURS-THIS-SEM-IN      TO HOURS-THIS-SEM-OUT.
           MOVE MAJOR-IN               TO MAJOR-OUT.
           WRITE REPORT-RECORD FROM OUTPUT-RECORD AFTER 2 LINES.
           READ STUDENT-FILE
               AT END MOVE 'DONE'      TO FILE-STATUS.
      *----------------------------------------------------------------*
       500-TERMINATION SECTION.
      *----------------------------------------------------------------*
           CLOSE STUDENT-FILE, REPORT-FILE.
```

Figure E.7 *Continued* An Illustration of the EXHIBIT Statement (Output)

a. Exhibited Results:

```
STUDENT-ID-IN = 343564321 MAJOR-IN = Csc
STUDENT-ID-IN = 555667777 MAJOR-IN = Mgt
STUDENT-ID-IN = 456789012
STUDENT-ID-IN = 353492761 MAJOR-IN = Eco
STUDENT-ID-IN = 376495268 MAJOR-IN = Fin
STUDENT-ID-IN = 000000001 MAJOR-IN = Gbu
STUDENT-ID-IN = 537903251 MAJOR-IN = Mgt
STUDENT-ID-IN = 486762389 MAJOR-IN = Csc
STUDENT-ID-IN = 474653790 MAJOR-IN = Eco
STUDENT-ID-IN = 502326955 MAJOR-IN = Mkt
STUDENT-ID-IN = 476329092
STUDENT-ID-IN = 442648942
```

Figure E.7 Continued on next page

Figure E.7 *Continued* An Illustration of the EXHIBIT Statement (Output)

b. Printed (Written) Results:

```
| Jimmy      Q. Anderson  | 343564321 | Gr | Csc |  00 | 219 |
| John       A. Booker    | 555667777 | Fr | Mgt |  15 | 035 |
| Matt       N. Carter    | 456789012 | Jr | Mgt |  08 | 094 |
| Anthony    R. Davidson  | 353492761 | Sr | Eco |  16 | 138 |
| David      Q. Eldridge  | 376495268 | So | Fin |  12 | 047 |
| Rose       V. Franklin  | 000000001 | Gr | Gbu |  12 | 189 |
| Kenneth    A. Garrison  | 537903251 | So | Mgt |  16 | 028 |
| Mark       C. Hamilton  | 486762389 | Jr | Csc |  18 | 096 |
| Matt       H. Issacs    | 474653790 | Sr | Eco |  18 | 120 |
| Harold     Q. Jefferson | 502326955 | Fr | Mkt |  18 | 018 |
| Floyd      R. Kennedy   | 476329092 | Jr | Mkt |  12 | 060 |
| Steven     O. Lincoln   | 442648942 | So | Mkt |  15 | 045 |
```

The TRACE Statement

TRACE is another statement that is often included in COBOL compilers but is not a part of ANS COBOL. The TRACE statement allows the programmer to determine the logical flow of a program from one procedure to another during execution of the program. Each paragraph or SECTION name encountered while the TRACE is active will cause the paragraph or SECTION name (or line number in the program) to be produced on the system output device (e.g., line printer). The TRACE statement is accompanied by two additional reserved words—READY and RESET. To initiate a trace of the procedure-names encountered during execution of a program, the programmer enters READY TRACE. An example of the tracing of the procedure-names is presented in Figure E.8. Notice that on the output of the program, the paragraph names that were reached while the trace was active (caused by the READY TRACE statement) are printed. Upon completing the 000-CONTROL-PROCEDURE paragraph, the programmer deactivates the trace by RESET TRACE. In the example, all the paragraphs of the program (except the 000-CONTROL-PROCEDURE paragraph) were subjected to the trace. However, if the program were longer and more complex, performing a trace from the beginning of the program to the end would not necessarily be desirable. The trace could be localized to concentrate on those areas of a program that are the likely source of the error. If several areas of the program are suspect, several sets of READY TRACE and RESET TRACE may be necessary to turn the trace ''on'' and ''off.'' This approach is generally more useful and does not overburden the programmer with a mass of unneeded tracing.

Figure E.8 An Illustration of the READY and RESET TRACE Statements

```
          1   1   2   2   2   3   3   4   4   4   5   5   6   6   6   7
   4   8  2   6   0   4   8   2   6   0   4   8   2   6   0   4   8   2

       *****************************************************************
        IDENTIFICATION DIVISION.
       *****************************************************************
        PROGRAM-ID.       PROCEDURE-TRACE.
        AUTHOR.           JOHN WINDSOR.
        DATE-WRITTEN.     JANUARY 1, 1989.
        DATE-COMPILED.    JANUARY 1, 1989.
       *    This program illustrates the use of the TRACE
       *    statement to provide the means for following the
       *    execution sequence of a program.
       *****************************************************************
        ENVIRONMENT DIVISION.
       *****************************************************************
       *---------------------------------------------------------------*
        CONFIGURATION SECTION.
       *---------------------------------------------------------------*
        SOURCE-COMPUTER. IBM.
        OBJECT-COMPUTER. IBM.
        SPECIAL-NAMES.    C01 IS TOP-OF-NEXT-PAGE.
       *---------------------------------------------------------------*
        INPUT-OUTPUT SECTION.
       *---------------------------------------------------------------*
        FILE-CONTROL.
            SELECT STUDENT-FILE ASSIGN TO UT-S-INPUT.
            SELECT REPORT-FILE  ASSIGN TO UT-S-OUTPUT.
       *****************************************************************
        DATA DIVISION.
       *****************************************************************
       *---------------------------------------------------------------*
        FILE SECTION.
       *---------------------------------------------------------------*
        FD  STUDENT-FILE LABEL RECORDS ARE OMITTED.
        01  STUDENT-RECORD.
            05 STUDENT-IDENTIFICATION-IN.
                10 LAST-NAME-IN          PIC X(10).
                10 FIRST-NAME-IN         PIC X(10).
                10 MIDDLE-INITIAL-IN     PIC X(01).
                10 STUDENT-ID-IN         PIC 9(09).
            05 FILLER                    PIC X(05).
            05 ENROLLMENT-INFO-IN.
                10 CLASSIFICATION-IN     PIC X(02).
                10 TOTAL-HOURS-IN        PIC 9(03).
                10 HOURS-THIS-SEM-IN     PIC 9(02).
                10 MAJOR-IN              PIC X(03).
            05  FILLER                   PIC X(35).

        FD  REPORT-FILE LABEL RECORDS ARE OMITTED.
        01  REPORT-RECORD                PIC X(133).
       *---------------------------------------------------------------*
        WORKING-STORAGE SECTION.
       *---------------------------------------------------------------*
        01  WORKING-VARIABLES.
            05  FILE-STATUS              PIC X(04).

        01  OUTPUT-RECORD.
            05 FILLER                    PIC X(03) VALUE ' *'.
            05 FIRST-NAME-OUT            PIC X(11).
            05 MIDDLE-INITIAL-OUT        PIC X(01).
            05 FILLER                    PIC X(02) VALUE '.'.
            05 LAST-NAME-OUT             PIC X(10).
            05 FILLER                    PIC X(04) VALUE ' *'.
            05 STUDENT-ID-OUT            PIC 9(09).
            05 FILLER                    PIC X(05) VALUE '  *'.
            05 CLASSIFICATION-OUT        PIC X(02).
            05 FILLER                    PIC X(06) VALUE '   *'.
            05 MAJOR-OUT                 PIC X(03).
            05 FILLER                    PIC X(08) VALUE '  *'.
            05 HOURS-THIS-SEM-OUT        PIC 9(02).
            05 FILLER                    PIC X(08) VALUE '     *'.
```

Figure E.8 An Illustration of the READY and RESET TRACE Statements

```
          1   1   2   2   2   3   3   4   4   4   5   5   6   6   6   7
  4   8   2   6   0   4   8   2   6   0   4   8   2   6   0   4   8   2
-----------------------------------------------------------------------
           05 TOTAL-HOURS-OUT                PIC 9(03).
           05 FILLER                         PIC X(03) VALUE '  *'.

       01  HEADING-RECORD.
           05 FILLER                         PIC X(23) VALUE SPACES.
           05 FILLER                         PIC X(22) VALUE
                                             'Student Semester List'.

       01  SEPARATOR-LINE.
           05 FILLER                         PIC X(01) VALUE SPACES.
           05 FILLER                         PIC X(79) VALUE ALL '*'.

       01  COLUMN-HEADING-1.
           05 FILLER                         PIC X(01) VALUE SPACES.
           05 FILLER                         PIC X(79) VALUE '*       Student
      -    'Name       * Student ID. * Class * Major *  Current    * Tota
      -    '1 *'.

       01  COLUMN-HEADING-2.
           05 FILLER                         PIC X(28) VALUE ' *'.
           05 FILLER                         PIC X(14) VALUE '*   Number'.
      *****************************************************************
       PROCEDURE DIVISION.
      *****************************************************************
      *---------------------------------------------------------------*
       000-CONTROL-PROCEDURE SECTION.
      *---------------------------------------------------------------*
           READY TRACE.

           PERFORM 100-INITIALIZATION.
           PERFORM 300-REPORT-HEADING.
           PERFORM 500-READ-RECORDS-PRINT-DETAILS
               UNTIL FILE-STATUS = 'DONE'.
           PERFORM 700-TERMINATION.

           RESET TRACE.

           STOP RUN.
      *---------------------------------------------------------------*
       100-INITIALIZATION SECTION.
      *---------------------------------------------------------------*
           MOVE 'START'                TO FILE-STATUS.
           OPEN INPUT STUDENT-FILE, OUTPUT REPORT-FILE.
           READ STUDENT-FILE
               AT END MOVE 'DONE'      TO FILE-STATUS.
      *---------------------------------------------------------------*
       300-REPORT-HEADING SECTION.
      *---------------------------------------------------------------*
           WRITE REPORT-RECORD FROM HEADING-RECORD AFTER
               TOP-OF-NEXT-PAGE.
           WRITE REPORT-RECORD FROM SEPARATOR-LINE AFTER 2 LINES.
           WRITE REPORT-RECORD FROM COLUMN-HEADING-1 AFTER 1.
           WRITE REPORT-RECORD FROM COLUMN-HEADING-2 AFTER 1.
           WRITE REPORT-RECORD FROM SEPARATOR-LINE AFTER 1.
      *---------------------------------------------------------------*
       500-READ-RECORDS-PRINT-DETAILS SECTION.
      *---------------------------------------------------------------*
```

Figure E.8 *Continued* An Illustration of the READY and RESET TRACE Statements

```
                1   1   2   2   2   3   3   4   4   4   5   5   6   6   6   7
    4   8   2   6   0   4   8   2   6   0   4   8   2   6   0   4   8   2

           MOVE STUDENT-ID-IN       TO STUDENT-ID-OUT.
           MOVE LAST-NAME-IN        TO LAST-NAME-OUT.
           MOVE FIRST-NAME-IN       TO FIRST-NAME-OUT.
           MOVE MIDDLE-INITIAL-IN   TO MIDDLE-INITIAL-OUT.
           MOVE CLASSIFICATION-IN   TO CLASSIFICATION-OUT.
           MOVE TOTAL-HOURS-IN      TO TOTAL-HOURS-OUT.
           MOVE HOURS-THIS-SEM-IN   TO HOURS-THIS-SEM-OUT.
           MOVE MAJOR-IN            TO MAJOR-OUT.
           WRITE REPORT-RECORD FROM OUTPUT-RECORD AFTER 2 LINES.
           READ STUDENT-FILE
               AT END MOVE 'DONE'   TO FILE-STATUS.
       *-------------------------------------------------------------*
        700-TERMINATION SECTION.
       *-------------------------------------------------------------*
           CLOSE STUDENT-FILE, REPORT-FILE.
```

Figure E.8 *Continued* An Illustration of the READY and RESET TRACE Statements (Output)

a. Tracing Results:

```
100-INITIALIZATION ,300-REPORT-HEADING ,500-READ-RECORDS-PRINT-DETAILS (00000013),700-TERMINATION
```

b. Printed (Written) Results:

Student Semester List

Student Name		Student ID. Number	Class	Major	Current	Total
Jimmy	Q. Anderson	343564321	Gr	Csc	00	219
John	A. Booker	555667777	Fr	Mgt	15	035
Matt	N. Carter	456789012	Jr	Mgt	08	094
Anthony	R. Davidson	353492761	Sr	Eco	16	138
David	Q. Eldridge	376495268	So	Fin	12	047
Rose	V. Franklin	000000001	Gr	Gbu	12	189
Kenneth	A. Garrison	537903251	So	Mgt	16	028
Mark	C. Hamilton	486762389	Jr	Csc	18	096
Matt	H. Issacs	474653790	Sr	Eco	18	120
Harold	Q. Jefferson	502326955	Fr	Mkt	18	018
Floyd	R. Kennedy	476329092	Jr	Mkt	12	060
Steven	O. Lincoln	442648942	So	Mkt	15	045

Index